Nineteenth-Century Literature Criticism

Guide to Gale Literary Criticism Series

For criticism on	Consult these Gale series
Authors now living or who died after December 31, 1999	*CONTEMPORARY LITERARY CRITICISM (CLC)*
Authors who died between 1900 and 1999	*TWENTIETH-CENTURY LITERARY CRITICISM (TCLC)*
Authors who died between 1800 and 1899	*NINETEENTH-CENTURY LITERATURE CRITICISM (NCLC)*
Authors who died between 1400 and 1799	*LITERATURE CRITICISM FROM 1400 TO 1800 (LC)* *SHAKESPEAREAN CRITICISM (SC)*
Authors who died before 1400	*CLASSICAL AND MEDIEVAL LITERATURE CRITICISM (CMLC)*
Authors of books for children and young adults	*CHILDREN'S LITERATURE REVIEW (CLR)*
Dramatists	*DRAMA CRITICISM (DC)*
Poets	*POETRY CRITICISM (PC)*
Short story writers	*SHORT STORY CRITICISM (SSC)*
Literary topics and movements	*HARLEM RENAISSANCE: A GALE CRITICAL COMPANION (HR)* *THE BEAT GENERATION: A GALE CRITICAL COMPANION (BG)*
Asian American writers of the last two hundred years	*ASIAN AMERICAN LITERATURE (AAL)*
Black writers of the past two hundred years	*BLACK LITERATURE CRITICISM (BLC)* *BLACK LITERATURE CRITICISM SUPPLEMENT (BLCS)*
Hispanic writers of the late nineteenth and twentieth centuries	*HISPANIC LITERATURE CRITICISM (HLC)* *HISPANIC LITERATURE CRITICISM SUPPLEMENT (HLCS)*
Native North American writers and orators of the eighteenth, nineteenth, and twentieth centuries	*NATIVE NORTH AMERICAN LITERATURE (NNAL)*
Major authors from the Renaissance to the present	*WORLD LITERATURE CRITICISM, 1500 TO THE PRESENT (WLC)* *WORLD LITERATURE CRITICISM SUPPLEMENT (WLCS)*

ISSN 0732-1864

Volume 146

Nineteenth-Century Literature Criticism

Criticism of the
Works of Novelists, Philosophers, and Other
Creative Writers Who Died between 1800
and 1899, from the First Published Critical
Appraisals to Current Evaluations

Russel Whitaker
Project Editor

THOMSON

GALE

Detroit • New York • San Francisco • San Diego • New Haven, Conn. • Waterville, Maine • London • Munich

THOMSON

™

GALE

Nineteenth-Century Literature Criticism, Vol. 146

Project Editor
Russel Whitaker

Editorial
Jessica Bomarito, Kathy D. Darrow, Jeffrey W. Hunter, Jelena O. Krstović, Michelle Lee, Ellen McGeagh, Joseph Palmisano, Linda Pavlovski, Thomas J. Schoenberg, Lawrence J. Trudeau

Data Capture
Francis Monroe, Gwen Tucker

Indexing Services
Sue Kelsch

Rights and Acquisitions
Margie Abendroth, Lori Hines, Emma Hull

Imaging and Multimedia
Dean Dauphinais, Robert Duncan, Leitha Etheridge-Sims, Lezlie Light, Michael Logusz, Dan Newell, Kelly A. Quin, Denay Wilding

Composition and Electronic Capture
Kathy Sauer

Manufacturing
Rhonda Williams

Product Manager
Janet Witalec

LIBRARY OF CONGRESS CATALOG CARD NUMBER 84-643008

ISBN 0-7876-8630-1
ISSN 0732-1864

Printed in the United States of America
10 9 8 7 6 5 4 3 2 1

Contents

Preface vii

Acknowledgments xi

Literary Criticism Series Advisory Board xiii

Preface

Since its inception in 1981, *Nineteeth-Century Literature Criticism* (*NCLC*) has been a valuable resource for students and librarians seeking critical commentary on writers of this transitional period in world history. Designated an "Outstanding Reference Source" by the American Library Association with the publication of is first volume, *NCLC* has since been purchased by over 6,000 school, public, and university libraries. The series has covered more than 450 authors representing 33 nationalities and over 17,000 titles. No other reference source has surveyed the critical reaction to nineteenth-century authors and literature as thoroughly as *NCLC*.

Scope of the Series

NCLC is designed to introduce students and advanced readers to the authors of the nineteenth century and to the most significant interpretations of these authors' works. The great poets, novelists, short story writers, playwrights, and philosophers of this period are frequently studied in high school and college literature courses. By organizing and reprinting commentary written on these authors, *NCLC* helps students develop valuable insight into literary history, promotes a better understanding of the texts, and sparks ideas for papers and assignments. Each entry in *NCLC* presents a comprehensive survey of an author's career or an individual work of literature and provides the user with a multiplicity of interpretations and assessments. Such variety allows students to pursue their own interests; furthermore, it fosters an awareness that literature is dynamic and responsive to many different opinions.

Every fourth volume of *NCLC* is devoted to literary topics that cannot be covered under the author approach used in the rest of the series. Such topics include literary movements, prominent themes in nineteenth-century literature, literary reaction to political and historical events, significant eras in literary history, prominent literary anniversaries, and the literatures of cultures that are often overlooked by English-speaking readers.

NCLC continues the survey of criticism of world literature begun by Thomson Gale's *Contemporary Literary Criticism* (*CLC*) and *Twentieth-Century Literary Criticism* (*TCLC*).

Organization of the Book

An *NCLC* entry consists of the following elements:

- The **Author Heading** cites the name under which the author most commonly wrote, followed by birth and death dates. Also located here are any name variations under which an author wrote, including transliterated forms for authors whose native languages use nonroman alphabets. If the author wrote consistently under a pseudonym, the pseudonym will be listed in the author heading and the author's actual name given in parenthesis on the first line of the biographical and critical information. Uncertain birth or death dates are indicated by question marks. Single-work entries are preceded by a heading that consists of the most common form of the title in English translation (if applicable) and the original date of composition.

- The **Introduction** contains background information that introduces the reader to the author, work, or topic that is the subject of the entry.

- A **Portrait of the Author** is included when available.

- The list of **Principal Works** is ordered chronologically by date of first publication and lists the most important works by the author. The genre and publication date of each work is given. In the case of foreign authors whose works have been translated into English, the list will focus primarily on twentieth-century translations, selecting those works most commonly considered the best by critics. Unless otherwise indicated, dramas are dated by first performance, not first publication. Lists of **Representative Works** by different authors appear with topic entries.

- Reprinted **Criticism** is arranged chronologically in each entry to provide a useful perspective on changes in critical evaluation over time. The critic's name and the date of composition or publication of the critical work are given at the beginning of each piece of criticism. Unsigned criticism is preceded by the title of the source in which it appeared. All titles by the author featured in the text are printed in boldface type. Footnotes are reprinted at the end of each essay or excerpt. In the case of excerpted criticism, only those footnotes that pertain to the excerpted texts are included. Criticism in topic entries is arranged chronologically under a variety of subheadings to facilitate the study of different aspects of the topic.

- A complete **Bibliographical Citation** of the original essay or book precedes each piece of criticism.

- Critical essays are prefaced by brief **Annotations** explicating each piece.

- An annotated bibliography of **Further Reading** appears at the end of each entry and suggests resources for additional study. In some cases, significant essays for which the editors could not obtain reprint rights are included here. Boxed material following the further reading list provides references to other biographical and critical sources on the author in series published by Thomson Gale.

Indexes

Each volume of *NCLC* contains a **Cumulative Author Index** listing all authors who have appeared in a wide variety of reference sources published by Thomson Gale, including *NCLC*. A complete list of these sources is found facing the first page of the Author Index. The index also includes birth and death dates and cross references between pseudonyms and actual names.

A **Cumulative Nationality Index** lists all authors featured in *NCLC* by nationality, followed by the number of the *NCLC* volume in which their entry appears.

A **Cumulative Topic Index** lists the literary themes and topics treated in the series as well as in *Classical and Medieval Literature Criticism, Literature Criticism from 1400 to 1800, Twentieth-Century Literary Criticism,* and the *Contemporary Literary Criticism* Yearbook, which was discontinued in 1998.

An alphabetical **Title Index** accompanies each volume of *NCLC*, with the exception of the Topics volumes. Listings of titles by authors covered in the given volume are followed by the author's name and the corresponding page numbers where the titles are discussed. English translations of foreign titles and variations of titles are cross-referenced to the title under which a work was originally published. Titles of novels, dramas, nonfiction books, and poetry, short story, or essay collections are printed in italics, while individual poems, short stories, and essays are printed in roman type within quotation marks.

In response to numerous suggestions from librarians, Thomson Gale also produces an annual paperbound edition of the *NCLC* cumulative title index. This annual cumulation, which alphabetically lists all titles reviewed in the series, is available to all customers. Additional copies of this index are available upon request. Librarians and patrons will welcome this separate index; it saves shelf space, is easy to use, and is recyclable upon receipt of the next edition.

Citing *Nineteenth-Century Literature Criticism*

When citing criticism reprinted in the Literary Criticism Series, students should provide complete bibliographic information so that the cited essay can be located in the original print or electronic source. Students who quote directly from reprinted criticism may use any accepted bibliographic format, such as University of Chicago Press style or Modern Language Association style.

The examples below follow recommendations for preparing a bibliography set forth in *The Chicago Manual of Style,* 14th ed. (Chicago: The University of Chicago Press, 1993); the first example pertains to material drawn from periodicals, the second to material reprinted from books:

Guerard, Albert J. "On the Composition of Dostoevsky's *The Idiot.*" *Mosaic: A Journal for the Interdisciplinary Study of Literature* 8, no. 1 (fall 1974): 201-15. Reprinted in *Nineteenth-Century Literature Criticism.* Vol. 119, edited by Lynn M. Zott, 81-104. Detroit: Gale, 2003.

Berstein, Carol L. "Subjectivity as Critique and the Critique of Subjectivity in Keats's *Hyperion.*" In *After the Future: Postmodern Times and Places,* edited by Gary Shapiro, 41-52. Albany, N. Y.: State University of New York Press, 1990. Reprinted in *Nineteeth-Century Literature Criticism.* Vol. 121, edited by Lynn M. Zott, 155-60. Detroit: Gale, 2003.

The examples below follow recommendations for preparing a works cited list set forth in the *MLA Handbook for Writers of Research Papers,* 5th ed. (New York: The Modern Language Association of America, 1999); the first example pertains to material drawn from periodicals, the second to material reprinted from books:

Guerard, Albert J. "On the Composition of Dostoevsky's *The Idiot.*" *Mosaic: A Journal for the Interdisciplinary Study of Literature* 8. 1 (fall 1974): 201-15. Reprinted in *Nineteenth-Century Literature Criticism.* Ed. Lynn M. Zott. Vol. 119. Detroit: Gale, 2003. 81-104.

Berstein, Carol L. "Subjectivity as Critique and the Critique of Subjectivity in Keats's *Hyperion.*" *After the Future: Postmodern Times and Places.* Ed. Gary Shapiro. Albany, N. Y.: State University of New York Press, 1990. 41-52. Reprinted in *Nineteeth-Century Literature Criticism.* Ed. Lynn M. Zott. Vol. 121. Detroit: Gale, 2003. 155-60.

Suggestions are Welcome

Readers who wish to suggest new features, topics, or authors to appear in future volumes, or who have other suggestions or comments are cordially invited to call, write, or fax the Product Manager:

Product Manager, Literary Criticism Series
Thomson Gale
27500 Drake Road
Farmington Hills, MI 48331-3535
1-800-347-4253 (GALE)
Fax: 248-699-8054

Acknowledgments

The editors wish to thank the copyright holders of the criticism included in this volume and the permissions managers of many book and magazine publishing companies for assisting us in securing reproduction rights. We are also grateful to the staffs of the Detroit Public Library, the Library of Congress, the University of Detroit Mercy Library, Wayne State University Purdy/Kresge Library Complex, and the University of Michigan Libraries for making their resources available to us. Following is a list of the copyright holders who have granted us permission to reproduce material in this volume of *NCLC*. Every effort has been made to trace copyright, but if omissions have been made, please let us know.

COPYRIGHTED MATERIAL IN *NCLC*, VOLUME 146, WAS REPRODUCED FROM THE FOLLOWING PERIODICALS:

American Literature, v. 74, June, 2002. Copyright © 2002 by Duke University Press. Reproduced by permission.—*American Quarterly*, v. 42, December, 1990. Copyright © 1990 The American Studies Association. Reproduced by permission of Johns Hopkins University Press.—*American Studies*, v. 31, fall, 1990 for "Anti-Individualism, Authority, and Identity: Susan Warner's Contradictions in *The Wide, Wide World*" by Isabelle White. Copyright © Mid-America American Studies Association, 1991. Reprinted by permission of the publisher and the author.—*English Language Notes*, v. 16, 1979. Copyrighted © 1979, Regents of the University of Colorado. Reproduced by permission.—*Essays in Literature*, v. 22, spring, 1995. Copyright © 1995, Western Illinois University. Reproduced by permission.—*Genders*, spring, 1989 for "Inside the Sentimental: The Psychological Work of *The Wide, Wide World*" by Nancy Schnog. Copyright © 1989 by the University of Texas Press. Reproduced by permission of the publisher and the author.—*German Quarterly*, v. 66, winter, 1993. Copyright © 1993 by the American Association of Teachers of German. Reproduced by permission.—*Germanic Notes and Reviews*, v. 27, spring, 1996. Reproduced by permission.—*Keats-Shelley Journal*, v. 27, 1978. Reproduced by permission.—*Keats-Shelley Memorial Bulletin*, v. 21, 1970. Reproduced by permission.—*Legacy*, v. 8, spring, 1991; v. 11, spring, 1994; v. 17, 2000. Copyright © 1991, 1994, 2001 by Legacy, A Journal, Inc. All rights reserved. Reproduced by permission of the University of Nebraska Press.—*Monatshefte für deutschen Unterricht, deutsche Sprache und Literatur*, v. 88, summer, 1996. Copyright © 1996 by The Board of Regents of The University of Wisconsin System. Reproduced by permission.—*Proceedings of the British Academy*, v. 75, 1989. Reproduced by permission.—*Representations*, winter, 1988 for "Sparing the Rod: Discipline and Fiction in Antebellum America" by Richard H. Brodhead. Copyright © 1988 by The Regents of the University of California, www.californiajournals.com. All rights reserved. Reproduced by permission of the publisher and the author.—*Selecta: Journal of the Pacific Northwest Council for Foreign Languages*, v. 18, 1997 for "Georg Büchner's Philosophy of Science: Totality in *Lenz* and *Woyzeck*" by Curt Wendell Nickisch. Edited by Craig W. Nickisch. Reproduced by permission of the author.—*Studies in American Fiction*, v. 25, spring, 1997. Copyright © 1997 Northeastern University. Reproduced by permission.—*Theatre Journal*, v. 44, March, 1992. Copyright © 1992, University and College Theatre Association of the American Theatre Association. Reproduced by permission of The Johns Hopkins University Press.—*Tulsa Studies in Women's Literature*, v. 18, spring, 1999 for "Homesickness in Susan Warner's *The Wide, Wide World*" by Sara E. Quay. Copyright © 1999, The University of Tulsa. All rights reserved. Reproduced by permission of the publisher and the author.

COPYRIGHTED MATERIAL IN *NCLC*, VOLUME 146, WAS REPRODUCED FROM THE FOLLOWING BOOKS:

Benn, Maurice B. From *The Drama of Revolt: A Critical Study of Georg Büchner*. Cambridge University Press, 1976. Copyright © 1976 by Cambridge University Press. Reprinted with the permission of Cambridge University Press.—Foster, Edward Halsey. From *Susan and Anna Warner*. Twayne Publishers, 1978. Copyright © by G. K. Hall & Co. All rights reserved. Reproduced by permission of the Gale Group.—George, Eric. From *The Life and Death of Benjamin Robert Haydon, Historical Painter: 1786-1846*. Oxford at the Clarendon Press, 1967. Copyright © 1967 Dorothy George. Reproduced by permission of Oxford University Press.—Grimm, Reinhold. From *Love, Lust, and Rebellion: New Approaches to Georg Büchner*. University of Wisconsin Press, 1985. Copyright © 1985 by The Board of Regents of the University of Wisconsin System. All rights reserved. Reproduced by permission.—Huxley, Aldous. From an introduction to *The Autobiography and Memoirs of Benjamin Robert Haydon (1786-1846)*. Edited by Tom Taylor. Peter Davies, Publisher, 2nd edition, 1926. Reproduced by permission of The Reece Halsey Agency.—Jones, Leonidas. From *The Life of John Hamilton Reynolds*. University Press of New England, 1984. Copyright © 1984 by University Press of New England. All rights reserved. Reproduced by permission.—Jones, Leonidas M. From an introduction to *The Letters of John Hamilton Reynolds*. Edited with an introduction by Leonidas M. Jones. Copyright © 1973 The University of Nebraska Press. All rights reserved. Reproduced by permission of the University of Nebraska Press.—Lindenberger, Herbert. From *Georg Büchner*. Southern Illinois University Press, 1964. Copyright © 1964 by Southern Illinois University Press. All rights reserved. Reproduced by permission.—Lukens, Nancy. From *Büchner's Valerio and the Theatrical Fool Tradition*. Akademischer Verlag Hans-Dieter Heinz, 1977. Reproduced by permission.—Marsh, George L. From *John Hamilton Reynolds: Poetry and Prose*. Humphrey Milford, 1928. Reproduced by permission of Oxford University Press.—Porter, Roger J. From "'In Me the Solitary Sublimity': Posturing and the Collapse of Romantic Will in Benjamin Robert Haydon," in *The Culture of Autobiography: Constructions of Self-Representation*. Edited by Robert Folkenflik. Stanford University Press, 1993. Copyright © 1993 by the Board of Trustees of the Leland Stanford Jr. University. Used with the permission of Stanford University Press, www.sup.org.—Reddick, John. From *Georg Büchner: The Shattered Whole*. Clarendon at Oxford University Press, 1994. Copyright © 1994 by John Reddick. All rights reserved. Reproduced by permission of Oxford University Press.—Richards, David G. From *Georg Büchner's 'Woyzeck': A History of Its Criticism*. Camden House, 2001. Copyright © 2001 David G. Richards. All rights reserved. Reproduced by permission.—Schmidt, Henry J. From *Satire, Caricature and Perspectivism in the Work of Georg Büchner*. Copyright © 1970 Mouton & Co., N. V. Publishers, The Hague. Reproduced by permission of Mouton de Gruyter, a division of Walter de Gruyter & Co.—Trubey, Elizabeth Fekete. From "Imagined Revolution: The Female Reader and *The Wide, Wide World*," NEMLA Conference, April 8, 2000, Buffalo, New York, NY. Copyright © Northeast Modern Language Association. Reproduced by permission.

PHOTOGRAPHS AND ILLUSTRATIONS APPEARING IN *NCLC*, VOLUME 146, WERE RECEIVED FROM THE FOLLOWING SOURCES:

Büchner, Georg, contemporary lithograph by A. Hoffman, photograph. The Granger Collection, New York. Reproduced by permission.—Haydon, Benjamin Robert, photograph. The Mary Evans Picture Library.—Reynolds, John Hamilton, engraving (c. 1830) after a miniature by Severn, photograph. Getty Images.—Warner, Susan, Photo by W. Kurtz. The Library of Congress.

Thomson Gale Literature Product Advisory Board

The members of the Thomson Gale Literature Product Advisory Board—reference librarians from public and academic library systems—represent a cross-section of our customer base and offer a variety of informed perspectives on both the presentation and content of our literature products. Advisory board members assess and define such quality issues as the relevance, currency, and usefulness of the author coverage, critical content, and literary topics included in our series; evaluate the layout, presentation, and general quality of our printed volumes; provide feedback on the criteria used for selecting authors and topics covered in our series; provide suggestions for potential enhancements to our series; identify any gaps in our coverage of authors or literary topics, recommending authors or topics for inclusion; analyze the appropriateness of our content and presentation for various user audiences, such as high school students, undergraduates, graduate students, librarians, and educators; and offer feedback on any proposed changes/enhancements to our series. We wish to thank the following advisors for their advice throughout the year.

Georg Büchner
1813-1837

(Full name Georg Karl Büchner) German playwright and novella writer.

The following entry presents criticism of Büchner from 1964 through 2001. For additional information on Büchner's life and career, see *NCLC,* Volume 26.

INTRODUCTION

Büchner is known for the few works he composed during his brief life: the novella fragment *Lenz* (1839) and the plays *Dantons Tod* (1835; *Danton's Death*), *Leonce und Lena* (1838; *Leonce and Lena*), and *Woyzeck* (first published in 1879). In these works Büchner rejected the idealism of the Romantic movement, which dominated German letters in the late eighteenth and early nineteenth centuries; instead, he sought to realistically depict what he saw as the hopelessness of life in a world where isolation, monotony, and suffering prevail and are perpetuated by deterministic historical and biological forces. This pessimistic view of life, along with the innovative techniques he used to obtain a sense of realism, gives Büchner a greater affinity with authors of the modern era than with those of the nineteenth century. Additionally, his link to several later developments in drama, among them Naturalism, the Theater of the Absurd, and Expressionism, has frequently been observed by scholars.

BIOGRAPHICAL INFORMATION

The eldest of six children, Büchner was born in Goddelau, Germany. His family moved in 1816 to nearby Darmstadt, the capital of the duchy of Hesse-Darmstadt. During Büchner's school years his father, a physician, encouraged him to study the sciences, while his mother nurtured in him a love of literature and art. He left for France in 1831 to study medicine at the university in Strasbourg. At that time Strasbourg was a refuge for German liberals seeking asylum from the widespread political repression in the German states following the Napoleonic Wars. Because of a law requiring all Hessian students to attend a native institution for at least two years in order to receive a degree, however, Büchner returned to Hesse in 1833. He continued his studies at the university in Geissing and there become involved in radical politics. Early in 1834 he and some fellow

students founded an underground revolutionary group, the *Gesellschaft der Menschenrechte* ("Society for the Rights of Man"), whose aim was to reform the Hessian government and social structure. Shortly thereafter Büchner wrote a seditious pamphlet in collaboration with Friedrich Ludwig Weidig, an aging liberal devoted to revolutionary causes. The pamphlet, *Der Hessische Landbote* (1834; *The Hessian Courier*), was distributed secretly among Hessian peasants and workers by the society but had very little effect on them. (Indeed, many of the copies were handed over to the police.) After returning to his parents' home in Darmstadt while authorities conducted an investigation into the pamphlet's distributors, Büchner began to write his first play, *Danton's Death,* in the early months of 1835. Hoping the play's publication would help finance his escape from Germany before his impending arrest, Büchner sent the manuscript to Karl Gutzkow, a young German man of letters who succeeded in selling it to a publisher. Before he received payment for the play, however, Büchner was forced to flee the country. Subsequently, he renounced all revolutionary activity and resumed medical studies in Strasbourg, where, after writing a well-received dissertation, *Sur le système nerveux du barbeau* ("On the Nervous System of the Barbel"), he obtained his doctorate. During this time he also composed *Leonce and Lena* for a romantic comedy contest, wrote *Lenz,* and began work on *Woyzeck* and possibly on *Pietro Aretino,* a play that has since been lost. In late 1836 he moved to Switzerland, where he taught at the University of Zurich. Early the following year, Büchner became ill with typhus. He died in February 1837 at the age of twenty-four. Following Büchner's death, his family would not allow his manuscripts in their possession to be published. Moreover, Wilhelmine Jaegle, to whom Büchner was secretly engaged in Strasbourg and who initially cooperated with Gutzkow by sending him *Leonce and Lena* and *Lenz* for publication in his periodical *Telegraf für Deutschland,* eventually became unwilling to surrender the other writings by Büchner that she owned. She destroyed all of her copies of his writings before she died in 1880. The first significant and complete edition of Büchner's works did not appear until 1879, when Karl Emil Franzos issued *Sämtliche Werke und handschriftlicher Nachlaß* after years of interviewing Büchner's acquaintances and collecting his manuscripts, letters, and papers. In the 1880s the popular German playwright Gerhard Hauptmann enthusiastically praised Büchner, and in 1902 and 1913, respectively, *Danton's Death* and *Woyzeck* were given their first stage productions.

MAJOR WORKS

In his early political pamphlet *The Hessian Courier,* Büchner and his co-author urged the lower classes to violently rise against the landed aristocracy, basing this exhortation on the grounds of radical socioeconomic reasoning for the period. The work had little tangible effect, although it has since been regarded as an original and innovative revolutionary manifesto. Büchner's first literary work, *Danton's Death* is frequently regarded as an expression of the author's subsequent disillusionment with radical politics. The play focuses on the last days of French Revolutionary leader Georges Jacques Danton, who, after the new regime had been established, became a proponent of peace and thus came into conflict with fellow insurrectionist Maximilien de Robespierre. Accusing Danton of trying to overthrow the government, Robespierre has him guillotined. Büchner depicts Danton as a passive hero who succumbs to the forces that oppose and torment him. These forces, ostensibly Robespierre and his adherents, are in the abstract a historical inevitability, what Büchner called in an often-quoted letter the "terrible fatalism of history." While the dialogue of *Danton's Death* makes explicit Büchner's deterministic views, the themes of his later writings are more implicitly expressed. In the comedy

Leonce and Lena, the title characters, the Prince of Popo and the Princess of Pepe, are unwilling victims of a mutually unsatisfying arranged marriage. They each attempt to escape their fate by running away, but they meet again, neither realizing the other's identity. Ultimately they fall in love and, when their identities are revealed, marry. Seemingly a derivative and light romantic comedy, *Leonce and Lena* features dark overtones of suicidal boredom, pessimism, and despair, themes that are also emphasized in Büchner's last, uncompleted play, *Woyzeck.* The title character of this later play is a poor young army private who, driven to madness by jealousy and his vision of a wretched and futile existence, murders his girlfriend and then commits suicide. Regarded as one of the first plays to portray a lower-class hero, *Woyzeck* is often perceived as a work of trenchant social criticism. The forces oppressing Woyzeck are represented by three grotesque figures from a higher social class, each deeply motivated by the repressed hopelessness and suffering that characterize the universe of Büchner's plays. These characters include the Captain, who continually berates Woyzeck; the Drum Major, who is having an affair with Woyzeck's girlfriend; and the Doctor, who uses the private as an experimental subject, feeding him nothing but peas in order to determine his minimal nutritional requirements. Büchner's only work of prose fiction, the novella fragment *Lenz,* is based upon an episode in the life of *Sturm und Drang* ("Storm and Stress") playwright Jakob Michael Reinhold Lenz. This work portrays the gradual deterioration of Lenz's mind, culminating in his total mental collapse. To achieve realism in the story, Büchner employs a complex technique of shifting viewpoints to render each subtle nuance of Lenz's situation. Within a given paragraph, Büchner will often begin by describing a scene from the viewpoint of an objective third-person narrator, then abruptly switch to Lenz's sensory and psychological perspective, a method deemed very effective by critics.

CRITICAL RECEPTION

Since the discovery of Büchner's works in the late nineteenth century, criticism has been for the most part positive, underscoring a shift in aesthetic sensibilities that has made his writings far more acceptable to modern literary tastes than those of Büchner's own time. While some commentators have pointed to the discursive, unrefined quality of his writings, arguing that they lack the polish achieved by more mature artists, most contend that Büchner attained a remarkable artistic and philosophical sophistication during his brief life. *Woyzeck,* despite its unfinished state, has generally been regarded as Büchner's masterpiece. Together with the somewhat more thematically transparent *Danton's Death,* this play is thought to evince Büchner's unique philosophical outlook, since recognized as a forerunner to twentieth-century Existentialism and the Theater of the Absurd. Equally noted by scholars are the aesthetic concerns and techniques displayed in these works. Büchner's forward-looking dramatic methods and theories, traced by a few commentators to the works of William Shakespeare and the *Sturm und Drang* playwrights, are more typically thought to anticipate techniques employed by twentieth-century playwrights, particularly Bertolt Brecht. Additionally, Büchner's novella *Lenz* has generally been considered a seminal piece of German prose fiction, and a work that demonstrates Büchner's break with the dominant literary aesthetics of his age. In an early part of the story, Lenz discusses his theories of art, attacking the idealism of the German Romantics. Lenz states, "I demand of art that it be life. . . . Let them try just once to immerse themselves in the life of humble people and then reproduce this again in all its movements, its implications, its subtle, scarcely discernible play of expression." While some critics have argued that this statement merely summarizes Lenz's views on art, most critics accept it as also epitomizing Büchner's aesthetic precepts.

PRINCIPAL WORKS

Der Hessische Landbote [*The Hessian Courier*] [with Friedrich Ludwig Weidig] (pamphlet) 1834

Dantons Tod [*Danton's Death*] (play) 1835

Leonce und Lena [*Leonce and Lena*] (play) 1838

Lenz (unfinished novella) 1839

Nachgelassene Schriften (plays and unfinished novella) 1850

Sämtliche Werke und handschriftlicher Nachlaß (plays and unfinished novella) 1879

*Woyzeck (unfinished play) 1879

The Plays of Georg Büchner (plays) 1927

Sämtliche Werke und Briefe. 2 vols. (pamphlet, plays, unfinished novella, translations, and letters) 1967-71

Georg Büchner: The Complete Collected Works (pamphlet, plays, unfinished novella, translations, and letters) 1977

*This play was first published in *Sämtliche Werke und handschriftlicher Nachlaß*.

CRITICISM

Herbert Lindenberger (essay date 1964)

SOURCE: Lindenberger, Herbert. "Forebears, Descendants, and Contemporary Kin: Büchner and Literary Tradition." In *Georg Büchner*, pp. 115-44. Carbondale: Southern Illinois University Press, 1964.

[*In the following essay, Lindenberger seeks to establish Büchner's position between neoclassical and modern European literature.*]

Büchner's revolt against a classicism gone stale was by no means the first such revolt in German drama. The Storm-and-Stress writers of the 1770's, in the name of spontaneity and truthfulness to nature, and with Lessing's criticism and Shakespeare's example to back them, had succeeded in clearing the German stage of its dreary, "correct" neoclassical drama—a development of the mid-eighteenth century which, as we now see it, never produced anything of lasting value anyway and whose best-known work, Gottsched's *Dying Cato* (1730), is nothing more than a pale, academic imitation of French and English plays on the same theme. One can, indeed, look at the history of German drama as a kind of alternation between relatively tight "classical" forms of one sort or another, and looser forms which derive much of their energy from their conscious revolt against an out-going theatrical tradition. Bertolt Brecht's demand for an "epic theater" can be interpreted as the latest of a number of war cries which have resounded in German dramatic criticism at various times in the last two hundred years.

Büchner's work bears only superficial resemblances to the major single achievement of the Storm-and-Stress drama, Goethe's *Götz von Berlichingen* (1773). Like *Danton's Death, Götz* presents a vast historical panorama composed of short, loosely connected scenes. Through their common attempt to render what they saw as Shakespeare's truthfulness to nature, both writers achieved a fullness and earthiness of detail and created a multitude of characters who seem to breathe with a life of their own. Yet two works could scarcely be more different in spirit than *Götz* and **Danton's Death,** for Goethe's play above all demonstrates the possibility of heroic action and meaningful human relationships—the very values toward which Büchner's work expresses the most uncompromising skepticism.

But there was one dramatist of the '70's for whom Büchner felt a fundamental affinity, and that was Lenz. Büchner was drawn to Lenz not only through the personal sympathy he obviously felt toward him, but also through his interest in his plays, especially *The Private Tutor* (1774) and *The Soldiers* (1776), which he mentions in his story on Lenz. These two plays are essentially like miniature paintings, if I may borrow a term which Brecht applied to *The Private Tutor,* a play he adapted for his Berlin Ensemble.[1] In their fusion of comic and tragic moods, in their uncondescending representation of ordinary people, above all, in the concreteness and fullness with which they depict a contemporary environment, they look forward to **Woyzeck** more than any other works in earlier German drama. In his slightly ridiculous, pathetic heroes—the young cloth merchant Stolzius in *The Soldiers,* the private tutor Läuffer—Lenz presents a type of passive hero which Büchner could later develop in the character of Woyzeck. Like Büchner, Lenz allows his characters to reveal themselves through their peculiarities of language; within a single play, in fact, he presents a generous selection of human beings, each asserting his individuality by his manner of speech. Lenz' characters often seem sharply individualized in the way Büchner suggested through the words he put into Lenz' mouth: "If only artists would try to submerge themselves in the life of the very humblest person and to reproduce it with all its faint agitations, hints of experience, the subtle, hardly perceptible play of his features."[2]

The discussion of aesthetics in Büchner's story, partly drawn as it is from Lenz' own critical pronouncements, provides some clues to the aims the two writers hold in common. Among other things, the discussion stresses the dignity and the poetry inherent in the lives of ordinary people. Speaking of the characters he had tried to create in *The Private Tutor* and *The Soldiers,* Büchner's Lenz calls them "the most prosaic people in the world, but the emotional vein is identical in almost every individual; all that varies is the thickness of the shell which this vein must penetrate." For the artist to capture the individuality of every being, he cannot create his characters according to conventional "types" or preconceived molds of any sort, but must observe concretely, indeed, "submerge himself" as he puts it, in his individual characters. The doctrine of realism which Büchner propounds is something far removed from the much more "scientific" doctrines of many writers in the later nineteenth century. For instance, Büchner's Lenz finds an attitude of love prerequisite to all successful artistic creation: "One must love human nature in order to penetrate into the peculiar character of any individual; nobody, however insignificant, however ugly, should be despised; only then can one understand human kind as a whole." By what seems a kind of paradox, a writer can create a world of autonomous human beings only through the love he feels for them; as soon as he begins to despise them, his characters lose their individuality and become mere puppets. The artist, in fact, plays a role analogous to God's, both in the plenitude and the variety with which he creates his world: "I take it that God has made the world as it should be and that we can hardly hope to scrawl or daub anything better; our only aspiration should be to recreate modestly in His manner." And, like God, the artist has the ability to breathe life into inert matter; indeed, the artist's central function lies in his life-giving powers: "In all things I demand—life, the possibility of existence, and that's all; nor is it our business to ask whether it's beautiful, whether it's ugly. The feeling that there's life in the thing created is much more important than considerations of beauty and ugliness; it's the sole criterion in matters of art." To illustrate his theories, Büchner's Lenz contrasts the two types of art—the one represented by the Apollo Belvedere and a Raphael Madonna, the other by two Dutch or Flemish genre paintings he had recently seen. He finds the former works too "idealized," and as a result "they make me feel

quite dead." The genre paintings, which he goes on to describe in detail, "reproduce nature for me with the greatest degree of truthfulness, so that I can feel [the artist's] creation."

Except for a few remarks here and there in his letters, the discussion of aesthetics in *Lenz* is Büchner's only commentary on his own artistic ideals. But this discussion by no means provides a full rationale for his work; what it tells us—and quite appropriately so—is the points of contact he must have felt with the real Lenz. The analogy which it sets up between their literary art and genre paintings itself suggests the limits within which one may profitably compare their work. Lenz' best plays have something of the charm and the unpretentiousness which we associate with genre art, but they do not attempt to reach beyond the social frame of reference in which they are so securely rooted. (At the end of *The Private Tutor* and *The Soldiers* Lenz, in fact, shamelessly draws a pedantic social moral from his tale—a moral which, in each play, is quite inadequate to account for the richness of life which the play had seemed above all to depict.) Still, Lenz knew better than to attempt to ask the existential questions which echo so naturally out of Büchner's world. The range of reference encompassed by Büchner's plays is immeasurably wider than that of Lenz'. The discussion of aesthetics in Büchner's story, though it provides a rationale for his dramatic objectivity and his richness of detail, takes no account of many elements fundamental to his work—for example, the grotesque characterizations in *Woyzeck,* the verbal complexity and virtuosity of all three plays, the images of an inverted world which emerge out of *Danton's Death* and *Woyzeck.* Though Büchner's critics often depend on the discussion of aesthetics in *Lenz* to provide a theoretical framework for his art, one wonders if the statement, "I take it that God has made the world as it should be" (a statement, incidentally, which Büchner drew from Lenz' *Notes on the Theater*—1774), is really applicable to a body of work which continually voices its despair at the results of God's creation.

"The idealistic movement was just beginning at that time"—with these words, so fateful for Lenz, Büchner begins the discussion of aesthetics in his story. In 1778, the time in which the story takes place, Goethe was already firmly entrenched in the courtly world of Weimar and was working on *Iphigenia in Tauris,* the first of his major plays in his so-called "classical" manner. The Storm-and-Stress revolt had by this time spent its force (except for Schiller's explosive early plays, which date from the early '80's). For Lenz the advent of the "idealistic" period meant the end of a world in which he could feel himself significantly creative; the very basis of his talent was an earthy realism which the new art-ideals which were to emanate from Weimar for the next generation could scarcely accommodate.

By the time Büchner began to write, the "idealistic movement" (which German literary historians have conventionally divided into two phases—Classicism and Romanticism, the latter itself subdivided into two phases) had also spent its force. It was only natural for Büchner to seek a model in a writer from an earlier era. But Büchner's obvious antipathy to the plays which the idealistic movement produced must not blind us to the real and enduring achievement which marks this drama at its best. The major dramatic works of German Classicism, Goethe's *Iphigenia* (completed in 1786) and *Torquato Tasso* (1789) and Schiller's *Wallenstein* trilogy (1799), though they are little known today outside Germany, can easily hold their own among the world's great dramas. But a contemporary audience can scarcely approach them without some conception of the artistic and cultural premises on which they are based. For one thing, these plays are part of Goethe and Schiller's attempt to found a national culture, of which they saw a national drama as an indispensable cornerstone. Unlike England, France and Spain during their major periods of dramatic writing, Germany lacked a vital popular theatrical tradition; as a result, the plays of Goethe and Schiller often seem a kind of hothouse growth, nurtured with a deliberateness and high-mindedness which can all too easily create a barrier to modern taste.

The dramaturgy on which these plays is based is far more closely related to that of French seventeenth-century drama than it is to Shakespeare, though it is by no means a slavish imitation of earlier models, as was the earlier type of German drama represented by *The Dying Cato*. Compared to the Storm-and-Stress plays and Büchner's work, the German Classical plays remain essentially within the Aristotelian dramatic tradition. Their characters are invariably of high station. Their chief dramatic effects emerge out of a carefully contrived, though often relatively simple plot. In striking contrast to the Storm-and-Stress drama, they cultivate an economy of means, with the result that they sacrifice richness of detail for a more austere, lofty effect. Whereas the Storm-and-Stress plays, like Büchner's, were generally in prose, most of the Classical dramas are in blank verse—a verse, indeed, of a rather formal sort, with a diction and syntax deliberately removed from those of ordinary conversation. A work such as *Wallenstein* (which, though publicized and translated into English verse by so powerful a voice as Coleridge's, is scarcely known today to English-speaking readers) succeeds in creating a type of effect quite foreign to that of the various German anti-Aristotelian dramas before and after it. For in *Wallenstein* Schiller, like the ancient Greek tragedians, is centrally concerned with the mysteries inherent in a man's relation to his destiny; his dramatic method, with its cunning contrivance of plot, its disdain for "extraneous" detail, and its careful balance of concrete situation and abstract idea, allows the larger metaphysical questions to emerge natu-

rally out of his fable with an intensity and singularity of effect which dramatists such as Büchner and Brecht have chosen to do without.

A sympathetic reading of the major German plays in the "classical" manner suggests that the distinction which Büchner's Lenz draws between "idealized" and "real" characters is not altogether fair to the actual practice of Goethe and Schiller. The characters of *Wallenstein,* for instance, are "idealized" only to the extent that they speak a somewhat heightened language and are not depicted in the informal situations in which Büchner customarily presents his characters. But Schiller's characters at their best are also concretely differentiated from one another and, once one accepts the premises of his dramatic method, the reader or audience quite naturally comes to believe in them as living beings. Büchner, like any artist confronting a mode of art antithetical to his own, probably did not bother to distinguish between Schiller at his best and at his worst: his two recorded comments on Schiller, both of them negative, attack him for being too "rhetorical" and for creating characters who are essentially "puppets with sky-blue noses and affected pathos, but not flesh-and-blood human beings."[3] And with the notable exception of *Wallenstein* (and perhaps also his uncompleted play *Demetrius*—1805), one must admit that Büchner's view of Schiller's "classical" plays is more or less a just one. In a play such as *The Bride of Messina* (1802), a much more conscious attempt than *Wallenstein* to re-create the effect of Greek tragedy, Schiller's high-mindedness comes to seem virtually unbearable. And, quite in contrast to *Wallenstein,* such later historical plays as *The Maid of Orleans* (1801), *Mary Stuart* (1800) and *William Tell* (1804) fail to embody their lofty central "idea" in any concrete dramatic situation in which a modern audience can honestly believe.

By the time Büchner wrote his first play Schiller had been dead for thirty years and was firmly entrenched as the chief classic of the German theater. Indeed, the rhetoric and the "affected pathos" of which Büchner complains had become standard conventions of German drama—conventions so deeply rooted that the major German dramatists of our century have felt a continuing need to challenge them. It seems only natural that writers like Gerhart Hauptmann and Brecht would look back to Büchner—as the latter looked back to Lenz—as a forerunner in their revolt against the Classical tradition in German drama.

But Büchner was not the first writer in his own century to challenge this tradition. At least two writers, Heinrich von Kleist and Christian Dietrich Grabbe, experimented with significantly new ways of dramatic expression. On the surface, at least, Kleist's plays seem to continue the Classical framework, for they utilize the basic conventions which Goethe and Schiller had established in their Classical plays. Kleist's major plays, *The Broken Jug* (1806), *Penthesilea* (1808), and *The Prince of Homburg* (1810), all maintain the formality of blank verse, and all are marked by the most rigorous economy of structure. Like the Classical plays before them, they are built out of a closely connected chain of events which lead up to the climax (the first two of these plays, though they are full length, each consist of a single, sustained act); and quite unlike Büchner's dramas they allow their central conflicts to develop through the direct confrontation of characters with one another.

Yet, despite his apparently traditional form, Kleist was far less an imitator than an innovator. His language, though elevated in diction, has a taut and breathless quality which, more than any other dramatic blank verse in German, creates the illusion of being spoken by living beings. Moreover, despite his Classical dramaturgy, which is predicated on the assumption that characters can express their conflicts with one another in verbal terms, his plays, like Büchner's, ultimately suggest the inability of human beings to communicate meaningfully at all. In *Penthesilea,* for example, the two chief characters appear to communicate with one another in an idyllic love scene, but the heroine, discovering that their relationship is based on a fundamental misunderstanding, ends up tricking her lover into a brutal death-trap. Kleist, one might say, exploits a dramatic method based on character relationships only to lay bare the deceptiveness inherent in these relationships. Like Büchner, Kleist was little known or appreciated in his own time; there is, in fact, no reason to think that Büchner discerned his real significance, if he read him at all. Yet despite their basic differences in dramatic technique, Kleist and Büchner share a certain kinship through the skepticism and the despair which their works voice with a notable lack of pretentiousness; and it hardly seems accidental that Kleist's plays, like Büchner's, achieved no general acclaim until our own century.

Grabbe, too, was little understood in his age. Although the quality of his achievement is considerably below that of Kleist and Büchner, his experiments in dramatic form anticipate much that Büchner was to develop in his own way. Grabbe's early plays are still largely in the grand style, and their blank verse betrays the staleness into which the language of Classical drama had fallen in the generation after Schiller. His heroes, quite in contrast to Büchner's, are also conceived in the grand manner; all, in fact, are men of titanic proportions—Napoleon, Hannibal, the Hohenstaufen emperors—who go to their doom through no fault of their own, but through the pettiness of a world which cannot support such titans. But Grabbe's later plays, above all *Napoleon or the Hundred Days* (1831) and *Hannibal* (1835), seem just as boldly "experimental" as **Danton's Death.**

Napoleon, which Büchner doubtless knew when he wrote his first play, presents a vast panoramic view of the events immediately leading up to Waterloo. Grabbe makes no attempt, as would a dramatist in the Classical tradition, to present these events in any causal chain. The play, in fact, is essentially a vivid and bounteous chronicle which focuses on such diverse phenomena as the crowds on the streets of Paris, soldiers in barracks on the eve of battle, the newly restored Bourbon court, and Napoleon vainly attempting to re-establish his past glory without realizing he lacked the means to do so. *Napoleon* is written in a terse and racy prose, a style which, unlike the verse of his earlier tragedies, is able to accommodate a wide variety of tones and to portray the historical milieu with a lively intimacy. In its mixture of comic and tragic elements, its technique of short, contrasting scenes, and its treatment of the common people caught up by vast historical forces, it may well have served as a model for **Danton's Death.** Though *Napoleon* still reads with a certain vitality, Grabbe did not, like Büchner, succeed in fusing the quite diverse components of his play to create a single, closely organized whole; and as a result, the play remains far more interesting in its individual details than in its totality. Above all, Grabbe lacks that quality of dramatic objectivity which I have tried to describe in Büchner's work. Karl Gutzkow tried to define this difference between the two writers in a letter he wrote to Büchner to encourage him in his work: "If one observes [Grabbe's] stiff, forced, bony manner, one must make the most favorable predictions for your fresh, effervescent natural powers."[4] If Gutzkow's statement is perhaps a bit unfair to Grabbe, it is also notable as the most powerful critical praise Büchner was to receive either in his lifetime or until half a century after his death.

II

It is a tribute to the richness and variety of Büchner's achievement that each of the writers who have felt his impact have absorbed a different aspect of his work. Gerhart Hauptmann, the first major figure whom Büchner influenced, shares Büchner's sympathy for the sufferings of lowly people. Hauptmann's career, which spans almost six decades, includes a vast variety of forms and themes, from contemporary social realism to symbolic fantasy to grand-style tragedy based on Greek myth. But Hauptmann seems closest to Büchner in his early, largely realistic period. His short story, *The Apostle* (1890), a study of a modern religious fanatic, attempts to imitate the narrative method of Büchner's **Lenz**; yet Hauptmann's interior monologue today reads like a somewhat dated technical experiment, while Büchner's retains a freshness and naturalness which belie its great distance from us in time. Hauptmann perhaps came closest to the spirit of Büchner's work in his drama *The Weavers* (1892) which depicts an actual peasant uprising of the 1840's such as Büchner might have stirred up in his Giessen days. But Hauptmann's play is no socialist tract, as its early audiences often thought. Like Büchner in **Danton's Death,** Hauptmann questions the value of revolution while at the same time showing a high degree of sympathy for the grievances of the common people he is portraying.

In two later plays, *Henschel the Carter* (1898) and *Rose Bernd* (1903), Hauptmann, like Büchner in **Woyzeck,** succeeds in giving a traditional tragic dignity to inarticulate and passive characters of humble background. Hauptmann goes much further than Büchner in attempting to paint a detailed and authentic social milieu; indeed, the Silesian dialect of the original version of *The Weavers* would have proved so difficult for German readers that he had to "translate" the play into a more easily comprehensible form. Hauptmann's figures often have the brooding, explosive quality that he doubtless discerned in many of Büchner's figures, perhaps even in Büchner himself, whose genius Hauptmann once characterized as "glowing lava hurled out of Chthonic depths."[5] The characters and backgrounds of Hauptmann's best "realist" plays still seem impressive today, though his dramaturgy, with its well-wrought plots and his carefully planned motivations and foreshadowings, seems somewhat old-fashioned next to Büchner's, which shares the disdain for traditional theatrical effect of much contemporary drama.

If Hauptmann drew largely from the realistic side of Büchner's work, Frank Wedekind drew from the "unreal" side of Büchner, above all, the grotesque element which he discerned in the doctor, captain and carnival figures in **Woyzeck.** In his early play, *The Awakening of Spring* (1891), a violent and impassioned protest against the suppression of sexual knowledge in the education of the young, Wedekind depicts his middle-class characters as the kind of grotesque, perverted beings Büchner had presented before him. But Wedekind's entire poetic world is made up of grotesque types: the naturalness and dramatic objectivity with which characters such as Büchner's Marie, Marion and Danton are presented were totally foreign to Wedekind's talent. Ideologically, however, Wedekind's plays attempt to propagate a doctrine of naturalness; thus, in his character Lulu, the heroine of *The Earth Spirit* and its sequel, *Pandora's Box* (1895), Wedekind created a symbol of amoral and instinctual nature. As a literary type, Lulu is perhaps less akin to Büchner's Marie than to his drum major, whom she resembles in the exaggerated manner in which her "naturalness" is depicted.

Wedekind's success as a dramatic artist, one realizes today, falls short of his success as a liberating force in German culture at the turn of the century; though he was often capable of crudely powerful effects, he rarely succeeded in finding an adequate dramatic embodiment for the new ideas he was so intent on disseminating. Even if one admires his integrity, his Lulu, one must admit, is a rather dated creature who lives less surely in

Wedekind's plays than in the opera which Alban Berg built around her. Through Wedekind, however, one side of Büchner—the rebel against bourgeois convention and the creator of the grotesquely extravagant language which Wedekind found in parts of **Woyzeck**—was transmitted to the Expressionist dramatists who followed him and, above all, to Bertolt Brecht.[6]

The fact that Berg's only two operas are based on **Woyzeck** and the Lulu plays is, I think, a testimony to the continuity which Berg's generation felt between Büchner's and Wedekind's work. Berg's setting (1921) of Büchner's play is itself an important instance of the impact of Büchner on our own century. Berg prepared his own libretto, and at first sight one feels amazed at how closely he followed Büchner's text. To be sure, he used only about two thirds of Büchner's scenes, and even these were sometimes pared down for economy's sake. But Berg stuck to the original dialogue to a relatively high degree and managed to retain much of the flavor of the play. His musical method, indeed, often succeeds in heightening Büchner's most original dramatic effects. For example, in Marie's repentance scene the music shifts back and forth in mood as Marie alternately reads from the Bible and expresses her own thoughts, and at the end of the scene it reaches a climax as piercing as any one might imagine from the text.

In its total effect, however, the opera seems a work of a very different kind from the play. Through the heavy orchestral commentary, which presents the composer's point of view on the events, the characters seem far less autonomous beings than they do in the original. The orchestra, in addition, serves to underline that sense of a malign fate which, because of the difference between the two media, hovers over the play in a far less distinct way. Indeed, the atonality of much of the music seems ideally suited to producing the eerie effects which Berg so obviously sought, especially in the final scenes. The character Wozzeck (whose name Berg spelled as it appeared in the Franzos edition of Büchner) seems even more passive and inarticulate than he does in the play. Among the passages which Berg cut out are those in which he asserts his dignity, for example the scene in which he gives Andres his belongings and reads his identification papers. Berg quite deliberately emphasized the abnormality and the suffering of his hero, who thus emerges as a helpless, crazed animal. Berg's version also stressed the economic degradation of the characters; in fact, the musical phrase which accompanies Wozzeck's words, "Wir arme Leut'"—"We poor folk"—is the chief leitmotif of the opera, achieving its fullest force in the long and powerful orchestral interlude which directly follows Wozzeck's suicide.

Berg's emphasis on the play's psychological and social aspects is accompanied by a lack of emphasis on the existential questions which Büchner poses so persistently throughout his work, for example in the complex mananimal imagery and in the grandmother's tale (of which Berg uses only a fragment). Büchner's existential questions depend, above all, on strictly literary means of expression for which Berg wisely did not seek a direct musical equivalent. Indeed, Büchner's basic dramatic method, with its loosely connected scenes which could seemingly be placed in several different combinations, in the opera becomes transformed into an entirely different mode of dramaturgy. Through the constant orchestral commentary, and, above all, through the interludes between scenes, each event seems to follow the last with the most frightening inevitability. Berg concentrates almost exclusively on the "main line" of plot and excludes everything that he must have thought subsidiary to it—for example, the carnival scenes, the conversation with the Jewish pawnbroker, in fact that whole crowded larger world which hovers around the edges of Büchner's play. Even the comic touches, grim as they are in the play, are almost missing from the opera; one is scarcely tempted to laugh during the scene between Wozzeck and the doctor, and largely, I think, because of the quite uncomic effect of the musical accompaniment (partly also because Berg, who was perhaps worried about getting his work performed, shifted the doctor's experiment from the excretory to the respiratory functions). The opera, as a result, has a kind of classical starkness and solemnity quite foreign to the spirit of the play. It seems to me symptomatic of Berg's classicism that every scene consists of a different musical form, each systematically different from the others. The following summary,[7] based on Berg's stated intentions, suggests the form-consciousness which governs the opera (scene numbers in parentheses, music in italics):

Act I. Exposition, Wozzeck and his relation to his environment / *five character sketches*: (1) the captain / *suite*; (2) Andres / *rhapsody*; (3) Marie / *military march and cradle song*; (4) the physician / *passacaglia*; (5) the drum major / *andante affettuoso (quasi rondo)*.

Act II. Dénouement, Wozzeck is gradually convinced of Marie's infidelity / *symphony in five movements*: (1) Wozzeck's first suspicion / *sonata form*; (2) Wozzeck is mocked / *fantasie and fugue*; (3) Wozzeck accuses Marie / *largo*; (4) Marie and drum major dance / *scherzo*; (5) the drum major trounces Wozzeck / *rondo martiale*.

Act III. Catastrophe, Wozzeck murders Marie and atones through suicide / *six inventions*: (1) Marie's remorse / *invention on a theme*; (2) death of Marie / *invention on a tone*; (3) Wozzeck tries to forget / *invention on a rhythm*; (4) Wozzeck drowns in the pond / *invention on a six-tone chord; instrumental interlude* with closed curtain; (5) Marie's son plays unconcerned / *invention on a persistent rhythm (perpetuum mobile)*.

Berg himself tells us that he chose such diverse forms to embody each scene in order to avoid the effect of musical monotony.[8] One must admit, surely, that even after repeated hearings the listener remains unaware of the nature of the various forms which Berg employs. Yet the form-consciousness which is manifest in the above chart is indicative, I think, of a kind of classicism peculiar to much of the art of the 1920's. It seems to me analogous, for instance, to the mythological framework and charts of correspondences around which James Joyce constructed *Ulysses*; T. S. Eliot's well-known description of the function of Joyce's mythological framework—"It is simply a way of controlling, of ordering, of giving a shape and a significance to the immense panorama of futility and anarchy which is contemporary history"[9]—is perhaps applicable to the function of the tight musical forms which Berg employs to contain the chaotic and characteristically modern materials that he found in Büchner's play. The resulting opera achieves a greatness that remains independent of that of the play; one recognizes it as a work of equal, though by no means kindred genius. Since Berg's work has made its way in recent years into the repertory of all the major opera houses, one hopes that the strong competition it offers will not exclude the play from theatrical performance, which, up to now, it has rarely achieved in the English-speaking countries.

Our sense of Büchner's modernity has been shaped to a large degree through his impact upon, and his affinities with the two most significant developments in European theater during the last few decades—the work of Bertolt Brecht, on the one hand, and the *avant garde* theater in Paris after World War II. It was only natural that Brecht should look back to Büchner as an example: not only did Brecht view Büchner as a fellow political revolutionary, but Büchner's work stood for many of the same values that Brecht throughout his life sought to articulate. Both writers, for instance, succeeded in creating a vital and glowing dramatic language by first refusing to be poetic in any traditional way. Like Büchner, Brecht created an idiom of his own, colloquial, earthy, ironical—an idiom, moreover, which appears to imitate the language of real men, yet which in its total effect has a richly poetic resonance. Brecht's, like Büchner's, is a realism which refuses to be pedantically realistic: the red moon which hovers menacingly over the murder scene in **Woyzeck** was conceived in something of the same spirit as the red moon which, at the end of Brecht's early play *Drums in the Night* (1919), turns out to be a Chinese lantern which the embittered hero angrily destroys.

Brecht's language is perhaps most directly imitative of Büchner's in his first play, *Baal* (1918), whose bohemian hero speaks a wildly extravagant language which Brecht, like Wedekind before him, developed from such examples as Woyzeck's descriptions of his visions and such caricatures as Büchner's doctor, captain and carnival figures. But Brecht's affinities with Büchner cannot be defined simply through such instances of imitation; one could argue, in fact, that the personal idiom he achieved in his more mature work, through its poise and control, has more in common with Büchner's language than anything in *Baal.* Both writers, moreover, attain much of their creative impulse through their conscious opposition to the conventions of the German Classical drama. For Brecht, as for Wedekind, Büchner served as a kind of liberating force, not only against the Classical drama, but against the middle-class values with which this drama was associated in their minds. The Schiller-like rhetoric which Büchner parodies in the speeches of the drunken stage-prompter Simon in **Danton's Death** is sustained through two full-length plays by Brecht, *St. Joan of the Stockyards* (1930) and *The Resistible Rise of Arturo Ui* (1941), whose intentionally pompous blank verse succeeds in parodying not so much the Chicago capitalists who are made to speak it as the middle-class Germans whose slavish awe of their theatrical classics was for Brecht a sure symptom of their false cultural values.

Not only must Brecht have discerned in Büchner a fellow enemy of theatrical rhetoric, but the forms of organization which Büchner developed in his three plays provided the most successful German example before Brecht of a non-Aristotelian serious drama. In certain crucial respects—for instance, in their disdain for linear plots and their stress on the relative independence of individual scenes—Büchner's plays can surely be seen as ancestors of Brecht's "epic" theater. But Brecht's much-publicized theoretical pronouncements on the nature of epic theater cannot be applied literally to Büchner's plays, nor, it could be argued, to Brecht's own best works; the so-called "alienation effect," whereby the audience is discouraged from believing in the literal reality of the events enacted onstage, is scarcely applicable to plays such as **Danton's Death** and **Woyzeck,** whose dramatic reality we are made to accept wholeheartedly and with whose heroes we sympathize to a high degree. Although Brecht attempted to create most of his heroes as didactic negative examples and to hold back the audience's sympathy with them, some of his greatest figures—for instance, the cowardly Galileo, the greedy vendor Mother Courage, the alternately hearty and sour Finnish businessman Mr. Puntila—despite their author's intentions, achieve something of the autonomous life and the sympathetic quality which we find in Büchner's Danton and Woyzeck.

Like Büchner, Brecht has a penchant for passive heroes who allow the world to shape them as it will; Brecht, indeed, has perhaps gone further than any major dramatist in exploring the psychology of passivity—for instance, in the well-meaning porter Galy Gay in *Man Equals Man* (1926), who is cajoled into assuming the

identity of another man and becoming a brutal soldier; in the hero of *The Life of Galileo* (1939), who compromises his principles for the sake of bodily comfort and privacy to pursue his writings; in the good soldier Schweik, who, transferred by Brecht from Jaroslav Hašek's novel (itself an extension of the comic possibilities in the character of Woyzeck) to a more modern setting in *Schweik in the Second World War* (1944), manages to survive and sometimes even to confound the Nazis by pretending to comply with them.

The essential humanitarianism which underlies both Büchner's and Brecht's work finds expression partly through their common skepticism toward older forms of humanitarianism which they see as false or stale. The skepticism with which Büchner treats the doctor's traditionally idealistic definitions of the human being finds its modern equivalent in such Brechtian formulations as the title and theme of *Man Equals Man,* which attempts to demonstrate that one human being *can* be changed into another, or Macheath's cynical refrain in *The Threepenny Opera* (1928):

> What does a man live by? By grinding, sweating,
> Defeating, beating, cheating, eating some other man
> For he can only live by sheer forgetting
> Forgetting that he ever was a man.[10]

The title of the parable play *The Good Person* [*Der gute Mensch*] *of Setzuan* (1940) seems almost an echo of the phrase which Büchner ironically puts into the captain's mouth time and again—"Woyzeck, du bist ein guter Mensch, ein guter Mensch"; the captain's phrase is as empty of real meaning as is the title of Brecht's play, whose parable attempts to demonstrate the impossibility of being "good" in the world as it is. Just as the work of both writers achieved a poetic quality only after their deliberate rejection of older, staler forms of poetic language, so it succeeds in expounding a humanitarianism through their tough-minded distrust of smug, traditional ethical statements.

It seems no accident that Büchner achieved his first major acclaim outside Germany in the French theater of the last two decades, for his plays anticipate many of the themes and techniques of the so-called "theater of the absurd." One might note, for instance, the following passage from the promenade scene in **Danton's Death** (Act II, Scene 2), in which Büchner records the conversation of two gentlemen walking along the street:

FIRST GENTLEMAN

> You know, it is the most extraordinary discovery! I mean, it makes all the branches of science look entirely different. Mankind really is striding towards its high destiny.

SECOND GENTLEMAN

> Have you seen that new play? There's a great Babylonian tower, a mass of arches and steps and passages,

and then, do you know, they blow the whole thing up, right into the air, just like that! It makes you dizzy. Quite extraordinary. [*He stops, perplexed.*]

FIRST GENTLEMAN

Why, whatever's the matter?

SECOND GENTLEMAN

Oh, nothing, really! But—would you just give me a hand—over this puddle—there! Thank you very much. I only just got over it. That could be extremely dangerous!

FIRST GENTLEMAN

You weren't afraid of it, were you?

SECOND GENTLEMAN

Well, yes—the earth's only a very thin crust, you know. I always think I might fall through where there's a hole like that. You have to walk very gently or you may easily go through. But do go and see that play—I thoroughly recommend it!

This passage could easily be mistaken for one of the random street conversations which one finds, say, in *The Killer* (1957) by Eugène Ionesco, who himself once listed Büchner, in company with Aeschylus, Sophocles, Shakespeare, and Kleist, as the only dramatist of the past whom he still found readable.[11]

Büchner, like Ionesco in similar passages, provides no context for this conversation: we are never told, for instance, what sort of scientific discovery the first gentleman is even talking about; much of the comic effect, indeed, comes from Büchner's deliberate failure to provide any context at all for the gentleman's pretentious remarks. Like the recent French dramatists, Büchner is concerned with exposing the emptiness inherent in the clichés with which people customarily express themselves ("Mankind . . . striding towards its high destiny"). By attempting to record conversation as it is really spoken—not, as in earlier drama, as it *ought* to be spoken—he exposes, as well, the absurdity of the transitions within ordinary human speech: the second gentleman, for example, moves unself-consciously from his enthusiasm for a new play to his fear of the hole in the street and then, at the end of the passage (which is also the end of the scene) directly back to the play in question. If one examines the transition (or lack of it) from the first to the second speech, one notes that the characters are shown talking *past* one another instead of *with* one another. Indeed, there is no real contact between them: the first is fully concerned with his statement about some scientific discovery, the second with his enthusiasm for a play he has seen. In thus demonstrating that human beings often fail to make contact even while they appear to be conversing, Büchner anticipates a technique that was not to be exploited to any great degree in drama until Chekhov and the recent French dramatists. The difficulty of human communication is not merely the theme of this small passage, but is, after all, one of the central themes of *Danton's Death* as a whole: one need only remember Danton's statement to his wife, on the first page of the play, of the impossibility of people really knowing one another. And it is a central theme, moreover, in such otherwise diverse contemporary plays as Arthur Adamov's *The Parody* (1947), Ionesco's *The Bald Soprano* (1948), and Beckett's *Waiting for Godot* (1952).

In fact, to catalogue the themes of the "theater of the absurd" is at once to catalogue many of Büchner's essential themes. The terror, absurd and frightening at once, which lurks behind Adamov's *The Large and the Small Maneuver* (1950) and *Each against Each* (1952) is similar in kind to the terror in the background of *Danton's Death,* which Adamov had himself translated into French a few years before completing these plays; moreover, the totalitarian political rhetoric which resounds in both plays is essentially a modern version of the brutally lifeless language of Robespierre's and St. Just's public pronouncements. The skepticism towards their self-identity which plagues the central characters of *Waiting for Godot* and Adamov's *Professor Taranne* (1951) has much in common with Leonce's skepticism in Büchner's comedy. The vaudeville routines which Beckett's clowns use to while away the time that hangs so oppressively on them corresponds quite precisely to the *commedia dell'arte* techniques employed by Leonce and Valerio to fulfill the same purpose.[12] Indeed, the very words with which Didi in *Waiting for Godot* voices his boredom and despair might easily have come from one of Danton's, or Leonce's, or Lenz' speeches: "We wait. We are bored. No, don't protest, we are bored to death, there's no denying it. Good. A diversion comes along and what do we do? We let it go to waste. Come, let's get to work! In an instant all will vanish and we'll be alone once more, in the midst of nothingness!"[13]

In the face of such an insight, voiced with equal emphasis by Büchner and Beckett, all human endeavor comes to seem futile, meaningless, and absurd. As Lee Baxandall has suggested in his essay on *Danton's Death,* the agonized lyricism of Büchner's first play "finds its closest modern counterpart" in *Waiting for Godot.*[14] And it is through this lyricism, one might add, that Beckett, more than any of his contemporaries, has captured that sense of mystery which ultimately stands behind the despair in Büchner's plays. Moreover, through its plotlessness, its vagueness of setting, and its lack of any real social framework, *Waiting for Godot* seems a kind of Büchner play with its narrative and its background removed. Or, rather, one could view it as a more radical step than the ones Büchner had taken in *Danton's Death* and *Woyzeck* to break down the canons of classical drama.

Yet a comparison of Büchner with the recent French dramatists also suggests some vital differences in purpose and form between his work and theirs. However strikingly Büchner's work may anticipate the significant experiments of our time, it also, for instance, employs certain traditional methods of characterization which the French dramatists have largely abandoned. Thus, Büchner attempted, as the French have chosen not to, to create the illusion of a full and varied world of real beings rooted in a real and recognizable environment. Marie in **Woyzeck** has a completeness and a reality that go well beyond her dramatic function in the play; when she sits before the mirror admiring her new earrings she gains our sympathy in a way that no character—except, perhaps, some of Beckett's—in any of the recent French plays can. Directly after the execution of the Dantonists, a woman passerby makes the sort of statement one often finds in Ionesco's plays: "I always say you ought to see a man in different surroundings; I'm all for these public executions, aren't you, love?" But the effect of these lines is shattering in a way that they could not be in Ionesco. Because of the interest and sympathy which Danton and his friends have aroused in us throughout the play, the passerby's statement causes us to feel at once the tragedy and the absurdity of their death. In contrast, the ironic statements made by the maid in Ionesco's *The Lesson* (1950) after the professor, in a fit of ire, has stabbed his pupil, suggest only the absurdity of the pupil's death. Ionesco, one might say, has dehumanized his characters in order to portray the precariousness and isolation in which they exist, while Büchner has demonstrated a similar precariousness and isolation by more traditional means—by first making us believe in the reality of his characters and their background. In the world of Büchner's plays we still feel the plenitude of creation, even if God's traditional beneficence is missing and his existence is, at most, a questionable thing.

III

The vitality and the fullness of vision which characterize Büchner's dramatic world have rarely been achieved by those whom he has influenced, perhaps only by Brecht, but these qualities are present in far greater abundance in the dramatist whose impact Büchner felt more strongly than that of any other, namely, Shakespeare. Shakespeare, indeed, is the one writer for whom Büchner expressed the highest and most unqualified admiration. "Poor Shakespeare was a clerk by day and had to write his poetry at night, and I, who am not worthy to untie his shoelaces, have a much easier time," Büchner wrote to his fiancée a few weeks before his death.[15] In his first letter to Gutzkow, when excusing himself for not being entirely true to history in *Danton's Death,* he consoled himself with the notion that "all poets, with the exception of Shakespeare, confront history and nature as though they were school-boys."[16]

The "fullness of life" which Büchner's character Lenz upholds so passionately as the central goal of art can be found only—thus we are told in the story—in Shakespeare and in folk poetry, and sometimes in Goethe—"everything else should be thrown in the fire." Like nearly all German writers for at least a generation before him, Büchner had been smitten by Shakespeare's plays since childhood; one of his Darmstadt schoolmates, in fact, testifies how Büchner and his friends would go to a nearby beech forest to read Shakespeare to one another on Sunday afternoons.[17]

The many verbal echoes from Shakespeare in Büchner's work have been scrupulously recorded by various scholars,[18] and I shall not attempt to add to their findings here. It seems no surprise to find that Büchner echoed *Hamlet* more than any other Shakespearean play, indeed more than any other literary work. The influence of *Hamlet* went considerably beyond the verbal level. In their passivity, their introspectiveness and their verbal ingenuity, characters like Danton and Leonce obviously have something of Hamlet in them, though they derive as much from the various Hamlet-like heroes of German Romanticism as from the character actually created by Shakespeare. In her pathos and madness Lucille, in **Danton's Death,** has certain affinities with Ophelia. The deathly atmosphere, moreover, which permeates Büchner's first play has much in common with the atmosphere of Shakespeare's play.

It is worth noting, furthermore, that Büchner sometimes resorted to Shakespeare during the tensest dramatic moments of his plays. When Lucille laments the death of her husband, she speaks like Lear on the death of Cordelia: "Dying—dying—! But everything lives, everything's got to live, I mean, the little fly there, the bird. Why can't he?" Woyzeck's last words, in turn, echo Lady Macbeth's feelings of guilt: "Am I still bloody? I better wash up. There's a spot and there's another." Only a dramatist in another language would dare echo such familiar lines at such crucial moments in his own work; for an English dramatist to do so would be to risk writing a parody.

More significant than such echoes is the fact that Büchner succeeded—better, perhaps, than any other German dramatist—in imitating Shakespeare's manner while at the same time integrating it fully into the contexts he himself was creating. His Shakespearean imitation is most fully evident in **Danton's Death,** and it becomes progressively less evident in each of his two other plays. The following passage, in which the carters standing outside the Conciergerie are waiting to take Danton and his friends to the guillotine, has a genuinely Shakespearean quality about it (more so, I might add, in the German than in translation):

SECOND CARTER

Well, who would you say was the best carters?

FIRST CARTER

Whoever goes farthest and quickest.

SECOND CARTER

Well, you old fool, you can't cart a man much further than out of this world, can you, and I'd like to see anyone do it in less than a quarter of an hour. It's exactly a quarter of an hour from here to Guillotine Square.

JAILER

Hurry up, you lazy slugs! Get in nearer the gate. Get back a bit, you girls.

FIRST CARTER

No, don't you budge! Never go round a girl, always go through.

SECOND CARTER

I'm with you there. You can take your horse and cart in with you, the roads are nice, but you'll be in quarantine when you come out again. [*They move forward.*] What are you gawping at?

A WOMAN

Waiting to see our old customers, dearie.

SECOND CARTER

My cart's not a brothel, you know. This is a decent cart, this is; the King went in this, and all the big nobs in Paris.

The bawdy and far-fetched jokes are obviously typical of the banter of Shakespeare's clowns and fools. But Büchner has not only captured the tone of this banter, he has also understood the dramatic function which this sort of banter has in a Shakespearean tragedy. Like the gravedigger scene in *Hamlet,* this passage creates a needed slackening of tension between the two anguished scenes in the Conciergerie immediately before and after it. Yet, also like the gravedigger scene, it functions as something more than "comic relief." Although we laugh at the jokes, the dramatic context in which they are placed powerfully qualifies the effect they have on us. There is something rather grotesque, after all, in the carter's concern for his social status ("this is a decent cart, this is; the King went in this") in the inverted world of the Reign of Terror: indeed, there is something even frightening about it, since he is about to cart the play's hero to his death. The fusion of comic and tragic which we see here and elsewhere in Büchner is a peculiarly Shakespearean one—a fusion, moreover, which is effected not only through the alternation of comic and tragic scenes, but through the multiplicity of levels (ironic, grotesque, pathetic, or whatever) with which a single speech, a single image even, may be interpreted. One could argue, in fact, that Büchner seems modern to us in many of the same respects in which he seems most Shakespearean. Through his use of comic tech-

niques to express the most desperate human situations, his plays as surely look backward to Shakespeare—for instance, to Lear's scenes with his fool—as they look forward to the clowning in *Waiting for Godot.*

Büchner's Shakespearean quality is discernible not only through his echoes and his conscious attempts at imitation, but in certain fundamental affinities he shares with Shakespeare. Büchner is Shakespearean, for instance, in the dramatic objectivity with which most of his characters are conceived and in the consequent impersonality he achieves in relation to his work. His talent is akin to that which Keats, in a famous passage from one of his letters, was trying to define when he distinguished his own and Shakespeare's mode from that of Wordsworth: "A Poet [by which Keats here means one like Shakespeare or himself] is the most unpoetical of any thing in existence; because he has no Identity—he is continually . . . filling some other Body—The Sun, the Moon, the Sea and Men and Women who are creatures of impulse are poetical and have about them an unchangeable attribute—the poet has none."[19] Like Shakespeare, Büchner expunges his own identity in favor of that of his characters, who seem to live with an autonomous and spontaneous life of their own. Of the major German dramatists before Büchner, only Goethe, I think, possessed this quality, though the severely classicist directions which Goethe's work, including his methods of characterization, took after his Storm-and-Stress years gave it an increasingly less Shakespearean character.

Büchner's most fundamental Shakespearean quality lies, perhaps, in his conception of a drama as a fully embodied poetic world of its own, relying as much on its richness of verbal texture as on its narrative to achieve its effects. The image of a crazy upside-down world which Büchner achieved in *Woyzeck* is comparable in kind, if not in degree, to the image out of which a play such as *King Lear* is built. The power that emanates from both these works is due as much to the atmosphere created by such indirect means as images and ironic thematic parallels as it is to the simple facts of "plot"; both plays, in fact, create their image of a distorted world partly, at least, through their constant insistence on the animallike nature of men—*Lear,* for instance, through its persistent imagery of wild animals, *Woyzeck* through such passages as the animal demonstrations in the carnival scenes. The non-Aristotelian conception of drama in which Büchner seems so conspicuously a pioneer is in certain respects, at least, a Shakespearean conception, as it was, indeed, for the German Storm-and-Stress writers, with whom Büchner felt such obvious affinities. Modern Shakespeare critics such as G. Wilson Knight and William Empson no longer read Shakespeare in terms of the expositions and dénouements with which their classicist-minded predecessors were all too often concerned, but attempt instead to describe and explore the larger poetic whole which they see in each play.[20]

Büchner, I think, discerned Shakespeare's dramatic method in something of the way we see it today, and to the extent that his plays achieve a Shakespearean thickness of texture and concentration of meaning, he seems to me the most Shakespearean of German dramatists.

IV

Even though Büchner's most striking affinities are with dramatists who lived long before or after him, in certain limited respects he is peculiarly of his own time. His work seems little related, however, to the German drama of the period; except for Grabbe . . . the significant dramatic writing of the 1830's took directions quite different from Büchner's. The work of the Viennese comic writers Ferdinand Raimund and Johann Nestroy derives directly from the popular theater of Vienna, the only German-speaking city which had maintained a living *commedia dell'arte* tradition. Franz Grillparzer, also a Viennese, succeeded in giving new life to the forms of the German Classical drama, which he was able to fuse with elements derived from Spanish drama and the Viennese folk tradition. If there was any contemporary dramatist for whom Büchner could feel any real affinities, it was one who did not write in German at all, namely Musset, from whom . . . he borrowed what he found useful, and no more.

Nor can one discern many significant relationships between Büchner and the German nondramatic writers of his time. When Büchner was mentioned by nineteenth- and early twentieth-century literary historians his name was usually lumped together with those of the Young Germany group, men such as Gutzkow, Heinrich Laube, and Ludwig Wienbarg—and for no better reason than that he was politically on the left and had been sponsored by Gutzkow. Even without Büchner's firm denial of sympathy with the aims and ideas of the Young Germans,[21] one need only set their works next to his to note a fundamental difference both in their essential thematic concerns and their artistic stature. Gutzkow's best-known work, his short novel *Wally the Doubter,* written in the same year (1835) in which Büchner began his correspondence with him, attempts, far more than any of Büchner's works, to deal with a characteristic contemporary problem, the "problem of the modern woman"; when we read it today, however, *Wally* seems less about any real woman than about a problem which Gutzkow lacked the means to embody in any artistically convincing way.

Of the most notable German poets writing in the 1830's—namely, Heinrich Heine, Annette von Droste-Hülshoff, and Eduard Mörike—only Heine shares something of Büchner's world. Büchner himself probably never appreciated Heine's real distinction, for he listed his name with those of the Young Germans (to whom Heine can be linked only superficially) whom he re-

jected.[22] The common spirit of the age which shapes the work of both manifests itself in their ironical perspectives and their ability to endow seemingly trivial and prosaic situations with poetic meaning; yet the sensibility that emerges from the writings of each—Heine's work is built around his personality, whereas Büchner's is notable for the deliberate absence of the author's personality—is as different as that of any two writers can be.[23]

The spirit of Büchner's age cannot be defined merely by the organized movements of the time—Young Germany, for instance, or Romanticism in France and Italy—but by the work of certain lonely figures who, in one way or another, were at war with their time. Büchner's closest contemporaries were perhaps less his fellow writers in German than such figures as Stendhal and Lermontov. Each of these, though rooted in the Romantic Movement within his particular country, is distinguished by the concretely real world he created in his fiction and by the steadfast ironic control he maintained over his material.

The major novels of Stendhal, who was thirty years older than Büchner, were written during the same decade which witnessed Büchner's brief career; Lermontov, who was a year younger than Büchner and died only four years after him, reached his artistic maturity in the last years of the decade. Both writers, like Büchner, have succeeded in making contact with our own century with an immediacy which few other nineteenth-century writers were able to achieve. Büchner was further removed from Romanticism (which had waned in Germany far earlier than in France or Russia) than were the authors of *Racine and Shakespeare* or the Byronic narratives that marked Lermontov's early period.[24] Yet it could be argued that each of these writers seems most modern to us in precisely those areas in which he found the means to distance himself from the various Romantic themes and conventions which he inherited. Pechorin, the protagonist of Lermontov's *A Hero of Our Time* (1840), speaks more directly to us than any of Byron's heroes (including even Don Juan) because Lermontov has created a recognizable social environment for him and, above all, has been willing to view him ironically from a number of points of view. We are willing to accept Julien Sorel, in *The Red and the Black* (1830), as a hero only because Stendhal has placed his heroic gestures in an environment in which they come to seem useless and absurd. At one point in this novel (Book II, Chapter XII) Mathilde looks back longingly to the heroic days of the Revolution and imagines her lover Julien in the role of Danton. Büchner, one might say, went one step further than Stendhal: the banality which Stendhal attributed to the world of the Restoration is much the same as the banality which Büchner discerned in the Revolution as well. The imaginary commonwealth which Stendhal depicted in *The Charterhouse of*

Parma (1838) is much akin—above all, in its attempt to hold on to long-outmoded institutions—to the grand duchy of Hesse in which Büchner grew up. If Büchner had lived on to write a drama or novel on Hesse, the image that might have emerged would, I think, have had more in common with Stendhal's ironic portrait of Parma than with the more simple-minded revolutionist's image of Hesse which Büchner presented in ***The Hessian Messenger.***

In Stendhal, Lermontov, and Büchner the modern reader recognizes a complexity of intelligence and a dramatic objectivity relatively rare in the work of their Romantic contemporaries and predecessors, whose virtues are of a different, less characteristically modern kind. The realism of these three writers is less amply detailed than that of Balzac or such later writers as Flaubert and Zola; yet it is a realism as surely rooted in their contemporary worlds as that of any writer who came after them. The ironical perspectives which govern the work of all three are centrally directed to laying bare pretensions and uncovering the shades of meaning that lie beneath pat assertions and dramatic postures. Büchner's skepticism, more than that of Stendhal or Lermontov, is a skepticism without poses; the dramatic form he employed (as well as the type of fiction with which he experimented in ***Lenz***) gave him little opportunity to put on masks of his own. His manner is perhaps less urbane than that of Stendhal or Lermontov; yet his irony is reinforced more powerfully than theirs by memorable images of terror and suffering. Whatever labels we ultimately attach to such writers—post-Romantic, say, or proto-Modern—their work leads us to question the conventional time divisions with which we have learned to look at literary history.

Notes

1. "Über das Poetische und Artistische," *Stücke* (Frankfort, 1959), XI, 216.

2. Walter Höllerer's analysis of *The Soldiers* (in Von Wiese's *Das deutsche Drama,* I, 127-46) includes some penetrating remarks on those aspects of Lenz' work which anticipate Büchner's.

3. Büchner, *Werke und Briefe,* ed. Fritz Bergemann [Wiesbaden, 1958], pp. 553, 400.

4. *Ibid.,* p. 523.

5. Quoted in Ernst Johann, *Georg Büchner in Selbstzeugnissen und Bilddokumenten* (Hamburg, 1958), p. 166.

6. Wolfgang Kayser defines several parallels between Büchner and Wedekind in their use of the grotesque in *Das Groteske,* pp. 141-43.

7. Adapted from Willi Reich's analysis of the opera, "A Guide to *Wozzeck,*" *Musical Quarterly,* XXXVIII (1952), 1-20. For a very different critical approach to the opera, see the chapter on *Wozzeck* and *The Rake's Progress* in Joseph Kerman's *Opera as Drama* (New York, 1959), pp. 219-49.

8. See Berg's note on the opera reprinted with Reich's analysis, pp. 20-21.

9. "'Ulysses,' Order, and Myth," in *Criticism: The Foundations of Modern Literary Judgment,* ed. Mark Schorer, Josephine Miles, and Gordon McKenzie (New York, 1948), p. 270.

10. Translated by Eric Bentley and Desmond Vesey, *The Modern Theatre* (New York, 1955), I, 168.

11. "Discovering the Theatre," trans. Leonard C. Pronko, *Tulane Drama Review,* IV (1959), 6.

12. Martin Esslin, in his study of the contemporary "absurd" drama, cites especially *Leonce and Lena* as an ancestor of this movement (*The Theatre of the Absurd*—New York, 1961—pp. 238-39).

13. *Waiting for Godot* (New York, 1954), p. 52.

14. "Georg Büchner's *Danton's Death,*" p. 148.

15. "Some Letters," trans. Maurer, p. 54.

16. Bergemann, p. 390.

17. *Ibid.,* p. 556.

18. See, for instance, the echoes and parallels cited by Heinrich Vogeley, *Georg Büchner und Shakespeare* (Marburg, 1934), pp. 30-51; Rudolf Majut, "Some Literary Affiliations of Georg Büchner with England," *Modern Language Review,* L (1955), 30-32; and Bergemann, p. 672. There is no evidence that Büchner read Shakespeare in English. His echoes are based on the standard German translation by Ludwig Tieck and August Wilhelm Schlegel.

19. *Letters,* ed. H. E. Rollins (Cambridge, Mass., 1958), I, 387.

20. See, for example, Knight's study of the imagery of *Lear,* "The Lear Universe," in *Wheel of Fire,* pp. 194-226, or Empson's study of the functions of a single word in the play, "Fool in *Lear,*" in *The Structure of Complex Words* (London, 1951), pp. 125-57.

21. Bergemann, p. 408.

22. *Ibid.*

23. Walter Höllerer, in *Zwischen Klassik und Moderne,* has made the best attempt thus far to define a common ground between Büchner and his contemporary writers in German, above all, Grabbe, Heine, Raimund, Nestroy, and Büchner's fellow Hessian writer, Ernst Elias Niebergall. (See the chapter on Büchner, pp. 100-42, and also pp. 36, 37, 63, 65, 67, 68, 80, 85, 151, 168, 169, 176,

178-79, 184, 189, 198-99.) Among the features which Höllerer distinguishes as common to most of these figures are a persistent skepticism, a fusion of wit and pathos, and the development of peculiarly terse ways of expression. Höllerer's fine argument does not deny the fact that Büchner has spoken to our age with a greater degree of contemporaneity than any of these other writers.

24. Despite his antipathies to German Romanticism, in a few respects his work represents a continuation of the aims and methods of this movement. *Leonce and Lena,* in its wordplay, its concern with boredom, and its attempt to reevoke the world of Shakespearean comedy, has something in common with Clemens Brentano's charming but impossibly diffuse comedy *Ponce de Leon* (1803), which, exactly thirty-five years before, had been submitted to the same competition for which Büchner prepared his play. Gutzkow, in fact, pointed out the parallel between the two plays in his memorial tribute to Büchner (in Bergemann, p. 595). Büchner's attempts, in *Danton's Death* and *Woyzeck,* to fuse comic and tragic elements and to break down the conventions of German Classical drama were among the central aims of the German Romantic school, which, however, was unable to produce a dramatist who could realize these aims. The apocalyptic grandeur with which the prisoners voice their despair in *Danton's Death* has something in common with the tone of *Night Watches* (1804) by Bonaventura (*pseud.*), one of a number of German Romantic works which anticipate the nihilistic attitudes of Büchner's characters. The grotesqueness of figures such as the captain and doctor in *Woyzeck* perhaps owes something to the grotesque characterizations of E. T. A. Hoffmann, with whose poetic world Büchner momentarily identified himself in one of his letters to his fiancée (in Bergemann, pp. 379-80). The sense of fullness with which Büchner characterizes the landscape in parts of *Lenz* ("he stretched himself out and lay on the earth, dug his way into the All") is perhaps the only aspect of his story which would keep it from being mistaken for a work of our own century. For studies of the relationship of *Leonce and Lena* with German Romanticism, see Armin Renker, *Georg Büchner und das Lustspiel der Romantik* (Berlin, 1924) and Gustav Beckers' *Georg Büchners "Leonce und Lena,"* pp. 73-102.

Henry J. Schmidt (essay date 1970)

SOURCE: Schmidt, Henry J. "Georg Büchner's Satiric Tendencies." *Satire, Caricature and Perspectivism in the Works of Georg Büchner,* pp. 104-14. The Hague, Netherlands: Mouton, 1970, 119 p.

[*In the following essay, Schmidt assesses the satirical and ironic nature of Büchner's literary temperament.*]

Ever since literary critics have been writing about Büchner, they have encountered unusual difficulty and frustration in defining his unique philosophy, aesthetics, and dramatic style. Definitions and labels proffered by one critic are quickly demolished by the next, who in re-examining the material, determines that designations such as "nihilist", "atheist", "revolutionary", or "realist" are not the last word and are too limited in scope to aid in grasping the thought and writings of Georg Büchner. A case in point: the two articles on Büchner in Benno von Wiese's *Das deutsche Drama*[1] are both specifically directed against a nihilistic interpretation of *Dantons Tod* and *Woyzeck,* of which von Wiese himself is a leading proponent. Each critical appraisal uncovers new complexities and finer shadings in Büchner's works, and there can be no better tribute to the genius of this man than the tendency to return constantly to the little that exists by him and assess its value anew. If there is to be a last word, it will necessarily be as cautious and ambivalent as Büchner himself was. Herbert Lindenberger writes: "Büchner poses far more questions than he attempts to answer; his very technique, to the extent that his dramatic situations are re-examined in one analogous situation after another, eschews any air-tight answers."[2] Critics need only turn to Büchner himself for an enlightened warning: we must not, like the Doctor, the Captain, or King Peter, escape complexity by retreating into the illusory security of formulas.

The coloration of Büchner's style is truly kaleidoscopic. The basic structural element of Büchner's dramaturgy, as Helmut Krapp points out, is the contrastive construction,[3] through which Büchner brings about the artistic re-creation of the "Schöpfung, die glühend, brausend und leuchtend . . . sich jeden Augenblick neu gebiert." (*Dantons Tod,* p. 40) Büchner's dramatic perspective is broad enough to accommodate a St. Just and a Marion, a King Peter and a Lena, a Doctor and a Marie, allowing these characters to exist on their own terms in their own environment. They are products of Büchner's intellect and intuition, which had to be extraordinary to produce such extraordinary figures.

In this respect critics face an even greater frustration. The sources for information on Büchner's personality are meager, and even the most important materials—Büchner's letters—are incomplete and inconclusive. Critics have attempted to construct a portrait of Büchner the writer, scientist, and politician from these sources, but such a portrait must necessarily remain a rough sketch. The sources are often unreliable: Büchner's letters to his parents were often designed to mislead them about his revolutionary activity; most of his letters have been extensively edited by Ludwig Büchner, and the originals are lost (see p. 753 of the 1922 Bergemann edition); many of the reminiscences about Büchner were written forty years after his death.

The purpose of this [essay] is to investigate the satiric tendencies in the personality of Georg Büchner as an extension of . . . textual analyses of his plays. Especially since the material on the playwright is so sparse, this [essay] cannot be much more than an appendix, for there is little in Büchnerian documentation . . . which would add to the interpretation of the plays. We aim at suppositions rather than at conclusions. This reappraisal of Büchner material is motivated by the conviction that there exist a number of misinterpretations and misapplications of these sources. . . .

Büchner's contrastive technique produces a constantly fluctuating attitude of affirmation and negation. Many interpreters have separated and analyzed the strands which constitute the fabric of his writings, and, while such investigations have greatly contributed to the understanding of the relationship between Büchner's studies in anatomy and medicine, his literary production, and his political activity, they occasionally create a false sense of proportion by giving too much weight to a chosen number of passages from his writings. This occurs most frequently in discussions of Büchner's aesthetic principles. By and large the discussions center on three sources: the "Kunstgespräch" between Camille and Danton in the scene, "Ein Zimmer" in Act II of *Dantons Tod*; Büchner's letter to his parents on *Dantons Tod,* written from Strassburg on July 28, 1835; and the "Kunstmonolog" in *Lenz*—all in all about five pages of text, not without repetition, having as a single theme the obligations of the artist to Nature. The three passages are of great relevance to the style and content of *Lenz* and the three plays, and they also shed light on Büchner's sympathies in the political sphere and on his anti-teleological position as set forth in his lecture, **"Über Schädelnerven"**. Yet there is, of course, much that is still unexplained,[4] and other texts are used to fill some of the gaps: the fatalism which dominates *Dantons Tod* and *Woyzeck* is traced primarily to the letter to Minna Jaeglé, written presumably in November, 1833; the satiric elements of the plays are said to have evolved from the "Spott des Hasses" mentioned in the fiery letter to his parents in February, 1834. But these sources are still too limited to be valid bases for appraisal of important aspects of Büchner's dramas.

We have seen how complex and varied are the motivations of the satirist. Judging from this evidence, it is an oversimplification to say, as Viëtor[5] and Mayer[6] and many others have done, that Büchner is acting as a social critic and not as a true artist when he created King Peter's court, the Doctor, and the Captain. Such a formulation is not only restricting but actually a disparagement of Büchner, for it implies that there is relatively little artistic merit in a considerable part of his dramatic production. . . . Using the remarks on the purpose and technique of satire as a basis, the extant documentation on Büchner will now be examined for clues which will hopefully yield further insight into the temperament which created these caricatures.

Büchner's pre-university life is especially difficult to reconstruct. There exists some derivative poetry of no particular significance, a few unrelated remarks collected by Karl Emil Franzos, some idle marginal scribbling in notebooks, and a few compositions. The marginal notes—those that are not quotations from Shakespeare—are private little outcries of a spirited student trapped in a boring class. To pass the time he pokes fun at his teachers. Already there is a seed of antipathy against empty pathos in the words: "Scharfsinn, Verstand, gesunde Vernunft! lauter leere Namen." (p. 458) The compositions dating from this period appear to be prescribed exercises, based on no particular convictions. This theory is strongly supported by Werner Lehmann's discovery that much of **"Heldentod der vierhundert Pforzheimer"** is copied from Fichte's "Rede an die deutsche Nation: Rede VIII".[7] It seems superfluous to elaborate upon the Fichtean influence upon this "Gymnasiast", for Büchner at this point can hardly be called an independent thinker. Nevertheless, the fervent idealism expressed in these essays was not totally without influence later on; although Büchner soon turned to the more pragmatic French thinkers, his political views during the years at Strassburg and Giessen reflected an idealized belief in universal freedom and equality.

The most penetrating glimpse into Büchner's life in Darmstadt is afforded by the memoirs of Friedrich Zimmermann (pp. 552-554) and Ludwig Wilhelm Luck (pp. 555-559). Concerning Büchner's temperament, Zimmermann speaks of Büchner's "mächtig strebender Geist" which followed its own inclinations, and he calls him "ein kühner Skeptiker".[8] Luck's more detailed description bears this out, and the character traits he saw in Büchner are strikingly similar to the temperament of a satirist. "Es war jedoch nicht seine Art, sich andern ungeprüft und voreilig hinzugeben, er war vielmehr ein ruhiger, gründlicher, mehr zurückhaltender Beobachter", reports Luck. However, he stresses that Büchner was by no means a cynic: "Wo er aber fand, dass jemand wirklich wahres Leben suchte, da konnte er auch warm, ja enthusiastisch werden." Büchner and the Zimmermann brothers employed their quick intelligence "zu allerlei kritischem und humoristischem Wetteifer in Beurteilung der Zustände", which Luck could appreciate but not take part in ("für den ich zu ernst und zu schwer war", he adds modestly). Büchner had a pronounced taste for parody, spoofing clergymen with Shakespearian quotations (p. 558) and making fun of lectures in his notebooks.[9] His sense of humor, which sustained him even in times of crisis, seems not to have been inherited from either parent. Büchner's father was a sober and dedicated physician, competent but unimaginative. His mother was of a far more sensitive, poetical nature, but she did not share her son's intellectual irony.[10]

Both Luck and Zimmermann mention Büchner's early interest in scientific, philosophical, and metaphysical questions. Luck notes an awakening of political consciousness, a growing awareness of the inequalities existing in the German states. The young Büchner seems to have been extremely active in the search for knowledge and mental stimulation, proceeding in many areas with the skeptical caution of the scientific observer. Whatever was assimilated was evaluated. Luck reports:

> In seinem Denken und Tun durch das Streben nach Wesenhaftigkeit und Wahrhaftigkeit frühe durchaus selbständig, vermochte ihm keine äusserliche Autorität noch nichtiger Schein zu imponieren. Das Bewusstsein des erworbenen geistigen Fonds drängte ihn fortwährend zu einer unerbittlichen Kritik dessen, was in der menschlichen Gesellschaft oder Philosophie und Kunst Alleinberechtigung beanspruchte oder erlistete.— Daher sein vernichtender, manchmal übermütiger Hohn über Taschenspielerkünste Hegelischer Dialektik und Begriffsformulationen, z.B.: "Alles, was wirklich, ist auch vernünftig, und was vernünftig, auch wirklich." Aufs tiefste verachtete er, die sich und andere mit wesenlosen Formeln abspeisten, anstatt für sich selbst das Lebensbrot der Wahrheit zu erwerben und es andern zu geben.

This passage provides a singularly appropriate commentary to the figures of King Peter, the Doctor, and the Captain. Luck continues: "Man sah ihm an, an Stirne, Augen und Lippen, dass er auch, wenn er schwieg, diese Kritik in seinem in sich verschlossnen Denken übte . . . Die zuckenden Lippen verrieten, wie oft er mit der Welt im Widerspruch und Streit lag." Büchner's critical outlook was so much a part of his nature that his uncompromising personality often provoked dislike in those who could not gain his friendship or understand his views. Carl Vogt, a witness to Büchner's unhappy days in Giessen, describes Büchner as an intelligent but unapproachable revolutionary. (pp. 559-560)

Büchner's letters span a period of little more than five years. Fritz Bergemann's summary of the insights they offer is apt: "Hier spricht der Dichter unmittelbar aus, was ihn bewegt, verstimmt, beschäftigt, hier lernen wir ihn als Menschen kennen in seiner sprühenden Laune und seiner sensiblen Reizbarkeit, in seinem sozialen Mitgefühl und seinem revolutionären Zorn, in seiner Naturfreude, seiner teilnehmenden Freundschaft und seiner trauten Zwiesprache mit der Geliebten, auch in seinem beruflichen Streben, seiner künstlerischen und politischen Meinungsbildung und seiner weltanschaulichen Gesinnung." (*Nachwort*, p. 602) The letters, like the plays, reflect a wide spectrum of interest and activity, as well as abrupt changes of moods. Already in the first extant letter there appears a perplexing Büchnerian twist. Almost as an afterthought, Büchner seems to deflate his own idealism. He describes the reception in Strassburg of the Polish General Ramorino, a leader in the recently suppressed Polish revolution. Ramorino was heralded as a symbol of the liberal freedom movement flourishing during the 1830's. Büchner was among the students who broke through police barriers to welcome Ramorino. His description of the event is coolly objective, and he concludes with the words: "Darauf erscheint Ramorino auf dem Balkon, dankt, man ruft Vivat—und die Komödie ist fertig." (p. 366) It does not seem likely that these words were meant to mislead Büchner's parents regarding his political interests, for he had just arrived in Strassburg, and political involvement would have had dangerous consequences only if Büchner were still in Germany. "Und die Komödie ist fertig" is in retrospect not as surprising as at first, for the tone of the letter is singularly dry. The phrase most probably indicates Büchner's dislike of ceremonies and demonstrations which have no practical results.[11] Büchner constantly strove toward the concrete goal; he demanded action which would effect lasting change—and herein lies his idealism. "Was nennt Ihr denn gesetzlichen Zustand?" he writes in 1833. ". . . dies Gesetz ist eine ewige, rohe Gewalt, angetan dem Recht und der gesunden Vernunft, und ich werde mit Mund und Hand dagegen kämpfen, wo ich kann. Wenn ich an dem, was geschehen, keinen Teil genommen und an dem, was vielleicht geschieht, keinen Teil nehmen werde, so geschieht es weder aus Missbilligung noch aus Furcht, sondern nur weil ich im gegenwärtigen Zeitpunkt jede revolutionäre Bewegung als eine vergebliche Unternehmung betrachte und nicht die Verblendung derer teile, welche in den Deutschen ein zum Kampf für sein Recht bereites Volk sehen." (p. 369) The latter statement is belied by Büchner's later revolutionary activity, but his basic attitude—the critical examination of every factor of a problem, the flexible perspective—never changed. Even ***Der Hessische Landbote,*** a tract of firm conviction and urgency, was not a blind gamble. August Becker stated in court: "Mit der von ihm [Büchner] geschriebenen Flugschrift wollte er vorderhand nur die Stimmung des Volks und der deutschen Revolutionärs erforschen. Als er später hörte, dass die Bauern die meisten gefundenen Flugschriften auf die Polizei abgeliefert hätten, als er vernahm, dass sich auch die Patrioten gegen seine Flugschrift ausgesprochen, gab er alle seine politischen Hoffnungen in bezug auf ein Anderswerden auf." ("Aus August Beckers gerichtlichen Angaben", p. 562.) The definitive manner in which Becker announces the termination of Büchner's political activity was designed to protect Büchner from arrest. Büchner continued his secret political agitation after his return to Darmstadt in August, 1834. Becker significantly uses the word "erforschen"; Büchner wrote and distributed the ***Landbote*** as an experiment so that he might observe the impact of his viewpoint (which differed from that of Weidig and other more moderate corevolutionaries) upon the masses. The experiment failed, but Büchner, proceeding in a scientific fashion, had gained valuable insight into his audience—a must for a political satirist who seeks to reform his public through his writings. Although the experience was a disappointment, Büchner remained level-headed enough to register a brazen complaint against the very authorities who were seeking to implicate him in revolutionary activity. (pp. 385-388) To this, too, Büchner might have added the epitaph, "und die Komödie ist fertig".

Despite Büchner's tendency to disparage his own beliefs, his antipathy toward the oppressors of the masses was unwavering. We have [elsewhere] spoken of the "Spott des Hasses" which Büchner directs against those who scorn those socially beneath them. The political situation in France, Büchner writes, "ist doch nur eine Komödie. Der König und die Kammern regieren, und das Volk klatscht und bezahlt". (Strassburg, December, 1832, p. 367) As for Germany: "Unsere Landstände sind eine Satire auf die gesunde Vernunft." (Strassburg, April 5, 1833, p. 368) Or, in a letter dating from Büchner's second sojourn in Strassburg: "Der König von Bayern lässt unsittliche Bücher verbieten! da darf er seine Biographie nicht erscheinen lassen, denn die wäre das Schmutzigste, was je geschrieben worden! Der Grossherzog von Baden, erster Ritter vom doppelten Mopsorden, macht sich zum Ritter vom Heiligen Geist und lässt Gutzkow arretieren, und der liebe deutsche Michel glaubt, es geschähe alles aus Religion und Christentum und klatscht in die Hände." (January 1, 1836, p. 407)

In these instances Büchner is writing with a satirist's pen. He demeans his victims with uncomplimentary appellations; he relies heavily upon irony and sarcasm, seeking out damaging contradiction, and he does not refrain from name-calling. In his words: "Es fällt mir nicht mehr ein, vor den Paradegäulen und Eckstehern der Geschichte mich zu bücken." (Giessen, November, 1833, p. 374) In the **Landbote,** he intensifies and animates his style through satiric imagery. In the letter of 1836, he is not being polemical, but he savors the ironies of political decrees and actions. His desire for direct action is sublimated into verbal ridicule.

In this connection it is especially regrettable that Büchner's drama about Pietro Aretino has never been found. According to a letter written less than two months before his death, Büchner informed his fiancée Minna Jaeglé that he was planning to publish **Leonce und Lena** and two other dramas. (p. 422) Franzos discovered the **Woyzeck** manuscripts in 1879, but the drama mentioned by Ludwig Büchner in his edition of his brother's works (1850) never appeared. Pietro Aretino (1492-1556) was a writer of comedies and satiric poetry—not a literary satirist, but a satirist with a vengeance. He used his wit as a powerful weapon, wielding it daringly for his personal advantage, unscrupulously, cynically, often obscenely. His talents enabled him to rise from a lowly origin to become the friend of Giovanni de' Medici, Francis I of France, and the pope. He became rich by extorting money from nobles by threatening them with the power of his satire. In his own estimation he was "divine" and the "scourge of princes".[12]

It is obvious why Büchner was attracted to Aretino: a poor man rises to challenge and dominate the aristocracy with the might of his pen; a satirist fearlessly exposes the weaknesses of an unjust society, disregarding conventional standards of order and morality. In personality and outlook the Italian and the German differed greatly, but both shared an *esprit libre* which could not be contained by their restrictive environments. There remains the fascinating question: how did Büchner mold Aretino into a Büchnerian hero?

Now that Büchner's satiric tendencies have been touched upon, it is necessary once again to point out that satire was not his primary goal, either artistically or otherwise, nor can he be called exclusively a satirist in temperament. Büchner was a great ironist, but the root of his irony was not based on an attacker-victim relationship. To repeat his words: "Man nennt mich einen Spötter. Es ist wahr, ich lache oft; aber ich lache nicht darüber, *wie* jemand ein Mensch, sondern nur darüber, *dass* er ein Mensch ist, wofür er ohnehin nichts kann, und lache dabei über mich selbst, der ich sein Schicksal teile." (pp. 377-378) This is more than satiric laughter. The satirist laughs *at* people, at their weaknesses, either out of personal enjoyment or out of the desire to improve his fellow men. Büchner's is a laughter of general despair, based on the recognition of the smallness of his own self, impotent against fate. This self-irony was, as we have seen, deeply rooted in his personality, and time and again he makes light of projects in which he was deeply involved. He speaks slightingly of his plays, calling them "Ferkeldramen" (p. 535; Gutzkow is apparently quoting Büchner in this letter), he makes fun of his projected lectures on philosophy: "Ich habe mich jetzt ganz auf das Studium der Naturwissenschaften und der Philosophie gelegt und werde in kurzem nach Zürich gehen, um in meiner Eigenschaft als überflüssiges Mitglied der Gesellschaft meinen Mitmenschen Vorlesungen über etwas ebenfalls höchst Überflüssiges, nämlich über die philosophischen Systeme der Deutschen seit Cartesius und Spinoza, zu halten." (p. 417) At one point he sees himself as a model for a grotesque caricature: "Ich hätte Herrn Callot-Hoffmann sitzen können"—a reference to E. T. A. Hoffmann, who had written *Phantasiestücke in Callots Manier,* based on the sketches of Jacques Callot (1592-1635). That this trait was more than just modesty is evident in that self-irony functions as a significant stylistic element in **Dantons Tod** and **Leonce und Lena.** Danton, his friends, Leonce, and Valerio are constantly holding up mirrors to themselves and laughing at their reflections. Their wit acts as a balm against the pain of existence; it lets them hold the world—and themselves—at a distance, whereby they preserve their conscious identities. For Büchner and his heroes, wit is activity—mental stimulation, a release from the chronic boredom which afflicts the perceptive individual. Danton and Leonce are for the most part dramatically inert—here they differ sharply from their spiritual cousin Hamlet—they are observers, as was Büchner himself. Yet neither of them is sure of his own vantage point. Self-doubt is made tolerable through self-irony. Self-deprecation is the only sure check against self-deception. A primary commandment of Büchnerian philosophy is that man must recognize his nature and live according to his potential; he cannot build existence upon an illusion. His fellow men are as he is, subject to the same painful mortality. Yet within this common fate there rests a powerful affirmation of existence: kinship and warmth among men. At one point in his correspondence Büchner elevates this attitude above the satiric with indisputable clarity: "Ich hoffe noch immer, dass ich leidenden, gedrückten Gestalten mehr mitleidige Blicke zugeworfen als kalten, vornehmen Herzen bittere Worte gesagt habe." (Giessen, February, 1834, p. 378) The balance is in favor of sympathy, not sarcasm, and Büchner's works bear this out. Their most remarkable feature is their depth of compassion for the human condition—the abandoned Lenz and Woyzeck, the doubting philosophers Danton and Leonce, the spontaneous warmth of Marion, Julie, Lucile, Lena, and Marie. Deep sensitivity and love suffuse Büchner's letters to Minna Jaeglé, and this "selige Empfindung" sustained him through periods of illness and mental depression. His scientific works reflect an admiration for the limitless diversity of nature. Those who have isolated themselves from the wholeness of life Büchner demolishes with the weapons of satire. Satire is in his works a servant of his affirmation of existence.

Notes

1. Walter Höllerer, "Dantons Tod", *Das deutsche Drama*, Vol. II, Benno von Wiese, ed. (Düsseldorf, 1960), pp. 65-88; Kurt May, "Büchner: Woyzeck" (same volume), pp. 89-100.

2. *Georg Büchner,* p. 94.

3. *Der Dialog bei Georg Büchner,* p. 145.

4. It is revealing that Helmut Krapp, who bases his analysis of Büchner's style largely on the principles outlined in the passages mentioned above, neglects entirely the characterizations which seem to come from another creative impulse (i.e., King Peter, the Doctor, the Captain, etc.).

5. *Georg Büchner,* p. 192.

6. *Georg Büchner und seine Zeit,* p. 438.

7. "Prolegomena zu einer historisch-kritischen Büchner-Ausgabe".

8. See also Büchner's diploma, where C. Dilthey, the school director, writes: "Den Religionsstunden hat er mit Aufmerksamkeit beigewohnt und in denselben manche treffliche Beweise von selbständigem Nachdenken gegeben . . . von seinem klaren und durchdringenden Verstande hegen wir eine viel zu vorteilhafte Ansicht, als dass wir glauben könnten, er würde jemals durch Erschlaffung, Versäumnis oder voreilig absprechende Urtheile seinem eigenen Lebensglück im Wege stehen." (p. 552)

9. According to Franzos, Büchner once rewrote Schiller's "Graf Eberhard der Greiner" in the Swabian dialect, but nothing more is known about this. (*Georg Büchner's Sämmtliche Werke,* xxiii.)

10. Hans Mayer, *Georg Büchner und seine Zeit,* pp. 32-39.

11. Mayer, p. 67.

12. "Pietro Aretino", *Encyclopaedia Britannica,* 11th ed. (1911), Vol. II, p. 456.

Maurice B. Benn (essay date 1976)

SOURCE: Benn, Maurice B. "*Leonce und Luna*" and "*Lenz.*" In *The Drama of Revolt: A Critical Study of Georg Büchner,* pp. 157-63; 186-93. Cambridge: Cambridge University Press, 1976.

[*In the following excerpts, Benn considers the tragic aesthetic of two works by Büchner,* Leonce and Lena *and* Lenz.]

LEONCE UND LENA

Leonce und Lena is exceptional among Büchner's works. Firstly because it is a comedy. Secondly because, more clearly than any of his other productions, it was prompted by an external occasion. On 3 February 1836 the publisher Cotta announced a prize for the best German comedy, and it was this competition that supplied the immediate impulse for the writing of *Leonce und Lena.* The deadline for Cotta's competition was 1 July 1836.[1] Büchner's manuscript arrived too late and was returned to him unopened, whereupon, it appears, he set himself to revise and improve the work. In a letter of September 1836, referring, presumably, to *Leonce und Lena* and *Woyzeck,* he wrote to his parents:

> Ich habe meine zwei Dramen noch nicht aus den Händen gegeben, ich bin noch mit Manchem unzufrieden und will nicht, daß es mir geht, wie das erste Mal. Das sind Arbeiten, mit denen man nicht zu einer bestimmten Zeit fertig werden kann, wie der Schneider mit seinem Kleid.

> (*An die Familie,* 2, 460)

In Zurich, in the last months before his death, Büchner was evidently still engaged in polishing and improving *Leonce und Lena,* for it was stated by Wilhelm Schulz in an obituary published in the *Züricher Zeitung* of 23 February 1837 that 'in the same period [i.e., the last period in Strasbourg] and later in Zurich he completed a comedy which exists in MS, *Leonce und Lena,* a work full of cleverness, wit and saucy humour'.[2] How near it was to being ready for publication is indicated by a sentence in what may have been Büchner's last letter to Minna Jaegle:

〈Ich werde〉 in längstens acht Tagen Leonce und Lena mit noch zwei anderen Dramen erscheinen lassen.

(2, 464)

After Büchner's death the MS mentioned by Schulz together with that of the fragment *Lenz* came into the possession of Minna Jaegle, who, as a reward for an article on Büchner in the *Frankfurter Telegraf* (June 1837), gave fair copies of these works, written by her own hand, to Karl Gutzkow.[3] *Leonce und Lena* was published by Gutzkow in the *Telegraph für Deutschland* in May 1838, the first Act being given in a fragmentary form together with Gutzkow's summaries of the omitted passages. The first nearly complete publication, based probably on an original MS, was in the *Nachgelassene Schriften* of 1850, edited by Büchner's brother Ludwig. Neither publication can be regarded as reliable. Gutzkow's . . . is incomplete and based on a copy which may well have been imperfect. Ludwig Büchner can be shown to have mutilated many passages out of 'prudery or negligence'[4] or out of 'political caution, literary incomprehension and pedantic arro− gance'.[5] As for the manuscript, only a few scraps of an earlier version are still extant. When criticizing and evaluating *Leonce und Lena* we must remember, not only that it lacked the author's finishing touches, but that it has been handed down to us in a corrupt form.

In his comedy Büchner is not so obviously in revolt against the tendencies of his time as in his serious plays. Whether, and to what extent, the spirit of revolt is present in *Leonce und Lena* also, is a question which must be further considered. But in the field of comedy there was certainly no classicism which could provoke Büchner's direct opposition as it was provoked by the classicism of Schiller in the field of tragedy. In Germany there was the comedy of the romantics, of Tieck and Brentano; in France the comedy of Musset. Büchner did not feel bound to combat either of these forms of comedy but rather, with whatever modifications, to continue and develop them, adopting an attitude comparable with Heine's—a disposition to extend and intensify romanticism to the utmost while infusing into it an element of scepticism, of irony and of parody which offsets and relativizes the romantic elements without completely annulling them. But inasmuch as irony, in

all its manifestations, was part of the tradition of German romanticism from the beginning, one must recognize that Büchner no more than Heine completely breaks with that tradition. Not, that is to say, so far as comedy is concerned; his serious works are a different matter.

On the whole, then, there is less of 'aesthetic revolt' in *Leonce und Lena* than in *Dantons Tod*; but, as we shall see, Büchner's modified romantic form still allows a good deal of scope for the expression of his political and metaphysical revolt.

Comparing his method here with that of *Dantons Tod, Lenz* and *Woyzeck,* we may note the significant difference that *Leonce und Lena,* unlike those tragic works, is not based on documentary records of real events. The course of the action does not reflect, and is not determined by, the actual experiences of a real historical figure. It is obviously suggested by the action, or by episodes of the action, of other literary works, particularly Brentano's *Ponce de Leon* (1801) and Musset's *Fantasio* (published in the *Revue des deux mondes* in May 1834). Brentano's hero has many traits in common with Leonce; he is described as 'a curious, capricious fellow who amuses everybody and is always bored—witty and shy, cruel and kind, for ever mooning around like a lover, making all the women one after the other fall in love with him and tormenting them with his coldness' (I. x).[6] Like Leonce, Ponce forsakes one of his mistresses (Valeria) and finds a hope of salvation in the arms of another (Isidora). Musset's *Fantasio* is the story of a princess (Elsbeth), who, like Büchner's Lena, is required for reasons of state to marry a prince whom she has never seen and who comes incognito to woo her. The extreme freedom with which Büchner has borrowed from these and other works of Brentano and Musset, as well as from Shakespeare, Tieck, Jean Paul and Heine, has not unnaturally resulted in his comedy being criticized as derivative. Gundolf found that 'the whole thing is a product of the literary imitation of Brentano, Tieck, Shakespeare',[7] and Hans Mayer similarly complained that the people in Büchner's comedy 'have read very many books', that they 'lead a life at second hand'.[8] This criticism has a plausibility which compels consideration and we shall have to return to it presently. Meanwhile it may be observed that, though the degree of *Leonce und Lena*'s dependence on other literary models may suggest a different relation to reality from that which obtains in *Dantons Tod,* it would be a mistake to infer that Büchner's comedy is merely a tissue of literary reminiscences with no basis whatever in real life. The substance of *Leonce und Lena* is in fact basically the same as that of *Dantons Tod, Lenz* and *Woyzeck.* It is the fund of experience which Büchner had acquired in his short but very intense life. It is the doubt and despair of his metaphysical speculations and historical reflections; his bitter awareness of the despotism and pettiness of the German principalities and of the agony and brutalization of the people; his sense of frustration, of the pointlessness and absurdity of his own endeavours; his endless boredom. But it is also his love for Minna Jaegle, that love which meant so much to him because he seemed to find in it what his restless tormented spirit most intensely longed for—peace.

All this is expressed in **Leonce und Lena** no less than in **Dantons Tod,** but it has to be expressed now in the tone of comedy. That Büchner should have attempted such an experiment was probably not only due to the external stimulus of Cotta's competition, but also to the fact that the first half of 1836 was a relatively happy period in his life. He had made good his escape from Germany; he was enjoying freedom and the company of his fiancée in his dear city of Strasbourg; his **Dantons Tod** had been enthusiastically acclaimed by Gutzkow; and he was making good progress with his scientific work. Under such circumstances it is understandable that he should have been willing to attempt a work in lighter vein, and in **Leonce und Lena** he certainly achieves a milder tone than in his other plays; in a number of passages there is at least the appearance of cheerfulness and high spirits. Yet the basic experiences underlying the work are, as we have remarked, for the most part grim and gloomy, and from such a source no very joyful laughter can spring. The motto which Büchner chose for Act I—

> O that I were a fool.
> I am ambitious for a motley coat
>
> *(As You Like It* II. vii)

is already ominous, for these are the words of the melancholy Jaques whose laughter springs from bitterness and for whom the freedom of folly is a means 'to cleanse the foul body of th'infected world.' Büchner himself was prepared to see in folly or madness a means of escape from intolerable suffering. Thus his Camille can say of Lucile:

> Der Himmel verhelf' ihr zu einer behaglichen fixen Idee. Die allgemeinen fixen Ideen, welche man die gesunde Vernunft tauft, sind unerträglich langweilig. Der glücklichste Mensch war der, welcher sich einbilden konnte, daß er Gott Vater, Sohn und heiliger Geist sey.
>
> **(Dantons Tod** IV v. 70)

And Valerio in **Leonce und Lena** is prepared at any time to barter his unprofitable reason for the flattering visions of megalomania (see I. i. 107).

In addition to the laughter of madness there are also other kinds of laughter which Büchner recognizes. There is the laughter that is prompted by an acute sense of the absurdity of the world, the futility of human endeavours including one's own endeavours, the ludi-

crousness of mankind including one's own ludicrousness. And there is the laughter that springs from hatred, the mockery with which Büchner relentlessly pursues those who, in their 'aristocratic' arrogance, feel entitled to make a mockery of others:

> Man nennt mich einen *Spötter.* Es ist wahr, ich lache oft, aber ich lache nicht darüber, *wie* Jemand ein Mensch, sondern nur darüber, *daß* er ein Mensch ist, wofür er ohnehin nichts kann, und lache dabei über mich selbst, der ich sein Schicksal theile . . . Ich habe freileich noch eine Art von Spott, es ist aber nicht der der Verachtung, sondern der des Hasses.
>
> *(An die Familie,* Februar 1834, 2, 423)

All these varieties of laughter are to be found in **Leonce und Lena**—the laughter of folly escaping from grief, the laughter of those who are overwhelmed by the absurdity of the human condition, the laughter which is Büchner's deadliest weapon in the struggle against aristocratic superciliousness. But it is obvious that all three represent, basically, a *negative* reaction to the world; they arise from suffering, not from joy. And occasionally in **Leonce und Lena,** particularly when Lena speaks, the bright veil of mirth is withdrawn and the dark background frankly revealed. More often the effect is of a kaleidoscope of tones, ranging in a 'chromatic phantasmagoria' from a cheerfulness that is *almost* happiness to a melancholy that is not far removed from despair. No doubt this iridescent effect was deliberately intended by Büchner, and it adds to the charm of the work as much as it challenges and perplexes the interpreter. Small wonder that **Leonce und Lena** has been so diversely understood and evaluated.

Borrowing Hölderlin's terminology, one may say that the *apparent* tone or 'artistic character' (*Kunstcharakter*) of the play is cheerful and comic, but that its *basic* tone (*Grundton*) is melancholy and almost tragic.[9] And one may suspect that it is precisely *because* the basic tone is so profoundly gloomy that the apparent tone has to be so fantastic, so bizarre, in many respects so unrealistic.

This may seem paradoxical in a writer so passionately committed to realism as Büchner professed to be, and at least one critic, Hans Mayer, finds that 'no greater disharmony can be imagined than that between all his other doctrine—the general tendency of his work—and this ironically romantic fantasy of the two royal children'.[10] But we must remember that the artistic principles which Büchner lays down in **Dantons Tod,** in **Lenz** and in his letters, are an incomplete statement of his aesthetic creed—there is no discussion of comedy in his extant writings; and the disharmony of which Mayer complains is after all not so difficult to understand. The truth is that for Büchner reality is essentially tragic. Consequently, in tragedy he can be fully realistic, in comedy not so. A fully realistic representation of life as he sees it would be incompatible with the tone of comedy. If he is to maintain that tone reality must somehow be modified, distorted, reduced, romanticized, burlesqued.[11] Its most intolerable aspects have to be suppressed or subdued and the emphasis placed on those of which the absurdity is not so painful as to forbid laughter. It is this tendency to dwell on the ludicrous and absurd aspects of life, with reduced realism, that has led some critics to see in *Leonce und Lena* a forerunner of the modern 'theatre of the absurd'.

Does this mean that in *Leonce und Lena* Büchner abandons the attitude of revolt? It would certainly mean this if Büchner had carried absurdity to its extreme, since absolute absurdity is incompatible with values, and without values there can be no revolt. When Büchner lets Danton say:

> Muthe mir nur nichts Ernsthaftes zu. Ich begreife nicht warum die Leute nicht auf der Gasse stehen bleiben und einander in's Gesicht lachen
>
> (*Dantons Tod* II. ii. 36)

we see the sense of absurdity carried to its extreme, and in such a state of mind, obviously, there is no value that can still command respect, no spring of action that is not broken. If Danton had *always* been of this mind he could never have been a revolutionary. And this is no doubt the reason why revolutionary and 'engaged' writers such as Brecht, Frisch, the later Adamov have been so critical of the absurd theatre or directly opposed to it. But Büchner does not carry absurdity to its extreme, not even in *Leonce und Lena.* Familiar as he was with that derisive mood which he ascribes to Danton, he never completely loses his sense of values. Even in *Leonce und Lena* there is still a feeling for political justice and political reason; there is still a feeling for the beauty of nature, and a suggestion, however hesitant, of the redemptive power of love. And so *Leonce und Lena* cannot be claimed for the absurd theatre. But in so far as its comic tone involves an evasion or distortion of reality it represents a movement in the direction of the absurd and consequently a weakening of the attitude of revolt. As we found the tone of the work wavering between the tragic and the comic, so we shall find the sense of it wavering between revolt and absurdity, the technique between realism and romanticism, the tendency between materialism and idealism. It is particularly the last of these antitheses that is suggested by the apocryphal utterances ascribed to Alfieri and Gozzi in the freakish 'preface' to the comedy:

> Alfieri: 'E la fama?'
> Gozzi: 'E la fame?'
>
> . . . . .

LENZ

The predominant influence on *Dantons Tod* and *Leonce und Lena* is clearly Shakespeare. In *Lenz* and *Woyzeck* the Shakespearian influence, though still latently present, is much less obvious and direct and Büchner's style becomes more individual and mature. This is one of the reasons and justifications for closely associating *Lenz* with *Woyzeck,* notwithstanding the fact that they are chronologically separated by *Leonce und Lena.* They are also alike in that they are primarily concerned with the life of poor and humble people, not, like *Dantons Tod* and *Leonce und Lena,* with that of kings and princes and famous historical figures. This development is consistent with Büchner's aesthetic principle that the artist must be prepared to immerse himself in the life of the lowliest of mankind, and with his political conviction that it was necessary to seek the formation of a new spiritual life among the *people.* If it had been given to him to live longer it is presumably in this direction— the direction initiated in *Lenz* and continued in *Woyzeck*—that his poetic and dramatic production would have proceeded.

It is not known with certainty when Büchner first conceived the idea of writing about Lenz. The collected works of this gifted and unfortunate poet appeared for the first time in 1828, edited by Tieck; and this edition may have come to the notice of Büchner even before his first visit to Strasbourg. In Strasbourg his circumstances were certainly calculated to nourish an interest in Lenz. Only a few years before, in 1826, J. J. Jaegle, the father of Büchner's fiancée, had delivered the funeral sermon on Jean-Frédéric Oberlin, the man who had once been Lenz's generous host and friend. In 1831 D. E. Stöber, the father of Büchner's friends August and Adolf Stöber, had published a biography of Oberlin in which Lenz's visit to Waldersbach was related. In the same year August Stöber had published in the Stuttgart *Morgenblatt* Lenz's letters to Salzmann and an account of his stay at Waldersbach based on a record by Oberlin which was to become the principal source of Büchner's Novelle. Evidence of continued interest in Lenz during Büchner's period in Giessen is to be found in the letter to Minna of March 1834 (2, 428), which contains a quotation from Lenz's poem about Friederike Brion, 'Die Liebe auf dem Lande':

> War nicht umsonst so still und schwach,
> Verlass'ne Liebe trug sie nach.
> In ihrer kleinen Kammer hoch
> Sie stets an der Erinnrung sog;
> An ihrem Brodschrank an der Wand
> Er immer, immer vor ihr stand,
> Und wenn ein Schlaf sie übernahm,
> Er immer, immer wieder kam . . .
> Denn immer, immer, immer doch
> Schwebt ihr das Bild an Wänden noch
> Von einem Menschen, welcher kam
> Und ihr als Kind das Herze nahm.
> Fast ausgelöscht ist sein Gesicht,
> Doch seiner Worte Kraft noch nicht,
> Und jener Stunden Seligkeit,
> Ach jener Träume Wirklichkeit,

Die, angeboren jedermann,
Kein Mensch sich wirklich machen kann.

The depth and persistence of Friederike's love for her faithless lover Goethe, so admirably expressed in these lines, explain the jealousy which Büchner ascribes to Lenz in the Novelle and which is such an important motif in it.

Although he had so long been interested in Lenz, it is not until May 1835 that we find the first indication of Büchner's intention to write a Novelle about him. On the 12th of that month Gutzkow writes to him:

> I presume your Novelle *Lenz* will be about the ship-wrecked poet, since Strasbourg suggests this subject.[12]

Then, on 28 September 1835, Gutzkow, eager for material for his projected journal *Deutsche Revue,* suggests that Büchner might be able to deal with Lenz more easily and quickly in the form of an essay:

> Give us, if nothing more for the beginning, *Recollections of Lenz*: you seem to have facts there which it would be easy to write up.[13]

And Büchner appears at first to fall in with this proposal, for he writes to his family in October 1835:

> Ich habe mir hier allerhand interessante Notizen über einen Freund Goethes, einen unglücklichen Poeten namens Lenz, verschafft, der sich gleichzeitig mit Goethe hier aufhielt und halb verrückt wurde. Ich denke darüber einen Aufsatz in der Deutschen Revue erscheinen zu lassen.
>
> (2, 448)

The material on which Büchner proposed to base his work was obtained largely, if not wholly, from August Stöber, and it included the manuscript of Oberlin's record of Lenz's visit. This record was published by Stöber for the first time in 1839 in the journal *Erwinia,* and a second time in Stöber's monograph *Der Dichter Lenz und Friederike von Sesenheim,* Basel, 1842, which contains the following footnote on Oberlin's report:

> On this essay is based the Novelle *Lenz* of my deceased friend Georg Büchner, which unfortunately remains a fragment. For a long time in Strasbourg he entertained the idea of making Lenz the hero of a Novelle, and I gave him as material all the manuscripts I possessed.[14]

To Gutzkow's inquiry of 6 February 1836: 'You were proposing once to write a Novelle *Lenz*' (*Eine Novelle Lenz war einmal beabsichtigt*) no reply has been preserved, and indeed Büchner makes no further mention of *Lenz* in any of the letters that have come down to us—unless we suppose that *Lenz* was one of the two 'dramas' referred to in Büchner's last letter to Minna which were to be published together with *Leonce und*

Lena. It is impossible to say precisely when the Novelle, in the form in which we have it, was written. It was evidently later than October 1835, since at that time Büchner was still proposing to deal with the subject in the form of an essay. And it was probably earlier than 1 January 1836, since *Lenz* was presumably one of the 'articles' which, as he remarks in his letter of that date, he was thinking of publishing in the *Phönix.*

. . . Gutzkow's valedictory article of June 1837 brought him as a reward from the hand of Minna Jaegle a fair copy of the manuscript of *Lenz* together with the copy of *Leonce und Lena.* Gutzkow published the Novelle in the *Telegraph für Deutschland* in 1839 under the title *Lenz. Eine Reliquie von Georg Büchner.* The next publication was by Ludwig Büchner in the *Nachgelassene Schriften* of 1850 under the title **"Lenz. Ein Novellenfragment."** The original manuscript and Minna Jaegle's copy have been lost, but some of the numerous errors and misprints in the first two publications can be corrected by reference to the record of Oberlin on which the Novelle is largely based.

It will have been observed that both August Stöber and Ludwig Büchner refer to the Novelle as a fragment; but it is now generally considered to be virtually complete. The conclusion, describing the condition of hopeless apathy and emptiness in which Lenz is sent away from Waldersbach and arrives in Strasbourg and in which he is doomed to go on living indefinitely (*So lebte er hin*), corresponds to the conclusion of Oberlin's record and is the logical end of Büchner's narrative. It is true that there is a lacuna in Büchner's text at the point where Oberlin describes his secret preparations for removing Lenz from Waldersbach, but Büchner has used the most interesting part of that description elsewhere and in the remainder there is little that could have seemed worthy to be incorporated in his Novelle. Yet it must be recognized that *Lenz* no less than *Leonce und Lena* lacks the author's final revision. There are some slight inconsistencies in the text and an occasional harshness in the grammatical constructions which Büchner might eventually have eliminated. Further difficulties are caused by the loss of the manuscript and the careless and incompetent editing already mentioned.[15]

The subject with which Büchner deals in *Lenz* could hardly be more serious. It is the story of the attempt of a young man of genius to escape the insanity that is overtaking him and of the failure of this attempt, the story of the gradual disintegration and destruction of his mind and soul. And Büchner deals with this subject in a tone as earnest as his theme. There is no ironical or whimsical diversion, as in *Leonce und Lena.* There are not even the touches of grim humour which occasionally relieve the tension in *Dantons Tod* and *Woyzeck.* The tragic reality is confronted simply and directly and rendered as it is, without distortion or mitigation. If in the remarks on literature and art which he puts into the mouth of Lenz we have the most perfect theoretical expression of Büchner's revolt against classicism and idealism, in the Novelle as a whole we have an admirable illustration of the consequences of that revolt for his literary and poetic practice. In this Novelle Büchner both preaches realism and practises it. He strives to render nature with the deepest truth, to seize and communicate that reality, that life, of which, as he lets his Lenz say, even the so-called realists had no conception and which was even more wretchedly travestied by the idealizers. He brings to the task the objectivity of a scientist as well as the imagination of a poet, and in his attitude of detached and uncompromising realism there is no doubt something of that implicit protest against Romantic illusions and chimeras, against Idealist dreams of perfection, which Hugo Friedrich has declared to be characteristic of nineteenth century realism in general.[16] But, as has already been observed in our discussion of Büchner's aesthetic revolt, one must be careful that one knows what one means when applying the equivocal word 'realism' to Büchner. Höllerer is no doubt right in his contention that Büchner's vivid compressed images often seem to anticipate the surrealists rather than the realists. But when he infers that 'Büchner, one of the fathers of realism, is at the same time one of the ancestors of so-called surrealism'; when he suggests that in some passages Büchner 'is nearer to surrealism and supranaturalism than to realism'; he appears to be introducing a dichotomy into Büchner's work which Büchner himself would have disclaimed.[17] It seems to be implied that Büchner is at one time a realist, at another time a surrealist or supranaturalist. But in truth Büchner is always a realist in the only sense that matters for him—in the sense that all his work is devoted to the one great aim of 'giving us nature with the utmost reality', of communicating his vision of reality with the utmost exactness, whether it be a vision of the external world or a vision of the human soul. He is not restricted in his choice of means; he can use exact descriptions or bold imaginative images:

> Auf dem kleinen Kirchhof war der Schnee weg, dunkles Moos unter den schwarzen Kreuzen, ein verspäteter Rosenstrauch lehnte an der Kirchhofmauer, verspätete Blumen dazu unter dem Moos hervor, manchmal Sonne, dann wieder dunkel.
>
> (84)

> [wenn] die Wolken wie wilde wiehernde Rosse heransprengten, und der Sonnenschein dazwischen durchging und kam und sein blitzendes Schwert an den Schneeflächen zog, so daß ein helles, blendendes Licht über die Gipfel in die Thäler schnitt.
>
> (79)

But one sees that the descriptions and the images serve the same purpose: the exact communication of the impression received, and the latter are no less necessary to this end than the former. This intentness on the precise impression seems to me to distinguish Büchner after all from the modern expressionists and surrealists, and to place him with Stendhal and Flaubert and Chekhov rather than with Barlach or Klee or Kafka. Camus's comparison of Melville and Kafka still holds good when Büchner's name is substituted for Melville's:

> Like the greatest artists, Melville has constructed his symbols out of concrete experiences, not out of the stuff of dreams. The creator of myths has a claim to genius only in so far as he inscribes them in the density of reality and not in the fleeting clouds of the imagination. In Kafka it is the symbol that gives rise to the reality described, the incident springs from the image; in Melville the symbol emerges from the reality, the image is born of the perception. That is why Melville always remains in contact with the flesh and with nature, which are obscured in Kafka's work.[18]

It is not his dreams that Büchner is trying to convey, nor any abstraction; it is no 'Wesensschau' or 'Tiefenschau'; it is the phenomena of life as he has experienced and observed them. And that is why, unlike the surrealists and expressionists, he is by no means averse to precise localization in space and time: the events of his Novelle occur to well known people at specific dates in a particular valley of the Vosges mountains. Present fashions should not tempt us to deny or minimize this strong realistic tendency which Büchner himself plainly and proudly recognized in his work.

It is this tendency which impels him once more, as in ***Dantons Tod*** and later in ***Woyzeck,*** to base his work on a careful study of historical documents. We have already noticed the relation of the Novelle to Oberlin's record of Lenz's visit. But that record is by no means the only source of Büchner's information. He has also taken many details from D. E. Stöber's biography of Oberlin, a work which he must have read attentively. In the Novelle as in the biography we are told how Oberlin was saved by an invisible hand from falling to his death from a bridge; how Oberlin counselled and comforted his parishioners and advised them on practical matters such as the construction of roads; how he heard mysterious voices and was interested in clairvoyance; how, in his childlike faith in God, he trustingly allowed his conduct to be determined by drawing lots.[19] And one may compare Büchner's sentence:

> Ein andermal zeigte ihm Oberlin Farbentäfelchen, er setzte ihm auseinander, in welcher Beziehung jede Farbe mit dem Menschen stände, er brachte zwölf Apostel heraus, deren jeder durch eine Farbe repräsentirt würde . . .
>
> (86)

with the following from Stöber:

> Le rouge signifie la foi; le jaune, l'amour; le bleu, la science . . . Chacun des douze apôtres de notre Seigneur et Sauveur Jésus-Christ a sa couleur, qui le distingue particulièrement.[20]

One may agree with Voss that by means of such details Büchner is able to give more plasticity to his portrait of Oberlin and at the same time communicate something of the religious, mystical and superstitious atmosphere of the Steintal.[21]

Goethe's *Werther* and Tieck's *Der Aufruhr in den Cevennen* (1826) are the fictional works which have most strongly influenced *Lenz.* Ludwig Büchner relates that when Minna Jaegle visited Büchner in Darmstadt in the autumn of 1834, he and she read Tieck's Novelle with great interest and pleasure;[22] and there are some striking parallels between particular passages in *Der Aufruhr in den Cevennen* and in *Lenz.* Büchner's account of the religious enthusiasm of the people of the Steintal may also have been influenced generally by Tieck's description of the religious fanaticism of the *Camisards.*

But more important than all these external sources are the personal experience and observation which Büchner has embodied in his Novelle. According to Ludwig Büchner, his brother 'found in Lenz's life and character spiritual conditions akin to his own, and the fragment is more or less a self-portrait of the writer'.[23] Without wishing to press this last assertion, one must agree that Büchner really had much in common with Lenz and that the extraordinary power and authority of his Novelle is largely due to this natural affinity. He had himself experienced the pantheistic raptures and sudden despairs which he ascribes to his hero, and he shared Lenz's passion for drama, his aesthetic principles, his sympathy for poor and oppressed people. Moreover, during the sickness and acute distress which he had suffered in Giessen in the winter of 1833-4 Büchner had experienced and had described in his letters states of mind which, as Landau remarks,[24] were not far removed from madness and not unlike those ascribed to the insane Lenz of the Novelle:

> Der erste helle Augenblick seit acht Tagen. Unaufhörliches Kopfweh und Fieber, die Nacht kaum einige Stunden dürftiger Ruhe. Vor zwei Uhr komme ich in kein Bett, und dann ein beständiges Auffahren aus dem Schlaf und ein Meer von Gedanken, in denen mir die Sinne vergehen . . . Meine geistigen Kräfte sind gänzlich zerrüttet. Arbeiten ist mir unmöglich, ein dumpfes Brüten hat sich meiner bemeistert, in dem mir kaum ein Gedanke noch hell wird.
>
> (*An die Braut,* März 1834, 2, 424 f.)

But Büchner's happier experiences also have found expression in *Lenz.* When, in the letter just referred to, he tells Minna that her image continually stands before him, that he sees her in every dream, we are reminded of Lenz's visions of Friederike Brion in the Novelle (*Er rettete sich in eine Gestalt, die ihm immer vor Augen schwebte*—89). And the Vosges mountains, which Büchner wandered over on foot in the summer of 1833 and described with so much enthusiasm in his letter of 8 July of that year—later he tells Gutzkow that he loves the Vosges like a mother and knows every peak and valley of them (2, 449)—provided him with the perfect and inevitable setting for the varying moods of his hero, the momentarily peaceful moods and the wildly tragic ones.

Notes

1. Ludwig Büchner, p. 37: 'Die Cotta'sche Buchhandlung hatte bis zum 1. Juli einen Preis auf das beste Lustspiel ausgesetzt.'

2. 'In derselben Zeit und später zu Zürich vollendete er ein im Manuskript vorliegendes Lustspiel, Leonce und Lena, voll Geist, Witz und kecker Laune.'

3. This is according to Gutzkow's account of the matter (*Werke,* ed. by Reinhold Gensel, vol. 11, p. 90). Lehmann (*Textkritische Noten,* p. 29) suggests that Gutzkow may have received an original MS of *Leonce und Lena* and, having mislaid or lost it, may only have pretended to have received a copy in order to conceal his carelessness. It seems improbable that Gutzkow would have dared to publish a statement which, as he must have known, Minna Jaegle would immediately recognize to be false. There is no reason to suspect Gutzkow of dishonesty. Lehmann himself remarks (ibid., p. 29) that Gutzkow frankly confessed to Louise Büchner that he had lost some of her brother's papers.

4. Bergemann, 1922, p. 687: 'aus Prüderie oder Unachtsamkeit'.

5. Lehmann, *Textkritische Noten,* p. 34: 'die von politischer Vorsicht diktierte, von literarischem Unverständnis und schulmeisterlichem Hochmut zeugende Redaktion Ludwig Büchners'.

6. '. . . ein wunderlicher, wetterwend'scher Kerl, der alle Leute unterhält und immer Langeweile hat, witzig und verlegen, hart und wohltätig, geht immer wie ein Verliebter herum, hat alle Weiber nach der Reihe in sich vernarrt und quält sie mit Kälte'.

7. Gundolf, p. 390: 'Doch das Ganze kommt aus der literarischen Nachahmung Brentanos, Tiecks, Shakespeares.'

8. Mayer, p. 310: 'Leonce aber, Lena, Valerio und alle die anderen Gestalten des Märchenspuks haben vor allem sehr viele Bücher gelesen. Prinz und Vielfraß, Prinzessin und empfindsame alte Jungfer führen ein Leben aus zweiter Hand.'

9. Hölderlin, 'Über den Unterschied der Dichtarten', StA 4, p. 266.

10. Mayer, p. 311: 'Größerer Mißklang ist nicht denkbar als hier zwischen Büchners sonstiger Lehre, der Gesamtanlage seines Werks, und diesem ironisch-romantischen Spiel von den beiden Königskindern.'

11. Cf. Fink, 'Leonce und Lena', Martens, 1965, pp. 500f.: 'Die nüchterne Wirklichkeit, wie er sie in seinem Dramen zeigte, war tieftraurig, ja tragisch, so daß sie keineswegs einer komischen Gattung hätte einverleibt werden können. Realismus und komödie sind in seinen Augen unvereinbar . . . Diese pessimistische Auffassung von der Wirklichkeit bringt als Gegensatz dazu die Unwirklichkeitder Komödie mit sich.'

12. 'Ihre Novelle Lenz soll jedenfalls, weil Straßburg dazu anregt, den gestrandeten Poeten zum Vorwurf haben?' (2, 479)

13. 'Geben Sie uns, wenn weiter nichts im Anfang, *Erinnerungen an Lenz*: da scheinen Sie Thatsachen zu haben, die leicht aufgezeichnet sind.' (2, 481)

14. 'Dieser . . . Aufsatz bildet die Grundlage der leider Fragment gebliebenen Novelle "Lenz" meines verstorbenen Freundes Georg Büchner. Er trug sich schon in Straßburg lange Zeit mit dem Gedanken, Lenz zum Helden einer Novelle zu machen, und ich gab ihm zu seinem Stoffe alles, was ich an Handschriften besaß.'

15. There are inconsistencies in the indications of dates at the following places in the *Novelle*: p. 93, l. 11; 94, 12; 94, 17; 95, 34; 97, 27; 100, 11 (cf. Landau, vol. 1, p. 108, Martens, 1965, p. 35). The grammar is strange or the text corrupt at 84, 29 ff.; and in the expression *leeres tiefes Bergwasser* (85, 26) one should probably read *reines* instead of *leeres*.

16. Cf. Höllerer, 1958, p. 423: 'Nach den Thesen von H. Friedrich ("Das antiromantische Denken im modernen Frankreich", München, 1935; "Die Klassiker des französischen Romans", Leipzig, 1939) entsteht Wirklichkeitsdichtung aus dem Absturz und als Gegenbild gegen alle Vollkommenheitsvorstellungen.'

17. Höllerer, ibid., pp. 134 f.: 'So wird Büchner, ein Vater des Realismus, gleichzeitig auch ein Ahnherr des sogenannten Surrealismus, sich stützend auf romantische Sprachbewegung.'

18. Camus, 'Hermann Melville', *Théâtre, Récits, Nouvelles,* 1962, p. 1901: 'Comme les plus grands artistes, Melville a construit ses symboles sur le concret, non dans le matériau du rêve. Le créateur de mythes ne participe au génie que dans la mesure où il les inscrit dans l'épaisseur de la réalité et non dans les nuées fugitives de l'imagination. Chez Kafka la réalité qu'il décrit est suscitée par le symbole, le fait découle de l'image, chez Melville le symbole sort de la réalité, l'image naît de la perception. C'est pourquoi Melville ne s'est jamais séparé de la chair ni de la nature, obscurcies dans l'œuvre kafkéenne.'

19. Stöber, *Vie de J.-F. Oberlin,* Strasbourg, 1831, pp. 116, 114, 182, 523, 547.

20. Ibid., pp. 533 f.

21. Voss, p. 6: 'Die Lebensgeschichte Oberlins, von Daniel Ehrenfried Stöber 1828 verfaßt, hat Büchner genau gekannt und ziemlich viele Einzelheiten in seine Novelle übernommen, um der Gestalt Oberlins die nötige Plastik zu geben und die religiöse Atmosphäre des Steintals besser zu zeichnen.'

22. Ludwig Büchner, p. 19.

23. Ibid., p. 47: 'In Lenzens Leben und Sein fühlte er verwandte Seelenzustände, und das Fragment ist halb und halb des Dichters eigenes Porträt.'

24. Landau, vol. 1, p. 113, Martens, 1965, p. 41.

Works Cited

Bergemann, Fritz: *Georg Büchner, Sämtliche Werke und Briefe,* Leipzig, 1922 (with critical apparatus omitted in later editions of this work).

Büchner, Ludwig: *Georg Büchner. Revolutionär und Pessimist,* Nürnberg, 1948. *Büchners Bild vom Menschen,* Nürnberg, 1967.

Camus, Albert: *L'Homme révolté* (1949), *Essais,* Bibliothèque de la Pléiade, Paris, 1965.

Gundolf, Friedrich: 'Georg Büchner', *Romantiker,* Berlin, 1930 (reprinted Martens, 1965, pp. 82 ff.).

Höllerer, Walter: 'Georg Büchner', *Zwischen Klassik und Moderne,* Stuttgart, 1958.

Landau, Paul: *Georg Büchners Gesammelte Schriften,* 2 Bände, Berlin, 1909.

Lehmann, Werner R.: *Textkritische Noten. Prolegomena zur Hamburger Büchner-Ausgabe,* Hamburg, 1967.

Martens, Wolfgang: *Georg Büchner,* hrsg. von Wolfgang Martens, Wege der Forschung, Bd. LIII, Darmstadt, 1965.

Mayer, Hans: *Georg Büchner und seine Zeit,* Wiesbaden, 1946. (Neue, erweiterte Auflage, Frankfurt a. M., 1972.)

Voss, Kurt: *Georg Büchners 'Lenz'. Eine Untersuchung nach Gehalt und Formgebung,* Bonn, 1922 (dissertation).

Nancy Lukens (essay date 1977)

SOURCE: Lukens, Nancy. "Introduction" and "Conclusion." In *Büchner's Valerio and the Theatrical Fool Tradition*, pp. 1-29; 192-95. Stuttgart, Germany: Akademischer Verlag Hans-Dieter Heinz, 1977, 221 p.

[*In the following excerpts, Lukens discusses the ironic function of Valerio in Büchner's* Leonce and Lena, *relating this character to the stage-fool tradition in European drama.*]

The first act of Georg Büchner's comedy **Leonce und Lena** (1836) is introduced by a motto from Shakespeare's *As You Like It* (II.vii.43-44):

> O wär ich doch ein Narr!
> Mein Ehrgeiz geht auf eine bunte Jacke.[1]

Surely it is no coincidence that Büchner should choose the melancholy Jaques of Shakespeare's creation to evoke the whole complex of attitudes toward reality and self that we sense in Leonce. In fact, Jaques' light-hearted counterpart Touchstone is also unmistakably present in Büchner's conception of Valerio, court fool in the fictitious kingdom of Popo, companion to the melancholy prince Leonce, and focal point of the present study. Just as Jaques envies Touchstone's gay yet "material" (i.e., pithy) wit (III.3.25), so Leonce depends on Valerio's ironic comments, facetious mockery and nonsense games to divert him from his perpetual idleness and abject boredom. Jaques' melancholy is an *ennui* not unrelated to that of Leonce. Both are restless and able to "suck melancholy" (*As You Like It* II.v.11-12) out of any object or situation, and the ultimate wish of both is to be freed of their present identity and to become something else. Leonce's central speech in the first scene of Büchner's play culminates in the exclamation: "O wer einmal jemand anders sein könnte! Nur 'ne Minute lang."[2]

This is a key passage for several reasons. First, it is reminiscent not only of the motto quoted above, but more generally of the spirit of Jaques' well-known set-speech in *As You Like It* on the "seven ages of man" (II.vii.140-165). For Leonce, life is a study in idleness, boredom and meaninglessness:

> —Müssiggang ist aller Laster Anfang.
>
> —Was die Leute nicht Alles aus Langeweile treiben! Sie studiren aus Langeweile, sie beten aus Langeweile, sie verlieben, verheirathen und vermehren sich aus Langeweile, und sterben endlich an der Langeweile, und—und das ist der Humor davon—alles mit den wichtigsten Gesichtern, ohne zu merken warum, und meinen Gott weiss was dabei.
>
> (I.i.106,6-12)

So far, before Valerio's entrance, Leonce's activity has been limited to bitter observation and reflection in this vein. Similarly, the image we get of Jaques wandering and reflecting in the Forest of Arden on man's foibles is that of a gloomy gentleman whose sole pleasure consists in embittered bemoaning of the world about him:

> All the world's a stage,
> And all the men and women merely players:
> They have their exits and their entrances;
> And one man in his time plays many parts,
> His acts being seven ages. At first, the infant,
> Mewling and puking in the nurse's arms.
> Then the whining school-boy, with his satchel
> And shining morning face, creeping like snail
> Unwillingly to school. And then the lover,
> sighing like furnace, with a woeful ballad
> Made to his mistress' eyebrow. . . .
>
> (II.vii.140-150)

But both Leonce's and Jaques' outlooks change radically under the influence of their gayer partners Valerio and Touchstone—and this points to the more important aspect of the passage in which we see Leonce's wish to be transformed, for it is here that we have the first indication of the essential function the fool will fulfill.

Normally sullen and antisocial of disposition, Jaques is beside himself with excitement as he tells the Duke of his meeting with Touchstone:

> A fool, a fool! I met a fool i' the forest,
> A motley fool; a miserable world!
>   . . . . .
> . . . When I did hear
> The motley fool thus moral on the time,
> My lungs began to crow like chanticleer,
> That fools should be so deep-contemplative;
> And I did laugh sans intermission
> An hour by his dial. O noble fool!
> A worthy fool! Motley's the only wear.
>
> (II.vii.12-24, 28-34)[3]

The ironic effect of the encounter depends in part on Shakespeare's device for conveying it dramatically through Jaques' second-hand account; in this way the fool's art works against Jaques even as he speaks positively of that fool. Not only has Touchstone enlivened Jaques, he has duped him in the process by playing up to his melancholy manner. With a note of parody Touchstone looks at the sundial "with lack-lustre eye" and makes dour observations about "how the world wags" (II.vii.21,23), thus playing his part by mirroring Jaques' own folly and himself remaining amusedly aloof, while Jaques is oblivious to anything but what he wants to see. Sensing in Touchstone something he himself would like to be, Jaques goes away from the encounter determined to acquire his own license to speak his mind and to "cleanse the foul body of the infected world" (II.vii.60).

Similarly, Valerio's first entrance in **Leonce und Lena** marks a sudden shift in tempo and mood from Leonce's ponderous reflections. In sharp contrast to the lack of dialogue or interaction between Leonce and the *Hofmeister* at the opening of the play, where Leonce simulates responses for his puppet-like tutor in order to continue his monologue, here Valerio initiates a rapid-fire exchange of absurdities which have the function simply of creating a relationship based on imaginative roleplay. Valerio appears, somewhat intoxicated, just as Leonce is expressing his desire to be transformed:

L.:

Wie der Mensch läuft! Wenn ich nur . . .

V.:

(stellt sich dicht vor den Prinzen, legt den Finger an die Nase und sieht ihn starr an): Ja!

L.:

(eben so): Richtig!

V.:

Haben Sie mich begriffen?

L.:

Vollkommen.

V.:

Nun, so wollen wir von etwas Anderem reden. (Er legt sich ins Gras.)

(I.i.106,25-31)

Without having any direct relationship with the life at court so far, the fool seems here to be a living mirror to its absurdity and pretentiousness. Leonce's "conversation" with the tutor evaporates into nothing for lack of opposition, and he falls into even deeper melancholy and self-pity for having to be aware of the rift between the serious, self-righteous mien of people around him and the spiritual vacuum it hides. Then suddenly Valerio's game snatches him out of this world and transports him to another—that of possibility—despite his resistance at first. After two responses addressing Valerio with condescending sympathy as one plagued with ideals like himself, Leonce then begins to identify with the fool, adopting the "du" form, and the game progresses with increasing familiarity and mutual intoxication until Leonce, too, is drunk on Valerio's fooldom:

L.:

Halt's Maul mit deinem Lied, man könnte darüber ein Narr werden.

V.:

So wäre man doch etwas. Ein Narr! Ein Narr! Wer will mir seine Narrheit gegen meine Vernunft verhandeln? Ha, ich bin Alexander der Grosse! Wie mir die Sonne eine goldne Krone in die Haare scheint, wie meine

Uniform blitzt! Herr Generalissimus Heupferd, lassen Sie die Truppen anrücken! Herr Finanzminister Kreuzspinne, ich brauche Geld! Liebe Hofdame Libelle, was macht meine theure Gemahlin Bohnenstange? Ach bester Herr Leibmedicus Cantharide, ich bin um einen Erbprinzen verlegen. Und zu diesen köstlichen Phantasieen bekommt man gute Suppe, gutes Fleisch, gutes Brod, ein gutes Bett und das Haar umsonst geschoren—im Narrenhaus nämlich—, während ich mit meiner gesunden Vernunft mich höchstens zur Beförderung der Reife auf einen Kirschbaum verdingen könnte, um—nun?—um?

L.:

Um die Kirschen durch die Löcher in deinen Hosen schamroth zu machen! Aber Edelster, dein Handwerk, deine Profession, dein Gewerbe, dein Stand, deine Kunst?

V.:

(mit Würde): Herr, ich habe die grosse Beschäftigung, müssig zu gehen, ich habe eine ungemeine Fertigkeit in Nichtsthun, ich besitze eine ungeheure Ausdauer in der Faulheit. Keine Schwiele schändet meine Hände, der Boden hat noch keinen Tropfen von meiner Stirne getrunken, ich bin noch Jungfau in der Arbeit, und wenn es mir nicht der Mühe zu viel wäre, würde ich mir die Mühe nehmen, Ihnen diese Verdienste weitläufiger auseinandersetzen.

L.:

(mit komischem Enthusiasmus): Komm an meine Brust! Bist du einer von den Göttlichen, welche mühelos mit reiner Stirne durch den Schweiss und Staub über die Heerstrasse des Lebens wandeln, und mit glänzenden Sohlen und blühenden Leibern gleich seligen Göttern in den Olympus treten? Komm! Komm!

V.:

(singt im Abgehen): Hei! da sitzt e Fleiz an der Wand! Fleig an der Wand! Fleig an der Wand! (Beide Arm in Arm ab.)

(I.i.107,13-108,8)

By the third scene of this act, in fact, Leonce has progressed so far in his ability to play the fool to his own role of puppet prince, that Valerio is prompted to comment: "Eure Hoheit scheint mir wirklich auf dem besten Weg, ein wahrhaftiger Narr zu werden" (I.iii.112,38-39).

Is this a fool figure that we recognize, whose dramatic function in relationship to the court we can adequately compare to that of the traditional Renaissance fool? We have seen a certain resemblance between Touchstone's and Valerio's manipulation tactics. Each mirrors the particular folly of his melancholy companion, and in so doing, implicitly points out the follies of society at large. But a striking difference remains between Touchstone's role in the idyllic (or mock-idyllic) world of the Forest of Arden, and Valerio's in the equally fantastic setting of the Kingdom of Popo. While both do assume an ironic, detached stance with regard to the values and ways of life of their respective worlds, this manifests itself in vastly different ways. Touchstone remains an observer, relatively uninvolved and unaggressive in the unfolding of the essential plot which centers around Orlando and Rosalind, reinforcing its themes in a sort of comic counterpoint to the serious undertones. Valerio, on the other hand, is clearly the moving force behind the "plot" in *Leonce und Lena,* if the movement here can indeed be called a plot. This question will be pursued further in another context. In any case, Valerio is no longer a tolerated misfit whose natural wit amuses the powers that be, but who represents no particular threat to their power or well-being; on the contrary, while the king remains a ridiculous caricature, the fool's antics and at first apparently nonsensical verbal feats assume a dramatic function which clearly outweighs that of any other character, including the title "hero" and "heroine."

What does this mean in terms of the original concept of the court fool's place in the king's household, and in terms of the subsidiary or at best complementary role he traditionally played in Shakespearean comedy and tragedy? In order to answer this and related questions, I shall . . . attempt to determine on the basis of the text of *Leonce und Lena* itself how Valerio's situation and character do compare to other well-known and lesser known plays in which a court fool figure plays a significant role.

Although we can use *As You Like It* as one point of reference, the configuration of king and fool figures and their power relationship in *King Lear* present an equally important side of the Shakespearean fool from which to observe traits essential to the understanding of Valerio's role. For here much more than in the comedy, we have the central theme of loss of identity in the ruler figure, one which also pervades Büchner's play, and which has direct bearing on our interpretation of the fool's part in the totality of the drama. Indeed, a major reason for having recourse to Shakespeare's models is the very direct correlation that seems to me to exist between his fool characters and the views of human power and human folly they help to convey, and on the other hand the views that Büchner puts forth through his own fool pair Leonce and Valerio.

My hypothesis is that Valerio, while resorting to many of the same devices of fooldom known to us through Renaissance figures such as Touchstone and Lear's Fool—word-play, impersonation and mockery, and varying extremes of nonsensical roleplay—at the same time presents a view of man, and fulfills a dramatic function radically opposed to that which we find implied in earlier plays. The very presence of the "all-licensed" fool in Shakespearean drama implies a political and social order which can tolerate the fool's arrows, a king who is human enough to need and appreciate the wit of a neutral subject such as his fool and yet whose role as representative of a higher order is not ultimately threatened. In the plays of Büchner as well as others to be considered in this study, the idea of any ultimate order is highly questionable. Thus the role of the fool is necessarily of different dimensions, and the relationship between king and fool by implication not one of give and take as before, but much more one-sided, with the greater degree of aggression on the fool's part. In fact, Valerio determines the course of "events" in *Leonce und Lena* to such a degree that King Peter's attempts to establish order appear utterly ridiculous and fooldom—whose nature we hope to determine in greater detail as we progress—proves the only way to preserve one's identity.[4]

At this point a perplexing question arises. If indeed we can talk about the problem of identity in the court fool of the modern stage—that is, in terms of his social relationships and his conscious role as a functioning member of the stage world—then the fool must have grown to new dimensions here from those of the types we encounter earlier. While the medieval and early Renaissance fool types were often recognizable as individuals, they did on the whole exist as representatives of chaos, evil, irrationality, or simple baseness rather than as complex beings involved in a real way in the dramatic action. The stage clowns of Shakespeare's day tended to improvise, even to the extent of becoming an attraction completely divorced from the tragedy at hand.[5] In fact, by the time the English Comedians found their way to the Continent in the early seventeenth century, with plays derived largely from Shakespeare, the total effect was burlesque. It was to rid the theater of all such influences that Gottsched caused Harlequin to be banned from the stage altogether, since it was felt he had no serious function in the drama of order and reason.[6] If the fool in Shakespeare had been intended to play an integral part in the dramatic universe, he had gradually become for the Germans of the Enlightenment a popular but distracting accessory.

From the time Harlequin was banished in 1724 until romantic playwrights such as Tieck and Brentano rediscovered his merits for their comedies, the fool remained unknown to the "high" theater of Germany. To be sure, there were isolated attempts by German enlightenment critics to rehabilitate the image of the stage fool, whether he be called Harlequin, Hanswurst, Skaramuz, or simply Narr. Lessing denounces Gottsched's action in both the *Siebzehnter Literaturbrief* (1759) and the *Hamburgische Dramaturgie, 18. Stück* (1767). In the former, he refers ironically to the banishment of Harlequin as "die grösste Harlequinade [. . .], die jemals gespielt worden."[7] It is interesting to note that it is in this same letter that Lessing speaks so enthusiastically of Shakespeare's dramaturgy. Undoubtedly Shakespeare's fool figures were not without influence on Lessing's hopes for the German theater, unfruitful though they proved to be in his own time. In the other instance Lessing makes reference to the comedies of Marivaux and insists that, although most would-be distinguished theaters in Germany had seemed to conform to the Gottschedian injunction, "im Grunde hatten sie nur das bunte Jäckchen und den Namen abgeschafft, aber den Narren behalten."[8]

Even earlier, in fact, the comic actor and playwright Johann Christian Krüger had defended Harlequin in the preface to his German translation of Marivaux (1747), and in 1761 Justus Möser had published a lengthy essay in his behalf, "Harlequin, oder Verteidigung des Grotesk-Komischen."[9] Here the true nature of the fool figure is recognized as one belonging neither to the crude burlesque comedies Gottsched abhorred, nor to the didactic bourgeois comedy of the Enlightenment, where his role is necessarily subordinated to complicated intrigues which point to an underlying moral code. Rather, Möser sees the opera as "das Reich der Chimären," which alone can provide the comic figure with the kind of *Spielraum* he needs. Möser's main thesis, put into the mouth of Harlequin himself, is that as a member of the king's payroll at court, the fool represents a legitimate and necessary rung in the hierarchy of the social and political order; in the aesthetic sense, that the grotesque-comic element is an indispensable component of the beautiful.[10] Möser appended to his treatise an original one-act comedy with many of the familiar *commedia dell'arte* types such as Harlequin, Scapin, Columbine, Isabelle and Valer, though even here the types are not given free rein to move outside the moral bounds of eighteenth-century taste.[11] So even the most outspoken proponents of a reinstatement of the fool figure in eighteenth century Germany was unable to create one who could fulfill a traditional function.[12]

Until the German Romantics rediscovered the world of the *commedia* and the masks it provided, the stage in Germany remained the poorer for the absence of the motley fool with his upside-down logic, his biting wit and crude sense of humor. Even in Tieck's *Verkehrte Welt* and *Prinz Zerbino,* and Brentano's *Ponce de Leon,* all of which Büchner knew and drew upon for his *Leonce and Lena,* the fool remains a type familiar from the Italian *commedia,* simply transported for the purpose of satirizing contemporary German society. Büchner's Valerio, on the other hand, seems to have a far deeper and more abysmal consciousness of his role as fool to the court's folly.

Is it possible, then, that Büchner is one of the first German dramatists since the seventeenth century whose fool figure again attains the stature of Shakespeare's by setting the dominant tone of the dramatic reality with his gruesome wit, and by entering into aggressive, personal relationship with the central figures? Valerio is no longer a distraction from or an amusing compensation for the basically tragic fabric of the drama: instead, like Lear's Fool, he reinforces it, and even more noticeably than Lear's Fool, he takes an aggressive role on behalf of his master. Not only does he reflect and dote on his master's folly to the delight and instruction of the audience; more importantly, he cultivates folly as a weapon against a society that deems itself reasonable.

To understand more fully what comprises this distinction in Valerio's character and his dramatic function is the chief task of this study. It is by no means a simple question, for Büchner clearly chooses to adopt some features of the traditions from which we have just begun to separate him. It is also difficult to compare such vastly different worlds as the grotesque-comic fairy-tale kingdom of Popo and the grimly realistic setting of Lear's dominion, for example, although in the abstract they are not so dissimilar. In fact, this similarity in the abstract—i.e., the scheme in which fool calls ruler's power into question and by turning the world of 'order' and 'reason' inside out actually brings new life to the court—is precisely the basis for our asking the central question about the modern fool's role. It seems to me that this very question constitutes a thrust of Büchner's dramatic effort which cannot be ignored. By trying to understand Valerio against the background of the tradition he represents, one can perhaps come closer to what Büchner is trying to say about tradition in general and about the nature of social man as he saw him in the third decade of the nineteenth century.

And yet the questions Büchner raises with the help of his fool are interesting to the modern reader and playgoer not only in this limited framework. They are universal. Not only does Valerio's function in *Leonce und Lena* have recognizable roots in tradition and new meaning for his own time, but his fooldom speaks a language rich in overtones and timeless gestures which lead today's audience to draw certain parallels, and in turn to play the fool by asking the same ultimate questions of himself and the powers that control his own society. Every organism, whether individual, corporate, natural or political, needs to be challenged and renewed continually in order to survive, and artists, in their portrayals of this process or its failure, have frequently assigned the role of harbinger of the process to a court fool figure of some sort, for reasons which should become clear in the course of this study.

As time goes on and social and political structures change, it is interesting to notice just how the dramatic artist chooses to portray this process of criticism and renewal within his compact, often symbolic structure of human relationships. Although for purposes of clarity I have chosen exclusively plays which deal directly with the king-court fool relationship, it should be kept in mind that this setting in more recent plays often serves merely as a historical veil for the playwright's views on such power relationships and social structures in general. This is the primary reason for including several twentieth century plays with prominent court fool figures in this study despite its primary focus on Valerio. Each of the plays since Büchner illustrates one or more aspects of the development of the fool's social and dramatic function already present in Valerio. Furthermore, the more recent playwright seems to be saying something about the fool-ruler or fool-society relationship which it is essential not to ignore if one takes Büchner seriously.

In Frank Wedekind's *König Nicolo—Oder so ist das Leben* (1901) we find a single figure in whom traditional concepts of the unjust ruler, the buffoon, and the prophetic wise fool are combined in an unusual fashion. Both internal evidence in the play and the playwright's own remarks about its reception point to the fact that the dramatist identifies himself with the king-fool figure.[13] In spite of dramatic weaknesses, which Wedekind himself recognized and attributed in part to this too close personal involvement with the central figure, *König Nicolo* does illustrate one direction the court fool figure of the modern theater can take, one which Büchner implies in Leonce and Valerio as well. This is that of the outcast, who discovers himself and his fool's mask only outside the bounds of his "normal" existence. Just as Valerio helps Leonce achieve ironic detachment from his designated social and political role as heir to a meaningless throne, so Nicolo moves through several states of detached self-examination until, with the help of his Hanswurst-companion Anna, he actually assumes the role of court fool to the king who had replaced him. While the exile of the fool and his companion in **Leonce und Lena** is voluntary and that of Nicolo and is daughter is forced, each pair's return to the court at the end of the play shows what their respective creators intended to say about the fool's role in the renewal of his society's values and structures. Not only this basic similarity between Wedekind's and Büchner's fool pairs, but other interesting interconnections as well will be pursued in the course of this investigation.

Another play of some interest to us in this same respect is Pär Lagerkvist's *Konungen,* "The King" (1932). The fool in this work is not such a central character as those in the other plays, yet his words and gestures are so expressive of the play's theme, so closely linked with the concerns of the main figure of the deposed and outcast king, and both in turn seem so clearly to have the playwright's sympathy, that again the parallels with Büchner are too striking to ignore. Both express revolutionary sympathies, and yet the dramatic solutions to similar questions are radically different in Lagerkvist. Both dramatists pose ultimate questions through their ruler and fool figures—i.e. What does the King really represent? What ultimate order and good does he bring to the people? How do the actions of king and fool as individuals define their identity with regard to the total order? Thus we are immediately alerted to watch for similarities and differences in the fool's position, as well as in the authors' unspoken assumptions about man's folly and ultimate order which are evident throughout each play.

Both Wedekind and Lagerkvist depict deposed rulers—as does Shakespeare in both *As You Like It* and *King Lear.* Each dramatist chooses his own technique of motivating the situation, but in each case the resulting relationship of king and fool is strikingly similar. In the comic setting of *As You Like It,* the deposition of the rightful duke is a temporary upset of the political order, which is restored with perfect symmetry and no dire consequences. On the other hand, the tragedy of *King Lear* shows dire consequences of the inner as well as outward upheaval in the king's domain, with ultimate healing nevertheless. Wedekind motivates the deposition within the framework of a just system. The deposed King Nicolo is seen as having violated the limits of his kingship by his arrogance, and the popular hero, the butcher Pietro who replaces him, is seen not as a usurper as in Shakespeare's comedy, but as a pragmatic and just ruler close enough to the political and economic needs of the people to maintain order better than the proud but blind Nicolo had done. Nicolo is in a situation not unlike Lear's, in that his own bad judgment has led to the undermining and overthrow of his kingdom. The fool in both cases is instrumental in reflecting the folly of the ruler which caused his inner chaos as well as actual upheaval in the kingdom. The interaction between King Lear and his fool shows the two figures to be intimately interconnected, even while appearing outwardly at opposite ends of the ladder of power. In Wedekind's play, king and fool are understood as two forces struggling for control within the one person of the king, and by implication in Everyman. In King Nicolo, true kingship is portrayed as being developed only by recognizing the foolishness of false royalty and by assuming the mask of the fool in order to convey truth to the court.

All of these variations on the deposed king motif have direct bearing on **Leonce und Lena,** and yet one cannot overlook the striking contrast. While the exposition of Shakespeare's and Wedekind's king-fool relationships relies heavily on substantial character development as well as on movement toward a recognizable dramatic climax, there prevails in Büchner's comedy an artificiality and a suspension that precludes any real interaction, or at least any dramatic development which the viewer could take seriously. Perhaps this suspension can be attributed solely to the absurdity of the image of

Peter as king. Leonce's desire to flee the kingdom is based not on outrage at any visible injustice as seen in *Lear, As You Like It* and *König Nicolo,* but on a vague feeling of desperation. The king and the kingdom are mere puppet and backdrop for the actual substance of the dramatic action in *Leonce und Lena,* which consists in the relationship between Valerio and the prince. The prince's absence from the throne—whether by flight or deposition—is not so much a motivating factor in a development toward renewed wholeness in the kingdom, but rather a mere pretext for tragi-comic contrast between the imagined ideal and the existing reality.

Even more acute than in the full-length plays of Shakespeare, Lagerkvist and Wedekind is the dramatization of the deposed king motif in the one-act play *Escurial* (1927) of the Belgian Michel de Ghelderode. Here again, the power play between the enthroned ruler and his court fool is of utmost importance; in fact, Ghelderode, by limiting his cast of characters to King, Fool, Priest and Executioner, shifts the attention completely away from extraneous persons and sub-plots which usually complicate both the *commedia dell'arte* and court drama, notably Shakespeare's. The spotlight falls not on a cross section of the universe, but exclusively on the tottering king and his grotesquely powerful fool Folial. Their exchange of roles is psychologically motivated on the one hand, insofar as both King and Fool contain projections of the other which influence their respective self-concepts and their attitudes toward the power balance. On the other hand, the outward motivation for purposes of dramatic development is again furnished by reference to an ancient religious and theatrical tradition of pre-Lenten religious rites in which an innocent man was invested with the symbols of royal power, made to reign splendidly on an illusory throne, then stripped of the symbols of power as suddenly as he acquired them, that he might be reminded of the lowly stature of every man. It is on the basis of this tradition that Folial the court fool proposes a "profound farce" to be executed between the king and himself. The implications of this roleplay are far-reaching, and will have no little bearing on our understanding of the importance of masked sooth-saying and assumed roles in *Leonce und Lena.*

In *Leonce und Lena,* the symbols of power in the scenes with King Peter are more subtly suggested. Peter's impotence is revealed not in a dramatic struggle with a threatening underling, but foremost in his very appearance as we first see him in I.ii. To be sure, Valerio's words and gestures ridicule the king long before we meet him, as will be shown later, but it is in this first glimpse of the king that Büchner uses tradition to say something new. Half-naked, His Majesty runs in circles around his dressing room, muttering absurd reflections to himself about his responsibility for the unthinking populace; meanwhile there is established in his confused and vacuous exclamations a direct relationship

between the physical and the moral or spiritual spheres of his existence—although this relationship undoubtedly escapes him:

> Jetzt kommen meine Attribute, Modificationen, Affektionen und Accidenzien: wo ist mein Hemd, meine Hose?—Halt, pfui! der frei Wille steht davorn ganz offen. Wo ist die Moral, wo sind die Manschetten? Die Kategorien sind in der schändlichsten Verwirrung. . . .

(I.ii.108,16-20)

This scene clearly has to do with the symbols of power; the sexual imagery is as blatantly and crassly comic with King Peter in *Leonce und Lena* as it is profound and drastic with Folial and the King in *Escurial.* King Peter, unknown to himself, enacts the farcical impotence of the role which he is; Folial and his king, on the other hand, are wholly conscious of their power struggle, which takes place on constantly shifting planes of reality and role-play. Surely it is no coincidence that in *Leonce und Lena* the viewer first sees the King of Popo in a mock-traditional setting, being enrobed by his valets and giving voice to his authority over his subjects. One need only look at the opening scene of Lagerkvist's highly symbolic drama for comparison. Here the high priest ceremoniously disrobes the king of his symbols of power—sword and tiara—for the duration of the religious festival. The king is visibly relieved to be freed of the very real responsibility these symbols represent. With King Peter, the enrobing scene serves only as a requisite of tradition to point up the desired contrast. There is no fool present as in Lagerkvist's *King* to remark that the disempowering and disenthronement of the king, and hence the turning upside down of the world, is indeed a welcome sight. But Valerio's function covers this territory as well, without his being present at every moment in which this process can be observed.

A sort of inversion of the thematic structure in the plays already mentioned is found in the more recent farce of Max Frisch, *Die Chinesische Mauer* (1947; revised version, 1955). Here, the fool, rather than constantly switching roles or hiding behind masks in order to mimic the emperor, to express unwelcome truths or to escape into holy madness, is in fact the only figure who speaks utterly straightforwardly as the so-called "Contemporary" (*der Heutige*). Emperor Hwang-Ti, like Büchner's King Peter in many respects, remains caught up in his own delusions of self-importance and his plans. He never perceives in the fool's behavior any threat to his integrity or any reflection of the kingdom's decrepit state. Instead, the drastic prophecies of *der Heutige,* like those of Wedekind's Nicolo returning to the new king in the capacity of official court fool, are regarded merely as amusing bits of madness and his "amusing" prophecies win him applause rather than serious attention. If the king does in fact detect a threatening note of reality about the fool, he tends either to wilfully misunderstand the fool as a misfit, or to punish and/or silence him completely. Whereas in Frisch's farce the situation is only postulated as an eternally recurring one in such situations of absolute power confronted by uncomfortable truth, in Ghelderode's *Escurial* this is carried out in a most morbid and drastic fashion. Here the tottering monarch succeeds in destroying his fool, only to be left to his laugh of despair and his fatal inner wound. The fate of Lear's Fool is called to mind as equally ambiguous; he is both cherished and chastised by the king, depending upon Lear's need for companionship or his willingness to hear the penetrating analysis of his moribund state. It is the Fool who remains closest to the demented ruler and most loyal to him in his utter dejection, and yet he disappears mysteriously early in the play.

Valerio, in a sense, fulfills the same function with Leonce; he is at once a merciless critic ("Ist denn Eure Hoheit noch nicht über die Leutnantsromantik hinaus?— II.iv.) and an indispensable, life-giving companion to Leonce. And yet, in contrast to Lear's Fool, Valerio is in no way subject to any real authority who could chastise or ban him; in fact, it is left to the fool himself to close the circle of farcical unreality in the final scene by appointing himself minister of state and dictating a new code of values which turns all conventional concepts inside out. It is he, in fact, who seems to determine the identity of the new king. It will be one of the aims of this investigation to explore the possibility that there might be a correlation between the king's identity crises and the acceptance or rejection of the fool; furthermore, that the identity of the two figures might at some times merge into one, and at other times be split.

The thematic connections of the Shakespearean motto "Motley's the only wear" and the intricate power relationship of wise fool and faltering king should thus become evident in the process of comparing these plays. In all of them are echoed the traditions of the court fool as both entertainer and prophet, companion and monster to the rulers and the society at court. Also incorporated into more than one of the plays is the carnival atmosphere with its sense of suspension of order and rationality and its inversion of conventional power relationships, such as prevailed in the medieval French carnival tradition of the Feast of Fools. This was a day designated by the church authorities as one on which clergy and simple townsfolk, priests and peasants, were free to exchange roles, subjecting rituals and sacred customs to grotesque ridicule as they joined in bawdy revelry under the elected Lord of Misrule. It is not insignificant that a contemporary American intellectual and theologian such as Harvey Cox should choose this tradition as a symbolic point of reference for his essay on festivity and fantasy as agents for inner and outward renewal of values in modern man.[14]

A thorough discussion of the transvaluation of values through the fool tradition is provided by Walter Kaiser in his book, *Praisers of Folly*. While his primary focus is on the Renaissance fool concepts of Erasmus, Rabelais and Shakespeare, he asserts that the fool figure of the theater actually originates in the medieval popular drama of the carnival. It is from the figures of *la mère Sotte* and *le Prince des Sots* in the French *sottie* that Erasmus and Rabelais derive prototypes for their figures of Stultitia and Panurge. In the anarchy of the religious festival humor, the prince of fools has unlimited license to play roguish tricks, to lead the crowd in the desecration of everything holy and authoritative, and the theme song of the fool's kingdom is "The World Turned Upside Down."[15]

The modern playwright has had recourse to this whole complex of tradition and social history with striking frequency. Lagerkvist's Fool in *Konungen* notes mysteriously amid the confusion after the ritual desecration of the King in the first act:

> Ha! Är det kanske inte bra att allt är upp- och nervänt! Är det inte välsignat att det n˙angang är nan ordning pa världen! Va!
>
> Allting upp- och nervänt! Och himlen full med eld![16]

It is not far from this state of affairs to that which prevails under Valerio's direction in the third act of ***Leonce und Lena***. Common to both is not only the sensual aspect of the carnival chaos, but the same social upheaval and the suspension of existing moral standards and social categories. As the fool's character and function in ***Leonce und Lena*** become clearer in the course of this study, we should be able to make more specific observations about his dependence upon and departure from such traditions, as well as to speculate on his validity as a channel of expression in the modern theater.

A note on the origin, scope and intent of the present study might be beneficial at this point. Lest the title be misleading, this is by no means an exhaustive study of Büchner, nor even of his comedy ***Leonce und Lena***. While I shall on occasion try to evaluate some of the findings of Büchner scholarship, my intent is not so much to elaborate on its accomplishments as to throw light on a particular aspect of Büchner's work, i.e., his use of the court fool figure, by means of the comparative approach. In concentrating on the court fool, specifically on the dynamics of his power relationship to the king or the courtly society, I am more or less eliminating related figures such as the circus clown or independent Harlequin types. Moreover, in using the 'theatrical fool tradition' as a frame of reference, I have no intention of compiling a history of the court fool type in the theater, although those aspects of the tradition which are most fundamental to this study will be discussed in some detail in connection with the fool figures of the seven selected plays. Finally, I am not primarily interested in establishing or tracing influences among the various authors and national literatures represented by the plays I have chosen. Such relationships do no doubt exist, most obviously in Ghelderode's and Büchner's debt to Shakespeare. However, I am more interested in the similarities of theme, situation and character relationships inherent in these plays than in actual literary correspondences or biographical data not intrinsic to the works themselves.

. . . [A] brief summary of recent scholarship reveals a growing awareness among critics, theorists and dramatists alike that the theatrical fool figure is experiencing a renaissance in modern drama. The current interest is not limited to literary criticism; one finds theologians and psychiatrists as well probing with equal fascination the phenomenon of the fool and the clown in modern art and literature, asking what it is about recent generations which attracts them back to the figure who had been banished from "respectable" theater centuries ago.[17] Period studies like Barbar Könneker's *Wesen und Wandlung der Narrenidee im Zeitalter des Humanismus* (Wiesbaden, 1966), Walter Kaiser's *Praisers of Folly* (Cambridge, 1963), [and] Wolfgang Promies' *Die Bürger und der Narr* (Munich, 1966), a study of the irrational element in the literature of German Rationalism, . . . complement each other well in their treatment of various historical and generic aspects of the fool, clown and Harlequin types and their domains in the theatrical world as well as in the circus and show business (Chaplin, Keaton, Valentin). The extremely comprehensive study by Robert Weimann of the sociological and dramaturgical aspects of the tradition of the folk theater, with special attention to its culmination in Shakespeare, also contains essential background material on the dramatic fool tradition. Weimann emphasizes the fool's relation to cult, myth, and mimesis from antiquity forward, as well as giving fascinating interpretations of Shakespeare from a critical standpoint which embraces the audience and its culture as a formative factor in the development of the fool tradition. Of major interest also in this vein is Wolfgang Kayser's *Das Groteske* (Hamburg, 1957), which in its discussion of the *commedia dell'arte,* the grotesque in German Romanticism (particularly Büchner), and the grotesque in modern drama (Wedekind), comes very near to the problems with which we will be concerned.

Works such as these provide informative as well as entertaining background to the topic at hand. But from this general acquaintance with the intriguing nature of the clown-fool type as a disruptive and yet regenerative force, several basic questions arise with specific reference to the theatrical fool in the narrower sense. For example, what becomes of the court fool figure in the theater when the reality of royal courts or professional fools no longer exists?[18] Moreover, is the fool tradition strong enough in the public mind that a literary figure can retain the same function in settings radically altered to suit a new socio-political context? That is, can the traditional power relationship of king and fool be portrayed effectively where there is no longer conscious belief in the integrity of royal authority? Most importantly, can the fool actually function as a force of renewal within his theatrical role, and if so, can a playwright effectively express his hopes for renewal, whether out of naïveté or disillusionment, through this figure?

It appears that modern dramatists (using the term loosely to refer to the theater from the 1830s to the present) might have rediscovered and begun to reimplement a traditionally effective theatrical form through which to voice their views of modern man and their political protests by creating modern equivalents of the Renaissance fool who can speak the unpleasant truth unabashedly and with impunity. Moreover, the fool figure seems more and more to be one with whom the politically conscious dramatist, the artist and the intellectual identifies himself, as one powerless except in this masked form to speak out and be heard. In this case one should ask whether the mask is a suitable one, or whether either individuality loses something in the process, making the play tendentious and contrived rather than allowing the fool his invulnerable position and universal wisdom. In the case of Max Frisch's *Die Chinesische Mauer,* for example, and his essay "Über die Höflichkeit," we get the impression that the writer feels the *Hofnarr* is definitely in a rather hopeless position, as one who is never taken seriously by those in power. In "Über die Höflichkeit" we read: "Ziel ist eine Gesellschaft, die den Geist nicht zum Aussenseiter macht, nicht zum Märtyrer und nichtzum Hofnarren, und nur darum müssen wir Aussenseiter unserer Gesellschaft sein, insofern es keine ist . . ."[19]—a statement which could be taken as the author's own comment on the role of the fool, *der Heutige,* in his tragic farce.

A view almost diametrically opposed to that of Frisch is expressed by Siegfried Melchinger in his article "Harlekins Wiederkehr."[20] Although Melchinger's concern is not so much with the figure of the court fool as with the traditional *commedia dell'arte* figures, he sees these as elementary forces of protest and social upheaval by virtue of their relationship to society and authority. Melchinger seems to feel, as does Priestley, that the modern Harlequin might have a similar function with regard to the rule of scientific technology to that of earlier fools in relation to their courtly rulers.

In a similar vein, but with more political emphasis, Günter Grass in the Princeton address previously cited wishes for the modern writer the power of the traditional court fool to change things in the world—"denn

Narren haben ein Verhältnis zur Macht, Schriftsteller selten."[21] He concludes that the modern artist must consent to being a simple craftsman, not the conscience of the nation, and if necessary must overturn his worktable and strive for compromises. For, as he declares, "das Gedicht kennt keine Kompromisse; wir aber leben von Kompromissen. Wer diese Spannung tätig aushält, ist ein Narr und ändert die Welt."[22]

A primary reason for focusing on Büchner . . . is that more than any other socially and politically conscious dramatist of modern times, he seems to me to be doing just this: grasping and acknowledging the paradoxical forces behind the illusory façades of social and political structures, and while assuming a cynical stance with regard to man's ability to change the course of history, nevertheless managing within the theatrical framework of his fool's mask to create a position of revolutionary truth amidst the paradoxes of the human situation. The irony and the cosmic humor fundamental to the fool's position make this stance both credible and attractive, and it remains . . . [to be seen] just how Büchner achieves this, and what, if any, far-reaching consequences his flair for fooldom has had with playwrights since his time or might have in today's theater.

·　·　·　·　·

Conclusion

Valerio is indeed the descendant of both Shakespeare's wise fools and the Italian harlequins; at the same time, though, he is the vehicle of a much greater force in the total conception of Büchner's comedy than were his predecessors in Shakespeare's dramas. This force is the all-encompassing irony of the fool Büchner, whose play is in itself a conscious masquerade of borrowed forms with which to fool the world, and at the same time to come to terms with his own questions about the masks of man by playing with them.

Büchner's irony is not of the same vintage as Shakespeare's, although it is certainly to a great extent informed by his wit. For while Lear's Fool and Touchstone use the ironic mask of folly out of loyalty to their respective masters and the kingdom—no matter how foolish—Valerio's irony is true only to itself and its own proliferation; it is a mask of confidence in conscious irony itself where even foolish loyalty would be a lie. Günter Grass' ironic title comes to mind once again: "Of the lack of confidence of writing court fools in view of non-existent courts." It is from behind the mask of irony that one has the confidence to point to the nothingness of the center of power in which one has lost confidence.

What, then, of the fool's power in weakness to act as a catalyst for renewal from within the order of the world? Grass' concluding statement in the Princeton talk ex-

presses the hope of the political activist in the possibility of enduring and transcending the tension that exists between the truth and the compromise of life: "Wer diese Spannung tätig aushält, ist ein Narr und ändert die Welt." For Büchner, the hope of folly lay not in the belief that it could effectively change the world on the level of the political order; for him, the tension was not between the truth as seen by fools and poets, and the reality in which kings live. Instead, it was a matter of choosing the right mask at the right time to create possibility out of stagnation on the level of play, embracing the nothingness of both fool and king. In the very act of creating Valerio, a court fool whose office consists of play rather than politically effective writing or action, Büchner showed that his own attitude as a "schreibender Hofnarr" was of a different order.

Büchner's contemporary to the North, Kierkegaard, formulated a description of the ironic process as embodied in Büchner's comedy which suggests a relationship between the Christian notion of holy folly for the sake of renewal and the conscious irony of Büchner's fooldom as a principle of survival:

> What the Christian talks about so much during agitated times,—to become a fool in the world—this the ironist realizes in his own fashion—except that he feels no martyrdom but the highest poetic enjoyment. But this infinite poetic freedom, already suggested by the fact that to become nothing at all is itself included, is expressed in a still more positive way, for the ironic individual has most often traversed a multitude of determinations in the form of possibility, poetically lived through them, before he ends in nothingness. For irony, as for the Pythagorean doctrine, the soul is constantly on a pilgrimage, except irony does not require such a long time to complete it.
>
> ·　·　·　·　·
>
> What costs the ironist time, however, is the care he lavishes on selecting the proper costume . . . In this matter the ironist has great skill, not to mention a considerable assortment of masquerade costumes from which to make a judicious selection.[23]

In choosing the masks he did for Valerio in his comedy, Büchner was indeed marking another step on his pilgrimage in search of freedom, and at the same time perhaps gleaning the poetic enjoyment of which Kierkegaard speaks from his positive attitude toward the threat of nothingness. But his brand of fooldom is in fact far removed from the kind of folly celebrated by Christians as a real source of renewal, because it begins from the feeling of having been cheated out of real meaning by the spirit of boredom which motivated God to create his puppet theater. Becoming a fool in the world in the Pauline sense, on the other hand, implies embracing the paradox that it is only as nothing that the fool is free to be someone in affirmation of the purpose of creation. One kind of fool refuses to live in the present reality, with its calculated pretense of reason and order. He senses that it is all a cosmic joke, and feels he can do better by imitating the joker and at least enjoying the game of exchanging roles with the creator of the carousel. The other kind of fool also refuses to live in the present reality, but in a different sense. It is because he senses another level of reality, for which the present one exists, that the fool in Christ refuses to seek ultimate meaning in the present order, but can nevertheless help it dance its way to the future. This kind of fooldom, like Valerio's, is a dynamic process of calling into question the appearance of order on any level, using the freedom that one's fantasy provides to unmask pretense.

Valerio's fooldom suggests a desperate attempt on the part of his creator to give positive, humorous form to his doubts about man's ability to recognize and implement divine order in the world, and by giving form to these doubts to divert himself from them. The automaton speech and the resolution of the comedy take place in the spirit of affirmative irony which seeks pleasure in imaginative possibility, but one senses that it is a certain *horror vacui* which produces this creative energy to defy the present order by playing with it in miniature.

Büchner's genius in his use of traditional forms to turn tradition inside out has certainly anticipated the efforts of many more recent playwrights to come to terms with the same struggles. The fascination and the ambiguous appeal of the fool figure served his purpose, as it now seems to be serving that of contemporary writers who necessarily see the questions somewhat differently.

Notes

1. Büchner uses the Tieck-Schlegel version of *As You Like It*. Where it seems important to consider the German text Büchner knew, citations will be from *Wie es euch gefällt* (Stuttgart: Reclam Verlag, 1957).

2. Throughout the text I will be quoting from the historical-critical edition of Werner Lehmann, *Georg Büchner: Sämtliche Werke und Briefe* (Hamburg: Christian Wegner, 1967), Vol. I. Here, I.i., 106, 20-21 (arabic numbers refer to page and line numbers in Lehmann's edition).

3. Note that the analogy is not perfect, since the gloomier comments of Jaques actually occur after his meeting with the fool.

4. I am using the term "fooldom" as an equivalent of the German *Narrentum*, referring to the act and practice of playing the role of the fool. It is distinct from folly (*Narrheit*), in that folly is not always conscious and does not often reign. It has nothing to do with foolishness or foolery. The word is consciously chosen to reflect the close relationship between the king's and the fool's domains.

5. Many critics read Hamlet's urgent warning to the players not to over-improvise (*Hamlet* III.ii.1-46) as an overt reference to a real problem encountered in contemporary actors of fools' roles. Cf. Friedrich Gundolf, *Shakespeare und der deutsche Geist* (Berlin: G. Bondi, 1923), p. 40.

6. Cf. Eckehard Catholy, "Komische Figur und dramatische Wirklichkeit: Ein Versuch zur Typologie des Dramas," *Festschrift Helmut deBoor* (Tübingen: Niemeyer, 1966), pp. 193-208.

7. Gotthold Ephraim Lessing, *Sämmtliche Werke*, ed. by Lachmann and Muncker (Stuttgart: Goschen, 1890, photog. reprod. 1968), VIII, 42.

8. *Ibid.*, IX, 256-57.

9. Reprinted in *Deutscher Geist*, ed. by Oskar Loerke, I (Frankfurt/Main: Suhrkamp, 1966), 44-63. See also Henning Boetius, *Harlekin—Texte und Materiatien mit einem Nachwort* (Bad Homburg: Gehlen-Verlag, 1968).

10. Justus Möser, cited by Loerke.

11. For more detailed discussion of this development see Horst Steinmetz, "Der Harlequin—Seine Rolle in der deutschen Komodientheorie und -dichtung des 18. Jahrhunderts," in *Neophilologus*, L (1966), 95-106. I am indebted to this source for much of the above discussion. See also Wolfgang Promies, *Die Bürger und der Narr oder das Risiko der Phantasie* (München: Carl Hanser Verlag, 1966).

12. August Wilhelm Schlegel suspected that even in the post-Shakespearean era, it was not a sign of refinement that the wise fool figure was missed on the stage. In his *Vorlesungen über dramatische Kunst und Litteratur*, he denounces the "enlightened" attitude of pitying one's ancestors for taking delight in such coarse amusement, putting forth his own explanation for the fool's disappearance: "Ich glaube aber vielmehr es wird an gescheidten Narren gefehlt haben, um die Stelle gehörig auszufüllen." Schlegel then continues, taking a more contemporary tack which is especially interesting in light of Büchner's caricature of reason in King Peter: "auf der anderen Seite ist die Vernunft, bei aller Einbildung von sich selbst, zu zaghaft geworden, um eine so verwegne Ironie zu dulden: Sie ist immer besorgt, der Mantel ihrer Gravität möchte aus seinen Falten kommen; und lieber als der Narrenkleidung einen anerkannten Platz neben sich zu gönnen, hat sie unbewu ter Weise die Rolle der Lächerlichkeit selbst übernommen, aber leider einer schwerfälligen und unerfreulichen Lächerlichkeit." (Quoting from August Wilhelm Schlegel, *Sämmtliche Werke*, ed. Eduard Bocking, Vol. VI: *Vorlesungen über dramatische Kunst und Litteratur*, Part II, 27th Lecture, pp. 201f.)

Schlegel's view is in full accord with several passages in Shakespeare: (1) In *As You Like It* I.ii., Celia responds to Touchstone's remark that "fools may not speak wisely what wise men do foolishly": "By my troth, thou sayest true: for since the little wit that fools have was silenced, the little foolery that wise men have makes a great show." (2) In *Twelfth Night,* Viola remarks that Feste is wise enough to play the fool, which indeed requires considerable talent, III.i.

13. For a well-documented discussion of the autobiographical elements in the play which at the same time points out that the personal scandal surrounding the work does not detract from its symbolic power, see Hector MacLean, "The King and the Fool in Wedekind's *König Nicolo,*" *Seminar,* V (Spring, 1969), 21.

14. Harvey Cox, *The Feast of Fools: A Theological Essay on Festivity and Fancy* (New York, Evanston and London: Harper and Row, 1969), pp. 1-6.

15. Walter Kaiser, *Praisers of Folly: Erasmus, Rabelais, Shakespeare* (Cambridge, Mass.: Harvard University Press, 1963), pp. 195-196.

16. Pär Lagerkvist, *Konungen* (Stockholm: Albert Bonniers Förlag, 1932), p. 11. English citation will be from Thomas R. Buckman's translation in *Modern Theatre,* ed. Thomas R. Buckman (hereafter *The King*) (Lincoln, Nebraska: University of Nebraska Press, 1966), p. 96: "Ha!—Do you suppose all's not well because things are turned upside down! Isn't it a blessing that for once there is some order in the world! Well? Everything turned upside down! And the heavens filled with fire!"

17. See Wolfgang M. Zucker, "The Clown as the Lord of Disorder," and Samuel H. Miller, "The Clown in Contemporary Art," both in *Theology Today,* XXIV (October, 1967), 306-317 and 318-328. Also, Joseph C. McClelland's *The Clown and the Crocodile* (Richmond, Va.: John Knox Press, 1970) uses the clown and fool figures as focal points for his theological essay on the comic vision in modern life and art. Harvey Cox' *The Feast of Fools* is a book-length essay with yet a stronger sociological dimension but with specific references to modern drama trends.

More comprehensive and more directly relevant to the purposes of this study is the excellent monograph by the psychotherapist and literary critic William Willeford, of the University of Washington, *The Fool and His Scepter* (Evanston: Northwestern University Press, 1969); see also Robert Weimann's *Shakespeare und die Tradition des Volkstheaters* (Berlin: Henschelverlag, 1967).

18. Günter Grass broaches this question ironically in connection with that of the role of the writer in an address given in Princeton in 1966, with the title: "Vom mangelnden Selbstvertrauen der schreibenden Hofnarren unter Berücksichtigung nichtvorhander Höfe," in *Über meinen Lehrer Döblin und andere Vorträge* (Berlin: Literarisches Kolloquium, 1968), pp. 67-72.

19. Max Frisch: "Uber die Höflichkeit," in *Auswahl deutscher Essays* (New York: Appleton Century Crofts, 1966), p. 199.

20. In *Merkur,* XI (November, 1957), 1023-1037.

21. From Grass, *Über meinen Lehrer Döblin,* p. 67.

22. *Ibid.,* p. 72.

23. Soren Kierkegaard, The Concept of Irony, trans. by Lee M. Capel (Bloomington: Indians University Press, 1965), pp. 298f.

Reinhold Grimm (essay date 1985)

SOURCE: Grimm, Reinhold. "'Cœur' and 'Carreau': Love in the Life and Works of Büchner." In *Love, Lust, and Rebellion: New Approaches to Georg Büchner,* pp. 79-100. Madison: University of Wisconsin Press, 1985.

[*In the following excerpt, Grimm comments on themes of love and eroticism in Büchner's dramas, particularly* Danton's Death.]

What [Büchner's] texts contain is clear—and clearly the critics, virtually without exception, have chosen to avert their eyes. Let us begin by simply listing what the reader encounters.

Two women commit suicide out of love for their men: one while in the grip of madness, the other through a conscious decision (decades before Wagner's *Tristan and Isolde,* she dies a veritable "love-death"). And there are men no less extreme in their passions: one drowns himself after having nearly strangled his lover; another attempts to take his own life in a similar manner—in a state of erotic intoxication, already anticipating ultimate fulfillment. A third, seized by blind despair, compulsively and methodically murders his woman, stabbing her to death in an almost ritualistic process of judgment and execution. All this in only three dramas, one of which is a sketchy fragment; dramas, moreover, teeming with true love and trollops, lovers and libertines, the most delicate tenderness and the most drastic lasciviousness, dramas in which flies mate on people's hands, curs couple in the streets, and we are confronted by the question: "Don't you feel like . . . tearing off your pants and copulating over someone's ass like dogs . . . ?"[1]

I am speaking of *Danton's Death,* of *Leonce and Lena,* of *Woyzeck.* I am speaking of Georg Büchner. Of all the many dozens of studies, monographs, and dissertations that have been devoted to this writer, not a single one actually deals with love; and among the hundreds of essays and articles on Büchner, there is, according to the existing bibliographies as well as the most recent handbooks and commentaries,[2] only one short article entirely devoted to this subject. It comes to us from Brazil, was authored by Erwin Theodor [Rosenthal], carries the title "Büchners Grundgedanke: Sehnsucht nach Liebe" ("Büchner's Fundamental Idea: The Longing for Love"), and was published in 1962 in the journal *Revista de Letras.*[3] Today, almost 150 years after the young writer's death, this is all that "the literature" has to offer regarding a theme which an insightful critic (one of the few) has described—albeit only in passing and in a manner which both exaggerates and is overly cautious—as functioning for Büchner as the "core [*Angelpunkt*] and meaning of life."[4]

The core and meaning of life for this writer? The scientist and revolutionary? The author of a seditious pamphlet? The fugitive conspirator who, at the age of twenty-three, died in exile in Switzerland, then the most proper and prudish of lands? His "fundamental idea," his overpowering "longing" was for love? But I must ask: What do we really know about Georg Büchner's view of love? What have we *dared* to know? In point of fact, we have only Rosenthal and a few scattered attempts.[5]

And yet, the very first scene of Büchner's first play begins with lines which unambiguously define the way this theme will be presented. A card game is in progress; and the figure who initiates the dialogue as well as the "love interest" is none other than Georg[es] Danton. He turns to his wife Julie and remarks: "Look at Madame over there—how sweetly she fingers her cards. She knows how, all right—they say her husband always gets the *cœur,* the others the *carreau.* You women could even make us fall in love with a lie."[6] The symbolic implications of the card suits mentioned by Danton are unmistakable. This is true of the "cœur," the heart, which traditionally has expressed a concept of love containing both Amor and Caritas. It is equally true of the "carreau" or diamond: here Büchner sets up a frivolous, obscene counterpart to the heart, using a sign the shape of which is decidedly suggestive. Contrary to one critic's ponderously naive thesis, it is surely not intended to serve as a metaphor for the "world theater."[7] Rather, what Büchner is referring to is something much more intimate, though no less universal. His friend Hérault develops and concretizes the reference when he takes the card names literally and declares that young ladies should not "play games like that. The kings and queens fall on top of each other so indecently and the jacks pop up right after."[8] (The reader will, I trust, forgive this Büchnerian smuttiness; the playwright could not have his "bandits"—to use his own hyperbolic term—talk like parsons' daughters, even though he himself was engaged to the daughter of a parson.)

What the duality of "cœur" and "carreau" conjures up from the very beginning is the entire range of the erotic: from the purest, indeed most chaste, affection as expressed by that ancient emblem the heart, all the way to the crassest carnality, which is denoted by the red diamond. And the two areas are not kept separate from one another but are closely bound together, in however daring, unbourgeois, and unstable a manner. Their common denominator is love—but not love as a mere concept or some anemic "fundamental *idea,*" but rather as an all-embracing fundamental *experience,* an experience which is at once joyous and overwhelming. For let us not forget that Julie and Danton, whose gentleness and kindness toward each other ("dear heart," she calls him)[9] culminate in Julie taking her own life for the sake of her beloved, exist alongside of Hérault and his promiscuous "queen of diamonds," a woman who can make a man fall in love with a lie. What is more, these two radically dissimilar couples are joined by Camille Desmoulins, who exhibits what is perhaps the most faithful and selfless love to be found in Büchner's works—yet it is precisely this figure who calls for the elemental "limb-loosening, wicked love" of Sappho, with "naked gods and bacchantes" and, again completely uneuphemistically, "Venus with the beautiful backside"![10] Unvarnished sexuality, the most tender affection, and a classical Greek sensuality which the declaration that Venus, along with Epicurus, is to become the "doorkeeper of the Republic"[11] clearly endows with emancipatory and even utopian traits: all this is present in Büchner's images and allusions, as well as in his invocations of Renaissance licentiousness. Attentive readers cannot fail to note that in the opening scene of his first drama the playwright sketches out a full panorama of the world of Eros; he develops, or at least alludes to, all its various manifestations, which not only recur in, and color the rest of, this drama of revolution, but also suffuse Büchner's comedy *Leonce and Lena* and, to an even greater extent, his proletarian tragedy, *Woyzeck.*

Yet there is more. This fundamental experience is not limited to Büchner's plays nor even to those of his writings which have been preserved. It can also be found in that "complete fragment," the novella (or story) *Lenz,* and must have been present in his play, apparently lost forever, **"Pietro Aretino"**—present, once again, unless all indications are wrong, in the most multifarious manner. What, after all, do we learn about that unhappy writer, Lenz? Does his breakdown not result in part, indeed primarily, from the collapse of his love for Friederike? Does he not fall apart because her "happiness," which always made him so "calm," no longer washes over him, and instead her "fate," as well as his own, lies on his heart "like a hundredweight"?[12] These are all direct quotes which, it must be added, occur directly before the central passage in which Lenz is seized by the "obsession" of resurrecting a dead girl, something he attempts to carry out with "all the misery of despair" and all the force of will he still possesses. It is surely no coincidence that the child at whom he vainly hurls his demented "Arise and walk!" also bears—or bore—the name Friederike.[13] And we find this blasphemous phrase repeated word-for-word in Leonce's frenzied ecstasy of love;[14] moreover, the underlying concept also crops up in Büchner's letters to his fiancée, Minna Jaeglé. In February of 1834, while at the university of Gießen, he wrote: "I am alone as if in a grave; when will your hand awaken me?" To this he added the highly allusive line: "They say I am mad because I have said that in six weeks I will rise again, but first I will ascend into heaven, in the diligence [to Strasbourg] that is."[15] Clearly, Büchner was not reluctant to mingle erotic allusions with references to Christianity and the Bible. This connection between his letters to Minna, his comedy, and his narrative dealing with Lenz can also be developed out of another passage in the story, the section which describes the religious ecstasy that the tormented writer experiences with such intensity after he preaches: "Now, another existence, divine, twitching lips bent down over him and sucked on his lips; he went up to his lonely room. He was alone, alone! Then the spring rushed forth, torrents broke from his eyes, his body convulsed, his limbs twitched, he felt as if he must dissolve, he could find no end to this ecstasy."[16]

Let us here carefully note Büchner's choice of words! Not only does he mention "ecstasy," he also causes the ᾿Ερως λυσιμελής of Sappho, referred to by Camille as "limb-loosening love" (*gliederlösende Liebe*), to spring from overheated piousness. It is important to see the connection here to the love scene in ***Leonce and Lena***[17] and, above all, to Büchner's "fatalism letter" of 1834, in which he tells Minna: "I glowed, the fever covered me with kisses and enfolded me like the arm of a lover. Above me there were waves of darkness, my heart swelled in infinite longing, stars forced their way through the gloom, and hands and lips bent down."[18]

The almost mystic undertones of this erotic fever-fantasy are as evident as is the startlingly erotic quality of Lenz's pietistic experience of transcendence. But even there, is not all "heavenly" love—if in fact such a thing is present in Büchner's writings—overshadowed by a love which is thoroughly worldly? When we seek to categorize the causes and effects of Lenz's madness, it is clear that those of a philosophical and social nature play an important role.[19] Yet should we not also look elsewhere, not so much in the area of religion—which lately has been stressed to the point of excess[20]—as in that of sexuality? Both in regard to Büchner in general, and in this context in particular, the emphasis on reli-

gious elements reveals itself as a highly dubious approach. Granted, certain remnants of Christianity are present in Lenz; after all, the man had studied theology. But are these remnants not thoroughly secularized by Büchner, just as he secularized so many other references to Christianity and the Bible? Indeed, to pose a rather heretical question, should not Lenz's mad attempt at resurrecting the dead Friederike be viewed as an attempt at reviving the bliss he experienced with the living Friederike? The shattered man, in the utter demise of his joy and happiness, prays "that God should grant him a sign and revive the child"![21] And Büchner chose these words, too, advisedly.

Or consider **"Pietro Aretino,"** Büchner's supposed "obscenity" dealing with the renowned eroticist of the Renaissance, a man who, like the Marquis de Sade, won for himself the cynical and yet admiring epithet, "the divine one." God knows, it is high time that the information which has been preserved or can be deduced[22] regarding this work is taken seriously, rather than being brushed aside with an embarrassed blush. Let us dare to admit that Büchner wanted to write about this man precisely on account of, and not despite, Aretino's having written the "*Sonetti lussuriosi*" ("Voluptuous Sonnets")—on "sixteen positions of a pair of lovers *in coitu*" after drawings by Giulio Romano—as well as the so-called *Ragionamenti,* his notorious "Conversations" among courtesans. Because, not in spite of, Aretino's "vigorous sensuality" in both life and art, the young German writer found him a fascinating figure. It is actually of little import whether the "legendary 'Aretino' drama" (thus Walter Hinderer)[23] was almost complete or only a conception, whether it was intentionally destroyed or lost in some other way. What is important is the subject matter and the fact that Büchner concerned himself with it. Quite recently, this work—or conception—has been the object of further speculation by a scholar, on the one hand, and a writer, on the other. According to the literary historian Hermann Bräuning-Oktavio, the drama would have been a historical "painting on a colossal scale," a gigantic fresco portraying the "power and greatness of human passions";[24] according to Gaston Salvatore, in whose play *Büchners Tod* ("Büchner's Death") the fevered deliria of the dying poet are haunted by Aretino,[25] Büchner would have linked the Italian not only to questions of revolution and class conflict but also to modern concepts regarding the problem of the intellectual's servile role in society—a favorite topic of Bertolt Brecht, by the way.[26]

It may well be that Bräuning-Oktavio's hypothesis possesses a certain validity; in any event, it is more convincing than Salvatore's notion of how Büchner would have portrayed this man who was known and feared by all Europe; who—for this reason—was showered with gifts, honors, and bribes; whom the great Ariosto apostrophized as the "scourge of the princes";[27] indeed, who liked to refer to himself proudly as "a free man by the grace of God" (*per divina grazia uomo libero*).[28] There is something colossal, almost monstrous, about this *condottiere* of the pen, something of a "Great Dane with dove's wings," to use the phrase which Büchner applies to Danton.[29] And yet, if one takes a closer look, it appears that in the case of Aretino, too, it was love that was of primary importance. Even a cursory glance at the Italian's life leads one to believe that the play dealing with him—as far as we know, Büchner's last or next-to-last work[30]—would have repeated and intensified, nay, virtually doubled, the theme of love which the young writer had developed in his previous literary efforts. In 1829 his contemporary, Christian Dietrich Grabbe, published *Don Juan und Faust,* and I for one am convinced that in 1837 Büchner would have followed suit by providing us with a work which would have amounted to a *Danton and Woyzeck.*

Aretino lends himself to an undertaking of this sort not only through his insatiable "affirmation of pleasure in every form," nor his endless "series of loves, love affairs, and love encounters" which, as was the case with Danton, caused him to be involved with women of all social strata, "the highborn and the low, those with intelligence and those with a price."[31] At the same time, he was also hopelessly in love with *one* woman who, having brought him great happiness, betrayed him—just as Marie betrays Woyzeck. For the rest of his life, Aretino was caught in the toils of an obsessive love from which he was unable to free himself even after this woman's death. His declarations of passion for the young Perina Riccia remind us, in their sensual intensity, of Danton's stammerings to Marion,[32] just as his searing lamentations at her deathbed recall Woyzeck's desperate grief as well as that felt by Lenz. We even hear echoes of some of Büchner's own statements.[33] (Salvatore, despite the many problematical aspects of his play, at least gives us some sense of all this when he has Minna appear before the feverish, sexually aroused Büchner as a courtesan.) In recent times, it has been regretfully noted that "we have not a single really good play about the Cinquecento."[34] It is my firm conviction that Büchner's **"Pietro Aretino,"** marked by both "cœur" and "carreau," was, or would have become, the work that could have filled this gap.[35]

But let us concentrate on the texts we possess, let us return to Büchner's first and most important work, ***Danton's Death.*** For I wish to commit yet another heresy by declaring that in this play the theme of love is no less central than that of revolution. Indeed, the two are inseparably intertwined. Even if we limit ourselves to the main characters, we see that this is true not only of Julie and Camille's wife, Lucile, but also of the "grisette" or "hetaera," Marion.[36] All three of the leading female figures in ***Danton's Death*** contribute—each in her own way—to the exemplary unleashing of both the dialectic of revolution, with all its contradictions, and of love "in every form."

As has been indicated, Julie and Lucile belong together, even more so at the end of the play than in the early scenes. Critics have noted that ***Woyzeck*** and ***Leonce and Lena*** exhibit elements of a circular structure in that their endings, to a certain extent, flow back into their beginnings.[37] However, something that has hardly been noticed, let alone investigated, is the circular construction of ***Danton's Death***[38] and the concomitant function which is assigned to the two female figures as well as to love. This oversight is the more surprising since all these elements are particularly noticeable in Büchner's drama of revolution. One need only compare the first scene ("Danton on a footstool at Julie's feet") with the last scene where Lucile sits "on the steps of the guillotine":

DANTON.

> No, Julie, I love you like the grave. . . . They say in the grave there is peace, and grave and peace are one. If that's so, then in your lap I'm already lying under the earth. You sweet grave—your lips are funeral bells, your voice my death knell, your breasts my burial mound, and your heart my coffin.

LUCILE.

> (*enters* . . .) I'm sitting in your lap, you silent angel of death. . . . You dear cradle, you lulled my Camille to sleep, you strangled him under your roses. You death knell, you sang him to the grave with your sweet tongue.[39]

The connection between these images, the cyclical way in which they anticipate and echo one another, can hardly be overlooked, especially since they are so boldly unusual. There can be no doubt that Büchner created this connection intentionally; the references to sweetness and love, peacefulness and silence, the correspondence established in both instances between a lap (*Schoß*, which can also mean "womb") and a grave— all this is simply too exact to be regarded as accidental. Even the cradle, which at first is missing from the opening scene, soon puts in an appearance. Before the next scene begins, we encounter the line, "having coffins for cradles,"[40] a phrase which clearly anticipates Lucile's speech at the end of the play; and, of course, the evocative rhyme of "womb" and "tomb," of "cave" and "grave," is something of which psychoanalysis has long been aware. In the programmatic writings of Norman O. Brown, to which I shall eventually return, one finds the laconic yet unambiguous words: "Birth, copulation, and death, equated."[41] This is precisely what Büchner accomplishes: "cradle," "womb" (*Schoß*), and "grave" are—as Danton himself declares—"one and the same." When Lucile utters the phrase "dear cradle," she is addressing the dreaded guillotine, the killing machine she also refers to as an "angel of death" and a "death knell"; and when Julie reaches for the vial of poison from which she imbibes her love-death, she does so with the words: "Come, dearest priest, your amen makes us go to sleep."[42] Both of these death scenes are love scenes, just as both figures are, above all else, women in love. True, it seems at first that Julie regards Danton's words as frivolous and shocking, for she turns away from him with an almost Kleistian "Oh." However, she quickly regains her composure, and with it her love for Danton, a love in which she henceforth abides with steadily increasing confidence and unreservedness until finally, with the words "sleep, sleep" on her lips, she follows Danton and the darkling world into the "slumber" of death.[43]

The same development can be discerned in Danton's much-cited loneliness: from his fatalistic and seemingly resigned declaration, "we are very lonely,"[44] to the fervent intimacy he shares with Julie in the aftermath of his agonizing nightmare. In the latter scene, which occurs in the second act, Danton is able to say, "Now I'm calm"—and are we not forced to envision him in his wife's arms, not just in her presence? "Completely calm, dear heart?" she asks, full of concern, and he replies: "Yes, Julie, come to bed."[45] That all this is connected to various aspects of the play's concluding scenes—for example, to the revolutionary's fear of the loneliness of death, a fear which is so difficult to reconcile with the philosophy he manifests in other situations,[46] and, above all, to Julie's actions and attitude, to the extraordinary love-sacrifice she offers—cannot be ignored. The correspondences extend even to specific words and phrases, something which is particularly evident in Danton's cry: "Oh Julie! If I had to go *alone*! If she would abandon me! And if I decomposed entirely, dissolved completely—I'd be a handful of tormented dust. Each of my atoms could find peace only with her. I can't die, no, I cannot die."[47] As a comforting answer, Julie has a messenger carry a lock of her hair to the imprisoned Danton: "There, bring him that and tell him he won't go alone. He'll understand. Then come back quickly. I want to read his looks in your eyes."[48] And, once again, Danton is freed from his agony. "I won't go alone," he says to himself as if he has been saved, "thank you, Julie."[49] Now he is able to face the guillotine, composed and calm.

Julie's love-sacrifice is indeed extraordinary. What renders it even more extraordinary and even more indicative of the importance Büchner attached to love is the fact that it has absolutely no basis in historical reality. It did not at all occur to the real Julie (who was actually named Louise) to accompany her Georges in death. Not only did she survive him by decades, but she had also no compunctions about remarrying—although, admittedly, this did not happen until she had mourned Dan-

ton for a few chaste (or, at least, relatively chaste) years.[50] The banality of these facts is sobering; yet it also serves to establish irrefutably that the heroic transfiguration effected by Büchner evinces his own concerns and conceptions. And then there is Lucile, who is presented as deriving a limpid, self-effacing happiness from the love she shares with Camille. Even with this character, Büchner departs from what he read in his history books. Instead of having her arrested, condemned, and executed on the basis of Laflotte's denunciation, which is what actually happened,[51] he causes her to provide a second example of transfiguration achieved by means of a luminous love-sacrifice. Like Julie, Lucile is cloaked in radiance. Or, as Maurice B. Benn puts it: "Against the dark background [of the play, these] two pure figures . . . appear in an almost radiant light."[52] Of course, Julie chooses death without hesitation and in the full freedom of her spirit, while Lucile, like Ophelia, falls victim to madness and is able to return to herself only at the very end of the play. Yet this ending, one of the most moving and magnificent in all of world drama, not only presents, in the words of Benn, "a sudden return of lucidity"[53] for Lucile; it also crowns and confirms the triumph, the limitless glorification of love in Büchner's drama of revolution. The passage in question is deceptively brief; it begins with the entrance of a militia patrol and then breaks off with Lucile being led away to her death:

A CITIZEN.

Hey—who's there?

LUCILE.

Long live the King!

CITIZEN.

In the name of the Republic! (*She is surrounded by the watch and led off.*)[54]

These lines must be read with the utmost attentiveness and exactitude. On the one hand, they serve to close the circle of the play's "love interest" which begins at the gaming table with the bantering about "cœur" and "carreau"; on the other hand, in testifying to the power of love, they also provide a final manifestation, indeed a proclamation, of the republic, and with it, the revolution. The part of the play's action which is connected to the revolution is encompassed by the theme of love. Even the scene in which Danton and his followers are executed, a scene in which their severed heads kiss "at the bottom of the basket,"[55] is framed by—and one might say, sublated into—this theme as it is developed in the two scenes devoted to Julie's and Lucile's acts of self-sacrifice and transfiguration. Yet, at the same time, the part of the play which deals with love is also subjected to a sublation. In that final scene, in which love shines forth one last time and reaches what could be termed its apotheosis, Lucile is, in a very literal manner, "surrounded" by the power of the revolution in its most concrete form.

The vividness of this action, which is truly theatrical in the best sense of the word, is no less striking than the imagery Büchner utilizes at the beginning and end of *Danton's Death,* or, for that matter, the basic circular structure of the play as a whole. Here, both themes are fused together in a relationship as inseparable as that of form and content. Comfort and hope, refuge from the present and assurances regarding the future, all are intertwined in Büchner's play. Truly, for individual human beings, love is all that remains. For humanity, however, there is the revolution. Although conservative critics would have us believe that the notion of progress and the linear movement of history is flatly rejected, and in its place a Spenglerian "circular movement of all history" is glorified,[56] this conclusion cannot be substantiated, regardless of whether one concentrates exclusively on *Danton's Death* or examines the young writer's entire oeuvre and biography.[57] Büchner was a man who despaired and yet continued to fight, a militant who founded the Society of Human Rights, wrote *The Hessian Messenger,* and yet admitted that he "felt as if [he] were crushed under the terrible fatalism of history."[58] If ever anyone had a right to lay claim to that dictum of Gramsci, "pessimism of the intellect, optimism of the will,"[59] then it was surely Büchner, a revolutionary in that most reactionary of times, the German Vormärz period. However, what sets him apart from Gramsci, and even raises him above the Italian's paradox, is the fact that he was a great writer and, both as a writer and a revolutionary, a man who loved. Büchner wanted "life and love" among human beings to be "one and the same"; he wanted love to be life and "life [to be] love."[60]

I believe that one can legitimately take these words, which come from a fragmentary scene not included in the final version of *Leonce and Lena,* and apply them in a general sense to Büchner's entire concept of love.[61] For are they not equally true of Marion, the third major female figure in *Danton's Death*? Does not this "grisette," in an exemplary manner, live a life of love? In her existence, are not life and love in fact identical? Admittedly, this is yet another heresy, and one especially offensive to those who, while not necessarily conservative in their political views, are nonetheless rigorously moralistic.[62] But have the numerous attempts to explain Marion with concepts such as "tragedy" and "guilt" really helped us to understand this figure? Should we deprive her of what she terms "the only thing,"[63] and instead burden her with "a dark, animalistic sadness," in effect, a bad conscience?[64] Ought we not instead approach both Marion and Danton as well as their relationship with one another—and, by extension, Georg Büchner's treatment of love in its entirety—with

very different concepts and values? That it is not enough simply to rattle off a few of the fashionable phrases of the playwright's era, such as the well-known "emancipation of the flesh," is, I would hope, obvious. It was no accident that Büchner repeatedly distanced himself from the Saint-Simonians and the Young Germans.[65] As for the latter group, their supposedly daring heroines[66] resemble, when compared with Marion, nothing more than "marionettes with sky-blue noses and affected pathos," the fleshless and bloodless constructs for which Büchner mocked the "so-called idealist poets."[67] But should we descend to the opposite extreme and—utilizing a word which carries with it the most repulsive of associations—see in Marion "something subhuman" (*Untermenschliches*)?[68] Neither this dubious concept nor the "uncontrollable animalistic lustfulness" which has been linked with it nor, by any stretch of the imagination, the insipid sensuality of the Young Germans can touch the essence of Marion's being; and the yammering and howling, the erotic spasms and convulsions which fill Peter Weiss's *Marat/Sade* also have very little to do with the serenity and delicacy, indeed the poetry of Marion and her scene.

Unfortunately, there is not enough space here to quote the love scene between her and Danton in its entirety. I can only point to the naturalness, the lyrical-idyllic simplicity and yet eloquence with which Marion—sitting "at the feet" of Danton, according to a telling stage direction—narrates the story of her life, which is to say the story of her love. "My mother was a smart woman. She always said chastity was a nice virtue." Thus Büchner, taking a sly jab at bourgeois morality, has Marion begin her account: "When people came to the house and started talking about certain things, she told me to leave the room. When I asked what they wanted, she said I ought to be ashamed of myself. When she gave me a book to read, I almost always had to skip over a couple of pages."[69] Marion goes on to recall how once, in springtime, while still a girl, she found herself "in a peculiar atmosphere," an atmosphere which "almost choked me." Luckily, a young man appeared who, though he often said "crazy things," was "good-looking." In time, Marion says, "we couldn't see why we might not just as well lie together between two sheets as sit next to each other in two chairs." Then, soon thereafter, she declares with calm frankness: "But I became like an ocean, swallowing everything and swirling deeper and deeper. For me there was only one opposite: all men melted into one body. That was my nature—who can escape it?"[70]

When the young man, who believed Marion was his alone, learned of her activities, he kissed her as if he wanted—again that word—to "choke" her: his arms wrapped tight around her neck; she was "terribly afraid." But he released her and then went off and drowned himself (an event which is conveyed to us only by Marion's indirect and highly evocative remarks; see chapter 5 below). "I had to cry," she admits, "that was the only break in my being."[71] Since then she has lived in complete unity and harmony with herself:

> Other people have Sundays and working days, they work for six days and pray on the seventh; once a year, on their birthdays, they get sentimental, and every year on New Year's Day they reflect. I don't understand all that. For me there is no stopping, no changing. I'm always the same, an endless longing and seizing, a fire, a torrent. . . . It's all the same, whatever we enjoy: bodies, icons, flowers, or toys, it's all the same feeling. Whoever enjoys the most prays the most.[72]

Marion's autobiographical account closes with this avowal, which clearly provides the philosophical, or ideological, highlight of the entire scene. Büchner was not, however, content to stop here. The ensuing dialogue between Marion and Danton provides yet another highlight—in this case, one which is lyrical-idyllic, even lyrical-utopian, in nature:

DANTON.

> Why can't I contain your beauty in me completely, surround it entirely?

MARION.

> Danton, your lips have eyes.

DANTON.

> I wish I were a part of the atmosphere so that I could bathe you in my flood and break on every wave of your beautiful body.[73]

It is at this point that Lacroix, loud-mouthed and vulgar, enters the scene. Accompanied by a pair of common whores, he fills the air with crude remarks; and thus the scene ends on a jarringly discordant note that tears apart the idyl briefly shared by the two lovers.[74]

I would like to ask: Could a playwright possibly express more in a single scene? Could a scene be any more unambiguous? How can it be that Büchner has been so completely misunderstood here by so many experts, by virtually the entire corps of critics? Or, phrased more maliciously: How is it possible to react to such a text—particularly when it is part of Büchner's drama of revolution—in a way which is so blind to history and so indifferent to art, so joyless and so dismally sanctimonious? It is perhaps not entirely accidental that the only voice which has been raised in favor of Marion comes to us from Sweden![75] Everything else one encounters reeks of puritanism and philistine narrow-mindedness. The eternal bourgeois (who, by the way, lurks not just in "bourgeois" critics) is not only repelled by a "soulless whore" or, at best, a "hetaera"; he finds her positively frightening. Indeed, Marion "is obviously a very dangerous person," we are informed in all seri-

ousness.[76] Critics' sensibilities—not to mention their senses—have failed to grasp this woman and her message even though, beginning with the very first scene and Camille's proclamation of Venus and Epicurus as the patron saints of the republic, it pervades the entire drama and stands inscribed as a secret motto over the events of the revolution. Of course, we also notice a marked heightening of the current of eroticism: Camille merely *demands* primal love and Greek sensuality, while Marion actually *manifests* these ideals, actually lives and proclaims them with her own flesh.

After Marion's scene, there can be no doubt that the erotic-utopian qualities which the play first presents in a purely theoretical manner or in broad outline, have now become elements of concrete praxis and thus must be recognized as a crucial dimension of the entire theme of revolution. And how could it be otherwise? Are not love and sensuality of every sort, as well as the achievement of full happiness in this life, integral and inalienable aspects of the complete and liberated human being, the *total* human being, and hence essential components of any full concept of revolution? If one draws on Camus, as does Benn, and speaks of Büchner's "threefold concept of revolution," which combines sociopolitical rebellion with metaphysical revolt and an overturning of established aesthetic norms[77]—then why not also acknowledge Büchner's liberation of Eros, that is to say, his sexual revolt? Are we not forced to do so by what we encounter in his works? I can no longer ignore the testimony of these texts. "Cœur" and "carreau" speak with a clarity that leaves little to be desired; what they say to us is far clearer and more convincing than any painstakingly assembled collection of quotations from Arthur Schopenhauer, whom some critics want to drag into the discussion of Büchner at all costs.[78] But so be it! If, in 1813, the year of Büchner's birth, this notorious reactionary and misogynist among German thinkers examined the "fourfold root of the principle of sufficient reason," then Büchner, the loving rebel among German writers, in **Danton's Death** dealt with the fourfold root of the principle of revolution. Indeed, it seems to me that even if one were to ignore the play, it still would be possible to establish the necessity of Büchner's support for a fourth revolt, the revolt of Eros:

> For what would it be this revolution
> Without universal copulation?[79]

Here we clearly have an area of intersection between Büchner and the author of *Marat/Sade,* regardless of how crude the latter's intentionally primitive slogans may seem when compared with Marion's scene. When Bo Ullmann, who is responsible for the aforementioned contribution from Sweden, refers to her message as a "utopia of unmutilated, total humanness," a "utopia of the erotic negation of both self and possession,"[80] he merely provides more restrained but, by the same token, considerably more apt formulations of what Weiss, his German-born countryman, has in mind.

But though it is an admirable virtue, the open-mindedness *in eroticis* displayed by Ullmann and Weiss is not in itself sufficient for a full understanding of Marion. The same is true of some "sisterly" insights; however knowing they may be, they remain incomplete or even lead to new varieties of misperception. Margaret Jacobs, for example, starts out on the right track when she writes of Marion: "In a special sense she is natural, but one must beware of assessing her as naive."[81] Precisely in its contradictoriness, this statement is directly on target. Unfortunately, Jacobs fails to perceive the full implications of her own *aperçu,* for she immediately lapses into a moralizing approach and decides that there is "something undeniably gruesome" about Marion. Even the moment of illumination provided by our Swedish critic flickers, dims, and finally disappears. In spite of all his accurate perceptions, Ullmann not only pushes Marion in the direction of "childishness" and "foolishness"[82] but feels compelled—even while acknowledging her "innocence" and "purity"—to describe her as "dirty"! Finally, he judges Marion to be "truly unfit for a utopia" because, as he goes on to inform us, she is "scarcely a person of this world"! (Wouldn't "although" make more sense?) Thus a utopian presence is registered, but only in order to be denounced as a failure. What seems to exert a certain fascination is not so much utopia itself as its supposed collapse. That this perspective involves a distortion, indeed almost an inversion of the concept of utopia is quite obvious. In actuality, Büchner is concerned neither with the "abandonment" nor with the "defense" of an erotic utopia, but rather with imagining and manifesting it. The fact that the present, even when it is revolutionary, fails to live up to the utopian goal does not refute the latter any more than the temporary collapse of the ongoing sociopolitical revolution refutes or even "compromises" its particular utopian vision.

However tempting it may be, one cannot connect Marion with Marie of the *Woyzeck* fragment;[83] nor can one view the proletarian tragedy as a necessary continuation of *Danton's Death,* much less its recantation.[84] This would presume, within Büchner's oeuvre, an evolution which has never been convincingly demonstrated. And if indeed one is willing to make the interpretive leap of associating the suicide of Marion's lover with the murder of Marie by the pond, why not link the young man's death with Leonce's loudly announced decision to plunge into the river and drown, a decision motivated not by despair, but rather by the ecstasy of love? In other words, one could just as easily concentrate on the laughable consequences of Marion's "terrible dangerousness" as on those which are somberly serious. Of course, it cannot be denied that she admits: "My mother died of grief, people point at me." But she

adds: "That's silly"[85]—a comment that Büchner meant to be taken seriously. Marion's mother, who is so ironically characterized as wise and moral, can hardly be regarded as tragic; if anything, she is to be pitied. And Marion's first lover is not only pitiable, he is comical. To say this obviously involves a degree of exaggeration—but is not the death brought on by grief a standard element of cheap melodrama? And does not the young man's impetuous suicide smack of a certain callow foolishness? The playwright, in any case, speaking through that incorrigible materialist, Valerio, describes such deeds as "lieutenants' romanticism."[86] Even the phrase "a foolish thing" is supplied by Büchner himself.[87] He refrains from condemning Marion morally—or, for that matter, in any way. She exists outside of the traditional value system which bases itself on Christian ethics and hence she cannot be defined in terms of its conception of morality. Marion does not have a faulty or corrupted conscience, she has no conscience at all. She is not an evildoer, not a sinner, not laden with guilt. In the final analysis, she is not even immoral. She can only be termed amoral. As both elemental nature and its utopian projection, she exists *before* as well as *after* and *above* all traditional, which is to say bourgeois, moral strictures and sexual mores. Marion is entirely natural and yet at the same time she presages a perfect utopia. The first of these aspects serves as an anticipatory manifestation, a poetic image, of the second aspect. Or, to draw on yet another notorious thinker, though he certainly was not always a misogynist: Marion, as a living revaluation of all the values of love, stands both before and beyond good and evil (and, by the way, completely removed from the world of work). She is the "restoration of nature, free from false moralism [*moralinfrei*]," to use Nietzsche's lapidary description of this condition.[88]

It is only through an appreciation of such paradoxes that we are able to understand Marion, her relationship to Danton, and the function of her scene. On the one hand, she is nature in its purest form and yet, on the other, she is not at all natural. Actually, she is caught between two sets of constraints: she is acutely susceptible to those of nature and she finds herself a prey of those of society. Only gradually is she able to overcome the double disharmony caused by these forces and mechanisms. This is revealed to us twice—here Büchner is quite exact—in the oppressive feeling of suffocation or choking which is so vividly visited upon Marion before she finally is able to become herself. In the midst of spring's luxuriance, it symbolizes the powerful drives of nature; in the enraged embrace of her disappointed lover, it represents society's insistence upon possession. For Marion, both issues now belong to the past; life and love have long since become one and the same. When this feeling of suffocation recurs at the end of the scene, it is no longer associated with her but instead with Danton. Coming on the heels of his strained debate with

Lacroix and Paris, it is symptomatic, both specifically and in a broad sense, of an external compulsion to "exertion" and "work," to purposeful "action" in general;[89] symptomatic, moreover, of the individual's renunciation of pleasure and obsession with productive accomplishment, as well as of that sad state of affairs in which people mutually oppress one another. Referring to his friends, Danton might well have repeated his line from the opening scene: "Their politics [i.e., their plans, their appeals, their demands] are getting on my nerves."[90] Marion, however, uses a different image in conveying this thought to Danton: "Your lips are cold, your words have stifled your kisses."[91]

Even in her lament, Büchner's grisette manifests, as a utopian projection, precisely that which Büchner's revolutionary, who is trying to blaze a trail to utopia, would like to achieve in historical reality: the realm of untrammeled pleasure. Marion is actually able to live the existence Danton demands, impatient and audacious—and hence burdened with guilt. She is able to be what he can only long for. The playwright has allowed her to rise above all constraints and enter that much sought-after realm. As Ullmann points out, Marion has attained complete and unmutilated "humanness" (*Menschennatur*); she has managed to transcend all notions of private property, an achievement which allows her to possess the entire world. Moreover, she has dissolved her sense of self; thus her existence, while totally unfragmented, is marked by infinite multiplicity. However, such fulfillment can only exist as the projection of a possibility; this perfect unity of being can only reside on the periphery of history, where origin and goal flow into one another. For the revolutionary who lives in the midst of a bloody reality, all this is unattainable. Danton, entangled in history, thoroughly caught up in the developments of each new day, must remain in a state of inner disharmony from which he can escape only for a few moments at a time. His agonizingly acute consciousness, which constantly disturbs his peace of mind, and Marion's seamless, almost unconscious, happiness are discordantly juxtaposed, their compatibility and loving encounter notwithstanding. Büchner's grisette manifests a tangible utopia, a concrete praxis of erotic liberation; in Büchner's revolutionary, we see a concretization of utopia's dependence on history and its concomitant contradiction of reality.

Yet the difference between Danton and Marion is not presented simply as a painful disharmony, but instead primarily in terms of a reconciliation. For this is the central meaning of the brief, lyrical exchange that consummates the idyl shared by the two lovers. Does it not almost resemble a duet? While it seems to begin so abruptly, the dialogue actually is a logical continuation of what has already been said, a final, poetically terse evocation both of the undistorted nature that preceded man's descent into history and of the erotic utopia that lies somewhere in the future. These lines are not intended to provide contrast; instead, they represent a culmination.[92] What does it mean when Danton voices his ardent desire to enfold Marion "completely" inside himself and feels a need to become "part of the atmosphere" so that he might "bathe" his lover in his "flood" and "break on every wave" of her "beautiful body"? And what are we to make of that seemingly cryptic line in which Marion reproachfully tells Danton that his lips have eyes? Should we follow the lead of formalist criticism and conclude that this is nothing more than a bold image that anticipates Rimbaud and the Dadaist Hans Arp? Should we accept the judgment of the critic and poet Walter Höllerer and view it as "surreal estrangement"?[93] But does not Hinderer offer a more convincing explanation when he speaks of a "metaphor for Danton's inability to turn off his consciousness"?[94]

Yet even this interpretation, while establishing a persuasive connection between form and content, provides only half the answer. The other half can be found in a book which makes no reference to Büchner, a book which carries the trendy—and yet appropriate—title, *Love's Body*. Experiences of the sort described by Marion are, the author emphatically informs us, "polymorphous perversity, the translation of all our senses into one another, the interplay between the senses," which is to say "the metaphor, the free translation."[95] And in truth, however suspicious we may be of faddish prophets and lecture-circuit revolutionaries, could we find a better description of Büchner's "new, previously unarticulated sensibility"[96] than this passage by Norman O. Brown? Does not the concept of "polymorphous perversity," the interplay of all the senses, provide, if not *the,* at least *a* key to Danton's lips that have eyes? Or, to phrase the question differently, is not the "metaphor" also a sensual reality? This notion, among others, is elucidated as Brown, proceeding in his inimitably eclectic manner,[97] issues a prophecy regarding an erotic utopia: "The human body would become polymorphously perverse, delighting in that full life of all the body which it now fears. The consciousness strong enough to endure full life would be no longer Apollonian but Dionysian—consciousness which does not observe the limit, but overflows, *consciousness which does not negate any more.*"

Does this not constitute a summation, and a rather detailed one at that, of both the dialogue and the relationship between Danton and Marion? Are they not, like the fervent disciple of Freud, though in a much more direct way, involved in the "complete abolition of repression" and the "resurrection of the body"? As if he were not only allowing Marion to reflect, but also seeking to outdo Danton's "laziness,"[98] Brown announces: "The riddle of history is not in Reason but in Desire; not in labor but in love." To be sure, Brown is indulging in extreme understatement when, in his earlier and better known book, *Life Against Death,* he refers to all this as "a little more Eros."[99] There is no denying that his writings run the risk of making an absolute of erotic liberation. Yet it is by no means mere eclecticism that leads him to draw not only on Nietzsche and, especially, Freud, but also on Marx, whose concept of the "total person" he blends with ideas taken from the other two thinkers.[100] (The concept, it will be remembered, first appeared in the *Economic-Philosophical Manuscripts* of 1844, that is to say, seven years after Büchner's death.) The necessity of connecting Marx and Freud, perhaps Nietzsche as well, and, in any event, Marxism and psychoanalysis, social and sexual revolution, was perceived long before Brown came on the scene. One need only think of Wilhelm Reich and, above all, Herbert Marcuse and his book, *Eros and Civilization.*[101] Actually, it is of secondary importance which of these thinkers one relies on for supporting testimony. What is crucial—as well as astounding—is the fact that in Büchner's works we encounter a thoroughly modern view of revolution, one which is not just twofold but actually fourfold; indeed, I would go so far as to say that in his oeuvre every conceivable variety of revolt is not only present but is developed to its fullest extent. Both love and revolution are here in all their various forms; both possess central importance and, at the same time, are inseparable from each other. Nowhere is this more evident than in the female figures of **Danton's Death,** and most of all in Marion.

Thus it is no exaggeration to say that Marion, the embodiment of sexual liberation, can be viewed as the pleasure principle incarnate: a notion which—let me make this point one last time—involves absolutely no value judgment. Nothing could be further off the mark than to dismiss Marion as an inferior variant of her partner by declaring, "[Her] insatiability . . . is a distortion, a vulgarization of Danton's."[102] For if one were carefully to compare the two figures, would it not emerge that the very opposite is much closer to the truth? Certainly, the playwright did not hesitate to underscore Danton's own naturalness and sensuality; in fact, he even relates these qualities to Marion's versions of them by having his protagonist anticipate, almost word-for-word, one of her key statements. Prior to the grisette's declaration, "that was my nature," her visitor has candidly announced, "That's my nature."[103]

Notes

1. Georg Büchner, *The Complete Collected Works,* translations and commentary by Henry J. Schmidt (New York: Avon Books, 1977). Hereafter *CCW* 48; cf. Georg Büchner, *Sämtliche Werke und Briefe.* Historisch-Kristische Ausgabe mit Kommentar, edited by Werner R. Lehmann (Hamburg: Christian Wegner Verlag, 1967-). Hereafter *HA* 35.

2. See Werner Schlick, *Das Georg-Büchner-Schrifttum bis 1965: Eine internationale Bibliographie* (Hildesheim, 1968) and Klaus-Dietrich Petersen, "Georg-Büchner-Bibliographie," *Philobiblon* 17 (1973): 89-115. Compare also Hinderer's *Büchner-Kommentar zum dichterischen Werk* (München, 1977), as well as Gerhard P. Knapp, *Georg Büchner* (Stuttgart, 1977).

3. Erwin Theodor [Rosenthal], "Büchners Grundgedanke: Sehnsucht nach Liebe," *Revista de Letras* 3 (1962): 201-13.

4. See Gonthier Louis-Fink, "Volkslied und Verseinlage in den Dramen Büchners," in Martens, pp. 442-87.

5. A few of them are quite useful. Particularly noteworthy, although by no means equal to each other in quality, are Bo Ullmann's chapter, "Marie und die Preisgabe der erotischen Utopie," in his *Die sozialkritische Problematik im Werke Georg Büchners und ihre Entfaltung im "Woyzeck": Mit einigen Bemerkungen zu der Oper Alban Bergs* (Stockholm, 1972), pp. 62ff. and 160ff., and Wolfgang Martens, "Zum Menschenbild Georg Büchners: 'Woyzeck' und die Marionszene in 'Dantons Tod,'" in Martens, pp. 373-85, as well as the studies of Swales and Reddick mentioned in the introduction, n. 86. I was unable to consult Ursula Segebrecht-Paulus, "Genuß und Leid im Werk Georg Büchners" (diss., München, 1969).

6. *CCW* 17; cf. *HA* 1, 9: "Sieh die hübsche Dame, wie artig sie die Karten dreht! ja wahrhaftig sie versteht's, man sagt sie halte ihrem Manne immer das cœur und andern Leuten das carreau hin. Ihr könntet einen noch in die Lüge verliebt machen."

7. Herbert Anton, *Büchners Dramen: Topographien der Freiheit* (Paderborn, 1975), p. 17—which means, as has been caustically noted, that the female lap (*Schoß*) is presented as a stage the masks of which conceal the "indestructible muttonhead" (*unverwüstlicher Schaafskopf*) of the masked god Dionysus (cf. Hinderer, p. 90).

8. *CCW* 18; cf. *HA* 1, 10: "Ich würde meine Tochter dergleichen nicht spielen lassen, die Herren und Damen fallen so unanständig übereinander und die Buben kommen gleich hinten nach."

9. Cf. *HA* 1, 41: "lieb Herz."

10. *CCW* 20; cf. *HA* 1, 11: "die gliederlösende, böse Liebe"; "nackte Götter, Bachantinnen [*sic*]"; "die Venus mit dem schönen Hintern." For the latter passage, see Hinderer, p. 93.

11. Ibid.: "Thürsteher der Republik."

12. Cf. *CCW* 124 and *HA* 1, 92-93: "Glückseligkeit"; "ruhig"; "Schicksal"; "centnerschwer auf dem Herzen."

13. *CCW* 125-26; cf. *HA* 1, 93: "fixe Idee"; "mit allem Jammer der Verzweiflung"; "Stehe auf und wandle!"

14. In one of the scattered fragments of *Leonce and Lena,* one finds the line: "Arise in your white dress and glide through the night and say to the corpse arise and walk!" (*Steh auf in deinem weißen Kleid u. schwebe durch die Nacht u. sprich zur Leiche steh auf und wandle!*) *HA* 1, 141.

15. *HA* 2, 423-24: "Ich bin allein, wie im Grabe; wann erweckt mich deine Hand? . . . Sie sagen, ich sei verrückt, weil ich gesagt habe, in sechs Wochen würde ich auferstehen, zuerst aber Himmelfahrt halten, in der Diligence nämlich."

16. *CCW* 117; cf. *HA* 1, 84-85: "Jetzt, ein anderes Seyn, göttliche, zuckende Lippen bückten sich über ihm nieder, und sogen sich an seine Lippen; er ging auf sein einsames Zimmer. Er war allein, allein! Da rauschte die Quelle, Ströme brachen aus seinen Augen, er krümmte sich in sich, es zuckten seine Glieder, es war ihm als müsse er sich auflösen, er konnte kein Ende finden der Wollust."

17. See *CCW* 160-61; cf. *HA* 1, 125.

18. *HA* 2, 426: "Ich glühte, das Fieber bedeckte mich mit Küssen und umschlang mich wie der Arm der Geliebten. Die Finsterniß wogte über mir, mein Herz schwoll in unendlicher Sehnsucht, es drangen Sterne durch das Dunkel, und Hände und Lippen bückten sich nieder."

19. See Knapp, *Georg Büchner,* pp. 75ff., who provides further bibliographical references.

20. In this regard, a particularly prominent role is being played by Wolfgang Wittkowski, who has launched a full-scale campaign to "Christianize" Büchner; see his contributions listed in chapter 5, n. 26. The weakness of Wittkowski's approach is revealed specifically with regard to *Lenz* in an article by Heinrich Anz (see chapter 3, n. 37).

21. *CCW* 126; cf. *HA* 1, 93: "daß Gott ein Zeichen an ihm thue, und das Kind beleben möge." Once again, *Leonce and Lena* provides a corresponding text; *CCW* 160 and *HA* 1, 124:

LENA.

. . . The moon is like a sleeping child, its golden locks have fallen over its dear face.—Oh, its sleep is death. Look how the dead angel rests its dark pillow and the stars burn around it like candles. Poor child, are the bogeymen coming to get you soon? Where is your mother? Doesn't she want to kiss you once more? Ah, it's sad, dead, and so alone.

LEONCE.

Arise in your white dress and follow the corpse through the night and sing its requiem.

(LENA.

. . . *Der Mond ist wie ein schlafendes Kind, die goldnen Locken sind ihm im Schlaf über das liebe Gesicht heruntergefallen.—O sein Schlaf ist Tod. Wie der todte Engel auf seinem dunkeln Kissen ruht und die Sterne gleich Kerzen um ihn brennen. Armes Kind, kommen die schwarzen Männer bald dich holen? Wo ist deine Mutter? Will sie dich nicht noch einmal küssen? Ach es ist traurig, todt und so allein.*

LEONCE.

Steh auf in deinem weißen Kleide und wandle hinter der Leiche durch die Nacht und singe ihr das Todtenlied.)

Thus the final version. But originally Leonce continued in a manner reminiscent of Lenz (cf. *HA* 1, 141).

22. See the summary provided by Hermann Bräuning-Oktavio, *Georg Büchner: Gedanken über Leben, Werk und Tod* (Bonn, 1976), pp. 41ff.; the following two quotes are also taken from this book.

23. See Hinderer, p. 172.

24. See Bräuning-Oktavio, p. 42.

25. Gaston Salvatore, *Büchners Tod* (Frankfurt, 1972), pp. 75ff.; for a "generic" background of sorts, see my survey essay, "Dichter-Helden: 'Tasso,' 'Empedokles' und die Folgen," *Basis* 7 (1977): 7-25.

26. See, for instance, *Brechts Tui-Kritik,* ed. Wolfgang Fritz Haug (Karlsruhe, 1976). "Tui" is a playful *chinoiserie* of Brecht's, derived from "*t*ellect-*u*el-in" = "*in*tellect*u*el."

27. The famous epithet, "the divine one," which has already been mentioned, also stems from Ariosto; see Peter Stafford's introduction to Pietro Aretino, *The Ragionamenti* (London, 1970), p. v.

28. See ibid., p. ix.

29. *CCW* 64; cf. *HA* 1, 49: "Dogge mit Taubenflügeln."

30. It appears that Büchner worked on his Aretino play in the summer or fall of 1836; see Knapp, *Georg Büchner,* p. 26 (who mistakenly writes "1837").

31. Bräuning-Oktavio, pp. 42, 46.

32. See *CCW* 31-32 and *HA* 1, 21-22; compare Aretino's declaration in Antonino Foschini, *L'Aretino*

(Milano, 1951), p. 137: "E tu mi fai lagrimar di piacere solo a pensarti."

33. See ibid., p. 139: "O Iddio, salva Perina, ché io l'ho amata, l'amo e l'amerò sempre, finché la sentenza del dí novissimo giudicherà le vanità nostre." Although those quotes are taken from a biographical essay which is strongly novelistic, their content and, to some extent, their wording are based on Aretino's letters.

34. Stafford, p. viii. It appears that the Englishman knows nothing of Büchner and has never heard of the interesting as well as shocking if, admittedly, less significant "cinquecento drama" by Oskar Panizza, *Das Liebeskonzil* (*The Council of Love*), which first appeared in 1895.

35. There is a certain irony in the fact that, instead of Büchner's own work, we have his translation of a play which the same English critic judges to be "probably the worst drama" dealing with this period: Victor Hugo's *Lucrèce Borgia*; cf. ibid. and compare *HA* 1, 193ff.

36. See *CCW* 16; cf. *HA* 1, 8 and Maurice B. Benn, *The Drama of Revolt: A Critical Study of Georg Büchner* (Cambridge: Cambridge University Press, 1976). Hereafter Benn, p. 135.

37. As to *Woyzeck,* compare in particular Klotz, *Geschlossene und offene Form im Drama,* p. 110 and Wilhelm Emrich, "Von Georg Büchner zu Samuel Beckett: Zum Problem einer literarischen Formidee," in *Aspekte des Expressionismus: Periodisierung · Stil · Gedankenwelt,* ed. Wolfgang Paulsen (Heidelberg, 1968), pp. 11-32. Both emphasize the circularity, the carrousel, the "world-wheel" (*Weltrad*) in the structure of *Danton's Death.* There are others, however, who reject this view or at least wish to modify it; see especially Benn, p. 254: "It has occasionally been suggested that the action of the play is circular, that the end is implicit in the beginning. This is evidently not so. The action has rather the form of a spiral ascending to an acme of tragic suffering." But he also states with regard to *Leonce and Lena:* "At the end of the play the situation—politically, psychologically, metaphysically—is still essentially the same as at the beginning" (ibid., p. 169). The same thesis is advanced by Richards, *Georg Büchner and the Birth of Modern Drama,* p. 114.

38. As for *Danton's Death,* there is a rather general reference to a "circular structure" (*struttura circolare*) in Giorgio Dolfini, *Il teatro di Georg Büchner* (Milano, 1961), p. 52. It is interesting to note that a similar structure can be detected in Heiner Müller's play *Germania Tod in Berlin;* see Schulz, p. 137.

39. See *CCW* 18, 95-96; cf. *HA* 1, 9, 75:

DANTON.

Nein Julie, ich liebe dich wie das Grab. . . . Die Leute sagen im Grab sey Ruhe und Grab und Ruhe seyen eins. Wenn das ist, lieg' ich in deinem Schooß schon unter der Erde. Du süßes Grab, deine Lippen sind Todtenglocken, deine Stimme ist mein Grabgeläute, deine Brust mein Grabhügel und dein Herz mein Sarg.

LUCILE.

(*tritt auf und setzt sich auf die Stufen der Guillotine*) Ich setze mich auf deinen Schooß, du stiller Todesengel. . . . Du liebe Wiege, die du meinen Camille in Schlaf gelullt, ihn unter deinen Rosen erstickt hast. / Du Todtenglocke, die du ihn mit deiner süßen Zunge zu Grabe sangst.

40. *CCW* 19; cf. *HA* 1, 11: "Särge zur Wiege haben."

41. Norman O. Brown, *Love's Body* (New York, 1966), p. 47; see also p. 42.

42. *CCW* 92; cf. *HA* 1, 72.

43. *CCW* 73; cf. *HA* 1, 73: "Schlafe, schlafe"; "Schlummer."

44. *CCW* 17; *HA* 1, 9: "wir sind sehr einsam."

45. *CCW* 55-56; cf. *HA* 1, 41.

46. It has been correctly pointed out that Danton's fears are "entirely inconsistent with his rational assumptions about death and what follows it" (cf. Richards, p. 55). When the same critic—in the same sentence, moreover—perceives in this an "essentially religious feeling," he errs grievously.

47. *CCW* 78-79; cf. *HA* 1, 61: "O Julie! Wenn ich *allein* ginge! Wenn sie mich einsam ließe! . . . Und wenn ich ganz zerfiele, mich ganz auflöste—ich wäre eine Handvoll gemarterten Staubes, jedes meiner Atome könnte nur Ruhe finden bey ihr. . . . Ich kann nicht sterben, nein, ich kann nicht sterben."

48. *CCW* 82; cf. *HA* 1, 64: "Da, bring ihm das und sag' ihm er würde nicht allein gehn. Er versteht mich schon und dann schnell zurück, ich will seine Blicke aus deinen Augen lesen."

49. *CCW* 85; *HA* 1, 67: "Ich werde nicht allein gehn, ich danke dir Julie."

50. See Hinderer, p. 90.

51. Ibid., p. 106; also, compare Josef Jansen, ed., *Erläuterungen und Dokumente [zu] Georg Büchner[s] 'Dantons Tod'* (Stuttgart, 1969), p. 10.

52. Benn, p. 138.

53. Ibid., p. 139.

54. *CCW* 96; cf. *HA* 1, 75:

> EIN BÜRGER.
>
> He werda?
>
> LUCILE.
>
> Es lebe der König!
>
> BÜRGER.
>
> Im Namen der Republik! (*Sie wird von der Wache umringt und weggeführt.*)

55. *CCW* 94; cf. *HA* 1, 74: "auf dem Boden des Korbes küssen."

56. See especially Helmut Koopmann, "Dantons Tod und die antike Welt: Zur Geschichtsphilosophie Georg Büchners," *Zeitschrift für deutsche Philologie* 84 (special issue, 1965): 22-41.

57. Clearly, the notions of a circular movement of history and a cyclical recurrence of that which has already been were not entirely foreign to the playwright. Not only the death of God and the rise of European nihilism, but also other elements of Nietzsche's thought were indisputably anticipated by Büchner. Yet can one proceed to read the "eternal recurrence of the same" (*ewige Wiederkehr des Gleichen*) into his works—especially since even Nietzsche's own use of the concept is far more complex than is commonly realized? It seems to me that one must be much more careful here and, in any event, differentiate with greater care, not only in regard to Büchner but also in regard to Heinrich Heine and Ludwig Börne, who are likewise forced into Koopmann's scheme.

58. *CCW* 306; cf. *HA* 2, 425-26.

59. Gramsci's *pessimismo dell'intelligenza, ottimismo della volontà* is also invoked—the text in question was first published in 1970—by Hans Magnus Enzensberger, *Palaver: Politische Überlegungen (1967-1973)* ("*Palaver: Political Considerations*") (Frankfurt, 1974), p. 129. It would seem to be no accident that, five years earlier, this same critic had edited the radical pamphlet, *The Hessian Messenger.*

60. See *HA* 1, 141: ". . . Leben u. Liebe eins seyn lassen, daß die Liebe das Leben ist, und das Leben die Liebe."

61. They constitute a response by Leonce to Valerio's ironic question, "Marry?" (*Heirathen?*) Büchner apparently realized that this was too serious, too weighty for a comedy for he later struck the words. However, the fact that they express one of his basic concerns is established by the ensuing line, which was not struck, but only slightly altered: "Do you know, Valerio, that even the most insignificant human being is so great that life is far too short to love him?" (*Weißt du auch, Valerio, daß selbst der Geringste unter den Menschen so groß ist, daß das Leben noch viel zu kurz ist, um ihn lieben zu können?*) In the initial draft, this passage read: "Do you know, Valerio, that even he who is most insignificant is so great that human life is far too short to love him?" (*Weißt du auch Valerio, daß auch der Geringste so groß ist, daß das menschliche Leben viel zu kurz ist um ihn lieben zu können?*) See *CCW* 162 and *HA* 1, 126, 142.

62. See especially Martens, "Zum Menschenbild Georg Büchners"; however, Benn has also adopted this view to a large extent. Its inversion, a nonmoralistic judgment which simultaneously stresses the notion of eternal recurrence à la Koopmann, was provided early on by Walter Höllerer, "Büchner: Dantons Tod," in *Das deutsche Drama: Vom Barock bis zur Gegenwart. Interpretationen,* ed. Benno von Wiese (Düsseldorf, 1958), 2, pp. 65-88; here, p. 73.

63. *CCW* 32; cf. *HA* 1, 22: "das Einzige."

64. See *Georg Büchner,* edited by Wolfgang Martens (Darmstadt: Wissenschaftliche Buchgesellschaft, 1965). Hereafter Martens, p. 375.

65. See, for example, *HA* 2, 451-52.

66. See especially Karl Gutzkow, *Wally, die Zweiflerin*; Theodor Mundt, *Madonna, oder: Unterhaltungen mit einer Heiligen* (both published in 1835).

67. See *HA* 2, 444: "Marionetten mit himmelblauen Nasen und affectirtem Pathos"; "sogenannte Idealdichter" (from a letter to his family of July 28, 1835).

68. See Martens, p. 376; this is also the source of the ensuing quotation. At the same time, Martens fully realizes that it is mistaken to speak of a "Young German sensualism" (*Jungdeutscher Sensualismus*) in regard to Büchner and his works (ibid., p. 380).

69. *CCW* 31; cf. *HA* 1, 21: "Meine Mutter war eine kluge Frau, sie sagte mir immer die Keuschheit sey eine schöne Tugend, wenn Leute in's Haus kamen und von manchen Dingen zu sprechen anfingen, hieß sie mich aus dem Zimmer gehn; frug ich was die Leute gewollt hätten so sagte sie mir ich solle mich schämen; gab sie mir ein Buch zu lesen so mußt ich fast immer einige Seiten überschlagen."

70. *CCW* 31-32; cf. *HA* 1, 21-22: "Ich gerieth in eine eigne Atmosphäre, sie erstickte mich fast. . . . Ein junger Mensch kam zu der Zeit in's Haus, er war hübsch und sprach oft tolles Zeug. . . . Endlich sahen wir nicht ein, warum wir nicht eben so gut zwischen zwei Bettüchern bei einander liegen, als auf zwei Stühlen neben einander sitzen durften. . . . Aber ich wurde wie ein Meer, was Alles verschlang und sich tiefer und tiefer wühlte. Es war für mich nur ein Gegensatz da, alle Männer verschmolzen in einen Leib. Meine Natur war einmal so, war kann da drüber hinaus?"

71. *CCW* 32; cf. *HA* 1, 22: "Er kam eines Morgens und küßte mich, als wollte er mich ersticken, seine Arme schnürten sich um meinen Hals, ich war in unsäglicher Angst. . . . Das war der einzige Bruch in meinem Wesen."

72. Ibid.: "Die andern Leute haben Sonn- und Werktage, sie arbeiten sechs Tage und beten am siebenten, sie sind jedes Jahr auf ihren Geburtstag einmal gerührt und denken jedes Jahr auf Neujahr einmal nach. Ich begreife nichts davon. Ich kenne keinen Absatz, keine Veränderung. Ich bin immer nur Eins. Ein ununterbrochnes Sehnen und Fassen, eine Gluth, ein Strom. . . . Es läuft auf eins hinaus, an was man seine Freude hat, an Leibern, Christusbildern, Blumen oder Kinderspielsachen, es ist das nemliche Gefühl, wer am Meisten genießt, betet am Meisten."

73. *CCW* 32-33; cf. *HA* 1, 22:

    DANTON.

    Warum kann ich deine Schönheit nicht ganz in mich fassen, sie nicht ganz umschließen?

    MARION.

    Danton, deine Lippen haben Augen.

    DANTON.

    Ich möchte ein Theil des Aethers seyn, um dich in meiner Fluth zu baden, um mich auf jeder Welle deines schönen Leibes zu brechen.

74. Ibid., pp. 21ff.

75. See Ullmann's study cited in n. 5 above.

76. Benn, p. 137. Even the charge of soullessness, which in this context is thoroughly odd, is flung at Marion by the otherwise perceptive critic (cf. ibid.): "But [Marion] has no soul." Many additional examples of this view could be adduced.

77. This is perhaps the place to state emphatically that my exacting and provocative criticism of the existing secondary literature on Büchner is not intended to obscure or denigrate its many significant accomplishments. I readily admit that I am indebted to other critics in various respects. However, a theme as complex and important as the one at hand must be pursued with complete freedom, indeed audacity, "wherever it may lead" (Benn, p. 3).

78. See Wolfgang Wittkowski, "Georg Büchner, die Philosophen und der Pietismus," *Jahrbuch des Freien Deutschen Hochstifts 1976* (Tübingen, 1976), p. 371: "Die Triebkraft des Unbewußten und die Begrenztheit des Erkennens fanden wir . . . bei Büchner. . . . Darüber hinaus praktizierte er letztere gegenüber Schopenhauer selbst (falls er ihn las)." Or ibid., p. 399: "In seiner Dissertation—leider [!] erst in der 2. Auflage nach Büchners Tod—kritisierte Schopenhauer . . ."—whereupon, as in the first instance, our critic blithely concludes that "perhaps here, too" (*vielleicht auch hier*) Büchner is speaking ironically from Schopenhauer's position. What speaks volumes is the use of "unfortunately" in regard to a text which was not even available "until . . . after Büchner's death" (assuming the latter 'failed' to find some way of reading it in spite of this).

79. Peter Weiss, *Dramen I* (Frankfurt, 1968), p. 244: "Denn was wäre schon diese Revolution / ohne eine allgemeine Kopulation." For the English version, see Peter Weiss, *Marat/Sade,* trans. Geoffrey Skelton, verse adaptation by Adrian Mitchell (New York, 1966), p. 92.

80. See Ullmann, pp. 64-65.

81. See Georg Büchner, *Dantons Tod and Woyzeck,* ed. with introduction and notes by Margaret Jacobs (Manchester, 1968), p. 119; the ensuing quotation is taken from the same source.

82. Regarding this and what follows, see Ullmann, pp. 64ff.

83. See especially the essay by Martens, "Zum Menschenbild Georg Büchners."

84. I should like to remind the reader that the relevant chapter in Ullmann's book is entitled, "Marie and the Abandonment of the Erotic Utopia"—as if the impossibility of realizing a utopia in the proletarian milieu of Woyzeck and Marie, that is to say, in the midst of the most extreme poverty and exploitation, could in any way refute this utopia!

85. *CCW* 32; cf. *HA* 1, 22: "Meine Mutter ist vor Gram gestorben, die Leute weisen mit Fingern auf mich. Das ist dumm."

86. *CCW* 161; cf. *HA* 1, 125: "Lieutenantsromantik."

87. *CCW* 32; cf. *HA* 1, 22: "ein dummer Streich." Büchner, however, does not apply the term to the

young man's suicide, but rather to his impulse, fed by passion and jealousy, to murder Marion, an impulse which he very nearly satisfies. Here again the "comic" parallel to *Woyzeck* is unmistakable.

88. See Friedrich Nietzsche, *Werke in drei Bänden,* ed. Karl Schlechta (München, 1954-56), 3, p. 739 (to which I have to resort in this case). Obviously, mine is a rather free, perhaps even daring, application of Nietzsche, who so conspicuously ignored Büchner. Nevertheless, I do not feel that this is unjustified. The two writers have far more in common than is generally supposed.

89. See *CCW* 21, 37, 45; cf. *HA* 1, 12, 25-26, 33: "Mühe"; "Arbeit"; "Handeln."

90. *CCW* 20; cf. *HA* 1, 12: "sie reiben mich mit ihrer Politik noch auf."

91. *CCW* 37; cf. *HA* 1, 26: "Deine Lippen sind kalt geworden, deine Worte haben deine Küsse erstickt." The image of suffocation is also employed by Lucile (cf. *CCW* 96 and *HA* 1, 75). It would be very useful to have detailed investigations of such clusters of words and images; see, for example, William Bruce Armstrong, "'Arbeit' und 'Muße' in den Werken Georg Büchners," in *GB III,* pp. 63-98.

92. For an opposing view, see Helmut Krapp, *Der Dialog bei Georg Büchner* (München, 1968), p. 141.

93. See Höllerer, p. 83 and, in a similar vein, Krapp, p. 141.

94. Hinderer, p. 98.

95. See Brown, p. 249.

96. Thus Krapp, *Georg Büchner,* p. 141; he is to be commended for having accurately recognized this aspect.

97. For the ensuing quotes, see Brown, pp. 307, 308.

98. *CCW* 51; cf. *HA* 1, 38: "Trägheit."

99. See Norman O. Brown, *Life Against Death: The Psychoanalytical Meaning of History* (Middletown, Conn., 1970), p. 322. The book was first published in 1959.

100. See Brown, *Love's Body,* p. 318.

101. First published in 1955. A brief report on Brown, Reich, and Marcuse as well as a massive condensation of their thought is contained in Jost Hermand, *Pop International: Eine kritische Analyse* (Frankfurt, 1971), pp. 72ff. Yet there are Marxist critics who take these trends very seriously; see, for example, the important study by the Czech theoretician Robert Kalidova, "Marx und Freud,"

in *Weiterentwicklungen des Marxismus,* ed. Willy Oelmüller (Darmstadt, 1977), pp. 130-89.

102. Simon, in his introduction to Georg Büchner, *Danton's Death,* p. 17.

103. *CCW* 20, 32; cf. *HA* 1, 12, 22: "Meine Natur war einmal so"; "Mein Naturellist einmal so."

James Martin Harding (essay date March 1992)

SOURCE: Harding, James Martin. "Integrating Atomization: Adorno Reading Berg Reading Büchner." *Theatre Journal* 44, no. 1 (March 1992): 1-13.

[*In the following essay, Harding presents a complex analysis of the aesthetic and social categories associated with materialist criticism of Büchner's* Woyzeck, *arguing that the drama resists a teleological interpretation of class conflict and is instead concerned with atomization and social fractionalization.*]

Roughly a year before his death in 1969, Theodor W. Adorno published a short work entitled *Alban Berg: Der Meister des Kleinsten Übergangs.*[1] The text could be considered marginal were it not for the substantial personal influence that Berg had on the young Adorno, and for the prominent position Berg occupies in Adorno's later writings on music and aesthetics. The text is also of interest because it contains the last link in a chain of readings that leads back to Georg Büchner's dramatic account of Johann Christian Woyzeck, an actual soldier who was executed after having murdered his lover (1821). Woyzeck's trial had attracted considerable attention because of a protracted medical inquiry into his mental stability. The results of this inquiry were published in a medical journal and subsequently adapted by Büchner for the stage.[2] Although Büchner died (1837) before completing the play, it was close enough to completion that it was later performed, and when Alban Berg saw the Vienna production, his response was so strong that he built his first opera around the script.

In the comments which follow, I examine how Theodor W. Adorno's interpretation of Alban Berg's operatic rendition of *Woyzeck* provides the basis for an as-yet-unexplored reading of Georg Büchner's unfinished drama. I contend that the critical strategies of Adorno's *Alban Berg* lay the foundation for a materialist analysis of *Woyzeck* in which the relation between particular and universal is reversed, the later being subordinated to the evolution of the former. I also contend that this reversal is consistent with Adorno's classic critique of Georg Lukács[3] and thus offers an implicit challenge to Lukács's own interpretation of Büchner's work, an interpretation that Lukács bases upon an analysis of class conflict. Lukács's reading of Büchner in "*Der faschis-*

tische verfälschte und der wirkliche Georg Büchner"[4] relies upon an hierarchical structure of mediation, a determination of the particular by a posited social whole, which, when considered in light of Adorno's arguments, is inadequate as an explanation of the complexities at play in Büchner's *Woyzeck.*

Adorno's analysis of Berg's *Wozzeck* provides the context for a three-fold analysis of Büchner's play. First of all, Adorno's reversal of the relation between particular and universal illuminates how conceptions of the social totality are reductive when it comes to understanding the complexity of the particular. For Adorno, such reductiveness and the discursive categories which sustain it inevitably lead to repression. He praises Alban Berg because Berg's compositions embody a particularity whose complexity is built upon resistance (and is thus a challenge) to accepted categories for understanding music. I argue that the complexity of Berg's operatic composition compliments a corresponding complexity in Büchner's *Woyzeck*—both in form and in the resistance that Büchner's play offers to the categories which ostensibly define the social totality mediating Woyzeck's experience. In Adorno's analysis of *Wozzeck,* conceptions of the whole constitute influential but not comprehensive dimensions within the constellations that make up the diversity of socio-historical situations. Correspondingly, conceptions of the social totality have an influential role in *Woyzeck,* but as a cornerstone, that is supposedly the determining factor of the particular, they cannot account for the complexity of the particular.

Second, after having explored how *Woyzeck* coincides with Adorno's attempts to reaffirm the complexity of the particular, I then examine how the emergence of this complexity in *Woyzeck* challenges attempts to define the "inevitable" path of history. The implied reference in these arguments is Lukács's belief that class conflict will eventually supersede itself. I argue that the lack of logical continuity from one scene to the next in *Woyzeck* gives each scene of Büchner's play a history of its own and that a unified or comprehensive "history" occurs only as a product of the reader's constructions.

Last but not least, my considerations of Büchner's play will show how the complexity of the particular is also questionable as a viable alternative to the limitations of analysis based upon a conception of the social totality. Thus, while *Woyzeck* coincides with the critique of Lukács which Adorno formulated in his classic article *"Erpreßte Versöhnung,"* the play also disrupts the presumptions upon which Adorno's critique is based.

I

Susan Buck-Morss has noted that the critical strategies which Adorno employs for social analysis often depart from the more traditional Marxist approach of analyses based upon class conflict.[5] Adorno's departure from traditional Marxist readings, however, does not altogether eliminate the issue of class conflict from his writings. Rather he subordinates the conflict to historical trends that—with unmistakably negative consequences—have circumvented the foundations upon which analysis of class conflict could serve as the basis for positive change. The departure is based upon a perception of rising social uniformity, which, according to Adorno and other members of the Frankfurt School, is slowly eroding the possibility for oppositional stance. According to these arguments, class conflict has succumbed to what Marcuse describes as "One-dimensional Society." Paradoxically, the one-dimensionality of society is sustained by an exacerbated fractionalization of it, a fractionalization foreshadowed in Woyzeck himself. The one-dimensionality can be seen when Woyzeck, too overwhelmed by divergent social demands to develop opposition to them, has not only to submit to the rigors of military discipline, but has simultaneously to submit to the constraints of being a specimen for scientific inquiry as well. In Woyzeck's case, the constraints of the doctor's experiment deny him the sustenance he needs to perform his other work. The two occupations are mutually exclusive, the one making him unfit for the other and vice-versa.[6] Fractionalization obstructs particularity because the avenues of Woyzeck's experience are predetermined. He has no time to develop distinctness because his time is consumed in a pathetic attempt to keep abreast of the requirements of his two jobs.

As society becomes more fractionalized, a stagnant uniformity becomes imminent. For Adorno, where society has become too fractionalized to oppose, particularity disappears. Yet, while society may be much too splintered to fit within the basic oppositions of class conflict, Adorno maintains that opposition, and thus particularity, has found an embattled respite in Art. This is because, according to Adorno, Art alone possesses the technical wherewithal to structure a mimetic opposition to increasingly divergent social trends. In the subtle ambiguities of Art, Adorno finds the last vestiges of opposition to the reified conscious structures that reinforce a one-dimensional society.[7]

When one peruses Adorno's writings on music, it becomes obvious that Adorno's high esteem for his previous music instructor, Alban Berg, stems from the complex technical sophistication in Berg's compositions, and especially in his two operas, *Lulu* and *Wozzeck.* These pieces, Adorno argues, demand such attention from the listener that they tax an individual's ability to comprehend. They resist "being understood by everyday consciousness."[8] But far from merely being obscurant, the achievement of Berg's work, according to Adorno, lies precisely in its having attained a level of composition which exhausts the tools of comprehension and perception. Adorno's praise rests upon what I would describe as his regard for an observed ability in Berg to "integrate atomization," i.e. an ability to orchestrate recognizable elements in such a manner that the limitations of these elements surface. Since the sophistication of Berg's work exhausts the structures of habitual perception, Adorno argues that the technique of atomization reaches back into nothingness:

> Furthermore, the level of composition proves itself—so superior that today it is hardly still perceived—precisely in the extremely conscious syntactical structure, which reaches from the whole movement to the status of each single note and leaves nothing out. This music is beautiful according to the Latin term *formosus,* that of the richness of forms. Its wealth in form shapes the music into eloquence, into a likeness with language. But the wealth has a special technique of calling, through their own development, the formed thematic structures back into nothingness.[9]

For Adorno, Berg's atomization, his calling themes back into nothingness, has a liberating effect, simultaneously exposing and resisting reification. On the one hand, the music incorporates general terms or themes, which, with development, begin to unravel and falter; in particular, the development of these incorporated themes exposes the contradictions which they otherwise obscure. The themes resemble language in that their development exposes how the forms that they assume in perception echo the structure or even ideological mediations a word imposes on its referent. On the other hand, Berg's compositions possess a uniqueness, a particularity, which—Adorno is delighted to admit—borders on defying description with general terms and which consequently affirms Adorno's own arguments that the particular is compromised when subordinated to a system or paradigm of the whole.

Adorno's appreciation of Berg is relevant to the study of Büchner because in terms of literary technique and effect, *Woyzeck* has a natural affinity with the style employed by Berg for composing. Indeed, this affinity can be seen in Adorno's own explanation of Berg's understanding of Büchner's play:

> He understood Büchner's drama of the tormented, paranoid soldier Wozzeck [sic], who lets out the injustice done to him on untamed Nature and kills his lover . . . in the same spirit that Karl Kraus, citing the expired word of humanity turned against the prevailing inhumanity, to which language fell victim.[10]

The allusion to Kraus in Adorno's explanation may result from the influence that Kraus's writing exercised not only on Berg but also on Berg's teacher, Arnold Schönberg, who claimed to have learned more from Karl Kraus than one man ought to if he still wanted to remain independent.[11] Both composers admired Kraus, and Berg arguably transposed into his music Kraus's ability to separate humanism from its tropes. The spirit

in which Berg understood *Woyzeck* corresponds to Kraus's ability to formulate a critical discourse which undercuts language that was once liberating and affirming of humanity but that now is expired and has become victimized by appropriation for inhuman ends. It is interesting that Adorno associates Berg's "understanding" of Büchner with Kraus's "use" of the spoken word because the association emphasizes the active, constructive role any reader has in understanding a text. Yet what I would like to suggest is that the spirit in which Berg understood *Woyzeck* was as much the result of the play itself as it was of Berg's critical powers.

Berg's spontaneous comments after having seen the first Viennese production of *Woyzeck* (May 5, 1914) are reported by Paul Elbogen to have expressed the need to set the play to music.[12] If this is in fact true, then Berg immediately recognized the play's compatibility with his own style of composing, a compatibility that Adorno attributes to the "language-like" technique in Berg's compositions. Not only are Berg's compositions marked by an "integration of atomization," so too is Büchner's play. Indeed, the thematic elements in *Woyzeck* follow a path similar to the musical themes in Berg's compositions whose development, Adorno claims, calls them back into nothingness. Like Kraus's use of the language of humanism in order to illuminate its appropriation for inhuman ends, *Woyzeck* employs a discourse of humanism, whose terms it dismantles by developing their implications, i.e. by pursuing them to their logical conclusions and by exposing their susceptibility to tyrannical, repressive agendas. The aesthetic technique of atomization, as it functions in Büchner's play, structures a critical stance against the regression of humanistic language into abstract ideals. Specifically, the atomization in *Woyzeck* undermines the causal relation between universal and particular.

Two examples illustrate the scope of the atomization active in *Woyzeck*. First of all, while Lukács would cite the character of Woyzeck as exemplary of a social whole in which the sufferings of the poor are the price with which others obtain the possibility to lead fulfilled lives, Woyzeck's suffering is not a point of camaraderie with his peers, not a point of common or shared misery which could lead to a revolutionary consciousness of the socio-economic whole. One need only consider that the scenes of Woyzeck's most extreme torment are either when he is alone, or more significantly, when these sufferings are foiled by the character of Andres, who passes the time whistling and singing folk songs and is apparently undisturbed by the social situation that he and Woyzeck share. The point is that while the two soldiers share the same abysmal circumstance, they are opposites in their experience of it. Not only does Andres appear to have found the means with which to deal with his situation, but he also maintains a compassionate relationship with Woyzeck: listening to Woyzeck, attempting to assist him when he is drunk and even spying for him on the Drum Major, the rival for Marie's affections.

While the social structure contributes to Woyzeck's misery, class structure alone is not sufficient as a concept to account for the whole of Woyzeck's suffering. In this respect, the atomization characteristic of the compositions of Berg and of the textual structures of **Woyzeck** reflect the social currents which preclude the foundations of class conflict, the link pin of Lukács's argument for revolutionary change. Andres constantly undermines Woyzeck's position as exemplary of the poor, and the consequent atomization questions whether categories founded in reductiveness can actually serve as the basis of critical change. Nonetheless, there is a disturbing correspondence between atomization as an aesthetic critical technique and the fractionalization of society as a repressive socio-historical phenomenon. Not only is atomization the means with which **Woyzeck** challenges the ideals and structures of social reform, but it is also a reflection of the social currents that are at the source of Woyzeck's repressive situation.

Insofar as atomization mirrors the fractionalization of society, it is not altogether a positive accomplishment, and this is the second example of atomization as a critical literary technique. While atomization may formulate an effective critical opposition to the repressive reductiveness that results from attempts to subordinate the particular beneath a rubric of the whole or of the universal, the calling of formed thematic structures back into nothingness is as often pernicious as it is positive. At the very least, it is indicative of equally repressive countercurrents within the oppositional stance assumed by atomization. For example, the *"ungebändigte Natur"* ("against Nature")—against which, according to Adorno, Woyzeck vents the consequences of the injustices done to him—by no means possesses the unmediated status that Adorno grants it. The same process of atomization that Adorno identifies applies to the concept of Nature as well. The play compares "Nature" to the "reason" of the trick-horse at the county fair. More importantly, the play incorporates "Nature" into the sadistic rationalizations of the doctor. Thus the striking out to which Adorno refers becomes a striking out at nothingness, at an absent space or a dearth—the fact of nothingness being the injustice itself.

If Berg's compositions were merely exercises in atomization, it is doubtful whether Adorno would have been as taken by them as he evidently was. There is, in fact, reason to believe that he was aware of the insufficiency of atomization as a panacea for social ills. In *"Erpreβte Versöhnung,"* Adorno exhorted against succumbing to the naive over-simplification of arguments whose strategies are to dismiss an object on the grounds that it "disintegrates into a series of incompatible parts."[13] The ex-

hortation can be seen as a recognition of the need for the process of atomization to be part of a larger critical dynamic. A response to this need distinguishes Berg's compositions, and Büchner's drama as well, from a mere reflection of an increasingly fractionalized society. Both employ atomization while not succumbing to the naiveté against which Adorno warns. While atomization uncovers the reductiveness and/or contradictions which sustain a fractionalized society, Berg's compositions are not solely marked by a technique of atomization. Integration is as important to the artistic achievement of Berg's work as is the technique of developing themes in order to expose their limits. Neither can stand alone.

Integration functions as both a counter to repressive social fractionalizations and to naive rejections of socio-historical determination. While the processes of atomization disentangle themes from forms that development exposes as reductive and stultifying, the integration of these processes into an unique and autonomous musical composition testifies to the particularity that atomization reinstates. Not only does the work expose reified structures, but its own complexity, i.e. its ability to integrate atomization, also affirms the particularity which is lost when reduced or confined to patterns of general and recognizable forms. The sophistication which Adorno observes in Berg's compositions is synonymous with its particularity, a particularity which becomes reified when not allowed to come to full fruition because it is trapped within dominant social patterns, however fractionalized these patterns might be. On the one hand, integration simulates a utopian function, achieving what the fractionalization obstructs. But on the other, the sophistication of Berg and Büchner, their ability to achieve particular integration amidst general fractionalization is what sustains their unique, un-reified status in the face of reified socio-historical currents toward an increasingly splintered society.

What distinguishes the technique of "integrating atomization" from its initial apparent utopian yearnings is that it abandons the attempt to alter the whole as a means of establishing the particular. The emergence of an utopian element in the aesthetic strategies of Berg and Büchner can be seen in much the same light as the parallels between atomization and the splintering of society. Inasmuch as atomization is a critical reflection of increasingly divergent socio-historical currents, so too does integration critically reflect the influence that conceptions of the whole have within these currents; and, just as integration keeps atomization from succumbing to the naiveté which Adorno denounces in *"Erpreβte Versöhnung,"* so too does atomization keep integration from progressing into the status of an absolute or universal. The tension between atomization and integration establishes what seems to me to be the central shared characteristic between *Wozzeck* and **Woyzeck,** a critical particularity which is based on a "levelling technique" that subordinates the universal (the whole) to the particular.

An ambivalent sense for the radical implications of this technique can be found in the more recent critical assessments of Berg's compositions. George Perle, for example, has argued that the integration found in Berg's *Wozzeck* maintains particularity in the unique dynamic it creates with the elements or themes that emerge in his work. But while Perle is correct about the strategies Berg employs, he is by no means comfortable with their implications. Perle writes:

> In Berg as in Mozart, a constant and inevitable order subsumes the dramatic details, but Berg's order [in *Wozzeck*], unlike Mozart's, is irrational, meaningless, non-human, indifferent, for it embraces the casual and the essential, the momentous and the trivial, with equal impartiality.[14]

In that Perle interprets Berg's impartial embrace of elements as irrational, meaningless and non-human, it seems to me that he demeans the critical significance of the technique which he so astutely observes. The particularity that emerges from Berg's impartial embrace pivots on the challenge that his work poses to the seemingly "universal" criteria for determining not only the momentous and the trivial, but rationality, meaning and humanity as well. The impartiality with which *Wozzeck* and **Woyzeck** embrace the momentous and the trivial emphasizes the distance these works place between themselves and the discursive categories which, supposedly, are "impartial" in their reinforcement of a perceived image of the social totality. One can see this distance in the juxtaposition of scenes: in **Woyzeck,** the impartial embrace places "acceptable" behavior and the effect it has on Woyzeck on a par with the brutality of his later attack on Marie. One can also see the distance in the individual scenes themselves: witness the contrast between the universal concepts of "morality" and "virtue" accepted by the captain and the particularization of these same concepts by Woyzeck as he shaves the captain. The captain's universal concepts do not encompass the particularity of Woyzeck's circumstance.

Rather than merely reflecting the progressive fractionalization of society, **Woyzeck** counteracts this fractionalization by incorporating it into itself, negating the repressive splintering of society through integration. Yet, Adorno argues that, in *Wozzeck,* atomization has the specific function of resisting, indeed not permitting a lasting resolution. The individual elements or impulses of the work, he argues, rebel against lasting resolution, against subordination to a greater whole.[15] The utopian element present in integration is challenged not only by **Woyzeck**'s own claim to particularity but also by the individual elements of the drama which in their devel-

oped uniqueness (their development into nothingness) resist incorporation into a stable, generalized "meaning" of the text. As Adorno argues in *The Philosophy of Modern Music*: "*Wozzeck* negates its own point of departure precisely in those moments in which it is developed."[16] The complexity of the particular is preserved only in resistance to that which attempts to account for or define the whole. What this means, then, is that **Woyzeck** and *Wozzeck* achieve particularity because the presence of both atomization and integration create a dynamic tension without resolution.

II

The irreconcilable clash between atomization and integration establishes what might be described as a particularity in dissonance. But the dissonance of **Woyzeck** is not only a description of the divergent literary tensions within the play. These tensions reflect a critical discord which **Woyzeck** develops in relation to the belief that past values can evolve with the times, still maintain their integrity and thus serve as the foundation upon which to base present and future ideals. The dissonance with this faith in continuity is perhaps most immediately evident in—though certainly not limited to—the random assortment of the different scenes within the play; it can be seen in the absence of clear logical continuity from one scene to the next. In its implications, the form of **Woyzeck** highlights a basic point of contention in the competing aesthetic views of Lukács and Adorno: while Lukács adheres to a belief that history leads toward a specific social *telos,* Adorno cautions against the pursuit of ideals whose relevance becomes increasingly suspect as time alters the situation to which they first responded.[17] This admonishment is implicit in Adorno's departure from analysis based upon class conflict. The admonishment echoes throughout Adorno's writings on art in general, and it seems to me, is at the source of his fascination with Berg's use of retrogrades and palindromes in *Wozzeck.*

In *Ästhetische Theorie,* Adorno writes: "The view that artistic technique advances in linear fashion, irrespective of substance, is beset by a false idea of continuity."[18] Adorno de-emphasizes innovation because the discussion of it implies a qualitative continuity in art that he argues is misguided. It defines art according to novelty rather than defining it as a critical response that is socio-historically determined. In this and similar passages of *Ästhetische Theorie,* Adorno challenges the historical integrity of concepts in general by challenging the continuity of Art in particular. It is a challenge which, as we presently will see, Adorno argued was central to Berg's opera. For Adorno, each socio-historical context demands a new (and thus nontranscendent) set of aesthetic values—values which discussions of progressive innovation overlook. The significance of aesthetic form or technique, Adorno argues, is solely contingent upon the relation it has to the society in which the work is produced. The point is that by contextualizing aesthetic values, Adorno implicitly questions values in general, and more importantly, he argues that art pivots on its ability to expose the social contradictions that accepted values obscure.

The techniques of composition which Berg used in *Wozzeck* demonstrate an acute sensitivity to Büchner's subversion of ossified social ideals. Adorno observes Berg's "*Neigung* [in *Wozzeck*] *für spiegel- und krebsartige Gebilde*"[19] [proneness to mirror-like and retrogressive patterns] and notes that "*musikalische Krebse sind antizeitlich*"[20] [musical retrogrades are anti-time]. As Douglas Jarman has pointed out, Adorno describes Berg's use of retrogrades and palindromes as "anti-time" because "they deny time by returning to the point at which they began and thus symbolically erasing [sic] what has taken place."[21] While the "symbolic erasure" is open to some debate, an arguable consistency exists between Adorno's "non-transcendent" aesthetics and his attraction to Berg's use of retrogrades and palindromes. First of all, the occurrence of palindromes in *Wozzeck* forces a contextualization of specific musical themes by "de-composing" them once the opera progresses beyond the context in which the themes initially emerge. More significant still is Berg's placement of these musical retrogrades: he places them in direct correspondence with the values that ***Woyzeck*** calls into question.

Jarman's reference to Adorno and to Berg's use of palindromes occurs in the midst of a discussion of the opening scene of the opera. While Woyzeck shaves the captain, the captain lectures to Woyzeck. He recommends that Woyzeck develop a sense of time, that Woyzeck proceed "*langsam*"[22] ["slowly"] and that he organize his life sequentially, taking things "*ein's nach dem andern*" ["one thing at a time"].[23] The captain supplements these recommendations with claims which imply that morality and virtue will only result from such a temporal ordering of one's life. Jarman notes that this first scene is one of the few in which Berg actually rewrites the original text. The revision is minimal: Berg frames the musical score of the captain's comments on time by having the captain end his advice with the same word with which he began, "*langsam.*" This framing orchestrates an abruptness which is reflected in the music's dissonance, i.e. in its not "leading" to the next scene. The abruptness clashes with the value that the captain places on letting one thing lead to another. The opera generates a critical non-identity to the captain's advice by following a path which is the exact opposite of that which he recommends.

The stakes in this opening scene of the play are frequently subordinated to a more immediate and understandable concern with the abjectness of Woyzeck's predicament. Yet the problem with such concerns—and

in this respect, one can take Lukács's reading of ***Woyzeck*** as an example—is that the concern with Woyzeck's abjectness consistently leads to arguments that, as "the most impressive representation of the 'poor' in Germany at that time" [*die großtartigste Gestalt des damaligen »Armen« in Deutschland*"],[24] the function of Woyzeck is to cultivate a sense of historical (and thus revolutionary) consciousness; in other words, the function of Woyzeck is to cultivate a sense of time. That the captain recommends to Woyzeck an attitude similar to that which, according to Lukács, the character of Woyzeck encourages aligns the revolutionary consciousness, which Lukács advocates, with perhaps the most repressive figure in the play—the figure who is not only the most vocal about morality and virtue, but who is also the most authoritarian.

There is, of course, the argument that the captain's frequent references to eternity suggest him to be the voice of the contradictions of bourgeois morality and not the voice of some more general conception of historical optimism. Yet, what most suggests a correspondence between the position of the captain and the arguments of Lukács is that the opening scene establishes an opposition between Woyzeck and an ethics whose foundation is chronology and sequentiality. The opposition contrasts the captain's faith that one thing will lead to another with the disjointed and non-sequential ordering of the play itself. This non-sequentiality is at the crux of the critical particularity of the play: a particularity based upon a form, the individual elements of which resist resolution within a greater whole. At the very least, the disjointed juxtaposition of scenes in ***Woyzeck*** demands the recognition that their resolution into a "unified" whole comes as an external imposition on the play and that such an imposition compromises the complexity of the particular scenes themselves. This last point is underscored in the exacerbation of Woyzeck's suffering by interaction with characters who attempt to dictate their behavior, and the behavior of others, according to a preconceived universals.

Based on the opening scene, Adorno's claim that "*musikalische Krebse sind antizeitlich*" can be seen not only to express the implications of the techniques which Berg employs in the opera, but also to indicate the dissonant currents within the play. By structuring an opposition between Woyzeck and the captain, Büchner places Woyzeck in opposition to a universalizing conception of time whose ramifications the play exposes as viciously detrimental. As the play progresses, the captain's maxim on virtue retrogresses into perversity, the negative image of the captain's claim. By the time the captain's opening lines find an echo in Woyzeck's own statements, the phrase "*ein's nach dem andern*" has become the signification of the social currents that wreck his existence. Inasmuch as the captain becomes the voice for a developed sense of time, so too does this sense have an increasingly repressive role in the play: the more comprehensive this sense becomes, the more it becomes systemically malignant.

III

Even an aesthetic technique like Berg's, which achieves particularity in an abreaction of one-dimensional social trends, has a conception of the whole. Indeed, Adorno argues that art is the negative knowledge of society.[25] The conception of the social whole that underlies Adorno's contentions about art presumes a comparability between the reified avenues of society and the ruts which develop in a frequently traversed path: while the ruts are constraining and increasingly difficult to avoid, they do not altogether preclude alternatives. But just as "atomization" is a critical reflection of the fractionalization of society and "integration," a critical reflection of utopian yearnings, so too is the emergence of dissonance as an aesthetic phenomenon reflective of the embattled position which art faces in modernity. Adorno argues: "Dissonance has had a momentous and far-reaching impact on modern art because the immanent dynamic of autonomous works of art and the growing power of external reality over the subject converge in dissonance."[26] Thus the social significance of aesthetic dissonance, this negative knowledge of society, lies in its ability to illuminate reified social furrows or patterns where they previously existed unperceived. More importantly, dissonance illuminates where previous paths of opposition have retrogressed into predictable ossified patterns.

The aesthetic dimensions of *Woyzeck* are not an exception to this argument, neither in the drama's ability to articulate a negative knowledge of society—which opposes the repressive presumptions of totality in both the captain's 'morality' and Lukács's historical materialism—nor in the drama's own potential to become a path too often traversed. As with Berg's style of composing, the aesthetic achievements of *Woyzeck* lie in its having circumvented social trends which generally obstruct particularity as a possibility, through having developed a form of dissonance to the reification within dominant social avenues. But the crux of this dissonance lies in circumvention. It defies the reified structures of society, yet is not actively *engaged* in, attempts to transform them. Indeed, the dissonance of the play is in marked contrast to the presumption which underlies Lukács's conceptions of art. To argue that what qualifies *Woyzeck* as art is its dissonance, rather than an *engagement,* is, according to the criteria which Lukács employs in "*Der faschistisch verfälschte und der wirkliche Georg Büchner,*" to disqualify the drama as art. An aesthetic of dissonance places the drama within the categories which Lukács denounces as indulgent and decadent.

Interestingly enough, Adorno's description of aesthetic dissonance occurs in the context of an affirmation of "*ästhetischen Hedonismus,*"[27] which arguably serves as

an indirect rebuttal to Lukács's rejection of decadence. Whereas accusations of decadence connote a certain prudishness, Adorno's affirmations of hedonism at first give the impression of being a defense of tolerance. But the differences between Adorno and Lukács with regard to hedonism are perhaps not as far apart as they initially would appear. The hedonism in Adorno's argument is offset by a rigid conception of the forms in which it manifests itself. This rigidity is perhaps most evident in the threat which, according to Adorno, looms ominously above the continued possibility of aesthetic expression:

> True modern art is polarized into two extreme forms: on the one side, there is a kind of unmitigated and sad expressivity that staunchly rejects any conciliatoriness whatever and becomes autonomous constructions; on the other side, there is pure construction without expression, signalling the impending eclipse of expressivity as such.[28]

It seems to me that, if Adorno's historicist analyses are so rigorous that even class conflict loses its stature as the basis for social criticism, then the social currents which he argues are approaching the disarmament of expressivity must be of such magnitude and momentum that they defy his implied personification of them. They defy goal-oriented attributes. In other words, these trends are as subject to retrogression as programs for social change and could not stop at precluding expressivity but would continue in their course until it too became a "*Krebsgang,*" generating enough chaos that expressivity once again becomes a possibility. So long as Adorno maintains that art is the negative knowledge of society and that form is a reflection of a society which precludes expressivity, then a nineteenth-century play like *Woyzeck* is more problematic than helpful to Adorno's arguments. A play which reflects these tendencies suggests not only the need for a new art altogether but also that Adorno is formulating arguments on the basis of anachronistic crises in form.

Despite other differences Adorno and Lukács have, the two critics share the view that the social environment mediates and thus determines the subject. This is ostensibly the basis of Adorno's warning about the pending loss of expressivity. Yet it is difficult to imagine exactly what Adorno means by expressivity if not that the individual subject emerges in (critical) response to sociohistorical mediations—a response decipherable in both words and deeds. Rather than citing portents of the coming impotence of expressivity as such, a focus on the coming impotence of expressivity as it was conceived in the nineteenth century would remain truer to the implied tolerance of "*ästhetischen Hedonismus.*" Furthermore, this shift would radically alter the stakes in Adorno's claim and, it seems to me, would move toward dislodging the mind set which obstructs the emergence of an art that offers a negative knowledge of contemporary society. In short, *"die heraufziehende Ohnmacht des Ausdrucks"* reflected in the structure of **Woyzeck** is not only historically different from that which is addressed by Adorno, but the drama's retreat into form also undermines the stagnant conception of expressivity which Adorno defends. When juxtaposed to Büchner's **Woyzeck,** the basis of Adorno's criticism betrays its dependence on a nostalgic conception of the subject which, ironically, collapses in the negative knowledge of society that is structured into Büchner's drama. The continued relevance of the play lies in its ability to raise questions about the agenda of arguments that pivot on the pending annihilation of expressivity altogether and about the hysteria these arguments are intended to cultivate.

At this point in the argument, it is, however, important to note that when Adorno speaks of the loss of expressivity, the implicit reference of his claim is to a pending loss of culture, the definition of which is what forces Lukács and Adorno into irreconcilable camps. For Lukács, culture can only emerge once a reconciliation of the contradictions of society has occurred—hence his reading of **Woyzeck** as a revolutionary text which pushes toward the possibility of culture. For Adorno, culture resides in the continued possibility to express disunity and opposition, i.e. in the continued possibility to express a negative knowledge of society—hence his reading of **Woyzeck** via Berg as one of the last vestiges of culture. Thus the brunt of Adorno's critique of Lukács is directed against what Adorno perceived as attempts to force a reconciliation that would eliminate the possibility of opposition and ultimately lead to a one-dimensional society, regardless of whose ideology justified its structure.[29]

This then is the consequence of eliminating class conflict as the motivating force behind history: that culture thrives in opposition to insurmountable social ills, so long as opposition to those ills is possible. When Adorno speaks of the impotence of expressivity, what he means is the absence of culture, a muted disunity, or an irreconcilability with society without a voice of opposition, either in form or content. Interestingly enough, by employing a technique of "integrating atomization," **Woyzeck** expresses a discomfort with both positions: the drama challenges Lukács's faith that egalitarian agendas, vigorously pursued, will not regress into repressive programs; at the same time, the drama emphasizes that the particularity which Adorno treasures is only procured in the continued one-dimensionality of Woyzeck himself.

Notes

1. Theodor W. Adorno, *Alban Berg: Der Meister des Kleinsten Übergangs* (Wien: Verlag Elisabeth Lafite, 1968). All translations are mine.

2. For a concise account of the case of Johann Christian Woyzeck, see "Anhang zum *Woyzeck,*" *Georg Büchner: Werke und Briefe,* ed. Werner R. Lehmann (München: DTV, 1980), 373-429. All citations from *Woyzeck* are taken from this same addition. It is also worth mentioning that Büchner's drama is extremely critical of the conclusions which Dr. Clarus draws in the original transcripts of his analysis of Johann Christian Woyzeck. Indeed, one would argue that the doctor in the play is a parody of the doctor who examined Woyzeck.

3. For further study of this critique see: Theodor W. Adorno, "Erpreßte Versöhnung," *Noten zur Literatur II* (Frankfurt am Main: Suhrkamp, 1961), 152-87 ["Reconciliation under Duress," *Aesthetics and Politics,* ed. Ronald Taylor (New York: Verso, 1977), 151-76].

4. Lukács wrote this article in commemoration of the hundredth anniversary of Büchner's death. It is included in *Deutsche Literatur in zwei Jahrhunderten* (Berlin: Luchterhand, 1964), 249-72. The primary focus of Lukács's article is on the drama *Dantons Tod,* but he uses his discussion of this play as the context for numerous comments about *Woyzeck.*

5. For a more detailed account of this departure, see *The Origin of Negative Dialectics* (New York: Free Press, 1977), 24-42.

6. I realize that this last point is a matter of some dispute, particularly in light of Alfons Gluck's arguments that the doctor is in collaboration with the military. Gluck argues that the doctor places Woyzeck on a diet of peas in order to establish the minimal nutrition requirements for sustaining an army. Gluck's hypothesis is an intriguing instance of speculation, but I would suggest that, even if correct, Woyzeck is still overwhelmed and the doctor's calculations are far from perfect. For the whole of Gluck's argument, see "Die Rolle der Wissenschaft in Georg Büchners *Woyzeck,*" *Georg Büchner Jahrbuch* 5 (1985): 139-82.

7. These arguments have not gone unchallenged and have been the source of controversy since the latter years of Adorno's life. For a brief but concise account of the early challenges to Adorno's claims, see Peter Hohendahl's "Looking Back at Adorno's *Ästhetische Theorie,*" *German Quarterly* 54.2 (1981): 133-48. For a more recent challenge to the absolutes in Adorno's argument, see Bruce Baugh, "Left-Wing Elitism: Adorno on Popular Culture," *Philosophy and Literature* 14.1 (1990): 65-77.

8. Baugh, 69.

9. Adorno, *Berg,* 8-9. "Vielmehr bewährt sich das Komponierniveau Bergs—so hoch daß es heute

kaum auch nur wahrgenommen wird—gerade in der äußerst bewußten syntaktischen Gliederung, die vom ganzen Satz bis in den Stellenwert jedes einzelnen Tons reicht und nichts ausläßt. Schön ist diese Musik nach dem lateinischen Begriff formosus, dem des Formenreichen. Ihr Formenreichtum prägt sie zur Beredtheit, zur Sprachähnlichkeit. Aber er verfügt über eine besondere Technik, die geprägten Thematischen Gestalten, durch ihre eigene Entwicklung ins Nichts zurückzurufen."

10. Adorno, *Berg,* 11. "Er hat Büchners Drama von dem gequälten paranoiden Soldaten Wozzeck [sic], der das Unrecht, das ihm angetan wird, an der ungebändigten Natur ausläßt und die Geliebte umbringt . . . im selben Geiste ergriffen wie Karl Kraus das vergangne Wort der Menschlichkeit zitierend gegen die herrschende Unmenschlichkeit wandte, der die Sprache zum Opfer fiel."

11. Buck-Morss, 13. For a more detailed analysis of the influence Kraus had specifically on Berg and his contemporaries, see Martin Esslin, "Berg's Vienna," *The Berg Companion,* ed. Douglas Jarman (Boston: Northeastern University Press, 1989), 1-12.

12. Paul Elbogen, "Firsthand reminiscence of a historic night," *San Francisco Chronicle* 27 October 1981, 40; cited in Douglas Jarman, *Alban Berg: Wozzeck* (Cambridge: Cambridge University Press, 1989), 1.

13. Adorno, "Erpreßte Versöhnung," 159 ["Reconciliation under Duress," 156].

14. George Perle, *The Operas of Alban Berg,* vol. 1 (Berkeley: University of California Press, 1980), 36.

15. Theodor Adorno, *Philosophy of Modern Music,* trans. Anne G. Mitchell and Wesley V. Blomster (New York: Seabury Press, 1973), 31-32.

16. Adorno, *Modern Music,* 31.

17. Adorno's stance here seems to me to correspond to Christopher Norris's argument that, for Adorno, "the only kind of truth now available is that which unmasks the delusive truth-claim of all aesthetic ideologies and other such falsely positive systems of thought." See, "Utopian Deconstruction: Ernst Bloch, Paul de Man and the Politics of Music," *Paragraph* 11.1 (1988): 45.

18. *Aesthetic Theory,* trans. C. Lenhardt (Boston: Routledge and Kegan Paul, 1984), 306-7. Theodor W. Adorno, *Ästhetische Theorie* (Frankfurt am Main: Suhrkamp, 1970), 320. "Mit einem falschen Begriff von Kontinuität operierte noch die Ansicht eines geraden Fortschritts der künstlerischen Technik, unabhängig vom Gehalt."

19. Adorno, *Berg,* 21.

20. Adorno, *Berg,* 21.

21. Jarman, *Alban Berg: Woyzeck,* 63.

22. Büchner, 164.

23. Büchner, 164.

24. Lukács, 265.

25. Adorno, "Erpreßte Versöhnung," 164 ["Reconciliation under Duress," 160].

26. *Aesthetic Theory,* 21. "Die unabsehbare Tragweite alles Dissonanten für die neue Kunst . . . rührt daher, daß darin das immanente Kräftespiel des Kunstwerks mit der parallel zu seiner Autonomie an Macht über das Subjekt ansteigenden auswendigen Realität konvergiert." Adorno, *Ästhetische Theorie,* 29-30.

27. Adorno, *Ästhetische Theorie,* 29 [*Aesthetic Theory,* 21].

28. Adorno, *Aesthetic Theory,* 63-64. *Ästhetische Theorie,* 70. "Stichhaltige Kunst polarisiert sich nach einer noch der letzten Versöhnlichkeit absagenden, ungemilderten und ungetrösteten Expressivität auf der einen Seite, die autonome Konstruktion wird; auf der anderen nach dem Ausruckslosen der Konstruktion, welche die heraufziehende Ohnmacht des Ausdrucks ausdrückt."

29. Gilian Rose has noted in her discussion of the Marxist dispute over modernism that for "Lukács the destruction of the possibility of culture is Adorno's criterion of the possibility of its existence." Whereas for Lukács culture is an autonomous unity which is lost in capitalistic society, the question for Adorno, Rose writes "is not whether culture has lost unity, but whether the possibility of expressing disunity may have been lost." See *The Melancholy Science* (London: Macmillan, 1978), 116.

Helga Stipa Madland (essay date winter 1993)

SOURCE: Madland, Helga Stipa. "Madness and Lenz: Two Hundred Years Later." *German Quarterly* 66, no. 1 (winter 1993): 34-42.

[In the following excerpt, Madland approaches Büchner's novella Lenz *as a generalized literary depiction of madness, rather than as a quasi-medical account of the insanity of the historical Jakob Michael Reinhold Lenz.]*

Lenz[1] lenzelt noch bei mir.[2]

The authoritative document on which literary history has based its perception of Lenz's madness is neither a report by a contemporary observer of the sick Lenz, nor Lenz's own description of his experience with mental illness, nor an assessment of it by medical authorities, but a 19th-century fictional text—Georg Büchner's novella *Lenz.* This famous piece of fiction, justifiably one of the most admired and respected works of German literature, is considered to be a model representation of schizophrenia in general, and a true description of Lenz's mental illness in particular.[3] Its authority resides in the perceived authenticity of Büchner's portrayal of mental illness, in a narration which is delivered from the perspective of a sympathetic observer whose voice is intermingled with that of the doomed sufferer. The persuasive power of Büchner's language is unmistakable. From an innocuous opening sentence—"Den 20. [Januar] ging Lenz durch's Gebirg"[4]—the narrative moves rapidly and spectacularly toward its intention: the linguistic representation of a deteriorating mind. Büchner has succeeded in transforming the structure of his protagonist's psychological state into language: short sentences are compressed, linked by commas and not separated by periods, without an attempt at using subordinate clauses. The resulting paratactic structure, the piling up of short sentences without relief from subordinating elements, gives the effect of breathlessness and confusion; it illustrates an inability to place hierarchy or order upon events and put them in their proper perspective. The effect is dazzling, as the following sample from the long opening paragraph demonstrates:

> Gegen Abend kam er auf die Höhe des Gebirgs, auf das Schneefeld, von wo man wieder hinabstieg in die Ebene nach Westen, er setzte sich oben nieder. Es war gegen Abend ruhiger geworden; das Gewölk lag fest und unbeweglich am Himmel, so weit der Blick reichte, nichts als Gipfel, von denen sich breite Flächen hinabzogen, und alles so still, grau, dämmernd; es wurde ihm entsetzlich einsam, er war allein, ganz allein, er wollte mit sich sprechen, aber er konnte nicht, er wagte kaum zu athmen, das Biegen seines Fußes tönte wie Donner unter ihm, er mußte sich niedersetzen; es faßte ihn eine namenlose Angst in diesem Nichts, er war im Leeren, er riß sich auf und flog den Abhang hinunter. Es war finster geworden, Himmel und Erde verschmolzen in Eins. Es war als ginge ihm was nach, und als müsse ihn was Entsetzliches erreichen, etwas das Menschen nicht ertragen können, als jage der Wahnsinn auf Rossen hinter ihm. Endlich hörte er Stimmen, er sah Lichter, es wurde ihm leichter, man sagte ihm, er hätte noch eine halbe Stunde nach Waldbach. Er ging durch das Dorf, die Lichter schienen durch die Fenster, er sah hinein im Vorbeigehen, Kinder am Tische, alte Weiber, Mädchen, Alles ruhige, stille Gesichter, es war ihm als müsse das Licht von ihnen ausstrahlen, es ward ihm leicht, er war bald in Waldbach im Pfarrhause. Man saß am Tische, er hinein; die blonden Locken hingen ihm um das bleiche Gesicht, es zuckte ihm in den Augen und um den Mund, seine Kleider waren zerissen. Oberlin hieß ihn willkommen, er hielt ihn für einen Handwerker.

I have quoted this rather extensive passage from the opening paragraph of the novella to demonstrate the force of Büchner's prose: it does *not,* for example, inform the reader that on the 22nd of January, two days after the disoriented walk through the mountains Büchner describes, the historical Lenz wrote a letter to Johann Kaspar Lavater in which there is no indication of mental confusion.[5] The novella overwhelms the reader through the power of Büchner's language, and the conclusion that insanity must be like this or, more specifically, the insanity of Lenz was like this is the result of Büchner's artistry, not necessarily of his knowledge or observation of mental illness. The illusion that the realist Büchner has created is so complete that readers find it difficult to distance themselves from the text and respond to it as a work of art, rather than as the authentic representation of the mental illness of Jakob Michael Reinhold Lenz.

I do not intend to argue that Lenz was not mentally ill, nor do I want to claim that the novella *Lenz* does not contain a convincing representation of insanity. Instead, I want to review the evidence on which the conclusion that Lenz was a schizophrenic is based, and make two related points: first, Büchner's novella *Lenz* is above all a work of fiction, and a reading of it for biographical purposes must be approached with extreme caution;[6] second, the sources on which assessments of Lenz's mental illness have been based are limited and need to be reexamined and reevaluated within a context of 18th-century discourse on insanity. The psychoanalytic Lenz biography called for by Rüdiger Scholz would be a useful beginning for such a project.[7]

BÜCHNER'S NOVELLA

Since Lenz's image, and particularly our understanding of his madness, has been profoundly determined by representations of his madness, it is pertinent that recent studies on late 18th- and early 19th-century literary representations and social perceptions of insanity enter into Lenz scholarship. The most distinguished work in this area is Michel Foucault's *Madness and Civilization.* Foucault theorizes that our perception of madness underwent significant changes during the 17th and 18th centuries. A brief summary of the history of insanity follows: During the Middle Ages, some madmen in Germany were confined in the so-called *Narrentürme,* but the majority were expelled, and many found a peripatetic home in the *Narrenschiffe* which roamed villages and seas. The *Narrenschiff* is, of course, a motif which figures prominently in literature, and the character of the fool as the speaker of truth has been known from antiquity to Shakespeare and beyond. The image of the madman, or fool, was used for didactic purposes, or even for amusement, but madness did not seem to be a particular embarrassment to the community, only an inconvenience inasmuch as the insane, like the indigent, required care. But as early as the 16th century, and increasingly in the 17th and, particularly, 18th centuries, madmen acquired a different role. Foucault argues that the insane ultimately assumed the place lepers had previously held in society, that is, the moral values attached to lepers, which made them function as outcasts and scapegoats, were transferred to the insane. The natural outcome of this development was the extensive confinement of the insane during the 18th century. For the age of reason, madness and other social deviances, in their utterly uninhibited display of the existence of unreason, were particularly uncomfortable and embarrassing, and hiding the evidence was a convenient solution.[8] Foucault stresses the fact that during the age of reason madness became linked to morality. A new work ethic, which arose out of changing economic conditions, severely condemned idleness, regarding it as the root of all evil, and created the so-called workhouses, in which "young men who disturbed their families' peace or squandered their goods, people without profession, and the insane"[9] were locked up together. In the classical age, "for the first time, madness was perceived through a condemnation of idleness."[10] Since an idle life was regarded as the ultimate rebellion against God, and madmen were included in the proscription of idleness, madness was no longer considered both a medical and moral problem, as had been the case in the Middle Ages and in antiquity, but only an ethical problem.

We must give serious consideration to the connection between madness and idleness if we are to understand Oberlin's evaluation of Lenz's behavior. There is, of course, no criticism of Lenz's life-style in Büchner's novella; quite to the contrary, it is an extremely sympathetic portrayal of him. But Oberlin's journal was the basis for Büchner's understanding of Lenz's insanity, and Büchner depended on its description and judgment of Lenz's conduct. In an essay with the thought-provoking title "Lenz Viewed Sane," published in 1974, Janet K. King argues that Büchner wanted to portray society, not Lenz, as insane. King notes that while "Oberlin's diary depicts a man deeply disturbed and emotionally unstable, the pastor's report does not use terms such as *wahnsinnig* or *toll*."[11] In the concluding sentence of his report, Oberlin refers to Lenz as "bedauernswürdiger Patient,"[12] but it is noteworthy that he uses the word "vergnügt" many times throughout the report, when describing either Lenz's condition or the manner in which time was spent. These many lighter moments seem to occur even more frequently than the serious episodes so well known from the novella, during which Lenz behaves irrationally and frightens everyone around him. They seem to indicate that Oberlin hesitated to associate Lenz with the insane who were confined to institutions and often chained and treated like animals. King points out that mystical experiences, not unlike those undergone by Lenz and related by Oberlin, were not unusual occurrences in the Steintal,

where Oberlin was pastor. Oberlin himself wrote a treatise entitled 'Berichte eines Visionärs über den Zustand der Seelen nach dem Tod,' and his comment about Lenz's efforts to raise a young girl from the dead was simply: "[es war] ihm aber fehlgeschlagen."[13] This, King argues, is an indication that he was not particularly dismayed by Lenz's behavior. Oberlin was, however, critical of Lenz's way of life and admonished him to honor his mother and father if he wanted to find peace of mind.[14] King notes that the tendency to disapprove of Lenz's way of life reappeared in his "obituary in the *Allgemeine Literaturzeitung* of May 1792 [which] simply judges him a misfit in a manner reminiscent of Kaufmann's reproaches which Büchner introduced into the novella."[15] The newspaper expresses the following opinion: "Er [Lenz] starb, von wenigen betrauert, und von keinem vermißt. Dieser unglückliche Gelehrte . . . verlebte den besten Teil seines Lebens in nutzloser Geschäftigkeit, ohne eigentliche Bestimmung."[16]

This link among the admonitions by Kaufmann, Oberlin, and the newspaper must be noted, for they are critiques of Lenz which resemble those by his own father. The 18th century's fear of idleness, the mortal sin of bourgeois society described by Foucault, is reflected in these attitudes. In an age which perceived madness "on the social horizon of poverty, of incapacity for work, of inability to integrate with the group,"[17] it must have been difficult to separate one condition from the other in a man as complex as Lenz. His existence in the economic margin was certainly one of the factors leading to the aberrant behavior first noted by Kaufmann in November 1777,[18] and then by Oberlin in January 1778. Possibly because of his inability to find permanent employment—a condition which certainly was not his alone, as the crowded workhouses attest—Lenz had "alienate[d] himself outside the sacred limits of its [the bourgeoisie's] ethics."[19] His friends and associates could very well have considered him to be mad.

When Georg Büchner chose the theme of madness as one of his central concerns, the perception of madness and, particularly, its treatment in literature had changed considerably. Madness had been celebrated by Cervantes and Shakespeare, but after the middle of the 17th century, it was expelled from most literary forms and confined to satire; Gottsched's banishment of Hanswurst from the German stage is symptomatic of this development.[20] During Romanticism, a preoccupation with the pathological returned with greater force, and madness in literature acquired a new function: it was no longer perceived as entirely negative, but came to be associated with artistry and even was, to a certain degree, idealized and glorified (Reuchlein 228, 230). By the time Büchner wrote **Lenz,** the Romantics' glorification of madness had been transformed by the sober positivistic appraisal of insanity as illness, a perception of madness which was reflected in literature by a demand for clinical descriptions. Responding to both romantic and realistic perceptions of insanity, Büchner combined the tradition of the *Künstler- und Wahnsinnsroman* while treating madness as an illness. His protagonist, like Tasso or the artist figures in romantic narratives, exists outside the bourgeois world, but his madness is not idealized, nor is it associated with his antibourgeois life-style. As Reuchlein perceptively observes, Büchner's major innovation, a move which differentiates his text from those of Romanticism and the 18th century, is his focus on madness itself, rather than on its effects or causes:

> Weitaus stärker als bis dahin üblich, steht im *Lenz* der Krankheitsprozeß als solcher und gleichsam für sich . . . im Zentrum des Erzählens. Demgegenüber verlieren über das Pathologische hinausweisende Momente transzendenter, genieästhetischer, erkenntnistheoretischer, zeitkritischer oder moralischer Natur etc., die die literarische Beschäftigung mit dem Wahnsinn im späten 18. wie im frühen 19. Jahrhundert eigentlich erst motiviert hatten, an Bedeutung und rücken in den Hintergrund. Insgesamt erreicht damit die, seit dem Beginn des 19. Jahrhunderts in der Psychopathologie wie in der Dichtung beobachtbare, Tendenz zur Konzentration auf die Symptomatik der Seelenkrankheit und auf deren Dynamik bei Büchner literarisch einen Kulminationspunkt.
>
> (Reuchlein 389)

Reuchlein identifies Büchner's innovation in the literary representation of madness as responsible for psychologists' and literary scholars' interest in this work as a case study. These interpretations, which have become a commonplace in Büchner scholarship (Reuchlein 389-96),[21] have had their echo in Lenz scholarship. One Lenz scholar writes: ". . . the temptation often arises to dismiss all his thoughts as the product of an unbalanced mind—which of course they were."[22] Yet it is understandable that critics would react to *Lenz* in this way, for Büchner's complicated narrative perspective, which blends the narrator's and the protagonist's voices and invites the reader's complete identification with the experience of the protagonist, gives the strong impression that his novella is just that—a case study. *Lenz* is, however, not an authentic medical report of mental illness in general, as many scholars have assumed, nor is it a true depiction of the mental illness of Jakob Michael Reinhold Lenz.

Notes

1. A shorter version of this paper was read at the meeting of the American Association for Eighteenth-Century Studies in Seattle, Washington, March 1992.

2. Letter from Lavater to Sarasin, August 1777. *Lenz in Briefen,* ed. Franz Waldmann (Zurich: Stern, 1894) 73.

3. See Walter Hinderer, "Georg Büchner: 'Lenz' (1839)," *Romane und Erzählungen zwischen Romantik und Realismus,* ed. Paul Michael Lützeler (Stuttgart: Reclam, 1983) 274.

4. Georg Büchner, *Werke und Briefe,* ed. Werner R. Lehmann, 5th ed. (Munich: Deutscher Taschenbuch Verlag, 1984) 68.

5. Jakob Michael Reinhold Lenz, *Werke und Schriften in drei Bänden,* ed. Sigrid Damm (Munich: Hanser, 1987) 3: 566-67.

6. Indeed, Timm Menke has recently argued that the novella belongs in Büchner scholarship and not in Lenz scholarship. See "'Durchs Fernglas der Vernunft die Nationen beschauen.' Lenz-Rezeption in den letzten Jahren der DDR: Christoph Heins Bearbeitung des *Neuen Menoza.*" Paper delivered at the International J. M. R. Lenz Symposium of 17-20 October 1992, held at the University of Oklahoma, Norman, Oklahoma.

7. See Rüdiger Scholz, "Eine längst fällige historisch-kritische Gesamtausgabe: Jakob Michael Reinhold Lenz," *Jahrbuch der deutschen Schillergesellschaft* 34 (1990): 212.

8. Michel Foucault, *Madness and Civilization: A History of Insanity in the Age of Reason* (New York: Vintage, 1988) 3-37, 199-220.

9. Ibid. 45.

10. Ibid. 58.

11. Janet K. King, "Lenz Viewed Sane," *The Germanic Review* 49 (1974): 148.

12. Büchner, commentary 366.

13. Ibid. 363.

14. The author of a medical dissertation on Lenz's schizophrenia also notes: "Für Oberlin besteht ein deutlicher Zusammenhang zwischen den Sünden, die Lenz begangen hat, und seinem Wahnsinn, der ihm als Strafe auferlegt worden ist." See Herwig Böcker, "Zerstörung der Persönlichkeit des Dichters J. M. R. Lenz durch die beginnende Schizophrenie" (Diss. U of Bonn, 1969) 217. Another medical study, which unfortunately has not been available to me, is by R. Weichbrodt, "Der Dichter Lenz, eine Pathographie," *Archiv für Psychiatrie und Nervenkrankheit* 62 (1920): 153-87. Böcker summarizes Weichbrodt's study as follows: "Die ersten Anzeichen des Wahnsinns treten in Weimar auf, vorher besteht kein Hinweis auf Krankheitssymptome. Weichbrodts Diagnose: Katatonie, Remission mit Restzustand, 1786 neuer Schub, rasche Verblödung. In seinen letzten Jahren habe Lenz nur noch vegetiert und 1792 sei er an seiner Katatonie gestorben." See 12. In a brief chapter on Lenz, K. R. Eissler says little to further

an understanding of Lenz. See *Goethe, eine psychoanalytische Studie,* trans. Peter Fischer (Basel and Frankfurt: Stroemfeld/Roter Stern, 1983) 57-73.

15. King 147-48.

16. Quoted by King 148.

17. Foucault 64.

18. M. N. Rosanow, *Jakob M. R. Lenz, der Dichter der Sturm- und Drangperiode: Sein Leben und seine Werke,* trans. C. von Gütschow (Leipzig: Schulze, 1909) 389.

19. Foucault 58.

20. Georg Reuchlein, *Bürgerliche Gesellschaft, Psychiatrie und Literatur: Zur Entwicklung der Wahnsinnsthematik in der deutschen Literatur des späten 18. und frühen 19. Jahrhunderts* (Munich: Fink, 1986) 50. Subsequent references appear in parentheses in the text. Other studies on this topic are by Jutta Osinski, *Über Vernunft und Wahnsinn: Studien zur literarischen Aufklärung in der Gegenwart und im 18. Jhdt.* (Bonn: Bouvier, 1983) and by Anke Bennholdt-Thomsen and Alfredo Guzzoni, *Der "Asoziale" in der Literatur um 1800* (Königstein: Athenäum, 1979).

21. Hinderer 270-78.

22. See Bruce Duncan, "A 'Cool Medium' as Social Corrective: Lenz's Concept of Comedy," *Colloquia Germanica* 8 (1975): 232.

John Reddick (essay date 1994)

SOURCE: Reddick, John. "The Desperate Mosaic." In *Georg Büchner: The Shattered Whole,* pp. 3-28. Oxford: Oxford University Press, 1994.

[*In the following excerpt, Reddick studies the fundamental tension between Büchner's scientific and literary perceptions of the world.*]

[Büchner] died at 23 (an age at which Goethe had not even produced *Werther*); he left the barest handful of texts; and he impinged little on the consciousness of the century in which he so briefly lived. Not for him the succession of definitive editions, the Eckermanns eager to immortalize each crumb of wisdom from his mouth. His œuvre, already slender enough, was further decimated by the disappearance, perhaps even the physical destruction, of the great majority of his letters,[1] his putative diaries, and possibly an entire play—the mysterious **"Pietro Aretino."**[2] Not one of his writings was published in his lifetime in authentic and definitive form; even his doctoral dissertation—a *mémoire,* in

French, on the cranial anatomy of an obscure fish—though printed just before his death, was not published until just after it.[3] For the rest, his work survives only in a more or less conjectural, fragmentary, or reconstituted form. Even today, more than a century and a half after his death, we wait in exasperation for a full historical-critical edition.

In sheer stature, then, Büchner is dwarfed by the monumental figure of Goethe. But monumental stature can exact a heavy price. Goethe looms on his plinth like Nelson on his column, but he is equally remote. For all his true merits, for all the magnificent vitality trapped in the cold stone, he has acquired the status of a curiosity, a monument at once deeply revered and largely ignored. With Büchner it is quite the reverse. This slender, provocative, sharp-edged figure lives more vitally amongst us than ever before. No other German writer before Kafka and Brecht so vividly catches the modern imagination. It is an extraordinary phenomenon that, whereas the nineteenth century was largely deaf to this man's voice, he seems to speak to us now with 'incendiary' force (Günter Grass)[4] and 'remarkable relevance' (Heinrich Böll)[5] as if he were alive and well in Munich or Berlin. Political protesters in the Federal Republic have daubed the war-cry of ***Der Hessische Landbote*** across a thousand banners and squatted houses: 'Friede den Hütten! Krieg den Pallästen!' (*Peace to the peasants! War on the palaces!*) His plays are a mainstay of the contemporary German theatre, and are regularly staged abroad. Werner Herzog, one of the most imaginative directors in the modern German cinema, made a powerful (if capricious) film of ***Woyzeck*** (and chose a quotation from *Lenz* as the epigraph for *Kaspar Hauser*). Erich Kästner described himself as Büchner's 'pupil and debtor'.[6] For Wolfgang Koeppen 'Büchner was always the closest star in the German firmament'.[7] In the eyes of Christa Wolf, 'German prose begins with Büchner's *Lenz*'; it is her 'absolute ideal', her 'primal experience' ('Ur-Erlebnis') in German literature.[8] For Wolf Biermann, Büchner is quite simply the greatest writer Germany has known ('unser größter Dichter').[9] And we should not forget the revolutionary and revelatory impact that the newly discovered Büchner had on earlier writers: on Gerhart Hauptmann and his fellow Naturalists, on the German Expressionists, on Wedekind and Brecht above all.

Undisputed though the strength and immediacy of Büchner's voice may be, however, there are wild and bitter disputes about what that voice is saying. This is not surprising, for several factors conspire to make him a natural focus of controversy. Most obviously, there is the sheer smallness of scale and the uncertain state of his output. Imagine the jousting ground that would have been afforded to critics if Goethe had left only *Götz, Urfaust,* and *Werther,* let us say, and if these had survived only in scrawled, incomplete, often illegible manuscripts, or in printed versions that were variously mutilated, truncated, bowdlerized, or garbled, as well as being largely posthumous and wholly unauthorized. Then there is the richly provocative nature of his concerns. Sex, religion, politics, these taboo topics for all decent folk, are amongst his most urgent preoccupations. From the first lines of *Dantons Tod* with their image of the pretty lady who gives her heart to her husband and her cunt to her lovers, Büchner's 'obscenities' have ensured him the status of *enfant terrible,* and in the process have served to betray the blinkered perspective of countless critics. Gods, God, and spirits are insistently invoked by his characters, to be denied, defied, condemned, entreated—and thus to serve as a constant challenge to believer, agnostic, and atheist alike. Büchner's politics are of course an especially fulminant issue. Here is a man who was one of the most radical left-wing thinkers of his age within the German lands, a proto-Marxian revolutionary who, although he entered the fray as a political publicist and activist for only the briefest of periods, remained committed throughout his life to the overthrow of what he saw as an illegitimate, parasitical, and effete ruling class, and the resurgence and emancipation of the cruelly exploited popular mass. Given the paucity both of direct evidence, such as Büchner's correspondence, and of indirect evidence, such as reminiscences of friends and acquaintances, there is much scope for argument even about his precise activities and stance within the political micro- and macro-realities of the time. The fiercest controversy, however, is inevitably provoked by his writing. At one extreme is the view exemplified by Georg Lukács: Büchner as an unswerving Jacobin essentially unaffected by the grim fiasco of *Der Hessische Landbote*: 'Büchner was at all times a rigorous revolutionary'.[10] At the opposite extreme, the view exemplified by Robert Mühlher: Büchner as a man whose abrupt and bitter insights propelled him into 'extreme or absolute nihilism', and in the process depoliticized him and 'thrust him for ever from the liberal and democratic camp'.[11]

The scant and uncertain status of the texts, the inflammatory nature of the issues they contain: these features of Büchner's work are themselves conducive to controversy. But their effect is greatly compounded by a third decisive element: the *manner* of Büchner's art, the language, modes, and structures that he uses to express his concerns. For the flickering image of the world that he evokes is profoundly un- and anti-classical, and consciously remote from the prevailing conventions and expectations of his age. Whether in language, mood, plot, or personae, he offers no steady development, no sense of anything rounded, resolved, or unified. Instead of unfolding in clearly measured rhythm, his works progress through a succession of kaleidoscopic convulsions, enacting what Walter Jens has called a 'law of discontinuity'.[12] Wholeness, when it appears, is always false—a pretence, an illusion, at best a transitory state.

It is *particles* that loom large; discrete elements that he highlights in startling isolation, or in disparate clusters and combinations that create a constant sense of paradox, multivalence, and mystery. This is a chief mark of his spectacular modernity: already in the 1830s he is doing the kind of thing that will seem outrageously new when practised by the most avant-garde painters, composers, and writers of the early twentieth century. But it also makes him especially difficult to interpret. In particular, it entails the problem of perspective: being so disparate and discrete, the elements in his work change their aspect and apparent importance quite radically when viewed from different vantage points.

How are we to deal with this systematic discontinuity? As a first step, perhaps, we need to take it seriously. This might seem an easy and obvious measure, but it has eluded many critics.

The most unsubtle way of not taking it seriously is that favoured by certain critics in the English tradition, who have patronizingly applied the yardstick of good old English common sense, and declared Büchner to be insufficiently mature. Thus A. H. J. Knight could assert that 'The perpetual changes of scene in *Dantons Tod* . . . reveal a not unnatural absence of practical dramatic sense in the young author'.[13] Ronald Peacock, likewise referring to *Dantons Tod,* descries a 'disunity . . . that is a symptom both of Büchner's philosophical and of his poetic-dramatic immaturity'.[14] This plain man's approach is severely reductive: the more challenging a complexity, the more likely it is to be branded a defect or mistake—a tendency hair-raisingly exemplified when Knight touches on the Marion episode, one of the most powerful and extraordinary moments in the mosaic of Büchner's work, and baldly dismisses it as 'contributing nothing to the theme of the play'.[15]

A more subtle and more common way of failing to do justice to Büchner's disjunctive and paradoxical mode is to behave as though it did not exist. It is all too easy to don spectacles of this hue or that, and to believe that the particular pattern that they reveal is the only one, or the only one that matters. The basic trouble perhaps is that critics have traditionally been the products of academe who were schooled chiefly or wholly in the traditions of classicism. We are accustomed to seeing works of literature as programmatic and exemplary, as vehicles purpose-built to embody and demonstrate an already fully developed view or ethos. We recognize in the late plays of Schiller, for example, a magnificent complexity, but a complexity like that of a baroque fugue with its rich and balanced elaboration of lucidly stated themes. Such an approach, or such a set of expectations, can only be reductive to the point of distortion when applied to Georg Büchner. He never writes to communicate solutions. Instead, his writing is a kind of happening, a constant search, a dynamic enactment of the very process of argument and conflict, of the collision and interaction of contrary possibilities. His works begin, but never at a beginning, and they come to an end, but not to a conclusion.[16] This means that we should never be tempted to seize on a particular discrete element and single it out as a summation of the whole, or as the definitive fixing of a position—though many critics have done so, hence the persistent misrepresentation of Büchner as being variously a programmatic pessimist and nihilist, a programmatic fatalist, a programmatic Christian, a programmatic Jacobin revolutionary. There is indeed an underlying consistency and unity in Büchner; but it will be found only *within* and *through* the paradoxes and multiplicities of his work—not despite them.

It helps for us to recognize what is perhaps the paradox of paradoxes in Georg Büchner: his disjunctive mode with its relentless insistence on fragments and particles is always the product of a radiant vision of *wholeness*. Again and again, in every area of his existence—his politics, his science, his aesthetics, his art—we find an ardent sense of wholeness, but a wholeness that is almost always poignantly elusive: it *was* but is no longer; or *will* be but isn't yet; or—most poignant of all—it *is* in the present, but can be perceived or possessed only partially or transiently. Büchner is thus forced to be a maker of mosaics. But the more jagged the fragments in these mosaics, the more strident they are in their invocation of the whole; a pattern that is perfectly epitomized in the earliest pages of his work when he has Lacroix define the quest of Danton amongst the whores in just such terms: 'Er sucht eben die mediceische Venus stückweise . . . zusammen, er macht Mosaik, wie er sagt'; 'Es ist ein Jammer, daß die Natur die Schönheit . . . zerstückelt und sie so in Fragmenten in die Körper gesenkt hat' (20-1;[17] *He's just trying to get the Medici Venus together again piece by piece, he's making a mosaic, as he puts it; It's a crying shame that nature has broken beauty into pieces and stuck it in fragments like that into different bodies.*) Minutes later the theme is echoed and intensified in Danton's yearning response to Marion with its double stress on 'totality': 'Warum kann ich deine Schönheit nicht ganz in mich fassen, sie nicht ganz umschließen?' (22; *Why can't I take your beauty wholly into myself, wholly enfold it within my arms?*) At the beginning of *Lenz* we find the same essential image, even to the extent of a verbal echo: 'er meinte, er müsse den Sturm in sich ziehen, Alles in sich fassen'; 'er wühlte sich in das All hinein' (79; *he believed he should draw the storm right into himself; he burrowed his way into the all*). In *Leonce und Lena* it is the wholeness of love that is fragmented: split asunder into the separate notes of a musical scale, split asunder into the separate colours of a rainbow. But, as always, the emphasis on fragments implies the conviction of wholeness—which indeed is made explicit here in the image of love *beyond* the differentiated spectrum

of the rainbow: as 'der weiße Gluthstrahl der Liebe'—a single shaft of white-hot radiance (112). And it is precisely Leonce's experience of a love-inspired totality of being that is celebrated in the fleeting climax of the play: 'Mein ganzes Sein ist in dem einen Augenblick.' (125; *All my being is in this single moment.*)

The force and central importance of Büchner's vision of wholeness become clearer still when we realize that it also lies at the heart of his work as a scientist-philosopher. Büchner spells this out in his Trial Lecture **'Über Schädelnerven' ('On Cranial Nerves')**,[18] which he delivered on 5 November 1836 (less than four months before his death from typhus), and which—astonishingly—he must have written at the very same time as he was working on **Woyzeck**. Trial Lectures were a ritualistic affair, not unlike the modern Inaugural except that they constituted a final hurdle *before* the victim's confirmation in a teaching post, in Büchner's case as a *Privatdozent* in Comparative Anatomy at the brand new University of Zurich. They encouraged a contender to demonstrate his stance as well as his standing; and with an audience of dignitaries that included Lorenz Oken, the University's founding *Rektor,* and one of the most influential and most controversial scientist-philosophers of the age within the German lands, Büchner goes to considerable lengths to define his general standpoint and frame of reference, before launching into his particular argument concerning the skull. And Büchner puts a quite remarkable emphasis in these prefatory pages on his sense of the natural world as an *organic whole* characterized by order, proportion, unity, and essential simplicity. The study of the natural world, he says, has taken on a new shape. Previously, botanists and zoologists, physiologists and comparative anatomists had been confronted by a monstrous chaos of irreconcilable, undifferentiated data—'ein ungeheures, durch den Fleiß von Jahrhunderten zusammengeschlepptes Material, das kaum unter die Ordnung eines Kataloges gebracht war'; 'ein Gewirr seltsamer Formen unter den abentheuerlichsten Namen'; 'eine Masse Dinge, die sonst nur als getrennte, weit auseinander liegende facta das Gedächtniß beschwerten' (ii. 293; *a huge mass of material, laboriously heaped up over the centuries, that had scarcely even been systematically catalogued; a confusion of weird forms under the wildest names; a mass of things that previously weighed heavily on one's memory as so many separate, unconnected facts*). But enormous progress has at last been made ('bedeutender Fortschritt'), and the chaos and confusion have resolved in consequence into simple, natural, exquisitely proportioned patterns: 'einfache, natürliche Gruppen', 'schönsten Ebenmaaß'. The essential thrust of this new understanding, in comparative anatomy as in the various kindred subjects, was towards a kind of unity, with all forms being traced back to the supremely simple primordial type, or archetype, from which they were developed: 'In der vergleichenden

Anatomie strebte Alles nach einer gewissen Einheit, nach dem Zurückführen aller Formen auf den einfachsten primitiven Typus.'

As we might expect, Büchner tells us that the whole picture in all its richness is not yet fully understood, but that coherent parts of it have taken shape: 'Hat man auch nichts Ganzes erreicht, so kamen doch zusammenhängende Strecken zum Vorschein'. In the similar but more vivid image conveyed earlier in the same paragraph: 'Hatte man auch die Quelle nicht gefunden, so hörte man doch an vielen Stellen den Strom in der Tiefe rauschen' (*Even though one had not found the wellspring, there were nevertheless many places where one could hear the river roaring down below.*) This has a familiar ring, for it echoes the kind of pattern generated in the poetic writing: there, too, the river is never reached, but its roaring can be heard. We have only the fragments of a mosaic, the separate notes of the scale, the scattered colours of the spectrum; but they imply and betoken a vibrant if elusive whole.

The supreme importance to Büchner of this sense of wholeness is evinced even more remarkably a little earlier in the Trial Lecture (ii. 292). What is it that paved the way for this new understanding of the physical world? It is the fundamental postulate that all things in nature are part of a *single organic complex,* a 'gesammte Organisation', and that this rich complex is governed and patterned according to a *single natural law,* a 'Grundgesetz'. Büchner had already begun to define his scientific-philosophical credo in the brief last paragraph of his doctoral dissertation earlier in 1836: his conviction that the grand richness of nature is not due to any kind of arbitrary functionalism, but is the elaboration of a design or 'blueprint' of supreme simplicity: 'La nature est grande et riche, non parce qu'à chaque instant elle crée arbitrairement des organes nouveaux pour de nouvelles fonctions; mais parce qu'elle produit, d'après le plan le plus simple, les formes les plus élevées et les plus pures.' (ii. 125). This is directly echoed, and intensified, in the Trial Lecture: the 'Grundgesetz', the all-informing law of nature, is an 'Urgesetz'—a kind of law-of-laws—'das nach den einfachsten Rissen und Linien die höchsten und reinsten Formen hervorbringt' (*that produces the highest and purest forms according to the simplest patterns and designs*). On this view, everything—form, matter, function—is governed by the one law: 'Alles, Form und Stoff, ist . . . an dies Gesetz gebunden'; 'Alle Funktionen sind Wirkungen desselben [Gesetzes]'. The astonishingly positive nature of Büchner's stance is radiantly clear in these lines. The primal law, the 'Urgesetz' that he sees as the matrix of all things, is to him nothing less than a law of *beauty,* 'ein Gesetz der Schönheit'. And since this law is so benign, and since all things in nature—functions as well as form and matter—are generated by it, the myriad workings of nature not only never conflict with each other:

they interact positively together to yield a *necessary harmony*: 'ihr . . . Aufeinander- und Zusammenwirken ist nichts weiter, als die nothwendige Harmonie in den Aeußerungen eines und desselben Gesetzes, dessen Wirkungen sich natürlich nicht gegenseitig zerstören.'

This paean of faith in a universal order of rich simplicity, engendered by beauty and resonant with harmony, can seem bewildering indeed, coming as it does from the pen of a man whom critics of different eras and very different persuasions have variously categorized as 'a most decided nihilist' (Viëtor),[19] 'perhaps the most uncompromising German Nihilist of the nineteenth century' (Closs),[20] an exponent of 'profound pessimism' (Hans Mayer),[21] of 'extreme or absolute nihilism' (Mühlher),[22] of 'an extreme form of pessimism' that is 'deeper and darker than any to be found in the previous history of German thought, with the possible exception of Schopenhauer' (M. B. Benn).[23] This long tradition of depicting Büchner as a nihilist or pessimist has rightly fallen into considerable disfavour.[24] But even if we doubt the many critics of this complexion, we are still faced with the strident paradox within the texts themselves: the beauteous harmony and order postulated with such faith and confidence in the Trial Lecture—and the bleak visions so frequently and so eloquently evoked in the poetic work: the terrifying cold isolation of Lenz at the end of the story, and of the child in the un-fairytale in **Woyzeck** (100-1; 151); the famous, or infamous, cry of Danton that the world is chaos, and nothingness its due messiah (72); the fear of Leonce that all we see may be mere imaginings masking a reality of blank, bare vacuity (118). Such examples could be multiplied.

Again we face the problem of how to cope with the unremittingly paradoxical nature of Büchner's writing; and again I would insist that we can only begin by taking it seriously. It evades the issue to suppose, as Knight did, that Büchner was simply changing his ground in the last phase of his life, and moderating from his alleged 'total pessimism'.[25] Hans Mayer does not get us much further when he sorrowfully maintains that there is a regrettable discrepancy, a 'dissonance', between Büchner's (radical) view of society and his (conservative) view of nature.[26] And it is quite mistaken, I believe, to allege that the radiant faith expressed in the Trial Lecture is some kind of bogus remedy, a 'nostrum', as J. P. Stern has asserted, hastily contrived 'to repair the shattered fabric of existence'.[27] Büchner's faith in abundant, vibrant wholeness was not a sudden new stance, nor a strange aberration, nor a convenient refuge in adversity: it was fundamental to his existence and to all his doings; and even the most raucous anguish in his writings—*especially* the most raucous anguish—is always born of it.

One of the most extraordinary paradoxes in Büchner is that, whereas the *manner* of his poetic writing is inexorably un- and anti-classical, the faith and vision that underlies it is classical almost to the point of anachronism: if he was spectacularly ahead of his time in the one respect, he was unspectacularly but distinctly behind it in the other. We get an inkling of this once we register the gross discrepancy between Büchner's reception as a writer, and his reception as a speculative scientist. As a writer, he notoriously remained largely unrecognized throughout the nineteenth century: there was no framework of reference or of expectations that could begin to accommodate the radical unconventionality of his work. *Dantons Tod,* the only one of his poetic works to appear during his lifetime, could do so only after it had been morally and politically sanitized—even so, it is a mystery how it slipped through the net of an oppressive and efficient censorship—and it met with almost no response at all, except for instance to be savagely castigated by a pseudonymous reviewer as 'filth', 'pestilential impudence', 'excrescences of immorality', 'blasphemy against all that is most sacred', 'degeneracy'.[28] As a comparative anatomist, on the other hand, Büchner was instantly admitted into the fold of international orthodoxy. His doctoral dissertation, **'Mémoire sur le système nerveux du barbeau,'** published in Strasbourg in April 1837, was immediately welcomed in authoritative circles in France, Germany, and Switzerland: its 'Partie descriptive' was hailed as 'very thorough' and 'entirely correct', and as 'extending knowledge with all desirable precision', while its 'Partie philosophique', containing Büchner's specific argument, was endorsed by Johannes Müller, a like-minded comparative anatomist, but also a physiologist who was to make advances fundamental to nineteenth-century science.[29] Büchner's Trial Lecture, in its turn, met with 'the widest approval' among its local but distinguished audience of established academics, and Oken himself not only made a point of recommending his new young colleague's classes, but sent along his own son.[30]

The problem with the particular scientific-philosophical position that Büchner embraced as wholeheartedly as he rejected its literary counterpart is that it was rapidly losing its predominance and credibility even as he entered upon it. There is an eloquent irony in the fact that, during the period that Büchner was immersing himself in his dissections and concretizing his received wholist vision of the natural world, Charles Darwin was busily collecting his data on the *Beagle.* By the time his ship returned to England in October 1836, just a few weeks before Büchner's lecture, Darwin had the makings of a theory that would help to make the world-view of which Büchner was such an ardent exponent seem antiquated and irrelevant, an apparent by-water remote from the mainstream of scientific progress—and a deeply suspect one at that. This suspect status was both demonstrated and sharply reinforced in Thomas Henry Huxley's famous Croonian Lecture of 1858, when he set out to discredit precisely that central tenet that lies at the heart of both Büchner's doctoral dissertation and his Trial Lec-

ture, namely Goethe's and Oken's vertebral theory of the skull. The triumphant, sabre-rattling tone is unmistakable when Huxley ridicules 'the speculator' for his conjuror's ability to 'devise half a dozen very pretty vertebral theories, all equally true, in the course of a summer's day', and calls for support from 'Those who, like myself, are unable to see the propriety and advantage of introducing into science any ideal conception, which is other than the simplest possible generalized expression of observed facts'.[31]

We need to appreciate the real enormity of the problems faced by life-scientists in the century or so before Darwin did for biology what Newton had done for physics almost two centuries earlier; even the very word 'scientist'—not coined (by Whewell) until 1840—is an anachronism that tends to beg essential questions. Büchner is not exaggerating when he speaks in his Trial Lecture of a monstrous chaos of disorderly, undifferentiated data. Referring to the great systematizer John Stuart Mill and his attendance at zoology lectures at Montpellier University in 1820, Sir Peter Medawar has remarked that 'there seems no doubt that his thought on methodology was strongly influenced by the study of a subject overwhelmed by a multitude of "facts" that had not yet been disciplined by a unifying theory'; and he continues: 'Coleridge described it [in 1818] as "notorious" that zoology had been "fully abroad, weighed down and crushed as it were by the inordinate number and multiplicity of facts and phenomena apparently separate, without evincing the least promise of systematizing itself by any inward combination of its parts".'[32] Biologists of this period found themselves battling through a teeming jungle of new knowledge. Behind them lay Aristotle-Land, with its clear but no longer adequate model of a fixed and static 'Ladder of Nature'; ahead of them somewhere was that magnificent vantage point that Darwin was ultimately to construct, with its momentous spectacle of an evolutionary pattern in nature both dynamic and explicable. Many crucial stations were established along the way by great speculative and/or systematizing minds like Linnaeus, Bonnet, Buffon, Lamarck, Cuvier; but being on the whole too closely modelled on the Aristotelian 'fixed-and-final' scheme, none of them could sufficiently order or accommodate the riotous growth of new facts and discoveries.

That there was a real fear in this period of being overwhelmed by the welter of 'facts and phenomena' is clear from the comments of Coleridge, and implicit in Büchner's use of language in the Trial Lecture ('ein ungeheures . . . Material, das kaum unter die Ordnung eines Kataloges gebracht war', 'ein Gewirr seltsamer Formen unter den abentheuerlichsten Namen', 'eine Masse Dinge, die . . . als getrennte, weit auseinander liegende facta das Gedächtniß beschwerten'). The fear was a complex one. At its most banal there was no doubt the professional fear of all scholars in all eras that their minds might not be equal to their material. At a much deeper level, the gathering confusion was bound to generate anxious perplexity in an age conditioned by the Enlightenment to believe that all things in existence are systematically patterned, and that man's mind can discern that pattern. At its deepest, however, the fear was existential: what was threatened was man's whole sense of the world in which he lived, and of his place within that world. The ultimate upshot is a matter of history: *On the Origin of Species by Natural Selection* resolved one kind of fear, but confirmed the other: it did discern a pattern, and it thereby revolutionized biology, and the sciences in general; but in the process it also profoundly affected man's conception of the world in all its dimensions—philosophical, religious, ethical, social, political. In the meantime, though, the earlier systematizers struggled to order the increasing chaos—seeking consciously or unconsciously to put upon it the most comfortable construction that they could.[33]

Both Büchner and Coleridge point to the gravest particular cause of fear: the real threat lay not so much in the sheer extent or bulk of the new 'facts and phenomena', but rather in their disorderliness and, above all, their discreteness: they were 'getrennte, weit auseinander liegende facta', they were 'apparently separate' and showing no promise of an 'inward combination of [their] parts'. This 'inordinate multiplicity' not only resisted Enlightened assumptions about an orderly progression towards the discernment of order in the *natural* world; it also very readily seemed to echo, to symbolize and even to compound the atomistic forces that were tending to disrupt progress towards a better order in the *human* world (as seen from a progressivist point of view), or alternatively to disrupt the human order already prevailing (as seen from a conservative point of view). For approximately a century, cataclysm after cataclysm ensured that no thinking person could easily sustain a clear and stable picture of the world: the devastating Lisbon earthquake of 1755 that so profoundly affected Voltaire; the incessant revolution in scientific data; the Industrial Revolution with its colossal social and economic repercussions; the French Revolution with its magnificent aspirations and horrific reality—precisely the setting of Büchner's first play; the international turmoil of the Napoleonic wars; the bloody spasms of social revolution in 1830 and 1848. This was by far the greatest and the most obsessive age of taxonomy and system-building in human history: like Büchner's Danton, they were 'making mosaics', feverishly trying to assemble the exploded pieces into sensible, significant order. And today we still live to some extent in the long shadow of the twin texts that were the towering culmination of these endeavours, texts that were equally dedicated to the ordering of classes, and to the modes of change to which those classes are subject: *On the Origin of Species*—and *The Communist Manifesto.*

Nowhere was the atomistic threat felt more acutely than in Germany. Not least because there *was* no Germany: in sharp contrast to France or England, there was no kind of political, economic, social, or cultural entity characterized by an 'inward combination of its parts' (to borrow Coleridge's words once again), but instead an 'inordinate number and multiplicity' of states and statelets—the atomization and attendant backwardness of particularism. The hundred years from about 1750 to 1850 saw an astonishing outpouring of genius in German thought and literature (not to mention music) that is without parallel in Europe since the Renaissance. But this great torrent welled up in a fragmented landscape that had lain barren in many respects since time immemorial, and which enjoyed nothing of the clear, well-established, centralized system of channels and reservoirs that offered an instant sense of direction, context, and common endeavour to the gifted Frenchman or Englishman. Referring particularly to literature, W. H. Bruford has observed that 'It is remarkable, as has often been pointed out, that Germany succeeded, in the absence of . . . a national tradition and of political institutions to support it, in producing a literature that came to be looked upon as classical, though it was, in Freytag's phrase, "the almost miraculous creation of a soul without a body".[34] It was indeed remarkable. But it would have been even more remarkable if the mighty talents of the age had *not* energetically built themselves elaborate constructs to compensate for what was missing.

But what kind of constructs? A fundamental disparity at once begins to appear between the German pattern, and the pattern elsewhere. At its simplest, it is the contrast between empiricism and idealism; between the inductive and deductive modes; between progression from matter to mind, and progression from mind to matter. Given the increasingly evident backwardness and atomization of the German reality, and the almost nonexistent role of the emergent intelligentsia, and its ideas, in the prevailing political structures and processes, it is scarcely surprising that the constructs of thinkers and writers came more and more to be built as it were on stilts, at a deliberate remove from narrow, intractable reality.

The decisive figure here was Immanuel Kant (a man who himself moved from 'matter' to 'mind' in the sense that he taught physics and mathematics before he changed to philosophy). What could the mind know, and how could it know it securely? Kant posited on the one hand a realm of essential reality, of 'things in themselves', of which we can know nothing whatever. But the position is profoundly different with regard to the world of phenomena, of things as they *appear.* Kant's 'Copernican revolution', as he himself described it, was truly revolutionary. Just as Copernicus had shown that the apparent motion of the heavenly bodies was due to the motion of the beholder on his mobile planet, so Kant argued that the world as we know it, the world of appearances, is a function of our vantage point, and is constituted solely by the interaction of our senses and our intelligence: every feature of it, even its thereness in space and time, is ascribed to it by the mind.

The radical epistemology of this 'Transcendental Idealism' took the giant first step towards establishing the mind as the giver of meaning, as the creator in a certain sense of the knowable world—and it thereby prepared the ground for a whole plethora of systems, philosophies, and ideologies that set the human mind or spirit (*Geist*) ever more intensely at the centre of the universe. In terms of philosophy itself, there are the 'Absolute Idealist' systems of Fichte, Schelling, and, above all, Hegel. In the domain of art, there is the High Romanticism of Friedrich Schlegel and Novalis. And in the realm of the natural world, there is *Naturphilosophie*—which is what particularly concerns us in the context of Georg Büchner.

We can enter the fray at a conspicuously benign moment. It is 1794. Goethe and Schiller, these twin giants of Weimar Classicism, are gravely estranged, thanks largely to Goethe's conviction that they are at 'diametrically opposite poles', and separated by such an 'enormous gulf' that there can be 'no question' of their ever being reconciled (x. 540[35]). But they happen to find themselves emerging together from a meeting of J. G. K. Batsch's 'naturforschende Gesellschaft' in Jena, and it is Schiller's criticism of the analytical, atomistic tone of this meeting that suddenly sparks their famous friendship. What Schiller objects to is the treatment of nature as so many separate fragments ('eine so zerstückelte Art die Natur zu behandeln', ibid.). Goethe agrees in deeply characteristic terms: instead of nature being regarded as an assemblage of separate bits and pieces, it can readily be shown to be vibrant and alive, carrying its wholeness through into all its parts ('nicht gesondert und vereinzelt . . . sondern . . . wirkend und lebendig, aus dem Ganzen in die Teile strebend', ibid.). What serves to unite these two diametrically different men, therefore, is a shared hostility to what they regard as an excessive and barren empiricism: a concentration on the part, on the particularity of discrete data, that forfeits all sense of the whole. Again there is the Coleridgean spectre of man's ordering mind being swamped by 'facts and phenomena'. This is why Goethe rejects Baconian science: it purports to collate the particular only in order to discern the universal ('Partikularien'/'Universalien'); but it loses itself so completely in individual data that life goes by and all energies are exhausted before any simple essence or any conclusion can be arrived at ('ehe man durch Induktion . . . zur Vereinfachung und zum Abschluß gelangen kann, geht das Leben weg und die Kräfte verzehren sich', xiv. 91). Goethe's crucial point, indeed one of his central articles of faith, is that the whole is always present within the part, and a single fact can therefore serve for thousands in that it contains their essence within itself, all being equally manifestations of the primordial type, the particular 'Urphänomen', that wholly informs them; to fail to grasp this, says Goethe, is to forgo all chance of a joyous or beneficial outcome ('Wer nicht gewahr werden kann, daß ein Fall oft tausende wert ist, und sie alle in sich schließt, wer nicht das zu fassen und zu ehren imstande ist, was wir Urphänomene genannt haben, der wird weder sich noch andern jemals etwas zur Freude und zum Nutzen fördern können.', xiv. 91-2).

In rejecting the Baconian absorption in empirical data, Goethe is by no means turning his back on reality. On the contrary, it is precisely his conviction that true reality is closed to Baconian (or Newtonian) empiricism, which forfeits any chance of seeing the wood through its exclusive concentration on the trees. It is only through a wholist approach, he believes, that one can apprehend reality. He insists on his 'obstinate realism' ('hartnäckigen Realismus', x. 541); and when he conjures up for Schiller his vision of nature as 'wirkend und lebendig, aus dem Ganzen in die Teile strebend', this is to him no abstraction, but something he sees and experiences with his own eye, as he might a table or a chair. Having meanwhile been carried by their conversation into Schiller's house, he not only *exposits* his notion of the metamorphosis of plants, but makes it palpable by actually drawing a 'symbolic plant' ('symbolische Pflanze', x. 540) for the other to physically see with his eyes. But this very nearly ends their friendship before it has begun, for it touches on that 'enormous gulf' that had always separated them: Schiller as a fully fledged Kantian ('ein gebildeter Kantianer', x. 541) cannot accept this assertion of experiential reality: '"Das ist keine Erfahrung, das ist eine Idee."' (x. 540; *'That is not an experience, it is an idea.'*) This was Goethe's self-confessed and blessed 'naïvety': that his thoughts and ideas were literally, palpably visible to his eye (xiii. 26-7). We do not have to be learned Kantians to recognize that Schiller is of course quite right: what Goethe envisions is to his own eye a lived reality, but it nevertheless remains a product of his mind, an ideal—not an inherent and necessary quality of objective reality itself.

This begins to define the central thrust of that contentious but widespread and persistent mode of scientific enquiry that was German *Naturphilosophie*. In essence, and at its best, it was an attempt to syncretize the epoch's two antithetical attitudes of Empiricism and Idealism in order to establish a middle ground in which mind and matter, instead of dominating and diminishing each other, came fully into their own in a kind of rich interplay. In its fundamental wholist tenets it is unquestionably idealist, even metaphysical. As T. J. Reed remarks in his 'Past Masters' book on Goethe: 'The—in some sense—divine ground and wholeness of the world are presupposed, and to that extent Goethe is a metaphysician.'[36] And Strohl has declared that mysticism is plainly the departure point of Lorenz Oken's wholist aspirations in his textbooks of *Naturphilosophie* (*Übersicht des Grundrisses des Systems der Naturphilosophie,* 1802; *Grundriß des Systems der Naturphilosophie,* 1804).[37] But far from rejecting reality and resorting to the pure abstractions and fantasies of the Idealist philosophers and the High Romantics, the *Naturphilosophen* used their idealist-metaphysical-mystical postulates as a vantage point from which to comprehend the real workings of the real natural world, to descry imaginatively but also precisely and specifically the order within the otherwise unmanageable chaos of data. Throughout all his scientific-philosophical speculations, Goethe never strayed from detailed and painstaking experimentation and analysis of specimens; Oken published no fewer than thirteen volumes of 'straight' experimental, descriptive 'Naturgeschichte' ('natural history'). But their approach in their laborious experimentation was always deductive and integrative, never inductive and atomistic: whereas the Baconian starts with the part (and in the view of the *Naturphilosophen* can never get beyond it), they begin with the whole—which indeed they believe to be always immanent in every least particle.[38]

By the time it came to Georg Büchner's brief spell in the realm of the sciences in the mid-30s, *Naturphilosophie,* though still predominant, was under severe threat, for the parallel and alternative mode of empiricism was rapidly moving towards that position of supremacy that it still holds to this day (the great dispute between Cuvier and Saint-Hilaire referred to in note 38 is one milestone in this momentous struggle for ascendancy). In the process of the gradual discrediting of *Naturphilosophie,* it attracted much disparagement and even ridicule. This is partly because of the hyperbolization in both expression and conviction that the battle of attitudes forced on its participants. It was engagingly symbolized on the occasion of Oken's Inaugural Lecture at Jena in 1807, a sensational and polemical affair in which Oken felt driven to the climactic and preposterous assertion: 'Der ganze Mensch ist nur ein Wirbelbein.' (*The entire human being is but a vertebra.*)[39]—a dictum that instantly spawned a derisive greeting among the local wags: 'Guten Tag, Herr Wirbelbein!'[40] The polemical intensity of the battle can be readily gauged from the scathing—and no less hyperbolic—tone of Justus von Liebig, the great chemist, who in 1840 attacked the *Naturphilosophen* and their doings as 'the pestilence, the Black Death, of the nineteenth century'.[41] Much later Liebig pronounced on *Naturphilosophie* in more moderate, but more devastating terms: 'We look back on German *Naturphilosophie* as though on a dead tree that bore the most beautiful foliage and the most magnificent flowers—but no fruit.'[42] It is no doubt true that some of the extravagances of *Naturphilosophie* were 'fantastic to the verge of insanity'.[43] And one of its most radical exponents was J. B. Wilbrand, professor of Comparative Anatomy, Physiology, and Natural History at Giessen from 1809—and the young Liebig's particular *bête noire* from the moment in 1824 that he took up his own chair in Giessen, where both men were still very active in their antagonistic camps when Büchner arrived to continue his studies in 1833.[44]

It is easy to mock at the excesses of *Naturphilosophie*: at Wilbrand's dogged and absolute denial of the circulation of the blood, and likewise of the interchange of oxygen and carbon dioxide in respiration; at his treatise succinctly entitled 'On the Connection between Nature and the Supernatural, and How a Thorough Study of Nature and its Phenomena Points Ineluctably to the Continuance of Spiritual Life after Death'; at the belief of Oken and others that light is the consciousness of God, ether his self-positing activity, and objects his concretized thoughts; at Goethe's repudiation of Newton's theory of light. For one thing, however, we might bear in mind that Liebig himself, the great empiricist, was trained by *Naturphilosophen,* remained a Vitalist throughout his life, and underpinned the physical with the metaphysical in the motto inscribed over his laboratory: 'God has ordained all things by measure, number, and weight'. It is as easy and convenient for us as it was for the protagonists in the polemic to distinguish categorically between sheep and goats, to see deductivists and speculative idealists on the one hand, and inductivists and rigorous empiricists on the other. In reality, as Popper and Medawar have persuasively argued, there are not two distinct camps in science, but a continuous spectrum linking the opposite and equally unfruitful extremes of 'an inventory of factual information' and 'a totalitarian world picture of natural laws'[45]—with all significant advances in science being made in that mid-range of the spectrum that involves the most fruitful interaction between speculative, imaginative intuition, and careful empirical testing. At its zaniest, *Naturphilosophie* did veer towards a ludicrously absolute and unproductive extreme. Even in its normal, median condition as a classical mode of scientific enquiry enshrined in all the universities of the land, its subordination of experiment to a priori ideology ensured that it could not survive against the professional scepticism, the questioning subjection of hypotheses to experimental testing, that increasingly became the hallmark of nineteenth-century science.[46] Nevertheless, *Naturphilosophie* did make a very real contribution to the development of science, both in the general and in the particular: it considerably extended the realm of the thinkable; and it either made, or provided the stimulus for, a whole range of specific discoveries. As to the general: its dare-to-speculate mentality greatly furthered science in its quantum leap from the physics-derived fixed-mechanism model of the world in the eighteenth century, to the transformational, evolutionary model so characteristic of the nineteenth. The out-and-out empiricists found this imaginative leap very difficult to make. Cuvier, for instance, clung tenaciously to his view of the biological realm as fixed and unalterable; faced with the fossil data produced by the revolutionary new science of palaeontology, his now comical explanation was that the world must have experienced a succession of great catastrophes, the last being the Flood, and the devastated areas had then been repopulated each time from parts of the globe as yet unknown to science. At the level of specifics: Oken with his doctrine of primordial 'sacs' ('Bläschen') paved the way for cell biology; Johannes Müller made great advances in physiology and embryology; Carus helped significantly to open up the new discipline of gynaecology; Schelling's principle of polarity led Schönbein to discover ozone, and considerably influenced Berzelius and Volta; Goethe's stress on comparative anatomy and 'morphology' (a word that he himself coined), as distinct from straight anatomy on the one hand, and Linnaean comparing of external characteristics on the other hand, was an important stimulus in the development of evolutionary theory.[47]

This, then, is the kind of context within which Büchner and his science-cum-philosophy belong, and within which we need to try to locate and understand him. Its most crucial characteristic is its 'continuous spectrum' quality: Büchner criticism has been—and continues to be—bedevilled and distorted by that inveterate tendency to polarization that sees only separate, mutually exclusive camps of empiricists-materialists-realists, and speculative idealists. Such a tidy dichotomy may conceivably be relevant to the realms of abstract philosophy and literary fantasizing, both of which offered an alluring refuge from reality during this period; but it is mischievously irrelevant to the realm of scientific enquiry—and hence also to the writing of Georg Büchner. For the beliefs and practices that inform his science equally inform his art. Not only in the commonplace sense that the laboratory dissector is also the literary dissector, but in the much more important sense that there is in both a profound and essential interaction of the Real and the Ideal. For the devotees of polarization, it has to be either/or, and what they inevitably do is to hustle Büchner into the empiricist-materialist camp, which is of course by definition anti-idealist. This is a tendentious travesty, whether in the crass form exemplified by Walter Müller-Seidel with his depiction of Büchner as wholly anti-idealist and wholly 'scientific',[48] or in the subtle form proffered by Raimar Zons with his claim that Büchner held to the notions of *Naturphilosophie*— but only as an expedient heuristic category, not a set of beliefs; only as a 'methodological postulate', a kind of handy toolkit to help him deal with the world.[49]

This surely is the crux, the teasing but critical question that every serious student of Büchner has to confront. Do we credit the radiantly positive vision—Goethean and *naturphilosophisch* in its essence—that he voices in the preamble to the Trial Lecture? Do we believe that

he believed in a primal law of beauty, in simplicity as the fount of rich complexity, in pure harmony as the necessary outcome of the primal law throughout the natural world? Or do we decide that the vision is uncharacteristic and illusory—a strategem perhaps, a piece of ritual rhetoric, a contrived nostrum, an act of calculated ingratiation, an inexplicable and dismissible aberration? Both alternatives are problematic. To take the latter is generally to find oneself in a familiar logical bind: Büchner is a fearless speaker of unidealized truth, therefore it cannot be the truth when he speaks of ideals. To prefer the other alternative is to collide at once with the fact that harmonious beauty and rich simplicity are scarcely the most resonant message of his poetic work. Nevertheless I believe this alternative to be incontrovertibly the right one: Büchner did mean every warm and positive word of his preamble; and so completely was he blessed and cursed by an inherited sense of natural harmony that even the slightest discord, the slightest departure from received pitch, was for him an agony. His misfortune—and in consequence our delight—is that he happened, like Hoffmann's Ritter Gluck, to be a man of richest harmonies in a world increasingly dominated by scratchers and scrapers and mechanical contraptions grinding out the same old cracked, broken, excruciating tunes.

Fanciful language, perhaps? But it echoes Büchner's own, in a memorable letter to his beloved Minna Jaeglé in March 1834 (ii. 424). Even the reference to Hoffmann is there (though not specifically to *Ritter Gluck*): 'Ich hätte Herrn Callot-Hoffmann sitzen können, nicht wahr' (*I could have sat* [as a model] *for Herr Callot-Hoffmann, couldn't I*).[50] So, too, is the strident duality of natural harmony and desperate mechanical grinding. He has just been outside in the open, he writes: 'Ein einziger, forthallender Ton aus tausend Lerchenkehlen schlägt durch die brütende Sommerluft, ein schweres Gewölk wandelt über die Erde, der tiefbrausende Wind klingt wie sein melodischer Schritt.' (*A single resonant tone from the throats of a thousand larks bursts through the brooding summer air, a heavy bank of cloud wanders over the earth, the booming wind rings out like its melodious tread.*) This is his vibrant, melodious present. But until the outside air served to free him and give him life again, he had been long transfixed by a kind of rigor ('Starrkrampf'), by a sense of being already dead ('Gefühl des Gestorbenseins'), so that he and all around him seemed like deathly puppets with glassy eyes and waxen cheeks. And at this point Büchner suddenly launches into a characteristically thrilling cadenza of despair (one wonders what poor Minna made of it all):

> und wenn dann die ganze Maschinerie zu leiern anfing, die Gelenke zuckten, die Stimme herausknarrte und ich das ewige Orgellied herumtrillern hörte und die Wälzchen und Stiftchen im Orgelkasten hüpfen und drehen sah,—ich verfluchte das Concert, den Kasten, die Melodie und—ach, wir armen schreienden Musi-

kanten, das Stöhnen auf unsrer Folter, wäre es nur da, damit es durch die Wolkenritzen dringend und weiter, weiter klingend, wie ein melodischer Hauch in himmlischen Ohren stirbt? Wären wir das Opfer im glühenden Bauch des Peryllusstiers, dessen Todesschrei wie das Aufjauchzen des in den Flammen sich aufzehrenden Gottstiers klingt?

and then, when the whole machinery began to grind away, with jerking limbs and grating voice, and I heard the same old barrel-organ tune go tralala and saw the tiny prongs and cylinders bob and whirr in the organ box—I cursed the concert, the box, the melody—oh, poor, screaming musicians that we are—could it be that our cries of agony on the rack only exist to ring out through cracks between the clouds and, echoing on and on, die like a melodious breath in heavenly ears? Could it be that we are the victims roasted in the belly of Perillus' bull, whose screams as they die ring out like the jubilant roars of the bull-god as it is devoured by the flames?

An unnerving antiphon: in nature—the wind and the larks and their liberating melody; among men—a deathly mechanical rasping, and tortured screams extracted perhaps by some distant deity for his melodious titillation. And it is precisely this drastic antiphon that Büchner uses nine months later to ring in the crescendo marking the grand-opera climax of **Dantons Tod**:

PHILIPPEAU.

Meine Freunde man braucht gerade nicht hoch über der Erde zu stehen um von all dem wirren Schwanken und Flimmern nichts mehr zu sehen und die Augen von einigen großen, göttlichen Linien erfüllt zu haben. Es giebt ein Ohr für welches das Ineinanderschreien und der Zeter, die uns betäuben, ein Strom von Harmonien sind.

DANTON.

Aber wir sind die armen Musicanten und unsere Körper die Instrumente. Sind die häßlichen Töne, welche auf ihnen herausgepfuscht werden nur da um höher und höher dringend und endlich leise verhallend wie ein wollüstiger Hauch in himmlischen Ohren zu sterben?

(etc.; 71)

PHILIPPEAU.

My friends, one doesn't have to stand very far above the earth to see no trace any more of all this shifting, shimmering chaos, and to behold instead a simple, great and godly outline. There is an ear for which the cacophony and clamour, so deafening to us, are a stream of harmonies.

DANTON.

But we are the poor musicians and our bodies the instruments. Are the ugly, vamping sounds bashed out on them just there to rise up higher and higher and gently fade and die like some voluptuous puff of breath in heavenly ears?

It would be easy to conclude—as innumerable critics have done—that Philippeau is simply a stooge, a foil of fatuous optimism serving to silhouette the 'true' nega-

tivity in the ensuing chorus of grandiloquent despair. But this would be quite wrong. For one thing . . . the chorus of despair is itself a desperate illusion. More to the point here: Philippeau's 'stream of harmonies' is profoundly real to Büchner. When he heard its melody among the wind and the larks in Giessen, it brought him back from figurative death (thus inaugurating a central topos of death and resurrection that runs throughout his work). And it is, above all, the measure that makes the sounds given out by the human 'instrument' seem by contrast so ugly, so raspingly mechanical.

The essential question is *why,* for Büchner, men have become so drastically, so agonizingly out of tune, so remote from the 'stream of harmonies', from that 'necessary harmony' that the primal law of beauty bestows so readily upon the rest of nature.

Notes

1. To date, only 11 autograph letters have come to light; the remainder are either lost, or else survive only in second-hand and excerpted form (i.e. as printed in Ludwig Büchner's 1850 part-edition of his brother's writings; the originals from which these letter-excerpts were taken were destroyed in a fire at the Büchners' home in 1851). Cf. Jan-Christoph Hauschild, *Georg Büchner. Studien und neue Quellen zu Leben, Werk und Wirkung* (Königstein, 1985), 101 ff.; Susanne Lehmann, 'Der Brand im Haus der Büchners 1851', in T. M. Mayer (ed.), *Georg Büchner Jahrbuch*, 6/1986-7, 303-13.—Since this note was written, two further autograph letters have been tracked down; see *Der Spiegel*, 36 (1993), 198-204, and E. Gillmann, T. M. Mayer, R. Pabst, and D. Wolf (eds.), *Georg Büchner an 'Hund' und 'Kater'. Unbekannte Briefe des Exils* (Marburg, 1993).

2. It was long supposed that Büchner must have left behind a complete or near-complete play manuscript on the subject of Pietro Aretino, and that his fiancée Minna Jaeglé must have destroyed it; it now seems much more likely that the project was planned rather than executed (the negative picture of Minna Jaeglé's attitudes and behaviour in the decades after Büchner's death has also been convincingly discredited). Cf. Hauschild, *Georg Büchner,* 57 ff.; Jan-Christoph Hauschild, 'Büchners Aretino. Eine Fiktion?', in Anon. (ed.), *Georg Büchner 1813-1837. Revolutionär, Dichter, Wissenschaftler* (Basel and Frankfurt, 1987), 353-5. Büchner's interest in Aretino is itself interesting: Pietro Aretino (1492-1556) was a self-styled 'scourge of princes' (*flagello dei principi*) who, besides many other activities including painting, and writing successful comedies and a tragedy, became notorious for his vitriolic satires and his

salacious exposés of corruption and carnality in high places, and also for his highly erotic poetry, notably the *Sonetti lussuriosi* (Lewd Sonnets).

3. See Hauschild, *Georg Büchner*, 372-3.

4. Anon. (ed.), *Büchner-Preis-Reden 1951-1971* (Stuttgart, 1972), 162.

5. Ibid. 183.

6. Ibid. 56.

7. Ibid. 116.

8. Christa Wolf, *Fortgesetzter Versuch. Aufsätze. Gespräche. Essays* (Leipzig, 1979), 64.

9. Wolf Biermann, 'Der Lichtblick im gräßlichen Fatalismus der Geschichte', *Die Zeit,* 25 Oct. 1991, 73. More recently, Biermann has compared Büchner to Shakespeare, and referred to him as a 'Weltgenie' (genius of world stature); see 'Geschichte kennt keine Moral. Wolf Biermann über die wiederentdeckten Briefe Georg Büchners und ihre Bedeutung für die Gegenwart', *Der Spiegel,* 36 (1993), 207.

10. Georg Lukács, 'Der faschistisch verfälschte und der wirkliche Georg Büchner', repr. in W. Martens (ed.), *Georg Büchner* (Darmstadt, 1965), 201. Lukács's polemic was originally written in Moscow in 1937.

11. Robert Mühlher, 'Georg Büchner und die Mythologie des Nihilismus', in Martens (ed.), *Georg Büchner,* 260.

12. Walter Jens, *Euripides. Büchner* (Pfullingen, 1964), 46.

13. A. H. J. Knight, *Georg Büchner* (Oxford, 1951), 80.

14. Ronald Peacock, 'A Note on Georg Büchner's Plays', *German Life and Letters,* NS 10 (1956-7), 191. Peacock's article proved influential, not least in serving as the explicit departure point for Dorothy James's monograph *Georg Büchner's 'Dantons Tod': A Reappraisal* (London, 1982)—a work that is repeatedly weakened by its premiss that *Dantons Tod* demonstrates Büchner's 'immaturity as a dramatist' (25).

15. Knight, 74.

16. Cf. Helmut Krapp in his seminal study of 1958, *Der Dialog bei Georg Büchner* (Darmstadt, 1958), 145: 'Büchners Position . . . ist kein "Entwurf" und keine "Lösung" im überlieferten Sinne, denn das Kontrastschema hat eigentlich keinen Anfang und kein Ende. Kontraste lassen sich unendlich aneinanderreihen' (*Büchner's position . . . represents neither a 'blueprint' nor a 'solution' in the traditional sense, for his contrastive scheme of things knows no real beginning or ending. Contrasts can be concatenated ad infinitum*).

17. Parenthetic page references relate throughout to the so-called Hamburg Edition (plain numbers refer to vol. i, numbers with the prefix 'ii' refer to vol. ii): Georg Büchner, *Sämtliche Werke und Briefe. Historisch-kritische Ausgabe mit Kommentar,* ed. Werner R. Lehmann: i. *Dichtungen und Übersetzungen mit Dokumentationen zur Stoffgeschichte* (Hamburg, 1967); ii. *Vermischte Schriften und Briefe* (Hamburg, 1971). Lehmann's edition has had a sorry and exasperating history. Four vols. were originally planned: the two vols. as published, and two vols. containing the critical apparatus and the promised 'Kommentar'. Not only did the project change publishers (transferring from Christian Wegner, Hamburg, to Carl Hanser, Munich), but the third and fourth vols. never appeared. Although it still constitutes the most authoritative and most widely available complete edition—and is accordingly used as the base-text throughout the present study—most of the main works have since been variously and separately published in editions considerably superior to Lehmann's. A truly historical-critical edition of the entire corpus is in preparation under the editorship of Thomas Michael Mayer; in the meantime we have to wait and make do.

18. The title is not Büchner's own. It was coined by Karl Emil Franzos for his 1879 edition of Büchner's works.

19. Karl Viëtor, *Georg Büchner. Politik, Dichtung, Wissenschaft* (Berne, 1949), 296.

20. August Closs, 'Nihilism in Modern German Drama. Grabbe and Büchner', in Closs, *Medusa's Mirror: Studies in German Literature* (London, 1957), 157.

21. Hans Mayer, *Georg Büchner und seine Zeit* (Wiesbaden, [1960]), 104.

22. Mühlher, 261.

23. Maurice B. Benn, *The Drama of Revolt: A Critical Study of Georg Büchner* (Cambridge, 1976), 61, 62.

24. Cf. Gerhard Knapp: 'Es hat sich im Grundsätzlichen erwiesen, daß die Kategorie des Nihilismus . . . für eine Annäherung an das Werk Büchners nicht in Frage kommen kann und sollte. Die Büchner-Forschung sollte diesen Interpretationsgang, der sich als Aporie erwiesen hat, endgültig ad acta legen.' (*It has become clear in all essential respects that the category of nihilism cannot and should not be called upon in any approach to*

Büchner. Büchner research should once and for all abandon this line of interpretation, which has shown itself to be a complete cul-de-sac; see also Knapp's endnote).—Gerhard Knapp, *Georg Büchner. Eine kritische Einführung in die Forschung* (Frankfurt, 1975), 120.

25. Knight, 69, 174-5.

26. Hans Mayer, *Georg Büchner und seine Zeit,* 372.

27. J. P. Stern, 'Georg Büchner: Potsherds of Experience', in Stern, *Idylls and Realities: Studies in Nineteenth-Century German Literature* (London, 1971), 35.

28. Felix Frei [pseudonym], in *Literarisches Notizenblatt der Dresdner Abendzeitung,* 28 Oct. 1835. Cf. Hauschild, *Georg Büchner,* 185 ff. Cf. also Thomas Michael Mayer, 'Büchner-Chronik', in H. L. Arnold (ed.), *Büchner I/II,* special number of *Text + Kritik* (Munich, 1979), 404. Mayer eloquently documents the virulent campaign of the period against 'subversive' writers, orchestrated by the Metternichian hatchet man Wolfgang Menzel—a campaign that culminated in the imprisonment of Büchner's new friend and patron, Karl Gutzkow (ibid. 397 ff.).

29. Cf. Jean Strohl, *Lorenz Oken und Georg Büchner. Zwei Gestalten aus der Übergangszeit von Naturphilosophie zu Naturwissenschaft* (Zurich, 1936), 59.

30. T. M. Mayer, 'Büchner-Chronik', 419.

31. T. H. Huxley, 'On the Theory of the Vertebrate Skull', in M. Foster and E. R. Lankester (eds.), *The Scientific Memoirs of Thomas Henry Huxley,* i. (London, 1898), 584-5. Sir Peter Medawar has described Huxley's 1858 lecture as one of the 'very few' cases in the history of science where a theory has been 'utterly discredited' (P. B. Medawar, *Induction and Intuition in Scientific Thought* (London, 1969), 30). But the position is not quite so clear-cut. It can be argued that Huxley's own hypothesis was not all that far removed from the one he so vigorously ridiculed. And even to this day, the theory of the vertebrate skull is still not entirely dead.

32. Medawar, 9.

33. One curious monument to this obsession with taxonomy is, of all things, Roget's *Thesaurus.* P. M. Roget, born 1779, was a doctor and natural scientist of considerable repute, a Fellow of the Royal Society and its Secretary for more than twenty years, who not only invented a 'system of verbal classification', but based it—as he explained in the Introduction to the first edition of 1852—on 'the same principle as that which is employed in the various departments of Natural History. Thus the sectional divisions I have formed, correspond to the Natural Families in Botany and Zoology, and the filiation of words presents a network analogous to the natural filiation of plants or animals.' (R. A. Dutch (ed.), *Roget's Thesaurus of English Words and Phrases* (London, 1981), pp. xxi, xxxv.)

34. W. H. Bruford, *Germany in the Eighteenth Century: The Social Background to the Literary Revival* (Cambridge, 1965), 292.

35. Volume and page numbers concerning Goethe refer to the 'Hamburg Edition', 14 vols., ed. Erich Trunz *et al.* (Hamburg, 1948-66).

36. T. J. Reed, *Goethe* (Oxford, 1984), 47.

37. Strohl, 12.

38. These contrary scientific positions are precisely epitomized by Goethe when he summarizes the attitudes of Cuvier and Saint-Hilaire, the two disputants in the great debate of 1830 in the Paris Academy of Sciences: xiii. 220.

39. Strohl, 11.

40. Cf. H. Bräuning-Oktavio, *Oken und Goethe im Lichte neuer Quellen* (Weimar, 1959), 49.

41. Cited by Walter Müller-Seidel, 'Natur und Naturwissenschaft im Werk Georg Büchners', in E. Catholy and W. Hellmann (eds.), *Festschrift für Klaus Ziegler* (Tübingen, 1968), 207.

42. Cited by Raimar St. Zons, *Georg Büchner. Dialektik der Grenze* (Bonn, 1976), 61.

43. Charles Singer, *A Short History of Scientific Ideas to 1900* (Oxford, 1960), 385.

44. It has long been customary in Büchner criticism to speak disparagingly—if at all—of Wilbrand. For a long-overdue reappraisal, see Christian Maass, 'Georg Büchner und Johann Bernhard Wilbrand. Medizin in Gießen um 1833/44', in Anon. (ed.), *Georg Büchner 1813-1837,* 148-54.

45. Medawar, 59.

46. The corrective or normative effect of internationalism is highly important here: German political, social and economic structures, and German philosophy and literature, developed in their own relatively isolated and idiosyncratic way in the 19th c.; but science increasingly transcended national frontiers, and the history of German science in the period is in a sense a history of accelerating internationalism.

47. Cf. Strohl, 28 ff.; Singer, 384 ff.

48. Müller-Seidel, 210 and *passim.* Müller-Seidel has his wires crossed throughout his confused and

question-begging essay, not least in his claim that Büchner is a cynical and fatalistic Schopenhauerian, but above all in his assertion that the approach that this entails reflects the general mood and practice of modern science as it was then evolving. The screams of anguish in Georg Büchner's works are those of a passionate, wounded idealist, not a cool, enquiring empiricist.

49. Zons, 69 ff. Cf. also T. M. Mayer, 'Büchner-Chronik', 419.

50. The 'Callot' is an allusion to Hoffmann's *Fantasiestücke in Callots Manier* (of which 'Ritter Gluck' happens to be the first).

Margaret T. Peischl (essay date spring 1996)

SOURCE: Peischl, Margaret T. "Büchner's *Lenz*: A Study of Madness." *Germanic Notes and Reviews* 27, no. 1 (spring 1996): 13-19.

[*In the following essay, Peischl summarizes the subject, action, style, and central conflicts of* Lenz.]

The reader who doesn't know in advance that Georg Büchner's novella **Lenz** deals with the mental decline of the *Sturm und Drang* writer, J. M. R. Lenz, is at least introduced immediately on the first page to a very tense and uncanny scene precluding healthy normality. The protagonist is portrayed from the start as an individual plagued by rapidly changing moods and with a strange manner of thinking: »Nur war es ihm manchmal unangenehm, daß er nicht auf dem Kopf gehen konnte.«[1] In the first five paragraphs of the novella Lenz demonstrates four different moods: he is successively indifferent, plagued, passionate, and greatly alarmed. Soon the reader notices that the landscape also appears sinister and awaits evidence of some kind of relationship between the man and nature, particularly when it is said of Lenz: »Es war ihm alles so klein, so nahe, so naß; er hätte die Erde hinter den Ofen setzen mögen.« (p. 65) This relationship is revealed as being intimate and complex: »Er meinte, er müsse den Sturm in sich ziehen, alles in sich fassen, er dehnte sich aus und lag über der Erde, er wühlte sich in das All hinein, es war eine Lust, die ihm wehe tat.« (p.65)

The steps of the wanderer Lenz are propelled by his anxiety; »Es faßte ihn eine namenlose Angst in diesem Nichts: er war im Leeren!« (p.66) to the degree that there can be no doubt of his pathological state. He is walking in the dark and feels as though madness were pursuing him on horses. When he sees the lights of the village, he feels better; when he reaches the home of his friend Oberlin, he becomes noticeably calmer. The protagonist's vacillating state of mind, his peace, and his fear are expressed in terms of poles such as light and darkness, human company and loneliness.

After his conversation with Oberlin, Lenz is given a room in the school house where he is again overcome by a nameless fear. He occurs to himself as a dream; it is stated that: »Er konnte sich nicht mehr finden; ein dunkler Instinkt trieb ihn, sich zu retten.« (p.67) It becomes increasingly apparent that the protagonist is schizophrenic and suffers from a struggle between his illness and his instinct for self-preservation. Büchner's use of reflexive constructions demonstrates how split the personality of his protagonist is. The subject and object are separated, as though they were two different individuals. Lenz stands outside of himself; he views his illness and makes attempts at rescuing himself. His flight-like hike through the mountains and his search for something »wie nach verlornen Träumen« (p.65) underlines this. His first night in the village is so unbearable for him that he throws himself into the well; he seems to find his conscious self through physical pain. Water means for him perhaps the possibility for a new, healthy life. Lenz later tells Oberlin that he had felt something of his own being when he was transported into a kind of somnambulistic state in the mountain water. Büchner explains that Lenz's half-hearted attempts to kill himself are less a wish for death than the attempt to bring himself back to himself through physical pain. The effect of the water is, in fact, beneficial. Despite the fact that Lenz appears in an improved state on the following day, one reads: »Mit Oberlin zu Pferde durch das Tal.« (p.67), and the missing subject and verb give the impression of the force of an unnamed power. It is not Lenz who voluntarily performs an action, but an unidentified »somebody« is driven to it. Here there is at work a powerful will to live which brings about the action; it is the healthy part of Lenz, who understands the value of activity and human companionship. This will to live gives him a strong impulse toward the external world. Oberlin has a calming effect on Lenz, but toward evening Lenz is seized by a strange fear so that he would have liked to chase after the sun. In the nighttime he seeks lights, which mean something healing to him, and he throws himself into the well again, for only in this way can he overcome the fear of being alone.

One day he experiences a special feeling of Christmas and he believes that his mother, who gave him that feeling, must be standing behind a tree. Later he preaches in the village church and feels a sweet pain as he participates in the suffering of the villagers. When he is later alone in his room, he cries and feels compassion for himself. Since his being at this time is better integrated, he can also tolerate himself better. He peacefully goes to sleep. On the following morning he calmly tells Oberlin that he had dreamed of his mother and her death, and he then moves on to a conversation about nature. He wishes for a direct relationship with various forms of nature. At this point he makes the impression of an appeased individual, if not one who is recovering. He again shows interest in his surroundings.

When his acquaintance Kaufmann visits the village, Lenz is reminded of earlier unpleasant circumstances and he fears he will lose his peace of mind. Kaufmann, the counterpart of Lenz, is an advocate of literary liberalism. Their conversation about art is the climax of the novella: Lenz's long monologue shows likewise the climax of his health. He speaks rationally and draws logical conclusions. His anthropocentric thoughts are evident, and he simultaneously demonstrates his love for his fellowmen. He expresses an affirmation of life which could not be expected from him at an earlier stage. He is able to build on satisfying experiences with the people in the village, with Oberlin and his family, in nature, and with religion. He has become somewhat more balanced. Büchner says of him at this point: »Er hatte sich ganz vergessen.« (p. 73)

Kaufmann's visit, however, actually leads to the catastrophe that Lenz had anticipated. A paranoiac inevitably believes in a hostile environment; thus Lenz becomes agitated when Kaufmann suggests to him that he should go home. To return to his earlier way of life would mean a defeat for him, and he is convinced that this is Kaufmann's desire. The accelerated tempo of his words and his many questions for which there are no answers express his mental disturbance more dramatically than at any earlier time. On the next day Lenz learns that Oberlin plans to take a trip and the former's schizophrenic condition again comes to the fore: » . . . er rettete sich in eine Gestalt, die ihn immer vor Augen schwebte.« (p.74) That Oberlin will leave him drives him to a renewed and stronger state of anxiety. Erna Kritsch Neuse maintains that this is the precise midpoint of the *erzählte Zeit* as well as of the *Erzählzeit*.[2]

From this point on Lenz's condition becomes increasingly worse and continues to deteriorate until the end of the narrative. Neuse points to a parallel between the two halves of the novella and demonstrates that every occurrence in the protagonist's life up to this time has a counterpart in the second part of the story.[3] The essential difference has to do with the deterioration of his condition after Oberlin leaves.

Lenz continues to hike on after he has accompanied Oberlin and Kaufmann for a part of their way. In the evening he comes to a hut in which he encounters people and a situation that are in striking contrast to Oberlin's family and circumstances. The cosy and peaceful atmosphere he had found in Oberlin's home are lacking. The family of the hermit living here communicates something disturbing and even frightening. The sick girl, the snoring woman, and the mystic with his »unruhigem verwirrtem Gesicht« (p.75) are contrasting figures to those in Oberlin's family. They have such a disquieting effect on Lenz that he spends a very disoriented night. The antitheses in the following passage attest to his excited and vacillating frame of mind: »Durch *das leise Singen* des Mädchens und die Stimme der Alten zugleich tönte das *Sausen* des Windes, bald *näher,* bald *ferner,* und der *helle,* bald *verhüllte* Mond warf sein wechselndes Licht traumartig in die Stube.« (p.75) Even when he is at home again, the impressions of the night remain with Lenz; he can neither eat nor sleep. He laughs and cries and »Ahnungen von seinem alten Zustande durchzuckten ihn und warfen Streiflichter in das wüste Chaos seines Geistes.« (p.76) He spends much time with Madame Oberlin so that he need not be alone.

When he is reminded of his foresaken sweetheart Frederike through the girl's singing, he breaks down and begins to experience guilt feelings that he considers as the root of his illness and his hallucinations. »Jetzt ist es mir so eng, so eng! Sehn Sie, es ist mir manchmal, als stieß' ich mit den Händen an den Himmel; o, ich ersticke!« (p.77) He senses pain in his left arm with which he had touched Frederike. His mental state becomes increasingly precarious: »Je leerer, je kälter, je sterbender er sich innerlich fühlte, desto mehr drängte es ihn, eine Glut in sich zu wecken.« (p.77) He is again like two people: one attempts to rescue the other. When he hears of a deceased child with the name of Frederike, he covers his face with ashes and dresses like a penitent, and he believes that if God gave him a sign, he could awaken the child from the dead. He is so plagued by guilt that he believes he must get rid of it through a great deed. As is frequently the case with mentally ill individuals, he thinks that he is the only person alive, that he alone participates in all human experiences and therefore also possesses superhuman power. Neuse compares this event with his earlier sermon, which is likewise a manifestation of Christian faith, but one that is much healthier.[4] Since his wish to revive the dead child remains unfulfilled, a strong deterioration of his condition follows. His religious enthusiasm is suddenly transformed into an annulment of it: »ein Triumphgesang der Hölle« (p.78) His disappointment and his rage at God are so powerful that they actually become atheistic assertions. On the following day, however, he is overcome by enormous anxiety over his sin. His hallucinations increase to such an extent that even Oberlin's mention of Lenz's parents affects Lenz as a rejection. He is reminded again of his imagined guilt in regard to Frederike; his fragmentary and irrational utterances reveal him more and more frequently as a completely disturbed and irrational individual. His feelings become so exaggerated that he even requests that Oberlin beat him. In the middle of the night he again throws himself into the well and calls Frederike's name in accelerated confusion and desperation.

Lenz remains in bed on the following day and for a long time does not react to Oberlin's presence. Then he complains about boredom and it is obvious that his illness has become so extreme that even his anxiety has become paralyzed. His increasing fears have separated him from the external world to the degree that he ultimately feels himself incarcerated alone with his anxiety. At those moments when his anxiety is greatest, he complains that he is being narrowed in. (Abutille maintains that the word »Angst« is etymologically related to the word »eng«.[5] As Lenz's illness grows worse, he becomes less and less able to deal with life; his activities decrease and his world becomes smaller. Instead of possessing a full and varied emotional life, his mental experiences become concentrated solely on his anxiety. Not even the strongest feelings can endure indeterminately, and without a connection to the outside world even Lenz's anxiety becomes numbed and turns into a void. As his inner life becomes flat and undifferentiated, so does his outer life: » . . . die Langeweile, die Langeweile! O, so langweilig! Ich weiß gar nicht mehr, was ich sagen soll, . . . ich mag mich nicht einmal umbringen: es ist zu langweilig!« (p.80) His capacity for differentiating and making distinctions, that was already weakened at the time of Oberlin's departure, (»es verschmolz ihm alles in eine Linie, wie eine steigende und sinkende Welle, zwischen Himmel und Erde; es war ihm, als läge er an einem unendlichen Meer, das leise auf und ab wogte.«) (p.74) diminishes more and more:» . . . wenn ich nur unterscheiden könnte, ob ich träume oder wache; . . . « (p.80)

Thus it appears at this point that it is no longer a matter of a conflict between health and illness, but rather of two different forms of pathology. Lenz has already stepped beyond the bounds of health; his hopeless condition is an undeniable fact. One can, however, still speak of a certain activity and passivity; insofar as he still experiences anxiety, a kind of resistance against a completely dark and mindless existence is at work. Inasmuch as he sees around and in himself a void and emptiness, however, his illness has already reached an advanced stage. Although he struggles against the catastrophe, his behavior must be viewed as manifesting insanity. By jumping out of the window, visiting the grave of the dead child, running away from his attendants, and ultimately declaring himself a murderer, he is again making attempts to rescue himself from himself. He wants to cling to the outer world, however unpleasant and painful it may be. When he suffers physical pain and when he does penance for his sins, his spiritual pains and his existential anxiety are somehow assuaged. The situation is thus the opposite of what it appears to be on the surface; when Lenz is active, he participates, if irrationally, in life; when he withdraws from the external world, however, all his experiences become empty and meaningless. There exists therefore a tension between two different aspects of his mental illness; »die

Welt, die er hatte nutzen wollen, hatte einen ungeheuern Riß; er hatte keinen Haß, keine Liebe, keine Hoffnung—eine schreckliche Leere, und doch eine folternde Unruhe, sie auszufüllen. Er hatte nichts.« (p.81)

It is clear how hopeless Lenz's condition has become when he tells Oberlin of Frederike's death. He believes he knows about it through hieroglyphics. Neuse indicates this assertion as a parallel to Lenz's earlier dream of his mother's death.[6] This second delusion is by no means within the confines of reality and is a far more exaggerated expression of his deteriorating state of mind than was the earlier dream.

The split in Lenz's personality is also illustrated through his behavior when he is alone. He becomes so desperately lonely that he talks to himself, cries out, and then is terrified again; it seems to him as if a strange voice had spoken with him. As is the case in schizophrenia, he recognizes no boundaries between himself and others. If he thinks of another person, it seems to him as if he were that person. His instinct for self-preservation drives him to want: »die Häuser auf die Dächer zu stellen, die Menschen an- und auszukleiden, die wahnwitzigsten Possen auszusinnen.« (p.82) The psychopathological urge to ignore all mental demarcations and differentiations is so threatening to Lenz that he must struggle against it in the most desperate, radical way. Any kind of mental activity, even if entirely absurd, is preferable to the void. The narrator makes an unequivocal explanation of Lenz's situation: »Er mußte dann mit den einfachsten Dingen anfangen, um wieder zu sich zu kommen. Eigentlich nicht er selbst tat es, sondern ein mächtiger Erhaltungstrieb: es war, als sei er doppelt, und der eine Teil suche den andern zu retten und rufe sich selbst zu . . . « (p.82)

Lenz now has attacks even in the light of day; the demarcations of daylight no longer help him. His pathology is now battling so energetically and successfully that he must utilize an equal amount of strength to preserve by any means any kind of mental health. He throws himself into Oberlin's arms, for the latter is the only being who is alive for Lenz. There is no further external world for him; everything seems cold and dream-like to him. Occasionally Oberlin succeeds in calming Lenz for a brief period of time, and the latter then yearns more and more for peace. He continues to make half-hearted suicide attempts and causes himself severe physical pain, all in an attempt to be able to return to himself. He complains about the weight of the air and the crying stillness. His perceptive faculties have been damaged to the extent that he no longer has any relationship with the outer world. Everything that he hears and feels is a projection of his inner being. The air is heavy for him because his inner spiritual struggle is so oppressive, and the cries which he allegedly hears are calls for help from his own psychological prison.

When commitment to a hospital finally becomes a necessity, Lenz is taken to Straßburg, and the contrast with the opening scene, i.e., Lenz's hike through the mountains is immediately obvious. This applies particularly in regard to Lenz's frame of mind: it is stated at the opening of the narrative that he was completely indifferent, even though there was not yet at that point unequivocal reasons to question seriously his sanity. Now it is perhaps easier to understand the beginning of the novella: the protagonist's condition was at that time already so endangered that nature, i.e., the external world is viewed solely as a projection of his inner state. The descriptions of nature disappear as Lenz's mental health is exacerbated in the second half of the narrative and as he becomes deeper confined in his own inner life. As he is being driven away to the hospital, a dull anxiety grows in him; he makes continued attempts at suicide, but gradually there is a terrible emptiness in him. He feels neither anxiety nor desire and his existence is an unendurable burden. That does not mean, however, that his inner conflicts are resolved, rather that the temporary peace is a deception and, as Baumann asserts, there remains in Lenz »eine bedrohliche, heillose Spannung.«[7]He states further: »Jetzt bietet sich eine verklärte Landschaft dar, dionysisch trunken, ein Strömen und Werben der Natur; allein sie mag den sich selbst Entfremdeten nicht in sich hineinziehen; keine Regung des Gefühls erwacht, stumm und starr in sich verschlossen verharrt der Wahnumfangenen seiner unheimlichen Spannung.«[8] This is a striking contrast to the opening scene where Lenz wants to wallow in nature and become one with it.

The conflict at the center of the novella manifests itself at first between an individual and his environment and then, in a markedly pathological fashion, within the individual himself. The first page of the novella already gives indications and a foreshadowing of a predominant dichotomy: words like »hinunter«, »herab«, and »auf-abwärts« occur frequently; nature is at one time impenetrable, at another accessible; Lenz's mood is very erratic, and the reader is given the impression of great discrepancies. At the beginning stages of Lenz's illness, it is a matter of a rift between a mentally imperiled individual and the wholesome external world. Lenz hopes that he will be able to recover at Oberlin's home, with the practice of his Christian faith, and in the company of simple, unpretentious villagers. It appears temporarily as though this might be possible. When Kaufmann reminds him, however, of a »hostile« outer world, Lenz's feelings of guilt surface again and an even stronger process of alienation begins for him. Now Lenz's instinct for self-preservation has a weaker relationship with his surroundings; instead he must struggle with his rapidly diminishing mental powers against an intangible internalization, a mental numbness, a non-being. Lenz is thus forced to give his world of madness some kind of validity so that he does not completely lose himself.

The only possibility for being consists for him in his insanity and feelings of persecution. In an analysis of the style of the novella Peter Hasubeck illustrates the relationship between Lenz's mental state and the language Büchner uses. The missing verbs, the frequent repetitions, the fragmentary sentences, and the predominant use of parataxis are viewed as indications of a deterioration of the protagonist's mental powers.[9] It is also evident how frequently reflexive constructions and doubling occur in the second half of the novella. The tension with which the novella is introduced is thus internalized and becomes more evasive; it continues, however, in an externally less perceptible fashion and thus it is said of Lenz at the conclusion of the novella: »So lebte er hin . . . «

Notes

1. Georg Büchner, *Werke und Briefe* (München: Deutscher Taschenbuch Verlag, 1968), p. 65. All quotations are taken from this edition.

2. Erna Kritsch Neuse, »Büchners *Lenz*: Zur Struktur der Novelle,« *German Quarterly,* XLIII (1970), 201.

3. Ibid., p.202.

4. Ibid., p.205.

5. Mario Carlo Abutille, *Angst und Zynismus bei Georg Büchner* (Bern: Francke Verlag, 1969), p. 119.

6. Neuse, p.206.

7. Gerhart Baumann, »Georg Büchner: *Lenz*; Seine Struktur und der Reflex des Dramatischen,« *Euphorion,* 52 (1958), 169.

8. Ibid., p. 167.

9. Peter Hasubeck, »›Ruhe‹ und ›Bewegung‹ Versuch einer Stilanalyse von Georg Büchners *Lenz*,« *Germanisch-Romanische Monatsschrift,* XIX (1969), 36ff.

Kathryn R. Edmunds (essay date summer 1996)

SOURCE: Edmunds, Kathryn R. "*Lenz* and *Werther*: Büchner's Strategic Response to Goethe." *Monatshefte für deutschen Unterricht, deutsche Sprache und Literatur* 88, no. 2 (summer 1996): 176-96.

[*In the following essay, Edmunds contrasts the narrative structure and effects of* Lenz *with those of Goethe's novel* Werther, *asserting Büchner's tacit rejection of Goethe's literary worldview in his novella.*]

In *Dichtung und Wahrheit* (Book XIV, published 1814) Goethe explicitly diagnoses Jakob Michael Reinhold Lenz's anti-social self-absorption as a result of his

Werther-like suffering: "[er] litt . . . im allgemeinen von der Zeitgesinnung, welche durch die Schilderung Werthers abgeschlossen sein sollte,"[1] but Goethe is careful to distinguish Lenz from the truly Werther-like "redliche Seelen" to the extent that Lenz's behavior seemed exaggerated and voluntary. Roughly twenty years later Georg Büchner also associates the Storm and Stress poet with Werther, although not so explicitly; and, whereas Goethe is openly critical of Lenz, Büchner is subtly critical of *Werther.* It is reasonable to assume, as others have, that Büchner wrote his ***Lenz*** against or at least in dialogue with Goethe's portrait of his former friend.[2] It is furthermore possible that Büchner exploits the familiarity of *Werther* to develop a foil (within his narrative) against which he can develop a subtle and sophisticated contrast between his conceptions of the individual self, fate and autonomy and those propounded in the "goethische Kunstperiode,"[3] particularly by Goethe himself. A comparison of ***Lenz*** with the intertexts *Die Leiden des jungen Werthers* and passages from *Dichtung und Wahrheit* contributes not only to our understanding of Büchner's world view but also to our appreciation of his literary craft.

Discussions of the similarities and differences between ***Lenz*** and *Werther* are not infrequent. Most often scholars note Büchner's use of "Storm and Stress" diction and syntax, resounding of *Werther,* as a means to situate Lenz in his own time period.[4] Very few authors are interested in comparing the structure of the two texts, probably because they are so obviously dissimilar.[5] Also frequently acknowledged are the particular passages in ***Lenz*** which seem to be deliberate allusions to *Werther,* such as when it is said that Lenz "ging mit sich um wie mit einem kranken Kinde" (17).[6] The protagonists have been contrasted in terms of secular martyrdom,[7] self-awareness,[8] ability to articulate,[9] in terms of their relationships to nature as an aesthetic landscape,[10] and in terms of the relative security each derives from a theistic world view on the one hand (pantheism and monotheism in *Werther*) or a weltanschauung based on human empathy, on the other hand.[11] Whereas these earlier studies argue for the similarity and dissimilarity of the two texts by pointing to the divergent use of common themes (e.g. nature, art, madness) and to the disparity between similar "protagonists," I compare and contrast the two narratives as wholes and argue that Büchner's strong evocation of *Werther* allows a critical reception of "Goethezeit" values and assumptions to emerge. Büchner's method of using familiar language evocative of certain ideologies in a slightly iconoclastic and somewhat provocatively paradoxical way has been noted before;[12] here I add his manipulations of voice, plot and structure to his repertoire of subversive narrative tactics.

Such textual echoing is thus not viewed as merely an aesthetic or literary exercise but is rather seen as Büch-

ner's deliberate attempt to highlight the disparity between his understanding of the socially and physiologically determined individual and the concept of the autonomous individual held by the Storm and Stress, pre-French-revolutionary writers and maintained by many, including the reactionary older Goethe, well into the nineteenth century. The aim of this article is not to seek out socio-historical or biographical influences on the two authors' thinking; instead, it aims to show how Büchner's political and philosophical agenda concerning the essential equality and ultimate insignificance (with respect to the fatalism of world history) of all people is carried out in his ***Lenz***-fragment largely on the basis of intertextual allusions to an earlier popular text.

Before turning to *Werther* it is worth noting how Büchner works with the portrayal of Lenz from *Dichtung und Wahrheit,* where Goethe's confidence in the individual's ability to determine him- or herself is particularly pronounced. Goethe portrays Lenz as wilful but whimsical, talented but undisciplined; he is supposed to have been an irritating, scheming scoundrel: "er [pflegte] sich immer etwas *Fratzenhaftes* vorzusetzen, und eben deswegen diente es ihm zur beständigen Unterhaltung. . . . [M]it seinen Vorstellungen und Gefühlen verfuhr er *willkürlich,* damit er immerfort etwas zu tun haben möchte" (HA 10: 8; my emphases). What is remarkable is the degree to which Goethe attributes purpose to Lenz's antics; both "vorzusetzen" and "damit" indicate that Lenz decided to behave as he does, even if he—as Goethe surmised—had no other "Zweck" than his own perverse entertainment.

Where Goethe emphasizes Lenz's deliberate machinations, Büchner presents a man who usually does not know why he does what he is doing and who apologizes remorsefully for having done something he did not intend to do.

> [Er] verwirrte sich ganz und dabei hatte er einen unendlichen Trieb, mit allem um ihn im Geist *willkürlich* umzugehen. . . . Er amüsierte sich, die Häuser auf die Dächer zu stellen, die Menschen an- und auszukleiden, die wahnwitzigsten Possen auszusinnen. Manchmal fühlte er einen unwiderstehlichen Drang, das Ding auszuführen, und dann schnitt er entsetzliche *Fratzen.* . . . Dann war er wieder tief beschämt.
>
> (27-28; my emphases)

The "willkürlich" and "Fratzenhaftes" from Goethe's description of Lenz are echoed here, but the impish intentionality is absent; instead, Lenz is subject to a "Trieb" and a "Drang" stronger than he is. Unlike the portrait of Lenz presented by Goethe, Büchner's Lenz does not choose to entertain himself and others with deliberate tomfoolery and does not purposefully seek "durch die verkehrtesten Mittel . . . seinen Neigungen und Abneigungen Realität zu geben" (HA 10: 8). The following comparison of *Lenz* and *Werther* explores the ways in which Büchner's text plays off of Goethe's work so as to undermine Goethe's view not only of Lenz in particular but also of individual autonomy in general.

In *Werther* a fictional editor presents a collection of letters in a book which he hopes will provide comfort to his readers. As is well-known, each of the letters presents a coherent episode or emotion, such as an experience of union with nature (10 May 1771), Lotte at the well (6 July 1771), Werther's visit to the town in which he was born (9 May 1772), or Werther's encounter with the insane flower-seeking man (30 November 1772). Toward the end of the novel, the editor interrupts the sequence of letters in order to offer a third-person account of the last days before the letter-writer ends his own life. The plot of the Werther-story is a clear causal sequence of love, frustration, attempts at consolation, followed by despair and suicide. This is framed by the editor's comments which present his own loss of a friend as potential consolation for his Werther-like readers.

Werther's despair of possessing Lotte in this world is neutralized by his confidence that he will have her in heaven; similarly, the editor's sadness at the loss of his friend is tempered by his anticipation that his "Büchlein" will serve as a friend to others, that the death will not have been meaningless. The editor intends for Werther's "Leiden" and death, like Christ's, to benefit somebody. Similarly, the protagonist died with the tentative belief that Albert and Lotte's "Frieden" could be restored through his departure: "O daß ihr glücklich wäret durch meinen Tod!" (HA 6: 121). Although he admits with what may be feigned humility, "das ward nur wenigen Edeln gegeben, ihr Blut für die Ihrigen zu vergießen und durch ihren Tod ein neues, hundertfältiges Leben ihren Freunden anzufachen" (HA 6: 123), he seems in fact to count himself among these few. His last meal of bread and wine and his confidence that he goes "zu [s]einem Vater" and that he and Lotte "werden sein . . . werden [sich] wiedersehen" (HA 6: 117) indicate that he—in the context of Christianity—situates his suicide as martyrdom rather than as an unforgivable sin. In his letter of November 15, 1772, Werther manages (in an idiosyncratic, indeed blasphemous manner) to deny Christ's intervention for himself without denying his existence or his sacrifice for the rest of humanity: "Wenn ich nun ihm [Christ] nicht gegeben bin? Wenn mich nun der Vater für sich behalten will?" (HA 6: 86) and in his letter of November 30, 1772, he compares his suicide to the prodigal son's return to the father and argues that "[ihm] ist nur wohl" in the presence of God (HA 6: 91). These references to Christianity establish a positive teleological trajectory against the text's negative trajectory toward suicide.[13] The trajectories give the novel direction and a goal. From the outset the reader

knows that Werther will die, but she does not know the cause and course of his suffering; she reads in order to find out. Thus, the reader, the editor and the letter-writer all act according to purposes, and presumably they all succeed in achieving their respective goals.

In contrast with *Werther*, *Lenz* seems to lack a plot and a protagonist[14] as these are commonly understood. The narrative doesn't have a particular goal or direction (other than to return to the point of departure); there is no particular story to tell, and therefore there is no suspense or anticipation.[15] Lenz's condition improves and then worsens, so we are told, but the descriptions of his activities remain similar throughout. As in *Werther* there are several episodic "scenes" presented chronologically; these include scenes such as Lenz's walk through the mountains; his vision of his mother; his sermon; the "Kunstmonolog"; his attempt to resurrect the child; the episode with the cat; his profane rejection of God as a non-saviour; his complaints about the heaviness of the air and the loudness of the silence; and finally, his passive departure. Common motifs, such as the frequent use of the words "Ruhe"[16] and "Gewalt" or the recurring attacks of "Angst" or "Wahnsinn," run throughout the narrative, giving it unity, but not a unified plot. The beginning and end are determined by Lenz's arrival in and departure from the valley; thus time and space—not a specific "Handlung"—delimit the narrative.

Although it is argued that Lenz becomes progressively worse (after an initial period of apparent improvement), one can also assert that his condition does not substantially change. His sense of well-being rises and falls, alternating with phases of fear, ennui, madness, and desperation. Nothing is permanent: after his "Triumph-Gesang der Hölle" (22) he is still able to pray; after the complaint of "Langeweile" and his lack of "behaglichen Zeitvertreib" (25), he immediately asserts that it would be worthwhile (and therefore not "langweilig") to investigate "ob [er] träume oder wache" (25); after the narrator describes him as "gleichgültig" and resigned, he is said to have tried to harm himself. Thematically, the emphasis is on regular cycles and irregular fluctuation, not on beginnings or ends: the waxing and waning of the moon, the shifting light and dark, the wave-like line of the mountain silhouettes, the ticking of a clock, the rise and fall of voices, the rhythm of imagined dressing and undressing. These rhythms are reinforced grammatically with pairs such as "auf- und ab-," "an- und aus-," "hin- und her-," and "bald . . . bald." Events themselves recur: Lenz bathes himself in the fountain at night on several occasions (8, 9, 24); he jumps from the window more than once (25, 30); he speaks of his beloved first with Frau Oberlin and later with Pastor Oberlin; his attempt to raise the dead child can be paired with the strange man's attempt to heal the sick girl; twice Lenz stays in bed for a long time and is visited there by Oberlin (24, 29); twice he is told to return home to his father—once by Kaufmann and once by Oberlin; twice Oberlin is irritated by Lenz's blasphemy (25, 29). These recurring events never lead us to believe that Lenz may recover and never allude to some sort of impending disaster, unlike the fairly frequent references to departure and suicide in *Werther.* In *Lenz* we don't anticipate anything; we observe. What we observe is not the story or "Schicksal" of one particularly extraordinary "Unglücklichen" but rather the pulses of nature as they are manifested in mountain landscapes, quiet valleys, small communities, and in the acts and thoughts of people.

The differences in the plots of the two works are emphasized by the differences in structure and narrative voices. The pronounced trajectories of the plot in *Werther* are supported by the linearity of the letter sequence and the neat, apparently arbitrary division of the book into two parts, "erstes Buch" and "zweites Buch." The series of distinct dated letters (month and day) makes the passage of time into a heavily-highlighted structural feature, while the division into two parts means that there are two end points toward which the reader reads, thus enhancing the focus on goals or resolutions. The two parts of the novel echo one another and emphasize the themes of expectation and disappointment and of departure and loss. The fact that each part ends with Werther's decision to leave Lotte subordinates all other alternations of hope and loss to this dominant drama; similarly, the timeless, tableau-like nature of many of the letters is absorbed by the movement of the story viewed over time. The editor's foreword and his final report place the whole Lotte-complex, the story told through letters, in a context emphasizing both the editor's relationship to the reader and the protagonist's quasi-martyrdom for the sake of similarly passionate and introspective individuals.

In contrast with this highly structured and purposeful epistolary novel, *Lenz* appears loosely impressionistic. Where *Werther* is structured linearly, like the Old and New Testaments with the anticipation and fulfillment of certain events, *Lenz* is structured circularly: various, perhaps unrelated episodes and vignettes form points along the circumference of a circle beginning and ending in more or less the same place. The opening description of Lenz wandering through the mountains is echoed in the closing description of him being driven away from the mountains; the earlier images of red climbing up on top of blue, of the earth becoming "klein wie ein wandelnder Stern" (6) are picked up again at the end by the images of mountains rising up "wie eine tiefblaue Kristallwelle" (30) into the evening's red horizon and of the earth "wie ein goldner Pokal" (31).[17] This subtle circularity is reinforced by Lenz's descriptions of the paintings mentioned in his conversation with Kaufmann.

Just as Werther's story of the young girl's suicide (August 12, 1771), or his stories of the "Bauerbursch" (May 30, 1771; September 4, 1772), and of the demented former-scribe (November 30, 1772) provide encapsulated versions of his own tragic drama, so too do the narrative-versions of Lenz's favorite paintings offer a small-scale pattern which the entire narrative follows. The description of the first painting begins "Es ist ein trüber, dämmernder Abend" (15) and ends, summarily, "so ist das Bild, mit dem einförmigen bräunlichen Ton darüber, dem trüben stillen Abend" (16). Before the description returns to this point of departure, Lenz presents a sequence of events, as if the painting had a temporal dimension: the stranger comes, speaks, breaks bread, the others recognize him, it becomes dark, "es tritt sie etwas Unbegreifliches an" (16), but this is not frightening. Lenz's description uses the same short paratactic clauses so characteristic of *Lenz* as a whole. The grammatical subject shifts from "er" (the stranger), to "sie" (the disciples), to the impersonal "es" in the same way that agency in the main narrative moves around among Lenz, other people, and impersonal forces.

The presentation of the second painting is quite similar. It begins, "Eine Frau sitzt in ihrer Kammer, das Gebetbuch in der Hand . . ." (16), and closes with this same image: "die Frau liest den Text nach" (16). Again the description consists of brief clauses; again Lenz "reads" more than could possibly be depicted visually—the woman couldn't go to church, but she could hear the bells and choir resounding over the landscape; again the presentation of the painting flows in a way similar to the flow of *Lenz* as a whole. The circularity of the narrative descriptions of the paintings undermines the strength of the temporal dimension (linearity) Lenz was able to project onto the atemporal scenes. This tension between linear chronology and a circularity resisting progression also characterizes *Lenz* as a whole, but because the first and final scenes of the essay are so similar, the tendency toward circularity dominates over the suggestions of progression.

Whereas in *Werther* the "wiederholte Spiegelungen" (HA 12: 322) pertain to the plot and themes, in *Lenz* they pertain to visual images, verbal motifs and narrative form. Of course, both paintings have a Christian theme, and Lenz's struggles with faith and blasphemy are a much-discussed aspect of Büchner's essay,[18] but in Lenz's descriptions, as in the text as a whole, the specific content is significantly less important than "eine unendliche Schönheit, die aus einer Form in die andre tritt, ewig aufgeblättert, verändert" (15). Thus, although *Werther* and *Lenz* could be compared with regard to the role of religion for each of the protagonists, I am only concerned with the Christian aspects of *Werther* to the extent that they enhance the linear, goal-oriented effect of the text. The Christian aspects of *Lenz,* such as Oberlin's unchallenged faith in a transcendental care-taker, do not lend linearity to the text as a whole, since the narrator does not indicate any particular bias toward the idea that life and death are endowed with some sort of divine purpose.

Goethe's text emphasizes progression and the possibility for positively influencing society and its values: a given sequence of events is recognized as a story which culminates with a suicide and with the question as to whether the Christian God, if not the Church, can accept the misunderstood iconoclast; also questioned are the social factors leading to this death. Büchner's text emphasizes non-development but not stasis, change but not progression: the text has no particular story, it asks no questions and it provides no answers. For Büchner, form, "das Gesetz der Schönheit" (2: 292), is all we can hold onto. This "Urgesetz," presented in "Ueber Schädelnerven" as a philosophical natural law, refutes the "Zweckmäßigkeit" of the teleological interpretation of phenomena. The "notwendige Harmonie" of *Lenz* results not from a uniform progression toward a known goal, but rather from the "einfachsten Rissen und Linien" (2: 292) of the narrated events and attitudes.[19] Whereas the structure and intratextual resonances of *Werther* rely on the fact that an individual chooses to act in certain ways and anticipates the consequences of these choices, Büchner's text relies on nature's rhythms and cycles and on the fact that people—even if they perceive themselves as autonomous and distinct—are as subject to the impersonal laws of nature (including "das Gesetz der Schönheit") as are all other phenomena.

Consistent with these disparate functions and effects of plot and structure are the differences in the narrative perspectives of *Werther* and *Lenz*. This stylistic variance has a profound effect on the way we view the content of the narratives, on the way we perceive the speakers, and, ultimately, on the way we understand the author's concept of self. Both Werther and the editor have fairly stable first-person points of view. The narrator of *Lenz* does not offer such stability of perspective, although he does offer some distance from Lenz.[20] Just as the editor comes in to "replace" Werther's voice once he is close to death, so too does the narrator of *Lenz* maintain a greater distance from the figure's perspective toward the end of the piece. However, the narrator of *Lenz* cannot be located and defined, which means that even though we move away from the dizzying perspective of Lenz, we are still not granted alternatively secure footing.

The extensive hypotactic sentence from the first paragraph of Büchner's generally paratactic text is frequently associated with *Werther* and encourages comparison and contrast of the two texts. Because the sentence is so long (twenty-five lines in Reclam) and because most readers are familiar with it, I do not cite

it in full. Lenz, the person through whom the landscape is focalized, does not appear until quite late in the sentence (in the seventeenth of the twenty-five lines), in the impersonal clause, "riß es ihm in der Brust" (6). Lenz's passivity is emphasized not only by the frequent use of impersonal "es" constructions but also, as David Horton has observed, by the sentences where abstractions (e.g. "Angst" and "Schmerz") act as subjects of transitive verbs.[21] The less often Lenz appears as the grammatical subject, the less we are inclined to think of him as a philosophical subject. Moreover, the narrator anthropomorphizes inanimate phenomena so much that Lenz—even when he is the grammatical subject—does not appear distinct from the scene he observes: the voices on the cliffs "awaken" and seem to want to "sing" to the earth; the clouds "jump" like horses; the sun, armed with a sword, comes and goes; red climbs onto blue. Lenz's "dehnen" and "wühlen," his "still stehen" and "Augen schließen" seem as premeditated or unpremeditated as the wind's lullaby or the storm's goading of the clouds. Because Lenz is described by a consciousness other than his own, he appears as elemental, as involuntary as other natural phenomena. While Raimar Stefan Zons, among others, argues that Lenz "versucht . . . am Anfang noch, einen Zugang zur Natur zu gewinnen,"[22] I argue that Lenz is not presented as distinct from "nature" (wind, sunlight, mountains as non-sentient nature); rather, he is part of the landscape, part of the natural sublimity. The creative and destructive forces Werther observes so fondly and so despairingly in the landscapes may not necessarily be visible *to* Lenz, but they are visible *in* him.[23]

In the clause "er meinte, er müsse den Sturm in sich ziehen" the verb "meinen" suggests consciousness and intention, but the "müssen" counters this by implying that Lenz felt compelled without choice and without reflection. We recall Büchner's passionate questioning after the "muß" of human nature: "Das *muß* ist eins von den Verdammungsworten, womit der Mensch getauft worden. . . . Was ist das, was in uns lügt, mordet, stiehlt" (2: 426). Something acts through Lenz; Lenz does not act.

The sobering sentence following the passionately accumulative one is this: "Aber es waren nur Augenblicke, und dann erhob er sich nüchtern, fest, ruhig, als wäre ein Schattenspiel vor ihm vorübergezogen, er wußte von nichts mehr" (6). The narrator's suggestion that Lenz arose as if a "Schattenspiel" had passed offers a parallel, as we shall see, to the "Schauspiel" Werther describes, but in *Lenz* the analogy to a performance is produced by the narrator, and it is unclear if the narrator is here "conceptualizing phenomena through the perspective of the protagonist"[24] or if he is organizing the phenomena in a way Lenz would be incapable of doing: as a coherent and meaningful performance. Here and throughout the text, the line between authorial and figural perspective is often blurred or obliterated, thus also blurring the distinction between subjectivity and objectivity, and even between subject and object. If, as Büchner's Lenz recommends, "man . . . senke sich in das Leben des Geringsten und gebe es wieder" (14), then what happens to one's own perspective and identity? Is selfhood something that comes and goes like light and shadow, or is it something fixed? In **Lenz,** such questions are solicited not only explicitly by statements referring to Lenz's loss of a single stable identity (e.g. "es war als sei er doppelt" [28]) but also—more subtly and more pervasively—by the narrator's tendency to slip in and out of Lenz's consciousness, as if there were no firm boundaries between the observer and the observed.

In *Werther,* on the other hand, readers are confident that Werther's identity is defined, even if he sometimes fears he has lost himself: "Wenn wir uns selbst fehlen, fehlt uns doch alles" (August 22; HA 6: 53).The stability of his identity results not from what he says and does, but from the narrative perspective of his letters and from the editor's comments. For contrast with the long "wenn"-sentence of **Lenz** just discussed, we can look at one of Werther's three extensive nature descriptions (May 10, 1771; August 18, 1771 and December 12, 1772):[25] the third offers, as Zons has noted,[26] the most similarities to Büchner's introductory description in **Lenz**:

> Nachts nach eilfe rannte ich hinaus. Ein fürchterliches Schauspiel, vom Fels herunter die wühlenden Fluten in dem Mondlichte wirbeln zu sehen, über Äcker und Wiesen und Hecken und alles, und das weite Tal hinauf und hinab *eine* stürmende See im Sausen des Windes! Und wenn dann der Mond wieder hervortrat und über der schwarzen Wolke ruhte, und vor mir hinaus die Flut in fürchterlich herrlichem Widerschein rollte und klang: da überfiel mich ein Schauer und wieder ein Sehnen! Ach, mit offenen Armen stand ich gegen den Abgrund und atmete hinab! hinab! und verlor mich in der Wonne, meine Qualen, meine Leiden da hinabzustürmen, dahinzubrausen wie die Wellen . . . O Wilhelm! wie gern hätte ich mein Menschsein drum gegeben, mit jenem Sturmwinde die Wolken zu zerreißen, die Fluten zu fassen! . . .
>
> Und wie ich wehmütig hinabsah auf ein Plätzchen, wo ich mit Lotten unter einer Weide geruht . . .—das war auch überschwemmt, und kaum daß ich die Weide erkannte! Wilhelm! Und ihre Wiesen, dachte ich, die Gegend um ihr Jagdhaus! wie verstört jetzt vom reißenden Strome unsere Laube, dacht' ich. Und der Vergangenheit Sonnenstrahl blickte herein, wie einem Gefangenen ein Traum von Herden, Wiesen und Ehrenämtern. Ich stand!—
>
> (HA 6: 98-99)

Werther intentionally goes out into the storm during the "menschenfeindliche[] Jahrszeit"; his "ich" stands prominently as a voluntary witness to the performance.

The first-person narration of Werther's letter suggests that he is aware of himself as actor in a staged scene. The environment is itself identified as "nächtliche[] Szenen"; Werther enters the stage. The details of how he stood, how he breathed, how he "wehmütig hinabsah," all contribute to the impression that he is describing his own performance. The fact that he reports of a past event, in the past tense, undermines any suggestion of spontaneous expression appropriate to the actual moment of intense feeling; the exclamation "Wilhelm!" combined with this use of the past tense directs our attention as much to the reflective narrating letter-writer as to the pained wretch desperate on the cliff's brink. The most remarkable details of Werther's self-description are the direct quotation of his own past thoughts: "Und ihre Wiesen, dachte ich, . . . wie verstört jetzt vom reißenden Strome unsere Laube! dacht' ich." If his intention were not self-dramatization, he would have at most reported his thoughts in indirect narration, or summary, if at all. The exclamatory expression of the thoughts (which is archetypical for Storm and Stress speech patterns) appears comical when set off with the sober inquit phrases "dachte ich." The fact that he quotes his thoughts directly and describes himself in such detail reveals that he finds himself and his thoughts worthy of an audience.

The details of Werther's self-descriptions are always (here and throughout the novel) pregnant with meaning; his behavior and gestures are intended to communicate to Wilhelm and us his inner state, but because he is always aware of his behavior as an act of communication, we begin to question its genuineness; he could perform *as if* he felt and thought a certain way, without actually feeling this way. Whereas the gestures and facial expressions in Büchner's text are included for their own sake, as if the narrator were following the advice of the fictional Lenz by including the "Zuckungen . . . Andeutungen, [das] ganz[] feine[], kaum bemerkte[] Mienenspiel" (14), those in Werther's letters are "zweckmäßig" (like the teleological explanations of natural phenomena discussed in the *Probevorlesung*) and carry a message the addressee is invited to decode. When he picks flowers, arranges them in a bouquet and tosses it in the river (August 10, 1771), we are not to overlook this mime as a chance detail included in his self-description; rather, we are to read it as a meaningful communication, suggesting perhaps his despair at not being able to keep Lotte (his picked flowers) or foreshadowing his suicide (perhaps an allusion to Ophelia's suicide). Similarly, gnashing teeth indicate fury and anger or impatience; walking "auf und ab" communicates restless nervousness. A tear in his or Lotte's eye means strong and admirable emotion. Such gestures very well could appear as unreflected and spontaneous communication if they were to be reported by someone other than Werther. However, because Werther includes such details in his letters, we suspect that he is a script-writer aware of how such gestures will be interpreted; he performs accordingly.

Werther is observed by Schiller to be a sentimental character, but Büchner's Lenz (insofar as he might be considered as having a definite, describable personality at all) would have to be regarded as naive.[27] Werther's incessant self-awareness and habitual writing undermine his attempts to be the natural unaffected and spontaneous hero of his own narrative. When he says he is losing his mind ("ich soll nicht zu mir selbst kommen" [November 30; HA 6: 88]); "ich [habe] keine Besinnungskraft mehr" [December 14; HA 6: 100]) we are perplexed by the paradoxical nature of the claim: how can he display such ability to analyze himself and write of himself if he has lost control over or contact with himself? He would like to lose control, but cannot. This is the determining characteristic of Werther's "sentimental" personality; his outpourings imitate spontaneous bursts of emotion, but they are rhetorically designed with a view toward their effect on the audience. He is never without control.

Werther's "I" is lost neither in nature (landscapes) nor in the overpowering love for Lotte; he is always conscious of his condition. His self-awareness and reflexivity help establish him as a stable subject. Obviously, this stability does not result from a consistency in attitude and outlook—which are all too labile—but rather arises from or becomes evident in the permanence of the letter-writing "ich." Because this "ich" is able to write effectively and well, the letters reflect the confidence from day to day and season to season that the "ich" is a definable self, with one consistent identity over time: "wie ich so wissentlich in das alles, Schritt vor Schritt, hineingegangen bin! Wie ich über meinen Zustand immer so klar gesehen . . . jetzt noch so klar sehe" (August 8; HA 6: 44). The fact that Werther reflects on his present behavior and relates it to his past behavior indicates a sense of continuous identity: "Bin ich nicht noch eben derselbe, der ehemals in aller Fülle der Empfindung herumschwebte [?] . . . und dies Herz ist jetzt tot" (November 3; HA 6: 84). As Peter Brenner observes in his study on the emergence, maintenance and disappearance of the subject in eighteenth century novels, "die Möglichkeit, sich zu sich selbst als einem immer Identischen zu verhalten, ist . . . eine Voraussetzung für das Erreichen nichtrestringierter Subjektivität."[28] For Werther, the non-restricted subjectivity—this incessant consciousness of himself—resists the possible dissolution of the self through total union with nature or with another aspect of the object-world. This self-awareness paradoxically reflects a unified self even when the self claims to be fragmented. Although Büchner's Lenz is treated as a single person with a continuous history, he is not depicted as aware of himself as "ein[] immer Identische[r]" (Brenner), and his "history" is less a story of his loss of sanity than it is an account

of the particular course of nature his life displays. Phases of lucidity and coherence alternate with phases of confusion, and each phase may be contaminated by traces of the other, just as for Werther perception of destruction and loss can be accompanied with a recollection of the previously perceived creativity and plenty. Werther, as letter writer, shows himself to be aware not only of his current reflection on the loss of previous joy but also of himself as the unifying constant linking the opposite perceptions in one consciousness: "Selbst diese Anstrengung, jene unsägliche Gelüste zurückzurufen, wieder auszusprechen, hebt meine Seele über sich selbst und läßt mich dann das Bange des Zustandes doppelt empfinden, der mich jetzt umgibt" (August 18; HA 6: 52). Büchner's Lenz, on the other hand, is presented as someone as victimized by his memories and intuitions as he is by the ephemeral circumstances determining his experience: "Ahnungen von seinem alten Zustande durchzuckten ihn, und warfen Streiflichter in das wüste Chaos seines Geistes" (20). Although one might argue that the mental chaos is responsible for Lenz's loss of a sense of identity, Büchner's text does not support the concept of an autonomous self-identified individual even apart from madness.

Werther's control and agency as a subject are primarily exercised and displayed linguistically. He is concerned with his ability to express himself and is impressed by the "Bauerbursch" because he has so much feeling in his "Erzählung" about his unattainable beloved (May 30, 1771). As if in order to acquire this force and fire of passion, Werther soon falls in love with Lotte and then writes about it to Wilhelm (June 16, 1771).[29] For Werther, Lotte's absence even more than her presence provides what he is looking for: an occasion to express his heartfelt joy and longing with language of his soul, with "den ganz wahren Ausdrücken der Natur" (May 4; HA 6: 7).

Lenz, in contrast, cannot be said to do anything so purposefully. The thought of his beloved does not haunt him until the maid's song of her distant "Schatz" unexpectedly recalls Friederike (not named in the text) to his mind: "Das fiel auf ihn, er verging fast unter den Tönen. . . . Er faßte sich ein Herz, er konnte nicht mehr schweigen, er mußte davon sprechen" (20).[30] Although the love-triangle mentioned very briefly in *Lenz* ("sie liebte noch einen anderen") might offer a point of comparison to *Werther* with regard to the protagonists' relative skill in coping with desire and guilt,[31] of more significance is, in my opinion, the fact that Werther chooses to fall in love, chooses to develop and sustain an obsession with Lotte, while Lenz responds apparently (in Büchner's text) without much reflection and without an awareness of optional responses to whatever stimulus presents itself: a vision of his mother incites the desire to preach; learning of the child's death compels him to try to resurrect her; hearing about a maid's distant beloved reminds him of his own.

When compared to Werther's control over his heart and his language, Lenz's difficulties with verbal expression are especially striking. Again, the fact that Werther writes and Lenz is written about plays a significant role in our perception of the characters and, in *Lenz,* of the narrator. Another hypotactic sentence from *Lenz* seems to echo one of Werther's highly controlled sentences, and serves, in its context, to highlight the contrast between Werther and Lenz with respect both to language and to the sense of lack. In the letter to Lotte of January 20th Werther writes: "Der Sauerteig, der mein Leben in Bewegung setzte, fehlt; der Reiz, der mich in tiefen Nächten munter erhielt, ist hin, der mich des Morgens aus dem Schlafe weckte, ist weg" (HA 6: 65).

Werther is capable of describing lack in language and syntax which reveal a fair amount of pleasure and finesse. The three parallel hypotactic clauses are measured and controlled: the subjects of the first two main verbs are metaphors for Lotte ("Sauerteig" and "Reiz") and the fact that the third main verb lacks its own distinct subject rhetorically recreates the situation described: "der Reiz" "ist weg." Werther's manifest pleasure in language belies the supposed apathy and emptiness.

A sentence from *Lenz* echoes this one of Werther's and resounds with the now familiar oscillating cadence:

> . . . alles was er an Ruhe aus der Nähe Oberlins und aus der Stille des Thals geschöpft hatte, war weg; die Welt, die er hatte nutzen wollen, hatte einen ungeheuren Riß, er hatte keinen Haß, keine Liebe, keine Hoffnung, eine schreckliche Leere und doch eine folternde Unruhe, sie auszufüllen. Er hatte *nichts.*
>
> (27)

The hypotaxis of the first clause imitates the first two clauses of Werther's statement cited above. The second clause exchanges the predicate expressing absence ("fehlt") in Werther's sentence for a predicate paradoxically expressing possession and deprivation simultaneously ("hatte" + "Riß," insofar as "Riß" is defined as a hole or rip). The *Lenz*-narrator then deserts the hypotactic syntax but continues with this model of "haben" plus negative (the three adjectives "kein," the paradoxical substantive "Leere," and the prefix "un-"), culminating with the "nichts" of the following sentence. Lenz's situation is fundamentally different from that of Werther both because that which is missing is much more comprehensive than an absent beloved, and, more significantly, because he can't talk about it. The narrator is responsible for the careful organization of the sentence; the narrator is capable, as is Werther, of achieving a

stable perspective on the current mental climate and of communicating this perspective in an orderly, controlled manner. As if in deliberate contrast with Werther's linguistic expertise, the *Lenz*-narrator describes Lenz's disturbed relationship to speech: "Im Gespräch stockte er oft, eine unbeschreibliche Angst befiel ihn, er hatte das Ende seines Satzes verloren; dann meinte er, er müsse das zuletzt gesprochene Wort behalten und immer sprechen . . ." (27). Moreover, Lenz is said to mistake his own voice for that of another person and to mistake himself for the chance people he thinks about. With the disturbed, uncontrolled relationship to language comes an inability to hold onto oneself as a definable, stable self.

While these close readings from each text point out differences between passages in Werther's voice and passages in the voice of the *Lenz*-narrator, they do not address the passages written in the voice of the fictional editor in *Werther.* The editor's section at the end of the *Die Leiden des jungen Werther* is, from a narratological standpoint, much closer to *Lenz* than are Werther's letters. The editor, like the narrator of Büchner's text, not only uses direct and indirect speech, but also occasionally uses a "dual voice" which merges his and his protagonist's voices. The following excerpts provide examples of this dual voice; the sentences which could express either Werther or the editor's thoughts are in italics:

> Da er durch die Linden mußte, um nach der Schenke zu kommen, wo sie den Körper hingelegt hatten, entsetzt' er sich vor dem sonst so geliebten Platze. *Jene Schwelle, worauf die Nachbarskinder so oft gespielt hatten war mit Blut besudelt. Liebe und Treue, die schönsten menschlichen Empfindungen, hatten sich in Gewalt und Mord verwandelt.*
>
> (HA 6: 95; my emphasis)

Because our perspective was determined for so long by what Werther reports in his letters, we are now inclined to view such evaluative assertions (e.g. "die schönsten menschlichen Empfindungen") as Werther's own. Once Werther arrives at the scene of the crime, we see through his eyes. Similarly, when Werther encounters the captured murderer we enter his thoughts: "Werther sah hin und blieb nicht lange zweifelhaft. *Ja! es war der Knecht, der jene Witwe so sehr liebte . . .*" (HA 6: 95; my emphasis).

Despite the fact that the editor of *Werther* uses some of the same techniques as the narrator of *Lenz* will use, we are not inclined to consider him or Werther as dreamy and borderless as Lenz and the narrator seem to be. This results primarily from the fact that the editor refers to himself and to his project, and he gives us direct access to his thinking and to his process of gathering information. Thus the editor of Werther's letters does not hide, while the narrator of *Lenz* refers to himself only once and in the first person plural ("uns" 9,9) as if he didn't mean himself specifically but rather all of humankind. If the *Lenz*-narrator unobtrusively "sinks" into the essence of those people and places he presents, the fictional editor of *Werther,* like Werther himself, projects ideas onto those he tries to understand. In the case of Lotte, for instance, he decides that he can project his own version of a female soul onto her in order to figure out what her thoughts would have been: "eine schöne weibliche Seele sich in die ihrige denken" (HA 6: 101). Büchner's Lenz, on the other hand, would become completely confused, were he to attempt to imagine or project a "soul" for another person: "dachte er an eine fremde Person, oder stellte er sie sich lebhaft vor, so war es ihm, als würde er sie selbst" (27). The fact that both Werther and the editor have well-defined identities and each speaks, at times, in the first-person means that in the few instances in which the editor allows his perspective to coalesce with Werther's we do not feel we have lost either person as a definable and defined self.

Werther, even in his most extreme conditions of self-alienation, even when the editor presents him as the victim of abstractions ("unüberwindlich bemächtigte sich die Teilnehmung seiner und es ergriff ihn eine unsägliche Begierde, den Menschen zu retten" [HA 6: 96]), even then Werther is in control and acts logically, with forethought. Sometimes this forethought is presented explicitly by the editor: "er hatte sich gesagt, es [suicide] solle keine übereilte, keine rasche Tat sein, er wolle mit der besten Überzeugung, mit der möglichst ruhigen Entschlossenheit diesen Schritt tun" (HA 6: 100). But sometimes the logic of Werther's thinking and actions is communicated through the simple conjunction "daß": "Er fühlte ihn so unglücklich, er fand ihn als Verbrecher selbst so schuldlos, er setzte sich so tief in seine Lage, *daß* er gewiß glaubte, auch andere davon zu überzeugen" (HA 6: 96; my emphasis). The "daß" presents Werther's confidence in persuading others as a result of his own strong feelings of empathy. In *Lenz* a remarkably parallel passage does not include the "daß," suggesting that Lenz's feelings and actions are not linked by deliberation and by awareness of cause and effect, but rather only temporally as consecutive experiences and grammatically as paratactic clauses of the same sentence: "Das Kind kam ihm so verlassen vor, und er sich so allein und einsam; er warf sich über die Leiche nieder; der Tod erschreckte ihn, ein heftiger Schmerz faßte ihn an, diese Züge, dieses stille Gesicht sollte verwesen, er warf sich nieder . . ." (22). While we are inclined to see Lenz's actions, like Werther's, as a result of his feelings, the causality is not explicitly stated.[32] Surprisingly, this lack of explicit causality ("daß") creates the effect of an even stronger causal relationship: throwing himself down on the small corpse is an automatic, instinctive response to the sense of

aloneness, the child's and his. A "daß" would imply a moment of reflection, a pause during which he could decide what to do.

Werther is not the only character the editor presents as an autonomous, purposeful individual, just as Lenz is not the only person presented in Büchner's text as lacking autonomy. In his discussion of Lotte's dilemma the editor presents her as someone aware of her freedom and able to make a choice: "Wie sollte sie ihrem Mann entgegengehen?" (HA 6: 118). The fact that the editor is able to speculate on a different outcome for the story reinforces the fact that he, at least, believes that people's free choices can affect the course of events: "Hätte eine glückliche Vertraulichkeit sie [Albert and Lotte] früher wieder einander nähergebracht . . . vielleicht wäre unser Freund noch zu retten gewesen" (HA 6: 119). In *Lenz* we are not invited to speculate in such a way about how events could be altered by the actions of the individuals affected by them: we have no convincing etiology for Lenz's illness, no clear motivation for his actions, and no suggestion as to how his situation could be improved. In fact, in *Lenz,* we are rarely shown alternatives or decisions at all. The result is that people as well as circumstance appear to be guided by "de[r] gräßliche[] Fatalismus der Geschichte"—the force Büchner felt operated behind the ineffectual revolutionary efforts of reformers during the French Revolution and which he felt destined all individuals to "eine entsetzliche Gleichheit."[33]

Because Lenz is going mad, it is perhaps invalid to combine observations concerning how the narrator presents him with those concerning how the narrator presents other people.[34] Nevertheless, it is important to consider the others in order to assess what might be considered "healthy" or mentally stable in this (con)text. If madness is solely responsible for the elusiveness of a defined self, then we could not argue that Büchner questions the autonomy and individual essence of all people. Oberlin is the most significant person in the text other than Lenz. In analyzing the presentation of Oberlin it should be recalled that Büchner's primary source was a first-person account written by Oberlin and that several passages from Büchner's text follow Oberlin's wording almost exactly, switching only the first-person focalization to the third-person. The effect of this switch is, above all, to suggest at least superficially that the narrator has no more or less access to Oberlin's consciousness then he does to Lenz's, since now both men are presented in the third-person. In Oberlin's text, we are given his thoughts and impressions directly, and we are not given Lenz's other than in what he is reported as having said. In Büchner's text this is almost reversed, such that we are allowed much more access to Lenz's mind than we are to Oberlin's. However, Oberlin's thoughts and actions are reported carefully, although without as much detail as are Lenz's and without as much coalescing of authorial and figural perspective.

Oberlin responds to whatever comes his way and he interprets the events according to his own world view, as if he were not even aware that there may be other ways of looking at things. He is said to have seen Lenz's arrival in Steintal as a "Schickung Gottes" (13); he accepts him and responds to him. Oberlin, like Lenz, is not depicted as having much autonomy: he draws lots to determine what he should do (10). In his own record Oberlin presents decisions in detail, explaining or suggesting why he chose as he did. His record is essentially an apology: he wants to explain why he took in Lenz and why he had him sent away. He explains that he knew Lenz (a theologian) was coming before Lenz actually arrived, and he explains how he makes sense initially of Lenz's bizarre behavior: "Herr K . . . liebt das kalte Bad auch, und Herr L . . . ist ein Freund von Hn. K . . ." (36);[35] he explains his need for a break from weekly preaching, before he says that Lenz held the sermon; he presents several instances of how Lenz was not in control of himself, thus justifying his decision to have Lenz guarded and then eventually transported to Strassbourg. In Büchner's text Oberlin is presented as responding but not as deciding to respond in a specific manner.

The only instance in Büchner's text in which Oberlin is aware of a choice is when he may choose whether or not to go with Kaufmann to Switzerland; even here the narrator says that Oberlin's desire to meet Lavater "bestimmte ihn," thus making Oberlin the grammatical object and minimizing the suggestion of actual volition (17). Otherwise Oberlin is presented as responding invariably, as if automatically, in accordance with what he regards as God's plan. In other words, I argue that he does not choose to reprimand Lenz for his aimless, godless life-style and does not choose to regard it as sinful. Rather, he simply does regard it as sinful, and he perceives it as his obligation to admonish Lenz: this is what the conditions of his upbringing and experience have made into necessity for Oberlin. Thus, I do not think that Büchner intends to criticize Oberlin any more than he intends to criticize Lenz.[36] Büchner's text does not pass judgment: it presents people as the involuntary and "necessary" products of nature and society.

Such refraining from judgment is not possible in *Werther*; here individuals are considered responsible not only for their actions and inactions (e.g. if only Lotte and Albert had talked with each other), but also, to a large extent, for their moods (cf. the discussion about "üble Laune," July 1; HA 6: 32). *Werther* presents the individual as unique and autonomous, capable of decisions whether they be influenced by strong emotion or by reason. The well-delineated voices and perspectives

of the editor and the letter-writer reinforce the underlying confidence in distinct, largely self-determining selves. These selves are not viewed entirely as products of external, or even internal circumstance, but as beings with souls—some aspect of which is inexplicably independent of natural and social influences—contributing voluntarily to their surroundings. *Lenz,* narrated by a perplexingly anonymous voice and from an instable perspective sometimes within and sometimes distanced from Lenz's consciousness, reinforces the elusiveness of what a previous generation might have called a self.

In "Aus Goethes Brieftasche" the young author of *Werther* mentions "de[r] geheime[] Punkt" where the necessary "Gang des Ganzen" and "das Eigentümliche unsres Ichs, die prätendierte Freiheit unsres Wollens" confront each other (HA 12: 226). Büchner's Lenz, in keeping with the thoughts of the historical model he represents, also mentions the realist's desire to find and depict this individual core of his subject: "in das eigenthümliche Wesen jedes einzudringen" (15). The Storm and Stress authors in general were unusually focused on the significance of the individual self and particularly horrified by the thought of its dissolution or annihilation through death or oblivion: "Für nichts gerechnet! Ich! Der ich mir alles bin, da ich alles nur durch mich kenne!" (HA 12: 224). However, Büchner himself, convinced that "wir durch gleiche Umstände wohl Alle gleich würden" (2: 422), not only rejects the notion of "Freiheit unsres Wollens" but also challenges the idea that there is an essential, innate quality specific to each being. Whereas Werther's letters and "Leiden" reflect "sein[en] Geist und sein[en] Charakter" (HA 6: 7), Lenz's wanderings and sufferings, as depicted by Büchner, are not to be read as specific to Lenz's character, but rather as indicative of the fact that the "Gang des Ganzen"—in this case the aberrant, but natural course of madness—does not encounter any meaningful or effective resistance from what might be called "das eigenthümliche Wesen" of Lenz's self. Where Goethe (in *Dichtung und Wahrheit*) had intended to present Lenz's "Charakter" in terms of his accomplishments ("Resultaten"), Büchner presents Lenz less as a particular man than as a sample human being, less as an odd case study of mental illness, than as a sample of nature's patterns and permutations. The frequent allusions to *Werther* and the less frequent evocations of Goethe's descriptions of Lenz establish a strong presence in *Lenz* of the very tradition Büchner's text rejects. The text does not present "the sufferings of young Lenz"[37]; in fact, it does not present Lenz as an individual at all: it presents "das Gesetz der Schönheit," the rhythms of which subject us, at times, to "Angst" too measureless for words and to voids, nadirs so "entsetzlich" when considered in isolation, but so paradoxically beautiful when viewed as the involuntary signature of animate and inanimate, conscious and oblivious nature.

Notes

1. Johann Wolfgang von Goethe, *Werke,* ed. Erich Trunz et al. (Hamburg: Wegener, 1958) 10: 8. All subsequent references to Goethe's works will be cited in the text and will refer to this edition (HA); in the case of Werther's letters both the dates of the letters and the page numbers will be given. The 1787 version is used here; it seems much more likely that Büchner would have read this later edition. References to Georg Büchner's works other than *Lenz* are to *Sämtliche Werke und Briefe,* ed. Werner R. Lehmann (Hamburg, Wegener, 1967). The quotations from *Lenz* are based on the "Studienausgabe," ed. Hubert Gersch (Stuttgart: Reclam, 1984).

2. For example, Hubert Gersch also sees Büchner's Lenz as a response to Goethe's description in *Dichtung und Wahrheit*; in "Georg Büchners Lenz-Entwurf: Textkritik, Edition und Erkenntnisperspektiven. Ein Zwischenbericht," *Georg Büchner Jahrbuch* 3 (1983): 15-24; for this reference p. 24.

3. The term is Heinrich Heine's (9). It refers to an "aristokratische Zeit der Literatur" (9) in which Goethe, "ein Indifferentist" (46), had reigned and which had ended with Goethe's death, only three years prior to when Büchner may have begun work on *Lenz*. Cf. *Die Romantische Schule,* ed. Helga Weidmann (Stuttgart: Reclam, 1976). In Büchner's *Lenz* even the literary period spanning the early part of Goethe's productive life is labeled as the "idealistische Periode" and is presented as aristocratic, although Goethe is himself acknowledged as having some tendencies toward real compassion and as being able to depict "Möglichkeit des Daseins" (14).

4. The similarities in style, diction (e.g. Storm and Stress and pietistic vocabulary) and syntax (e.g. "wenn-Periode") are discussed by many, including Gerhart Baumann, *Georg Büchner, Die Dramatische Ausdruckswelt* (Göttingen: Vandenhoeck & Ruprecht, 1961) 32-49; Peter Hasubek, "'Ruhe' und 'Bewegung': Versuch einer Stilanalyse von Georg Büchners 'Lenz,'" *Germanisch-Romanische Monatsschrift* 50 (1969): 33-59; Roy Pascal, "Büchner's Lenz-Style and Message," *Oxford German Studies* 9 (1978): 68-83; and Dennis F. Mahoney "The Sufferings of Young Lenz: The function of Parody in Büchner's Lenz," *Monatshefte* 76 (1984): 396-408.

5. Baumann is an exception to this generalization. He notes that the "Rückbezüge" and "Durchblicke" of Werther's letters create a highly structured text with thematic links allowing the organizing "Geist des Dichters" (124) to be visible, while *Lenz,* according to Baumann, lacks "Spannung" (135) and emphasizes the present moment rather than connections between similar moments (124). This is discussed further below.

6. This representative allusion to *Werther* is noted by Benno von Wiese, "Lenz" in *Die deutsche Novelle* II (Düsseldorf: Bagel, 1962) 117. Walter Hinderer further notes that both protagonists express interest in "die geringen Leute" (166) that both combat feelings of indifference (168), and that the health of each progressively worsens (170) (*Büchner-Kommentar zum Dichterischen Werk* [München: Winkler, 1977]). The common theme of "Wahnsinn" is noted by Paul Landau, among others (Paul Landau, "Lenz" [1909], rpt. in *Georg Büchner,* ed. Wolfgang Martens [Darmstadt: Wissenschaftliche Buchgesellschaft, 1965] 32-49). Other points of comparison are the facts that both protagonists are involved in an unhappy love triangle; both emphasize the importance of "Mitleid"; both may be described as a homeless "Wanderer"; both express a desire for "Ruhe" and fear the threat and experience of nothingness; both display paranoid and masochistic behaviors; both may be identified as "artists"; and both fear separation from the stabilizing person (Lotte; Oberlin) to whom they cling. These similarities in personality assume that the characters and authors share a common existential confidence in "identity" and "individual"; as soon as we see that Büchner's text assumes no such thing, the points of similarity become points of contrast.

7. Walter Hinderer, "Pathos oder Passion: Leiddarstellung in Büchners 'Lenz,'" *Wissen aus Erfahrung,* ed. Alexander Bormann (Tübingen: Niemeyer, 1976) 484.

8. Baumann 121.

9. Ilse Stephan and Hans Gerd Winter, *"Ein vorübergehendes Meteor"? J. M. R. Lenz und seine Rezeption in Deutschland* (Stuttgart: Metzler, 1984) 82 ff.

10. Raimar Stefan Zons, "Ein Riß durch die Ewigkeit/ Landschaften in 'Werther' and 'Lenz,'" *literatur für leser* 4 (1981): 65-78.

11. Mahoney 404. While Mahoney's argument may be compelling on some levels, it appears severely flawed by the apparent hypothesis that the historical Lenz modeled his behavior on Werther's. In this paper it is assumed that the Werther-Lenz parallels are invented by the author and that the similarities of Lenz's activities in Waldbach as recorded by Oberlin to those presented in Werther's letters are only coincidental.

12. Rosemarie Zeller discusses Büchner's perception of the ambivalence, equivocalness, and "Widers-

pruch" of language and his method of using (in *Dantons Tod* and *Leonce und Lena*) this inherent ambiguity to contrast words with the disparate reality they are supposed to signify; cf. "Das Prinzip der Äquivalenz bei Büchner," *Sprachkunst* 5 (1974): 211-30. Heinrich Anz speaks of "ein poetisches Verfahren der Umdeutung" (164) with which Büchner uses pietistic terminology to criticize the theology usually expressed with these very terms; cf. "'Leiden sey all mein Gewinnst' Zur Aufnahme und Kritik christlicher Leidenstheologie bei Georg Büchner," *Georg Büchner Jahrbuch* 1 (1981): 160-68. Büchner's criticism of the freedom-championing "Formeln der Aufklärung" (146) is observed to be carried out by using these very phrases in contexts revealing how little they have to do with political and social reality; cf. Silvio Vietta, "Sprachkritik bei Büchner," *Georg Büchner Jahrbuch* 2 (1982): 144-56. Peter Horn speaks of how the "Volk" depicted in Büchner's *Dantons Tod* must resort to blasphemous "Umfunktionier[ung]" of the "vorgegebenen Diskurs" (216) in order to achieve any insight into its desperate situation; cf. Peter Horn, "'Ich meine für menschliche Dinge müsse man auch menschliche Ausdrücke finden': Die Sprache der Philosophie und die Sprache der Dichtung bei Georg Büchner," *Georg Büchner Jahrbuch* 2 (1982): 209-26.

13. Herbert Schöffler disputes the Christian interpretation of this text and argues instead that it is the first piece of pantheistic literature in the German language. Herbert Schöffler, *Deutscher Geist im 18. Jahrhundert* (Göttingen: Vandenhoeck & Ruprecht, 1956) 155-81. I argue, however, that while the last line, "Kein Geistlicher hat ihn begleitet," may be a criticism of the Church, it is not necessarily a criticism of the faith. It seems more likely, in fact, whatever Goethe's own beliefs may have been, that this last sentence—consistent with the editor's desires to apotheosize Werther—would serve to point out how the Church (like most social institutions) fails to recognize the extraordinary value of this unorthodox individual, while God, who is beyond mundane rules and who might serve as an imagined role model for the "gute Seele" reading the novel, would not reject Werther.

14. Maurice Benn regards Lenz as an "unconventional protagonist" in a text which seems as much like a scientific study as a work of literature (Maurice Benn, *The Drama of Revolt* [London: Cambridge UP, 1976] 200 ff.). However, for lack of a better term, I refer to Lenz as the protagonist, despite the fact that this term implies (as a result of its usual connotations in today's usage) both that the person is a particular "character" and that the text in which he appears has a delineable plot.

15. This argument is disputed by those who regard the essay as a novella or a "Halbnovelle" and who seek the "Wendepunkt" in the sermon, in the "Kunstgespräch" or in Oberlin's departure (cf. Pongs, Neuse, Jansen) or the "sich ereignete unerhörte Begebenheit," which some (cf. Himmel) locate prior to the beginning of the "Halbnovelle" with the onset of Lenz' madness. Cf. Hermann Pongs, "Büchners 'Lenz,'" in: *Georg Büchner,* ed. Wolfgang Martens (Darmstadt: Wissenschaftliche Buchgesellschaft, 1967) 138-50; Erna Kritsch Neuse, "Büchners *Lenz,* Zur Struktur der Novelle," *The German Quarterly* 43 (1970): 199-209; Peter K. Jansen, "The Structural Function of the Kunstgespräch in Büchner's *Lenz,*" *Monatshefte* 67 (1975): 145-56; and Hellmuth Himmel, *Geschichte der deutschen Novelle* (Bern, 1963) 152 ff. For a thorough survey of approaches to the structure and plot as well as themes of *Lenz,* see Walter Hinderer "*Lenz.* 'Sein Dasein war ihm eine notwendige Last,'" in: *Interpretationen. Georg Büchner* (Stuttgart: Reclam, 1990) 70-82.

16. For discussions of the central motif of "Ruhe" see Hasubek and Mark Roche, "Die Selbstaufhebung des Antiidealismus in Büchners *Lenz,*" *Zeitschrift für deutsche Philologie* 107 "Sonderheft" (1988): 136-47.

17. Both Heinz Fischer (*Georg Büchner, Untersuchungen und Marginalien* [Bouvier: Bonn, 1972] 37) and Zons compare the first and last nature descriptions. They argue that Lenz is unable to appreciate the landscape during his departure and that this loss marks the most advanced stage of his illness presented in the text. Although it is true that Lenz is described as apathetic and that the narrative perspective here is not through Lenz as it was in the beginning, it seems presumptuous to assume that this final episode is meant to depict a terminally extreme condition. Rather, I contend that the oscillations which have been presented throughout the narrative will continue, and that the "so lebte er hin" refers not to Lenz's indifference, but to the pronounced oscillations between states of indifference and engagement, unrest and tranquility.

18. Cf. Walter Hinderer (1976) and Dieter Sevin, "Die existentielle Krise in Büchners *Lenz,*" *Seminar,* 15 (1979): 15-26. Obviously not only the question of Lenz's faith (as presented by Büchner) is discussed; Büchner's own attitudes toward organized religion, particularly Christianity, are a favorite topic for Büchner-scholars, and thus *Lenz* is often regarded as the showcase in which Büchner displays his own criticism of religion.

19. Zons applies these concepts from the *Probevorlesung* to his discussion of the landscapes in *Wer-*

ther and *Lenz.* Lenz does not view nature as aesthetically pleasing *for* him (which would correspond to the teleological purpose of nature's beauty); rather nature is beautiful "an sich," while Lenz is "unendlich abgesondert" from nature, because of his "Geist" and his "ästhetischen Blick" (73ff.). Zons reads *Lenz* as "Exposition des Naturverlusts" (77). However, I argue that *Lenz* is presented as part of nature, not distinct from it, and that the "Gesetz der Schönheit" is shown to work through him as well as through the other natural phenomena presented in the text.

20. For analyses of the narrator in *Lenz* see Martin Swales's "Lenz" in *The German Novelle* (Princeton: Princeton UP, 1977) 105 ff.; Pascal; and, particularly, David Horton "Modes of Consciousness Representation in Büchner's *Lenz,*" *German Life and Letters* 43 (1989): 34-48.

21. David Horton, "Transitivity and Agency in Georg Büchner's *Lenz*: A contribution to a stylistic analysis," *Orbis Litterarum* 45 (1990): 236-47.

22. Zons 74.

23. The episode in which Lenz and the cat lock each other's gazes until Madame Oberlin physically interferes provides a particularly clear example of how Lenz *is* nature, and of how scholarly discussions of his maintaining or losing his contact with or appreciation of the landscapes and nature are essentially irrelevant. In this context it is worth noting Wackenroder's description of one of the artists in *Herzensergießungen eines kunstliebenden Klosterbruders.* (That *Lenz* reflects influence by Novalis, Tieck and Wackenroder is discussed [among others] by Raleigh Whitinger, "Echoes of Novalis and Tieck in Büchner's *Lenz,*" *Seminar* 25 [1989]: 324-38.) In the section about the peculiar artist Piero di Cosimo one reads: "Der Künstlergeist soll, wie ich meyne, nur ein brauchbares Werkzeug seyn, die ganze Natur in sich zu empfangen, und, mit dem Geiste des Menschen beseelt, in schöner Verwandlung wiederzugebähren. Ist er aber aus innerem Instinkte, und aus überflüssiger, wilder und üppiger Kraft, ewig für sich in unruhiger Arbeit; so ist er nicht immer ein geschicktes Werkzeug,—vielmehr möchte man dann *ihn selber* eine Art von *Kunstwerk der Schöpfung* nennen" (Wilhelm Heinrich Wackenroder, *Sämtliche Werke und Briefe,* ed. Silvio Vietta und Richard Littlejohns. [Carl Winter: Heidelberg, 1991] 1: 105; my emphases). Like Cosimo, Büchner's Lenz is presented not so much as a mimetic artist turning nature into art, but as himself an aesthetically pleasing, if powerfully disturbed and disturbing, natural phenomenon.

24. Horton (1989) 43.

25. This letter is December 12 in the 1787 edition. In the 1774 edition (the edition Zons uses for his study) it is dated December 8 and precedes the interruption by the editor. The displacement of this letter in Goethe's revision is significant, but is beyond the scope of this paper.

26. Zons 69: "Diesen letzten Naturbezug Werthers . . . zitiert Büchner herbei, aber nicht als End-, sondern als Ausgangspunkt einer Entwicklung. . . ."

27. Friedrich Schiller, *Über naive und sentimentalische Dichtung,* in: F. S. *Werke und Briefe* VIII: Theoretische Schriften, Rolf-Peter Janz. (Frankfurt a.M.: Deutscher Klassiker Verlag, 1992) 772 and *passim.*

28. Peter Brenner, *Die Krise der Selbstbehauptung* (Tübingen: Niemeyer, 1981) 114.

29. Peter Pütz also observes that the relationship of Werther to the "Bauerbursch" is like his relationships to literature; he forms himself consciously according to an external model; "Werthers Leiden an der Literatur," *Goethe's Narrative Fiction,* ed. W. J. Lillyman (New York: Walter de Gruyter, 1983): 55-68 (here p. 67).

30. This scene in which Lenz sits with Madame Oberlin and plays with her child evokes the letter of December 4, 1772, in which Werther, with one of Lotte's siblings on his knee, listens to Lotte play on the piano the melody which apparently throws Werther into a fit.

31. Cf. Baumann 134.

32. Baumann refers to the fact that in *Lenz* "kausale Verbindungen [werden] ausgespart" (144), by which he means that there are often no logical connections between the distinct episodes of the essay.

33. Büchner, letter to Minna Jaeglé (March 10, 1834; II, 425).

34. Not everyone agrees that Lenz is depicted as mad or as going mad. For alternative perspectives see Janet K. King, "Lenz viewed sane," *The Germanic Review* 49 (1974): 146-53, and Pascal 76, note 2.

35. Oberlin's report is reprinted in the "Studienausgabe" of *Lenz* (cf. note 1). The page reference refers to this edition.

36. Sabine Kubik, however, argues that Büchner criticizes Oberlin for not being sensitive to Lenz's individual needs; *Krankheit und Medizin im literarischen Werk Georg Büchners* (Stuttgart: M & P Verlag für Wissenschaft und Forschung, 1991) 60-61; *passim.*

37. Mahoney.

Curt Wendell Nickisch (essay date 1997)

SOURCE: Nickisch, Curt Wendell. "Georg Büchner's Philosophy of Science: Totality in *Lenz* and *Woyzeck*." *Selecta* 18 (1997): 37-45.

[*In the following essay, Nickisch outlines Büchner's thematic conceptualization of totality—the integration of all elements of human existence and all aspects of the natural world—as exemplified in* Lenz *and* Woyzeck.]

Karl Georg Büchner, a seminal and anachronistic dramatist, wrote only three plays, one of which remains unfinished, and a prose piece. A brilliant scientist, Büchner completed a dissertation on ichthian neurology and joined the University of Zurich faculty as a Reader in Comparative Anatomy. He died in February 1837, at the age of 23.

Georg was born to a family of physicians. Besides his public education, he was also instructed at home in reading, writing and contemporary literature by his mother, Caroline.[1] At the age of eighteen he left for the University of Strasbourg to study medicine, and the new location proved to be a rich experience for Büchner. Strasbourg, even within the school of medicine, was a hotbed of philosophical discussions and political activity. There Büchner's already strong political interests and awareness only intensified.

After two years Büchner was required to continue his studies in Gießen, which after Strasbourg seemed a political backwater. But Büchner became involved in local political circles and helped found a political society. He co-authored a subversive pamphlet, *Der hessische Landbote,* which encouraged peasants and laborers to revolution. Most of the pamphlets were seized by authorities, and Büchner hastened to Darmstadt to escape prosecution.

There Büchner wrote his first play, *Danton's Death,* set during the French Revolution. Upon its completion he returned to Strasbourg, where he wrote the prose piece *Lenz* and the comedy *Leonce and Lena* and completed his dissertation. The University of Zurich granted him a doctorate in 1836, and Büchner joined the university's faculty in November after delivering his much-discussed *Probevorlesung,* entitled **"On Cranial Nerves,"** which drew unsettling philosophical conclusions from scientific observations. There he began *Woyzeck,* which survives as an unfinished play.

Büchner's medical and scientific studies exerted a profound impact on his *Weltanschauung,* and those studies appear as critical components in his literary works. Büchner understood that science cannot alone explain the external (much less one's internal!) world, and he valued science instead in its relation to other interconnected elements—socioeconomic, spiritual, philosophical and physiological. Büchner developed what may be termed a philosophy of *totality,* which classifies science as an integral, but not exclusive, component of human thought; it must be combined with other equally important elements to arrive at valid conclusions or successful results. That, for its time, was fresh thinking indeed.

Büchner's theory formed the background for his singular approach to writing, to which German literature's realism and naturalism owe much. Still, Büchner's work should not be mistaken for unvarnished realism; for him, human existence and the natural world are made up of various and often contradictory interrelated components. The end result is a complex, but intrinsically whole entity. In both *Lenz* and *Woyzeck* Büchner enriches the documented, factual histories of mentally disturbed individuals with artistically conjectured emotions, thoughts and even events. This rare fusion, which would be significantly less effective without Büchner's experience in the natural sciences, arrives at an aesthetic foundation of writing which was wholly different from the romanticism and idealism popular in his day. It is not surprising, then, that Büchner's works were not fully appreciated until a half century or more after his death.

LENZ

Although *Lenz* is Büchner's only prose piece, its events, characteristically, are based on documented material, and its protagonist is an actual person. In the piece, which has been labeled both a novella and a short story, Büchner provides us with insight into a brief but paramount period in the life of the poet Jakob Michael Reinhold Lenz.[2] Büchner begins and halts his presentation abruptly and seemingly arbitrarily; this is no *Bildungsroman.* But by no means can *Lenz* be classified as either a fragment or a "slice of life." While it does leave the reader, in the words of one critic, with the "open wound of despair," it portrays a decidedly rich and telling string of events.[3]

Jakob Lenz is of course the poet of the Storm-and-Stress, and while relatively short-lived, the period profoundly influenced German literature. The young Schiller became an instant success with his play *Die Räuber,* and Goethe's *Werther* is a hallmark of the vibrant period, which valued emotional and subjective responses to one's environment, as well as rebellion against the given hierarchies of the time.[4] Büchner himself, a lone figure within the literary context of his time, owes more of his literary models (if any may reasonably be ascribed) to this period than to any other.

While other Storm-and-Stress poets matured, Jakob Lenz remained a holdout. Notoriously passionate and emotional, he fell in love with Goethe's sister, and later even with Friederike Brion. While Goethe did his best to guide the rambunctious poet, Lenz remained turbulent and unpredictable, which eventually earned him the nickname "Goethes Affe."[5] After a suicide attempt, Lenz lived in January and February of 1778 in the Alsatian mountain home of Pastor Johann Friedrich Oberlin (after whom the Ohio institution is named).[6] Büchner's *Lenz* encompasses this brief period of the poet's life. Lenz then returned to his home in Lithuania; he regressed into insanity and was found dead on a Moscow street in 1792.

A major portion of *Lenz* is based on Pastor Oberlin's diaries. Büchner fuses the more objective documentation (straightlaced Oberlin never achieved significant insight into Lenz the person) with his own projections of Lenz's turbulent thoughts and emotional experiences. Far from conventional historical fiction, Büchner's text possesses a rare grasp of the mind of a mentally disturbed individual. Thus the narrative achieves a haunting, landmark portrayal by incorporating both reality and fiction into the total work.

Note that Büchner's protagonist is no traditional tragic figure. Lenz is a poet, to be sure, but one who has outlived his literary fame, and his value to others is so depreciated that he is personally ridiculed. Büchner peers into the secret world of this other human. Just as he examined basic anatomical building blocks of fish, systematically establishing philosophical ramifications as a scientist, here Büchner peers into the nature and structure of the human mind in relation to the outside world—drawing a philosophical extension.

At the outset of the piece, Lenz is traveling in the mountains, an image reminiscent of philosophers or truthseekers. Absent from the opening of the work is all exposition typically required: "On the twentieth of January Lenz went across the mountains. The summits and the high slopes covered with snow, gray stones all the way down to the valleys, green plains, rocks, and pine trees" (37). On first reading the uncomplicated descriptions might hint of later literary movements, but Büchner soon strays from convention. The second sentence contains no verb at all, and subsequent images utilize strikingly abstract language: "mist rose . . . so lazy, so awkward," and "All seemed so small to him, so near, so wet" (37).

Then comes a jolt: "He felt no tiredness, only sometimes it struck him as unpleasant that he could not walk on his head" (37). The third-person narration seems based on familiar ground, yet it incorporates an intimate perspective, wherein we can "hear" Lenz's thoughts as the narrator moves deftly between reality and perception. Thus a certain empathy for Lenz germinates, one much stronger than that experienced in reading Oberlin's diaries.

Büchner achieves this dual awareness stylistically as well. While concepts like head-walking may derail one's orientation, statements such as "he could not understand why so much time was needed . . . to reach a distant point; he thought that a few paces should be enough to cover any distance" somehow become more accessible distortions of reality (37).

If Büchner challenges his audience to draw a strict line between sanity and insanity, i.e., between the reader and Lenz, alas, a well-defined line is impossible to establish. Consequently, Lenz's condition is not viewed as an isolated and impenetrable outbreak of irrationality, but rather as a fluctuation, an imbalance within Lenz of already-extant facets of human psychology. Büchner examines them within the parameters of the scientific method: he studies documentary materials, and from his data he projects a hypothesis, an explanation for the observed events.

Lenz's confusion subsides when he approaches Oberlin's village, Waldbach. From this point forth, much of the material is lifted from Oberlin's diaries. Yet Büchner retains his established narrative style and maintains the creative tension between fiction and history. At the start of Lenz's stay with Oberlin, he is stabilized by human contact, much as a boat remains righted by its keel. Although shy, Lenz interacts with others reasonably comfortably and enjoys human conversation: "To Oberlin his conversation gave much pleasure, and Lenz's graceful and childish face delighted him" (41). Indeed, the author's reference to childhood is particularly adept, for Lenz grows fearful, "like children left to sleep in the dark," after the daylight dwindles (41). Oberlin, the well-meaning pastor, is convinced that religion is the most appropriate avenue for Lenz's recuperation. Lenz however attempts to arrive at answers in a more arbitrary manner; "like a child he would cast dice whenever he did not know what to do" (42).

Christoph Kaufmann, a visitor to Waldbach, converses with Lenz, who acts as Büchner's mouthpiece, amiably scorning the idealist movement: "Even the poets of whom we say that they reproduce reality have no conception of what reality is, but they're a good deal more bearable than those who wish to transform reality" (43). Another of Lenz's comments is significant: "I take it that God has made the world as it should be . . . our only aspiration should be to re-create modestly in His manner" (45). This notion, which Büchner may have encountered in Lenz's *Remarks about Theater,* is certainly in consonance with Büchner's idea of totality.[7] The world does not exist as a teleological, sequential entity, but rather as one which changes, its pieces continually articulating and converging, while it remains externally a constant whole.

Kaufmann suggests to Lenz that he return to Lithuania, and with this reminder of the world outside of Waldbach begins Lenz's adolescent stage. When Kaufmann departs, Oberlin decides to accompany him for a visit to Lavater, the Swiss theologian.[8] Lenz, who calls himself a "sick child," fears the departure of the paternal figure. Lenz does tag along for a distance, and on his return he encounters a cottage with eccentric inhabitants. Frightened and lonely, Lenz senses that his home at Waldbach no longer constitutes a sanctuary. The appearance of elements from outside the village home—the mention of Lithuania and even the mystical people in the cottage—impress on Lenz that the world, and thus his well-being, is in dynamic flux.

Lenz tries to cope with this adolescent awareness, which sparks memories of his love for Friederike Brion. His reflections are subsequently regressive: he muses, "she was wholly a child," and he remembers feeling like one, too (52). In his deteriorating sanity, he yearns for the stability of an earlier, innocent time.

Büchner introduces here a subtle parallel drawn directly from medicine. Lenz, heartsick for Friederike, feels pain diagnostic of a heart attack: ". . . physical pain, there, in the left side, in my arm with which I used to hold her" (52). Büchner demonstrates again that human existence is manifest in many different interrelated and specialized structures.

Lenz learns of the death of a child, whose name is Friederike, and fixates on the fact. After fasting, he goes to see the child's body, and after a time commands the corpse: "Arise and walk!" (53). As soon as he recognizes failure, he loses his remaining stability and flees into the mountains, his mental equilibrium fluctuating wildly.

Pastor Oberlin returns, and a fascinating incident occurs which metaphorizes Büchner's totality concept. Lenz gives Oberlin a bundle of birch switches and begs to be whipped. After taking them from Lenz, Oberlin kisses him, and says, "These are the only strokes I can give you" (55). Lenz, longing to be purged of his condition, perceives no discrimination between physical or mental health. Stolid Oberlin, who has begun feeding Lenz stock advice like "Honor thy father and thy mother," entertains no such creative solution (54). To him, a mental problem must be solved in the mind—a simple teleological extension. Lenz's thoughts and actions, however, illustrate that an equilibrium is at stake, not a faulty component.

One morning the pastor finds Lenz naked in bed and tries to cover him, but Lenz cries out that "all was so heavy, so very heavy! that he did not think he could walk at all, that never before had he felt the immense weight of the air" (60). Later he asks Oberlin: "Can't you hear the terrible voice that is crying out the whole length of the horizon and that is usually known as silence?" (61).

Lenz makes some reluctant attempts at suicide, not to die, it seems, but to remind himself of his physical presence. He feels a "blank calm that bordered on non-existence" (60). After a break in Büchner's narrative (the original manuscript is lost) the final scene depicts Lenz in a coach on his way to Strasbourg. Unlike his behavior in the opening scene, where he felt emotions ranging from ecstasy to torment, now Lenz acts remarkably detached and lifeless.

Lenz achieves singular insight into the psychological currents of the human mind by establishing coexisting conventional and unconventional perspectives. Instead of discarding all of the aesthetics of romanticism or idealism, Büchner couples some of them, for instance a developmental theme, with thoroughly unorthodox qualities such as the "straddling" narrator and the absence of customary coherence. Although the story may seem to open with vague circumstances and close with unresolved issues (Lenz still suffers from his disorder), close analysis reveals a familiar progression. Such plot as exists is thus restricted to the top of the dramatic arch, leaving the reader to extrapolate the background and project the conclusion.

So, in its totality, is a human life. This story begins with birth, as the sound of human voices and community calm the bewildered, lonely Lenz. Limited to the small circle he joins, he lives contentedly and without torment. References to childhood pepper the narration. Pastor Oberlin's departure, however, introduces Lenz to elements of the world outside of Waldbach. Lenz's "adolescence" affords him a deeper view into his own condition, and he struggles violently with it. He yearns for the stability of childhood and searches for answers. Oberlin's return does not replenish the calming effect that once existed. Instead, he appears more patronizing than ever, like an affectionless father. Lenz eventually fails at his attempts to regain sanity, and he submits to "cold resignation," a virtual death (61). The top of the dramatic arch encompasses life itself.

Much of Büchner's genius lies in establishing an effective duality. A less gifted writer might disregard all elements of conventional prose, and effect a simple polarization which would likely achieve little. Instead, *Lenz* thrives on its apparent paradox.

WOYZECK

Although *Woyzeck* is a dramatic fragment, it counts as Büchner's most influential work. Boldly attacking the class system and simplistic cause-and-effect explanations, *Woyzeck* searches for "uncolored reality" in portraying the tragic Franz Woyzeck and reaches a conclusion supporting Büchner's notion of totality.[9]

As in *Lenz,* this unfinished play features a mentally disturbed individual as a blatantly anticlassical protagonist. This protagonist is not even a fallen poet; he is a member of the proletariat and a murderer. The character Woyzeck is in fact based on the cases of three soldiers who murdered their mistresses.[10] Büchner's Woyzeck carries the temper of Johann Diess, the perplexity of Daniel Schmolling and the victimization of the historical Johann Christian Woyzeck.

Büchner's strong scientific bent allowed for a successful incorporation of these actual figures into the character Woyzeck. Just as he developed a philosophical concept from his observations of fish nerves, Büchner drew a conclusion from the nature of murder cases. Where a less complex scientist might have concluded that the three very similar murderers were each afflicted with a specific disease or disorder, Büchner, the total scientist, discerns that the murders were sparked by a number of factors, including socioeconomic and psychological ones. He achieves a *scientific* perspective with an unmistakably *human* voice.

The first soldier from which Franz Woyzeck was created is one Daniel Schmolling. Well liked and absent of any indication of mental disturbance, he stabbed his girlfriend a single time during a walk in the woods. He planned to stab himself as well, but was frightened by approaching people. He confessed and then asked his dying girlfriend's forgiveness. The second killer was one Johann Diess, who had a history of aggressive behavior and suicide attempts. He stabbed his lover repeatedly on a street after an argument.

The third actual murderer, a certain Johann Christian Woyzeck, occupies the middle ground. Infatuated with a widow who only halfheartedly answered his devotion, Woyzeck grew insanely jealous. After she rejected him for another soldier, Woyzeck stabbed her to death in her doorway, although later it appeared that the murder may have been premeditated. Woyzeck had previously displayed emotional outbursts, but whether he was mentally ill remains a question.

Dr. J. C. A. Clarus, a physician, was summoned by the court to examine the defendant for any mental illnesses but could discover nothing extraordinary. He repeated his investigation at the behest of the court when witnesses testified that Woyzeck was psychologically unsound. Clarus' views failed to change and in his second report he judged Woyzeck as a "man, who in the course of an uncertain, desolate, thoughtless, and indolent life sank from one level of moral degeneration down to the next, who finally in the dark tumult of primitive emotion destroyed a human life, shall now, rejected by society, lose his own on the scaffold by human hand."[11] Johann Christian Woyzeck was beheaded in a Leipzig square on 27 August 1824.

The execution generated a whirlwind of controversy, and Büchner's father was in possession of all three case histories. Not only were they accessible to Georg, but one critic speculates that they were likely discussed in the Büchner home.[12] The timely occurrence of the timeless debate offered the writer a rich opportunity to voice a striking statement about the nature of the murderers and the society which, in Büchner's view, drove them to commit the crimes. Büchner's vision penetrates so deeply because he does not content himself with passing moral judgments or recycling formulaic explanations.

The unfinished text remains problematic (Büchner died in the midst of revisions). While considerable debate has arisen concerning even the proper order of the scenes, one can reasonably surmise that Büchner would have concluded the play with Woyzeck's trial and execution. Dr. Clarus had indicated that Woyzeck's death was to be an example, and one might imagine that Büchner's depiction of the execution would have been an example indeed.

The play opens with Franz Woyzeck, a soldier, in a field with his aloof confidant friend and fellow soldier, Andres. Woyzeck hallucinates, and he remarks how hollow the earth feels (an observation Lenz could have made just as easily). The second scene shows Woyzeck's lover Marie, with whom he has a child, in the town. These two starkly different settings immediately establish a tension between nature and society. Marie sings nursery rhymes and folk songs, and in looking from her window, is physically attracted to the Drum Major. When Marie is criticized by her neighbor Margret, the reader is granted a glimpse of Marie's materialistic inclinations. The reader also learns that Marie knows of Woyzeck's hallucinations.

Marie's desire for money becomes increasingly apparent. When a sergeant pulls out a watch for a demonstration at a fair, she is mesmerized: "This I've got to see" (184). Someone, presumably the Drum Major, gives her a pair of earrings. Her monologue as she peers into the fragment of a mirror demonstrates that she is aware of the association between wealth and class: "The likes of us only have a little corner in the world and a little piece of mirror, but my mouth is just as red as the great ladies with their mirrors from top to toe and their handsome lords who kiss their hands" (184). She feels guilt for her longings, however, when Woyzeck gives her some of his meager pay. But she quickly rationalizes that: "Everything goes to hell anyhow, man and woman alike" (185). Infidelity is inevitable.

Consecutive scenes of the play introduce a physician and the captain of Woyzeck's company; here contrasts and tensions are created between the middle and working classes. Woyzeck appears in a subservient role, shaving his captain. The officer's speech is pocked with pedestrian humor and lackluster rationale. Woyzeck seems detached until the Captain accuses him of lacking morality. Woyzeck replies, "Us poor people. You see Cap'n—money, money. If you don't have money. . . . Just try to raise your own kind on morality in this world" (186). The Captain is also unable to bridge the socioeconomic gap between himself, a member of a more privileged class and Woyzeck, a representative of the oppressed, exploited, military proletariat of the time.

The subsequent scene depicts Marie with the Drum Major in her room. She finds him attractive, and while her accessibility to, say, the Captain would be difficult, the Drum Major offers Marie a reasonable improvement in status and income. Woyzeck senses her emotionless resignation (reminiscent of Lenz's "cold resignation") in the next scene, and he foreshadows the murder by saying: "You are as beautiful as sin. Can mortal sin be so beautiful?" (188).

As a despicable character, the physician is critical to the thrust of Büchner's attack on societal conventions. Büchner does not criticize medicine or science in themselves, he criticizes specific *practices* of medicine and scientific experimentation. He feels that strictly scientific pursuit without human consideration neglects other fundamental aspects of collective human nature. Büchner spares no scorn in criticizing this type of scientist.

The Doctor has put Woyzeck on a diet of peas in a study which will, he says, revolutionize science. This physician is utterly unfeeling and one-dimensional. "Who would get excited about a human being, a human being?" he asks (190). Woyzeck reports that he has heard voices and follows with this very Lenzian thought: "The toadstools, Doctor. . . . Have you seen how they grow in patterns? If only someone could read that" (190). The Doctor immediately (and shallowly) makes a diagnosis: "a marvelous *aberratio mentalis partialis,* second species, beautifully developed" (190). When the physician calls Woyzeck "Subject Woyzeck," he is calling him a scientific subject just as much as he is a class subject.

Woyzeck feels lost because Marie is the only aspect of his existence which he values, and Marie seems lost to him. Their conversations, though oblique, can at least be categorized as communication. The extra money he makes from the Doctor's experiment and from shaving the Captain are invested in Marie. She is the only "good" he possesses; if he loses her, he loses everything.

Psychosomatic effects become apparent in Woyzeck. He complains of how hot he feels, the same adjective he uses to describe Marie when he is jealous. He is restless; things twirl in front of his eyes. After he sees the Drum Major and Marie dancing and hears her gaily shout "on and on!" Woyzeck's rage and frustration sur-

face in an angry speech. In a mechanism we have since come to associate with Brecht, an apprentice outside preaches "all that is earthly is passing, even money must eventually decay."[13] Back in an open field, as at the beginning of the play, and lying on the ground, Woyzeck hears voices which tell him to stab her.

The next day, a grandmother, an unmarried couple and several children are together on the street. The children play games and sing songs and nursery rhymes, symbolic and stylistic reflections of the Doctor's and Captain's attitude toward humans as puppets or toys. The Grandmother tells a story:

> Once upon a time there was a poor little child with no father and no mother, everything was dead, and no one was left in the whole world. Everything was dead and it went and searched day and night. And since nobody was left on the earth, it wanted to go up to the heavens, and the moon was looking at it so friendly, and when it finally got to the moon, the moon was a piece of rotten wood and then it went to the sun and when it got there, the sun was a wilted sunflower and when it got to the stars, they were little golden flies stuck up there like the shrike sticks 'em on the blackthorn and when it wanted to go back down to earth, the earth was an upset pot and was all alone and it sat down and cried and there it sits to this day, all alone.
>
> (199)

It is, of course, a tale of false expectations and utter betrayal. The child discovers that goals it strove for were nothing but perversely disappointing illusions. We suspect that Woyzeck will find Marie so, and eventually she would come to find the parading Drum Major equally disappointing.

After the Grandmother's story Woyzeck takes a walk with Marie—outside the town—and stabs her to death. His psychosomatic symptoms continue, notably as body temperature, the hot and cold symbolic of life and death. The end of the (unfinished) play is the Court Clerk's chilling statement: "A good murder, a real murder, a beautiful murder. As good a murder as you'd ever want to see. We haven't had one like this for a long time" (204).

Woyzeck is a logical extension of Büchner's earlier works, inasmuch as it combines the psychological study of *Lenz* with the political passion of *Der hessische Landbote.* The drama's disjointed style and economical, powerful language come across as thoroughly contemporary, even for a late 20th century audience. *Woyzeck* remains consistent with Büchner's literary and scientific writings, because it further explains, in dramatic form, his concept of totality. Büchner would, we may suspect, finally exculpate Woyzeck; he saw in the barber and soldier a victim of society and ill fortune. Forced to sell his health in order to earn a little money, Woyzeck still could not avoid losing the one being he valued and who lent him value, Marie.

But more problematic is the pivotal story of the Grand-mother. Does the absence of solace and hope signify only the danger of idealizations and simplified projections, or is it truly representative of the world, implying more of what we have since encountered in naturalism? The latter answer would seem to signify a departure for Büchner from his totality theory.

The answer is housed in Woyzeck's action. Though he would himself die, he killed Marie, thus choosing active suicide over passive disintegration. Significantly, he takes to the woods, away from the city and society, to kill her. Unlike the materialistic Marie, he does not resign to notions of fatalism. Although he felt deeply threatened and was mentally ill, he still discovered a way to express himself; tragically, society offered only one avenue. In final analysis, Woyzeck could not neglect cogent components of his total person.

Georg Büchner is a singular figure, well in advance of his time, and we may be pleased to find that this student of history, philosophy, politics and medicine found the concept of totality integral to his literary productivity. Science plays an important role in offering reason, analysis and the art of observation, with which certain facts and truths can be defined. Science alone, however, is of little value, as evidenced by the physician in *Woyzeck.* It must be accompanied by other human aspects such as compassion, socio-economic awareness and physical and mental health, in order to claim validity and manage beneficial effects. Despite the fact that Büchner did not live to finish the play, the theme of totality is clearly evident in the dramatic fragment.

In Conclusion

Georg Büchner, the political activist, scientist and writer, possessed a piercing insight and astute ability in each field. His understanding of science, combined with his interests in philosophy and politics, provided for a unique approach to the writing of literature. His concept of totality is a vastly intuitive vision: each component of human existence and the natural world is an integral, yet independent piece in a self-contained whole. Faithful to the concept, Büchner arrives at the depiction of ultimately human protagonists in *Lenz* and *Woyzeck,* for each element of their existences is inexorably and complexly interdependent with the rest. Büchner's characters are in themselves whole: complex arrangements of mutually dependent components.

Notes

1. Hilton, p. 6.

2. Schmidt, p. 319, and Hamburger, p. 95.

3. Schmidt, p. 328.

4. Baumann and Oberle, pp. 114-115.

5. Hamburger, p. xi.

6. Schmidt, p. 319.

7. Hilton, p. 41.

8. Lavater is the Swiss theologian to whom Büchner referred in *Die Probevorlesung.* See Knapp, p. 227, and Schmidt, p. 319.

9. Büttner, p. 94.

10. Schmidt, p. 362.

11. Schmidt, p. 368.

12. Hilton, p. 114.

13. The play, as those of Brecht, is intended to make a political statement. See Schmidt, p. 194.

Works Cited

Abutille, Mario Carlo. *Angst und Zynismus bei Georg Büchner.* Basler Studien zur deutschen Sprache und Literatur. No. 40. Ed. Heinz Rupp and Walter Muschg. Bern: Franke, 1969.

Baumann, Barbara, and Birgitta Oberle. *Deutsche Literatur in Epochen.* München: Max Hueber, 1985.

Büttner, Ludwig. *Büchners Bild vom Menschen.* Nürnberg: Hans Carl, 1967.

Hamburger, Michael, ed. and trans. *Georg Büchner—Leonce and Lena, Lenz, and Woyzeck.* Chicago: U of Chicago P, 1972.

Hilton, Julian. *Georg Büchner.* NY: Grove Press, 1982.

Knapp, Gerhard P., ed. *Georg Büchner, Gesammelte Werke.* 7. Aufl. München: Goldmann, 1990.

Schmidt, Henry J., ed. and trans. *Georg Büchner: The Complete Collected Works.* New York: Avon Books, 1977.

David G. Richards (essay date 2001)

SOURCE: Richards, David G. "Recent Criticism: 1980-1999." In *Georg Büchner's 'Woyzeck': A History of Its Criticism,* pp. 111-42. Rochester, N.Y.: Camden House, 2001.

[*In the following excerpt, Richards surveys criticism of* Woyzeck *published in English and German during the last two decades of the twentieth century.*]

Two events mark the beginning of a new period in Büchner scholarship: the founding of the Georg Büchner Gesellschaft in May 1979 and Gerhard Schmid's publication of a facsimile edition of *Woyzeck* in 1981. Also in 1981, in a second special volume of *Text und*

Kritik devoted to Georg Büchner, Thomas Michael Mayer, a founder of the Georg Büchner Society, announced in a review entitled "Some New Tendencies of Büchner-Scholarship" that the society's annual publication, the *Georg Büchner Jahrbuch,* would "serve as an organ for taking stock of the current state of scholarship and for new contributions, for reflection and debate, for the documentation of sources, the rapid mediation of controversy and communication of new findings," and would be comprehensive in its inclusion of debate and the results of research (265).

In a study published in 1980, Albert Meier summarizes and continues the trend of the politically oriented seventies to emphasize the socially critical content of *Woyzeck.* Meier sees the play not as a fragment but as an analytical model of a historically determined situation as it relates to an individual. In his view, it is a politically and dramaturgically radical attempt to "represent the historical totality" of Büchner's time (16).

In a brief discussion of the manuscripts Meier concludes that Büchner changed his conception of the play after writing the first sequence of scenes, nearly all of which relate to jealousy and murder. Only the carnival scene and some lines spoken by a barber go beyond this basic plot. With the exception of the figures appearing in the last scene (H1,21), all the figures in this version are from the same social class. The second group of scenes introduces representatives from other social levels, and the various relationships of the figures to each other make possible the "very exact placement of each one into a social system of coordinates." In this context Woyzeck's abnormal behavior no longer appears to be the result of his "sickly exaggerated jealousy" but rather of his social situation, the forces of which do not allow him any autonomy and compel him to work constantly to support his family (24-27).

Whether H2 represents a change in conception or a filling of the gaps does not seem particularly relevant for Meier's interpretation, since he considers H4 to be a synthesis of H1 and H2. In this final version Büchner presents Marie's infidelity, intensifies Woyzeck's jealousy, and at the same time develops their social conditions. Appearing for the first time in this version, Meier claims, is a psychologically accurate connection between unhealthy jealousy and the social situation. Meier finds support for this interpretation in scene H4,4, in which Marie admires her new earrings for the effect they have on her appearance and for their intrinsic value. Woyzeck loses her for two reasons: he cannot acquire social recognition for her, and his work prevents him from being able to spend time with her. He can meet neither her material nor her physical demands. According to Meier, Woyzeck's thought of killing Marie derives not merely from jealousy but also from the social causes of his jealousy and from his ever-increasing isolation. Marie's infidelity undermines his social position and subjects him even more to the ridicule and abuse of his social superiors (30-31).

Also contained in scene H4,4 is Marie's use of "psychoterror" on her son, by which Meier means her reference to the sandman, which is meant to force the child to self-discipline by creating fear of supernatural punishment. To escape this danger, the child must continually control himself, thus internalizing the supernatural force and becoming accustomed to being controlled by it. This supposedly hinders his ability to resist real danger. Marie thus contributes to the continuation of oppression of her own class; to get her own pleasure she must deprive others of theirs (36).

. . . . .

Ingrid Oesterle claims in a 1984 article that *Woyzeck* is related to, but not a pure example of, "Schauerliteratur" (thriller or Gothic literature) and the tragedy of fate. Büchner found inspiration and sources in the works of Ludwig Tieck, E. T. A. Hoffmann, and other romantic writers. Characteristic of this genre is the shift from dominance of vision and the eye to involvement of all the senses: hearing, smelling, touching, and the awareness of temperature and physical pain. Since the source of suffering and anxiety is obscure, mysterious, and incomprehensible, dialogue and communication decrease in importance and language is simplified and loses its literary quality (1984, 169-74, 186-87). From her analysis of the play's first scene, Oesterle demonstrates that *Woyzeck* shares the following structural elements and motifs with Gothic literature: disagreeable and fateful places, bewitched nature (ghostly light phenomena and optical illusions with deadly consequences), the terror of seemingly unnatural appearances and forces such as the Freemasons, terrible stillness, and the sudden change from deathly silence to deafening noise and from darkness to visionary brightness (189-96).

In another article published in 1984, Heinz-Dieter Kittsteiner and Helmut Lethen object to interpretations that seek a "hidden center" and that fill the "empty spaces" beneath the "semblance of a plot," as do Wolfgang Wittkowski (by supplying a Christian content) and Albert Meier (by applying Ingarden's aesthetics). Kittsteiner and Lethen intend, on the other hand, to heed Mercier's advice from *Dantons Tod* and "to follow the phrases to the point they become embodied," that is, to look at what actually is, rather than at what supposedly lies hidden. In their view, Büchner's accomplishment was to "destroy linguistically the meaning-centers around which the thinking of his time circled," an accomplishment that is itself a product of his time, in which thought patterns that were common in the eighteenth century were losing their validity. Büchner rejects the thinking and theories of the Enlightenment and idealism in favor of an "anthropological materialism" (240-42).

In comparison with the historical Woyzeck, who belonged to and wanted to be a part of bourgeois society but was incapable of internalizing bourgeois morality, Büchner has deprived his figure of many of Woyzeck's bourgeois attributes, write Kittsteiner and Lethen. Thus, in disagreement with those interpreters who identify a conflict of conscience in Woyzeck, Kittsteiner and Lethen argue that Woyzeck does not reflect upon his situation and on what is right or wrong; rather, he responds to inner voices and their projection onto the outside world. Büchner agrees with the Romantics in their devaluation of the moral influence of conscience on action and in their recognition of angst as internalized conscience. In depriving Woyzeck of his bourgeois attributes, Büchner does not portray Woyzeck's supposed madness as medical pathology but as a mode of perceiving and understanding the world. The revolutionary implications disappear from this "magical-apocalyptic world view": Woyzeck does not experience a call to rebellion but simply the command to kill (249-52).

According to Kittsteiner and Lethen, the bourgeois ego, which Woyzeck does not possess, views its actions from a moral-philosophical perspective, according to which the world must be thought of as a system of goals in the pursuit of which there is no insurmountable gap between nature and freedom. The world as history is a place for the future realization of morality. History is linear, goal-oriented, and progressive. Büchner appears to adapt an earlier view of history as cyclical. Or perhaps more accurately, his thinking about history is paradoxical, in that, as Maurice Benn and Reinhold Grimm have claimed, he considers it to be both linear and cyclical. The Doctor and the Captain in *Woyzeck* represent these opposing views (255-57).

The Captain suffers from the cyclical nature of time, the eternal and hopeless repetition of the same or similar actions as represented for him by the turning of the mill wheel. He has a "feudal" relationship to time but, seen existentially, he is also modern in his melancholic reaction to the passing of time and in his awareness of the absurdity of life. As indicated by his attempts to slow down Woyzeck and the Doctor, he wants to reduce or escape from the consequences of passing time (258-64). The Doctor, in contrast, is always in a hurry. He wants to move with time and to contribute to the progress of time and history. In the Doctor's view, the Captain and Woyzeck are anachronisms (265-66). According to Kittsteiner and Lethen, the representation of the restive motion of Woyzeck's body shows the conflict in him of the cyclical and linear orientations to time and his lack of an inner regulator that could reconcile the opposing tendencies (266-67).

In a study of accountability in works by E. T. A. Hoffmann and Büchner published in 1985, Georg Reuchlein views *Woyzeck* as a reaction against the fundamental assumptions of restoration psychology and justice upon which Dr. Clarus's evaluations are based, especially the belief that, except in certain extreme cases, people are able through reason and free will to determine their fate and control their actions. Whereas the judicial system in the eighteenth century had tried to separate morality and religion from the administration of justice, lawyers and psychiatrists in the 1920s criticized the separation of moral and juridical judgments. Woyzeck's case provided grist for the mills on both sides of the question. A year after their publication in 1824, Clarus's conclusions were attacked by the Bamberg court physician Dr. Carl Moritz Marc and defended against Marc's attack by Dr. Johann Christian August Heinroth, who, like Clarus, considers the loss of reason to be the consequence of sin and therefore punishable. By caricaturing and criticizing morality, religion, and indeterminism, Büchner discredits and disqualifies the philosophical, ideological foundation of Clarus's and Heinroth's juridical and medical assumptions (55-57).

It can be determined from Büchner's play that Woyzeck is not sane and accountable for his violent action, Reuchlein writes, but the actual state of his mind cannot be determined. In the first stage of composition, the signs of Woyzeck's madness follow his discovery of Marie's infidelity and could be considered products of his passion. In H2 and H4, which Reuchlein sees as belonging together in the second stage of composition, these signs precede the discovery and are therefore pathological, a fact that is of such importance that it becomes the focus of the beginning scene of the second version (H2) and, in revised form, of the final one as well. Like the Doctor, Marie and Andres, too, note Woyzeck's disturbed mental state. If Woyzeck is not actually mad, he is at least, as Kanzog writes, psychically stigmatized. In either case, he is not as Clarus sees him. On the other hand, Büchner's depiction of him also departs from the historical facts. Unlike the historical Woyzeck, Büchner's obtains a knife only after he hears voices commanding him to kill Marie, and Büchner's Woyzeck hears the command repeatedly, whereas the historical Woyzeck heard voices only once. Büchner thus emphasizes the compulsive element of the murder (61-63). Because he makes his Woyzeck more moral than the historical murderer, Büchner's text could not have changed the official judgment of Woyzeck, Reuchlein concludes, but it could have had an impact on the public, which was unfamiliar with the factual details. Furthermore, Büchner raises questions about causes, which he finds not only in the individual but also in social relationships. While definite causal relationships cannot be determined—we don't know, for example, what the effect of Woyzeck's diet of peas is—it is clear that blame lies, or also lies, with the social order (69-71, 74-75).

The primary goal of John Guthrie's 1984 study of the dramatic form of plays by Lenz and Büchner is to demonstrate that these playwrights do not have as much in common as has generally been assumed and that Büchner's plays do not fulfill the theoretical demands of the open form of drama as defined by Krapp, Klotz, and others. Guthrie considers it ironic that the theories of the open form of drama, which have influenced subsequent editors and interpreters of the text, were based on Bergemann's edition, whose editorial principles, according to his critics, were based on the closed form of drama. While it is true that Bergemann's edition has been criticized for the contaminations undertaken to strengthen causal connections, this in itself does not result in a text representative of the closed form of drama. Nor should it be assumed, as Guthrie does, that all editors and critics who "assign the play as a whole to the category of the open form" place theory ahead of analysis (121).

At issue here is not the assignment of the play "as a whole" to a particular category, but the identification and analysis of the characteristics peculiar to different and in some ways opposing traditions and forms of drama, namely, the classical and the Shakespearean, the closed and open form, the linear and episodic, or whatever designations one might choose to give them. Klotz does not presume to prescribe what characteristics the forms *must have*: rather, on the basis of his analysis of a number of plays of each type, he identifies characteristics he considers peculiar to each form. Klotz's procedure certainly has greater methodological validity than the one proposed by Guthrie, which is based on his "conviction that theories such as that of the open form do not substantially contribute to an understanding of the play's real, that is to say, dramatic structure" (121).

In opposition to presumed implications of the theory of the open form of drama, Guthrie argues that *Woyzeck* does not consist of a sequence of static images or independent and autonomous scenes that can be rearranged at will without affecting the meaning of the whole (121). But Klotz does not claim that scenes can be rearranged at will. As noted above, those who advocate the arbitrary rearrangement of scenes tend to represent the standpoint of theatrical production and directorial creativity. Likewise, the argument for the play's open ending does not mean, as Guthrie implies, "that a number of endings are possible and can be supported by internal evidence" (121). It means, rather, that no ending is given and none unequivocally foreshadowed by internal evidence. The play ends as it begins: *in medias res.* There are a number of possibilities for what could follow the break in the action, but none of these is specified by the author.

In a scene-by-scene analysis, Guthrie attempts to demonstrate that the plot follows a clear line of development, with each scene having its proper and foreor-

dained place, and that the play therefore belongs to the closed form of drama. "It is argued," he writes, "that because the open form of drama knows no exposition," because scenes are supposedly interchangeable, and because each scene anticipates the conclusion in the same way, it is possible to begin the play "with any, or at least a large number of scenes," an argument that supposedly has been used to justify beginning the play with H4,5, in which Woyzeck shaves the Captain. But Guthrie's assumptions about the implications of the open form are not accurate and the explanation he offers apodictically for the placement of H4,1 is based on subjective criteria: "if one looks carefully at the justification for using H4,1, apart from its authorization in the manuscripts, one finds that it is justified not at all from the point of view of a theory but because it is the best scene to commence with in every conceivable way." And: "In view of the scenes Büchner has left us, however incomplete, this one cannot be bettered as exposition" (122).

In his discussion of the fair scene, Guthrie identifies the middle section between the Barker's speech outside the booth and the Showman's performance inside, that is, the moment in which contact is made between Marie and the Drum Major, as the "most important part of the scene" and "its real body," because it is significant for the development of the plot. "The actual content of the 'Marktschreier's' ranting does not matter as much as this does." Compared to the "serious foreground action," Guthrie claims, the meaning of the Barker's words comparing Woyzeck to a monkey (words actually spoken by the "Ausrufer" rather than the "Marktschreier") "cannot conceivably be evident to an audience at this stage, for the simple reason that we have not seen enough of the main character." The impact of the speeches in this "quasi-episodic element in the plot" differs in nature from that of the rest of the scene, Guthrie claims. "One may suggest that it is a less intense impact, analogous to comic relief in Shakespeare, preparing us for the main point of the scene" (128-29).

Here and elsewhere, Guthrie appears to contradict his own argument by acknowledging the existence of episodic elements in the play, that is, elements peculiar to the open form as defined by Klotz. He identifies H4,9 (Captain. Doctor), for example, as a "pendant-like scene" that "does not forward the plot in the most direct way possible" (134). Likewise, some of scene H1,14 (Margret [= Marie] with Girls in Front of the House) is "not, strictly speaking, part of the development of the plot" (146). Furthermore, some of Guthrie's assumptions regarding the forms of drama are not accurate: he argues, for example, that the scenes are not independent and autonomous because there are manifold connections between them (126), but such interconnection is described by Klotz and others as not only typical of, but essential for the open form of drama, since such connections—Klotz's "metaphorische Verklammerung," and the recurrence of various types of motifs—help create dramatic unity where some of the unifying devices of the closed form of drama are lacking.

More convincing is Guthrie's opposition to the claim that the play's end is implied in every scene or that the structure of the play is circular. As he, and more recently Burghard Dedner have demonstrated, the plot is characterized by a tight linear and chronological development.

Burghard Dedner joins Guthrie in arguing against the commonly accepted view that *Woyzeck* is an example of the open form of drama and in deploring what he considers to be attempts by editors to make their editions comply with this form. Dedner acknowledges that Büchner follows Shakespeare rather than the classical drama, but with the retention of linear plot development and the strict and condensed sequence of scenes that is characteristic of the latter. Taking exception to the comparison of the structure of *Woyzeck* to the form of a ballad, which he attributes especially to Viëtor, but which, in fact, was quite common in criticism before Viëtor, Dedner claims that the play is not non-linear and does not progress through stations or separate episodes, and that the scenes were not written "helter skelter" (*bunt durcheinander*), as Viëtor maintains, but in sequence. "If the open drama has no continual, uninterrupted plot development," he argues, then the form of *Woyzeck* is closed (1988/89, 163-165). However, by admitting to the inclusion of remnants of folk life such as folk songs and some of the events involving children, and of a number of "interior scenes" such as H4,2, in which Marie observes the Drum Major, H4,3, in which she observes the Barker, and H4,17, in which Woyzeck surveys his life and possessions, Dedner, like Guthrie, undermines his own argument (169). And to his examples could be added others such as the Grandmother's tale and the banter of the journeymen.

Dedner bases his argument on conclusions drawn from what he considers to be a complete manuscript: in his view, the plot as contained in H4 and H1,14-21—with the possible inclusion of H3,2—is complete as it stands and does not require further supplementation from earlier drafts (147). In H1 he sees a causally connected sequence of scenes with some passages left open, whether intentionally or not. This manuscript consists of a closed sequence of scenes focusing on the murder and its aftermath and connected by two principles he identifies as "haste" (Hetze) and a "tendency to simultaneity" (Tendenz zur Simultaneität). The scenes are connected by Woyzeck's scurrying from one activity to the next and by an increase in the tempo toward the end. Simultaneity or near simultaneity can be found in several instances where scenes overlap or appear to be taking place at the same time: for example, after Marie has been stabbed in H1,15, her dying sounds are heard by the people coming in H1,16; and scene H1,18 with the children may be taking place at the same time as the inn scene, H1,17. In Dedner's view, both of these "connecting principles" are more developed in H2 and H4, though he admits that some are actually eliminated in the revision of earlier scenes for inclusion in H4 (147-51).

According to Dedner's calculations, the action of the play takes place in as little as forty-eight hours and in no more than three days, which is in keeping with the unity of time of the classical drama. He argues against the transposition of H1,18, which was introduced by Franzos, retained by Lehmann and Poschmann, and defended by Kanzog. In his response to Lehmann's argument that the children would not be up at such a late hour, Dedner echoes an observation made by Patterson in a 1978 study of the play's duration, which Patterson estimates to be four days, namely, that it "depends on a rather middle-class view of bringing up children" (Patterson 1978, 120). Not all children are so disciplined as to be in bed two hours after dark, Dedner argues, and that would be especially true on an evening in which the news of a murder would spread quickly through crowded quarters, creating a special situation in which the children would likely share the excitement and desire to witness the murder scene. As indicated above, H1,18 could be taking place at the same time as H1,17, and it establishes a connection between H1,16 (the arrival of people at the pond and discovery of the murder) and H1,19, in which people responding to the news of the murder arrive at the pond and scare off Woyzeck, who has returned to the scene of the crime. Furthermore, Dedner continues, H1,18 reflects the immediate, sensational reaction to the murder, which would have diminished somewhat by the following morning, and it gives Woyzeck time to get from the inn to the pond (Dedner 155-57).

As for other problematic passages, Dedner notes that even though the Captain's reference to Marie's infidelity in H2,7 is represented in H4,6, he still thinks it probable that Büchner would have added Woyzeck's appearance in H4,9, but he would have had to change it to agree with the new situation in which Woyzeck has already seen the Drum Major with Marie or leaving her house (154-60). Dedner seems to agree with Poschmann that H3, or at least H3,2 (The Idiot. The Child. Woyzeck) was written after H4, that H3,2 authorizes the murder sequence H1,14-21, and that it corresponds to an increasing tendency on Büchner's part to "individualize figures from the folk." In Dedner's view, H3,2 should follow H1,20, Woyzeck's entry into the pond, to which the Idiot supposedly refers with his finger-counting game. With respect to H3,1, The Doctor's Courtyard, Dedner agrees with Müller-Seidel, Paulus, and Richards that this scene cannot be placed before the end of H4, where it no longer has any purpose. Since the comic content of H3,1 is on a lower level than that of H4, it appears that H3,1 precedes H4 and was superseded by it (161-63).

In a paper presented at a 1987 colloquium at the University of Aalborg, Denmark, and published in 1988, Swend Erik Larsen identifies three components in the phenomenon of power and powerlessness in *Woyzeck* and *Lenz*:

> —the concrete *event* in which power and powerlessness meet and where the strength of power is tested,
>
> —the *structures* that determine the forms of confrontation,
>
> —consciousness which the parties or persons involved possess of the connection between structure and event.
>
> (1988, 176; author's emphasis)

Larsen claims that reflection about oppression and the abuse of power emanates from every sentence in the play. The event he chooses to analyze in detail is the scene in which Woyzeck shaves the Captain (H4,5). In this scene Woyzeck is clearly inferior and subordinate to the Captain, who demonstrates his superiority in various ways: he gives orders, comments on Woyzeck's private life, makes fun of him, and instructs him. During the course of the scene, however, Woyzeck gains the upper hand, which distresses and confuses the Captain. His replies to the Captain, which are at first short and automatic, become longer, and his participation in the dialog becomes more active. He gives an unexpected twist to the Captain's religious allusions, for example, and raises the issue of money in relation to morality (176-77).

The Captain's loss of ground is manifest also in the use of personal pronouns. He begins addressing Woyzeck in the third person singular "Er" rather than with the "Du" or "Sie" that would be used with a person of similar status. Accepting his inferior role, Woyzeck avoids the use of pronouns in addressing the Captain: to refer to the Captain as "Sie" would presuppose considering himself as an "ich," Larsen claims, as a person with a right to speak. Only when Woyzeck begins to seize the initiative in the conversation does he address the Captain as "Sie" and begin, tentatively at first, to assert his own individuality: after first speaking about poor people in general and using the plural pronoun "wir" and the impersonal "man," he finally speaks in the first person singular. The scene ends with the Captain apparently accepting the "partial identity" between himself and Woyzeck, both of whom are "good men." Thus the hierarchy breaks down on the verbal level, according to Larsen, and, because his power stands on shaky feet, the Captain identifies with Woyzeck. Woyzeck does not

take advantage of the Captain's weakness in order to undermine his power, however, but to define his own difference and in a subjective way to confirm the hierarchy of power. Woyzeck is conscious of and accepts his position in the power-structure (177-78).

Because of their cynical arbitrariness, writes Larsen, the representatives of power are dangerous, and because of their neurotic narrow-mindedness, they are also ridiculous. They possess real power, but it is power they have not earned and do not deserve. It is a "perverse-routinized extension" of a power that may once have served a useful purpose but has now lost its meaning and function in a new and different social context, where it continues to function for its own sake. When power is no longer part of a total structure and no longer contains any vision, Larsen writes, those who exercise that power live in a "partial universe" that only includes themselves and not the totality. Hence we experience them in the "here and now" where they are threatened by that which they would dominate, the Captain by Woyzeck and his craftiness, the Doctor by nature and arbitrariness. For his part, Woyzeck also identifies with the Captain, Larsen maintains, and behaves like him as the master in his own partial world. And just as the Doctor views Woyzeck as his property, so Woyzeck views Marie as his. When Marie asserts her independence, Woyzeck's identification with the other persons of power moves him to kill her (179-81).

Conclusions similar to Larsen's are reached by Richard T. Gray, who, borrowing a phrase from Max Horkheimer and Theodor Adorno, analyzes the "dialectic of enlightenment" in Woyzeck. While the Enlightenment purports "to provide the means for the emancipation of humanity from the obscurity of myth," according to Horkheimer and Adorno, it "ultimately reveals itself to be a more insidious manifestation of myth itself" (1988, 79). Büchner had similar insight, Gray maintains, and this manifests itself in his skepticism toward the transition from a holistic science to the purposive-rational approach that was coming into prominence in his time. He finds confirmation for his "worst suspicions about the potential inimicality of reason to life" in Clarus's report on Woyzeck, which was not only the source of Büchner's play but the "true impetus behind the entire conception of the work." Büchner is less interested in Woyzeck himself than in the way Clarus portrays him. The aim of Büchner's fragments, Gray writes, "is to reflect critically on the 'dogmatism of reason' as manifest in the Clarus report with the goal of bringing enlightenment to reflect on itself" (80-81).

In his diagnosis of Woyzeck's motivation to commit murder, Clarus asserts the dominance of reason over emotion in the same absolute manner as Büchner's Doctor, a caricature of Clarus. Like the Doctor in *Woyzeck,* Clarus valorizes "freedom of will" and "the free use of reason" without ever questioning the appropriateness of these values for the uneducated and underprivileged Woyzeck; he condemns Woyzeck based on Enlightenment conceptions about human beings. Clarus assumes that Woyzeck is capable of reasonable thinking and that his will is free, but that he misuses his reason in a perverse manner. Whereas pure insanity, the complete absence of reason, may be accepted, the hybrid between reason and unreason, the "confusion of subjective feelings with objective conceptions," in the words of Clarus, undermines the integrity of reason itself and threatens to overturn the relationship between subject and object on which scientist reason is based (81-82).

Clarus's position, Gray argues, "can be read as an unwitting condemnation of the socioeconomic order responsible for Woyzeck's 'limited means.'" Clarus objects to Woyzeck's "inherently underprivileged status in society, his lack of formal education, his poverty, his 'moralische Verwilderung' [moral degeneration]." According to Gray, Clarus reveals in his report that he is possessed of the very qualities he condemns in Woyzeck, namely, a specific set of prejudices, false judgments, and errors. Consequently, when he passes judgment on Woyzeck as a curious hybrid of reason and unreason, he is also passing judgment on himself. He exemplifies the "merging of myth and enlightenment, or the reversion of enlightenment to myth" that is the central thesis of Horkheimer's and Adorno's critique of enlightenment (82-83).

Gray suggests that Büchner's reading of Clarus's report was similar to his own reading based on theories of Horkheimer and Adorno. In *Woyzeck* Clarus's pedagogical and scrutinizing gaze is itself subjected to a scrutinizing gaze, "the gaze of dramatic spectatorship." Büchner's drama "assumes the spectatorial gaze of enlightened reason only in order to turn it against this reason itself." In this regard the carnival scenes are of central importance. Carnival inherently involves inversion and destabilization of authoritative values, and it possesses revolutionary potential. In his carnival scenes Büchner introduces dominant societal values in a context that mocks and overturns them. Clarus's idealized vision of rational human beings is mocked by the grotesque hybridization of reason and unreason as represented by a variety of trained animals. The Barker's ironic praise of reason in this scene is simultaneously its denunciation. This figure therefore embodies the "dialectic of enlightenment" in the same way Clarus does and provides skeptical comment on the attitudes he represents. The "self-ironization and self-condemnation of reason is put on display" in this scene, and the audience is "invited to witness this event in all its grotesqueness." The Captain and the Doctor are non-carnivalesque counterparts of the Barker and represent in stylized exaggeration the enlightened bourgeois values of Clarus (84-85).

When we critically overturn Clarus's metaphysical privileging of reason in the classical duality of reason and unreason, free will and necessity, "then Woyzeck's hybridization ceases to signify the failure of enlightenment and instead indicates its incipient and insidious victory." Woyzeck's murder of Marie does not indicate the failure of reason to control passion, Gray argues, but becomes an expression of the enlightened will to mastery. Woyzeck thus represents the "attempted coming to enlightenment of myth." Following a different line of argument, Gray reaches a conclusion similar to Larsen's: in reaction to his exploitation and oppression Woyzeck appropriates the "same structures of mastery and control under which he suffers as a strategy for his own liberation." Marie's behavior toward her child constitutes a similar attempt at mastery and control. It is behavior characteristic of most of the figures in the play: the oppressed become the oppressors (88-90, 94).

An increasing tendency among critics who emphasize the play's socially critical content has been to identify Dr. Clarus as a callous, inhumane, and morally rigid practitioner of medicine and as a servant of the state and the people with power who stand to benefit from keeping the common people poor and powerless. In the extreme, this criticism has considered the Doctor in *Woyzeck,* and by implication the historical figures he caricatures—the anatomist Johann Bernhard Wilbrand and the chemist Justus Liebig, both of whom were professors at the University of Giessen when Büchner was a student there, as well as Clarus himself, who was also a university professor—as precursors of the doctors who carried out grotesquely inhumane experiments on people in Nazi concentration camps. Dorothy James places this matter in the proper perspective in a 1990 essay by considering Clarus's judgment and the positions represented by him and by Büchner's Doctor in the context of the time in which Büchner was writing. While the play's form belongs more to the twentieth century than to Büchner's time, she writes, it contains "real and documentable threads" that connect it to both time periods (119), a claim she supports with ample documentation.

Woyzeck was indeed an "interesting case" in his own time, James argues, a time in which the nature of man and his behavior was the topic of considerable disagreement and debate. On one side of the issue was Dr. J. C. A. Heinroth, a supporter of Dr. Clarus's conclusions, who was convinced that man stands above the animals because he has reason and can choose to be free. Consciousness and reason can lead him to God; if he does not take this path, it is his own fault and a sin. Heinroth considers illness to be the result of sin, which agrees with Clarus's conclusion that Woyzeck's dissolute life led to his downfall. When he committed the murder, Woyzeck was not controlled by a "necessary blind and instinctual drive," that upset his "free use of reason,"

Clarus concluded. He therefore exercised free will and was responsible for his action (113-14).

Clarus and Heinroth represented a minority position even in their own time, according to James, who cites Professor Johann Christian August Grohmann as a leading proponent of the opposing side of a heated debate. Grohmann maintained that the human being is not "essentially free" or "essentially rational." He may have raised himself above the animals by virtue of his intellect and reason, but he has not eliminated the animal forces in himself. His animal nature is particularly evident in the various drives aimed at the survival of the species. The will is influenced by physical as well as intellectual needs: circumstances can brutalize men and incline them to the bestial side of human nature. In such circumstances, the human being no longer exercises free will but is rather the victim of sickness that attacks not only the body but also the spirit and the will, upon which it has a brutalizing effect. "Is the death penalty possible in such circumstances as punishment," he asks, "or is the animal simply to be sacrificed?" Grohmann disagreed with Clarus's verdict on Woyzeck, and he certainly opposed the punishment, which was described by J. B. Friedrich, a contemporary authority on criminal justice, as "a terrible judicial murder" (115-16).

James notes that the diagnosis of Woyzeck provided by Büchner's Doctor is not unreasonable in the context of contemporary systems of classifying mental disease, though his "outspoken relish in pronouncing his diagnosis to the disturbed man himself" is unreasonable, even grotesque. "Fixed ideas" were considered at the time to be partial mental disturbances or madness. Particularly in the early part of the nineteenth century they were associated with melancholy, which was defined by the French authority Dr. Philippe Pinel as a "delirium attached to an object." As James writes, fixed ideas "involved a confusion of the subjective and the objective, the subject being convinced that a given fantasy attached to an object was literally true. It was much debated whether a person's derangement could really be limited to one area or object." If so, could a person be considered sane in all other aspects of his life? If a person suffered from partial or periodic insanity associated with fixed ideas, he presumably could not be held accountable for acts committed when in that state, but what about behavior during the periods in which the person's behavior appeared to be normal and responsible? Clarus addressed this point in his report and concluded that Woyzeck's reason was never overpowered by "an incorrect or over-wrought concept of the objects of the physical or transcendental world or by the conditions of his own physical and moral personality" such that the "free perspective for other conditions was distorted and the proper assessment of them obscured." In other words, he did not suffer from fixed ideas and was

therefore accountable for his actions. Had Clarus's diagnosis agreed with that of Büchner's Doctor, Woyzeck's life would have been spared, which is not to say that Büchner is not mocking the Doctor and his disregard for the well-being and humanity of his fellow men (105-107).

James proposes an additional model for Büchner's Doctor, the one he was closest to and knew best: his own father, who also functioned as a court doctor and wrote expert opinions for the court, some of which were published (109-110).

Finally, James discusses the debate taking place in Büchner's time concerning the nature of animals, in particular the seemingly human attributes of animals that perform tricks, as do the animals in Büchner's carnival scene. Do animals have souls, imagination, feeling, free will, a form of language, or are they simply machines? This debate connects to the emerging evolutionary theory that appalled defenders of free will such as Heinroth and Clarus (117). "It is not a coincidence," James writes,

> that Grohmann, who viewed Woyzeck as a victim of social and environmental circumstances and of physiological determination, was "evolutionary" in his thinking, rejecting as early as 1820 teleological explanations of evolution which Büchner later mocked in his *Woyzeck,* and which he seriously combatted in his lecture "Über die Schädelnerven."
>
> (118)

As a number of critics have pointed out, the focus on Woyzeck given by the play's title is an editorial construct, since there is no mention of a title in the manuscripts or any of Büchner's letters. It is conceivable that Büchner's title for the play would have included Marie's name along with Woyzeck's, as is the case with ***Leonce und Lena.*** And while Woyzeck has certainly been at the center of most criticism, a number of critics have recognized the tragic dimension of Marie's fate and have exonerated her and placed the blame on Woyzeck and society, which has instilled in him the notion of erotic possessiveness. Those efforts have not been enough for feminist critics, however, who consider criticism of the play to be unbalanced in favor of Woyzeck and a patriarchal view of the world, and who turn their attention to Marie.

Taking her cue from a performance of the play in Sydney, Australia in which the actor playing Woyzeck rammed his knife up between Marie's legs and later commented in an interview that "it felt good to kill Marie in this manner because he, Woyzeck, had been dependent on Marie's sexuality for too long" (294), Kerry Dunne sets out in an article published in 1990 to demonstrate that Marie is as much a victim as Woyzeck. In her sexuality Marie is subject to the demands of her nature just as Woyzeck is when he pisses on the wall or when he creates a child without the blessings of the church. In addition, she is also a victim of her sexual attractiveness and desirability. In Dunne's view, Büchner's aim is to rehabilitate sexuality as a meaningful and natural part of human existence, but to do so would have required that Woyzeck be brought to trial and sentenced, which would have repudiated the societal values upon which the murder was based, namely, the assumption that women are men's possessions (294, 304-7).

Noting the recent attention given to love and sex in Büchner's works and to the female figures as those most clearly linked with love and the depiction of sexuality, Dunne intends to fill what she considers to be the need for a more detailed study of the play's sexual imagery. She considers Marie to be a parallel figure to the Drum Major and the Sergeant: each uses animal imagery and refers to parts of the body in responding to the physical appeal and animal vitality of the other. Marie's reference to the Drum Major's beard, for example, has symbolic associations with male virility and public hair, Dunne maintains, which betray the erotic nature of her interest. The Sergeant's comment about her heavy dark hair shows he is "responding to her sensual appearance and his statement that its weight could pull her down, indicates not only the abundance of hair, but is also perhaps an indirect expression of his desire to see her lying beneath him." The Sergeant's stress on the blackness of Marie's eyes suggests "the physiological response of enlarged pupils during sexual arousal," Dunne interprets rather fancifully. The reference to her hair dragging her down also implies that her sexuality could be her downfall, and the reference to her black eyes introduces the notion of death (296-97).

The Drum Major amplifies on his colleague's implied innuendoes when he compares looking into her eyes with looking into a chimney or a well, "images which suggest an underlying image of the vagina." Also having vaginal connotations, according to Dunne, are references to Marie's mouth and lips. As he is about to kill her, Woyzeck refers to her hot lips and the attraction they still have for him. Earlier, when he begins to suspect her, he refers to her red mouth and looks at her lips for a blister that would be evidence of her infidelity. "Blisters are traditionally a symbol of deceit," Dunne writes, but could also be an allusion to a lesion from a sexually transmitted disease. In killing Marie, Woyzeck is not inflicting punishment for sin—he says he would forgo heaven in exchange for kissing her—he is acting out of sexual jealousy, as is indicated by his repeated stabbing of her body with the knife, which also suggests to Dunne "the phallic revenge on female sexuality that has castrated the owner (by preferring another lover)" (296-99, 304).

Most of these images point to a positive view of sexuality, Dunne writes. Since the imagery used in connection with Marie is similar to that used for the Drum Major, one cannot say that Marie or women are denigrated in Büchner's portrayal. His view of Marie and her fate is also indicated by his choice of her name, which refers both to Mary Magdalene and to the Virgin Mary. The choice of this name "suggests an authorial caution to the reader/viewer against the division of women into the pure and the carnal." It has been suggested that Marie exploits her attractiveness and sexuality, the only bargaining power a poor woman has in a class-ridden, patriarchal society, to gain financial support from Woyzeck and to better her social standing through the Drum Major. But while Marie has indeed exploited her sexuality to obtain financial support from Woyzeck, Dunne argues, the images she uses to describe the Drum Major indicate that her involvement with him is not motivated merely by a desire to better herself but also by her sexual needs (298-99).

Dunne identifies two different types of cultural knowledge that determine the moral views of the play's characters: one derived from folk-songs, in which the existence of female sexuality is acknowledged and in part celebrated, and which reflect "the existence and power of sexuality in a relatively playful, non-judgmental manner," and one derived from Christianity, which regards female sexuality as threatening and evil. It is the latter that prevents Büchner from rehabilitating the physical and sexual. Woyzeck and the Drum Major share the Christian view: the Drum Major asks whether the devil is in her, and Woyzeck views her as a sinner. Licentiousness, evil, and destruction are linked in Woyzeck's vision of Sodom and Gomorrah in the beginning scene, in his reaction to seeing Marie and the Drum Major dancing, and in his linkage of female sexuality with the devil in the final inn scene. The reason Woyzeck kills Marie rather than the Drum Major, Dunne writes, is that he acts not merely out of jealousy but as the instrument of punishment in a patriarchal society that considers female sexuality to be especially sinful and threatening and in which women are regarded as possessions. Even Marie herself is unable to embrace her sexuality in an unfettered way, as Marion does in *Dantons Tod.* Following her conflict with Margret, her neighbor, she accepts society's attitude toward her in referring to her child as a "whore's child," and following Woyzeck's discovery of her with the earrings she calls herself a whore (*ein schlecht Mensch*). And when she cannot resist the Drum Major's advances, she longs in vain to be able to follow the example of the repentant Mary Magdalene (295, 300, 302-6).

Countering the devaluation of the physical and sexual within society is the admonition by the Barker to accept our animal nature. Woyzeck is torn between the two views: in defending himself against the Captain and the Doctor, he considers his poverty and the demands of his nature to be excuses for his "immoral" behavior, but he

accepts the views of society as represented by his oppressors when he punishes and takes revenge on Marie
for her sin. Without explaining how or why, Dunne
claims that if Woyzeck were to have been "brought to
trial and sentenced, then not only would the overall importance of societal values be different but Woyzeck
would be punished," an outcome resulting in a view of
sexuality more in accordance with that represented by
Marion (302-306).

Writing in the same year as Dunne, Elisabeth Boa, too,
notes the incongruity between Woyzeck's appeal to nature in defense of his performance of bodily functions
and his inability to see Marie's transgression in the
same light, namely, as nature "in revolt against a life
denuded of pleasure," but Boa places greater blame on
class structure and social conditions. In her view, both
Marie and Woyzeck are subject to brutal assertions of
power by those who treat them as instruments to be exploited: the power of knowledge and science represented by the Doctor and the power of a repressive morality represented by the Captain. Another contributing
factor is the "antithetical structuring of masculinity and
femininity," which includes the sexual division of labor
in which Woyzeck and Marie are caught up—he to provide for his family, she to mother their child—and the
sexual antagonism that is created by this division. In a
patriarchal society, men have exclusive right of ownership of the female body, and mothers are not supposed
to feel sexual desire. The allocation of power to men
provokes Marie's reaction and her willingness to use
her sexuality as a vehicle of power, though internalized
religious teachings make her feel guilty. Furthermore,
Boa writes, the sexually active woman in a patriarchal
society provokes a violent reassertion of male dominance and the barbaric reassertion of his masculinity, as
is the case when Woyzeck murders Marie. As long as
the sexes remain divided, social justice is impossible
(1990, 174-77).

Contrary to Dunne's reading of the folk songs as an affirmation of sexuality, Laura Martin sees them in an article published in 1997 as representing an ideology according to which loose women represent a social
problem. Martin claims that Marie's sexual promiscuity
"indicates her belief in herself as a free agent," which
goes against patriarchy's ownership of women. Woyzeck
is not destabilized by his diet of peas or the other abuse
he suffers as a poor man but by Marie's refusal to be
controlled by him, or by "her ignorance that she is to
be considered his property, his chattel" (436). The contribution of Christianity is not different from that of the
folk songs, according to Martin, though it is less light-
hearted, and it introduces the concept of sin and retribution. In applying the Biblical concepts, Woyzeck becomes "the prophet of the apocalypse" (436-37).

With reference to René Girard's book *Violence and the
Sacred,* Martin considers Marie to be an example of the
scapegoat whose sacrifice Girard considers to be the
foundation of every religion. The scapegoat must be
similar to the real or potential perpetrators of violence
in order to substitute for them, but it must also be different enough not to threaten the commonality. "What
better victim, then, than a woman?" Martin asks. "A
woman is the same, but different, other." The scapegoat
must be sufficiently other for its sacrifice not to require
revenge, a demand fulfilled, Martin claims, by the loose
woman. The "sacrificial crisis" preceding the act of sacrifice is a communal situation in which distinctions
have been erased, according to Girard. Martin finds
such a loss of distinctions in the play's repeated equation of animal and human, and in the supposed loss, or
at least confusion, of class distinctions that occurs here
in the false application of bourgeois morality to a member of the proletariat. The Doctor's and Captain's "nagging" of Woyzeck is inappropriate and misplaced, Martin maintains, "for it assumes a sameness of outlook
and lifestyle between these two classes which simply
does not exist." In fact, Marie and Woyzeck have no
need to be as "moral" as the Doctor and the Captain,
since "Kantian moral free will is . . . contingent on
class and upbringing." Finally, distinction between the
sexes also begins to blur: Marie is "uncharacteristically
active for a woman character." She is closer to Faust
than to Gretchen in her masculine will to experience
pleasure. Woyzeck, on the other hand, is passive, lacking in will power, and effeminate. He is easily victimized by the real men in what Martin calls their "thirst
for violence" (437-38, 441).

Martin weakens her argument by pointing out that the
act of sacrifice in Girard's sense is a communal activity,
whereas Woyzeck acts alone. "The Girardian sacrificial
crisis cannot ever be resolved in the play, for there is
no unanimity in the choice of the victim: at times it appears to be Woyzeck himself, yet he chooses his own
victim in the form of Marie." Thus the choice of Marie
as scapegoat, which Martin has considered so obvious,
is

> not unproblematic, and it is in fact on this paradox that
> the play turns. Only if all those involved were to agree
> on the necessity of her death could the play be a trag-
> edy in the ancient sense of that word. All the evils
> threatening the social order would be heaped upon
> Marie's shoulders and Woyzeck would be the hero for
> ridding society of the unclean thing.
>
> (439)

But of course Woyzeck himself is an outcast whose
deed is not celebrated by society but condemned and
punished. In our time of "objective justice," the sacrifice of an ignorant and unstable fool like Woyzeck can
no longer be accepted as a legitimate means of eliminating violence from society. Thus, neither Woyzeck
nor Marie can serve as a proper scapegoat. The conclu-

sion, then, with respect to Girard's theory is that it is impossible to find the perfect victim in a society that lacks "consensus and a community of faith" (439).

Martin nevertheless tries to defend her hypothesis by claiming that Marie succeeds in her role as victim. She is the only one of Woyzeck's tormentors to accept any guilt for the effect her actions have on him, and in saying that she could stab herself, she reveals a readiness for self-sacrifice. Readers and audiences seem willing to recognize her suitability as a sacrificial victim: "violence against a woman is disapproved of, yet understood, and therefore actually effectively condoned." The community that condemns Woyzeck is the same one that spurred him on to the deed. Marie's spilt blood becomes a purifying libation to the gods. She becomes "the scapegoat for crimes not committed by her, but by her supposed social superiors, if anyone. *Woyzeck* then is not so much about the victimization of the hero as it is the portrait of the development of the violent criminal—or of the accession to manhood in our rotten society" (439-40, 442).

In a study of Woyzeck published in 1991, Edward McInnes comes closer to Boa than to Dunne in the emphasis he places on the social dimension of Marie's attraction to the Drum Major. With his fine clothing and ability to give her a valuable gift—she thinks the earrings could be gold—he represents for her a higher social standing and affirms her view of herself as equal to the grand ladies. According to McInnes, the Drum Major senses from the beginning a strong impulse of revolt in Marie's responses to him, and he is able to exploit it for his own ends. In strutting before her and referring to the Prince's admiration of his manliness, he impresses on her that he is socially sophisticated and successful and that he is at ease in all strata of society. The gift of the earrings confirms his status as a man of some means. In seducing her, he is able to take advantage of her dissatisfaction with her social status and her frustration with her narrow and demeaned existence. In yielding to his seduction, McInnes argues, Marie not only expresses her strong sensuality, she also reveals a strong impulse of social rebellion and revolt (1991, 21-23).

As opposed to his emphasis on the social dimension of Marie's situation, McInnes considers the murder to be an entirely personal matter concerning Woyzeck and Marie alone, and he downplays the importance of the Captain and the Doctor as vehicles of social protest. They may be seen to "embody a strong socially enforced authority," he writes, but "both are in reality anguished men, each in his own way ravaged by a deep sense of existential horror and apprehension." They are "torn by feelings of inner emptiness and of their estrangement from a world in which they can see no ultimate sustaining meaning." Büchner seeks through them "to lay bare a disabling sense of metaphysical desolation which neither can fully articulate much less confront" (31, 47).

In his 1994 *Georg Büchner: The Shattered Whole,* the first book-length study of Büchner published in English since the 1970s, John Reddick follows a trend of recent scholarship to establish more fully and accurately the intellectual, cultural, social, and political contexts that provide a background for evaluating and interpreting Büchner's works. Reddick discusses in four introductory chapters some of the primary elements of Büchner's thought and art. Although Büchner's artistic vision is disjunctive with its insistence on fragments and particles, he believed in the fundamental unity and wholeness of nature, and this, Reddick claims, locates him in the German tradition of *Naturphilosophie,* which was already outdated at the time (9). Consequently, Reddick considers Büchner to be "hopelessly remote from the prevailing spirit of his time" in his "reliance on idealist, poetical, mystical notions" and his rejection of rationalist philosophy and mechanistic science (39-40). The manner of his writing is "inexorably un- and anti-classical," but "the faith and vision that underlies it is classical almost to the point of anachronism" (13). Reddick considers Büchner to be involved in a "Rearguard Action," as his second chapter is entitled, and dismisses Büchner's often-quoted pronouncement on fatalism as "the sonorous trumpeting of a transient mood" (29), a reading that is based not on evidence from the text but on the fact that Büchner did not cease his political activity after supposedly gaining this shattering insight. He identifies a similar contradiction or paradox in the discrepancy between Büchner's scornful dismissal of intellect and learning and his relentless pursuit of knowledge. Reddick finds similar inconsistencies in the main figures of Büchner's works; they appear to be part of the fullness and quickness of life Büchner wants to capture in his art and that he opposes to the marionettes of idealist art, whose mechanistic obsessions and behavior he caricatures in such figures as King Peter in *Leonce und Lena* and the Doctor and the Captain in *Woyzeck* (50).

Fundamental to Büchner's thought, Reddick writes, is his affirmation of life and his emphasis on the individual, each of which is a valuable manifestation of a primal law and exists in and of itself. ("Everything that exists, exists for its own sake" [II.292].) He is antagonistic to every kind of anti-life force or process. King Peter in *Leonce und Lena* is satirized for his anti-life philosophizing, the Doctor, Büchner's "most savagely satirical stooge," for his "anti-life scientizing" (43, 46). The Doctor sacrifices his patients to an excess of science. He is not interested in helping suffering individuals but rather in promoting his own self-interest. At the same time, he is also a laughable victim, who is demented by his own version of the fixed idea he diagnoses in Woyzeck. In speaking of freedom of will to the man he has enslaved, he contradicts and refutes his own theories, as he does also in praising individuality while denying the existence of individuals, who for him are reduced to the status of specimens or cases (46-49).

The Captain represents a variant on the comic model of power, according to Reddick. He plays a role similar to King Peter's: both figures occupy the supreme power position within their respective plays, Reddick writes, "but in comic contrast to the might and mantle of their positions, both of them are puny and petrified, and utterly dwarfed by their ostensible victims." Both are easily thrown into confusion, and they share a sense of fear, which is at once existential and the product of thinking. As has been frequently pointed out, the Captain is more complex and interesting than the Doctor, since he is "stricken by glimpses of an abyss that in varying forms critically affects the destinies of all Büchner's central characters." Because he fears infinitude and eternity, time appears monstrous to him. As opposed to Woyzeck, he behaves as an abject coward in his avoidance of the abyss and in his attempts to seek refuge in artificial constructs such as specious morality and a measured routine of unhurried activity (50-52).

Reddick cautions against taking any particular speech or argument as the play's ultimate truth. The statements by Woyzeck and Marie relating to poverty, for example, are not sufficient, in his view, to characterize the play as a social drama. In fact, Büchner's Woyzeck is much better off than his historical counterpart: he has some income, a place to stay, and a familial relationship with Marie and their child, none of which was true for the historical Woyzeck. The first draft of the play contains no sign of poverty, the second, not much more. In H4 Büchner thematizes poverty and projects it in class terms, but it is not a central issue. Furthermore, Reddick continues, Woyzeck contradicts himself no less than does the Doctor: in defending himself against the Captain for his illegitimate child and against the Doctor for his inability to control his bladder, he cites the demands of nature, but, as the feminist critics point out, he condemns and punishes Marie for yielding to the demands of her nature. Likewise, the words of the Barker relating to the animal nature of man and the words of the Journeyman concerning the teleological view of life are not meant to be swallowed whole. At issue in the play, according to Reddick, are "questions of civilization as against nature; moral choice as against animal compulsion; responsibility and accountability; crime and punishment; sin and retribution." Büchner conjures up a context that "challenges the very idea of humanity, society, civilization" (304-308).

Büchner's concern is with the nature of man; the whole play can be seen as a kind of "*Ecce homo.*" According to Reddick's count, the word "Mensch" (man, mankind), which, apart from proper nouns and titles, is the most frequently used noun in all Büchner's poetic writings, appears 78 times in **Woyzeck,** which is considerably more than in **Dantons Tod** (29 times) and **Leonce und Lena** (34 times). The personae are not presented as "quirky individuals caught up in the specificity of their particular personality and history, but emblematically, as archetypes" (336). (Reddick sees the interspersion of song fragments as a device that encourages us to see the story in archetypal terms [337-44].) Woyzeck's story can be understood in the terms of the child's questions in the Grandmother's tale as to the what and the why of man. He is more profoundly tormented than any other of Büchner's protagonists by the gulf "between thinking and knowing, between subject and object, between the lonely, errant, solipsistic mind and the objective reality of the world outside" (350).

It is not surprising, given Büchner's background and the direction of his study, that illness, especially psychological illness, appears in all his works and is of primary importance in **Lenz** and **Woyzeck.** Analysis of the illnesses he portrays and their treatment, or lack of it, and the relationship of Büchner's position to the medical knowledge and practice of his time has been the object of two published dissertations in the nineties: Sabine Kubik's *Krankheit und Medizin im literarischen Werk Georg Büchners* (Sickness and Medicine in the Literary Works of Georg Büchner) was written as a dissertation at the Ludwig-Maximilians University of Munich in 1990 and published in 1991; and *Büchner and Madness: Schizophrenia in Georg Büchner's Lenz and Woyzeck* by James Crighton, a retired medical doctor, was presented as a dissertation at the University of Leicester in 1994 and published in 1998.

Kubik agrees with Dorothy James that Büchner's play was not written merely as a counterargument to Clarus but also and even more as a critique of the scientific view of medicine and the scientific method of investigation that were becoming predominant at the time. According to Kubik, Woyzeck is not presented unequivocally as organically sick or as a psychopathic murderer. The play contains no explicit diagnosis of Woyzeck's condition, and the question of his accountability remains open. In his awareness of the complexity of human behavior, determined as it is by hereditary and social factors, Büchner does not consider a clear judgment to be possible, and he is therefore critical of the unequivocalness that is a central postulate of forensic and juridical discourse. Emphasizing the inadequacy of the means of evaluation in those fields, he begins his investigation or presentation where medicine and justice reach their limits (167-70).

Kubik finds support for her argument in her study of the sequence of manuscripts, from which she concludes that Büchner gives greater emphasis in the second stage of the play's composition (H2) to Woyzeck's pathology and the origins of his illness. Through the introduction of the Captain and especially the Doctor, Büchner establishes a causal connection between Woyzeck's illness, the severity of which is increased in H2, and the socially superior figures who exploit and abuse him. The Doctor's interest in Woyzeck is limited to his diagnosis of Woyzeck's illness and to the contribution he may be able to make to the progress of science. He makes no attempt to treat or heal him. On the contrary, his experiments contribute significantly to Woyzeck's destabilization, Kubik assumes. Unfortunately, Kubik relies for most of her evidence on two scenes whose inclusion in the final version is questionable, namely, H2,7, in which the Doctor makes Woyzeck the victim of his scientific observations, and H3,1, in which Woyzeck is treated no better than an animal, and in which his symptoms can "undoubtedly" be attributed to the diet of peas the Doctor has subjected him to (64-71).

In his lack of humanity and medical ethics, the Doctor represents a type of scientist that was not uncommon in an era when positivistic, empirical scientific investigation was replacing the romantic, speculative *Naturphilosophie* as the dominant mode of discovery and in which science was becoming less human. Kubik refers to the similarity between Justus Liebig's nutritional experiments on soldiers and the Doctor's experiment on Woyzeck, and she also cites the example of doctors who dissected their own relations, including one Philip Meckel who dissected three of his own deceased children and used his eight-year-old nephew as his assistant (181-83, 189).

Though Büchner is seen by many critics as a precursor of modern literature, and though his influence on writers in the twentieth century has indeed been widespread and profound, Büchner belonged very much to his own time in dealing with actual problems of the new positivistic science, according to Kubik. His doctor is the first in German literature to be oriented to the natural sciences, and he is the only one in the century to be treated critically, Kubik claims: the other doctor figures in this period are heroized and idealized in keeping with the new faith in the progress of science. Not until the expressionists in the twentieth century were doctors again seen with a similarly critical eye (250-58).

James Crighton's study is similar to Kubik's in its historical review of philosophical and medical theories of madness and of the occurrence of madness in works of literature. In keeping with his medical background and his diagnosis of Woyzeck, however, he gives greater emphasis to the symptoms and medical descriptions of what later became known as schizophrenia. Unlike Kubik, he does not consider the Doctor, who is but one part of Woyzeck's threatening and unfathomable world, to be responsible for Woyzeck's breakdown. According to Crighton, the roots of Woyzeck's madness lie in his "resistance (defiance would be too strong a word) to the relentless forces which have shaped the world he lives in and which have condemned him to subjection." Andres and Marie inhabit the same world, but they are protected by their passivity. Woyzeck attempts to understand the world and to cling to the woman who gives his life meaning and stability. In his attempt to find meaning in life and in nature, he is driven ever deeper into unreason. Finally he sees only chaos in the world and he sees himself devoid of all freedom. In what he calls "double nature" Woyzeck perceives an unbridgeable gap between appearances and reality, most painfully in the person of Marie. His suffering is "caught in this gulf between the essence of things and their appearance," a gulf also evident in his relationship to Marie, his mate and the mother of his child, in whom he discovers a whore (284, 275-76).

Works Cited

Boa, Elizabeth. "Whores and Hetairas. Sexual Politics in the Works of Büchner and Wedekind." In *Tradition and Innovation: 14 Essays,* ed. Ken Mills and Brian Keith-Smith, 161-81. Bristol: U of Bristol P, 1990.

Crighton, James. *Büchner and Madness: Schizophrenia in Georg Büchner's* Lenz and Woyzeck. Bristol German Publications, Vol. 9. Lewiston, NY: The Edwin Mellen Press, 1998.

Dedner, Burghard. "Die Handlung des Woyzeck: wechselnde Orte—geschlossene Form." *Georg Büchner Jahrbuch* 7 (1988/89): 144-70.

Dunne, Kerry. "Woyzeck's Marie 'Ein schlecht Mensch'?: The Construction of Feminine Sexuality in Büchner's *Woyzeck*" Seminar 26 (1990): 294-308.

Gray, Richard T. "The Dialectic of Enlightenment in Büchner's *Woyzeck.*" *The German Quarterly* 61 (1988): 78-96.

Guthrie, John. *Lenz and Büchner: Studies in Dramatic Form.* Frankfurt: Lang, 1984.

James, Dorothy. "The 'Interesting Case' of Büchner's Woyzeck." In *Patterns of Change: German Drama and the European Tradition: Essays in Honour of Ronald Peacock.* Ed. Dorothy James and Sylvia Ranawake, 103-19. New York: Peter Lang, 1990.

Kittsteiner, Heinz-Dieter and Helmut Lethen. "Ich-Losigkeit, Entbürgerlichung und Zeiterfahrung. Über die Gleichgültigkeit zur 'Geschichte' in Büchner's *Woyzeck.*" *Georg Büchner Jahrbuch* 3 (1983): 240-269.

Kubik, S. *Krankheit und Medizin im literarischen Werk Georg Büchners.* Stuttgart: M. & P. Verlag für Wissenschaft und Forschung, 1991.

Larsen, Svend Erik. "Die Macht der Machtlosen. Über Lenz und Woyzeck." In *Georg Büchner im interkul-*

turellen Dialog. Eds. Klaus Bohnen and Ernst-Ulrich Pinkert, 176-94. Copenhagen: Verlag Text und Kontext; Munich: Fink, 1988.

Martin, Laura. "'Schlechtes Mensch/gutes Opfer': The Role of Marie in Georg Büchner's *Woyzeck.*" *German Life and Letters* 50 (1997): 427-44.

Mayer, Thomas Michael. "Zu einigen neueren Tenden-zen der Büchner Forschung. Ein kritischer Literaturber-icht (Teil II: Editionen)." In *Georg Büchner III.* Special issue in the series *Text und Kritik,* ed. Heinz Ludwig, 265-311. Munich: edition text + kritik, 1981.

McInnes, Edward. *Büchner, Woyzeck.* Glasgow: U. of Glasgow French and German Publications, 1991.

Meier, Albert. *Georg Büchner: "Woyzeck".* Munich: Fink, 1980.

Oesterle, Ingrid. "Verbale Präsenz und poetische Rück-nahme des literarischen Schauers. Nachweise zur ästhe-tischen Vermitteltheit des Fatalismusproblems in Georg Büchners *Woyzeck.*" *Georg Büchner Jahrbuch* 3 (1983): 168-99.

Patterson, Michael. "Contradictions Concerning Time in Büchner's 'Woyzeck.'" *German Life and Letters* 32 (1978-79): 115-21.

Poschmann, Henri. *Georg Büchner: Dichtung der Revo-lution und Revolution der Dichtung.* Berlin, Weimar: Aufbau Verlag, 1983.

——. "Büchner ein Klassiker?" In *Büchner. Zeit, Geist, Zeit-Genossen,* 73-88. Darmstadt: Technische Hochschule Darmstadt, 1989.

Reddick, John. *Georg Büchner: The Shattered Whole.* Oxford: Clarendon Press, 1994.

Reuchlein, Georg. *Das Problem der Zurechnungs-fähigkeit bei E. T. A. Hoffmann und Georg Büchner: Zum Verhältnis von Literatur, Psychiatrie und Justiz im frühen 19. Jahrhundert.* Frankfurt: Lang, 1985.

Wetzel, Heinz. "Die Entwicklung Woyzecks in Büch-ners Entwurfen." *Euphorion* 74 (1980): 375-96.

FURTHER READING

Criticism

Bamforth, Iain. "Writing with a Scalpel: Georg Büch-ner." *PN Review* 26, no. 16 (July-August 2000): 17-26.

Includes a partial English translation of Büchner's *Lenz* preceded by a brief biographical introduction to the novella.

Bohm, Arnd. "Büchner's Lucile and the Situation of Celan's 'Der Meridian.'" *Michigan Germanic Studies* 17, no. 2 (fall 1991): 119-27.

Traces similarities of theme in Paul Celan's "Der Meridian" and *Danton's Death.*

Constabile, Carol Anne. "Christa Wolf's Büchner Prize Acceptance Speech: An Exercise in *Sprach-* and *Kul-turkritik.*" *Germanic Notes* 22, no. 1-2 (1991): 58-61.

Mentions *Lenz* as part of a discussion of the mod-ern contradiction between scientific and literary language.

Del Caro, Adrian. "Paul Celan's Uncanny Speech." *Philosophy and Literature* 18, no. 2 (October 1994): 211-24.

Explores the concept of "the uncanny" (*das Unheimliche*) in literature, applying this idea to works by Büchner, Paul Celan, and others.

Hermand, Jost. "Deepest Misery—Highest Art: Alban Berg's *Wozzeck.*" *Houston German Studies* 8 (1992): 173-92.

Calls Alban Berg's *Wozzeck* "the greatest opera of the twentieth century" and explores the work's re-lationship to its literary source, Büchner's drama *Woyzeck.*

Horton, David. "Georg Büchner's *Lenz* in English." *Ba-bel* 41, no. 2 (1995): 65-85.

Examines four English translations of *Lenz,* prob-ing stylistic affinities between these texts and the German original.

Martin, Laura. "'Schlechtes Mensch/Gutes Opfer': The Role of Marie in Georg Büchner's *Woyzeck.*" In *Gen-dering German Studies: New Perspectives on German Literature and Culture,* edited by Margaret Littler, pp. 51-66. Oxford: Blackwell Publishers, 1997.

Feminist analysis of *Woyzeck* that discusses what Martin considers the hypocritical male scapegoat-ing and sacrifice of Maria in the drama.

Müller-Sievers, Helmut. "Büchner-Cult." *MLN* 112, no. 3 (April 1997): 470-85.

Offers discussion and favorable reviews of Jan-Christoph Hauschild's biography *Georg Büchner* and John Reddick's critical study *Georg Büchner: The Shattered Whole.*

Perraudin, Michael. "Towards a New Cultural Life: Büchner and the 'Volk.'" *Modern Language Review* 86, no. 3 (July 1991): 627-44.

Assesses Büchner's representation of common people (*das Volk*) in his dramas.

Richards, David G. *Georg Büchner and the Birth of the Modern Drama.* Albany: State University of New York Press, 1977, 289 p.

Study of Büchner's seminal influence on modern theater.

Stern, Sheila. "Truth So Difficult: George Eliot and Georg Büchner: A Shared Theme." *Modern Language Review* 96, no. 1 (January 2001): 1-13.

Suggests the possible thematic influence of *Lenz* on George Eliot's novel *Adam Bede.*

Walker, John. "'Ach die Kunst! . . . Ach, die erbärmliche Wirklichkeit!' Suffering, Empathy, and the Relevance of Realism in Büchner's *Lenz.*" *Forum for Modern Language Studies* 33, no. 2 (April 1997): 157-70.

Describes the tension between human empathy and philosophical idealism illustrated in Büchner's *Lenz.*

Additional coverage of Büchner's life and career is contained in the following sources published by Thomson Gale: *Concise Dictionary of World Literary Biography,* **Vol. 2;** *Dictionary of Literary Biography,* **Vol. 133;** *European Writers,* **Vol. 6;** *Literature Resource Center;* *Nineteenth-Century Literature Criticism,* **Vol. 26;** *Reference Guide to Short Fiction,* **Ed. 2;** *Reference Guide to World Literature,* **Eds. 2, 3; and** *Twayne's World Authors.*

Benjamin Robert Haydon
1786-1846

English autobiographer, essayist, critic, and diarist.

INTRODUCTION

Aspiring to achieve greatness as a historical painter, Haydon never attained the success he envisioned. Instead, the tumultuous figure is remembered more for his autobiographical writings, which reveal his flair for romanticized and exalted language; his tremendous ambition and pride; his disputes—both public and private—with his many "adversaries," including London's Royal Academy; and his never-ending anxiety over his professional failures and financial troubles. Not considered a major writer during his lifetime, Haydon attracted attention as a literary figure after his death with the publication of the three-volume *Life of Benjamin Robert Haydon, Historical Painter, from His Autobiography and Journals* (1853), which was printed at the request of his wife. A highly abridged version of his personal writings, the *Life* exhibited such literary merit that it has been reissued in modified forms several times since its original publication.

BIOGRAPHICAL INFORMATION

Haydon was born in Plymouth in January of 1786 to Benjamin Robert Haydon, a bookseller and printer, and Sarah Cobley Haydon. At age six he began drawing, and by age eighteen, certain of his love for art, he left his father's business and enrolled at the Royal Academy. Though beset in childhood with an eye disease that permanently damaged his vision, Haydon was driven by an intense determination to succeed. He found inspiration in famed English portrait painter Sir Joshua Reynolds's *Discourses on Art* (1769-91) and hoped to paint in the mode of the great Renaissance painters Raphael and Michelangelo. Devoted to what he referred to as the masters's "high art," he wished to replicate their reverence for religion, their precision of form, their sense of patriotism, and their emotional expressiveness—qualities he vehemently set in contrast to the work of the "carrot painters," those artists whose still lifes, portraits, and small-scale landscapes were so loved by the uninformed public. Arriving at the Royal Academy in 1804, Haydon achieved success with his first commissioned work, *The Assassination of Dentatus* (1808), which in 1810 won a premium for historical

painting from the British Institution for the Promotion of the Fine Arts. This also marked the beginning of a lifelong conflict with the Royal Academy, triggered by a dispute over the display of the painting in the Academy. Some of Haydon's other early works—*The Judgment of Solomon* (1814) and *Christ's Entry into Jerusalem* (1820)—garnered high prices, and for a short time he was even called by some critics England's finest historical painter. Haydon quickly accumulated massive amounts of debt, however, as he spared no expense with materials and models while spending enormous amounts of time on the massive works. He temporarily maintained solvency only through the generosity of friends and by borrowing money. These continued financial difficulties would contribute significantly to his downfall.

During this same time the Elgin marbles, a collection of ancient Greek sculptures and inscriptions, was brought to England from Athens by Lord Elgin, who hoped that they would be purchased by the English government.

Haydon, who had first seen the marbles in 1808, quickly became a proponent of the purchase and became embroiled in an intense public dispute with connoisseur Richard Payne Knight, director of the British Gallery, who claimed the marbles were inauthentic and inartistic. Haydon attacked the detractors in his first publication, *The Judgment of Connoisseurs upon Works of Art Compared with That of Professional Men* (1816), which brought about widespread notoriety for the author. Haydon became further incensed at the fact that, even though his name had been submitted as a "friendly witness," he was never called by Parliament to testify as to the artistic value of the marbles. Haydon's public status reached its height when he was awarded an honorary membership in the Russian Imperial Academy. Around this time Haydon's friends included the Hunt brothers (John, Leigh, and Robert), Charles Lamb, John Keats, and William Wordsworth, the latter two sharing Haydon's ambitious artistic goals. Keats and Wordsworth, in fact, both wrote sonnets to their friend.

Haydon's quarrel with the Royal Academy extended to the areas of art instruction for the public and governmental funding for artists, causes that he returned to repeatedly over the course of his life. He claimed that the Royal Academy had "subtly and insidiously abandoned its most sacred obligation, that of providing sufficient art instruction for the people." Thus, he established a private school of his own, which operated from 1815-23, and opened the doors to artisans, mechanics, and traditional artists. Haydon's mantra was that design was crucial to any aesthetic undertaking, and his school focused heavily in this area. "My object," he stated, "was to make design as cheap as ABC, that the merest door-painter might paint the human figure."

A year after his success with *Christ's Entry into Jerusalem,* Haydon married the widow Mary Cawrse Hyman. She already had two children, and four more were born in subsequent years. Mounting debts only increased, and a series of imprisonments resulted for Haydon, who could no longer escape the money lenders and creditors. By 1824 Haydon was forced by his legal adviser to submit to a new methodology: the artist had to start painting portraits and could not work on the massive canvasses he had previously desired. In effect, Haydon became one of the detested "carrot painters." For the next several years he painted portraits, including an 1842 portrait of Wordsworth and *Mock Election,* completed during one of his many stays in debtor's prison. He busied himself with trying to convince the government to subsidize historical painters and also began a career as a public lecturer, speaking in London, Edinburgh, and the northern cities, particularly Liverpool. Though popular and enjoyable as a lecturer, Haydon was never able to break from poverty. In early 1846, he arranged another exhibition of his works, featuring two final paintings entitled *The Banishment of Aristides* and *The Burning of Rome by Nero.* The showing was a complete failure. Impoverished and despondent, Haydon attempted to set his affairs in order. Overwhelmed, he shot and stabbed himself in the throat. The medical examiner listed "insanity" as the cause of death.

MAJOR WORKS

Haydon began writing his autobiography in 1841, writing for two years and stopping his chronicle at 1820. His journals fill in the years both before and after that period. Totaling twenty-six folio volumes, his highly dramatic journal entries begin in 1808 and are filled with letters and documents, sketches, gossip about contemporaries, literary criticism, talk of English politics, his views on debtors' laws, newspaper cuttings, his anguish over his constant financial woes, and descriptions of his paintings. Writings in both his autobiography and journal reflect his grandiose ideas about his own artistic talent and his aspirations to elevate the artistic preferences of the general marketplace and his almost desperate desire to see his own country achieve the same respect in painting as it had in poetry. Reflecting, too, his emotional intensity, his writings continually emphasize the "ceaseless oppositions" that he felt characterized his entire life, highlighted by his feeling that the London art establishment never accorded him the honor and respect he deserved and the subsequent resentment and bitterness he fostered throughout his career. Conversely, his jottings also exhibit his knack for simplicity and humor, evidenced in particular in the anecdotes of his friendships with Wordsworth and Keats, the former whom he admired for his skill at using the written word to convey emotions, and the latter for whom he felt a devoted kinship. Both of these writers, in Haydon's estimation, would forego life if their lofty artistic goals were not reached. In addition, the journals reveal Haydon's great admiration for Dante, Milton, Shakespeare, and Homer, and allusions to these literary giants fill his writings. Religion is also a major component of the works; at one point, Haydon, an orthodox Christian, claimed that, except for religion, "I should have gone mad."

CRITICAL RECEPTION

From the start, Haydon was criticized for his lack of judgment where his own artwork was concerned; in fact, Haydon was criticized for extolling his own artwork in such publications as *Annals of the Fine Arts* and *The Examiner* (these pieces were often published anonymously). As early as 1926, English novelist and critic Aldous Huxley claimed that Haydon "had absolutely no artistic talent" and that he had missed his true calling as a romantic novelist, citing his keen powers of observation, his comic style, his strength in storytelling, and his verbal dexterity. Biographer Eric George, too, declared that "Haydon chose to be a painter, but it is through the pen and not the brush that he is most likely to be remembered." Critics have stressed that Haydon's writings contain characteristics of the Romantic writers and that he possessed an extraordinary gift for drama. One of the areas of interest to scholars is the fact that even though Haydon professed that he was bound to tell the truth, almost all his writings are colored by his distorted and grandiose view of himself and of his work. Haydon's endless self-analysis and indulgence in obsessive melancholy, both evident in his writings, have also inspired critics to speculate on his motives for penning his life story.

PRINCIPAL WORKS

The Judgment of Connoisseurs upon Works of Art Compared with That of Professional Men; in Reference More Particularly to the Elgin Marbles (criticism) 1816

New Churches Considered with Respect to the Opportunities They Afford for the Encouragement of Painting (essay) 1818

Description of Mr. Haydon's Picture of Christ's Triumphant Entry into Jerusalem, Now Exhibiting (prose) 1820

A Descriptive Catalogue of Mr. Haydon's Great Picture of the Raising of Lazarus, Now Exhibiting at the Egyptian Hall (prose) 1823

Explanation of the Picture of Chairing the Members, a Scene in the Mock Election, Which Took Place at the King's Bench Prison, July, 1827 (prose) 1828

Some Enquiry into the Causes Which Have Obstructed the Advance of Historical Painting for the Last Seventy Years in England (essay) 1829

Painting, and the Fine Arts: Being the Articles Under These Heads Contributed to the Seventh Edition of the Encyclopedia Britannica [with William Hazlitt] (essays) 1838

Thoughts on the Relative Value of Fresco and Oil Painting, As Applied to the Architectural Decorations of the Houses of Parliament (essay) 1842

Lectures on Painting and Design. 2 vols. (lectures) 1844, 1846

Life of Benjamin Robert Haydon, Historical Painter, from His Autobiography and Journals. Edited and Compiled by Tom Taylor, of the Inner Temple, Esq. 3 vols. (autobiography) 1853; revised as *The Autobiography and Memoirs of Benjamin Robert Haydon (1786-1846).* 2 vols. (autobiography and memoirs) 1926

Benjamin Robert Haydon: Correspondence and Table-Talk. With a Memoir by His Son, Frederic Wordsworth Haydon. With Fascimile Illustrations from His Journals. 2 vols. (letters) 1876

Autobiography of Benjamin Robert Haydon (autobiography) 1927

The Autobiography and Memoirs of Benjamin Robert Haydon, 1786-1846, Compiled from his "Autobiography and Journals" and "Correspondence and Table-Talk" (autobiography, memoirs, and letters) 1927

The Autobiography and Journals of Benjamin Robert Haydon (autobiography and journals) 1950

The Diary of Benjamin Robert Haydon. 5 vols. (diary) 1960-63

Invisible Friends: The Correspondence of Elizabeth Barrett Browning and Benjamin Robert Haydon, 1842-1845 (letters) 1972

CRITICISM

Aldous Huxley (essay date 1926)

SOURCE: Huxley, Aldous. Introduction to *The Autobiography and Memoirs of Benjamin Robert Haydon (1786-1846)*, by Benjamin Robert Haydon, edited by Tom Taylor. Vol. 1, pp. v-xix. London: Peter Davies, 1926.

[*In the following excerpt from his introduction to the 1926 edition of Haydon's* Autobiography, *Huxley insists that Haydon wasted his creative energy on painting when it was as a writer—in particular as a romantic novelist—that Haydon's true talent lay.*]

Haydon was something more than a bad and deservedly unsuccessful painter. He was a great personality to begin with. And in the second place he was, as I like to think, a born writer who wasted his life making absurd pictures when he might have been making excellent books. One book, however, he did contrive to make. *The Autobiography* reveals his powers. Reading it, one realises the enormity of that initial mistake which sent him from his father's bookshop to the Academy schools. As a romantic novelist what might he not have achieved? Sadly one speculates.

There were times when Haydon himself seems to have speculated even as we do. "The truth is," he remarks near the end of his life, "I am fonder of books than of anything else on earth. I consider myself, and ever shall, a man of great powers, excited to an art which limits their exercise. In politics, law, or literature they would have had a full and glorious swing. . . . It is a curious proof of this that I have pawned my studies, my prints, my lay-figures, but have kept my darling authors." The avowal is complete. What genuine, born painter would call painting an art which limits the exercise of great powers? Such a criticism could only come from a man to whom painting was but another and less effectual way of writing dramas, novels, or history.

It is, I repeat, as a novelist that Haydon would best have exhibited his powers. I can imagine great rambling books in which absurd sublimities ("a Sphinx or two, a pyramid or so") and much rhapsodical philosophising would have alternated in the approved Shakespearean or Faustian style with admirable passages of well-observed, naturalistic comic relief. We should yawn over the philosophy and perhaps smile at the sublimities (as we smile and yawn even at Byron's; who can now read *Manfred,* or *Cain*?); but we should eagerly devour the comic chapters. *The Autobiography* permits us to imagine how good these chapters might have been.

Haydon was an acute observer, and he knew how to tell a story. How vividly, for example, he has seen this tea-party at Mrs Siddons's, how well he has described it!

> After her first reading (from Shakespeare) the men retired to tea. While we were all eating toast and tingling cups and saucers, she began again. It was like the effect of a Mass bell at Madrid. All noise ceased, we slunk to our seats like boors, two or three of the most distinguished men of the day with the very toast in their mouths, afraid to bite. It was curious to see Lawrence in this predicament, to hear him bite by degrees and then stop, for fear of making too much crackle, his eyes full of water from the constraint; and at the same time to hear Mrs Siddons's "eye of newt and toe of frog," and then to see Lawrence give a sly bite and then look awed and pretend to be listening. I went away highly gratified, and as I stood on the landing-place to get cool, I overheard my own servant in the hall say, "What! is that the old lady making such a noise?" "Yes." "Why, she makes as much noise as ever." "Yes," was the answer, "she tunes her pipes as well as ever she did."

There are, in *The Autobiography,* scores of such admirable little narratives and descriptions.

Haydon's anecdotes about the celebrated men with whom he came in contact are revealing as well as entertaining. They prove that he had more than a memory, a sense of character, an instinctive feeling for the significant detail. Most of the anecdotes are well known and have often been reprinted. But I cannot resist quoting two little stories about Wordsworth, which are less celebrated than they deserve to be. One day Haydon and Wordsworth went together to an art gallery. "In the corner stood the group of Cupid and Psyche kissing. After looking some time, he turned round to me with an expression I shall never forget, and said, 'The Dev-ils!'" From this one anecdote a subtle psychologist might almost have divined the youthful escapade in France, the

illegitimate daughter, the subsequent remorse and respectability. The other story is hardly less illuminating. "One day Wordsworth at a large party leaned forward in a moment of silence and said: 'Davy, do you know the reason I published my "White Doe" in quarto?' 'No,' said Davy, slightly blushing at the attention this awakened. 'To express my own opinion of it,' replied Wordsworth."

Merely as a verbal technician Haydon was singularly gifted. When he is writing about something which deeply interests and excites him, his style takes on a florid and violent brilliance all its own. For example, this is how, at the coronation of George IV, he describes the royal entrance. "Three or four of high rank appear from behind the throne; an interval is left; the crowd scarce breathe. Something rustles; and a being buried in satin, feathers and diamonds rolls gracefully into his seat. The room rises with a sort of feathered, silken thunder." He knows how to use his adjectives with admirable effect. The most accomplished writer might envy his description of the Duke of Sussex's voice as "loud, royal and asthmatic." And how one shudders at the glance of a "tremendous, globular and demoniacal eye!" How one loves the waitresses at the eating-house where the young and always susceptible Haydon used to dine! When they heard that he was bankrupt, these "pretty girls eyed me with a lustrous regret."

Haydon could argue with force and clarity. He could be witty as well as floridly brilliant. The man who could talk of Charles Lamb "stuttering his quaintness in snatches, like the Fool in *Lear,* and with as much beauty," certainly knew how to turn a phrase. He could imply a complete criticism in a dozen words; when he has said of West's classical pictures that "the Venuses looked as though they had never been naked before," there is nothing more to add; the last word on neoclassicism has been uttered. And what a sound, what a neatly pointed comment on English portrait-painting is contained in the following brief sentences! "Portraiture is always independent of art and has little or nothing to do with it. It is one of the staple manufactures of the Empire. Wherever the British settle, wherever they colonise, they carry, and will every carry, trial by jury, horse-racing and portrait-painting." And let us hope they will every carry a good supply of those indomitable madmen who have made the British Empire and English literature, English politics and English science the extraordinary things they are. Haydon was one of these glorious lunatics. An ironic fate decreed that he should waste his madness in the practice of an art for which he was not gifted. But though wasted, the insanity was genuine and of good quality. *The Autobiography* makes us wish that it might have been better directed.

Clarke Olney (essay date March 1934)

SOURCE: Olney, Clarke. "John Keats and Benjamin Robert Haydon." *PMLA* 49, no. 1 (March 1934): 258-75.

[*In the following essay, Olney discusses Haydon's influence on the young John Keats during the mid-1810s, when the two men shared an intense devotion to art. Haydon encouraged Keats to undertake themes considered by Olney to be more "grand" and "powerful" than the poet's earlier subjects.*]

The friendship between John Keats and Benjamin Robert Haydon is one chapter in the life of the poet which has never been satisfactorily written. A biography, like a novel, must needs have a villain; and in Haydon, Keats's biographers have one ready made. He was an egoist, a fanatic, and—worst of all—a failure; and surely, one is likely to think, whenever Haydon and Keats disagreed, Keats must have been right.[1] The fact is that Keats and Haydon were intimate friends during the greater part of Keats's active creative life, and that each held the other, as an artist, in the highest regard. The purpose of the present study is to examine in some detail the course of this friendship and tentatively evaluate the importance of the influence of the painter on the poet.[2]

At the time Keats met Haydon, late in 1816, the painter had been for some years a friend and intimate of Leigh Hunt who had an undoubted genius for friendship—and extraordinarily good judgment in the choice of his friends. On December 1, 1816, less than a month after his introduction to Haydon, Keats met Hunt for the first time when he called to thank the editor of the *Examiner* for the "Young Poets" article, published that very day.[3] The *Examiner* had previously noticed Keats's promise by publishing his sonnet on "Solitude" earlier in the year. But Hunt's article was so liberal in its praise that Keats appears to have brought the editor this thanks in person. Once the acquaintance was made, Keats soon became a favorite member of the Hunt circle.

The mildly convivial and pleasantly sentimental activities of these kindred spirits, the bouts at sonneteering, the commemorative dinners, are familiar matters. One of the dinners, in honor of the composer Haydn, was described by Mary Russell Mitford in a letter to Sir William Elford, the recipient of many of her best and most intimate letters. She had the story from "a great admirer of Mr. Haydon's and a friend of Leigh Hunt's"; it was too good, she felt, to keep. The story concerned Haydon's misapprehension of the purpose of the dinner: he had been informed that the group was celebrating his birthday.[4] But not all the meetings of the group were so innocent. The liberty which Hunt and his friends advocated so vocally was religious as well as political. Like most "enlightened" men of the period, they were deistic—or worse. Haydon, a militant and orthodox Christian, soon found himself baited on every side. His bout with Shelley, at Horace Smith's, is one of the most spirited and amusing passages in the *Autobiography*.[5] And Mrs. Mitford, again writing to Sir William Elford, reported another incident of Haydon at bay among "some of the cleverest unbelievers of the age,"[6] including Leigh Hunt. These meetings occurred, of course, after Haydon had met Keats. Their significance in the relations between the two men will appear presently.

The time and place of Keats's introduction to Haydon have not been definitely determined. Haydon records in the *Autobiography* that they met at Hunt's;[7] but Keats's letters seem to show otherwise; and as Haydon's recollection of details is often faulty, the letters probably offer the best evidence. While not conclusive it may be summarized as follows. In an undated note, which Forman assigns to 31 October 1816, Keats wrote to Charles Cowden Clarke:

> My daintie Davie,
>
> I will be as punctual as the Bee to the Clover. Very glad am I at the thoughts of seeing so soon this glorious Haydon and all his creation . . .

The plan seems to have been to visit Haydon at his painting room in Great Marlborough Street; but the visit had to be postponed. In another undated note, written apparently a day or two later, Keats informed Clarke that Haydon had written his regrets for that evening as he had "an order for the Orchestra to see Timon ye Misantrophas."[8] The next of the letters is addressed to Haydon and is dated November 20, 1816. "My dear Sir—" Keats wrote. "Last evening wrought me up, and I cannot forbear sending you the following"; and he added the sonnet beginning "Great spirits now on earth are sojourning." Haydon must have returned his answer to this by the same post; for a second letter from Keats, dated "Thursday afternoon, 20 November 1816," follows.

> My dear Sir,
>
> Your letter has filled me with a proud pleasure, and shall be kept by me as a stimulus to exertion—I begin to fix my eye upon one horizon. My feelings entirely fall in with yours in regard to the El[l]ipsis, and I glory in it. The Idea of your sending it to Wordsworth put me out of breath—you know with what Reverence I would send my Well-wishes to him.

The reference to "last evening" in Keats's first letter of November 20 points clearly to a meeting—possibly their first—on the preceding day. Miss Lowell, in fact, does not scruple to describe the scene in Haydon's painting room, the evening which inspired "Great Spirits."[9] Another sonnet, "Addressed to Haydon," usually associated with this, which Colvin says was written "after an evening of high-talk at the beginning of their acquaintance,"[10] Miss Lowell feels was written before the two men had actually met. This sonnet, beginning "Highmindedness, a jealousy for good," she finds, has less fire and feeling than "Great spirits"; and the fact that it was not sent Haydon along with the other seems to support her judgment.[11]

It has been generally assumed that Keats was acquainted with Leigh Hunt before he met Haydon. There seem to be grounds for doubting this. Keats, of course, knew Hunt's poetry and admired it; he also admired Hunt's political fortitude, as his sonnet "Written on the day that Mr. Leigh Hunt left Prison" (February 2, 1815) shows. But if one accepts the date arrived at by Edmund Blunden, Hunt's most recent biographer, Keats did not meet Hunt until December 1, 1816, at least ten days after his first visit to Haydon's.[12] Again Keats was accompanied by Charles Cowden Clarke,[13] and again an intimate friendship resulted. Hunt celebrated the new intimacy with the sonnet beginning

> 'Tis well you think me truly one of those,
> Whose sense discerns the loveliness of things;[14]

and Keats seems to have responded with his "Keen, fitful gusts." In the friendliness of Hunt's "little cottage" and in the painting room of "glorious Haydon," Keats found ready inspiration and encouragement for the poetic aspirations which had already enticed him away from his medical studies.

The friendship of Haydon, Hunt, and Keats was not to continue long, but at the beginning of 1817 it was in full swing. Keats's intimacy with the painter was of rapid growth; and during the winter of 1816 and the spring that followed he was a constant visitor at Haydon's studio. Early in their acquaintance Haydon seems to have made the life mask of Keats which is usually ascribed to him, with a technique already perfected by his mouldings of Wordsworth and Wilkie. There was much eager talk during these visits. Haydon, of whom Hazlitt is reported to have said, "'He talks well, too, upon most subjects that interest one, indeed better than any painter I have met',"[15] was also an excellent listener, and Keats must have found both stimulation and encouragement in the painter's company. Haydon was thirty-one, Keats ten years his junior: both were young and passionately intense in their love for beauty. Haydon had, moreover, already made a name for himself as an advocate and practitioner of High Art. His *The Assassination of Dentatus,* completed eight years before, had won the premium for historical painting at the British Institution. His *Macbeth,* although still unsold, had caused a profound, if not altogether favorable impression. *The Judgment of Solomon,* exhibited at the Water-Colour Society in 1814, had brought him seven hundred guineas. Haydon was definitely making his mark, and was already considered by many the greatest historical painter whom England had produced. But he had already involved himself in ever-mounting debts which were to bring about his ruin. His devotion to art could not be seriously doubted: he had risen to an almost single-handed defense of the Elgin Marbles against the Connoisseurs and the Royal Academicians, to the vast injury of his prospects. And Keats's clear intelligence must early have perceived the high and earnest seriousness of Haydon's poetic taste in contrast with the shallow facility of Hunt's.

Early in March appeared the first of Keats's published volumes, the *Poems* of 1817. Leigh Hunt was charmed and wrote a long and laudatory criticism of the volume in the *Examiner.* Haydon was also impressed and wrote an equally favorable review, unsigned, which appeared in the *Champion* for March 9. In this article, "the very earliest review of Keats's book to be published,"[16] Haydon particularly praised "Sleep and Poetry." He concluded his article with a bit of inevitable self-advertisement, which is somewhat less offensive when one realizes that the painter was a man of established reputation and that Keats was virtually unknown.

> We have had two Sonnets presented to us, which were written by Mr. Keats, and which are not printed in the present volume. We have great pleasure in giving them to the public, as well on account of their own power and beauty, as of the grandeur of the subjects; on which we have ourselves so often made observations.[17]

The two sonnets which Haydon reproduced were the familiar "To Haydon, with a sonnet written on seeing the Elgin Marbles" and "On Seeing the Elgin Marbles," which he had received only a few days before. His letter acknowledging the receipt of these sonnets is an interesting example of both the deficiencies of Haydon's poetic taste and the genuineness of his affection and respect for Keats.[18] The third sonnet to Haydon and that "On Seeing the Elgin Marbles" were the immediate results of a visit to the British Museum under Haydon's guidance. On this visit, if one may trust Haydon's later recollection, the two enthusiasts were accompanied by John Hamilton Reynolds.[19] The marbles made a profound impression upon Keats; and with Haydon as his guide it is little wonder, for he, better perhaps than any man in London, loved the marbles and had mastered their meaning.

Haydon's influence upon Keats during this period was probably at its greatest. Not only were Haydon's talk and his works inspirations; the painter realized as well the value of object lessons. Of these the visit to the Elgin Marbles was one; another was the presentation copy of Goldsmith's *History of Greece* with the inscription in the first volume, "To John Keats, from his ardent friend, B. R. Haydon, 1817."[20]

Meanwhile Haydon's dissatisfaction with the religious views of Hunt and his friends had become acute. Shelley had been, no doubt, the worst offender, but the religious obliquity of the other members of the group was almost equally annoying. Haydon was, moreover, worried about the effect of these subversive ideas upon Keats. Already, in March, in a remarkably passionate outpouring of his affections, he had written Keats his concern lest the poet's "ardor might lead [him] to disregard the accumulated wisdom of the ages in moral points." But in his letter of May 11, Haydon was even more outspoken in his warnings:

> I love you like my own brother. Beware, for God's sake, of the delusions and sophistications that are ripping up the talents and morality of our friend [Leigh Hunt]! He will go out of the world the victim of his own weakness and the dupe of his own self-delusions, with the contempt of his enemies and the sorrow of his friends, and the cause he undertook to support injured by his own neglect of character.

Keats's reply to this cannot entirely have reassured his friend, but at least the growing disaffection for Hunt which he expressed must have been satisfactory. Haydon appears to have been steadily winning Keats away from the influence of Leigh Hunt and his friendly circle. It was no doubt high time. Hunt had been a loyal friend and advocate; but Keats had already outgrown him. Hunt could offer Keats the pleasures of gay and whimsical companionship, the encouragement of a man of taste and ready learning. But Keats no longer needed these. "He of the rose, the violet, the spring, the social smile, the chain for Freedom's sake" was being rapidly and inevitably supplanted in Keats's regard by him "whose steadfastness would never take a meaner sound than Raphael's whispering." For "mighty workings" were afoot. *Endymion* had been commenced that spring, and Keats had little inclination for the easy and facile friendliness of the Hunts. Haydon had written in the letter just quoted:

> I think you did quite right to leave the Isle of Wight and being quite alone, after study you can now devote yourself eight hours a-day with just as much seclusion as ever. Do not give way to any forebodings. . . . Every man of great views is, at times, thus tormented. . . . *Trust in God* with all your might, my dear Keats. This dependence, with your own energy, will give you strength, and hope, and comfort.

And Haydon's advice at that moment must be allowed to have been excellent.

On Keats's return from his spring vacationing on the Isle of Wight, at Margate, and at Canterbury, he resumed his intimacy with both Hunt and Haydon; but

Haydon continued to warn him against Hunt, advising him particularly not to show Hunt his *Endymion* "on any account or he will have done half for you."[21] Haydon was making but little progress with his *Christ's Entry into Jerusalem,* which he had begun in 1814. During the summer he had moved into larger quarters in Lisson Grove North; the Hunts moved into the same street shortly afterward. According to Keats, Hunt came frequently to the painting room to inspect the painting and always found something in it to criticize adversely.[22] Haydon, however, was as active socially as ever, and Keats must have found interesting company at the painting room. There he became acquainted with William Bewick, Haydon's promising pupil who was just Keats's age, and the two became friends. Bewick was being greatly impressed by the social splendors of his master's studio. On May 30 he wrote his brother: "At Mr. Haydon's I am daily, and here I am introduced to all kinds of known characters, authors, poets, painters, sculptors, &c., not only of this, but of every country of Europe."[23] Among the frequent visitors to Haydon's about this time were Hazlitt, Clarke, and Reynolds. Charles Lamb dropped in occasionally; Wordsworth whenever he came up to London.

The quarrel which had been brewing for some time between Haydon and Hunt broke late in the year. Keats, who was not involved, reported the immediate cause to his brothers in his letter of January 13, 1818.

> The quarrel with Hunt I understand thus far. Mrs. H[unt] was in the habit of borrowing silver from Haydon—the last time she did so, Haydon asked her to return it at a certain time—she did not—Haydon sent for it—Hunt went to expostulate on the indelicacy &c.— they got to words and parted for ever. All I hope is at some time to bring them all together again.

Incidentally, the "silver" over which the quarrel started is interpreted by Colvin as "money"; Miss Lowell renders it "spoons."[24] Of course from what one knows about Mrs. Hunt, it might have been either. But the real causes of the quarrel probably lay deeper. It is quite conceivable that Keats himself, or rather the rivalry for primacy in Keats's friendship, may have been at the root of the trouble. Haydon seems to have felt very definitely that Hunt was having a bad influence upon his friend. Keats himself, in fact, had already begun to recognize Hunt's limitations, in matters of taste if not of morals. On September 21, 1817 he had written to Reynolds: "What a very pleasant fellow he is, if he would give up the sovereignty of a Room pro bono. What Evenings we might pass with him, could we have him from Mrs. H." In his letter to Bailey some three weeks later he half agreed that Haydon's warning about showing *Endymion* to Hunt was justified; and by the end of 1818 he had little respect left for his former friend. At that time, writing to George and Georgiana Keats, he said:

Hunt . . . is certainly a pleasant fellow in the main when you are with him—but in reallity he is vain, egotistical, and disgusting in matters of taste and in morals. He understands many a beautiful thing; but then, instead of giving other minds credit for the same degree of perception as he himself professes—he begins an explanation in such a curious manner that our taste and self-love is offended continually. Hunt does one harm by making fine things pretty and beautiful things hateful. Through him I am indifferent to Mozart, I care not for white Busts—and many a glorious thing when associated with him becomes a nothing. This distorts one's mind—make[s] one's thoughts bizarre—perplexes one in the standard of Beauty.

The comment is, no doubt, severe; but perhaps, from Keats's point of view it is essentially just. And surely it does a great deal to account for Keats's preference for Haydon. The painter, at least, was not one to be guilty of making "fine things pretty" or "beautiful things hateful." His soaring, if sometimes ill-controlled imagination and enthusiasm, his ideal of grand and dignified beauty Keats must have found much more to his taste than the prettiness and preciousness of Leigh Hunt. Haydon, who was a good hater, and who had definitely broken with Hunt, must have been even more violent in his strictures, if his scurrilous letter to Sir Walter Scott, written ten years later, may be accepted in evidence.[25] Haydon also quarreled with Reynolds about this time, and as Reynolds remained one of Hunt's intimates, the break with the Hunt circle was virtually complete. Keats, however, was not involved, and maintained at least a nominal friendship with all the persons concerned. His explanation of the Reynolds-Haydon quarrel appears in his letter to George and Thomas Keats, dated January 13, 1818.

The attacks by "Z" on "the Cockney School of Poetry," which appeared in *Blackwood's* during 1817 and 1818 were directed chiefly at Leigh Hunt and John Keats. Haydon escaped with only incidental mention in the August, 1818, article, where "Z" referred to him, in connection with Keats's sonnet "Addressed to Haydon," as:[26]

> that clever, but most affected artist, who as little resembles Raphael in genius as he does in person, notwithstanding the foppery of having his hair curled over his shoulders in the old Italian fashion.

Later attacks became more personal, and John Scott, in his article in the *London Magazine* on "The Mohock Magazine," protested at "Horae Scandicae" for referring to the artist, "a gentleman of clean and rather careful habits," as "'greasy-pate Haydon.'"[27]

Sometime before the end of 1817, Keats was first introduced to Wordsworth, probably by Haydon, but probably not at the painter's "immortal dinner."[28] The description of this dinner, which "came off" on December 28, occupies several pages in Haydon's *Autobiography* and is one of the most familiar passages in that work.[29] Keats's version of the event may be found in his letter to his brothers on January 5, 1818.

In September, 1817, began an affair which threatened for a time to wreck the friendship between Haydon and Keats. It started in a letter which the painter wrote to Keats at Oxford in which he asked the poet to look up a young art student whose work Haydon had thought promising during a recent visit to the university. Haydon was willing, he said, to train the young man "with no further remuneration than the pleasure of seeing him advance." Keats obliged, and wrote a full and favorable account of the student, whose name, he reported, was Crip[p]s. "He does not," Keats wrote, "possess the Philosopher's stone—nor Fortunatus' purse, nor Gyges' ring . . . [but] I have a great Idea that he will be a tolerable neat brush." Meanwhile Keats and his friend Bailey were going to try to plan some means of enabling Cripps to benefit by Haydon's apparently generous offer. Matters dragged for some weeks. When Keats returned to London early in October, he asked Haydon to dine with him on a Sunday in order to get the affair settled. The painter begged off on an excuse of ill health; and Keats felt certain that he would never come. Haydon appeared to have lost interest. In November Keats was still concerned over the affair, and on the twenty-second he wrote Bailey commiserating him on an unpleasant letter which Haydon had written him about "poor Crip[p]s."

> . . . To a Man of your nature such a Letter as Haydon's must have been extremely cutting. . . . As soon as I had known Haydon three days I had got enough of his character not to have been surprised at such a Letter as he has hurt you with. Nor when I knew it was it a principle with me to drop his acquaintance . . . I wish you knew all that I think about Genius and the Heart . . . Men of Genius are great as certain ethereal Chemicals operating on the Mass of neutral intellect—by [*for* but] they have not any individuality, any determined Character . . .

By January 5, 1818, Cripps may have been in London, for on that date Keats wrote to his brothers from Devonshire: "I received a short Letter from Bailey about Crip[p]s and one from Haydon ditto—Haydon thinks he improves very much." By the middle of the month friendly relations between Keats and Haydon seem to have been fully restored, and Keats wrote the painter about the advisability of having Cripps bound to him as an apprentice. This arrangement was the usual one between Haydon and his pupils, and Keats's failure to suggest it earlier may have accounted for Haydon's sudden coldness toward the idea of becoming Cripps's master.[30] Keats concluded his letter on a note of warm praise:

> Your friendship for me is now getting into its teens—and I feel the past. Also every day older I get—the

greater is my idea of your achievements in Art: and I am convinced that there are three things to rejoice at in this Age—The Excursion, Your Pictures, and Hazlitt's depth of Taste.

And he signed himself, "Yours affectionately." Haydon was pleased and replied in kind:

> I feel greatly delighted by your high opinion, allow me to add sincerely a fourth to be proud of—*John Keats' genius!*—This I speak from my heart.—You and Bewick are the only men I ever liked with all my heart, for Wordsworth being older, there is no equality tho' I reverence him and love him devotedly—and now you know my peculiar feelings in wishing to have a notice when you cannot keep an engagement with me; there can never be as long as we live any ground of dispute between us. . . .

The Cripps incident was almost closed. About January 19 Keats made further mention of it in a letter to his brothers. On the twenty-third, writing to Bailey, he spoke of his efforts to raise money for Cripps's binding and added, with some humor,

> Cripps is improving very fast. I have the greater hopes of him because he is so slow in devellopment—A Man of great executing Powers at 20—with a look and a speech almost stupid is sure to do something.

On February 5 Cripps made his final appearance in Keats's correspondence, and I can find no further mention of him anywhere. Keats may have been somewhat disillusioned with Haydon, as his letter to Bailey already quoted seems to suggest; but their friendship was not seriously interrupted. And surely the details of the affair are not sufficiently clear to warrant any condemnation of Haydon for his part in it.

Endymion had been finished in November 1817. The following January, Book One was sent to the press; the entire poem was published in April. Haydon had been unfailing in his encouragement. On January 23 Keats wrote to his brothers:

> Haydon is struck with the 1st Book. I . . . received a letter from him, proposing to make, as he says, with all his might, a finished chalk sketch of my head, to be engraved in the first style and put at the head of my Poem, saying at the same time he had never done the thing for any human being, and that it must have considerable effect as he will put the name to it.

This particular drawing was, apparently, never made.[31] There are, however, at least three representations of Keats's head from Haydon's pencil: the one in *Christ's Entry,* the sketch reproduced in Haydon's **Correspondence and Table-Talk,** and a sketch from memory in a letter from Haydon to Elizabeth Barrett.

The social gatherings at Haydon's continued through 1818. Bewick was still enthusiastic, and proud to be a disciple of the painter. On February 11 he wrote to his brother and sister:[32]

I have been at two or three very intellectual dinners since I came. Amongst the company were Horatio Smith (author of *Rejected Addresses*), Keats the poet, Hazlitt the critic, Hunt the publisher [probably John, whom Haydon always liked and respected], &c., &c.

Coleridge was also an occasional visitor about this time,[33] as was Severn, who relates the amusing incident of Haydon's duping the vegetarians.[34]

In February Haydon was in Devonshire. In March Keats journeyed thither to be with his brothers, George and Thomas. When he arrived there on the fourth, Haydon had apparently already left. On the day of Keats's arrival Haydon dashed off a breathless note regarding a gold ring and seal which had been found "in a field that belonged to Shakespeare" and which apparently bore his initials. Keats replied on the fourteenth, beginning: "In sooth, I hope you are not too sanguine about that seal—" and including "some dogrel" ("For there's a Bishop's teign") and "a bit of B——hrell" ("Where be ye going, you Devon Maid?"). The concluding passage of this letter is the familiar one praising Hazlitt's merits as a "damner."

Haydon, in his letter of March 25, expressed his pleasure at the "bi——ell" and advised Keats not to miss going to Plymouth, offering him letters of introduction. *Jerusalem* was progressing, he reported; "God grant [*Endymion*] the most complete success, and may its reputation equal your genius." Keats continued the correspondence on April 10, writing Haydon of his proposed trip to the north of England and to Scotland. "I am nearer myself," he wrote, "to hear your Christ is being tinted into immortality. Believe me Haydon your picture is part of myself."

On the eighth of May, Haydon wrote his congratulations on *Endymion*. "I have read your delicious Poem, with exquisite enjoyment, it is the most delightful thing of the time. . . . Success attend you my glorious fellow." Leigh Hunt, incidentally, was much more critical. In a letter previously quoted from, Keats had written: "Hunt . . . allows it not much merit as a whole; says it is unnatural and made ten objections to it at the mere skimming over." There is a gap in the correspondence until September 25 when Haydon, visiting his sister at Bridgewater in the hope of improving his eyes, dictated a note expressing his desire for a speedy return to London.

The intimacy between Keats and Haydon seems, on the whole, to have been on the wane during 1818. True, their addresses were as cordial as ever; but their meetings were much less frequent. Without any sign of a quarrel, they seem to have grown apart. Both were away from London for considerable periods during the year. Keats, on his return to Hampstead from his northern tour, saw almost no one. Tom was dying; Keats's own health was none too good; and he had no desire for society under the circumstances. Haydon was away on several trips during the year. One knows that he visited Devonshire in the spring and was with his sister in the fall. It is also probable that he visited Wordsworth at Rydal Mount during the summer.[35]

The year 1819 saw the breaking up of the intimacy between Keats and Haydon. They continued friends to the last, but the spirit had gone out of their relationship. The trouble arose, as it so frequently did where Haydon was concerned, over money. The letters which passed between the two men tell all that can be known of the story, a story which has often been related by the biographers of Keats to Haydon's discredit. But a careful and dispassionate examination of the evidence makes the painter's sole guilt in the matter much less certain. The incident, too, had its tragi-comic aspects which should not be overlooked. Toward the end of 1818, Haydon evidently approached Keats regarding a loan, for on December 22 Keats wrote:

> Believe me Haydon I have that sort of fire in my heart that would sacrifice every thing I have to your service—I speak without any reserve—I know you would do so for me—I open my heart to you in a few words. I will do this sooner than you shall be distressed: but let me be the last stay—Ask the rich lovers of Art first—I'll tell you why—I have a little money which may enable me to study, and to travel for three or four years. I never expect to get anything by my Books. . . . Try the long purses—but do not sell your drawing[s] or I shall consider it a breach of friendship.

Haydon replied at once in a long and effusive letter:

> I approve most completely [of] your plan of travels and study, and [s]hould suffer torture if my wants [in]terrupted it—in short they shall not [m]y dear Keats. I believe you from my soul when you say you would sacrifice all for me; and when your means are gone, if God give me means my heart and house and home and every thing shall be shared with you—I mean this too. It has often occurred to me but I have never spoken of it. My great object is the public encouragement of historical painting and the glory of England in high Art—to ensure these I would lay my head on the block this instant.

But the patience of his friends was exhausted, he said; his health was poor; and the lovers of art offended his sensitive soul by their delays and considerations.

Keats evidently called on Haydon soon after, for there are notes which plan a meeting. In the meantime, it is quite possible that Haydon renewed his trials upon the "long purses." Keats's note of January 2, 1819, was more than ordinarily affectionate, calling the painter "one who has been my true friend" and promising an all-day visit when "we will hate the profane vulgar and make us Wings."

Haydon's attack upon the "rich lovers of Art" was apparently unavailing, for on January 7, probably not much more than two weeks after his first request for a loan, he wrote:

> I now frankly tell you I will accept your friendly offer. . . . I am disappointed where I expected not to be and my only hope for the concluding difficulties of my Picture lie[s] in *you*. . . . Do let me hear from you how you are, and when I shall get my bond ready for you, for that is the best way for me to do, at two years.

Keats replied hopefully: "I will be in town early tomorrow, and trust I shall be able to lend you assistance noon or night." But he was evidently over-sanguine, for a second note followed a day or two later:

> I shall have a little trouble in procuring the Money and a great ordeal to go through—no trouble indeed to any one else—or ordeal either. I mean I shall have to go to town some thrice, and stand in the Bank an hour or two—to me worse than any thing in Dante . . . do not be at all anxious, for *this* time I really will do, what I never did before in my life, business in good time, and properly. With respect to the Bond—it may be a satisfaction to you to let me have it: but as you love me do not let there be any mention of interest, although we are mortal men—and bind ourselves for fear of death.

Haydon found this letter "every thing that is kind, affectionate, and friendly. I depend upon it; it has relieved my anxious mind." But there were further delays. Keats found the guardian difficult. The money, which had been Tom Keats's, was, the poet discovered, somewhat encumbered.

There the matter rested. The money which Keats had so blithely hoped to advance early in January and upon which Haydon had depended, was not forthcoming. More than a month later, Keats was still writing his encouragements to Haydon: "Nor must you think I have forgotten you. No, I have about every three days been to Abbey's and to the Law[y]ers." That was mailed on March 8. Haydon replied on the tenth, urging his immediate need of Keats's "promised assistance," before the twentieth if at all possible. A month later Haydon wrote again, but this time his patience was at an end. One who realizes his continual financial straits will hardly be surprised. He upbraided Keats for holding out "delusive hopes" and blamed him for the increase of his financial difficulties:

> I am sensible of the trouble you took—I am grateful for it, but upon my Soul I cannot help complaining because the result has been so totally unexpected and sudden—and I am floundering where I hoped to be firm.—Don't mistake me—I am as attached to you as much and more than to any man—but really you don't know how [you] may affect me by not letting me know earlier.

In his reply, Keats tried again to make the difficulty of his position clear. Toward its close his letter took on an almost querulous note:

I am doubly hurt at the slightly reproachful tone of your note and the occasion of it . . . now you have maimed me again; I was whole, I had began reading again—when your note came I was engaged in a Book . . .

Between April 13, the date of this letter, and June 17, 1819, the loan was evidently consummated, for on the latter date Keats wrote Haydon asking repayment.[36] It is quite evident, then, that Haydon had had the money no longer than two months, and under the very conditions of the loan, Keats must have known that it would be virtually impossible for Haydon to repay it so soon. The painter was quite frankly living on borrowed money in expectation of the success of his *Jerusalem.* All his friends must have known that: he made no secret of the fact. He had no income and could expect none until his picture was finished and exhibited; and yet Keats was seriously disgruntled when Haydon did not repay him his two months' loan. On September 17 he wrote to George and Georgiana Keats:

I have a few words to say about Haydon. Before this Chancery threat had cut of[f] every legitimate supp[l]y of Cash from me I had a little at my disposal Haydon being very much in want I lent him 30£ of it. Now in this se[e]-saw game of Life I got nearest to the ground and this chancery business rivetted me there so that I was sitting in that uneasy position where the seat slants so abominably. I applied to him for payment—he could not—that was no wonder; but goodman Delver, where was the wonder then, why marry, in this, he did not seem to care much about it—and let me go without my money with almost non-chalance when he ought to have sold his drawings to supply me. I shall perhaps still be acquainted with him, but for friendship that is at an end. Brown has been my friend in this—he got him to sign a Bond payable at three Months.

One wonders, from this, just what had happened to Keats's injunction to Haydon that he was not to sell his drawings "or I shall consider it a breach of friendship." And the bond—which Haydon had suggested be drawn up "at two years" and which Keats had been willing to accept because "it may be a satisfaction to you to let me have it"—the bond had been made payable at three months! The insignificance of the sum, thirty pounds, is, of course, apparent to anyone who has read Haydon's own accounts of his epic borrowings in the **Autobiography** and in his Journals.[37] It is surely ironic that Haydon's most intimate and important friendship should have come to grief over such an amount. It has always been assumed that Haydon never repaid this loan, although there is no evidence on the point one way or the other. If this assumption be true, it is doubtless another stone with which to damn Haydon. It should be remembered, however, that by the time the profits from *Jerusalem* were in (November 4, 1820), Keats had already sailed for Italy; and Haydon, with £1298, 2s to his credit, was paying it out to his creditors in handfuls, for, as he said, "everybody to whom I owed a shilling took it into their heads that they had only to press me to get their cash."[38]

Forman prints four more letters from Keats to Haydon; two from Haydon to Keats. Keats's letter of October 3 was quite as full of admiration as ever, but it had, as Forman points out, a "certain reserve of tone."[39] There was, however, no definite coldness: Keats had apparently forgiven if not forgotten the injury. The other three Keats notes, all of August, 1820, are of slight importance. Two of them refer to Haydon's copy of Chapman's *Homer* which Keats had borrowed and lost, and ultimately had to replace. Haydon's two letters managed to express much the same feeling of affection and respect as those of earlier times. The first, written probably in July, 1820, showed Haydon's genuine concern over Keats's illness. In it Haydon recommended his own physician and long time friend, Dr. George Darling.[40] The other, dated July 14, 1820, is of no particular interest.

In addition to the letters, there is further evidence of continued friendly relations in the publication of Keats's "Ode to the Nightingale" and the ode "On a Grecian Urn" in Haydon's own particular mouthpiece, the *Annals of the Fine Arts.* This was in 1819. On the twenty-fifth of March, 1820 Keats showed his good will toward Haydon by attending the private view which preceded the exhibition of the long heralded *Christ's Entry into Jerusalem.* Keats did this in spite of wretched health and, according to Haydon, stood in a corner with Hazlitt, "really rejoicing."[41]

Too great emphasis should not be placed upon the failure of the intimacy between Keats and Haydon during 1820. The rapid progress of Keats's illness, the intensity of his passion for Fanny Brawne kept him more and more to himself. "If I cannot live with you I will live alone," he had written her. Brown and Severn were the only ones among his old friends who saw much of him. In January he wrote to Georgiana Augusta Keats:

You said in one of your letters that there was nothing but Haydon and Co in Mine. There can be nothing of him in this, for I never see him or Co. . . . To me it is all as dull here as Louisville could be. I am tired of the Theatres. Almost all parties I may chance to fall into I know by heart. I know the different styles of talk in different places, what subjects will be started how it will proceed. . . . If I go to Hunt's, I run my head into many times heard puns and music. To Haydon's worn out discourses of poetry and painting. The Miss Reynolds I am afraid to speak to for fear of some sickly re-iteration of Phrase or Sentiment.

And in June he wrote to Charles Brown another letter which showed all too clearly how dim the flame was burning:

I met —— in town, a few days ago, who invited me to supper to meet Wordsworth, Southey, Lamb, Haydon, and some more; I was too careful of my health to risk being out at night.

The last meeting between Keats and Haydon took place in the early autumn of 1820, not long before Keats's departure for Italy. On August 14, Keats had written:

> I am glad to hear you are in progress with another Picture. Go on. I am afraid I shall pop off just when I [*for my*] mind is able to run alone.

In another note, which Forman assigns to the same date, Keats expressed the hope of seeing Haydon shortly. Haydon evidently called soon afterward. He was profoundly affected. His report of the visit in his Journal describes, with, no doubt, some overemphasis, Keats's depressed state and his own dismay at his friend's condition.[42]

The recollections of Keats which Haydon left in his *Autobiography,* his Journals, and his letters have been widely quoted by the biographers of Keats. Some of his comments may be accounted among the finest and most discriminating things ever said about the poet; others, less favorable to Keats, have aroused a great deal of protest. But the purpose of this study is not to evaluate the reliability of Haydon's judgments; it is rather to relate in some detail the course of the friendship between Haydon and Keats and to estimate the influence of the painter upon the poet.

The determination of the influence of one artist upon another must always be somewhat tentative, even when the artists are working in the same medium. When one attempts to demonstrate that a painter has influenced a poet, however, the problem requires an even more cautious approach. It may be assumed, first, that whatever influence Haydon exerted upon Keats was confined to the development of the poet's conceptions of the quality and functions of art, and applied not at all to the particular technical problems of poetry. Not that Haydon did not care for poetry. He "gloried in it." His Journals were crowded with his enthusiasms for Shakespeare and Homer. If impetus had been needed for Keats's appreciation of "the realms of gold," Haydon would have supplied it. "I have enjoyed Shakespeare more with Keats," he wrote in his Journal, "than with any other human creature."[43] Haydon, in fact, considered poetry an art of equal merit to his own; they were closely allied. "Painting," he said, "is only the means of exciting poetical and intellectual associations. Poetry and painting require the same minds, the means only are different."[44] But in regard to poetry, Haydon must be considered an enthusiast rather than a critic.

Keats, then, could meet Haydon on an equal footing as an artist. True, Haydon was ten years older and had already achieved some measure of success. The painter, too, was somewhat domineering; but he spoke with authority, and Keats seems to have been willing, during their early friendship at least, to become the disciple and to absorb with eagerness Haydon's ideas and enthusiasms. A great many of the artistic causes to which Haydon devoted himself, such as his attack on the Royal Academy and his agitation for the national patronage of art—causes largely social—had little interest for the poet; but Haydon's ideas on the nature of art, ideas which Keats could apply to his own poetical compositions, seem to have exerted a more direct influence.

Haydon's ideals for art were the "bold," the "masculine," the "grand," and the "powerful."[45] The highest art, he felt, must concern itself only with the grandest, the most sublime themes. In this belief Haydon followed the theories of David and of Sir Joshua Reynolds, who held that historical and religious subjects were those most likely to excite the loftiest emotions in the beholder. For the great artist, then, the choice of "High Art" was inevitable; for there "every hour's progress is an accession of knowledge; the mind never flags, but is kept in one delicious tone of meditation and fancy."[46]

It would be injudicious to make too much of Haydon's influence upon Keats's poetry. It does seem reasonable, however, to suppose that Haydon's ideas and example may have encouraged Keats to attempt his more "bold," more "grand," and more "powerful" *Endymion*; and one does know that Haydon encouraged him throughout its composition. Keats's genius and temperament were unsuited for the handling of strictly historical or religious themes. He did, however, after the publication of the 1817 *Poems,* turn rather definitely from the present to the past for his subjects. For this, Haydon's influence may very well have been partly, although perhaps not solely, responsible.

Perhaps the most definite influence which Haydon exerted upon Keats's poetry is to be discerned in its increase in masculinity. Here, too, other causes were doubtless at work—developing maturity, sorrow, and hopeless love—but intimacy with Haydon must have hastened the growth. It would not be in order here to discuss the influence of Leigh Hunt on Keats's poetic style; but it is sufficiently apparent that Hunt's example is to blame for the almost smirking delicacy of some of the phrasing in the 1817 volume. This influence Keats never entirely outgrew, but for its diminution Haydon is probably chiefly to be thanked. Haydon, like so many men of small stature, was intensely masculine: determined, combative, and self-assured. Somewhat earlier he had achieved a reputation for violent swearing, surprising in one of his religiosity; but he seems to have outgrown this.[47] Throughout his life, however, Haydon continued pugnacious and self-assertive, in contrast to Leigh Hunt, who prided himself on his refinement and languor. Art to Haydon was an enormously serious matter, something to be fought for; Hunt's attitude toward it was more dilettantish, more feminine. And when Keats came more fully under Haydon's influence, his poetical calling took on new significance, new dignity, the grand, calm beauty which Haydon had shown him in the Elgin Marbles. *Endymion* and the poems of 1820 sound deeper notes and richer harmonies than Leigh Hunt's facile example could ever have inspired.

On the whole, then, Haydon's influence upon Keats was wholesome; for by showing him the seriousness and dignity of the poet's calling, he helped make Keats dissatisfied with the trivialities of the Cockney school.

Notes

1. "A gentleman of oblique vision, given to profuse statement" is, for example, one of the kindest of Amy Lowell's remarks on the painter. *John Keats* (Boston and New York, 1925), I, 253.

2. The source of all quotations in this study not otherwise noted is the most recent edition of *The Letters of John Keats,* edited by Maurice Buxton Forman (Oxford Press, 1931). I have also accepted the dates assigned by Forman to doubtful letters.

3. I have adopted here the date arrived at by Edmund Blunden in his *Leigh Hunt* (London 1930), p. 107.

4. The Rev. A. G. K. L'Estrange, *The Life of Mary Russell Mitford, Told by Herself in Letters to Her Friends* (New York, 1870), I, 320.—Sir William, of course, knew Haydon, being a fellow townsman and one of the purchasers of *The Judgment of Solomon* in 1814.

5. The *Autobiography* is not clear on the place of this meeting. Haydon's son, however, puts it at Horace Smith's. Frederic Wordsworth Haydon, *Benjamin Robert Haydon: Correspondence and Table-Talk* (London, 1876), II, 72, *n.*

6. *Op. cit.,* I, 273-274.

7. Aldous Huxley, ed., *The Autobiography and Memoirs of Benjamin Robert Haydon* (Edited from his Journals by Tom Taylor) (New York, n.d.), I, 251. See also Clarke's "Recollections of John Keats," *Gentleman's Magazine,* Feb. 1874, p. 198.

8. Amy Lowell notes that *Timon of Athens* was on at the Drury Lane for the ten days beginning on Monday, October 28, 1816. *Op. cit.,* I, 202.

9. *Ibid.,* pp. 206-207.

10. Sidney Colvin, *John Keats: his Life and Poetry, his Friends, Critics, and After-Fame,* 2nd ed. (London, 1918), p. 64.

11. Lowell, *op. cit.,* I, 204.

12. *Op. cit.,* p. 107.—H. B. Forman places Keats's introduction to Hunt in the spring of 1816. M. B. Forman, *Op. cit.,* I, xxix.

13. See Charles and Mary Cowden Clarke, *Recollections of Writers,* (New York, [1878]), pp. 132 ff.

14. H. S. Milford, ed., *The Poetical Works of Leigh Hunt,* (Oxford Press, 1923), p. 243.

15. Thomas Landseer, *Life and Letters of Wm. Bewick* (London, 1871), I, 129.

16. Roberta D. Cornelius, "Two Early Reviews of Keats's First Volume," *PMLA,* XL, 193-210, reprints this review in full.

17. *Ibid.,* p. 199.

18. This letter, reproduced in somewhat garbled form in the *Correspondence and Table-Talk,* II, 2, is corrected by Forman (*op. cit.,* I, 14, *n.*). Throughout the present study Forman's version of Haydon's letters to Keats has been preferred over Frederic Wordsworth Haydon's as being more accurate and more complete. H. B. Forman had access to Haydon's Journals, which are now, unfortunately, not available.

19. *The Athenaeum,* Feb. 19, 1898, p. 248.

20. *Ibid.,* p. 285.

21. Forman, *op. cit.,* I, 54-55.

22. *Ibid.*

23. Landseer, *op. cit.,* I, 40.—Bewick was less favorably inclined toward Haydon when, in 1823, he found himself involved in his master's financial ruin.

24. Colvin, *op. cit.,* p. 254: Lowell, *op. cit.,* I, 138.

25. In Wilfred Partington, *The Private Letter Books of Sir Walter Scott* (London, 1930), pp. 174-175.

26. *Op. cit.,* III, p. 520.

27. *London Magazine,* II (December, 1820), 667-668; 682.

28. Amy Lowell has well summarized the evidence regarding the circumstances surrounding this meeting. *Op. cit.,* I, 542-543.

29. Huxley, *op. cit.,* I, 268-271.

30. From Haydon's *Journals* it would appear that the usual fee was around two hundred guineas (Huxley, *op. cit.,* II, 681-682). Keats mentions a subscription for Cripps of between £150 and £200.

31. See Lowell, *op. cit.,* I, 551-552.

32. Landseer, *op. cit.,* I, 41.

33. See F. W. Haydon, *op. cit.,* I, 110.—Coleridge was also listed in the *Annals of the Fine Arts,* IV (1920), 131, as among the distinguished company which

"honored the private day" of the exhibition of drawings of the Raphael Cartoons by Haydon's pupils.

34. William Sharp, *The Life and Letters of Joseph Severn* (London, 1892), p. 33.

35. William Knight, *The Life of William Wordsworth* (Edinburgh, 1889), II, App. V, p. 409.

36. Miss Lowell makes much of the supposition that Keats did not ask "the return of the whole loan, he merely asked for 'some' money" (*op. cit.,* II, 263-264). What Keats actually wrote was "Do borrow or beg some how what you can for me." And considering the insignificance of the sum borrowed, it would seem that Miss Lowell's distinction is not important. She then continues with passionate inaccuracy, "Haydon's capacity for borrowing was inexhaustible, but he never paid his debts . . ." (*loc. cit.*).

37. Huxley, *op. cit., passim.*

38. *Ibid.,* I, 288.

39. *Op. cit.,* II, 472 *n.*

40. From an inscription, signed by Haydon, in a copy of the first volume of his *Lectures on Painting and Design* (London, 1844), in the writer's possession, it would appear that the painter had known Dr. Darling since 1810.

41. Huxley, *op. cit.,* I, 282.

42. *Ibid.,* p. 302.

43. *Ibid.*

44. F. W. Haydon, *op. cit.,* II, 255.

45. *Ibid.,* I, 88.

46. *Ibid.,* p. 141.

47. James Greig, ed., *The Farington Diary* (Lond., 1923-28), V, 171-172. Haydon may have acquired this habit from Fuseli, Keeper of the Academy, who was notoriously profane.

Varley Lang (essay date July 1947)

SOURCE: Lang, Varley. "Benjamin Robert Haydon." *Philological Quarterly* 26, no. 3 (July 1947): 235-47.

[*In the following essay, Lang portrays Haydon as a reformer in the field of the arts, focusing in particular on the painter's lobbying for increased public support of the arts and his belief that all English manufacturers and artisans should combine excellent workmanship with high artistic skill. In addition, Lang compares Haydon's ideas with those of later English art reformers, including Matthew Arnold, William Morris, and John Ruskin.*]

Whenever reforms in English art of the nineteenth century are mentioned, whether they concern standards of beauty in things of utility, or the social and economic influence upon art in handicrafts and manufactures, or the national, moral, and spiritual implications of art, one thinks immediately of Morris, of Ruskin, and of Arnold. It is usually taken for granted that the suggestions for improvement in the arts and in the attitudes of people toward the arts were either original with them or were first warmly and powerfully encouraged by them. But Benjamin Robert Haydon, before any of the latter reformers had ever uttered a word on art, had fought most of his life for, and given powerful expression to, the ideas which they were later to defend and promulgate. Haydon was not a great artist, but he was a first class fightin' man; because he thought he was right, he fought unselfishly in a fight that brought him nothing but calumny and suffering: "For thirty years I have urged the point of public encouragement of art . . . and all our great men seemed absolutely abroad on the subject. Even Canning was not at all aware of the connexion of art and manufacture, or the moral importance of High Art."[1] In such beliefs he stood alone, no one else having the courage or desire to sympathise with his views, except for a very few personal friends; and their support was covert and private. He fought until he was tired and could fight no longer; until misery, want, persecution, and exhausting labors had made life unendurable for him; he admitted his defeat as an individual by killing himself, but he never for a moment conceded that his ideas could be anything but right and capable of victory if acted upon.

For the sake of greater clarity, I shall examine, first, Haydon's views concerning handicrafts and manufactures, and compare them with Morris's; then, secondly, his views concerning the social, moral, and economic implications of art in general, and compare them with those of Morris, Ruskin, and Arnold. The two must, of course, overlap somewhat.

When Haydon began to be known in London as a painter, about 1804, he was brought sharply into contact with the idea, even then generally held, that the English people had very little taste in works of utility and that artists were scarcely fit for anything but flattering portraits of eminent personages.[2] From the beginning Haydon urged reforms to raise the taste of the people and to increase the beauty of articles of utility. He saw that older artifacts, even of the commonest sort, were excellent in form and design; why should they have become so inferior in his day?

Haydon was ahead of his times. Looking upon commerce and industry as something more than a mere matter of sale and purchase, but rather as pursuits in which high skill, sound knowledge, and efficient organization must be combined with excellence in workmanship, he aimed at so educating England's manufacturers and artisans in the true principles of art and design as to secure for her a supremacy in manufacture which could only be attained by beautiful pattern as well as make. As early as 1808 Haydon argued:

> We are inferior to French and Italians of the fifteenth and sixteenth centuries; beyond all conception inferior to the Greeks; and not even equal to the Ancient Egyptians in our designs for manufactures. And why? Because our pursuits in Art are low. Because we do not cherish that style as a nation which is the basis of excellence in those departments of art. And because we do not strive to raise the taste of the nation, but keep it down to the level of personal vanities, and pecuniary success.[3]

Furthermore, Haydon was keen enough to know that in a country where the profit motive was at the basis of society, he must appeal to the pockets of the manufacturers. "But to do this I must touch their pockets. I must show them it may be made a great means of material success."[4]

But how attain to excellence in the manufacture of artifacts? How make them beautiful? Haydon believed he had the answer. It was necessary to educate the whole people, but especially the artisans, in the true principles of art, particularly in the branch of designing. To do this, he wished to establish schools of art and design throughout England, since the Royal Academy, the only existing means of spreading a knowledge of art, "had subtly and insidiously abandoned its most sacred obligation, that of providing sufficient art instruction for the people."[5] He aimed "at making the humblest workman acquire a scientific knowledge of the principles of his work."[6] This workman must also be given a broad background in the general principles of art; indeed Haydon wished no separation between artist and artisan to be made, as far as instruction is concerned.[7] That he was perfectly sincere in his belief that artisans, if industrial art were not to remain vulgar, must have a thorough education in the general principles of high art, is proved by his conceiving and opening in 1837 a Society for Promoting Practical Design. He had at last convinced the government that education of artisans was necessary and opened his school when he found that the National School of Design was neglecting the instruction of workmen and narrowing the curriculum. To Haydon's school "mechanics were invited, and came in large numbers. Drawing from the antique was taught, and lectures . . . on anatomy, design, color, fresco, etc., were delivered."[8] "My object," said Haydon, "was to make design as cheap as ABC, that the merest door-painter might paint the human figure." For him, as for Morris, design was the basis of all art, "and a basis of such breadth that manufactures as well as Art rest in its excellence."[9] There must be no artificial distinctions raised among the arts.

In 1884, thirty-eight years after Haydon's death, the Art-Worker's Guild was formed with Morris as a member. The Guild was to consist of Handicraftsmen and Designers in the Arts, and "the central idea was the principle of the Unity, the Interdependence, the Solidarity of all the Arts."[10] Haydon had deplored the neglect of contemporary art for old masterpieces[11] and complained that the exhibitions at the Royal Academy were not truly national or representative.[12] The members of the Guild worked out a scheme for exhibitions really representative of all contemporary art; this scheme became known as the Arts and Crafts' Exhibition Society. "The movement of these prominent artists made itself immediately felt, and in the autumn of 1888 a scheme was formed for a National Association for the Advancement of Art in Relation to Industry."[13] What a pity Haydon could not have been present at the meeting of this society which, together with the Guild, was founded on principles he had fought a lifetime to establish.

Let us see what Morris, the most prominent member of these societies, said concerning the things which had been dear to Haydon's heart. In the first place, Morris repeated the painter's criticism that the French are superior to the English in design and thought it due in part to the superior training of the former. And good, original design, Morris pointed out to the Royal Commission on Technical Instruction, is necessary for business merely as a commercial affair.[14] He complained also of the superiority of the French in textile designs, as did Haydon; and he employed his argument for good design, even if more expensive, when he claimed better art is also commercially better.[15] In order to compete with French art in design, Morris wanted what Haydon had advocated, a thorough training for workmen:

> What I want to see really is, and that is the bottom of the whole thing, an education all round of the workman, from the lowest to the highest, in technical matters as in others; and that this should be obtainable in the several centers of industry; that is, a man should not be obliged to have to come to London to learn his work.[16]

As to how designers were to be trained, Morris is again at one with Haydon: "My view is that it is not desirable to divide the labor between the artist and what is technically called the designer, and I think it desirable on the whole that artist and designer should practically become one."[17]

Haydon believed art must rest upon old examples of good art, such as the Elgin Marbles, and upon nature, especially the human form. After having fought for thirty years for schools of design, he, as has been seen, was dissatisfied with those set up by the government. Therefore he introduced his own school with instruction on the principles he advocated: "Mechanics were invited, and came in large numbers. Drawing from the antique was taught, lectures by Haydon [and others] on anatomy, design, color, fresco, etc., were delivered, and Haydon introduced a fine female model and set workingmen to draw from her. The school became immensely popular."[18]

Morris, when questioned by the Commission as to the best curriculum for a school of art, replied:

> There are two chief things that would have to be thought of, in providing facilities for study of art design. However original a man may be, he can not afford to disregard the works of art that have been produced in times past . . . ; he is bound to study old examples, but he is also bound to supplement that by a careful study of nature . . . getting the habit of knowing what beautiful forms and lines are: that I think is a positive necessity . . . The designer wants to be taught to draw thoroughly.[19]

And Morris, like Haydon, was definitely of the opinion that the English textiles had suffered in competition with other countries from the absence of school training in design.[20]

Both the earlier and the later reformer had excellent reasons for insisting upon such a broad curriculum for art instruction, for they realized the danger of mere mechanical skill resulting from too narrow an application. The artisan must be an artist, not a soulless mechanic. It has been seen that the government schools of design did not come up to Haydon's expectations. Part of the reason for his dissatisfaction can be made clear by the following extract from a letter written to his son by "a competent authority":

> Schools of Design have not done what was expected of them, mainly, I believe, because they have been led into the wrong road by the teaching of South Kensington, which has encouraged an exaggerated mechanical precision of finish, instead of designing on the large and true principles such as your father would have insisted on.[21]

So Morris, as late as 1882, was telling the Commission on Technical Instruction that art education must be put on a broader basis; industrial art must get rid of "a certain high finish, and what I should call shop-counter look."[22] To be sure, Morris insisted always that the conditions of production of artifacts must be changed, especially the division of labor; whereas Haydon lived earlier when this division had not advanced so far, and either did not observe it closely or was more taken up with the other reforms which we have so far considered; nor had he the advantage of having read Karl Marx.

So far, rather special art reforms and ideas concerning the progress of the arts have been considered. But Haydon's fiery spirit and energetic mind could not rest on only one phase of the subject. He understood, for example, that the problem was not one concerning a single class in society itself, not a group, such as the Royal Academy, within the nation, but the entire country. Like Ruskin and Morris, Haydon saw intuitively that true art must be national and touch the lives of all: "A knowledge of the beauties, capabilities and actual practical utilities of Art, Haydon maintained, was essential to the general interest of England and more or less applicable to every situation and circumstance of her national life."[23] This web-like interrelation, this connection of art with all things, from the highest to the lowest, is familiar as one of Morris's most powerfully expressed tenets. Haydon had a strong sense of the web-like quality of art covering all things, and throughout his life gave private and public utterance to it. In one of his public lectures on Painting and Design, for example, he gave it as his purpose "to advance his listeners' taste, refine their feelings for High Art, prove its connection with their various callings, rekindle the lost feeling for its national importance, and prove its immense value to manufactures."[24] For this reason the mechanic as well as the portrait painter must be informed of the true principles of art. The cabinet and many members of the upper class were against Haydon because he desired to educate the artisan like the artist. "Why educate a journeyman above his class?" it was asked. The painter's answer was fearless and steadfast: Art is the concern of everyone, artisan as well as artist, the bricklayer's and My Lord's, too. Morris would have approved.

For giving some idea of the state of art in England during Haydon's time, and indeed in Morris's also, the following by the painter's son is a plumped nutshell:

> The administration of public affairs, upon which High Art relies, was entirely in the hands of a few great families . . . These families had a low conception of what patronage for art really meaned [*sic*]. The best of them—those who, in public opinion, held first place as lovers of art—were not remarkable for their depth or breadth of view upon the subject. They loved art so far as it contributed to their pleasure, but they had no notion of the public function of art. They collected foreign pictures, and like the Romans of old formed galleries in competition with one another . . . and as the Romans in their day neglected and despised their own native art for foreign specimens, so did the English nobility.[25]

Haydon, from first to last, attacked the monopoly of art by the Royal Academy and the pernicious, narrowing influence of an ignorant patronage. Art is for My Lord too, not for My lord only:

> It is not surprising that a desire to please their rich patrons should come in time to be exclusively considered by Academicians to the neglect of the principal object of their institution, viz., the training and education of all classes, in the true principles of art and design. I

fear the low taste of the patrons. Art is looked upon as nothing but a sort of gilding for their drawing rooms and chimney pieces. They have no conception of its public function.[26]

All the critics blamed the artists annually for want of talent, elevated conceptions, and subject matter; but Haydon knew the painters were not completely to blame. After all, the exhibitions in London showed, not the works the artists wished to paint, but what they were obliged to paint. "They bring to market the goods which will sell."[27] A further result is the formation of too many societies of narrow tastes, too much prejudice—all this, as far as art is concerned, is entirely owing to the art being thrown on the protection of individuals: a patronage of art by riches, in other words.[28] Later, Morris was to ask whether art must remain forever the slave of riches, limited to a narrow class who only care for it in a languid way, or was it to become the solace of a whole people? Certainly Haydon had wished it to be so, for he continually struggled to make art a public possession.[29] It must be public, must be national, if it is to be healthy, vigorous, significant. Haydon, like Morris and Ruskin, knew instinctively that great, sustained art must spring from the *whole* people. Haydon writes:

> From the people, and the people alone, must great art spring; let them be instructed and educated, and they must react on privileged classes; if . . . schools of design be soundly established, and professors at the universities, art will begin to bud on a solid foundation. . . . Statesmen must themselves be taught good art and given principles of good taste; it must be a truly national movement, from beginning to end.[30]

And just as Arnold preached in *Culture and Anarchy* that what makes a country great is spiritual greatness, so Haydon writes: "It appears to me no country was ever great, or ever will be, where native art was not the prime object of King, nobility and people."[31]

Now, if Morris believed firmly in anything, it was that art must depend, ultimately, upon the people, the nation as a whole. It is necessary for a population to be able to see beauty before it can produce it, and the artist cannot live amongst a people careless of the arts. The aim of art is to make life happy and dignified for all people, says Morris:

> To succeed in such an aim, is it not necessary that it should both spring from and be cherished by the people at large? Believe me, if today it seems otherwise, if Art has taken refuge altogether among the highest intelligences and the greatest cultivation, it is because it has for the moment ceased to be progressive, and rests upon the memory of the popular energy of past times.[32]

On another side, Haydon is much more like Ruskin than Morris. This pioneer combined a belief in the power of art to be morally elevating with his instinct

that it must be national, and arrived at large principles of the growth and decay of art like those later expounded by Ruskin. Haydon considered a close connection to exist between the moral temper and the cultural, aesthetic, intellectual development of a country:

> Is taste in Art not essential to the intellectual condition and moral and material improvement of a country? *The highest departments of Art cannot be adequately fostered by the liberality of individuals alone.* . . . A love of High Art neither in Greece nor in Italy preceded the genius of the artists or the patronage of the government, but was the consequence of the development of both.[33]

And in another place he comes still closer to Ruskin; he practically affirms that the animating principle of art is spiritual, that the art of a people is a spiritual expression of their common culture and intellectual development. In 1832 he writes:

> The ancient artists were idolaters, and believed that on the perfection of their works depended their ultimate happiness. This is the great reason of their superiority. Every touch was a compliment to a deity, and a chance of translation to heaven. So it was with the Roman Catholic painters of the fifteenth century. They were animated also by religious enthusiasm and worked under its powerful influence. The enthusiasm of the English people is of another description. It is political, not religious. But I see no reason why he who is animated by awe for the liberties of the human race cannot be actuated by the same elevation as the ancient Greek or more modern Italian.[34]

It is only a step from realizing the connection between society and the arts to a criticism of society for its adverse influence upon the arts. It was natural for Haydon to take this step, for he had a quick sense of social injustice, a true sympathy for the lower classes, and a fiery indignation fearless of consequences.[35] He believed that vital art and its appreciation must spring from the people; but how, when they "individually are occupied, taxed and struggling"?[36] And although the people are alive to the importance of grand art in England and have always flocked anywhere that such art has been displayed, yet the enthusiasm of the people has never been seconded by the state, says Haydon; and the great works "successively produced these last fifty years . . . are hidden from the public eye . . . in cellars, or lost in private collections. It naturally occurs to every foreigner, what is the reason? [of bad art in England] *The reason is to be found in the various influences of our social condition.*"[37]

After all his struggles for art, Haydon began to feel strongly the hopelessness of his individual efforts in a country where, sociologically and morally, good art was extraordinarily hampered. He assigns the failure of the arts, not to this small thing or that accident,[38] but to the moral temper of the people, especially those who have wealth: "It is shocking," he writes, to me to see Hallam proposing in the decoration scheme [proposed decoration of the Houses of Parliament] a law be laid down that the artists should not choose their own subjects, but the choice be made by . . . the Treasury . . . ! Now, the position of the British painter in the estimation of these men is coming out. He is a cipher, a suitor, a beggar, a serf. The aristocratic principle means to assert its superiority. They pay, therefore they must select . . . England is not worthy the naked majesty of genius. Next to the curse of being born, is the disgrace . . . of belonging to a class in a country where you are looked upon as a slave of a set of men, who in one year waste more money in vice, in folly, and in extravagance than would suffice to develop the struggling talent of a nation.[39]

But there are broader sociological reasons. How can great art flourish in a country where injustice and hypocrisy of all kinds are permitted under pretense of securing private property, Haydon continues:

Independence of mind is a fiction amongst us. . . . Obedience to law, custom, and precedent . . . has debauched and debased the minds of all to such an excess, that all classes unite in permitting any injustice, any despotism, under pretense of security to property, or respect to the dignity of authority. . . . I declare to God there is actually more suffering, more ruin, more injustice, more corruption, more hypocrisy in England than in any other country in Europe.[40]

Haydon did not believe art could live or prosper in such a social atmosphere, any more than did Morris or Ruskin[41] after him. And again, the sociological reason is given. Art is tied up with the rest of society; and if society is corrupt, art must suffer:

The British people are a fine people, but so borne down by habits of proper submission to authority, that every proposition independent of some authority, is looked on like the emanation of a lunatic. Genius is an impertinent intrusion on the established order of things. They don't want Genius. Property is endangered by an original conception and the Crown and the Altar will go to rack if a Painter insists that portraits should not be made to stand upon tiptoes.[42]

But Haydon sees a revolution in the offing:

A moral revolution is far advanced. Society dines and dances, and grows rich, and goes to court, and doesn't see it. . . . Exactly as the moral and intellectual revolution advances will the curses of our present unnatural social Conditions become apparent. As the rich wax richer the poor will lapse into greater poverty, capital and labour will quarrel. . . .[43]

As long as there is social injustice, as long as a large portion of the population must live in want and ignorance, as long as art is considered a mere decoration for drawing rooms, mere items in some obscure collection, as long as it is not believed capable of moral elevation as a result of narrow patronage by a few wealthy and influential people, so long must art be and remain on a lower level and taste with it. Is not this, in effect, what Morris and Ruskin represented so forcibly again and again? In condemning an Exhibition of the Royal Academy as "a piece of wretched twaddle" Morris gives the reason for its failure as social. "What, I say, is to feed the imagination, the love of beauty of the artists today while all life around them is ugly; sordid poverty on the one hand, insolent or fatuous riches on the other?"[44] Under such circumstances the great arts, however they may be practiced for a while by a few "great minds and wonder-working hands" are bound to lose the vitality and dignity of popular arts and become what Haydon had earlier complained they were, "nothing but dull adjuncts to unmeaning pomp, ingenious toys for a few rich and idle men."[45] In another place Morris sums up the situation neatly—"Rich men won't have art, and poor men can't."[46]

Haydon cried out against commercialism in art, the smug evaluation of art in terms of pounds and shillings, as did Morris and Arnold later. He gives a satirical presentation of the Philistine viewpoint:

That professional man in England who prefers excellence to profit is considered an anomaly; a rogue who cannot in the nature of things pay his bills, and ought not to be trusted or supported. What, prefer excellence in your art to emolument! "A fellow, Sir, who does this, is a man out of the circle of commercial taste"— the only principle of taste acknowledged with us.[47]

And here is a bitter indictment of a social injustice excoriated by Morris also: "No people," Haydon writes, "are less prepared to respect Genius alone than the English. A man of the greatest Genius, gifted by God with the greatest variety of power, without property, or authority, or rank, is regarded in England with little more respect than a pauper."[48] Morris says again and again that injustice is a great enemy to art; injustice, social and political. Sound, good art must be popular, of the people, and it must have a foundation in fairness to all, "the careful and eager giving his due to every man," regardless of his rank or property. On the political side, suffering must, as far as possible, be eliminated, "particularly the dreadful contrast between waste and want."[49]

Often Haydon strikes a blow at blind, money-grubbing Philistinism in language so much like Arnold's that at least one quotation may be interesting:

I cannot conceive how our nobility can go abroad, see every church, hall, gallery, teeming with pictures and come back and forget all, and bury immediately their feelings and their taste in junction railways, and mining speculations for copper or coal . . . Here we must look into our steward's accounts, here we must examine the premium of our shares.[50]

And Haydon's remedy is culture, too. Let man be taught in the institutions of learning as well "utility and refinement, knowledge and love of beauty, nature and fine arts."[51]

I do not mean to say that Morris, Ruskin, and Arnold are indebted directly for many important ideas to Haydon. As a matter of fact, I can find no evidence that Morris, for example, had ever heard of Haydon, though his **Lectures on Painting and Design** were fairly popular, and any of the three men may have come across the two volumes. Also the painter's correspondence, journal, and conversation with a long memoir by his son came out in 1876, in time, perhaps, to have some influence. By this time, and even before, Haydon's ideas were no longer thought to be peculiar and unheard of. He himself writes, in 1844: "All that I attacked the Academy for in 1812 is now acknowledged to be just, and the press itself is oozing out my former sentiments."[52] And Haydon's son observes: "It is amusing now, in 1875, forty years after Haydon's . . . labours, to read the addresses of our public men upon the want of our knowledge of design, as if it were a new discovery."[53] I wish merely to make a tribute to a pioneer who, without pay or reward, devoted his time and energy, sacrificed personal aggrandizement and honors for the vigorous promulgation of an important truth. In this aim he never faltered once, though harassed by staggering privations and hardships, and left almost alone in his efforts. I believe he deserves to have his name inscribed with the three great reformers in the field of arts who came after him.

Notes

1. B. R. Haydon, *Lectures on Painting and Design,* (1844), I, vii, 330. He delivered twelve lectures on this subject in most of the principal cities of England in 1835. Seven of these lectures were printed in 1844; a second volume, containing the other five, appeared in 1846, the year of Haydon's death.

2. B. R. Haydon, *Correspondence and Table Talk,* with a memoir by his son, F. W. Haydon, (1876), I, viii.

3. *Ibid.,* I, xii.

4. *Ibid.,* I, 203.

5. *Ibid.,* I, 62-3.

6. *Ibid.,* I, 193.

7. *Ibid.,* I, 198, 256.

8. *Ibid.,* I, 198.

9. *Ibid.,* I, xii, 76.

10. May Morris, *William Morris, Artist, Writer, Socialist* (1936), I, 184.

11. *Lectures on Painting and Design,* II, 24.

12. *Op. cit.,* I, x.

13. May Morris, *William Morris,* I, 94.

14. *Ibid.,* I, 206.

15. *Ibid.,* I, 209.

16. *Ibid.,* I, 210-11.

17. *Ibid.,* I, 211.

18. *Correspondence and Table Talk,* I, 198. The government schools were forced, at least temporarily, to reform. Haydon dissolved his school, his purpose accomplished.

19. *William Morris,* I, 211. In another place Morris said: "My own view is that drawing should be taught more or less from drawing the human figure . . ." (*Ibid.,* I, 222); see also *Ibid.,* XII, 20.

20. *Ibid.,* I, 220-21. Haydon writes (*Correspondence and Table Talk,* II, 227): "Our Manchester cottons were refused in Italy at the conclusion of the war of 1816, because their design was tasteless."

21. *Correspondence and Table Talk,* I, 195, note.

22. *Op. cit.,* I, 151.

23. *Correspondence and Table Talk,* I, xii, 76.

24. *Ibid.,* I, 193. Given at London Mechanic's Institution, 1835.

25. *Ibid.,* I, 24.

26. *Ibid.,* I, 256.

27. *Lectures on Painting,* II, x-xi.

28. *Correspondence and Table Talk,* I, 97.

29. *William Morris,* XXIII, 143ff. See Haydon's letter to Leigh Hunt on the Waterloo Monument, *Correspondence and Table Talk,* I, 258.

30. *Lectures on Painting,* II, 99-106.

31. *Ibid.,* I, 39.

32. *William Morris,* XXIII, 195, 199.

33. *Correspondence and Table Talk,* II, 224. Italics Haydon's.

34. *Ibid.,* II, 357. Cf. *Stones of Venice,* I, ch. i; II, ch. vi. But for a still earlier expression, see *The Poetry of Architecture,* 225, note: "It is utter absurdity to talk of building Greek edifices now; no man ever will, or ever can, who does not believe in the Greek mythology. . . . The architectural appurtenances of Norman embrasure or Veronaic balcony must be equally ineffective, until they can turn shopkeepers into barons, and schoolgirls into Juliets."

35. *Ibid.,* p. 227; p. 283. He was a friend of Leigh Hunt and his brother John, and was in sympathy with their liberalism.

36. *Lectures on Painting,* II, 40.

37. *Ibid.,* II, 96-7. Italics mine.

38. For example, the adverse influence of climate on art and genius in England. England is in the northern latitudes, cold, foggy, misty: these conditions handicap art in many ways. The idea is old, but assumes particular importance in England during the eighteenth century as an element in the growth of the historical point of view in criticism: that is, different climates, different kinds of art, different qualities of art. The idea that countries, such as England, which lie in a cold, foggy climate are at a disadvantage in the productions of the imagination is persistent in the eighteenth century. To cite a few examples: 1720, Sir Richard Blackmore, *The Nature of Man,* Book I; 1748, Thomas Grey, *Alliance of Education and Government,* pp. 84-7. To these may be added many more references to the influence of climate of a more general nature; some, even, are of the opinion that the English climate is favorable to the productions of geniuses. (P. Stockdale, e.g., *Inquiry into the Nature and Genuine Laws of Poetry,* 1788, p. 60.) But I had supposed that after the eighteenth century climate was no longer employed in art criticism, at least not in the sense that it is written of here. It is interesting to find that Haydon thought the idea of such importance as late as 1835 to speak often and vigorously against adverse climatic influence. Often, like Stockdale, he asserts that the climate of England is favorable to art: "I love my country; I glory in its poetry, its philosophy . . . its mechanical power. Why should we not place art on a level . . . with these great departments? Is there any just reason? O, yes!—the climate is foggy . . . I answer the climate of England is more adapted for great effort than any other in the world." (*Lectures,* I, 40.) See also *Ibid.,* I, 37, 197, 328; *Correspondence,* I, viii-ix; II, 307.

39. *Correspondence and Table Talk,* II, 214-15.

40. *Ibid.,* II, 215.

41. Ruskin proclaimed that great art can flourish only in a society worthy of it, and that decay in social morality leads to degradation of art. See *Stones of Venice.* The whole book is virtually an elaboration and proof of this idea. See also *The Seven Lamps of Architecture,* vii, 8. In *The Poetry of Architecture,* 225, note, Ruskin writes: "Let the national mind be elevated in its character, and it will naturally become pure in its conceptions; let it be simple in its desires, and it will be beautiful in its ideas; let it be modest in feeling, and it will not be insolent in stone."

42. *Ibid.,* p. 280.

43. *Ibid.,* II, 280-81; see also pp. 339 and 341.

44. *William Morris,* I, 215ff.

45. *Ibid.,* XXII, 4.

46. *Ibid.,* XXII, 114.

47. *Correspondence and Table Talk,* II, 339.

48. *Ibid.,* II, 341.

49. *William Morris,* XXII, 47-8.

50. *Lectures,* II, 149-50. Cf. *Culture and Anarchy,* ed. Wm. S. Knickerbocker (New York), 1929, pp. 46-8.

51. *Lectures,* II, 149-50. Cf. *Culture and Anarchy,* ed. Wm. S. Knickerbocker (New York), 1929, pp. 46-8.

52. *Op. cit.,* II, 206. To attempt to trace these "oozings" would be to broach another whole subject, the gradual growth of ideas given telling and finished and more or less complete statement later on by Morris and others. But from a casual examination of three or four leading journals up to the time of Haydon's death in 1846, and even after, I should say "the press" oozed very few of the painter's sentiments. Almost all notices of Haydon are adverse, except those of Hunt in the *Examiner*; and none show an understanding of his true aims. To give an example, the *Athenaeum* (Nov. 9, 1844, pp. 1025-27) in a review of the first volume of Haydon's *Lectures on Painting and Design,* finds him "smart, startling, anecdotal, conceited and unsound." It is an adverse review from beginning to end; and I can easily see why the reviewer found Haydon startling, for he shows no sign of understanding the reformer's criticism of art from the sociological standpoint, or even of having grasped his more immediate criticism of especial abuses. In the same publication, for July 18, 1846 (pp. 737-39) the same reviewer discusses the second volume of the *Lectures,* but this time in a more friendly spirit, perhaps because Haydon had just killed himself and was no longer able to "startle" the world of art with "unsound" criticism. This review shows a little consciousness of the sociological import of Haydon's *Lectures,* but misses many of his ideas and displays no understanding of their far-reaching significance. The reviewer writes: "Another tenet of ours often propounded—(I cannot find that he propounded these ideas anywhere in the *Athenaeum*) the tendency of the Middle Class patronage to bring

about a Middle Class species of Art, we find here insisted on. The author's eighth and ninth chapters are eloquent attempts to rescue painting from the boudoir and the cabinet and the ground floor, the citizen's and the squire's state-apartments . . . and to raise it into large national receptacles. Government he thinks bound to become a substitute for princely patrons and princely palaces." This is *all* he has learned from Haydon's *Lectures,* and this he has not altogether understood; but, at any rate, he is catching on, and probably others were too.

53. *Correspondence and Table Talk,* I, 203.

Eric George (essay date 1967)

SOURCE: George, Eric. "Haydon on Haydon." In *The Life and Death of Benjamin Robert Haydon, Historical Painter: 1786-1846.* 1948. Reprint, with additions by Dorothy George, pp. 374-84. Oxford: Clarendon Press, 1967.

[*In the following essay, George, using as his source W. B. Pope's* Diary of Benjamin Robert Haydon *(1960-63), the first publication of the full text of Haydon's* Journals, *focuses on Haydon's entries describing his "darker side"—the anguish over his own sanity, and those feelings of anxiety and despondency that plagued the artist throughout his entire career.*]

> Painters & Poets are liable to the erruptions of different feelings
>
> (Oct. 1809).

Does Haydon's darker side, the hypochondria and the fits of despair, editorially muted by Taylor, affect the question of his sanity? He brooded on insanity as he brooded on suicide, expected Leigh Hunt to die insane, feared the same fate for Frank, and thought Frank's instability inherited from himself. Hypochondria, like suicide, he attributed to indigestion. 'What machines we are. Digestion is the great cause of every virtue & every vice . . .',[1] he wrote in June 1845. A few months earlier he had prayed; 'Spare me, O God from a failing brain.'[2] The preservation of his sanity he ascribed to marriage and to his religion, and the direct intervention of the Almighty. But for religion, he told a clergyman, 'I should have gone mad.'[3] And, 'It is wonderful to me I have held out so long to 56. Had I been debauched or drunken I never could, and the Religion of my mind has saved my intellect often.'[4]

Haydon's religion, intertwined with superstition, was a lifeline, a talisman, his prayers an incantation, and a blend of entreaty and confession and self-justification ('Thou knowest . . .') that became a necessity. In the

aggregate they fill many many pages. The superstition he admitted: 'Men of Genius are considered superstitious, but the fact is, the fineness of their nerve renders them more alive to the supernatural than ordinary men.'[5] Thus in 1830. Ten years later, 'Danger is the very basis of Superstition. It produces a searching after help, supernaturally, when all human means are no longer supposed to be available.'[6] His frequent resort to the *sortes Biblicae* he did not regard as superstitious. The comforting text always turned up, just as—till the very end—the timely cheque or commission seemed a direct answer to prayer.

His religion was peculiar and highly characteristic. He was a pragmatist, yet had a mystical sense of communion with the Almighty. 'God be praised! If this perpetual belief in the protection of God be a weakness, it is a weakness that tends to great good.'[7] 'Carry me through the ensuing week, the ensuing month, the ensuing Year!' he prayed in 1845. 'In *thee* I trust with an unfailing splendour of Vision in my brain, as if I saw a light mortals cannot see, & heard a harmony that makes me faint.'[8] His horror of scepticism was not fundamentalist. On the contrary: 'I have known Deists, Atheists, Sceptics, Baptists, Protestants, Unitarians & catholics, & always found the Catholics ready with damnation & never wrong, but all the rest acknowledging that they could not explain, candidly.'[9]

After much musing on the problem of evil he came to the conclusion that the Almighty was not omnipotent. On his fifty-first birthday, 'I find now my judgment matured—conviction at last arrived at that the Deity cannot eradicate Evil, & that the Mortal can only check or compromise with it. But that is no reason it should not be opposed, or checked, resisted & turned aside, if possible.'[10] In a bitter mood in 1842: 'Evil certainly has more power than good, is a match for virtue, & though it cannot overturn, it seems as if it maliciously *baffled* the Almighty.'[11] What shook his confidence in the justice of God was not his own manifold injuries (as he thought them) but the massacre of 500 men, women, and children in Algeria, which 'really shakes one, as to the moral justice of the Great Creator, to allow so many innocent people to be butchered in so horrid a way. It is a mystery. Prayed to be eased of agonising doubts.[12]

Haydon was saved (till 22 June 1846) by his faith and by his vitality and his natural resilience and buoyancy. His capacity, not only for putting a good front to the world, but for enjoying simple pleasures in the middle of adversity, was remarkable. In July 1845, 'Dined with my dear Friend Peter Fairbairn, & he took me to the play. I had not been so long I laughed & cried like a child.'[13] And, three weeks later, that dinner at Greenwich with his boys—'I enjoyed myself immensely.'

There are wild outbursts of misery that seem less than sane, but, strangely, only in 1824, a year of domestic bliss and relative freedom from money troubles, owing to Kearsey (pp. 173-6) and portraits. One of these Taylor quotes, deleting the more extreme passages, and it is quoted here (p. 171). It ends: 'Adieu for ever, unadulterated happiness! purity of thought! ardour of heavenly love! & welcome bloody, bawdy madness! endless, torturing, fierce, ungovernable agony,—welcome!'[14] More wild, more raving, is a long passage some months earlier which is worked up to a climax of surrealist nightmare. It begins: 'Of what use is my Genius—to myself or others? It has brought me to prison—of what use is that fame which a breath may destroy as a breath has created it? . . . My Youth is gone! . . . I am ruined! I wonder my frame has born this so long—the mere agitations of the conceptions one's mind has flushing one's brain with blood, & bathing one's body in perspiration, must wear it, and then in addition the necessities of poverty are dreadfull. If I were alone again I would leave my Country for ever—buried in Italy or Greece, I would pass my days in the lowest avocations, could I get peace! ay, peace!' Finally, imagining himself sinking into 'the sloth & superstition, the dreary praying, the solemn imbecility of a cowled monk!', he would plunge into the wild, vent his rage on trees, stones, birds, and animals, and 'glory with ecstatic rapture to meet a *solitary human being without defence*', whom he would murder in the most savage, ghastly, and gory way. 'Ah, ah, Revenge, Revenge, thou dear, dear, dear passion! . . . Genius! the nectar of a soul parched & dried up by poverty & ruin! Curses, Curses, Curses, endless, withering, Hellish, from that lower Hell where the most Hellish rebels down are deeper thrown—light [? blight], blast, scathe those who could dim a brain so brilliant & a heart so tender to such bitter, bitter, solace. B. R. Haydon.'[15] (Abridgement here mitigates the savagery.) Was this a brainstorm, or fantasy, or a safety-valve? Haydon describes his distress (in 1824) at seeing a rabbit shot.[16]

The summing up of the year on the last day of December is also strange. Taylor prints the optimistic reflections—'My domestic happiness is doubled. . . . My mind calmer, my principles of honour firm, & Religion deeper than ever.' But then comes a wild despairing cry on the human condition which he omits: . . . 'ye came into breath without consciousness and ye go out cursing your fate that ye possess it! Heroes, Poets, Painters, Mathematicians, Fanatics, Priests, or what ye may be! . . . Oh humanity, humanity, can there be a being who can . . . bear to hang over thy filth! who is alive to lovely thoughts? can bear thy murders, thy malice, thy base desires.' There is much more. The entry ends, 'Pardon me if too Presumptuous, Worldly, & vain. Amen. I leave all to thy mercy. Amen.'[17] The contrast between Haydon in his ***Journals*** and in contact with the world is pointed by an undated letter of about December 1824, printed by Taylor. 'I must own that the comforts and ease and tranquillity which attend por-

traits and the misery and insults which have always attended my history-painting, begin to affect me.'[18]

The note of wild despair is never struck again. (It was in 1824 that he told Miss Mitford (p. 7) '. . . die I shall at last from the agonies of racked ambition'.) 'I do not think any man on Earth ever suffered more agony of mind than I have done, & so would the World think if it knew why, and yet I always had an abstracting power, & that saved my mind & made me look down & meditate, as it were, on my own sufferings. They became a matter of curious speculation.'[19] Haydon called himself 'of a sanguine disposition' (***Autobiography***) and 'naturally happy tempered'.[20]

The despair was doubtless caused by the realization—sometimes allusively recorded—that with a family and without his large lofty painting room,[21] his dream of greatness was but a dream. 'What I could produce if seconded by Public encouragement! I dread to dwell on it! It pains me so.' (The occasion was an abortive proposal to paint a Crucifixion for Liverpool Town Hall.)[22] 'I look back on the glories of my past life with desponding enthusiasm. Here I am now in a snug carpeted parlour!—but alas! where is now the magnificent grandeur of my solitary & extended Painting Room! . . . My feelings perhaps are deeper now, perhaps higher, but I look back & ever shall (though then unblessed by Mary's face) with desponding remembrance to days & nights which are passed—*for ever*!' And he breaks into free verse beginning 'Solitude—Farewell!' and ending '. . . Would human / Effort fail if not roused by hoping / To do more than it can do?'[23]

'I am one of those beings born to bring about a great object through the medium of suffering', he wrote in 1829. 'I shall accomplish what I was born for, and die in all probability without sharing its worldly benefits. I only hope, if I should, my Children will not be forgotten by my Country.'[24] He compares his hypochondria to Johnson's: 'O God, assist me to get rid of this insane condition of mind. I take it, I feel the want of *discipline* in my early life. I was an only son, & ever had my own will, like Byron, & left to my own impulses. This has produced all the good and all the vice of my character.'[25] 'Whenever I have been encouraged I have met it by desperate exertion, but I have been so ill used and so cruelly treated that my feelings are melancholy & exasperated, and I have occasional fits of sluggish disgust. My face, with its energy & colour conceals my feelings. My Mary only knows them.'[26] (Apart from specific grievances, by ill treatment or cruelty Haydon means the absence of commissions for High Art.) He was again upset by reading—passionately—Bourrienne's *Memoirs,* 'the Boswell of Napoleon'. 'Remembering him as I do from 1796, it is peculiarly interesting to me, and I awoke this morning despising myself for my present pursuits [he was painting *Punch*] and agitated by all my former ambitious feelings.'[27]

In 1834, distraught by financial dangers and family troubles, 'I must "who aspire to greatness" shew form of being able "*greatly* to suffer". . . . I fear a curse hangs over me, for leaving my Father to pursue Art—whenever I touch "high Art" it seems in force.'[28] A few days later, after a timely cheque, 'These anxieties are proper corrections! They keep the creature dependant to his Creator. . . . Continued prosperity would make me impudent, voluptuous & ungrateful. I see the value of affliction to a character like mine, if he has a soul to be saved.'[29] And, in the desperate plight of 1836 (from which he was to be extricated by Newton). 'Though more hopeless than ever in situation, I despair less than ever and trust in thee O god, with all my Soul, & know I shall be delivered. Amen.'[30]

All this Taylor omits, as he does expressions of pure pessimism. Even in the early raptures of marriage, after 'indigestion': 'Such is human Nature!—sleeping, rising, eating, drinking, purging, propagating, suffering, dying & rotting!—but there is one little matter in "Life's else bitter cup distilled" that makes us bear the rest.'[31] 'Next to the agony of being born is the horror of belonging to *such a species!*', he writes, on realizing that though he had wept bitterly at the death of his baby Fanny, he 'did not feel less hungry of my dinner.'[32] In the bitter aftermath of the cartoon contest, after revelling in sea-bathing at Dover, 'swimming always braces me—but then comes this calamity—Life.'[33] Nine days later, 'Rubbed in Uriel, but harrassed so much my brain becomes turgid with apprehension.'[34]

In these days of 'torturing petty anxieties' as well as of anguish—'I feel I have suffered so much my Imagination is diseased about ruin'[35]—optimism has a forced note and is largely omitted by Taylor. 'Weather, indigestion, a glass of wine beyond my three, oversleeping, not working hard—all these causes help to depress the physique & then the mental—yet what a Blessing is life!'[36] A year later, 'Who for fear of Pain would lose their intellectual being? If there be happiness on earth it is mine. To sit, with a Sketch one side, my Literature the other, & a grand work before me—meditating alterations & improvements—"Seeing Him who is invisible" & hearing Immortal Chauntings no Earthly Ear can Catch.'[37]

Haydon prided himself on his courage—his bottom—but not, apart from his tenacity in pursuing high art, on strength of character. 'The same follies, the same weaknesses, the same want of self-command, the same——.'[38] And, 'I am the same Man as ever, 30 years [ago] I had just the same feelings, the same delusions!'[39] One impulse which he knew to be a weakness, and which became an addiction, was the urge to polemics in the press. Tempted by 'a pompous announcement in the Times . . .' 'After a struggle I conquered my evil Genius.' 'Writing to me is no trouble; it is pouring out

my thoughts only, as I would talk, but the consequences are deep. I tell too many truths, make enemies, & lose my time.'[40] After spending a week on 'a memorial for Lord Grey, about the Academy, which has disturbed my thoughts. . . . Why cannot I, as Buckingham said, consider myself blessed by God with high gifts & be content to exercise them—why cannot I indeed?'[41] 'O God restore my intellect to its sound condition', he prayed, 'its passion for painting, root out this appetite for Controversy & writing, except on subjects of Art, calm & useful, for Jesus Christ's sake, Amen.'[42] 'Wrote, but neither drew or painted, I regret to say, I ought never to write, because if I say what I know to be truth, I hurt myself, if I do not I hurt my conscience.'[43] 'Many years more of effectual practice I can hardly expect', he reflected in 1844, 'and is it not time to think only of my dear Art, and let her do her duty by the Pencil alone—as well as my family. The fact is, the Cause is so linked up with me, that both Pencil & pen I fear will ever go together.'[44] In 1845 Haydon sketched in his *Journal* a pen and a palette and brush, which he called 'The bane & Antidote', with the comment, 'Unless I am constantly Painting, I give vent with the pen. The moment my mind is not excited by the brush, it turns right round & pours out a torrent of thought for the pen.'[45] How different his life would have been if he had never embarked on his polemical career with those two articles in the *Examiner* in 1812 (p. 45).

Haydon came to deplore his intervention in politics over Reform which he regarded as a public desertion of the Tories in favour of the Whigs. His politics were peculiar and characteristic—a complex of concern for the Art, self-interest, public spirit, Academy-phobia, regard for rank, Radical leanings, John-Bullishness, hero-worship of Wellington, then, admiration (this side idolatry) for 'dear Lord Grey'. In 1827 he had declared himself a Reformer, 'that is, a man whose abstract notions of right & wrong are too intensely strong to yield to the whispers of self-interest! or be blind to the sophistry of Power!'[46] Haydon's zeal for Reform (which makes a first appearance in the *Journals* in December 1819) was based on hatred of the corrupt corporation—embodied of course in the Academy—and therefore of the nomination borough. He told Lord Althorp that the Academicians were 'the Boroughmongers of the Art'.[47] The 'Radical Junior'[48] letters of which he was so proud (p. 211) were anonymous. 'I would wish to keep well with all in hopes of getting some of the Rascals to do something for Art.'[49]

The Reform Banquet picture changed that. Haydon's expectations soared. 'The immortality conferred upon me by Lord Grey in giving me a Picture connected with Reform—the glory of that night at Guildhall—the return of fortune . . . but I regret to say the materials I have to work with for Art—King, Nobility & People—are materials from which little good can be expected.'[50] The abortive Newhall Hill picture (p. 206) had inspired more spontaneous enthusiasm. Here are his conflicting views on the Radicals. 'If we were left to the Radicals, God help Art, science, knowledge or honour.'[51] Some five years later, 'The Radicals, men of honest, abstract Virtue, despise worldly ways, & leaving principles to act for themselves, fall before Men less honest, who know the World better'.[52] His social attitude had similar conflicts: '*I should be happy to enlighten* the lower classes but not to *dine* with them [he must have been thinking of Johnson]. . . . This is, I daresay, wrong, but I cant help it. I prefer Tasso or Virgil, Propinque maribus, champagne, & the order of the Bath. I know it is wrong, & in reality perhaps I don't, but "*the ribbon paints well*". Times are coming when it won't be the thing, & I don't see why the Queen [Adelaide] should have 100,000 a year. There is Poetry in the *People,* but there is also Poetry in *nobility,* the Elect, the Choice, the Adorned, the Refined. I can't deride [? decide] & yet I can. The Rights of Thousands, & the privileges of some.—"an ounce of civet".'[53] (One of Haydon's favourite quotations from *Lear.*)

Haydon can hardly be called a *staunch* Tory. 'If the English People again submit to the Tories', he wrote in May 1833, 'may they be ground to dust & crushed to atoms, may Russians, Prussians & Austrians help to enslave, and may their old enemies the French come in at the Crisis & complete their destruction . . . [etc. etc.] these things & worse is my ardent prayer. Amen.'[54] (How little his verbal explosions could mean. He feared a popular upheaval and blamed it on Tory policy after 1815.) With less extravagance: 'Church & King—means pluralities & the Pension List', but annotated it four years later, '1838 October. This was Radical cant. It does not mean that in essence, but it comes often to that in abuse.'[55] In essence, Haydon was a Church and King man.

Disillusion with the Whigs set in. Talking to his friend, William Hamilton, 'I said I did not think the Whigs so fit for business as the Tories, and I found a great deal of Aristocratic feeling among the Whigs. Lord Grey would leave me to go to lunch & never ask me, though he knew I must be feeling faint. Lord Mulgrave always made me frankly dine, breakfast & lunch with him, and yet Lord Grey knew it was my habit, because when he left town he gave orders for my having a lunch at the time I painted in Downing Street.'[56] 'I never dined but once with a Whig, and yet the Tories, with all their pride, were always having me at their tables, and the only Minister who has invited me to dine during the fever for me is a *Tory (Palmerston)*—curious, certainly. Johnson said the first Whig was the Devil. Why? From a love of Liberty—no. From a hatred of controul, & a passion to rule others. This is the secret of Whiggism.'[57]

'Lord John's saying that an open Window was enough air & exercise for a Prisoner has shewed me the real despotism of his nature, & the conduct of the Whigs to me in settling the School of Design that I first proposed, never consulting me, & putting no Artists but Academicians has disgusted me much. It shews they have no real desire to open a new Aera, and that if they could have helped it, they never would have passed the Reform bill.'[58] Two weeks later, 'The Whigs are evidently sinking . . . they will go without regret from any body. This comes from playing *Tories* . . . As to myself, I have been rightly served for belying my real heart & rushing forward to honour them because I believed they passed the Reform bill, when I found on close contact they were as much annoyed at being obliged to do it almost as the Tories themselves.'[59]

'The Unfortunate Banquet! it ruined me, has ruined the Engraver, & thus my enthusiasm for the cause, which they never would have carried except for *the people,* and which they have lamented carrying *ever since, has been my bane!*'[60] By 1838 Haydon was violently anti-Whig, hated the new Poor Law, resented and dreaded their foreign policy. 'I am in a devil of a rage with the Whigs for the want of decision they display in every thing but keeping their places.' This ends a long, extravagant tirade in the vein of the anti-Tory explosion.[61] In 1839, 'I *do certainly* regret the part I took about the Reform Bill'. (This is annotated 'I do not (1841). I would do it again, if the Duke acted so again.') 'I believe it was more revenge for ill usage & spirit because the Duke said *no Reform* was necessary than genuine Patriotism. *I do not know.* . . . I hate Radicalism & Whiggism. I hate Intermediation, & believe I shall end my Life a Conservative Reformer. If the Duke comes to sit & gives me a commission, I am done for! At any rate *this* is honest. . . . The real truth, I court all Parties to get one [or] other to do *something* for the Art, but I am more a Duke's man than any other, and under every other pretence *have always been so,* and *that* is from my *heart*! . . .'[62]

But he thought himself committed to the Party. 'It is impossible for me now after my devotion & enthusiasm for the Whigs, after the absurd Catalogue I wrote about them (pp. 209-10) ever to mingle again in political matters without deserved Ridicule. It is the Duke's fault. . . .'[63]

By 1841 Haydon was veering to the Whigs. 'If there be a dissolution what shall I do? The Whigs have not done *all* I could wish, but they have done a great deal. Will Peel do as much? I fear not. . . . The Whigs granted me a Committee . . . [Ewart's]. They have formed a Central School as I advised in my evidence. They have begun branch Schools, as I recommended. Ought I not to be grateful & pleased?'[64] Peel's ministry is mentioned (1 September) without enthusiasm, and after that politics are submerged by a complex of anxieties— Mary, Orlando, Frank, the cartoons. He remarks in 1842, 'The reign of the Tories has always been a curse to me. I never get employed when they are uppermost.'[65] Not that Haydon lost interest in public events. On the eve of the fatal last exhibition: 'The Victories of the Punjaub are the grandest thing since Waterloo, & by Pupils of that illustrious Man!' He prophesied that 'its entire civilization & final Christianity will be the result.'[66]

Thrice Haydon recorded his political creed. First, a plea for Church and monarchy, '& the Nation will gradually arrive at an Amalgamation of Classes, without blood, violence or folly'.[67] Then, twice, in almost identical terms. 'Of the Two Evils, Monarchy is preferable to Democracy [still a word of ill-repute]. It is an evil that any given number of human beings should be fed & pampered & made believe it is the duty to feed & pamper them, but when property & religion & Liberty are more secure under a Sovereign as an abstract head of the Law than under a plurality of Tyrants as abstract heads of Democracy, Monarchy in the long run will be the selected Government of the Earth.'[68]

Though the **Autobiography** shows a vivid memory for details of early life, there are strange lapses in the **Journals.** Haydon says (in 1845) that his name 'had been down 4 times [for the Academy,] 1810 & 1811, 1826, 1827—& never had a single vote'.[69] He told the Ewart Committee that he had been rejected for the Associateship in 1810, 1811, and 1820 (p. 214). The minutes of the R.A. confirm what the reader of the **Autobiography** and the **Journals** suspects, that he applied only in 1810 and 1827.[70] Then, when Mary went to Brighton for her health in March 1846 (p. 281)—'My dearest love who has never left me for 25 years'; he forgot that other momentous first separation, after eighteen years, when Mary went to Oxford to see Orlando.

Haydon was torn by conflicts ('I try to like Portrait, & I try not to like it')[71]—between solitude and family life, between the People and the elect, between life as a calamity and life as a blessing, between a death-wish and desire for long life. Two of Haydon's musings on suicide demand quotation. In 1835 in a verse on 'The Painter's Blessings' addressed to Mary: 'Oh hail my three blessings of Life, / My pencil, my Book, & my Wife, / Never mind the alloy, / While these I enjoy, / I defy both the bullet and knife.' This was the outcome of prolonged musings on mind and body, immortality, Revelation, and suicide induced by reading Brougham's *A Discourse of Natural Theology.* The book 'threw my mind entirely off its balance for painting . . .'.[72] In 1842:

> Nothing is so dreadful as the inexorability of Time! The half of the Year was last week. . . . Oh Time, Time—dreadful. If the falls of Niagara were near, I would go over them shouting to put an end to this horror of living *here!* Would it put an end? *Here* it might, but where would you *wake?*

This is sheer '*stomach strain*' from foul air & anxiety.

I am ashamed of myself, but such is life!—and such is a Lord of Creation when his *stomach* is deranged—that's the power after all, the identical thing which can & does baffle the mind—is surely the strongest of the two, and regulates its deductions. I am not well & do not know how it will all end. Let us draw the Curtain—& all to meditation.[73]

Notes

1. [*The Diary of Benjamin Robert Haydon,* ed. W. B. Pope, Harvard University Press, 5 vols. (1960-3),] v. 456.

2. v. 402, 6 Dec. 1844.

3. iv. 525, 2, 3, 4 Oct. 1838.

4. v. 152, 9 May 1842.

5. iii. 429, 12 Mar. 1830.

6. iv. 619, 6 Apr. 1840.

7. iii. 181, Jan. 1827.

8. v. 448, 25 May 1845.

9. v. 37, 10 Mar. 1841.

10. iv. 401, 25 Jan. 1837.

11. v. 119, 10 Jan. 1842.

12. v. 464, 20 July 1845.

13. v. 467, 28 July 1845.

14. *Diary* ii. 499, 6 Oct. 1824.

15. ii. 474-5, 26 Apr. 1824.

16. iii. 107, 30 June 1826.

17. *Diary* ii. 502-7.

18. *Autobiography and Memoirs [of Benjamin Robert Haydon (1786-1846),* edited from his *Journals* by Tom Taylor, Peter Davies, Publisher] (1926), i. 358.

19. iii. 38, 13 Aug. 1825.

20. iii. 117, 10 July 1826.

21. It still exists, or did recently, called Welbeck Hall, and is used as a chapel by a group of Plymouth Brethren at 1 Rossmore Road. ii 129 n.

22. iii. 8, 21 Feb. 1825.

23. iii. 94-95, 30 Apr. 1826.

24. *Diary* iii. 334, 15 Jan. 1829.

25. iii. 359, 10 May 1829.

26. iii. 373, 21 June 1829.

27. iii. 390-1, 25-27 Aug. 1829.

28. iv. 221, 30 Aug. 1834.

29. iv. 221, 30 Aug., 3 Sept. 1834.

30. v. 373, 27 Aug. 1836.

31. ii. 377, 19 Aug. 1822.

32. *Diary,* iii. 582-3, 22 Nov. 1831.

33. v. 373, 6 July 1844.

34. v. 376, 15 July 1844.

35. v. 310, 16 Sept. 1843.

36. v. 383, 15 Aug. 1844.

37. v. 465, 22 July, 1845.

38. iv. 449, 14 Nov. 1837.

39. iv. 493, 16 June 1838.

40. iii. 395, 10 Sept. 1829.

41. iv. 23, 15 Dec. 1832. B is James Silk Buckingham.

42. *Diary* iv. 578, 26 Aug. 1839.

43. v. 208, 3 Oct. 1842.

44. v. 361, 8 May 1844.

45. v. 440, 13 May 1845.

46. iii. 231, 6 Nov. 1827.

47. iv. 16, 25 Nov. 1832.

48. 'Junior' because of a series of influential letters in *The Times* from December 1830, signed Radical. They had been attributed to Lord Durham, but were by Lt.-Col. Leslie Grove Jones.

49. iii. 570, 22 Oct. 1831.

50. *Diary,* iv. 27, 31 Dec. 1832.

51. iv. 126, 26 Aug. 1833.

52. iv. 486, 3 June 1838.

53. iv. 33, 24 Jan. 1833.

54. iv. 84-85, 20 May 1833.

55. iv. 242, 26 Nov. 1834.

56. *Diary* iv. 245, 21 Dec. 1834.

57. iv. 195-6, 31 May 1834.

58. iv. 403, 8 Feb. 1837.

59. iv. 407, 22 Feb. 1837.

60. iv. 442, 29 Oct. 1837.

61. iv. 492-3, 16 June 1838.

62. iv. 556, 19 May 1839.

63. iv. 557-8, 28 May 1839.

64. v. 52-53, 24 May 1841.

65. v. 134, 28 Feb. 1842.

66. v. 528, 3 Apr. 1846.

67. v. 40, 23 Mar. 1841.

68. v. 277, 28 May 1843. The entry for 16 Sept. 1842 is almost the same.

69. *Diary* v. 438-9, 11 May 1845.

70. I am much indebted to Mr. Hans Fletcher for this information.

71. iii. 355, 2 May 1829.

72. iv. 321, 3 Nov. 1835.

73. v. 173, 27 June 1842. Haydon adapts *Henry VI, Part II,* III. iii. 32-33.

Colbert Kearney (essay date 1978)

SOURCE: Kearney, Colbert. "B. R. Haydon and *The Examiner.*" *Keats-Shelley Journal* 27 (1978): 108-29.

[*In the following essay, Kearney attempts to prove that Haydon was the author of several anonymous letters and articles published in the Hunts' paper* The Examiner *during the early 1800s, using entries in Haydon's* Diary *to validate his argument and maintaining that the published pieces attest to the close relationship between Haydon and the Hunts during that time.*]

Writing in *The British Press* for 3 July 1823, "An Observer" claimed that Haydon the historical painter—then in the King's Bench Prison for debt—had written critiques of his own work in *The Examiner* and in the *Annals of the Fine Arts.* Haydon complained of this to the editor of the *Annals,* James Elmes, who replied in a letter that was clearly intended to be shown to anybody who doubted Haydon's denial of the original charge:

> I have no hesitation to avow that, during the five years that the *Annals of the Fine Arts* were published, of which I was sole editor and part proprietor, no criticisms or praises on your own works, or on those of others that were printed, were written by you, or even seen by you, till in print.

(Without looking further than Haydon's ***Autobiography,*** this can be shown to be a lie.) Elmes went on:

> Of the *Examiner,* of course, I know nothing, but the similarity of Mr. Robert Hunt's initials, R. H., to yours, B. R. H., may have led some careless readers to the conclusion you complain of; but I am certain I have heard Mr. Robert Hunt declare a number of times that

you never wrote criticism in the *Examiner* on your own, or other works, except such as had your name at length, or your initials in full.[1]

Haydon then wrote to John Hunt and received the following reply:

You ask "Am I, or was I ever, the author of any criticisms on modern works of art, signed R. H. in the *Examiner*?" and "Did I ever in my life criticise a modern picture, or influence you or your brother, Mr. Robert Hunt, directly or indirectly to give favourable or unfavourable opinions of any modern picture or any modern artist?" In reply, I have to state that you certainly never wrote any articles in the *Examiner* under the signature of R. H. (which were written by my brother Robert), that you never criticised any modern picture or artist in that paper, and that you never to my knowledge, directly or indirectly, induced any writer in the *Examiner* to give favourable or unfavourable opinions respecting works of art or their authors.[2]

One is reluctant to question the word of a man who chose imprisonment rather than compromise, yet the cold precision of John Hunt's letter reminds one of an honorable lawyer with a dubious brief. There is no indignation or emotion of any kind and he is clinically careful to answer only the questions he has been asked. It is as if he knew more than he wished to reveal in the circumstances.

It was widely felt then (as it is now) that Haydon's connection with *The Examiner* was more intimate than John Hunt's letter would suggest and it is Haydon's contribution to *The Examiner* that is the subject of this essay. It will facilitate our understanding of his writings if we begin by recalling some of the more important details of his early career.

The first number of *The Examiner* appeared on Sunday, 3 January 1808. It was an important month for Haydon, for it was in the same January that he had his first sight of the Elgin Marbles.

Haydon had come to the Royal Academy in 1804 and had soon made an impression as a diligent student who had a burning ambition to make a name for himself (and for his country) in historical painting. There was a popular belief at the time that Britain would soon produce an outstanding artist in "high art"—as opposed to the "lower" forms; landscape, portrait, and still life—and Haydon was not slow to see his own ambition in the light of this historical necessity. Almost everything tended to increase his optimism. Only two years after his arrival, with no notable work to his credit, he was commissioned to paint a historical picture, *The Assassination of Dentatus,* for Lord Mulgrave. Before starting on this he painted a trial-picture of *Joseph and Mary Resting on the Road to Egypt* which he exhibited successfully at the Academy in 1807 and sold to Thomas

Hope. As work on *Dentatus* came to a close, Haydon received yet another commission, this time for a picture of *Macbeth* for Sir George Beaumont.

However, though he must have seemed to be the darling of Fortune, Haydon was not everybody's favorite. His contempt for the "lower" forms of painting was not calculated to endear him to the majority of R.A.'s who lived by portraiture. Nor were the members of the Academy pleased when Haydon led a group of students who made a presentation to Fuseli in 1807. Haydon was anything but the docile student sitting at the feet of his elders: he simply ignored advice that did not coincide with his own opinions. For example, he believed that anatomy, including dissection, was an essential part of the historical student's study, while the Academy held that a superficial knowledge of the subject was sufficient; Haydon continued to dissect. His innate determination was strengthened by an essay which he read in 1805, John Foster's "On Decision of Character." Foster maintained that "a resolute mind is omnipotent; difficulty is a stimulus and a triumph to a strong spirit."[3] Problems arose which would have given pause to any ordinary student but for Haydon they were merely opportunities to display his "decision of character."

When *Dentatus* was not given pride of place at the Exhibition of 1809, Haydon withdrew the painting and accused the Academy of trying to sabotage his career. The British Institution, which awarded *Dentatus* a premium in the following year, seemed to sanction Haydon's behavior and led him to hope for a power struggle between the Academy and the Institution for the leadership of British art in which the Institution would emerge successful. Soon, however, Haydon was feuding with one of the leading members of the Institution, Sir George Beaumont, who had commissioned *Macbeth*. Haydon had increased the dimensions of the work without consulting Beaumont; when Beaumont complained, Haydon behaved in a very highhanded fashion and went so far as to publicize his correspondence with Beaumont. He continued the painting "animated by the most determined resolution to produce a picture that Sir George could not refuse."[4] A great deal depended on this work. Haydon was extravagant in his use of models and materials and when, in 1810, his father ceased to support him, he began to borrow. To remain solvent, he simply had to win the Institution premium and sell the painting to Beaumont.

But to return to the appearance of *The Examiner* in January 1808. It was a Sunday paper, the work of the three Hunt brothers, John, Leigh, and Robert, and its objective was the radical reform of all aspects of British life. On a wide range of topics from royal morality and army discipline to current politics and letters, the paper spoke out with courage and vivacity. Generally speaking, John was the manager and Leigh Hunt the chief writer. Robert Hunt, who wrote the Fine Arts column, had been apprenticed to an engraver and had done some painting: perhaps his family hoped that art would bring him the financial security it had brought his uncle, Benjamin West, P.R.A., who had frequently helped the Hunt family in distress and who was invariably referred to as "the venerable President." The paper was quite a success, achieving a notoriety among the upper classes and a wide circulation throughout the country.

Fellow student David Wilkie introduced Haydon to Leigh Hunt late in 1807.[5] Although Hunt does not figure in Haydon's *Diary* until the summer of 1811, they had become increasingly friendly since their first meeting. Hunt jested at Haydon's anxiety when bringing *Dentatus* to the fateful Exhibition of 1809, and Haydon was Hunt's guest at Christmas dinner the following year.[6] The silence of the *Diary* is telling. Haydon was essentially a jingoistic Tory and had, from 1806 onwards, enjoyed the patronage of two aristocrats, Mulgrave and Beaumont; his chances with the upper classes would not have been enhanced by his connection with radicals. However, by 1811, he had alienated himself from "rank and fashion" and had little to lose and a good deal to gain from his association with the generous Hunts.

From the beginning there is evidence of Haydon's influence on the Fine Arts column of *The Examiner.* Of course it is difficult to prove this for the Hunts were far from ignorant of the arts and their views may have coincided with Haydon's rather than have come from him.[7] Nevertheless, the accumulation of similarities between the opinions of R. H. in *The Examiner* and those of Haydon in his *Diary* is, to say the least, striking. An early example concerns the efforts of Charles Bell to secure the Professorship of Anatomy at the Academy in 1808. Haydon had enormous respect for Bell and, together with Wilkie, canvassed support for him. Haydon was not very optimistic because Bell's opponent was Anthony Carlisle who did not advocate a deep study of anatomy for the students but who knew, in Haydon's words, "the effect good dinners have on half starved Academicians."[8] When Carlisle was chosen, *The Examiner,* which had supported Bell, claimed intrigue and jobbery and mentioned the dinners that Carlisle had lavished on the electors; later on, Carlisle's lectures were reported with a blatant partiality. We may assume that Wilkie was not the type to advocate such methods and Bell actually wrote to *The Examiner* to dissociate himself from the remarks about the dinners; we must conclude that the impulsively belligerent Haydon provided much of Robert Hunt's fire. Certainly Hunt never wrote anything which was not in line with Haydon's ideas, and an article "On the Benefits to the Arts from Government Encouragement" is almost a paraphrase of Haydon's frequently expressed opinion on this theme.[9]

This seemed an ideal arrangement: Haydon's opinions were aired while he himself was not seen to be personally involved. But the Elgin Marbles were a different matter and Haydon felt that a portion of his future fame would be owed to his heroic defense of the sculpture that Lord Elgin had brought from the Parthenon in the hope that the government would buy it for the nation. Of the artists who examined the Marbles in London, all were impressed but none nearly so much as Haydon who considered them the finest sculpture ever.[10] There was some opposition: the prominent connoisseur Richard Payne Knight did not rate them very highly, while some, notably Byron, denied Elgin's right to remove them from Athens. The hostility of Payne Knight is difficult to understand; perhaps he was envious and trying to defend his position as *arbiter elegantiarum* by abusing a rival collection. Haydon reports that in 1806 Knight told Elgin that his collection was not Greek but Roman, "of the time of Hadrian, when he restored the Parthenon," and that even if they were Greek, they were not the work of Phidias who, according to Knight, never worked in marble.[11] It was almost certainly Knight who wrote the Introduction to the first volume of *Specimens of Antient Sculpture,* produced by the Society of Dilettanti in 1809, in which the following occurred:

> Of Phidias's general style of composition, the friezes and metopes of the Temple of Minerva at Athens, published by Mr. Stuart and since brought to England, may afford us competent information; but as these are merely architectural sculptures executed from his designs and under his directions by workmen scarcely ranked among artists . . .[12]

Meanwhile, Byron, in *English Bards and Scotch Reviewers,* 1809, and in *The Curse of Minerva,* 1814, presented Lord Elgin as a rapacious barbarian committing sacrilege in an oppressed land.

Haydon's studies had led him to see the Marbles as superior to all other antique sculpture and he was not the one to keep his opinions to himself. On 22 September 1809 he had the full story of the Marbles from Elgin himself and noted it down in his *Diary.*[13] In *The Examiner* for 8 October 1809, following Robert Hunt's piece, there was a letter from *An English Student* that set out to refute derogatory remarks on Lord Elgin in a recent book, *Letters from an Irish Student in England to his father in Ireland.* The writer of the letter was Haydon and the pseudonym was one that he used again; the letter echoes Elgin's narrative and defends the acquisition of the Marbles. Haydon does not mention this contribution in his *Autobiography* where, with his usual sense of style, he implies that his first adventure into print was one that caused some stir in *The Examiner* late in 1811.

By the summer of 1811, Haydon was spending more and more time in the company of Leigh Hunt to whom he described the "principles" that he was evolving from his anatomical studies and his examination of the Elgin Marbles. There was one aspect of these "principles" that did not appeal to Hunt. Haydon followed Charles Bell in believing that there was a formal gradation from the lower animals to the finest sculpture; in this gradation the Negro physique was thought to contain more "brutal characteristics" than that of the European and the physiological difference, they argued, was in proportion to a difference in intellectual capacity. *The Examiner* supported the current agitation for the abolition of slavery and Leigh Hunt used the arrival of a ship with an all-black crew at Liverpool as a springboard for a condemnation of those who believed in the inferiority of the Negro. To Haydon this was an attack not on slavery but on his aesthetic theories; he felt obliged to reply.[14]

Signing himself *An English Student,* he wrote four letters to *The Examiner* which appeared on 1, 15, 22, 29 September 1811. The argument itself and the manner in which it was conducted are of little interest today. Haydon's application of art theory to the physiology of race almost succeeds in amusing: for example, in his second letter, he expounded at length on the Elgin Marbles. Another correspondent, *Niger,* was intrigued by the logic of it all; with total seriousness, Haydon urged him to read certain extracts from *The Works of James Barry,* a historical painter. By now Haydon is rampant and the nominal subject of the debate is forgotten. If art students read these extracts from Barry's *Works,* "we shall soon see high art blaze forth on such an 'adamantine' foundation, as will ever secure it against the 'stream of time.'" This is what is of interest: the sheer enjoyment Haydon found in such release and his inability to resist the temptation to indulge himself in irrelevant didacticism. This weakness proved costly. It was one thing for *An English Student* to defend Lord Elgin, as he did again in a letter on 1 December 1811; it was quite another to embroil himself with the big guns of British art as he did early in the following year in a three-part letter entitled **"To the Critic of Barry's Works in the Edinburgh Review, Aug. 1810."** This had lasting consequences and it is worthwhile examining its background.

There is a gap in Haydon's *Diary* between the end of the third folio in September 1811 and the beginning of the fourth in November 1811. The latter pages of the third folio contain nonjournal writings which the editor, W. B. Pope, took to be drafts of (*a*) marginalia that Haydon wrote on William Hamilton's *Memorandum on the Subject of the Earl of Elgin's Pursuits in Greece,* and of (*b*) the letter Haydon wrote to *The Examiner.* I have my doubts as to the idea of drafting marginalia; my own reading of the manuscript led me to believe that there is no simple division in the material. It is

confused and untidy, written in moods of angry frustration and with publication in mind. The only unity is in the constant desire to hit out. Why?

The account given many years later in the **Autobiography** is unsatisfactory. There Haydon wrote that when he heard Beaumont's decision not to buy *Macbeth* (28 January 1812) he decided to attack the Academy.[15] However, the first part of the letter was published in *The Examiner* on 26 January and, as we have seen, he was meditating such action toward the end of the previous year. Perhaps a clue is to be found on page 172 of the third folio where Haydon anticipates the objection that his anger will be attributed to his failure in the Academy elections. It was the custom of the Academy to elect associate members in November; Haydon had applied in 1810 but had not received a single vote—hardly surprising after his performance at the exhibition of *Dentatus* in 1809. Many years later Haydon claimed that he had also sought election in 1811, with similar results, but this is not recorded in the minutes of the Academy. Now Haydon's devotion to the truth could never be described as fanatical, but was he likely to fabricate such a story without some basis in fact? Somehow I do not think so. There is a possible resolution: if we assume that, chastened by his total refusal in 1810, Haydon, rather than risk another in 1811, tried to canvass some support. In his eyes, his failure to find any would have amounted to another rejection by the Academy. Why he should have hoped for better results in 1811 is hard to imagine; perhaps it was a gesture of desperation rather than hope. At any rate, it would go some way toward explaining the interruption in the *Diary.*[16]

By the end of 1811 then, Haydon was in a corner. Of his own genius and of the importance of historical painting he had no doubts; yet the Academicians, the majority of whom were portrait painters, seemed hostile to both. (Haydon identified his own cause with that of historical painting.) The British Institution seemed more enlightened and had honored him and *Dentatus*; yet one of its foremost members was Sir George Beaumont who had, in Haydon's opinion, behaved so unsympathetically during the painting of *Macbeth.* The treatment of the Elgin Marbles was symptomatic: the artists were cautious, others were denigratory, the government uninterested. Perhaps even more offensive in Haydon's mind was Benjamin West's claim to have understood the principles on which the Marbles were executed; this knowledge was Haydon's preserve. The drafts in the journal show him swiping in all these directions: he denies West's claims, abuses the Academy for neglecting historical painting, urges the Institution to continue its support for "high art" and, finally, launches into a diatribe against the main opponent of the Marbles, Richard Payne Knight.

I would guess that the wild belligerence sprang from two main causes: the negative response to his "feelers" for support within the Academy and his rising doubts regarding his painting of *Macbeth* and Beaumont. Unable to make peace on his own terms, he demonstrated his "decision of character."

> While animated by some magnanimous sentiments which he has heard or read, or while musing on some great example, a man may conceive the design, and partly sketch the plan, of a generous enterprise; and his imagination revels in the felicity, to others and himself, that would follow from its accomplishment. The splendid representation always centres in himself as the hero who is to realize it.[17]

Haydon recalled a review that Payne Knight had written of James Barry's *Works* for the *Edinburgh Review*; the piece had been unsigned but the identity of the writer had become widely known. The subject and the author suited Haydon's purposes: in spite of his shortcomings as a painter in Haydon's view, Barry was a martyr for the cause of historical painting in England, while Payne Knight was the leading sinner against the light of the Elgin Marbles.

The modern reader is inclined to see Haydon's letter as "merely a piece of gratuitous quarrelsomeness."[18] This is not quite fair: an examination of the original review shows that not only was Payne Knight out of sympathy with the personal behavior of Barry but also with the academic theory for which Barry stood. It must also be remembered that the Royal Academy paid lip service to the ideals for which Barry (and later Haydon) suffered; Payne Knight's review contradicted several important Academic tenets. For example, Barry had said that he would have nothing to do with any painters other than the Roman masters; Knight retorted that Rubens, Vandyke, and Rembrandt were among

> the greatest masters of the art, considered abstractedly as the art of painting,—that is the art of employing colours to imitate visible objects with the greatest possible degree of skill, judgement, taste and effect.[19]

Haydon had enormous respect for the technical skill of these artists but could not countenance Knight's elevation of technique above the intellectual aspect and he was merely repeating traditional doctrine when he wrote that Michelangelo and Raphael "excelled in the intellectual excellencies of the art, and therefore excelled in the highest."[20] Again, Barry's refusal to tolerate small works was typical of the blunt extremism of the man; Knight's contention that Michelangelo and Raphael would have been better occupied on easel-works was nevertheless nothing short of heretical. In short, Payne Knight's review provided a less ardent spirit with an opportunity to write a rejoinder that would have defended the academic position against such revisionism. For Haydon, however, the supremacy of large historical

paintings was more than an element of academic theory: it was the basis of his existence. The silence of the Academy was but another indication of its decadence. Payne Knight had advised young artists against putting too much trust in their own powers; this for the disciple of "decision of character" was typical of the mental mediocrity against which the student of genius was pitted.

The first part of Haydon's letter is relatively controlled and free of rancor but gradually the argument goes to Haydon's head and the second and third parts often verge on the hysterical. All is done in the name of historical painting for which Haydon speaks with messianic zeal:

> The grand style is the style which alone can give rank to 'this England in art' and which only wants rank in such matters to be the greatest nation the world has yet seen.[21]

He turns on the Academy and accuses it of hindering the elevated style it was founded to cultivate; against his own idea of the great artist creating the taste by which he is admired, Haydon places the Academic portrait.

> To see a head without bone, raw, husky, and flimsy, stuck on shoulders without a neck, enveloped in splashes of white for a cravat, and a hand dashed about in senseless ostentation, as much incapable of motion as if it were paralysed;—to see this, is to see a perfect example of Royal Academical execution.[22]

What began as a defense of the faith developed into a display of rant, abuse, and paranoia.

On 3 February David Wilkie, A.R.A., complained to Haydon that he had been exempted from the general censure of the Academicians in such a way as to suggest that he had been a party to the letter, and he noted that one might be forgiven for suspecting that Haydon was trying to ingratiate himself with the Institution by praising it as much as he disparaged the Academy. Haydon, in *The Examiner* for 16 February, absolved Wilkie from any responsibility; he did not take up Wilkie's other point, which was obviously on target. The same issue carried a review of *Macbeth*, then hanging at the Institution: Robert Hunt lavished praise on it, considering the picture an honor to the Institution and the country, an astonishing work from one "who styles himself a student." With an embarrassing lack of subtlety, he urged the Institution to be proud of having supported Haydon in the past.

It does not surprise one to learn that the campaign in *The Examiner* defeated itself. It cannot have helped Haydon when, as a result of an article in the issue for 22 March, John and Leigh Hunt were convicted of libeling the Regent and sentenced to two years in gaol. The Institution could not award a premium to Haydon without seeming to endorse his behavior with Beaumont and his attack on the Academy. (Haydon's pseudonym did not afford any protection.[23]) When the Institution decided against awarding any premiums, Leigh Hunt himself wrote of the travesty of justice but Haydon needed more than indignation.[24] He now found himself without support and with an expensive painting left on his hands. His reaction was to write another letter to *The Examiner*: at the end of the fourth folio of the *Diary* there is a draft to "Mr. Examiner" asking for "one column more" in order to expose the villainy of a man who stands "high in reputation." The man is easily recognized as Beaumont but the letter, if submitted, was not published; perhaps Haydon (or the Hunts) had seen the error of such ways.[25]

With limitless faith Haydon continued with *The Judgement of Solomon*. The Hunts, who began their sentence in February 1813, managed to keep Haydon and the paper going. I suspect that Haydon was the author of an open letter to the President of the Academy, published in October 1812 and signed *A Student*, that criticized the recent ruling that only students who had won medals should be allowed to make drawings of the Elgin Marbles. This letter must remain a doubtful ascription; the same is not true of another on 7 February 1813, signed *An English Student*, dealing with **"The Prospect of Efficient Patronage to the Arts from Princess Charlotte."** Haydon had read that the princess had bought a painting at the British Institution.

> The moment I read it my heart expanded, and I was soon lost in the beaming wanderings of my fancy; I saw the ceilings decorated, the palaces painted, and the churches filled; I saw the nobility and the people stand with awe before representations of the great actions of the great Heroes of the World; I saw her Royal Highness . . . giving scope to the genius of the country. . . .

He awoke to the very different reality but retained his optimism; eventually this optimism was to a great extent rewarded when he finished, exhibited, and sold *Solomon* in 1814. This triumph re-established his reputation and—of more pressing importance—his credit. He acknowledged the assistance of the Hunts by bringing the painting to the prisons where they were (separately) serving their sentences. Nor did he forget the Hunts when, to celebrate his success, he traveled to France with Wilkie. He wrote them full descriptions of his tour and the Hunts were quick to see the appeal of these letters. The result was three articles in *The Examiner* in August and September 1814 over the signature of *E[nglish]. S[tudent]*. Haydon was a zestful tourist and visited all the sights, especially those with Napoleonic associations. His keen awareness of self and scene, his dramatic "musing," and his own style of patriotism all combine to transport the reader with considerable panache.[26]

The success of *Solomon* had brought Haydon and Beaumont together again and Beaumont hoped that Haydon would refrain from public writing. Haydon assured him that since his 1812 polemic (which he stood by) he had not "written one line in attack."[27] Despite this assurance (given in July 1815) I am inclined to attribute to Haydon two letters that appeared in *The Examiner* in 1814 and that were critical of the Academy. The first must remain a very doubtful ascription: this was a letter on 2 October, signed *A Visitor,* condemning the lack of library facilities at the Academy. Three weeks later there was a letter that I would attribute to Haydon with something approaching confidence: it was signed *Echo* and concerned the **"Singular Advantage of Being an R.A."** *Echo* told how a French guard had confiscated the sketchbook of a Royal Academician in Paris; having mocked the subservience of the Academician, *Echo* adds that he would have smashed the guard's nose and, in a postscript—Haydon was addicted to postscripts— expresses his suspicions that the R.A.

> had not quite recovered from an overwhelming overflow of the bile, with which he was unfortunately attacked while looking at HAYDON's *Judgement of Solomon*, at the last Spring-gardens Exhibition.

The bumptious attitude to the French and the willingness to seize on the slightest opportunity to abuse the Academy are typical of Haydon. The pseudonym is not one he used elsewhere but he would hardly have praised his own work—another tendency in his pseudonymous writings—over a recognizable name.

Signing himself *E. S.,* Haydon contributed two letters to *The Examiner* in late 1815. In the first of these, **"On the probable formation of a School of Art at Plymouth,"** he advocated that his own methods of dissection and anatomical analysis be used. (He was a native of Plymouth and later, in January 1818, when he heard that an Academy was to be built there, he wrote to *The Examiner* to express his delight.) The second of the 1815 letters concerned the memorial to be built to celebrate the battle of Waterloo; it appeared on 31 December and was addressed **"To Members of Parliament, the Prince and the Nation."** Haydon asked that native artists be employed on the project and that the Academy "as a body" should not be consulted, on the grounds that "as a body" it was pernicious.

During these years of success, from 1814 to 1820, Haydon is the special concern of Robert Hunt's column: readers are kept informed of his progress with *Christ's Entry,* and there are times when it is clear that Hunt is writing with Haydon, literally or metaphorically, beside him. For example, in the *Diary* for 29 November 1815, Haydon described Canova examining the Elgin Marbles:

> "Come e sentito" he kept saying as he put his hand with the dash of experience on all the principle [sic] beauties of the body. . . .

In *The Examiner,* Robert Hunt praised Canova and "the way in which he dashed about his hand when pointing out the beauties of the Elgin Marbles." He, like Haydon, commented on Canova's willingness to accept the supremacy of the Marbles after a lifetime committed to the "old antique," and he also mentioned the edition of Milton that Haydon had presented to Canova.[28]

With Waterloo and the subsequent relaxation of political tension, the debate on the future of the Elgin Marbles arose again. It was a debate in which Haydon wished to play a prominent part for he considered himself to be *the* expert on the sculpture. Lord Elgin had nominated him to give evidence to the Select Committee which collected evidence from 29 February till 13 March 1816; one can understand his feelings when he heard that, "out of delicacy to Knight," he would not be heard.[29] After all, Haydon had been the most vociferous if not the most diplomatic champion of the Marbles. Not to be silenced at the crucial juncture of the campaign, he wrote an essay **"On the Judgement of Connoisseurs being preferred to that of Professional Men,"** which was published in *The Examiner* (and also in *The Champion,* a rather similar paper edited by his friend John Scott) on 17 March 1816; the essay was also issued as a pamphlet. It attacked the supposition that people versed in classical literature were automatically competent to appraise works of art, mentioned Payne Knight as a case in point, and presented Haydon's appreciation of the Marbles. He claimed that he wrote the essay in the fear that Payne Knight would influence the Committee against the Marbles and he maintained that it played a vital part in the decision of the Committee. It is difficult to agree. In the first place, Payne Knight did not have much influence; the evidence of the majority was overwhelmingly in favor of the Marbles while, in the *Report,* Payne Knight appears rather silly. Asked if he had examined the Marbles, he replied: "Yes, I have looked over them." Secondly, the essay came too late to have any real effect. Yet Haydon had done an enormous amount in the previous eight years and one sympathizes with his desire to be associated with the triumph. I suspect he was the author of an unsigned notice in *The Examiner* for 19 May 1816, which confidently anticipated government purchase of the Marbles despite the opposition of Payne Knight. Two other contributions on the subject of the Marbles may be attributed to him. The first, which appeared on 24 November 1816, signed *R.,* poked fun at the Academicians by describing them in an imaginary debate as to whether they should acquire casts of the Marbles; the other, an unsigned notice on 19 January 1817, expressed indignation that the Academy had allowed a restoration of one of the Elgin casts that showed an arrogant ignorance of the principles on which the Marbles were executed.

The years between 1814 and 1820, when he was working on *Christ's Entry into Jerusalem,* mark the zenith of Haydon's career. He was quite a celebrity, the painter of *Solomon,* the successful champion of the Elgin Marbles, the associate of some of the most notable literary figures of the day. He established a school in opposition to the Academy. Between 1816 and 1820 he put a great deal of his literary energy into the quarterly *Annals of the Fine Arts,* but he continued to write for *The Examiner.*

If, in Haydon's eyes, there was a pictorial equivalent of the Elgin Marbles, it was the collection of seven cartoons by Raphael, then at Hampton Court and now in the Victoria and Albert Museum. The Academy had copies of these works which were used more or less as set texts during the lectures. Haydon boasted that it was as a result of his efforts that the originals were included in the British Institution Exhibitions between 1816 and 1819. He prayed that, together with the Elgin Marbles, the Raphael Cartoons would inspire a great era in English art; at the same time he could not contain his glee at going one better than the Academy in providing *his* school with the originals to copy and study.[30] The reviews of the Cartoons which he wrote for *The Examiner* were reprinted in the *Annals.*

As a rule, Haydon opens with a brief history of the works and then sets out to provide a literal script for the *muta poesis.*

> I beg all Fathers and Mothers, all tender Lovers and gentle Mistresses, all sweet Girls and interesting young Gentlemen, to look forward, and with this paper in their hands, alternately read the paper and look at the Picture.[31]

Continuing in this intimate style, he spells out the story behind the work, quoting the texts on which the scene is based, glossing difficult points such as the details of the ritual involved in *The Sacrifice at Lystra.* The kernel of the review is an account of his own intense reaction which seeks to elicit a similar enthusiasm from the reader. Normally the critique contains a short discourse on some technical aspect—such as composition or invention—of which the Cartoon in question was thought to be a fine example.

Raphael was considered to be the master of "expression" in painting and Haydon tries to transcribe into language what the artist has done with line and color. For example, there is Elymas

> deprived of his sight; his eyes shut, his hands out grasping for some object to guide him; his foot cautiously creeping for fear of falling; his whole figure betraying an eager, timid apprehension, a miserable helplessness searching for support.

Here we see that Haydon's approach is more emotional than analytical and hinges on his ability to re-enact the event portrayed. His style is nowhere more apparent than in his reading of the healing of the lame beggar in *The Beautiful Gate*. Having indicated how Raphael presented the tentative joy of the cured man, Haydon recalls his own feelings on regaining his sight after a period of childhood blindness:

> Ye who have been blind, and remember when ye first saw light glimmer through the dreary darkness, and then feared to open your eyes again lest your rapturous anticipation prove delusive; ye who recall the slow, cautious, trembling, terror, with which you tried your powers of vision before you burst forth in fulness of gratitude to God; bear witness to the truth, the intense truth of nature, here simply told.

The tone is not always quite so solemn: equally typical of these writings is a slightly mawkish lyricism in the description of females. He attached a great deal of importance to the role of female figures and was inclined to believe that all formal beauty was based on the female form.[32] He marveled at the success of *Christ's Charge to Peter* in which no female was portrayed, and wrote of a girl in *The Beautiful Gate*:

> Her head is turned over her shoulder, her lustrous eyes are looking out, and her delicate breathing mouth is half open; she seems as if she had dropped from heaven on a May morning!

Although Haydon hoped that the Cartoons would effect a great improvement on the national taste, he became quite petulant when the Academy sought to borrow one. Signing himself *R.,* he complained in *The Examiner* for 1 December 1816 that the Academy students would abuse it, adding that the delegation which had gone from the Academy to Hampton Court had been more interested in fishing than in the Cartoons. *Student* rejected Haydon's accusations and had the better of a brief controversy. Haydon's peevishness is inexcusable but is understandable when one recalls that he was at this time convinced that it would be possible to end the supremacy of the Academy. The Academy succeeded in borrowing *Ananias* in late 1816; when, after it had been exhibited at the Institution in 1817, it was taken back to the Academy, Haydon wrote a letter of condemnation which was printed in *The Examiner* for 24 August 1817. On 16 November 1817 *The Examiner* reprinted from the *Annals* an account of how three of Haydon's pupils, who had followed the Cartoon to the Academy, had to cease drawing there because of constant interruption. Appended to the reprint is a rhetorical call from Haydon to all young artists, urging them not to travel abroad but to stay at home; nowhere else would they find the Elgin Marbles, the Raphael Cartoons, "such cherub children, such proportioned men, or such beautiful women." Despite interruptions, real or imaginary, Haydon and his pupils made life-size drawings from the Cartoons and exhibited them with considerable success in early 1819; Haydon advertised the success in a letter to *The Examiner,* signed *B. R. H.,* on 28 February 1819.

Haydon's was not the only pen used in the politics of painting. Perhaps the most notorious document was a *Catalogue Raisonee* (sic) of the 1816 Exhibition at the Institution, a piece of crude and malicious satire. This work was anonymous but many, including Haydon, were convinced that it came from the general direction of the Academy. *The Examiner* for 6 October 1816 reprinted from the *Annals* a piece entitled "Review of a Catalogue Raisonne of the Pictures exhibiting in Pall Mall." In his ***Autobiography,*** Haydon claimed this as his own and I am inclined to agree with him although the *Annals* would suggest that he was not the author. The review was unsigned in the *Annals* and contained a sketch of an Academician, Owen, "by a friend of our's, a clever fellow." The clever fellow is none other than Haydon and the sketch is one of five drawn in his ***Diary*** for 5 May 1815.[33] Despite this false lead, the style of the writing leads one to attribute it to Haydon. At any rate, he was confident that he would vanquish the Academy just as he had squashed the authors of the *Catalogue.*

> The *Catalogue Raisoneers* have had their day; the day of glory for History is coming, and they well know, as Historical feeling rises in the country, they must sink.[34]

He could never resist the temptation to swipe at the Academy: in *The Examiner* for 12 April 1818 we find him—over the signature *R.*—mocking the Academicians who were angry at being satirized in the *Annals.* He was nevertheless sensitive to criticism himself, especially by those who did not reveal their identities. With the indignation of wounded innocence he wrote two letters to *The Examiner,* on 7 and 14 March 1819, defending himself and the editor of the *Annals* from pseudonymous attack.

Haydon's contributions to *The Examiner* during these years of success were not confined to the Elgin Marbles, the Cartoons, and the *Annals.* I am confident that he it was who wrote in the issue for 13 April 1817 that the American Congress had voted historical paintings for the decoration of the Capitol and added that this was the kind of patronage badly needed in England. (There was no signature apart from four asterisks.) I would also attribute to him a letter which appeared in the subsequent number, signed *B.,* supporting a plan to erect a replica of the Parthenon on Primrose Hill. Again on the subject of state patronage, his essay (also produced as a pamphlet) on ***New Churches considered with respect to the opportunities they afford for the encouragement of Painting*** was printed on 1 March 1818, over his full name.

The one book review that he did for *The Examiner* is of particular interest for readers of the ***Diary*** who cannot but notice Haydon's strange admiration for Napoleon. On 27 April and 4 May 1817 there appeared two articles by him on the recently published *Manuscrit Venu de St. Hélène, d'une Manière Inconnue*. This purported to be Napoleon's autobiography but was in fact the work of Lullin de Chateauvieux. The point of Haydon's review was to judge the authenticity and he decided that it was a genuine autobiography: he argued that this self-portrait of a man of genius was so accurate that nobody—except Shakespeare—could have faked it. The implication of Haydon's argument is that he himself has this same quality of genius and is therefore fitted to vouch for the truth of the book.

Haydon and Leigh Hunt frequently clashed on the question of religion and by 1818 they had ceased to be friends. Haydon seems to have remained on good terms with John Hunt until 1823 and, as we have seen, continued to write for their paper which still took a special interest in him and his work. Despite certain reservations, *The Examiner* thought *Christ's Entry*—finally completed and exhibited in 1820—superior to *Solomon* and, in the following year, it lavished praise on *Christ's Agony in the Garden*—a feat of partial criticism for the work is utterly devoid of merit.

In May 1821 Haydon attended a sale at Christie's of works by Reynolds and described it in a letter in *The Examiner* for 3 June, commenting on Reynolds' style and expressing satisfaction at the keen bidding for paintings by an English artist. Money was very much on his mind at the time: *Christ's Entry* had not been sold and on 22 June 1821 he was placed under temporary arrest for debt. He pushed ahead with his painting of *Lazarus* but in an atmosphere of desperation that did not encourage him to write for the public press. However, in *The Examiner* for 9 December 1821, there is a note, signed *W.*, on a cartoon by Michelangelo. There is no circumstantial evidence to suggest Haydon as the author and the signature is not one he used elsewhere; yet the criticism of Michelangelo is similar to that often expressed by Haydon and the writer quotes, as Haydon frequently did, Fuseli's description of Michelangelo's females as "moulds of generation." On 15 December 1822 the paper carried a letter from Haydon that described a low relief by Michelangelo that Haydon had seen two days previously in the house of its owner, Sir George Beaumont. Haydon flatters Beaumont without compromising his own estimate of Michelangelo by remarking that it was the finest thing to come into the country since the Elgin Marbles and was of the artist's earlier and purer period, before he lapsed into "manner."

This was the last piece that Haydon wrote for the paper while it was owned by the Hunts. *The Examiner* hardly survived the departure of Leigh Hunt for Italy in 1821 and it passed out of their hands in 1825. Meanwhile it did not forget Haydon: it praised *Lazarus* highly in 1823 but praise could not prevent the financial disaster that Haydon had courted for so long. He was impris-

oned for debt in May 1823. *The Examiner* for 25 June referred to the petition that Brougham had presented to Parliament on Haydon's behalf but this imprisonment cut Haydon's last real tie with the paper; he was bitterly disappointed when John Hunt did not reply to his request for books.[35]

After 1825 *The Examiner* continued to be sympathetic but Haydon did not respond as he had done to the Hunts. In the issue for 27 January 1828 Haydon wrote in praise of his protégé, the sculptor John Graham Lough. In May 1830 the paper contrasted the talents of Haydon, again in prison, with the faults of which his enemies accused him. On 20 May there was a letter from *Your Constant Reader,* absolving Haydon from all charges. The writer is undoubtedly Haydon himself: the opening paragraph is his on grounds of style and content, there is a tone of personal distress in the letter, and, finally, Haydon pasted the cutting into his journal. (Before 1823, Haydon kept almost no record of his occasional writings, but after his imprisonment he began to keep cuttings in his journal, frequently identifying himself as the author of pseudonymous letters to the press. This is the chief means of tracing his contributions to periodicals during the remainder of his life.) He wrote two other letters to *The Examiner,* which were printed on 11 and 17 September 1836, the first concerning the price he had received for a painting, the second appealing for patronage for historical painting; but these cries of a desperate man bore little resemblance to the confident critiques, polemics, and essays in propaganda which he had written when *The Examiner* was almost a personal weapon in his various campaigns.

To return to John Hunt's letter which was quoted at the outset. An examination of Haydon's contributions to *The Examiner* tends to confirm an earlier suspicion: that Haydon and Hunt were being very careful in this exchange of letters. For example, it seems clear that Haydon influenced Robert Hunt in his writings on Anthony Carlisle, but Hunt's denial of Haydon's influence on Robert Hunt only went as far as "any modern picture or artist." Hunt seems on shakier ground when he agrees that Haydon never criticized "any modern picture or artist." Perhaps Haydon did not specifically denigrate any artist or picture but he did not conceal his low opinion of the Academicians (excepting Wilkie) and their style of painting. However, Hunt's defense would probably stand up in court. It is obvious that the terms of the correspondence mask the most important element: that Haydon was, during the greater part of the paper's life under the Hunts, on particularly close terms with the Hunts, that they showed a sympathy with and a willingness to publish his ideas and objectives, and that, as radical journalists, they welcomed his broadsides against the art establishment. What of the contributions that were disguised under unusual signatures? There is no evidence that the Hunts were or were not aware of such a practice but the precise caution of John Hunt's letter leaves one with the impression that he knew more than he wished to comment on.

CHECKLIST OF CONTRIBUTIONS

8 October 1809, p. 652f. Untitled letter, signed *An English Student,* in defense of Lord Elgin.

1, 15, 22, 29 September 1811, pp. 566ff., 596ff., pp. 611ff., p. 628f. Four letters to the editor, the first untitled, the others headed "Negro Faculties," signed *An English Student,* attempting to prove the Negro inferior to the European.

1 December 1811, p. 773f. Letter entitled "Grecian Marbles," signed *An English Student,* in defense of Lord Elgin.

26 January, 2, 9 February 1812, pp. 60ff., pp. 76ff., pp. 92ff. Three-part polemic, entitled "To the Critic on Barry's Works in the Edinburgh Review, Aug. 1810," introduced by a letter to the editor signed *An English Student.*

16 February 1812, p. 105. Letter to the editor, signed *An English Student,* absolving Wilkie from any part in writing of previous polemic.

*25 October 1812, p. 683. Open letter entitled "The Elgin Marbles. To Benjamin West, Esq. P.R.A. and H.P.H.M.," signed *A Student,* criticizing restriction of drawing from Elgin Marbles. [* Denotes doubtful attribution.]

7 February 1813, p. 90f. Letter to "Mr. Examiner," entitled "The Prospect of Efficient Patronage to the Arts from the Princess Charlotte," signed *An English Student.*

21, 28 August, 4 September 1814, pp. 530ff., p. 547f., pp. 562ff. Three articles, entitled "Extract of a Private Letter from Paris, dated June 6, 1814," "Excursions in the Neighbourhood of Paris," and "Paris and Excursions in its Neighbourhood," signed *E. S.*

*2 October 1814, p. 632f. Open letter "To the Members of the Royal Academy," signed *A Visitor,* criticizing poor library facilities at Academy. [* Denotes doubtful attribution.]

23 October 1814, p. 684f. Letter to "Mr. Examiner," entitled "Singular Advantage of Being an R.A.," signed *Echo,* relating anecdote of an R.A. in Paris.

26 November 1815, p. 762f. Notice entitled "On the Probable Formation of a School of Art at Plymouth," signed *E. S.,* stressing the importance of the study of anatomy.

31 December 1815, pp. 843ff. Open letter "To Members of Parliament, the Prince, and the Nation," signed *E. S.,* urging patronage of native artists.

Notes

Author's note: When a quotation from Haydon's *Examiner* work is not footnoted, necessary publication information will be found in the checklist at the end of this article; the checklist is in chronological order and publication date is followed by pagination, as in *8 October 1809,* p. 625f.

1. *Benjamin Robert Haydon: Correspondence and Table-Talk,* ed. F. W. Haydon, 2 vols. (London: Chatto and Windus, 1876), I, 357. Hereafter cited as F. W. Haydon.

2. F. W. Haydon, I, 358.

3. John Foster, *Essays in a Series of Letters to a Friend,* 2nd ed., 2 vols. (London: printed for Longman, Hurst, Rees, and Orme, 1806), I, 219.

4. *Autobiography of Benjamin Robert Haydon,* ed. Edmund Blunden (London: Oxford University Press, 1927), p. 141. Hereafter cited as *Autobiography.*

5. See *Autobiography,* p. 159f. On 27 January 1828, Haydon wrote to Walter Scott that he had been introduced to the Hunts by Wilkie; see National Library of Scotland MS.3906, fol. 35.

6. Unpublished letter owned by W. B. Pope, editor of the *Diary.* I am grateful to Prof. Pope for permission to study and quote from his large collection of MSS.

7. See Ian Jack, *Keats and the Mirror of Art* (Oxford: Clarendon Press, 1967), pp. 1-22.

8. *The Diary of Benjamin Robert Haydon,* ed. W. B. Pope, 5 vols. (Cambridge, Mass.: Harvard University Press, 1960-63), I, 22. Hereafter cited as *Diary.*

9. *The Examiner,* 2 October 1808, p. 638.

10. Their views are to be found in the *Report of the Select Committee of the House of Commons on the Earl of Elgin's Collection of Sculptured Marbles* (London, 1816).

11. *Autobiography,* p. 276.

12. *Specimens,* p. xxix.

13. *Diary,* I, 85-89.

14. Charles Bell, *The Anatomy and Philosophy of Expression as connected with the Fine Arts* (London, 1806), *passim.*

15. *Autobiography,* p. 164.

16. See Eric George, *The Life and Death of Benjamin Robert Haydon,* 2nd ed. with additions by Dorothy George (Oxford: Clarendon Press, 1967), p. 384. George is wrong when he accuses Haydon of neglecting to state in his *Autobiography* that Beaumont eventually bought the *Macbeth* (p. 42); Haydon does mention this on p. 325.

17. Foster, I, 130.

18. George, p. 45.

19. *The Edinburgh Review,* 32 (1810), 293.

20. *The Examiner,* 26 January 1812.

21. *The Examiner,* 2 February 1812.

22. *The Examiner,* 9 February 1812.

23. See *Autobiography,* p. 166, and also p. 6018 of the full transcript of the *Farington Diary* in the British Museum.

24. *The Examiner,* 21 June 1812.

25. See *Diary,* I, 244.

26. The tour is also described at length in the *Autobiography* and *Diary.* For the letters to the Hunts, see F. W. Haydon, pp. 270-282.

27. F. W. Haydon, p. 289.

28. Compare *Diary,* I, 485, and *The Examiner* (1815), p. 793.

29. *Autobiography,* p. 309.

30. See *Diary,* I, 4, and *Autobiography,* p. 341.

31. *The Examiner,* 1 June 1817.

32. B. R. Haydon, *Lectures on Painting and Design,* 2 vols. (London: Longman, Brown, Green, and Longmans, 1844-46), II, 283.

33. See *Diary,* I, 433.

34. *The Examiner,* 1 June 1817.

35. *Diary,* II, 423.

Roger J. Porter (essay date 1993)

SOURCE: Porter, Roger J. "'In *me* the solitary sublimity': Posturing and the Collapse of Romantic Will in Benjamin Robert Haydon." In *The Culture of Autobiography: Constructions of Self-Representation,* edited by Robert Folkenflik, pp. 168-87. Stanford, Calif.: Stanford University Press, 1993.

[*In the following essay, Porter attempts to pinpoint the reason why Haydon felt the intense need to chronicle his life in his autobiography and in his journals.*]

On June 22, 1846, moments before he committed a kind of double suicide by shooting himself and slashing his throat, Benjamin Robert Haydon, historical painter, would-be savior of British art, and friend to both generations of romantic writers, wrote the final words in the diary he had kept for 38 of his 60 years: "'Stretch me no longer on this tough World'—Lear."[1] With a symmetrical gesture he could hardly have been conscious of making, Haydon was closing a parenthesis of allusion around his life. In 1808, at the beginning of what he envisioned—no less than did his companion Keats—as a grand and illustrious calling, Haydon noted in the first entry of his journal that he stood upon the cliffs of Dover where "Lear defied the storm" (1:3) and when a storm actually broke over the coast Haydon fancied himself as the great white-haired king blasted by nature and fiendish daughters; he was moved to reread the play, and thus began a series of identifications with Lear that were to linger through thousands of pages of journal and hundreds of autobiography. At Dover Haydon envisioned a colossal statue of Britannia looming over the sea and facing France, as if in challenge to that country's art. We can take that defiance and heroic posturing at the start of his career, and its self-dramatizing end, as coordinates in his life and the signs and motives for his writing, which in both its magnitude and its obsessive self-aggrandizements became the rival of, if not the substitute for, his painting. With the exception of Van Gogh, there may be no other visual artist whose need to write—out of self-justification and compensation—was as great as Haydon's, and who created as extended a literary self-portrait as an alternate life to the one that brought him such grief.[2]

Virginia Woolf said of Haydon, "we catch ourselves thinking, as some felicity of phrase flashes out or some pose or arrangement makes its effect, that his genius is a writer's. He should have held a pen."[3] There is an amplitude to his journals that corresponds to the grandiose scale of his historical paintings, their sheer size and the heroism of their subjects, those he actually painted and those he only desired to paint: Achilles, Christ, Samson, Adam, Solomon, Antigone, Orpheus, Lear, Andromache, Macbeth, Caesar, Hercules. His writing similarly refuses to be narrowly focused; a partial list of topics might include meditations on the Bible; literary criticism of Homer, Dante, and Milton; discussions of human and animal anatomy; treatises on the Elgin marbles; character analyses of Wordsworth, Keats, and Napoleon; technical discussions of oil painting; attacks on debtors' laws (Haydon was imprisoned three times for debt); stories of betrayal by those whose patronage he had expected; gossip about other artists, M.P.'s, and critics; detailed descriptions of his progress on a given painting; critiques of English and continental politics; meditations on fleeting fame; endless self-analysis; attacks on the art establishment and its institutions; and long prayers to carry a painting to completion. But

Haydon's *Diary* and his *Autobiography,* despite their sprawl and catch-all nature, have what we might call an autobiographical plot; I mean this not merely in the sense of a theme or cluster of related themes that we can trace through the life, whether they were composed with hindsight by the autobiographer or with relative spontaneity in the dailiness of the diary. I mean rather "plot" in the sense of its author's motive for writing, as De Quincey in *Confessions of an English Opium-Eater* urges us to understand a motif as a motive "in the sense attached by artists and connoisseurs to the technical word *motivo,* applied to pictures."[4] The themes reveal Haydon's motive for writing, and indeed he makes the impelling need to write the dominant theme of autobiography. Writing stands beside painting, if it does not virtually displace it, in Haydon's own order of importance.

Haydon was born at Plymouth on January 26, 1786. He began serious sketching at 6, and although an inflammation of his eyes permanently and early dimmed his sight he pursued his profession as if possessed. From an early age he assiduously read biographies of ambitious men and prophesied his own fame, drawing up a list of painterly subjects that would bring about this result. He was the first English artist to see the importance of the Elgin Marbles, and they greatly influenced him all his life. He soon entered into embattled relations with the Royal Academy, which he had attended as a boy, especially chagrined at not being elected to membership. His continuously disputatious life led to numerous fights with patrons over financial matters, alienated friendships, and a belief that the entire art establishment was bent in opposition to him. His life was a constant oscillation between an obsessive devotion to the cause of British historical painting and a history of debt. In between his stays in debtors' prison, he set up a school to rival the Academy, fought rancorous battles with everyone, and continued to rail against portrait painting as insufficiently heroic. He finally received substantial requests for work, but five of his children died, and the loss of commissions to decorate the Houses of Parliament rendered him particularly bitter. When he committed suicide, the coroner's report included a verdict of insanity.

At 22 Haydon started the journal that was to last throughout his life, and he made almost daily entries in 24 volumes. When he was 53 he began writing his *Autobiography,* and labored several years on the work, carrying his life only to 1820, 26 years before his death at 60. It is likely that writing about the succeeding years would have caused too much pain; to describe and analyze the difference between his early glory and the later neglect, or at least what he had come to perceive as a lifetime of failed promise and constant oppression from an unappreciative public and a system of reluctant patronage, would doubtless have frayed an already delicate psyche. It was difficult enough for Haydon to record on a daily basis his defeats and embattled status; to place the events in a structure of impending disaster would have been too anguishing. But the large questions remain: why did he write at all, and why was he so committed to some form of autobiography? What function did it serve, and what is its relation to his art?

Walter Jackson Bate, in his biography of Keats, has described Haydon's "vivid, simple-hearted energy" and his "endless, booming confidence."[5] These traits do emerge from Haydon's writing, especially in his heroic claims to outdo the greats of the past. One of the dominant voices is that of the young man staking his place in history:

> People say to me: "You can't be expected in your second picture to paint like Titian and draw like Michel Angelo"; but I will try; and if I take liberties with nature and make her bend to my purposes, what then? "Oh yes, but you ought not to do what Michel Angelo alone might try." Yes, but I will venture—I will dare anything to accomplish my purpose. If it is only impudent presumption without ability I shall find my level in the opinion of the world; but if it be the just confidence of genius I shall soon find my reward.[6]

Even his endless prayers to God for blessings have the self-assured tone of a man who, if he cannot cajole the deity to shower talent upon him, at least is on intimate and easy terms with that authority. Much of the autobiographical writing is a trying out of such attitudes, and even towards the end Haydon persists in his confident address to the world: "My position still is solitary and glorious. In *me* the solitary sublimity of High Art is not gone" (5:407).

The *Autobiography* and the *Diary* are filled with assertions of his own greatness and immortality, the devotion to a high calling almost as if it were a divine mission. When the serious eye disease he suffered as an adolescent left him temporarily blind, Haydon defiantly proclaimed he would be the first great sightless painter. Later he described the cure as if it were the work of destiny, and his own spirit as if it were sanctified: "It would have been quite natural for an ordinary mind to think blindness a sufficient obstacle to the practice of an art, the essence of which seems to consist in perfect sight, but 'when the divinity doth stir within us,' the most ordinary mind is ordinary no longer" (*Autobiography,* p. 15). Much of the *Autobiography* takes the form of a *Bildungsroman,* with Haydon the hero who overcomes the obstacles of disease, official resistance to his youthful bravado, the Academy's timidity toward historical painting, and its insistence that artists conform to the vogue of portraiture that Haydon detests. There is a description of a ritual moment of stocktaking as he begins his first painting, an allusion to the close of *Paradise Lost* as the world of promise opens before him, a prophecy that he will bring honor to England with his art, and a characteristic belief that difficulties are stimulants that discourage only the indolent. Again and again we hear of his monumental labors, the anticipation of glory, greatness and fame, and his posturing in the style of Julien Sorel.

> I was so elevated at . . . the visit of crowds of beauties putting up their pretty glasses and lisping admiration of my efforts, that I rose into the heaven of heavens, and believed my fortune made. I walked about my room, looked into the glass, anticipated what the foreign ambassadors would say, studied my French for a good accent, believed that all the sovereigns of Europe would hail an English youth with delight who could paint a heroic picture.
>
> (*Autobiography,* p. 104)

Every encounter is a test, every creative act a competition with past greatness, and Haydon uses the *Autobiography* to convince himself that he is correct in his defiance, or if he misjudges things, that he is nonetheless heroic in his convictions. There is an ebullience and daring in his self-congratulation: "I had proved the power of inherent talent, and I . . . had shown one characteristic of my dear country—bottom. I had been tried and not found wanting. I held out when feeble, and faint, and blind, and now I reaped the reward" (*Autobiography,* p. 199).

When Haydon wrote this passage, describing the reception of his work "The Judgement of Solomon," it was 1844 and the painting was gathering dust in a warehouse. Haydon sees its ignominy as a metaphor for his own decline in popular and official esteem, but prophesies "shame on those who have the power without the taste to avert such a fall; who let a work which was hailed as a national victory rot into decay and dirt and oblivion! But it will rise again; it will shine forth hereafter, and reanimate the energy of a new generation" (*Autobiography,* p. 236). This challenge corresponds to Haydon's motives for autobiography: vindication in the Rousseauean mode; and a nostalgic reliving of past greatness from a perspective in which, as he moves towards the close of the autobiography, his powers and fame are waning. Autobiography sanctions Haydon's struggles not by merely recording them but by elevating them to a heroic status in spite of, or rather because of, the difficulties they brought upon himself. Haydon deeply overestimated the greatness and originality of his own work, and this misjudgment makes his condemnation of his critics suspect, unlike the way Van Gogh's self-justification gains our credence. Nevertheless, despite the fact that, as Haydon's biographer has argued, the "myth of ill-usage was one he cultivated assiduously throughout his life,"[7] the autobiography reveals how Haydon refused to "bear affliction and disappointment" and often acted in a self-destructive way against all his better judgment. He claims his work can

serve as a guide to the young, who will exercise more caution and avoid the fatal consequences arising from reckless behavior, but Haydon's tone suggests he also relishes those actions, and relived them as much for his own morbid pleasure as to convince the world of his integrity.

As he writes the *Autobiography* his own life is gradually crumbling about him—several children have died, he has spent months in debtors' prison, he fears his creative juices may be drying up, his work has been attacked in the press, and even former supporters have deserted him. To compose autobiography is to risk further pain, perhaps even to cultivate this pain as a sign of stoical resignation and ultimately of heroic courage. The most common psychological move that Haydon makes throughout both the *Autobiography* and the *Diary* is to embrace struggle and difficulty as a sign of superiority. He encounters "ceaseless opposition" from the first, and there is a kind of energizing joy in confrontation with his enemies, a power that only contentiousness confers. Indeed controversy and conflict are the very animators of his writing. In an argument with Leigh Hunt, Haydon determines to get the better in print; Hunt is a dangerous opponent because he is editor of the *Examiner,* in whose pages they will do battle. In the *Autobiography* Haydon's punning metaphor draws the fight with Hunt into Haydon's own domain: "Though this is not the first time Leigh Hunt is mentioned it is the first opportunity I have had of bringing him fairly on the canvas. . . . This controversy consolidated my power of verbal expression and did me great good. . . . I resolved to show I could use the pen against the very man who might be supposed to be my literary instructor" (*Autobiography,* pp. 142, 144). Failure is a great stimulus for Haydon, a kind of tempering mechanism to test his invincibility. There is a determination not to be defeated in any competition. To complete a painting under trying circumstances is analogous to composing autobiography itself: ruthless honesty through the analysis of emotional complexity or foolish action testifies to a willingness to face difficult home truths and to avoid easy evasions. Too luxurious a climate would encourage indolence; too uncomplicated a romance would undermine the value of the love; too charmed a life would dull its vigor. "Some faculties only act in situations which appall and deaden others. Mine get clearer in proportion to the danger that stimulates them. I get vigour from despair, clearness of perception from confusion, and elasticity of spirit from despotic usage . . . want and necessity, which destroy others, have been perhaps the secret inspirer of my exertions" (2: 397-98).

How does conflict produce this feeling of well-being? In Haydon's case it creates the illusion that he has, in the very act of facing difficulty, justified his life and reached down into deeper resources of being. It is true that Haydon avoids excessive difficulty, arguing, for example, that his painting keeps him from madness and pain, and dulls his sensitivity to really disastrous experience; he even inserts into his journal a bit of doggerel claiming a purgative function for painting, writing, and love. The last line anticipates inadvertently the twin weapons of his suicide, as if he were invoking them as a talisman to ward off what later happens.

> Oh hail, my three blessings of Life,
> My pencil, my Book, and my Wife,
> Never mind the alloy,
> While these I enjoy,
> I defy both the bullet & knife.

> (4: 321)

Yet he constantly writes about difficulty as a catalyst for creativity, and links this strategy with the trope of heroic identification. Napoleon and Nelson are only two of many figures Haydon views as different from the run of ordinary men (as presumably Haydon himself is) exactly because to men of genius insurmountable difficulties are stimulants to action.

> Nelson is an illustrious example of what persevering, undivided attention to one Art will do; of how far a restless habit of enterprise will carry a man; to what a length never resting in indolent enjoyment after exertion will go. He began the war unknown . . . and concluded it famous throughout the World. . . . The same eagerness, the same enthusiasm, the same powers, the same restlessness, the same determination to go on while in existence, in any art, will carry a man the same length, because such conduct begets a confidence in others, as well as yourself.

> (1: 284)

Throughout his work Haydon wavers between the egotistical sublime of heroic self-assertion and the negative capability of self-effacement or identification with other men, primarily Napoleon, Wellington, and Michelangelo. It would seem that the latter impulse is no less self-projecting, since Haydon takes on the identities of triumphant figures. Nevertheless, I would suggest this strategy is an ironic form of self-denigration, in that the identification implicitly asserts the failure of originality and the need to subsume other selves. Unlike such autobiographical writers as the Keats of the *Letters,* writers who playfully try out a series of roles, inventing spiderlike from within themselves, Haydon often defines himself by taking on the personae of historical or artistic figures. Haydon's autobiographical writing meets the problem of unavailable originality by allowing him to assert a range of identifications, as though mimicry could substitute for genius, if not validate it.

Bate has elsewhere described the burden such demands for originality placed on writers and painters by the end of the eighteenth century:

> The eighteenth-century "Enlightenment" had created, and had foisted upon itself and its immediate child . . . an ideal of "originality": sanctioned both officially (theoretically, intellectually) and, *in potentia,* popularly. As a result the vulnerability of the [artist], already great enough, was accentuated by having his uneasiness now given a "local habitation and a name." For the first time in history, the ideal of "originality"— aside from the personal pressures the artist might feel to achieve it anyway—was now becoming defined as necessary, indeed taken for granted.[8]

That pressure on Haydon comes not from external sources but from within himself. Again and again he declares he will be the salvation of British art by raising it to a level formerly attained only in ancient Greece and Renaissance Italy. He aspires to the achievements of Raphael and Michelangelo (Haydon literally dreams that the latter comes to him; in a Wordsworthian echo he muses: "I certainly think something grand in my destiny is coming on, for all the spirits of the illustrious dead are hovering about me," 3: 510), and he will not bow to any contemporary or obey any obsolete rule if it will inhibit the value of his work. "Genius is sent into the world not to obey laws but to give them" (*Autobiography,* p. 95). A decade later, in 1815, he expresses the feeling of power and buoyant self-assertion in an entry suggesting not merely confidence but something like a self-apotheosis:

> Never have I had such irresistible, perpetual and continued urgings of future greatness. I have been like a man with air balloons under his arm pits and ether in his soul. While I was painting, or walking, or thinking, these beaming flashes of energy followed and impressed me! . . . Grant that they may be the fiery anticipations of a great Soul born to realize them. They came over me, & shot across me and shook me.

> (1: 430)

And in a letter to Keats, Haydon sounds like both Prospero and a Hotspur of the creative spirit, the elements of water and earth substituting for the fire and air of the previous passage: "I have no doubt you will be remunerated by my ultimate triumph. . . . By Heaven I'll plunge into the bottom of the sea, where plummets have now never sounded, & never will be able to sound, with such impetus that the antipodes shall see my head drive through on their side of the Earth to their dismay and terror."[9] What disturbs about the autobiographical writing, however, is Haydon's continual need to identify himself with other beings or with forces of nature. To be sure, it is hard not to admire the Tamburlaine-like desire to seize upon elements outside the self and to absorb and incorporate them as a way of vitalizing his longed-for power. And yet, on another view of the case, each identification undermines the very claims Haydon makes for originality and implies the need to compensate for disappointment or uncertainty with an endless series of self-dramatizations. As part of the autobiographical motive this process answers the twin needs to be original and to be like others, especially like persecuted men. The irony is that while Haydon desired to join himself to greatness, whether in the role of Wellington, Michelangelo, Achilles, or Christ, he never could make his influence felt. When the news of Haydon's death reached Hunt he remarked, "I looked upon [Haydon] as one who turned disappointment itself into a kind of self-glory,—but see how we may be mistaken" (5: 561).

Throughout the *Diary* and the *Autobiography* Haydon's view of himself veers between those of a misunderstood, martyred man (the oppressors include patrons, critics, rival painters, the general public, and the Royal Academy), and of a successful, dominating will. Haydon's identification with satanic energy ("Give me the sublimity of chaos, give me the terror of Hell, give 'Hail, horrors, hail . . . and thou profoundest hell receive thy new possessor,'" 1: 309) appears as a Romantic strategy to achieve power while it recoils against orthodox Christian beliefs. The impulse here is to equate greatness with suffering wherever it can be found, but the seminal figure behind both the *Autobiography* and the *Diary* is not Satan but Rousseau.

Often Haydon asserts the absolute sincerity of his efforts as autobiographer; he will not be outranked on this score: "There I will defy any man, let him be Raffaele himself, to beat me" (*Autobiography,* p. 90). He is talking not about painting but about honesty and confessional integrity. The "Author's Introduction" to the *Autobiography* bears a striking resemblance to the famous opening paragraphs of Rousseau's *Confessions*; Haydon claims that his writing originates from a sense of unjust persecution, and that although he has made occasional mistakes, and has even been sinful, his sincerity, decent intentions, and perseverance will serve to exonerate him in the eyes of his readers. But sincerity is not the real issue. Haydon's deeper instinct is for a Rousseau-like cultivation of suffering, which he hopes will testify to a misunderstood genius; indeed he is self-congratulatory about his willingness to acknowledge anguish: "I am one of those beings born to bring about a great object through the medium of suffering. . . . Adversity to me, individually, is nothing" (3: 334). Haydon's aspiration to be raised above the world gradually gives way to an awareness of futility and a corresponding nurturing of defeat, almost as if it were an alternate proof of greatness.

In a crucial diary entry Haydon distinguishes between sublimity and the pathetic. Sublimity is unconnected with the earth, freed from mundane emotions; it speaks to the imagination and genius, unavailable to the mass of mankind; pathos speaks to the heart and is common. The sublime corresponds to what he calls "the grand conception," ambition and glory. Pathos contains the realization of heart-aching failure, the impossibility of achievement, and the recognition that he might be "born the sport and amusement of Fortune" (2: 362).

Both aspects of personality—heroic genius and ill-usage—receive their due in the writing; it is difficult to say which myth gives Haydon more pleasure in the recording. There is a curious luxuriating in the numerous long passages documenting and expanding upon the instances of persecution and official neglect, almost as if oppression itself were a valid sign of genius. Each mode produces its characteristic rhetoric of hyperbole, whether in the high Romantic sublime or in the Rousseauean complaint.

In 1824, after losing commissions, being rejected for membership in the Academy, getting arrested for debt with no help from patrons, and failing to persuade influential M.P.'s to appropriate government funds for the support of painting, Haydon laments: "Of what use is my Genius—to myself or to others? . . . All this was bearable when I was unknown because the hope of fame animated me to exertions in order to dissipate my wants; but now, what have I to hope? My youth is gone! every day and year will render me more incapable of bearing trouble; at an age when I ought to have been in ease, I am ruined!" (2: 474). It would be absurd to claim that Haydon simply takes pleasure in his losses or enjoys the sensation of defeat; nevertheless the self-dramatizing easily adheres to whatever the situation, and "the glories of a great scheme" are no more ecstatically described than "the troubles, the pangs, the broken afflictions, the oppressions, the wants, the diseases of life" (*Autobiography,* p. 165). Haydon stands simultaneously inside and outside his life, not only a public man concerned with the impact of art on the social body, or a private man tracing each particular nervous agitation in the self, but one who dramatizes a self for the public even as he speaks to himself within the privacy of his journals.

Haydon seems drawn to the most dramatic gyrations of fortune, the sinusoidal curve of his life providing evidence of both sensitivity and recovery. Even here the exemplary figure is Napoleon, advancing on Moscow, retreating, escaping from Elba, defeated once again. The pleasure of triumph, says Haydon, is that we no longer look up (we are there) but down (Haydon longs to excite envy); and yet looking down already anticipates an inevitable decline to the grave. Haydon was of two minds regarding Napoleon: he revered his titanic power and aloofness from ordinary men, yet was comforted by Napoleon's ordinariness and vulnerability. This fascination with the swings of fortune appears throughout Haydon's writings: he receives a commendatory sonnet from Wordsworth that cheers him; immediately after he relapses into melancholy. He walks the streets in grief, and within moments enters a drawing room "like a comic hero in a farce." Following an arrest for debt he goes from the bailiff's house into a room full of beautiful women and elegant pictures. "What a destiny is mine! One year in the Bench, the companion of Demireps & Debtors—sleeping in wretchedness & dirt, on a flock bed, low and filthy, with black worms crawling over my hands, another, reposing on down & velvet, in a splendid apartment, in a splendid House, the guest of Rank & fashion & beauty!" (3: 167).

The inconsistencies of his own personality intrigue "that mysterious, incomprehensible, singular bit of blood, bottom, bone, & genius, B. R. Haydon" (2: 273). The same perplexity of human character not surprisingly attracts him to Shakespeare's mixed style and juxtaposition of character types (this of course is a common Romantic attitude). The **Diary** is filled with instances of incongruity, such as the laughter in his infant son's sleep at the moment Haydon's wife is lying in agony in the next room. Haydon appears drawn to rather than dismayed by these turns and violent contrasts; his autobiographical writing stands in opposition to the classical certitude and careful planning of a life such as Gibbon's, who perceives his existence as a work of art given compositional grace and symmetrical order corresponding to schemata ordained by prudence. For Haydon there are no models to follow with confidence, for even the ostensible exemplars are patterns of inconsistency.

Haydon holds a mirror to himself, but each event witnessed, every book read, seems to reflect a different self. In 1844 he had painted some 25 portraits of Napoleon, and while there was an economic motive for this obsession, it also reflects his penchant for finding infinite variations in an emulated figure, and thus a desire to be many different persons—an indirect version of Rembrandt's life-long series of self-portraits. Haydon's journals fight against the tendency of autobiography to freeze the self into a fixed image; they express not merely the implicit fragmentation we expect from journal writing, but a subtle pleasure in the act of creating multiple perspectives.

> This book is a picture of human life, now full of arguments for religion, now advocating virtue, then drawn from chaste piety, & then melting from a bed of pleasure, idle & active, dissipated & temperate, voluptuous & holy! burning to be a martyr when I read the Gospel! ready to blaze in a battalion when I read Homer! weeping at Rimini and at Othello. Laughing & without sixpence, in boisterous spirits when I ought to be sad & melancholy when I have every reason to be happy!
>
> (2: 273)

The irony of this dissipation of self is that once again the powerful impulse toward ego does not hold. Whether we call him a manic-depressive or a doubt-

ridden genius, there is continual self-qualification that undermines the foundations of his own confidence and makes the autobiographical writing less Cellini-like than might otherwise be the case.

Perhaps the roots of this fragmentation are to be found in Haydon's dwelling on fleeting fame, passing time and loss. In a world that presents to him so many images of frustrated ambition, unexpected suffering and diminished power, it is not surprising that the self appears unstable. Frequently at the end of a calendar year Haydon identifies the year's passing with death in terms imaged as either an eternal waterfall churning into a gulf below or an irresistible tide sweeping everything away in its wake. We are vulnerable children, and neither our hopes, raptures, calculations nor our art can prevent us from sinking into sorrow. In other passages time is a reptile devouring men, who are born to putrefaction, or a Conqueror who exceeds Napoleon for power. At such moments Haydon's voice is that of an evangelical preacher, or of Leonardo da Vinci in the *Notebooks,* foreseeing universal ruin in the deluge, the swirling and anarchic water of our helpless condition. This is a sublime, visionary moment: "The sun shines, winds blow, ships are wrecked, men are drowned, children are born, women are in labour, youths in love, in one ceaseless round! . . . Matter & events seem to be in one eternal reaction & destruction" (2: 347). Haydon struggles to affirm existence, for he cannot bear this ceaseless round: despondency takes over, and he sees himself as a desperate chaser of an unattainable happiness that diminishes as he approaches it, and an overrater of joy that lies just ahead but is darkened by folly and wickedness. What appears sweet and beautiful on the outside is revealed as "bitter & corky & putrid & full of ashes."

Like an Old Testament prophet, Haydon dramatizes his vulnerability and isolation, and then turns and acts out an imaginary retribution, as if retaliating against all the authorities who have humiliated him. His fragile sense of self, controlled by a susceptibility to natural process and social attack, finds a reprieve in fantasy. In one of the most melodramatic passages, he imagines himself a self-exiled Romantic wanderer.

> If I were alone again I would leave my Country for ever—buried in Italy or Greece, I would pass my days in the lowest avocations, could I get by it peace! ay, peace! I would lie out in the Acropolis and hail the ruins about me, as congenial to my own destroyed hopes. I would wander in the Alps, sleep in ravines, and be lulled by the invisible roar of foaming floods, and be waked by echoing screech of soaring eagles! I would willingly have footed, scrambled over rugged barks, fallen pines, and climb sharp cutting flinty rocks, & plunge with the flood, & rise from its depths, & lie panting & breathless on its banks, till Nature recovered sensation, & my desolation returned to me! Or I would . . . vent my rage on the trees, the stones, the birds,

the animals, & glory with ecstatic rapture, to meet a *solitary human* being *without defence* on whom I might vent my hatred of human nature! and gratify my tiger feelings by tearing out his heart & drinking his blood! and then strip my body, my half clothed & ragged body, & paint it with grinning faces in the blood yet warm and unclotted by the air! Ah, ah, Revenge, thou dear, dear, dear passion!

(2: 475)

This passage, with its powerfully suggestive echo of Milton's Satan, implies that within the confines and shelter of the ***Diary*** he can enact his fantasies of retribution without having to confront his adversaries. He can play out with impunity a range of roles, allowing him to justify himself and to appear as oppressed scapegoat. These strategies find a place in the privacy of the book, but even as we witness the Romantic will sublimely asserting itself against all opposition, we also see the luxury of self-effacement. For Haydon, autobiography simultaneously permits a therapeutic assertion and an unembarrassed diminution of self.

In designating the ***Diary*** and ***Autobiography*** as shelters I am claiming that his writing (especially in the ***Autobiography,*** where the events have occurred at least two decades earlier) is part of an elaborate process of image formation. He is pleased to be thought a fighter, and the autobiographical writings are filled with verbatim letters and essays in which his career and public self is launched against others. Haydon revels in his status as pariah because within the writing he is free to vindicate his actions without public consequence. Haydon may relive his experiences but he need not account to others for his actions. There is no evidence that he intended publication of either the journals or the autobiography during his lifetime. He took great pleasure in the force of his attacks upon painters, critics, and patrons, the very strength of the offended opposition confirming him to himself as a man of convictions.

But if aggrieved outrage regarding a painting hung in a dimly lit exhibition space, or a patron who reneged on a commission, marks one pole of Haydon's sensibility, reckless self-destruction marks another. There are numerous litanies of self-accusation:

> I had always a tendency to fight it out, a tendency most prejudicial to artists, because it calls off his mind from the main point of his being—perfection in his art. . . . My will had not been curbed, or my will was too stubborn to submit to curbing; Heaven knows. Perhaps mine is a character in which all parts would have harmonised if my will had been broken early. The same power might have been put forth with more discretion, and I should have been less harassed by the world
>
> (***Autobiography,*** p. 116)

These sentiments contrast with the more vituperative ones directed outward against the world. Harold Bloom has remarked how, according to Freud, part of the ego's own self-hatred is projected onto an outward object but part remains in the ego. Such a description precisely fits Haydon's situation.[10] "The heart . . . sinks inwardly in itself & longs for a pleasure calm & eternal, majestic, unchangeable. I am not yet 40 and can tell of a Destiny melancholy and rapturous, severe, trying, & afflicting, bitter beyond all bitterness, afflicting beyond all affliction, cursed, heart burning! heart breaking! maddening, not to be dwelt on lest its thought scathe my blasted heart and blighted brain." (2: 499). There is as much self-hatred as loathing of the world in this entry. Puritanical disgust and guilt for not working harder or achieving greater stature dominate his writing in the middle years. But Haydon's fundamental strategy is to escape the implications of his particular, idiosyncratic behavior by lamenting both a crippled self and the disappointments of living. Chastened by his growing awareness that he is simply not as great a painter as he had thought, he cannot bear to acknowledge that truth, even to himself within the confines of writing. Instead, he turns on the world and on the general state of human misery without facing the possibility of self-delusion regarding his own skill. Autobiographical writing defers the problem by allowing endless options for the perpetuation of ambivalence towards himself. All Haydon could hope for was that his sufferings alone would vindicate him, but the more he stresses them the more it appears he has brought them on himself.

Haydon's biographer Eric George claims that Haydon's ultimate tragedy would have been not to be noticed, and that all his efforts were bent on avoiding that final humiliation. But one can also argue that Haydon knew, as all the Romantics did, the impossibility of fulfillment, and that the autobiographical writing testified to what could not be avoided. This awareness seems to have come early to Haydon, whose endless prayers for the energy to conquer obstacles soon turned into prayers to bear up under stress and defeat. Loss of power and the crises brought by its realization were Haydon's subject from the start, as if in his desperate need to find models in history for his desire, he envisioned a radical emptiness even as he projected a powerful libido.

When he is most critical of a life without design, when most ashamed of his drift, the prose becomes fragmented, as Haydon dramatizes the disconnected moments in the life.

> My mind fatuous, impotent—drewling over Petrarch—dawdling over Pausanias—dipping into Plutarch. Voyages and Travels no longer exciting—all dull, dreary, flat, weary, & disgusting. I seem as if I should never paint again. I look at my own Xenophon, & wonder how I did it—read the Bible—gloat over Job—doubt Religion to rouse my faculties, and wonder if the wind be East or S. S. West—look out of the window and gape at the streets—shut up the shutters, & lean my hand on my cheek—get irritable for dinner, two hours

before it can be ready—eat too much, drink too much—and go to bed at nine to forget existence! I dream horrors, start up, & lie down, & toss & tumble, listen to caterwauling of cats, & just doze away as light is dawning. Delightful life!—fit attendents on Idleness. With my Ambition! my talents! my energy! Shameful.

(3: 549)

The *Diary* can be read as the gradual recognition that hope is less salvation than nemesis, in the sense that it not only holds out impossible illusions but, if miraculously gratified, is followed by inevitable disappointment. For Haydon all dreams are enchantments; the nearer we get to their fulfillment the less desirable they become. We live in a world of time and imperfection, but deceive ourselves that we can remedy our plight. There are moments of relief, when Haydon endows his Muse-like precursor painters, his friends, a beloved, and of course his creative work with the potential to redeem his despair. He even declares that similarly wretched men "shoot themselves—but not me" (5: 412). Nevertheless he seems to know that nothing will come of his hopes, that all "grand conceptions" and "elevated sensations of an ambitious and glorious soul" (*Autobiography,* p. 165) are flimsy constructions, much like love objects who can never make good the expectations with which we have freighted them.

Haydon's reluctance to submit to the reality of events and to the diminution of his life in its contingencies has its analogy in his attack on realism and portrait painting, and on the need for a heroic scale. There is something almost visceral in his passionate commitment to painting that is heroic in both size and subject matter, as if his very being could not tolerate limitation. He constantly seeks a form of transcendence, and the sheer scale of his work becomes the measure of escape from the trivial and mundane aspects of existence. In his public life Haydon craved largeness of scale as if to proclaim his greatness; smallness (or portrait painting) was equated in his mind with obscurity. When he painted large canvases he felt important and significantly controversial. His *Autobiography* in fact concludes with a description of his beginning to work on a painting of Lazarus, "determined to make it my grandest and largest work" (*Autobiography,* p. 345), and the *Autobiography* breaks off not after a description of the work or its execution, but after a meditation on size per se: "I always filled my painting-room to its full extent; and had I possessed a room 400 feet long, and 200 feet high, and 400 feet wide, I would have ordered a canvas 399-6 long by 199-6 high, and so have been encumbered for want of room, as if it had been my pleasure to be so" (*Autobiography,* p. 346). The painter, hemmed in and striving to create a gigantic world, is a Titanic figure wrestling with resistant material. The desire to transcend limits is a projection of heroic striving into both the principal figures of the painting: the Christ

who performs a miracle, and the Lazarus who achieves his rebirth. (From the vantage point of the composition of the *Autobiography,* two decades after this scene from 1820, Haydon no doubt saw Lazarus as a symbol of his own hoped-for rebirth after twenty years of public defeats and private unhappiness.) Painting is a form of combat "because [in the eyes of a misguided public] Reynolds beat West in force, depth & color, Portrait Painters beat Historical Painters" (3: 118). Losing the game is inevitable, because "the Historical Painter, whatever be his talent . . . is considered half cracked or completely mad" (3: 311). In the face of public disdain, Haydon turns to the autobiographical writings, where the intensification of these struggles magnifies his sense of being both victim and scourge.

Paul de Man's acute observation about autobiography applies to Haydon's need to live within the writing: "We assume the life *produces* the autobiography as an act produces its consequences, but can we not suggest, with equal justice, that the autobiographical project may itself produce and determine the life and that whatever the writer *does* is in fact governed by the technical demands of self-portraiture and thus determined in all its aspects, by the resources of its medium?"[11] Haydon's life was partly shaped by the achievement of the writing, in that autobiography granted him a certain freedom to experiment in his life by trying out and anticipating within the security of the writing all possible consequences of his action. Then, as he confronted lost commissions and official neglect, he turned to the autobiographical project for solace, the very privacy of the writing compensating for and justifying his unacknowledged work. A myth of self-defeat emerges as the dominating one, as in a remark appended to an earlier entry where an inner voice urges him not to miss out in proposing designs for the Nelson Monument: "And yet it ended in nothing, & here my old voice deceived me" (4: 525). Triumph or even desire inevitably turns to loss, and the writing unfolds this design as if Haydon—against his will—were both compelled actor and composing author of his tragedy.

Haydon, both sinned against and sinning, finds the causes for disappointment wherever he can—in the public world, in his own misapprehensions, in the way life is. He bows to a course of ineluctability, even as he asserts that he will not submit to suicide; time is inexorable and surrender is half-sweet in the contemplation. He alleges he would plunge over the falls of Niagara if he could, those sublime torrents that always stand for the deadly rush of time. Reading through great stretches of the *Diary,* we see that passages of calm and ordinary experience inevitably give way to passages of hysteria and nightmare: whether Haydon meditates on his own self-destructive impulses, his dreams of revenge, his marriage as the ruination of his art and of those whom he drags down with him, or the overestimation of his chances for greatness, he is aware of a tragic arc to his life, yet unable to accept it. The autobiographical writing, veering as it does between hope and despair, expresses the instability of its author as he attempts both to write himself into tranquility and to lash out against the failures he can no longer deny.

In a moment that looks like melodrama but really suggests a fascination with the course of his own psyche, we see why Haydon could never let any emotional problem rest without examination: "I do not think any man on Earth ever suffered more agony of mind than I have done, & so would the World think if it knew why, and yet I always had an abstracting power, & that saved my mind and made me look down & meditate, as it were, on my own sufferings. They became a curious speculation" (3: 38). Haydon reveals both a therapeutic benefit from self-exploration and also a morbid excitement from his own pain. Writing brings peace—it helps dispel the uncertainty of things—but it also intensifies the anguish as he relives it and explores every detail. He is unable to escape from the circle of curiosity he has drawn.

Haydon claims he writes to show the reader how to "bear affliction and disappointment" (*Autobiography,* p. 164); it is an autobiographical commonplace for a writer ostensibly to address his work to an audience who will benefit from his wisdom, but Haydon, like so many autobiographers, writes largely to console himself and to assert an irrepressible claim for his own genius. We have noted that early in the *Diary* he imagines himself as a figure of fiery greatness: "I have been like a man with air balloons under his arm pits and ether in his soul. While I was painting, or walking, or thinking, these beaming flashes of energy followed and impressed me! . . . Grant that they may be the fiery anticipations of a great Soul born to realize them" (1: 430). Twenty-six years later he is still unquenchable, his imagery equally Promethean. "Had a most glorious idea of Genius at 4 this morning. I awoke saying what is Genius? It is a spark from the Deity's Essence which shoots up into the Heavens fiery & blazing over an astonished World, & when it has reached its elevation, drops back into his Being like lava from a Volcanic Mountain" (5: 82). The Romantic ego expressed here is in the high mode of natural supernaturalism and self-renovation. But the defeated dross of nature, unresponsive society, and an unwilling self combine to check those enthusiasms. Nevertheless, Haydon celebrates the self even in and through its defeats; autobiography replaces the painted self-portrait (he did only one), and expresses a belief that in his solipsism he can gather strength against his detractors and assert a radical "I am" even as he slowly kills himself with recrimination.

But, ironically, Haydon's problem is that he can never fully turn inward, at least without extreme self-consciousness; too often he has his eyes on others, on their judgments and their determination of his fortune. Haydon enacts what Bloom calls the first stage or Promethean mode of the "internalized quest-romance," defined as an "involvement in political [and] social . . . revolution, and a direct, even satirical attack on the institutional orthodoxies of . . . English society."[12] Haydon's condemnation of the Royal Academy and of misplaced patronage figures here. But he is ultimately fixated on these issues—he can never shake free of a preoccupation with the accusing voices, even when he internalizes them. He needs others' condemnation in order to assert himself; trapped in the process, he becomes fully absorbed with defense of his worth. His obsession with avatars suggests that he cannot separate himself from the past and from judgment. (Does Michelangelo in the dream come to inspire or to judge?) It is not surprising that he was unable to paint in an original style.

Just as he can never turn from his elders, so he exhibits an adolescent petulance in his life-long insistence that he is better than anyone else. The *Diary* and the *Autobiography* express his attempt to re-beget himself and to assert an identity without the defining imperatives of others, but Haydon cannot sustain this posture. Defiance is as crucial as achievement; indeed one is impossible without the other. Frustrated or defeated creativity is mandatory for self-assertion. "In reading over my journals of 1818, I gloried to see how I suffered . . . how I vanquished," and "It is my destiny to perform great things, not in consequence of encouragement, but in spite of opposition, & so let it be. . . . 'Impossibility is the Element in which he glories.'—Hazlitt" (5: 447, 430).

He is plagued not only by the expectations of others, but also by his own heroic demands, the images he must live up to. Here is Haydon's essentially oxymoronic position: it is in a purgatorial mode, expressing hopeful labor and fear of entrapment. Autobiographical writing is both an escape from sorrow and the net that enmeshes him more tightly in his grief; that writing is not merely reflective, composed at the end of a long life, but an almost daily tracing of the torment of his failure to meet his own expectations. Self-absorption becomes a tragic game in Haydon's hands, his writing both the vantage point from which to perceive his life's slow dying, and the virtual instrument of that death.

Notes

1. *The Diary of Benjamin Robert Haydon,* ed. Willard Bissell Pope, 5 vols. (Cambridge, Mass.: Harvard University Press, 1963), 5: 553. Further references to this edition by volume and page number will be in parentheses following the passage.

2. Midway between these entries Haydon described the birth of his first son like Lear pronouncing on

the inevitable doom in store for the child: "I had been sitting on the stairs, listening to the moaning of my love, when, all of a sudden, a dreadful, dreary outcry, a tortured, passionate, dull, & throttled agony, gasping, breathless, & outrageous, announced intense suffering, and then there was a dead silence, as if from exhaustion, and then a puling, peaked cry, as of a little helpless living being, who felt the air, & anticipated the anxieties, & bewailed the destiny of his irrevocable humanity" (2: 392). Heroic defiance, prophetic doom, and exhaustion are all characteristics Haydon assigned to his own Lear-like being.

3. Virginia Woolf, "Genius," in *The Moment and Other Essays* (New York: Harcourt, Brace, 1948), p. 191.

4. *The Collected Writings of Thomas De Quincey,* ed. David Masson, 14 vols. (London: A. and C. Black, 1897), 3: 233.

5. W. Jackson Bate, *John Keats* (New York: Oxford University Press, 1963), pp. 98, 101.

6. *The Autobiography and Journals of Benjamin Robert Haydon,* ed. Malcolm Elwin (London: Macdonald, 1950), p. 94. Further references to the *Autobiography* will be in parentheses following the passage.

7. Eric George, *The Life and Death of Benjamin Robert Haydon* (Oxford: Oxford University Press, 1967), p. 92.

8. W. Jackson Bate, *The Burden of the Past and the English Poet* (New York: Norton, 1970), pp. 106-7.

9. *The Letters of John Keats,* ed. Maurice Buxton Forman (London: Oxford University Press, 1952), p. 278, letter from Haydon to Keats, Jan. 23, 1819.

10. Harold Bloom, "The Internalization of Quest-Romance," in Harold Bloom, ed., *Romanticism and Consciousness* (New York: Norton, 1970), p. 12.

11. Paul de Man, "Autobiography as De-Facement," *Modern Language Notes,* 94 (1979): 920.

12. Bloom, "The Internalization of Quest-Romance," p. 11.

FURTHER READING

Criticism

Barlow, P. J. "Benjamin Robert Haydon and the Radicals." *The Burlington Magazine* 99, no. 654 (September 1957): 311-12.

Records Haydon's unsuccessful attempt to paint the May 1832 scene at Newhall Hill in which the Birmingham Political Union gathered to celebrate the success of Reform.

Brooks, E. L. "An Unidentified Article by Benjamin Robert Haydon." *Keats-Shelley Journal* 6 (1957): 9-12.

Proposes that Haydon was the source of an article in John Scott's *A Visit to Paris in 1814* (1815), in which the author reported on his reactions to a visit to the Louvre.

Cummings, Frederick. "B. R. Haydon and His School." *Journal of the Warburg and Courtald Institutes* 26 (1963): 367-80.

Describes the contributions to nineteenth-century art and art education of Haydon's private school (1815-23), discussing Haydon's teaching method, his artistic theory, his curriculum, and two of his most notable students, Sir Edwin Landseer and Sir Charles Lock Eastlake.

Davis, Norma S. "Wordsworth, Haydon and Beaumont: A Change in the Role of Artistic Patronage." *Charles Lamb Bulletin* 55 (July 1986): 210-24.

Examines the differences in attitude toward Sir George Howland Beaumont shown by William Wordsworth and Haydon, who were both recipients of financial assistance from the art patron.

Haydon, Frederic Wordsworth. Preface to *Benjamin Robert Haydon: Correspondence and Table-Talk.* Vol. 1, pp. vii-xix. London: Chatto and Windus, 1876.

Attempts to clarify some of B. R. Haydon's more controversial views and opinions.

Hunt, Bishop C., Jr. "Wordsworth, Haydon, and the 'Wellington' Sonnet." *Princeton University Library Chronicle* 36, no. 2 (winter 1975): 111-32.

Describes the revision history of Wordsworth's "On a Portrait of the Duke of Wellington Upon the Field of Waterloo, by Haydon" (1842) and the poet's relationship during that time with Haydon, whose painting *Wellington Musing on the Field of Waterloo* inspired the sonnet.

Jones, Stanley. "Haydon and Northcote on Hazlitt: A Fabrication." *Review of English Studies* 24, no. 94 (May 1973): 165-78.

Claims that the 3 August 1826 entry in Haydon's diary contains numerous falsehoods about English historical painter James Northcote and English essayist William Hazlitt.

——. "B. R. Haydon on Some Contemporaries: A New Letter." *Review of English Studies* 26 (1975): 183-89.

Reprints an 1824 letter written by an angry Haydon to his friend Mary Russell Mitford a few years after Wordsworth refused to lend the painter a sum of money.

Woof, Robert. "Haydon, Writer, and the Friend of Writers." In *Benjamin Robert Haydon, 1786-1846: Painter and Writer, Friend of Wordsworth and Keats,* by David Blayney Brown, Robert Woof, and Stephen Hebron, pp. 25-64. The Wordsworth Trust, 1996.

Studies in detail the relationships Haydon maintained with such writers as Wordsworth, Percy Bysshe Shelley, John Keats, Charles Lamb, and Elizabeth and Robert Browning.

Additional coverage of Haydon's life and career is contained in the following sources published by Thomson Gale: *Dictionary of Literary Biography,* **Vol. 110; and** *Literature Resource Center.*

John Hamilton Reynolds
1794-1852

English poet, satirist, critic, and playwright.

INTRODUCTION

Reynolds is best remembered as a close friend and correspondent of the Romantic poet John Keats, whose letters to Reynolds constitute a significant body of his poetic thought. At the time of their friendship, however, Reynolds was regarded as a poet with as much promise and talent as Keats himself. He published widely in literary periodicals, and his critical writings reveal a discriminating appreciation of poetry, particularly in his admiration for William Wordsworth at a time when the elder poet was not widely respected. While Reynolds became successful as a satirist later in his career, the poetic talent heralded by Lord Byron and Leigh Hunt remained unfulfilled.

BIOGRAPHICAL INFORMATION

Reynolds was born in Shrewsbury to George Reynolds and Charlotte Cox Reynolds. His father was a school teacher; his mother was related to the Hamilton family (from which Reynolds received his middle name), which included the Gothic writer William Beckford. Reynolds attended the Shrewsbury school where his father taught, then enrolled at St. Paul's in London when the family moved in 1806. He graduated from St. Paul's in 1810, completing his formal education. He took a junior clerkship in an insurance office, the Amicable Society for Perpetual Insurance, working there at least through 1816. In the meantime, he pursued his self-education by reading widely in classical and English literature and also began writing poetry. He was encouraged in his literary interests by his friend John F. M. Dovaston, a former student of Reynolds's father. Reynolds's first published poem, "Ode to Friendship, Inscribed to J. F. M. Dovaston of West Felton," appeared in *Gentleman's Magazine* in 1812. He continued publishing poems and articles in such periodicals as *Repository of Literature, Arts, and Sciences, Gentleman's Magazine,* and *Ladies' Museum,* then released his first major work, the long poem *Safie; An Eastern Tale,* in 1814. Only twenty years old at the time, Reynolds received favorable notice from a number of critics and poets, including Lord Byron, whose work Reynolds had closely imitated. Later that year, he published *The Eden*

of Imagination, this time imitating Wordsworth, who also encouraged the younger writer. He published these poems under the auspices of his friend John Martin, who also hired Reynolds as a poetry editor for the *Inquirer.* In 1815 Reynolds moved on to the *Champion,* where he was the literary and theater editor until 1817. Both journals provided Reynolds with a ready forum for his poetry, literary criticism, and theater reviews. With the publication of *The Naiad: A Tale. With Other Poems* in 1816, Reynolds took a step forward in his poetry by moving away from purely imitative efforts. Also during this period, Reynolds became associated with a literary circle formed around a family of young women in Devon. Mary, Sarah, and Thomasine Leigh often entertained Reynolds's friends Benjamin Bailey and James Rice, and Reynolds joined the group sometime in 1815. The friends warmly encouraged Reynolds as the true poet of the group, which spent hours together writing, copying verses, and discussing poetry. His friend Leigh Hunt also supported his writing and introduced him to another young poet Hunt greatly admired, the then unknown John Keats. Keats and Reynolds became fast friends, encouraging and challenging each other in their quest for literary recognition. In 1816, Reynolds took the bold step of leaving his clerkship to live solely by his writing. This endeavor was short lived, and by late 1817 Reynolds began practicing law when his friend Rice took him on as a partner in his father's firm. Biographers speculate that Reynolds's decision was motivated by his plans to marry Eliza Powell Drewe and the need to set up a household with a reliable income. Nevertheless, he continued writing and published *Peter Bell,* a parody of Wordsworth, in 1819; *The Fancy* in 1820; and *The Garden of Florence and Other Poems,* the fruit of his friendship with Keats, in 1821. He also wrote for several periodicals, including the *Yellow Dwarf, London Magazine, Edinburgh Magazine,* and the *Edinburgh Review.* After a lengthy engagement, he married Eliza Drewe in 1822, which led to a friendship and literary collaboration with her brother-in-law, Thomas Hood. Together the two wrote several comic and satirical pieces, signed and unsigned, the most popular of which was *Odes and Addresses to Great People* (1825). This was Reynolds's last publication in book form during his lifetime. He began writing non-literary prose for the magazine *Athenaeum* and produced a handful of theatrical scripts. Money was becoming a problem, as his attention to his primary career, the law, was sporadic at best, and tragedy struck in 1835 when his ten-year-old daughter Lucy died. He was bankrupt in 1838 but continued eking out a small income writing for *Bentley's Miscellany,* the *New Monthly,* and other magazines. In 1847, Reynolds gave up the law completely and subsequently moved to the Isle of Wight to work as an assistant clerk in a county court. Most biographical accounts suggest that at this point in his life Reynolds was depressed and drinking heavily, although he was not without friends and admirers to the end. He died in Newport on the Isle of Wight in 1852.

MAJOR WORKS

Reynolds best known poetic works are derivative of the canonical poets of his age. Chief among these is *Peter Bell,* a parody of a poem by Wordsworth. As a lyric poet, Reynolds was indebted to Wordsworth, and his comic mockery of the greater author demonstrates that he was not an unthinking or uncritical admirer. His parody exaggerated the least appealing aspects of Wordsworth's poetry, particularly his expressions of self-satisfaction and his romanticizing of the lower classes. *Peter Bell* was a tremendous success for Reynolds when it was first published and continues to be his most widely read work. His other satirical works, particularly *The Fancy* and *Odes and Addresses,* also won the favor of contemporary audiences, but their subjects—obscure figures in London society and sports—are generally too topical to allow modern readers to enjoy them. A num-

ber of critics and scholars have advocated that greater attention be given to Reynolds's serious poetry, which has been overshadowed by his association with his close friend Keats and by his imitations of Wordsworth. His strongest collections are *The Eden of the Imagination,* which owed much to Wordsworth's *An Evening Walk,* and *The Garden of Florence.* The latter collection features one of Reynolds's best serious poems, "Devon," a reflection on his time among the Rice-Bailey-Leigh circle. *The Garden of Florence* also contains "The Romance of Youth," a poem written during his intense collaboration with Keats, marking the high point of Reynolds's ambitions to be a serious poet. A prolific periodical contributor, Reynolds did not make a lasting name for himself as a prose writer, although he proved to be an astute and witty literary critic. Two 1816 essays from the *Champion* stand out: "The Pilgrimage of Living Poets to the Stream of Castaly" and "Boswell's Visit." Reynolds also wrote a series of fictitious letters on current events for *London Magazine* from 1820 to 1824. The letters of "Edward Herbert" were extremely popular in their time, even if, like most journalistic writing, they now hold little interest for any but the most serious scholars. Reynolds's personal correspondence remains his most significant contribution to literature, not for its own intrinsic merit but for Reynolds's ability to illuminate the lives of Keats and other writers of the time.

CRITICAL RECEPTION

Early reviews of Reynolds's works predict the position he would eventually occupy in literary history: a poet of great potential that was never realized. Critics of *Safie* and *The Naiad* were quick to point out Reynolds's failures of imagination and poetic craft, but they did so while encouraging the poet to improve upon his faults and publish again. With some exceptions, modern critics have focused primarily on the Keats connection. One of Reynolds's first twentieth-century champions was George L. Marsh, who also edited a collected edition of Reynolds's works. Marsh identified several unsigned periodical contributions as those of Reynolds, and through his research was able to pull together several details of Reynolds's biography. His assessment of Reynolds's career suggests that although Reynolds was inconsistent as a poet, the body of criticism, satire, and poetry he produced have earned him a literary ranking higher than that of merely "Keats's close friend." In the second half of the twentieth century, the scholar Leonidas M. Jones published multiple studies heralding the importance of Reynolds in the study of early nineteenth-century literature. Jones completed the work of Marsh, releasing a full biography of Reynolds as well as a collection of Reynolds's letters, further detailing the portrait of Reynolds as a central figure in the literary scene of his time. Both Jones and John Barnard have also argued that although Keats was perhaps the greater talent, the influence and encouragement of Reynolds was a factor in Keats's artistic development. Despite the assertions of Marsh and Jones that Reynolds deserves to be more highly esteemed for his own works, comparatively little scholarship exists that does not emphasize either Reynolds's artistic ties to Wordsworth or his friendship with Keats, and his correspondence continues to receive at least as much attention as his best literary writings.

PRINCIPAL WORKS

The Eden of Imagination (poetry) 1814
Safie; An Eastern Tale (poetry) 1814
The Naiad: A Tale. With Other Poems (poetry) 1816
One, Two, Three, Four, Five; By Advertisement (play) 1819
Peter Bell. Lyrical Ballad [as W. W.] (satire) 1819
The Fancy (satire) 1820
The Garden of Florence and Other Poems (poetry) 1821
Gil Blas (play) 1822
The Youthful Days of Mr. Mathews (play) 1822
Odes and Addresses to Great People (satire) 1825
Miss Kelly's New Entertainment Entitled Dramatic Recollections (play) 1833
Confounded Foreigners (play) 1838

CRITICISM

Monthly Review (essay date September 1814)

SOURCE: Review of *Safie; An Eastern Tale. Monthly Review* 75 (September 1814): 60-5.

[*In the following essay, the reviewer praises the talent Reynolds demonstrates in his first major work but faults the poet for too closely imitating Lord Byron.*]

We believe that this is Mr. Reynolds's first appearance at our tribunal, and we congratulate him on that introduction being sanctioned by a dedication to Lord Byron, whose style and manner it appears to be his principal aim to copy. If with the style and expression the noble Lord's genius and power of thought could be successfully attained, no object could be more worthy of a young author's ambition: but it must never be forgotten that *originality* is of itself one primary constituent of genius, and that the most successful copy can never be

equal to its original. The finishing may even be higher, the colouring brighter, the effect in every respect more laboured and complete: but the want of freedom and boldness will of itself give a character of inferiority. The very defects and inequalities of genius are essential to its existence, though a copyist would justly deem it wrong to adopt them. Unfortunately, however, some defects are so easily caught, that an imitation generally preserves more of the faults than the beauties of its prototype; and this is precisely the case with the little work before us. The style of declamation, the abrupt and irregular expression, and the long and involved sentences, which we pointed out as faults in our review of *The Corsair,* are to be found in every page of *Safie*; while we look in vain for that forcible, yet correct, display of the human heart for which Lord Byron's productions have been so sadly remarkable. With all this, however, we discern traces of genius, of bold and nervous diction, of glowing but correct painting, of touches at once animated and pathetic, in this little poem; which convince us that Mr. Reynolds is capable of doing much better, if he had chosen a subject and a style less exclusively imitative.

In poetry, as in painting, we have the great antient masters as models for every student to follow. It is true that we have seen, in both pursuits, artists who have dared to depart from those models, and who have charmed by such departure; and we are far from censuring such boldness: on the contrary, reliance on its own powers is one of the surest pledges of genius:—but, if a writer does not feel "that within him" which emboldens him to execute something entirely new and original, we think that he is not justified in deviating from those standards which, after all that has been done in imitation or in contempt of them, remain unrivalled monuments of the perfection of the arts to which they belong.

It is not a little singular that the Tales of Dryden have met, in the present day, with so few imitators. With scarcely more than one successful exception[1], their style has not been adopted since the time of Parnell. Goldsmith may not be considered as imitating, but as affording a beautiful variety of this species of composition; and the originality even of Crabbe has most advantageously displayed itself by selecting the same style. To this old standard-style of poetry, even Lord Byron, after some daring aberrations which success may have amply justified, has returned in his last (and perhaps best) production, "The Corsair;" and this part of his Lordship's example we would most particularly recommend to the imitation of the young author now before us.

The story of *Safie* is perfectly simple, and without intricacy. The heroine, the favourite mistress of Assad, a Persian, is torn from his Haram by an unknown Turk; who, with his followers, attacks that retreat, and in the contest which ensues disables Assad from immediate pursuit. Unable, however, to recover that peace of mind of which the loss of his favourite has deprived him, Assad sets out with a chosen band of men, resolved to discover whither Safie has been carried, and to repossess himself of her person. In the progress of his journey, he arrives under the walls of a Turkish Haram towards evening, and stops, attracted by the sounds of music and revelry; when, to his astonishment, he hears the well-known voice of his lost mistress singing to another the song which formerly charmed and delighted him. Stung with this proof of her faithlessness, he immediately attacks the Turkish Haram, and a furious battle commences, in which Assad is wounded and taken prisoner. In the course of the succeeding night, he stabs himself in his dungeon; leaving a scroll of pathetic reproach for the unworthy object of his passion. This relique being delivered to Safie, it so affects her that she gradually sinks under the mixture of remorse and sorrow which it occasions.

To the poem are prefixed some introductory stanzas, addressed to the 'Land of the East.' We give a specimen of this introduction:

> 'Thine is the land for love! the land for soul!
> For hearts of ardour, and for beauty bright;
> Love lives and roves with thee without controul,
> Smiles in the air and in the laughing light:
> Oh! Woman's frown is like a moonless night,
> When every cheering ray from earth is driven;—
> Her glance is promise to the gazer's sight,
> Her lively smile bestow'd is rapture given,—
> And oh! her feeling heart is ever Eastern heaven.'

From the subsequent passage, nearly at the opening of the tale, we have the first glimpse of what is to follow;

> 'Yes! she was dear as living light,
> As angel pure,—as morning bright;—
> Her heart could love—Oh! Assad tell,
> Awhile how faithfully! how well!—
> 'Tis even sweet, though years are past
> Since Safie look'd and sigh'd her last;—
> 'Tis even sweet to think upon
> The semblance of those beauties gone,—
> To meditate most silently
> Upon that form—that heart—that eye;—
> And yet, amid the soft reflection,
> At times a sadden'd recollection
> Of Safie's sorrow darts its pain
> Across the meditating brain,—
> And makes it dread to think again.
> Yet, loving still, the memory scorns
> To shun the object that adorns;
> But ponders still—and still admires,—
> And loves the shade with living fires:
> Till one sad thought, more dread than hate,
> Glares on the mind—the maiden's fate!'

Mr. R. thus delineates Assad's death:

> 'The slave hath said who saw him die,—
>   That not for worlds would he again

> View the last look of such an eye:—
>   It glancing spoke of inward pain,—
> Of faded hope—of baffled hate,—
> Which blood would glad, and nought but death could sate.
>   And might he once but live again,
> The same dread deeds so dared of late,
> Again he'd venture for his mate;—
> And sorrow—love—revenge would wait,
>   To lead him on, yet lead in vain.
> The slave hath said,—while life was leaving
>   In dark red streams his mangled breast,
> The causes of his death,—his grieving,
>   Upon his thoughts tumultuous prest.
> He dash'd his arm upon the floor,
> So wet, so stain'd with his own gore;
> He writhed his body,—struck his wound,
> And scatter'd wide the blood around;—
> But towards the last his strength grew tame,
> And languor mark'd a weaken'd frame;—
> His thoughts—his love were still the same;—
> While dying, lovely Safie's name
> In murmurs from his pale lips past;
> One groan he utter'd:—'twas his last!
> Yet still upon his pallid face,
> Revenge the vassal's eye could trace,—
> Which living feelings first imprest,—
>   Which Death had fix'd with his cold touch;—
> And oh! that faded front exprest
>   Of unextinguished hate so much,
>   The slave could scarce believe that such
> Was the last look of one at rest!'

This is spirited; indeed, it is open to the charge of being a little overdone, but that is a fault on the right side. We must, however, remark that the word 'Mate,' used in this and in several other places in the poem, is not sanctioned by the best examples, and is too low an expression. We can afford room for only one extract more, and we take the lines which immediately succeed the last quotation. As it is a passage on "the loveliest theme, that ever filled a poet's dream," it is at least a fair specimen of the author's manner:

> 'Oh, love! what art thou? Sadly sweet!
> A grief the bosom pants to meet;—
> A weary source of restlessness,
> That makes all other woes seem less:—
> Thy charms are such, that, syren like,
> Upon the tranced heart they strike:—
> Thy hapless victims all admire
>   The gilded ray of future ruin:—
>   For darksome woe waits present wooing,
> As blacken'd embers follow fire.
> 'Tis thine to lead the ardent soul
> To deeds that spurn a cool controul;—
> Through scenes of varied woe and joy,
> To break the spirit and destroy.
> 'Tis thine to pause, retreat, and range,—
> To promise truth, and yet to change;—
> To lead to poverty and care,—
> To bondage,—madness,—and despair!'

In making these citations, it is but fair to say that we have taken some of the most favourable parts of the work, and that our readers must not expect the whole to be equal to these samples. The poem has merit enough, however, to justify us in recommending a perusal of it, and in expressing a strong hope that the author will improve in his next attempt.

With the expectation of meeting Mr. Reynolds again, we shall take the trouble of a little verbal criticism; to which, in general, we are much averse. We know not any such word as 'reseeks,' p. 12; and we object to the frequent introduction of foreign words, as 'Caftan,' 'Bizestien,' and 'Talpack,' p. 13. 'Tophaike,' p. 21. and 'Ataghan,' in several places. 'The spurs were lanced' is an incorrect expression for denoting that the horse's sides were lanced. The recurrence of rhymes too nearly resembling each other is also a fault, as in pages 20, 21, and 22, where many rhymes are long *i*'s; and again in p. 23, six lines in succession end with syllables rhyming with a long *a*. The prevailing fault through the poem is the introduction of unnecessary lines for the sake of rhymes; as 'when like a log the ship remains,' (a vulgar expression in itself,) 'and ne'er her trackless travel gains;' which last line has three faults; it is not sense, it is unnecessary, and it contains a bad alliteration. 'East' and 'west' (p. 29.) are almost as far from each other in the rhyming dictionary as on the mariner's compass. The omission of the article and pronoun (seldom a beauty, though frequently practised by Mr. Scott and his followers,) is carried to a ridiculous length in the passage descriptive of Assad's behaviour after the rape of his favourite: viz.

> 'Did voice speak madness loud and dire?
> Did eye flash rage revengeful fire?
> Was bosom beat? Was garment rent?

Some instances of plagiarism occur; as, in two places, of Goldsmith's beautiful idea expressed in the line, "And drags at each remove a lengthening chain;" and at p. 67. 'Strange that lips so sweetly glowing, should set the tide of promise flowing,' which is too like a passage in one of the Irish Melodies.

Note

1. "The Four Slaves of Cythera," by the Rev. Robert Bland, one of the authors of the elegant "Collections from the Greek Anthology."

British Critic (essay date October 1817)

SOURCE: Review of *The Naiad: A Tale. With Other Poems. British Critic* 8 (October 1817): 415-20.

[*In the following essay, the reviewer admires the story, imagination, and versification of* The Naiad, *but suggests that Reynolds falters by adopting Wordsworth as his model.*]

This is really a pleasing little poem; the story of it is tastefully chosen, and told with lightness; the descriptions which it contains are given in a wild and fanciful

manner, and in a versification which, though unequal, is upon the whole agreeably tuned. We could indeed wish that these merits were not so often thrown into the shade, by prettynesses, and simplenesses, and sillinesses, and all those other childish affectations, which the imitators of Mr. Wordsworth are so apt to suppose inseparable from the other qualities of his poetry; and, but that the present is, we imagine, our poet's first appearance before our tribunal, we should perhaps feel disposed to be less lenient than we intend to be. We should be sorry to discourage an author of promise, even though his merits may possibly be only of a subordinate quality; more especially when, as in the present instance, his faults are not inherent in his genius, but merely the accidental fruits of having injudiciously chosen his model. We do not mean to say, generally, that Mr. Wordsworth is an improper model of poetry; though unquestionably he will be found a very dangerous one; we only mean, that when a writer is induced to model his compositions upon those of another, he should select one whose genius is cast in a mould similar to his own. To emulate a writer, simply because we admire him, is a very unsafe proceeding. Nothing can be more natural than to feel admiration for the beautiful qualities of Mr. Wordsworth's mind, and nothing more easy than to imitate the occasional childishness and affectation of his manner; but a person must not suppose himself like Alexander, merely because he can walk with his neck awry. Our author's genius is as distinct from Mr. Wordsworth's as is well conceivable; lightness and playfulness of fancy are the qualities which he should principally cultivate, as they seem to be those which are most within his reach; and these qualities, we should imagine, may be studied almost any where, rather than in the "Lyrical Ballads." But this is not the place for a critical dissertation.

The poem professes to be founded upon an old Scotch ballad, which the author procured from a young girl of Galloway, who delighted in treasuring up the legendary songs of her country. As our author says so, we conclude this to be the fact; but the subject of the tale is so exactly similar to that of Goëthe's "Fisherman," that we can hardly keep ourselves from suspecting the "young girl of Galloway" and the "German Baron of Weimar" to be, what one cannot easily understand how two such dissimilar characters should be, one and the same person. However this be, we have no right to accuse our author of plagiarism, for he himself points out the coincidence.

> "One of the ballads of Goëthe, called 'the Fisherman,' is very similar in its incidents to it: Madame de Stael, in her eloquent work on Germany, thus describes it. 'A poor man, on a summer evening, seats himself on the bank of a river, and as he throws in his line, contemplates the clear and liquid tide which gently flows and bathes his naked feet. The nymph of the stream invites him to plunge himself into it; she describes to him the delightful freshness of the water during the heat of

summer, the pleasure which the sun takes in cooling it-self at night in the sea, the calmness of the moon when its rays repose and sleep on the bosom of the stream: at length the fisherman attracted, seduced, drawn on, advances near the nymph, and for ever disappears.'"

P. viii

Except that the "Fisherman" is changed into a young and handsome braon, riding along the banks of the stream, attended by a page, on his way to meet his beautiful bride, who is supposed to be waiting his arrival with all the preparations of music and dancing, the above extract will at once put our readers in possession of the sum and substance of the poem which we are now desirous of making them acquainted with.

The following lines, descriptive of the scenery through which the road of Lord Hubert and his page lay, are pleasing, in spite of the conceits and affectations with which they are sprinkled. We shall just note the particular expressions we allude to by italics, in order to let our readers perceive the nature of the faults we before animadverted upon.

> "'Twas autumn-tide,—the eve was sweet,
>   As mortal eye hath e'er beholden;
> The grass look'd warm with sunny heat,—
>   Perchance some fairy's glowing feet
>   Had lightly touch'd,—and left it golden:
> A flower or two were shining yet;
> *The star of the daisy had not yet set,—*
> It shone from the turf to greet the air,
> Which *tenderly* came breathing there:
> And in a brook, which lov'd to fret
>   O'er yellow sand and pebble blue,
>   The lily of the silvery hue
> All freshly dwelt, with white leaves wet.
> Away the sparkling water play'd,
>   Through bending grass, and blessed flower;
>   *Light, and delight* seem'd all its dower:
> Away in merriment it stray'd,—
>   Singing, and bearing, hour after hour,
>   Pale, lovely splendour to the shade.
> *Ye would have given your hearts to win*
>   A glimpse of that fair willow'd brook:
>   The water lay glistening in each leafy nook,
> And the shadows fell green and thin.
> As the wind pass'd by—the willow trees,
>   Which lov'd for aye on the wave to look,
>   Kiss'd the pale stream,—but disturb'd and shook,
> *They wept tears of light at the rude, rude breeze.*
> At night, when all the planets were sprinkling
>   Their little rays of light on high,
> The busy brook with stars was twinkling,—
>   And it seemed a streak of the living sky;
>   'Twas *heavenly* to walk in the autumn's wind's
> sigh,
> And list to that brook's lonely tinkling."

P. 2

The next specimen with which we intend to present our readers, will form a continuation of that which we have already given; but it is, in point of style, much less exceptionable.

> "For a moment with pleasure his bridle hand shook,
> And the steed in its joy mock'd the wave on the brook,
> It play'd—and danced up for a moment—no more—
> Then gently glided on as before.
> Now forth they rode all silently,
> Beneath the broad and milky sky,
> They kept their course by the water's edge,
> And listen'd at times to the oreeking sedge;
> Or started from some rich fanciful dream,
> At the sullen plunge of the fish in the stream;
> Then would they watch the circle bright,—
> The circle, silver'd by the moonlight,—
> Go widening, and shining, and trembling on,
> Till a wave leap'd up, and the ring was gone.
> Or the otter would cross before their eyes,
> And hide in the bank where the deep nook lies;
>   Or the owl would call out through the silent air,
> With a mournful, and shrill, and tremulous cry;
> Or the hare from its form would start up and pass by;
>   And the watch-dog bay them here and there.
> The leaves might be rustled—the waves be curl'd—
> But no human foot appear'd out in the world."

P. 8

The lines, in which our author describes the rising of the Naiad from the stream, possess great merit; the picture which he presents to our imagination is fancifully conceived, and very poetically painted. The first eight or nine lines are feeble, but the remainder of our extract will, we are sure, afford pleasure.

> "Lord Hubert look'd forth;—say, what hath caught
>   The lustre of his large dark eye?
> Is it the form he hath lov'd and sought?
> Or is it some vision his fancy hath wrought?
>   He cannot pass it by.
> It rises from the bank of the brook,
> And it comes along with an angel look;
> Its vest is like snow, and its hand is as fair,
> Its brow seems a mingling of sunbeam and air,
> And its eyes so meek, which the glad tear laves,
> Are like stars beheld soften'd in summer waves;
> The lily hath left a light on its feet,
> And the smile on its lip is passingly sweet;
> It moves serene, but it treads not the earth;—
> Is it a lady of mortal birth?
> Down o'er her shoulders her yellow hair flows,
> And her neck through its tresses divinely glows;
> Calm in her hand a mirror she brings,
> And she sleeks her loose locks, and gazes, and sings.

"The Naiad's Song"

> "'My bower is in the hollow wave,
>   The water lily is my bed;
> The brightest pearls the rivers lave
>   Are wreath'd around my breast and head.
>
> "The fish swims idly near my couch,
>   And twinkling fins oft brush my brow;
> And spirits mutely to me crouch,
>   While waters softly o'er them flow.
>
> "Then come thee to these arms of mine,
>   And come thee to this bosom fair;

And thou mid silver waves shalt twine
   The tresses of my silky hair.
"I have a ring of the river weed,
   'Twas fasten'd with a spirit's kiss;
I'll wed thee in this moonlight mead,—
   Ah! look not on my love amiss.'"

                                                    P. 11

As our author has succeeded so well in the lines descriptive of the "Sprite's" introduction to our hero, possibly our readers will not be displeased to read our author's conception of the song with which she tempted Lord Hubert to forget his earthly bride and follow his new acquaintance under the wave.

   "'Oh! come, and we will hurry now
   To a noble crystal pile;
Where the waters all o'er thee like music shall flow,
And the lilies shall cluster around thy brow.
We'll arise, my love! when morning dew
Is on the rose-leaf, soft and new;
We'll sit upon the tawny grass,
And catch the west winds as they pass;
And list the wild birds while they sing,
And kiss to the water's murmuring.
Thou shalt gather a flower, and I will wear it;
I'll find the wild bee's nest, and thou shalt share it;
Thou shalt catch the bird, and come smiling to me,
And I'll clasp its wing, and kiss it for thee.'"

                                                    P. 20

Lord Hubert would not appear to have been insensible to the charms of this poetical invitation; our poet continues,

   "She step into the silver wave,—
And sank, like the morning mist, from the eye;
Lord Hubert paus'd with a misgiving sigh,
   And look'd on the water as on his grave.
But a soften'd voice came sweet from the stream,
Such sound doth a young lover hear in his dream;
   It was lovely, and mellow'd, and tenderly hollow:—
   'Step on the wave, where sleeps the moon beam,
Thou wilt sink secure through its delicate gleam,
   Follow, Lord Hubert!—follow!'
He started—pass'd on with a graceful mirth,
And vanish'd at once from the placid earth.

"The waters prattled sweetly, wildly,
Still the moonlight kissed them mildly;
All sounds were mute, save the screech of the owl,
And the otter's plunge, and the watch-dog's howl;
But from that cold moon's setting, never
Was seen Lord Hubert—he vanish'd for ever:
And ne'er from the breaking of that young day
Was seen the light form that had passed away."

                                                    P. 22

We cannot afford room for further extracts; indeed, considering the shortness of the poem, and the modesty of its pretensions, we think we have paid it no little compliment in extracting from it so largely. What remains

to be told, may be said in a few words. The reader is taken to the castle of the father of Angelina (for such is the name of Lord Hubert's intended bride) where of course both she and the guests wait in vain for the bridegroom. He makes his appearance, however; but it is not until all the guests have separated for the night; and then his appearance is under somewhat unwelcome circumstances. His watery bride, we must suppose, had rather disappointed his expectations; for the very same night he returns to his earthly allegiance, and leaves his "noble chrystal pile," in order to come and claim his original mistress. But however much the latter may have lamented her lover's fickleness, she would not seem to think that the matter was at all mended by the proof he gives her of his posthumous fidelity.

   "'Thy arms around me press'd
   Like bands of ice upon my breast,
   Are fresh now from the chilling water,
   To me they come like silent slaughter.'"

                                                    P. 31

We are sorry to end our extracts with such four notably absurd lines; but our author has no reason to complain; for we have overlooked many that would as little redound to his credit.

George L. Marsh (essay date 1928)

SOURCE: Marsh, George L. Introduction to *John Hamilton Reynolds: Poetry and Prose*, pp. 9-48. London: Humphrey Milford, 1928.

[*In the following excerpt, Marsh characterizes Reynolds as a writer whose taste in poetry exceeded his talent.*]

The rocket-like career of John Hamilton Reynolds has in it much that is puzzling, or at best uncertain; much that is pathetic, verging on the tragic. Here is one who at nineteen attracted Byron's attention as a clever young disciple; who at twenty-two was bracketed with Shelley and Keats as one of the young men destined to carry forward the torch of English poetry, and became thenceforth one of the closest and most intimate friends and correspondents of Keats. Later, though he had become a solicitor, he was associated with Lamb, De Quincey, Hazlitt, Hood, and lesser lights on the staff of the most brilliant magazine of the day, and he continued intermittently to maintain relations with important literary men in a divided allegiance between law and literature. Yet, for reasons that we only partly know and partly guess, he failed to justify the promise of his youth and gradually dropped from notice, dying at fifty-eight—a disappointed, prematurely old man, after some years of exile in the Isle of Wight—an exile, it is to be feared, painfully resembling that of Burns at Dumfries.

Shrewsbury was his birthplace; September 9, 1794, the date; thus he was a little more than a year older than Keats. The *Dictionary of National Biography*, without statement of authority, made the year 1796; but the Register of St. Mary's Parish, Shrewsbury, contains a record of the baptism on September 29, 1794, of John Hamilton Reynolds, son of George and Charlotte Reynolds. This earlier date is in harmony, and 1796 is not in harmony, with Leigh Hunt's understanding that Keats was the youngest of the three 'young poets'—Shelley, Reynolds, and Keats—whom he attempted to introduce to a reluctant public in 1816, and with all other contemporary indications as to Reynolds's age.

George Reynolds, the father, was a schoolmaster, an expert in the then famous Bell, or Madras, system of education—a question-and-answer method devised by the Reverend Andrew Bell, who became Superintendent of the Madras Male Orphan Asylum in 1789. It has long been known that the senior Reynolds was writing master in Christ's Hospital at the time of the intimacy of his family with Keats, but most of the following details are the results of investigations by the editor of this volume.

According to Christ's Hospital records, George Reynolds, 'only son of Noble Reynolds of St. Michael, Cornhill, who was a freeman of the City of London and of the Barbers' Company,' was baptized on January 20, 1765, at St. Olave, Hart Street. From March 16, 1774, to October 13, 1779, George Reynolds was a pupil at Christ's Hospital. What further education he may have received, and when or where he began to teach, we do not yet know; but the Shrewsbury Parish Register already cited describes him as 'writing master' in a record of the baptism of his daughter Eliza in 1799, and as 'school master' in a like record for his daughter Charlotte in 1802.

The entrance of John Hamilton Reynolds in St. Paul's School, London, on March 4, 1806, seems to indicate the removal of the family from Shrewsbury before that date; and during the years up to 1817 George Reynolds apparently held positions in several different institutions. Before his permanent appointment as writing master to Christ's Hospital in May 1817, he served the 'blue-coat school' for seven years as usher in its writing school; but the record does not show whether these seven years were before or after, or partly before and partly after, his residence in Shrewsbury. In 1809, however, Christ's Hospital paid him '£20 for visiting the Hertford school and introducing there Dr. Bell's system of education;' and in the same year he published *The Simple Rules of Arithmetic, in Questions and Answers . . . on Dr. Bell's Plan.* Three years later, when his *Teachers Arithmetic . . . on the Rev. Dr. Bell's System* appeared, he was described on the title-page as 'Master of the Lambeth Boys' Parochial School, and Writing Master to the Female Asylum, Lambeth'. And the latter position, at least, he held for some time after his permanent appointment in Christ's Hospital, as a letter written by his son in 1820 shows. In 1813, 1818, 1822, and finally in 1838, he published school books, all on arithmetic except *The Madras School Grammar,* which was dedicated to the Archbishop of Canterbury in 1813. This, by the way, is not an English Grammar, but deals in catechism style with methods of organizing and teaching classes—the Bell system.

George Reynolds continued as writing master in Christ's Hospital from May 1817 till March 1835, when he was retired on a pension at the age of seventy. He did not die, however, till July 29, 1853, outliving his son by several months and passing the age of eighty-eight.

Charlotte Reynolds, the wife of George, whose maiden name was Cox, seems to have been older than he; born in 1761 according to Buxton Forman's information from her daughter Charlotte. She also lived to an advanced age, until May 13, 1848. After passing sixty-five years she fell victim to the family's bent toward authorship, publishing in 1827, under the pseudonym Mrs. Hamerton, a moral tale for children called *Mrs. Leslie and her Grandchildren,* about which Lamb wrote to Hood as follows: 'We have all been pleased with Mrs. Leslie: I speak it most sincerely. There is much manly sense with a feminine expression, which is my definition of ladies' writing.'

In the preface to her book the fictitious Mrs. Hamerton declared herself to have 'bred up nine daughters to womanhood'. Whether or not this is literally true of Mrs. Reynolds, only four of her daughters are known to us, but three of these are of real interest. Of the two who corresponded with Keats, Jane married Thomas Hood and Marianne became mother of Charles and Townley Green, artists of some note. Charlotte, the youngest of the family so far as we know, survived, a spinster, till 1884 and gave considerable information to Buxton Forman. She it is who used to play for Keats by the hour and whose music is supposed to have inspired the song, 'Hush, hush! tread softly!'

The first known record of the boy John Hamilton Reynolds after that of his baptism is of his entrance at Shrewsbury School in 1803; next, three years later, of his entrance at St. Paul's School, then in St. Paul's Churchyard. In one of the primary sources of information about Reynolds—an article signed 'T. M. T.' in *Notes and Queries* for 1856, and evidently written by some one with personal knowledge—it is said that after completing his education at St. Paul's School he became a clerk in the Amicable Insurance office. This assertion is supported by indications in the records of the 'Amicable Society for a Perpetual Assurance Office', now in possession of the Norwich Union, which absorbed the 'old Amicable' in 1866. According to Amicable minutes, three clerks were employed in the office early in 1810, the names of two of whom appear, but not that of the third. 'For some time prior to July 1810', however, 'practically all the declarations . . . were witnessed by the second clerk, John Griffin, but on 18th July 1810 a declaration was witnessed by J. H. Reynolds. After this date most of the declarations were witnessed by Mr. Reynolds until 1816 when some were witnessed by J. H. Reynolds and some by W. B. Wedlake. The last declaration witnessed by Mr. Reynolds that we can trace is dated 24th April 1816. It appears therefore that Mr. Reynolds entered the service of the Amicable not later than July 1810 and remained with the Society at any rate until April 1816.'[1] A specimen signature is like the writing in the few known manuscripts by Reynolds.

His junior clerkship in the Amicable Society, then, was Reynolds's main employment when he first burst into literature very early in 1814, seven months before he was twenty, as an imitator of the most popular poetic idol of the day, in *Safie, an Eastern Tale.* Of this poem he evidently sent a copy to Byron, to whom it was dedicated and who wrote of it as follows in his Journal for February 20:

> 'Answered—or rather acknowledged—the receipt of young Reynolds's poem, *Safie.* The lad is clever, but much of his thoughts are borrowed—whence, the Reviewers may find out. I hate discouraging a young one; and I think,—though wild and more oriental than he would be, had he seen the scenes where he has placed his tale,—that he has much talent, and, certainly fire enough.'

Byron's letter to Reynolds of the same date, after thanks and good wishes, comments thus:

> 'The poem itself, as the work of a young man, is creditable to your talents, and promises better for future efforts than any which I can now recollect. Whether you intend to pursue your poetical career, I do not know and have no right to inquire—but, in whatever channel your abilities are directed, I think it will be your own fault if they do not eventually lead to distinction.'

Then follows some advice as to the best attitude toward criticism which reads oddly enough from the pen of the author of *English Bards and Scotch Reviewers.* This is a part of it:

> 'The best reply to all objections is to write better, and if your enemies will not then do you justice, the world will. On the other hand, you should not be discouraged; to be opposed is not to be vanquished, though a timid mind is apt to mistake every scratch for a mortal wound.'

The kindness of Byron to his young disciple went still farther, for on February 28 he wrote as follows to his friend Francis Hodgson:

> 'There is a youngster, and a clever one, named Reynolds, who has just published a poem called *Safie,* published by Cawthorne. He is in the most natural and

fearful apprehension of the Reviewers; and as you and I both know by experience the effect of such things upon a *young* mind, I wish *you* would take his production into dissection, and do it *gently.* I cannot, because it is inscribed to me; but I assure you this is not my motive for wishing him to be tenderly entreated, but because I know the misery, at his time of life, of untoward remarks upon first appearance.'

Within a short time after the appearance of *Safie* one of its publishers, John Martin of Holles Street, Cavendish Square, started a periodical called *The Inquirer, or Literary Miscellany,* in the first number of which, dated May 1814, are three contributions signed 'J. H. R.', who beyond any reasonable doubt was John Hamilton Reynolds. Two of these are poems; the third is a prose article **'On the Character of Hamlet'**. The last number of the short-lived *Inquirer,* dated January 1815, contains another poem signed 'J. H. R.'; and in both this and the other numbers there are unsigned articles on the contemporary stage which, in view of Reynolds's known later employment as a dramatic critic and his evident relations with Martin, the publisher, one is tempted to ascribe to him.

In August 1814 Martin and the other publisher of *Safie,* James Cawthorn, brought out a second little book for their young poet, *The Eden of Imagination,* in which the influence of Wordsworth supersedes the influence of Byron.

The *Notes and Queries* article already mentioned attributes to Reynolds 'an Ode on the Overthrow of Napoleon'. No such work appears in the British Museum Catalogue in connexion with Reynolds's name, nor has an inquiry for it brought any reply as yet; but in the *Anti-Jacobin Review and True Churchman's Magazine* for April 1815 there is a review headed and beginning as follows:

> **'An Ode.'** 8vo. pp. 18. Martin, Holles-street. 1815.
>
> 'The lines which bear this laconic title are the substance of a soliloquy of the tyrant of Elba, previous to his return to the scene of his crimes.'

Nearly sixty lines of the **'Ode'** are quoted, the citations making up almost the whole review. From the fact that Martin of Holles Street was one of the two publishers of Reynolds's little books of 1814 and was the sole publisher of *The Inquirer,* it seems probable that this review is of the poem meant by 'T. M. T.'

Late in 1815, when our young Amicable clerk was a little past twenty-one, he appears to have made a connexion with the *Champion* Sunday newspaper which was to be very important for about two years. Keats's letters provide evidence of Reynolds's connexion with *The Champion* during 1817, and with this as a starting-point it is easy to go back through the files and identify a large amount of material in that newspaper as by Reynolds. The earliest *Champion* article that can be confidently assigned to him is a prose appreciation of Wordsworth, thoroughly in harmony with *The Eden of Imagination,* signed 'R.' in the issue of December 10, 1815; and from the beginning of 1816 both prose and poetry signed 'R.' or 'J. H. R.' appear frequently, besides innumerable unsigned theatrical notices of which the vast majority were probably by him as the regular dramatic critic of the journal. A number of the *Champion* poems signed by initials were later reprinted in one or another of the collections known to be by Reynolds, and there are various other bits of evidence that all contributions signed 'J. H. R.' were his, and at least several of those signed 'R.'

One of the 'J. H. R.' articles, in *The Champion* of April 7, 1816, entitled **'The Pilgrimage of Living Poets to the Stream of Castaly'**, is a decidedly interesting 'vision of poets' in which Wordsworth is particularly exalted, and begins with the following sentence which is startlingly prophetic of what came to be Reynolds's attitude toward his own work in poetry:

> 'I am one of those unfortunate youths to whom the Muse has glanced a sparkling of her light—one of those who pant for distinction, but have not within them that immortal power which alone can command it.'

Besides all his newspaper work, Reynolds also published, before the autumn of 1816, *The Naiad: a Tale, with Other Poems.* This collection was issued anonymously; but the last two pieces had appeared in *The Champion* as by 'J. H. R.' and it was *The Naiad* and its companions that Hunt had in mind when he discussed Reynolds with Shelley and Keats. Moreover, Reynolds sent a copy of the little book to Wordsworth with a request for criticism which the Lake poet took all too seriously to hold his young admirer's personal allegiance. A letter from Wordsworth to Reynolds, dated at Rydal Mount, November 28, 1816, first published by Mr. Henry C. Shelley in *The Lamp* in 1904 and later in his *Literary By-Paths in Old England,* contains the following comments:

> . . . 'Your poem is composed with elegance and in a style that accords with the subject, but my opinion on this point might have been of more value if I had seen the Scottish ballad on which your work is founded. You do me the honour of asking me to find fault in order that you may profit by my remarks. . . . I will not scruple to say that your poem would have told more upon me, if it had been shorter. . . . Your fancy is too luxuriant, and riots too much upon its own creations. Can you endure to be told by one whom you are so kind as to say you respect that in his judgment your poem would be better without the first 57 lines (not condemned for their own sakes), and without the last 146, which nevertheless have in themselves much to recommend them? The basis is too narrow for the su-

perstructure, and to me it would have been more striking barely to have hinted at the deserted Fair One and to have left it to the imagination of the reader to dispose of her as he liked. Her fate dwelt upon at such length requires of the reader a sympathy which cannot be furnished without taking the Nymph from the unfathomable abyss of the cerulean waters and beginning afresh upon terra firma. I may be wrong but I speak as I felt, and the most profitable criticism is the record of sensations, provided the person affected be under no partial influence.'

However sound this criticism may be, however studiously polite the letter, it may easily be understood to have had a chilling effect upon the recipient. Reynolds was still very young; he had been for at least two years a great admirer of Wordsworth, whom he obviously imitated in some of the work of this volume; he was brilliant, very ambitious, impetuous and temperamental—no wonder if henceforth he could not look upon Wordsworth with the enthusiasm displayed in *The Eden of Imagination*; no wonder that in a little over two years he could write the 'ante-natal *Peter Bell*'.

Publication of *The Naiad* by Taylor and Hessey, who are remembered chiefly because they gave the world Keats's volumes of 1818 and 1820, began a relationship of Reynolds with that kindly firm which lasted a good many years; but a more important event of 1816 for Reynolds was his introduction to what we now call the Keats circle, though at the time it bore an evil name to many as the Hunt circle. Besides Leigh Hunt, radical editor of *The Examiner,* the painter Haydon was at the moment the most conspicuous member of this group. To him on November 20, 1816, Keats sent his sonnet beginning,

> 'Great spirits now on earth are sojourning';

and the next day Reynolds addressed a **'Sonnet to Haydon'** which appeared in *The Champion* on November 24. On Sunday, December 1, Hunt published in *The Examiner* his famous article on Shelley, Reynolds, and Keats as the most promising young poets in the field; and on December 8 Reynolds attempted payment by printing in *The Champion* a sonnet complimentary to Hunt's *Story of Rimini*. The *Examiner* article calls Reynolds 'John Henry', but by the remark that 'his nature seems very true and amiable' implies personal acquaintance. *Safie* and *The Naiad* are the only writings of Reynolds that Hunt mentions. The first twenty-seven lines of the latter poem are quoted and other extracts are promised for the future—but never given. Whatever interest Hunt had in Reynolds seems quickly to have subsided, for after this first winter of their acquaintance they seldom mention each other, and there are in later letters distinctly unflattering remarks of each about the other.

But with Keats the case was very different. He and Reynolds apparently met this autumn or early winter of

1816, probably at Hunt's, soon were fast friends, and remained such to the last. Though there came a time when the Reynolds sisters ceased to please Keats, nothing in his correspondence indicates other than the friendliest feelings toward their brother John, who in his turn remained steadfastly one of the most valued and useful friends of Keats. It should be remembered, too, that a young man of a mean or jealous spirit might have found Reynolds's position no easy one. He was older than Keats and to some extent an accepted poet when Keats began to publish; but he seems immediately to have recognized his friend's superior genius, and, though for more than a year he continued to cherish ardent poetical ambitions for himself, not the slightest indication of envy or jealousy on his part is known. While Reynolds was still on the staff of *The Champion,* contributing to its columns most of the original poetry they contained, a correspondent wrote to the newspaper as follows:

> 'I have seen some lines in your paper, occasionally, signed J. H. R., which have pleased me much. I think that the writer (whoever he is) can furnish something much better than your favourite Mr. Keats, whom my perverseness of taste forbids me to admire.'

Two weeks later *The Champion* printed Keats's 'Sonnet on the Sea', with the comment that the editor considered this sonnet—

> 'quite sufficient . . . to justify all the praise we have given [the author]—and to prove to our correspondent . . . his superiority over any poetical writer in the *Champion.*—J. H. R. would be the first to acknowledge this himself.'

It is altogether likely that this comment was made with Reynolds's knowledge and consent; at any rate it had no evident effect on his attitude toward Keats. 'I set my heart on having you high,' he once wrote to Keats, 'as you ought to be. Do *you* get Fame, and I shall have it in being your affectionate and steady friend.'

The best biographers of Keats have duly stressed the services rendered him by Reynolds: the happy rewriting of the preface to *Endymion* that was caused by Reynolds's criticism of the first draft; the defence of Keats against the *Quarterly* which Reynolds printed in an Exeter newspaper and Hunt reprinted in *The Examiner*; perhaps above all the sympathy of a kindred spirit which Keats's letters indicate he found in Reynolds. A large part of his most significant discussion of his art is to be found in those letters to Reynolds.

More potent than Keats in the life of this friend, however, was a certain dark-eyed girl of Exeter with whom Reynolds seems to have fallen in love not long after his acquaintance with Keats began. Under the spell of her and the beautiful Devon scenes in which she dwelt, and

of poetic rivalry with his ardent young friend Keats, the modest and never too steadfast genius of Reynolds made its most notable efflorescence. This is revealed especially in **'The Romance of Youth'** and such shorter poems as **'Devon'** in *The Garden of Florence* collection, as well as in several charming songs and sonnets. This Exeter girl was Miss Eliza Powell Drewe, of whom little is known except that at the time of her marriage she was described as 'eldest daughter of the late W. Drewe, Esq., of South street'; that she had dark hair and eyes; that she (or her worldly-wise family) persuaded her literary lover to become a solicitor. Reynolds's poems of 1817 indicate a quick and happy courtship. For a considerable part of the summer he was in Devon, evidently near the sea, and about the end of the year he visited at Exeter, as we know from Keats's acting for him as dramatic critic of *The Champion.*

Evidently Reynolds did not return to *The Champion* on coming back to London, for there is no indication of work by him in that newspaper in 1818, and in a letter of January 23 Keats mentions Dilke's 'having taken *The Champion* theatricals'. During February 1818, according to Keats, Reynolds contributed to *The Yellow Dwarf,* a short-lived periodical issued by Leigh Hunt's brother John; but anything like his literary activity of the preceding years was prevented by a serious illness which Keats frequently mentions in letters between February 21 and June 10. During, or perhaps just before, this illness, Reynolds evidently made that 'great renunciation' of which he several times wrote with a charming mixture of regret, misgiving, and loving if reluctant acceptance of the supposedly prudent decision. The 'Farewell to the Muses' that Reynolds inscribed in the volume of Shakespeare he gave to Keats, and in which Keats afterward wrote his 'Bright star' sonnet, is dated February 14, 1818; and George Keats's comment of March 18 on Reynolds's illness as 'deadening his hopes of . . . advance in business' seems to imply entrance into 'business' before that date. Our most exact information on this matter comes from Dilke, who succeeded Reynolds on *The Champion* (as has been noted) and many years later was associated with him in proprietorship of *The Athenæum.* 'Rice'—says Dilke, as quoted by Forman—'suggested that he should become a lawyer, and his relation, Mr. Fladgate—himself a literary man in early life and editor of the "Sun" newspaper—consented to receive him as an Articled Pupil, and dear generous noble James Rice—the best, and in his quaint way one of the wittiest and wisest men I ever knew—paid the fee or stamp or whatever it is called—about £110 I believe—and promised if he ever succeeded to his father's business to take him in partner. He not only kept his word, but in a few years gave up the business to him.'

When Keats, then, writes to Reynolds from Scotland in July 1818, he makes jocular remarks about 'you and

Frank Floodgate in the office' (the Mr. Fladgate mentioned above had a son Frank who also was an 'articled clerk') and declares that 'now one of the first pleasures I look to is your happy Marriage'. But, though Reynolds spent six weeks in Devon during September and October and gave Keats the impression of being 'almost over-happy' and 'going on gloriously' (letter to Dilke of September 21), his marriage was yet far in the future, and we do not know why unless it was deemed prudent to wait till he became well established in business. It was during his rather long holiday for a would-be solicitor that he contributed to an Exeter newspaper the important defence of Keats against the *Quarterly* to which Hunt gave the more general publicity afforded by reprinting in his *Examiner.* Toward the end of the year Reynolds went again to Devonshire because of 'a great Misfortune in the Drewe Family—old Drewe has been dead some time; and lately George Drewe expired in a fit'. (So Keats wrote in the chronicle letter to his brother and sister-in-law which he finished January 4, 1819.) Presumably George Drewe was a brother of Reynolds's sweetheart.

Whatever good intentions of settling down to business Reynolds may have had when he renounced the Muses on St. Valentine's Day of 1818, he seldom managed for any considerable period of time to refrain from literary indulgence in some form. In October, as already noted, he published his long article in defence of Keats. By the end of the year, according to Keats, he had 'become an Edinburgh Reviewer'. In April 1819 he dashed off his famous 'ante-natal *Peter Bell*'; and in July and at intervals for some months thereafter his *One, Two, Three, Four, Five: by Advertisement; a Musical Entertainment in one Act,* was played with considerable success. Early in the next summer he published *The Fancy* (1820); still earlier in 1821 *The Garden of Florence*; and with the August number for the latter year his prose articles in the *London Magazine* began. All these lapses from strict attention to solicitorship occurred before his marriage.

Reynolds's brilliant biographical sketch of Peter Corcoran, pretended author of *The Fancy,* suggests a possible explanation of his own Jacob-like service for his Devon love. Some details as to Peter Corcoran are certainly true of Reynolds himself (e. g. birth at Shrewsbury in September 1794, and study of the law); but some are not true (e. g. attendance at Oxford and early death). Nevertheless, when Mr. John Masefield reprinted *The Fancy* in 1905, he accepted as substantially autobiographical the whole story of Corcoran's passion for sport, his trouble with his sweetheart because of it, his neglect of his profession and even of poetry. If this view were sound, however, there should be more support for it in the contemporary comments on Reynolds, especially in the letters of Keats and other friends. These show, as we have seen, the most intimate relations with the Drewe family to the end of 1818, and the letters of Keats give no hint of excessive devotion to sport on Reynolds's part. Moreover, he was too busy: throughout 1817—the year in which Peter Corcoran is said to have become a continual visitor at the Fives-Court—Reynolds was an industrious dramatic critic and was in friendly competition with Keats in ardent devotion to poetry; and the literary accomplishments summarized in the preceding paragraph, plus the study necessary to make him a solicitor by 1822 or earlier, seem incompatible with anything like the absorption in sport that is attributed to Peter Corcoran. No doubt Reynolds's long connexion with the stage brought him into contact with the 'night life' of the metropolis, and he obviously obtained an expert reporter's knowledge of the activities of 'the fancy'. He may have felt at times that he enjoyed such frivolities too much—may even, like many another gay young lover, have been reproved and disciplined by his *inamorata*; but there is no contemporary evidence that as self-portraiture his characterization of Peter Corcoran contains more than a germ of truth.

However, so much literary activity after an alleged 'Farewell to the Muses' may well have displeased the young lady and her family as not aiding that progress in business necessary for the support of a wife; and if along with this there was even a little tendency toward over-enjoyment of sports, a period of estrangement may have occurred. In Keats's remarks to and about Reynolds after the letter that was completed January 4, 1819, there is no further mention of matrimonial prospects—a fact which may or may not be significant. But in September 1820 Reynolds wrote to Taylor from Exmouth in gay spirits except for some worry about Keats. And at any rate by the time of the publication of *The Garden of Florence* the estrangement, if there had been one, was ended, for in the library of the Marquess of Crewe there is a copy of that little volume bearing in Reynolds's hand the following inscription at the top of the fly-leaf: 'Eliza Powell Drewe from her affectionate J. H. Reynolds 25th June 1821.'

The long-delayed marriage occurred finally August 31, 1822. In a brief notice in the *London Magazine* for October the bridegroom is described as 'J. H. Reynolds, Esq., Solicitor, of Great Marlborough-street, London'. James Hessey, of Taylor and Hessey, who were then publishers of the *London Magazine,* wrote enthusiastically to the peasant poet John Clare as follows:

> 'Reynolds is gone off to Exeter to be married, tomorrow is the happy day that is to witness the union of as interesting a couple as I ever met—a fine sensible high-spirited generous warm-hearted young fellow in the prime of youth and health and a pretty, intelligent, modest, interesting young girl, warmly attached to him as he is to her.'

Hood left a 'humourous account of Reynolds's wedding drawn up in the form of a State procession', which may be seen in full in Henry C. Shelley's *Literary By-Paths in Old England.* There is thus every indication that, whatever caused the delay, the final consummation of the wedding was a completely happy event.

Before proceeding with the career of Reynolds as a married man and solicitor, it is desirable to pick up a few scattered threads of biography, mainly literary, from the years of bachelor servitude to his 'dark lady'. The first has to do with the real 'hit' of his career—his 'run-away ring at Wordsworth's *Peter Bell*', which Shelley called the 'ante-natal Peter' because published before the real one. Early in April 1819 London newspapers carried an advertisement to the effect that 'in a few days will be published, Peter Bell, a Tale in Verse, by William Wordsworth, Esq.' Reynolds heard of this announced poem and, according to Keats's account, 'took it into his head to write a skit upon it called Peter Bell. He did it as soon as thought on, it is to be published this morning [April 15] and comes out before the real Peter Bell.' Accordingly the following advertisement appeared April 16: 'This day is published, in octavo, price 2*s.* 6*d.*, *Peter Bell:—a Lyrical Ballad.* "I do affirm that I am the real Simon Pure." Taylor and Hessey.' And this anticipatory parody Keats reviewed for Hunt's *Examiner* of April 25.

Samuel Taylor Coleridge, watchful friend of Wordsworth, saw an advertisement of the alleged 'Simon Pure' *Peter Bell* and wrote at once to the publishers, saying that he knew of *Peter Bell* as a poem of Wordsworth's, but had not heard of its publication. He protested against an attack on a work still in manuscript and asked for an opportunity to see the parody. The publishers at once sent him a copy of the little book and a letter containing the following interesting explanation and comment, which is in essential harmony with the views of Keats and a good many other admirers of Wordsworth at his best. Taylor and Hessey wrote:

> 'It was written by a sincere admirer of Mr. Wordsworth's poetry, by a person who has been his advocate in every place where he found opportunity of expressing an opinion on the subject, and we really think that when the original poem is published he will feel all the intense regard for the beauties which distinguishes the true lover of Mr. Wordsworth's poetry. The immediate cause of his writing this burlesque imitation of the "Idiot Boy" was the announcement of a new poem with so untimely a title as that of "Peter Bell". He thought that all Mr. Wordsworth's excellencies might be displayed in some work which should be free from those ridiculous associations which vulgar names give rise to, and as a Friend he felt vexed that unnecessary obstacles were thus again thrown in the way of Mr. Wordsworth's popularity.
>
> . . . . .
>
> 'We are placed in a situation which enables us to see the effect of those peculiarities which this writer wishes Mr. Wordsworth to renounce, and we must say that

they grieve his friends, gladden his adversaries, and are the chief, if not only, impediments to the favourable reception of his poems among all classes of readers.'

The whole of Taylor and Hessey's letter, as well as Coleridge's reply, may be seen in Mr. H. C. Shelley's *Literary By-Paths in Old England.*

The striking success of the anonymous ***Peter Bell*** is indicated by the fact that a second edition was advertised within two weeks of the publication of the first. Everybody seems to have enjoyed the *jeu d'esprit* except ardent admirers of Wordsworth who were unwilling to take a joke; and from this time Reynolds, in verse, was mainly a joker.

His 'musical entertainment' of 1819 received its odd name, ***One, Two, Three, Four, Five: by Advertisement,*** from the fact that the principal actor, a mimic, answering an advertisement, impersonates and imitates five noted figures on the stage of the day. Trivial as it seems, this effort was played as part of the bill at the English Opera House, London, more than fifty times, beginning July 17, and was the means of launching John Reeve upon a very successful career as a comedian. Keats was encouraged by this and by the periodical writings of Reynolds to think that he might make a living by his pen—Reynolds obviously could if he had not taken up the law, why not Keats?

Reynolds the humourist, the parodist, the burlesquer, is predominant in ***The Fancy*** of 1820; but during the summer of 1821 Reynolds, the friend of Keats, put into a little volume all that he cared to preserve of the serious poetry which for the most part he had written three or four years previously in a sort of rivalry with the friend now dead. This is ***The Garden of Florence and Other Poems*** by 'John Hamilton'.

In 1821, also, began the connexion with the *London Magazine* which 'T. M. T.' in *Notes and Queries* declared to be 'the only true period of his literary life. He now became associated with Charles Lamb, Hazlitt, Allan Cunningham, George Darley, Barry Cornwall, Thomas Hood, and others, who met regularly at the hospitable table of the publishers [Taylor and Hessey], and by whom his wit and brilliancy were appreciated; and he was at that time one of the most brilliant men I have ever known.' Another acquaintance, writer of the obituary notice of Reynolds in *The Athenœum* for November 27, 1852, said: 'In every number of the *London* the traces of his light and pleasant pen were visible; and at every social meeting of the contributors . . . his familiar voice was heard, followed by a laugh as by an echo.'

It is not now possible to identify work by Reynolds in 'every number'; but from the testimony of Hood, assistant editor of the magazine at this time, we know that he wrote the series of prose articles purporting to be by 'Edward Herbert'. These are letters from a Londoner to a country family, the Powells (note that Reynolds's fiancée was Eliza *Powell* Drewe), dealing with such topics as the coronation of George IV, Greenwich Hospital, the green-room of a theatre, the inside of a stage-coach, the cockpit royal, etc. Apparently these 'Edward Herbert' articles attracted considerable attention, even in a magazine that was running the *Essays of Elia* and *Confessions of an English Opium-Eater*; for advertisements indicate a plan to publish them in book form 'with etchings by George Cruikshank'. The book seems never to have been issued, but two of Cruikshank's etchings for it were said by the late Bertram Dobell to have been in existence as late as 1906. Between August 1821 and February 1824 there were eight of these 'Edward Herbert' articles in the *London Magazine.*

Meanwhile, married man and solicitor though he was, Reynolds had thrust his finger into other literary pies. 'T. M. T.'s' often quoted article of 1856 says that he 'had a hand in preparing more than one of Mathews' monologues'. These were entertainments given year after year, single-handed, by the very popular actor Charles Mathews, who impersonated a whole series of comic characters in an evening, usually calling his entertainment, 'Mr. Mathews at Home'. According to some unsigned reminiscences in the *New Monthly Magazine* for 1838 under the title, 'The Manager's Note-Book', Mathews's entertainment for 1822, first produced March 11 and called 'The Youthful Days of Mr. Mathews', was written by 'Messrs. Peake and H. Reynolds' (that is, Hamilton Reynolds, as he came to be called frequently). The next year Mathews was in America, and after his return he gave an entirely new 'monopolylogue' entitled 'A Trip to America'—'written by Mr. J. Smith, assisted by Mr. J. H. Reynolds.' And on March 10, 1825, Mathews gave another new 'at home' called 'Memorandum Book', 'from the pens of two gentlemen who had before so ably assisted him, Messrs. Peake and Reynolds.' This last statement finds support in a letter of January 8, 1825, from Mathews to his wife: 'I am delighted at the coöperation of Peake and Reynolds; but I hope they will work.' Mrs. Mathews in a foot-note says that the Reynolds meant is 'author of *The Garden of Florence*, etc., a charming writer'. She also cites a letter by Peake, who was a minor dramatist of the period, in which he mentions 'my worthy colleague J. H. Reynolds'. Neither Mrs. Mathews's *Memoirs* of her husband nor the *New Monthly* article gives any hint of further participation by Reynolds in the Mathews entertainments, but Hood had a part in some later ones.

Soon after Reynolds's first work for Mathews he seems, according to a tradition in the Hood family, to have had a hand with Hood, and apparently Peake, in 'the operatic drama of Gil Blas', which was played at the English Opera House more than thirty times beginning August 15, 1822—a little more than two weeks before Reynolds's wedding. A notice of the piece in *The Mirror of the Stage* for August 26 includes this comment: 'This then is the product of two or three, or more authors, and a *summer's preparation.* We regret that its attainment is so little profitable. The *material* of the piece is ascribed to Mr. Peake; and this we can easily discover, by the frequent attempts at punning.' Hood's daughter, however, declared, 'My father also assisted my uncle Reynolds in the dramatising of Gil Blas'; and though she is wrong as to the date and the place of presentation, she is likely to be right as to the fact of collaboration. Moreover, the contemporary comments indicate several authors; the amount of attention given the piece in the *London Magazine* suggests a friendly attitude toward it; and certainly 'attempts at punning' are no bar to Reynolds and Hood as co-authors, whatever may have been the reputation of Peake in that regard.

Reynolds's most important and successful collaboration with Hood came some years later, in the ***Odes and Addresses to Great People,*** published anonymously early in 1825 and reaching a third edition the next year. This book was generally considered the best collection of humourous and satirical verse since the *Rejected Addresses* of 1812, and Coleridge paid it the high compliment of insisting in letters to Lamb that he could think of no living person but Lamb who could have written it. A considerable majority of the poems have generally been attributed to Hood, and the whole collection has been reprinted in editions of Hood's works. Hood himself, however, in a copy of the book formerly in the possession of Buxton Forman, indicated that Reynolds was the author of the five following poems:

> Ode to Mr. M'Adam,
> Address to Mr. Dymoke,
> Address to Sylvanus Urban,
> Address to R. W. Elliston,
> Address to the Dean and Chapter of Westminster;

and that both he and Reynolds participated in the

> Address to Maria Darlington.

But a copy given by Reynolds to Richard Monckton Milnes (afterward Lord Houghton), and now in the possession of the Marquess of Crewe, contains very circumstantial indications of authorship in Reynolds's hand, agreeing with Hood as far as the six poems mentioned above are concerned, but claiming for himself a share with Hood in five other poems, namely:

> Ode to Mr. Graham,
> Ode to Joseph Grimaldi,
> Address to the Steam Washing Company,
> Ode to Captain Parry,
> Ode to W. Kitchener, M.D.

It is possible that the somewhat disgruntled Reynolds of his later years, having failed to live up to the promise of his youth, claimed a larger share than was really his in the most successful book in which he had a hand; yet his attitude in his correspondence with Milnes (as will be seen) was modest in relation to his own attainments, and his statements as to authorship must be considered to carry a certain weight.

The fact seems to be that for a number of years Reynolds, having a supposed gainful occupation as a solicitor, rather freely aided Hood in various ventures and paid little heed to credit for himself. *Whims and Oddities,* the *Comic Annual, Hood's Own,* all contain poems identifiable as by Reynolds yet usually printed with Hood's works. The two men seem to have met in 1821, probably through the connexion of both with the *London Magazine.* In his *Literary Reminiscences* of 1839, commenting on his editorial duties in the heyday of that magazine, Hood wrote: 'How I used to look forward to Elia! and backward for Hazlitt, and all around for Edward Herbert!' The earliest of Hood's longer poems, *Lycus the Centaur,* appeared in the *London Magazine* in 1822; and when, five years later, it was put into a book with *The Plea of the Midsummer Fairies* and other poems, a dedication to Reynolds read as follows:

> 'My dear Reynolds: You will remember "Lycus".—It was written in the pleasant spring-time of our friendship, and I am glad to maintain that association, by connecting your name with the Poem. It will gratify me to find that you regard it with the old partiality for the writings of each other, which prevailed in those days. For my own sake, I must regret that your pen goes now into far other records than those which used to delight me. Your true Friend and Brother, T. Hood.'

And again in 1831, when Hood made an illustrated book of *The Dream of Eugene Aram,* he honoured his brother-in-law with a dedication.

Hood had married Reynolds's sister Jane in 1825, and his published letters indicate very happy relations with his wife's family. With the somewhat peppery 'J. H. R.' indeed there came sometime, according to Hood's daughter, a misunderstanding; but her language is vague, being merely an expression of regret that the friendship of the two men 'did not survive to the end'. For many years, nevertheless, there were close relations, both personal and literary—relations so intimate, in fact, that the *Athenæum* obituary notice remarked of Reynolds, 'With him has probably passed away the person most competent to write the Life now wanted of Thomas Hood.'

The literary activities thus far indicated were by no means all in which Reynolds engaged. According to the friends who wrote about him in *The Athenæum* and in *Notes and Queries* within a short time after his death,

he contributed to the *Edinburgh Review,* the *Retrospective Review,* the *Westminster Review.* Keats, about the end of 1818 (as has been noted), mentions his becoming 'an Edinburgh Reviewer'; and a letter by Hazlitt indicates that the opportunity came through Hazlitt's intercession with Jeffrey. Precisely what article or articles he contributed, however, has not yet come to light; and the same is true with regard to the other reviews mentioned. Keats also writes of an offer to Reynolds by 'Constable, the bookseller', of 'ten guineas a sheet to write for his Magazine—it is an Edinburgh one, which Blackwood's started up in opposition to'. The old *Scots Magazine* is meant; and in its numbers for October 1819 and August 1820 are articles entitled **'Boswell Redivivus, a Dream'**, and **'Living Authors, a Dream'**, which are only slightly different from contributions by 'J. H. R.' to *The Champion* during 1816. Somebody evidently discovered the way in which Reynolds was earning his 'ten guineas a sheet', for in the *Scots Magazine* for October 1820 appeared the following 'Notice':

> 'A Correspondent has brought a charge of plagiarism against the writer of **"Living Authors, a Dream"**, which appeared in one of our late numbers. We have too high an opinion of the writer's originality to suppose that any other person ever dreamed his dream; but, like people who are fond of repeating their dreams, he may, for anything we know to the contrary, have related it before. We wish, to put the matter out of doubt, that he would send us his *third* dream, without delay, and, if it is akin to the former, and has never been seen elsewhere, the accusation will be laid to rest.'

Apparently this ended the relations of Reynolds with Constable.

His most important connexion with a periodical after the days of the *London Magazine* was with *The Athenæum,* of which he was one of the original proprietors when it was founded in 1828. He 'retired from proprietorship' in 1831, but continued to write for the journal occasionally for most of the rest of his life. The reminiscences of C. W. Dilke, who also was one of the original proprietors, include some letters by Reynolds— one of February 15, 1831, for example, protesting against the lowering of the price of single numbers of *The Athenæum* from eightpence to fourpence. Poems identifiable as his are to be found in this journal at intervals from 1832 to 1848, and he contributed many reviews. Early in 1832 appeared what was apparently intended for the beginning of a new series of 'Edward Herbert' letters; but from the lack of others we must conclude either that the name had lost its potency or that the author failed to provide the letters.

During the latter thirties and the forties Reynolds sustained intermittent relations with other magazines. 'Hamilton Reynolds' appears as a contributor to both *Bentley's Miscellany* and the *New Monthly Magazine* in

1837 and 1838. Running through four numbers of *Ainsworth's Magazine* for 1844 is **'Oriana and Vesperella, or The City of Pearls'**, a story of oriental setting, said to be by 'John Hamilton'—which had been Reynolds's transparent *nom-de-plume* for **The Garden of Florence**; and farther on in the same volume of *Ainsworth's* is **'An Odelet to Master Izaak Walton'**, also by 'John Hamilton', which later provided the subject for an etching by the young Whistler. And again in *Bentley's Miscellany*, as late as 1847, were poems, this time signed by Reynolds's full name, entitled **'The Two Enthusiasts'**.

He continued also to be interested in the stage. On January 6, 1838, a farce called **Confounded Foreigners** was first acted at the Theatre Royal, Haymarket, and was favourably noticed in *The Athenæum* of January 13 as 'the joint production of Mr. George Dance and Mr. Hamilton Reynolds'; but a week later a signed letter by Reynolds was printed, saying that Dance suggested 'the idea of the subject', but that the 'construction of the plot and the entire dialogue' were the writer's own. During the same year this piece was printed as by 'J. H. Reynolds, Esq.', in volume three of *The Acting National Drama,* 'edited by Benjamin Webster, Comedian'.

Reynolds's name was also considered worth mention on the title-page, along with Hood's, as a contributor to *Sporting,* a handsomely illustrated volume of 1838, edited by the then famous person who called himself 'Nimrod'. Reynolds's sole identifiable contribution to the book is a poem in *ottava rima* stanzas on two foxhounds belonging to a certain sporting member of Parliament.

Details of Reynolds's legal career are almost wholly lacking. At the time of his marriage in 1822, J. H. Reynolds, Solicitor, was of Great Marlborough Street; later London directories give the following addresses: in 1832, 27, Golden Square; in 1836-8, 10, Great Marlborough Street; in 1841-2, 10, Adam Street, Adelphi; and letters of 1846 from him to Richard Monckton Milnes give his address then as 88, Guildford Street, Russell Square. There seems to be no reason to doubt the statement of Dilke, who from his long acquaintance with Reynolds and their association on *The Athenæum* must have known the facts, that Reynolds 'threw away this certain fortune' offered by the partnership given him by Rice. Presumably he neglected business for the sake of writing and failed to 'make a go' of either. Possibly also convivial habits, of which there are at least hints in his palmiest days—and more than hints if he should be identified thoroughly with 'Peter Corcoran'—became an increasing handicap. The nearly contemporary notices, already so often quoted, in *The Athenæum* and in *Notes and Queries,* contain the following significant comments:

> *Notes and Queries*: 'J. H. Reynolds was a man of genius, who wanted the devoted purpose and the sustain-

ing power which are requisite to its development; and the world, its necessities and its pleasures, led him astray from literature. . . . Reynolds, though full of literary energy at that time, was always hurried and uncertain. He indeed played the old game of fast and loose between law and literature, pleasure and study.'

> *The Athenæum*: 'This divided duty, however, is rarely successful:—the law spoiled his literature, and his love of literature and society interfered with the drudging duties of the lawyer. The contest ended only with his life.'

On his personal and family life we have just one tragic flashlight, in a letter from John Taylor to John Clare dated January 9, 1835: 'Our Friend Reynolds . . . has lost a Child—but she was his only Child, a Daughter, ten years of age, & I understand he grieves for her Loss.' . . .

Probably the most striking characteristic of Reynolds as a writer is the extent to which he was a weathercock. He began with a school-boyish imitation of Byron's Eastern romances, and later (in 'The Fields of Tothill' in **The Fancy**) attempted the style of *Beppo* and *Don Juan.* He wrote nature poetry and ballads of humble life (in **The Naiad** volume) in direct and serious imitation of Wordsworth; then turned and, in the very amusing **Peter Bell,** parodied Wordsworth's most pedestrian manner. In **'The Naiad'** he elaborated a Scotch ballad in a style almost equally compounded of Scott and Hunt. He wrote a good many sonnets and versified stories from Boccaccio in friendly competition with Keats; and during the same period he undertook a long Spenserian poem which, though essentially autobiographical, has its points of relationship with Beattie's *Minstrel* and Shelley's *Alastor.* After success with **Peter Bell** and his reputation among his friends had convinced him that he was chiefly a wit, he joined Hood in punning verses on contemporary celebrities.

In prose also he tried nearly all kinds of writing. His earliest known prose article is **'On the Character of Hamlet'**, and during the brief period of his life when he was, as we may assume, exclusively a writer, he was dramatic reporter for a Sunday newspaper. To that paper he contributed also a good deal of literary criticism—on Wordsworth, Chaucer, and others—and some 'vision papers' that were largely critical. His sketch of 'Peter Corcoran' in **The Fancy** is good biographical narrative. The 'Edward Herbert' papers in the *London Magazine* are fluent sketches of current events and interesting places about town. For *The Athenæum* he did journeyman reviewing of new books; and he beguiled the tedium of solicitorship by undertaking magazine fiction. His several dramatic attempts, though containing songs, are mostly prose.

Of all this prose the criticism is most worth resuscitation. What he had to say of Wordsworth, both seriously and in satire, is of distinct interest; and his defence of Keats against the *Quarterly* is one of the most penetrating and valuable of the early comments on that abused young poet.

The young Reynolds was in some respects amazingly like the young Keats—eager for sense impressions, enthusiastically devoted to poetry, bent upon writing—writing—whether or not he had anything to say. Considering its very simple story, **Safie** is spun out to surprising length; displays, for the product of a lad of nineteen, remarkable ingenuity in saying a little with all possible variety. Wordsworth's comments (quoted on page 17, above) indicate how **'The Naiad'**, likewise, was padded. The later narratives from Boccaccio have more action, move more directly, are less compounded of 'words, words'; but the tendency toward over-elaboration is as marked in **'The Romance of Youth'** as it is in *Endymion.*

The fault seems to have been primarily a lack of power of selection. Words, images—sometimes even thoughts—crowded in and were heaped up beyond measure. He dashed off what occurred to his fertile mind and had not enough patience in revision or power of self-criticism to prune down and perfect his work. Very often there are striking expressions; phrases, lines, or short passages of genuine beauty or power; but too seldom is the poetic mood sustained. In brief, fixed forms, such as the sonnet, Reynolds frequently did well; but even here he shows deficiency in ability to polish.

In early life, when he spent much time in Devon near the sea, he had a genuine Wordsworthian love of the beautiful nature about him, and expressed that love worthily and well in such poems as **'Devon'** and **'The Wood'**. There is fanciful charm in his treatment of fairy lore and real lyrical beauty in several songs. Such songs as the one with the refrain, 'And think of me', and the one beginning, 'By the river' (pages 143 and 153), surprise the reader by their foretaste of Tennyson's early work, as in the handling of double rimes, especially with verb forms in 'eth'.

Curiously enough, some of Reynolds's best poetry expresses his renunciation of poetry—the sonnets from the preface to **The Fancy**; the 'Farewell to the Muses' inscribed in the copy of Shakespeare which he gave to Keats; the lighter but in some parts charming verses of dedication in **The Garden of Florence.**

Of his satirical and humorous verses little need be said. **Peter Bell** speaks eloquently for itself; it is still, as it always was, one of the best parodies of Wordsworth. But the wit of such work as the **Odes and Addresses,** which deal mostly with persons and events now forgotten or known only to specialists in the period, is sadly dulled. Reynolds wrote, too, in an age when even so

great a man as Lamb considered punning to be a large element of wit, and the effect of that view on lesser men is not always pleasant to contemplate.

All in all, however, though the imperfections of Reynolds's work be granted, he scarcely deserves remembrance solely as a friend to whom Keats wrote important letters. He was a real personality in his time, even among men far greater than himself; and he wrote a considerable amount of both prose and verse of decided value to students of literature because of the ways in which it reflected current movements, and of interest, also, to readers—'few, though fit'—who have learned or are willing to learn that even the minor poetry, the minor prose, of a past epoch has its qualities.

Note

1. From a letter by W. W. Williamson, Assistant Actuary of the Norwich Union, to the editor of this volume, dated March 18, 1927.

Peter F. Morgan (essay date winter 1962)

SOURCE: Morgan, Peter F. "John Hamilton Reynolds and Thomas Hood." *Keats-Shelley Journal* 11 (winter 1962): 83-95.

[*In the following essay, Morgan discusses the literary collaboration of Reynolds with his brother-in-law Thomas Hood.*]

In this paper I intend to give a chronological account of the relationship between Keats's friend, John Hamilton Reynolds, and Thomas Hood, bringing to light aspects of their careers not dealt with in previous studies.[1]

In June 1821, soon after becoming an assistant to Taylor and Hessey in editing their *London Magazine,* Hood became acquainted with Reynolds, who had for some time been a contributor to it. On 2 November Taylor wrote to John Clare, "I hope you will like our old Friend Peter in his new Capacity of Shewman of the City *Lions* as the Curiosities of this great Capital are called—There is another Peter who resembles him so much as to be sometimes taken for his Brother, his name is Incog. but you shall see him when you come."[2] "Our old Friend Peter" was "Peter Corcoran," the author of **The Fancy,** that is, Reynolds, and "Incog.," Hood, two of whose contributions in the November *London,* for example, were followed by this abbreviation; it appears that they were both contributing to the often facetious editorial "Lion's Head."

The two attended the Magazine dinner on 6 December, at which Reynolds, with Charles Lamb and James Rice, was "particularly lively and facetious."[3] In a paper signed "Cogin" in the *London* for January 1822 it was undoubtedly Hood who recorded this his first dinner with "my ingenious and respected friend R. . . . I was delighted with his right merrie conceites, and the happy tone of his conversation; and I wished, which has since been realized, that the born friendship of that night might be of age in somewhat less than twenty-one years."[4] On 12 January Taylor's father referred to the two side by side, "How does Mr. Reynolds stand the cut up in the Drama—Is Mr. Hood in this number."[5]

In the autumn of this year 1822, Reynolds went down to Exeter to be married. On 30 August Hessey wrote to Clare, "tomorrow is to be the happy day. . . . Each of us is to send him a letter on his Wedding, and you must contribute your offering in Poetry or Prose or both."[6] Hood's contribution was a mock description of the wedding procession.[7] In October the "Lion's Head" growled that "A welcome paper from the *late* Mr. Edward Herbert . . . has just given us a very pleasant evidence of his continued existence."[8] On 8 October Hessey wrote to Taylor, "Theodore is very well, riding his Hobby . . . unmercifully. . . . I have not seen Reynolds lately. He has married a wife etc.—" The next day however he wrote, "Reynolds was here this morning—he is very well and comfortable."[9]

Throughout this year Hood's intimacy with Reynolds had put him on close terms with the latter's family—particularly with his sister Jane, to whom he became engaged in the autumn.[10] In the November *London* Reynolds introduced into his "Edward Herbert" letter to Exeter friends an engraving of a cockfight and exclaimed, "I wish your cousin Theodore were here; he would make the cocks crow again!"[11] Perhaps the high spirits of the two friends together were sometimes too much for Hessey; on 22 February 1823 he wrote to Taylor, "Thomas will tell you whether Reynolds can come—if he does not you may as well bring Hood with you, but it would not be comfortable to bring them purposely together."[12]

In April Hood and Reynolds were listed in a letter Clare wrote to Hessey concerning his *Village Minstrel,* "I would like to make your London friends a present of a Copy Cunningham & Reynolds & Hood"[13]; on 2 September Thomas Bennion, one of Clare's chief London correspondents and Taylor and Hessey's servant, referred to as "Thomas" above, wrote to Clare, "i [sic] have remembered you to Mr Hood and to Mr Reynolds & cc"[14]; but it is easy to infer that they were not really interested in the country poet. Hood and Reynolds were also mentioned together in an imploring letter to Hessey from T. G. Wainewright, who had been ill, "Don't like to teize Mr Taylor personally but persuade him as a good work to come with you today. . . . Allan [Cunningham] writes me word *he* is ill too which I truly regret I hoped to have seen Reynolds but he [verb omit-

ted] a similar excuse. So you see I have nobody besides yourself and whoever you will bring. I have some things to shew Hood I think he will like."[15]

The *London* for October contained **"A Chit Chat Letter . . . from Ned Ward, jun. a Fellow in London, to Anthony Wood, Jun. a Fellow at Oxford."** "Ned Ward, jun." was a pen-name of Reynolds and Wood sounds like Hood. The author wrote in doggerel verse to his friend:

> who (so dreaming thought will be!)
> May now be tilting pens with me. . . .
> 'Tis getting late:—Oh, that's no matter—
> Here! stay—there's brandy—there's the water.[16]

Brandy and water, it seems, remained an enthusiasm of Reynolds until late in life.[17] He was in fact away from London at this time. On 9 October Hessey wrote to Taylor, "on my way home from the Coach I called at Reynolds' where I learned that Mrs. R. was very unwell and that Hood was *very well* & had been there the previous Night. He has taken [word illegible] I suppose for he has not been near me. . . . Reynolds has not even written to his own family ever since he went—he has been living in Cottage near to Plymouth enjoying complete freedom & forgetfulness of all London Matters."[18] Eleven days later Hessey wrote again, "Reynolds is returned to Town, but I have not seen him yet—he told Hood he should send something."[19]

There are no contributions in the *London* identified as Hood's after July 1823; it is likely that he left soon after this date.[20] Reynolds did not leave until the autumn of 1824.[21]

Hood's tasks for Taylor and Hessey had not been altogether contributory and menial; a letter from Bernard Barton dated 11 February 1823 shows that he was working on a miscellany for them.[22] On 2 October that year Hood wrote, probably to Archibald Constable, referring both to the miscellany and to his own poems:

Lower Street, Islington

Oct 2 1823

Sir

When I had the pleasure of meeting you in town,—you were kind enough to express a desire to serve me, and accepting your offer as frankly as it was made, I will tell you where I think it lies in your power to do me a kindness.—My friends Messrs Taylor & Hessey & myself are partners in a work which I am to edite,—it is intended to consist of Poems by Living Authors,—and it is important to our undertaking that we should have something by Sir Walter Scott.—I have written to himself to request this favour & judging that you possess some interest with him, I shall feel much obliged by any thing you will do in aid of my application.—I have already obtained the assistance of many of my Friends here Mr Procter,—Mr Allan Cunningham,—Mr Lamb.—Mr Reynolds—John Clare etc. & if you can help me to obtain such a name as Sir Walter Scott's it will go far towards my success.—Perhaps at the same time you might be able to render me a like assistance with Mr Wilson or others of your Northern Poets—but I will not trespass too much upon your kindness.

I propose to publish, in the ensuing year—a Collection of my own Poems etc.—& if I should not print them on my own account I may trouble you to look at them.—I owe you many thanks for the friendly interest you have expressed towards me, & which I beg you to accept.

I am Sir

Your mo obedt St.

Thos. Hood[23]

Unfortunately, nothing immediately came of these suggestions.

After Hood left the *London* he worked with Reynolds on their **Odes and Addresses,** which were published in February 1825. Attributions among these are not made easier by three listings in addition to those hitherto well-known.[24] John Payne Collier reported in his *Old Man's Diary* a conversation with Reynolds of 27 October 1833 in which Hood was allowed the authorship of the poems concerning only Martin, Grimaldi, Sylvanus Urban, Parry, and Ireland.[25] On the other hand, Hannah Lawrance, an old friend of Hood, reminiscing in the *British Quarterly,* October 1867, attributed to Reynolds the poems on Sylvanus Urban, Elliston, and Darlington, and to Hood that on Ireland.[26] Finally, the late Mr. Tage Bull kindly informed me that he had a copy of the **Odes and Addresses** which once belonged to Frederick Locker-Lampson, and that "it appears from a note written by Frederick Locker that he had in his library a copy of this book, which was stated on the fly-leaf to have been presented to 'J. Wright, Esq. from Thomas Hood' who had written at the end of each poem the initials of the author. These Locker copied into the present copy." The attributions here are the same as those given by Walter Jerrold and Maurice Buxton Forman, except that the "Ode to Bodkin" is labelled "Joint."[27]

At this point, may it be said in qualification of the statement of a previous writer[28] that Hood's *Plea of the Midsummer Fairies,* published in August 1827, was not entirely the subject of contemporary critical disapprobation. In the *Literary Gazette,* 11 August, the book was likened to "a lovely summer day, sunny, not scorching; placid, enchanting, its airs balmy and refreshing, its various aspects delicious, and even its clouds delightful; so that all minister to enjoyment,"[29]—an opinion endorsed by Letitia Landon in letters to William Jerdan, editor of the *Gazette,* and to Hood himself.[30] The critic of the *Atlas* on the 26th thought Hood "closely resembles the cold wits of the

reign of CHARLES the First . . . [his work possessing] a certain *cobwebby* delicacy and fineness of imagination."[31] In the *Literary Chronicle* and in Hone's *Table Book* the day before, Edward Moxon published a sonnet eulogizing Hood as the author of the *Plea,*[32] and in the *Table Book* three weeks later Charles Lamb inserted "The Defeat of Time," what he called "a meagre, and a harsh, prose-abstract" of Hood's title-poem, concluding with a quotation from *Love's Labours Lost,* that "the words of Mercury are harsh after the song of Apollo."[33] The critic of the *Examiner,* 16 September, thought the *Plea* contained the general merits of "fancy, feeling, and elegance"; the poetry, though languorous, displayed "imagination and poetical feeling . . . indicative of powers of description and fancy from which greater things may be expected."[34] The *Sphynx* a month later thought that "Mr. Hood, in the volume before us, has taken very high ground amongst living poets; and that he has shewn himself imbued with the spirit of our older poetry, and particularly of our rich and overflowing drama."[35]

Four years later, in his *Literary Souvenir* for 1832, Alaric Watts wrote, "although the public will not allow a dependant upon its smiles, who is skilful in one kind of performance, to attempt another with any chance of success, it is a truth, of which all who will refer to his 'Plea of the Midsummer Fairies' may easily satisfy themselves, that [Hood] is entitled to take a high rank as a writer of serious poetry. Barring a few affectations of the quaintnesses of our early poets, I scarcely know a more graceful and imaginative poem, than the one referred to."[36]

Literary cooperation and crossfiring was a pastime dear to Hood and Reynolds, as it had been to Reynolds and Keats.[37] This has been suggested in the letter from "Ned Ward, jun." quoted above, and it has been shown in the **Odes and Addresses.** Such cooperation may have produced "Faithless Sally Brown," published in the *London* for March 1822.[38] Though this poem is marked in Reynolds' copy of the *London,*[39] "T Hood," Hood later referred to "my part in the following Ballad,"[40] and Reynolds' sister Charlotte claimed that the two contributed alternate stanzas.[41] In the *Literary Gazette,* 15 March 1828, Reynolds published a gay poem to Hood under the pseudonym of "Sam Wildfun," to which "Timothy P. Hunter," perhaps Hood, replied the next week.[42]

Reynolds contributed a poem to Hood's annual, the *Gem,* which appeared at the end of 1828. It must have been Reynolds who wrote to Hartley Coleridge about the *Gem* after May the next year, for Coleridge wrote to his mother, "I have received a letter from Mr. Hood's Brother, informing me, that Mr. Hood has declined the Editorship of that work."[43] Besides his contributions to Hood's first *Comic Annual,* Reynolds designed a tailpiece for the fifth.[44] In the *Athenaeum* he reviewed the first two *Comics* and that for 1836, and in that paper, 19 January 1833, Hood's "Sketch on the Road" was immediately followed by Reynolds' **"Ryghte Conceyted Verse toe Master Hoode on his new Boke of Jestis."**[45] In the issue for 7 July 1832 Hood's "Miss Fanny's Farewell Flowers" had been followed by Reynolds' **"Lines to Miss F. Kemble."**[46] At the end of 1837 both Hood and Reynolds contributed to "Nimrod"'s *Sporting*.

Reynolds' concern in the *New Sporting Magazine* can now, following the hint of Professor Edmund Blunden,[47] be pursued further. He was among the earliest contributors when R. S. Surtees began the magazine in 1831. Surtees' reminiscences on this point deserve to be quoted:

> We were indebted to the Hon. Fitzroy Stanhope for procuring us a capital racing contributor in the person of the late Mr Hamilton Reynolds, well known in racing as well as in literary circles. . . . The worst of Reynolds was that there was no getting him to work. He put everything off till the very last moment. . . . When he did sit down he went at a pace and with a power that I never saw surpassed. His accounts of Newmarket, Epsom, and Ascot Races in the opening numbers of the work are perfect models for beginners in that line on which to form their style. I cannot say the same for the shape in which he sent in his MSS. I shall never forget seeing his manuscript arrive at the printers' at the last moment: it would be delivered in the most extraordinary state of confusion—scribbled on letter-backs, old play-bills, anything he could get hold of,—written in a hand that seemed impossible to decipher. After several attempts to read it I was obliged to give it to the printer, with, I confess, no great expectation of its merit. Most agreeably surprised I was to find it read so well. Hamilton Reynolds—there were two Reynolds—was a very clever fellow.[48]

The witty articles to which Surtees refers occur in the *New Sporting* for May, June, and July 1831.[49] As he opined in the character of Jorrocks in the magazine for September 1835, "the werry best account I ever read of Epsom races was in the first volume of the New Magazine."[50]

It was surely Reynolds who introduced Hood to the *New Sporting*. In the number for February 1832 the *Comic Annual* was reviewed, and the March number contained Hood's ballad, "Jarvis and Mrs. Cope."[51]

In contrast with his sympathetic personal relations with Hood, and his activity for the *New Sporting,* Reynolds was not altogether successful in his professional life as a lawyer: witness his relations with members of the Keats circle.[52] A remark on his convivial character which has a ring of perceptiveness was confided by John Payne Collier to his diary on 27 October 1833, "Reynolds has lost his position and his money very much by sitting up late at night. He is very cheerful company, but somewhat prone to satire. . . . He is too much in the habit of thinking that conversation is only good as a vehicle for ridicule; consequently he makes no friends, though few want them more."[53] Collier points the relation between Reynolds and Hood in his account of a dinner which took place on 26 July 1832, and at which Hood was responsible for a parody: "This was voted very good for the extemporaneous attempt of a bashful versifyer, who spoke so low that he could not do justice to his own performance. Hamilton Reynolds wrote it down, and read it aloud."[54] When James Hogg visited London at the beginning of the next year he linked the two men: "Hood, from whom I expected a continued volley of wit, is a modest, retiring character. Reynolds more brilliant."[55]

When Hood quarreled with his wife's relatives at her bedside in January 1835 he did not include Reynolds among them. Reynolds had just lost his daughter, aged ten. Hood wrote to Charles Dilke on 8 February, "I have still a wife—a comfort I would have poor J. H. R. hug to his heart as I do—poor fellow, I pitied him in the midst of my own seeming calamity."[56]

Soon after this Hood sailed for Germany, fleeing from bankruptcy. He left his wife staying with her brother, and wrote to her on 13 and 15 March, referring in friendly terms to Reynolds. In the second letter he wrote, "I hope Reynolds may be able to beat the receivers about the house."[57] However, after Jane joined him she wrote to her sister Charlotte on 25 August, "John is vexed at not hearing which I wonder at—for he must know the reason—Hood is now so very busy that [he] cannot write to him I fear—or else I should wish him to do so, as I forgive his treatment of me not liking to nourish anger against those I love when we are so far apart."[58] In spite of this family unpleasantness, Hood made friendly reference to Reynolds in a letter to Dilke of January 1836.[59]

The following accounts, showing Reynolds having trouble in his personal relations and in financial affairs, are not cheerful. They were sent to Hood abroad by John Wright, the engraver who was Hood's business collaborator over the *Comic Annuals*. On 17 March 1837 he wrote, "Reynolds and I are friends again but that says all. Dilke has been very serious with me on this matter and says if I ever put my neck into nooses again I ought to suffer he said he should set me down as past redemption but concluded by gravely saying 'but you will, now if I asked you to accept a bill, you'd do it directly'!" On 31 May Wright mentioned a Mr. Coghlan, "Reynolds and him are friends again." And on 8 September he wrote, "I have been sorry to hear that John Reynolds is in some scrape about Price's affairs. I do not know how but hear that he had become possessed some time since of 7 or 800 pounds in the business which the creditors now claim to be divided it was money in Chancery and paid over by the court I believe to John and he now has to refund it. Fy! Now! poor John sooner or later you must break up, your friends all foresee it and almost wish it in the hope that it may clear away the mist that has so long obscured you."[60] Reynolds was not entirely in the confidence of Hood himself, for the latter had written to Wright on 30 April concerning his drawings for *Up the Rhine,* "You may show them to Harvey if you like—but mind—not J. H. R."[61]

On 21 April 1838 Mrs. Dilke wrote that Mrs. Reynolds was ill, "I fear it is worry—for she talks of Persons *not* paying *their* Bills to Reynolds—and then how is he to pay *his*."[62] In fact he was not able to do this. A fiat was issued against him on 14 May, and eight days later his bankruptcy was gazetted. He underwent meetings and examinations in May and July. A certificate of bankruptcy was allowed on 26 October; there was another meeting for auditing in November. A dividend of one shilling and ten-pence was declared on 13 June 1839.[63] After all this, he wrote drily to Hood on 13 March 1840, "I am now,—or rather my new Residence is—undergoing repair and whitewashing:—I wish I could undergo repair myself; the *whitewashing* I have gone through."[64]

Surtees had given up the editorship of the *New Sporting* at the end of 1836. Who now became editor is uncertain. C. J. Apperley, "Nimrod," was offered the job early in 1838.[65] That Reynolds' connection with the magazine about this time was slight is suggested by the comments of a review in it concerning an article by Reynolds; this, entitled **"Epsom Races,"** was published in "Nimrod" 's *Sporting*. The reviewer wrote that the article "ought properly to have appeared in a book for the entertainment of sentimental young ladies."[66] That "Nimrod" 's editorial connection with this compilation was nominal is shown by his own unfriendly comments in *Fraser's Magazine,* December 1842, "it was a sad mistake to put a London lawyer to write the article on Epsom races. Some terrible trash is also introduced by another apparently Cockney writer, about the Talbot hound. . . . I trust . . . if these spirited publishers bring forth such an expensive work at a future time, they will not, for the sake of obliging friends, suffer persons to contribute to it who know little or nothing about the subjects on which they write."[67] From August 1838 the *New Sporting* contained no contributions from "Nimrod" and sharp criticisms of him. That Reynolds about now had an editorial interest is suggested by a letter of his belonging to February 1839. He wrote:

Sunday Night

Dear Sir,

I send you *all—but Turfiana*—I wish you would let all be calculated—so that I may temper the length of *T.* to the space remaining. I am tired to death.

You will find the list now as the annexed list on the other side tells you—& the *star* shews that the M.S. is now with you. I think the Varieties & Notes of the Month may exceed what I have reckoned. Let me hear from you at the Office as soon as possible

Yours truly

J. H. Reynolds

P.S. Get the correspondence in one page by small type.[68]

The list contains the contents of the *New Sporting* for March, which however does not include "Turfiana."

That Reynolds continued editorial activity through 1839 and 1840 is shown in Hood's dealings with the magazine. The number for November 1839 contained the "Sonnet on Steam," extracted from *Hood's Own,* and the numbers for January and February following contained extracts from *Up the Rhine*.[69] On 13 March Reynolds wrote to Hood, "I will arrange with Mr. Speirs about the magazines,—and pray let me have the promised paper at your earliest convenience—as the month is careering on again to its close. I do seriously believe that the Months are very unlike cherubs, and consist *only* of *Latter Ends.* I am no sooner out of the frying pan of one magazine,—but I am in to the fire of the one immediately following."[70] In the April number appeared the first part of Hood's "Fishing in Germany."[71] On the seventeenth of that month Hood wrote sulkily to his wife, "I take for granted JHR. has not sent the Sporting Magazine & I take equally for granted that as *I have done the articles* I now shall not have them."[72] To the July number he contributed the conclusion of "Fishing in Germany," and also "An Autograph." In the August number it was stated editorially, "Mr. Hood promises us, 'health and weather permitting,' to cruise with us again next month."[73] But he did not. In December a new series of the *New Sporting* was announced, and in January 1841 "Nimrod" returned. It seems as though Reynolds would by then have retired.

In 1840 Hood entered into a litigious quarrel with his publisher, A. H. Baily. On 16 May Reynolds as Hood's solicitor applied to Baily for proper accounts to be furnished. His letter three days later may be quoted as displaying perhaps characteristic acerbity:

Your letter requiring me to attend you after two or three days notice . . . has just reached me. . . . I consider that the earliest explanation of what are asserted to be erroneous accounts should have been afforded me here I cannot ask to open a settled account nor do I but I apprehend you are mistaken as to their [sic] being one I can and do however require to have a correct account rendered to Mr Hood if the statements at present in my hands are not such as Messieurs Baily & Co intend to abide by your extract from Mr Hoods of the 18th of February refers only to errors discovered on such a perusal of the accounts as the "time permitted" and does not therefore even infer a satisfaction which your quotation would seem to intimate—If I were to answer you by extracts from letters I think Messrs Baily & Co would regret that such a mode of dealing with their accounts was resorted to—My course will be very straight forward with your Clients if I am not immediately satisfied as to the statements made to me and I will venture to say that more extraordinary accounts were never issued from a publishing house I shall commence proceedings against Messrs Baily and C^o for the considerable balance due to Mr Hood and I presume you will appear to process for Messrs Baily & Co, tomorrow morning at noon I shall require to have the stock delivered up and such as they withhold I shall also take the proper measures to obtain

In these demands Reynolds was quite unsatisfied. After further developments he wrote a similarly toned letter on 26 March 1841:

> It is strange that Messrs Alfred Head Baily & Co can give no account of the quantity of stock attached by Mr Follett on or about the day on which the writs were issued against the former at the suit of Mr Hood and respecting which attachment Messrs Alfred Head Baily & Co the Agents of Mr Hood gave no intimation or information to him however an explanation of the facts can be obtained—The request I addressed to you to be allowed to examine the account was made in consequence of the report given by Dr Elliot of Stratford[74] of a conversation had between himself and Mr Baily in which the latter said that he had never known that his accounts were questioned and that his books were always open to inspection—These accounts are so full of errors that I should presume Messrs Alfred Head Baily & Co would be at once ready to see them right but your letter forbids this presumption—I have again therefore to ask you whether Messrs Alfred Head Baily & Co will permit a proper enquiry into the accounts and an adjustment of them.[75]

On the last day of the month Reynolds was sent a statement of the stock attached, but was not allowed an enquiry. From June it was St. P. B. Hook who corresponded on Hood's behalf with Baily and his solicitors.[76] It may be that a difference over the proper conduct of Hood's affairs led to the breaking off of a twenty-year-old friendship, for Reynolds does not again appear in the later biography of Hood.[77]

In this paper I have been concerned merely to add to the knowledge of the relations between Reynolds and Hood. But perhaps in a concluding paragraph an attempt may be made to give an impression of the whole. Reynolds and Hood had laughed together, in private and in print, at the pretensions and oddities of the world. They both endured serious financial difficulties, and were able to laugh at them. They differed, however, in their response to the challenge of social life: Reynolds became a clubbable, sporting lawyer, who dabbled in literature; Hood, shy and sickly, retired into himself and the bosom of his small family, and found compensation for a certain social isolation in his writing, at times brilliantly witty and penetrative. An advantage he held over Reynolds was that he had sufficient creative power to live by literature. It might be said that Reynolds had the geniality to consort with poets, but not the genius wholly to be one. At times he must have felt his life as a continuing decline from the incandescent days of his friendship with Keats. Hood, on the other hand, had the self-respect of a consistently productive man of letters; he kept a steady fire burning, which emitted occasional inspired gleams. Hood lives in literary history as a poet and comic genius; Reynolds lives as the friend of a great poet. They both deserve to be remembered just as men.

Notes

1. See particularly by George L. Marsh: "New Data on Keats's Friend Reynolds," *MP* [*Modern Philology*], XXV (1927-1928), 319-329; "The Writings of Keats's Friend, Reynolds," *SP* [*Studies in Philology*], XXV (1928), 491-510; *John Hamilton Reynolds. Poetry and Prose* (London, 1928); "Newly Identified Writings by John Hamilton Reynolds," *K-SJ* [*Keats-Shelley Journal*], I (January 1952), 47-55. See also Alvin Whitley, "Keats and Hood," *K-SJ*, V (Winter 1956), 33-47; Leonidas M. Jones, "New Letters, Articles, and Poems by John Hamilton Reynolds," *K-SJ*, VI (Winter 1957), 97-108.

2. British Museum Egerton MS. 2245 f. 374.

3. Richard Woodhouse, "Notes of Conversations with Thomas De Quincey," in the latter's *Confessions of an English Opium-Eater*, ed. Richard Garnett, (London, 1885), p. 213.

4. Walter Jerrold, *Thomas Hood: his Life and Times* (London, 1907), p. 100—hereafter cited as Jerrold; *London Magazine*, V, 52.

5. I am grateful to the Executors of H. C. Brooke-Taylor, deceased, for permission to publish this and following items from MSS in their possession.

6. British Museum Egerton MS. 2246 f. 97, quoted by Edmund Blunden, "New Sidelights on Keats, Lamb, and Others," *London Mercury*, IV (June 1921), 147.

7. Henry Charles Shelley, *Literary By-Paths in Old England* (Boston, 1909), pp. 324-326.

8. *London Magazine*, VI, 291.

9. Brooke-Taylor MSS. Theodore was Hood's nickname: see Jerrold, pp. 127, 131, 157. When Hessey wrote "lately" he must have meant "for the last five days," for he had written to Taylor on the preceding day that he had seen Reynolds on 3 October: *The Keats Circle, Letters and Papers, 1816-1878*, ed. H. E. Rollins (Cambridge, Mass., 1948), II, 423.

10. Jerrold, p. 124.

11. *London Magazine,* VI, 393. I am grateful to Mr. Leonidas M. Jones for pointing this passage out to me.

12. Brooke-Taylor MS. The month and day of this letter are supplied by the writer, and its year by a reference he makes to "Dramaticle." "Dramaticles" appear in the *London Magazine,* VII (February and March 1823), 181, 297, and VIII (July 1823), 10.

13. *Letters of John Clare,* ed. J. W. and Anne Tibble (London, 1951), p. 145.

14. British Museum Egerton MS. 2246 f. 235.

15. This and following MSS at the University of California Library, Los Angeles, are quoted by permission.

16. *London Magazine,* VIII, 361-364. That Reynolds wrote this piece is shown by Leonidas M. Jones, *K-SJ,* VI, 103.

17. See Edmund Blunden, *Keats's Publisher* (London, 1936), p. 222.

18. Brooke-Taylor MS.

19. *The Keats Circle,* II, 450. Reynolds' reputation about this time is shown by an unremarked reference in *John Bull,* 11 January 1824, p. 13: "We have read of the COCKNEY School of Poetry, but the HACKNEY School of Critics, for the first time, rears its head"; the writer goes on to list Fox, Robinson, Sothern (sic), Aspland and Bowring as sons of Bentham: "the writers in the late LIBERAL are to unite their forces with this new phalanx. We have heard that MR. REYNOLDS and MR. PROCTOR [sic], and MESSRS. THOMPSON and FEARON, who are dealers in gin, cordials, and compounds, on Holborn Hill, are also to contribute," with Kitchener, to the new *Westminster Review.*

20. See *Memorials of Thomas Hood,* ed. his daughter [Frances Freeling Broderip] (London, 1860), I, 8—hereafter cited as *Memorials.*

21. *The Keats Circle,* II, 459.

22. Jerrold, pp. 120-122.

23. National Library of Scotland MS. 3072 f. 40, reproduced by permission. The letter is addressed to J. (?) Constable.

24. See *The Works of Thomas Hood,* ed. his son and daughter (London, 1869-1873), X, 545, V, 20—hereafter cited as *Works;* Jerrold, pp. 163-165; *The Letters of John Keats,* ed. M. Buxton Forman, 4th ed. (London, 1952), p. xxxix; *John Hamilton Reynolds. Poetry and Prose* (London, 1928), p. 31; Alvin Whitley, *K-SJ,* V, 36.

25. John Payne Collier, *An Old Man's Diary* (London, 1872), IV, 61—hereafter cited as Collier.

26. "Recollections of Thomas Hood," *British Quarterly Review,* XLVI (October 1867), 333.

27. Mr. Bull's letter.

28. Alvin Whitley, *K-SJ,* V, 47.

29. *Literary Gazette,* 11 August 1827, p. 513.

30. *Works,* V, 292, 296.

31. *Atlas,* 26 August 1827, p. 538.

32. *Literary Chronicle,* 25 August 1827, p. 543. *Table Book,* 25 August 1827, p. 239.

33. *Table Book,* 15 September 1827, pp. 335-339.

34. *Examiner,* 16 September 1827, p. 581.

35. *Sphynx,* 14 October 1827, p. 235.

36. *Literary Souvenir,* 1832, p. 245.

37. See Mabel A. E. Steele, "The Woodhouse Transcripts of the Poems of Keats," *HLB* [*Harvard Library Bulletin*], III (1949), 248.

38. *London Magazine,* V, 202-204.

39. At the Keats House, Hampstead.

40. *Works,* V, 124.

41. *Letters of John Keats,* pp. xxxix-xl.

42. *Literary Gazette,* 15, 22 March 1828, pp. 171, 189. Jerrold, p. 187, misdates the volume 1827. The attribution of the first poem to Reynolds is made by Leonidas M. Jones, *K-SJ,* VI, 104-105.

43. *The Letters of Hartley Coleridge,* ed. G. E. and E. L. Griggs (London, 1936), p. 100. Coleridge's letter can be roughly dated by the fact that the *Court Journal,* referred to elsewhere in his letter, first appeared on 2 May 1829.

44. Reynolds possessed what he called "a very remote uneducated turn for sketching." This phrase occurs in his "Greenwich and Greenwich Men," published in *Bentley's Miscellany,* VII (March 1840), 282, and reprinted in *Tales from Bentley,* (London, 1859), 9.

45. George L. Marsh, *SP,* XXV, 503, 505, 506, lists these *Athenaeum* items, except for the review of the *Comic* for 1836, which was attributed to Reynolds by Hood's friend, John Wright: see *Letters of Thomas Hood from the Dilke Papers in the British Museum,* ed. L. A. Marchand (New Brunswick, 1945), p. 56—hereafter cited as *Letters.*

46. *Athenaeum,* 7 July 1832, p. 436. The exchange at pp. 66, 114 of the *Athenaeum,* between the authors of "Reply to a Pastoral Poet" and "Answer to Pauper," was not, as Hood's son at first thought, between Reynolds and Hood, but between B. W. Procter and Hood: see the latter's *Works,* VI, 225, X, 547. Oddly enough, the "long duel about the respective merits of 'eyes of black' and 'eyes of blue'," to which Hood's son refers as between Reynolds and Hood, was between Reynolds and Keats: see Mabel A. E. Steele, *HLB,* III, 248.

47. George L. Marsh, *K-SJ,* I, 55.

48. *Robert Smith Surtees by himself and E. D. Cuming* (Edinburgh, 1924), pp. 65-66.

49. *New Sporting Magazine,* I, 17, 113, 198.

50. The same, IX, 357. It is noteworthy that articles with extracts from the *New Sporting* in the *Athenaeum,* 18 June, 31 December 1831, pp. 395, 847, are marked as by Reynolds in the editorial file of that periodical: see George L. Marsh, *SP,* XXV, 504, 505.

51. *New Sporting Magazine,* II, 230, 323. See *Robert Smith Surtees,* p. 125. The *Athenaeum,* 18 January 1834, p. 50, extracted from the *New Sporting* an "Ode to Crockford," which began with a quotation from Hood.

52. See for example *More Letters and Poems of the Keats Circle,* ed. H. E. Rollins (Cambridge, Mass., 1955), pp. 31-32, 38-41, 58, 67, 70-72.

53. Collier, IV, 62. With Collier's estimate of Reynolds may be compared that of Alfred Bunn who, in *The Stage* (London, 1840), III, 156, linked him with John Poole; he considered Reynolds "a d———d good judge," one of those who has "more stuff in his little finger than is to be found in the heads, put together, of half of those he is compelled to associate with."

54. Collier, II, 19.

55. James Hogg, *A Series of Lay Sermons* (London, 1834), p. 83. Hood refers to Reynolds in letters to W. B. Cooke and A. H. Baily about this time: these are at the University of California Library, Los Angeles.

56. *Letters,* p. 21.

57. *Memorials,* I, 57, 62, and MS at the Bristol Reference Library.

58. MS at University of California Library, Los Angeles: referred to indirectly by Alvin Whitley, *K-SJ,* V, 37.

59. *Letters,* pp. 47, 60.

60. MSS at the Bristol Reference Library.

61. MS at the University of California Library, Los Angeles.

62. Bristol MS.

63. See *Perry's Bankrupt and Insolvent Weekly Gazette,* XI, 322, 335, 365, 402, 445, 453, 492, 653, 679, 706; XII, 327, 354, 445. For verifying these references I am grateful to Mr. Eric Blake.

64. *Bookman,* LXIV (September 1923), 277.

65. Charles James Apperley, *My Life and Times* (Edinburgh, 1927), p. 303.

66. *New Sporting Magazine,* XIV (January 1838), 62. Reynolds' authorship of "Epsom Races" is established by Leonidas M. Jones, *K-SJ,* VI, 105-106.

67. *Fraser's Magazine,* XXVI, 675, reprinted in Apperley, p. 210.

68. Typescript copy in the possession of Mr. J. M. Cohen, to whom I am grateful for permission to publish it.

69. *New Sporting Magazine,* XVII, 317; XVIII, 4, 86-90.

70. *Bookman,* LXIV, 277.

71. *New Sporting Magazine,* XVIII, 253-257.

72. Bristol MS.

73. *New Sporting Magazine,* XIX, 19-26, 49-51, 70.

74. A close friend of Hood, and his physician.

75. These two letters were copied into Hood's Bill of Complaint against A. H. Baily, filed on 22 May 1843, and now at the Public Record Office.

76. These items are also gathered from the Bill of Complaint.

77. In "The Reynolds-Hood Commonplace Book: A Fresh Appraisal," *K-SJ,* X (Winter 1961), 43-52, Mr. Paul Kaufman prints a poem "To T. Hood on hearing of his sickness," indicating that it is by Reynolds and transmitting the suggestion that perhaps the poem effected a reconciliation between the two men when Hood was on his death-bed. Mr. Kaufman does not give any evidence for assigning the poem to Reynolds, nor do I know of any evidence of a reconciliation.

Leonidas M. Jones (essay date 1970)

SOURCE: Jones, Leonidas M. "Reynolds and Rice in Defence of Patmore." *Keats-Shelley Memorial Bulletin* 21 (1970): 12-20.

[*In the following essay, Jones relates the details of a legal case that illuminates both Reynolds's career as an attorney and the intense rivalries among the periodicals for which Reynolds often wrote.*]

Charles Brown wrote to Keats on 21 December 1820: 'I know you don't like John Scott, but he is doing a thing that tickles me to the heart's core, and you will like to hear of it, if you have any revenge in your composition. By some means (crooked enough I dare say) he has got possession of one of Blackwood's gang, who has turned King's evidence, and month after month he belabours them with the most damning facts that can be conceived;—if they are indeed facts, I know not how the rogues can stand up against them'.[1]

Brown's guesses were shrewd. Scott had in effect secured 'possession of one of Blackwood's' former regular contributors, Peter George Patmore, though there was nothing 'crooked' in engaging him. After a succession of protests in letters to *Blackwood's* against its scandalous abuse, Patmore had shifted his allegiance to the *London Magazine* and had grown so close to Scott that he planned to become assistant editor. Brown was also astute in anticipating that an editor of *Blackwood's* could not endure Scott's attacks. John Gibson Lockhart challenged Scott to a duel; Scott declined to fight when Lockhart refused to disavow his editorship of *Blackwood's*; Lockhart's second, Jonathan Henry Christie, insulted Scott in a letter; Scott challenged Christie; and Christie wounded Scott mortally.

In an earlier article I have described the indirect involvement of John Hamilton Reynolds in the quarrel.[2] As an old and trusted friend since 1815 when Reynolds served on the staff of Scott's *Champion,* Scott turned to him for assistance to set his affairs in order in case of his death. He requested Reynolds to deliver his final letters to his widow and brother-in-law; to write an account of the dispute to his ally against *Blackwood's* in Edinburgh, John R. McCulloch; and to provide temporary directions for the principal contributors to the *London Magazine.*

Another link between Reynolds and the fatal controversy, which has hitherto gone unrecognized because of the anonymity of Reynolds' early contributions to the *London,* is that Scott had thought at first that Reynolds should have written the chastising attacks on *Blackwood's.* At the beginning of the November article, Scott announced that he intended to give the matter much more serious treatment than jocular sparring between two magazines: 'Our principal quarry is a higher one than the New Monthly, or the Old Monthly, or the European, or the Gentleman's—or Blackwood's, which is *not* the Gentleman's'.[3] In a footnote Scott added, 'This is borrowing an arrow from the quiver of another—a dead shot—who ought to have saved us this trouble, and then we shouldn't have pilfered from him. As it is, we hope he will excuse our making free with what he can so well spare'. The 'dead shot' Reynolds' article, from which Scott pilfered, was **'The Jewels of the Book'**, printed in the *London* two months earlier, where

Reynolds protested banteringly against objections to his writing pugilistic articles for the *London* simply because *Blackwood's* had published pugilistic essays earlier. If absolute originality were required, Reynolds had concluded, 'who would commence a magazine *now* (for in this particular, there are about fourteen . . .)—or who would *ever* have commenced one after the *Gentleman's*'.[4] Probably Scott thought that Reynolds should have written the frontal assault because he was so certain of Reynolds' strong antipathy to *Blackwood's,* a certainty which he had expressed in 'Lion's Head' of August.[5] And perhaps Reynolds had reported to Scott, as he had to Benjamin Bailey, that 'poor Keats attributed his approaching end to the poisonous pen of Lockhart'.[6]

But once resolved to assume the task which Reynolds had not performed, Scott entered into the unpleasant duty so energetically that he sacrificed his life as a result. After Scott's death, the law firm of Reynolds and Rice participated in the ensuing litigation to an extent which is of considerable interest to students of the Keats circle since it is the only example we have of the successful exercise of their legal abilities in an important case. Scott's second, Peter George Patmore, engaged the law firm to defend him in the legal proceedings. Having been acquainted in all probability since 1816 when Reynolds wrote for Scott's *Champion,* Patmore and Reynolds undoubtedly encountered each other often during the year that both contributed actively to the *London,* and, as we have seen, both were close to Scott during the days immediately preceding the duel. There is no evidence that Patmore had met James Rice before, though it would not be unlikely since both were very sociable.

The first step by Reynolds and Rice was to spare Patmore from arrest by sending him to Calais, where he remained for several weeks under the name of P. G. Pitt. Reynolds, Rice, and a third young lawyer, who was a friend of Scott but not retained in the case (probably Thomas Noon Talfourd), attended the inquest held at Chalk Farm Tavern from 5.30 p.m. until 12.30 a.m. on 1 March before the coroner, Thomas Sterling of Middlesex, and his jury. When a member of the jury challenged their presence, Reynolds identified himself as a friend of Scott and a solicitor for a person involved, while Rice explained that he too was a legal representative.[7] When a member of the jury suggested that the names of the suspected participants be mentioned to refresh the memory of a witness, they objected and succeeded in preventing it.

The first day began safely enough for Patmore, as well as for Christie and his second, James Traill. The carpenter Thomas Smith and the hostler James Ryan, who had helped to carry Scott to the Chalk Farm Tavern where they had been employed, testified very minutely as to details, but they pretended to a laughable igno-rance of names. They identified men only by apparel—the man in the white coat, the man in the blue coat, the man in the red coat, but no, I believe it was plaid—in such a confusing way as to endanger no one. But later the landlord, Hugh Watson, while posing no threat to Christie or Traill, implicated Patmore by name repeat-edly. He recognized Patmore in the tavern after the duel because he had known him before; indeed he had known Patmore's father for twenty years. He reported that a pistol brought in after the duel was Patmore's and that Peter Patmore, Sr. had offered a reward for the recovery of the pistols. All this was dangerous enough, but the real bombshell came when Dr. Darling read the follow-ing memorandum, reporting Scott's account to him on the day after the duel:

> 'This ought not to have taken place: I suspect some great mismanagement: there was no occasion for a sec-ond fire'. After a short pause, he proceeded—'All I re-quired from Mr. Christie was, a declaration that he meant no reflection on my character: this he refused, and the meeting became inevitable. On the field Mr. Christie behaved well, and when all was ready for the first fire he called out—"Mr. Scott, you must not stand there; I see your head above the horizon; you give me an advantage": I believe he could have hit me then if he liked. After the pistols were re-loaded and every thing ready for a second fire, Mr. Trail called out—"Now, Mr. Christie, take your aim, and do not throw away your advantage as you did last time". I called out immediately, "What! did not Mr. Christie fire at me"? I was answered by Mr. Patmore, "You must not speak: 'tis now of no use to talk; you have now nothing for it but firing". The signal was immediately given; we fired; and I fell'.[8]

Not having understood a word of Traill's statement ex-cept Christie's name, Patmore had guessed mistakenly that Traill was blaming Scott for firing too soon, and that Scott was on the verge of a bitter argument: 'What! did not Mr. Christie fire at me' [at the same time I fired at him]. The duel had been fought in foggy moonlight, Christie had levelled his pistol in the general direction of Scott, and Patmore had had no way of knowing that Christie had missed intentionally. Patmore had therefore stopped what he misunderstood as heated argument to avoid making pacification more difficult in case one of the duellists should be slightly wounded in a later fire. But on the first day of the coroner's inquest, Dr. Dar-ling's memorandum thrust the whole weight of the blame for the second, fatal fire upon Patmore, and pub-lic sentiment against him raged unabated for several weeks.

The second day of the inquest, which began at 5.30 p.m. on 2 March, went somewhat better for Patmore. To be sure, the surgeon Thomas J. Pettigrew revealed that Patmore had engaged him, and he placed Patmore on the field during the duel, but he also presented Pat-more's case in the misunderstanding about the first fire. He described the altercation between the seconds after Scott was wounded when Patmore had insisted angrily to Traill that he knew nothing of Christie's firing wide on the first exchange. And he testified that Patmore had visited him several days after the duel to reaffirm his complete ignorance after the first fire that Christie had missed intentionally. Nevertheless at 12.30 a.m. the jury delivered its verdict: 'Wilful murder against Christie, Patmore, and Trail[l]'.[9]

Seeking to temper the effect of Dr. Darling's testimony on public sentiment, Rice inserted an advertisement in the *Morning Chronicle,* urging that people not be mis-led by partial evidence but that they wait for further de-velopments to clear Patmore.[10] Reynolds pressed his de-sire to protect Patmore by quieting public feeling rather too far when he attempted to postpone a notice in the *London Magazine* soliciting funds for Scott's family with the argument that it would be inflammatory, but fortunately for Caroline and the Scott children Robert Baldwin printed the notice despite Reynolds' objection.

Reynolds and Rice worried about the influence of pub-lic opinion on the jury, but they were even more con-cerned about the legal status of Darling's memorandum. It had been admitted at the inquest because of the rather flexible rules for evidence at the preliminary hearing, but it might be possible to bar it from the trial. The law held that the statement of a dying man was admissible only if he knew at the time he made it that death was imminent, the reason being that the knowledge of ap-proaching death substituted for an oath to insure verac-ity. Reynolds succeeded admirably in developing this aspect of the case. He secured Caroline Scott's report that her husband had thought he would recover at the time he spoke to Dr. Darling. He won the same admis-sion from Dr. Darling after telling him straightforwardly that Patmore's life was at stake. And he received cor-roboration from Dr. Guthrie, who had been most opti-mistic in the first few days after the wound.

Caroline Scott presented a serious problem. At first she refused to see Rice, who was a stranger to her, but Rey-nolds managed to see her readily since she had known him a long time as a friend of her husband. Reynolds also made tactful and effective use of their mutual friend, Mrs. Basil Montague, to persuade her to co-operate fully. The problem was not that she was reluc-tant to shield Patmore; her friendship remained very warm, and she wished him to emerge from the affair with his reputation unblemished. She discounted Dr. Darling's testimony strongly; Scott could not have said it, or, if he had, he was delirious. She blamed Traill bit-terly for not stopping the duel after the first fire, and she resented the great reputation which Christie had won. She was more than willing to testify in order to clear Patmore and blast Traill, but the problem for Pat-more's attorneys was whether to have her testify.

At a conference of legal authorities retained for counsel on 21 March, John Adolphus and a Mr. Curwood advised Reynolds and Rice not to call Caroline Scott as a witness because of the emotional effect her appearance might have on the jury. The appearance of the widow on the stand might press the jury to convict all the defendants as an example against the evil of duelling. We can infer the strategy adopted by Reynolds and Rice from Reynolds' and Caroline Scott's letters to Patmore and from the newspaper accounts of the trials. They would concentrate on barring Dr. Darling's evidence from the trial; in this they could hope for co-operation from Christie's and Traill's attorneys. Although the Darling memorandum represented Christie and Traill favourably, it also placed them on the field and described their participation in a duel. Admitting it virtually guaranteed as a minimum a verdict of manslaughter for all three defendants. On the other hand, if there were no clear identification of Christie and Traill, they might be acquitted. Reynolds and Rice evidently decided to hold Caroline Scott in reserve: not to use her if Darling's evidence were barred, but to call her to counter the Darling evidence if it should be admitted.

Reynolds and Rice worked thoroughly for Patmore's welfare. Rice attended to most of the practical details: arranging to send him a passport, referring him to an influential French friend at Calais in case of need, visiting his parents and his uncle, and effecting the assignment of his £10,000 estate to prevent forfeiture in case of a conviction for manslaughter or worse. Reynolds tried unsuccessfully to negotiate an agreement with Mr. Minshull, magistrate at Bow Street, so that the police would not seek to arrest Patmore on his return if he agreed to surrender for trial. Reynolds succeeded, however, in negotiating with Mr. Brown, the keeper of Newgate prison who knew Rice well from earlier dealing, to insure that Patmore's confinement would be as agreeable as possible if it were necessary. The lawyers explained the danger frankly and left the final decision to Patmore on whether to risk return for trial.

Early in April Patmore returned secretly to London, communicating with Caroline Scott and conferring with his attorneys.[11] At this time he wrote a carefully argued apologia intended for publication.[12] At first Caroline Scott concurred with Patmore in thinking that he ought to make it public, but she soon bowed to other advisers who persuaded him to withhold it. As a whole, it was an enlightening document which would have cleared away some misunderstanding about Patmore's conduct. Why was it not published? Patmore clung doggedly to the conviction that until after the second fire Scott had not 'the most distant suspicion' that Christie had fired wide the first time. Publication would certainly have caused heated controversy with Dr. Darling and his

friends and with Christie, Traill, and their friends. Bitter public argument would have weakened the chances of all three defendants in court.

As the trial approached on 13 April, Reynolds and Rice and their learned consultants, Adolphus and Curwood, faced a decision. They wanted to make whatever arrangements would guarantee Patmore the best chance of acquittal or light sentence, and they were not faced with hostility from any quarter. Scott's family had instigated the legal investigation leading to the trial,[13] and Caroline Scott was extremely sympathetic toward Patmore. Reynolds had determined 'that the feeling of the prosecutors is known to be . . . favourable'.[14] In the light of subsequent events, it seems probable that Reynolds and Rice conferred with Christie's and Traill's attorneys to reach an agreement whereby Christie's and Traill's lawyers would not press for admission of the Darling memorandum in exchange for a guarantee that Reynolds and Rice would prevent Patmore from surrendering for the first trial. Christie's and Traill's attorneys could elicit from the surgeon Pettigrew all the evidence they needed: Christie's firing wide the first time, his remorse, his humane concern for the wounded Scott, and Scott's judgment that all had been fair and honorable. Pettigrew's testimony insured that Christie and Traill would receive no more than a verdict of manslaughter, and the exclusion of Darling's memorandum might make possible an acquittal, for Pettigrew could not after the foggy night view identify either Christie or Traill. But Pettigrew must identify his old acquaintance Patmore as a participant on the field, and a conviction of Patmore would pose some danger to Christie and Traill, since a jury might wish to avoid the appearance of partisanship. The sensible solution would be an agreement by all parties to drop Darling's evidence and to have Patmore refrain from surrendering, while Christie and Traill were tried.

The degree to which the first trial was arranged in advance must remain speculative, but Patmore's reason for not surrendering is fact. An advertisement in the *Times* informed the public that Patmore refrained from surrendering, on the advice of counsel, to avoid the risk of endangering Christie and Traill.[15] Before the trial, Patmore moved from London to Witney, Oxfordshire, where he remained in hiding under the name of P. G. Preston.[16]

The first trial went off like clock-work on Friday, 13 April, at 10.00 a.m. before the Lord Chief Justice Abbott and Justice Park. The court was crowded with 'persons of distinction', as Mr. Walfourd presented the case for the prosecution and Mr. Gurney the case for the defence. It would be impossible to find a more sympathetic prosecutor than Mr. Walfourd, who glowed with emotion for Christie and Traill:

> . . . it was difficult for him to find adequate language
> to convey any idea of the painful feelings with which

he rose to state the evidence which he had to adduce in support of the indictment against the gentlemen at the bar. It was impossible for him, when he recollected the rank in society in which these gentlemen moved, and when he reflected upon the fatal consequences which might come to them upon this trial—it was, he repeated, impossible for him to behold their situation without emotion. The man who, standing there, could do so, must have firmer nerves than he possessed.[17]

This was the *prosecutor*. The mild case he presented was exactly what one would expect after that maudlin preamble. He drew from Pettigrew all the evidence favourable to Christie including Christie's statement that he had fired wide, except that Pettigrew unfortunately forgot to add what he had reported at the coroner's inquest—that Christie had been forced to shoot Scott in self-defence. But the alert defence attorney, Mr. Gurney, immediately prodded his memory, and that too went into the record. The prosecutor then called Pettigrew's assistant Morris, Hugh Watson, and James Ryan to establish the order of events on the fatal night. None of them could identify Christie or Traill as participants on the field. Lawyers and spectators alike were doubtless startled when Thomas Smith departed from the script to say, 'The prisoner Traill was one of the gentlemen in the field'. But the real climax came when Dr. Darling testified. After he and Dr. Guthrie explained that Scott had not believed he was dying when he made the statement, the judges conferred for a few minutes at the bench and then pronounced the evidence inadmissible.

The defence offered only a long succession of character witnesses for the defendants, who were attired in deep mourning. Justice Abbott did Lord Chief everything he possibly could for the prisoners, at one time even indulging in a mental hand-spring with possibility: 'It was possible, he said, that the real perpetrators of the crime might have escaped from the field before the arrival of Mr. Pettigrew, and that the prisoners at the bar might have appeared accidentally at the moment'. No one could have been much surprised when the jury returned the report, 'Not Guilty'.

According to Caroline Scott, Reynolds was chiefly responsible for representing Patmore's interests *in absentia* during the first trial.[18] She was present in court, but there was no occasion for her testimony since Dr. Darling's statement was barred and since Pettigrew had protected Patmore by mentioning the altercation between the seconds and by quoting Patmore's outburst, 'Why was it not communicated to me—I knew nothing of it'.

Rice directed the defence when Patmore eventually surrendered for the second trial on 8 June before Justice Bayley. Since Pettigrew was an old acquaintance of Patmore's who had been sympathetic toward him throughout the affair, it seems certain that what happened was planned as a neat legal manœuvre. Both Pettigrew and Morris, who were the only witnesses able to identify Patmore as a participant on the field, refused to testify on the grounds that they might incriminate themselves.[19] The other witnesses merely repeated their testimony from the first trial. 'Without the slightest hesitation', the jury reported the verdict, 'Not Guilty'.[20]

Caroline Scott was strongly dissatisfied with the conduct of the case by Reynolds and Rice and by her own attorney, Watkins. She had wanted them to clear Patmore's name without a shadow of a doubt and at the same time to preserve her husband's character as stainless. One can infer from her letters to Patmore that she had wished to testify herself. But surely Reynolds and Rice were wiser than she. The widow's testifying might well have influenced the jury emotionally and caused them to make an example of all three defendants. Lengthy and detailed justification of Patmore, moreover, might have required at least some disparagement of Scott, and such an attack on the dead would have also been a very dangerous risk with a jury. The acquittal for a man against whom the public had been incensed only a few weeks before was no small achievement.

Notes

1. Hyder E. Rollins, ed., *The Letters of John Keats,* 2 vols. (Cambridge, Massachusetts, 1958), II, 364-365.

2. 'The Scott-Christie Duel', *Texas Studies in Language and Literature,* XII (Spring, 1970).

3. *London,* II (November 1820), 509. The principal quarry of course was to be Sir Walter Scott's son-in-law Lockhart.

4. *London,* II (September 1820), 268.

5. II, 123.

6. Hyder E. Rollins, *The Keats Circle,* 2 vols. (Cambridge, Massachusetts, 1965), I, 232.

7. *Morning Chronicle,* 2 March 1821. The names of Reynolds and Rice are not given, but they fit the descriptions exactly. That the third man was Talfourd is supported by the fact that he was a barrister; Talfourd had been admitted to the bar on 10 February 1821, and Reynolds had attended his dinner to celebrate the occasion. All the subsequent information on the first day of the inquest is drawn from the *Morning Chronicle,* which reported the first day's proceedings more fully than *The Times* in a joint report of both days on 3 March.

8. *Times,* 3 March 1821. I quote from *The Times* rather than the *Morning Chronicle* because the latter garbled one line of the statement.

9. *The Times,* 3 March 1821, provides a fuller account of the second day of the inquest.

10. The facts in this paragraph and the following four paragraphs are drawn from Reynolds' letters to Patmore, Basil Champneys, *The Memoirs and Correspondence of Coventry Patmore,* 2 vols. (London, 1900), II, 420-425.

11. Ibid., II, 415. Caroline Scott wrote of his having been in London.

12. Ibid., II, 426-429.

13. So the prosecutor Walfourd said at the trial, *The Times,* 14 April 1821.

14. Champneys, II, 424.

15. *The Times,* 14 April 1821.

16. Derek Patmore, 'A Literary Duel', *Princeton University Library Chronicle,* XVI (Autumn 1954), 16.

17. *The Times,* 14 April 1821. Subsequent quotations from the first trial derive from the same source.

18. Champneys, II, 418. She writes of Reynolds being responsible 'on the first occasion' and of Rice's being responsible 'in the last'.

19. That Pettigrew was in no real danger of prosecution was evident from the coroner's jury's refusal to indict him after he explained that he had merely done his duty by responding to a call for professional service.

20. *Morning Chronicle,* 9 June 1821.

Leonidas M. Jones (essay date 1973)

SOURCE: Jones, Leonidas M. Introduction to *The Letters of John Hamilton Reynolds,* pp. ix-xxxvi. Lincoln: University of Nebraska Press, 1973.

[*In the following excerpt, Jones presents an overview of Reynolds's literary career.*]

JOHN HAMILTON REYNOLDS AND THE KEATS CIRCLE

John Hamilton Reynolds's father's family background entitled him to his place as a member of the Cockney school of English poetry. His great-grandfather, Thomas Reynolds, was a tanner of Tottenham, and his grandfather, Noble Reynolds, a barber of the same parish.[1] His father, George, after attending Christ's Hospital from 1774 to 1779, taught school for most of his long life in London at the Lambeth Boys Parochial School, the Lambeth Female Asylum, and at Christ's Hospital, though from the early 1790s until about 1806 he left

the city to teach at Shrewsbury School. Active in his profession, he was a specialist in the Bell system of education, who was once sent by Christ's Hospital to introduce the plan at Hertford School, and he published six school books,[2] one of which the *Edinburgh Review* listed in the same announcement of new books as Keats's *Endymion.*[3] In his family life, however, he was quiet and unassertive; Keats does not mention him even once during all the time he visited in his houses. His son delicately refrained from informing him when he interceded to try to prevent a reduction of his salary in 1820.[4] His "rooted objection to having his personal appearance delineated in any way" frustrated all Thomas Hood's attempts to have him sit for a portrait.[5]

Clearly the stronger spouse throughout their long life together was Charlotte Cox Reynolds, whom he married on 7 January 1790.[6] Four years older than her husband when she married at what was then the rather late age of twenty nine, she came from a family with pretensions superior to those of his humble origin. She was related by marriage to a distinguished Hamilton family whose descendents included the famous William Beckford and the sprightly writer on hunting, Peter Beckford, and she showed her pride in her connections in the middle names of two of her children, John Hamilton and Eliza Beckford Reynolds. Her only brother, William Beckford Cox, who established himself financially during military service in India and the East Indies, was the father of the sophisticated "Charmian" of Keats's letters.[7] While her husband remains almost unobserved in the wings, Mrs. Reynolds's more forceful personality figures prominently on stage in the records of Keats and Hood. And yet one ought to guard against exaggeration of her strong will which might result from Keats's reaction against her or from Hood's bitter quarrel with her in 1835. John F. M. Dovaston's "Lines to Mrs. Reynolds of Lambeth with a Goose" testifies to the happy home which she maintained for her husband as well as her children.[8] The character of Mrs. Morton in Reynolds's Edward Herbert essays, with her subordination of herself to her beloved husband despite her superior intellect, hints that Charlotte Reynolds was wise enough to treat her husband's ego carefully.[9] And Hood's early letters reveal that she was as loving and lovable as she was firm in the control of her household.

The single known record of George Reynolds in the years immediately following his graduation from Christ's Hospital in 1779 shows only that on 5 February 1788 he lived at Kingsland in the area of Hackney and Tottenham;[10] probably by that time he had already begun his long career of teaching in London schools which have not been identified. He was still in London on 28 November 1791, because the baptism of his first child, Jane, is recorded on that date.[11] Thereafter he moved the family to Shrewsbury, where he taught in the school and where his first and only son, John Hamilton Reynolds, was born on 9 September 1794. Three other daughters were later born at Shrewsbury: Mariane[12] on 23 February 1797, Eliza Beckford in 1799, and Charlotte in 1802.

From his ninth through his twelfth years (1803-1806), John Hamilton Reynolds attended the Shrewsbury School, where his father taught. Two poems in the *London Magazine,* signed with Reynolds's pseudonym Ned Ward, Jr., cast some light on what life was like there for the young students.[13] In May 1823 Reynolds wrote **"A Parthian Peep at Life, an Epistle to R———d A———n,"**[14] recalling joyously their shared schoolboy activities, but by the next year the friend had died and in **"Stanzas to the Memory of Richard Allen,"**[15] he lamented the schoolmate who had been buried in a "country church-yard" under trees beneath which he had played as a boy. Although no Shrewsbury School record has been accessible to check on Richard Allen's attendance, it seems safe to conclude that in general Reynolds drew on his own experience at school, though nostalgia and poetic license may have colored some details. The activities recounted are by no means surprising—indeed, they are what one would expect of the usual schoolboys—but they are particular enough to deserve being specified. In **"A Parthian Peep,"** he recalls playing on the walls, shooting marbles on the playground under the trees, reading romances in the shade, playing at the river's edge (the Severn), looking for birds' nests, stealing crab apples, and attending a school party with country dancing. Repeating some of the items like the marbles and searching for linnets in **"Stanzas to the Memory of Richard Allen,"** he adds recollections of "wild Thursday afternoon" (evidently a half holiday), hunting, fishing, swimming, playing ball and prisoner's base, rolling hoops, climbing trees, and stealing apricots for a "pillow treat."

The poem **"Old Ballads"** included in a *London* essay[16] probably refers to Shrewsbury School too, though the experience may have occurred during his later attendance at St. Paul's. After reading the ballads "under the play-ground tree," he would tell the stories to the other boys, undoubtedly interesting them the more because he was breaking the rule as he related the tales of *Chevy Chase* and Richard Plantagenet. The picture which emerges from the poems is one of a normal and happy school life.

The fullest account of life at Shrewsbury School at this time appears in **The Fancy** (1820), but one must be warier in dealing with the experiences of Peter Corcoran described there than was John Masefield, who accepted them all as Reynolds's own.[17] Although Peter Corcoran echoes Reynolds's life in many ways—both were born in September 1794, both were sent to Shrewsbury School, both had an avid interest in sports, and both were aspiring poets—the book is mock autobi-

ography. Its theme, treated both comically and sentimentally, is the moral decay of Peter Corcoran, ending in rejection by his beloved and his death because of his increasing addiction to sports, especially the unsavory boxing. Anticipation of that theme undoubtedly led Reynolds to exaggerate some of his own misconduct and to add offenses of which he was innocent: young Peter tore grammars, broke bounds, pilfered orchards, fought, and swore. As the traditional servant to an older boy, he cleaned shoes, set the tea utensils, and prepared special treats for his supper. Also for his boy-master, he would slip out of the bedroom window at night to steal fruit for his tart, and he would carry the older boy's fighting cocks in a bag to a nearby field. Like Huck Finn and Tom Sawyer, he was very active at night, stealing out by moonlight to fish for trout and swim in the Severn. Because he did not study industriously, the headmaster punished him frequently with the rod, but his tutor, the Reverend Mr. S———, who was third master, was both kind and assiduous in counseling him and caring for him.[18] Although we cannot know which experiences were Reynolds's own, a summary of these activities in a biographical sketch is valuable because, after discounting the degree of misconduct, we are left with a sense of what life was like at Shrewsbury School when Reynolds attended.

Three other features of Peter's development at Shrewsbury are especially important because the appearance of the same traits in the later Reynolds argue that they were indeed based on personal schoolboy experience: the writing of verse, the desire for fame, and the sharp wit. Peter began writing verse at this early period: he lampooned his boyish enemies and he penned melancholy and heroic songs. Deeply gratified by the applause these efforts won from his schoolfellows, he was stirred early by a craving for fame. In like manner, his fighting with schoolmates was for glory, as well as for love of battle. His wit also began to win notice; no one could surpass him in smart remarks to the master's daughter or the maid.

It is certain that by 1809 the Reynolds family had returned from Shrewsbury to London because the Christ's Hospital record for that year includes a payment to George Reynolds of "£20 for visiting the Hertford school and introducing there Dr. Bell's system of education."[19] But probably the family had made the move earlier, in 1806 when John Hamilton finished at Shrewsbury School and enrolled at St. Paul's, where he remained until 1810. Later in life Richard Harris Barham, author of *The Ingoldsby Legends,* reported that Reynolds had been "an old schoolfellow of mine at St. Paul's School,"[20] but Barham probably did not know Reynolds at the school well, if at all, since he was six years Reynolds's senior and he left the school the year after Reynolds's arrival to enter Oxford in 1807. Richard Bentley, the same age as Reynolds, was evidently more nearly contemporary at St. Paul's, but the strictly businesslike tone of Reynolds's later letters to him in this volume argues that at most their acquaintance in school could have been slight.

Graduating from St. Paul's in 1810, Reynolds secured a junior clerkship in the Amicable Society for a Perpetual Assurance office not later than 18 July, the date on which he signed his first document. He continued to perform this clerical work until about 24 April 1816, the date of his last signature in the record.[21] The office was small as compared with Lamb's great East India House with its numerous clerks and huge tomes of accounts; the Amicable Society usually employed only three clerks at a time, among whom were John Griffin in 1810 and W. B. Wedlake in 1816. Reynolds evidently performed this mundane work capably from his sixteenth through his twenty-second year, if the fact that he signed most of the documents from 1810 through 1816 can be taken as evidence of his competence.

During some of his free time, Reynolds kept in touch with an old friend in Shropshire, John F. M. Dovaston, who had been his father's student in Shrewsbury School.[22] Dovaston was a lawyer who showed his affection for his London friends by including in *Fitz-Gwarine, with Other Rhymes* a sonnet to John and "Lines to Mrs. Reynolds of Lambeth with a Goose." Reynolds returned the affection with an **"Ode to Friendship, Inscribed to J. F. M. Dovaston of West Felton"** in the *Gentleman's Magazine* for 1812, his first known poem, and later in 1814 dedicated his much more ambitious *The Eden of Imagination* to him.

As early as 1798 one John Dovaston of West Felton (presumably the father of J. F. M. Dovaston) had founded the Breidden Society near Shrewsbury for the purpose of celebrating an annual festival on Breidden Hill with eating, drinking, smoking, poetry reading, toasting, singing, dancing, and—if the record is to be believed—much kissing sparked by the traditional kissing of a stone.[23] Until his death in 1808, John Dovaston conducted the summer festival every year without any formal organization. In 1809 Thomas Yates, who succeeded as president, arranged for written rules, which were recorded by J. F. M. Dovaston. Every year thereafter the president named his successor for the following year before leaving the hill, and "the president's will being by him signified" was "in all cases [to] be held decisive law." But the president had to pay for those prerogatives since he alone was "at the whole Expence, and Trouble of providing a plain cold dinner; Rum, Brandy, and Beer." No laurel being available in the area, a poet laureate could not be created; instead, the abundant fern on the hill led to the substitution of the august position of poet ferneat, a post which vied in importance with that of queen of the hill, which the president filled by solemn pronouncement each year af-

ter selecting from the fair revellers. J. F. M. Dovaston was president, poet ferneat, and recorder in 1810; vice-president and poet ferneat in 1811; and poet ferneat in 1812.

Although there is no certain evidence, it seems highly probable that Reynolds attended these festivities with his friend Dovaston while he lived in Shrewsbury, until 1806, while the affairs were being conducted by the elder Dovaston, and he may well have come over from London for such happy occasions in later years. In 1813 Reynolds himself served as poet ferneat, as the following extract from the minutes reveals:

> July 12, 1813
>
> The day was fine and the company numerous. At one o'clock upwards of sixty sat down to dinner, soon after which the usual convivialities began. The annual tribute of the Poet Ferneat M[r] John Hamilton Reynolds of Lambeth was received with heartfelt applause, and he being absent his cup was crowned with the Ferne.

The poem which Reynolds sent shows that he was familiar with the customs of the occasion:

The Reflections of Mirth, On the Eve of the Breidden Festival, for the Year 1813.

To Morrow's dawn shall scarcely light
The ferny brow of Breidden's height,
    Ere souls of wit and worth
Will rise to sip at Pleasure's rill,
And to make that *"heaven kissing hill"*
    A *kissing* hill of *earth*.

That morn shall find each roseate streak
Reflected bright in many a cheek,
    It's light in many an eye:
The gladsome smiles of day shall grace
The festive scene, and many a face
    Will shine as brilliantly.

Wit and song the scene shall crown,
I the corpse of Care will drown,
    And give the wine a zest.
The sun shall view the gen'rous feast
When first he rises in the east,
    And when he leaves the west.

Time shall throw aside his scythe then;
Time shall bless the feast of Breidden,
    While gay the gambols pass;
Time shall lose his grating pow'r,
Shall disregard the *sandy* hour,
    And only use the *glass*.

Then quickly fly, ye shades of night,
And quickly come, O morning bright,
    In all thy colours fair;
Every lov'd one, every friend,
Around my favour'd circle blend,
    While I support the chair.

                            John H. Reynolds

Occupying the chair which his poem, read in absentia, supported was Henry Langley, president of the society for that year. The punning evident in the poem, which Reynolds loved all his life, culminated in 1825 in *Odes and Addresses to Great People,* written jointly with Hood. Perhaps it is not too obvious to explain that the "favour'd circle" of the next to the last line refers not only to his many friends in the society gathered for the occasion, but to his wine glass, which he knew would be ceremonially crowned with fern. The reference anticipates happily the many years of convivial imbibing which he would enjoy, but also unhappily the very heavy drinking of his last half-dozen years.

Like Lamb, whom he knew well, Reynolds continued with his clerical duties and produced literary work in his spare time. After following Dovaston's lead by submitting several pieces to the *Gentleman's Magazine* in 1812 and 1813, he expanded to more ambitious efforts in 1814. Through the publishing firm of his friend John Martin, he issued *Safie, an Eastern Tale* in an attempt to capitalize on the vogue of Byronic Oriental tales in verse. Byron was favorably impressed with the book, as can be seen from the entry in his journal, his letter to Reynolds, and his letter to Francis Hodgson recommending a favorable review. Not only did he make these efforts to encourage the author and foster the book; he also met personally with Reynolds over "a vegetable dinner."[24] Later in the same year Reynolds published, again through Martin, *The Eden of Imagination,* an elaborate imitation of Wordsworth, chiefly in the manner of *An Evening Walk.* Martin's short-lived periodical the *Inquirer* also furnished him with an outlet for several poems and prose pieces.

His satisfaction with these promising early achievements was clouded darkly late in 1814 by the death of an unidentified girl whom he loved, a tragedy over which he grieved repeatedly in numerous poems dating from January 1815. But in late 1815 he had recovered sufficiently to take several steps up the journalistic-literary ladder by joining the staff of John Scott's influential *Champion,* an association which he continued through December 1817. He increased the volume of his production markedly during these years with a steady flow of literary essays, theatrical reviews, and verse, including, aside from his abundant contributions to the *Champion,* **"An Ode"** (1815) on the overthrow of Napoleon published by Martin.

Perhaps it was through his publisher, John Martin, that Reynolds met Benjamin Bailey and James Rice, Jr., since Martin's sister married Bailey's brother.[25] Rice, two years older than Reynolds, was a junior attorney in his father's London office; Bailey, three years older than Reynolds, was a serious young man with strong moral and religious inclinations and a "loquacious pen" (as he described it) who resided in London where he had come from his native Cambridgeshire. Rice, whose bad health remained chronic, traveled often to Sidmouth in Devon for relief. In the summer of 1814, he took with him his new friend Bailey, and there the two first met Mary, Sarah, and Thomasine Leigh.[26] A warm friendship developed quickly with the sisters and their cousin Maria Pearse, who spent much time at their home, Slade Hall. Visiting them at Slade about a dozen times from 1814 to 1817, and meeting them at least once at Clifton near Bristol, Rice and Bailey established close bonds with all these "adopted sisters," to whom they supplied abundant verse and glowing prose celebrations of friendship. Bailey fell in love with the youngest, Thomasine, and waxed most sentimental about his adored "Zilia," but she never returned his love, and he came to realize that she was not just displaying maidenly modesty. In 1817 she settled the matter finally by marrying Lieutenant John Carslake of the Royal Navy.

Two of their friendly projects may give some of the flavor of their intimate association. In the spring of 1815, they planted six sweetbriars in the garden at Slade to commemorate their reunion and to represent their growing friendship. In March of the same year, after reading and copying into commonplace books Wordsworth's "Poems on the Naming of Places," they made a walking tour of the coast, naming six rocks of the Dunscombe Cliffs for each of the group and adding a seventh "Union Rock" to symbolize their closeness.

By 25 March 1815 Eliza Powell Drewe from Exeter had joined the group. Bailey was considerate in easing her into this "very dear circle of friends" when she at first imagined that he "thought lightly of her" as an outsider.[27] Despite a certain ponderousness and stiffness of manner, Bailey emerges from the voluminous records as a rather attractive person. Though usually more sentimental or moral than gay, he was capable of high-spirited congeniality. Rice emerges as a man who refused to permit recurring illness to repress his warm affection, his lively wit, and his playful teasing and joking.

Thanks to Clayton E. Hudnall's admirable study of the Leigh Browne-Lockyer Collection, an old error has been corrected, and we now know that Reynolds did not join Bailey and Rice in their visits to Slade during the first two years. The first date by which we can be certain that Reynolds had met Bailey was 18 February 1815, when Bailey wrote a poem on his introduction to Reynolds's sisters,[28] but the two young men may have known each other for some time before Reynolds introduced his friend to the family. The first recorded date by which Reynolds knew Rice was 17 June 1815, the date in a book presented by Reynolds to Rice, who in turn presented it to Thomasine Leigh.[29] It seems virtually certain, however, that Rice, who was so close to

Bailey, would have met Reynolds soon after Bailey did, if indeed it was not Rice who preceded Bailey as Reynolds's friend.

Bailey and Rice sang the praises of this young published poet whose two 1814 volumes had been reviewed rather widely and favorably, and the Leigh girls were so impressed that they welcomed any of his verses which they could secure for their commonplace books. In October and November 1815 Rice and Bailey wrote two letters from London which describe vividly the kind of life that they and Reynolds were living at the time. The three frequently spent their evenings together after Rice had finished his legal duties and Reynolds his clerical work. First Rice on 9 October 1815:

> . . . when the Evening closes in & we "stir the fire & wheel the sofa round and draw the curtains close" when "we retire the world shut out."[30] Then it is that We Bailey Reynolds & myself in all the luxury of mental relaxation indulge our fancies our feelings & our humors, & without any of the prescriptions of form, ramble over the fields of imagination running after every butterfly subject that starts up before us.—You will of course suppose that he [Reynolds] is no stranger to our delightful & dear Sisterhood of Slade—but do not therefore for a moment think that we profane your names to those to whom you ought to be Strangers or in whose actual acquaintance we are not confident you would be pleased.—We have always some project on the carpet, some game ever afoot—Either Reynolds or Bailey have ever got the Muses Spur in their side that will not allow them rest or respite—& very sad things their productions *may* be for ought I know—but they give up pleasure & make us every now & then cry "excellent" & that serves our turn you Know as well as if they were better. Reynolds has made progress in a Tragedy that according to my own judgment (if it be not particularized) bids fair to stamp his name with very current reputation.—Within this week too we have bethought of us turning that delightful little tale of Louisa Venoni[31] into an Opera for which it has ever seemed to me admirably suited—I have bargained to furnish the plot & some of the humour & Reynolds the serious & sentimental—or as a Satirist would quiz it, he is to be the Quack & I the merry Andrew of the Piece—no matter if these Our Plans never come to anything or change once a month like the Moon, like her too they serve to enliven our Nights whilst they *do* last.—[32]

Then on 24 November 1815 Bailey described their joint composition of a poem to celebrate Sarah Leigh's birthday:

> I told you in my letter of yesterday that we kept or were to keep your birthday at my rooms. . . . On the other side is our *playfulness of affection* [the poem]. Reynolds late in the Evening regretted that we had not sooner thought of writing a Poem on the occasion in *triplets* Each person writing a line. . . . I therefore immediately produced the paper, and wrote the first line. . . . They were all written in whirlwinds of laughing. For it was our delight so to change the thought of

the person who wrote last as to puzzle him to convert it into anything like agreement or sense with his own, and then to laugh and make what noise we could to interrupt the unhappy artist who was doomed to scratch his head for a thought. . . . I wish you could see Reynolds whose lines are so superior in this little thing to ours—[33]

Toward the middle of 1816, when *The Naiad* neared publication, Reynolds felt secure enough to abandon his clerical work at the Amicable Assurance Society. After Taylor and Hessey issued the poem in August, he left with Rice for a long vacation in Exeter and Sidmouth. During the visit at Slade Hall from 31 August through 11 September, he met the Leighs in the company of Eliza Powell Drewe of Exeter, whom he later married. His letters to Benjamin Robert Haydon reveal that he did not, as has long been supposed, meet Eliza through the Leighs. When he wrote Haydon on 26 August, five days before the visit to Slade, he already knew the Drewes. He was evidently visiting in their house in Exeter; he certainly knew them well enough to ask Haydon to send his letters to their address.[34] He had probably met Eliza and her family through the Drewes' London relative, Mrs. Butler, a friend of the Reynolds family in Lambeth.[35]

Proud of *The Naiad: A Tale with Other Poems,* which combined imitation of Scott and Wordsworthian overtones in the title poem, with Wordsworthian influence even more apparent in the short pieces, he sent the revered Wordsworth himself a copy for judgment. With candor and directness, veiled only thinly by concern for the young poet's feelings, Wordsworth replied with considerable censure and only limited praise. Reynolds must have been disappointed.

His disappointment over Wordsworth's letter was more than compensated for by the greatest good fortune from another direction, as he welcomed Keats into the circle which included Haydon and Leigh Hunt. By the time of his return from the vacation in Devonshire, his friendship with Haydon was well established. Although he admired the painter's achievements and expressed his admiration enthusiastically, he was not overawed by the older man's towering ambition and immense confidence in his own ability, as the mock attack and joking tone of much of the two letters he wrote from Exeter reveal. In October 1816 he spent a great deal of time with Hunt and with Haydon, whose temporary quarters at 7 Pond Street, Hampstead, allowed him to visit constantly with Hunt. After Charles Cowden Clarke introduced Keats to Hunt in the week of 13 October[36] and Keats presented Hunt with the sheaf of selected poems as a sample, Reynolds was one of those friendly critics among whom the poems circulated for judgment, as can be seen from Haydon's verses to Reynolds.[37] Aware of his own ability, and ambitious as he was for *The Naiad,* a copy of which he had already sent Hunt, he saw immediately that Keats's poetic potential was clearly superior to his own, and he told Haydon so forthrightly. He could not be envious of one whom he sensed at the outset as the greatest poet of his generation. Furthermore, he was immediately attracted by the extraordinary personality of Keats the man: he dined with Keats at Haydon's in Hampstead on 20 October 1816 and with Keats at Hunt's on another evening in October.[38] From that beginning developed the friendship which was to be Keats's closest outside his family for the next remarkable three years.

Soon Reynolds introduced Keats to his family, who by 22 November 1816 had moved from Lambeth to 19 Lamb's Conduit Street, where Keats visited them often. George Reynolds continued his service of more than seven years for Christ's Hospital, a position which he combined with that of writing master to the Female Asylum in Lambeth. After he was appointed head writing master in 1817,[39] he moved in early 1818 to one of the master's houses near Christ's Hospital in Little Britain.[40] Like Haydon before him, Keats was quickly welcomed by Reynolds's sisters; on 9 March 1817 he wrote of the "kind sisters." He was understandably more attracted to the older girls, Jane, twenty-six, and Mariane, twenty, than he was to the younger sisters. For almost two years he was thoroughly sympathetic, writing them gay and affectionate letters, while they reciprocated by entertaining him in their home and preserving drafts of his poems in their commonplace books. In October 1818 a reaction against their sentiment which had been accumulating climaxed in his disapproval of their jealous treatment of Mrs. Reynolds's niece, Jane Cox, and during his last months in England he was infuriated with both mother and daughters because of their disapproval of Fanny Brawne. But none of this later dislike of mother and sisters seriously affected his close friendship with the son and brother.

Through Reynolds, either directly or indirectly, Keats met most of the other friends who are now such familiar members of the Keats circle. By 17 March 1817 he knew Charles and Maria Dilke, and through the Dilkes he met Charles Brown. By about 12 April 1817 a transfer had been arranged from Keats's unsatisfactory first publisher to John Taylor and James A. Hessey, Reynolds's friends who had published *The Naiad*; significantly, Keats wrote his first letter to Taylor and Hessey from the Reynolds house. Before he left for the Isle of Wight on 14 April 1817, he had met Rice, and about the same time he met Bailey, when the sudden death of a friend brought him to London from Oxford, where he had matriculated on 19 October 1816 to read for holy orders. Keats called John Martin friend by August 1817 and saw him frequently thereafter. Through either Reynolds or Taylor and Hessey, he met Richard Woodhouse, to whom our debt is very great for preserving so much Keatsian material.

Reynolds's services to Keats are so familiar as to require only summary here. He stimulated Keats's writing of *Isabella, Robin Hood,* the espistle *To J. H. Reynolds, Esq.,* and numerous short pieces. His discussions and correspondence evoked some of Keats's finest letters on poetry. He championed Keats's reputation vigorously, reviewing *Poems* of 1817 and *Endymion* favorably, encouraging sympathetic reviews from others, and preventing him from publishing the first brash preface to *Endymion.* Throughout the friendship Reynolds was clear-sighted and unselfish. Though Hunt had praised Reynolds equally with Keats and Shelley in the "Young Poets" article in the *Examiner* of 1 December 1816, Reynolds never confused his own great talent with his friend's genius. He wrote Keats prophetically, "Do *you* get Fame,—and I shall have it in being your affectionate and steady friend."[41] The same modest disavowal of hope for fame appeared also in **"The Pilgrimage of Living Poets," ** in **"Farewell to the Muses,"** and in two fine sonnets in **The Fancy.**

Despite Reynolds's diffidence, the association with Keats stimulated his own work, as he continued to produce a large volume of material for the periodicals, and at the same time wrote the poems which went into **The Garden of Florence and Other Poems** (1821). Probably because he had resolved on marriage to Eliza Powell Drewe in 1817 (Keats does not speak of an engagement until 13 July 1818, but he treats it as a matter long settled[42]), he turned to a steady source of income to replace the salary from the clerical work which he had resigned the preceding year. Rice encouraged him to enter law, generously paying for him the fee of £110, and promising to take him in as a partner if he ever succeeded to his father's business—a promise which he fulfilled faithfully.[43] On 4 November 1817 Reynolds became an articled pupil in the office of Francis Fladgate, a relative of Rice, and thereafter divided his efforts between literature and the law in such a fashion that both his interests eventually suffered. He vacillated between objection to the dreariness of the law and interest in it: five months after his entry Keats is obviously replying to his complaints about the law when he reassures him that all knowledge, including even dull civil law, has value,[44] but after another year Keats reports, "Reynolds is completely limed in the law: he is not only reconcil'd to it but hobbyhorses upon it."[45]

During the three years after his entry into law, Reynolds's resolution to concentrate on it was partially thwarted by recurring illness and partially broken by heavy contributions to periodicals and by other writing. He wrote for the *Yellow Dwarf,* the *Alfred,* Constable's *Edinburgh Magazine,* and the *Edinburgh Review.* His reputation rose to such a height that William Blackwood went to surprising lengths to seduce him away from his liberal friends. On a visit to London Blackwood sought him out: Keats reports that "Blackwood wanted very much to see him—the scotch cannot manage by themselves at all—they want imagination."[46] John Gibson Lockhart flattered him by praising him above Hazlitt: "The only enlivening things in it [Constable's *Edinburgh Magazine*] are a few articles now and then by Hazlitt, and a few better still by a gay writer of the name of Reynolds. . . . Mr. Reynolds, however, is certainly a very promising writer, and might surely do better things than copying the Cockneys."[47] Blackwood's ally in the enemy camp, Peter George Patmore, brought to its climax this campaign to make Reynolds abandon his friends and turn his coat; on 7 April 1819 he wrote Blackwood:

> I dined with Reynolds a few days ago—and talked with him about writing for you—but, as I expected, from his friendship with Hunt and Hazlitt, he has a feeling about the Magazine which prevents him—otherwise I know he would like to do so—for I was pleased to find that he didn't scruple to speak very highly of the general talent with which the work is conducted. He was very much pleased with the liberal offer you made him—to choose his subject and name his own terms.[48]

In the light of Reynolds's financial need and the startling offer to name his own price, it is very much to his credit that he resisted all advances and remained just as determined as Keats not to "Mortgage [his] Brain to Blackwood."[49]

In addition to contributions to periodicals, Reynolds also produced during his association with Keats the splendid parody of Wordsworth's *Peter Bell* on 15 April 1819; a farce entitled ***One, Two, Three, Four, Five: By Advertisement*** on 17 July 1819, which Robert Gittings has recently suggested may be worthy of revival; the pseudo-autobiographical memoirs of Peter Corcoran called ***The Fancy*** in 1820; and ***The Garden of Florence and Other Poems*** in 1821. Gittings has observed of the last volume what is certainly true, though unremarked before—its similarity in general pattern to the *Lamia* volume. Both include imitations of Boccaccio, which had of course originally been planned for a joint volume. Just as *Hyperion* is a fragmentary major achievement, so **"The Romance of Youth"** is a fragmentary major effort. Reynolds's sonnets and lyrics correspond with Keats's, though Reynolds's volume has nothing approaching the massive great odes.[50] While this is not the place for extensive criticism of Reynolds's poetry, I would recommend a poem which other critics have passed over. It is not so much the title poem that is successful, nor the earnest **"Romance of Youth,"** interesting as it is, but **"The Ladye of Provence,"** which inclines toward the Chaucerian in its curious treatment of the sentimental and macabre (the heroine is tricked by her husband into eating the heart of her would-be lover). Though not so fascinating as *Isabella*, which it surpasses in weaknesses, it is a strange and

partially successful poem with just a hint of irony that leaves a teasing question as to precisely what the poet's attitude was toward his material.

While Keats lived, Reynolds reacted against three members of the Keats circle with whom he had initially been very friendly: Haydon, Bailey, and Hunt. These relationships require some consideration.

The two letters from Reynolds to Haydon in this volume complement Haydon's doggerel invitation to Reynolds to dine with Keats[51] to show clearly that by the autumn of 1816 the friendship was strong and unreserved on both sides. Like Keats, Haydon was received into the Reynolds home, as we know from his sending his best wishes to Reynolds's sisters. Reynolds's friendship with Haydon continued unabated as Keats's grew even to surpass it in 1817. But after 28 December 1817 Haydon exploded when Reynolds neither attended the immortal dinner nor gave any explanation as to why he did not attend. Reynolds could not brook that explosion because of Haydon's long history of being highhanded about appointments and other obligations. Although Reynolds's letters to Bailey have not been preserved, it seems a certain inference that Reynolds was in no mood to treat Haydon gently because Haydon had just behaved irresponsibly toward his older and closer friend, Bailey, who was courting his sister Mariane. Haydon had at first made magnanimous promises to accept an impecunious young painter named Cripps as a student without charge, then suddenly turned cool after Bailey and Keats responded to the proposal, and finally insulted Bailey with a "cutting" letter.[52] Though the Cripps affair had been smoothed out, the memory of it must have rankled. When it came to cutting, Reynolds could always give better than he or his received; he was second only to his idol, Hazlitt, in that department. He replied to Haydon with "one of the most cutting" letters Keats had ever seen, blasting all his faults and weaknesses.[53] Though Keats thought Reynolds should have been more tolerant, he conceded that Reynolds was "on the right side of the question." Of course the friendship ended, and the two were never reconciled. With the passage of time, however, Reynolds's anger cooled so that by the time he reviewed *The Conversations of James Northcote* twelve years later he was impartial enough to defend Haydon in part from Hazlitt's printed attack.[54]

The letters from Rice and Bailey to the Leigh sisters quoted above have revealed the high degree of intimacy between Reynolds and Bailey in the early period. After Bailey began his study for the clergy, the close friendship continued undiminished. Keats's extremely high praise of Bailey is matched by Reynolds's praise of him in the *Yellow Dwarf*.[55] Whenever Bailey could get to London from Oxford, he spent much time in the hospitable Reynolds home and became a paragon of all the virtues for the Reynolds women. No subject could be mentioned without mother or daughters dragging in Bailey's name: "If you mentioned the word Tea pot— some one of them came out with an a propos about Bailey—noble fellow—fine fellow!"[56]

Without the sex appeal of Reynolds, Rice, or Keats, Bailey was passionate by nature, "the slave of passion" to use his own phrase,[57] but less likely to be able to satisfy his desires irregularly, and, even if opportunities offered, he could not as a prospective clergyman easily permit himself such misconduct. Older than his friends by several years, he realized, it seems clear, that he needed a wife. He had tried Thomasine Leigh and failed. He turned to an eligible relative of John Martin's and was again rebuffed. Nothing daunted, he selected Mariane from the Reynolds sisters and paid his addresses to her. His peculiar combination of piety and passion is revealed by Keats's account of his wooing her "with the Bible and Jeremy Taylor under his arm."[58] After sustained courtship, he made his declaration, but Mariane demurred, either genuinely not in love with him as Keats thought when he reported that she loved him like a brother, or with pre-Victorian delicacy lest she be supposed to leap at a proposal. Bailey failed to play the expected part of patient and determined suitor who perseveres until he wins the heart of the modest maiden. One can hardly blame him much when he recalls that Bailey had been through all that before, pining away for three years until Thomasine Leigh married another. He was not to be frustrated again. He turned swiftly to the sister of a college classmate, found in Hamilton Gleig a woman not disposed to play at cat and mouse, and married her, after making only a stiff bow to rectitude by returning Mariane's letters and requesting the return of his own.[59]

For an ordinary man, all circumstances considered, Bailey's conduct seems perfectly understandable. But the trouble was that the Keats circle had not looked upon Bailey as an ordinary man—they, Keats included, had regarded him as godlike, and now he was revealed to be merely human. Keats was appalled. After thorough examination of the evidence, Rice decided that he would break with Bailey entirely. Reynolds must have been equally indignant over the supposed callousness to his sister. The sequel to the story, however, shows that neither Keats nor Reynolds was adamant. After time had calmed tempers, Keats wrote to congratulate him on his marriage, and when Bailey came down to London in 1820, Reynolds met him and talked with him.[60] It speaks well for Reynolds's character, as well as for Keats's, that he did not harbor an unrelenting grudge. Mariane did not suffer any serious damage; within a few years she fell in love with her future husband, H. G. Green, and was no doubt happier than she would have been if she had married Bailey and migrated to Ceylon.

Quite friendly with Leigh Hunt early in his career, Reynolds paid him an enthusiastic compliment as a poet in a footnote to *The Eden of Imagination* (1814). On 7 April 1816 he presented him favorably in **"The Pilgrimage of the Living Poets to the Stream of Castaly."**[61] When he visited the Leigh sisters in September 1816, he respected Hunt enough to copy in a commonplace book Hunt's manuscript sonnet before it was published.[62] During the first year of his friendship with Keats, he spent much time socially in Hunt's company, exchanged complimentary sonnets with him, and was grateful, we can assume, for Hunt's high praise in "Young Poets." On 10 September 1817 Reynolds's attitude toward Hunt shifted when he met Hunt in the pit at Drury Lane, where he had gone to review for the *Champion* and Hunt for the *Examiner.*[63] When he told Hunt that Keats was progressing toward the completion of four thousand lines of *Endymion,* Hunt replied possessively: "Ah! . . . had it not been for me they would have been 7,000!"[64] Since he was still very close to Haydon, Reynolds's sympathy had been deflected away from Hunt by Haydon's quarrelling with him. Haydon had warned that Hunt was jealously seeking to preserve the idea that Keats was his protégé, and now Hunt's statement confirmed Haydon's assertion. Reynolds wrote Keats at Oxford of the incident, whereupon Keats conjured up an image of the scene in the theater, "I think I see you and Hunt meeting in the Pit,"[65] and launched into combined disparagement and praise of Hunt.

Thereafter Reynolds's attitude toward Hunt increased in antipathy. Although but one of his letters to Keats has survived, it is easy to understand why so many of Keats's attacks on Hunt were written to Reynolds: Keats was sure that Reynolds would be a receptive reader. Reynolds did not abandon his own liberal views—he contributed to John Hunt's *Yellow Dwarf* and he allowed Leigh Hunt to reprint his defense of *Endymion* in the *Examiner*—nor did he compromise his political principles by writing for the Tory press, but he sensed the danger to Keats's literary reputation posed by continued association in the public mind of Keats's name with Hunt's, and he sought to prevent it. He remonstrated successfully against a plan for publishing *Hyperion* in a joint volume with a work by Hunt.[66] When he reprinted the revised version of the early **"Pilgrimage of the Living Poets"** in 1820 as **"Living Authors: A Dream,"** he quietly omitted the favorable treatment of Hunt, compensating only slightly by adding in a footnote condescending praise of the *Indicator* as "a very clever little periodical work."[67] Even more strongly than Keats, he reacted against Hunt's personal traits, writing John Taylor of "the vain and heartless eternity of Mr Leigh Hunt's indecent discoursings" and of "the irksome, wearing consciousness of a disgusting presence, than which I know of nothing more dispiriting."[68] It is not surprising that Reynolds's savage private attacks cloaked by public civility left Hunt so baffled that he wrote Hazlitt, "Reynolds is a machine I don't see the meaning of."[69]

Many years later Charles Cowden Clarke, who remained unswervingly loyal to Hunt, noted that "Reynolds poisoned him [Keats] against Hunt—who never varied towards Keats."[70] But that remark is only a partial truth; Clarke's love of Hunt led him to overstate the case. Reynolds reenforced a change in Keats's attitude, as Keats realized for himself Hunt's limitations and weaknesses.

After Reynolds's death, Charles W. Dilke wrote from general recollection that "in every number of the London the traces of his light and pleasant pen were visible."[71] The new letter to John Scott in this volume refines upon Dilke's memory by showing the date and circumstances of Reynolds's beginning his contributions, as well as identifying the long two-part essay "On Fighting" in his best lively and jocular manner.

As a contributor to the *London,* he became involved indirectly in the duel which led to the death of its first editor, John Scott, and he and Rice served as attorneys for Scott's second, Peter G. Patmore, in the legal action that followed. After Taylor and Hessey acquired the magazine in 1821, for three and a half years he assisted with the editing and wrote most of the theatrical reviews, epistolary articles under the pseudonym Edward Herbert, other literary articles, reviews of current books, and poems. Although Dilke's statement that these years were "the only true period of his literary life"[72] is inaccurate because it neglects his achievement during Keats's lifetime, it serves to emphasize the success he enjoyed with the *London.* He published prose worthy to be printed along with the greatest prose geniuses of the period, Lamb and Hazlitt, and he joined Lamb, Hazlitt, Thomas De Quincey, Bryan Waller Procter, John Clare, and other contributors at the convivial dinners given by John Taylor.

His long-delayed marriage to Eliza Powell Drewe on 31 August 1822, accompanied by the jubilation of many old members of the Keats circle as can be seen from Thomas Hood's comic progress to celebrate the event, led to many years of domestic happiness. Though he had lost Keats, he gained Hood, who married his sister Jane in 1825, and the second literary friendship flourished too.[73] What life was like in the Reynolds home at this time can best be seen in a passage from Hood's letter to Mrs. Reynolds about January 1823 when he was engaged to Jane:

> I shall need all my strength if you expect me to come and romp with your grandchild [Eliza Reynolds Longmore's baby]. My dear Jane writes that owing to Mr. Acland's delay, it is likely that they may not come up till the week after next. Pray make use of the interval in double-bracing your nerves against "the little sensible Longmore." She will put you to your Hop-Tea. I expect she will quite revolutionise Little Britain. The awful brow of Mariane, the muscular powers of Lottie, the serious remonstrances of Aunt Jane, the maternal and grand-maternal authorities will be set at naught with impunity. As for Green [Mariane's suitor] and I, we shall come up empty about dinner-time, and in the hubbub, be sent empty away. The old china will be cracked like mad; the tour-terelles, finger-blotted and spoiled; the chintz—now *couleur de rose*—all rumpled and unflounced! . . .
>
> Think of your good and clever daughters, who paint sea nymphs, and sing, and play on the piano; and of your son John, dear to the Muses. I think few families have been dealt with so well, if, indeed, any. There's Jane, and Eliza, Mariane, and Lottie,—four Queens; and John,—you must count "two for his nob."[74]

The scene here depicted supplements Keats's more fragmentary references to suggest the appeal of this cultured and hospitable home five years before to John, George, and Tom Keats, Rice, Bailey, Woodhouse, and Charles and Maria Dilke.

When he left the *London,* Reynolds's comic and satirical gifts continued, first in a sparkling attack on John Wilson in the *Westminster Review* and then in his greatest popular success in 1825, **Odes and Addresses to Great People,** the work produced anonymously with Hood which Coleridge was certain that no one but Lamb could have written. From 1828 through 8 June 1831 he owned part of the *Athenaeum,* but he unfortunately sold his share to protest Dilke's cutting the price in half. He must have regretted that step sorely as Dilke's judgment proved sound and the magazine prospered, while his own financial situation grew ever more desperate. He managed, however, to supplement his income from law by contributing steadily to the *Athenaeum* through 1837; as pedestrian as much of that work was, he deserves credit for leading Dilke's campaign against the corrupt puffing of new books. Theatrical writing also augmented his income: to the operetta **Gil Blas** of 1822 and the **Mathews** monologues of the twenties, he added in the thirties **Fanny Kelley's Recollections** (1830), **A New Entertainment** (1833), and **Confounded Foreigners** (1838).

The Garrick Club, which he joined as a charter member in 1831, provided an opportunity to meet socially with Thackeray and Richard Harris Barham, both of whom sought to assist him in placing his work in periodicals. The new Garrick Club letters in this volume display some small but attractive facets of his character. He shows his solicitousness for Eliza by ordering special meat for her in her illness. He reveals his kindliness toward the old porter, whom other members wanted discharged because of senility, by requesting that he be given the convenience of a chair and a rug.

After more than a decade of family harmony in his close and happy association with Hood, in 1835 Hood quarreled bitterly with the Reynolds family, as Jane lay desperately ill. Although Hood specifically excepted Reynolds from the angry blasts that he fired at the other members of the family, Reynolds must have been sorely grieved by this family friction. In the same year his life was darkened further by the death at the age of ten of his daughter, Lucy, the only child surviving after the death of an infant years before.[75]

On 26 October 1838 a long history of financial difficulties resulted in a certificate of bankruptcy. The increasing need for money pressed him to cease contributing to the respected *Athenaeum* and to turn instead to the less dignified but more lucrative *New Sporting Magazine,* which he edited through 1840. After long service as Hood's attorney, he was dismissed in 1841, and that abrupt action probably marked a break in the old friendship.[76] During his last decade, he clung precariously to the small prestige of a free-lance author by contributing to *Ainsworth's Magazine,* the *New Monthly,* and *Bentley's Miscellany.* The letters to Richard Bentley, new in this book, identify another series of essays in the *Miscellany,* including copious paraphrases of Latin verse, though neither prose nor verse is superior in quality to his late work which has long been known.

Abandoning private legal practice in 1847, he secured a position as assistant clerk of the county court at Newport in the Isle of Wight, where he spent his last five years. Having procrastinated his own life of Keats for twenty-five years, he was pleased to cooperate enthusiastically with Richard Monckton Milnes in preparing the first extensive biography. In other respects his last years were gloomy. Although Lord Ernle may have exaggerated somewhat in calling him "a broken-down, discontented man . . . whose drunken habits placed him beyond the pale of society,"[77] since he did function responsibly and earn the respect of many in the Isle of Wight,[78] it is clear that he drank heavily and that he was usually unhappy and depressed before he died on 15 November 1852. Lord Ernle meant to damn him by charging that he went to his grave a "professed . . . Unitarian and a bitter Radical," but for that integrity Hazlitt would have been proud of his old comrade on the *Yellow Dwarf* in the campaign against autocratic kings and self-serving prelates.

Notes

1. Guildhall Library, London, MS 5266, vol. 4; MS 5265, vol. 5; MS 5257, vol. 10; and MS 5257, vol. 11, as recorded in Robert Gittings, "The Poetry of John Hamilton Reynolds," *Ariel,* I (1970), 8-9 (hereafter cited as Gittings).

2. George L. Marsh, *John Hamilton Reynolds: Poetry and Prose* (London: Oxford University Press, 1928), pp. 10-11 (hereafter cited as *J. H. R.: Poetry and Prose*).

3. *Edinburgh Review,* XXX (June 1817), 260.

4. See p. 17 below.

5. Henry C. Shelley, *Literary By-paths in Old England* (Boston: Little, Brown, and Co., 1906), pp. 222-23 (hereafter cited as Shelley).

6. Phyllis G. Mann, "The Reynolds Family," *Keats-Shelley Journal,* V (1956), 6.

7. Gittings, pp. 9-10.

8. John F. M. Dovaston, *Fitz-Gwarine, with Other Rhymes* (Shrewsbury, 1813).

9. Leonidas M. Jones, ed., *Selected Prose of John Hamilton Reynolds* (Cambridge, Mass.: Harvard University Press, 1966), pp. 309-11 (hereafter cited as *Selected Prose*).

10. Guildhall Library, MS 5265.

11. Mann, "The Reynolds Family," p. 7. Many records erroneously report the date of her birth as 1792.

12. I follow Hyder Rollins in spelling the name as her son always spelled it. Keats and others spell it variously and inconsistently.

13. Leonidas M. Jones, "New Letters, Articles, and Poems by John Hamilton Reynolds," *Keats-Shelley Journal,* VI (1957), 103.

14. *London Magazine,* VII (May 1823), 525-26.

15. Ibid., IX (January 1824), 35-36.

16. Ibid., IV (July 1821), 8-9.

17. John Masefield, ed., *The Fancy* (London: Elkin Mathews, 1905).

18. *Selected Prose,* pp. 261-63.

19. Marsh, *J. H. R.: Poetry and Prose,* p. 11.

20. Richard Harris Barham, *The Garrick Club* (New York: privately printed, 1896), p. 42.

21. Marsh, *J. H. R.: Poetry and Prose,* pp. 12-13.

22. Gittings, p. 10.

23. A manuscript book of the constitution, laws, and minutes of the society is in the Houghton Library at Harvard.

24. *Selected Prose,* p. 252. This was the only logical time for the meeting between them which Reynolds reported.

25. Gittings, p. 12.

26. Clayton E. Hudnall, "John Hamilton Reynolds, James Rice, and Benjamin Bailey in the Leigh

Browne-Lockyer Collection," *Keats-Shelley Journal,* XIX (1970), 13 (hereafter cited as Hudnall).

27. Ibid., p. 17.

28. Ibid., p. 18.

29. Ibid., p. 38.

30. Cf. Cowper, *The Task,* IV. 36-37.

31. By Mr. M'Kenzie in the *New Novelist's Magazine,* 1786, pp. 151-55.

32. Hudnall, pp. 31-32.

33. Ibid., p. 34.

34. See p. 4 below.

35. Gittings, p. 11, reports the friendship of the Reynoldses and Butlers and states that the Butlers had lived in Lambeth. Eliza's father and brother George (and presumably also her mother) having died before the wedding to John, Mrs. Butler represents for Eliza's side "The Head of the Family" in Hood's progress celebrating the wedding (Shelley, p. 325); she was therefore especially close to Eliza.

36. On the much discussed question of the date of the first meeting, Robert Gittings has the last, and I believe accurate, word in *John Keats* (Boston: Little, Brown, and Co., 1968), p. 83.

37. Hyder E. Rollins, ed., *The Keats Circle,* 2d ed., 2 vols. (Cambridge, Mass.: Harvard University Press, 1965), I, 4-5 (hereafter cited as *KC*).

38. Gittings, *John Keats,* pp. 92-93.

39. Mann, "The Reynolds Family," p. 6.

40. Shelley, p. 326.

41. See p. 13 below.

42. Hyder E. Rollins, ed., *The Letters of John Keats,* 2 vols. (Cambridge, Mass.: Harvard University Press, 1958), I, 325 (hereafter cited as *Letters*).

43. Marsh, *J. H. R.: Poetry and Prose,* pp. 21-22.

44. *Letters,* I, 276-77.

45. Ibid., II, 78.

46. Ibid.

47. John G. Lockhart, *Peter's Letters to His Kin-Folk,* 2d ed., 2 vols. (Edinburgh, 1819), II, 227-28. Published before 19 July 1819, when Sir Walter Scott acknowledged receipt of his copy.

48. Alan Lang Strout, "Knights of the Burning Epistle," *Studia Neophilologica,* XXVI (1953-54), 85.

49. *Letters,* II, 178-79.

50. Gittings, p. 13.

51. *KC,* I, 4-6.

52. *Letters,* I, 183.

53. Ibid., I, 205.

54. *Selected Prose,* pp. 414-15.

55. Ibid., p. 215.

56. *Letters,* II, 67.

57. Hudnall, p. 25.

58. *Letters,* II, 67.

59. Ibid., II, 66.

60. *KC,* I, 232.

61. *Selected Prose,* p. 48.

62. Hudnall, pp. 20-21n.

63. *Letters,* I, 162, 169. Files of the two newspapers reveal the date and place. Reynolds wrote no review for 7 September 1817. For 14 September 1817 Reynolds and Hunt reviewed the same performance, and both mention attending on the same night, 10 September.

64. Ibid., I, 169.

65. Ibid., I, 162.

66. See p. 66 below.

67. *Selected Prose,* p. 256n.

68. See p. 22 below.

69. Percival P. Howe, *The Life of William Hazlitt,* 3d ed. (London: Hamilton, 1947), p. 291.

70. *The Novello-Cowden Clarke Collection* (University of Leeds, 1955), p. 9.

71. *Athenaeum,* 27 November 1852, p. 1296.

72. *Notes and Queries,* 4 October 1856, p. 275.

73. For detailed accounts of the Reynolds-Hood relationship, see Alvin Whitley, "Keats and Hood," *Keats-Shelley Journal,* V (1956), 33-47, and Peter F. Morgan, "John Hamilton Reynolds and Thomas Hood," *Keats-Shelley Journal,* XI (1962), 83-95.

74. Shelley, pp. 329-30. For non-cribbage players, the nob is the jack, held in the hand, of the same suit as the card turned up. It counts one in the game; Hood shows his admiration for Reynolds by doubling his nob. Keats occasionally called him Jack too.

75. *KC,* I, cxxi.

76. Morgan, "John Hamilton Reynolds and Thomas Hood," pp. 90-91.

77. Rowland E. Prothero, Lord Ernle, *The Works of Lord Byron, Letters and Journals,* 6 vols. (London: John Murray, 1898-1901), III, 46n.

78. Willard B. Pope, "John Hamilton Reynolds, the Friend of Keats," *Wessex,* III (1935), 3-15.

Leonidas M. Jones (essay date June 1979)

SOURCE: Jones, Leonidas M. "Reynolds' 'The Romance of Youth,' Hazlitt, and Keats's *The Fall of Hyperion.*" *English Language Notes* 16, no. 4 (June 1979): 294-300.

[*In the following essay, Jones compares poems by Reynolds and Keats, noting their similarities and arguing that Reynolds's work came first.*]

Noting the marked similarity between Keats's encounter with Moneta in *The Fall of Hyperion* and Reynolds' poet's confrontation with the visionary female in **"The Romance of Youth,"** Robert Gittings suggested that Reynolds' passage was a rather tame and pale echo of the intense and poetically charged imagery of his great friend.[1] Since **"The Romance of Youth"** was not published until May 1821, that is the normal inference which anyone would make faced by the apparently earlier composition of Keats's poem. But Gittings could not know of Clayton E. Hudnall's revelation in his excellent study of the Leigh Browne-Lockyer Collection that in January 1817 Reynolds copied into commonplace books Stanzas 30, 31, 35, 92, and 93 of **"The Romance of Youth,"** as well as two partial stanzas that were not published.[2]

Hudnall's revelation, combined with Reynolds' prose introduction to the published poem, shows that Reynolds had almost certainly completed his fragment before Keats began *The Fall.* Reynolds reports in his introduction that "The plan of this poem came suddenly on the Author's mind some few years back, at a time when he was passing his hours in a most romantic part of the country, and when all his feelings were devoted to poetry";[3] that is, from 31 August through 11 September 1816 when he, James Rice, and his future wife Eliza Powell Drewe were visiting the Leigh sisters at Slade Hall in Devonshire. The strong probability is that he virtually completed the fragment in the three and one-half months before he returned to Slade Hall to copy the selected stanzas in January 1817. The fragment has 104 stanzas, and Stanzas 92 and 93, which he copied, lead directly into the final eleven stanzas. In the ensuing months, he doubtless did some revising of the first draft, as the rejection of the partial stanzas from the final version indicates, but he probably had the initial draft finished by January 1817. Even if he continued to work on it for a period after that date, it is highly unlikely that he extended the process for almost two years until Keats had completed the Induction to *The Fall* in October 1818.[4]

In the prose introduction to the published fragment, Reynolds stresses that he did not revise the version written years ago, and there was no conceivable reason why he should lie since Keats's *The Fall* was not published and Reynolds could not expect that it ever would be. In the light of all these clear facts, it is a safe conclusion that **"The Romance of Youth"** preceded *The Fall of Hyperion.*

After finishing the first canto of **"The Romance of Youth"** in 1817, Reynolds set it aside for a multitude of other activities: a flood of prose for *The Champion* and *The Yellow Dwarf* and thousands of lines of other verse. On 4 November 1817 he committed himself to becoming a lawyer, a step about which he remained ambiguous for the rest of his life. Sometimes he could be enthusiastic about it, but most of the time he hated it for distracting him from achieving the great dream of his life—to become a major poet. In the spring of 1818 when he was seriously ill with rheumatic fever for several weeks, he became depressed and reflected morosely upon what seemed to him the death of his earlier poetic hopes. Since almost none of Reynolds' letters to Keats have survived, we have to infer what Reynolds wrote from Keats's replies, but in this case the inference is easily made. On 3 May 1818 Keats wrote:

> I see no reason, because I have been away this last month, why I should not have a peep at your Spencerian—notwithstanding you speak of your office, in my thought a little too early, for I do not see why a Mind like yours is not capable of harbouring and digesting the whole Mystery of Law as easily as Parson Hugh does Pepins—which did not hinder him from his poetic Canary—[5]

The "Spencerian" was **"The Romance of Youth,"** which was written in the Spenserian stanza. Reynolds evidently had been sensitive and reticent about it during the year and a half that he had come to know Keats so intimately, not showing it to Keats because so much of his poetic dream rested upon it. But now in his illness he took it out once again and wrote Keats dejectedly that he would have to abandon it because the dreary study of the law required all his time and attention.

Keats's counter argument that Reynolds might combine mastering of the law with continuing development as a poet did not succeed; Reynolds did not continue the poem beyond the first canto. But it seems highly probable that Keats must have followed through with his expectation and read the manuscript of **"The Romance of**

Youth" on his return to London. When a few months later he turned to his own major effort and wrote the Induction to *The Fall of Hyperion* in September and October of 1818, the most graphic and memorable image from Reynolds' major effort recurred to him, either consciously or unconsciously, and he varied it and intensified it masterfully in his depiction of the encounter with Moneta.

Reynolds had written:

XCII

The distant world now wooed the boy, who knew
Nought of its deadly sorrows; . . .

XCIV

But oft his sleep gave gloom;—and one night, late,
A strange and dreary vision did arise:
That in the forest deep he lay with musing eyes;

XCV

That when he lifted them—before him stood
A figure tall, and in a shadowy dress:
It was as some lone spirit of the wood,
With eyes all dim, and fixed with distress,—
And sunken cheeks,—and lips of pallidness,—
Standing with folded arms, and floating hair,
The shadow of a woman!—but a tress
Was sometimes lifted by the gusty air,
And now the waved robe a heaving breast did bare.

XCVI

He gazed—his hand paused on a turning leaf,
And his blood ran in coldness to his heart:—
He gazed—but still his eyes felt no relief;
For that dim lonely form would not depart:
It stood—as prison'd there by mystic art,
Looking upon him steadily;—he tried
To utter speech, but not a word would start
From his weak lips—her very feelings died,
And he beheld the spirit of melancholy pride!

XCVII

"I know thee, boy—and thou wilt know me better
"Ere many years be past,"—the spirit said;
"Of late thou hast pined to wear an earthly fetter,
"And wish'd these woods by thee untenanted.
"I've read thy inmost mind; and I have sped—
"My wing is rapid as the wing of Time—
"To wreak thy wish: the fault be on thy head;
"Since 'tis thy will those bounding hills to climb,
"And pass into the world, I'll crown that wayward
  crime.

XCVIII

"Thou knowest not the happiness that lies
"In this romantic home, or thou would'st not
"Seek in cold cities for it; thy young eyes
"Have seen no other than a guileless spot,
"A wood as peaceful as a fairy grot,—
"Leaf-canopied,—and peopled all with deer,
"And birds: the world thou seek'st will change thy
lot;
"There wilt thou meet with bitterness and fear,
"And in thy very heart,—the form thou seest here!"

XCIX

It vanish'd—and his slumber vanish'd too;
But not with that the frightful recollection:
The shape—the shadowy hair—the snowy hue
Of the dooming lip—the desolate dejection
Of the whole form, sank him in mute reflection
Day after day. He sought his friend, and told
The terrors of his mind; but no election
Was left him to depart or stay, for old
And cunning scoff that friend before him did unfold.[6]

Several months after he read this passage, Keats wrote:

But yet I had a terror of her robes,
And chiefly of the veils, that from her brow
Hung pale, and curtain'd her in mysteries
That made my heart too small to hold its blood.
This saw that Goddess, and with sacred hand
Parted the veils. Then saw I a wan face,
Not pin'd by human sorrows, but bright blanch'd
By an immortal sickness which kills not;
It works a constant change, which happy death
Can put no end to; deathwards progressing
To no death was that visage; it had pass'd
The lily and the snow; and beyond these
I must not think now, though I saw that face—[7]

I have quoted at length from Reynolds because copies of the poem are now rare and because it is important to show that the basic positions of the two poems are similar, though they have different emphases. Both poems indicate the superiority of a poetry based on worldly experience and human suffering over the sensuous and fanciful dreaming of the pastoral and romantic. However, in **"The Romance of Youth"** Reynolds presents the naive dreaming over the flowers, woods, streams, birds, and fairies of the rural scene as appealing, while in *The Fall of Hyperion* Keats is harsh and scathing in his disparagement of the poet as dreamer. But Reynolds is no less certain than Keats that it is essential for the poet who matures to pass beyond "the realm of Flora, and old Pan" to treatment of "the agonies, the strife / Of human hearts." He regrets that the poet must leave the unsophisticated world of dreaming, but he knows that it is inevitable if the poet is to advance to great poetry. In his prose introduction to the poem he calls his glowing depiction of the rural dream "the mere picture" of poetry, and he promises, if the first canto is favorably received, to continue with "the passion itself of poetry" concerned with the hard reality of human experience.

Keats would have been interested to read this view of poetic development so close to his own by his "co-scribbler" Reynolds, but he must have snapped to attention when he saw that the cynical friend in the last four lines of the quoted passage scoffed at any suggestion that a worthy poet could remain in the realm of dream and accepted as inevitable the poet's proceeding to worldly experience and human suffering. Again it is necessary to quote at length from **"The Romance of Youth"** to identify the friend:

LXXXVI

And he did find one friend whose heart was brave
With doubt; who ample questionings could muster,
Which would with clouds inclose a mind of purest
lustre.

LXXXVII

How is it that the minds of mortals jar
In what should be their music and their joy?
The spirit, which might make itself a star,
Doth wrap itself in clouds, and all destroy
The innocent and lofty heart, and toy
With idle questionings of serious things?—
Is it that men were made themselves to annoy
With dreams of ill, and mystic ponderings,
And doubts of old religion, and the bliss she brings.

LXXXVIII

The friend was stern to all save him, and cold
With high wrought caution,—full of fancies strange;
A lover of the heathen times of old,—
A questioner of all things in the range
Of lofty hopes,—a worshipper of change
In human practices—a denizen
In scenes which he reviled:—he would estrange
Men from their faith;—and smooth his words were,
when
Such were to win the hearts and thoughts of quiet
men.

LXXXIX

This world was all he credited,—which gave
To his retired hours a dreariness;
Oblivion was the spirit of the grave,
And chance lent life its ills and happiness,—
So deem'd he,—ah! how sore was his distress
By night, and in his meditative hours!—
Hope had for him no soft blue eye—no tress
Of golden hair—no fair and lovely bowers;
The soul was mortal all, like Summer's heedless flow-
ers.

XC

This wise friend marr'd the youngster's innocence,
Put poison in the cup of his content;
Made him no more a joyer in the sense
Of forest comfort;—turn'd his mental bent
To other scenes,—ah! scenes how different!
And did estrange him from the oak and pine.—
"Was it for such as he,"—the friend would vent
His converse thus,—"to keep a mind supine,—
"A mind that might among the great and lofty shine!"

XCI

And then he set the young thoughts straying wide,
Through metaphysic labyrinths,—which none
Have ever yet explored;—and then the pride
Of youth he did awaken with a store
Of flatteries,—and promises of more
From learned men in cities of the wise. . . .

Some of these characteristics could apply to a number of men who were Reynolds' friends: the attack on religion, the general skepticism, the love of heathen times, and the worship of change could refer to Hunt or even to Keats himself. But other features point unmistakably to Hazlitt, and to Hazlitt alone. The sternness, coldness, and "high wrought caution" with all except his friends describe the saturnine Hazlitt exactly. "A denizen / In scenes which he [the young poet] reviled" refers to Hazlitt's flagrant patronizing of brothels, which was notorious. The "metaphysic labyrinths" recall *The Principles of Human Action* and Hazlitt's life-long pride in his philosophical ability. The confidence in Reynolds' ability and the assurance that Reynolds might command the admiration of learned and wise men come as a surprise to those unfamiliar with the Reynolds-Hazlitt relationship, but these items, too, fit Hazlitt precisely. Hazlitt always had a high regard for Reynolds' ability. He secured Reynolds as his chief collaborater on the one journal that he conducted himself, *The Yellow Dwarf.* He was so impressed with Reynolds' successful imitation of his own prose style that he called Reynolds *"alter et idem"* with himself.[8] He read an entire poem by Reynolds at a public lecture, while merely quoting briefly from Keats: one suspects indeed that Hazlitt fell into one of his rare lapses in discrimination by actually valuing Reynolds over Keats. The promises of admiration from learned and wise men may sound exaggerated to twentieth century readers, if learned and wise are understood to apply to Francis Jeffrey and the regular contributors to the *Edinburgh Review,* but one must recall the enormous prestige of the *Edinburgh* at the time. And Hazlitt in a sense fulfilled that promise: he did in fact arrange to have Reynolds contribute to the *Edinburgh Review.*[9]

It seems impossible that Keats would have had to ask Reynolds who the friend was when he read the manuscript of **"The Romance of Youth"**; he would recognize the clear outline of the critical giant who was as much his mentor as he was Reynolds'. And the impact on Keats of the friend Hazlitt's expression of his final view would have had to be strong. Hazlitt's scoffing at the poet as dreamer may well have contributed its part to the sharpness, even the bitterness, of Keats's attack in *The Fall of Hyperion.*

Notes

1. Robert Gittings, "The Poetry of John Hamilton Reynolds," *Ariel,* 1 (1970), 14-15.

2. Clayton E. Hudnall, "John Hamilton Reynolds, James Rice, and Benjamin Bailey in the Leigh Browne-Lockyer Collection," *Keats-Shelley Journal,* 19 (1970), 21.

3. All Reynolds' poems are long out of print; we need new editions badly. I quote from photocopy of the typescript of "The Poetical Works of John Hamilton Reynolds," ed. George L. Marsh, in the University of Chicago Library—six weeks after I submitted this article, Donald H. Reiman published in *The Romantic Context: Poetry* series *The Garden of Florence, The Press, and Odes and Addresses to Great People* (New York, 1978). Romanticists should be grateful to Professor Reiman for his very valuable service in providing texts for a wide range of significant poets.

4. I have argued for this new dating in my "The Dating of the Two *Hyperions,*" *Studies in Bibliography,* 30 (1977), 120-135.

5. Hyder E. Rollins, ed., *The Letters of John Keats,* 2 vols. (Cambridge, 1958), I, 276.

6. Photocopy of George L. Marsh, ed., "The Poetical Works of John Hamilton Reynolds." Here and in the later quotation, I have corrected obvious typing errors silently.

7. H. W. Garrod, ed., *The Poetical Works of John Keats* (London, 1939), p. 514, I, 251-263.

8. P. P. Howe, ed., *The Complete Works of William Hazlitt,* 21 vols. (London, 1930-1934), XVIII, 353.

9. Leonidas M. Jones, "Hazlitt, Reynolds, and the *Edinburgh Review,*" *Studies in Bibliography,* 29 (1976), 342-346.

Leonidas M. Jones (essay date 1984)

SOURCE: Jones, Leonidas M. "The *Champion*—1816-1817." In *The Life of John Hamilton Reynolds,* pp. 80-96. Hanover, Vt: University Press of New England, 1984.

[In the following essay, Jones highlights Reynolds's years as a literary critic writing for Champion.*]*

Before beginning an account of his friendship with Keats, it will be well to consider what Reynolds's prose in the *Champion* reveals about his reading, critical views, and intellect. When he joined the staff of the weekly newspaper in December 1815, he could read Latin and Italian, and he had taught himself a little Greek. His wide reading in English literature in the five years after he left St. Paul's School, done in the evenings after work between dinner and midnight, was systematic and thorough enough to prepare him to be an informed critic.

His knowledge of English literature began with Chaucer, whose most striking achievement, he believed, was vividness in describing external nature: "A leaf is described by him so clearly, that its crispness and glossy greenness come directly before the sight."[1] He valued especially Chaucer's ability to portray "internal feelings as connected with external nature"; instead of merely observing a landscape, the reader caught the mood and entered into the feelings of the author. Chaucer's most characteristic mood was happiness, and descriptions of the morning, colored by that mood, he found particularly appealing: "Chaucer is the clear and breathing Poet of the months of April and May—of morning—of meadows, and birds and their harbours. . . . Chaucer delights to be up and out, before the sun—while the stars are coldly light in the cold white sky—while the trees are still, and the waters are looking through the silent air to heaven, and the dew is twinkling, and all the world seems wrapt in cheerful and quiet thought."

He praised Chaucer's subtlety in bringing characters to life; a veiled reference to the Friar's conduct, for example, struck off the essence of his character in two brief lines:

> He had ymade ful many a marriage,
> Of young women at his owen coste.

Although he found that Chaucer's low characters had more "pure bold strength" than those of any other writer, the tales of romance impressed him more than the fabliaux. He praised lavishly the magnificent vestments and the marvels of "The Squire's Tale." He found Chaucer's versification harmonious and praised his ability to fit the sound to the sense. Far from taking Chaucer's apparent simplicity at face value, he saw both the humor and the artistry of it.

He was especially pleased, as was Keats, with "The Flower and the Leaf," mistakenly attributed to Chaucer at the time. His favorite passage was the celebration of the nightingale, a subject which always made him "feel a kindness" toward any poet who treated it. Chaucer's two faults he judged to be grossness of language and a lack of selectivity.

He greatly admired all the major Elizabethan and Jacobean dramatists, but he literally worshiped Shakespeare. Reynolds frequently used religious terms to express the extent of his devotion, on one occasion describing Shakespeare as the "divinity of the world of imagination."[2] In a review of a contemporary play, he carried the analogy further:

> For our own parts, liberal and tolerant as we are in our sentiments on ordinary occasions, we must confess ourselves bigots of the right Spanish breed in matters of this kind.—Were we exalted to the Papal Chair of criticism (and critics possess the same attribute of infalli-

bility with his holiness) we should certainly pronounce against these heresies in taste, the same sentence that our holy brother used in religious differences of opinion, only reversing the *order* of the punishment—we would have them *damned here* and trust their being *burnt hereafter.*—Since however we live in so tolerant an age, that it would be in vain for us to preach up persecution against the whole sect of these dissenters from the Shakespearian Orthodoxy, it would be unjust to attack one for the offences of the whole.[3]

He was joking in part, but the reference to "Shakespearian Orthodoxy" was revealing. Such an attitude virtually precluded adverse criticism. "We feel that criticism has no right to purse its little brow in the presence of Shakespeare. He has to our belief very few imperfections,—and perhaps these might vanish from our minds, if *we* had the *perfection* properly to scan them." Consequently, the only value judgment he could make was to determine the degree of praise to be bestowed upon each of Shakespeare's works. After discussing the limitations of the historical plays, he declared: "We hate to say a word against a word of Shakespeare's,—and we can only do so by comparing himself with himself."[4]

Like Coleridge, Schlegel, and Hazlitt, Reynolds concentrated on psychological analyses of the characters. Since he considered Shakespeare the foremost "anatomist of the human heart," he felt that the critic's primary duty lay in interpreting personalities and motives. He insisted repeatedly that the characters in the plays were real people, and not merely "the idle coinage of the Poet's brain."[5] Although this device was a common Romantic method of paying tribute to Shakespeare's genius, few other critics approached the extreme to which Reynolds took it. Almost all his discussions of Shakespeare have some variation of his statement that "Macbeth, and Lear, and Othello are real beings."[6] Arguing from this premise, he eventually arrived at the strange conclusion that Shakespeare lost control over the characters after he created them.[7]

Since he was primarily interested in psychological interpretation of Shakespeare's characters, he had little use for most of the earlier critics, who "preyed only on the expressions of Shakespeare, and wholly disregarded his spirit and feeling" with their "little questionings of words and phrases . . . petty cavillings about black-letter books, or worn-out and worthless customs."[8] The only two critics whom he considered worthy of the subject were Schlegel and Hazlitt. He did not know Coleridge's similar criticism because none of Coleridge's lectures delivered before 1818 were published until 1849 and later. He regarded Schlegel's lectures, which he read in the translation of John Black, as the first significant criticism of Shakespeare.[9]

An even greater influence on his Shakespearean criticism was Hazlitt, his idol as a periodical essayist, whom he knew personally at least by 2 June 1816, when he wrote of him, "We also know one writer of the present day, who delights his readers with the most able and ingenious speculations, and who is never so eloquent as when he speaks of his own feelings. He then seems to rise above this earth, and to float in an air and in a light of his own:—his youth comes back upon him. His heart lives in a vision. He talks the purest poetry."[10] Reynolds saw Hazlitt often and for long periods of time, as we know from his glowing account of Hazlitt in the letter to Mary Leigh of 28 April 1817.[11] The two had much in common. Both had spent their early years in Shropshire, Reynolds in Shrewsbury and Hazlitt in nearby Wem. Both were theatrical and literary reviewers and essayists, and both supported themselves by their journalism—Hazlitt, indeed, wrote occasionally for the *Champion.* Because of their shared interests and because of Reynolds's charming personality and lively conversation, they became fast friends, Hazlitt offering a sympathetic and very high appraisal of Reynolds's ability and Reynolds becoming Hazlitt's disciple in literary matters. From Hazlitt Reynolds derived many of his most cherished ideas; he imitated his style, quoted him often, repeated his quotations from the old poets, and adopted his critical terms and catch phrases.[12] He seldom called Hazlitt by name in the *Champion,* but the reader of his essays soon learns to identify Hazlitt with almost any anonymous reference to a gifted writer of prose. Hazlitt is "an able writer," "a great authority in these matters," and "the critic of the *Times.*"[13]

When Hazlitt's *Characters of Shakespeare's Plays* appeared in 1817, Reynolds reviewed it at length in two installments and paid Hazlitt the highest possible tribute: "This is the only work ever written on Shakespeare, that can be deemed worthy of Shakespeare;—some remarks in Schlegel's German lectures only excepted. Now this is a sweeping assertion,—and yet it is true." He described his personal reaction to the book: "The work before us is one, of all others, which we longed to see written,—and now it is come we must make the most of it." His description of it as "a sort of mental biography of Shakespeare's characters" would have been equally applicable to his own Shakespearean criticism. He included large extracts accompanied by praise, and in only one case did he express a reservation about Hazlitt's treatment of his subject. The essay on Hamlet did not quite live up to his expectations, but he absolved Hazlitt of any blame by declaring that the subject was too sublime for even the greatest of critics.[14]

Another contemporary critic who influenced Reynolds's Shakespearean criticism was Charles Lamb, whose "Theatralia, No. 1. On Garrick and Acting; and the Plays of Shakespeare, considered with reference to their fitness for Stage Representation" (the title as Reynolds read it instead of the more familiar one given it in Lamb's *Works* of 1818), Reynolds read in the fourth

and last number of Hunt's *Reflector* of 1812. He studied that short-lived periodical carefully, sent Dovaston
copies of it, patterned the *Inquirer* on it, and copied one
article from it before sending Dovaston the issue.[15] He
did not say which one he copied, but it may well have
been the most famous one in the magazine, in which
Lamb argued that Shakespeare cannot be represented
adequately on the stage. Reynolds never mentioned
Lamb by name, perhaps because he did not know who
wrote the anonymous article, but he echoed it clearly:

> We wished the other evening, at the theatre, for the
> presence of three friends [Mary Leigh, Eliza Drewe,
> and probably James Rice], to whom we had been lately
> reading the first part of *Henry the 4th*—and to whom
> we had been also asserting that Shakespeare's plays
> suffered in the representation. They would, we feel as-
> sured, have been convinced of the truth of our asser-
> tion,—for the performance of this admirable play made
> wondrous havoc with the wit, and spirit, and poetry,
> which are so excellent and evident on a perusal. We do
> not much like to see Shakespeare tortured on the
> stage:—what has he done to deserve it?[16]

Although the review including this passage was Reynolds's fullest exposition of the argument that Shakespeare's plays cannot be represented satisfactorily on
stage, the idea was almost always present in his mind
when he reviewed the contemporary productions of
Shakespeare. On 14 December 1817, for example, he
began a review of *Hamlet,* "What has Hamlet done, that
he should be held up to mockery on an unfeeling stage,
and all his utmost and most passionate sensations turned
into pageants and the shews of grief?"[17]

Less overawed than in his criticism of Shakespeare,
Reynolds was a judicious critic of Ben Jonson. Examining the traditional charge that Jonson's pedantry had
overpowered his imagination, he admitted that the criticism had an element of truth, but he argued that the old
generalization required qualification: *The Alchemist* and
Volpone showed "a richness of character, added to a
conversational humour, that cannot be surpassed."[18] He
quoted several richly imaginative passages from Jonson's plays and masques to substantiate his claim. One
such passage from *The Sad Shepherd,* in which an old
shepherd instructs Robin Hood's followers in the art of
finding witches, shows his early love of the Robin Hood
legend, which later led him to write the two fine sonnets that he sent to Keats. Another quotation from *The
Alchemist,* Sir Epicure Mammon's extravagant description of the exotic foods on which he planned to feast
after he discovered the secret of alchemy (II, ii, 72-87),
is typical of the richly sensuous poetry that he found
especially appealing. He quoted the same passage with
similar praise in a later article for the *Scots Magazine.*[19]
Though he was never able to achieve a comparable
richness in his own verse, his admiration of it prepared
him to appreciate Keats.

In an essay devoted entirely to Jonson, he used as a
point of departure a statement by John Aikin in *Vocal
Poetry* that the exquisite gem from *The Silent Woman,*
"Still to be neat, still to be drest," was "one of the few
productions of this once celebrated author, which by
their singular elegance and neatness, form a striking
contrast to the prevalent coarseness of his tedious effu-
sions."[20] Such an assertion, said Reynolds, could prove
only one of two things: Dr. Aikin's ignorance of Jonson's works or a total lack of taste. He readily admitted
that many passages in the comedies were indelicate, but
he found it difficult to believe that a critic could find
"singular elegance and neatness" a rare quality in Jonson. In his earlier essay he had discounted the customary charge that Jonson's pedantry and love of polish
had stifled his imagination, but he considered that over-
statement more tolerable than Dr. Aikin's general censure of coarseness. Quoting William Cartwright's remark that Jonson polished until "the file would not
make *smooth* but wear,"[21] he regretted that too often the
bold and vigorous in Jonson was also bare and naked.
Nevertheless, he felt that in an unusually large number
of poems Jonson had struck the perfect balance between imagination and restraint to produce incompa-
rable classic lyrics. Passing over "Drink to me only
with thine eyes" and the lyrics in *The Sad Shepherd,*
which he supposed were already well known to his
readers, he selected for quotation several beautiful, but
less familiar lyrics from *The Gipsies Metamorphosed*
and *The Forest and Underwoods.* In conclusion he declared that any composer might bring honor to himself
by setting Jonson's lyrics to music, though in most
cases because of the excellent modulation of the verse,
music would be superfluous.

Reynolds's analyses and judgments of the other Elizabethan dramatists, who he thought occasionally approached Shakespeare and Jonson, need not be particu-
larized. Contemporary revivals of Massinger and
Beaumont and Fletcher provided opportunities for
thoughtful studies at some length. In his second theatrical review, he recommended that John Ford be revived,[22]
and, when his recommendation went unheeded, he devoted his greatest attention to his favorite Ford in the
second essay **"On the Early English Dramatists."**[23]
Marlowe, Marston, and Dekker he discussed generally
and briefly.

Reynolds was either indifferent to, or contemptuous of,
the revivals of the tragedies of the Restoration and eighteenth century like those of Thomas Southerne and
Nicholas Rowe, but he had a high regard for the comedy. Congreve and Farquhar, Goldsmith and Sheridan,
he used frequently in his theatrical reviews as models
of wit to contrast with the dull writers of his own day.
John Gay's *The Beggar's Opera* was one of the first
plays that he saw as a boy, and it remained a favorite
throughout his life. He referred to it more often than to

any other work except the plays of Shakespeare. Very much interested in boxing, he filled his essays with figures of speech based on the sport. Since boxing was illegal in his time, the participants and many of their followers were a part of the underworld. The lives of these people, which he later depicted in **The Fancy,** fascinated him, and the scenes in *The Beggar's Opera* often reminded him of them.

Dramatists received most of Reynolds's attention because of his position as theatrical critic, but he also criticized nondramatic poets in the literature section of the newspaper. During his connection with the *Champion,* he and Benjamin Bailey engaged in friendly rivalry over the relative merits of Spenser and Milton. Reynolds championed Spenser; Bailey, Milton. Each wrote a sonnet on his idol for the *Champion,*[24] and Reynolds addressed another sonnet to Bailey in which he said, "Milton hath your heart,—and Spenser mine."[25] Though Reynolds did not write a separate essay on Spenser, he frequently praised Spenser's rich sensuousness. Reynolds's part in the argument, however, was more the exercise of ingenuity than the expression of firm conviction. Though partial to Spenser, he never failed to recognize the sublimity of Milton, often coupling Milton with Shakespeare and on one occasion paying Milton the highest tribute: he said that he had met with only three or four intelligent readers who did not think Milton as great a genius as Shakespeare.[26]

On two occasions Reynolds published comprehensive essays evaluating many of the poets of the period. To the miscellanea department of 7 April 1816, he contributed **"The Pilgrimage of Living Poets to the Stream of Castaly."**[27] Pretending to be apprehensive about his boldness in passing judgment on the successful poets of the day, Reynolds introduced the printed essay with an apology for his own limitations: "I am one of those unfortunate youths to whom the Muse has glanced a sparkling of her light,—one of those who pant for distinction, but have not within them that immortal power which alone can command it. There are many,—some, Sir, may be known to you,—who feel keenly and earnestly the eloquence of heart and mind in others, but who cannot, from some inability or unobtrusiveness, clearly express their own thoughts and feelings." When he published this passage, the twenty-two-year-old Reynolds had written a large amount of verse, but was uncertain as to whether he was destined to become a genuine poet. The disclaimer of ability, however, must not be taken entirely at face value. He admired Chaucer, and there are several indications that he followed the pattern of Chaucer's dream visions in this essay. As we have seen, he admired Chaucer's irony in pretending to be a simple person; he was fond of "my wit is shorte, ye may well understand."[28] A repetition of the pose later in the essay sounds even more Chaucerian than the introduction: "I have a great desire to attempt giving pub-

licity to my dream, but I have before told you how limited are my powers of expression;—so I must rely upon your goodness, in receiving the crude description, or not." The expression of modesty was largely a pleasant Chaucerian convention, for he knew perfectly well that the *Champion* would print the article. He had been a regular member of the staff for over four months.

In the body of the essay, Reynolds pretended that he walked forth one evening to the side of a brook, where he sat down to read one of the old poets. Falling into a deep sleep, he dreamed that, while walking through a romantic valley, he met a beautiful female figure who was the guardian of the stream of Castaly. The Spirit explained that, because of Reynolds's love of her favorite Spenser, she would allow him to see the annual procession of living poets who came to obtain water from the Castalian stream. The treatment of a selection of them will show the nature of the satire. The first was a melancholy figure bearing a Grecian urn, whom Reynolds recognized from his look of nobility as Lord Byron. After shedding tears, which purified the water into which they fell, he declared that he would preserve his portion untouched for several years. He had hardly finished speaking, however, before he allowed several drops to fall carelessly to the ground. The second poet, whose breastplate and rough plaid contrasted strangely with his dress shoes and silk stockings, proved to be Walter Scott. Although the old helmet in which he collected his portion was very shallow, the water received a pleasant sparkle from the warlike metal shining through it. Scott announced that he had already arranged to dispose of his share on advantageous terms. Southey, whose brow was encircled by a wreath of faded laurel, appeared bewildered and could hardly find his way to the stream of inspiration. Though chanting the praises of kings and courts, he dropped several poems which were opposite in tone from those he was singing. After scooping up only a little of the water in his gold vessel, he mounted his horse and rode off at an uneven pace toward St. James's.

Walking toward the stream together, Coleridge, Lamb, and Lloyd (the close friend who had published with them) conversed about the beauties of nature, its peaceful associations, and the purity of the domestic affections. The conversation turning to poetry, Lamb and Lloyd spoke simply, but Coleridge soon became confused by the abstruseness of his own observations. When he mentioned his plan of writing a metaphysical poem in a hundred books, Lamb remarked that he would prefer one of Coleridge's fine sonnets to all the wanderings of his mind. Reynolds directed the most effective satire of the piece against Coleridge:

> Lamb and Lloyd dipped in a bright but rather shallow part of the stream;—Coleridge went to the depths, where he might have caught the purest water, had he

not unfortunately clouded it with the sand which he himself disturbed at bottom. Lamb and Lloyd stated that they should take their porrengers home and share their contents with the amiable and simple hearts dwelling there;—Coleridge was not positive as to the use to which he should apply his portion of the stream, till he had ascertained what were the physical reasons for the sand's propensity to mount and curl itself in water.

His praise of Leigh Hunt was warm and friendly: "Next came Hunt, with a rich fanciful goblet in his hand, finely enamelled with Italian landscapes; he held the cup to his breast as he approached, and his eyes sparkled with frank delight. After catching a wave, in which a sun-beam seemed freshly melted, he intimated that he should water hearts-ease and many favourite flowers with it. The sky appeared of a deep blue as he was retiring." Though he found no fault with Hunt's work, he did not place him among the first order of poets, complimenting him for gracefulness and geniality rather than more serious qualities.

With the entrance of the last poet, the tone of familiarity with which he had treated the other contemporaries vanished. Wordsworth appeared almost like a god:

> Last came a calm and majestic figure moving serenely towards the stream. . . . It was Wordsworth! In his hand he held a vase of pure chrystal,—and, when he had reached the brink of the stream, the wave proudly swelled itself into his cup:—at this moment the sunny air above his brow, became embodied,—and the glowing and lightsome Spirit shone into being, and dropt a garland on his forehead;—sounds etherial swelled, and trembled, and revelled in the air,—and forms of light played in and out of sight,—and all around seemed like a living world of breathing poetry. Wordsworth bent with reverence over the vase, and declared that the waters he had obtained should be the refreshment of his soul;—he then raised his countenance,—which had become illumined from the wave over which he had bowed,—and retired with a calm dignity.

Reynolds found some faults with Wordsworth later, but he never doubted that along with Keats he was the preeminent poet of the age.

After he had observed the procession of poets to the true Castalian stream, Reynolds noticed another brook nearby where the poetasters were splashing around like a flock of gabbling geese. William Hayley, John Wilson, and Amos Cottle were among the group who mistakenly believed that they were drawing the genuine water of inspiration from the false stream. Most foolish of all was William Lisle Bowles, who "laboriously engaged in filling fourteen nutshells." Bowles improved the joke by taking umbrage and writing an indignant letter to the *Champion* proclaiming the merit of his sonnets.[29]

Reynolds's second comprehensive appraisal of the contemporary poets appeared in **"Boswell's Visit."**[30] He was well prepared for his work as a critic for the *Cham-*

pion by a close reading of the periodical essayists of the preceding century, including Johnson's *Idler*. His greatest interest in Johnson, however, was in the man and critic as seen in Boswell's *Life of Johnson*. In an essay on egotism in literature, he had written, "Dr. Johnson was a thorough egotist: his misgivings—his asperities—his downright, *adamant* assertions—his weighty reasonings—his charitable kindnesses—were all egotistical. He was, however, on the whole, a melon of human nature,—for under a rough outside he had the very kindliest feelings at heart."[31] In his second comprehensive article on contemporary poets, he devised a clever anachronism in which Dr. Johnson and other members of the Literary Club judged the poets of the early nineteenth century.

In **"Boswell's Visit,"** Reynolds described himself returning home weary after the theater to prepare his review of the play, only to find that the printer's devil had called to warn him that copy was due the next morning. Worrying for some time about the deadline, he fell asleep and dreamed that James Boswell visited him and solved his problem. Boswell presented him with a record of the conversation of Dr. Johnson, Edmund Burke, and Sir Joshua Reynolds at the Literary Club, which had continued to meet in the shades after the death of the members, and Reynolds pretended that he transcribed the paper from memory after awakening. Those with strong interests in both the Johnson circle and Romantic poetry can hardly fail to be pleased by Reynolds's success in re-creating in an unexpected way minor disagreements between Johnson and Boswell, Johnson's lofty abstractions and balanced sentence structure, and his dogmatic assertion. The critical judgments of George Crabbe, Samuel Rogers, Robert Southey, and Walter Scott in the first installment follow logically and amusingly from Johnson's literary principles and tastes.

Reynolds devoted most of the second installment to Coleridge, Byron, and Wordsworth. The frame he had chosen proved most suitable for criticism of Coleridge: the common sense of the imaginary Dr. Johnson was ideal for satirizing metaphysics and mystification. Boswell began the discussion.

> I stepped forward and asked the Doctor what he thought of Coleridge.
>
> Johnson—"Why Sir, I think him a strange fellow."
>
> Boswell—"But do you think him a better metaphysician than a poet?"
>
> Johnson—"Sir, it is impossible to separate his fancy from his ponderous logic. He has made negus of his poetry and his metaphysical prose. I have read some of his early poems with pleasure, because they were written before he had bewildered himself with the intricacies of philosophy. He is very rich in the good gold of feeling,—but he hoards it up. Two or three of his Odes are lofty."

Boswell—"But have you read his Christabel, Sir?"

Johnson—"I have Sir—and it is a very dull enigma. He has put nonsense into fine words, and made her proud. I do not like to be puzzled to no purpose:—and it is a downright insolence in Mr. Coleridge to pester us with his two incomprehensible women. Sir, Geraldine is not to be made out:—she may be Joanna Southcote for all I know. Then what can be said of the dreams. They are arrant stuff. If Coleridge annoys us with more, the world will wish him a dreamless sleep. Sir, he might as well kick you."

Burke—"His politics appear to be very changeable."

Johnson—"Yes Sir, but he seems to be wise in his late opinion on that head."

Sir Joshua—"I think his description of the shadow of pleasure's dome floating midway on the waves of a river, gives you a grand idea of the size of the structure. It seems to me very picturesque."

Johnson—"But, Sir, I can make nothing of the dream. Any man may say an occasional good thing, but that will not embalm his eternal follies. He talks of a *sunny* dome, with caves of *ice*;—Sir, such a building could not exist. Fancy turns away with disgust from such an absurdity."

Boswell—"Lord Byron has spoken well of the poems, Doctor."

Johnson—"Sir, if he chuses to say a silly thing, I am not bound to abide by it. He may write an eulogy on Idiotcy, but I shall be bold to deem him mad, Sir, he may write ten yards of complimentary prose, or ten inches of insane poetry, if he likes; and I will neither read the first, nor admire the last. Let us hear no more of Coleridge."

Despite his objection to Byron's praise of Coleridge, the imaginary Dr. Johnson's opinion of Byron was generally favorable. He preferred *Childe Harold* to his other work because of its serious tone and intellectual content, but he found its hero almost as objectionable morally as the leading characters of Byron's Eastern romances. He declared the Giaour, Lara, and the Corsair to be black villains. Though he considered the descriptions of the natural landscapes pleasing, he thought Byron unwise to devote so much attention to scenery, since men and the affairs of society were more interesting and valuable subjects.

Although Reynolds had the fictitious Johnson express great admiration for Wordsworth, the criticism is brief and general. Dr. Johnson wished that he might write the life of "the glorious poet," and he compared the tone of his poetry to Milton's. In this case Reynolds probably saw that if Dr. Johnson's principles were applied to Wordsworth's poetry strictly, the resulting appraisal would have fallen short of his own high conception of the poet's genius. Consequently, he avoided the difficulty by treating Wordsworth briefly.

Except for the two general articles just discussed, Reynolds's criticism of the contemporary poets was scattered throughout the *Champion* in literary articles, reviews, and theatrical notices. His criticism there of Wordsworth is significant enough to merit detailed consideration.

As we have seen, Reynolds early in life recognized Wordsworth as the greatest poet of the age. His friendship with Haydon and contact with John Scott, editor of the *Champion,* confirmed his commitment. Haydon had been a friend of Wordsworth's for years, and Scott knew him personally and corresponded with him regularly from 14 May 1815 through 19 June 1816. Reynolds looked forward to *The Excursion* as a great philosophical poem in which Wordsworth would put behind him the simplicities that limited some of his earlier work,[32] and he valued the work so highly when it appeared that he wrote a guide to assist readers in their progress through its loosely arranged and uneven attractions.[33]

His earliest prose contribution to the *Champion* was an epistolary essay entitled **"Mr. Wordsworth's Poetry."**[34] The subject, he wrote, was of the utmost importance to the literary world, for the very character of the age would depend to a large extent on its reception of Wordsworth's poetry. In intellectual content he found Wordsworth's work comparable to that of Milton and Jeremy Taylor. He admitted that Wordsworth lacked the popular appeal of many of his contemporaries, having neither the haughty melancholy and troubled spirit of Byron, the melodious fancy of Moore, nor the "gentlemanly prettinesses" and touches of antiquity of Walter Scott. Nevertheless, Reynolds believed, his descriptions of nature mingled with philosophy would continue to live after the fame of the others had receded. In discussing genre, Reynolds distinguished between the true and artificial pastoral. He considered the pastorals of the eighteenth century coldly conventional with little intellectual and no emotional appeal. As an example, he cited Shenstone, who in his opinion deserved the sharp criticism of Gray and Johnson, since he "would make us believe that the fields are for ever green, the sheep for ever feeding, and that the shepherds have nothing to do but to make love and play on a pipe." With the publication of *Lyrical Ballads,* Wordsworth had begun a revolution against the artificial system. Though strongly opposed by many, his innovations had been welcomed from the first by a few intelligent readers, and they had gained further support through the years. Pleased to find that Wordsworth was aware of the extent of his own powers, Reynolds closed with a quotation from the "Essay Supplementary" to the preface of *Poems* of 1815, in which Wordsworth declared his conviction that his work was destined to endure.

In the issue of 18 February 1816, Reynolds continued his praise with his sonnet **"To Wordsworth,"** a graceful but conventional and undistinguished poetic tribute. He mentioned the solace and gratification which he had received from Wordsworth's poetry and wished that the beauties of nature might continue to inspire him. Wordsworth was mildly pleased by the poem, though he showed no curiosity about the author. After mentioning the *Champion* in a letter to John Scott dated four days after the issue in which Reynolds's sonnet appeared, Wordsworth wrote, "Thank you for the verses—I have the satisfaction of not infrequently receiving tributes of the same kind. What numbers must find their way to your namesake! and to the 'bold bad bard Baron B.'"[35]

In subsequent articles, Reynolds referred to Wordsworth's poetry frequently. In a theatrical review, for instance, a discussion of stage pastorals led to a comment on Wordsworth's descriptions of nature.[36] The affected simplicity of the actors and the obvious artificiality of the scenery made "a rural opera" ridiculous. The beauties of nature, he contended, could be portrayed most successfully in poetry. The two authors who had been best able to describe the woods and the fields were Chaucer and Wordsworth: Chaucer delighted the reader with his freshness and spontaneity, while Wordsworth cast a different kind of charm over his descriptions by introducing reflections and moral philosophy.

After his return from Exeter in early October 1816, Reynolds wrote two essays in which he included his most extensive appraisal of Wordsworth's genius. Wordsworth published his *Thanksgiving Ode* on the victory at Waterloo earlier in the year, and the *Champion* was late in reviewing it. In the first article, **"Popular Poetry—Periodical Criticism, & c"** on 13 October 1816, Reynolds explained that he would have noticed the poem earlier except for "personal circumstances of interruption," a reference to his six-weeks vacation in Devonshire.[37] He devoted the first article to a discussion of general principles that were to serve as an introduction to the specific criticism of the second essay. For his major thesis he returned to "Essay Supplementary" to the preface to *Poems* of 1815, quoted in his first article on Wordsworth, and selected a passage in which Wordsworth maintained that new poetry should not be judged by its popularity. Reynolds agreed that inferior poets were likely to have a wider appeal because their work required very little of the reader. In developing the idea, he pointed out that the general advance in education had altered conditions for the poet. During earlier periods, the number of readers had been small, but those who could read were well prepared to appreciate poetry of the highest order. The number of readers had increased greatly in his own day, but their learning was so superficial that they were incapable of judging properly. Progress was also a mixed blessing in other respects: "Modern improvements are excellent things,—as every one who has lately bought stoves or dining tables must know: but we have the convenient in lieu of the

romantic." Country houses, shooting-boxes, curricles, and gigs had been acquired at the expense of old moated castles and coaches and six.

Another unfortunate concomitant of the advance of society, Reynolds maintained, was that the proper relation between poetry and criticism had been reversed. In earlier times the poet had preceded the critic, and the critic had derived his principles from great poetry. In his own age the reviewers were violating the natural order by attempting to prescribe for poets. The rules might be applied correctly to minor poets, but they could not possibly have any bearing on the productions of an original genius, whose work must be, by definition, an exception to the general rule. Yet Reynolds did not attack all contemporary criticism indiscriminately; he admitted that the *Edinburgh Review* had done much toward developing the public taste, and he showed considerable respect for its editor Francis Jeffrey's judgment. Despite his attack on Wordsworth, Reynolds believed that Jeffrey himself appreciated the true nature of Wordsworth's genius.

In Reynolds's opinion, however, the *Edinburgh* was an exception to the poor quality of the contemporary periodicals, which had reduced criticism to "giving rules by the observance of which Mr. Higgins may write well to his correspondents, and his wife may deliver her opinion like a sensible woman at a tea table." With cant phrases and pert remarks the journalists were attacking works of real genius because they were incapable of understanding them. Unable to comprehend larger meanings, they selected petty faults in lines and phrases and applied "dictionary interpretations to the imagination's abstractions." Furthermore, they were inconsistent in their condemnation of lowly details, for they ridiculed Wordsworth's Wanderer as a Scotch pedlar, while they overlooked the fact that Spenser had made his "lovely ladie" ride upon a "lowly asse." According to Reynolds, one of the greatest offenders was the *Quarterly Review,* which he admonished, "To him, for instance, who favoured the public with the egregious criticism of *The Tale of Rimini* that appeared in the *Quarterly*! What would they say to the phrase in the second line that follows?

> 'The noble hart, that harbours vertuous thought,
> And is *with child* of glorious great intent.'"[38]

How dare small-minded critics object to what they call lowly details when Spenser had used the simple bodily image of pregnancy for his powerful line.

The danger of such criticism as that in the *Quarterly,* Reynolds believed, was its tendency to draw poets down to the level of critics. Since the great majority of readers in fashionable society were only superficially educated, they relied upon the periodicals for their critical opinions. Hence, there was strong pressure upon any poet who wanted monetary or social success to conform to the standard of the critics.

In the second article, entitled **"Wordsworth's Thanksgiving Ode,"** Reynolds returned to his principal theme of the preceding week: "Mr. Wordsworth . . . is not a popular poet:—we are very sure he is an admired one; and as to popularity, though it is a desirable thing for any weekly newspaper, yet we do not know that it is absolutely necessary for the Cartoons or the Samson Agonistes."[39] That Wordsworth's poem was occasional seemed of little importance to Reynolds, for he maintained that Wordsworth was never dependent on his subject. The chief reason for Wordsworth's success lay in his depiction of his own imagination, no matter what the subject. After quoting the opening stanza of Wordsworth's ode, Reynolds indulged in transparent mystification: without mentioning the author or title, he included a long passage from *Samson Agonistes* and declared it was by an earlier author who had been just as unpopular as Wordsworth. He apologized with mock seriousness for inserting such "tedious" lines and pretended to fear that the publisher of the paper would object when he found that they had been included. Then, shifting his ground, he promised that if any reader could admit the sublimity of the extract by the unnamed author, and at the same time deny any merit to Wordsworth's ode, he would renounce all pretensions to criticism.

By praising Wordsworth, Reynolds was running counter to a strong current of literary opinion even as late as 1816. He reported that a lady had written from Edinburgh to ask whether he really believed that Wordsworth had ever written anything as fine as Campbell's *The Pleasures of Hope*. He admitted, moreover, that some of his friends did not agree with him. One had been puzzled about Wordsworth's meaning, and another had asked sarcastically whether Harry Gill's teeth were still chattering. Despite these objections, Reynolds was firmly convinced that Wordsworth was the great poet of the age—he had barely met Keats. The only reservation in his praise of the *Thanksgiving Ode* was to its reactionary political tone. Although he joined Wordsworth in rejoicing over the victory at Waterloo, he was not nearly so satisfied with conditions in England. He took exception, though somewhat cautiously, to Wordsworth's "excess of saintly rapture" in having the angels welcome the hideous defeat of the French and declared that his own political opinion was closer to that which Wordsworth had held earlier in life than to that which he professed in the *Thanksgiving Ode*.

Reynolds's error of judgment in overvaluing the *Thanksgiving Ode*, which posterity has forgotten, undercuts these two essays for the twentieth-century reader. But despite the serious error, much that is valuable remains in the two critiques, for though he was wrong about the particular poem, he was right about Wordsworth.

Notes

1. The Reader, No. IV, *Champion,* 26 May 1816, p. 160. *Selected Prose,* p. 53. [Leonidas M. Jones, ed., *Selected Prose of John Hamilton Reynolds* (Cambridge: Harvard University Press, 1966).]

2. Review of Hazlitt's *Characters of Shakespeare's Plays, Champion,* 20 July 1817, p. 230. *Selected Prose,* p. 114.

3. "The Broken Sword," *Champion,* 13 October 1816, p. 326. *Selected Prose,* pp. 157-58.

4. "Richard Duke of York," *Champion,* 28 December 1817, p. 413. *Selected Prose,* p. 207.

5. "Hamlet," *Champion,* 14 December 1817, p. 397. *Selected Prose,* p. 204. He borrowed the phrase from Hazlitt's *Characters,* P. P. Howe, ed., *The Complete Works of William Hazlitt,* 21 vols. (London: J. M. Dent, 1930-34), IV, 232.

6. "Manuel," *Champion,* 16 March 1817, p. 85. *Selected Prose,* p. 178.

7. Review of Hazlitt's *Characters, Champion,* 20 July 1817, p. 230. *Selected Prose,* p. 114.

8. Review of Hazlitt's *Characters,* p. 230. *Selected Prose,* p. 113.

9. *A Course of Lectures on Dramatic Art and Literature,* by Augustus Wilhelm Schlegel, Translated from the Original German by John Black, 2 vols. (London: no publisher, 1815).

10. The Reader, No. V, *Champion,* 2 June 1816, p. 174. *Selected Prose,* p. 62.

11. *Letters of R,* p. 9. [Leonidas M. Jones, ed., *The Letters of John Hamilton Reynolds* (Lincoln: University of Nebraska Press, 1973).]

12. The manner in which he echoed Hazlitt, perhaps unconsciously, can be seen from a comparison of two passages. Hazlitt wrote in *The Round Table:* "A journeyman sign-painter, whose lungs have imbibed too great a quantity of white-lead, will be seized with a fantastic passion for the stage" (*Complete Works of Hazlitt,* IV, 59). In describing a similar situation, Reynolds used many of the same words and phrases: "We remember seeing a Mr. Edwards, a journeyman sign-painter we believe . . . his voice fainted from his lips, overcome with turpentine and white lead" ("King Richard. Mr. Fisher," *Champion,* 7 December 1817, p. 389).

13. *Champion,* 16 February, 14 December 1817, pp. 53, 397. For the latter, *Selected Prose,* pp. 204, 205.

14. Review of Hazlitt's *Characters, Champion,* 20, 27 July 1817, pp. 230-31, 237. *Selected Prose,* pp. 113-19.

15. R to Dov, 30 September 1813. Richardson, p. 107. [Joanna Richardson, *Letters from Lambeth* (London: Boydell Press, 1981)]

16. "The First Part of Henry the Fourth. Mr. Stephen Kemble in Falstaff," *Champion,* 13 October 1816, p. 325. *Selected Prose,* p. 153.

17. *Champion,* 14 December 1817, p. 397. *Selected Prose,* p. 203.

18. "Essay on the Early Dramatic Poets," *Champion,* 7 January 1816, p. 6. *Selected Prose,* p. 34.

19. "Mr. Hazlitt's Lectures," *Scots Magazine,* December 1818, p. 548. *Selected Prose,* p. 243.

20. John Aikin, *Vocal Poetry* (London: J. Johnson, 1810), p. 166n., quoted in R's "Ben Jonson," *Champion,* 4 May 1817, p. 14. *Selected Prose,* p. 108.

21. William Cartwright, "In the Memory of the Most Worthy Benjamin Jonson," l. 104, included in *Jonsonus Virbius* (1638).

22. *Champion,* 17 December 1815, p. 405.

23. *Champion,* 3 March 1816, p. 70. *Selected Prose,* pp. 42-44.

24. Reynolds's "To Spenser," *Champion,* 10 March 1816, p. 78. Bailey's "To Milton," *Champion,* 30 June 1816, p. 206.

25. "Sonnet to a Friend," first published in the *Athenaeum,* 7 July 1832, p. 432, but dated 1817.

26. "Mr. Kemble," *Champion,* 29 June 1817, p. 206.

27. *Champion,* 7 April 1816, p. 110. *Selected Prose,* pp. 45-50. He had evidently written a first version of the article several years earlier, for a letter of Thomas Winstanley of Liverpool to Dovaston on 20 April 1816 contains on a separate sheet in a different hand an extract from another version of the article containing lavish praise of Dovaston not in the *Champion* version (Dovaston Collection, Shropshire County Record Office). Winstanley was a close friend of William Roscoe, Ralph Rylance's mentor and close friend since boyhood. Rylance regularly sent Roscoe a large volume of his own poetry and prose. Apparently when Rylance and Reynolds were warm friends, Rylance sent Roscoe a manuscript copy of the Reynolds essay sometime before the spring of 1814 when the Reynoldses broke all communication with Rylance. When Winstanley became acquainted with Dovaston in 1816, he sought to please him by sending the lavish praise from the manuscript essay in the Roscoe family papers. After his friendship with Dovaston faded, Reynolds deleted the passage in praise of Dovaston.

28. R's quotation from the General Prologue, l. 748 in *Champion,* 26 May 1816, p. 166. *Selected Prose,* p. 58.

29. *Champion,* 12 May 1816, p. 151. *Selected Prose,* pp. 51-52.

30. *Champion,* 1, 15 December 1816, pp. 381-82, 397-98. *Selected Prose,* pp. 84-96.

31. The Reader, No. V, *Champion,* 2 June 1816, pp. 173-74. *Selected Prose,* p. 62.

32. R to Dov, 30 July 1814. Richardson, p. 120.

33. Hudnall, p. 21.

34. *Champion,* 9 December 1815, p. 398. *Selected Prose,* pp. 25-27.

35. Ernest de Selincourt, ed., 2nd ed. revised by Mary Moorman and Alan G. Hill, *The Letters of William and Dorothy Wordsworth, the Middle Years* (London: Oxford University Press, 1970), p. 283.

36. *Champion,* 21 April 1816, p. 125.

37. *Champion,* 13 October 1816, pp. 326-27. *Selected Prose,* pp. 70-76. John Scott wrote Wordsworth on 29 May 1816 that he planned to review the *Thanksgiving Ode* himself (MS in Dove Cottage), but the review five months after his statement could not be his because its author wrote that "our publisher will see it [a long quotation] with grief of soul" (p. 79), and Scott was the publisher, who was in Paris and would not see it until after publication. Mr. Patrick O'Leary, who is preparing a biography of John Scott, notes that in a number of cases Scott's stated intentions to write pieces went unfulfilled. I am grateful to Mrs. Winifred F. Courtney and Professor Robert Woof of the University of Newcastle upon Tyne for helpful correspondence in this matter.

38. *The Faerie Queene,* I, v, 1-2. R supplied the italics. Keats quoted the same lines, *Letters of Keats,* I, 134.

39. *Champion,* 20 October 1816, pp. 334-35. *Selected Prose,* pp. 76-84. The cartoons were paintings by Raphael.

John Barnard (essay date 1989)

SOURCE: Barnard, John. "Keats's 'Robin Hood', John Hamilton Reynolds, and the 'Old Poets.'" *Proceedings of the British Academy* 75 (1989): 181-200.

[*In the following essay, Barnard discusses Keats's debt to Reynolds as evidenced by the former's Robin Hood poems.*]

Much of this lecture will be taken up with an exposition of the important letter which Keats sent, with two accompanying poems, to John Hamilton Reynolds on Tuesday, 3 February 1818. Two larger points are involved. First, Keats's individual letters, even more perhaps than has been realized, need to be read in the fullest possible assembly of the texts, both prose and poetic, which generate them, and with attention to their effect on subsequent Keatsian texts. In the case of the letter to Reynolds this evidence happens to be particularly fully preserved. Second, Keats's own unsure taste, coupled with that of the poetry reading public's, was further enforced by the vulnerability of a youthful writer faced by the achievements of his older contemporaries. Keats's letters to Reynolds at this particular point in his development provided an insulated space for exploration and 'private' experiment. The *letter* to Reynolds is, like all of Keats's most important letters, a private *locus* in which different texts compete with one another. In that space Keats's own poetic texts already have an audience of one, but they can hardly be said to be fully published. Indeed they may remain semi- or partly private, even if printed by Keats in his lifetime.

'Robin Hood', which Keats chose to publish in his final volume *Lamia, Isabella, The Eve of St. Agnes, and Other Poems* (1820), dates back to February 1818 when he was copying out the second book of *Endymion*. The poem, like the three other 'rondeaus' with which it is printed in the 1820 volume, now seems markedly inferior to the other poetry in the book. Yet one of the first readers of the volume, the *Eclectic Review*'s critic, praised the 'light and sportive style' of both 'Robin Hood' and 'Fancy'.[1] The anonymous reviewer characterizes 'Fancy', the first of the 'rondeaus' accurately enough, and is right, up to a point, about 'Robin Hood'. What the reviewer misses is a level of seriousness in the latter poem. That is not at all surprising. 'Robin Hood', as its sub-title 'To a Friend' indicates, belongs to a larger exchange, much of it private, which was necessarily excluded from the volume published by Taylor and Hessey in the summer of 1820. The background to the lines explains why Keats published this poem and 'Lines upon the Mermaid Tavern' next to one another in 1820, and demonstrates the signal importance of Reynolds's poetic friendship to Keats at this stage in his career.

Morris Dickstein, the lone modern critic to admire the 'fine lines' on 'Robin Hood', is quite right to read the poem as a critique of capitalist society, offering a jocular parallel to the more famous attack in stanzas 14 to 16 of *Isabella*.[2] The Robin Hood of Keats's poem has a political dimension. Robin Hood's liberation from the popular tradition of broadsheets and garlands began with Percy's *Reliques of Ancient English Poetry* in 1765. However, the rehabilitation of the folk hero was, essentially, the scholarly work of Joseph Ritson in his

Robin Hood: A Collection of all the Ancient Poems, Songs and Ballads, now extant, relative to that celebrated English Outlaw published in 1795. As R. B. Dobson and J. Taylor say, Ritson not only believed in the existence of an historical Robin Hood, but was 'the first writer to convert Robin Hood into a thoroughgoing ideological hero'.[3] Ritson, a Jacobite who, remarkably, became a Jacobin, published his work during the highly politicized years of the 1790s. Robin Hood was, for Ritson,

> . . . a man who, in a barbarous age, and under a complicated tyranny, displayed a spirit of freedom and independence, which has endeared him to the common people, whose cause he maintained, (for all opposition to tyranny is the cause of the people,) and, in spite of the malicious endeavours of pitiful monks, by whom history was consecrated to the crimes and follies of titled ruffians and sainted idiots, to suppress all record of his patriotic exertions and virtuous acts, will render his name immortal.[4]

Dobson and Taylor note that Ritson was 'one of the few Englishmen to adopt the French Revolutionary calendar', and that Ritson's sentiments were those of the Revolution and of Paine. They also note that the two main novels concerned with Robin Hood, Scott's *Ivanhoe* and Peacock's *Maid Marian*, were written in 1818. The first did not appear until 1819, and it is unlikely that Keats knew of Peacock's work, not published until 1822, but the motif was one which seems to have been in the air.[5] The publication of Keats's poem in July 1820 probably prompted Leigh Hunt to publish his four poems on Robin Hood in the *Indicator* in November 1820. These celebrate the greenwood outlaw's fight against oppression both of church and state, as well as the good living in the natural forest. They give a clear, if simplistic, expression to Hunt's political feelings.

Keats wrote to Reynolds from Hampstead on Saturday, 31 January 1818, sending him several poems including an 'old song' 'O blush not so, O blush not so'.[6] When he next wrote to Reynolds, who was staying in Little Britain, Keats acknowledged the receipt of two sonnets on Robin Hood, included his answering poem along with the 'Lines on the Mermaid Tavern', and arranged to meet at four o'clock the following day, when he hoped to show Reynolds the newly copied Book II of *Endymion*. 'Robin Hood' was clearly written before he turned to his letter. 'Lines on the Mermaid Tavern' were composed a few days earlier.

Reynolds's sonnets were printed, along with an additional sonnet, shortly after in *The Yellow Dwarf* on 21 February 1818, and reprinted in 1821 in his **Garden of Florence**. *The Yellow Dwarf*, a short-lived liberal periodical, was edited by John Hunt, the brother of Leigh Hunt. The first *published* text of the two poems sent to Keats was as follows:

To a Friend, on Robin Hood

The trees in Sherwood forest are old and good,—
The grass beneath them now is dimly green;
Are they deserted all? Is no young mien,
With loose slung bugle, met within the wood?
No arrow found,—foil'd of its antler'd food,—
Struck in the oak's rude side?—Is there nought seen,
To mark the revelries which there have been,
In the sweet days of merry Robin Hood?
Go there with summer, and with evening,—go
In the soft shadows, like some wandering man,—
And thou shalt far amid the Forest know
The archer-men in green, with belt and bow,
Feasting on pheasant, river fowl, and swan,
With Robin at their head, and Marian.

                                        J. H. R.

To the Same

With coat of Lincoln green, and mantle too,
And horn of ivory mouth and buckle bright,—
And arrows wing'd with peacock-feathers light,
And trusty bow, well gathered of the yew,—
Stands Robin Hood:—and near, with eyes of blue
Shining through dusk hair, like the stars of the night,
And habited in pretty forest plight,
His greenwood beauty sits, young as the dew.
Oh, gentle tressed girl! Maid Marian!
Are thine eyes bent upon the gallant game
That stray in the merry Sherwood? Thy sweet fame
Can never, never die. And thou, high man,
Would we might pledge thee with thy silver can
Of Rhenish, in the woods of Nottingham.

                                        J. H. R.

Reynolds's two sonnets are part of an exchange between two young poets trying to establish their own voice. Taken together Reynolds's sonnets and Keats's letter and poem form part of a continuing conversation between the two men.

Reynolds's sonnets are really a nostalgic lament for a lost past, but the first sonnet, which begins by asking whether Sherwood Forest has lost the era of Robin Hood irrecoverably, ends by claiming that if the reader goes to the forest he or she will 'know' the 'archer-men . . . / Feasting . . . / With Robin at their head, and Marian'. The second describes Robin and Maid Marian, claims that their fame can never die, and concludes by wishing that 'we might pledge thee [Robin] with thy silver can / Of Rhenish. . . .' The first poem believes that the spirit of Robin Hood and his company lives on for those with imaginative sympathy, and both sonnets try to recreate their lost world. There is one important difference between the copy of the second sonnet sent to Keats and the printed version. The printed version describes Maid Marian as 'His greenwood beauty . . . young as the dew' (1.8): in the manuscript which Keats received the last phrase read 'tender and true'.

Keats's answering poem was written and sent off on the day he received Reynolds's sonnets, Tuesday, 3 February. Woodhouse notes that these arrived 'by the 2^{dy} [twopenny] post'. Keats sent his letter, including copies of his two poems, that same day, in the hope that Reynolds might read his 'Scribblings' in the evening.[7]

When the poem was published in 1820 it was titled 'Robin Hood To a Friend'. The letter is more specific (as are the extant manuscripts), 'To J. H. R. In answer to his Robin Hood Sonnets'. The text of the poem sent to Reynolds differs both from Keats's first draft and that finally published (a point to which I shall come back). In what follows I shall quote from the version of 'Robin Hood' (and that of 'Lines on the Mermaid Tavern') which Reynolds actually received.

Keats's poem is indeed an answer to Reynolds's sonnets: it is also less sentimental and more political. Keats begins by denying that it is any longer possible to call up the past:

> No! those days are gone away,
> And their hours are old and gray,
> And their minutes buried all
> Under the down-trodden pall
> Of the leaves of many years . . .

The stanza concludes by placing Robin Hood in a distant precapitalistic past:

> Many times have winter's shears,
> Frozen north, and chilling east,
> Sounded tempests to the feast
> Of the forest's whispering fleeces,
> Since men [paid no Rent and] leases.
>
>   (ll. 6-10)[8]

In addition to attacking the cash nexus and property Keats may also be reminding Reynolds that his new profession, the law, was antipathetic to poetry (as indeed proved the case). Keats later pictures how Robin Hood and Maid Marian would respond to the modern world if they were to see it—

> She would weep, and he would craze:
> He would swear, for all his oaks,
> Fall'n beneath the dockyard strokes,
> Have rotted on the briny seas;
> She would weep that her wild bees
> Sang not to her—strange! that honey
> Can't be got without hard money!
>
>   (ll. 42-8)

Keats is attacking both the navy and commerce here, but in opposition to Reynolds's sentimentality, he insists that the modern world is irrevocable—'So it is!' All that the contemporary poet can do is to honour the past in a catalogue of their names and attributes (ll. 50-60). The last two lines turn to Reynolds, and their exchange of poems—

Though their days have hurried by
Let us two a burden try.

Keats's vision of 'outlawry' is clearly related to that of Ritson (though there is no evidence that he had read Ritson). It also echoes the tradition which linked the greenwood world of Robin Hood with the classical Golden Age. The description of the Golden Age at the beginning of Ovid's *Metamorphoses* could indeed be a source for some of the details in Keats's poem. Ovid like Keats looks back to a time preceding man-made laws, and prior to the exploitation and cultivation of nature:

> Aurea prima sata est aetas, quae vindice nullo,
> sponte sua, sine lege, fidem rectumque colebat.
> poena metusque aberant, nec verba minantia fixo
> aere legebantur, nec supplex turba timebat
> iudicis ora sui, sed erant sine iudice tuti.
> nondum caesa suis, peregrinum ut viseret orbem,
> montibus in liquidas pinus descenderat undas,
> nullaque mortales praeter sua litora norant;
> nondum praecipites cingebat oppida fossae;
> non tuba directi, non aeris cornua flexi,
> non galeae, non ensis erant: sine militus usu
> mollia securae peragebant otia gentes.
> ipsa quoque immunis rastroque intacta nec ullis
> saucia vomeribus per se dabat omnia tellus,
> contentique cibis nullo cogente creatis

> (I. 89-103)

(In the beginning was the Golden Age, when men of their own accord, without threat of punishment, without laws, maintained good faith and did what was right. There were no penalties to be afraid of, no bronze tablets were erected, carrying threats of legal action, no crowd of wrong-doers, anxious for mercy, trembled before the face of their judge: indeed, there were no judges, men lived securely without them. Never yet had any pine tree, cut down from its home on the high mountains, been launched on the ocean waves, to visit foreign lands: men knew only their own shores. Their cities were not yet surrounded by sheer moats, they had no straight brass trumpets, no coiling bass horns, no helmets and no swords. The peoples of the world, untroubled by any fears, enjoyed a leisurely and peaceful existence, and had no use for soldiers. The earth itself, without compulsion, untouched by the hoe, unfurrowed by any share, produced all things spontaneously, and men were content with foods that grew without cultivation.)[9]

The men of Sherwood Forest are their own soldiers, and they spend their time in leisure 'Idling in the "grenè shawe"' (1.36)[10] with their 'fair hostess Merriment' (1.29). This is clearly related to Keats's dislike of standing armies and soldiers ('The scarlet coats that pester human-kind').[11] He had told Reynolds in April 1817 of his 'disgust' at the presence of a military barracks, 'a Nest of Debauchery', in 'so beautiful a place' as the Isle of Wight.[12]

Further, Keats's letter makes explicit the connection with Shakespeare's *As You Like It* where the Duke and his 'merry men . . . live like old Robin Hood of England . . . as they did in the golden world' (I. i). Shakespeare's comedy identifies Robin Hood and his greenwood world with *As You Like It*'s own pastoral. So Keats links the great 'old' Elizabethan poets with Robin Hood's England, the values of both of which were, in his view, denied by the modern world—and by modern poetry.

This context gives Keats's letter a clear shape. As always, he writes with a particular correspondent in mind, but this high-spirited letter, even more than usual, assumes mutual sympathy and an intimate knowledge on Reynolds's part of Keats's current thinking. When Keats signs himself, 'Y^r sincere friend and Coscribbler', he means it. They are 'Coscribblers' in that they share the same poetic values, are both as yet unsuccessful poets standing outside the dominant modes of contemporary poetry, and both look back to a lost 'English' past.

The letter begins indeed with a greenwood compliment which is part of an involved running joke. In April 1816, almost two years earlier, Reynolds had mocked William Lisle Bowles's sonnets, picturing Bowles as 'laboriously engaged in filling fourteen nut-shells'. Keats's request on 31 January 1818 for Reynolds to send 'a refreshment' (that is, some poetry) with his next letter led to the first two Robin Hood sonnets, which themselves took leave from Keats's references to the outlaw in 'Lines on the Mermaid Tavern'.[13] Hence Reynolds's sonnets are 'Filberts' because they are as full of real poetry as a nut (unlike Bowles's), yet cheap because carried by twopenny post:'

> My dear Reynolds,
>
> I thank you for your dish of Filberts—Would I could get a basket of them by way of desert every day for the sum of two pence—Would we were a sort of ethereal Pigs, & turn'd loose to feed upon spiritual Mast & Acorns—which would be merely being a squirrel & feed[ing] upon filberts. for what is a squirrel but an airy pig, or a filbert but a sort of archangelical acorn.

Keats's bantering opening immediately picks up a key pastoral theme. The forest has no cash economy: its herds of swine feed on the mast (or nuts) provided by the forest-trees. At the same time, Keats self-mockingly inverts proverbial wisdom. 'Pigs might fly' indeed! The joke opposes wishful thinking against actuality, fiction against fact. An 'airy pig' is as improbable as an archangelical acorn: if so, where does that leave the 'etherial' status of poetry? But the joke is also a form of modesty on behalf of himself and Reynolds, for Keats *does* believe in the value of Reynolds's sonnets. He immediately goes on to use the accurate archery of Robin Hood and his men to praise the 'ready drawn' simplicity of Reynolds's poetic archery:

> About the nuts being worth cracking, all I can say is that where there are a throng of delightful Images ready drawn simplicity is the only thing.

Keats then gives his comments on the two sonnets. These reveal Keats's taste and suggest what he himself was trying to do in his own poem (and the related 'rondeaus').

> . . . the first [sonnet] is the best on account of its first line, and the 'arrow—foil'd of its antler'd food'—and moreover (and this is the only word or two I find fault with, the more because I have had so much reason to shun it as a quicksand) the last has 'tender and true' [i.e., l.6]—We must cut this, and not be rattlesnaked into any more of the like—. . .

Keats, as he had from the beginning of his career, sees 'a throng of delightful Images' as a sign of true poetry, but he particularly values 'simplicity'. This is represented in Reynolds's poetry by the monosyllabic directness of the opening line of the first sonnet, 'The trees in Sherwood Forest are old and good', while the image of the arrow 'foil'd of its antler'd food' is presumably praised because it unexpectedly takes up the arrow's viewpoint. Keats's objections to 'tender and true' seems to have some personal reference: what that was is unclear, though 'tender' is a favourite word in Hunt's poetry. Sentimentality is surely his target here (and Reynolds followed Keats's advice, changing the phrase to 'young as the dew' in the printed version).

At this point Keats introduces modern poetry itself as a subject. This topic occupies the long middle of the letter, until Keats concludes by copying out his two poems for Reynolds and arranging to meet him the next day. Quite clearly, he sees Reynolds's poems and his own as opposed to what is taken as serious poetry by his contemporaries. The middle section is an effort to claim space for their aims, and to align support for their kind of work against modern poetry, specifically modern pastoral poetry:

> It may be said that we ought to read our Contemporaries. that Wordsworth &c should have their own due from us. but for the sake of a few fine imaginative or domestic passages, are we to be bullied into a certain Philosophy engendered in the whims of an Egotist— Every man has his speculations, but every man does not brood and peacock over them till he makes a false coinage and deceives himself—

Throughout what follows Keats famously contrasts Wordsworth (and later Hunt) with the Elizabethans, setting Elizabethan simplicity against what he regards as the subjectivity of modern poetry, which, he believes, tyrannizes over its readers and their 'speculations' ('false coinage' damningly picks up the attack on 'rents and leases' in 'Robin Hood'). As the subsequent discussion of 'Two April Mornings' proves, 'the fine imaginative or domestic passages' are those in Wordsworth's poems depicting everyday incidents. In them Keats feels that Wordsworth, an 'Egotist' who has developed his own 'Philosophy', denies the possibility of alternative interpretations. Yet every man, whether Sancho Panza or Keats, has his own speculations and 'halfseeings', which could be written down:

> Many a man can travel to the very bourne of Heaven, and yet want confidence to put down his halfseeing. Sancho will invent a Journey heavenward as well as any body.

Wordworth's poetry denies truth to anyone but himself. Keats then makes one of his best known remarks about poetry, 'We hate poetry that has a palpable design upon us—and if we do not agree, seems to put its hand in its breeches pocket'. But when he goes on to say that 'Poetry should be great & unobtrusive' he maintains the pastoral imagery, setting the Elizabethans and the Robin Hood world against modern poets:

> Poetry should be great & unobtrusive, a thing which enters into one's soul, and does not startle it or amaze it with itself but with its subject.—How beautiful are the retired flowers! how would they lose their beauty were they to throng into the highway crying out 'admire me I am a violet! dote upon me I am a primrose!' Modern poets differ from the Elizabethans in this. Each of the moderns like an Elector of Hanover governs his petty state, & knows how many straws are swept daily from the Causeways in all his dominions & has a continual itching that all the Housewives should have their coppers well scoured: the antients were Emperors of vast Provinces, they had only heard of the remote ones and scarcely cared to visit them.—I will cut all this—I will have no more of Wordsworth or Hunt in particular—

Keats, since there is no reason to believe he was flattering Reynolds, must have thought that Reynolds's sonnets were examples of objective poems taken up only with their subject. Certainly they draw no moral, are made up of statements and images, avoid the first person, and enjoin the reader to participate in creating the experience. Reynolds in his turn thought of Keats as an objective nature poet. Reviewing Keats's first volume in *The Champion* on 9 March 1817 he had written, 'He relies directly and wholly on nature. He marries poesy to genuine simplicity'. (Yet Reynolds's demonstration of his point is based on the belief that 'In the simple meadows [Keats] has proved that he can

> "—See shapes of light, aerial lymning,
> And catch soft floating[s] from a faint heard hymning.'"
>
> [*Sleep and Poetry*, ll. 33-4][14]

These are precisely the kind of visions which Reynolds's sonnets try to evoke, and which Keats's 'Robin Hood' denies.)

The reference to the modern Elector of Hanover places Wordsworth and Hunt in the role of petty tyrants (and given Hunt's power as a publicist and editor, there is a real point here). If this seems far-fetched the very next sentence reinforces the possibility:

Why should we be of the tribe of Manasseh, when we can wander with Esau?

Esau is linked with Robin Hood: both are hunters, and Esau shot 'venison' with his bow for his father (Keats passes over the negative aspects of Esau's story—unless he thought, as well one might, that Esau was cheated of his birth-right). The reference to the tribe of Manasseh must in the first place be to the elder but less important of the tribes of Israel descended from Joseph which provided men for Gideon's defeat of the Midianites. But Keats is likely also to be thinking of Manasseh, the seventh century king of Judah.

> His reign of fifty-five years was marked by a reaction against the reforming policy of his father, and his persistent idolatry and bloodshed were subsequently regarded as the cause of the destruction of Jerusalem and of the dispersion of the people.[15]

The poetry of Keats and Reynolds, then, is on the side of freedom and against tyrants: it speaks for true English rights denied by both the present day government and by the various dominant literary tastes.

At the same time Keats conceives of true poetry as reaching a higher level of truth: the pursuit of the 'ethereal' remains a theme:

> . . . why should we kick against the Pricks, when we can walk on Roses? Why should we be owls, when we can be Eagles? Why be teased with 'nice Eyed wagtails,' when we have in sight 'the Cherub Contemplation'?—Why with Wordworths 'Matthew with a bough of wilding in his hand' when we can have Jacques 'under an oak &c'—

The contrast is between the natural richness of Shakespearian creativity and the limitations and constricted achievements of modern poets. Leigh Hunt uses the phrase 'the nice-eyed wagtails' in 'The Nymphs', a poem which Keats had seen in manuscript in May 1817,[16] and which was to be published in *Foliage* in 1818. Keats's reference to the 'cherub Contemplation' in Milton's *Il Penseroso* (l. 54), where the cherub is the chief of the muses 'Guiding the fiery-wheeled throne' of poetry, sets the seventeeth-century greatness of Milton looking to heaven for his inspiration, against the limited ambitions (and false diction) of Leigh Hunt, satisfied with a wagtail for his muse. Similarly, Wordsworth's didactic anecdotes of modern life are set against the creativity and richness of Shakespeare. The greenwood pastoral of *As You Like It,* in which Jacques's meditations 'Under an oak' on the dying deer are at once richly comic and moving, has a range and complexity entirely missing in modern poetry.

Keats's dislike of Wordsworth's 'The Two April Mornings' is consistent with his attitude elsewhere. Wordsworth's poem reports a meeting with a now-dead village schoolmaster, Matthew, whose only daughter died in childhood, and ends by recalling him holding a 'bough / Of wilding in his hand'.[17] The cause of Keats's antipathy is made clear in the account of the poem which follows:

> The secret of the Bough of Wilding will run through your head faster than I can write it—Old Matthew spoke to him some years ago on some nothing, & because he happens in an Evening Walk to imagine the figure of the old man—he must stamp it down in black & white, and it is henceforth sacred. . . .

Keats's objection is that Wordsworth's 'forest' pastoral (signalled by 'the Bough of Wilding') imposes Wordsworth's reading of the incident on the reader and excludes other interpretations. I suspect that he also disliked the fact that the poem dwells on death, is about contemporary rural society, and finds no explicit way of transcending or accommodating its pathos: it is far from being 'joyful' in any Keatsian sense.

Keats goes on to allow the achievement of Hunt and Wordsworth before reiterating his belief in the 'old Poets' and giving himself the opportunity to attack another subjective modern poet, Byron:

> I don't mean to deny Wordsworth's grandeur & Hunt's merit, but I mean to say we need not be teazed with grandeur & merit—when we can have them uncontaminated & unobtrusive. Let us have the old Poets, & robin Hood Your letter and its sonnets gave me more pleasure than will the 4th Book of Childe Harold [published April 1818] & the whole of any body's life & opinions.

Keats's claims for the two sonnets by Reynolds are then that they are 'uncontaminated', 'unobtrusive' and objective. These, therefore, are the qualities which he is pursuing in his own poetry. 'Old poetry', like Robin Hood, is also on the side of freedom.

The letter then moves towards its conclusion with a return to woodland imagery:

> In return for your dish of filberts, I have gathered a few Catkins, I hope they'll look pretty.
>
> To J. H. R. In answer to his Robin Hood Sonnets. "No, those days are gone away &c"—
>
> I hope you will like them they are at least written in the Spirit of Outlawry.—Here are the Mermaid lines.
>
> "Souls of Poets dead & gone, &c"—. . . .

Keats's two poems are 'catkins' because, unlike Reynolds's compact sonnets, they dangle down the page, and because hazel catkins fertilize filberts. The 'Spirit of Outlawry' places Keats and Reynolds outside the differing kinds of poetic taste represented by Hunt and Wordsworth, or indeed Byron, and indicates Keats's political stance.

Keats's letter concludes with practical arrangements:

> I will call on you at 4 tomorrow, and we will trudge together for it is not the thing to be a stranger in the Land of Harpsicols. I hope also to bring you my 2ᵈ book—In the hope that these Scribblings will be some amusement for you this Evening—I remain copying still on the Hill
>
> > Yʳ sincere friend and Coscribbler
> >
> > John Keats.

The reference to the 'Land of the Harpsicols [harpsichords]' is probably to a musical evening at the Novellos', but while Keats writes dismissively of his 'Scribblings' it is clear that for him and for his 'Coscribbler' Reynolds, these ideas about Robin Hood and the 'old Poets' were a serious matter, and ones which gave a vantage point allowing them to elude the pressure exerted by contemporary poetic taste. It will also be clear that in placing these two poems together in the middle of *Poems* (1820) Keats was making a statement about his poetic and political allegiances as well as demonstrating his technical and tonal variety.

Keats's admonition was taken seriously by Reynolds, and prompted the third (and best) sonnet published by Reynolds in *The Yellow Dwarf*, **'To E—, with the foregoing Sonnets'**. 'E—' is probably Eliza Drewe, Reynolds's future wife.

> Robin, the outlaw! Is there not a mass
> Of freedom in the name? It tells the story
> Of clenched oaks, with branches bow'd and hoary
> Leaning in aged beauty o'er the grass:—
> Of dazed smile on cheek of border lass,
> List'ning 'gainst some old gate at his strange glory;—
> And of the dappled stag, struck down and gory,
> Lying with nostril wide in green morass.
> It tells a tale of forest days—of times
> That would have been most precious unto thee,—
> Days of undying pastoral liberty!
> Sweeter than music of old abbey chimes,—
> Sweet as the virtue of Shakespearian rhymes.—
> Days, shadowy with the magic greenwood trees!
>
> > J. H. R.

This is more a reply to Keats's letter and poem than a sonnet addressed to Reynolds's fianceé. It shows Reynolds learning from Keats's letter and poem, and makes more explicit Keats's stance. The phrase 'undying pastoral liberty' is an optimistic formulation of the values which Keats wishes to support.

Reynolds's three sonnets appeared one and a half years before Keats chose to publish his Robin Hood poem. It is worth noting that *The Yellow Dwarf* published very little poetry. Most of its space was given over to politics. It did, however, show an interest in literary politics. Coleridge's lectures on Shakespeare were reported in the issue for 21 February 1818, in particular Col-

eridge's claim that Caliban was 'an original and caricature of Jacobinism'. In reply Coleridge was violently attacked for his own earlier Jacobinal views, and for criticizing Maturin's *Bertram* because his own drama, *Zapolya,* had failed: as to Caliban, he 'is so far from being a prototype of modern Jacobinism, that he 'is strictly the legitimate sovereign of the island, and *Prospero* and the rest are usurpers . . .'[18] It is easy to see why Reynolds's sonnets might appear in *The Yellow Dwarf.* The appearance of the Hymn to Pan from *Endymion,* over seventy lines of verse, in the issue for 9 May 1818, less than two weeks after the poem was published, may reflect John Hunt's wish to help the sales of his brother's protégé. It also gave further support to the contemporary Tory reviewers' recognition that *Endymion* had a bearing on contemporary religion and politics. Wordworth's negative reaction to the Hymn, like that of the Tory reviewers of the poem as a whole, was a response to Keats's serious effort to imagine a 'natural religion'.[19]

When Keats wrote his letter to Reynolds on 3 February 1818 and when he composed 'Robin Hood' he was still working on *Endymion,* copying out the final draft. Only four days earlier he had sent his publisher, John Taylor, the very important new opening lines to the 'Pleasure Thermometer' passage (I. 777-81):

> Wherein lies Happiness? In that which becks
> Our ready Minds to fellowship divine;
> A fellowship with essence, till we shine
> Full alchymized and free of space. Behold
> The clear Religion of heaven—fold—& c.—[20]

The ambition apparent in these lines—*Endymion* hoped to describe no less than 'the clear Religion of heaven'—is as remarkable as the slightness and apparent flippancy of 'Robin Hood' when it appeared in *Poems* (1820). One explanation of 'Robin Hood's' tone is obvious: the prolonged commitment to *Endymion*'s 4,000 lines had taken up all Keats's energies. But the poem, like 'Lines on the Mermaid Tavern', deals with themes close to the heart of Keats's poetry, and their slightness is a form of self-defensiveness.

The 'Lines' were composed extemporaneously during an evening spent with Horace Twiss and Horace Smith at the tavern, and Keats is reported as saying that 'Reynolds, Dilke, and others, were pleased with this beyond any thing I ever did.[21] This awkward little poem celebrates the 'old Poets' and their conviviality, a conviviality firmly linked to 'bold Robin Hood', Maid Marian and venison pies: 'Souls of poets dead and gone' cannot have known any 'elysium' superior to that of the Tavern. The second verse turns on a comic version of Keats's belief (explored at length in *Endymion*) that poets write stories which somehow inscribe themselves in the heavens, and are then available for later poets to draw on:

I have heard that on a day
Mine host's sign-board flew away,
Nobody knew whither, till
An astrologer's old quill
To a sheepskin gave the story,
[Says] he saw you in your glory,
Underneath a new old sign
[L]ipping beverage divine,
And pledging with contented smack
The Mermaid in the zodiac.

The discovery among the observations of an ancient astrologer of an additional 'new old' constellation in the Zodiac, provides the dead Elizabethan poets with an appropriate, if fanciful, Elysian hostelry: their 'beverage divine' is a heavenly version of the *Nightingale*'s 'true' and 'blushful Hippocrene'.

In sending these two poems, which he claims were 'at least written in the Spirit of Outlawry' to Reynolds, Keats knew that they would find a sympathetic reader. And Keats's two poems can now be most fully and sympathetically understood within the friendly argument conducted between Reynolds's and Keats's texts, and their struggle against competing texts written by previous poets and by their contemporaries. Both poems need, that is, the assistance given by Keats's letter of 3 February 1818 and by Reynolds's sonnets: equally, the letter cannot be properly understood without also listening to the alternative texts and voices which it invokes.

Yet, while Keats and Reynolds needed one another's poetic companionship and support at this time to free them from the pressure of Hunt's influence and status, the distinction between what they were doing and Hunt's poetry is a necessary fiction. When Keats remarks 'I will have no more of Wordsworth or Hunt in particular' he may refer to both poets equally, or more particularly to Hunt. The difficulty for both Keats and Reynolds was that their own taste had been formatively influenced by Hunt, and remained very close to his. Indeed, Keats and Reynolds had met through Hunt by October 1816, and both shared Hunt's admiration for Greek mythology, the poetry of Boccaccio, Chaucer, Spenser, and the Elizabethans, as well as being political liberals. Consequently, when Reynolds and Keats tried in the course of 1817 and 1818 to separate their work from Hunt's, the differences are not, seen retrospectively, particularly well-marked. As Keats himself told Reynolds on 9 April 1818 when responding to the anxiety caused by the original preface to *Endymion*, 'I am not aware there is any thing like Hunt in it, (and if there is, it is my natural way, and I have something in common with Hunt) . . .'.[22] The parenthesis is essential to an understanding of Keats's difficulties. In so far as he learnt from Hunt, the older poet was likely to have preoccupied Keats's ground. The same was true for Reynolds, older than Keats, but younger than Hunt.

Indeed, Hunt's *Foliage*, probably published between 4 February and 10 March,[23] a little after Keats's and Reynolds's exchange, must have been particularly threatening to Keats. 'The Nymphs', the first poem, was, like *Endymion*, a modern reusing of classical mythological figures. Not only had Keats's diction been heavily influenced earlier by Hunt, but Hunt's Preface develops, at far greater length, his own version of Keats's attack on the French school published a year earlier in 'Sleep and Poetry' (ideas Keats had learnt from Hunt in the first place). Hunt also notes the 'revived inclination for our older and great school of poetry' (the Elizabethans), and uses exactly the same phrase, the 'beautiful mythology of Greece',[24] which Keats was to use in his revised preface to *Endymion* in early April. Further, *Foliage*, although it has no Robin Hood poems, is cast in a greenwood mode. *Foliage, or Poems Original and Translated* is divided into two parts. The first is called 'Greenwoods, or Original Poems' with a separate title page which contains 'greenwood' and other retirement epigraphs from Ben Jonson, Shakespeare, Lorenzo de Medici and Ludovico Paterno (sig. B1ᵃ). The second part is entitled 'Evergreens; or Translations from Poets of Antiquity . . .' (sig. 2A1ᵃ). Hunt's volume clearly claims as its direct poetic forebear Ben Jonson's division of his poems into 'The Forest' and 'The Underwood'. It also seems that from at least 1815 Hunt preferred his books to be bound in green, 'the colour of the fields'.[25] Keats cannot but have been aware of Hunt's interests. Keats's letter to Reynolds needs to misrepresent the close relation between Hunt's example and their own poetry, and to claim a difference which is hard to justify except as a manœuvre to create the imaginative space essential to the two younger writers.

In the privacy of his letter to Reynolds, Keats gives unambiguous expression to his poetic antagonism to Hunt. Yet the two men were meeting regularly. The day after Keats wrote to Reynolds, the very day on which he hoped to hand over the fair copy of Book II of *Endymion*, Keats took part with Hunt and Shelley in a competition to write a sonnet on the Nile in fifteen minutes.[26] More than that, Keats must have brought the original draft of 'Robin Hood' with him, either giving it to Hunt or leaving it at his house—Shelley's draft of his sonnet 'To the Nile' is actually written on the same piece of paper as Keats's draft of 'Robin Hood'.[27] It is hard to believe, in consequence, that Keats had not brought the draft poem for Hunt's inspection, despite what he and Reynolds were saying to one another in private.

In effect, Keats's poem has its genesis in a private exchange with Reynolds, but the subsequent textual history of 'Robin Hood', like that of 'Lines on the Mermaid Tavern', is of early manuscript circulation among the Keats circle, accompanied by a process of revision spread over the next year and a half. If 'Lines on the

Mermaid Tavern' were originally inspired by an evening with Twiss and Horace Smith and 'Robin Hood' by Reynolds's sonnets, the original drafts of both were subsequently revised by Keats—in the case of 'Robin Hood' later the same day when he copied them into his letter. In January 1820 George Keats took copies of both poems back to America, 'Lines on the Mermaid Tavern' being copied out fair in his notebook by Keats himself.[28] However, the published texts of both poems follows no extant manuscript. Both poems, then, were first 'published' in manuscript copies for a select group of readers including Reynolds, Charles Dilke, Charles Brown, George Keats, and (probably) Hunt.[29] The texts of the *poems* were, strictly speaking, never private. Rather Keats used his friends as sounding-boards at this early stage in their existence. The final version of both poems printed in the 1820 volume derives from a fresh look at the poems by Keats, or his publishers, or by both together.

The uncertainty of Keats's own poetic taste seems implicit in his disarming description of them as pretty 'Catkins'. Even after revision, the poems stand apart from most of those in the 1820 volume. They stand out because they are, along with the two other 'rondeaus', the poems most directly related to the tastes of Reynolds and Hunt.

The distinction between Keats and Hunt lies in the seriousness which led Keats to undercut Reynolds's sentimentality, denying that the 'archer-men' of Robin Hood's band can be 'known' by the modern visitor to Sherwood Forest. But, for all that, *Endymion* had tried to make Greek myth work again in modern poetry, and had used it for 'speculation'—as he assured Taylor, 'when I wrote [the 'Pleasure Thermometer passage], it was a regular stepping of the Imagination towards a Truth'.[30] Keats's seriousness is absent from both Reynolds's and Hunt's verse: Robin Hood, nymphs, goddesses and fairies are, for them, in the end, no more than a poetic *façon de parler*, no more than fanciful.

The closeness and ultimate distance between Keats and Reynolds is evident in the self-mocking introductory verse Reynolds wrote for **The Garden of Florence and Other Poems** (1821), when he had given up 'drawling verse for drawing leases':

> There is some talk of fairies in my book,
>   (Creatures whose bodies have doubtful title)
> I once believed in them—and oft have shook
>   My boyish heart with thoughts that made me sigh,
>   till
> Years stood like shadows in each leafy nook,
>   To parcel out the wilds in rood and pightle;
> There is some talk, I must confess, of fairies,—
> I knew no better,—boys will have vagaries.
>
>   (p. vii)

Reynolds's is a witty, and in the circumstances, sad, farewell to poetry. The free forest world of his 'boyish'

poetic fancies has been parcelled out, measured, and disowned by his adult lawyer's mind. Keats, however, in a sense held on to the 'boyish' beliefs which he had taken from fashionable poeticizing, ultimately fusing Huntian diction and poetic fancies into the yearning scepticism of his later woodland pastoral, the 'Ode to a Nightingale':

> Already with thee! tender is the night,
>   And haply the Queen-Moon is on her throne,
>   Cluster'd around by all her starry Fays;
>   But here there is no light. . . .

That imaginative 'vision' is able to accommodate, as Hunt and Reynolds could not, the admission that the 'elf' of imagination might be a cheat:

> Adieu! the fancy cannot cheat so well
>   As she is fam'd to do, deceiving elf.

Fancy's 'elf' may be no more than the product of wishful thinking, may be, in the end, an 'airy pig'.

Notes

1. Reprinted in *The Young Romantics and Critical Opinion 1807-1824,* ed. Theodore Redpath (1973), p. 506.

2. *Keats and his Poetry: A Study in Development* (Chicago, 1971), pp. 159-61.

3. R. B. Dobson & J. Taylor, *Rymes of Robyn Hood: An Introduction to the English Outlaw* (1976), p. 55. See also J. C. Holt, *Robin Hood* (1982). Holt refers to Keats's poem (pp. 185-6).

4. *Robin Hood* (1795), Vol. 1, pp. xi-xii.

5. Ibid., p. 57.

6. *The Letters of John Keats,* ed. Hyder E. Rollins (Cambridge, Mass., 1958), Vol. 1, pp. 219-22.

7. Ibid., Vol. 1, pp. 223-5.

8. *The Poems of John Keats,* ed. Jack Stillinger (Cambridge, Mass., 1978), p. 228. All further quotations of Keats are based on this edition. Square brackets mark the readings of the earlier versions of the two poems sent by Keats to Reynolds.

9. I am grateful to Hermione Lee drawing my attention to the broader context of Keats's *topoi.* See her *Willa Cather: A life Saved Up* (1989), p. 203.

10. The quotation from Chaucer's *Friar's Tale* seems to be decorative rather than functional.

11. 'To My Brother George', 1.130 (*Poems,* edn cit., p. 59).

12. 17-18 April 1817, *Letters,* edn cit., Vol. 1, pp. 131-2.

13. See Leonidas M. Jones, *The Life of John Hamilton Reynolds* (Hanover, Vt., and London, 1984), pp. 138-9, and *Letters,* edn cit., Vol. 1, p. 219.

14. Reprinted in *The Young Romantics and Critical Opinion 1807-1824,* p. 451.

15. *Encyclopædia Britannica,* 11th edn (1911).

16. Letter to Hunt, 10 May 1817, *Letters,* edn cit., Vol. 1, p. 139. For the quotation, see *Foliage: or, Poems Original and Translated* (1818), p. xxxiii.

17. *William Wordsworth: Poems,* ed. John O. Hayden (Harmondsworth, 1977), Vol. 1, p. 383.

18. *The Yellow Dwarf,* pp. 60-1.

19. *The Keats Circle: Letters and Papers,* ed. Hyder E. Rollins (Cambridge, Mass., 1958), Vol. 2, p. 144.

20. 30 January 1818, *Letters,* edn cit., Vol. 1, p. 218.

21. *Letters,* edn cit., Vol. 1, p. 225, from E. F. Madden, *Harper's New Monthly Magazine,* IV (1877), 361. Madden reports that he was shown the letter by George Keats's daughter, Mrs Philip Speed.

22. *Letters,* edn cit., Vol. 1, p. 266.

23. Hunt's sonnet, 'The Nile', written in competition with Keats and Shelley (see *Letters,* edn cit., Vol. 1, pp. 227-8) was printed in *Foliage* (1818), p. cxxxiv. Mary Shelley reports that the Shelleys left London for the Continent on 12 March 1818 after seeing the Hunts on 10 March (*The Journals of Mary Shelley, 1814-1844,* ed. Paula R. Feldmann & Diana Scott-Kilvert (1987), Vol. 1, p. 197). Shelley wrote to Hunt from Lyons on 22 March 1818 congratulating him on *Foliage,* and calling 'The Nymphs' a 'delightful poem' (*The Letters of Percy Bysshe Shelley,* ed. Frederick L. Jones (Oxford, 1964), Vol. 2, p. 2). Shelley went so far as to call 'The Nymphs' 'truly poetical'. The timing suggests that Shelley must have taken the printed volume with him. Mary Shelley's *Journal* does not record when Shelley read Hunt's book.

24. *Foliage,* (1818), p. 220.

25. See Charles & Mary Cowden Clarke, *Recollections of Writers* (1878), pp. 193-4, which quotes a letter dated 7 November 1815 in which Hunt complains that the binder has, contrary to instructions, bound a gift copy to Clarke of *The Descent of Liberty* and *The Feast of the Poets* in red instead of green. Clarke records that he was played the same trick when *Foliage* was bound in 'bright *blue*' instead of green. However, Clarke's copy, now in the Brotherton Collection (Novello-Cowden Clarke Collection) is now a greeny-blue. Its binder was W. Hickley, 4 Upper James Street, Golden Square, according to the label inside the front cover.

26. See *Letters,* edn cit., Vol 1, pp. 227-8.

27. Jack Stillinger, *The Texts of Keats's Poems* (Cambridge, Mass., 1974), p. 166. The manuscript is now lost, but was described by Forman.

28. Ibid., p. 168.

29. Ibid., pp. 166-9, and *Poems,* edn cit., pp. 228-31, 592-4.

30. *Letters,* edn cit., Vol. 1, p. 218.

FURTHER READING

Bibliography

Marsh, George L. "The Writings of Keats's Friend Reynolds." *Studies in Philology* 25, no. 4 (1928): 491-510.
Chronological lists of Reynolds publications, including uncollected poems and essays.

Biography

Jones, Leonidas M. *The Life of John Hamilton Reynolds.* Hanover, Vt.: University Press of New England, 1984, 371 p.
Provides a critical biography.

Criticism

Clarke, Micael. "A Mystery Solved: Ainsworth's Criminal Romances Censured in *Fraser's* by J. Hamilton Reynolds, Not Thackeray." *Victorian Periodicals Review* 23, no. 2 (summer 1990): 50-4.
Argues that an unsigned review of William Harrison Ainsworth's novel *Jack Sheppard* was written by Reynolds.

Clubbe, John. "The Reynolds-Dovaston Correspondence." *Keats-Shelley Journal* 30 (1981): 152-81.
Reprints letters from a young Reynolds to his friend John Dovaston that reveal Reynold's early interests and thoughts on writing.

Gittings, Robert. "The Poetry of John Hamilton Reynolds." *Ariel* 1, no. 4 (October 1970): 7-17.
Evaluates Reynolds's poetic career and suggests that a lack of self-confidence ultimately prevented the poet from fulfilling his early potential.

Hudnall, Clayton E. "John Hamilton Reynolds, James Rice, and Benjamin Bailey in the Leigh Browne-Lockyer Collection." *Keats-Shelley Journal* 19 (1970): 11-37.

Examines the manuscripts, correspondence, drawings, and other materials collected from Reynolds's time with Rice, Bailey, and the Leigh sisters.

Kaier, Anne. "John Hamilton Reynolds: Four New Letters." *Keats-Shelley Journal* 30 (1981): 182-90.
Reprints letters to Leigh Hunt and the illustrator George Cruickshank.

Kaufman, Peter. "A Keats Circle by the Sea." *English Miscellany* 22 (1971): 173-213.
Examines the poetic and personal relationships among Reynolds, James Rice, Benjamin Bailey, and the Leigh sisters.

Lange, Donald. "A New Reynolds-Milnes Letter: Were There Two Meetings Between Keats and Coleridge?" *Modern Language Review* 72, no. 4 (1977): 769-72.
Suggests that Reynolds's letter casts uncertainty onto certain aspects of Keats's life.

Luke, David. "Keats's Notes from Underground 'To J. H. Reynolds.'" *Studies in English Literature* 19 (1979): 661-72.
Considers a Keats letter to Reynolds as illustrative of his Romantic aesthetic.

Marsh, George L. "New Data on Keats's Friend Reynolds." *Modern Philology* 25, no. 3 (1928): 319-29.
Updates several details of Reynolds's biography.

————. "Newly Identified Writings by John Hamilton Reynolds." *Keats-Shelley Journal* 1 (1952): 47-55.
Identifies several unsigned or initialed articles as Reynolds's using the Leigh-Browne-Lockyer collection at the Keats Museum.

McMullin, B. J. "John Hamilton Reynolds and Archibald Constable & Co., 1819-1821." *Keats-Shelley Journal* 43 (1994): 19-24.
Discusses correspondence illuminating Reynolds's relationship with Constable, publisher of *Scots Magazine*.

Richardson, Joanna. "The Reynolds Family and J. F. M. Dovaston: A Postscript to *Letters from Lambeth*." *Keats-Shelley Review* 33 (1982): 62-5.
Produces two new letters regarding the failure of the friendship between Reynolds and Dovaston.

Rollins, Hyder E. *The Keats Circle,* 2 vols. Revised edition. Cambridge: Harvard University Press, 1965.
Includes letters and poems from the literary circle that included Reynolds, Rice, Bailey, Hunt, and Hazlitt.

Sperry, Stuart M. "Keats's *Epistle to John Hamilton Reynolds*." *ELH* 36, no. 9 (1969): 562-74.
Examines Keats's poem to Reynolds as evidence of his developing poetics.

Additional coverage of Reynolds's life and career is contained in the following sources published by Thomson Gale: *Dictionary of Literary Biography,* Vol. 96; and *Literature Resource Center.*

The Wide, Wide World

Susan Warner

The following entry presents criticism of Warner's novel *The Wide, Wide World* (1850). For discussion of Warner's complete career, see *NCLC*, Volume 31.

INTRODUCTION

One of the most widely read American novels of the nineteenth-century, *The Wide, Wide World* established Susan Warner as the nation's preeminent sentimental novelist. Bearing Warner's pseudonym Elizabeth Wetherell, the novel spawned a series of similar works published by "the author of *The Wide, Wide World*," a contrivance that would allowed Warner, as one of America's first bestselling writers, to largely maintain her anonymity. Noted for its accurate portrayal of the social limitations imposed upon nineteenth-century women, *The Wide, Wide World* traces the maturation of a young girl, Ellen Montgomery, from childhood to adolescence. Though generally valued less for its literary merit than for its historical significance, the work is considered one of the earliest examples of the domestic novel—a genre focused on the lives of ordinary women that became extremely fashionable after 1850. Frequently dismissed by the majority of twentieth-century critics as overly sentimental, the novel was "rediscovered" more than a century after its first publication by feminist scholars who have begun the process of evaluating it as an outstanding, if long since marginalized, example of popular literature written by women.

BIOGRAPHICAL INFORMATION

Born in New York City in 1819, Warner was the daughter of a prominent and ambitious lawyer, Henry Whiting Warner. Educated by private tutors, she studied literature, music, French, and Italian. In 1828 her mother died, and her paternal aunt moved into the household to care for Warner and her younger sister Anna. Her father's successful investments in real estate enabled the family to move several times to successively more affluent neighborhoods, and Warner frequently attended fashionable social gatherings as a young woman. However, an economic downturn in 1837 forced the family to retreat from their mansion at St. Mark's Place to an old farmhouse on Constitution Island. During the next

ten years, her father's failing law practice and his involvement in several lawsuits over his property furthered the family's financial difficulties. In 1848, urged by her aunt, Warner began work on *The Wide, Wide World* with the hope that the novel would serve as a source of income. After being rejected by several publishers, *The Wide, Wide World* was issued in a limited edition in 1850. Demand for the book exceeded the initial expectations of the publisher; reissued through fourteen editions in the next two years, *The Wide, Wide World* established an unprecedented record for sales. Encouraged by the success of her first novel, Warner wrote *Queechy* (1852), another novel portraying the development of a young girl. Throughout the next three and a half decades, Warner remained on Constitution Island and continued writing, producing more than thirty works of her own and six in collaboration with her sister, Anna. None of Warner's subsequent novels, however, achieved the same level of popular success as *The*

Wide, Wide World, which remained in print for almost 80 years and was widely translated. In 1987, after decades of public neglect, the novel was reissued by the Feminist Press in an enlarged edition that featured a concluding chapter written by Warner but dropped by her original publisher.

PLOT AND MAJOR CHARACTERS

At the beginning of *The Wide, Wide World* young Ellen Montgomery's father has lost a lawsuit, and the family doctor has prescribed a vacation for Ellen's severely ill mother. Because of the family's limited resources, her father, the unfeeling Captain Montgomery, decides to leave Ellen with her aunt in a small, rural village while taking his wife on a business trip to Europe. Separated from the love of her tender and devout mother, Ellen is mistreated by her spiteful aunt, Miss Fortune Emerson, who denies her requests for a formal education and withholds her mother's letters. Ellen suffers from the undeserved punishments and neglect of her aunt, yet obtains support and spiritual guidance from Alice and John Humphreys, the children of a local minister. A devout Christian, Ellen finds solace with the Humphreys and later goes to live with them in order to take care of Alice when she falls ill. Alice dies, as does Ellen's mother, and Captain Montgomery forces his daughter to move to Scotland and enter the household of the Lindsays, relatives of her deceased mother. Proving themselves even crueler than Aunt Fortune, the Lindsays treat Ellen as little more than property. They force Ellen to relinquish her identity as an American and criticize her faith. Nevertheless, she continues to find strength in her resilient Christian piety and in her correspondence with John Humphreys in America. Eventually, John arrives in Scotland with assurances that her life will be happy again if she becomes his wife upon reaching the proper age. With the suggestion that Ellen and John will marry, Warner's novel, as originally published, ends. In a concluding chapter, restored in the 1987 edition, Ellen returns to America, and she and John are presented as a married couple.

MAJOR THEMES

Since the action of *The Wide, Wide World* focuses on Ellen Montgomery's emotional, intellectual, and spiritual maturation from young girl to adult woman, critics have frequently viewed the work within the generic context of the *bildungsroman,* with its defining themes of personal and social development. In addition to being a narrative of Ellen's growth, however, the novel also features a strongly Christian message as Ellen, after suffering a reversal of financial fortune, the loss of her mother, exile from her homeland, and ill treatment at the hands of others, learns to overcome her feelings of vulnerability and helplessness by finding strength in her insurmountable religious devotion. In this sense, critics have viewed *The Wide, Wide World* as a sort of primer in Christian morality, observing that Ellen's sufferings eventually bring rewards as she learns to trust in her unshakable faith. Similarly, the novel has also been interpreted as an example of Christian allegory, analogous to that found in John Bunyan's *Pilgrim's Progress,* a work that, after the Bible, is Ellen's most treasured book. Additionally, *The Wide, Wide World* illustrates a collection of more properly sentimental or domestic themes centered on Ellen's circumscribed role as a young, middle-class woman living in the mid-nineteenth century. With only an extremely limited control over the direction of her own fate, she must accept and endure the choices made by her father until she finds another man (in this case, the admirable John Humphreys) willing to save her by making her his wife. Such elements of the novel have been of particular interest to contemporary feminist critics eager to explore the acculturated gender dynamics and historical realities of women's lives depicted in the *The Wide, Wide World.*

CRITICAL RECEPTION

Extraordinarily popular in the United States and England upon its publication, *The Wide, Wide World* elicited a broad range of responses, with many reviewers admiring its respectable heroine, charming storyline, and steadfastly Christian content. Generally appealing to dominant Victorian sensibilities, the novel was extremely well received by most. Some critics, however, took exception to the immoderate emotionalism of Warner's novel, as characterized by the excessive weeping of its heroine, and to the fervid religiosity of the work. A few criticized the author's verbose prose style and other stylistic shortcomings, and some dismissed the work outright. Such negative perceptions of *The Wide, Wide World* predominated for much of the twentieth century, during which time the novel's heavy reliance on the tropes of feminine sentimentality and religious allegory provided ground enough to condemn the book. Nevertheless, a number of more recent scholars have emphasized the difficulty of properly interpreting the nineteenth-century religious and moral values expressed in the work from a contemporary perspective. Recent critics have also remarked on changes in taste over the decades, with twentieth-century scholars admiring Warner's skilled evocation of New England local color as exemplified in the diction of her rural characters, an aspect of the work that Victorian audiences tended to dislike in favor of Ellen's genteel—but to the modern ear stilted—English. Likewise, Ellen's unswerving and self-assured religious faith has frequently struck critics as making her seem unintentionally smug or sanctimonious. Infrequently read, and its interest restricted almost exclusively to feminist scholars, *The Wide, Wide World* has become a central text in the contemporary discourse on nineteenth-century women's fiction in America, with commentators examining the dynamics of oppression delineated in the story, and disputing whether or not religion functions as a submission to patriarchal authority in the novel. In most cases, modern critics have focused on gendered themes in the work and concluded that the control exercised over Ellen by her father, husband, and other relatives represents an accurate portrayal of the constraints imposed upon nineteenth-century women in making decisions governing their own lives. Given these qualities, *The Wide, Wide World* serves critics as a valuable historical and literary document of nineteenth-century female experience.

PRINCIPAL WORKS

The Wide, Wide World [as Elizabeth Wetherell] (novel) 1850

American Female Patriotism: A Prize Essay (essay) 1852

Queechy [as Elizabeth Wetherell] (novel) 1852

Carl Krinken: His Christmas Stocking [with Anna Warner] (children's literature) 1853

The Hills of the Shatemuc (novel) 1856

Say and Seal [with Anna Warner] (novel) 1860

Hymns for Mothers and Children (children's literature) 1861

The Golden Ladder: Stories Illustrative of the Eight Beatitudes [with Anna Warner] (children's literature) 1862

The Old Helmet (novel) 1863

Melbourne House (novel) 1864

Daisy (novel) 1868

Daisy in the Field (novel) 1869

Opportunities (novel) 1871

"What She Could" (novel) 1871

The House in Town (novel) 1872

Sceptres and Crowns (novel) 1874

Bread and Oranges (novel) 1875

The Flag of Truce (novel) 1875

The Gold of Chickaree [with Anna Warner] (novel) 1876

The Rapids of Niagara (novel) 1876

Wych Hazel [with Anna Warner] (novel) 1876

Diana (novel) 1877

My Desire (novel) 1879

The End of a Coil (novel) 1880

The Letter of Credit (novel) 1881

Nobody (novel) 1882

Stephen, M. D. (novel) 1883

A Red Wallflower (novel) 1884

*Daisy Plains (unfinished novel) 1885

**This work was completed by Anna Warner.

CRITICISM

Prospective Review (review date 1853)

SOURCE: Review of *The Wide, Wide World*. *Prospective Review* 15 (1853): 314-39.

[*In the following excerpt, the reviewer describes* The Wide, Wide World *as an excellent example of morally didactic literature for children but critiques some of its stylistic qualities.*]

Except *Amy Herbert*, we never read a child's story to compare in interest with the **Wide, Wide World**; and as it has gone far through the wide worlds of England and America, and received a large share of attention from the readers of fiction here and there, it claims, we think, with its sister story, some notice at our hands. We have lately spoken of the important influence acquired by fiction, and the functions of the critic respecting it. But if he is called upon to interpret its deep truths, and explore its hidden meanings, and detect its subtle beauties, and if he is to determine the laws of taste that should be observed by creative genius, no less certain is it, that he should endeavour to expose the moral fallacies and religious errors which appear to him to mar the perfection of a noble and life-like production, and to make the valuable ally of reverence and reason, to some extent at least, the generator of false sentiment or unreal doctrine.

We enter upon the criticism of these books with no narrow prejudice or sectarian animosity; we have been delighted as well as instructed by them. None could read them without benefit. They move the heart and charm the imagination, and prove themselves, on every page, to be the productions of women of singular power and high character. Were we to say all that we have felt during their perusal, we should be believed to be still in our childhood, and carried away by a sympathy as young and enthusiastic as Ellen Montgomery's. What we shall have to object to in the main is confined almost exclusively to the more popular of these productions, which contains grave and serious error, not natural to the creating mind, but the artificial graft of an orthodox education.

Before entering, however, upon this ground, let us express our real joy and satisfaction in meeting with books for the young, so high in tone and so truly religious. It is not because they are so that we have any fault to find. We could wish nothing better for the rising generation, than that it might possess a whole library of fictitious productions such as these, (not of course unmingled with a much larger amount of other reading,) provided their general tone and religious teaching were of a healthier description than such as the **Wide, Wide World** presents, and savoured less of bibliolatry and what is called evangelical Christianity. It may seem narrow in us to object to a story on account of the theological views of the writer; but when those views are brought prominently forward, and didactically pressed upon our notice, and urged as the proper principles of action, and the sources from which peace is to come, to young and old alike, then we must step forward, however reluctantly, and as the friends of truth and reality, declare what we deem false and prejudicial, in works otherwise so beautiful and attractive.

It will interest our readers to know, what an American review has told us, that Elizabeth Wetherell and Amy Lothrop are sisters—two Miss Warners; the elder one is the author of the **Wide, Wide World** and **Queechy**. In many respects she shows more power than the authoress of *Glen Luna*. The former delights in describing sentiment and passion, the latter avoids "scenes," and keeps upon the still waters and quiet ways of domestic life. The one revels in the pathetic, and probably loves to excite, and be excited, to tears, since she describes them as so abundant in her little heroine. She takes an orphan each time for her central figure. Her sister, on the contrary, (who probably considers that some virtue consists in controlling all outward emotion,) draws characters mainly of reserved and subdued feeling, whose affections (though almost equally sensitive) are more deep than passionate, more self-conscious than violent and impulsive. We do not mean to say that there is any disagreeable self-consciousness in the characters of *Glen Luna*; by no means; quite the contrary; the book appears to us entirely free from this defect, so painfully characteristic of our age, and not altogether absent from the tales of her sister: we only mean that she gives to her characters not more intellect perhaps, but more reflection; and, consequently, self-knowledge and reason keep the feelings under admirable restraint and control; whereas the impulsive and less thoughtful minds which her sister delights to describe, full of intellectual perception and curiosity, with lively instincts and enthusiastic tendencies, unbalanced by meditative power and the clear reasoning of common sense, are perpetually convulsed with anger, sorrow, or despair. The **Wide, Wide World** we should judge to be the swift production of an open demonstrative character, ready of imagination, and fluent in speech as in writing. Miss Warner writes *too* easily; she is too diffuse. She has plenty to say, and does not care to condense her narrative. She gives you variety of scene, and a good deal of incident, but is quite heedless as to the space-filled, and the pe-

riod required for perusal. It demands more labour and time to write tersely and briefly, *multum in parvo,* and this labour and time Miss Warner cannot or will not give. Her sister has, unquestionably, a less ready invention. There is a good deal less variety of scene and incident in her tale; and if it is long and tedious (which we did not feel it to be), it is more from this cause, the sameness of the narrative, than from that diffuseness of style observable in the **Wide, Wide World.** We could wish the younger Miss Warner would sometimes write at *more* length. She is perfectly enigmatical in many of her conversations. We laid down her book with no complaint except of the sad labour occasionally required to make out what her speakers were referring to, or how they slipped so strangely into this or that subject, or what in the world they were driving at. We could not help thinking that these parts were written at a late hour of the night, when the mental powers were in a hazy balance between sleeping and waking, or partially occupied a wool-gathering. The story of *Glen Luna* is otherwise unexceptionable. Its style though less vigorous and strongly marked than that of the **Wide, Wide World,** is more delicate and graceful, and bears more signs of careful and studied composition. It is more peculiarly the writing of a refined and tasteful mind, of the true feminine stamp: full as essentially religious as her sister's book, but the religion is more unobtrusive, and given after a less didactic fashion: and this is one of its charms. We like to see religion rather underlying the structure of a tale, and spontaneously breaking forth, now and then, in a full stream to the surface, than brought forward systematically, or by officious efforts of the will, as if the writer were bent upon preaching of duty, and not occupied with the simple unfolding of character. In another respect also we think that *Glen Luna* claims precedence, as not being anywhere marked in the least degree with the prominent and rather disagreeable tendency of the age, of which some slight traces are to be found in the **Wide, Wide World.** The tendency we allude to is that of loving to dwell upon exaggerated or at least uncommon states of sensibility and passion, while self-consciousness is close at hand. In Mr. Kingsley's tales, to some extent, this tendency is perceptible, but in *Jane Eyre, Shirley,* and *Villette,* it is dominant. The authoress of these books draws passion with a keen self-consciousness; and while her heroines, bound indeed by an iron will under the great law of duty, but subdued by no feminine instincts, and chastened by no religious love, show themselves prematurely open to the advances of their passionate despots, the ardour revealed on the one side or the other, or both, being regarded from within as well as from without, a painful consciousness is produced in the reader as of the presence of unrefined and coarse elements in the life presented to him; and however much he may own the breadth and power of the painter's brush, he has an unpleasant sense of the colours being by no means clear or clean. That these two inharmonious human tendencies do not always appear in the same character, matters nothing: they appear in the book; they are contiguous in the writing; they mingle their streams together, and the precipitate is dark. Look at Louis Moore, one of the brothers in *Shirley*; in him you have the very sediments of an earthly nature, and self-consciousness strongly active. The **Wide, Wide World,** and **Queechy,** are not to be compared with these novels for a moment. But truly sensitive and impulsive as Miss Warner's heroines are, and never without pure and feminine instincts, their womanly attachments are too early developed, not without a show of consciousness in them, and some want of delicacy occasionally in the writer: but the least agreeable points of mental character, and those most nearly resembling what we have been referring to, are to be found in the delineation of her cool, self-conscious, and despotic heroes. She never speaks of their true character, or indeed seems to know or understand it; but it is apparent from the first. We had heard so much female adoration expended on Mr. John Humphreys, that we anticipated making the acquaintance of some more exalted Edmund Bertram or Frederick Wentworth, before whom the heroes of *Mansfield Park* and *Persuasion* would pale and be forgotten. What was our disappointment then to meet with a thoroughly disagreeable personage; we use this substantive advisedly; he *is* a personage essentially; important, and authoritative, and most instructive, bearing all the appearance of a schoolmaster who has been spoiled by his profession, and almost as stupendously dignified as Dr. Blimber himself, without any of that gentleman's native simplicity. He is declared religious by his author, but, in our view, does not really prove himself so at all, though eminently moral; not religious, i.e. if religion consist, as we believe, in the pious devotion, love, and humility of the heart, and not in the dogmatism of the creed, or the iron rule of the will. Mr. John Humphreys is not merely proud, but proud in the worst way, *spiritually* proud. He assumes that he has found the true way of life, that he can show it to whom he will, that he may command the mind and heart of any one more *ignorant* or less evangelical than himself, as if the knowledge of the right, the instinct of duty, and the willingness of affectionate obedience, were entirely the lessons of learning and experience or biblical theology, and not of nature and conscience, i.e. of God. Ellen Montgomery is truly religious by nature, and continues so under all her little errors and struggles, whether her dictator be at hand or not. But *his* self-satisfaction and self-reliance is anything but religious. *She* loves, and looks up, and clings to higher natures, or those she regards as such, and bows her soul before the spiritual being whom she serves and adores; *he* looks down or around him, that is, on his inferiors or equals, but spontaneous reverence and affection are no parts of his nature. It is quite a mistake to say that he could be interesting as a preacher.

He might do good; he might rouse the moral sense; but a man so ungenial, so arbitrary, so self-conscious, could never move any soul to penitence or devotion. He moves about through the story like a performer on the stage; he is always dramatic and "effective," inasmuch as he is aiming to produce effects, moral though they be. It is surprising to find how very popular, with the gentler class of readers, these magisterial, despotic heroes appear to be. With ourselves, we must say, that Mr. Rodney Collingwood (the hero of *Glen Luna*), though less sharply sketched—slightly indistinct perhaps—finds much more favour. He is every way more of a Christian and a gentleman.

A brief passage from the **Wide, Wide World** may serve as an example of that self-contented condition of mind, proper, in his own opinion, to a true Christian believer, to one who, as is elsewhere shown, places his confidence in the efficacy of Christ's sacrifice and death, or in his own belief in that efficacy. We italicise a few words, to direct attention to them.

> "I wonder," said Alice, after a pause, "how those can bear to love, or be loved, whose affection can see nothing but a blank beyond the grave."
>
> "Few people, I believe," said her brother, "would come exactly under that description; most flatter themselves with a vague hope of reunion after death."
>
> "But that is a miserable hope—very different from ours."
>
> "Very different indeed! and miserable; *for it can only deceive, but ours is sure.* 'Them that sleep in Jesus will God bring with him.'"

Why is the hope of any human being to be thus tossed to the winds? Happily the Infinite One may do what He will with his own; and as the less narrow heart of a poet has written,—

> *We* think and feel—but will the *dead*
> Awake to thought again?
> A voice of comfort answers us
> God doeth nought in vain:—
> He wastes no flower, no bud, no leaf,
> No wind, no cloud, no wave;—
> Nor *will He waste the hope* which grief
> Hath planted in the grave!

To Mr. Humphreys, sen., no objection can be made; he is slightly sketched, but the circumstances of his life make his quiet and reserve natural. The best male character in this story is Mr. Van Brunt. Few delineations could be better, more graphic, or more true to life. The authoress is, however, more generally successful in describing her own sex. In Aunt Fortune, and Alice Humphreys, and Nancy Vawse, in the invalid Mrs. Montgomery, and in the last sketches of Scottish Ladies, there is hardly a line that does not tell, and is not drawn from life. Perhaps little Ellen Chauncey is as sweetly and excellently described as any character in the book, and is most beautifully, with true artistic tact, introduced as a contrast to her pensive friend, the heroine of the tale, upon whose history and inner life is lavished a skill and power truly admirable.

We believe, however, that in writing for children it is very undesirable to take a theme so exciting and sad as the struggles of a desolate orphan child. Falling into the hands of children, the book is as likely to be prejudicial to their healthy life as novel reading, of an exciting kind, to older minds. It is true that such a position as her heroine's enables the writer to manifest the use of religion more easily, just as many preachers find that sermons of consolation for sorrow and bereavement are more easily written than sermons for the ordinary conditions of life. But is it advisable to draw upon the sensibilities of children? Decidedly we believe not. Those of a natural tenderness and sympathy need no extra excitement of this kind. It does them harm, and not good: they need bracing for action; they need to be strengthened by pictures of courage and scenes of cheerfulness, not to be melted into tears. While with others of a harder nature, if capable of perceiving the beauty of a character like Ellen, without sharing their sensitiveness at all,—an unnatural and lamentable sentimentality may too readily be induced that cannot be again uprooted. We have been rejoiced to find that there are still many natural spontaneous healthy-minded children to be met with, who have neither suffered too keenly with poor Ellen Montgomery, nor striven, against their natures, to resemble her. *Glen Luna* is a story hardly suited to young children at all, but eminently more healthy for all who can enter into it. It describes the struggles of the *outer* life such as it is everyway *wholesome* to contemplate, and does not lay bare the tender heart, with the acute sufferings of solitude and bereavement. The consequence is, that the one tale braces the mind to energy and duty, while the other schools the soul into submission. If this latter virtue were one commonly required of children; if their natures were usually mature in affection at an early age, and their lives generally so forlorn and isolated as that of an orphan child of peculiar sensibility must be; then we might admit that the *Wide, Wide World* was one of the most useful books that had ever been written: but all will allow that this is not the case. Where one child is constituted so keenly sensitive and tender-hearted, as to suffer from separation and bereavement with all the intensity conceivable in the young, a dozen will be found more hardly constituted. At all events, circumstances are not often so unfortunate, thanks to a gracious Providence, as to try the young very severely by a lot of loneliness and unbefriended affection; and, therefore, as we used to object to the novel-like tales of Mrs. Hofland, we cannot but regret that powers so remarkable as Miss Warner's have been spent upon a tale of struggle and grief, so calculated to excite prematurely the deeper feelings of the

young heart, which cannot be too sacredly kept for real life, and must be in danger of injury, if too early expended upon fiction. If the *mature* nature suffers (through its vivid appreciation of human wants and weaknesses and trials) by too frequent a perusal of exciting stories, more dangerous is it, a great deal, to draw much upon the tender sympathies of *childhood* by pictures of life, rousing the whole inner nature, and yet *pictures* only. It must cherish an early taste for the morbid enjoyments of sentiment through the imagination, by no means to be coveted for the young. Their tales, we think, should owe their interest to difficulties and struggles arising rather from without than from within; calling for energy, and courage, and self-denial, and honesty, and forbearance, more than for religious resignation and trust. And the best parts of the *Wide, Wide World* are those which have *that* object rather than *this*. The exercise of forbearance towards Aunt Fortune, and forgiveness towards Nancy Vawse, is among the most useful and excellent portions of the discipline through which Ellen Montgomery has to pass. It is premature to ask for *deep* reliance in a spiritual being at so early an age. We do not deny that, to some extent, religious trust will often be developed in childhood, and certainly in a character of Ellen's innate sensitiveness, reverence, and affection. But we grow up *gradually* into trust in God, out of trust in humanity; and it is plain enough that even Ellen's trust is really in the Humphreys, and only very partially in her Saviour. We would not be understood to say that children are incapable of being religious, of being possessed with an idea of the presence of God; far from it. But it is impossible that at so unripe an age, they should be brought to throw themselves, with all their troubles, and cares, and perhaps anguish, upon the bosom of the Unseen. They need some visible arm, some human breast, on which to lay their aching heads and sob out their griefs; the youthful imagination cannot grasp—the untried affections cannot compass—the all-pervading spirit; and Time only can lift up the soul gently and gradually to that condition wherein it shall be easy to "commit all its griefs and ways" into the gracious hands of Him who is "over all, and through all, and in all."

Nor is the difficulty removed, though it may be lessened, by removing the object of reliance (granting this to be admissible) from the all-pervading Father to his realised image in Christ his Son. It is quite true that Jesus of Nazareth, the companion of Peter and James and John, the friend of Mary and Martha, the healer of disease, the feeder of the multitude, the restorer of the dead, may be comprehended and loved by the young reader of the gospels, where no adequate conception of the great Life-giver can be attained. He who took little children up in his arms and blessed them, who washed his disciples' feet, and was bowed in agony in the garden, and remembered his mother, and prayed for his enemies, and spoke peace to his fellow sufferer on the cross, presents to every mind, even in youth, a reality of existence, and an idea of perfection, that more or less can be grasped and understood. But still we do not think it possible, for most children, if for any, to be able to cast themselves in thought upon his help and care, as if he were a human being close at hand, and anxious to assist them. Imagination must be *very* vivid, and Faith *very* keen, in one whose heart, as yet timid and inexperienced, prone to cling to the strong hand of protection, and the kind look of love, can find solace and support in the merely *mentally-conceived* image of one whom it has never known. This may be possible, not to say easy, to one who has for years studied that divine character, and unconsciously drawn forth all its real greatness and wonderful beauty by the mingled processes of mental study and personal experience. But children must have the realities of knowledge to hold by, and the parent, sister or friend must *train them up* to a love and reverence for Christ, by fixing their intuitive sympathies first upon what is *visibly* good, or almost virtually *made* visible by the living efforts of the human mind, through eye and ear, to convey its impressions to the untaught soul. We question much whether *any* use of the Bible to a child really alone in spirit, debarred from all outward help, and teaching, and sympathy on religious subjects, would prove any effective source of strength and comfort. It was through Mrs. Montgomery and the Humphreys that Ellen's high principles were really cultivated, and in sending her to the Scripture and the Saviour, they only sent her to cultivate her higher sympathies with themselves. So prayer comforted her, mainly perhaps because she was occupied as they wished. A child's conscience may be early cultivated. Very soon do children know right from wrong; it is a deeply-seated instinct of our nature, of which we become aware long before we know what it means, or why it must be obeyed. But reliance upon God's help and blessing under trouble and temptation is of much later growth; and though it is desirable doubtless early to teach some simple form of prayer, the deep *realities and uses* of prayer *cannot* be known and felt at a tender age.

And further; though to a mature mind, thoroughly imbued with orthodox views, the **Wide, Wide World** might prove simply instructive and beautiful, we do not believe that to any child with a clear mind and a simple heart, there can be any truthful reality in the relation there described as existing between man and Jesus Christ, or in the manner in which our duties towards him are inculcated. There in the New Testament is set before us a great prophet, mighty in power and solitary in holiness; he is described as dependent on God, though constantly in communion with Him. He is a character of unequalled excellence; but his life and death are parts of the world's history, and all his existence is linked with the past or associated with our unearthly future. It is only long culture in the popular theology that can lead the mind to identify this great Teacher and Prophet of the Jews, with the eternal Creator. The one is a human being belonging to a certain age and country, the other a spirit independent of all time, the source, and centre, and controller of all things. That Jesus was immortal does not prove him omnipresent even to our globe,—and the simple reader of Scripture would not certainly come away thence with the idea, that our great Master and Exemplar, who passed his life between Galilee and Judea, was now to be the daily refuge of the soul, the answerer of prayer, and the giver of peace, and the saviour from sin. At any rate whatever may seem natural to children trained by Trinitarian parents, we must deprecate the influence of these ideas amongst those who hold the humanity of Jesus Christ. There is a tendency in the present day among Unitarians to forsake the simple ground of real conviction, for fanciful sentiments and pleasing theories. We should be the last to desire a return to the old, hard, unreverential view of Christ's life and character. We do not think of him, with Mr. Parker of America, as a distinguished Hebrew reformer, but as the express image of the Father, the word of God made flesh, the revealer to the world of God's character and will. But this he was by the grace of God, who gave to him, His spirit without measure. He was a created being. A Hebrew of the Hebrews, he executed his divine mission; cast upon the world his glorious revelation, and then returned to the Father's bosom. Historical in his birth, in his life, in his death, he bears to the Father of All, the relation we bear ourselves, that of a child, a son. We *know* that *God* encompasses us behind and before. *His* presence is essential to the maintenance of life, to the very existence of the air we breathe, the light by which we see,—the ground we tread,—the landscape we admire, the human forms we love. We feel assured that we could not raise our arm, or our eyelid, or move one step, or feel one beating of the pulse, if His power were not present,—His will momentarily operative around and within us. If our Lord is the same being with this Almighty One, then we may, indeed, fly to Jesus, and lay our troubles at his feet, for we must ever feel him near. But if this be but the arbitrary assumption of the fanciful theologian, then why confound the all-sustaining personality of God, with the prophet of a past age, albeit risen and glorified? When shall we learn deeply to love, and highly to revere, and meekly to imitate the excellencies of our Lord, without flying off into exaggerated sentiments, and making a God, virtually or really, of the Son who was sanctified and sent into the world? Where is our proof that he abides with us individually, and will hear our cry if we call to him, and stretch out his hand for our rescue? To put him in the place of God as our daily ally and refuge,—is it not to put imagination in the place of conviction, and to turn from the inherent Spring of all life, to the peculiar Inspirer of the world about eighteen centuries ago? from the Independent

Fountain of all things, to one of earth's dependent beings whose life is among the records of history, however truly it may be declared the brightest and the best, and lifted heavenward by divine attributes and a constant communion with the Eternal?

To keep upon the firm ground of *reality,* and not dream until we mistake imagination for truth, and truth for imagination, is surely one of the first requisites for a deep and vital religion. We do approach God through Christ; because our minds can form no image of the Father so pure and perfect, so moving to the deepest love and veneration of the heart, as that with which the Gospels supply us in our Lord. But because he is the channel or mediator through which our thoughts ascend on high, he does not, therefore, become, in *any* sense, the *present* friend and sanctifier of the soul: and it appears to us purely visionary and self-deceptive, to believe in his spiritual presence with us, and to seek his counsel and support. He came to show us how the filial relation of a human being to the great Father could be perfectly sustained, not to bid us set that filial relation aside, and take a new Parent. The relation to God into which he was born, was precisely that of which we also are conscious, and his example of perfection is lost upon us, if that relation is to be changed through the nature of his mission, or the consequences of his exalted fidelity. Nor do we think that an opposite conclusion is to be established on the reading of a few texts of scripture. With regard to this, two things have to be considered; the almost inevitable unexactness of many of the reported sayings of Jesus; and the place, time, and circumstances in which they were uttered. What can be established from a single text in a single gospel, like that of Matthew xviii. 20? It might be addressed exclusively to his immediate disciples; it might refer only to the presence amongst his earnest followers, assembled as such, of that holy spirit which he had awakened and fostered; or it might be the Evangelist's version of some saying of Jesus, misunderstood by him or indistinctly heard. We must not forget these possibilities. It is not at all probable that the words of Jesus were taken down as they fell from his lips, and many a sentence must have been modified in its meaning, and certainly given to us in other words, in the course of its transmission to our present Gospels. Who can suppose that all the latter chapters of St. John's Gospel (admitting that it was certainly written by him) give us word for word the discourse of Christ? The supposition is plainly absurd, even were there no reason to believe that it was the latest composition of the Evangelist. The more carefully we study the sacred records, the more are we convinced that we must *not* rely on the strict verbal accuracy of our Scriptures at all, but, contented with their general truthfulness, rejoice to be able to draw forth the *spirit* of their teachings throughout. Great mischief is done by taking texts away from their context, and giving to them a general application, in place of that special one

evidently their own, and the only one of which they will fairly admit. We take an example of this error from the ***Wide, Wide World***; the passage occurs near the commencement of the story, and will furnish a good specimen of Miss Warner's style. Ellen Montgomery is about to be separated from her mother, who is consumptive, and going to Europe for a voyage, the little girl remaining behind; the morning had been spent in making purchases for Ellen.

> When dinner was over, and the table cleared away, the mother and daughter were left, as they always loved to be, alone. It was late in the afternoon, and already somewhat dark, for clouds had gathered over the beautiful sky of the morning, and the wind rising now and then, made its voice heard. Mrs. Montgomery was lying on the sofa, as usual, seemingly at ease; and Ellen was sitting on a little bench before the fire, very much at *her* ease indeed—without any seeming about it. She smiled as she met her mother's eyes.
>
> "You have made me very happy to-day, mamma."
>
> "I am glad of it, my dear child. I hoped I should. I believe the whole affair has given me as much pleasure, Ellen, as it has you." There was a pause.
>
> "Mamma, I will take the greatest possible care of my new treasures."
>
> "I know you will. If I had doubted it, Ellen, most assuredly I should not have given them to you—sorry as I should have been to leave you without them. So you see, you have not established a character for carefulness in vain."
>
> "And mamma, I hope you have not given them to me in vain, either. I will try to use them in the way that I know you wish me to; that will be the best way that I can thank you."
>
> "Well, I have left you no excuse, Ellen. You know fully what I wish you to do and to be; and when I am away, I shall please myself with thinking, that my little daughter *is* following her mother's wishes. I shall believe so, Ellen—you will not let me be disappointed?"
>
> "Oh, no! mamma," said Ellen, who was now in her mother's arms.
>
> "Well, my child," said Mrs. Montgomery, in a lighter tone, "my gifts will serve as reminders for you, if you are ever tempted to forget my lessons. If you fail to send me letters, or if those you send are not what they ought to be, I think the desk will cry shame upon you. And if you ever go an hour with a hole in your stocking, or a tear in your dress, or a string off your petticoat, I hope the sight of your workbox will make you blush."
>
> "Workbox, mamma?"
>
> "Yes. Oh! I forgot—you've not seen that."
>
> "No, mamma! What do you mean?"
>
> "Why, my dear, that was one of the things you most wanted; but I thought it best not to overwhelm you quite this morning; so, while you were on an exploring expedition round the store, I chose and furnished one for you."

"Oh! mamma, mamma!" said Ellen, getting up, and clasping her hands, "what shall I do? I don't know what to say. I can't say anything. Mamma, it's too much."

So it seemed, for Ellen sat down, and began to cry. Her mother silently reached out a hand to her, which she squeezed and kissed with all the energy of gratitude, love, and sorrow; till, gently drawn by the same hand, she was placed again in her mother's arms, and upon her bosom; and in that tried resting-place she lay, calmed and quieted, till the shades of afternoon deepened into evening, and evening into night, and the light of the fire was all that was left to them.

Though not a word had been spoken for a long time, Ellen was not asleep; her eyes were fixed on the red glow of the coals in the grate, and she was busily thinking, but not of them. Many sober thoughts were passing through her little head, and stirring her heart; a few were of her new possessions, and bright projects—more of her mother. She was thinking how very, very precious was the heart she could feel beating where her cheek lay; she thought it was greater happiness to lie there than anything else in life could be; she thought she had rather even die so, on her mother's breast, than live long without her in the world—she felt that in earth, or in heaven, there was nothing so dear. Suddenly she broke the silence.

"Mamma, what does that mean, 'He that loveth father or mother more than me is not worthy of me?'"

"It means just what it says. If you love anybody or anything better than Jesus Christ, you cannot be one of his children."

"But then, mamma," said Ellen, raising her head, "how *can* I be one of his children? I do love you a great deal better; how can I help it, mamma?"

"You cannot help it, I know, my dear," said Mrs. Montgomery, with a sigh, "except by His grace, who has promised to change the hearts of his people—to take away the heart of stone, and give them a heart of flesh."

"But is mine a heart of stone, then, mamma, because I cannot help loving you best?"

"Not to me, dear Ellen," replied Mrs. Montgomery, pressing closer the little form that lay in her arms; "I have never found it so. But yet I know that the Lord Jesus is far, far more worthy of your affection than I am; and if your heart were not hardened by sin, you would see Him so; it is only because you do not know Him that you love me better. Pray, pray, my dear child, that He would take away the power of sin, and show you Himself; that is all that is wanting."

"I will, mamma,' said Ellen, tearfully. 'Oh, mamma! what shall I do without you?"

Alas! Mrs. Montgomery's heart echoed the question—she had no answer.

"Mamma,' said Ellen, after a few minutes, "can I have no true love to Him at all, unless I love Him *best?*"

"I dare not say that you can," answered her mother seriously.

"Mamma," said Ellen, after a little, again raising her head, and looking her mother full in the face, as if willing to apply the severest test to this hard doctrine, and speaking with an indescribable expression, "do *you* love Him *better than you do me?*"

She knew her mother loved the Saviour; but she thought it scarcely possible that herself could have but the second place in her heart; she ventured a bold question, to prove whether her mother's practice would not contradict her theory.

But Mrs. Montgomery answered steadily, 'I do, my daughter;' and, with a gush of tears, Ellen sunk her head again upon her bosom. She had no more to say; her mouth was stopped for ever as to the *right* of the matter, though she still thought it an impossible duty in her own particular case.

I do, indeed, my daughter," repeated Mrs. Montgomery; "that does not make my love to you the less, but the more, Ellen."

"Oh, mamma, mamma!" said Ellen, clinging to her, "I wish you would teach me! I have only you, and I am going to lose you. What shall I do, mamma?"

With a voice that strove to be calm, Mrs. Montgomery answered—"I love them that love me; and they that seek me early shall find me." And after a minute or two she added, "He who says this has promised, too, that He will gather the lambs with His arm, and carry them in His bosom."

By the ingenuity of the orthodox mind, these two sentences are quoted as the words of Jesus Christ, the one from Proverbs (viii. 17), the other from Isaiah (xl. 11); the one consisting of words put by the writer into the mouth of personified Wisdom, the other a declaration made by the Prophet concerning the gracious kindness about to be manifested by Jehovah to his people. "Behold the Lord-God will come with strong hand, &c.," is the commencement of the passage, and supplies the subject of the pronoun *He*: yet, showing that there is no mistake as to the reputed source of these declarations, little Ellen quotes the first of the two later on in the story, and "remembers" that her mother had said that they were "the Saviour's words."

Now we must earnestly protest against the doctrinal contents of this passage. Miss Warner boldly grapples with the difficulty she perceives, and puts the whole dilemma forward through her heroine's simple observations. Now, did not the authoress feel how grievously she was violating innate human instincts, and human nature generally, if not Scripture also, by first demanding an impossibility from the young and loving heart, and then attributing its incapacity to comply with that demand, to the effect of original sin? We were not aware that hearts could be subdivided; and that that which was human and affectionate in one direction, could be (without any provocative cause of deadness or hostility, and with an obvious cause for reverence and love) hard and icy in another. That Ellen had a tender and feeling heart, and only needed mental growth and experience, together with the culture she received, to feel the full claim of Jesus Christ on her admiration, veneration, and attachment, is amply proved. What, then, is the writer's ground for accusing her of having a "heart of stone, hardened by sin?" Simply that she did not love her Lord better than her Mother, in deference to the authority of the quoted text.

The textual question is easily settled. The words of Jesus, spoken to his immediate followers and apostles, to whom the great work was committed of preaching the Gospel far and wide over the earth, and who had been privileged to enjoy a close and confidential intercourse with their heavenly Master, cannot bear to us that *peculiar* force, and admit of that *literal* explanation which belonged to them in their first utterance. But at the same time they have a clear application to ourselves, and undoubtedly imply that in cases where some *antagonism* arises between parental claims and those of our divine Teacher, we must prefer *duty* to filial obedience or devotion. More than this we believe is not demanded in the text. And it appears to us quite suicidal towards those innate affections implanted in our souls by our Creator, to demand that, as soon as ever we become conscious of duty, we shall bring the spiritual reverence and devotion that we owe to our unknown Lord, into immediate comparison with our personal human affections, and set ourselves down as guilty creatures, if our hearts are not more strongly knit to him than to our relatives and friends. Whatever may be possible for the mature, we think that to ask this of children, is nothing less than monstrous. To whom are they really most indebted? To the Christ of whom they have heard or read in Scripture, or to the parents, guardians, or friends who have nursed them from infancy, shielded them from cold and heat, danger and death, satisfied their natural wants, opened their minds and hearts, and blest them with every species of culture and love? Christianity has herein its peculiar sanction as a divine religion, that it is every way calculated to *develope,* in the most natural and orderly manner, the native principles and dispositions of the uncorrupted heart of infancy. It does not remove a "heart of stone" and replace it by a "heart of flesh;" it nurtures and elevates the innate dispositions of the fleshly heart, and out of human affection generates, gradually and harmoniously, the love of Christ and God. But it is necessarily some time before human attachment, and spiritual reverence and affection, can be brought to assimilate. This is the slow process of years;—as we learn by broken ties to associate the earthly with the heavenly, and by prayer and faithfulness of will to bring down to earth our conceptions and our love of Heaven. To bring before us a child so essentially loveable and good as Ellen Montgomery, and represent her to the reader as already separated from God and her Saviour, by a mean and earthly nature spoiled by sin, is to invent a foul blot for humanity, and pretend, at the expense of all reality and truth, that it is deforming the fair beauties of God's holiest creation, which it is felt in nowise to injure or affect. What better instance could we have than this, of the essential antagonism between Calvinistic or so-called evangelical Christianity, and the teaching of him who said, "Suffer little children to come unto me and forbid them not, for of such is the kingdom of God?"

Another thing we find fault with in this book is the writer's occasional indulgence in that indiscriminate moralising often employed towards the young, but tending to produce prejudicial effects, through deception and consequent disappointment. Singularly enough she devotes the greater part of her story to proving the utter falseness of the following homily. Ellen is to live with a half sister of her father's, a certain Aunt Fortune, already mentioned, who, up to the very last, shows herself inexcusably unjust and unkind towards her devoted and forgiving little niece. Ellen regrets that the relationship between her aunt and herself is not closer. Her mother asks the reason:—

> "I'm afraid (says Ellen) she will not be so likely to love me."

> "You mustn't think so, my child. Her loving or not loving you will depend solely and entirely upon yourself, Ellen. Don't forget that. If you are a good child, and make it your daily care to do your duty, she cannot help liking you, be she what she may; and, on the other hand, if she have all the will in the world to love you, she cannot do it, unless you will let her—it all depends on your behaviour."

A little further on she adds—

> "It will be your own fault if she does not love you, in time, truly and tenderly."

And again—

> "You can make her love you, Ellen, if you try."

Now, as soon as we read this passage, before we made Miss Fortune Emerson's acquaintance, we felt how one-sided a mis-statement it contained. If it is only given to prove that Mrs. Montgomery was a weakminded woman, we have nothing more to urge. But this does not appear. Now in this particular case, the opposite would have been very much nearer the truth, indeed it would have been the truth; for it really depended *entirely* on Aunt Fortune, whether any mutual love were possible. Ellen's heart was open and tender to a fault. The most commonplace kindness would have made her captive at once. But even in any ordinary case, it is manifest that two persons being concerned, the responsibility cannot rest entirely with one. Supposing this wise apophthegm had been pronounced to Miss Emerson by Mr. Van Brunt, while it was falling from Mrs. Montgomery's lips, there is no reason to bring why it would not have been as appropriate in the one case as in the other. Yet to what absurdity are we then reduced. Mutual love between A. and B. is declared by C. to depend "solely and entirely" upon A.; by D. it is declared to depend "solely and entirely" upon B.;—which (after Euclid's phraseology) is absurd. This unmeaning kind of language is too often indulged in towards children, and nothing but disappointment and misery can come of it. The serious though often disheartening truths of life should be at once boldly confessed and stated. Truth before all things.

One other fault we have to find with the authoress of the *Wide, Wide World* before we close our observations of disparagement. We think she insists upon an obedience too unlimited. She seems to approve of Ellen's calling herself Ellen Lindsay, and the daughter of her uncle, in direct opposition to the fact, as well as to her own instincts and inclination, because she had been so commanded by him. And where she is courageous enough to speak the truth respectfully, she is made to repent as of some wrong action, and to apologise accordingly. And in one or two places in the early part of the story, Ellen shows a readiness to keep things secret from her father, and afterwards from her Aunt Fortune, that appeared to us unsatisfactory, and quite needless to the tale, and inconsistent with her conscientious disposition. Her one fault in our eyes is her prudery.

The descriptive parts of the story are well written and vivid, though in this respect we think *Queechy* shows signs of increased power, and additional care and pains. The following passage from the *Wide, Wide World,* describing Ellen's journey in Mr. Van Brunt's ox-cart from Thirlwall to her aunt's house, gives an interesting picture both of the country and the child:—

> Slowly, very slowly, the good oxen drew the cart and the little queen in the arm-chair out of the town, and they entered upon the open country. The sun had already gone down when they left the inn, and the glow of his setting had faded a good deal by the time they got quite out of the town: but light enough was left still to delight Ellen with the pleasant look of the country. It was a lovely evening, and quiet as summer; not a breath stirring. The leaves were all off the trees; the hills were brown; but the soft, warm light that still lingered upon them, forbade any look of harshness or dreariness. These hills lay towards the west, and at Thirlwall were not more than two miles distant, but sloping off more to the west as the range extended in a southerly direction. Between, the ground was beautifully broken. Rich fields and meadows lay on all sides, sometimes level, and sometimes with a soft, wavy surface, where Ellen thought it must be charming to run up and down. Every now and then these were varied by a little rising ground, capped with a piece of woodland; and beautiful trees, many of them, were seen standing alone, especially by the roadside. All had a cheerful pleasant look. The houses were very scattered; in the whole way they passed but few. Ellen's heart regularly began to beat when they came in sight of one, and "I wonder if that is Aunt Fortune's house!"—"perhaps it is!"—or, "I hope it is not!" were the thoughts that rose in her mind. But slowly the oxen brought her abreast of the houses, one after another, and slowly they passed on beyond, and there was no sign of getting home yet. Their way was through pleasant lanes, towards the south, but constantly approaching the hills. About half a mile from Thirlwall, they crossed a little river, not more than

thirty yards broad, and after that the twilight deepened fast. The shades gathered on field and hill: everything grew brown, and then dusky; and then Ellen was obliged to content herself with what was very near, for further than that she could only see dim outlines. . . . They plodded along very slowly, and the evening fell fast; as they left behind the hill which Mr. Van Brunt had called "the Nose," they could see, through an opening in the mountains, a bit of the western horizon, and some brightness still lingering there, but it was soon hid from view, and darkness veiled the whole country. Ellen could amuse herself no longer with looking about; she could see nothing very clearly but the outline of Mr. Van Brunt's broad back, just before her. But the stars had come out!—and, brilliant and clear, they were looking down upon her with their thousand eyes. Ellen's heart jumped when she saw them, with a mixed feeling of pleasure and sadness. They carried her right back to the last evening, when she was walking up the hill with Timmins; she remembered her anger against Mrs. Dunscombe, and her kind friend's warning not to indulge it, and all his teaching that day; and tears came with the thought, how glad she would be to hear him speak to her again. Still looking up at the beautiful quiet stars, she thought of her dear far-off mother—how long it was already since she had seen her—faster and faster the tears dropped—and then she thought of that glorious One who had made the stars, and was above them all, and who could and did see her mother and her, though ever so far apart, and could hear and bless them both. The little face was no longer upturned—it was buried in her hands, and bowed to her lap, and tears streamed as she prayed that God would bless her dear mother, and take care of her. Not once nor twice—the fulness of Ellen's heart could not be poured out in one asking. Greatly comforted at last, at having, as it were, laid over the care of her mother upon One who was able, she thought of herself and her late resolution to serve Him.

Here we must take leave of Miss Warner for the present. Her other work suggests a variety of criticism on American life, and manners, and characters, that we cannot enter upon here, and we, therefore refrain from quoting from its lively and interesting pages. Our warmest thanks are due to the lady who has so delicately and powerfully delineated the true and tender heart of a most interesting orphan child.

Southern Literary Messenger (review date April 1854)

SOURCE: Review of *The Wide, Wide World. Southern Literary Messenger* 20, no. 4 (April 1854): 214-16.

[*In the following excerpted review, the critic calls* The Wide, Wide World *"the most delightful tale that has probably ever been written."*]

We have no intention of criticising any production of [Susan Warner's] pen, and only fear that we shall be guilty of extravagance in speaking of her writings. We well recollect our first perusal of the *Wide Wide World,* and we then predicted its success. It deserved to succeed if a pure and beautiful work of Art, full of the most exalted piety, and as true to life and human nature as reality itself, deserve success. *Queechy,* which followed it was its twin sister; and if the features were somewhat more arch and changeable and inviting, there was no such difference in the heart. The two books were dedicated to a single idea, and surely a grand idea! In both the object is to paint every-day life with its pleasures and annoyances, its sunshine and shadow, its joys and sufferings: and then, as a frame to the picture, a burden to the strain, to indicate the source from which humanity may gather strength to resist the trials of the world. Many sermons are preached in other places than the pulpit. We think that Miss Warner's works are among the strongest and most beautiful. Certain critics have taken exception to the variety of gifts united in her pictures of children, and, so, called the work unnatural. We dissent from this opinion, totally, in every point; but without pausing to discuss what is scarcely to our purpose, we may say without fear of dissent from any reader whatsoever, that the "moral" of these books is beyond criticism. We use the word *moral* in its familiar sense, and mean that Miss Warner's books make the reader purer, clear the atmosphere around him, open the blue sky above as the wind does when it sweeps away the clouds and vapors; when the purity and beauty of the world seems to revive, rising from sleep; when all is brighter for the clouds of trial. In the case of "Ellen," in the first work, the trial was in the form of a violent temper, and a tormentor who assailed the child on that weak-side with a relentless, never ceasing persecution. Against this persecution, assailing her systematically throughout every hour of the day, and driving her nearly mad with the conflict of emotions, pride and passion and self-condemnation—the child had her Bible only. Still that was quite enough. And how she at last overcame everything is all written there in the most delightful tale that has probably ever been written.

Edward Halsey Foster (essay date 1978)

SOURCE: Foster, Edward Halsey. "The Perils of Apostasy." In *Susan and Anna Warner,* pp. 34-53. Boston: Twayne Publishers, 1978.

[*In the following excerpt, Foster surveys the content and reception of* The Wide, Wide World, *considering the book "one of the first, and certainly the most famous domestic novel" in America. The critic continues by probing the reasons for its popularity in the nineteenth century as well as the principal sources of contemporary interest in the work.*]

> [*The Wide, Wide World*] was written in closest reliance upon God: for thoughts, for power, and for words. Not the mere vague wish to write a book that should do

> service to her Master: but a vivid, constant, looking to him for guidance and help [sic]: the worker and her work both laid humbly at the Lord's feet.
>
> —Anna Warner, *Susan Warner*[1]

I A BOOK THAT WOULD SELL

Susan and Anna Warner spent most of their lives from 1838 until their deaths many decades later, in the old farmhouse, "Woodcrags," on Constitution Island. It was here that most of their books were written. The first was begun in the winter of 1847-48. Anna wrote it as part of a children's game, *Robinson Crusoe's Farmyard,* which she had devised to teach natural history to children. The game included twenty-four hand-painted cards with pictures of animals, and the accompanying book described the animals and gave answers to questions printed on the backs of the cards. The publisher was George P. Putnam, who was later to make a fortune by publishing *The Wide, Wide World* and *Queechy.*

Robinson Crusoe's Farmyard provided the Warners, who were nearly destitute, with greatly needed funds, yet if the family was to survive, it would be necessary, they knew, to find other sources of income. One evening during the winter when Anna was writing her book, Aunt Fanny, turning to Susan, remarked, "I believe if you would try, you could write a story." As Anna later wrote, her aunt had meant a story "That would sell"—a means of lifting the family out of poverty.[2] Anna believed that her sister began *The Wide, Wide World* that evening. It was completed a year and a half later but, at first, was not offered to any publisher. When the book finally was offered to publishers, the results were discouraging. Virtually every major publisher refused it. The reader at Harper's scribbled "Fudge!" on one of the pages, and at Carters, which later became one of the Warners' major publishers, no one bothered to read the manuscript. Finally it was taken to George P. Putnam, who did not read it himself but asked his mother, who was visiting him at the time, for her opinion. "If you never publish another book," Mrs. Putnam said, "publish this!"[3] But Putnam remained unconvinced, and although, at his mother's urging, he agreed to publish it, he decided to print only 750 copies.

The Wide, Wide World was issued in December, 1850. To Putnam's considerable surprise, it received extraordinarily favorable reviews, one of which concluded that the author had "few equals, and no superiors, on either side of the Atlantic," while another claimed that the book was "capable of doing more good than any other work, other than the Bible."[4] The first edition sold out quickly, and Putnam, still cautious and a little incredulous, issued a second of 750 copies. This, too, sold out quickly, and a third edition of 750 or 1,000 copies was proposed. By the end of 1852, the book was heading toward its fourteenth edition and its reputation as one of the greatest publishing successes of all time. With the sole exception of *Uncle Tom's Cabin,* it was the most famous and popular book of the day, and it continued to find enthusiastic readers and reviewers and to sell astonishingly well for more than half a century.

II A CHRISTIAN TRAINING

The heroine of *The Wide, Wide World* is Ellen Montgomery, a young girl who has grown up in New York City in relatively fashionable and comfortable circumstances. Her father, at the beginning of the novel, has recently lost an important lawsuit and with it much of his fortune. In addition, his wife is in poor health, and in the hope of finding new sources of income and a place where her health will improve, he has decided to take her and travel abroad. Since his funds are limited, he has decided to leave his daughter in America and has arranged for her to live with his sister, Miss Fortune Emerson, in Thirlwall, a rural village far from the city. The opening chapters concern Ellen's separation from her mother and the subsequent journey to Thirlwall. Aunt Fortune or, as she is also called, Miss Fortune (the pun here is intentional) has little love for Ellen and considers her largely a nuisance until Ellen, during one of her aunt's illnesses, shows herself efficient and competent in running her aunt's domestic affairs. Meanwhile, Ellen is befriended by a neighboring farmer, Bram Van Brunt, who manages Aunt Fortune's farm and who later marries her. Among Ellen's other friends are Alice Humphreys and her brother John, a divinity student. They are the children of a local minister. Through the Humphreys, Ellen becomes friends with their relatives, the Marshman family, local gentry whose cultivated and cultured lives are compared by the author to the rustic lives and customs of Miss Fortune and her friends. A large portion of the book is spent contrasting a social "bee" at Miss Fortune's with the Marshman's elegant means of entertaining at Christmas.

Alice Humphreys dies, and Ellen, in obedience to one of Alice's last wishes, goes to live with Mr. Humphreys and his son in the hope of being daughter and sister to them. While abroad, Ellen's mother and father have died but have left a request that Ellen be sent to Scotland to live with her mother's family, the Lindsays. Ellen is sent to Scotland but hopes to return eventually to her friends in America and particularly to John. The concluding paragraph of the book suggests that eventually she will return to him and that they will be married.

The book is almost entirely lacking in dramatic incident or conflict. The narrative will inevitably seem discursive, rambling, to any reader unaware of the author's religious purpose or objective in writing the novel, for *The Wide, Wide World* is, first of all, a religious allegory, a sort of *Pilgrim's Progress* (a book that, notably, is among Ellen's favorites). The book traces Ellen's

education as a Christian, and many of the central characters are models or emblems of such Christian virtues as patience, charity, and willing submission to divine purpose. Each character either contributes directly to Ellen's Christian education or tests that education by exposing Ellen to worldly values. Aunt Fortune and the Lindsays are as important to Ellen's education—and the narrative—as are Alice and John Humphreys, for it is in her conflicts with the former that she is able to prove herself as obedient and forgiving as the Humphreys have taught her to be. *The Wide, Wide World* is essentially a didactic novel; its purpose is to teach religious and moral values.

Susan's moral and religious values were those of nineteenth-century evangelical Christianity: charity, forbearance, sobriety, and submission to divine will and biblical authority, among others. In turn, these values dictated much of the novel's plot and characterization—a situation very different from that in the fiction of such contemporaries as, say, Nathaniel Hawthorne. In Hawthorne's works, a moral stance is used to *interpret* rather than *dictate* plot and characterization. This point is worth emphasizing, for it is basically this which, aside from differences in strictly literary merit, distinguishes *The Wide, Wide World* from books like *The Scarlet Letter.* In subject matter, both are, after all, religious novels, but Warner's is didactically so. Hawthorne interpreted his narrative from a moral perspective, but Warner began by devising a narrative that schematically illustrated her moral and religious beliefs. Even in her later books, which were all solidly based on historical incidents, narrative and characterization were shaped to didactic ends.

The Wide, Wide World traces its heroine's progress from a concern solely with worldly love—suggested by her devotion to her mother—to a concern with higher or spiritual love—suggested by, among other things, her devotion to the minister John Humphreys. Perhaps no passage in the book is liable to seem more extraordinary or incredible to modern readers than that in which one of the Marshmans tells the heroine that God has taken her mother from her because Ellen, in loving her mother so intensely, "was in danger of forgetting him, and he loved you, Ellen; . . . and now he says to you, 'My daughter, give *me* thy heart.'"[5] *The Wide, Wide World* contends that the true Christian will absolutely, unquestioningly, and unhesitatingly submit himself to divine will, especially divine will as revealed in the Bible. Above all, the Christian will allow no human affection to interfere with his devotion to his God.

III THE DOMESTIC DILEMMA

The nineteenth century, as recent historical studies have shown, was preeminently an era of domesticity and close family life. Philip Aries and his followers have documented some of the effects that family life had on individual lives and civilization in general.[6] While historians may not agree on the reasons why family life became as important as it did, all agree that for the nineteenth century, domestic life was of overwhelming importance—a fact reflected in the literature of the time and a major concern of *The Wide, Wide World.* Susan Warner personally left no doubt that she, like her contemporaries, considered family life not only important to social life but central to an individual's spiritual and moral existence, and although she herself never married, her most famous novel is a didactic tale that preaches the values of family life.

Ellen's mother has no affection for her husband (nor does he have any for her), but neither she nor, for that matter, the author questions his absolute authority over his wife. Paul in his epistle to the Ephesians demanded, as Susan, of course, well knew, that wives "submit [themselves] unto [their] own husbands, as unto the Lord" and that children be similarly obedient to their parents.[7] Biblically, neither wife nor child is given the right to question the authority of the husband or father. Ellen has no love for her father and, after his death, remembers her experiences with him as "the least agreeable" part of her life.[8] Her father has neither her love nor his wife's affection, but he has their absolute obedience.

As part of her education, Ellen is told that she must learn to submit her will to her elders as unhesitatingly as her mother has submitted her will to her husband. Ellen must learn never to contradict her elders—or, eventually, her husband—even when she believes they are wrong. The novel suggests, however, that while Ellen may not contradict the will of an elder, she might conceivably disobey him if she believed that his will did not accord with some higher, divine purpose. For example, in the closing chapters of the novel, Ellen is sent to Scotland to live with her uncle and his family. The uncle insists that Ellen give him the respect and obedience that would be due a father, and Ellen agrees—with a condition. She is willing to be docile, obedient, and submissive to her uncle unless his will conflicts with what she knows, particularly as the result of studying her Bible, to be a higher purpose. She is willing to submit herself unconditionally only to men like John Humphreys, who wants to escape from the world and "the signs of man's presence and influence," and who is seldom content except when contemplating spiritual matters.[9]

Although *The Wide, Wide World* continually reasserts the importance of family life and particularly the absolute authority of the husband and father, the book also insists that this authority is his only when it does not conflict with what his wife and children consider divine will. In effect, he has no more free will or free choice than they, and his authority is valid only when it reflects God's purpose.

IV CHRISTIAN NURTURE

As we have seen, Susan's theological training was largely in evangelicalism, which insisted on an individual's attention to biblical authority and absolute submission to divine will. Her religious perspective was that of her minister, Thomas Harvey Skinner; and there is no record that she ever dissented from his opinions. She followed him even in defending religious ecumenicity—a relatively unpopular but open and liberal movement of the day. Certainly this movement deeply influenced her religious attitudes.

There were other sources for her theological premises. Among the theologians whom she read was Horace Bushnell, a liberal Congregationalist minister whose *Christian Nurture* (1846) argued that religious conversion could result not from a sudden awareness or awakening to divine grace—a theological point argued by Charles Grandison Finney and other influential revivalist ministers—but from a life-long training in Christian principles and attitudes. In turn, *The Wide, Wide World,* which was written and published during the years *Christian Nurture* was being widely condemned by conservative theologians, portrays the sort of religious training that Bushnell described. Ellen becomes a Christian not through a sudden awareness of divine grace but through an extensive education in Christian behavior—an education begun by her mother and carried out by members of the Marshman and Humphreys families. In terms of Protestant theological thinking at the time the novel was published, *The Wide, Wide World* must have seemed liberal indeed. *Christian Nurture,* after all, so upset the conservative clergy that Bushnell was very nearly tried for heresy.

V RELIGION AND SALES

With good reason, readers today may wonder why a novel so intensely moralistic and pietistic should also have been one of the most extraordinarily popular books ever published. Of course, religious novels can still be found on best-seller lists, but these novels are generally more concerned with religious, usually biblical, history than with theological matters such as those that dictated so much of the narrative and characterization in *The Wide, Wide World.*

The best sellers of the nineteenth century, particularly the latter half of the century, are often marked by biblical and theological concerns no less abstruse than those that concerned Susan Warner. *The Gates Ajar* by Elizabeth Stuart Phelps sketched out with much theological pedantry a materialistic heaven to which any middle-class American could aspire, and E. P. Roe's *Barriers*

Burned Away (1872) used an exceedingly melodramatic plot involving the Chicago Fire to make more palatable (or exciting) what was essentially a sermon on Christian values. Charles M. Sheldon's *In His Steps* (1896) taught its readers to make in their lives the sort of decisions that Christ would have made. Novels based on biblical history also enjoyed huge audiences. Lew Wallace's *Ben Hur* (1880) sold two-and-a-half million copies. Earlier best-selling biblical novels included Joseph Holt Ingraham's *The Prince of the House of David* (1855). In addition, domestic novelists, like Susan Warner, were often religious novelists as well, and their worship of domesticity was tied to a belief in the religious values that domestic life was supposed to entail. Maria Cummins's *The Lamplighter* (1854) and Augusta Jane Evans's *St. Elmo* (1867) are very nearly as drenched in religiosity as *The Wide, Wide World.* Most of what we consider best in nineteenth-century American literature is also largely concerned with moral or religious problems. *Moby-Dick* and *The Scarlet Letter,* to cite two of the more prominent examples, are as concerned with morals and metaphysics as any of the more popular novels of the time.

VI A Sense of Time and Place

The Wide, Wide World's religious orientation was responsible for much, perhaps most, of the critical attention that it received, but critics, especially those who wrote for literary journals like *The North American Review* and *The Literary World,* also had considerable praise for its detailed descriptions of rural life. This second factor, the novel's local color, still attracts literary attention today. *The Wide, Wide World* depends heavily for its sense of time and place on the author's knowledge of Yankee and upstate New York customs and dialect. As a record of New England life, the novel was in fact matched by no contemporaries and few successors. The book's didactic lessons are dramatized through highly realistic details of characterization. Ellen, Alice, John, and some of the other characters may seem too ideal, too pure to satisfy readers, but these improbably perfect figures are balanced by others—particularly Aunt Fortune, Mr. Van Brunt, and the townspeople in Thirlwall—who are graphically and realistically characterized. Intended primarily as emblems of spiritual and moral values, figures like Alice and John have no psychological vitality—or validity—but Aunt Fortune and others like her are realistically portrayed in terms of regional dialect and manners.

The Wide, Wide World continues to receive critical attention largely because it is one of the earliest and best examples of local-color writing, but unlike most local color fiction, it is unsympathetic to the rural life and manners it portrays. In general, local colorists approached regional customs with nostalgia. Sarah Orne Jewett, for example, lovingly described rural values and customs which had been usurped by urban values and customs which she found distasteful. But Susan Warner, like Edith Wharton a half-century later, considered rural New England to be morally barren—a region of practical, utilitarian thought where human affection had no place.

Susan Warner's knowledge of New England (and her dislike of it) resulted from childhood experiences. When she was a young girl, she was sent, against her will, to spend her summers at the old Warner homestead not far from the Massachusetts border in upstate New York. But, for a young lady of fashion, this was unwelcome exile. Her experiences in the country deserve special attention, since they not only provided her with much valuable material for her fiction but also determined that aversion to Yankee life that is found in most of her local-color writings.

VII A New Canaan

The large, rambling farmhouse where the Warner children spent several summers had been built by their grandfather, Jason Warner, and was located in Canaan, New York. The Warners had been among the town's earliest settlers and had prospered there as farmers. Jason left the town briefly to serve with his father in the Revolutionary War and later represented his region in the state legislature, but most of his life was spent in Canaan. It was the only town in which Susan Warner's father lived before he left for college and his subsequent legal career in New York. The Warners were closely identified with Canaan, but it was an identification which Susan, as a fashionable young lady, at times wished to hide or forget. Much more to her taste were the mansion and elegant estate of her grandfather Bogert.

The Warners were descended from Pilgrim and Puritan colonists, and although the Canaan homestead was technically located in New York State, the few miles that separated the house from the Massachusetts border did not prevent the family from thinking of themselves as Yankees or New Englanders. When they moved to Canaan in 1764, they brought with them their New England Calvinism. Members of first the Congregational and later the Presbyterian church, the Warners had little reason, in either religion or ancestry, to consider themselves New Yorkers. They had little contact either with Dutch New Yorkers or with the Dutch Reformed and Anglican churches that prevailed in most of New York. As late as 1909, when Anna Warner was in her eighties and had never lived more than a few months within New England's geographic boundaries, she described herself as a New Englander.[10]

Canaan itself was essentially a New England village. To the east, the town bordered on Massachusetts, and only by geographical accident were the Canaanites Yorkers rather than Yankees. When Susan wrote about Canaan, as she did in both *The Wide, Wide World* and *Queechy,* she wrote in effect about a New England town, and it is as a New England local colorist that she should be studied. The first of the New England local colorists—and Susan Warner's only major predecessor—was Catharine Maria Sedgwick, who wrote about Stockbridge and other Massachusetts villages twenty miles to the east of Canaan. Stockbridge and Canaan were similar in so many respects—heritage, customs, dialect—that the two authors found themselves utilizing virtually the same materials in their fiction. But there was this major difference: while Miss Sedgwick, at least in her later works, wrote with affection and nostalgia about New Englanders, Susan Warner generally treated them with disapproval or condescension.

The worlds she preferred were to be found in books and New York drawing-rooms. The heroines of *The Wide, Wide World* and *Queechy* spend much time walking in the meadows and woods, but when visiting her grandfather, Susan Warner had always preferred to stay inside with her books. "Her nervous imagination," Anna recalled, "fostered this indoor life; with slippery hills, and creeping things, and strange wayfarers along the road,—all sorts of unknown possibilities everywhere— the sheltering walls of the house seemed delightful, and she left them as little as she could."[11] After spending the summer at her grandfather's when she was seventeen, she wrote, "I do not love Canaan very much most certainly, and shouldn't care much if I thought we should not spend another summer here."[12] A visit to the Shaker community in the neighboring town of Lebanon had been proposed, but it held no interest for her: "How much better worth it is to stay quietly at home and read Cowper, than to see all the Shakers in the world."[13] (And this from an author who was to describe the Shakers at length many years later in *Queechy.*)

After her grandfather's death in 1841, the sisters no longer visited Canaan, and over the years, her attitude toward rural New England softened, although her condescension toward New Englanders never completely vanished. Ten years after *The Wide, Wide World* was published, she visited a friend in Lenox, a small Massachusetts village a few miles east of Canaan. "What air! what lakes and hills! what Canaan reminiscences!" she wrote. "It is lovely out of doors and in; . . . It is all so good to us!"[14] One would not guess that the same writer had once "cared not very much for the natural world" but had instead been "eagerly fond of society."[15] Susan Warner never escaped entirely her prejudice against Yankees and New England, but the Yankees in her last novels—notably the heroine of *My Desire*—are treated at times with a respect that no one who has read *The Wide, Wide World* might expect.

VIII Reality and Fiction

Contrary to what some of its first reviewers assumed, *The Wide, Wide World* is not autobiographical. She did, however, draw heavily on her memories of life in Canaan and on her grandfather's farm. The Emerson farmhouse is, for example, based on her grandfather's. She turned the house on its axis to face east rather than west and extended the distance from house to town by a few miles, but in other respects she described her grandfather's house and its setting with photographic fidelity. Likewise, she faithfully recorded Canaan customs and dialect, particularly in Chapters twenty-four and twenty-five. These chapters concern Aunt Fortune's "bee," at which the townspeople, in return for food and drink, help her with various farm chores. The following passage is representative of the dialogue in this episode. The setting is Aunt Fortune's house, and the speakers are her guests.

> "Girls! girls!—what *are* you leaving the door open for!"—sounded from the kitchen, and they [Ellen and a neighbor, Nancy Vawse] hurried in.
>
> "'most got through [paring apples], Nancy?" inquired Bob Lawson. . . .
>
> "Ha'n't begun to, Mr. Lawson. There's every bit as many to do as there was at your house t'other night."
>
> "What on airth does she want with such a sight of 'em," inquired Dan Dennison.
>
> "Live on pies and apple-sass till next summer," suggested Mimy Lawson.
>
> "That's the stuff for my money!" replied her brother; "'taters and apple-sass is my sass in the winter."
>
> "It's good those is easy got," said his sister Mary; "the sass is the most of the dinner to Bob most commonly."
>
> "Are they fixing for more apple-sass down stairs?" Mr. Dennison went on rather dryly.
>
> "No—hush!"—said Juniper Hitchcock,—"sassages!"
>
> "Humph!" said Dan, as he speared up an apple out of the basket on the point of his knife,—"ain't that something like what you call killing two—" [He means here that people at a "bee" should be assigned one task, not two as is the case here.]
>
> "Just that exactly," said Jenny Hitchcock, as Dan broke off short and the mistress of the house walked in. "Ellen," she whispered, "don't you want to go down stairs and see when the folks are coming up to help us? And tell the doctor he must be spry, for we ain't a go'ng to get through in a hurry," she added, laughing.[16]

When Susan was writing about the people of Thirlwall, her own diction became at times more natural and colloquial than in the rest of the novel. Among the colloquial expressions that she introduced are "no sooner said than done," "neat as a pin," "neat as wax," and "apple-pie order."[17] A hearth is "clean swept up"; a room full of people is "in a complete hurly-burly"; and another room is "as neat as hands [can] make it."[18] Ellen is "fevered with [a] notion"; Alice is "chatting away"; and Ellen's grandmother talks "as much as she [has] a mind."[19] Mr. Van Brunt is "no mean hand; his slices of ham [are] very artist-like, and frying away in the most unexceptionable manner."[20] One person is said to be "all eyes," while another's face is "a real refreshment," and another's is "very dead-and-alive."[21] Ellen is "kept on the jump a great deal of the time"; eggs are "scrambled to a nicety"; and a particular incident is "enough to set the whole neighbourhood a wondering."[22]

There is nothing consistent about the colloquial diction; it may be found on one page and not on the next. With few exceptions, however, the colloquialisms are limited to passages dealing with Aunt Fortune and the townspeople, and there is good reason to believe that the author's shift to colloquial diction in these passages was entirely unplanned and unconscious. Certainly her contemporaries did not approve of the colloquialisms, which one reviewer called "certain specimens of homeliness in diction," "sad blemishes" on the book.[23] In fact, the book makes plain the fact that the author herself considered colloquial language disagreeable. Alice, for example, is distressed whenever Ellen uses poor English or colloquial language, and John corrects Ellen when she says she has "fixed [herself] . . . nicely on the sofa," when she should have said "arranged" or "established."[24] John and Alice would surely have been distressed to find their author saying of Mr. Van Brunt that "he was beating his brains the whole way to think of something it would do to say."[25] No less distressing would have been the "sentence," "Then fell a fumbling in his pocket."[26] The statement is understandable and effective in the passage in which it occurs, but Alice and John (and, had she thought about it, the author herself) would have been distressed by the fact that it is both colloquial and grammatically incorrect. As contemporary reviews of *The Wide, Wide World* suggest, the colloquial language that readers now consider colorful were then thought to be in very poor taste.

Alice always speaks what the author felt was perfect English. Much is made of Alice's having grown up in England where her language was not tainted by Yankee expressions, yet today that language seems stilted and impersonal. In one episode, Alice, concerned that her father may be wondering where she is, tells Mr. Van Brunt, "I shall be greatly obliged if you will be so kind as to stop and relieve my father's anxiety."[27] It is refreshing, by contrast, to hear Aunt Fortune tell her niece, "Well, ask [your question] then quick, and have done, and take yourself off. I have other fish to fry than to answer all your questions."[28]

IX YANKEE VS. YORKER

Aunt Fortune and Mr. Van Brunt conform, respectively, to two folk types common to nineteenth-century American literature: the Yankee and the Yorker. James Fenimore Cooper's *Satanstoe* (1845), for example, has much to say about Yankees and Yorkers (at the Yankees' expense), and in Washington Irving's "The Legend of Sleepy Hollow" (1820), the schoolmaster Ichabod Crane is Yankee, and his rival, Brom Bones, is a Yorker. Yankees in American fiction are descendants of the early New England settlers, from whom (although this is not the case with Aunt Fortune) they often inherit a highly religious and superstitious nature. They are also shrewd, crafty, and practical, and they are usually good businessmen. Like other Yankees in fiction, Aunt Fortune is remarkably efficient and businesslike. Her farm is well run. She allows herself no frills and is practical and shrewd in all her undertakings. Her dislike for her niece is tempered only by Ellen's willingness to help with the housework, and she marries Mr. Van Brunt because it is more efficient to run their respective farms as a single operation.

By contrast, Mr. Van Brunt, like other Yorkers in American fiction, is warm and sympathetic. He has inherited the generosity, honesty, and affectionate nature of his ancestors, the original Dutch settlers of New York. He shares Aunt Fortune's practicality and good business sense—indeed he is the better businessman—but never allows financial or practical matters to interfere with his friendship with Ellen or other people in Thirlwall. Nonetheless, his country manners place him in a category far below Alice, John, and Ellen, and the novel treats him with much condescension. In one episode, in which he takes Ellen by ox-cart from the center of the town to Aunt Fortune's farm, he is called "he of the ox-cart" and the "rough charioteer."[29] Ellen, accustomed to genteel city life, is distressed to find Mr. Van Brunt, a common farmer, eating with her at the same table—a distress that the fastidious author undoubtedly thought justified.[30] Characterization eventually triumphs over didacticism, however; Mr. Van Brunt's practicality and rugged honesty may seem today far more attractive than Ellen's smug idealism or Alice's perfect manners and stylized diction.

X THE RIGHT PEOPLE

Alice and John Humphreys and their father provide Ellen with examples of moral and spiritual ideals, while Mr. Van Brunt offers practical examples of honesty and kindness. In addition, the Marshman family is used to illustrate hospitality, social grace, courtesy, and other social values. The Marshmans, who may have been based on Susan's mother's family, are the author's ideal aristocrats—people of exquisite manners and fine moral sensibilities.

The Marshman estate, Ventnor, is apparently situated (the exact geography is vague) near the Hudson in Dutchess or Columbia County—a region which for more than a century had been widely known for its vast country estates, most of which were owned by the Livingston family, with whom the Warners were good friends. (The Livingston estates also provided the settings for *Wych Hazel* and *The Gold of Chickaree,* which Susan and Anna later wrote together.[31]) However, the Christmas celebration that Ellen attends at Ventnor may well have been drawn after similar celebrations at the Bogert family estate in Jamaica, Long Island.

Mr. and Mrs. Marshman are "of stately presence, and most dignified as well as kind in their deportment"—a description that accords well, incidentally, with what we know of Cornelius Bogert and his wife.[32] One of the Marshman daughters, Mrs. Chauncy, is "a lady with a sweet, gentle, quiet face and manner," while another, Mrs. Gillespie, has "her mother's stately bearing," and the third, Sophia Marshman, is "lively and agreeable and good-humoured."[33] One imagines that in various Bogerts can be found these aristocratic women, that, for example, Susan's mother may have been the model for Mrs. Chauncy, and that Mrs. Chauncy's daughter, Ellen, is the author's idealized portrait of herself as a young lady.

The Marshmans' generosity and hospitality are extended to all who share their good breeding and manners. They treat Ellen as an equal, and neither do they display pride in their wealth and ancestry, nor do they ever use these things as yardsticks to measure social class. Above all, they share their good fortune with others—or at least with those whose conduct defines them as ladies or gentlemen. Their world of perfect manners is the social equivalent of the Humphreys' ideal moral and spiritual realm.

XI The Critics

The Wide, Wide World's moral and religious ideals were immediately and widely praised by critics. The *Literary World* concluded that the novel's "religious teachings are worthy of all praise from their gentleness and earnestness, and the happy manner in which they are introduced."[34] John S. Hart compared aspects of the novel with the works of Daniel Defoe, then went on to say that this book was "the only novel in which real religious truth, at least as understood by evangelical Christians, is exhibited with truth."[35] Even reviewers who were generally unfavorable to the book spoke well of its religious intentions. In *Holden's Dollar Magazine,* the reviewer took issue with Alice and John's lengthy homilies and Ellen's "incessant blubbering"—in fact, she spends much of her time in tears. He hoped that the author's next book would "contain less dry logic and more dry land," yet he also insisted that the book was "wholly and unmistakably good . . . moral and religious instruction."[36] There were few who agreed, at least in print, with the reviewer who thought that this novel and *Queechy* were offensive in their "too frequent and even violent introduction of peculiar religious sentiments."[37]

Among the novel's admirers was Henry James, who described it favorably in an 1865 issue of *The Nation.* He was especially interested in the novel's realistic evocation of rural life, and he thought that as a transcription of local color, it was more successful than the novels of Flaubert. There are surely few who would defend James's conclusion today, but it does suggest the enormous critical esteem that *The Wide, Wide World* once enjoyed.[38]

Frank Denham, discussing the novel several years ago in the *New York Times Book Review,* said that "Miss Warner thought herself a realist, but her characters were not real people because she never let herself know what people were really like."[39] The statement is a curious one, unsupported by a close reading of the novel. James was accurate in noting the book's excellent sense of local color and realistic detail. Among recent critics, Henry Nash Smith finds, "amid the interminable tears and prayers," "well-executed genre scenes";[40] another has said that "it is essential to read some of [Warner's books] in order to have a complete picture of American social life in the nineteenth century."[41]

Although nineteenth-century critics almost universally agreed that the novel was a masterpiece, twentieth-century critics have violently attacked it, particularly for its piety and sentimentality. Van Wyck Brooks dismissed it as "malarial," "a swamp of lachrymosity,"[42] while Frank Luther Mott said it fit a "Home-and-Jesus formula" and was, "at best, mawkish in its sentimentality and pious to a repulsive degree."[43] Such extreme reactions tell us more about the prejudices of the critics involved than about the book itself; they are also the exceptions. Neither Matthew Arnold nor Charles Kingsley, it is true, thought highly of the book (Kingsley called it *The Narrow, Narrow World* and retitled its successors *Squeeky* and *The Hills of the Chattermuch*),[44] but there have been other critics who have strongly or warmly defended it. George Saintsbury recalled the book "with pleasure,"[45] and the American critic Brander Matthews listed it, together with works by Sir Walter Scott, Charles Dickens, and George Eliot, as one of the "hundred Best Novels in English."[46]

XII The Readers

In a recent article on the Warners, Grace Overmyer claims that *The Wide, Wide World* was "the first American best seller,"[47] and even though the records of book selling in the nineteenth century are notoriously incomplete and unreliable, the novel's success in this country was apparently unprecedented. Overmyer's claim is not entirely accurate—there were, of course, many American novels before 1850 that were best sellers, but certainly no American book had ever sold so well.

The book was also very popular abroad. More than two dozen English publishers issued separate editions. Since publishers' records in Britain, like those in America, have been lost or destroyed, the total sales will never be known; but we know that one publisher, Routledge, sold eighty thousand copies, an astonishing figure for the time. The book remained popular with all classes; and forty years after it first appeared, it was, with the Bible, "one of the four books most widely read in England."[48] One investigator who set out to discover "what . . . English peasants read" concluded that *The Wide, Wide World* was, together with *Pilgrim's Progress* and *Uncle Tom's Cabin,* among their favorite books.[49] According to a poll taken in 1886, English schoolgirls rated Susan Warner's novels above those by George Eliot, Harriet Beecher Stowe, William Makepeace Thackeray, and Charlotte Brontë. *The Wide, Wide World* and *Queechy,* one critic wrote, "give place to no books in the English language for popularity among girls old and young."[50] The book was translated several times, and editions appeared bearing the titles, *Heimwarts: oder Führung durch die Weite Welt, Den Vide, Vide Verden,* and *Le monde, le vaste monde.* In 1876, a contributor to *The Nation* commented that Frenchmen and Germans who claimed to know something about American literature often turned out to have read only *The Wide, Wide World.*[51]

XIII Why It Sold

Neither its author nor its publisher anticipated the novel's success, and its popularity is still difficult to explain. If nineteenth-century reviews and comments are a reliable index to popular opinion, *The Wide, Wide World* was admired and read because of its evangelical bias, its attitude toward family life, and its record of rural American life and customs. The novel's didacticism was far more important to its popular reception than was its literary value, and the thematic ingredients that insured its popular success were soon recognized by other writers. Evangelical Christian doctrine, local color, and domesticity are central to many later best sellers, including novels by Maria Cummins, Augusta Jane Evans, and E. P. Roe which, like *The Wide, Wide World,* sold in the hundreds of thousands.

Hiram Haydn, one of the most respected editors of our time, once read several of Lloyd C. Douglas's religious novels in order to discover why they "sold by the carloads."[52] He discovered a "passionate conviction . . . manifest on every page" that not only "persuaded the reader" but also sold the books.[53] A similar "passionate conviction" is characteristic of Susan Warner's novels and, for that matter, the novels of most best-selling, nineteenth-century religious writers. Without that conviction, didactic religious fiction is often dry, obviously schematic, and unconvincing. Didactic fiction does not transcribe human nature realistically but arranges characterization to illustrate principles or ideas. If, however, a "passionate conviction" underscores those principles or ideas, the novel may convey an intensity that compensates for weak plotting and improbable characterization.

The Wide, Wide World should not be criticized according to twentieth-century standards: both its purpose and its reception can be understood only within its historical setting, but presentist critics—critics, that is, who interpret past literatures in terms of present-day standards and interests—have, from time to time, offered ingenious explanations for the book's popular success; on close examination, these explanations, however, prove themselves textually and historically questionable. One critic—whose sense of nineteenth-century cultural history is generally excellent—falls into the presentist trap by declaring that *The Wide, Wide World* was popular because, among other things, it "provided its ready audience with every one of the five Jungian archetypes"[54]—an explanation that may satisfy few except Jungian critics. The book has also been misread as a popular appeal to a nascent feminist sensibility, and because the book is central to an understanding of women's literary and cultural history, this interpretation deserves particular notice.

XIV Women's Rights

Helen Waite Papashvily suggested in her study of domestic novels, *All the Happy Endings* (1956), that *The Wide, Wide World* responded to the sensibilities of women who believed themselves dominated, against their wills, by husbands, brothers, fathers, or other men. Papashvily's book is widely respected and has influenced subsequent studies of domestic novels. *All the Happy Endings* is an exceptionally important study of nineteenth-century American culture, but Papashvily is mistaken in including *The Wide, Wide World* among feminist novels. Susan Warner's attitude toward the social and domestic position of women was, as we have seen, quite different from what Papashvily suggests.

All the Happy Endings argues that while mid-nineteenth-century feminists were rallying around the Seneca Falls "Declaration of Sentiments" (that extraordinary document that claimed that throughout history men had tried to establish "an absolute tyranny" over women), their more conservative sisters were reading domestic novels which, however innocuous they seemed on the surface, were "a witches' broth, a lethal draught brewed by women and used by women to destroy their common enemy, man."[55] Papashvily suggests that *The Wide, Wide World* was part of that "lethal draught" and that the novel is at least in part about an unjustifiable submission of women to men. Nothing could be further from the truth.

Some of the domestic novels, particularly Mrs. E. D. E. N. Southworth's, seem to fit Papashvily's formula; but throughout Susan's works, she insisted that traditional husband and wife relationships were virtuous and just, because biblically sanctioned. Papashvily is correct in assuming that the readers of *The Wide, Wide World* were largely women; but if these women, as she assumes, read the book because of its message, they sought a lesson in obedience, submission, and sobriety. In fact, since evangelical Christianity, which made of obedience a virtue, pervaded the nineteenth century, it is likely that the lesson that the novel taught was a lesson its readers had already learned well.

The Wide, Wide World is of major significance to an understanding of America at mid-century. It is tempting, but ultimately misleading, to interpret the era in the conflicting terms of Emersonian optimism and Melvillian skepticism. The extraordinary, sympathetic reception that *The Wide, Wide World* received implies a substantial audience which shared neither extreme—an audience which, above all, valued sobriety, temperance, and obedience to divine will. And the book's great popularity also suggests that the Seneca Falls "Declaration of Sentiments" was historically a far more eccentric document than some historians, in retrospect, would make it seem.

XV THE DOMESTIC NOVEL

The Wide, Wide World is one of the first, and certainly the most famous, domestic novel—a type of didactic novel that preached the virtues of family life and that became a staple of best-seller lists in the second half of the nineteenth century. Read principally by women, these novels were directed at a Protestant audience which considered the family ideally a moral bastion. Evangelical morality and piety were usually preached, although occasionally a writer like Mrs. Southworth was too busy with her sensational or melodramatic plots to worry about moral or metaphysical implications. Most domestic novels, including *The Wide, Wide World* showed the influence of eighteenth-century sentimental fiction, Hannah More's didactic tales, and the evangelical, Low-Church novels popular in England. Low-Church novels, it is true, were frequently more sensational and sentimental than their American kin, and they were also more explicitly didactic, but they shared an evangelical bias and invariably interpreted experience morally.

The earliest American domestic novelist was Catharine Maria Sedgwick. In the 1820s and 1830s, she combined domestic life with local color to create novels whose success was as unexpected as the success of *The Wide, Wide World*. Miss Sedgwick wrote, however, from a Unitarian perspective which stressed freedom of the individual conscience rather than obedience to authority. The moral position was unacceptable both to Calvinism and evangelicalism; and the novels, although widely praised and admired for their pictures of American life, never had sales as spectacular as those of *The Wide, Wide World*.

Susan Warner's novel is in some respects similar to Miss Sedgwick's *A New-England Tale* (1822). Indeed, in broad terms, the plots are almost identical—and both novels make considerable use of New England local color. In both books, an unquestionably moral young girl is left an orphan shortly after her father loses his fortune. Both girls are then cared for by aunts who are blind to their nieces' moral natures and unfairly accuse them of wrongdoing. In the end, however, both heroines are married to men as virtuous as they and are promised an ideal family life. Susan Warner, of course, develops her plot to illustrate moral principles that her predecessor would have found unacceptable; yet there are so many similarities between the two novels that *A New-England Tale* seems almost certainly to have been a model for *The Wide, Wide World.*

Miss Sedgwick's novel, it is true, was published a quarter of a century before Susan Warner began work on hers, but she may have remembered the book from childhood; for in its day, *A New-England Tale* would have seemed, along with the works of Maria Edgeworth and Hannah More, appropriate didactic fare for children.

Although *A New-England Tale* may have been a model for *The Wide, Wide World* Susan did not, however, read Miss Sedgwick's other domestic novels, *Redwood* (1824) and *Clarence* (1835) until *The Wide, Wide World* was finished and being set in type. She read the novels at her publisher's suggestion. Putnam was then issuing a uniform edition of Miss Sedgwick's writings; and in his wife's phrase, he considered her to be "a piece of perfection."[56] Mrs. Putnam did not agree—nor, after reading these novels, did Susan. "Miss Sedgwick's novels are *inexpressible*," she told her sister; these two books in particular were "dismally poor."[57]

The many parallels, both in subject matter and literary treatment, between Miss Sedgwick's novels and *The Wide, Wide World* make this harsh criticism appear startling and unexpected. Certainly Miss Sedgwick had cleared the literary ground that Susan occupied, but theologically they stood opposed to each other, and from Susan's moral stance and religious position, Miss Sedgwick's novels could only seem morally weak or misleading. In the end, a book's value, for people like

Susan, was to be judged solely on religious and moral, not literary, grounds.[58]

Notes

1. *Anna Warner, Susan Warner ("Elizabeth Wetherell")* (New York, 1909), p. 264.

2. Ibid., p. 263

3. Ibid., p. 283

4. Ibid., pp. 344-45. The first of these comments is quoted from the *Edinburgh Witness,* the second from the *Newark Daily Advertiser.* The *New York Times* is quoted as saying that ". . . one book like this is not produced in an age."

5. Susan Warner, *The Wide, Wide World* (New York, 1850), I, 84-85.

6. Philip Ariès, *Centuries of Childhood: A Social History of Family Life* (New York, 1962). The literature on the history of the family is huge; among the best recent books on the subject is Edward Shorter's *The Making of the Modern Family* (New York, 1975).

7. *Ephesians* V: 22.

8. *The Wide, Wide World,* II, 102.

9. Ibid., I, 340.

10. *Susan Warner,* p. iii.

11. Ibid., pp. 124-25.

12. Ibid., p. 166.

13. Ibid., p. 166.

14. Ibid., p. 423.

15. Ibid., p. 177.

16. *The Wide, Wide World,* I, 308.

17. Ibid., I, 133, 153, 198, 302; II, 83.

18. Ibid., I, 229, 304; II, 118.

19. Ibid., I, 308, 221; II, 82.

20. Ibid., II, 82.

21. Ibid., II, 115, 117.

22. Ibid., II, 47, 63.

23. Caroline Kirkland, review of *The Wide, Wide World, Queechy,* and *Dollars and Cents; The North American Review,* LXXVI (January, 1853), pp. 120-21.

24. *The Wide, Wide World,* II, 219.

25. Ibid., II, 72.

26. Ibid., I, 333.

27. Ibid., I, 247.

28. Ibid., I, 167.

29. Ibid., I, 121, 116.

30. Ibid., I, 135.

31. Susan and Anna numbered various Livingstons among their childhood friends; and, even after the sisters were living in virtual poverty, they maintained an acquaintance with Mrs. David Codwise—a Livingston by birth. They were also friendly with Miss Mary Garretson, daughter of Catharine Livingston and niece of Chancellor Robert Livingston. Catharine married the Reverend Freeborn Garretson, a noted Methodist preacher. On Livingston land in Dutchess County, they built a modest but substantial house and surrounded it with a magnificent estate known as Wildercliff. The Warners visited there extensively; and in all probability, it was while visiting there and at other estates nearby that they got background details for *Wych Hazel* and *The Gold of Chickaree.* This was, in any case, good literary country. Not far from Wildercliff was an estate where Henry James as a boy spent much time with relatives, and just down the hill from Wildercliff was a large Gothic mansion at which Edith Wharton spent a portion of her childhood.

32. *The Wide, Wide World,* I, 342.

33. Ibid., I, 343.

34. Anonymous, review of *The Wide, Wide World,* VII (December 28, 1850), 525.

35. John S. Hart, *Female Prose Writers of America* (Philadelphia, 1852), p. 387.

36. Anonymous, review of *The Wide, Wide World, Holden's Dollar Magazine,* VII (March, 1851), 136-37.

37. Anonymous, review of *The Hills of the Shatemuc, Putnam's Monthly,* VIII (November, 1856), 539.

38. Henry James, "The Schönberg-Cotta Family," *The Nation,* I (September 14, 1865), 345.

39. Frank Denham, "How to Drive the Sheriff from the Homestead Door," *New York Times Book Review* (December 24, 1944), p. 8.

40. Henry Nash Smith, "The Scribbling Women and the Cosmic Success Story," *Critical Inquiry,* I (September, 1974), 66.

41. Marion Lochhead, "Stars and Striplings: American Youth in the Nineteenth Century," *Quarterly Review,* V (April, 1959), 184.

42. Van Wyck Brooks, *The Flowering of New England* (New York, 1936), p. 427.

43. Frank Luther Mott, *Golden Multitudes* (New York, 1947), pp. 122, 123.

44. Charles Kingsley, *The Water-Babies* (London, 1903), p. 174.

45. Mott, *Golden Multitudes,* p. 124.

46. Arthur Penn [Brander Matthews], *The Home Library* (New York, 1883), p. 45.

47. Grace Overmyer, "Hudson River Bluestockings—the Warner Sisters of Constitution Island," *New York History,* XL (April, 1959), 137.

48. F. S. D. [sic], "Tears, Idle Tears," *The Critic,* XXI (October 29, 1892), 236.

49. Anonymous, untitled note, *The Illustrated London News,* XCIX (September 12, 1891), 342.

50. Edward G. Salmon, "What Girls Read," *The Nineteenth Century,* XX (October, 1886), 524.

51. Anonymous, review of *Wych Hazel, The Nation,* XXII (June 8, 1876), 370. One sign of the book's popularity was the publication of *Lyrics from "The Wide, Wide World"* (New York, 1853) with words by W. H. Bellamy (based on passages in *The Wide, Wide World*) and music by C. W. Glover. An advertisement of the day claimed, "In the '*Wide, Wide World*' cannot be found better undergarments and hosiery than at James E. Ray's, 108 Bowery." (*Susan Warner,* p. 345.)

52. Hiram Haydn, *Words and Faces* (New York, 1974), p. 20.

53. Ibid., p. 20.

54. Carl Bode, *Antebellum Culture* (Carbondale, Ill., and Edwardsville, Ill., 1970), p. 176.

55. Helen Waite Papashvily, *All the Happy Endings* (New York, 1956), p. xvii.

56. *Susan Warner,* p. 293

57. Ibid., pp. 313, 305.

58. The plot of *The Wide, Wide World* is reminiscent, at least distantly, of Charlotte Brönte's *Jane Eyre* as well as *A New-England Tale*. All three books deal in part with orphans at the mercy of tyrannical aunts. It is worth noting that Susan closely identified with the heroine of the Brönte novel. Visiting with Mrs. David Codwise, she wrote home to her sister in April, 1848, "Mrs. Codwise has just run through Jane Eyre. Do you know she says I am so much like her, and wanted to know if you did not think so. I did not tell her that *I* thought so, but I do, as you know" (*Susan Warner,* p. 267). Susan was working on *The Wide, Wide World* when she wrote this letter, and one might assume that the character of Jane Eyre in part de-

termined the character of Ellen Montgomery—but in fact the two characters are quite dissimilar. If the Brönte novel did influence Susan's work on *The Wide, Wide World,* the influence was distant and weak.

Richard H. Brodhead (essay date winter 1988)

SOURCE: Brodhead, Richard H. "Sparing the Rod: Discipline and Fiction in Antebellum America." *Representations,* no. 21 (winter 1988): 67-96.

[*In the following excerpt, Brodhead explores the acculturated psychodynamics of Ellen's reliance on her mother, and the effects of the latter's death.*]

Susan Warner's **The Wide, Wide World** (1851), which went on to become one of the four or five most widely read American novels of the whole nineteenth century, is often cited as the first of the new bestsellers. And it is Warner's book that offers the most impressive recognition of discipline through love as a culture-specific historical formation. **The Wide, Wide World** is a historical novel in a systematically restricted sense of the word. Throughout the book Warner poses the extradomestic world outside of her sphere, in a place unavailable to her literary knowing. Its initial harmony devastated by a lawsuit, neither the book's characters nor the book itself can get access to the transprivate world in which they could know what the suit's occasion was. Through the same strict observation of the limits of her sphere, Warner makes *history* in the usual sense unavailable to her knowing: what is going on in the world outside of certain family spaces is, in this book, a sealed book. But if she fails to locate her characters' private lives in relation to any sort of generalized process of collective change, part of Warner's power as a writer is that she implicitly grasps the households she represents as historically different formations of the domestic sphere. Aunt Fortune, to whose grumpy care Warner's child heroine Ellen Montgomery is shipped off after the book's opening crisis, plays the role in **The Wide, Wide World** of fairy-tale's cruel stepmother. But Warner registers her milieu quite concretely—and registers it not in idiosyncratic or local-color detail only, but in such a way as to grasp its surface features' relation to its sociohistorical form. While this point is never commented on overtly, every feature of Aunt Fortune's household exemplifies the logic of the old-style household economy: Fortune is always busy, because this home is a place of work; her house is smelly and noisy, because this house is still a scene of production; her coverlets are of linsey-woolsey, because the necessities of life are still homemade in her world; she scorns Ellen's desire to go to school, because in her world knowledge means knowing how to do practically productive tasks; entertainment at her house takes the form of an apple-paring and pork-packing bee, because in her world entertainment is not disconnected from the household's economic productivity; and so on through a legion of comparable details. The other households in the book differ from Aunt Fortune's on every count. But they differ not just because they are the homes of other people, but because they embody different social formations of the home's place and work: the more genteel (and less productive) formation of a historically later phase, in the case of Alice and John Humphreys; the altogether leisured, pleasure-oriented formation of a Europeanized gentry class, in the case of the aristocratic Lindsays.

While this point too is never registered in any abstract form, Warner's picturing strikingly represents the discipline of love as inhering in a differentiated way in one of these social formations. In contrast to Aunt Fortune's, the household associated with Ellen's mother and Ellen's exemplary friend Alice is characterized by a raised threshold of decency and comfort. (Its furniture is tastefully ornamental, not only functional; Ellen's traumatic experiences at Aunt Fortune's suggest that she is used to indoor plumbing.) In it women are conspicuously exempted from productive functions. (Alice does the more delicate baking, but has a maid to do heavy housework; Ellen's mother, with the wearying exception of one shopping trip, does nothing at all.) Its forms of entertainment are mentally uplifting, and also unproductive and privatized. (Where Aunt Fortune has a bee, these women read.) And this household is also and indistinguishably two more things: it is affectionate, so much so that the cultivation of close relations might be said to *be its* productive activity; and it is pious, specifically in a way that makes its female heads feel called to the work of improving others' spiritual characters. (When Ellen first meets Alice, Alice at once picks up the task of revivalistically reforming Ellen's temper that her mother had left incomplete.) This reformatory lovingness is profoundly different from any disciplinary method seen elsewhere in the book. Aunt Fortune, untender and impious, is too busy to *care* about Ellen in Alice's and Mrs. Montgomery's way, let alone to care about her moral nurture; her discipline is confined to occasional bouts of highly arbitrary authoritarianism, backed up (in one instance) by blows.[1] The Lindsays, more genial but quite secular, try to make Ellen sleep late, drink wine, cut back on religious reading, and be more fun at parties: theirs is another discipline entirely, training for life in the very different gentry world. Moralizing lovingness is confined to scenes that have all the marks of the new middle-class feminine domesticity. Warner knows *that* discipline as *that* social formation's pastime and work; she knows *that* discipline as forming the *self that* world aims to reproduce.

Part of the distinction of *The Wide, Wide World* is that it specifies the cultural location of this *scheme* of acculturation so precisely. Another of its distinctions is that it plots the actual psychological transactions this scheme entails with unmatched precision and care. The novel begins, thus, by showing what it would mean, in human terms, to be encompassed with tenderness as this plan requires. Ellen Montgomery lives with her mother at the novel's opening, but this phrase does not begin to describe the form of their attachment. It would be more accurate to say that she lives *in* her mother, in the *Umwelt* her mother projects. Her mother is always with her, her mother is the whole world available to her (when her mother sleeps Ellen looks out the window, but the world outside the window is inaccessible to her; hired food preparers and even Ellen's father sometimes intrude on this domesticity, but when they withdraw "the mother and daughter were left, as they always loved to be, alone"; 1:43). Enclosed within her mother's emotional presence, Ellen has been bred to a reciprocating strength of love that makes her feel each event first in terms of how it will bear on her mother's frame of mind. And this other-centeredness or (as we say) *considerateness* is what makes her responsive to the authority of her mother's codes. As she surrounds her child with her highly wrought emotionality, Mrs. Montgomery also fills the world so centered with moral prescription. She has a rule for everything, a rule in each case absolutely and equally obligatory: "Draw nigh to God" is her religious requirement for her daughter, but her rules of etiquette, even of fashion—one must never ask the names of strangers; girls' cloaks must be of medium-grade merino wool, and not green (1:26, 65, 56-57)—are put forward as binding in no less a degree. And as the beginning of the novel (a little pathetically) demonstrates, Ellen's love for this authority figure—her continual impulse to think of her mother before she thinks of herself, and the absolute imperative she feels under to maintain her mother's favorable emotional atmosphere—makes Ellen, in and of herself, want to do and be what her mother would require of her. While her mother pretends to nap in the first chapter, Ellen makes the tea and toast, not only makes them but makes them *just so,* with a ritualistic precision of observance. And she performs this labor and follows this tight prescription because the tea is for her mother, and she is driven by "the zeal that love gives" (1:14). Crushed to hear that her mother (quite incomprehensibly) must abandon her and move with her father to Europe now that the lawsuit is lost, Ellen is required to suppress her grief in consideration of her mother's fragile state—"Try to compose yourself. I am afraid you will make me worse," the tyrannically delicate Mrs. Montgomery says. This injunction is hard for the aggrieved Ellen, but the stronger emotion of "love to her mother" has "power enough" to make her "exert all her self-command" (1:13).

What the opening of *The Wide, Wide World* really dramatizes is the primitive implantation of moral motivation, as discipline by intimacy specifies that practice. Made into a compulsive love seeker, Ellen shows how the child so determined becomes driven, by her heightened need to win and keep parental favor, not just to accept but really to *seek out* the authority of the parent's moral imperatives. What the rest of the novel then dramatizes is the ongoing career of authority seeking this primal scene initiates. Two facts, not one, constitute Ellen's initial world: the fact that the world is centered in the mother, and the fact that the mother is going to be lost. The news that inaugurates this narrative, the news that the lawsuit is lost and Ellen must be abandoned, carries a powerful sense of women's victimization by the nondomestic masculine economic world they are now dependent on but shut out from knowledge of. (When the separation scene finally arrives Ellen is viscerally wrenched from her mother by the disruptive stranger who is her father.) But in another sense the separation crisis that inaugurates this novel simply recognizes that oneness with the mother is what one cannot *not* lose—a fact that the child's new centrality to the mother's life in middle-class domesticity makes in new measure traumatic.

What the plot of this novel then shows is how an acculturation system like Ellen's makes this newly intensified grief of separation a psychic resource for the disciplining of the subject. In *The Wide, Wide World* to love one's mother is to wish to do things her way, but to love her and lose her is to have this wish heightened into full-fledged moral imperative. Loving and losing her mother commits Ellen to a career of seeking for substitutes for this lost beloved. But since the mark of others' substitutability for the mother is that they simultaneously give warm baths of affection and impose strict codes of obligation, this way of repairing an emotional breach drives Ellen deeper and deeper into the territory of psychological regulation. (The final beloved regulator, John Humphreys, does not even tell Ellen his final requirement of her, "but whatever it were, she was very sure she would do it!"; 2:333.) Coached by such surrogates, Ellen's achievement as the novel plots it is to move toward ever more perfect internalizations of parental authority—an achievement whose psychic payoff, as the book shows it, is to restore oneness with the mother now lost.[2] Conscience, at last grown strong enough to make her obey even the most outrageous of Aunt Fortune's commands, lets Ellen hear an inner voice that she knows as coming from "her mother's lips" (1:317). When she then undergoes the conversion her mother had covenanted her to, Ellen at once accepts the authority of her mother's religious system and recovers, through participation in that system, felt contact with the mother herself: after her conversion "there seemed to be a link of communion between her mother and her that was wanting before. The promise, written and believed in by the one, realized and rejoiced in by the other, was a dear something in common, though one had in the mean while removed to heaven, and the other was still a lingerer on the earth" (2:72).

Jane Tompkins, the strongest recent champion of Warner's novel, writes in a fine phrase that "a text depends upon its audience's beliefs not just in a gross general way, but intricately and precisely."[3] This is exactly the relation *The Wide, Wide World* has to the living-scenario adumbrated in the philosophy of disciplinary intimacy: proof that the world this novel knows and speaks is by no means only the (in her formulation apparently universal) mid-nineteenth-century American evangelicalism that Tompkins has nominated as its cultural context, but the quite particular middle-class world (evangelical Protestantism was one of its constituents) that coalesced around this socializing strategy in the antebellum years. The suspicion that *The Wide, Wide World*'s intricate reflection of this culture's patterning of experience was a source of this book's *popularity* is supported by another case. The ultimate mass-circulation novel of the 1850s, the book that far exceeded the circulation records set by *The Wide, Wide World* a year before, is *Uncle Tom's Cabin* (1852). And *Uncle Tom's Cabin* is the book that deploys the disciplinary conceptions I have been discussing with greatest profundity and force.

Notes

1. Susan Warner, *The Wide, Wide World*, 2 vols. (1851; New York, 1856), 1:193. Numbers after subsequent quotations from the novel refer to pages in this text.

2. My understanding of what might be called motivation-by-reunion has been helped by Nancy Schnog's unpublished essay "A History of Sentiment: Susan Warner's *The Wide, Wide World* in Psychosocial Perspective."

3. Jane Tompkins, *Sensational Designs: The Cultural Work of American Fiction, 1790-1860* (New York, 1985), 156. The social undifferentiatedness of the context Tompkins proposes is evident throughout her otherwise useful chapter on Warner, "The Other American Renaissance": revivalism thus has "'terrific universality'" (149; the undisowned phrase is Perry Miller's); evangelical thought "pervaded people's perceptions" (156), informed "how people in the antebellum era thought" (158), and so on. For a striking reading of the function of evangelicalism in nineteenth-century middle-class emergence see Ryan, *Cradle of the Middle Class*, chaps. 2 and 3.

Nancy Schnog (essay date spring 1989)

SOURCE: Schnog, Nancy. "Inside the Sentimental: The Psychological Work of *The Wide, Wide World*." *Genders*, no. 4 (spring 1989): 11-25.

[*In the following essay, Schnog declares that* The Wide, Wide World *is a complex, psychological portrait of feminine sentiment.*]

In the past few years Susan Warner's sentimental novel *The Wide Wide World*, one of nineteenth-century America's most popular novels and the nation's first best-seller, has been at the center of some of the most provocative and detailed discussions of the mechanics and politics of sentimentality.[1] A decade ago, on the margin of this revival, Warner's novel was typically regarded as a subliterary fiction that peddled comfortable dreams and cheerful platitudes to a large and undemanding middle-class readership.[2] More recently, in the wake of feminist re-evaluations of nineteenth-century women's fiction, scholars have begun to uncover Warner's multivocal handling of social and political themes as well as her positive imaging of female independence and self-assertion. Once thought to advocate an "ethos of conformity" and women's "unquestioning submission to authority,"[3] *The Wide Wide World* is now more often perceived as projecting and celebrating models of female autonomy and power.[4] In the latest and perhaps most sophisticated analysis of this theme, Jane Tompkins has shown how Warner actively encouraged the ideal of female self-determination by teaching her readers to capitalize on their delegated roles and exploit them in their own self-interest.[5]

This essay also uses *The Wide Wide World* as a case study through which to examine the nineteenth-century sentimental novel's narrative mechanics and cultural power. It differs from its contemporary predecessors, however, by turning away from the theme of female power and giving emphasis to a more intimate, private dimension of the novel: female sentiment. Indeed, to read *The Wide Wide World* is to become enmeshed in a novel whose line of action unfolds as an emotional landscape. Along with Ellen Montgomery, the novel's adolescent heroine, readers follow, if not empathetically undergo, the series of deep attachments and traumatic separations which take Ellen first from her mother, then from Alice Humphrey, and later from a life she loves in America. In the past these tearful scenarios have merely confirmed hostile and cynical interpretations of the sentimental novel as a debased literary form, purveyed by women writers and dedicated to the exaggeration and distortion of human feelings. This essay challenges this perspective. It shows to the contrary that Warner's novel, like many other sentimental novels of the period, used sentimental discourse in an effort to represent and analyze significant and real emotional and psychological experiences. Whereas one critic of Warner's novel cast Ellen Montgomery as "a weeper of artesian resources,"[6] this essay suggests, in a vein less contemptuous of feelings, that Ellen's tears were a valid and authentic response to traumas well known to a large segment of Warner's nineteenth-century readership, although no longer visible or familiar to us today.

Warner's serious interest in the exploration of female sentiment is evident in her novel's reproduction of an emotional and psychological terrain particular to the lives of many middle-class women in mid-nineteenth-century America. Accordingly, Part 1 of this essay will show how the intimate experiences of Warner's female heroines mirror and repeat some of the most important emotional events known to this class of women over a century ago. Part 2 will suggest the "therapeutic" function of Warner's psychological realism. Here we will see how Warner's novel not only represents shared points of crisis in women's emotional lives but also tries to reduce their traumatic significance by showing women readers how to prepare for and manage them.

1

Warner's recreation of a mid-nineteenth-century psychosocial landscape begins with what Warner pinpoints as the core of women's emotional being: mother-daughter attachment. Opening with a sequence of scenes that highlight the warm and dependent ties which unite mother and daughter, Warner writes:

> The mother and daughter had had the Sabbath to themselves; and most quietly and sweetly it had passed. They had read together, prayed together, talked together a great deal; and the evening had been spent together in singing hymns; but Mrs. Montgomery's strength failed here, and Ellen sang alone . . . She [Mrs. Montgomery] listened—till she almost felt as if earth were left behind, and she and her child already standing within the walls of that city where sorrow and sighing shall be no more, and the tears shall be wiped from all eyes forever.[7]

Warner's description of Ellen and her mother on a Sabbath evening, prior to the news of Mrs. Montgomery's departure, conveys the affective climate within the feminine sphere. At home, "themselves," without Mr. Montgomery, the mother and daughter establish their own private and exclusive world of personal contentments. As the four repetitions of "together" suggest, Ellen and her mother derive their contentment through their symbiotic attachment and mutual will.[8] Intimate communion is a central feature not only of the mother-daughter relationship but also of the activities the women choose to engage in. Reading, talking, praying, and singing hymns are themselves systems which foster union between a practitioner and another person, an author, or God. By foregrounding the importance of communal activity, Warner locates the distinctive character of the feminine sphere in the value it places on the primacy of relation. As opposed to the virtues of individualism and nonconformity that Emerson expounds in the pages of "Self-Reliance," experience in this milieu is judged by its potential to foster close and mutually dependent ties.

Although characters like Ellen and her mother have been regarded by twentieth-century critics as "inert puppets whom no one really believed in,"[9] nineteenth-century audiences to the contrary recognized Ellen and her mother not as "puppets" but as symbols of a pervasive and deeply felt experience among women. In a study of nineteenth-century women's correspondences and diaries, Carroll Smith-Rosenberg has demonstrated that mother-daughter relationships, as well as female friendships, were characterized by especially intense patterns of female bonding.[10] Diaries attest to the overwhelming attention women paid to other women as well as to the trauma that resulted from the interruption of contact through either geographical separation or death. Rosenberg maintains that "for nearly a century . . . women played a central emotional role in each other's lives, writing time and again of their love and of the pain of separation."[11] Expressions of "emotional dependency" and "confessions of loneliness" were typical of the *cri de coeur* of middle-class women in the nineteenth century.[12]

Social conditions and emotional imperatives sustained this female world. Rigid gender segregation as well as limitations placed on male-female social interactions spawned a severing of spontaneous relations between the sexes while encouraging the formation and meaningfulness of homosocial bonds. At the same time, female love nourished women's emotional needs. It allowed women to share their personal concerns with empathetic listeners and through those interactions to develop and strengthen qualities of personal dignity and self-confidence. Immersed in intimate mother-daughter, kin, and other female relations, women, deprived of opportunities to achieve power and self-fulfillment in the public sphere, were able to gain a sense of their own importance through the experience of loving and feeling loved by others. Warner echoes this sentiment when she has Alice Humphrey remind Ellen that "it is not beautiful things nor a beautiful world that make people happy—it is loving and being loved" (164, VII).

Although *The Wide Wide World* opens with scenes that foreground the close attachments between mother and daughter, it is noteworthy that the same sequence of scenes closes with a scenario that belies a suggestion of domestic harmony. From the beginning of the novel, stable domestic relations are challenged by the threat of separation. Mrs. Montgomery's trip to Europe prefaces the novel and is the condition which sets the novel underway; Ellen must be informed of her mother's immanent departure and of the separation that will necessarily follow. As a scene which joins the currents of dependency and loss, the Sabbath scene capitulates the larger structure of Warner's novel, in which scenes of attachment and separation flow one into another, comprising the book's narrative action. Indeed, by making the dynamics of dependency and loss ubiquitous in the novel, Warner fashions dramatic action as psychological movement. Within this context female experience can be seen as fundamentally active—a modus operandi that demands the continual mediation of conflicting affective forces. It also establishes attachment and separation as a transition of such emotional potency for women that it becomes the unit of experience around which women organize and posit meaning in their lives.[13]

Warner dramatizes the centrality of attachment and separation by delimiting action in *The Wide Wide World* as a woman's confrontation with either one of two events: geographical separation or death. Warner signals the preeminent experiential value of geographical separation by employing it as the internal measure of Ellen's development: Ellen's early life is marked by her removals from New York to Thirwall, from her Aunt Fortune's to the Humphrey parsonage, from the Humphrey parsonage to the Lindsays' in Scotland. This is equally true of the role of death in the novel, in which Ellen's despair over the loss of her mother and her "adopted sister," Alice, comprises two distinct periods of emotional transition in Ellen's life. From this perspective accusations, such as Edward Foster's, that Warner's scenes are "almost entirely lacking in dramatic incident and conflict" reveal a misperception of the realm of action in the novel.[14] By presenting emotional events as the substance of women's experience, Warner posits affective movement and change as untiring sources of drama and conflict in women's lives.

In addition, Warner illustrates how the loss of a primary love object, which breaks the female world of love, provokes an enduring source of pain for women. Representative of a plethora of such communications in the novel, a letter Mrs. Montgomery writes to Ellen describes her response to their interrupted contact: "I have missed you my dear child very much. There is not an hour in the day, nor a half hour, that the want of you does not come to my heart; and I think I have missed you in my very dreams. This separation is a very hard thing to bear. But the hand that has arranged it does nothing amiss; we must trust Him my daughter that all will be well" (274, VII). This style of writing has inspired the acerbic criticisms against the sentimental novel as preoccupied solely with the peddling of sentiment and piety. Such passages have become the prooftext of interpretations which cast Ellen as an unregenerate weeper and Mrs. Montgomery as a mouthpiece for Warner's overt and unrelenting religious teachings.[15] Yet these views overlook the serious representation of female sentiment within these passages as well as the documentation of pain and trouble within this sphere. While the rhetoric of piety is undeniably a predominant feature in Warner's writing and one which she applies to her own therapeutic aims in the course of the novel, the rhetoric of emotional survival in this passage is just as strong. Away from Ellen, Mrs. Montgomery leads a new existence in which mourning plays an integral part. As this unhappy missive shows, the consequences of separation result in a pervasive and enduring experience of loss.

Those consequences are made painfully clear to Ellen in the wake of Mrs. Montgomery's absence and Alice's untimely death. Having taken up the care of the Humphrey parsonage, Ellen finds herself in an environment antithetical to her other homes. Now Ellen is alone. The passages describing this period return repeatedly to the theme of Ellen's isolation: "When John was gone and her morning affairs were out of the way, Ellen brought out her work basket and established herself on the sofa for a quiet day's sewing, without the least fear of interruption. But sewing did not always hinder thinking. And then certainly the room did seem very empty, and very still; and the clock, which she never heard the rest of the week, kept ticking an ungracious reminder that she was alone" (205, VII).

In the same scene Ellen spends Saturday evening contemplating Alice's death, followed by Sunday, which was "another lonely time" (207). With a day of sewing at home the only thing before her, Ellen's thoughts travel to her solitary condition and to the losses of the women who shared and enlivened the domestic sphere in the past. The image of Ellen's aloneness at the parsonage is the antipode of the Sabbath scene, the world of female love that opens the book. While it was Ellen's choice to fill Alice's place at the parsonage, it is, nonetheless, a painful one; without Alice there is no partner with whom to establish a continuum of intimate exchange and ritualized duty. In portraying these opposing portraits of female experience—female support networks and Ellen's solitary confinement—Warner articulates two of the most frequently voiced poles of feeling established by Smith-Rosenberg's study: emotional dependency and utterances of loneliness. Although the self-created world of female love enhanced the quality of women's lives part of the time, it was not a fully enduring solution to a cultural situation that increasingly stripped middle-class women of their productive functions and confined them to the home.

Furthermore, Warner shows how interruptions of primary female dependencies were complicated further by social conditions which were making communications "across the spheres" increasingly difficult. This can be clarified by way of reference to converging economic and social conditions which individually and collectively exerted pressures that divided the interests of men and women while bringing women into closer and more dependent relationships with each other. Mary Ryan has summarized these structural changes in nineteenth-century society in terms of "the divergence of private and public life," "the separation of male and female spheres," and "the emergence of the cult of domesticity and the parallel masculine ideal of the self-made man."[16] With the ebbing of household production and the formalization of distinctions between the workplace and the home, primary economic and social responsibilities became newly divided along gender lines. As guardians of the home, women were expected to oversee their children's development and the domestic economy, while men, as entrepreneurs of the marketplace, were expected to make money and conduct secular affairs. These separate provinces of activity and responsibility were equally overlaid with social meanings. A "canon of domesticity" imaged women as "wives and mothers" whose duty was "to nurture and maintain families, to provide religious example and inspiration, and to affect the world around by exercising private moral influence."[17] While women were cast as ministering angels, men, on the other hand, were conceived of in terms of their "selfishness, exertion, embarrassment, and degradation of soul" that resulted from their secular pursuits.[18] The dichotomies that established the male sphere as public, secular, and aggressively self-assertive and the female sphere as private, sacred, and passionately self-denying deepened a rift between the sexes by separating male and female experiences, interests, and conceptions of value.

Warner characterizes interpersonal relations across the spheres as fraught with tensions and imbalances. This breakdown in heterosexual communication is illustrated in the second half of the Sabbath evening scene in which Mr. Montgomery arrives home and announces to his wife that Ellen will have to leave the next day. Too distraught to sleep that night, Mrs. Montgomery lies in bed fearfully anticipating the morning:

> The fear of Ellen's distress when she would be awakened and suddenly told the truth, kept her in agony . . . The captain, in happy unconsciousness of his wife's distress and utter inability to sympathize with it, was in a sound sleep, and his heavy breathing was an aggravation of her trouble: it kept repeating, what indeed she knew already, that the only one in the world who ought to have shared and soothed her grief was not capable of doing either.

(72)

While the expectation of Ellen's departure causes intense upset for Mrs. Montgomery, Warner alerts us to the other source of her despair: Mr. Montgomery's complete irresponsiveness to his wife's condition. Mr. Montgomery's "happy unconsciousness" and "utter inability to sympathize" remind his wife of the paucity of emotional exchange within their marriage. For Mrs. Montgomery, it is not her husband who has tended to her emotional needs but Ellen. As a source of compassion, Mr. Montgomery is useless—he neither shares nor soothes—and as "a man not readily touched by anything" promises little hope of change. In recognizing the immutable space between her husband and herself, Mrs. Montgomery bares the "unhappy consciousness" of disappointment in a failed marriage.

Warner characterizes the relationship between Ellen and her father as similarly deficient in vital affective connections. In the disturbing conclusion to the Sabbath evening scene, Mr. Montgomery demonstrates his equal disregard of his daughter's feelings. Here Mr. Montgomery forbids his wife to spend the last hours before Ellen's departure with her daughter. He insists that his daughter's interests will be better served by a good night's sleep as well as a cool and sudden parting. That decision becomes the focus of Ellen's musings later the next day: "She went over again in imagination her shocked waking up that very morning—how cruel that was!—the hurried dressing—the miserable parting" (82). Instead of recognizing the need between mother and daughter to wean themselves slowly from each other, Mr. Montgomery orchestrates a jarring finale to the most important single relationship in each of the women's lives.

Moreover, Ellen's feelings of distance toward her father are not simply a response to her father's role in the "cruel" departure. The division between father and daughter, as with husband and wife, cuts more deeply into the very shape and development of the family history. Upon hearing of the possibility of her father's death in a shipwreck, Ellen reflects on how little this loss means to her: "Ellen rather felt that she was an orphan than that she had lost her father. She had never learned to love him, he had never given her much cause. Comparatively, a small portion of her life had been passed in his society, and she looked back to it as the least agreeable of all" (102, V. II, bk). The close ties which characterize Ellen's relationship with her mother have no counterpart in her father, since her father's absence has rendered impossible the nurturance of similar bonds. Like the relationship between wife and husband, father-daughter relations have failed to provide daughters with meaningful or even positive contact.[19]

2

In reaction to these sources of emotional crisis and to a culture that remained largely indifferent to the quality of women's personal needs, Warner shows evidence of building into her text a response to this neglected realm of women's psychological well-being. This has the effect of transforming what appears to be Warner's purely spiritual concerns into an extended dialogue on attachment, loss, and the dynamics of survival after the loss of a primary caretaker. This transformation reveals the broadened scope of Warner's story and her preoccupation with issues that transcend Ellen's spiritual training. For within what at one level operates as a spiritual training narrative there lies another pattern of development which is equally prominent, a progress in affective communion, or the daughter's symbolic journey of return to the mother. If it is separation between mothers and daughters that was the unraveling thread of women's emotional existence, then Warner attempts to rectify these conditions by creating strategies that could help daughters overcome the pain of separation by having them preserve their feelings of connection to the mothers they loved.

In the past critics frequently assessed the story of Ellen's religious and moral education as a polemic designed to impress upon women the correctness of self-sacrifice and piety and the justice of their abased position in the world. Because the novel portrays pictures of obedient womanhood (mothers and female mentors who educate their female dependents in the "hard" doctrine of self-denial and submission), traditional critics pointed to these images as proof of their thesis without questioning the way this ideology may have served the needs of women. In *The Wide Wide World* traditional ideologies help women because they come to the reader not separated from but inextricably tied to the emotional realities of the world of female love; in other words, conventional religious and social ideologies are accommodated by Warner into systems, or therapeutic strategies, that attempt to reduce women's vulnerability to dependency and isolation. Through the manipulation of familiar cultural myths, Warner conveyed a message to her audience that transcended an admonition to "submit and obey." Rather, Warner softened the ethic of obedience by reformulating sacred and secular ideologies as a language that spoke directly to women's needs.

While in *The Wide Wide World* the female mentors, like Mrs. Montgomery, Mrs. Vawse, and Alice, present to the daughters, like Ellen, the absolute necessity of submission to worldly and divine authorities, it has been less readily apparent how this ideology became a special vehicle of communication among women; an ideology that could be used as a substitute to or replacement for the primary world of female interactions. This becomes clear by focusing not on the novel's didacticism but on the whole context through which Warner's conventional ideology is conveyed. For in the novel the medium is very much a part of the message; the attachment to and love for the mother is just as if not more important than her words and teachings. Because the novel is so thick in religious description and so committed to the fervor of its evangelicalism, it has been easy to interpret the role of the mother as a disembodied mouthpiece for the promulgation of Christian values. In the meantime this assessment has divorced the religion of the mothers from what Warner has clearly delimited as the book's psychosocial frame. In other words, a full interpretation of the religion of the mothers must take into consideration the social context of the female world of love—the mutually dependent interests of mothers and daughters—as well as the emotional imperatives that evolved as a consequence of those relations.

Warner's religious females were not the duped buyers of a system of belief that exacted their submission and obedience; to the contrary, they were the generators of a system of belief that was designed to respond to the separations and consequent isolation that so often characterized women's lives. When Mrs. Vawse, the novel's symbol of female health and autonomy, describes what has allowed her to achieve a perfect contentment in her hermetic existence on a mountaintop, she locates religion as the source of her freedom. Yet as she extols the benefits of her religion, she mentions solely her religion's consolatory power, which enabled her to survive personal experience with attachment and loss: "It is not until one looses one's hold of other things and looks to Jesus alone that one finds how much he can do. 'There is a friend that sticketh closer than a brother;'—but I never knew all that meant till I had no other friends to lean upon—nay, I should not say no other friends;—but my dearest ones were taken away" (228). Here religion is projected as a response to an emotional dilemma. Not a description of religious dogma alone, Mrs. Vawse's words radically alter the theology of her faith by reducing it to two main considerations—the permanence of Jesus and the evanescence of earthly love. This is illustrated in Mrs. Vawse's interchanging references to Jesus and to loss, to the "friend that sticketh closer than a brother" and to the "dearest ones [who] were taken away." By constricting religious doctrine to these two features, Warner relates the importance of Jesus as a religious symbol and the importance of attachment and loss as a human predicament. Indeed, by the very nature of their juxtaposition and propinquity, the two principles emerge as mutually dependent ideas. In Mrs. Vawse's conception of religion, one which is shared and espoused by all the religious female characters in the book, there is no such thing as a religious stricture that is imposed from outside and divorced from female needs. Turning to Jesus is a solution to loneliness rather than a religious precaution against sin or evil. Mrs. Vawse's religious counsel is presented not as a jeremiad aimed at controlling female behavior but as a consolatory myth whose attractiveness and power lie exclusively in its ability to respond to women's painful feelings of loss.

The blurring of the edges between religious rhetoric and "female" rhetoric, or the language which appears in the novel to express the problematic affective conditions within the world of female love, is a pervasive trend in Warner's novel and one that plays continually on building an association between divinity and womanhood. On the one hand, Warner makes this association an implicit part of her story by having the book's female mentors—Mrs. Montgomery, Mrs. Vawse, and Alice—become identified personally with the conventional ideologies they espouse. The identities of these female mentors are linked to the conservative doctrines they practice and teach; to invoke womanhood in this novel is essentially identical to invoking religion and vice-versa. Warner makes this association explicit by having Ellen learn, just after the separation from her mother, the standing between motherhood and the divine:

> In the first place, it is not your mother, but he, who has given you every good and pleasant thing you have en-

joyed in your whole life. You love your mother because she is so careful to provide for all your wants: but who gave her the materials to work with? She has only been, as it were, the hand by which he supplied you! And who gave you such a mother?—There are so many mothers not like her:—who put into her heart the truth and love that have been blessing you ever since you were born? It is all—all God's doing from first to last.

(87)

This passage exhibits in its quintessential form the mixed rhetoric of divine motherhood. While Ellen's religious teacher, who we later discover is the Humphreys' friend Mr. Marshman, takes pains to separate in the child's mind the divine and maternal realms, his line of argumentation paradoxically undercuts his intentions. Whereas the content of his speech renders motherhood as the transparent medium through which God works, as God's ministering agent, the emphasis in the language, which keeps returning to the theme of ideal motherhood, ends by placing maternity on a level with God. This is established through a linguistic pattern in which the shuttling back and forth between subjects—"she" and "he," mother and God—equates rather than separates the image of divine power. Even though mothers are characterized as the "hand" by which "truth and love" are carried to human beings on earth, they are empowered simultaneously in being singled out as God's representatives and as actors who work in full syncopation with God's will. While Mr. Marshman is intent upon proving that the source of all good is God, his inability to lose sight of the maternal presence simply reinforces the reader's perception of the mother as ubiquitous and divine. Despite the eulogy to God's unique strength, Mr. Marshman's words deify two subjective presences, mothers and God.

The link between divinity and motherhood is an association that Ellen becomes aware of through spiritual advisors like Mr. Marshman, but more importantly Ellen is educated into this school of thought by her female mentors themselves. It is this special twist, the fact that mothers were inculcating a theology of divine maternity in their daughters, that makes religion such a potent ideology in the novel and one that works so ingeniously against the problematics of female dependency and loss. The relationship between Ellen and her mother is a strong example of the way religion becomes transformed into a vehicle of connection between mother and daughter, an ideology which has the power to sustain their "primacy of relation," although at a secondary or imaginative level, despite separation or death. Mrs. Montgomery's inscription in Ellen's Bible reveals her interest in passing on to Ellen a conception of divine maternity. On the flyleaf of the Bible which Mrs. Montgomery provides for Ellen before their separation, Mrs. Montgomery writes: "I love them that love me; and they that seek me early shall find me" with the afterthought, "I will be a God to thee, and to thy seed after thee" (49). The significance of these phrases lies in the ambiguous use of the first person, an ambiguity which makes it impossible to determine whether the speaker of these words is in fact Mrs. Montgomery or God.[20] Although this phraseology mingles suggestions of maternity and divinity, the heavy assertiveness of the "I will be a God to thee" takes divinity into the hands of the mother and reshapes maternity as the divine. Mrs. Montgomery writes herself into Ellen's Bible as source, not agent. Through the act of inscription, Mrs. Montgomery initiates a dual transformation; she joins herself with God and invests Ellen's Bible with words that become the lasting symbolism and legacy of maternal divinity.

Hence, it is no great surprise that, after her mother's death, the object Ellen gravitates toward most immediately is the Bible. While before the death Ellen had not been able to grasp the meaning of her mother's inscription or to appreciate the significance of her Bible, in the wake of her mother's death Ellen becomes alert to religion's healing potential. For Ellen discovers in her burgeoning religiosity "a link of communion between her mother and her that was wanting before. The promise written and believed in the one, realized and rejoiced in by the other, was a dear something in common, though one had in the meantime removed to heaven and the other was still a lingerer on the earth" (69, VII). In this passage Warner shows that Ellen's spiritual awakening is exciting and positive, not because she is entering an exclusive relationship with Jesus or with God, but because religious faith opens up to Ellen "a link of communion" between her mother and herself. Connecting her to her mother's desire and will, religion helps Ellen preserve the primacy of relation, or symbiosis of being, that characterized the mother-daughter attachment. Ellen's new faith provides a space in which an enclosed system of communion can be maintained between Ellen and her mother—Mrs. Montgomery's hopes can be rejoiced in and acted out by her daughter—despite Mrs. Montgomery's death. By responding to her mother's desires for her own salvation, Ellen adopts not solely a pious Christian demeanor and outlook upon the world but an ideology so thoroughly permeated with the maternal presence that her own mimetic expression of that ideology translates into a form of imaginative reconnection with her mother.

Hence, Warner advocates a theory of association as a strategy of response against female isolation and loneliness. For the power of association, as a process of imaginative union between subject and object, is what Warner holds out to her readers as their greatest and most readily available source of protection against separation and the problematics of dependency. The therapeutic value of this religious ideology is reinforced for Ellen through the parallel lessons of her four religious

mentors, all of whom instruct Ellen to invest her affections in divine over human relations.[21] Alice's words reflect the beliefs of the group when she advises, "Don't lean upon me, dear Ellen; remember you have a better friend than I always near you; trust in him; if I have done you any good, don't forget, it was he who brought me to you yesterday" (202). Similar to Mrs. Vawse's speech, Alice's words remind Ellen of the source of her salvation, Christ, yet like so many of the religious passages in the book, Alice's advice contains a subtext that deals more with emotional than spiritual reality. Here the terms of the promise of salvation, which demand of a communicant devotion to Christ above all, are adapted by Warner into a system of transference whereby women are taught and encouraged to invest their earthly affections in an image of the divine. Yet this process, which commands women to transfer human feelings from a love object to an abstract religious ideal, is really a strategy which helped women establish a durable sense of relation with the women they loved. Encouraging the deflection of attachments from the earthly to the divine allowed women to experience continuity in their feelings of love because the concept of divinity women were taught to submit to was already defined in terms of maternity. While a message like Alice's teaches the displacement of affections, this displacement does not so much force women to capitulate to a difficult religious precept as secure for them, paradoxically, a more private and lasting form of attachment to a woman whose image has been projected as the divine. Consequently, this strategy of "divine reliance" helped women combat emotional disruptions in the world of female love in two ways: it gave women a means of dealing with and speaking about the issue of separation early on in a female friendship and provided a method so that when separations approached women would be equipped with conceptions, objects, or patterns of behavior that could elicit sentiments of reconnection with the lost but beloved figure.

This strategy, and Ellen's access to it, is the issue at stake in the scene in which Ellen, during her stay in Scotland, struggles to maintain her prayer hour. Another scene once regarded as clear evidence of Warner's purely religious interests, the prayer hour conflict is important not as an experience of communion with Christ but as an experience which recalls a set of affective attachments to the people and places Ellen has loved in the past. When Mr. Lindsay, Ellen's authoritarian uncle, threatens to take away Ellen's prayer hour, he is denying Ellen something much more crucial to her well-being than a moment of pious expression. He is, instead, refusing Ellen her "recipe against loneliness" (303, VII). In denying Ellen her prayer hour, Mr. Lindsay suppresses the "link of communion" discovered by Ellen in the sharing of her mother's religion. It is this negation which prompts Ellen's passionate defense of her private morning hour and her first overt act of self-assertion against male authority. Ellen insists: "I want some time to myself . . . I cannot be happy if I do not have some time" (295, VII). This demand follows from the fact that it was Ellen's "special delight to pray for those loved ones she could do nothing else for . . . and that though thousands of miles lie between the petitioner and the petitioned-for, the breath of prayer may span the distance and pour blessings on the far-off head" (294, VII). In Scotland, where Ellen is removed from the people, the traditions, and the country she loves and is treated as "a darling possession—a dear plaything" by her uncle's family, the prayer hour becomes an especially valuable vehicle for establishing connections with a cherished past (292, VII). Hence, the prayer hour reflects Ellen's devotion to a self-interested act of personal rejuvenation rather than a religious example of Ellen's "submission to divine will and biblical authority."[22]

As this rendering of Ellen's prayer hour shows, Warner responds to the dilemma of female isolation by underscoring the individual's ability to activate within herself a series of associations that foster imaginative union with loved ones despite temporary or permanent separations. As John Humphrey explains to Ellen:

> "When two things have been in the mind together, and made any impression, the mind associates them; and you cannot see or think of the one without bringing back the remembrance or the feeling of the other. If we have enjoyed moonlight happy hours, with friends that we loved . . . it yet brings with it a waft from the feeling of the old times—sweet as long as life lasts . . . This power of association is the cause of half the pleasure we enjoy."
>
> (221-222, VII)

This passage shows how meaningful experiences can become, through associations with enduring symbols, lasting and recurrent aspects of our everyday lives. As the passage suggests, a phenomenon, like moonlight, as an ever-present part of nature is liable to change through the power of imagination. Weaving connections between an object and human feelings, the power of association connects inherently separate phenomena until they appear to the senses as identical. This is the premise around which Ellen's religion functions: "the power of association" fuses the ephemeral experience of the mother-daughter relationship with the durable mythology of spiritual faith. In Ellen's mind, religion recalls motherhood, while motherhood recalls faith. In both cases, memorable experiences of love, either with friends or family, activate these associations and the conversions which turn secondary objects into extraordinarily powerful symbols of interpersonal communion. Because the power of association was private, accessible, and resistant to outside control, Warner could present this mental power as a stable source of emotional sustenance for women.

Given these circumstances, it is possible to comprehend why Ellen would be so ready to adopt her mother's, Mrs. Vawse's, and Alice's religion and style of behavior. Her readiness is derived not from the imposition of external regulations which force Ellen into untiring obedience but from an internal love and admiration for women that she wants to be like. For example, when Ellen takes over Alice's place at the Humphrey parsonage after Alice's death, Ellen adopts Alice's self-sacrificing mode of behavior not strictly as a capitulation to societal demands but as an assertion of love and connection to Alice: "Whatever she [Ellen] did was done with her best diligence and care; and from love to both the dead and the living, Ellen's zeal never slackened" (198, VII). In this context duty and service are cast as inner propulsions, as acts which cannot be understood properly unless they are seen as expressive of ties to the female world of love. The performance of duty fulfills Ellen by pleasing the living Humphreys, but just as importantly it pleases Ellen because she can do "whatever Alice would have wished" (193, VII). In this context Ellen's adoption of conventional behavior has little to do with the strictures of a society that disempowers her. Rather, she practices this pattern of behavior as an acting out of an allegiance to Alice, bridging the distance between her adopted sister and herself. As a mode of being, obedient womanhood—like religion or moonlight—stimulates Ellen's feelings of connection to her female mentors and therefore serves as an enduring "link of communion" with the female world of love.[23]

In sum, to regard *The Wide Wide World* as a narrative of overindulged sentiments is to overlook the emotional and psychological levels at which Warner's novel operates. While Warner's religious and moral preaching may strike the contemporary reader as of dubious literary value, the book is nonetheless invaluable as a cultural document whose primary concern is womanhood. Few other texts offer such sustained and elaborate portraits of women's psychosocial conditions in the nineteenth century. Like women's journals and correspondences, the sentimental novel was a form in which women authors could distill and study feminine experience. Warner portrays this world by making her subject matter conform to the shape of women's sphere. This explains the thoroughly feminine character of her book—the lives of heroines, the recurrent descriptions of home, and the intensive focus on female relationships. Even more suggestively, Warner represents the psychological and emotional issues that faced many middle-class women in her time. Patterns of homosocial bonding, the sincere and unhampered connections between mothers and daughters, and the problems of attachment and separation are features of our foremothers' experience which, due to the misreading and suppression of the sentimental tradition, have been lost to us today. Nevertheless, the sentimental novel is an enduring testimony to the deeply felt interior experiences of women in the nineteenth century.

Notes

1. I would like to thank Richard Brodhead for taking the time to discuss and challenge my ideas for this essay and Laura Wexler and Jane Tompkins for their insightful and helpful editorial comments.

2. This perspective has been memorably set forth by Henry Nash Smith, "The Scribbling Women and the Cosmic Success Story," *Critical Inquiry* 1 (September 1974); John T. Frederick, "Hawthorne's 'Scribbling Women,'" *New England Quarterly* 48 (1975). Aligned to this viewpoint is Ann Douglas, *The Feminization of American Culture* (New York: Avon, 1977).

3. Smith, "The Scribbling Women," 51.

4. Presently, critical debates around the sentimental novel have divided into three identifiable camps: the conservative view, which casts the sentimental novel as an unconscious perpetuator and supporter of women's traditional roles; the subversive view, which treats the sentimental novel as a handbook on rebellion and liberation for women readers; and a third, more recent view, which attempts to work through the complicated interactions between these opposing perspectives. For examples of the former, see Alexander Cowie, "The Vogue of the Domestic Novel, 1850-1870," *South Atlantic Quarterly* 41 (October 1942); Smith, "The Scribbling Women." The liberation arguments are presented by Helen Waite Papashvily, *All the Happy Endings: A Study of the Domestic Novel in America, the Women Who Wrote It, the Women Who Read It, in the Nineteenth Century* (New York: Harper and Bros., 1957); Dee Garrison, "Immortal Fiction in the Late Victorian Library," *American Quarterly* 28 (Spring 1976). For critics whose arguments yoke together elements of both perspectives, see Mary Kelley, "The Sentimentalists: Promise and Betrayal in the Home," *Signs* 4 (Spring 1979); Nina Baym, *Woman's Fiction: A Guide to Novels by and about Women in America, 1820-1870* (Ithaca: Cornell University Press, 1978); Jane Tompkins, *Sensational Designs: The Cultural Work of American Fiction, 1790-1860* (New York: Oxford University Press, 1985).

5. Tompkins, *Sensational Designs,* 147-185. Tompkins's treatment of *The Wide Wide World* is to date one of the most detailed case studies of the internal dynamics and cultural function of sentimentality. While her argument focuses mainly on the theme of female power, it also discusses and prepares the way for further considerations of the role of intimacy, mutual support, and emotional experience in the sentimental novel.

6. Frederick, "Hawthorne's 'Scribbling Women,'" 235.

7. Susan Warner, *The Wide Wide World* (New York: George P. Putnam, 1850), 67. All subsequent references to this edition appear directly in the text.

8. As the following historical sections of this essay will show, Warner's representation of a close and dependent mother-daughter relationship, at the center of a broader female support network, replicates what Carroll Smith-Rosenberg describes as a "female world of love and ritual." See Carroll Smith-Rosenberg, "The Female World of Love and Ritual: Relations between Women in Nineteenth Century America," *Signs* 1, no. 1 (Autumn 1975). Interestingly, the opening scenes of *The Wide Wide World* aim to establish the absolute primacy of the mother-daughter relationship. Likewise, Smith-Rosenberg writes: "An intimate mother-daughter relationship lay at the heart of this female world. The diaries and letters of both mothers and daughters attest to their closeness and mutual emotional dependency" (15).

9. Smith, "The Scribbling Women," 68.

10. As suggested above, Smith-Rosenberg's research offers an invaluable theoretical frame for interpreting the sentimental novel's intensive focus on women's emotional experience and homosocial attachments. For other important historical examinations of "women's sphere" in nineteenth-century America, see Carroll Smith-Rosenberg, *Disorderly Conduct* (New York: Alfred A. Knopf, 1985); Mary Ryan, *Cradle of the Middle Class: The Family in Oneida County, New York, 1790-1865* (Cambridge: Cambridge University Press, 1981); Barbara Epstein, *The Politics of Domesticity: Women, Evangelism, and Temperance in Nineteenth Century America* (Middletown, Conn.: Wesleyan University Press, 1981); Carl Degler, *At Odds: Women and the Family in America from the Revolution to the Present* (Oxford: Oxford University Press, 1980); Nancy Cott, *The Bonds of Womanhood: "Woman's Sphere" in New England, 1780-1835* (New Haven: Yale University Press, 1977); Barbara Welter, *Dimity Convictions: The American Woman in the Nineteenth Century* (Athens: Ohio University Press, 1976); and Kathryn Kish Sklar, *Catherine Beecher: A Study in American Domesticity* (New York: W. W. Norton and Company, 1976).

11. Smith-Rosenberg, "The Female World of Love and Ritual," 4.

12. Ibid., 26.

13. In her recent work on gender identity Nancy Chodorow discusses the problematic depths of

mother-daughter identification and separation in cultures which define mothering as a specifically female activity. Chodorow writes: "It seems likely that from their children's earliest childhood, mothers and women tend to identify more with daughters and to help them to differentiate less, and that processes of separation and individuation are made more difficult for girls." Although one wants to be careful not to generalize psychological phenomena over time, Chodorow's theory of gender personality has special implications for my argument. It suggests that in addition to "a female world of love and ritual," which strained women's experiences of loss, psychological factors, originating in girls' early and continuous identifications with their mothers, may well have deepened and complicated this already highly charged and difficult experience. For Nancy Chodorow's discussion of gender personality, see "Family Structure and Feminine Personality," in *Woman, Culture, and Society,* ed. Michelle Rosaldo and Louise Lamphere (California: Stanford University Press, 1974). For the classic discussion of the role of separation in child development, see the "fort-da" thesis in Sigmund Freud, *Beyond the Pleasure Principle* (New York: W. W. Norton and Company, 1961), 8-11.

14. Edward Foster, *Susan and Anna Warner* (Boston: Twayne Publishers), 36.

15. See Frederick, "Hawthorne's 'Scribbling Women,'" 235.

16. Ryan, *Cradle of the Middle Class,* 155.

17. Cott, *The Bonds of Womanhood,* 8.

18. Ibid., 67.

19. In the novel Mr. Montgomery's preoccupation with public concerns, like his lost lawsuit, and indifference toward his private concerns, like his wife and daughter, offer the clearest example of the "divided spheres," especially as they functioned to intensify and disturb female dependencies. Although outside the scope of this essay, Warner's novel depicts and explores several other models of heterosexual interaction and communication.

20. This observation has been discussed at length by Jane Tompkins in her thorough textual analysis of *The Wide Wide World.* Tompkins interprets Warner's feminine theology as a by-product of a fundamentally political issue, women's powerlessness in society, and views that theology as a way in which women reconciled their "needs for power and status with a condition of economic and political subservience" (see Tompkins, *Sentimental Designs,* 165). My view of the role of religion and

female capitulation to the strictures of conservative cultural ideologies differs crucially from this point of view, in that I perceive the theology of maternal divinity as a system that aims to ameliorate women's psychosocial needs—needs which were produced because of the particular social structure of female relations in the nineteenth century—rather than as a system exposing Warner's concern with female power. Similarly, I view the act of submission to conventional ideology as less important for the self-mastery or the "assertion of autonomy" (162) that it paradoxically involved than for the way it enabled daughters to fulfill the maternal will and therefore experience a link of communion or form of connection with the mother.

21. In order to impress this point upon her reader, Warner has Mrs. Montgomery (68), Mrs. Vawse (228), Alice (202), and John (225, VII) tell Ellen that her best interests will be served by privileging her affections to Christ and suppressing her dependence on human relations. Here we see other examples of passages that read like religious polemics on the surface yet contain a latent discourse on the problem of durable versus transient relations.

22. Foster, *Susan and Anna Warner,* 36.

23. For a reading of these relationships as complicit in a cultural system of social discipline as opposed to my own theory of emotional reunion and recuperation, see Richard Brodhead, "Sparing the Rod: Discipline and Fiction in Antebellum America," *Representations* 21 (Winter 1988): 67-96.

Isabelle White (essay date fall 1990)

SOURCE: White, Isabelle. "Anti-Individualism, Authority, and Identity: Susan Warner's Contradictions in *The Wide, Wide World.*" *American Studies* 31, no. 2 (fall 1990): 31-41.

[*In the following essay, White places* The Wide, Wide World *in the ideological context of nineteenth-century America and states that the work represents the conflict between the individual and authority during a period of developing capitalism.*]

During the 1850s, the decade that culminated in the Civil War, competing interests struggled to shape a definition of America. Issues at stake were whether the national identity would be defined by slave states or free states, by agrarian interests or industrial-capitalist interests, and by what were coming to be perceived as men's interests or women's interests. Popular fiction, perhaps most clearly among literary texts, reflects such issues. And at least sometimes, it goes beyond simply endorsing readers' values and validating their world views to crystalize issues and to attempt to influence the values that will determine the direction the culture takes.[1] Susan Warner's *The Wide, Wide World* (1850), the first American novel to sell more than a million copies, made such an attempt.[2]

This book, which has been said to "represent in its purest form an entire body of work that this century's critical tradition has ignored," promoted an ideology that combines domesticity and evangelical Christianity and which on its surface opposes the individualism and materialism basic to an expanding market economy.[3] Warner's ideology of course did not prevail against industrialist-capitalist values. But Warner's relation to the values becoming dominant was not one of simple opposition followed by defeat. Because those who shared Warner's values also shared economic disadvantage and thus dependence on the dominant culture, her work became implicated in the very individualism and materialism against which she argued. Further, the religion that was the foundation of these ideas was itself changing. Domesticity and evangelical Christianity came to be identified with non-dominant groups and thus became marginal in American life. Warner's position is further complicated by her presenting her argument through the novel, a commercial genre with strong ties to individualistic ideas. Thus Warner's novel, though it argued against increasing individualism and materialism, in some ways fostered the movement of the culture in those directions.

The development of commercial capitalism was a major factor in the polarization of nineteenth-century men's values and women's values. As Barbara Epstein has argued, the interests of middle-class women of this period came to be pitted against those of men.[4] Men and women were responsible for different activities, which required different and conflicting values. To compete in commercial capitalism, men "had to learn to separate morality and sentiment from self-interest, while women, in legitimizing their own domestic activity, called upon the values of the society that commercial capitalism was engaged in destroying." Men and women of the period clashed not just as individuals but as "representatives of antagonistic cultures."[5] The values generally associated with men and the values generally associated with women thus came to represent competing social orders.

That Warner would have been particularly sensitive to the stresses generated by the developing capitalist order is understandable in the context of her personal situation, which illustrates the changing patterns of prestige and authority in the larger culture. Warner was born

into an elite family that traced its ancestry back to colonial Ipswich, but the panic of 1837 undermined her lawyer father's financial security and status, and his efforts to recoup his losses were unsuccessful.[6] Privileged as a child, a maturing Warner watched a new and different order become dominant, an elite based not on inherited status and moral-religious authority but on money earned in a market economy, an economy from which women were automatically excluded.

Warner's endorsement of domesticity and evangelical Christianity, which was a response to these changes, served both the interest theory function and the strain theory function of ideology as described by Clifford Geertz. "In the interest theory, ideological pronouncements are seen against the background of a universal struggle for advantage; in the strain theory, against the background of a chronic effort to correct sociopsychological disequilibrium."[7] The interest theory suggests that the function of ideology is to "pursue power," while the strain theory, which "refers both to a state of personal tension and to a condition of societal dislocation," has as its function the relief of anxiety.[8]

As Geertz says and Warner's response illustrates, the two functions of ideology, the promotion of the advantage of a particular group and the relief of anxiety generated within its members, are not mutually exclusive. Warner's ideology promoted what she saw as the interests of the family and religion. At the same time, her assertions both reflected and relieved the anxiety concurrent with the uncertain status of family and religion in a changing culture. Her ideology accepted and reinforced the authority of the family, which was located primarily in the husband and father and the authority of the patriarchal God of evangelical Protestantism. Warner believed that young women should submit to these authorities and should subordinate their own wishes to those of others. She believed that the sacrifices made in this world would be more than compensated for in the next. Her efforts on behalf of this ideology were ultimately unsuccessful for reasons that Warner's experiences did not enable her to foresee. Her beliefs were at odds with crucial economic changes that were determining the direction of shifts in power and therefore had little chance of acceptance except among marginal groups.

The principle focus of *The Wide, Wide World* is the conflict between the individual and authority, and Warner's characters generally exist apart from the market economy. However, Warner gives brief negative glimpses of the world of commerce. One such incident occurs early in the novel. A clerk at first disregards and then tries to cheat Ellen Montgomery, the novel's protagonist, who is shopping for her sick mother. Though this scene reveals Warner's view of the world of commerce, it is incidental; her characters generally are set apart from that world. Women are of course excluded from competitive business on the basis of their gender, and Warner's major men characters live on money from some unspecified source or they are ministers. Characters who perform other work do so in rural, agrarian settings. Warner's anti-individualistic and anti-materialistic ethic was more compatible with the contexts of home and religion than with the capitalist economy.

The novel records Ellen Montgomery's learning to subject herself to the authority of others, specifically the interrelated authorities of her father, of her Aunt Fortune, of John Humphreys, of her Scottish uncle, and of the novel's thoroughly patriarchal God. Ellen's submission to these secular and religious authorities, however, is entangled with the individualism it counters. Warner reinforces traditional authority, but does so in such a way as to ultimately give authority to the individual.

Ellen's first lesson in submission comes from her unfeeling father. Mr. Montgomery separates the child from her dying mother, emphasizing his control by withholding until the last day information regarding when Ellen is to be sent away to live on a farm with his sister. The aptly-named Miss Fortune is a stand-in for Ellen's father; because she is single and has property, she is identified with the masculine world of power. She requires hard labor, refuses to arrange for Ellen to go to school, and withholds from Ellen her mother's letters. Ellen, however, must learn to submit to this aunt, whose authority at times is totally arbitrary.

Lessons in submission continue. The gentle Alice Humphreys befriends and counsels Ellen, but the forceful, demanding John, who is studying for the ministry, becomes her major teacher. He directs Ellen's reading, instructs her in drawing and riding, and, most importantly, gives her religious guidance. Being subject to this man's authority, however, does not free Ellen from that of her father. Though her father has been dead for some time and Ellen is behaving as a responsible adult managing the Humphrey household, she and the Humphreys agree that she must go to live with her mother's family in Scotland, as prescribed by a letter that had been concealed by Ellen's aunt. The authority of the father is absolute; after his death it is enforced by others. Mr. Montgomery's plan places Ellen at the mercy of still another authority figure, her wealthy Scottish uncle. Compared to the deprivations of life with Aunt Fortune and even with the comforts provided by the Humphreys, Ellen's life in Scotland is privileged; but her uncle is perhaps the harshest authority that Ellen encounters. Demanding that she forget her past, he insists that he is her father and wants to possess her entirely.

One of the conventional criticisms of mid-nineteenth-century popular fiction is that its heroines are unbelievably good children. But "goodness" (which in this con-

text means submissiveness) is not inherent, and, at least in this case, is not easily attained. Ellen requires repeated and harsh lessons in subduing the self; only with great difficulty does she learn to give up her own desires for the sake of others. A scene which takes place at her aunt's combination apple and sausage "bee," (a major social event at which the community helps with work and is entertained) reveals that Ellen is making progress in her moral development. A crisis arises when Ellen, for whom pleasurable occasions are especially rare at this time, is given the last portion of an unnamed but immensely popular dish. But before she can enjoy it, her attention focuses on Nancy, a mischievous girl whose friendship she has rejected. Ellen experiences conflict but knows what she should do. She graciously gives the treat to Nancy. It is more difficult for Ellen to learn the further lesson of eradicating her anger and her sense that she is being personally wronged. A strong-willed child, Ellen becomes "vexed" over and over again. At times she resists her aunt, she resists John, and she resists her uncle. But the lessons are repeated and repeated until finally Ellen learns that anger will not get her what she wants and that she must do as she is told by the authority figures in her life.

Both her mother and Alice have guided Ellen in learning to subdue her desires and her temper, but most of the authorities to whom she submits are men. And each man's authority is linked with that of another and linked, finally, to the authority of a patriarchal God. John reinforces the control of Ellen's father when he says Ellen must obey her dead father's instruction that she go to live with her Scottish relatives. Her Scottish uncle's discipline erases what is left of Ellen's willfulness. Although it is not the uncle's intent, his discipline prepares Ellen for eventual marriage to John and for the discipline of a Christian life. And John, who frees her from other masters, becomes almost synonymous with God. Warner's ideology did not, however, require all women to submit to all men; for her, authority was located not in men in general but in the father as representative of God. Warner also did not argue for a separate sphere for women. *The Wide, Wide World* teaches women self-sacrifice, but it argues that the whole world should be organized on this principle.

Ellen's lessons in submission would perhaps not have seemed unduly harsh or unusual to nineteenth-century readers in the light of current child-rearing practices. Carl Degler has recorded an episode in which family discipline was used for a similar purpose.[9] Francis Wayland, a prominent minister and later President of Brown University, described for a religious journal his experience in disciplining his fifteen-month-old son, who had refused to accept food from him. The child was isolated and not fed, until, after twenty-four hours, he finally accepted food from his father. But the child continued to refuse to go willingly to his father's arms. After further isolation, broken by an hourly visit from his father, he became subdued and welcomed his father. Wayland reported that thereafter his son was extremely attached to him. Through the process of disciplining, the father reinforced his authority in the family and also prepared his son to submit to God. Wayland interpreted the episode as illustrating the value of submitting to Christ, thereby linking his authority as father with religious authority.

Ellen likewise learns submission early in life so that she can finally submit to God's authority. Warner's God requires and will reward the heroine's total devotion; by taking away what stands in the way, God brings her closer to him. Her mother has told Ellen that God is separating them because Ellen loves her too much. The child learns to submit to this loss, as she must later submit to the loss of her mother-substitute, Alice Humphreys. Ellen's mother tells her that God doesn't punish because he wants to; he punishes for her own good. When Ellen responds appropriately, the punishment will end. Warner's reasoning was that when Ellen is no longer angry, when she accepts loss and draws closer to God, it will no longer be necessary for God to punish her by subjecting her to further losses. To today's reader who does not share Warner's faith, this religion sounds at best like a way of rationalizing suffering and at worst like masochism. But to Warner (and her readers) the belief served a valuable purpose. It organized for them both this world and the next, and it allowed them to live with conditions they could not change and to look forward to another world in which their values would prevail.

The ultimate goal of family discipline in the nineteenth century, as Degler says, was internalization of standards. But once the individual has successfully internalized controls, she becomes the authority. And at that point, external sources of authority are likely to be questioned. Warner's ideology, however, precludes the conflicts that to modern readers seem inevitable. The end of *The Wide, Wide World* comes close to presenting conflicting authorities, to putting Ellen in a situation in which her sense of right and wrong (not just her sense of being personally offended) is violated by the authority of the Scottish relatives with whom she is living—by, in other words, her family. The Lindseys live a much more worldly life than Ellen had been accustomed to in America, and her uncle insists that Ellen adopt their ways. When Uncle Lindsey insists that she drink a glass of wine, Ellen, who has followed the Humphreys' example in refusing wine, appears to be faced with a serious moral conflict. Her uncle insists that he is her father and must be obeyed. Ellen obeys, though the example of the Humphreys has led her to believe that drinking is wrong. Warner, however, later explains away this potential conflict. When Ellen reports the incident to him, John assures her that drinking wine is not

"a matter of great importance."[10] He encourages Ellen to do as her new family says, as long as they do not ask her to do something wrong. Two father figures at first appear to disagree, but Warner's belief in the necessity of authority kept her from actualizing this conflict.

But later, a more serious conflict threatens to develop. Ellen's grandmother, who objects to the girl's religious "notions" because she believes they are spoiling her for the "world," orders that Ellen not be permitted time alone in the morning for reading her Bible. Ellen's uncle, however, comes to her rescue; because Ellen has gradually and with difficulty learned to submit to him, he is willing to use his authority to arrange for Ellen to have her room again. This restores Ellen's privacy, her opportunity for self-nurture.

Thus Warner paves the way for reconciling two authorities, Ellen's uncle and her future husband. Though he has earlier tried to erase even her memories of the people in her past, Lindsey eventually allows Ellen to write to John, who has proved his forcefulness and authority in an initially unwelcome visit. From the time she first meets John, the reader suspects that Ellen is intended to marry him and in the final chapter of the novel as originally published, John makes two requests of Ellen and tells her that another will come later. Warner continues that "for the gratification of those who are never satisfied" she will add that Scottish discipline continued to improve Ellen's character and that she then "went back to spend her life with the friends and guardians she best loved."[11] An additional chapter published for the first time in the 1987 Feminist Press edition of the novel makes explicit what the originally published version of the ending implies.

In the full ending of the novel, Warner still subjects Ellen to external authority, that of her husband John. But Warner emphasizes that John understands Ellen thoroughly. Ellen marvels at John's ability to find "the very knot of her thoughts" and untie it.[12] John, like God, knows her better than she knows herself. Like Christ as he was newly interpreted by nineteenth-century Protestantism, John becomes the friend that exists within. His will therefore does not conflict with Ellen's own wishes. Warner thus effects a reconciliation—at the end of the novel Ellen is no longer in a hierarchical arrangement in which she is always subjected to external authority. She has internalized authority by making it her own in a relationship that will not violate her integrity.

In her new home, Ellen's inner room of her own symbolizes the identity she has achieved. John has furnished the room with heirlooms and works of art, and the entrance to the room is through his study. Ellen, however, "may set open" this door whenever she likes, and she is free to make "additions" to the room. Unlike the Victorian parlor, Ellen's room reflects the private rather than the public self; it has been furnished with an "utter carelessness of display." While the room contains a wide variety of objects, Warner emphasizes that there is nothing incongruous about the room: "all was in keeping though nothing was like anything else."[13] Ellen's room thus reflects an existence characterized by fullness and by freedom from both conflict and the need to please others. Ellen has ironically attained the selfhood symbolized by this room through learning to subdue her own will to that of others. The contradictory process by which Ellen finds her identity is a female version of Emerson's process of finding the essential self through losing superficial egotism. By becoming passive, Warner's protagonist, like Emerson's persona, ironically becomes more powerful.

Protestantism, Warner's major source of external authority, ironically becomes a means of giving authority to the individual. The history of Protestantism in America reveals a shift from outward to inner authority. The Puritans hoped to be chosen by God; nineteenth-century Protestants felt that the individual had the power to choose (or not choose) God. In spite of efforts by the established clergy, the focus of religious authority was shifting from the ministers of the established churches to the individual worshipper. Warner does not depict the church as being central even in the lives of John Humphreys and his minister father; they are portrayed almost exclusively in a domestic context. Ellen rarely goes to church. What is more important to her than attending services is time alone to read her Bible, time that provides, on a secular level, the opportunity for self-nurture. While Warner's theology had not moved entirely away from the idea of God as harsh punisher, the major focus had shifted to Christ as internalized friend and guide. Since the individual was now interpreter of the Bible and Christ as he exists within the person, submitting to religious authority began to approach learning to rely on oneself.

Through the very act of writing her novel, Warner was herself assuming authority not previously available to women. Ann Douglas, in her exploration of the alliance between popular women writers and the clergy, has noted that Warner and other writers were also competing with theological and religious work in direct ways, that they "could and did by-pass clerical sanction even while they usurped clerical authority."[14] It has been argued persuasively that popular culture (of which Warner's novel is of course a highly representative artifact) has taken on the function once served by religious institutions. Peter Homans in *Theology after Freud* concludes that ". . . what is usually called popular culture is at once the result of the collapse of a theological dimension in human life and also an attempt to recover some sense of religious form."[15] Warner's novel may be a great distance from traditional Protestant theology, but she clearly intended Ellen as a model of religious character formation for her readers.

The traditional function of Christian faith, according to Peter Homan's extension of Philip Rieff's argument, is that through a primarily unconscious process it "'superintends' personality organization and social relatedness." It is, in other words, central to both personal and social identity. Its function is to pattern "internal energies in the direction of moral passion and social cohesion." But because Ellen's identity develops under the influence of a religion that is in the process of losing its external referent, she is at the end of her development alone, though in a comfortable room of her own. Ellen's final isolation thus prefigures the modern "therapeutic" type for whom, according to Homans, "well being . . . replaces moral passion and social commitment."[16]

Both Warner's domesticity and her evangelical Christianity thus retreated from the larger world at the same time they opposed its tendencies. Warner participated in the evangelical movement during the 1850s, a time when, as Sandra Sizer says, "evangelical religion generally became part of a private sphere, a matter of the individual's heart, having little to do with the larger communal structures of the society."[17] Her resistance to individualism (to the extent that she does resist it) did not lead Warner to a vision of people joining together with those beyond the immediate family. The focus came to be on change within the individual, perhaps because attempts to change the outside seemed futile. Unlike Harriet Beecher Stowe, who argued that changes inside the individual will lead to changes in the world, Warner's attention was limited to the destiny of her protagonist. And she did not, like Stowe with the Quakers of *Uncle Tom's Cabin,* create a vision of ideal community. As Jane Tompkins has observed, the character in *The Wide, Wide World* who has the most satisfying life is Mrs. Vawse, a self-sufficient woman who lives alone on top of a nearly inaccessible mountain.[18] Warner in this respect is again like Emerson. Both avoided social problems; and, like Warner, Emerson used the imagery of domestic retreat, saying that "every spirit builds itself a house." Emerson advised readers to build their own worlds through their minds; this, he wrote, will bring about "correspondent revolution in things" in which "disagreeable appearances, . . . mad-houses, prisons, enemies, vanish."[19] The disagreeable outer world has vanished for Ellen. Although she is a minister's wife at the end of the novel, she focuses not on a life of service but on her household. And even within her household, she can retreat to her own sanctuary.

If American Protestantism was changing, so was Warner's other source of authority, the patriarchal family. Degler finds through his examination of letters and journals that the roots of the modern, democratic family go back to the period between the Revolution and 1830. Alexis de Tocqueville had commented on the weak patriarchal authority in America in the 1830s, and Degler observes that while many of the child-rearing books of the time continued to insist that the father was the head of the household, they at the same time recognized a central role for women in child-rearing. In arguing for the authority of the father, Warner argued for an authority that was diminishing, partly, as Degler says, because fathers were simply not present in the home as much as they had been in the past.[20]

Warner's concern with teaching self-control and encouraging the internalization of authority places her in the tradition of much nineteenth-century writing. Order at mid-century was threatened in countless ways; those interested in promoting their version of the public good attempted to encourage self-control as the external controls of religion, community and family lost their power. Warner's work responded to the same anxieties surrounding personal and social identity in the same manner as numerous advice manuals of the period. Karen Halttunen has argued that those advice manual writers, believing that youth was very malleable and that the republic would be in danger if young people abandoned virtue for luxury and sin, wrote particularly for young men alone—those without their families present to guide them. Writers emphasized the importance of fixed principle as a guide in a world that to many Americans appeared to be a "giant, threatening game of hazard."[21] Certainly the world appeared as such to Warner, whose financial security and chances for a "good" marriage had been lost with her father's money. But rather than presenting a young man going to the city to seek his fortune, Warner chose to give us a young woman alone; she orphaned her heroine and thrust her out into a "wide, wide world" at a time when both the family and religious institutions were losing much of their power to shape children's lives.

Warner's ideal of selflessness has its individualistic component; her ideal of spirituality is likewise not immune to the materialism that it resists. Ellen's spiritual growth is rewarded by material goods. Deprived during her time with Aunt Fortune (who is not poor but is ungenerous), Ellen enjoys a life of comfort with the Humphreys and of luxury with her Scottish relatives. Married to John (in the Feminist Press final chapter), Ellen has overall responsibility for the household, but a trusted and efficient housekeeper will allow her to spend her time in her interior room, where "nothing had been spared which wealth could provide or taste delight in." Perhaps the most impressive object in this room is an elaborate secretary with a concealed drawer "well lined with gold and silver pieces and bank bills."[22] John assures Ellen that he will never ask how the money was spent and that the drawer will be perpetually re-filled. Representing spiritual reward by material goods is of course not peculiar to Warner; the practice permeates Hebraic-Christian tradition and reveals the difficulty the economically disadvantaged have in maintaining an anti-materialistic stance.

The contradictions Warner's ideology involved her in are further seen in her complex relation to the genre in which she worked. In her effort to communicate her message and to support herself and her sister, Warner used the genre available to her as a writer without an elite education—a genre that was also marketable. The form of the novel, however, is not consistent with her overt message. The novel is "organically individualistic," even when it attacks individualism. It is "always about the unitary self versus the others."[23] And in crucial ways, the novel encourages individualism. Reading novels has always been a private, personal experience; no institution mediates between novel and reader. Reading empowers individuals as surely as expanded political freedoms do; and novels, along with newspapers and magazines, were the reading material of those without elite educations.[24] The fierce opposition with which political, social and religious leaders greeted the earliest American novels had abated by the time Warner wrote, but those who protested the novel were nonetheless correct in seeing the novel as a form subversive of their authority.[25]

When John visits Ellen in Scotland, he leaves her with two requests—that she write to him and that she not read novels. Warner thus used *The Wide, Wide World* to criticize novel-reading and to dissociate herself from the genre in which she worked. This action was not a hypocritical effort to make her work more acceptable to readers who might be suspicious of the moral effects of fiction; rather it was a way of emphasizing her seriousness of purpose. Critics ranging from Nathaniel Hawthorne in Warner's own time to Ann Douglas in our time have underestimated Warner (and other popular women writers) by believing that they merely echoed platitudes developed out of their own self-interest.[26] Warner's thinking on cultural values was not systematically worked out nor was it explicitly stated. But there is no reason to doubt the sincerity of feeling behind Warner's claim that she wrote *The Wide, Wide World* on her knees; this perception of her writing as religious practice reveals that she was writing about what was vitally important to her.

But if the use of the novel genre undermined her position, Warner in turn undermined the novel form by her non-conformity to generic expectations. The genre from its beginning required individualized characters; and by the mid-nineteenth century, the novel was coming more and more to be valued by critics on this basis. Individualism as discussed here is of course not synonymous with individuality; to say that Warner's ideology denied that authority is inherent within each person is not to say that she resisted the idea that each person is unique. Nonetheless, the concepts are related, and Warner did not value individuality as highly as do twentieth century readers. It is not surprising that later critics (and some of her contemporary reviewers as well) praise her minor characters as being clearly and realistically drawn while rejecting her major characters, whom she used as representative (not perfect) models. Uninterested in psychological analysis, Warner made explicit her lesson but not her characters' thoughts.

Market-place values were of course victorious in the mid-century struggle to define America. Their victory is evident even in the terminology I have chosen—"anti-individualism" and "anti-materialism" define that which they oppose. In her later years, Warner apparently recognized that she had fought a losing battle. Her final journal entry reads: "'The world is on one side, and we on another—with our Lord'."[27] As the dominant culture became more firmly established, readers could no longer take Warner's ideology seriously, could no longer appreciate the conflict she depicted. Her works therefore became less appealing to general readers. Critics too have turned away from works such as **The Wide, Wide World,** devaluing them because of our strong tradition of individualism, which as Nina Baym has pointed out, has defined the "Americanness" and thus the value of our national literature.[28] Part of my argument has been that the interest Warner shares with other nineteenth-century writers in the problem of identity in a changing world and her complicity in promoting individualism indicate that she was not as removed from the mainstream as has been assumed. But the greater significance of this examination of the non-dominant ideology and its appeal for the mass of readers from the middle to the end of the nineteenth century is that it contributes to an understanding of the struggle to define dominant American values and reveals one way in which the beliefs of those without economic and political power are subsumed by the beliefs of those with these kinds of power.

Notes

1. Joanne Dobson, "The Hidden Hand: Subversion of Cultural Ideology in Three Mid-Nineteenth-Century American Women's Novels," *American Quarterly* 38 (Summer 1986), 223-42. Dobson also uses the book as an example of popular fiction that "clearly coalesces the issues." She says that readers "probably read for a literary experience that affirmed the ideology structuring their lives," but that the book communicates on a second level which recognizes the cost to women of that ideology (228).

2. Susan Warner, *The Wide, Wide World,* ed., Jane Tompkins (New York, 1987).

3. Jane Tompkins, *Sensational Designs: The Cultural Work of American Fiction, 1790-1860* (New York, 1985), 145.

4. Barbara Epstein, *The Politics of Domesticity: Women, Evangelism and Temperance in Nineteenth Century America* (Middletown, Connecticut, 1981).

5. *Ibid.,* 62.

6. Mary Kelley, *Private Women, Public Stage: Literary Domesticity in Nineteenth-Century America* (New York, 1984), 31.

7. Clifford Geertz, "Ideology as a Cultural System," in *The Interpretation of Cultures* (New York, 1973), 201.

8. *Ibid.,* 203.

9. Carl Degler, *At Odds: Women and the Family in America from the Revolution to the Present* (New York, 1980).

10. Warner, *Wide World,* 562.

11. *Ibid.,* 569.

12. *Ibid.,* 581.

13. *Ibid.,* 572-575.

14. Ann Douglas, *The Feminization of American Culture* (New York, 1977), 86.

15. Peter Homans, *Theology after Freud* (Indianapolis, 1970), 227.

16. *Ibid.,* 152.

17. Sandra Sizer, *Gospel Hymns and Social Religion: The Rhetoric of Nineteenth-Century Revivalism* (Philadelphia, 1978), 85.

18. Warner, *Wide World,* 165.

19. Ralph Waldo Emerson, "Nature," in *Selections from Ralph Waldo Emerson,* ed., Ralph E. Whicher (Boston, 1960), 56.

20. Degler, *At Odds,* 75, 82.

21. Karen Halttunen, *Confidence Men and Painted Women: A Study of Middle-class Culture in America, 1830-1870* (New Haven, 1982), 19.

22. Warner, *Wide World,* 574, 582.

23. Myra Jehlen, "Archimedes and the Paradox of Feminist Criticism," in *The Signs Reader: Women, Gender and Scholarship,* ed., Elizabeth Abel and Emily Abel (Chicago, 1983), 89.

24. Cathy Davidson, *Revolution and the Word: The Rise of the Novel in America* (New York, 1986).

25. Nina Baym, *Novels, Reader, and Reviewers: Responses to Fiction in Antebellum America,* (Ithaca, New York, 1984). Baym concludes on the basis of original reviews in widely-read periodicals that the educationally elite of the period she studies no longer resisted the novel genre but rather tried to "establish some control over novels" (30).

26. Hawthorne's remarks about the "damned mob of scribbling women" are well known; and while Douglas claims to be sympathetic, her tone is disdainful.

27. Kelley, *Private Woman,* 295.

28. Nina Baym, "Melodramas of Beset Manhood," *American Quarterly* 33 (Summer, 1981), 123-139.

Susan S. Williams (essay date December 1990)

SOURCE: Williams, Susan S. "Widening the World: Susan Warner, Her Readers, and the Assumption of Authorship." *American Quarterly* 42, no. 4 (December 1990): 565-86.

[*In the following essay, Williams remarks on Warner's initial resistance to being labeled a sentimental novelist.*]

I

"Sue, I believe if you would try, you could write a story." Thus, according to her sister Anna, did Susan Warner's Aunt Fanny unceremoniously suggest that she write a novel. Anna then qualified this anecdote: "Whether she added 'that would sell,' I am not sure; but of course that was what she meant."[1] The less pragmatic version of this account appeals to the image of Warner as a sentimental novelist. It seems appropriate to locate the genesis of her authorship in a conversation between aunt and niece that, in its emphasis on success through "trying," tacitly encodes the virtues of discipline and self-suffering that inform Warner's *The Wide, Wide World.* Fanny's implicit assumption about marketability, however, is equally important to an understanding of this genesis. "Susan had always had literary ambitions," reported George Haven Putnam, son of Warner's original publisher, "but it was the pressure for money that constituted the immediate incentive to the writing of *The Wide, Wide World.*[2]

The financial constraints that prompted Warner to write continued to influence her throughout her career. Her financial stability depended on her success as a sentimental novelist, a success due in turn to her responsiveness to the desires of her readers. These readers expressed their desires in letters to Warner that conflated the character of Ellen Montgomery—the heroine of *The Wide, Wide World*—with Warner herself, thereby initiating a legacy of Warner scholarship that frequently has equated Warner with Ellen. The manuscript of *The Wide, Wide World,* however, reveals that Warner was more worldly than Ellen Montgomery: that she *chose* to write in the sentimental mode and to invest Ellen with the virtues of piety and self-discipline venerated within the domestic "woman's sphere."[3] In addition, her family history, particularly her relationship with her sister Anna, made her attentive to competition between women that theories about this "sphere" tend to overlook. An understanding of Warner's construction of this sphere challenges critical assumptions about her authorship.

The financial difficulties that induced Warner to write began when her father, Henry, a prosperous lawyer in Manhattan, lost much of his fortune in the Panic of 1837. Before the Panic, the Warners had been a socially prominent family with a fashionable address at St. Mark's Place. John Jacob Astor and Samuel Ward (father of Julia Ward Howe) lived nearby. Susan and Anna spent their childhood in a round of social visits and lessons in singing, dancing, French, and Italian; they were expected to marry well.[4] Henry Warner's losses, however, forced the family to move to Constitution Island, a small New York island situated on the Hudson across from West Point. Warner's losses continued in a legal battle over a dam he had built on the Island, and it was then that Aunt Fanny suggested that Susan begin to write. (Warner's wife had died soon after Anna's birth.) It had become incumbent upon the sisters to help stabilize the family finances. Anna already had created and sold a natural history game that had been fairly successful. The family, nonetheless, had to auction off many of its possessions, including a piano and some valuable engravings. "When at last the men and the confusion were gone," Anna wrote, "then we woke up to life" (*SW,* 279).

Anna entitled Susan's completed novel *The Wide, Wide World,* and Henry Warner took it to New York to find a publisher. At first he had little success. Harper's returned it inscribed with the word "Fudge!" and Robert Carter, the religious publisher who would later become the Warners' primary backer, refused to read it.[5] Its eventual publisher, George P. Putnam, also first wanted to reject it. He received it from one of his readers with the report that it was "pleasantly written, with good character studies; . . . wholesome in purpose and earnest in its religious feeling; but it was not dramatic, and the story was in no way sensational, and there was the further objection that it was very long."[6]

He took it home to Staten Island, however, where his mother read it and said, "George, if you never publish another book, you must make '*The Wide, Wide World*' available for your fellow men."[7] Putnam then published seven hundred and fifty copies of the novel as a Christmas book in December 1850. Three years later, twenty-two editions of it had appeared. Now, there are at least one hundred and thirty editions of *The Wide, Wide World,* including translations into French, German, Polish, and Dutch.[8] Its sales in the mid nineteenth century were surpassed only by those of *Uncle Tom's Cabin.* Clearly, Aunt Fanny had been right about Warner's ability to write a story.

Warner's journal entries, however, reflect not so much a concern with the story as with the money it brought: she never forgot her original impetus for writing. Waiting anxiously to see whether the book would sell, she asked: "Alas, my poor little book—art Thou too big?" (*SW,* 327). When she received her own copies, she was most impressed by their appearance. She exulted in one "lovely red-edged copy" and later was almost as excited by the gilt ornament on the books as by their favorable reviews (*SW,* 333, 340). She was also happy that copies were selling at $2.50 each (*SW,* 343). However, these sales did not alleviate her financial worries. As soon as she had finished proofreading *The Wide, Wide World,* she began her second novel, *Queechy.* Anna began to write too; her first novel, *Dollars and Cents,* was published along with *Queechy* in 1852. The next year, the Warners produced their first collaborative work, *Carl Krinken: His Christmas Stocking.*

Together, the Warners eventually wrote more than eighty-five novels, short stories, essays, biographies, and religious tracts that went to well over eight hundred editions.[9] This enormous output still did not give them economic security; they used income from the books as soon as they received it, often selling their rights at the outset rather than waiting for royalties.[10] As Anna noted, "We never dreamed of dressing or living up to the standard of my childish days" (*SW,* 351). Writing was for them not a means to luxury; it was a necessity for financial stability. Decreasing revenues increased the will to write. In 1860, for instance, Susan was "mortified" that *Say and Seal* "should not have done greater things." She described being

> taken aback by Lippincott's statement of $1,500 due to us. I had looked for something like a thousand more. Greatly taken down for a little, and shewed it. I said God's will be done, and felt it—but the loss of my visions of a little rest and ease and elbow-room, I also felt. This must set me to work.
>
> (*SW,* 406)

As this comment shows, Warner conceived of her work as simultaneously obeying the will of God and facilitating her dream of greater "ease." Material incentives accompanied her religious devotion.

Warner aimed to write four pages a day and filled her journal with reports of her daily production. She and Anna routinely began writing at 5:00 a.m. and often

would work through dinner, pausing only to drink tea. "Trying" to write stories, for both of the Warners, demanded much discipline, will, and energy. Anna described this regimen, as Jane Tompkins notes, with a combination of "self-discipline and delectation that marks both their writing and their lives":[11]

> I was generally up by half past four; and by the time my sister came down the fire was burning, the kettle near the boiling point . . . and the green-shaded student lamp gave out its soft invitation to write. A delicious cup of tea with the much-relished bread and butter, came first however; and then two busy (but silent) pens kept company in the delightful work. . . . The fire sang and snapped, the coals dropped softly; the noiseless pens covered sheet after sheet of paper with their black marks.
>
> (*SW* 381-82)

Anna depicted this scene in 1909, well after her sister's death and just after finally achieving economic security with the sale of Constitution Island for $150,000. In such a position of nostalgia and ease, it would have been easier for her to include the "delectation" of the scene than it would have been in the 1850s. There is also evidence that Susan was never as content with this scene of domestic collaboration as was her sister. Economic necessity forced her to play her part in it, but it always remained for her somewhat of a part, a role that her social and economic status sanctioned and that her large and passionate audience of readers applauded and demanded. She played the role so well that she has descended to us in it: only recently have critics such as Tompkins and Mary Kelley begun to explore her image as a pious spinster who was content to live a reclusive life on Constitution Island with her sister, who was simultaneously her family, friend, and professional collaborator.[12]

Although this depiction is not entirely inaccurate, a more precise one would be of a passionate, bright, and cultured socialite whom financial problems forced to relinquish the friends and husband she early had anticipated. She turned to writing, a vocation that began as a way of earning money but that eventually precluded a return to the way of life which that money was intended to achieve. Warner wrote *The Wide, Wide World* as a story about a young girl's increasing self-control, discipline, and faith in God, and certainly those values sustained her own life. They also helped market the novel. It is striking that George Haven Putnam remembered the reader at his father's publishing house as initially rejecting the novel not because of its "religious feeling" but because of its length and lack of drama. Putnam also recalled that the first major order for *The Wide, Wide World* came from the Baptist Sunday School in Providence, Rhode Island, after a group of ministers there had recommended it.[13] The novel's success was founded on its religious message. This very success, however, led Warner's readers to demand that she continue to write in the sentimental mode, thereby establishing her in a career that she had begun in order to recover some of her father's financial losses. The need to continue earning money encouraged her to depend on the support and assistance of her sister and increasingly her public, despite some discomfort with her role as a sentimental novelist.

II

The *New York Times'* reviews of *The Wide, Wide World* over the course of its history summarize changing critical attitudes toward the Warners, particularly the *Wide, Wide World.* When the novel first appeared, the *Times* raved that "one book like this is not produced in an age" (*SW,* 344). By 1915, the year of Anna's death, it was lamenting that the book was not still read:

> The novel was thoroughly wholesome in theme and treatment, without a touch of melodrama, and pictured life as the authors saw it. . . . It is not likely that the books of the Warner sisters are still widely read. But they were familiar to readers of all ages a few generations back, and their pictures and studies of life helped to enrich and support the social fabric of those days. It has been remarked that it seems scarcely possible that the children and grandchildren of those who read and enjoyed the Warner books are today the advocates of social destruction.[14]

This "social fabric" is spun from the virtues of piety, purity, and submissiveness associated with the cult of "true womanhood" or domesticity.[15] In the same issue of this *Book Review,* George Haven Putnam describes Anna Warner in terms of this ideal. She was, he writes, "a conscientious and capable author, an earnest Christian, a useful citizen, a loyal woman."[16] Both Putnam and the anonymous reviewer value the Warners primarily for their cultural authority.

By 1944, *The Wide, Wide World* had become a "forgotten best seller" that stood little chance of being resurrected. "Its language, characters, and motivations seem as unreal to us as something from the Hindustani," reviewer Frank Denman stated. "Today the most devout would find [its] excessive piety wearing." Again, Denman agreed that it "reflected the attitude of the period;" its popularity stemmed from the Warners' knowledge of "the trivia wherewith their [audience's] mental apartments [were] furnished."[17] In 1987, Sally Mitchell's review of the Feminist Press edition of the novel put that "trivia" in psychoanalytic terms. "The readers' tears," she wrote, "are for the lonely children within themselves who, (like Ellen) are misunderstood, crave mothering, feel melancholy. . . ." Warner's "magic" stems from her ability to evoke rather than merely to describe emotions.[18]

The novel evokes such emotions in part through a plot that constructs a series of potential but transitory mothers for the heroine, Ellen Montgomery. It opens with

the catastrophic separation of Ellen from her mother (and father) following the loss of an unspecified lawsuit. She is shipped to her Aunt Fortune's house, where she struggles with the coarseness and labor of country living and receives word of her mother's death. She finds solace in her spiritual advisor and "adopted sister," Alice Humphreys, and goes to live with Alice and her brother John, only to witness Alice's death and be sent to Scotland. There she lives with her aristocratic maternal grandparents, the Lindsays, until John eventually rescues her. In this series of moves, Ellen encounters various domestic spheres that successively inculcate her with the virtues of piety, self-discipline, and maternal affection.[19]

This emphasis on the power of maternal affection is central to the cult of domesticity that critics have used to explain the popular success of *The Wide, Wide World* in the nineteenth century. This cult began to shift the internal order and experience of nineteenth-century middle-class family life from "patriarchal authority" to "domestic affection." This shift weakened the idea of fatherhood and gave the bond between mother and child "central place in the constellation of family affection." At the same time, the ideological distinction between the public and private spheres grew larger: the "streets" became more masculine and dangerous, while the "home" became more feminine and safe.[20]

Conduct books advised women about their duties within their "oasis." One that appeared in the same year as *The Wide, Wide World,* Mrs. L. G. Abell's *Woman in Her Various Relations,* establishes the moral importance of this private realm in its opening words:

> We are living when the allotments and responsibilities of Woman, in her own *appropriate* sphere, should be brought before the mind in their true *weight* and *importance.* . . . Woman, as mistress of a family, occupies a station where her influence is deeply, if not widely felt. She is the center flower, the main-spring, the pendulum that keeps all the delicate machinery in regular motion.[21]

Mrs. Abell then enumerates the swings of that pendulum, from housekeeping and care of parlors to female piety and the worth of affection. Her views toward the latter reflect her stance toward women's domestic importance: "It is the easy and voluntary manifestation in the voice and manner, showing the condition of the *feelings,* that makes either the blessedness or wretchedness of home."[22]

Women, however, were not the only writers dictating the parameters of their "appropriate sphere." T. S. Arthur, for example, wrote *Woman's Trials* "with the end of creating for woman . . . sympathy and true consideration, as well in her own sex as in ours. We are all too much engrossed in what concerns ourselves. . . ."[23]

This work focuses especially on women's kindnesses to women less wealthy than they. One story depicts a woman who thinks she is overworked egregiously until she listens to the experiences of her washerwoman. Arthur suggests a larger fact about the cult of domesticity: it was generally directed to women of leisure and gave them a goal and a vocation at a time when some of their traditional labors were no longer necessary. Susan Warner grew up in such a household; one of the largest changes resulting from her father's lost wealth was that she had to "turn housekeeper." Her diaries record the slow and painful process of learning to skim milk, make butter, sew, and make johnny-cake and pudding sauce (*SW*, 181).

It was into this environment of conduct books and sentimental novels that Warner presented *The Wide, Wide World.* It is not clear how many of such novels she herself had read. She definitely read Catharine Sedgwick's *Clarence* and *Redwood* at the Putnams' while proofreading *The Wide, Wide World* and found them "dismally poor" and "*inexpressible*" (*SW*, 305, 313). Mostly she steeped herself in British authors—Scott, Austen, the Brontës, Defoe, Boswell, Cowper—along with volumes of Tasso and *Plutarch's Lives.* In a letter to Anna in 1848, Warner explicitly compared herself to Jane Eyre (*SW*, 267). She was a sentimental novelist, but that did not preclude a preference for other genres.

Despite Warner's interests beyond domestic fiction, recent criticism has tended to categorize her as a "literary domestic"[24] and has focused on the ways in which the novel's subtext undermines the traditional goals of domesticity. In these readings, Mrs. Montgomery is not just an ideally pious, submissive woman, but also, by buying her daughter a writing desk with funds received from the sale of her ring, an embodiment of "female hostility to male power over women and female desire for independence."[25] John Humphreys, the brutal horsebeater and Ellen's eventual husband, and Ellen's father, Morgan Montgomery, become incompetent villains who covertly reveal the strength and competence of the female characters. Indeed, the entire domestic ethos of the novel becomes a showcase for feminine power.[26] It is, however, a paradoxical power, one which derives from self-suppression rather than protest or escape.[27] Meanwhile, a few critics have continued to see feminine "power" in the novel in its nineteenth-century terms: as a rock of support or hope of "cosmic success" for everyone experiencing confusion as a result of social change.[28]

Thus, although interpretations of the shape, power, and intent of domesticity in *The Wide, Wide World* have varied, no one has questioned that the text centers around that domestic ethos. In confining Warner, like Ellen, to the domestic sphere, however, these interpretations do not address the authorial distance involved in her construction of the character of Ellen.

III

Warner's contemporary readers, far from questioning her domesticity, completely collapsed the distinction between author and character and praised both in an enormous outpouring of letters. At first, Warner, who published *The Wide, Wide World* under the pseudonym of Elizabeth Wetherell, resisted such contact. In 1851, when Lydia Sigourney asked to meet her after awarding her a $50.00 prize for an essay on female patriotism, Warner wrote in her journal: "I humbly beg leave to decline and keep my incognito" (*SW*, 339). In 1852, when John Hart published his *Female Prose Writers of America,* he had to identify Wetherell simply as the author of *The Wide, Wide World,* despite the public's desire "to know something of the author." Already Hart was establishing her in the public persona she would retain: an author who had the power to "warm the heart with thoughts and instances of goodness" and whose novel exhibited "real religion . . . with truth."[29] Moreover, Hart sanctioned the prevailing view that women authors were more "knowable" than male ones, because text and author were so intertwined:

> . . . in the case of most female writers, the subjects of which they write, are chiefly of an emotional nature, carrying with them on every page the unmistakable impress of personal sympathy, if not experience. Women, far more than men, write from the heart. Their own likes and dislikes, their feelings, opinions, tastes, and sympathies are so mixed up with those of their subject, that the interest of the reader is often enlisted quite as much for the writer, as for the hero, of a tale.[30]

Warner's fan letters confirm Hart's statement, as they praise her own conformity to and "personal sympathy" with the domestic and Christian ideals she depicted in *The Wide, Wide World.* If, in her later novels, Warner appeared to be deviating from these ideals, her readers quickly complained. They also suggested ideas for new novels and variations on endings of old ones—ideas which continually reaffirmed Warner in the mode she had chosen initially.

One of the most striking features of these letters is the passion with which they were written, suggesting that the cult of domesticity not only organized social spheres but also evoked deep emotion. Interestingly, however, these letters were not all from women, nor from Americans: the public that affirmed and supported Warner extended well beyond middle class Northeastern women.[31] These writers claimed an emotional and private tie with Warner through her writing. "I think you have preached many sermons, and done much good for the world. I feel as if I knew you and you were my personal friend," wrote one.[32] Years earlier, Cordelia Darrach had addressed Warner simultaneously as a confidant and an object of veneration, asking for her autograph to go with her "treasures of Irving and Cooper and Longfellow and Halleck and Gould and Sigourney . . . not one of which have ministered to the highest and noblest feelings of my nature *so much as yourself.* . . . I feel strongly impelled to pour out to you my most earnest heartfelt thanks."[33]

And so the praise continued, and Warner abandoned her "incognito." J. P. Morgan's wife Frances wrote to tell of Lord Esher's comment at a London dinner party that he "read through *Queechy* once a year, I find so much pleasure in it."[34] Missionaries in Minnesota and China wrote gratefully about using *The Wide, Wide World* in their schools. A child wrote "longing to thank" Warner for the "pleasure" and guidance she had given her.[35] Ministers praised the way she had made "religion a matter of daily life interest" and caused "the adversary [to] tremble."[36] Most of the writers would have agreed with Clarence Booth that their "desire to write was too strong to be resisted" and with Jonathan Burdick that the Warners' works were "not only the most interesting works of the present day—but at least *equal* to the productions of the old novelists."[37] In the 1850s, Edward Hale, clergyman and author of *The Man Without a Country,* put *The Wide, Wide World* on a list of "ten great novels which form the religious character of the young." Also on the list were *Robinson Crusoe, Emma, Pride and Prejudice,* and *Jane Eyre.*[38]

Warner evoked great longings and desires, but she also commanded her public's respect as a writer. By 1864, an aspiring young writer in Kentucky, Eugenia Sadler, had turned to Warner for advice on preparing a manuscript. "I have aspirations, but they are to occupy such a position as yours," she wrote.[39] That position also was linked inextricably with preaching and pastoral care; the letters reflect the conviction that literature should be endowed with high moral and religious purpose. In this context, some young Austrian parents found it appropriate to send Susan a photograph of their daughter, who had just died: "The last earthly wish of our dear Maria was to have another of your works—She is no more and she is gone where she sees clearly what you brought to her mind."[40]

Once the Warners' readers had put them on such literary and divine pedestals, they were quick to notice if the sisters began to step off. One woman scolded Susan for using the words "deuced," "cursed," and "devil" in *Stephen, M.D.* (1883).[41] A Chicago woman, Mattie P. Halsey, complained about a character in Anna's novel *Patience* (1890): "How could you make the manly, straight-forward, easiest Christian character of Ross Ingram degenerate into that of a weak, heartless trifler?"[42] Earlier, a Canadian reader had given the Warners perhaps their worst condemnation. After reading *Wych Hazel* (1876), a joint work about a wealthy orphan's debut into society, this reader wrote: "If you ever loved the Savior, it is to be feared you have yielded to worldly influences."[43]

Clearly, "worldly influences" were not what readers expected when they opened a Warner novel, and, on the whole, the Warners did not disappoint them. Both sisters were associated primarily with *The Wide, Wide World,* and it seemed as if the passions that Ellen always sought to quell were displaced into readers' therapeutic compulsions to "pour out" their thoughts.[44] Although they did not explicitly inspire Warner to write *The Wide, Wide World,* those compulsions probably did encourage her and Anna to continue writing in the same vein. Their writings were expected to be as dependable as the books they already had produced. As a young woman wrote from England, those books sat "smiling side by side in a cosy corner of my book shelf; and they come down one after the other in turn, sweet as the first days of our acquaintance."[45] Peter Carter, of Robert Carter and Brothers, the Warners' primary publisher after the Civil War, expected a similar regularity: "Each one goes just about like his fellows and *Stephen, M.D.* has started quite as well as any of his predecessors. Aside from the profits it is a very great *pleasure* to us to have them. They are all books very dear to us."[46]

Following the popular approval of *The Wide, Wide World,* the Warners never would publish anything other than what their publishers and readers had come to expect. They were held to the form that Susan had first found to be profitable. Their readers influenced the terms of their writing and, at times, appeared to suppress a literary will toward increased worldliness.

IV

Nina Baym has suggested that in cases of authors such as the Warners, "the move from their books to their lives must necessarily be indirect, since social criteria for women's literary production intervene between the felt life and the word."[47] A compelling example of such mediation lies in the revisions Warner made to the episode in *The Wide, Wide World* in which Ellen, *en route* to Miss Fortune's farm, is befriended by a kind gentleman on board her boat, later revealed to be George Marshman. In the published version, this man consoles Ellen with a pious sermon about fulfilling the will of God, who "knows every wish and throb of your heart" (*WWW,* 74-75). In a manuscript version of the same episode, however, this man does not quote Scripture or hymns; he does not even mention God. He dries Ellen's tears, and "a long conversation followed"—the conversation that fills nine pages in the published version.[48] Indeed, in this earlier version, the fact of the conversation nearly is forgotten as Ellen and Mr. Marshman take an extensive tour of the boat. In the published version, this tour receives two sentences.

The plots of the two versions are identical, but in the first Warner shows the impulses that made her love the naval exploits of works such as Cooper's *The Red Rover.*

She wrote to Anna from the Putnams' after reading it: "O the inexpressible charm of the sea, and its thrilling adventures and chances, and the display of fine character in intelligence, coolness, and command! The interest of the love-story is absolutely nothing—it is the fine naval characters and doings" (*SW*, 317). Warner's characters did travel on sea voyages, but in *The Wide, Wide World,* she omitted the most naval of their doings, transforming a boat into a sort of travelling home.

The manuscript, however, gives striking evidence of her acknowledgement of potential disruptions within that home. For example, while standing in the pilot box, Ellen is intrigued by Mr. Marshman's story about a naval accident in which a ship was split in two.

> As we suddenly rounded a headland, I saw a little sloop ahead standing just across our track and so near I thought the pilot must have lost his wits. I sprang to the bow and got there just in time to see how we cut her in two. She went down instantly.
>
> (MS, 11)

The crew is saved, but the tale evokes a possibility of disaster through lack of control that has no parallel in the published text.

After leaving the pilot box, Ellen examines the boiler room and hears Mr. Marshman's ruminations about danger: "There is some danger. There is danger everywhere, but it does not happen very often" (MS, 11). The description of the furnace room, with its fires, steam pipes, coal dust, sooty engineer, and other machinery is anything but "domestic." Suddenly the reader is in a world more like that of *Moby-Dick,* which was published in 1851, just after *The Wide, Wide World.* Ellen is, as usual, timid around the dirt and potential danger. Here, however, Mr. Marshman does not affirm her timidity, but rather smiles at her fears. They finish the tour, she sleeps on his arm, and they eat chicken together—still with no sermon.

Warner seems to have consciously domesticated this "Red Rover" version of the episode, as she transformed the original action—"a long conversation followed and then he asked Ellen if she would like to look over the boat"—into a carefully elaborated treatise about why Ellen should not miss her mother (MS, 10-11). A gap clearly exists here between Warner's impulses and those she deemed appropriate for Ellen Montgomery.

A second example of such mediation involves an unpublished ending to *The Wide, Wide World* that Tompkins included in the 1987 edition. Tompkins notes that Putnam may have cut this chapter because he thought it did not contribute substantially to the novel, which was already too long.[49] What is puzzling, however, is why Warner or Putnam never published it subsequently, despite frequent requests from Warner's readers that she amplify the ending. Even as late as 1891, a few years after Susan's death, one reader, Mrs. O. J. Hollister, still was exhorting Anna to write a sequel. "We want to see Ellen back in the old home in dear America. It would make us all young again," she wrote.[50] This unpublished chapter does indeed return Ellen and John to America, but the Warners never fulfilled their readers' requests to publish just such an ending.

The worldliness of the chapter is striking. Putnam and the Warners may have sensed that such worldliness might disrupt the moral message that their readers admired. Most of the chapter is devoted to a description of Ellen's room, which John has decorated as a shrine to high culture, complete with paintings, statuary, copies of the "wonders of the world," antique furniture, easy chairs, and books. It also contains a glorified version of the writing desk that Ellen's mother had purchased for her years before: an "escritoire" with "beautiful workmanship," "costly antique garniture," and a drawer full of "gold and silver pieces and bank bills" (*WWW*, 575, 581-82). Although one of the paintings is a portrait of a Madonna and child, and John quotes hymns and Scripture, when Ellen says, "I am satisfied. . . . I want no more," her satisfaction seems to reflect more than spiritual fulfillments. This room gives her the freedom that Baym defines as "being left alone, protected and comfortable, to pursue one's own interests."[51]

In her Afterword to *The Wide, Wide World,* Tompkins reiterates this point and relates the chapter to Warner's own fantasies. "In using the last chapter to supply herself, in imagination, with the luxury and the protection she longed for, Warner has become aware, at some level, that the dream of wealth and comfort does not jibe with her hard-won resolve to accept the Lord's will" (*WWW*, 603). Warner's biography justifies reading this ending as a wistful glance back at her childhood among the wealthy of Manhattan. Yet Tompkins's analysis of the disjunction between such a glance and Warner's religious views deemphasizes the possibility of authorial choice. This chapter was never published and that can be seen as evidence of Warner's desire to strengthen the sentimental mode of the novel. Here, as in the manuscript version of the scene on the boat, she seems to have considered and then dismissed narrative alternatives to this mode.

V

In addition to the worldliness of the unpublished ending, there are signs of material opulence within the published version of *The Wide, Wide World* as well. Ellen's work box with its satin crimson lining, her red leather Bible, the detailed description of the contents of the Christmas stocking she receives at Ventnor, her distaste for the coarse sheets she must endure at Aunt Fortune's—all bespeak Ellen's attraction to worldly luxury.[52] She also often tries to ascertain her own "worth." She learns, for instance, that her mother loves her "better" than the ring which she has sold to buy the work box but loves the Lord even more (*WWW*, 29, 38). The unpublished ending expresses Ellen's fantasy of luxury and protection more overtly than the rest of the novel, but it is not wholly anomalous; Ellen early learns to intertwine her religious devotion with an attention to material worth.

Equally striking is the way in which the novel allies this attention to material worth with female competition. Some of Ellen's most anxious moments about her material possessions occur in the presence of another girl, Ellen Chauncey, with whom she spends Christmas while living with the Humphreys. Although critics have identified the tensions which subvert the men, or wielders of power, in the novel, it is also important to examine the tensions underlying Ellen's relationship with her female friends. A compelling yet overlooked distinction of the novel is that its problems of power exist, not solely between male "villains" and feminine "heroines," but also among the "heroines" themselves.

Warner initially constructs a sense of uncanny doubling in the scene when the two Ellens meet at Ventnor:

> "We have both got the same name," [Ellen Chauncey said], "how shall we know which is which?"
>
> "Why," said Ellen laughing, "when you say Ellen I shall know you mean me, and when I say it you will know I mean you. I shouldn't be calling myself, you know."
>
> "Yes, but when somebody else calls Ellen we shall both have to run."
>
> (*WWW*, 284)

This doubling soon assumes competitive overtones. We watch as the two Ellens agonizingly supervise the division of a bag containing pieces of Moroccan leather. On Christmas morning, both Ellens worry that they will be unable to distinguish their stockings and are relieved that one reads "Ellen Mon." They lift out each item in the stockings in turn and compare the gifts to certify that neither has been slighted, even noting the ribbons and pictures on their respective packages of sugar plums. They laugh throughout their comparisons, but the elaborate detail of the scene reflects the gravity of the enterprise. After that Christmas, whenever Ellen Chauncey visits the parsonage or Ellen Montgomery visits Ventnor, they enjoy a camaraderie "unclouded by a shade of discontent or disagreement on either brow" (*WWW*, 339). One wonders, however, what might have happened had one package of sugar plums not had a ribbon. In general, the Ventnor Christmas is incongruous: on this Christian holy day, in the middle of an ex-

plicitly Christian novel, there is no word about Jesus. It is a secular day of stockings, food, and playing "The Old Curiosity Shop"; and Ellen goes to bed, not with a prayer, but with a last look at her presents. The two Ellens compete to be what Ann Douglas terms the "symbol of expenditure" in the economy of the novel.[53]

If Ellen Chauncey—for all the light-heartedness and happiness she inspires in Ellen Montgomery—nonetheless poses a threat should their precarious equality cease, Ellen Montgomery's other "sister," Alice Humphreys, poses a different sort of threat: that of complete mastery through knowledge. Here again, the scene of introduction is paradigmatic. When they meet, Alice confuses Ellen by knowing her name; she has known Ellen's identity long before Ellen even thinks to question Alice's. Later, this knowledge expands: Alice knows the proper uses of grammar and diction and chastises Ellen for her mistakes. She also knows how to make tea cakes and hot chocolate; Ellen does not. She watches Ellen constantly, and Ellen looks to her as the source of everything she lacks.

This relationship makes explicit the threat of domination that remains hidden in the "sisterhood" of the two Ellens; Alice is always in control. She teaches Ellen the virtues of self control, but her power over Ellen essentially robs her of a self to be controlled. Only when Alice dies can Ellen assume such a self, although that self is in many respects a new Alice. Ellen manages Alice's house and eventually marries her brother, thereby simultaneously legitimating a potentially incestuous bond and subsuming Ellen into Alice's void. In this respect, the relationship between Alice and Ellen is the most fully realized bond of power in *The Wide, Wide World.*

Anna Warner wrote that, when she first read *The Wide, Wide World,* she had taken Alice's death as a figure for Susan's death: "the thought took possession of me that my darling had written those pages to gently prepare me for *her* going. No one knew it: but in secret I half wept my heart away" (*SW*, 265). This comment suggests the power of Anna's dependence on Susan, a dependence parallel to that of Ellen on Alice. Anna frequently stated that as a child, she had felt inferior to Susan, who was eight years older. She was especially aware of her sister's closeness to their father and felt that Susan loved him more than she did Anna (*SW*, 108). As an adult, Susan received more letters from her readers and was the better writer of the two, but by this time Anna felt that their religion had given them equal status. In 1844 they joined the Mercer Street Presbyterian Church, an evangelical congregation that emphasized conversion and faith over doctrine.[54] Their religion put them, in Anna's words, "on ground where neither years nor knowledge went for much." It knit between them a bond "which should outlast all time" (*SW*, 204).[55]

Yet Anna's identifying Alice with Susan suggests that this bond was not always one of equality but, rather, like that between Ellen and Alice, of superiority and domination. Anna's novel *Dollars and Cents* gives another example of the conflict inherent to sisterly bonds. The work chronicles the lives of two sisters as their father, embroiled in a lawsuit, watches his fortune steadily dissolve. The older sister, Kate, eventually marries, while Grace, the younger sister who narrates the novel, finds this marriage traumatic:

> There was no place for the something [her reaction to the marriage] which at last began to assert its power, as I sat by Kate looking up and listening—happy in spite of that weight. And yet it deepened; and as it were spread over all my heart,—a very film of ice . . . my heart was full. Of sorrow for myself—of joy for them,—of mingled sorrow and joy for the dear friend who had wished just such successors; and turning away, I wept some of the bitterest, sweetest tears, that ever fell from my eyes.[56]

Grace's ambivalence toward losing Kate through marriage suggests the powerful and conflicted nature of the bond between them. Kate's marriage disrupts their sisterly bond, and this disruption, although bringing joy to Kate, leaves Grace sorrowful and envious. The unpublished final chapter of *The Wide, Wide World* portrays marriage not just as a disruption but as a release from sisterly bonds. Ellen's marriage to John Humphreys allows her to achieve the financial and spatial freedom she desires, a freedom restricted by her previous bonds with women. Ellen's marriage is finally more freeing and empowering than her female bonds have been. This revelation of the competition behind sisterly bonds challenges the doctrine of a special "woman's sphere" in which women banded together to encourage and support their own exalted status.

Within such a sphere, it is easy to assume that the Warners lived in an aura of mutual support and dependence, always sitting at the table under the green lamp, lovingly writing the pages of their stories. One might picture them in a sisterly marriage similar to that attributed to Alice and Phoebe Cary, who rejected "offers of marriage in order to stay together, quite literally creating a domestic life based on sisterhood."[57] However, the Warners do not fit the sisterhood mold quite so readily. The downturns in family fortune and social status were certainly significant factors in their remaining single,[58] and they both continued to seek society away from the home. Their success as authors did reestablish some of the social activity they had known before the Panic of 1837. "In time, all this [publishing] broke up our solitude," Anna wrote, "and both friends and strangers began to remember and look for us" (*SW*, 360).[59]

In the early 1850s, they spent many evenings with the Putnams, where they saw "Thackeray one night, and Lowell another" (*SW*, 373). Throughout her life, Susan made visits away from home; her letters to Anna tell of attending a lecture by Catherine Beecher, hearing a concert by Jenny Lind, and viewing Niagara Falls (*SW*, 232, 287, 449). During the Civil War, Susan commented that there was "no man or boy to be had, for love or money" (*SW*, 443), and after the War she began a Sunday afternoon Bible class for the cadets at West Point, who rowed across the Hudson to attend. The sisters clearly were devoted to one another, and Anna, in particular, gained much intellectual and emotional stimulation from her elder sister. Yet they also sought society away from the writing table on Constitution Island.

In the manuscript of *The Wide, Wide World,* Ellen Montgomery does not want to remain in the pilot's box as she travels down the Hudson, but Susan Warner might have chosen differently. Unlike Ellen, she perceived the problems inherent to a mutually dependent sisterhood and the attractions of a separate course. The manuscript warns about the dangers that pilots face even as it recognizes the attraction of their position; Warner restricts a potential valorization of independence by inserting a cautionary tale into Mr. Marshman's story. The pilot, he says, "must keep a good look out . . . to steer through all these vessels without running over some of them" (*MS*, 11). An undisciplined and uncircumscribed course brings the danger of annihilation. We might appropriate this tale as a paradigm of Warner's own construction of authorship. She herself appears to have navigated through competing impulses before finally settling on the narrative route she wished to take, a route in which she ran over or deleted no moral lesson for Ellen Montgomery, such as Mr. Marshman's sermon, and thereby created a work of great sentimental power.

This trope of the pilot recurs in the unpublished ending of the novel, where Ellen uses it to represent her willingness to rely on John. "I often launch out upon a sea where I dare not trust my own navigation, and am fain to lower sail and come humbly back to shore," she admits, "but now I will take the pilot along . . . and sail every whither" (*WWW*, 577). Ellen's relinquishment of authority here emphasizes the value of community and self-abnegation that she has learned from her mother, Alice, and John. Again, however, we might take it as an allusion to Warner's own continuing struggle between a need for independence, both personal and authorial, and a need for acceptance and public support. Working within this struggle, she did not write a naval adventure, even though she might have found it engaging; neither did she write about a worldly, cultural paradise, even though a desire to regain its trappings had made her begin writing. The narratives Warner chose to tell are powerful in themselves, but the choice out of which they grew is crucial to an understanding of her authorship and the power it entailed.

Had Warner not had financial problems and thus been answerable to a particular public, she might not have written at all. She would have had no impetus to begin or, once begun, no impetus to continue. Once she did begin writing, however, the act brought her at times to unexpected possibilities: to visions of naval adventures, secularized opulent Christmasses, powerful and manipulative men *and* women, and a room of her own. It led her, in other words, momentarily in directions other than the sentimental mode with which we now associate her. Thus, an understanding of the motivations underlying Warner's choice of a literary mode becomes particularly important, especially since it suggests the degree to which the support of her readers helped to construct the terms of her literary career and to convert an initial choice into a permanent vocation. It also becomes incumbent upon critics to consider what factors made her so responsive to the demands of that public—factors originating in the nexus of financial, familial, and social pressures that defined her existence on Constitution Island—but perhaps extending beyond it to include Warner's acknowledgment of the "cultural work," to borrow Tompkins's term, that she could exert on that public.

Such considerations reveal that the world in which Warner wrote was a wide one. Her social world, though never again as fashionable as the one she had known at St. Mark's Place, extended well beyond the tea table on Constitution Island, eventually including an international group of readers who regularly wrote to her. Over the course of her career, these readers encouraged her to restrict the scope of her literary world, depending upon her to write books that were rooted in the domestic sphere of the sentimental novel. In *The Wide, Wide World,* however, Warner gives some critique of that sphere by portraying the competition inherent to female bonds. Moreover, the manuscript of *The Wide, Wide World* shows Warner envisioning an escape from these bonds, as she imagines Ellen exploring a ship and entering a marriage that promotes some individual freedom. By not publishing such moments of freedom from female bonds, Warner strengthened the sentimental power of *The Wide, Wide World* and thereby successfully assumed her role as a sentimental novelist.

Notes

1. Anna B. Warner, *Susan Warner [Elizabeth Wetherell]* (New York, 1909), 263. Hereafter references to this work will be cited as "*SW*" within the body of the text.

2. George Haven Putnam, "The Warner Sisters and the Literary Association of the Hudson River Valley," *Fourth Report and Year Book of the Martelaer's Rock Association* (1920-23): 23-24.

3. For a discussion of "woman's sphere," see Nancy F. Cott, *The Bonds of Womanhood: 'Woman's Sphere' in New England, 1780-1835* (New Haven, 1977), esp. 197-206.

4. Edward Halsey Foster, *Susan and Anna Warner* (Boston, 1978), 20-21, 57-59. See also Jane Tompkins's biographical sketch of the Warners in her "Afterword" to Susan Warner, *The Wide, Wide World,* ed. Jane Tompkins (New York, 1987), 587-91. All references to *The Wide, Wide World* will be taken from this edition and will be cited as "*WWW*" within the text.

5. Foster, *Susan and Anna Warner,* 34-35.

6. Quoted by Putnam in "The Warner Sisters," 25.

7. Ibid., 25-26.

8. For a complete listing, with the exception of the 1987 Feminist Press edition, see Dorothy Hurlbut Sanderson, *They Wrote for a Living: A Bibliography of the Works of Susan Bogert Warner and Anna Bartlett Warner* (West Point, N. Y., 1976), 17-20.

9. Ibid., 1.

10. Foster, *Susan and Anna Warner,* 24; and *SW,* 491.

11. "Afterword" to *The Wide, Wide World,* 605.

12. See Jane Tompkins, *Sensational Designs: The Cultural Work of American Fiction, 1790-1860* (New York, 1985); and Mary Kelley, *Private Woman, Public Stage: Literary Domesticity in Nineteenth-Century America* (New York, 1984).

13. Putnam, "The Warner Sisters," 25, 27. Putnam describes the religious appeal of the novel as preceding its literary one: "The religious reviewers finally came to understand the wholesome purpose and the valuable influence of the book, and then the literary critics discovered that it was not merely wholesome, but that it was real literature" (27).

14. "Causerie," *New York Times Book Review* (31 Jan. 1915): 36.

15. This particular list of "cardinal virtues" was formulated by Barbara Welter in "The Cult of True Womanhood, 1820-1860," *American Quarterly* 18 (Summer 1966): 152.

16. *New York Times Book Review* (31 Jan. 1915): 37.

17. Ibid. (24 Dec. 1944): 8.

18. Ibid. (10 May 1987): 16.

19. For a discussion of maternal affection as a form of discipline, see Richard H. Brodhead, "Sparing the Rod: Discipline and Fiction in Antebellum America," *Representations* 21 (Winter 1988): 67-96.

20. Mary Ryan, *Cradle of the Middle Class: The Family in Oneida County, New York, 1790-1865* (New York, 1981), 231-35.

21. Mrs. L. G. Abell, *Woman in Her Various Relations* (New York, 1851), iii, 9.

22. Ibid., 42.

23. T. S. Arthur, *Woman's Trials* (Philadelphia, 1856), 3.

24. The term is Mary Kelley's. See *Private Woman, Public Stage,* especially viii-xiii.

25. Beverly R. Voloshin, "The Limits of Domesticity: The Female *Bildungsroman* in America, 1820-1870," *Women's Studies* 10 (1984): 289-91.

26. See Frances B. Cogan, "Weak Fathers and Other Beasts: An Examination of the American Male in Domestic Novels, 1850-1870," *American Studies* 25 (Fall 1984): 6-7; Joanne Dobson, "The Hidden Hand: Subversion of Cultural Ideology in Three Mid-Nineteenth Century American Women's Novels," *American Quarterly* 38 (Summer 1986): 230-31 (Dobson looks at Warner's subverted critique of power generally and includes Aunt Fortune in the "villain" category); and Mary Kelley, "The Sentimentalists: Promise and Betrayal in the Home," *Signs* 4 (Spring 1979): 442-43. The first scholar to see Warner as a latent feminist was Helen Waite Papashvily, who, in *All the Happy Endings* (New York, 1956), states that "those pretty tales" were "a witches' broth, a lethal draught brewed by women and used by women to destroy the common enemy, man" (xvii).

27. Tompkins, *Sensational Designs,* 176-77.

28. See, for instance, Henry Nash Smith, "The Scribbling Women and the Cosmic Success Story," *Critical Inquiry* 1 (Sept. 1974): 47-68; and Foster, *Susan and Anna Warner,* esp. 51-52.

29. John S. Hart, *The Female Prose Writers of America* (Philadelphia, 1852), 387.

30. Ibid., vii-viii.

31. My analysis is based on a study of the letters in a collection given by the Constitution Island Association to the United States Military Academy Library. This collection consists primarily of letters received by the Warner sisters and is by no means complete. Nevertheless, it holds a diverse group of letters from clergy, editors, friends, West Point cadets, and fans. Of the more than fifty fan letters in this collection, slightly less than half are from men.

32. Ella K. Blake to Susan Warner, 9 Feb. 1879, Constitution Island Association Warner Collection, Special Collections, U. S. Military Academy, West Point, NY. Hereafter letters from this collection will be cited as "Warner Collection."

33. Cordelia E. Darrach to Susan Warner, 26 April 1852, Warner Collection.

34. Frances T. Morgan to Susan Warner, 12 Nov. [n.y.], Warner Collection.

35. Mary Barnes to Susan Warner, n.d., Warner Collection.

36. E. Bedell Benjamin to Susan Warner, 5 Jan. 1864, Warner Collection; and Thomas H. Skinner to Susan Warner, 24 June 1851, Warner Collection.

37. Clarence Booth to Susan Warner, n.d., Warner Collection; and Jonathan Burdick to Susan Warner, 2 May 1861, Warner Collection.

38. Edward E. Hale to Anna Warner, 28 Oct. 1903, Warner Collection. Hale is remembering a list composed in the 1850s.

39. Eugenia Sadler to Susan Warner, 6 July 1864, Warner Collection. Fanny Fern satirizes such requests for favors in *Ruth Hall,* where Ruth's fans write asking for money, academic compositions, and her hand in marriage. See Fanny Fern, *Ruth Hall and Other Writings,* ed. Joyce W. Warren (New Brunswick, N. J., 1986), esp. 180-82, 188-90.

40. W. Novvak to Susan Warner, 20 Sept. 1878, Warner Collection.

41. Mrs. C. J. Pickford to Susan Warner, 9 May 1884, Warner Collection.

42. Mattie P. Halsey to Anna Warner, 21 March [n.y.], Warner Collection.

43. L. Guning to Susan Warner, 22 Feb. [n.y.], Warner Collection.

44. For a discussion of the structures of therapeutic consolation within *The Wide, Wide World,* see Nancy Schnog, "Inside the Sentimental: The Psychological Work of *The Wide, Wide World,*" *Genders* 4 (Spring 1989): 11-25.

45. Mary Barnes to Susan Warner, n.d., Warner Collection.

46. Peter Carter to Susan Warner, 10 Oct. 1883, Warner Collection.

47. Nina Baym, "Rewriting the Scribbling Women," *Legacy* 2 (Fall 1985): 10.

48. This manuscript version was published under the title "A Journey By Steamboat Up the Hudson in 1850" in the *Constitution Island Association An-*

nual Report 63 (1979): 9-13. References taken from it will be given in the text as "MS."

49. See Tompkins's "Note on the Text" in *WWW*, 8.

50. Mrs. O. J. Hollister to Anna Warner, 14 April 1891, Warner Collection.

51. Nina Baym, *Woman's Fiction* (Ithaca, 1978), 150.

52. Ann Douglas also emphasizes the complexities of Ellen's "otherworldiness," noting her "obvious love of the act of possession" and identifying the "underlying question of her saga" as "who can prove the best right to this jewel of a girl?" See *The Feminization of American Culture* (1977; reprint, New York, 1988), 64.

53. Ibid.

54. Foster, *Susan and Anna Warner,* 28.

55. Tompkins also sees Susan's journal as giving the sense "that she thought she was Anna's superior," and her religious conversion as changing their relationship and giving Susan a "reason for living" (*WWW*, 591).

56. Anna B. Warner, *Dollars and Cents* (Philadelphia, 1897), 514-15.

57. Judith Fetterley and Marjorie Pryse, "Alice Cary," *Legacy* 1 (Spring 1984): 1-3.

58. Kelley, *Private Woman, Public Stage,* 35, 152.

59. The following excerpt of a letter of apology for cancelling a visit reflects the fullness of Susan's social schedule and her concern with the forms of social acceptance:

> It was not my will or intention to treat your invitation so. But somehow, hindrance upon hindrance has come. . . . Since the cool weather began, we ourselves have been on the go, or with a houseful of company. We have but just got home, four days ago. . . .
>
> (Susan Warner to Mrs. Monell, 2 Dec. 1854, Collection of American Literature, Beinecke Rare Book and Manuscript Library, Yale University, New Haven, Conn.)

Grace Ann Hovet and Theodore R. Hovet (essay date spring 1991)

SOURCE: Hovet, Grace Ann, and Theodore R. Hovet. "Identity Development in Susan Warner's *The Wide, Wide World*: Relationship, Performance and Construction." *Legacy* 8, no. 1 (spring 1991): 3-16.

[*In the following essay, the critics read* The Wide, Wide World *as a sophisticated rendering of feminine identity construction that has been falsely dismissed by many as mere sentimental fiction.*]

I. READING THE SENTIMENTAL

Recent critical readings of the 1850 bestseller ***The Wide, Wide World*** disagree on whether Susan Warner's frequent depictions of tears of grief, rage, helplessness or joy—scenes which seem so emotionally excessive to many readers today—convey a critique of patriarchal domination or a justification for feminine submission to it. But these readings agree in that they all treat such sentimental scenes as Warner's attempt at a direct or transparent transcription of feminine behavior. Ellen's character, in short, is seen primarily in terms of emotional responses to events or circumstances.[1]

This literal reading of sentimental characterization fails to do justice to the narrative and psychological complexity of the novel. It is true that Warner, like many other women writers, presents a stark opposition between feminine emotion and masculine instrumental power. But in the treatment of the interaction between these oppositions there exists a highly complex, often subtle portrayal of psychological development that requires a different kind of critical focus than that applied to masculine narratives of the identity quest such as "Nature," *Moby-Dick*, "Song of Myself," or *Walden*. While the masculine narratives treat identity primarily in terms of the autonomous self in relation to nature, transcendent reality or inner depths, Warner depicts identity as a process that is constructed or scripted out of the mediation between conflicting desires to reveal or hide subjective experiences that accompany maturation.[2] Hence images of masking, costuming and voicing—the appurtenances of both stage and feminine public life—carry the depths of meaning which the well-known works of the American Renaissance assign to images drawn from nature (the white whale, Walden Pond, the poet's body) or to cultural artifacts (Prometheus, Biblical place names, Plato). When critical attention is shifted to Warner's images of "performance," one can see that the model of psychological development that she presents clearly defines female identity in terms of relationship to others and involves the movement from an undifferentiated to a mediated acceptance of self and others. The model consists of three stages, the first involving the development of a relational self in childhood. At this stage the individual only minimally discriminates between self and others and bases her self concept on being accepted by others. The second stage is a passage from the relational self to the adolescent performing self. During this stage, the individual, now beginning to distinguish between self and role expectations, starts experimenting with various roles (i.e., performing) and willingly masks self-expression that causes others' disfavor or disapproval. Finally, the third stage is a movement from the performing self to the adult constructing self during which the individual engages in a positive and on-going negotiation between the needs of expressing self, meeting role expectations and pleasing others. The development of voice accompanies the movement through the psychological stages as Ellen progresses from silence to "feminine conversation" in the relational stage, to the "dual voice" of the performing stage, to the brink of dialogue in the constructing stage. Ellen's inability to sustain her position at the last developmental stage constitutes Warner's perceptive analysis of the way masculine vision silences feminine voice and constitutes material for yet another study.

In terms of developmental models, however, one of the remarkable things about Warner's novel is the light it casts on contemporary research on moral and psychological development, particularly that of Carol Gilligan and her associates. Although it might appear anachronistic to apply contemporary models of psychological development such as Gilligan's to a nineteenth-century work of fiction, in actuality Warner's narrative throws considerable light on these models because of its grounding in the social and economic realities which shaped white middle-class culture in America. Nina Baym and Jane Tompkins have convincingly demonstrated how Warner's understanding of this emerging culture grew out of her own experience of American economic and social realities. A privileged and indulged adolescent who was accustomed to private tutors and a luxurious life, she awoke at age nineteen to poverty and need. Her father's financial mismanagement and the Panic of 1837 meant the way of life she had known and the social opportunities she had taken for granted ceased to exist for her. For this reason, she had to forge a new identity for herself out of the available resources. Thus in 1844, she and her sister became members of the Mercer Street Presbyterian Church, a move which involved a religious conversion that Tompkins describes as a "necessary strategy for survival" (591). She was, moreover, obliged to find a way to financially support herself and the family. Her decision to write *The Wide, Wide World,* then, underscored her perception that the young woman needed to pay attention to her outward resources as well as her inner ones. As Susan Williams points out, Warner "*chose* (Williams's italics) to write in the sentimental mode and to invest Ellen with the virtues of piety and self-discipline venerated within the domestic 'woman's sphere'" in order to respond to readers' desires and demands (566). For these reasons, Warner's novel is one of the central documents in understanding how social and economic realities shaped the image of the feminine self which emerged in white middle-class culture.

Because *The Wide, Wide World* presents such a detailed account of psychological and moral development and its disruption, it constitutes one of the key missing texts in the story of white middle-class women's efforts to construct a meaningful identity in American culture. In so doing, this text also casts a flood of light on the degree to which such patterns of female development rely on interdependence over autonomy and the voice of transforming power rather than the vision of transcendence.[3]

II. THE COLLAPSE OF AUTHORITY AND THE EMERGENCE OF A FEMALE IDENTITY

Warner's focus on identity development was not unusual during the first half of the nineteenth century. A widespread concern with psychological and moral development emerged in America during this period as ministers and educators perceived the unraveling of traditional authority structures under the impact of social and economic modernization (Degler 90). Warner relentlessly depicts the disintegration of traditional organic relationships brought about by these disruptions. Ellen's native city is a Dickensian nightmare of rain, darkness, dirt and threatening figures like the "bold, ill-bred, and ill-humored" store clerk who eventually assaults her (31). Ellen's father, Captain Montgomery, symbolizes the break-up of the organic social forms; like the "absent father" whom Carl N. Degler describes as symptomatic of America's modernization in the nineteenth century, he is gone from home much of the time searching for the business deal that will solve the family's perpetual financial problems (77). When he is home, he is aloof, capricious and dictatorial. Thus Ellen only wants her father "to go away" again so that she can be alone with her mother (27).

But for financial and other reasons, this is not to be. Captain Montgomery's loss of a lawsuit compels him to seek employment abroad, and in an ultimate act of abandonment he takes the ailing Mrs. Montgomery with him and leaves Ellen behind to make her way with his hitherto-unheard-of stepsister, Miss Fortune Emerson. Thus the unraveling of traditional authority structures and the vicissitudes of the market economy immediately affect Ellen's life. At the age of ten or eleven, in fact, she is left virtually alone, a point Warner emphasizes in several ways. The Dunscombs, acquaintances of her father's only, grudgingly assent to letting Ellen accompany them to the rural Northeast where her father's stepsister lives. They are rude and inhospitable to her during the trip and simply desert her, unaccompanied and unattended, at Thirlwall, where her Aunt Fortune is supposed to meet her. No Aunt Fortune appears; Captain Montgomery has not even written to inform her of his decision to foist Ellen off on her. When the young child is finally deposited at Miss Fortune's door, her surly Aunt is upset because Ellen took the place in the ox-drawn cart intended for flour and produce. Indeed, for the ten year old to survive her infancy in the "wide, wide world" of fragmented relationships, economic disruption and cultural commodification, she must find some way of sustaining belief in the importance of connectedness and care, which—in addition to a Bible, a work box and a writing desk—is the major legacy her mother is able to leave her.

III. RELATIONAL IDENTITY AND FEMININE CONVERSATION IN A NINETEENTH-CENTURY CONTEXT

Warner has thus set the scene for depicting Ellen's psychological and moral development in a world devoid of legitimate authority and social continuity. Ellen becomes the prototypic American girl who must on her own develop a "proper sense of self" and, in her mother's terms, "improve [herself] by every means" (31). In psychological terms, Ellen's immediate need is to maintain a sense of being cared for and connected to others, despite her feelings of abandonment and isolation. Merely to survive her losses and the overall pull toward alienation, she has to find an approach to life that satisfies relational needs while engaging in what Nancy Schnog calls the "dynamics of survival" (17). Warner depicts Ellen's success at establishing a relational identity in terms of women's legacies, first her mother's and then her mother surrogate's.

In the first instance, upon her arrival at Thirlwall, Ellen draws as close as possible to the memory of her mother, whom she loves "a great deal better" than Christ himself (38). Ellen thus sees her own identity as an extension of her mother's. "People would think strangely of *her*" (the mother), she remarks, "if I didn't behave well" (240). One of the major ways she remains connected is through letter writing and correspondence.

Significantly, before she left, Mrs. Montgomery had impressed on Ellen the importance of maintaining communication with each other. Defying her husband's stinginess, her doctor's concerns and her own attachment to her mother's ring, Mrs. Montgomery sells the latter and purchases a writing desk for Ellen. Warner—who devotes a full four pages to describing the purchase and appearance of the desk—ends by having the mother admonish the daughter to "[i]mprove yourself by every means, and especially by writing to me" (32-33). Voice and narrative, in short, are to provide "a link of communion" in spite of sundered physical bonds. Furthermore, communication through letter writing will provide Ellen her first chance to "author" herself, i.e., to create an identity through telling her own story to her mother (111-12).[4]

When both death and Aunt Fortune rob Ellen of open channels of communication with her mother, however, Ellen must find another way to survive. Warner, like Harriet Beecher Stowe and numbers of other women during this period, found in Christocentrism—a highly personal belief in Jesus—a way to survive the deaths and separations and hardships they continually faced in white middle-class society. Schnog has admirably ana-

lyzed how Warner pictures Christocentrism as a "link of communion" not only between herself and God but also between herself, her mother and the community of like-minded women. In addition to Schnog's analysis, Susan Juster's study of "conversion narratives" in America provides a valuable insight into how a Jesus-centered religious faith not only served the relational needs of white middle-class women separated from the bond of family and community but also affirmed the value of women's voice and created the concept of "transforming power" as opposed to masculine hierarchical power.

Juster illustrates how these women took their relationship with God out of the cathedrals of patriarchy and into the intimacy of heart and home. In male conversion narratives, she explains, legalistic terminology pervades: God is "king," "mediator," "tribune" or, above all, "sovereign." As she explains, "The role of lawgiver rather than that of father or friend predominates, and the metaphor of government displaces that of family" (42). In contrast, in women's conversion narratives the image of God is "portrayed . . . most often as that of a family member or friend." God is "endowed with human qualities and capable of expressing human affection and sympathy" (40-42). Sin is thus not looked upon as a violation of the law but as "a consequence of failed or flawed attachments" (41)—the same kind of flaws that Carol Gilligan and her colleagues discuss in terms of detachment and "not listening." In Juster's terms, "a tyrannical, unloving Father" is an appropriate symbol of "the anti-God of the women's spiritual drama" (44).

In a striking fashion, Warner portrays how Ellen responds to the image of God as an intimate friend and to the concept of power as transforming rather than authoritative. She dismisses the traditional image of God as the powerful lawgiver by tersely remarking that the concept of the Day of Judgment "is dreadful" (242). In addition, her desire that her father "go away" symbolically expels the patriarchal "anti-God"; Ellen and female authors of conversion narratives replace the authoritative power figure with the image of God as mother or loving family member or friend. For Ellen, one of the most important features of belief in a personal Jesus is what psychologists today call "silent communication." As described by Carl D. Schneider, silent communication acknowledges that

> The child . . . needs the company of an adult in the privacy of her world. God [or Jesus] . . . is the supreme being whose constant presence is available to the child in case of need. God knows the child internally and is a constant witness to her experiences.
>
> (202)

It is important to note here that whereas the transcendent God of traditional religion sees every sinful thought and deed, this Jesus knows every "wish and throb" of the heart. Thus in Warner's narrative, God is no longer the transcendent sovereign who *sees* into the darkest corners of self but a loving presence in this world with whom one *speaks*.

Ellen's religion privileges what women—through their diaries, conversion narratives and novels—tell us they experienced and valued, confident that such voicing of relationship and care could serve well their developmental needs. In a revealing passage, Warner emphasizes how the relational ethic of this religion spills over into social as well as spiritual life. Alice Humphreys, one of Ellen's surrogate mothers, takes her to visit an elderly lady, Mrs. Vawse. Alice is filled with loneliness because her only brother has left home to continue his education. Mrs. Vawse, her spiritual mentor, gives her religious counsel such as, "There is a friend that sticketh closer than a brother; but I never knew all that meant till I had no other friends to lean upon" (189). Alice replies: "you have comforted me already. The sound of your voice always does me good. I catch courage and patience from you I believe." Then, "drawing their chairs together, a close conversation began" (189). As this scene vividly demonstrates, informal peer relations based on shared experiences rather than power or authority mark women's approach to Christ as well as to each other. In being included in the circle of "communicants," Ellen experiences a confirmation of the value of relationship. The scene also explains how "silent communication" spills over into the public use of voice.

One is tempted to interpret Ellen's relational identity based on Christocentrism and voice as Warner's subversive female alternative to the masculine psychology of domination. As a closer reading reveals, however, Warner sees that the Christocentric model in itself does not provide the means to survive the approaching demands of adolescence and adulthood. Elizabeth Abel accurately points out that in nineteenth-century fiction an inability to make developmental transitions is often represented by the death of female protagonists who refuse "to accept an adulthood that denies profound convictions and desires" (2). Like Eva in *Uncle Tom's Cabin* and Beth in *Little Women,* Alice Humphreys in **The Wide, Wide World** cheerfully dies from consumption because it frees her from the adult social and moral conflicts which interfere with her relationship with Jesus.[5] Ellen does not die. Instead, she confronts the developmental tasks that await her in adolescence. More specifically, she begins to attempt to extend the ethos of non-authoritarian care beyond the close circle of like-minded believers. To do this, she will meet with types of indifference and even opposition that test her ethos of care and force her to assert herself in some way. From the relative silence or intimate conversation of childhood, Ellen begins to move toward the challenge of discovering how to insert her voice into the cultural dialogue as, for example, by insisting she be allowed to maintain her practice of praying despite her new guardians' opposition. Torn between the desire for a relational identity like the one she has experienced with her mother and Alice and her need to make her way in the world, Ellen is the perfect example of Abel's contention that in fiction written by women "the heroine's developmental course is more conflicted, less direct: Separation tugs against the longing for fusion . . ." (2).

The significance of Ellen in the story of women's development is not that she finds a solution to the conflict which destroys so many other fictional women. Rather it is in Warner's portrayal of how Ellen, as she moves into adolescence, constructs an identity out of the conflict between relationship and autonomy by adopting "performance" as a mediator between the two. Warner thereby provides us with a critical insight into the nature of women's identity in modern America and defines related moral issues, especially those associated with role expectations regarding women's selflessness and goodness.

IV. The Performing Self

Ellen's need for self-expression becomes the ground of battle in her second and more complicated adolescent phase of growth. At about age fourteen, Ellen gets jolted out of her known environment and moved to Scotland where proud, authoritarian relatives take control of her. Though kindly intended, her grandmother's and uncle's possessive interpretation of "care" means that Ellen must jump to meet their expectations, whether or not such action violates her sense of self or goes against her own desires. Their expectations, of course, are premised on the normative cultural script that presumes women's role is to sacrifice herself to serve the needs of others. Ellen is eager enough to extend the relational network she had developed during childhood in America to some by trying to please her relatives (and to be cherished by them), but not to any extent. The Lindsays's concept of being good, i.e. being selfless, includes their demand that she deny her own identity as well as former friends and faith. "Forget that you were American, Ellen," Mr. Lindsay declares, "you belong to me; your name [a most fundamental identity marker] is not Montgomery anymore,—it is Lindsay . . . you are my own little daughter, and must do precisely what I tell you" (510).

Lindsay's demand puts Ellen in a conflict she had not yet experienced and is all the more interesting because it involves the need for her to develop a voice suitable for a public role more expansive than the intimate conversational circles of her childhood. She feels that she herself—and not just the authority figures around her—has something to say about what is best for her. Her emerging assertiveness is directly linked to the sense of individual worth and value of relationships she developed during her relational phase. But saying that Ellen learns to speak up for herself does not mean that she speaks openly for herself. In fact, one of the ways in which Warner most clearly anticipates current developmental literature on women is in her incisive presentation of Ellen's dual voice (inner and public) and dual self (private and performing). In depicting Ellen at this phase of development, Warner cunningly foregoes the rhetoric of authenticity and self-assertion common in masculine identity narratives and, instead, introduces a new concept of identity that centers on performance (necessarily a "connected" activity) and the difficulties in finding a more public voice. As part of this concept, she probes the ways in which equivocation, disguise, mask and shame figure into women's developmental histories.

In the framework of autonomy so valued in the masculine identity quest, Ellen's course of action with the Lindsays would be clear. To borrow Jane Attanucci's useful distinction between the "me" and the "I" of self (201), she would simply resolve the tension between the "me" that wants to meet the Lindsay's social expectations and the "I" that wants to retain her own interests and values by rebelling. She would separate herself from the power and influence of guardians, journey outward to where she could discover her authentic self and then build her identity upon it. But such a course of action is both impossible and distasteful to Ellen. She wants to assert her right to a private life, it is true, but she also wants to extend the relational ethos to the Lindsays. Thus

> [s]he could not help loving her uncle; for the lips that kissed her were very kind as well as very peremptory; and if the hand that pressed her cheek was, as she felt it was, the hand of power, its touch was also exceeding fond. And as she was no more inclined to despite his will than he to permit it, the harmony between them was perfect and unbroken.
>
> (510)

What Ellen discovers in trying to have "both selves" is that she must learn to perform, which involves understanding when and when not to speak up, and even when and when not to tell the truth. The latter comes into play in one of the first episodes in which she asserts herself. Feeling oppressed by the constant surveillance of the Lindsays, she wants to escape them by going to church. She intuits correctly, however, that they will resist this "Americanism" on her part. Hence she resorts to concealment and lie: she wants to go to out, she says, because she has not "seen enough of Edinburgh yet" (531). As many child psychologists point out, equivocation can be seen as a necessary first step in identity formation. According to Michael F. Hoyt, "the child's first successful lie breaks the tyranny of the parental omniscience . . . the child begins to feel that it

has a mind of its own, a private identity unknown to its parents" (Darnton 63). In Ellen's case, the lie she uses to get to church frees her to express herself once there. Leaning "forward as much as possible to screen herself from observation" of other church goers, "she burst into an agony of tears." Warner makes it clear that this act is more one of self-expression than grief by commenting: "It was a great relief to be able to weep freely; at home she was afraid of being seen or heard or questioned; now she was alone and free, and she poured out her very heart in weeping . . ." (531-2). In other words, she has her own felt need and she expresses it. Predictably, she feels conflicted by this first evasion of truth, torn by the desire to express herself freely while at the same time fulfilling the Lindsays's expectations.

Her Christocentric religious feelings provide the stimulus for her more open assertion of her desire to be "alone and free." This desire, in turn, leads to her recognition of the need to mask desire, for the Lindsays are opposed to private religious exercises. Since she arrived at their home, she has cherished the "precious hour alone" with her Bible before the rest of the household woke up. Here the silent communication of her relational phase nurtures an inner sense of self that has to be repressed the rest of the time: "The burden of thoughts and affections gathered during the twenty-three hours was laid down in the twenty-fourth; and Ellen could meet her friends at the breakfast-table with a sunshiney face. Little they thought where her heart had been . . ." (540). However, her grandmother, with Mr. Lindsay's consent, orders Ellen to give up her morning hour on the grounds that she is "spoiling herself for life and the world by a set of dull religious notions" (542-3). For once, Ellen openly asserts herself and with great difficulty works out a compromise which enables her to regain the hour of silent communication. But her guardians' actions teach her that she must hide her religious belief from them and "be more careful of her private hour" (532).

Episodes like this dramatically illustrate the failure of twentieth-century critics to read the sentimental novel with insight into its psychological acuity. Even the most sympathetic and sensitive of them have failed to see how Warner pictures deception and concealment in episodes like the church scene as a necessary part of feminine identity development. As such she conveys a much more complex and ambiguous portrait of human psychology than that contained in the portraits of the "authentic self" common in the male *bildungsroman*. In order to be "alone and free," Ellen cannot simply light out to the territory ahead—"the world elsewhere," as Richard Poirier characterizes it. She has to construct with costume and mask a public persona behind which she can conceal her own thoughts and feelings. "Less keen observers," the narrator informs us, are convinced that "Ellen is just what she seemed, without the shadow of a cloak in anything." But in reality the Lindsays's possessiveness and control give rise to "sundry thoughts . . . which she kept to herself" (504-5). For example, when Mr. Lindsay tells her that she must forget that she was an American and a Montgomery, Ellen responds with an outward "Yes," but inwardly she says something much different: "'I shall do precisely what he tells me of course,' she said to herself . . . 'but there are some things he cannot command; nor I neither;—I am glad of that! Forget indeed!'" (510). In another noteworthy scene, Warner depicts how Ellen learns to conceal her thoughts and feelings behind the mask of feminine charm and happiness. On New Year's Eve, Ellen is sad with the memory of her absent American friends, particularly John. While helping her dress for the night's festivities, the maid overcomes Ellen's sadness by reminding her that her guardians will expect her to look happy as well as pretty:

> I beg your pardon, Miss Ellen, but you know it's your grandmother that must be satisfied, and she will have it just so . . . she won't be pleased if you carry such a soberish face down stairs,—and what will the master say! Most young ladies would be as bright as a bee . . . if you can, don't look as if it was a funeral.
>
> (557)

Ellen responds by donning the appropriate mask: "For a minute tears flowed; then they were wiped away; and the smile she gave Mr. Lindsay when she met him in the hall was not less bright than usual" (588). Ellen has thus learned that in order to maintain her sense of self—a self, incidentally, that wants to extend relational values to individuals as haughty as her aunt, Lady Keith—she must wear a mask that conceals her inner thoughts and emotions. Ironically, then, Ellen's belief that the highest form of Christian behavior is "self-denying performance" is the one that best protects and stimulates her sense of self.

But performance is not without its attendant conflicts. The need to maintain a dual voice—one for the "I" of the inner self, the other for the "me" of social role—forces Ellen into an identity confusion Warner represents in one of Ellen's few open confrontations with Mr. Lindsay. Knowing that he wants her to claim to be his daughter and yet resisting this identification, she hesitates to identify herself by the name Lindsay rather than Montgomery (524). In so doing, she knows that she has displeased her uncle/father and yet feels righteous, too. Moreover, she is acutely aware of the doubleness of her position. "Self" urges her to rebel against his demands openly: "Pride said indeed, 'do no such thing [as apologize]; don't go to making acknowledgements when you have not been in the wrong; you are not bound to humble yourself before unjust displeasure.'" Later, however, when Mr. Lindsay confronts her—"What were you thinking of last night?

What made you answer . . . in the way you did?"—then Ellen finds "her prepared speech . . . no longer possible." With averted face, she says, "I did not know what to say" (525-6).

With the "averted face" here and the many other scenes of "downcast eyes" that characterize Ellen's behavior, Warner introduces yet another dimension of conflict in the performing phase of women's development which also has been overlooked by critics, namely, the presence of shame. Seldom does Ellen decide to perform—to put on the sunshiney face—that she does not feel the tension between her outward and inward states. Because her guardians are so insistent on their version of her, she fears exposing her inner self. Hence, Warner suggests that, at the same time as Ellen feels pride in her efforts to voice at least inwardly her own sense of self, she also experiences a nagging sense that there is something shameful about that self. Ellen "cover[s] her face with her hands" in several scenes because she is so "ashamed of [her] own unworthiness" (575). In this regard, Warner illuminates one of the less explored aspects of identity development that only today is engaging the attention of contemporary psychologists. Donald L. Nathanson, for example, contends that shame is a critical indicator of growth, especially among individuals who—like Ellen—live in an environment where others are interested in them only to the extent that these individuals please them (80).

Ellen's sense of shame, in fact, anticipates the third phase of identity development—the constructing self. According to experts on identity development such as Nathanson and Léon Wurmser, the need to alleviate the sense of shame created by an inner sense of self at odds with parental (or guardian) expectation stimulates the individual to disclose the inner self—not openly but through the semiotics of performance. As Wurmser explains,

> [P]erceptual-expressive interaction is the one area that is cardinally important for the development of the core of our identity. Only in seeing and being seen, in hearing and being heard, can the matching occur between our own self-concept and the concept others have of us.
>
> (92)

What Wurmser does not point out, however, is the great difficulty such interaction poses for the female because of her commitment to a relational identity. Earlier we remarked on several scenes where Ellen begins to speak up (or cry out). The significance of her mother's insistence on the importance of communication begins to take shape as the act itself becomes more complicated. In whose voice is Ellen to speak? The subjective voice of the relational self she hopes to extend to the Lindsays? The objective voice of the role(s) she is expected to perform? Whereas in the first, relational phase, Ellen made no distinction between self and role, in this phase of performance she becomes ever more aware of the tensions that exist between them, most especially because those in power over her seek to silence self for the sake of role. Lacking as yet a strong core identity, a female adolescent like Ellen has a difficult time deciding which self to articulate. Thus, when asked her name by a French riding master, she replies, "Monsieur, je m'appelle Ellen M——." "She stopped short," Warner tells us, "in utter and blank uncertainty what to call herself; Montgomery she dared not; Lindsay stuck in her throat" (524). Montgomery is the name with which she inwardly identifies; Lindsay is the one she associates with the performing self. Understandably, for one trained in pleasing others, the performing self constantly threatens to submerge the inner self at this stage. Her uncle overhears the exchange with the riding master and insists that she identify herself as Ellen Lindsay. "Again Ellen hesitated, in great doubt how to answer, but finally, not without starting tears, said 'Oui, Monsieur'" (524-5).

Her uncle's unwillingness—perhaps inability—to acknowledge Ellen's sense of self creates an environment that makes it very difficult for her to express it at this stage of development. Her desire to be pleasing and good in order to preserve the relational self is so strong that, as Warner notes, she prefers "her plodding walk around the ring to any putting herself forward" (536). Performance thus of necessity entails disguise, i.e., equivocation rather than expression. The self speaks in two voices, the one inner, the other outer, with the latter clamoring for the lead part that reaffirms one's goodness and willingness to sacrifice self.

That Ellen becomes increasingly aware of the tensions between the two voices of inner self-expression and outward performance marks her readiness to move from performance to the constructing phase of development. In order to do this she has begun to voice her interests and to understand how the balance of power between herself and her guardians must shift sufficiently for her to enter into adult dialogue. When they do not "hear" her or let her participate in the adult dialogue, she utilizes the strategies of performance, equivocation and concealment rather than directly challenging or offending them. To understand and empathize with this type of identity construction requires us to free ourselves from traditional notions of moral development. From the perspective of the Emersonian authentic self, mask and performance are the tribute that vice pays to virtue. In the words of Richard Poirier, it is a surrender to the duplicitous "environment of costume" (30). But from Ellen's standpoint, "sin is failed or flawed attachment" (Juster 41). Thus her ethic of responsibility and care outweighs her need to extract her own private script from the cultural dialogue. Mask and performance, in

fact, help deconstruct boundaries between inner and outer, private and public selves. Nevertheless, if Ellen is to continue to grow morally and psychologically, she must cross the threshold of performance and enter a new phase in which inner and outer voices unite into a single one participating in the cultural dialogue of adulthood.

V. THE SELF: CONSTRUCTING AND DISMANTLING

The concluding chapter of **The Wide, Wide World,** left out of the original version by the publisher, carries Ellen from adolescence in Scotland to early adulthood in America. Warner initiates the transition from the performing self to the constructing self positively enough. Ellen begins to develop a single voice when, without seeking the Lindsays's permission, she draws the newly-arrived John Humphreys into her private chamber and—through her ever-copious tears—truthfully tells him the story of her life with the Lindsays. She gains even more control over her adult identity when she openly asserts that there are some things she will not allow the Lindsays to demand (previous dissent had been behind the mask, silent). In this regard, the basis for Ellen's behavior begins to change: truth counters the tendency toward equivocation and shame that the performance phase engendered. Even more significantly, once she stops crying she is able to enter into a dialogue with John as an equal rather than as a former pupil. John's comment at the end of their conversation is apt: "You are grown, Ellie . . . you are not the child I left you" (562).

The sense that Ellen is moving into the adult community through dialogue with it intensifies in the early section of this chapter. The conversation with John marked her ability to enter into discussion, expecting to be heard on her own terms as well as to listen to others on their terms. Moreover, once married to John and leaving for America, Ellen is able to secure her relationship with the Lindsays, solidifying their regard for her even while establishing a separate identity. Thus Ellen appears to be able to transcribe the relational network of her youth into the dialogic network of "the wide, wide world," and Warner seems to be providing the reader with the classic happy ending. But again, encoded into the text are a series of conflicts probing the developmental difficulties of constructing an adult identity that acknowledges the importance of a relational identity as well as the need for self-expression.

New problems begin for Ellen as soon as she returns to America and enters the house John has provided. In Scotland, the ancient aristocratic allegiance to social forms provided a stage on which Ellen could experiment with various personae and in the process shield her emerging self from the eyes of her guardians. In America, however, most social forms had been wiped away by political and economic transformations. Whereas the Lindsays expected Ellen to maintain a "sunshiney face" and fit into the social milieu, John—acting out the "rights" of the intense individualist—privatizes Ellen. For example, he virtually ignores the public parlor of their house and introduces her, instead, to a private study behind the staircase, the hall, and his own room. He has selected for her every piece of furniture, every artifact, and even the desk and writing materials. In that Ellen's adult development depends on how successfully she can participate in constructing and voicing her own identity (rather than just performing one scripted by him), her reaction reveals her inability to deal with the environment John has constructed. After showing her the room, John, as a kind of afterthought, remarks that though he thinks the room complete, "it will be for you to do . . ." any additions. Ellen's response is to "cover her face with her hands," to protest that he does too much for her, to claim she would never want to add anything, and—most revealing of all—to admit that "[y]ou make me ashamed of my own unworthiness" (575). From the standpoint of the cult of domesticity, Ellen's response might be interpreted as meeting the pious ideal of submissiveness and passivity. From Warner's psychological standpoint, however, it is simply a regression into the performing self she had learned at the Lindsays.

That Warner is indeed critical of Ellen's behavior rather than an uncritical purveyor of the domestic ethic of self-effacement becomes strikingly clear as the last chapter continues to unfold. She links John with the modern propensity to treat the outward world, including human beings, as mere signs of a deeper level of reality which must be "unmasked." To use Lionel Trilling's summary, this "unmasking trend" in modern culture rests upon

> the firmly entrenched belief that beneath the appearance of every human phenomenon there lies concealed a discrepant actuality and that intellectual, practical, and (not least) moral advantage is to be gained by forcibly bringing it to light.
>
> (142)

In this modernist fashion—one is tempted to say psychoanalytical fashion—John's "quick eye" constantly works to "see through" or unmask Ellen as a way of controlling her. Early in the novel, Warner signaled how objectionable she found such prying. When Ellen sought to discover the name of the old gentleman who had rescued her from the store clerk, her mother chided such curiosity: "It is very dishonourable to try to find out that about other people which does not concern you, and they wish to keep from you" (55). John has few scruples along this line and although Warner unmasks him for the tyrant he is—he is described by those who know him best as the "grand Turk," "the biggest gob-

bler in the yard" (316)—she concentrates on Ellen's response to his penetrating gaze. Following the scene in which she submits to John's conscription of her room, her responses become more and more regressive in developmental terms. At one and the same time, however, they also become more complex and devious. Knowing that he will "see through" the performing of roles that sustained—and enlarged—her relational world at the Lindsays, she seizes upon a more subtle kind of mask. Warner discloses the origin of this mask through one of John's "art" lessons.

After showing Ellen her private room, John leads her to "two little pictures," one of the Magdalen by Correggio and the other of the Madonna by an unnamed Renaissance artist. John tells her that the Magdalen represents "beauty that is merely physical; there is only the material outside." The Madonna, in contrast, is transparent: the picture "serves but the purpose of a clear glass through which what is behind ["the eternal model of right"] may be the more easily and perfectly seen" (578). The implications for women's identity are unmistakable. For John, or any male committed to "seeing through," the woman who insists upon her own identity is a "worldling" like the Magdalen because she draws attention to her own individuality rather than erasing it so that the observer can see "what is behind." In contrast, the true Christian woman, like the Madonna, tries to become transparent: through self-sacrifice, she erases her individual identity and physical presence so that through her will shine the "beauty which endures" (580). She thus makes herself into a transparent sign of male vision and desire.

As John continues his lesson, however, he unwittingly gives Ellen a clue to the new mask she can wear when he is trapped into admitting that transparency can be faked. This admission comes about when Ellen naively, but logically, concludes that the painter of the Madonna must have been a highly spiritual person since he was directly in contact with the divine shining through her. He "ought to have been a good man," she muses, since "he must have understood and felt so much of the good and true." John, who is as committed to factual truth as to God, hurriedly admits that this is probably not true; the transparency of the Madonna is really an illusion, an artistic convention, mastered by numerous Renaissance painters who are not, he is afraid, "much the better for it . . ." (580). In other words, transparency can be "per-formed." It is not really a window opening unto a higher spiritual reality, but an image of transparency. With this scene, therefore, Warner has effectively exposed the falseness of John's version of the feminine ideal, a version widely accepted in the culture of the period.[6]

Ellen takes this lesson to heart. Like the Renaissance artist, she can create the appearance of the transparency which John so much admires. But such artifice comes only at the price of abandoning self-expression (being the dreaded Magdalen) for the sake of pure performance. She thus responds to "his quick eye" with a "look that seemed in its self-renunciation to gather up all the past and lay it and herself with it at his feet" (576). Read with the nineteenth-century feminine ideology of submissiveness and passivity in mind, such passages show an "ideal" Ellen. Read as a developmental case study, however, such passages signal Ellen's pathetic failure to mature as she joins in the false game of transparency. As she puts it, all she has longed for is a return to "those old times" (583) and John, forgetting his praise at the Lindsays about her having grown up, remarks that "You are the same child you used to be . . ." (580). In short, she regresses to childish silence and unquestioning acceptance of authority. For example, when Ellen is puzzling about "what I ought to be and do," John shamelessly offers to tell her, or when he claims he knows her "perfectly," she remains "silent" and then moves on to a safer topic (582-3). Their "conversation," in fact, becomes a kind of picture-reading: he claims that her "eyes and mouth have their own language" (583). Thus, with Ellen's compliance, John-the-critic interprets his Madonna-like artifact. As significantly, Ellen, heeding his interpretation, appears to erase whatever script she had begun at the Lindsays in order to mirror his desire. Thus she engages in what Jane Tompkins describes as a *bildungsroman* in reverse (598) by resisting the growth pattern Warner has inscribed into the narrative.

One of the most overlooked aspects of Warner's novel is this complicity on the part of Ellen in John's repression of her identity. Contrary to critical interpretations that stress Warner's approving portrayal of selflessness, Ellen's behavior is neither innocent nor harmless. During Ellen's stay at the Lindsays, she generally resolved the tension between self-identity and social role, as we have seen, in favor of being perceived by others as good and pleasing. This implicated her in the use of a dual voice: the inner arguing for her identity and desires, the outer using, on occasion, silence, equivocation and mask. Jane Attunucci explains how the next developmental phase would ideally come about: there would be a "growing awareness of the deception inherent in the feminine role of selflessness and the destruction to self and other which that deception breeds" (207). Borrowing from Carol Gilligan, Attunucci further contends that "the critical transition for adult women is the transition from a conventional feminine role in which 'goodness' is equated with self-sacrifice, toward a truthful acknowledgment of oneself as deserving of the consideration one grants others. . . . Women, having achieved this transition from goodness to truth . . . acknowledge their interdependence as caring individuals, including themselves in the circle of those for whom they care" (207).

Ellen's willingness as John's adult wife to continue to perform, albeit wearing the grave mask of transparency (579) rather than the "sunshiney face of sociability," implicates her in the process. She allows John to transform her into a symbol. As long as Ellen agrees—and this in keeping with John's interpretation of the Madonna figure—to evade the truth of her own reactions and to silence her interpretations, then she is refusing to enter into the adult world of constructivist dialogue. In so doing, she regresses from the identity she had begun to forge in her guardian's home and sinks into silence and invisibility. At the same time, she encourages John to continue seeing the world as the signs and symbols of his own ego, thus tipping the balance of power back to an authoritative rather than transformational mode. In the scene alluded to earlier where Ellen silently acquiesces to John's bold declaration that he knows her "perfectly," Ellen not only helps sustain the psychology of mastery, but develops a sophisticated form of cover-up and equivocation. Together, then, both John and Ellen erect an edifice of moral illusion which marks the besetting limitation of American middle-class life and which seriously, perhaps fatally, handicaps the identity development of the individual right up to the present moment. The fact that Warner so effectively dismantled John's lecture on transparency makes it clear that she was not unaware of the implications of her protagonist's regression into silence.

It is this unstated awareness that enabled Warner to construct an unforgettable portrait of the conflicted course of women's psychological and moral development as they face the realities of modern culture. It is perhaps not too much to say that Warner virtually creates a modern feminine self that is as significant as Emerson's creation of the self-reliant man.

Notes

1. Nancy Schnog, for example, argues that Warner's novel directly represents "significant and real emotional and psychological experiences," and that "Ellen's tears were a valid and authentic response to traumas well-known to a large segment of Warner's nineteenth-century readership" (12). David Leverenz also sees the tears as a direct representation, but argues that they were meant to teach Ellen and Warner's readers the necessity of submitting to patriarchal domination. Schnog (Note 4, 23) and Leverenz (Note 21, 340-1) provide a helpful summary of the way critics such as Helen Waite Papashvily, Nina Baym and Jane Tompkins have dealt with the question of whether or not Warner is presenting a critique or a justification of patriarchal domination.

2. For helpful descriptions of the masculine identity quest, see Abigail Solomon-Goudeau and Elizabeth Abel. We are indebted to Abel's useful dis-

tinction between women's novels of "apprentice-ship" and "awakening." We agree with her that the apprenticeship years such as Warner covers constitute but one psychological cycle of moral and psychological growth. As we will argue elsewhere, the three-phase developmental scheme illuminates awakenings that occur in later life as well as initiations in the early years.

3. We concur with Joan Scott and others that Gilligan's ahistorical and essentialized gender model tends to ignore the political and social contexts of psychological identity. Nevertheless, the model provides a way of interpreting feminine identity that illuminates many aspects of fictional portrayals of women in nineteenth and twentieth-century novels. We are thus throughout this study indebted to the work on women's psychological development that she and her colleagues at the Center for the Study of Gender, Education and Human Development at Harvard University have provided, particularly as presented in *In a Different Voice* and *Mapping the Moral Domain*. James MacGregor Burns's distinction between transaction and transformation power is also illuminating. To him, leadership is a subset of power and can be used as a medium of exchange (transactional) or as a means of empowering others through dialogue, conflict resolution and affirmation.

4. Mark B. Tappan and Lyn Mikel Brown have demonstrated the importance of "authoring" oneself to psychological and moral development.

5. The death-prone behavior of young women continues to this day. Gilligan points out that today's startling increase in eating disorders has its roots in problems of survival and regeneration. Anorexia nervosa and bulimia frequently signal the wish not to grow up. *Mapping the Moral Domain* (156-57).

6. Karen Halttunen's study of nineteenth-century conduct manuals reveals how pervasive this feminine ideal of transparency had become in middle-class culture by mid-century. Conduct manuals, like John, urge the "true woman" to be "constitutionally transparent . . . with heart on her lips and her soul in her eyes" (57).

Works Cited

Abel, Elizabeth. Introduction. *The Voyage In: Fictions of Female Development.* Hanover: UP of New England, 1983.

Alcott, Louisa May. *Little Women.* 1868-69. New York: Modern Library, 1983.

Attunucci, Jane. "In Whose Terms: A New Perspective on Self, Role, and Relationship." *Mapping the Moral Domain: A Contribution of Women's Thinking to Psychological Theory and Education.* Ed. Carol Gilligan, Janie Victoria Ward and Jill McLean Taylor. Cambridge: Harvard UP, 1988. 201-24.

Baym, Nina. *Woman's Fiction: A Guide to Novels by and about Women in America, 1820-1870.* Ithaca: Cornell UP, 1978.

Burns, James MacGregor. *Leadership.* New York: Harper and Row, 1978.

Darnton, Nina. "Understanding Kids' Lies." *Newsweek* 2 Oct. 1989: 62-63.

Degler, Carl. *At Odds: Women and the Family in America from the Revolution to the Present.* New York: Oxford UP, 1980.

Gilligan, Carol. *In a Different Voice: Psychological Theory and Women's Development.* Cambridge: Harvard UP, 1982.

Gilligan, Carol, Janie Victoria Ward, Jill McLean Taylor, eds. *Mapping the Moral Domain: A Contribution of Women's Thinking to Psychological Theory and Education.* Cambridge: Harvard UP, 1988.

Halttunen, Karen. *Painted Women and Confidence Men: A Study of Middle-Class in America, 1830-1870.* New Haven: Yale UP, 1982.

Juster, Susan. "'In a Different Voice': Male and Female Narratives of Religious Conversion in Post-Revolutionary America." *American Quarterly* 41.1 (1989): 34-62.

Leverenz, David. *Manhood and the American Renaissance.* Ithaca: Cornell UP, 1989.

Nathanson, Donald L. Introduction. "A Mature Sense of Shame." By Carl D. Schneider. *The Many Faces of Shame.* Ed. Donald L. Nathanson. New York: Guilford, 1987. 194-96.

Poirier, Richard. *A World Elsewhere: The Place of Style in American Literature.* New York: Oxford UP, 1966.

Schneider, Carl D. "A Mature Sense of Shame." *The Many Faces of Shame.* Ed. Donald L. Nathanson. New York: Guilford, 1987. 196-213.

Schnog, Nancy. "Inside the Sentimental: The Psychological Work of *The Wide, Wide World.*" *Genders* 4 (Spring 1989): 11-25.

Scott, Joan. "Gender: A Useful Category of Historical Analysis." *American Historical Review* 91 (1986): 1053-75.

Solomon-Goudeau, Abigail. "Going Native." *Art in America* (July 1989): 118-29; 161-63.

Tappan, Mark, and Lyn Mikel Brown. "Stories Told and Lessons Learned: Toward a Narrative Approach to

Moral Development and Moral Education." *Harvard Educational Review* 59 (1989): 182-205.

Tompkins, Jane. Afterword. *The Wide, Wide World.* By Susan Warner. New York: Feminist, 1987. 584-608.

Warner, Susan. *The Wide, Wide World.* New York: Feminist, 1987.

William, Susan. "Widening the World: Susan Warner, Her Readers, and the Assumption of Authorship." *American Quarterly* 42.4 (1990): 565-86.

Wurmser, Léon. "Shame: The Veiled Companion of Narcissism." *The Many Faces of Shame*: 82-92.

Veronica Stewart (essay date spring 1994)

SOURCE: Stewart, Veronica. "The Wild Side of *The Wide, Wide World*." *Legacy* 11, no. 1 (spring 1994): 1-16.

[*In the following essay, Stewart characterizes Nancy Vawse as a subversive trickster figure in* The Wide, Wide World *who provides a vital commentary on the use of power as represented in the novel.*]

In Susan Warner's popular nineteenth-century novel, ***The Wide, Wide World,*** aged Mrs. Vawse supplies the most pertinent clue to a comprehension of her incorrigible granddaughter's role in the text when she informs us that Nancy Vawse does not return home "if there's a promise of a storm" (193). As a wild, unpredictable child of storm, aligned with nature and natural passions rather than with the dominant social conventions, Nancy escapes the cultural imperatives that require a self-willed command of all desires from the text's heroine, Ellen Montgomery. In keeping with the most articulated precepts of the "cult of domesticity," as well as with the rhetoric of religious conversion that generally accompanied it, Ellen's rite of passage to womanhood involves a complete resignation to what Jane Tompkins calls an "ethic of submission" (162). Throughout Warner's novel, Ellen's adult advisors insist upon the need for her to curb every natural sentiment. These textual restraints on Ellen's behavior also reflect Warner's compliance with the accepted feminine ethos, the "stringently delimited terms [of expression] designed to reinforce conservative cultural assumptions about woman's identity" that, according to Joanne Dobson, restricted most nineteenth-century American women writers (*Dickinson and the Strategies of Reticence* 2). Critical readings focused on Warner's biographical circumstances, however, suggest that the author only invested self in one character of ***The Wide, Wide World,*** i.e., her heroine, Ellen.[1] This limited vision of the creative process, particularly in regard to the complicated relationship between author and text, both denies the author a multi-faceted unconscious and refuses to consider the myriad ways in which that complexity may emerge in her creation.[2] If Ellen's acceptance of the cultural terms prescribed by domestic ideology implies a reticence on the author's part, then Nancy Vawse's defiant rebellion against those constructs must enact a more subversive and creative dimension of Warner's personality and work.[3]

To the extent that she resists what Mikhail Bakhtin calls the authoritative "word of the father" ("Discourse in the Novel" 342) that limits both Warner and her protagonist, Nancy's character represents an innovative, alternative stance, a female "other" who undermines and disrupts, however briefly, the novel's dominant ideological message. Through Nancy, a forceful, unembarrassed, outspoken female, Warner disturbs the stereotypical constructs of woman's identity that eventually overpower her heroine, lending a stylistic and aesthetic complexity to her narrative that might not otherwise have developed. Rather than mark a simple clash between direct opposites, with a good girl heroine struggling against her "bad-girl double" (Leverenz 189), the confrontations between Ellen and Nancy reveal several strata of dialogic, and therefore complementary, relations at work in the text. From a psychological perspective, Nancy's interactions with Ellen highlight conflicts taking place within the heroine herself. As a manifestation of Ellen's (and Warner's) unconscious and/or "unofficial" responses to external authority,[4] Nancy's presence allows a dialogue to emerge between Ellen's deliberate attempts to conform to the principles of domestic ideology and her suppressed discomfort with the total abdication of self required of her. In this respect, Nancy's role corresponds with traditional trickster figures in literature and folklore, and seems particularly compatible with Carl G. Jung's definition of the trickster as an archetypal "shadow figure" of the unconscious, as a configuration of the psyche that confounds the "ego-personality" by personifying suppressed character traits ("Trickster" 262-66).[5]

Unlike Freudianism, which Volosinov/Bakhtin condemns as an ahistorical perception of the unconscious that disengages the individual psyche from its ideological content and context,[6] Jungian psychology proposes an essentially dialogic "system of relations" among the unconscious and conscious aspects of human personality, as well as between "individual consciousness and society" ("Anima and Animus" 81, 84.)[7] Nancy's character reveals Ellen's inner conflicts at the same time that she provides the heroine with the potential to actualize her individuation process by differentiating and developing self in compensatory relation to an "other," a sociological perception of the psyche's interconnections with community that both Jung and Bakhtin posit as a required condition for self-awareness.[8] Moreover, Nancy's alignment with the unconscious (specifically the feminine unconscious) and nature is also connected to Nancy's socio-economic status, opening up the potential for yet another dialogue in Warner's text, in this case between classes. Nancy's role as a trickster figure grants her the latitude to disrupt the status quo from both a psychological and cultural standpoint. Nancy's "otherness" in *The Wide, Wide World,* then, serves as a relatively flexible dialogizing element that energizes the novel's discourse, introducing difference so urgently that her presence, almost singlehandedly, keeps Warner's text from falling into a strictly monologic, dogmatic presentation of its heroine.

A storm announces Nancy's textual birth, an omen of her turbulent opposition to some of the suffocating circumstances imposed on Ellen. Her first appearance in the novel coincides with a spell of bad weather that has imprisoned Ellen in her Aunt Fortune's kitchen for several days:

> With nothing to do, the time hanging very heavy on her hands, disappointed, unhappy, frequently irritated, Ellen became at length very ready to take offence, and nowise disposed to pass it over or smooth it away. She seldom showed this in words, it is true, but it rankled in her mind. Listless and brooding, she sat day after day, comparing the present with the past, wishing vain wishes, indulging bootless regrets, and looking upon her aunt and grandmother with an eye of more settled aversion.
>
> (114)

In direct contrast to the heroine's subdued demeanor in this scene, Nancy bursts into the text on the heels of the same tempest that both physically and mentally immobilizes Ellen. Just as we begin to think of Ellen as doomed to a static, unproductive consideration of her own pathetic condition, Nancy pierces through the monotony and diverts our attention. Her presence also diverts the heroine's attention, interrupting her prolonged, unhealthy self-absorption by introducing a stranger, an outsider who stimulates both Ellen and the reader's curiosity. Like the breeze of a fresh summer storm, Nancy sweeps away the stagnant gloom and boredom pressing down on Fortune's kitchen, Ellen's mind, and the reader's imagination.[9] It is as if Ellen's stifled frustrations spawn an untamed child of storm who, unlike Ellen, sweeps into the text equipped with the audacity to formulate her thoughts into "words."

With no fear of adult authority, without so much as a civil knock on the door to herald her arrival, Nancy marches into Aunt Fortune's kitchen, strides up to the heartless spinster who intimidates Ellen, and demands a pitcher of milk. When Ellen's aunt hesitates, Nancy coaxes the stingy woman into compliance, beguiling Fortune with sugary compliments. Her cunning deception succeeds, but Ellen, who "did not understand" the knowing "look" Nancy gave her, fails to grasp the sig-

nificance of Nancy's message—Fortune can be easily manipulated through flattery (114-15). While Ellen finds it impossible to assert herself without bursting into tears, Nancy milks language as a means to impose her will and gain power over others. At another point in the text, Nancy "scornfully" chides Ellen for not being able to discern whether her "tongue is [her] own or somebody's else" (119). Warner might well have posed this question to herself. Given the extent to which nineteenth-century women authors were expected to compose fiction that submitted to culturally determined definitions of woman's identity, Warner might wonder whether or not her "tongue" (her writing) was her "own or somebody's else." Warner circumvents that problem through Nancy, who functions outside of the cultural terms that restrict Ellen's prerogative to verbalize dissatisfaction without experiencing punishment or guilt.[10] Though Warner observes the narrative and ideological conventions imposed upon her by allowing several characters in the text to condemn Nancy's behavior and by developing Ellen as a saintly, obedient woman, she nonetheless creates in Nancy a female character who permits her some latitude to experiment with aesthetic freedom and narrative play.

Nancy comes into the narrative already empowered with an authority based primarily on her command of details about others. During Miss Fortune's canning bee, for example, Nancy provides information and opinions about the guests from a standpoint that seems to exceed her years. Her comprehensive social commentary ranges from commonplace gossip to shrewd condemnations of specific lifestyles and temperaments (250-51). Nancy's peculiar talent lies in her exceptional powers of observation, a skill she shares with her author-creator, whose realistic descriptions in *The Wide, Wide World* provide a wealth of information for scholars to draw on as they try to reconstruct the everyday life and concerns of the period.[11] Nancy displays a knack for sifting through her immediate environment, screening out superfluous information, and compiling the essential data required to exist on the margins of society, all capacities for self-reliance that Ellen never develops. Functioning as a centrifugal, subversive force, Nancy seems connected with Warner's artistic impulses, with that part of self engaged in a novelistic discourse that resists, whether consciously or unconsciously, sanctioned behaviors for women in the society.

Warner's creative investment in Nancy's character emerges most clearly during Nancy's first encounter with Ellen in Fortune's kitchen. While Miss Fortune fills Nancy's pitcher with milk, the two girls use the opportunity to study each other:

> Ellen's gaze was modest enough, though it showed a great deal of interest in the new object [Nancy]; but the broad, searching stare of the other seemed intended to

take in all there was of Ellen from her head to her feet, and keep it, and find out what sort of a creature she was at once. Ellen almost shrank from the bold black eyes, but they never wavered, till Miss Fortune's voice broke the spell.

(115)

Nancy's intense desire to study Ellen mirrors the kind of posturing an author might assume in the creative function of imagining her character. Her probing, consuming gaze during this scene marks a point in the narrative where the author, as creator, retreats from within her heroine and contemplates her through the eyes of another. As Bakhtin suggests, "*aesthetic* form" emerges in the text "from within the *other*," from the "author's *creative* reaction to the hero[ine] and [her] life" ("Author and Hero" 90, original italics). Until Nancy appears in the text, the reader's attention has been riveted on Ellen Montgomery's suffering, an indication, perhaps, of the author's own preoccupation with developing her heroine. Warner's aesthetic impulse, her "creative reaction" to her own submissive, naive heroine generates Nancy, who dwells somewhere outside the cultural standards that demand Ellen's humble acceptance of intolerable conditions. Nancy's presence gives Warner as creator a new authorial stance apart from her heroine, and this aesthetic distance from her subject enables her to "take in all there was of Ellen," i.e., to break out of the quasi-autobiographical fusion with her subject that has, at least in part, conveyed Ellen to such a narrative *cul-de-sac* in Fortune's kitchen.[12]

Through Nancy's spellbinding "bold black eyes," Warner as author takes a long "searching stare" at the demure "creature" she is in the process of creating, and her protagonist can hardly bear up under such intense scrutiny. Nancy's creative force disrupts the ideologies that produce Ellen, creating new values, including that of speaking one's own mind, of being true to oneself.[13] "Brooding" quietly in Aunt Fortune's kitchen, Ellen represses her tempestuous passions, while Nancy, as well as Warner's narrative as a whole, thrives on them. Resistance against androcentric social conventions, particularly the gender-determined split between public and private spheres, works as a propelling force in Warner's fiction; a fundamental discontent with family structure as it was articulated in domestic conduct manuals initiates the narrative plot, whisking Ellen Montgomery away from her natural parents and launching her out into *The Wide, Wide World*.[14] To rewrite her grandmother's pronouncement, Nancy, the barometer of Warner's creative power, materializes whenever "there's a promise of a storm," whenever an opportunity appears to subvert either the heroine's conservative worldview or the cultural terms used to form Ellen's character.

Nancy seems drawn to whirlwinds of psychic turbulence in the text. Not surprisingly, then, her second appearance follows Ellen's furious overreaction to Mr. Van Brunt's harmless request for a kiss, her subsequent "storm of anger" against Aunt Fortune, and her guilt over the prospect that such uncontrolled rage must displease Jesus (116-17). Nancy's propensity for showing up on the scene whenever Ellen tries to contain her passions, or whenever she experiences doubts about her salvation as an elect saint, suggests that Nancy, as trickster, works in a "complementary relation to the 'saint'" (Jung, "Trickster" 256), compensating for Ellen's imbalances on the conscious level. Neither Nancy nor Ellen fit neatly into polar oppositions; they each reveal aspects of the "other" at various places in the text. Nancy relieves the built-up pressure of Ellen's submerged desires, a consequence of the heroine's insufferably restrictive conditions. At the same time, Ellen's eventual identity as an elect saint derives in part from her response to Nancy, that is to say, from the sundry methods Ellen uses to control, through denial or suppression, her own desires whenever they attain what seems to be an autonomous expression through Nancy.

In their second encounter, Nancy tempts Ellen away from home to ramble freely about the countryside, a concrete realization of Ellen's own desire to escape confinement. Throughout their forbidden adventure, the text cloaks Nancy in an aura of mystery, avoiding any mention of her name and referring to her instead as "she of the black eyes," "companion," "other," and "stranger." All these nameless identities assigned to Nancy arouse suspicion about her, creating an unsettling apprehension about possible impending and ominous consequences of the difference she embodies. Like a cautious animal stalking its prey or an ethereal, and perhaps demonic, supernatural being materializing out of thin air, this nameless entity sneaks up behind Ellen so well that the heroine hears no "footsteps drawing near," remaining completely unaware of Nancy's presence until "a voice spoke almost in her ears" (117-21).[15] Nancy's "voice," which at first seems to emanate from within Ellen's own mind, poses a series of probing questions to Ellen, all designed specifically to elicit a confession of her hatred for Aunt Fortune (118). This disconcerting interrogation leaves the heroine feeling ill at ease because Nancy's queries verbalize Ellen's most hidden thoughts, another instance of Nancy's disturbing knowledge of other characters in the text. The reader knows that Ellen has already privately expressed the fear that she might "get to hate" Fortune (117), that Nancy's questions merely reiterate Ellen's own dark speculations about her unsatisfactory relationship with her aunt. In this minor altercation with Nancy, however, she refuses to acknowledge these feelings as her own, choosing instead to condemn Nancy for this improper "kind of talk" (119). Because Ellen denies her own emotions, because she repudiates, on a conscious level, her own repressed desire to rebel against the restrictions placed on her by authority figures, Nancy retains the power to afflict her.

When articulating Ellen's resistance to authority fails to raise the heroine's consciousness, Nancy tries to remove Ellen physically from the cultural environment that obstructs an apprehension of her inner self. With all the "wildness, wantonness, and irresponsibility of paganism" that Jung assigns to trickster figures ("Trickster" 258), Nancy lures Ellen into an alternate reality, an enchanting region of nature where "every thing," every remembrance of suffering past and present can be "forgotten in delight." Like a "bird out of a cage," Ellen travels with her shadow figure into the dark recesses of her unconscious, a deeply wooded area where the terrain becomes increasingly difficult for the dainty city girl to navigate: "Gradually the ground became more broken, sinking rapidly from the side of the path, and rising again in a steep bank on the other side of a narrow dell." They descend the deep embankment to a charming brook, arriving at a "wild little place" where Ellen can "scarcely contain herself at the magnificence" of the scene (118-22). Free from the restrictive atmosphere inherent to the domestic sphere, liberated from chores, rules, and obligations, Ellen experiences, for the first and last time, an unchecked, uninhibited enjoyment of nature's beauty:

> Often by the side of the stream there was no footing at all. . . . It was ticklish work getting along over these stones; now tottering on an unsteady one; now slipping on a wet one; and every now and then making huge leaps from rock to rock. . . . But they laughed at the danger; sprang on in great glee, delighted with the exercise and fun; didn't stay long enough anywhere to lose their balance, and enjoyed themselves amazingly. There was many a hair-breadth escape; many an *almost* sousing; but that made it all the more lively.
>
> (122-23, original italics)

Through a precarious journey along the intricate, labyrinthine path of the winding brook, with its "foam[ing] and fum[ing] and frett[ing]" waters, its "noisy and lively" waterfalls, and its "tiny cascades" (122-23), Ellen experiences a momentary harmony with Nancy and with nature, which frees her to experience spontaneous, childlike pleasure with herself and her environment.[16]

In Warner's text, Nancy substitutes for Ellen's unconscious nature, enticing the heroine to follow the twisting, non-linear (and therefore deviant), creative stream of her imagination. Ellen's sojourn with her stormy, dark companion into the woods of her shadowy unconscious elicits a primordial, animalistic, instinctive joy. Nancy, as trickster, specifically as Ellen's suppressed nature, reveals the heroine's internalized predisposition to escape oppressive social conventions by tapping a

sense of connection with nature's beauty. Ellen frequently imagines the possibility of alleviating her problems through a relation with the earth. During a moment of extreme anguish, for example, she "cast[s] herself down upon the moss, lying full length upon the cold ground, which seemed to her childish fancy the best friend she had left" (148). In another instance, a walk in the woods removes all memory of "Miss Fortune and all in the world that was disagreeable" (337). However, Nancy, as a representation of unconscious nature, of nature as it stands indifferent and detached from phallogocentric concepts in the novel, also has it in her power to disrupt idealistic illusions about nature's supposed sympathy with human events, to unleash destructive forces capable of unsettling any sense of order or security Ellen might achieve.

This subversive element of Nancy's character both figuratively and literally throws Ellen off balance at the conclusion of their excursion along the meandering brook. Although Nancy unlocks the portal to the imaginative realm and instigates a burst of playful, creative energy in the text, as trickster she also releases a scurrilous force that seeks amusement through atrocious deeds, through a "fondness for sly jokes and malicious pranks" (Jung, "Trickster" 255). Ellen falls victim to one of these tricks when Nancy urges her to cross the water by walking barefoot on a log:

> Slowly and fearfully, and with as much care as possible, she set step by step upon the slippery log. Already half of the danger was passed, when, reaching forward to grasp Nancy's out-stretched hand, she missed it,—*perhaps* that was Nancy's fault—poor Ellen lost her balance and went in head foremost. The water was deep enough to cover her completely as she lay, though not enough to prevent her getting up again.
>
> (125, original italics)

Jung argues that "annoying accidents," events we generally attribute to "defects of the conscious personality," actually originate in the unconscious realm of the shadow ("Trickster" 262). Just as Ellen begins to think she will make a successful crossing, Nancy withdraws her hand. In a sense, then, Warner, as author, also withdraws her hand, permitting her heroine to fall back into guilt for her disobedient actions, reminding her of the reprisals she will likely suffer at the hand of Aunt Fortune. Ellen's "accidental" slip into the water dampens her spirits, effectively dousing any fantasies Ellen might have entertained of a prolonged escape from social responsibilities through a puerile, romantic fusion with idyllic nature.

Warner's text also plunges the reader into the harsh social realities of the communities depicted in *The Wide, Wide World,* refusing to validate any sentimental illusions about the world. The politics of Nancy's psychological and aesthetic trickster role in the narrative center on a power struggle between classes. Nancy's coarse language, crude syntax, and rough manners denote a poor education, and her unfamiliarity with the kind of plush carpeting that Ellen compares to soft moss affirms Nancy's lower-class status (120-21).[17] Her position as a poverty-stricken, uneducated, rustic girl places Nancy's affiliation with nature in a particular historical framework, within a culturally determined understanding of nature's role as it finds its expression in social, religious, and philosophical constructs. The different ways in which Nancy and Ellen respond to nature during their journey into the woods provide a condensed version of the larger cultural issues that surround and submerge nature throughout the text. Specifically, the tensions between Nancy and Ellen uncover the novel's philosophical bias for polished, urbane, genteel learning over unaffected connectedness with nature. Ellen's enthusiasm about nature's beauty, for example, animates her longing to penetrate and master all of nature's secrets. She wants, as she informs Mr. Van Brunt elsewhere in the text, to "know the reason" for everything that occurs in nature (132), so she questions Nancy about the strange vegetation she finds growing on rocks and about the migratory habits of ducks. Her urge to exact some "truth" from nature, her penchant for possessing, cataloguing, and demystifying nature completely baffles Nancy (120).[18] Nancy resists this quantifying and hence authoritative discourse on nature.[19] On one textual level, Nancy's lower-class status excludes her from this learned discourse, but, beyond this, her own instinctive affinity with the indiscriminate, catastrophic force of storms precludes any desire to impose logical, unalterable natural laws on a naturally capricious, transient, and mutable universe.

Ironically, Nancy's alignment with unconscious nature as a trickster figure, the very source for her power and freedom in the text, simultaneously assures her continued exclusion from any economic, religious, or social power structures. The threat she represents to cultural order amounts to nothing less than the menace of an unmanageable, illiterate, poor female who fits both Jung's description of the trickster in its iconoclastic role ("Trickster" 255) and Bakhtin's delineation of carnival liberation from "established order" (*Rabelais and His World* 10). Julia Kristeva expands both of these definitions by aligning the carnivalesque with her concept of an essentially feminine semiotic.[20] Nancy's carnivalesque discourse shares the repressed (but not necessarily maternal) feminine drives of Kristeva's semiotic. Additionally, as trickster, Nancy "breaks through the laws of a language censored by grammar and semantics," while simultaneously voicing a "social and political protest" (Kristeva, *Desire* 65). However, while Nancy personifies feminine drives repressed by the symbolic in a capitalistic society, her connection with nature already situates her on the margins of the socially symbolic system, limiting her ability to make any per-

manent change within it.[21] In Warner's text, Nancy's alignment with unconscious feminine nature reduces her subversive antics to fleeting, apparently ineffective disturbances of authoritative discourse. From the perspective of the creative process, however, these disturbances are not in vain. The ongoing dialogue between Nancy's unconscious (yet ideologically motivated) semiotic and Ellen's socially symbolic discourse generates a significant subversion of authoritative power in Warner's novel.

Despite the transient aspects of her struggle for power in *The Wide, Wide World,* Nancy expends most of her energy on efforts to penetrate the status quo, to bring her disruptive natural storms to bear on domestic ideology. She makes repeated attempts to infiltrate the inner space of Ellen's foster home, brazenly barging into aunt Fortune's kitchen, rudely pressing her face against Fortune's windowpanes to eavesdrop on private conversations (231), and impudently arriving at Fortune's bee despite the fact that she has been expressly forbidden to attend (247). She even threatens to smuggle herself into Ellen's bedroom when least expected by entering through the window at night (209-10), a terrifying prospect for Ellen. Her most successful intrusion into Ellen's domestic space, however, occurs while the heroine is in a weakened and vulnerable condition, recovering from a prolonged illness. Still needing Ellen's unconscious permission to materialize, Nancy invades Ellen's room in response to the bedridden heroine's repressed desire for a visitor:

> After two weeks Ellen began to mend, and then she became exceedingly weary of being alone and shut up to her room. It was a pleasure to have her Bible and hymnbook lying upon the bed, and a great comfort when she was able to look at a few words; but that was not very often, and she longed to see somebody, and hear something besides her aunt's dry questions and answers.
>
> (207)

Ellen's unspoken discontent with the comfort to be received from God's Word in the Bible, the most valued authoritative word in Warner's text, summons the "other," the trickster, into the narrative again.

Under the pretense of assuming Fortune's place as Ellen's nurse, Nancy wrecks Ellen's tidy sick room, haphazardly rummaging through the heroine's personal belongings for ways to create havoc in Ellen's orderly existence:

> Nancy was in great glee; with something of the same spirit of mischief that a cat shows when she has a captured mouse at the end of her paws. While the gruel was heating she spun round the room in quest of amusement; and her sudden jerks and flings from one place and thing to another had so much of lawlessness that Ellen was in perpetual terror as to what she might take it into her head to do next.
>
> (208)

Nancy's chaotic "lawlessness" does no permanent damage to either Ellen or her possessions, but it does break apart several stereotypical notions about female identity propagated by domestic ideology. Nancy, an earthy creature linked with the feminine unconscious, demonstrates no natural instinct for mothering.[22] Instead, she makes a cruel mockery of nursing, transforming proper sickroom deportment into sadistic burlesque. After binding her weak victim into bed by tucking sheets all around her, Nancy laughs as she tries to force-feed Ellen some poorly prepared gruel. With no sign of remorse, she continues her perverse laughter when Ellen bursts into tears, and proceeds to torment the sick girl further by tickling Ellen until she writhes hysterically (211-12).

The sheer madness and collapse of order that Nancy triggers, however, reflects more than concern with mothering as a gender-determined function; it embraces class struggle as well.[23] As the granddaughter of a poor, unemployed immigrant widow, Nancy probably does not own anything like the array of fine dresses, ruffles, hoods, and capes she discovers in Ellen's trunk, nor would she ever be likely to attain such niceties. By daring to handle, inspect, and criticize every piece of Ellen's clothing, and then carelessly toss each precious item in a heap on the floor (210-11), Nancy's chthonic nature violates Ellen's privacy, profanes property laws, challenges boundaries, and defies materialistic value systems.

The trickster figure in Warner's text thus presents a formidable danger to an unjust economic hierarchy, to a society that requires humility, patience, and obedience from the poor to maintain class distinctions. Moreover, her presence jeopardizes Warner's ability to write a text that stays neatly within the accepted margins of literature written by women in nineteenth-century America. The confrontations between Ellen and Nancy, whether we formulate their conflicts in psychological, politically aesthetic, or historical terms, represent an ongoing struggle in Warner's text between novel and society, between that which could be called novelistic (the creative, heterogeneous, revolutionary) and sanctioned social conventions. Nancy's nature must be subdued in the text for Warner to write an acceptable woman's novel, for her to privilege Ellen's traditional religious conversion to sainthood and her socialization as a woman/mother.

Ostensibly, Nancy's assimilation into the community transpires because of Ellen's charity. Despite the ill treatment she receives at Nancy's hands, Ellen wins permission for Nancy to attend the bee, and this one generous act supposedly tames Nancy's rebellious spirit (248-49). Eventually, Nancy enters Fortune's home with her permission, though not as daughter, but as hired help. This new position uproots Nancy from her ties with nature, transplanting her, rather abruptly, indoors.

On the lowest rung of the domestic ladder, as a slave to the everyday drudge work involved with keeping house, Nancy obviously loses her potential to destabilize social norms. She does commit one crucial last rebellious act, however, robbing her employer of the letters Aunt Fortune had kept from Ellen. Stealing Mrs. Montgomery's letters to her daughter, Nancy uses her apron to carry them to their rightful owner, tucking the repressed communications of a silenced (because deceased) woman into the folds of the garment that most emphatically signifies her own diminished authority in the text. As Ellen surrenders herself gradually to the male logos, Nancy's power, the force of the creative, feminine unconscious, begins to recede, but it does not disappear from the text completely.

Ellen's struggle with the aspects of her unconscious that most conflict with definitions of woman conceived to please man continues in more subtle ways throughout the text. The male character Ellen most wants to please, who she must, in fact, please if she aspires to be his wife, is John Humphreys, a virile young man studying for the ministry. Humphreys' relationship with Ellen takes many shapes: he becomes Ellen's adopted brother, her religious mentor, and, eventually, her husband. Throughout the novel, however, Humphreys articulates the authoritative word that both discounts Nancy and overwhelms Ellen. He demands that Ellen "read no novels" (564). This tyranny over her reading signifies the extent to which the creative dialogic forces of novelistic discourse threaten to dismantle the monophonic, authoritative word of histories and religious texts, which John uses to train Ellen into submission. His sullen desire for the apocalyptic end of the world as foretold in Revelation places him in direct opposition to nature and all things natural. With little or no faith in humankind's capacity to amend its sinful ways, Humphreys longs morbidly for the Last Judgment, when the "heavens shall be wrapped together as a scroll," when they "shall vanish away like smoke, and the earth shall wax old like a garment;—and it and all the works that are therein shall be burned up" (312). Because of her connection with nature and the creative impulses of novelistic discourse, Nancy's personification of a feminine unconscious shares the earth's fate in John's religious philosophy and Warner's text.

Ellen must wrap up all desire to enjoy nature, must incinerate her natural instincts, and shift to a delight in the word of God as it is imparted and interpreted by John. As Humphreys guides Ellen through a study of John Bunyan's *Pilgrim's Progress,* dominating her reading of the text so thoroughly that he refuses her permission to pick the book up without him, that transition begins. In her biographical account of her sister, Anna Warner notes that their father conducted "evening readings" of literature to "furnish safe fuel for [Susan's] imagination," refusing either of his daughters permission "to touch the work then in hand" (90). Warner, as author-creator, unconsciously relates Ellen's religious conversion, which occurs as a direct result of John's reading, with a suffocating patriarchal control over literature that suppresses woman's creative imagination. From the very first session John's readings from *Pilgrim's Progress* have a startling effect on Ellen:

> Her attention was nailed; the listless, careless mood in which she sat down was changed for one of rapt delight; she devoured every word that fell from the reader's lips; indeed they were given their fullest effect by a very fine voice and singularly fine reading.
>
> (351)

Warner emphasizes the ravenous condition of Ellen's spiritual being with this graphic image of the young girl gorging herself on the life-giving nourishment of Bunyan's allegory as it flows from John's lips. As the chief provider of her famished soul, John becomes the nurturing parent of Ellen's rebirth, the male mother of her spirit. He plays a key role in Ellen's spiritual conversion, acting as intermediary between her and God. The consequences of Ellen's complete submission to John's symbolic texts do not, however, become fully evident until the end of Warner's novel.

In her final and originally suppressed chapter, Warner divides the two discourses that have worked in complementary relationship throughout the novel into two separate pictures. Ellen and John Humphreys, now newly wed, compare two pieces of art: a "fine copy of Correggio's recumbent Magdalen" and a picture of the Madonna and Child (578). The narrative frames, and therefore contains, the seductive, capricious, and potentially destructive components of the feminine unconscious in the picture of Magdalen. The picture of the Madonna and Child, however, indicates that Ellen's function as wife will also be contained, fixed within the limited framework of the paternal law that, as Judith Butler notes, requires women to be portrayed primarily through their maternal roles ("Body Politics" 175). In response to her own first impulse, Ellen admires the engraving of the prostitute, Magdalen, for its "perfect graceful repose," for its depiction of woman experiencing the "entire, natural abandonment of every limb." Her critique of the picture gives voice to the wholesome desire of a new bride for a natural, total abandonment to physical pleasures, for sexual fulfillment void of embarrassingly awkward or artificial postures. Humphreys, on the other hand, favors the Virgin Mother and Jesus for its "grave maternal dignity and love," for its "moral beauty" (578). The picture he admires does not even include woman's body, showing only the heads of mother and child. As his wife, Ellen's submission to John requires more than a renunciation of her own physical pleasure, a surrender of her body to his pleasures. She must also substitute his limited construct of

woman as mother in place of natural female sexuality. Ellen's defense of the Magdalen engraving signifies the last gasp of feminine nature in Warner's text, the last gasp of Warner's dialogic creativity; Humphreys' victory in this scene, on the other hand, marks the end of Ellen's unconscious desires and, by extension, the end of Warner's novel.

Notes

1. As several critics point out, Warner's life parallels many of the circumstances she creates for Ellen in the novel. In her afterword to *The Wide, Wide World,* Jane Tompkins makes unmediated comparisons between Susan Warner's biography and Ellen Montgomery's fictional life: "The endlessly demanding attempt to achieve self-sacrifice that is the principle of Ellen's education in *The Wide, Wide World* also governed Susan Warner's life" (586). In another such reference to Warner's life, David Leverenz points out similarities between Ellen's relationship with "her God and her father" and Warner's own "intensity of submission" to these patriarchal figures (189). Neither of these perspectives permits Warner a repressed unconscious with the potential to rebel against authority. Mikhail M. Bakhtin's early work on narrative interrelationships, "Author and Hero in Aesthetic Activity," stresses that arguments that confuse the "author-creator (a constituent in a work) with the author-person (a constituent in the ethical, social event of life)" fail to comprehend the "creative principle in the author's relationship to a hero[ine]" (10).

2. As Bakhtin points out, the "artist's struggle to achieve a determinate and stable image of the hero[ine] is to a considerable extent a struggle within [her]self ("Author and Hero" 6). I do not, by any means, wish to suggest that we can psychoanalyze Susan Warner, the person, through a study of the behaviors exhibited by Nancy, Ellen, or any of the other characters in the text. On the contrary, I maintain, with Bakhtin, that a "work's author is present only in the whole of the work, not in one separate aspect of this whole, and least of all in content that is severed from the whole" (*Speech Genres* 160). In novelistic discourse "all characters and their speech are objects of an authorial attitude" and "dialogic relations are possible between them" (*Speech Genres* 116). However, I do wish to emphasize Warner's creative investment in Nancy, a point that has heretofore gone unrecognized in criticism, and I am formulating Warner's relation with both Nancy and Ellen as a dialogic element in the text.

3. Although Nancy is the focus of this study, her character is not the only manifestation of uncon-

scious subversion in *The Wide, Wide World.* See Dobson's essay, "The Hidden Hand: Subversion of Cultural Ideology in Three Mid-Nineteenth-Century American Women's Novels," for an exploration of the ways in which tyrannical authority figures in Warner's text also undercut the feminine ethos underlying Ellen's self-sacrifice.

4. In his Marxist critique of Freudianism as a bourgeois psychology, Bakhtin refers to Freud's delineation of the unconscious as the *"unofficial conscious"* (*Freudianism: A Critical Sketch* 3, original italics), a remark that suggests ideological motivation governing the unapproved, and therefore suppressed contents of the psyche.

5. In *Woman's Fiction*, Nina Baym claims that a "Jungian perspective" explains the typical heroine's development in women's fiction during the nineteenth century, since most of the heroines of these tales must negotiate a movement from being an "undifferentiated child through the trials of adolescence into the individuation of sound adulthood" (12). Baym does not, however, delineate any specific Jungian function of unconscious subversion at work in her section on *The Wide, Wide World,* nor does she discuss Nancy Vawse's role in Ellen's differentiation process (140-50).

6. In their book *Mikhail Bakhtin,* Katerina Clark and Michael Holquist argue for Bakhtin as the "sole author" of *Freudianism: A Critical Sketch* (147). However, the text remains a disputed work since it was originally published under V. N. Volosinov's name, but we can claim with certainty that Bakhtin contributed heavily to this piece. See both the foreword and the translator's introduction to I. R. Titunik's translation of the text.

7. Although Bakhtin never mentions Jung by name, his last "Notes Made in 1970-71" begin to sketch out a way to incorporate Jung's concept of the collective unconscious into dialogics. In a short, fragmented passage, Bakhtin argues that our connectedness with the past, with the "collective unconscious," is "fixed in the memories of languages, genres, and rituals" (*Speech Genres* 144). The note suggests that Bakhtin was preparing to argue for the collective unconscious as a learned cultural product rather than a psychic legacy genetically inherited by each individual. In that case, the suppression of any portion of the collective memories into the "unconscious" would be informed by an individual's dialogic relation to the culture at large. Novelistic discourse, were we to push his obviously incomplete thoughts on the subject even further, transmits what Jungians presently term the collective unconscious.

8. In *Freudianism,* Bakhtin suggests that any "motivation of one's behavior, any instance of self awareness . . . is an act of gauging oneself against some social norm. . . . In becoming aware of myself, I attempt to look at myself, as it were, through the eyes of another person . . . (86-87). Similarly, in his "Anima and Animus" piece, Jung argues that "for the purpose of individuation, or self-realization, it is essential for a [wo]man to distinguish between what [s]he is and how [s]he appears to [her]self and to others" (84).

9. My argument is partially in response to David Leverenz's assertion in *Manhood and the American Renaissance* that "we focus on Ellen alone" throughout the text (184).

10. Ellen's character seems to operate as a locus for what Bakhtin calls the "centripetal forces of language," i.e., her silent submission functions as an attempt toward "ideological unification and centralization," a desire, in this specific social situation, to ignore the heteroglossia that shapes domestic ideology. Nancy, on the other hand, brings "centrifugal" forces to bear in Warner's text, which break down any illusion of social or historical unity, emphasizing the diverse cultural stratifications permeating domestic ideology ("Discourse in the Novel" 270-72). Neither force can be privileged over the other since it is through the dialogic struggle between them that meaning emerges.

11. See Glenna Matthew's references to recipes and canning techniques in *The Wide, Wide World* as an example of Warner's close attention to minute details (*"Just a Housewife"* 15-17). In "The Hidden Hand," Dobson points out that Warner's graphic writing style creates a "thoroughly realized New England farming community and lively believable minor characters" (229).

12. In "Author and Hero in Aesthetic Activity," Bakhtin covers this problem rather thoroughly: "If there is only one unitary and unique participant, there can be no *aesthetic* event. An absolute consciousness, a consciousness that has nothing transgredient to itself, nothing situated outside itself and capable of delimiting it from outside—such a consciousness cannot be 'aestheticized'. . . . An aesthetic event can take place only when there are two participants present; it presupposes two non-coinciding consciousnesses" (22).

13. Bakhtin suggests that "aesthetic form cannot be founded and validated from within the hero[ine], out of [her] own directedness to objects and meaning, i.e., on the basis of that which has validity only for [her] own lived life." Novelistic discourse, then, can only occur when the author "produces values that are transgredient in principle to the hero[ine] and [her] life." To accomplish this

end, Bakhtin argues that the author "must become another in relation to [her]self, must look at [her]self through the eyes of another" ("Author and Hero" 90, 15).

14. Since both Ellen's father and mother fail in their cultural assignments, Warner's text emphasizes the weaknesses, hypocrisies, and incongruities embedded within such diametrically opposed constructs. In *Woman's Fiction,* Baym suggests that "surrogate family" arrangements in nineteenth-century women's writing, like Ellen's adoption into the Humphreys' family circle in Warner's text, represents "allegiance to the family ideal at the same time that [they] embod[y] a bitter criticism against families as the characters (and their authors) have really known them" (149). In Bakhtin's terms, such conflicts reveal dialogic tensions between centripetal and centrifugal forces involved in personal, cultural, and textual formation.

15. These mysterious depictions of Nancy heighten a sense that she could be something either more or less than human, that she could be "both sub-human and super-human, a bestial and divine being," as Jung says of the trickster (263). Such heterogeneous features strengthen Nancy's capacity as a dialogizing element in the text.

16. In her biography of her sister, Anna Warner points out that Susan suffered from a "nervous imagination" about coming to harm or falling, which kept her from "climbing hay mows, mounting ladders, swinging, racing" and rambling, as Anna did, along the "brook" near their home (123-25). In this scene, Ellen participates in an activity that Susan Warner avoided because of unconscious fears, marking a textual instance where the author-creator's imagination runs wild in ways that Warner, as author-person, seems not to have done.

17. The derogatory remark Ellen makes about the size and shape of Nancy's nose also implies a racial bigotry against non-English immigrants (124).

18. Ellen shares this desire to control nature through knowledge with Alice Humphreys, the devout minister's daughter who initially undertakes responsibility for Ellen's formal education. Alice owns a cabinet of curiosities that contains, among other items, "dead moths," "empty beetle-skins," and "butterflies' wings" (163), strong evidence of her dominance over nature. Alice's scientific knowledge of nature's laws, however, neither checks her love for nature's beauty, nor contradicts her religious tenets. Quite the contrary, this knowledge reinforces her competence as a rational, intelligent, and educated person in the text, lending further credibility to her religious teachings.

19. Michel Foucault identifies the "true discourse" of phallogocentric language as that which seeks to "base itself in nature" by sketching "out a schema of possible, observable, measurable and classifiable objects" ("The Discourse on Language" 218-19).

20. Kristeva defines the feminine semiotic as a "fragmentary" phenomenon that has been "kept in the background" of the "history of signifying systems," as an event that both "underscore[s] the limits of socially useful discourse" while it "attest[s] to what it represses" (*Revolution* 16), a description that seems to correspond perfectly with Nancy's dialogic role in Warner's text.

21. In her critique of Kristeva, Judith Butler notes that the "subversive effects" of Kristeva's concept of the semiotic never amount to "more than a temporary and futile disruption of the hegemony of the paternal law" ("The Body Politics of Julia Kristeva" 164). Diane Price Herndl stresses a related concern about the efficacy of polyphonic feminist discourses when she suggests that the "space which has been opened for feminist criticism [in academic institutions] may be merely a carnival provided by institutional authority" ("The Dilemmas of a Feminine Dialogics" 20). However, that which is temporary need not be futile, and disruptive discourse, when considered in its historically grounded dialogical function, cannot help but have some effect on authoritative discourse. In this specific historical event, i.e., in the production of *The Wide, Wide World,* Nancy's disruptive force, however fleeting it may be, provides readers with a different perspective on the ideologies Warner's text seems to be reinforcing through Ellen.

22. Nancy Vawse is not the only female in the text who "fails" at mothering. Aunt Fortune, for example, performs every duty of nursing for Ellen efficiently, yet leaves out love, and more important for Warner's religious agenda, spiritual comfort. Proper mothering does not rely on gender identity in *The Wide, Wide World.* Rather than a natural instinct, mothering is an art one learns, and that responsibility can only be performed well by a regenerate woman married to a converted man, an ideal condition that Warner's text only hints at in the final suppressed chapter.

23. Leverenz suggests that "Ellen's kindnesses to Nancy . . . bear a cloying touch of noblesse oblige" (189); her fear of Nancy, however, also emanates from Ellen's higher position on the social and economic ladder.

Works Cited

Bakhtin, M. M. "Author and Hero in Aesthetic Activity." *Art and Answerability: Early Philosophical Essays.* Ed. Michael Holquist and Vadim Liapunov. Trans. Vadim Liapunov. Austin: U of Texas P, 1990. 4-276.

———. "Discourse in the Novel." *The Dialogic Imagination: Four Essays.* Ed. Michael Holquist. Trans. Caryl Emerson and Michael Holquist. Austin: U of Texas P, 1981. 259-442.

———. *Rabelais and His World.* Trans. Helene Iswolsky. Cambridge: M.I.T. Press, 1968.

———. "From Notes Made in 1970-71." *Speech Genres and Other Late Essays.* Ed. Caryl Emerson and Michael Holquist. Trans. Vern W. McGee. Austin: U of Texas P, 1986. 132-58.

Baym, Nina. *Woman's Fiction: A Guide to Novels By and About Women in America, 1820-1870.* Ithaca: Cornell UP, 1978.

Butler, Judith. "The Body Politics of Julia Kristeva." *Revaluing French Feminism: Critical Essays on Difference, Agency, and Culture.* Ed. Nancy Fraser and Sandra Lee Bartky. Bloomington: Indiana UP, 1992. 162-76.

Clark, Katerina and Michael Holquist. *Mikhail Bakhtin.* Cambridge, Belknap Press, 1984.

Dobson, Joanne. *Dickinson and the Strategies of Reticence: The Woman Writer in Nineteenth-Century America.* Bloomington: Indiana UP, 1989.

———. "The Hidden Hand: Subversion of Cultural Ideology in Three Mid-Nineteenth-Century American Women's Novels." *American Quarterly* 38.2 (1986): 223-42.

Foucault, Michel. "The Discourse on Language." *The Archaeology of Knowledge.* Trans. A. M. Sheridan Smith. New York: Pantheon, 1972. 215-37.

Herndl, Diane Price. "The Dilemmas of a Feminine Dialogic." *Feminism, Bakhtin, and the Dialogic.* Ed. Dale M. Bauer and S. Jaret McKinstry. Albany: State U of New York P, 1991. 7-24.

Jung, Carl G. "Anima and Animus." *Aspects of the Feminine.* Trans. R. F. C. Hull. Extracted from Vol. 7 of Hull's translation of *The Collected Works.* 1959. Princeton: Princeton UP, 1982. 77-100.

———. "On the Psychology of the Trickster-Figure." *The Archetypes and the Collective Unconscious.* Vol. 9, Part 1 of *The Collected Works.* Ed. Gerhard Adler, et al. Trans. R. F. C. Hull. Princeton: Princeton UP, 1959. 255-72.

Kristeva, Julia. *Desire in Language: A Semiotic Approach to Literature and Art.* Ed. Leon S. Roudiez. Trans. Thomas Gora, et al. New York: Columbia UP, 1980.

———. *Revolution in Poetic Language.* Trans. Margaret Waller. New York: Columbia UP, 1984.

Leverenz, David. *Manhood and the American Renaissance.* Ithaca: Cornell UP, 1989.

Matthews, Glenna. *"Just a Housewife": The Rise and Fall of Domesticity in America.* New York: Oxford UP, 1987.

Tompkins, Jane. *Sensational Designs: The Cultural Work of American Fiction 1790-1860.* New York: Oxford UP, 1985.

Volosinov, V. N./Bakhtin, M. M. *Freudianism: A Critical Sketch.* Ed. I. R. Titunik and Neal H. Bruss. Trans. I. R. Titunik. Bloomington: Indiana UP, 1976.

Warner, Anna B. *Susan Warner.* New York: G. P. Putnam's Sons, 1909.

Warner, Susan. *The Wide, Wide World.* 1850. New York: The Feminist Press, 1987.

Veronica Stewart (essay date spring 1995)

SOURCE: Stewart, Veronica. "Mothering a Female Saint: Susan Warner's Dialogic Role in *The Wide, Wide World.*" *Essays in Literature* 22, no. 1 (spring 1995): 59-74.

[*In the following essay, Stewart compares* The Wide, Wide World *with John Bunyan's* Pilgrim's Progress, *and asserts that Warner's novel is an allegorical, proto-feminist spiritual journey that confronts the dominant literary and religious ideologies associated with nineteenth-century Anglo-American domesticity.*]

According to Anna Warner, one of the first reviews of her sister's novel praised **The Wide, Wide World** (hereafter **WWW**) as a book "capable of doing more good than any other work, other than the Bible" (344). Unfortunately, twentieth-century scholarship on Susan Warner's unprecedented bestselling novel rarely progresses beyond this oft-quoted *Daily Advertiser* review, reading both the novel and its author as simple embodiments of the most conservative and religious Victorian ideals (Tompkins, "Afterword" 585-86). Ironically, this limited assessment of the novel and its author emerges out of ground-breaking attempts on the part of gender-concerned scholars to rescue nineteenth-century women's fiction from obscurity and denigration. Rather than respond directly to critics who "trash" these so-called sentimental texts as inferior literary performances, Jane Tompkins, for example, sets aside "stylistic intricacy, psychological subtlety, [and] epistemological complexity" as inapplicable criteria for a study of Warner's first novel or Harriet Beecher Stowe's *Uncle Tom's Cabin.* Instead, she labels them "political" enterprises motivated and formed entirely by a particular "set of religious beliefs" (*Sensational Designs* 124-27). In an effort to establish the revolutionary potential of *WWW* and several other previously neglected novels by women, Nina Baym contends that they lack "formal self-consciousness," as well as serious "esthetic" dialogue with a "grand tradition," since the authors think of themselves as "lay ministers" writing "evangelical sermons" in order to "spur conversion" (32, 44).[1] By concentrating on Warner's text as a strictly socioreligious rather than literary project and focusing exclusively on formal plot characteristics shared with work by other women of the period, early Warner scholarship forfeits any consideration of *WWW* as an imaginative novel with a discrete form emerging from Warner's unique dialogic engagement with prevailing ideologies and established literary conventions.

The general lack of critical concern with aesthetic form in Warner's novel emanates, at least in part, from a tendency to draw unmediated parallels between the author's biographical circumstances and her fictional text. Warner's personal life as a converted member of the Mercer Street Presbyterian Church, for example, leads critics to ascribe the unrelenting "ethic of submission" imposed on her heroine, Ellen Montgomery, to Warner's own religious and moral principles (*Sensational Designs* 161). Anna Warner's biography of her sister, which includes excerpts from Susan's journals, seems to encourage such biographical interpretations, for Anna describes her sister's writing process as a devotional exercise rather than an aesthetic act, affirming Susan's intimacy with God so thoroughly that He seems to play an active role as co-author of *WWW*:

> It was written in closest reliance upon God; for thought, power, and for words. Not the mere vague wish to write a book that should do service to her Master; but a vivid, constant, looking to him for guidance and help: the worker and her work both laid humbly at the Lord's feet. In that sense, the book was written upon her knees: and the Lord's blessing has followed it, down to this day. How many of whom even I have heard, trace their heart conversion straight to that blessing on [its] pages.
>
> (264)

This depiction of Susan's writing process as a pious act has been accepted without question, yet the propensity Anna displays for extravagant applications of religious rhetoric suggests the need to approach some aspects of her biographical project with the same caution one might bring to Cotton Mather's *Magnalia Christi Americana*. In this passage, she draws on all the power traditionally invested in spiritual conversion to establish divine, and therefore unquestionable, authority for Warner and her novel. Rather than offer irrefutable facts that can be used to develop a critical reading of *WWW*, Anna's description of the religious motives underlying this novel articulates a popular, culturally-sanctioned

device through which to empower a woman writer's work. In fact, this characterization of Warner and her project functions as a direct response to specific inquiries Anna had received from her sister's nineteenth-century readers.

In the introduction to her biography, which begins with a brief note addressed to her deceased sister, Anna emphasizes the reading public's incessant demand for evidence of Susan Warner's personal faith: "My love, they want me to tell about you. . . . They write me from England and America that back of such books as yours there *must* be a faith worth hearing about, a life that should be told" (emphasis added). Anna designs her text to satisfy this desire on the part of readers for detailed information about Susan's spirituality, ending her prefatory remarks with the hope that "nothing irrelevant" to this explicit purpose appears in her biography (ix). Her account of Susan's fan mail supports Susan Coultrap-McQuin's contention that nineteenth-century readers and literary critics of women's novels did not trouble themselves to distinguish clearly between an author and her text (15). Richard Brodhead identifies this tendency to link writers with their work as a "buried commercial publicity operation," which created the "sense that a rare 'life' lies veiled inside the most public of performances" and encouraged audiences to pursue a simulation of that life through further "consumption" of art (63). As an accomplished author in her own right, Anna's rhetorical strategies perpetuate a vision of her sister as an exemplary, elect saint worthy of emulation, and as a result, her biographical account improves the market for her sister's publications. Twentieth-century studies that continue the practice of making direct correlations between Warner's life and her work, however, fail to advance critical interest in Warner's novel. Instead, information pulled out of context from Anna's biography only augments an already operative predilection to characterize nineteenth-century religious women as unimaginative truthsayers and all religious narrative as simplistic work.

Anna's biography (as well as Susan's novel) proves to be far more self-reflexive as a narrative act than previous criticism suggests. Anna begins, for example, by stressing that she was "*not* willing" to write about their "strange, extraordinary life," describing herself as a naturally "secretive person" (iii). Although this self-portrait may register sincere reservations on her part, it nevertheless gives expression to what Joanne Dobson elaborates as an acceptable feminine ethos for nineteenth-century women authors, which reinforced "conservative cultural assumptions" that women write only with extreme "reticence" under duress (*Strategies* 2). The savvy rhetorical maneuvers Anna uses in her preface to enhance her own credibility also underscore her remarkably studied control of approved formulas for women's writing, a talent she shares with her sister.

Anna tries in her preface to prevent any doubt about her veracity as a "faithful chronicler" of Susan's life by encouraging readers to assume that a female "believer," who claims to have no "cause to cover [her] face" before the "dear Lord," would not have the wherewithal to conceal, alter, or exaggerate information as it suits her needs (iii). In terms of their writing, both Warner sisters demonstrate a capacity to indulge the powers-that-be to gain authority for their work. They grasp the standard prescriptions required of them as women authors, and on occasion find good reason to laugh about the need to strike a humble pose in relation to their craft. As Anna informs us, when Susan wrote a "playful" letter to her editor, Mr. Putnam, out of "natural impatience" for remuneration after her novel's publication, she obliquely skirted the issue by asking if there was reason to "hope she might thenceforth live by the pen?—or should she betake herself to needle and thread?" The sisters "made merry over the letter at home, laughing at the idea of [Susan's] minute and painstaking stitches . . . earning daily bread" (346). This account of the joke they shared not only compares Susan's writing style with painstaking, careful stitches, but also marks a finely-tuned sense of humor about the unpretentious posture required of professional women writers.

Apart from Anna's single-minded commentaries on her sister's piety, nothing in her biography or her sister's journal entries provides substantial evidence to conclude that Susan Warner lived by the unbearable restraints required of her heroine. Instead of resigning themselves to the unexpected turn of events that hurled them into poverty or depending on their father to reverse his financial situation, both Warner sisters displayed extraordinary self-reliance and intense determination in their efforts to earn money for the family through writing and other creative activities. Rather than force her into a submissive posture, Susan Warner's religious sentiments intensified her aspirations to succeed in the literary world. Although she prays frequently in her journal that her "talent might be thoroughly sanctified" (*SW* 342), this particular entry (and all others like it) comes in response to accolades Warner received about her first novel, connecting her expressed desire for sanctification with an equally fervent longing for continued material success.[2] Furthermore, the Warner sisters were not compelled to undergo a "stiff formula" to join their church. Anna Warner's description of their religious examination emphasizes the ease with which they were admitted, despite the fact that Susan could not answer her examiners satisfactorily about whether or not she loved "holiness" (202-3). Given Warner's own lack of preparation for close scrutiny by churchmen, combined with their apparently generous response to her indecisive answers, it is clear that Ellen Montgomery's long, tedious training for spiritual conversion under the rigid scrutiny of authority figures in *WWW*

does not emerge directly from Warner's personal religious experience. From a Bakhtinian perspective, studies that confound the "author-creator (a constituent in a work) with the author-person (a constituent in the ethical social event of life)" fail to comprehend the "creative principle in the author's relationship to a hero-[ine]" ("Author and Hero" 10). Although Warner no doubt draws from persons and events in her own life to compose *WWW,* she writes fictional renditions of such autobiographical material and creates numerous, textual counter-responses to the rigid indoctrination inflicted on her heroine.[3]

Rather than produce a monoglossic religious education manual, Warner's text offers significant resistance to both secular and religious restrictions imposed on its heroine, especially prior to Ellen's conversion experience. As I argue elsewhere, suffocating textual restraints on the heroine generate Nancy Vawse's rebellious character, which functions as a centrifugal force in the text, disrupting the novel's authoritative discourse through the dialogic tensions her presence creates (1-2). According to Joanne Dobson, Warner's novel also undercuts Ellen's ultimate submission by inflating the abusive tyranny this young heroine suffers at the hands of authority figures (*Strategies* 20-21).[4] Cultural and linguistic ambiguities embedded within the discourses of both domestic ideology and religious conversion, as well as the author's own psychological complexities, prevent Warner's novel from becoming a simple iteration of some preordained set of sanctioned beliefs.[5] Although Ellen's resignation to authoritative discourse keeps Warner's text safely within the limited boundaries established for women's writing, the author's aesthetic interaction with her text cannot be understood through exclusive concentration on either Ellen or her religious conversion experience.[6] As Bakhtin points out, the "author is present only in the whole of the work, not in one separate aspect of this whole, and least of all in content that is severed from the whole" (*Speech Genres* 160). Rather than fuse entirely with Ellen's character or align herself completely with the authoritative discourse represented in her text, Warner engages in a unique, dialogic relationship with her heroine, a relationship which reveals Warner's own struggle, as author-creator, to reconcile inherent conflicts between traditional religious imperatives and the newly-defined role of mothers in nineteenth-century American society.[7]

Although the cult of domesticity and the religious conversion rhetoric that generally accompanies it are crucial factors for an historically aware reading of *WWW,* these components neither preclude the text's sophistication as an aesthetic act nor diminish Warner's concern with form. More than just an "analogue" of Warner's novel (Tompkins, *Sensational Designs* 183), John Bunyan's *Pilgrim's Progress* plays an intricate role in her text, providing the infrastructure for Ellen's journey toward spiritual, emotional, and physical maturity and serving as the inspirational text responsible for the heroine's religious conversion.[8] Warner's attempt to integrate the language, themes, and structure of Bunyan's exemplary allegory with nineteenth-century concepts of the ideal mother as the primary caretaker of religious salvation results in an unresolved textual struggle between the two sanctioned means for women to authorize their creative social and literary enterprises: motherhood and religious conversion. During the early nineteenth century, as several scholars have documented, the responsibility for educating and disciplining children in both sacred and secular matters shifted primarily to mothers, while men, who could avail themselves of higher education or technical apprenticeship, left the home to earn a living. Women's conduct manuals and essays on domesticity obscured the economic and political rationales underlying such arbitrary divisions of labor, primarily through the agencies of traditional religious "motives" and spiritual conversion "rhetoric" (Cott 65). By empowering mothers as the designated guardians of national morality in terms derived from androcentric religious imperatives, discourses of domesticity bequeathed women the prerogative to determine socio-religious projects, an aspect of domestic ideology that Tompkins's study of sentimental power explores fully. Yet instead of giving expression to the "religious propaganda" of an American jeremiad sermon, as Tompkins suggests, Warner's novel underscores blatant discrepancies between the nation's sacred and secular agendas.[9] Warner's portrait of Ellen's family exposes gender-determined spheres of activities, particularly in relation to spiritual matters, as hypocritical camouflage designed to conceal an overall patriarchal failure to consummate the myth of America as a nation of elect saints. Ellen's separation from her parents, which inverts the circumstances surrounding Christian's departure from his family in Bunyan's text, emphasizes the disastrous effects that can occur when only one parent bears responsibility for the spiritual well-being of the family.

In *The Pilgrim's Progress,* Christian flees his wife and children to seek eternal life, running away from them without turning back, with his "fingers in his ears" to avoid hearing their cries (41). His voluntary separation from his family symbolizes the spiritual distance between an elect saint seeking assurance of grace and the sinners he leaves behind. Ellen's journey toward maturity also begins with her removal from her family, but her involuntary separation from her mother transposes Christian's situation, marking the distance between her unconverted and her mother's elect soul. Much critical attention has been devoted to Captain Montgomery's deficiencies as both a husband and father, indicating that Warner's novel refuses to mitigate adversities caused by unconverted males.[10] Captain Montgomery's unsatisfactory relationship with his wife, however, stems from the fact that their cultural assignments place them in direct opposition with each other. In keeping with conservative articulations of domestic ideology, Ellen's mother functions as the "chief minister" of her family's religious salvation, the sole parent responsible for rearing "all under her care to lay up treasures, not on earth, but in heaven" (Beecher 19). Just as Captain Montgomery proves inept at navigating the public sphere of high finance, Mrs. Montgomery fails to carry out her most crucial social function as wife and mother. Of course, when the narrative begins, Ellen's mother is already completely incapacitated by the prolonged illness which will eventually end her life, so any shortcoming on her part tends to be excused or overlooked. Nonetheless, Mrs. Montgomery's failure to convert either husband or daughter serves as a crucial element in Warner's text, for it not only initiates the plot but also raises serious doubts about each woman's individual capacity to perform her role as the family's sole religious instructor, challenging the overall efficacy of religious domesticity.

Through a dialogue with Charity, Bunyan clears Christian of any further responsibility for his family's spiritual welfare, for they proved "themselves to be implacable to good" by loathing Christian's "righteous" actions (84-85). While Christian manages to dissociate himself with relative ease from his family at the outset of his pilgrimage, Ellen's removal from home produces the opposite effect, strengthening her attachment to her saintly mother. In contrast to Bunyan's text, Warner's novel represents Ellen's foremost spiritual debility as her unwillingness to relinquish ties with her mother. The heroine confesses this particular weakness in an exchange with one of several characters who function like the Evangelist in Bunyan's allegory, serving as spiritual guides on her road to salvation. The first evangelist Ellen meets is a pious gentleman who befriends her on the boat voyage to her Aunt Fortune's farm. After he asks several probing questions to discern why this sweet young girl cannot say that she loves Jesus, Ellen responds: "Mamma said I could not love him at all if I did not love him best; and oh, sir . . . I do love mamma a great deal better" (70). The counsel she receives from this gentleman stranger gives voice to the lesson Ellen must master to achieve both physical and spiritual adulthood:

> You love your mother because she is so careful to provide for all your wants; but who gave her the materials to work with? [S]he has only been, as it were, the hand by which he supplied you. [A]nd who gave you such a mother?—there are many mothers not like her;—who put into her heart the truth and love that have been blessing you ever since you were born? It is all—all God's doing, from first to last.
>
> (72)

For all intents and purposes, religious domesticity provides Warner with the ideological "materials" to create "such a mother" as Mrs. Montgomery, for the possibility of a converted woman presenting so perfect a model for Christian behavior that she supersedes her child's love for God would have been an unthinkable concept in traditional, male-oriented religious rhetoric. More important, Warner uses this revolutionary concept of an ideal mother as an integral component of her narrative strategy in this text.

Warner relies on the significance of the mother's new role in the conversion process to generate her plot. If Mrs. Montgomery had converted her husband, he would have shared her values, making it inconceivable for him to consider separating his naive, helpless daughter from her dying mother.[11] By pushing the mother's crucial role in relation to her family's spirituality to its most radical consequences, however, Warner's novel undermines the premise that ideal, perfect mothers serve the status quo. Mrs. Montgomery's presence hinders rather than facilitates her daughter's conversion experience, a situation that overturns the most articulated religious goals of domestic ideology. To the extent that the figure of a converted mother obstructs her daughter's vision of God, it constitutes the "original" sin in Warner's novel. Since she removes Mrs. Montgomery from the narrative prior to her death, Warner gives her heroine reason to hope for her mother's return, protracting Mrs. Montgomery's capacity to stand between her daughter and an essentially patriarchal God until the conversion chapter, which does not occur until midway through this rather lengthy novel. Warner's plot, therefore, impedes the heroine's religious conversion, following the standard form of conversion narrative in which potential converts relate the tribulations and doubts suffered prior to the moment when they discover assurance of saving grace. In addition, however, all the attributes assigned to God in the evangelist's diatribe also describe the author's creativity in this text, for Warner's "hand" not only creates "such a mother" but removes her from the narrative as well. In this respect, the author's creativity, as well as her attempt to stay true to conventional forms of spiritual autobiography, rivals God's power. Warner's aesthetic relationship with her heroine thus corresponds with the position her novel assigns to Ellen's mother, providing a creative force outside the narrative that temporarily eclipses God. Both Mrs. Montgomery and the author-creator function as absent mothers who temporarily block the heroine's complete submission to a patriarchal authority. The evangelist's invective, which several tyrannically kind-hearted characters concerned with Ellen's well-being iterate throughout the text, gives voice to the authoritative discourse that seeks to reduce Mrs. Montgomery's behavior, as well as Warner's creative activity, to manifestations of God's will, a resignation of power that the first half of Warner's narrative resists successfully.

Rather than signify Warner's personal religious perspective, the text's repeated stress on Ellen's need to submit to patriarchal authority underscores the fact that both the heroine and her author (for different but related reasons) refuse to surrender their investment in the mother. The "contours" of *WWW,* particularly in relation to its "emphasis on submission," are not, as Cynthia Schoolar Williams suggests, "dictated" entirely by its heroine's "personality" (15). Warner depends upon her heroine's resistance to submission to shape her narrative, for the author's creative space in this novel emerges through an ongoing dialogic tension between the mother's newly-acquired role in social formation and traditional religious imperatives. The author's unique aesthetic involvement with her heroine forms around the function ascribed to Ellen's mother in this novel, but Warner's creative participation in the dynamics of this mother/daughter relationship collides with her equally crucial literary and social obligation, as both author and "mother," to assure her child heroine's religious conversion experience. Since the heroine's affection for her mother supplants her love of Jesus, Ellen, as well as the narrative, must relinquish the mother before the heroine's spiritual rebirth through Christ can transpire.

Being born of woman and refusing to break loose from this attachment hardly represents an original problem in Western patriarchal society, but the predicament usually occurs in religious narratives as a specifically male dilemma. In his *Confessions,* for example, Augustine includes a rebellion against weaning among his first possible offenses against God: "What then was my sin? Was it that I hung upon the breast and cried?" (3). In Augustine's seminal spiritual autobiography, male desire for a mother's nurturing care amounts to a grievous sin against the Father. By linking his continued longing for nourishment at his mother's breast with an innate depravity of the human condition, Augustine draws attention to guilt associated with his own lingering separation anxieties, recording the troubled, yet rationalized response of a socialized son who must repress such connections with his mother. Puritan ministers in the New England colonies try to gain a similar kind of control over a fundamental dependence on female biological functions through the rhetoric of Christianity, specifically the conventional metaphor of religious conversion as a rebirth of soul in Christ. In traditional Puritan conversion rhetoric, mothers produce only vile, unregenerate flesh, and pious fathers/ministers labor to (re)produce regenerate souls.[12] Early American sermons reflect an intense desire to appropriate reproduction from the female through descriptions of the male's role in the conversion process. For the sake of brevity, Cotton Mather's funeral sermon for his father, Increase, provides an abridged summary of the female imagery Puritan ministers applied to themselves: "Such Ministers are your Mothers too. Have they not Travailed in Birth for you, that a Christ may be formed in you? Are not their Lips the Breasts Thro' which the sincere Milk of the Word has pass'd unto you, for your nourishment?" (22-23). In his socio-psychological study of this phenomenon, David Leverenz concludes that the highly visible presence of female and stereotypically feminine imagery in first generation Puritan sermons "encouraged a shared fantasy . . . that sons could rescue the father's authority by being reborn of the greater Father, without a mother's help, and suckled and raised by Him alone" (*Language* 4).

The feminization of American culture, defined by Ann Douglas as a propagation of devotion based on "potentially matriarchal virtues of nurture, generosity and acceptance," was already in place before the collaboration between ministers and women that Douglas locates in nineteenth-century America (10). All the elements we might expect of a feminist theology—passion, explicitly feminine soul identity, androgenous or female God-language, female reproductive imagery, and mothering metaphors—pervade the writing of seventeenth-century Puritan males, facilitating their essentially patriarchal religious agendas.[13] In that respect, the "story of salvation through motherly love," which Tompkins identifies as the empowering narrative in nineteenth-century American women's novels (*Sensational Designs* 124-25), involves a problematic return to some of the most troublesome sexual politics of the original Puritan project. Puritan sermons written by male preachers used images of female reproduction and mothering to transcend a fundamental gender conflict stemming from their desire to unite passionately with a male godhead.[14] The same rhetoric, however, which domestic ideology retrieves for women, creates problems for Warner as a woman author writing about a specifically female conversion experience at a time when women were expected to play a vital role in the conversion process. As a novelistic, female pilgrim's progress, Warner's text ventures into previously unexplored aspects of religious conversion narrative. No traditional male religious rhetoric provides a precedent for Ellen to give up her mother that would not simultaneously damage the integrity of Mrs. Montgomery's character as mother or her status as an elect saint, the two elements upon which Warner, as author-creator, establishes her textual authority.

Conventional methods and language used to unwork mother/child attachments in religious narratives written by males naturally approach this problem in relation to mother/son ties, depending almost exclusively on male fear, hatred, or envy of the mother's role in reproduction to achieve separation from her. Augustine's need to differentiate between himself and his mother, for example, plays out the misogyny inherent in conventional male socialization processes; he must reject the mother and all things stereotypically feminine to achieve manhood.[15] Ellen's social maturation, on the other hand, involves a replication rather than rejection of her moth-

er's lifestyle, adhering to the dynamics of mother/daughter relationships in bourgeois, nuclear family constructs developing during the nineteenth century.[16] Unlike Christian in *The Pilgrim's Progress,* whose estimate of his family members as distinct from himself works to justify his detachment from them, Ellen never differentiates completely from her mother. In Warner's text, the heroine's symbiotic bond with her earthly mother defers her desire to seek union with an ethereal heavenly Father; no description by her spiritual mentors of this patriarchal godhead as a mothering, nurturing Being can convince Ellen to prefer His supposedly loving discipline to her mother's immediate kindness.[17] As long as Mrs. Montgomery remains alive, sustaining the possibility that she could return to the narrative at any time, the heroine and her author-creator resist the problematic language of a supposedly matriarchal theology initiated originally by men to expedite their spiritual unity with a male godhead.[18] Instead, the text explores three potential surrogates for the heroine's mother: Fortune Emerson, Alice Humphreys, and Mrs. Vawse. A brief character study of these women reveals that they each serve, in rather discrete ways, to keep the memory of Mrs. Montgomery alive in the text.

Ellen's Aunt Fortune defies every principle Mrs. Montgomery embodies in Warner's novel. As an independent spinster who performs all household chores herself and who has no use whatsoever for religion, Fortune's "stock Yankee character" and her "provincial doings" contrast sharply, as Leverenz observes, with the novel's representation of women's lifestyles in more refined, cultured homes (*Manhood* 182, 189).[19] Her stormy relationship with Ellen, who has been placed unceremoniously in her care, stems in part from Fortune's awareness of the class distinctions between herself and Ellen's mother. After refusing to make arrangements for Ellen to attend school, Fortune lambasts higher education as the source of Mrs. Montgomery's problems: "If she had been trained to use her hands and do something useful instead of thinking herself above it, maybe she wouldn't have to go to sea for her health just now; it doesn't do for women to be bookworms" (140). Although some readers characterize Fortune as the equivalent of a "fairy tale's cruel stepmother" (*Brodhead* 30), she expresses indignation over the fact that she is cast in that role against her will: "One might as good be a stepmother at once, and done with it" (178). Her complaint suggests a self-reflexive aspect of Warner's novel that has been previously neglected, for the anger Fortune acts out against her niece almost always relates to the self-reliant spinster's apprehension concerning her inability to satisfy some predetermined, but unspoken standard for good mothering. Warner's narrative stacks the deck against Ellen's aunt because she is unconverted, and this hard-working woman seems acutely aware of that judgment call, suffering humiliation from even the slightest insinuation that she falls short of being a proper surrogate mother for Ellen.

Fortune lashes out enviously against Mrs. Montgomery and Alice Humphreys, the two characters who interfere most with her attempt to raise her niece in a strictly pragmatic fashion. She derides Alice, a minister's daughter and evangelist in her own right, for meddling in other people's affairs, referring sarcastically to the pious young woman as a snobby "piece of perfection" (159). Alice's prestige in the community makes it impossible for Fortune to prevent her from speaking with Ellen, but Fortune exercises far more control over communications between the heroine and her mother. By hiding Mrs. Montgomery's letters to her daughter, Fortune tries to intercept any further missives from the absent mother. Such efforts to reduce Mrs. Montgomery's influence on Ellen miscarry, for each attack Fortune launches against Mrs. Montgomery fortifies Ellen's loyalty, intensifying the heroine's (as well as the reader's) longing for her mother's return to the narrative. Alice's character temporarily assuages this desire by picking up the heroine's spiritual and secular education where her mother left off. Just as Fortune suspects, Alice's talks with Ellen include lessons on how good Christians should "forgive" people like Aunt Fortune (164-67), an awkward topic for Ellen to disclose to her unregenerate relative. Although the text does not allow much room to feel sympathy for Aunt Fortune's plight, she correctly assesses every threat to her status as primary caretaker for Ellen.

Even though Alice Humphreys repeats Mrs. Montgomery's admonitions to her daughter, warning Ellen not to "lean" on her, but to put all her "trust" in God (167), this gentlewoman's loving protection amplifies Ellen's memory of her mother, extending the heroine's (as well as the narrative's) capacity to defer submission to God, matriarchal or otherwise. Not unlike Fortune, however, Alice expresses the fear that she makes a "poor substitute for [Ellen's] mother" (238), giving voice to a valid, self-reflexive comment on her limitations as a mother figure in the narrative. During their first visit together to Mrs. Vawse, Alice begs the solitary old widow for a "lesson of quiet contentment" to help her "get over" her brother "John's going away" to study for the ministry, a tearful confession of spiritual weakness on Alice's part that "surprise[s]" Mrs. Vawse and Ellen (188-89). The young evangelist cannot bring Ellen to a conversion experience because she shares the heroine's particular imperfection; Alice cannot endure separation from loved ones any better than her child protegé can. Woman's propensity for connectedness, expressed in this novel through an undying love for others and a dynamic involvement in the social and spiritual needs of her community, clashes with the emotional detachment from family and world mandated by traditional religious discourse.

Mrs. Vawse's spiritual lessons pose an ambivalent method for resolving this conflict since the gratification she claims to receive through "Jesus alone" only occurs after every person she ever loved has died: "But now I think I can say with Paul, 'I have learned in whatsoever state I am therewith to be content.' I think so; *maybe that I deceive myself*; but they are all gone, and I am certain that I am content now" (188-89, my italics). The model for female conversion presented by Mrs. Vawse's character suggests that a mother's engrossed concern with family members outweighs any sense of fulfillment she might achieve by turning to God prior to their deaths. More important, since Mrs. Vawse's capacity to be "content now" hinges on the removal of all her loved ones, her profound serenity in Jesus does indeed involve some self-deception on her part. Despite her repeated declaration that "not one" of her dear relatives or friends remains alive (189), Mrs. Vawse is sole guardian of her feisty granddaughter, Nancy. The old woman puts her formula for spiritual tranquility into play a bit prematurely, neglecting her granddaughter's presence in the world.[20] By fixing her attention steadfastly on her "home" in "heaven" (189), Mrs. Vawse manages to ignore Nancy, a young miscreant who runs wild during the first half of the narrative, creating havoc wherever she turns up.[21] Warner's text undercuts Mrs. Vawse's potential as a surrogate mother through the widow's apparent failure to control her granddaughter's behavior, thus preserving the unnarratability of an ideal mother capable of producing a spiritual conversion in her female progeny, situating this desired mother outside the parameters of the novel's world, beyond the heroine's lived experience.

None of the female proxies for Mrs. Montgomery in the narrative alleviate the ongoing dialogic tension between the absent mother's role in Warner's text and traditional forms of religious narratives, the conflict that stymies the heroine's spiritual progress. Yet after the text conclusively eliminates the absent mother's potential to reunite physically with her daughter by communicating news of Mrs. Montgomery's death, Ellen's spiritual transformation occurs posthaste. In the compressed space of one chapter centered exactly midway through this long novel, the young heroine learns of her mother's death, falls into a deep slough of despond, listens to readings of *Pilgrim's Progress*, undergoes a religious conversion, and experiences a spiritual affinity with her mother. In a matter of just a few pages, Ellen (as well as the reader) traverses a broad range of emotion, moving from the depths of paralyzing grief to peaks of spiritual ecstasy in an incredibly rapid fire, cathartic sequence of events.

John Humphreys, Ellen's adopted brother and future husband, controls her reading of Bunyan's allegory and functions as the agent of her conversion. Unlike the converted women characters in Warner's text, Humphreys's theological stance enables him to modify

Ellen's attachment to her mother, for his saturnine fixation on the apocalypse prophesied in Revelations keeps him aloof from intense worldly connection (312). Although Ellen asks Humphreys to interpret several sections of *Pilgrim's Progress* for her as he reads, Warner's text recounts only one of her questions, drawing special attention to the scene "where Christian loses his burden at the cross" (351). In Bunyan's allegory, Christ's death redeems Christian, for this divine sacrifice relieves the pilgrim of sins that weigh upon his soul. When Ellen asks her spiritual mentor to decipher the mark Christian receives on his forehead at the cross, Humphreys tells her it signifies the "mark of God's children—the change wrought in them by the Holy Spirit . . . that makes them different from others, and different from their old selves" (352). After pondering this standard explanation of Bunyan's symbolism for one brief evening, the young heroine discovers signs of spiritual change within herself, surrendering to the phallocentric word of God presented in Bunyan's work and translated in Humphreys's exegesis.

The heroine's dramatic shift in perspective, then, coincides with an equally striking alteration in the novel's intertextual exchange with *The Pilgrim's Progress*. Prior to Mrs. Montgomery's death, Warner's text interacts on a more creative and subtle level with Bunyan's work, modifying stock aspects of his exemplary Christian allegory to accommodate precepts of domestic ideology and gender-determined distinctions dictated by a specifically female conversion narrative. After Ellen's conversion experience, the text returns again to this sophisticated interplay with Bunyan's allegory, depicting Ellen's prolonged sojourn with the Lindsays, her relatives in England, as the complicated, psychological struggle of an economically dependent, female convert with the urban temptations of Vanity Fair.[22] During the conversion chapter, however, Warner's novel suspends heteroglossic exchange with Bunyan's work by treating *The Pilgrim's Progress* as a sacrosanct text. Novelistic discourse comes to an abrupt halt in Warner's conversion chapter, allowing the stilted conditions required for what Bakhtin calls the monoglossic "word of the father" ("Discourse in the Novel" 342) to emerge without resistance. In this respect, Humphreys's role in Ellen's conversion seems minor by comparison with the part the author plays in this event, for Warner relinquishes the narrative play that emanates from her active participation in a mother/daughter dynamic with Ellen to assure her heroine's conversion.

Although some contemporary, feminist readers find the heroine's ultimate surrender to God appalling, the artificial conditions Warner must create in this chapter for a conversion to occur reveal the arbitrariness of cultural and artistic imperatives on women, particularly in relation to definitions of ideal mothering. Moreover, when read within the context of the entire narrative, Ellen's conversion marks Warner's superb control over form.

By postponing Mrs. Montgomery's death in the narrative and refusing to let other characters serve as adequate surrogate mothers, Warner reserves the prerogative to initiate her own heroine's conversion through an aesthetic act. Warner generates Mrs. Montgomery's death from outside narrative, not only providing the traumatic coincidence that stimulates her heroine's conversion, but also giving her heroine the temporary freedom she needs to hear the word of God without further interference. To enact the ideal of motherhood propagated by domestic ideology without foregoing her heroine's spiritual conversion, Warner temporarily sacrifices her own creativity, exposing religious domestic ideology as an unnatural imposition on women in the society. Through this gesture, however, Ellen Montgomery's author-creator also consummates the perfect act of motherly love proposed but unfulfilled by characters in her narrative, allowing her heroine to proceed on her journey as a converted Christian.[23] In a society demanding that women "mother" if they hoped to gain a significant voice in public realms of activity, Warner never married or had a child of her own, but she nonetheless performed her cultural responsibilities as mother, as well as all the difficulties emanating from that role, through the imaginative birth of her artistic child, *The Wide, Wide World*.

Notes

1. Susan K. Harris provides a complete history of major critical trends in this field of study in the introduction of her book.

2. Baym reads Anna Warner's remark about Susan writing her book "on her knees" as evidence that the author "was praying for success" (142), but this conclusion applies more smoothly to Susan's journal entries than to Anna's biographical comments, which concentrate exclusively on Warner's text as a divine venture. Warner's personal entries, on the other hand, rarely fail to meld her sacred and secular desires.

3. Since her heroine's father, Captain Montgomery, experiences a financial catastrophe modeled on Henry Whiting Warner's actual circumstances, critics also try to use Montgomery's portrait as a clue to Warner's personal relationship with her own father. Because Warner agreed to let her father handle all the profits from her work, David Leverenz argues that the author suffered from the same "intensity of submission" toward father figures enacted by her heroine (*Manhood* 189). Yet Warner's narrative condemns the character fashioned after her father, depicting Captain Montgomery as an inept, heartless, unconverted male, completely indifferent to the emotional and spiritual needs of his family (60, 63). Brodhead on the other hand, argues that Warner's text is limited to "different formations of the domestic sphere" because the author had no specific information about

her father's business affairs (30). Anna Warner's account of her father's failed business ventures, however, indicates that both sisters were quite well-informed about the real estate lawsuits plaguing their father (196-98, 206-07), so the limitations Warner places on her heroine's knowledge of the public realm do not reflect the author's own personal awareness of this sphere of activity.

4. Dobson covers this aspect of Warner's text more thoroughly in "The Hidden Hand: Subversion of Cultural Ideology in Three Mid-Nineteenth-Century American Women's Novels."

5. Tompkins speaks of *WWW* as the "Ur-text" of the nineteenth century because "it embodies, uncompromisingly, the values of the Victorian era," perpetuating an "ideology of duty, humility, and submission to circumstance" and insisting on the "imperative of self-sacrifice." She concludes that the text, therefore, lacks "moral and epistemological ambiguity" (585-86).

6. In his early work on "Author and Hero in Aesthetic Activity," Bakhtin covers this problem thoroughly: "Aesthetic form cannot be grounded and validated from within the hero[ine], out of [her] own directedness to objects and meaning, i.e., on the basis of that which has validity only for [her] own lived life." Novelistic discourse, then, occurs when the author "produces values that are transgredient in principle" to those of her heroine (90).

7. As Bakhtin points out, "the artist's struggle to achieve a determinate and stable image of the hero[ine] is to a considerable extent a struggle within [her]self" ("Author and Hero" 6).

8. According to her earliest journal entries, Warner was telling original "stories" and reading *The Pilgrim's Progress* when she was only twelve years old (*SW* 94), two activities she melds in her first novel.

9. Tompkins argues that nineteenth-century women's novels use "religious conversion as the necessary precondition for sweeping social change." Instead of turning to conversion narrative or spiritual autobiography as the literary forms upon which *WWW* would, therefore, most likely be patterned, Tompkins aligns women's novels with the religious propaganda of the jeremiad sermon as defined by Sacvan Bercovitch (*SD* 125-27). Bercovitch's study of *The American Jeremiad,* however, concentrates almost exclusively on the works of elite ministers and male literary figures, ignoring all voices that do not reaffirm the dominant discourse upheld by the jeremiad. Warner's novel shares more in common with personal narratives where unresolved conflicts between political and spiritual matters emerge than with the monopho-nic rhetoric of political sermons. In her text, dialogic tensions appear between sacred and secular agendas, at precisely the juncture where jeremiads claim homogeneity.

10. As Leverenz argues, Warner "quickly multiplies her portraits of insensitive, commanding men during the opening chapters of her novel" (*Manhood* 185) through her characterizations of Mr. Montgomery, the deceptive Dr. Green, and the pompous store clerk, Mr. Saunders.

11. Brodhead approaches Captain Montgomery's exclusion from the close relationship between his wife and daughter as evidence of the "psychological transactions" of a general "scheme of acculturation" in which children develop an inner conscience by being "enclosed within the mother's emotional presence" (32). His argument, however, tends to lose sight of the fact that the acculturation process in Warner's novel relates specifically to mother/daughter bonding. Her text critiques a social system in which only female parents are held responsible for the religious concerns of the family and nation, and by extension, only female children must undergo religious conversion to perform their adult function in the community.

12. Anne Bradstreet's brief spiritual autobiography, "To My Dear Children," which she wrote in letter form to her children, may be one of few extant precursors of the female tradition of religious rhetoric explored by some nineteenth-century American women novelists. Bradstreet makes a highly unorthodox bid in the most conventional terminology to lay claim to a motherhood reserved for establishing the authority of the male in her society, retrieving the religious language of female reproduction for women: "As I have brought you into the world, and with great pains, weakness, cares and fears brought you to this, I now travail in birth again of you till Christ be formed in you" (241).

13. While males and females had a shared experience of the sacred, they had disparate connections with the task of founding a society in New England. Even though male preachers appropriated the language one might associate with a matriarchal theology, these concepts never extended to include equity between the sexes in their communal tasks, as John Cotton's views on public ministry make clear: "The female sex [falls] short of power, which Christ has given to the brother-hood. . . . I suffer not a woman to teach, nor to usurp authority over the man, but to be in silence" ("The Way" 47).

14. This Puritan expression echoes sentiments found in the religious writing of twelfth-century Cister-

cian monks. According to Caroline Walker Bynum, monks in the Middle Ages applied maternal imagery to "male religious authority figures, particularly abbots, bishops and the apostles, as well as to God and Christ," registering a "need, felt especially by males for a view of authority that balances discipline with love," along with a new "concern for evangelism and an approachable God" (111). The "discipline through love" theory, which Brodhead posits as a novelistic phenomenon specific to the needs of middle-class, nineteenth-century education (18-35), draws from long-established religious formats initiated by males.

15. Augustine's description of his escape from his mother characterizes her as an overprotective female who suffocates her son. She "bewailed" his journey and "followed [him] as far as the sea," forcing him to deceive her so that she would not interfere with his plans: "I feigned that I had a friend whom I could not leave till he had a fair wind to sail. And I lied to my mother, and such a mother, and escaped" (31).

16. Nancy Chodorow's work in *The Reproduction of Mothering* has been criticized for its tendency to universalize the conditions endemic to white, middle-class family dynamics, but since Warner's text presents a fictionalized version of that specific family model at its inception, several parallels exist between Warner's depiction of Ellen's relationship with her mother and Chodorow's revision of Freudian psychology, specifically in relation to the "prolonged symbiosis and narcissistic overidentification" between mother and daughter (104).

17. Grace Ann and Theodore R. Hovet note that "Ellen and female authors of conversion narratives replace the authoritative power figure with the image of God as mother or loving family member or friend," drawing on Nancy Schnog's discussion of Christocentrism as Ellen's means to form relations not only "between herself and God but also between herself, her mother and the community of like-minded women" (Hovet and Hovet 6). Both the Hovet piece and Schnog's work, however, ignore Ellen's steadfast resistance to God as a matriarchal figure in Warner's text, as well as the author's aesthetic role in relation to that defiance.

18. Several scholars provide insightful readings of Ellen's psychological relationship with her mother, concentrating specifically on the famous "link of communion" (353) Ellen ultimately attains with her mother in Warner's conversion chapter. For example, see Brodhead's *Cultures,* 32-35 and Tompkins' *Sensational Designs* 163-65. Neither of these critics, however, note that the figure of the mother generates dialogic tension in the text

by offering a means to resist God, explore how that conflict relates to Warner's concern with form, or demonstrate the author-creator's complicity with the mother's role in this text.

19. As Brodhead points out, Fortune demonstrates the "logic of the oldstyle household economy," thinking of her home as the central workplace in the community (31).

20. Leverenz argues that Warner intended "Mrs. Vawse as a model for Ellen's conversion from resentment to serenity" (*Manhood* 180), but Ellen's own religious conversion neither relieves her of obligations nor removes her from the world.

21. See my article, "The Wild Side of *The Wide, Wide World,*" for a thorough exploration of Nancy Vawse's rebellious character in relation to socioreligious, psychological, and aesthetic concerns in Warner's text.

22. See the Hovet article for an insightful, psychological study of Ellen's spiritual and social survival during her stay with the Lindsays as female performance art grounded in relational identity.

23. Bakhtin speaks of an author's "creative reaction" to her heroine as a gift of "aesthetic love" for an "other," i.e., as a formal, textual event that transfigures the character, transposing the "recipient of the gift to a new plane of existence" ("Author and Hero" 90).

Works Cited

Augustine. *The Confessions. Great Books of the Western World.* Ed. Robert Maynard Hutchins. Chicago: Encyclopedia Britannica, 1952, Vol. 18, Book I.

Bakhtin, Mikhail M. "Author and Hero in Aesthetic Activity." *Art and Answerability: Early Philosophical Essays.* Ed. Michael Holquist and Vadim Liapunov. Trans. Vadim Liapunov. Austin: U of Texas P, 1990. 4-276.

————. "Discourse in the Novel." *The Dialogic Imagination: Four Essays.* Ed. Michael Holquist. Trans. Caryl Emerson and Michael Holquist. Austin: U of Texas P, 1981. 259-442.

————. "From Notes Made in 1970-71." *Speech Genres and Other Late Essays.* Ed. Caryl Emerson and Michael Holquist. Trans. Vern W. McGee. Austin: U of Texas P, 1986. 132-58.

Baym, Nina. *Woman's Fiction: A Guide to Novels By and About Women in America, 1820-1870.* Ithaca: Cornell UP, 1978.

Beecher, Catherine E. and Harriet Beecher Stowe. *The American Woman's Home or Principles of Domestic Science.* 1869. Hartford: The Stowe-Day Foundation, 1985.

Bercovitch, Sacvan. *The American Jeremiad.* Madison: U of Wisconsin P, 1978.

Bradstreet, Anne. "To My Dear Children." *The Works of Anne Bradstreet.* Ed. Jeannine Hensley. Cambridge: Belknap Press, 1967.

Brodhead, Richard H. *Cultures of Letters: Scenes of Reading and Writing in Nineteenth-Century America.* Chicago: U of Chicago P, 1993.

Bunyan, John. *The Pilgrim's Progress.* Ed. Roger Sharrock. New York: Penguin Books, 1983.

Bynum, Caroline Walker. *Jesus as Mother: Studies in the Spirituality of the Middle Ages.* Berkeley: U of California P, 1982.

Chodorow, Nancy. *The Reproduction of Mothering.* Berkeley: U of California P, 1978.

Cott, Nancy. *The Bonds of Womanhood: "Woman's Sphere" in New England 1780-1835.* New Haven: Yale UP, 1977.

Cotton, John. "The Way of Congregational Churches Cleared." London, 1648.

Coultrap-McQuin, Susan. *Doing Literary Business: American Women Writers in the Nineteenth Century.* Chapel Hill: U of North Carolina P, 1990.

Dobson, Joanne. *Emily Dickinson and the Strategies of Reticence: The Woman Writer in Nineteenth-Century America.* Bloomington: Indiana UP, 1989.

———. "The Hidden Hand: Subversion of Cultural Ideology in Three Mid-Nineteenth-Century American Women's Novels." *American Quarterly* 38.2 (1986): 223-42.

Douglas, Ann. *The Feminization of American Culture.* New York: Knopf, 1977.

Harris, Susan K. *19th-Century American Women's Novels: Interpretive Strategies.* New York: Cambridge UP, 1990.

Hovet, Grace Ann and Theodore R. "Identity Development in Susan Warner's *The Wide, Wide World*: Relationship, Performance and Construction." *Legacy* 8.1 (Spring 1991): 3-16.

Leverenz, David. *Manhood and the American Renaissance.* Ithaca: Cornell UP, 1989.

———. *The Language of Puritan Feeling: An Exploration in Literature, Psychology, and Social History.* New Brunswick, NJ: Rutgers UP, 1980.

Mather, Cotton. "A Father Departing." Boston, 1723.

Schnog, Nancy. "Inside the Sentimental: The Psychological Work of *The Wide, Wide World*." *Genders* 4 (Spring 1989): 11-25.

Stewart, Veronica. "The Wild Side of *The Wide, Wide World*." *Legacy* 11.1 (Spring 1994): 1-16.

Tompkins, Jane. *Sensational Designs: The Cultural Work of American Fiction, 1790-1860.* New York: Oxford UP, 1985.

———. "Afterword" in *The Wide, Wide World* by Susan Warner. New York: Feminist P, 1987.

Warner, Anna B. *Susan Warner.* New York: Putnam, 1909; cited in text as *SW*.

Warner, Susan. *The Wide, Wide World.* 1850; New York: Feminist P, 1987.

Williams, Cynthia Schoolar. "Susan Warner's *Queechy* and the *Bildungsroman* Tradition." *Legacy* 7.2 (Fall 1990): 3-16.

Catherine O'Connell (essay date spring 1997)

SOURCE: O'Connell, Catherine. "'We *Must* Sorrow': Silence, Suffering, and Sentimentality in Susan Warner's *The Wide, Wide World*." *Studies in American Fiction* 25, no. 1 (spring 1997): 21-39.

[*In the following essay, O'Connell illuminates narrative tensions between Ellen's feminine subjectivity and the directives of male-gendered authority figures—a conflict that precipitates the protagonist's suffering in* The Wide, Wide World.]

Since its "rediscovery,"[1] Susan Warner's **The Wide, Wide World** has posed a challenge to critical readers: what is the meaning of the relentless, excruciating focus on the suffering of the young female protagonist in this record-setting bestseller?[2] The novel is structured around the trials of Ellen Montgomery and her subjective experience of pain. Suffering is a crucial narrative element of **The Wide, Wide World** and must be accounted for in any interpretation of the novel.

All recent critical considerations of **The Wide, Wide World** suggest theories about its depiction of suffering, and arguments about the novel's ideological meaning turn on how one understands the role of female suffering within the text. Jane Tompkins argues in *Sensational Designs* that through her suffering, the child Ellen learns a lesson in religious transcendence. By accepting suffering, Ellen supplants earthly patriarchal authority with divine: "So 'submission' becomes 'self-conquest' and doing the will of one's husband or father brings an access of divine power." According to Tompkins, the novel establishes that self-abnegation is really empowerment because women ally themselves with the most powerful possible authority. A quite different interpretation of the novel's emphasis on female suffering is put forward by Richard Brodhead in his essay "Sparing the Rod: Discipline and Fiction in Antebellum America." He finds that the novel's emphasis on obedience and submission reinforces patriarchy, both within and outside the narrative. Brodhead argues that the novel both represents and incites painful emotions, "indeed brings those feelings to a high pitch of outrage and grief. But the interest it thus excites involves us in its representation of *this same* disciplinary structure as sacredly founded and morally immitigable." In other words, the very power of the representation of suffering strengthens the imperative to obey the authority that is the ultimate source of the suffering. Tompkins and Brodhead represent poles in the debate over the narrative importance of female suffering and its relationship to the novel's politics.[3]

Because the novel reemerged as part of a feminist recovery of women's writing, there has been a good deal of interesting debate over the novel's gender politics. The novel insists unstintingly on absolute female submission as a social and religious imperative, even while recording the extreme psychic costs of compliance with that imperative. If one focuses on the first part of the equation—insistence on submission—disagreement about political implications becomes almost inevitable; is this emphasis subtle coercion of readers, as Brodhead alleges, advocacy of an empowering self discipline as Tompkins believes, or perhaps a pragmatic recognition of real-world limitations on women, as Nina Baym suggests?[4] If, on the other hand, one sees a subversive subtext emerging through the simultaneous endorsement of female submission and endless iteration of the suffering it produces, the novel comes to appear more ambiguous, indeed strongly divided against itself. Emphasis on narrative tension characterizes the approaches of Joanne Dobson and Susan Harris.[5] This essay will also assert that *The Wide, Wide World* is in conflict over the fundamental questions it engages. It will focus in particular on the novel's privileging of female subjectivity through its depiction of female suffering, and its simultaneous compromising of other, competing sources of narrative and cultural authority.

Ellen Montgomery's suffering is a central narrative element not because the story explicitly legitimizes the authority figures who cause this suffering (although it does), but because suffering provides her with a compelling means of self-expression. The emphasis on suffering thus constructs two competing sources of authority within the narrative: the literal authority figures who are responsible for female suffering, and the women themselves who suffer. The narrative also appeals to and constructs the reader as a domestic woman, one who is expected to identify with Ellen and whose own emotional experiences are implicitly validated by the narrative attention given to Ellen's.

In addition to granting narrative authority to affective experience, the novel undercuts its own endorsement of female submission by subtly rendering grotesque the moral features of its primary patriarchal authority figure, John Humphreys. While the novel carefully records the emotional life of the child Ellen, establishing the importance of her sentimental interiority, it compromises John Humphreys by drawing analogies between John and other characters directly acknowledged as threats to Ellen. Humphreys occupies virtually every position of "legitimate" male authority in his relations with Ellen: adopted brother, minister, teacher, and ultimately husband. To the degree that it implicitly condemns John through a kind of character condensation, the novel destabilizes all "rightful" male authority. These two lenses subtly but profoundly reshape the image Warner's text projects; the first magnifies Ellen's suffering and the second creates a prismatic or split image of John. Through them, it becomes possible to see beneath the surface image showing the necessity of female submission, a murkier image of the pain caused by such social relations.

The condemnation of the novel's authority figures is never made explicit. Neither characters within the novel or the narrator overtly question the prerogatives of patriarchal power. Yet silence is eloquent in this novel. When Ellen is forcibly silenced we witness her acute suffering. The narrator uncharacteristically refrains from commentary or interpretation when the story line includes abuses of power perpetrated not only by John Humphreys, but by the other "legitimate" authority figures as well.[6] This prohibition against direct speech charges even greater narrative energy to the novel's careful depiction of emotions.

The opening lines of the novel illustrate the crucial link between silence and sentiment. Ellen is facing separation from her beloved invalid mother due to her father's improvident business dealings. She inquires anxiously about the status of a crucial lawsuit in the novel's first line and is immediately silenced by her mother: "I cannot tell you just now. Ellen, pick up that shawl, and spread it over me."[7] Mrs. Montgomery deflects the question by appealing to Ellen's tender solicitude. Mrs. Montgomery's silencing gesture underscores the organic connections between affect, silence, and "woman's sphere."

The fact that the novel opens with this exchange about a lawsuit is paradoxical because such public matters are virtually excluded from the novel's purview. We (and Ellen) never learn the details of the lawsuit that sets in motion the action of the novel. The lawsuit here metonymically represents public, male discourse; its introduction and immediate exclusion define the novel's discursive parameters and its absolute immersion in the female sphere of domesticity.[8] This initial reference to a lawsuit also establishes the power of the public sphere as an absent cause in the novel; it will determine the fates of the women, but will be visible only as refracted through their suffering.

Mrs. Montgomery further sets down the discursive rules for the novel in this first scene when she tells Ellen: "though we *must* sorrow, we must not rebel" (12). This statement makes the possibility of rebellion explicit, even while forbidding it. Because grief and revolt are alternate possible responses to injustice, Mrs. Montgomery's statement tacitly acknowledges that it is unjust for her husband to separate her from her child. Moreover, the conjunctive joining of sorrow and rebellion suggests that the two acts are of equal importance and perhaps are even the same: sorrow, expressed intensely enough, becomes rebellion.

This scene is paradigmatic both for what is said and what is not said; it emphasizes the importance of the suffering that the mother and daughter experience, but cannot directly attack its source. While the irresponsibility of the patriarchal figure is clearly suggested, explicit narrative recognition of this fact, and any active resistance such recognition might occasion, cannot find expression within *The Wide, Wide World*. Nevertheless, the novel underscores the imperative to feel the full amplitude of emotion and recognize the importance of the sorrow. The intensive and extensive representation of emotional anguish allows meanings to emerge that are far different from the ones put forward by the novel's many official authority figures.

There is fundamental narrative tension between the sentimental construction of Ellen Montgomery's subjectivity through her passionate emotional life and the directive from every authority figure in the novel to abandon her sense of self and live for the will of others. The novel follows these two divergent trajectories simultaneously. Although the novel purports to chronicle the victorious journey of the Christian to self-renunciation, it provides an increasingly powerful expression of female subjectivity through the medium of unrelenting oppression and suffering. The more we see Ellen suffer, the more powerfully she dominates the novel, even while the "lesson" she is learning from her suffering is self-erasure.

The concurrent and contradictory assertion and destruction of Ellen's selfhood is often figured in the novel through the literal muting of Ellen's voice and recording of her resulting suffering. We see this dynamic in the narrative treatment of Ellen's silencing by her Scottish relatives, who are the most physically intrusive of the many authority figures who control her:

> Mrs. Lindsay touched her lips; a way of silencing her that Ellen particularly disliked, and which both Mr. Lindsay and his mother were accustomed to use.
>
> (p. 541)

Authority figures succeed in literally sealing Ellen's lips, but the narrative also insists on communicating Ellen's subjective response to that silencing process, thus paradoxically giving her voice.

Ellen's subjectivity is not, and cannot be, asserted through the usual modes of speech or action. In terms of the plot, she is much less subject than object, acted upon by every authority figure in the novel. She can never revolt, but she can suffer and she does so exquisitely. Feeling becomes the means of establishing narrative authority and authenticity not only more than speech or action, but frequently in opposition to them.[9]

The novel's most detailed descriptions of Ellen's suffering immediately follow moments when she has been ignored or her perspective discounted. The narrative emphasis on the reality and intensity of her suffering counterbalances (and implicitly condemns) the responses of those who overlook her. The moments when Ellen's agony is described in greatest detail tend not to be the classic tableaux of sentimental suffering such as deathbed scenes—although the novel certainly contains its share of these—but moments when other characters cannot see her as important or appreciate her emotional perspective. This emphasis is important for two reasons. First, it underscores the novel's central premise that the emotional life of the female child matters; significant narrative energy must go to countervene assumptions to the contrary. Second, this emphasis on Ellen's agony at being overlooked suggests that being erased as a subject is, for her, a calamity almost greater than the death of a loved one. Ellen agonizes over being treated as negligible, and the narrative both endorses this response and ministers the corrective of treating her with unfailing attention.

After Ellen has parted from her mother and is in the indifferent care of a fashionable woman, she experiences the humiliation of being laughed at because her bonnet is not stylish. One might expect that a narrator firmly dedicated to Christian discipline would chide Ellen for such vanity, but her suffering is taken seriously.

> If a thunderbolt had fallen at Ellen's feet, the shock would hardly have been greater. The lightning of passion shot through every vein. And it was not passion only; there was hurt feeling and wounded pride, and the sorrow of which her heart was full enough before, now wakened afresh. The child was beside herself.
>
> (pp. 66-67)

The narrator details all the components of Ellen's agony to make sure that its nuances are precisely registered. It is ironic that later critics pool all Ellen's many tears together, when we are informed by an exacting narrative titration how and why Ellen is suffering each time she cries.[10]

Ellen's only venture into the commercial marketplace teaches her definitively that in the "wide world" she is invisible. Again, the narrator compensates through an intimate description of Ellen's response to being ignored in a large department store.

> Clerks frequently passed her, crossing the store in all directions, but they . . . did not seem to notice her at all, and were gone before poor Ellen could get her mouth open to speak to them. She knew well enough now, poor child, what it was that made her cheeks burn as they did, and her heart beat as if it would burst its bounds.
>
> (p. 45)

The narrative places itself squarely on the side of the "poor child" and records in excruciating detail just how it feels to be vulnerable, to be absolutely incapable of making the world pay attention. The narrator, however, is paying rapt attention, recording every sign and symptom of Ellen's suffering and recognizing her feelings as meaningful.

There are occasions when Ellen's suffering is not caused by human cruelty but it remains a means of expressing her subjectivity. The narrative gives a detailed account of Ellen's sense of ennui and confinement when she is sick in bed. The degree of detail in this description suggests the importance of Ellen's subjective responses even—or perhaps especially—when she is incapable of any interaction with the "wide world." Given the extent to which invalidism was part of female identity and experience during the antebellum period, this narrative insistence seems particularly significant.[11]

> "I used to lie and watch that crack in the door at the foot of my bed," said Ellen, "and I got so tired of it I hated to see it, but when I opened my eyes I couldn't help looking at it, and watching all the little ins and outs in the crack till I was as sick of it as could be. And that button too that fastens the door, and the little round mark the button has made, and thinking how far the button went round. And then if I looked toward the window I would go right to counting the panes, first up and down and then across; I didn't want to count them, but I couldn't help it."
>
> (p. 220)

Warner creates a strong sense of the claustrophobia and hyperacucia induced by the endless repetition of interior scenes that marks the life of the invalid only more forcefully, not differently, than the life of the domestic woman.

Ellen's obsession with the details of the room eerily prefigures Charlotte Perkins Gilman's 1892 short story "The Yellow Wallpaper." Gilman's "madwoman in the attic" is similarly trapped in a restrictive female identity and a confined domestic space.[12] In both works, the subjectivity of the confined woman is privileged. Her perceptions and emotions are accorded extensive attention and the emphasis on her perspective precludes another from dominating the story. The subversive effects of Gilman's intense focus on the suffering female subject have been recognized for a number of years now; the effects of Warner's more sustained use of this figure are at least as powerful.

The narrative centrality of Ellen's experience is reinforced by the novel's inscription of a reader who, like Ellen, understands the particular pressures of a confined life, the significance of emotional interactions, and the symbolic meaning of the minutiae of domestic life. The reader is interpellated into the text as a domestic woman who will recognize the emotional power of Ellen's suffering, and who will play the assigned role of intense sympathizer.[13]

The intimacy the novel structures between its readers and Ellen is crucial because without a responsive reader, Ellen's trials and the attention paid to them become a listless litany of petty grievances. The painful events in Ellen's life are "trifles," as Susan Glaspell uses the term; the small details signaling the intense suffering of the submissive woman can only be decoded by those who understand the psychic costs of such a life. In contrast to the Glaspell play, however, *The Wide, Wide World* does not describe this discovery within the text but inscribes a reader who will make the connections.[14]

The narrative describes Ellen's domestic work in great detail, thus assuming a reader who knows and cares about the difficulty and importance of such work. Ellen is not usually shown doing hard manual labor, but rather the affective, nurturing work most commonly associated with domesticity.

Early in the novel, Ellen is described ritualistically preparing her mother's tea in a scene that critics have focused on as evidence of the power of female community.[15]

> She used in the first place to make sure that the kettle really boiled; then she carefully poured some water into the tea-pot and rinsed it, both to make it clean and to make it hot; then she knew exactly how much tea to put into the tiny little tea-pot, which was just big enough to hold two cups of tea, and having poured a very little boiling water into it, she used to set it by the side of the fire while she made half a slice of toast. How careful Ellen was about that toast! The bread must not be cut too thick nor too thin; the fire must, if possible, burn clear and bright, and she herself held the bread on a fork, just at the right distance from the coals to get nicely browned without burning. When this was done to her satisfaction (and if the first piece failed she would take another), she filled up the little tea-pot from the boiling kettle, and proceeded to make a cup of tea. She knew, and was very careful to put in, just the quantity of milk and sugar that her mother liked; and then

she used to carry the tea and toast on a little tray to her mother's side, and very often held it there for her while she eat [sic].

(p. 13)

This lengthy description is premised on the recognition that care taken in domestic tasks signals deep emotional attachment. In addition, the careful, almost instructional, recreation of these intimate obligations assumes and constructs a reader who can both understand and feel the psychic demands of life within the claustrophobic confines of domestic space.

The novel carefully courts its readers and takes any opportunity to ingratiate Ellen into their affections. Displays of Ellen's fortitude and virtue are often played out without any audience other than the reader. One scene describes Ellen having "done all she had to do, and set the supper table with punctilious care, and a face of busy happiness it would have been a pleasure to see if there had been any one to look at it" (p. 468). This passage both laments the lack of recognition for much of Ellen's domestic labor and at the same time rescues Ellen from this obscurity by being there "to look at it." The act of careful description sets up someone there to see it, even while the narrator's point is the pathos of Ellen's isolation. The narrative maintains the fiction that only those within the novel can respond to Ellen, even while it employs all possible devices to elicit a response from the reader.

The insistence on an engaged reader response and the privileging of Ellen's perspective combine to make appreciation of the novel contingent on one's willingness to identify with Ellen. To a much greater degree than for most novels, evaluations of *The Wide, Wide World* have rested on whether or not readers will consent to fill the role set out for them. Jane Tompkins alludes to this attribute of the novel when she remarks that the novel's power emerges from "our" having shared Ellen's painful experiences: "Ellen Montgomery is a vulnerable, powerless, and innocent person victimized by those in authority over her. Since we have all at one time or another been in her position, we cannot help sharing her emotional point of view."[16] While the novel encourages this identification, acceptance of Ellen's emotional point of view is not a natural or necessary consequence of reading the novel.

The critical history of *The Wide, Wide World* shows that many readers resent and resist its designs on them. One practitioner of the anti-sentimentality criticism of the early twentieth century calls the novel "a swamp of lachrymosity. It was a malarial book."[17] His choice of metaphor recognizes that the emotional temper of the novel is contagious; the book does not merely represent sentiment and suffering but attempts to "infect" the reader. Even though pejorative, the pathogen metaphor is useful: *The Wide, Wide World* works to involve readers viscerally in an experience that can be quite painful.

The sentimental focus on Ellen Montgomery's feelings grants narrative authority to the anger and suffering of the powerless, and implicitly questions the rightful authority of the powerful who cause such suffering. The novel further challenges its own authority figures through compromising the character of John Humphreys.

The delegitimation of John Humphreys is crucial to the novel's validation of Ellen's perspective and experience. The child Ellen eventually comes under the complete legal and psychological control of this man, and if the novel is seen as depicting his control as right and good, then the ending appears definitively to settle all questions of appropriate female behavior; Ellen's Christian forbearance is rewarded with the perfect marriage. Not surprisingly, if one reads the novel as unambiguously endorsing John's authority, it appears to be a manual for acceptance of or survival under patriarchy.[18]

However, the novel reveals in a number of subtle ways that John ought not to be entrusted with limitless power over a vulnerable young woman. John Humphreys is clearly shown to have a propensity for violence, and he is linked to a male figure who physically threatens Ellen. Violence as a method of control is anathema in women's sentimental novels of the antebellum period, as Richard Brodhead has convincingly demonstrated,[19] so the association of John Humphreys with violence is especially meaningful, particularly given the extent of the power he comes to hold over Ellen.

When Ellen first meets John, her impression of him is mediated through the perspective of his adoring sister, Alice. The problem with this source of information, in addition to obvious sibling bias, is that the relationship between Alice and John is shown from the beginning to be peculiarly erotic. This attribute becomes more obvious and troubling later in the book when Alice falls sick and is determined to have Ellen replace her as John's "sister," and John then goes on to marry Ellen. The incestuous overtones of the relationship between Alice and John Humphreys have been traced carefully by G. M. Goshgarian, who is interested in them as examples of the Freudian "family romance."[20] If one is focusing on Ellen's subjective experiences and vulnerability, the erotic bond between Alice and John has the effect of compromising even saintly Alice as a loving mentor to Ellen, since Alice's major contribution to Ellen's life is to transfer her to John.

On a brief holiday sojourn with the Humphreys family, Ellen and the reader receive information about John that is not filtered through Alice and shows him in a very different light. These good friends of the Humphreys have frightening things to say about John. The children of the household call him "King John the Second" (p. 315) and "The Grand Turk" (p. 316). The adults allude to John's violent side. One man reports that "I was not a match for him a year ago. . . . I do not know precisely . . . what it takes to rouse John Humphreys, but when he *is* roused he seems to me to have the strength enough for twice his bone and muscle" (318). This "friend" goes on to compare John to gunpowder in volatility. Neither the reader or Ellen ever gets the history of this physical fight, but the force of John's fury is unmistakable. Since the narrator has by this point carefully taught the reader to pay attention to Ellen's suffering, the lack of explanation for the behavior of Ellen's new "brother" is a problematic lacuna.

Later in the novel, the female members of this family report on John's propensity for horse beating. They have given Ellen a pony and are surprised by her reaction when they suggest she use a whip on him.

> "Hasn't John taught you that lesson yet?" said the young lady;—"he is perfect in it himself. Do you remember, Alice, the chastising he gave that fine Black horse of ours we called the 'Black Prince?'—a beautiful creature, he was,—more than a year ago?—My conscience! he frightened me to death." . . .
>
> "What did he do that for?" said Ellen. . . .
>
> "My dear Ellen," said Alice smiling, though she spoke seriously,—"it was necessary; it sometimes is necessary to do such things. . . . It was a clear case of obstinacy. The horse was resolved to have his own way . . . and as John has no fancy for giving up, he carried his point—. . . partly, I confess, by a judicious use of the whip and spur."
>
> (pp. 376-77)

Ellen, who is at this point increasingly coming under John's control, finds this story distressing, and the other women laughingly recognize that Ellen is making the connection between herself and the horse. The potentially serious implications of John's behavior are, once again, glossed over by Alice.

The role of horse beating as a metaphor for male domination becomes more striking—and more disturbing—in an agonizing scene in which horse beating stands in for rape. In an emergency, Ellen must ride to town alone to find a doctor. This is only the second time Ellen ventures into the "wide, wide world" by herself, and not only is this foray as disastrous as her much earlier trip to the department store, but she is tortured by the same man. On her return from town, she is accosted by the clerk from New York City who was cruel to her years previously and who has (very improbably) been transplanted to the small town upstate where Aunt Fortune lives. The unlikely return of Saunders, coupled with the slow, torturous pace of the scene, creates a nightmarish quality that accentuates the scene's metaphoric meaning. Saunders appears as a recurrent symbol of male exploitation of female vulnerability.

Saunders grabs Ellen's pony and threatens to whip him while she begs him not to: "'Please don't do anything with it,' Ellen said earnestly;—'I never touch him with a whip, . . . he isn't used to it; pray, pray do not!'" (p. 397). The scene continues for several pages with Ellen in an agony of apprehension and Saunders relishing her terror and helplessness. Throughout this scene and elsewhere Ellen is identified with her quiescent little pony.

The climax of the scene comes when, out of nowhere, John Humphreys appears to rescue Ellen. What is most striking about this "rescue" is not the difference it establishes between Saunders and John, but the essential similarity in the way the violence of the two men is treated. John is not just Ellen's savior from Saunders, he is also another incarnation of the threat Saunders represents. The conflation of Saunders and John undercuts the novel's support for John's authority. If we read this scene as a straight rescue, John's growing authority over Ellen is endorsed and the appropriateness of her submission to him is underscored. David Leverenz, who finds the novel essentially conservative, reads the scene this way: "When John saves Ellen from the ubiquitous Mr. Saunders, the contrast between the right kind of man and the wrong kind becomes obvious."[21] However, if we see Saunders as a stand-in for John, any distinction between them necessarily collapses.

John arrives on the scene and is outraged by the liberties Saunders is taking with Ellen. In his usual commanding way, he asserts his power over Saunders.

> "Take your hand off the bridle!"—with a slight touch of the riding-whip upon the hand in question.
>
> "Not for you, brother," said Mr. Saunders sneeringly;— "I'll walk with any lady I've a mind to. Look out for yourself!"
>
> "We will dispense with your further attendance," said John coolly. "Do you hear me? do as I order you!"
>
> The speaker did not put himself in a passion, and Mr. Saunders, accustomed for his own part to make bluster serve instead of prowess, despised a command so calmly given.—Ellen, who knew the voice, and still better could read the eye, drew conclusions very different. She was almost breathless with terror.
>
> (p. 400)

While Saunders' potential for violence frightens Ellen, John's leaves her "breathless with terror." The sexual connotations of this encounter are underscored by Saunders' comment that he will entertain himself with "any lady I've a mind to." This pony beating/rape sequence intially displaces male sexual violence onto the minor character of Saunders, but later merges him with John by having both practice the exact same form of violence (horse beating) and having both elicit a similar emotional response from Ellen.

Although the threat of violence destabilizes John's claim to rightful authority, his control of Ellen is not manifested through direct recourse to violence but rests primarily on his absolute power as religious advisor and tutor. However, these more indirect methods of control are premised upon the ever-present threat of violence and are more insidious because his domination is disguised or naturalized; Ellen is a child and John the adult who must guide her. John's more subtle psychological control over Ellen is also compromised within the novel, again through splitting or the "twinning" of John and a more obviously destructive figure.

Just as John's violence links him by a principle of transitivity to an acknowledged threat, his psychological demands on Ellen link him to another character who is explicitly criticized within the text: Ellen's Uncle Lindsey. Through a series of plot twists, Ellen's Scottish uncle, whom she has never met, adopts her during her teen years and brings her to live in his household. He demands humiliating degrees of intimacy and compliance from her, keeping her constantly at his bidding. He is obsessed over whether she truly loves him and willingly does as he instructs (she has no chance to resist actively). It is an extremely intrusive relationship and causes Ellen great suffering.

Almost as soon as Ellen arrives in Scotland, her uncle realizes he must struggle with John for power over her. Although Ellen is an adolescent, he forces her to call him "Father" and orders her to let others believe that she is his biological daughter (p. 526). His relationship with her, again like John's, has disturbingly erotic overtones.

The struggle between John and Mr. Lindsay over Ellen's psyche is not a veiled or coded one; Mr. Lindsay orders Ellen to stop thinking of John and referring to him as her brother.

> "I am not satisfied to have your body here and your heart somewhere else."
>
> "I must have a poor little kind of heart," said Ellen, smiling amidst her tears, "if it had room in it for only one person."
>
> "Ellen," said Mr. Lindsay inquisitively, "did you *insinuate* a falsehood there?"
>
> "No, sir!"
>
> (pp. 534-35)

Mr. Lindsay knows what Ellen evidently does not: that the control he and John demand does not allow for any sharing. Ellen does not understand that the kind of relationship sought by John and Mr. Lindsay is one of such power and erotic possessiveness that indeed there is "only room in it for one person."

The obsession with control in purportedly loving familial (and pseudo-familial) relationships and the blurring of lines between sexual and paternal affection muddy the novel's advocacy of female submission; there are too many strange demands made on the devoted domestic woman in these families. This tangle of family relationships, turgid and turbid, gives the novel a Gothic hue that further undermines its defense of patriarchal authority. The innocent female is courted, and metaphorically seduced (or raped), by dangerous men who possess unlimited legal and psychological power over her.

Eventually Mr. Lindsay concedes that John has greater power and gives up the fight for jurisdiction, but while the narrator gives the victory to God, there is ample evidence that John's will to dominate is personal. He tells Ellen to "humble yourself in the dust before him [God]—the more the better" (p. 297), but what we see is his insistence that she be humbled before John himself. The surface story of the Christian's journey toward resignation to the absolute power of God both masks and serves as a metaphor for the story of the young vulnerable female's inevitable submission to a man who has godlike power over her.

If John can be seen as arrogating to himself the divine right to adoration and blind obedience, his status within the novel becomes more precarious; he is even potentially diabolical or idolatrous. Ellen acknowledges that while she could disobey her Uncle Lindsey's orders if they should violate her conscience, she could not go against any of John's: "I could not have disobeyed *him* possibly!" (p. 519). The implication is that Ellen could not defy John even if she believed him to be wrong, or that she could never adjudge right and wrong for herself when he is present. Although the novel presents John's instructions to Ellen as coextensive with her personal conscience, the fact that John destroys Ellen's ability to make moral determinations is highly problematic in a novel that emphasizes so strongly the responsibility of individuals to consult and abide by their own consciences.

The narrative merging of God's will and John's accounts for the pervasive understanding of the novel as celebrating the Christian's victory over a sinful self. However, even those who argue most strongly for the power of the novel's representation of religious transcendence recognize its conflation of Christian submission to God with female submission to male authority. For instance, Jane Tompkins notes: "In sentimental fiction, the vocation to be mastered is Christian salvation, which, translated in to social terms, means learning to submit to authorities society has placed over you."[22] This "translation" or slippage is precisely what I wish to emphasize: while using the language of religious experience, *The Wide, Wide World* is describing social, political, and economic power relations.

John wins the struggle for Ellen's soul, but his penultimate demand when they are eventually reunited in Scotland (marriage being implied as the ultimate) further problematizes the novel's endorsement of his authority over her and her willingness to accept it. John orders her to: "Read no novels," and she immediately assures him that, "I never do, John. I knew you did not like it, and I have taken good care to keep out of the way of them" (p. 564). John wants to insulate Ellen from the "dangerous" effects of novels, and his hostility toward novels echoes a number of paternal authority figures of the late eighteenth and early nineteenth centuries.[23] However, it is odd to have the protagonist of a novel vow so earnestly to eschew the dangerous influence of novels.

Warner avoided the most obvious contradiction of this statement by never calling her own works novels, but her denial only complicates the question; why were novels so dangerous that she could not acknowledge writing them or allow her character to read them?[24] In the late eighteenth and early nineteenth centuries, public concern about the dangers of novel reading focused specifically on women, and the fear was that novels would lead women into indolence and moral corruption. Yet novels of the period appear to endorse extremely conservative female behavior and firmly to punish any deviance. In discussing seduction novels in *Revolution and the Word*, Cathy Davidson suggests that the "danger" of novels was that they offered women serious consideration of the injustices intrinsic to female life, albeit without advocating rebellion. By acknowledging that women suffered inordinately, novels questioned the social order consigning women to such self-defeating roles.[25] The novels Davidson discusses belong to an earlier generation of women's writing, but her observations apply to Warner's novel as well. Indeed, the effect is intensified in *The Wide, Wide World*; its emphasis on the subjectivity of the suffering woman, coupled with the fact that she does not eventually have to be vilified as a "fallen woman," greatly increases the power of the covert oppositional discourse.

It is ironically appropriate that John Humphreys, who both perpetrates and obfuscates psychic crimes against an innocent young woman, should fear the lessons sentimental novels teach young women about their mistreatment. John's prohibition and Ellen's acquiescence highlight the central tension in *The Wide, Wide World* and other women's sentimental novels; the depiction of female submission to patriarchal authority is ubiquitous but coexists with, and is necessarily undermined by, the constant attention paid to the suffering of the women who submit. The novel ultimately privileges female subjectivity even, or especially, when its women are prohibited from the most basic forms of expression and volition such as choosing when and what to say, do, or even read.

Notes

1. *The Wide, Wide World* was republished in 1987 by the Feminist Press. Although Warner's novel never entirely disappeared from view, for most of the twentieth century it was discussed, and dismissed, as a negative example of women's sentimental fiction. Nina Baym's *Woman's Fiction: A Guide to Novels By and About Women in America, 1820-1870* (Ithaca: Cornell Univ. Press, 1978) marked the first serious critical consideration of *The Wide, Wide World* and other works in the genre. Jane Tompkins' *Sensational Designs: The Cultural Work of American Fiction, 1790-1860* (New York: Oxford Univ. Press, 1985) contains an extended discussion of the novel.

2. Although publishing data from this period are notoriously unreliable, it seems indisputable that *The Wide, Wide World* was an unprecedented success, whatever the actual numbers of copies sold. On the commercial event that the publication of *The Wide, Wide World* became, see Edward Halsey Foster, *Susan and Anna Warner* (Boston: Twayne, 1979); Dorothy Sanderson, *They Wrote for a Living: A Bibliography of the Works of Susan Bogert Warner and Anna Bartlett Warner* (West Point: Constitution Island Association, 1976); and James D. Hart, *The Popular Book: The History of America's Literary Taste* (Berkeley: Univ. of California Press, 1950).

3. Tompkins, p. 163; Richard Brodhead, "Sparing the Rod: Discipline and Fiction in Antebellum America," *Representations* 21 (1988), 91.

4. Baym observes that overt forms of resistance were not available to Warner or her characters. She reads the novel's frequent tears as "therapy" and the "safe expression" of emotions which could otherwise not be expressed: "rage and frustration may not be openly voiced by the powerless without unfortunate consequences for them" (p. 144). "The story would have been different, of course, could she [Ellen] (or her author) have broken through to gestures of defiance more pleasing to the twentieth century" (p. 145).

5. In her essay "The Hidden Hand: Subversion of Cultural Ideology in Three Mid-Century American Women's Novels" (*AQ* [*American Quarterly*] 38 [1986], 223-43), Joanne Dobson describes "a strong emotional undertow that pulls the reader in the opposite direction" (p. 230) from the values the novel purports to endorse. In *Nineteenth-Century American Women's Novels* (New York: Cambridge Univ. Press, 1990), Susan K. Harris views women's novels of the 1850s as subversive "Janus-faced texts" (p. 30) that both endorse and undercut conservative models of female behavior.

6. Dobson observes that the novel's attribution of cruelty to authority figures helps to undercut its overt message: "The subversion of Warner's lesson in obedience comes in a manipulation of characterization that subtly undercuts the message: every official authority figure during the course of the story abuses Ellen in ways she experiences as traumatic" (p. 230).

7. Susan Warner, *The Wide, Wide World,* ed. Jane Tompkins (New York: The Feminist Press, 1987), p. 9. Hereafter cited parenthetically.

8. While historians remind us that the so-called cult of domesticity was never an absolute category, that the distinction between private/female and public/male was more ideological than actual, this division is rigidly enforced in *The Wide, Wide World,* attesting both to the power of the idea of separate spheres in antebellum America and the extreme depiction of powerlessness in *The Wide, Wide World.* Although ideals of domesticity pervade most women's novels of this period, few isolate their heroines from the world to the extent that Warner's novel does. For a comparative analysis of a large number of works of the period, see Nina Baym. For a discussion of the problematizing of the category of separate spheres, see Linda Kerber, "Separate Spheres, Female Worlds, and Woman's Place: The Rhetorics of Women's History," *Journal of American History* 75 (1988), 9-39.

9. This argument that subjectivity is established without or in counterdistinction to voice suggests that representations of female subjectivity, particularly in this generation of women's writing, may appear in more forms than previously assumed. For example, Barbara Bardes and Suzanne Gossett in *Declarations of Independence: Women and Political Power in Nineteenth-Century Fiction* (New Brunswick: Rutgers Univ. Press, 1990) define female subjectivity in terms of voice in their analysis of fictional representations of women in the early 1850s. They argue that "by speaking, a woman was claiming her place as *subject* rather than *object,* as self rather than other. . . . [I]t is a political gesture" (p. 69). In *The Wide, Wide World,* sentimentality complicates this picture tremendously; the narrative focus on emotions compromises the authority of speech and ruptures the association of subjectivity with the ability to speak.

10. For instance, Fred Lewis Pattee in *The Feminine Fifties* (New York: D. Appleton-Century, 1940) reports the exact number of times Ellen cries in the novel, not to illuminate the presentation of the child's emotional life, but to trivialize it: "By actual count there are 245 tear-flows in 574 pages of the novel" (p. 57).

11. Invalidism was a serious problem among middle-class, white antebellum women. Catharine Beecher crusaded against the deplorable state of women's health, attributing it to a lack of education, ignorance about domestic management, and restrictive clothing. In her essay "The Evils suffered by American Women and American Children" (New York: Harper and Brothers, 1846) Beecher asserts that "A perfectly healthy woman . . . is so infrequent among the more wealthy classes, that it may be regarded as the exception, and not as the general rule" (p. 13). For more information on Catharine Beecher, including her work on behalf of women's education and women's health, see Kathryn Kish Sklar, *Catharine Beecher: A Study in American Domesticity* (New York: W. W. Norton, 1973).

12. Gilman's 1892 short story chronicles the gradual descent into insanity by a woman forced by her doctor-husband to undergo the "rest cure" made infamous by Dr. S. Weir Mitchell, who treated Gilman during a period of mental crisis in her own life. The term "madwoman in the attic" comes from Susan Gilbert and Sandra Gubar's now-classic study of women's writing, *The Madwoman in the Attic: The Woman Writer and the Nineteenth-Century Literary Imagination* (New Haven: Yale Univ. Press, 1979).

13. I am here using Althusser's term for the construction of subjectivity, which suggests that functioning as a subject requires an awareness of one's position within the discourse that calls that subject position into being. In Warner's novel, female subjectivity is constituted both through a recognition of powerlessness within male-dominated discourse and through the emotional experience of suffering. See Louis Althusser, *Lenin and Philosophy* (New York: Monthly Review Press, 1971), pp. 170-77.

14. Susan Glaspell's *Trifles* tells the story of a murder investigation in which a wife is accused of killing her husband. The wives of the officials in charge of the case notice domestic details that provide evidence of her guilt along with evidence of her husband's extreme cruelty. They decide not to share their discoveries because as domestic women they understand what the woman endured and their husbands could not. Their common experience as women supersedes their allegiance to the law.

15. Jane Tompkins reads this scene as demonstrating the "sacramental power" of women's respectful focus on the rituals of their own domestic work and argues that the communal values symbolized by the communion of tea and toast constitute "the

reward [the novel] offers its readers for that other activity . . . the control of rebellious passion" (p. 170).

16. Jane Tompkins, "Afterword" to the Feminist Press edition of *The Wide, Wide World*, p. 585. However, Tompkins realizes that actual readers do not necessarily respond this way; she describes the hostility of critics to the novel and their designation of its concerns as frivolous or negligible (*Sensational Designs*, pp. 147-48).

17. Van Wyck Brooks, *The Flowering of New England 1815-1865* (New York: E. P. Dutton, 1937), p. 416.

18. The argument that the novel teaches women how to survive the very real difficulties of their lives is put forward primarily by feminist critics, for example Nancy Schnog, "Inside the Sentimental: The Psychological Work of *The Wide, Wide World*," *Genders* 4 (1989), 11-25; Isabelle White, "Anti-Individualism, Authority, and Identity: Susan Warner's Contradictions in *The Wide, Wide World*," *American Studies* 31 (1990), 31-41; Nina Baym; and Jane Tompkins. Those critics who argue that the novel is essentially an endorsement of patriarchy include Richard Brodhead in "Sparing the Rod" and David Leverenz in *Manhood in the American Renaissance* (Ithaca: Cornell Univ. Press, 1989); both assert that John's authority over Ellen is absolutely endorsed within the narrative.

19. See Brodhead, "Sparing the Rod."

20. G. M. Goshgarian, *To Kiss the Chastening Rod: Domestic Fiction and Sexual Ideology in the American Renaissance* (Ithaca: Cornell Univ. Press, 1992). For example, Goshgarian reads Alice and John's decision that Ellen will replace Alice as John's adoring and obedient sister when Alice dies as part of both Alice and Ellen's lurking incestuous desires. "Coupling with his 'sister,' John couples with his sister . . . shielded by those inverted commas, Ellen embraces the father she never really had" (p. 97).

21. Leverenz, p. 187.

22. Tompkins, *Sensational Designs*, pp. 176-77.

23. In *Private Woman, Public Stage: Literary Domesticity in Nineteenth-Century America* (New York: Oxford Univ. Press, 1984), Mary Kelley quotes Thomas Jefferson's serious reservations about the effects of novel reading on young women. He feared that the "inordinate passion prevalent for novels" fostered in female readers "a bloated imagination, sickly judgment, and disgust toward all the real business of life" (p. 117).

24. Jane Tompkins reports that Warner "never referred to her books as 'novels' but called them stories,

because, in her eyes, they functioned in the same way as Biblical parables . . . that is, they were written for edification's sake and not for the sake of art, as we understand it" (*Sensational Designs*, p. 149). Warner's ambivalence about novels runs deeper, however, than a simple aversion to art without religious content. Warner found the reading of novels a dangerous temptation in her own life. Anna Warner's biography of her sister, *Susan Warner* (New York: G. P. Putnam's Sons, 1909), quotes an excerpt from Susan's journal as an adolescent in which she asserts her determination to "keep clear of novels for one while at least; I get punished for it when I meddle with them, and I am sure they are about as bad for me as any thing I need wish to have" (p. 165). Despite this belief that novels were bad for her, Warner not only continued to read them but identified with their characters. While she was writing *The Wide, Wide World*, Susan wrote to her sister Anna that she considered herself very like Jane Eyre (*Susan Warner*, p. 267).

25. In *Revolution and the World: The Rise of the Novel in America* (New York: Oxford Univ. Press, 1986), Davidson explores the ideological content of the early nineteenth-century novel of seduction, arguing that seduction became a metaphor for women's dangerously unstable position in republican America. Davidson shows that the novel of seduction took seriously the dilemmas women faced through such narrative elements as the sympathetic portrayal of the fallen woman and the emphasis on her powerlessness: "many of these novels question the efficacy of the prevailing legal, political, and social values, even if the questioning is done by innuendo rather than by actual assertion of a contrary view" (p. 140).

Sara E. Quay (essay date spring 1999)

SOURCE: Quay, Sara E. "Homesickness in Susan Warner's *The Wide, Wide World*." *Tulsa Studies in Women's Literature* 18, no. 1 (spring 1999): 39-58.

[*In the following essay, Quay relates Warner's use of nostalgia and loss in* The Wide, Wide World *to emerging nineteenth-century middle-class consumerism.*]

Taken as a whole, Susan Warner's best-selling novel, **The Wide, Wide World** (1850), is about the experience of loss.[1] In fact, the novel might be said to have been generated from the profound loss its author, as a young woman, experienced when her family moved from their home in New York City to an isolated existence on Constitution Island in upstate New York. A result of the family's financial ruin, the move separated Susan Warner from the life she had known to that point.[2] She wrote in her journal soon afterward: "we have nothing to do with the world. Every human tie . . . is so broken and fastened off."[3] As if in response to this experience, Warner's novel, written while she lived on the island, centers around the losses undergone by its main character, Ellen Montgomery. After depicting early scenes in which Ellen is nestled safely at home with her mother, the novel goes on to record an extraordinary number of dislocations and separations. Warner's focus on loss was not just a personal preoccupation, but reflected a cultural one as well. The period in American history during which Warner wrote was marked, as Michael Rogin notes, by "a powerful sense of loss,"[4] a result of geographical distance between family members and loved ones as well as of incurable illnesses and early, often unexpected death. Ellen's experiences would have been familiar to many of the novel's readers, who would have empathized, for instance, with her poignant expression of pain after her separation from her mother: "I cannot reach her," she cries, "she cannot reach me!" (p. 148).

The Wide, Wide World foregrounds Ellen's losses but also works to resolve how individuals can both endure and recover from such experiences.[5] More specifically, the novel works to solve the problem in mid-nineteenth-century America of nostalgia. Defined in contemporary terms, nostalgia is "a form of melancholia caused by prolonged absence from one's home or country; severe home-sickness."[6] As the definition suggests, nostalgia characterizes the cultural affect of the mid-1800s in two ways. First, the term registers the challenge of maintaining the integrity of "one's home" or domestic space in the face of vulnerable interpersonal relationships and frequent geographic moves. Second, the term points toward the early-nineteenth-century wave of immigrants who, after leaving their country of origin, or national "home," arrived in America to secure a new one.[7] In both cases, homesickness is the affective corollary to the literal and figurative longing for home that shaped so much of mid-nineteenth-century American culture. In particular, it reflects the experience of loss the newly established American middle class underwent as it made the transition from a collection of individuals—from different national, geographic, and familial backgrounds—to a coherent group.[8] The search for "home," in other words, stands as a metaphor for the middle-class search for its identity. Conversely, the recuperation of home is marked by the cessation of nostalgia, which is replaced not only with a literal home in which to live, but a national and class-based sense of home defined by feelings of comfort and belonging.[9]

Warner's antidote to nostalgia—and to the losses the term connotes—lies in a particular relationship to the material world, one that marks the cultural shift from the Age of Homespun to full-fledged consumerism. As Ann Douglas has remarked, sentimental novels such as Warner's appear to embrace consumerism; they are "courses in the shopping mentality," and Ellen in particular represents the "quintessential pleasure of the consumer."[10] Upon closer investigation, however, *The Wide, Wide World* does not condone consumerism as eagerly as Douglas asserts. In fact, the novel actively resists the emerging ideology of commodity culture, representing it as a system that contributes to, rather than mediates, the problem of homesickness. Objects under consumerism are reified: they are evacuated of any human origins and become instead valued in and of themselves. Commodities may temporarily distract Ellen from the pain she feels in her longing for home, but they will never help her to recover from that pain because they threaten to replace the search for home with a search for material things. At the same time, however, the novel does not counter consumerism by embracing a return to the residual ideology of utilitarianism that defined the receding Homespun Age. In preconsumer society, objects are meant to serve only practical uses; they have no emotional meaning and, therefore, can be of no help in overcoming the state of homesickness that Ellen experiences.

In contrast to what the novel sees as these fundamentally flawed understandings of material things, *The Wide, Wide World* offers a third alternative, one which stands at the juncture between the overdetermined value of objects under consumerism and the purely practical value of things in the Age of Homespun. The difference lies in the type of meaning attributed to material things. As Ellen learns, by investing objects with affect, by imagining them as repositories of emotion connected with her home, she can overcome the pain—the nostalgia—of modern life. In doing so, she creates keepsakes—objects invested with the ability to maintain connections, to maintain quite literally a sense of home in the face of loss. Warner's sister, Anna, illustrates the way that keepsakes help alleviate homesickness when she writes in her biography of Susan that, after the family left their home in New York, "more and more the girl [Susan] brought up in general luxury, found in books, pictures, and her piano, the only tokens of what had been" (p. 206). The objects the Warner family brought with them from their city existence to their life on the island were the only connections they had to their previous home. As a result, such things reminded Warner of "what had been," providing her with a means by which she could remember, and perhaps even recover a sense of, the home she had left. Although keepsakes have been viewed as a defining trope of novels like Warner's, included in the genre of domestic or sentimental fiction, how and why they play so central a role has been only tangentially addressed. By examining the way that nostalgia is mediated through objects like keepsakes, this function can be clarified, not only within *The Wide, Wide World,* but in terms of the broader category of domestic fiction as well.[11]

The importance of material objects is evident in the early chapters of *The Wide, Wide World,* which are striking because of their preoccupation not only with Ellen's impending separation from her mother but with her acquisition of things. In preparation for their split, a result of Mrs. Montgomery's illness requiring her to go abroad without her daughter, Ellen and her mother embark upon a shopping trip. In keeping with Douglas's thesis that Ellen is the quintessential representation of nineteenth-century consumerism, the girl's initial response to the stores she visits is to be "completely bewitched" (p. 32) by "so many tempting objects" (p. 31). "From one thing to another she went," Warner writes, "admiring and wondering; in her wildest dreams she had never imagined such beautiful things. The store was fairyland" (p. 32). While Douglas sees Ellen's fascination as evidence of Warner's uncritical stance toward consumerism, she overlooks the critique inherent in this same scene. Mrs. Montgomery tells her daughter "I am a little afraid your head will be turned" (p. 31) by the objects in the store, and the scene warns against the blinding allure that commodities can have. As Ellen, with "flushed cheek and sparkling eye" becomes engrossed in the act of choosing a Bible—comparing the "advantages of large, small, and middle-sized; black, blue, purple, and red; gilt and not gilt; clasp and no clasp"—"everything but the Bibles before her" is completely forgotten. Most significantly, and problematically, Mrs. Montgomery herself is overlooked. Warner writes, "Her little daughter at one end of the counter had forgotten there ever was such a thing as sorrow in the world; and she at the other end was bowed beneath a weight of it that was nigh to crush her" (p. 30).

Although Ellen is clearly at risk of succumbing to the preoccupation with objects that Douglas accuses her of, Mrs. Montgomery counters this tendency by continually reminding her daughter that the items for which they shop have a particular purpose. She does so by instructing Ellen in the way that objects can hold meaning not because they are "beautiful things," but for the emotional meaning with which they can be imbued. More specifically, whereas the objects in the store threaten to seduce Ellen away from her mother—make her forget that her mother is even with her—they can also serve a different, more connective purpose. The first stop of the excursion, a pawn shop, acts as Ellen's first lesson. For at the shop Mrs. Montgomery sells a ring that once belonged to her own mother. When Ellen sees her mother sell "grandmamma's ring," she wonders how her mother can part with an item she "loved so much" (p. 29).[12] Mrs. Montgomery qualifies her action by stating: "You need not be sorry, daughter. Jewels in themselves are the merest nothings to me; and as for the rest, it doesn't matter; I can remember my mother without any help

from a trinket" (p. 29). The issue seems to be resolved, yet Warner writes, "there were tears . . . in Mrs. Montgomery's eyes, that showed the sacrifice had cost her something; and there were tears in Ellen's that told it was not thrown away upon her" (p. 29). Although she assures Ellen that she can do without the ring, Mrs. Montgomery's tears suggest that to sell the ring is to lose something, "the rest" of the object's meaning.

The function the ring serves is that of a sentimental object or keepsake: it helps Mrs. Montgomery "remember [her] mother" from whom she has been separated. Warner describes the process by which objects are invested with memory and affect as follows:[13] "When two things have been in the mind together, and made any impression, the mind *associates* them; and you cannot see or think of the one without bringing back the remembrance or the feeling of the other . . . (p. 479, italics Warner's). Evoking the tenets of eighteenth- and nineteenth-century associationism, Warner claims that through an initial association with a person, place, or thing, an object can stand as a tangible marker of an intangible connection; it recalls both the memory of what is absent and the emotions connected with it.[14] That the above discussion takes place in relation to a book is no coincidence; in fact, the first recorded use of the word "keepsake" was in reference to a book exchanged between two women.[15] This etymology suggests that objects that serve mnemonic functions can, like books, be read: they are attributed with narrative, imbued with the story of the past. Ellen exemplifies this relationship between memory and narrative when she tries to recollect an old acquaintance by "reading memory's long story over again" (p. 449). In a culture preoccupied with the power of reading, from novels, magazines, and manuals, to phrenological bumps and physiological characteristics, it is not surprising that objects too should be viewed as readable.[16]

With the lesson of the ring fresh in her mind, Ellen embarks with her mother on the next stage of the shopping trip. Together they purchase a long list of items, most importantly a writing desk, "dressing-box" (p. 32), "an ivory leaf-cutter, a paper-folder, a pounce-box, a ruler . . . a neat little silver pencil . . . some drawing-pencils, India-rubber, and sheets of drawing-paper" (p. 35). Each of these objects is meant to keep Ellen's relationship with her mother alive when they are separated. Although they initially stand in the store as commodities, Warner illustrates how such objects develop a more personal function, how they can be invested with emotional meaning. When Mrs. Montgomery later packs them into Ellen's trunk, Warner writes that

> it went through and through her heart that it was the very last time . . . she would ever see or touch even the little inanimate things that belonged to her [Ellen]. . . . It was with a kind of lingering unwilling-

ness to quit her hold of them that one thing after another was stowed carefully and neatly away in the
trunk. She felt it was love's last act. . . .

(pp. 59-60)

Ellen's objects evoke almost as much emotion in Mrs.
Montgomery as does Ellen herself. They emphasize her
love for her daughter and the reality that, after their
separation, "sight, and hearing, and touch must all have
done henceforth for ever" (p. 60). The writing desk,
dressing box, and other objects will provide the only
connection between mother and daughter—between
Ellen and her home—once they are parted.

Just as the sight of Ellen's things causes her mother to
feel pain "through and through her heart" because they
emphasize their impending separation, so are the objects meant to mitigate the pain such separation involves. In *The Body in Pain* (1985), Elaine Scarry explores the connection between pain and objects, yoking
the alleviation of physical suffering with the existence
and structure of material things. Taking the example of
a chair, Scarry argues that the chair will "accommodate
and eliminate the problem" of body weight, for in and
through its very form the chair "perceives" and thereby
works to relieve the pain of a tired body.[17] The shape of
the chair mimes the body, becoming the antithesis of
the body in pain. The chair, in other words, holds two
positions at once: evoking the presence of pain and its
promised absence. Although Scarry is interested in
physical pain, the ability of objects to symbolize both
presence and absence can be applied to emotional pain
as well. For here too objects become the shape, or perhaps more appropriately the hope, of "perceived-pain-
wished-gone." They do so not by structurally miming
the body in pain, but by structurally representing the
memory of what has been lost. When an object is given
to one person by another, it becomes a symbol of the
relationship between them. If they are then separated,
the object becomes the marker of both the pain of that
separation and its hoped-for-relief.[18]

This process becomes clear when Ellen and her mother
return home from their shopping excursion. When Ellen
examines her packages, she is overwhelmed by excitement: "One survey of her riches could by no means satisfy Ellen. For some time she pleased herself with going over and over the contents of the box, finding each
time something new to like" (pp. 40-41). But Ellen has
learned the underlying purpose of these gifts, and in the
midst of her pleasure she suddenly processes the knowledge that the objects she now holds signify the relationship she is about to lose:

At length she closed [the work-box], and keeping it
still in her lap, sat awhile looking thoughtfully into the
fire; till turning toward her mother she met her gaze,
fixed mournfully, almost tearfully, on herself. The box
was instantly shoved aside, and getting up and bursting

into tears, Ellen went to her. "Oh, dear mother," she
said, "I wish they were all back in the store, if I could
only keep you!"

(pp. 40-41)

Warner is palpably aware that objects cannot actually
replace people, yet she also knows that they can temporarily ease the pain of separation. And although Ellen
would rather "keep" her mother and return the boxes to
the store, she also knows that she must make do with
what she has, using her new objects to maintain the
about-to-be severed mother-daughter bond. For when
she asks Mrs. Montgomery, "Is there no help for it,
mamma?" her mother simply replies: "There is none"
(p. 41).

Although Ellen seems to have learned the difference between objects that sever and those that maintain connections, this lesson is reinforced when she goes on a
second shopping trip, this time alone. Her experience is
completely different when the act of shopping is undertaken outside of the emotional context that characterizes the previous excursion. Warner writes that once in
the store, Ellen

stood irresolute in the middle of the floor. . . . Clerks
frequently passed her, crossing the store in all directions, but they were always bustling along in a great
hurry of business; they did not seem to notice her at
all. . . . She felt confused, and almost confounded, by
the incessant hum of voices, and moving crowd of
strange people all around her, while her little figure
stood alone and unnoticed in the midst of them; and
there seemed no prospect that she would be able to
gain the ear or the eye of a single person.

(p. 45)

When Ellen finally gathers the strength to approach the
clerk behind the counter, she is further overwhelmed by
the way that a consumer culture impedes, distracts from,
and thwarts interpersonal interactions. The clerk is condescending toward her requests and impatient with her
uncertainty, so that Ellen quickly "wish[es] herself out
of the store" (p. 46). In contrast to the earlier shopping
trip, in which objects are sought in order to maintain interpersonal connections, this scene represents the way
that commodity culture can leave individuals feeling
isolated and alone. Here objects are more important
than people and the pursuit of them seems to drain even
the most basic forms of civility from human interactions. In response to this hostile culture, Ellen is left
"confused" (p. 45) and with "feelings of mortification"
(p. 48) that are reflected in "one or two rebel tears" (p.
48). Her experience reinforces her mother's warning
against her "head being turned" by the vast array of objects available for purchase. The feelings of alienation
Ellen undergoes in the store anticipate those that she
will experience throughout the novel when she is separated from her loved ones. The world of consumer cul-

ture, like the homesickness she is about to experience, stand in negative contrast to the comfort and meaning with which keepsakes are invested.

By showing the ways that consumerism can both dissipate and reinforce feelings of comfort and connection, Warner reveals that it is not shopping that Ellen loves, but rather the experience of purchasing objects that are to be invested with meaning. The meaning is not only emotional, however, but social as well, for Ellen loses not just any home, but a middle-class home marked by certain emotional and social conventions. As a result, her objects are meant to recall the characteristics of home as much as they are meant to reduce her feelings of homesickness. Her mother informs her: "My gifts will serve as reminders for you if you are ever tempted to forget my lessons. If you fail to send me letters . . . I think the desk will cry shame upon you. And if you ever go an hour with a hole in your stocking . . . I hope the sight of your work-box will make you blush" (p. 37). Mrs. Montgomery's words describe the type of home that Ellen must remember in and through her objects. In Richard Bushman's words, "Ellen has the skills of a well-bred young woman,"[19] and her objects will help to remind her of these middle-class ideals. Ellen understands and agrees to the terms, assuring her mother: "I will try to use them in the way that I know you wish me to; that will be the best way I can thank you" (p. 37). From that point on, her possessions remind Ellen of the values that define the home she is about to lose and the standards according to which the recuperation of that home must stand. Her possessions do not simply perform useful and practical functions—such as holding items of clothing or writing utensils—but emotional and, here, even social functions, representing the tenets of middle-class life—its values, refinements, and customs.

The objects serve their purpose immediately when Ellen leaves her home and journeys to her Aunt Fortune's farm. Upon her arrival, Ellen recognizes that her aunt's home is very different from the one she has just left. The comparison is based on the objects Ellen sees around her. Fortune's things are meant to serve only the most basic of functions. Her room, for instance,

> looked to Ellen very comfortless . . . [it] was very bare of furniture. . . . A dressing-table, pier-table, or whatnot, stood between the windows, but it was only a half-circular top of pine board set upon three very long, bare-looking legs. . . . The coverlid . . . came in for a share of her displeasure, being of homemade white and blue worsted mixed with cotton, exceeding thick and heavy.
>
> (p. 102)

As the critique inherent in the word "comfortless" expresses, Ellen correlates the physical comfort, or refinement, of objects with the emotional comfort she defines

as home. The adjectives that characterize her aunt's things—"comfortless," "bare," "bare-looking"—emphasize the fact that those things are practical and functional: they serve the purpose for which they were made and nothing more. As Ellen notes, "her tea-spoon was not silver; her knife could not boast of being either sharp or bright; and her fork was certainly made for any thing else in the world but comfort and convenience, being of only two prongs, and those so far apart" (p. 106). Absent from her aunt's possessions is the refinement that Ellen has learned marks meaningful objects. The purely functional and "homemade" aspects of the house are what Ellen rebels against.

Ellen measures her aunt's home not only by what it contains, but by whether or not her own objects belong in it. As she tells Alice Humphreys, a neighbor with whom she becomes friendly: "Mama gave me a nice dressing-box before I came away, but I found very soon this was a queer place for a dressing-box to come to. Why, Miss Alice, if I take out my brush or comb I haven't any table to lay them on but one that's too high, and my poor dressing-box has to stay on the floor" (p. 175). That her aunt's is a "queer place" for Ellen's "neat little japanned dressing-box" (p. 32) "to come to" underscores the incompatibility between her aunt's home and the one Ellen recalls through her possessions. Ellen's personification of her things suggests that not only does her dressing box not belong at her aunt's, but she does not either.

In response to her recognition that certain types of objects correspond with certain types of homes, Ellen uses her mother's gifts to recreate the comfort she misses at her aunt's. Her "books, writing-desk, and work-box were then bestowed very carefully in the one" closet and "her coats and dresses" in the other (p. 144). Finally, "the remainder of her things were gathered up from the floor and neatly arranged in the trunk again" (p. 144). After she has arranged her things about the room, "Ellen's satisfaction was unbounded" (p. 144); she has used the objects that her mother gave her to restructure the "comfortless" environment around her, creating a semblance of the home she has lost and to which she so painfully longs to return. In doing so, she invests her surroundings with meaning, with physical and emotional comfort, a process that her aunt metaphorically tries to reverse when she dyes Ellen's white stockings and "nice white darning-cotton" "slate colour" (p. 113), so that they do not need to be regularly washed. Ellen is so distressed at her aunt's action that she "seemed in imagination to see all her white things turning brown" (p. 113), an image that records the larger fear that her upbringing will be tarnished by her stay on the farm. Sensing that her mother would disapprove of her aunt's definition of material things, Ellen resolves to "keep her trunk well locked up" (p. 113), as if by protecting her things, she can protect her middle-class sentiments from the less-refined influence of country life.

While Fortune's home is unlike Ellen's ideal because it defines things in the residual terms of use, terms that are opposed to the store-bought objects to which Ellen is attached, another home offers her a different contrast. The Marshmans, a local family, befriend Ellen and invite her to spend the holidays with them, in their large and inviting home. Unlike her aunt's house, the Marshman residence and its objects more closely resonate with Ellen's sense of what a home should be. As Warner writes:

> The room to which her [Ellen's] companion led her was the very picture of comfort. It was not too large, furnished with plain old-fashioned furniture, and lighted and warmed by a cheerful wood-fire. The very old brass-headed andirons that stretched themselves out upon the hearth with such a look of being at home, seemed to say, "You have come to the right place for comfort."
>
> (p. 287)

Finding an apparent match between the type of objects and the type of home that offer "comfort," Ellen at first feels safe and happy with her new friends. While such comforts would seem to correspond with Ellen's ideal of home, however, she is faced with yet another test of what home really means. Whereas Fortune's home is marked by its paucity of comforting objects, the Marshman home is noteworthy for its surplus. After dinner, for instance, Ellen "munch[es] almonds and raisins, admiring the brightness of the mahogany, and the richly cut and coloured glass, and silver decanter stands, which were reflected in it" (pp. 283-84). Though these two homes take different forms, the basic problem is the same. While Fortune's objects lack emotional meaning because they are purely functional, the Marshmans' things preclude affect because, rather than helping maintain memories or relationships, they are valuable in and of themselves. The result is that the Marshman home, too, lacks the precise feeling that Ellen seeks; emotional meaning is ultimately evacuated from it. Indeed, over the course of the Marshman chapters, Ellen begins to succumb to her earlier fascination with things. After a "day of unbroken and unclouded [Christmas] pleasure," Warner writes, "Ellen's last act [i]s to take another look at her Cologne bottle, gloves, pincushion, grapes, and paper of sugar-plums" (p. 305) before going to bed. Ellen is seduced by the objects around her, by the very idea that she possesses them. As a result, she becomes more interested in her objects than in the people around her.

Ellen's seduction is checked, however, in a scene that evokes the early, anxiety-ridden shopping trip. When another Marshman guest suggests that Ellen would

"give a great deal" (p. 318) to have received a pair of earrings like those the guest has been given for a Christmas present, Ellen replies: "I don't think I care much for such things,—I would rather have the money" (p. 318). The other children taunt her for saying so, for claiming to desire money over more personal gifts, and inform Mr. Marshman, their host, of her request. On New Year's Day, Ellen arrives at the breakfast table to find the table napkins "in all sorts of disorder,—sticking up in curious angles, some high, some low, some half folded" (p. 326). Ellen's own napkin, however, "lay quite flat" (pp. 326-27) and while the other napkins hide small gifts, Ellen finds under hers "a clean bank-note" (p. 327). As in the humiliating trip to the fabric store, "the blood rushe[s] to her cheeks and the tears to her eyes," as she stares at the "unfortunate bank-bill, which she detested with all her heart" (p. 327). Unwilling to accept the "gift," Ellen asks Mr. Marshman to take back the bill and, moreover, not to think of her as someone who would want "money for my present" (p. 327). The bank-note, a type of Marxian super-commodity, is the most offensive "gift" Ellen can imagine. Not only is it impersonal and uninvested with emotional meaning, but it completely undermines the sense of home that objects have come to symbolize for her. Far from reinforcing interpersonal connections, money, because it is not invested with affect, actually distances people from one another. Mr. Marshman acknowledges as much when he, in turn, feels ashamed of having given a piece of money as a present. When Ellen gives him her gift—a needlecase she made herself—he says with chagrin that Ellen has "come and made me a present" (p. 328) and that he has none to give her.

Despite these unsuccessful attempts to find an approximation of the home she longs for, Ellen eventually does find what she seeks. Her friend, Alice Humphreys, lives in a more suitable environment, one notably filled with objects with which Ellen can immediately identify:

> The carpet covered only the middle of the floor; the rest was painted white. The furniture was common but neat as wax. Ample curtains of white dimity clothed the three windows, and lightly draped the bed. The toilet-table was covered with snow-white muslin, and by the toilet-cushion stood, late as it was, a glass of flowers.
>
> (pp. 163-64)

Alice's possessions remind Ellen of her own, for they tell a similar story and evoke in the young girl similar feelings. Here the "ample" curtains, the bed drape, the toilet-table cover, and the unseasonable "glass of flowers" all suggest to Ellen something more than the functionality of her aunt's possessions, yet something simpler (more "common") than those of the Marshmans. The Humphreys' home is modest yet comfortable; the objects in it do not overwhelm the family but create an environment in which people and relationships can flourish. Their middle-class status marks a happy medium between her aunt's and the Marshmans' situations and is characterized by its ability to balance physical and emotional comfort, by its possession of refined things that are not only physically pleasing, but emotionally comforting as well. Ellen finds here the semblance of the home she seeks, a discovery Alice encourages when she tells Ellen: "I want you to know it [her room] and feel at home in it; for whenever you can run away from your aunt's this is your home,—do you understand?" (pp. 162-63).

Alice's offer foreshadows the time when Ellen adopts Alice's home as her own, becoming a honorary member of the Humphreys family after Alice dies. Still later Ellen takes her place as a full member of the home as John Humphreys's wife. Before she can do so, however, before she can reclaim a personal home for herself, the novel redefines Ellen's search as one for a national home as well. In fact, just as she is moving into the Humphreys parsonage she is forced to relocate once again, this time to Scotland. She does so in response to her mother's dying request that Ellen live with her maternal relatives, so that the "old happy home of my childhood will be yours, my Ellen" (p. 489). By leaving America, Ellen traces the history not only of her fictional family, but of the individuals who gave up their national "home" to move to America during the early 1800s. Ellen's personal experience of homesickness thereby takes on the broader definition of nostalgia for one's country, for what Hawthorne called "Our Old Home." *The Wide, Wide World* is striking for its emphasis on the different nationalities of its characters—Swiss, Scottish, British, Dutch—who have only recently immigrated to America.[20] Ellen herself is a first generation American, and her mother's desire that she visit her extended family abroad underscores the emotional import attached to one's country of origin. Mrs. Vawse, a woman of Swiss origin who lives in a home built far up in the mountains, embodies the nostalgia for one's native country that permeates the novel. When Ellen and Alice travel to see Mrs. Vawse, Ellen notices right away that the house and the woman who occupies it are "not American" in appearance (p. 190). Mrs. Vawse has reconstructed a Swiss-style home on the New York hillside, and when Ellen asks her, "why you loved better to live up here than down where it is warmer," the old woman answers: "It is for the love of my old home and the memory of my young days. . . . If I have one unsatisfied wish . . . it is to see my Alps again; but that will never be" (p. 192). Fending off a homesickness for her native country, Mrs. Vawse uses the material things around her to recreate her "old home" as she adapts to her new.

Although Ellen's transatlantic trip symbolically retraces the steps of early-nineteenth-century American immigrants, her experience in Scotland ultimately reverses the direction of the nostalgic impulse present throughout the novel. It does so by identifying home not as a country other than America, but as America itself. The expectation is that, in moving to Scotland and joining her mother's relatives, Ellen will give up her American identity. As one friend asserts, "So you are going to be a Scotchwoman after all" (p. 494), and Ellen's Scottish relatives do their best to persuade Ellen to give up her ties to America. They attempt to do so, in part, through the objects she has brought with her from America, especially the Bible her mother gave to her when they parted and a copy of *Pilgrim's Progress* given to her by her future husband, John. Knowing that these books contain memories of, and therefore a connection to, Ellen's American life, her relatives try to erase the associations that such objects hold by taking away *Pilgrim's Progress* and threatening to confiscate her Bible as well. They also try to convince Ellen to give up her American name. Her uncle tells her that "it is right to love" her American friends "if they were kind to you, but as your aunt says, that is the past. It is not necessary to go back to it. Forget that you were American, Ellen,—you belong to me; your name is not Montgomery anymore,—it is Lindsay" (p. 510). Not only do they want to "adopt" Ellen, but they disdain America in general, describing it as "the backwoods" and asserting that Ellen "must learn to have no nationality but" theirs (p. 505).

Despite these efforts to make her abandon her American identity, Ellen refuses to do so. To her uncle's command that she "forget" that she is American, Ellen silently rebels, saying to herself, "Forget indeed!" (p. 510). More than simply national identities, Ellen thinks of the difference between Scotland and America in terms of her definition of a personal and familial home. Warner writes: "Alone, and quietly stretched on her bed, very naturally Ellen's thoughts went back to the last time she had had a headache, *at home,* as she always called it to herself" (p. 529, Warner's italics). As she had done at her aunt's, Ellen uses her keepsakes to create a semblance of home in her grandparents' house: "Her beloved desk took its place on a table in the middle of the floor. . . . Her work-box was accommodated with a smaller stand near the window" (p. 527). While arranging her "little sanctum till she had all things to her mind," she realizes that it lacks "a glass of flowers" (p. 527), a decoration that recalls her first glimpse of Alice's home, the place to which Ellen feels she belongs. Ellen's nostalgia for her own "old home" signifies a new generation identified specifically with America. By representing Ellen's nostalgia for America, *The Wide, Wide World* provides its readers with a medium through which their own identification with their new home might take hold. By distancing the novel's readers from America, in other words, Ellen's return to Scotland evokes a homesickness not for their native countries, but for America itself.

This representation of nostalgia helps to define the difference between the novel's two endings: the chapter that Warner originally intended to end her work and the chapter that was ultimately published as the novel's conclusion. In the published ending, read by Warner's contemporaries, John promises to retrieve Ellen from her ancestral home in Scotland and return her safely and happily to her national and familial home as his wife. Despite its optimistic outlook, however, the published ending is somewhat surprising. Although the narrative moves insistently toward a recovery of home for Ellen, in this version that return home is not described; Ellen is never shown returning to America or to the parsonage she thinks of so fondly. Yet Warner did complete a chapter in which a more satisfying conclusion takes place, one that would have put her readers at ease about Ellen's search for home, for a place in which her objects and she belong. In this ending Ellen returns to America as John's wife and as the mistress of his house. Moreover, as Ellen enters her new home, she utters "an exclamation of surprise and fond pleasure" (p. 571):

> around her, on every hand, were the very loved things she had been used to see at the Carra-Carra parsonage. . . . There stood the dear old book-case with its books—the sofas, the cupboard, the pictures,—yes, even Alice's cabinet of curiosities,—the same table in the middle of the floor. Ellen stood fixed, with clasped hands of pleasure and tender recollection, and eyes that were making too feeling a recognition of its objects.
>
> (p. 571)

This ending is clearly cathartic: Ellen is restored not only to America and to her home, but to the objects that hold meaning for her, which make home what it is. Midway through the chapter Warner marks the end of Ellen's homesickness. As Ellen embraces her father-in-law, Mr. Humphreys, Warner writes that Ellen "felt that the old wound was healed at last" (p. 574).

Although this chapter provides closure—not only to Ellen but to the novel's readers—it was never published; the nineteenth-century editions of the novel end with the deferral, literally, of home and, consequently, the continuance of nostalgia. Although the omission of Warner's intended ending may have been simply the result of an editorial attempt to limit the novel's length, the decision to end the work with Ellen's return home still pending may have ensured *The Wide, Wide World*'s successful reception by readers. The reason lies in the function of nostalgia itself. While it persists, nostalgia maintains a longing for home and, therefore, maintains an active pursuit of, and connection to, the past. Conversely, without the homesickness that nostalgia creates, the desire and therefore the effort to return home are

not only given up, but also in some way forgotten; the past recedes and the present becomes permanent. Objects, for instance, take on different functions when they are not used for sentimental or nostalgic purposes, as the unpublished chapter reveals. Upon her marriage to John and her return to America, Ellen receives an "old escritoire" (p. 581) with "beautiful workmanship and costly antique garniture" (p. 582). A reminder of the smaller writing desk, the keepsake once meant to maintain Ellen's bond with her mother and therefore her home, the desk has altered not only its form but its function. As John explains, "This piece of furniture . . . belonged to my father's mother and grandmother and great-grandmother, and now it has come to your hands" (p. 583). An heirloom, as opposed to a keepsake, the desk tells not the story of loss or a search for home, but of the stability and permanence of John's family, which will continue its advancement through Ellen's possession of its material things. As George Kubler asserts in *The Shape of Time: Remarks on the History of Things* (1962): "From . . . things a shape in time emerges. A visible portrait of the collective identity, whether tribe, class, or nation, comes into being. This self-image reflected in things is a guide and a point of reference to the group for the future, and it eventually becomes the portrait given to posterity."[21] In functioning as an heirloom rather than a keepsake, the desk marks the past as a memory not to be sought and regained, but to be carried into the future. Nostalgia is thus eliminated; the past becomes not something to mourn or recapture—to feel homesick for—but something with which to define one's identity and to propel oneself forward. Echoing the heirloom's meaning, John says to Ellen: "our happiness has a foundation and may stretch into the future far forward as faith can look" (p. 583).

In other words, if the novel had included Warner's original ending, thereby doing away with Ellen's search for home, it would have also done away with the nostalgic impulse so crucial to the novel's emotional weight, an experience also central to the novel's readers. As a form of processing tremendous change, nostalgia is a self-protective way to move gradually into the future while psychologically letting go of the past. The need for nostalgia lessens as a new identity evolves and takes hold. For a class in the throes of self-formation, to give up the longing or memory of home that the novel allows them to experience would be to give up part of its identity, a process it was moving toward but not entirely ready to complete.[22] In contrast, by letting the hoped-for return home ambiguously remain still in the future, the novel leaves in place the feeling of nostalgia that pervades its pages, refusing completely to relieve it while simultaneously anticipating that relief. Readers could thereby continue to negotiate their transition from their old home to new, from non-American to American, from past to present.

The Wide, Wide World itself became a type of keepsake—an object, in the form of a book—which helped to mediate its reader's experience of nostalgia or loss. Given the original reference of the term "keepsake" to a book and the contemporary popularity of keepsake gift books—"literary annuals consisting of collections of verse, prose, and illustrations"—the idea that a novel like Warner's could serve an affective function makes tremendous sense.[23] The novel was certainly imbued with emotional import by Warner and her family, who seem to have viewed it as a way to help them overcome the experience of being separated from their home. As Warner writes after she had distributed the first copies of the novel: "One lovely red-edged copy I gave to Anna for a Christmas present; and she said she had seen nothing in a long while that had so reminded her of old Christmas times as the look of those red edges" (Anna Warner, p. 333). The book in its mere physical "red-edged" form calls to Anna's mind the family history of "old Christmas times"; the novel connects Anna to a prior moment in her life, a time identified with the emotions of home. Eventually, letters from admiring readers made their way into the Warner household, further connecting the novel's author to its readers. Anna writes, "in time, all this broke up our solitude, and both friends and strangers began to remember and look for us" (p. 360). The book quite literally helped the Warners reunite with their old, familiar world.

The novel served a similar function for its middle-class readers by connecting them to one another. The extent of those connections is revealed in one admirer's letter to Warner:

> It is now nearly a year . . . since I first met with your incomparable work, *The Wide, Wide World,* which I read with the most heartfelt sympathy and delight. I immediately purchased it as a suitable gift for the thirteenth anniversary of *my* Ellen,—and recommended it to every one with whom I took the slightest interest,—and now every *reading* friend I have possesses a copy, and enjoys it as I do. During an illness of my husband (a grave man of fifty-seven), I read it aloud to him. . . . My oldest daughter of twenty (not very fond of reading) is charmed with it, and my Ellen (its owner) has read it three time alone, and as many times aloud, to a deeply interested circle of auditors.

> (Anna Warner, p. 355)

The author of the letter articulates the way that Warner's novel bound its readers together. It did so, like a keepsake, through the act of exchange, both physically between family members and verbally through word-of-mouth recommendations.

Those recommendations are qualified, however, by the author's statement that they were made "to every one in whom I took the slightest interest," the implication being that not everyone should have access to the novel or to the story it tells. In addition, the emphasis placed by the letter's author on "every *reading* friend" implies a distinction between reading and nonreading persons. These statements suggest what Anna Warner recorded other people stating outright: "not to have read the book is not to be in fashion," or, as a "woman of fashion" exclaimed with "an expressive gesture," "'My dear, you know, one must read it'!" (pp. 359, 345). Just as Ellen's objects are invested with social value, so too is Warner's text. To own and, more importantly, to have read *The Wide, Wide World* was a marker of social standing, creating a community of readers that identified itself in part through its familiarity with Warner's popular novel.[24]

Sentimental novels like Warner's, then, might be characterized not only by the recurrent use of keepsakes in their pages, but as keepsakes themselves that register a range of losses and assist their readers in the recovery from them. Those losses are primarily thought of in terms of the loss of home—or the sense of home—that the experience of nostalgia identifies. Harriet Beecher Stowe's *Uncle Tom's Cabin,* for instance, can be seen as an object that negotiated the loss accompanying abolition by using the home as its central and recurrent motif. As Philip Fisher argues in another context, "the key detail [to the book] . . . is that . . . Tom no longer lives in the cabin and never returns there. It is therefore . . . the home he doesn't occupy, but to which all of his thoughts are directed as the home to which he would return if he could. The title therefore asserts his homelessness, his possession of a home that he has not yet reached."[25] A metaphor for the sense of "homelessness" that would accompany the abolition of slavery, Uncle Tom's cabin and *Uncle Tom's Cabin* helped readers to process the urgent, though overwhelming change that resulted. The preoccupation with home and the attention to objects in other sentimental novels such as Fanny Fern's *Ruth Hall,* Louisa May Alcott's *Little Women,* and Caroline Kirkland's *A New Home, Who'll Follow?* reinforce the assertion that nostalgia for the home is central to the sentimental novel, and that nostalgia is resolved through the attribution of affect to the material world.[26] In fact, sentimentalism might be defined in these very terms: as the tangible representation of the past, a representation that permits an individual or a group to negotiate an irretrievable but necessary loss.[27] That the form of mediation takes place through the possession of objects, including books, helps to account for the widespread popularity of domestic fiction among middle-class Americans, who seem to have used such things as a way to process the alienation and loss that permeated the historical moment in which they lived.

Mid-nineteenth-century American culture was marked by a homesickness or nostalgia that, in her search for both a familial and a national home, Susan Warner's character Ellen embodies. Like the fictional Ellen, the middle class negotiated its experience of loss by correlating the emotional comfort of "home"—as both a physical and psychological site—with the physical objects available to them through the material world. Middle-class people imagined such objects as being invested with emotion and memory, with meaning that distinguished their function from the utilitarianism of the Homespun Age and the reification of emerging consumerism. Standing at the juncture between these two distinct cultural definitions of material things, keepsakes became the focus of middle-class life because they represented emotional continuity in the face of great personal and social change. This investment of objects with affect included an attachment to books like Warner's that evoked and even encouraged their readers to feel nostalgia, to experience a longing for home, in order to overcome those same feelings. Like Ellen, who uses the keepsakes given to her by her mother as a way to guide and gauge her search for a new home, the newly established middle class was able to absorb the process of its formation—and the loss that formation entailed—through the physical object, the keepsake, of *The Wide, Wide World.*

Notes

1. Susan Warner, *The Wide, Wide World,* afterword by Jane Tompkins (New York: The Feminist Press, 1987). All quotations from the novel will be from this edition and will be cited parenthetically in the text. I would like to thank Nancy Armstrong, Michael T. Gilmore, and Cynthia B. Ricciardi for their helpful comments on earlier drafts of this essay.

2. For more on Susan Warner, see Edward Halsey Foster, *Susan and Anna Warner* (Boston: Twayne Publishers, n.d.); Mary Kelly, *Private Women, Public Stage: Literary Domesticity in Nineteenth-Century America* (New York: Oxford University Press, 1984); Olivia Stokes, *Letters and Memories of Susan and Anna Bartlett Warner* (New York and London: G. P. Putnam's Sons, 1925); Anna Warner, *Susan Warner* ("Elizabeth Wetherell") (New York, 1909).

3. Anna Warner, *Susan Warner,* p. 333; subsequent references will be cited parenthetically in the text.

4. Michael Paul Rogin, *Fathers and Children: Andrew Jackson and the Subjugation of the American Indian* (New York: Alfred A. Knopf, 1975), p. 103.

5. For recent criticism of *The Wide, Wide World,* see Erica R. Bauermeister, "*The Lamplighter, The Wide, Wide World,* and *Hope Leslie*: The Recipes for Nineteenth-Century American Women's Novels," *Legacy: A Journal of American Women Writers,* 8, No. 1 (1991), 17-28; Richard H. Brodhead,

"Sparing the Rod: Discipline and Fiction in Antebellum America," in *Cultures of Letters: Scenes of Reading and Writing in Nineteenth-Century America* (Chicago and London: The University of Chicago Press, 1993), pp. 13-47; Joanne Dobson, "The Hidden Hand: Subversion of Cultural Ideology in Three Mid-Nineteenth-Century American Women's Novels," *American Quarterly,* 38, No. 2 (1986), 223-42; Grace Ann Hovet and Theodore R Hovet, "Identity Development in Susan Warner's *The Wide, Wide World*: Relationship, Performance, and Construction," *Legacy: A Journal of American Women Writers,* 8, No. 1 (1991), 3-16; Nancy Schnog, "Inside the Sentimental: The Psychological Work of *The Wide, Wide World,*" *Genders,* 4 (1989), 11-25; Jane Tompkins, *Sensational Designs: The Cultural Work of American Fiction 1790-1860* (New York: Oxford University Press, 1985); Tompkins, Afterword, *The Wide, Wide World,* pp. 584-608; Isabelle White, "Anti-Individualism, Authority, and Identity: Susan Warner's Contradictions in *The Wide, Wide World,*" *American Studies,* 31, No. 2 (1990), 31-41; Susan Williams, "Widening the World: Susan Warner, Her Readers, and the Assumption of Authorship," *American Quarterly,* 42, No. 4 (1990), 565-86; Helen Papashvily, *All the Happy Endings* (New York: Harper and Brothers Publishers, 1956).

6. *The Oxford English Dictionary* (New York: Oxford University Press, 1993) p. 535.

7. On the influx of immigrants between the years 1840 and 1860, see Maldwyn Allen Jones, *American Immigration* (Chicago: The University of Chicago Press, 1974), and Philip A. M. Taylor, The *Distant Magnet* (London: Eyre and Spottiswoode, 1971).

8. For scholarship on the culture of sentiment and the nineteenth-century middle class, see Stuart M. Blumin, *The Emergence of the Middle Class: Social Experience in the American City, 1760-1900* (New York: Cambridge University Press, 1989); Richard L. Bushman, *The Refinement of America: Persons, Houses, Cities* (New York: Vintage Books, 1993); Karen Halttunen, *Confidence Men and Painted Women: A Study of Middle-Class Culture in America, 1830-1870* (New Haven and London: Yale University Press, 1982); T. Walter Herbert, *Dearest Beloved: The Hawthornes and the Making of the Middle-Class Family* (Berkeley: University of California Press, 1993); David Marshall, *The Surprising Effects of Sympathy: Marivaux, Diderot, Rousseau, and Mary Shelley* (Chicago and London: The University of Chicago Press, 1988); Mary P. Ryan, *The Cradle of the Middle Class: The Family in Oneida County, New*

York, 1790-1865 (Cambridge: Cambridge University Press, 1981); Shirley Samuels, ed., *The Culture of Sentiment: Race, Gender, and Sentimentality in Nineteenth-Century America* (New York and Oxford: Oxford University Press, 1992); Carroll Smith-Rosenberg, *Disorderly Conduct: Visions of Gender in Victorian America* (New York: Oxford University Press, 1986); Barbara Welter, *Dimity Convictions: The American Woman in the Nineteenth Century* (Athens: Ohio University Press, 1976).

9. For more on nostalgia, see Peter N. Carroll, *Keeping Time: Memory, Nostalgia, and the Art of History* (Athens and London: The University of Georgia Press, 1990); Rogin, *Fathers and Children: Andrew Jackson and the Subjugation of the American Indian*; Christopher Shaw and Malcolm Chase, eds., *The Imagined Past: History and Nostalgia* (Manchester and New York: Manchester University Press, 1989); David C. Stineback, *Shifting World: Social Change and Nostalgia in the American Novel* (Lewisburg: Bucknell University Press, 1976).

10. Ann Douglas, *The Feminization of American Culture* (New York: Anchor Books, 1977), p. 64.

11. Dobson has claimed that the keepsake is the formal trope of the sentimental novel. See "Reclaiming Sentimental Literature," *American Literature,* 69, No. 2 (1997), 263-88. In addition, critics have tended to analyze the relationship between sentimental objects and sentimental novels in terms of Harriet Beecher Stowe's *Uncle Tom's Cabin.* I have chosen Warner's novel in order to examine the way readers of sentimental fiction might have seen themselves not in terms of abolitionism, but of their own identity as a class. For criticism on Stowe, see Gillian Brown, "Sentimental Possession," in *Domestic Individualism: Imagining Self in Nineteenth-Century America* (Berkeley: University of California Press, 1990), pp. 39-60; Philip Fisher, *Hard Facts: Setting and Form in the American Novel* (New York: Oxford University Press, 1987); Lynn Wardley, "Relic, Fetish, Femmage: The Aesthetics of Sentiment in the Work of Stowe," in *The Culture of Sentiment: Race, Gender, and Sentimentality in Nineteenth-Century America,* pp. 203-20.

12. In a different analysis, Tompkins views the ring as a symbol of "the tacit system of solidarity that exists among women" (*Sensational Designs,* p. 163).

13. For information on exchange and gift theory, see Lewis Hyde, *The Gift: Imagination and the Erotic Life of Property* (New York: Vintage Books, 1979), and Marcel Mauss, *The Gift: Forms and Functions of Exchange in Archaic Societies,* trans.

Ian Cunnison (New York: W. W. Norton and Company, Inc., 1967).

14. For more on eighteenth- and nineteenth-century associationism, see theorists like David Hume, *A Treatise of Human Nature* (1739), or the works of David Hartley.

15. "She sent me a little neat pocket volume, which I accept . . . as just the keepsake," in *The Oxford English Dictionary,* p. 377.

16. For more on reading in nineteenth-century America, see Nina Baym, *Novels, Readers, and Reviewers: Responses to Fiction in Antebellum America* (Ithaca and London: Cornell University Press, 1984); Bushman, *The Refinement of America*; Brodhead, *Cultures of Letters: Scenes of Reading and Writing in Nineteenth-Century America*; Cathy Davidson, *Revolution and the Word: The Rise of the Novel in America* (New York and Oxford: Oxford University Press, 1986).

17. Elaine Scarry, *The Body in Pain: The Making and Unmaking of the World* (New York: Oxford University Press, 1985), p. 289.

18. In a different context, Hannah Arendt argues that "in order to become worldly things, that is, deeds and facts and events and patterns of thoughts or ideas, they must first be seen, heard and remembered and then transferred, reified as it were, into things. . . . The whole factual world of human affairs depends for its reality and its continued existence, first, upon the presence of others who have seen and hear and will remember, and second on the transformation of the intangible into the tangibility of things," in *The Human Condition* (Chicago: The University of Chicago Press, 1958), p. 95. Although Arendt is talking specifically about works of art, and not what she calls "consumer goods" or "use objects," the principle is similar to what I am arguing here. In order to make something real, even an absence, it must first be made present through a tangible object. For the importance the mere presence of things holds, see Robert Plant Armstrong, *The Affecting Presence: An Essay in Humanistic Anthropology* (Urbana: University of Illinois Press, 1971), and *The Powers of Presence: Consciousness, Myth, and Affecting Presence* (Philadelphia: University of Pennsylvania Press, 1981); George Kubler, *The Shape of Time: Remarks on the History of Things* (New Haven and London: Yale University Press, 1962).

19. Bushman, p. 288.

20. Even the Humphreys are "English born," though, as Alice tells Ellen, "you may count me half American if you like, for I have spent rather more

than half my life here" (p. 174). The qualification of "half" is what the novel, in part, moves to erase, making all immigrants fully part of their new "home."

21. Kubler, p. 9.

22. Perhaps another reason the original ending was withheld was because it incorporates the world of consumerism into the novel in a way that is resisted throughout the rest of the book. Inside the inherited desk is "a certain concealed drawer" (p. 582), which contains "gold and silver pieces and bank bills" (p. 582). "[H]ere, Ellie," John states, "you will always find what you want in this kind. I shall never ask you how you spend it. . . . You are to be my steward in all that concerns the interior arrangements of the household" (p. 582). Just as the need for keepsakes evaporates, and just as Ellen finally recovers the home she has remembered and sought, the symbols of consumerism—against which she has fought throughout the entire novel—return. Money does enables Ellen to maintain the home that she has so arduously sought, yet the very function objects have played throughout the novel begins to come undone, suggesting the corrosive effects consumerism has on the material world as a place of affect. In one of the last lines of the book, Ellen marks this shift. Looking at the inherited desk she muses: "How long such an insignificant thing . . . outlasts its more dignified possessors" (p. 583). That the desk is now "insignificant" stands in stark contrast to Ellen's focus on objects, including her own writing desk, throughout the novel. The final chapter, then, naturalizes the rise of consumer culture; it is complicit in encouraging consumer culture's role both in middle-class existence and nineteenth-century life.

23. *Oxford English Dictionary,* p. 377.

24. Among the many indexes of the novel's popularity is its appearance in Louisa May Alcott's *Little Women,* read by the heroine, Jo March. See also Ronald J. Zboray and Mary Aracino Zboray, "Books, Reading, and the World of Goods in Antebellum New England," *American Quarterly,* 48, No. 4 (1996), 587-622. This essay documents the way that sentimental novels functioned as meaningful objects, though it does not suggest why they do.

25. Fisher, *Hard Facts,* pp. 119-20. The idealistic presence of the Quaker settlement exists, as Fisher also points out, in contrast to the continual absence of the cabin; see p. 111.

26. For an excellent analysis of Caroline Kirkland's novel, see Lori Merish, "'The Hand of Refined Taste' in the Frontier Landscape: Caroline Kirk-

land's *A New Home, Who'll Follow?* and the Feminization of American Consumerism," *American Quarterly,* 45 (1993), 485-523.

27. As Dolf Sternberger writes, sentimentalism conceives of the novel as "precious memento" "because it painfully relives the sweet sensations and once again sheds the long-dried tears, in short, because it evokes the totally bygone 'scenes' and lends the genre an admittedly specious permanence . . . the scene and the pathos alone do not suffice; here the desire for giving permanence to the scene and the pathos in the locked-up interior, for making sighs and tears repeatable till the end of life, giving introspection a tangible possession—that device, the memento, has once again become the scene," in *Panorama of the Nineteenth Century* (New York: Urizen Books, 1977), p. 62.

Suzanne M. Ashworth (essay date 2000)

SOURCE: Ashworth, Suzanne M. "Susan Warner's *The Wide, Wide World,* Conduct Literature, and Protocols of Female Reading in Mid-Nineteenth-Century America." *Legacy* 17, no. 2 (2000): 141-64.

[*In the following excerpt, Ashworth explains the thematic significance of Ellen's voracious reading and finds that this characteristic is an important mechanism of identity construction in* The Wide, Wide World.]

"THE EYES OF HER MIND": READING WITH SELF-APPLICATION

If [nineteenth-century] women readers were to begin with the interchangeable maxims "read with purpose" and "read no novels," then they were supposed to end with an eye to their own betterment, translating purpose into self-application—into a regimen of self-examination and self-correction that was inspired by select texts and interpretive exercises. In archetypal terms, reading with self-application was supposed to create cultivated icons of ideal femininity. In the process, this trajectory of self-improvement quelled the threat of women's reading with the rubric of middle-class female virtue: piety, submissiveness, and benevolence. With successive portraits of its heroine reading, **The Wide, Wide World** intervenes in this mode of psychic construction, dramatizing the interplay between the eyes of Ellen Montgomery's mind, the book before her, and conduct-book calls for self-correction. Through it, we glimpse the makings of an ideal.

Because reading was such a volatile activity for women, advice manuals advocated close surveillance of women readers. Indeed, the manuals themselves served as instruments of that surveillance. As they mastered a selfproctored domestic curriculum, women were instructed to turn the conduct book's censorious vision on themselves. "Would my young reader belong to the model class of women?" Wise queries in representative tones. "Then she must turn the eyes of her mind upon herself . . ." [Harvey Newcomb, *Newcomb's Young Ladies Guide,* 1846, 186]. Belonging to "the model class of women" required a self-command that encompassed a woman's capacity to rise early, to wear clean underclothes, to wash every part of her skin daily, to chew food properly, to resist displays of irritation or anger, and to remain resolutely focused on her domestic and social duties. As Margaret Coxe writes, "We have thoughts to regulate, imaginations to control, tempers to subdue, a body of sin to destroy, appetites to bring into subjection; but how can we proceed in our work, and learn our weak points in order to guard against them, unless we turn our serious and constant attention to what is passing there?" (57). In essence, conduct books turned a woman's vision inward, and viable self-cultivation depended on her ability to survey herself for weak or ungoverned elements of her psychic and social character. This unrelenting system of self-examination effectively closed the gap between individual and cultural dimensions as productive self-examination wielded assessments of self that mirrored cultural notions of admirable and appropriate femininity.[1]

Actively negotiating this aspect of conduct book ideology, *The Wide, Wide World* establishes an intimate correlation between reading, self-examination, and self-correction. In one instance, for example, Ellen's reading suffuses a self-punishing internal monologue as she repents a display of anger directed toward William Gillespie, an adolescent guest in the Marshman household at Christmastime: "'[I]t was not a bit like peacemaking or meek at all,' Ellen said to herself. She had been reading that morning the fifth chapter of Matthew, and it ran in her head, 'Blessed are the meek,'— 'Blessed are the peace-makers: for they shall be called the children of God'" (317). The scripture "in [Ellen's] head" becomes a vehicle of self-surveillance and regulation as she strives "to get back a pleasant feeling toward her young companions, and pray[s] that she might not be angry at any thing they should say" (317). In this responsive act, Ellen takes the Word inside herself, and reading—specifically Bible reading—becomes an instrument of behavior modification, an interior gauge of right conduct, right mind, right womanhood.[2]

Predictably, the Bible occupies a sacrosanct position within the conduct of female reading, and Ellen is clearly modeling "good" reading behaviors in this scene. Newcomb, for instance, devotes an entire chapter to Bible reading in his *Young Lady's Guide,* and Wise urges women to "Adopt [the Bible] for your daily companion. Read it thoroughly, patiently, carefully. Read a portion of it daily, on your knees, pausing at each sen-

tence, and asking its great Author to teach you its import" (192). More significant, Newcomb argues that women should read scripture "with self-application": "Whenever you have discovered any truth ask what bearing it has upon present duty," he writes; "If it relates to spiritual affections, compare it with the state of your own heart. If it relates to the spirit and temper of Christians, in their intercourse with one another, or with the world, compare it with your own conduct" (84). The verse in Ellen's head encodes the process of reading with the self-application that Newcomb endorses—a process in which women were schooled to inhabit the meaning of the text, measure their own self-worth accordingly, and infuse private thoughts and public deeds with its dictates.

Reading with self-application was such a valued interpretive strategy within advice manual rubrics that it extended beyond Biblical bounds to define appropriate textual engagements with English and American history, natural philosophy, biography, geography, and French—the principle genres deemed suitable for women within the conduct of reading (history and biography consistently ranking highest among them). In graphic terms, *The Wide, Wide World* represents how this devotional reading practice was employed in secular textual engagements. For example, engaging an exemplary text in an exemplary fashion, Ellen reads a biography of British Admiral Horatio Nelson, and as she relates her appreciation of his character to John, the novel deploys the founding tenets of reading with self-application: "'I like Nelson very much; don't you?'" Ellen asks John. "'Yes,'" he returns, "'as well as I can like a man of very fine qualities without principle'" (478). John warns Ellen that her assessment of Nelson is clouded by her admiration for his persona, and he instructs her to reread the book "'with a more critical eye'" (478). The conduct of reading teaches that cultivating this "critical eye" means reading history and biography from a highly moral vantage point; it means employing practices that defined Bible reading and occupying a secular text as a commentary on right conduct. As a result of this teaching, when she is asked to comment on Nelson's character later in the novel, Ellen responds, "I don't think, sir, I ought to like a man merely for being great unless he was good" (516). This idealized mode of response depends on a critical sort of empathy with a hero, an identification that subordinates emotional readerly responses to edifying lessons. Holding to this principle, as he prepares women to read secular history, Newcomb writes, "you must maintain, in the midst of your reading, a constant spirit of prayer" (222). "Whenever you take up a good biographical work," Coxe advises, "endeavor to make it subservient to your own improvement; study the errors of others, not that you may talk of them, but that you may learn to correct your own" (171). The immediate moves to self-application afforded by biographies and histories rendered them idealized objects of study within the conduct of reading. Implicitly, they served as secular scripture, and the reading postures they required, according to advice manual maxims, necessitated both self-examination and self-correction. Such active contemplation of the text insures that it functions as a productive catalyst to moral reflection; it insures that, as John Humphreys puts it, "fine qualities" do not obscure right "principles" in the reader's mind.

Given its emphasis on self-correction and improvement, then, reading with self-application attempted to suppress the more individualizing aspects of the female reading experience. It sought to contain the activity of reading and the creation of meaning within a nexus of self-imposed disciplines and a gaze—the eyes of a woman's own mind. The end of this regimen of self-cultivation was a normative way of being. In essence, reading with self-application enlists the reading process in the production and maintenance of a "model class of women"—domesticated, self-denying, and self-regulating women; including Ellen Montgomery, who is perfectly suited to the sphere of white, middle-class, American womanhood.

Mothered Reading

In broad terms, *The Wide, Wide World* is bent on producing the same breed of femininity. In fact, Shirley Foster and Judy Simon argue that *The Wide, Wide World* is ultimately concerned with "what constitutes ideal womanhood," and within the context of the novel, the "highest level of womanly perfection" incorporates "virtues of submission, self-forgetfulness, loving-kindness, and piety" (42). Maternal influences play a pivotal role in forging that ideal: Alice Humphreys, as Foster and Simon note, continues Mrs. Montgomery's earlier lessons "of self-control and submission" to God (44). Still, scholarship on *The Wide, Wide World* has yet to identify mothered reading practices as a prominent vehicle of those lessons. Indeed, mothers not only ensure that their daughters learn the principles of "womanly perfection," they also model reading postures that initiate the internalization of those principles. With an analysis of these maternal practices, we can see the role that mothered reading behaviors play in the female reader's social conditioning, in the formation of her interior vision, and in the dissemination of class-specific ways of reading.

Although advice manuals sanctioned an intense regimen of self-examination, women were simultaneously positioned within a larger field of vision that subjected them to the evaluative gaze of their immediate social relations. In *The Young Lady's Friend* (1837), for example, Eliza Farrar delineates appropriate deportment before parents, teachers, friends, servants, siblings, female friends, and gentlemen. Within the context of this deline-

ation, self-cultivation was ultimately social capital—valuable as a form of cultural currency or as an entrée into white, middle-class arenas. Thus, the ability to read with self-application was the mark of a self-in-relation—a female ideal located entirely within the social order and its eyeline.

In light of this positioning, young women readers were not to trust the eyes of their minds alone, and mothers were primarily responsible for monitoring their daughter-readers. In *The Mother's Book* (1831), for example, Lydia Maria Child states that "children, especially girls, should not read anything without a mother's knowledge and sanction" (92). Images of reading in *The Wide, Wide World* document the psychological and social import of this maternal sanction, revealing how easily maternal approbation translates into maternal modeling. For example, in the scene that opens this essay, when Ellen's mother asks her to read the twenty-third psalm aloud to her, the novel dramatizes the emotional power that a mother deploys with exemplary reading postures: "Long before she had finished, Ellen's eyes were full, and her heart too. 'If I only could feel these words as mamma does!' she said to herself" (15). Ellen's identification with her mother makes her want to identify with text or "feel these words" as she does, and thus her mother embodies a reading identity that Ellen yearns to emulate.

More pointedly, as Ellen reads *for* her mother, and, ultimately *like* her mother, reading becomes a catalyst of both emotional connections and moral mandates. In fact, the novel represents the definitive aspects of "feeling these words" in a later instance, as Ellen again reads Bible passages aloud to her mother. After Mrs. Montgomery directs Ellen to verses that speak of heaven, the novel details how "her mother's manner at length turned [Ellen's] attention entirely from herself" (27). Captivated by her mother's responsive gestures, Ellen observes that "Mrs. Montgomery was lying on the sofa, and for the most part listened in silence, with her eyes closed, but sometimes saying a word or two that made Ellen feel how deep was the interest her mother had in the things she read of, and how pure and strong the pleasure she was even now taking in them . . ." (27). The gratification that Mrs. Montgomery finds in scripture stands in direct opposition to Ellen's more troubled emotional state at this juncture. Up to this point, Ellen has been unable to accept separation from her mother with calm resignation despite her mother's counsel that "'[T]hough we must sorrow we must not rebel'" (18). Mrs. Montgomery's readerly interest in the midst of her grief and illness reflects her steadfast reliance on the printed word of God, her ability to enter the text, inhabit it, and modify her behavior accordingly. Feeling the words quells rebellion, and it constitutes a reading experience that Ellen must learn to pattern and replicate. Thus, before she leaves her mother's care, Ellen has internalized both her moral code and the way of reading that advances it.[3]

In her mother's absence, Alice Humphreys figures as another able mother of reading, guiding Ellen's studies when her solitary attempts fail, and in keeping with Mrs. Montgomery's exemplum, Alice actively reinforces reading behaviors that work through self-application. For example, as they read a hymn centered on the individual's "charge" to glorify God, Alice informs Ellen that her Christian duty requires that she be "'faithful, patient, [and] self-denying'" (239). Like Mrs. Montgomery before her, Alice uses reading to endow Ellen with the comportment and character of a true woman. Ultimately, Ellen's mother-readers go beyond the simple "knowledge and sanction" that advice manuals advocated to assume the role of the conduct book itself, shaping Ellen into a receptive and pliant daughter-reader and ensuring the transmission of socially appropriate values and behavior.

Gender norms are not the only measure of what's appropriate for a true reading woman, and images of mothered reading in *The Wide, Wide World* also comment on the class and race conditioning at work in the construction of the daughter-reader. One way to understand this bourgeois maternal legacy is to turn to the one mother figure in the novel who represents a counter-class culture. Significantly, Ellen's agrarian Aunt Fortune refuses to mother her desire to read, and she has no use for the women within the middle-class sphere. "'[I]t doesn't do for women to be bookworms,'" she grumbles when Ellen asks for the opportunity to resume her education. "'That's the way your mother was brought up I suppose,'" Fortune determines; "'If she had been trained to use her hands and do something useful instead of thinking herself above it, maybe she wouldn't have had to go to sea for her health'" (140). Fortune deems reading and studying a frivolous activity in her farming household, and she will not indulge Ellen's predilection for it. In contrast, the more leisured Alice Humphreys prominently displays her books and proudly claims possession of them: "'But here, Ellen, . . . is my greatest treasure—my precious books. All these are mine'" (164). In the opposition between Alice and Aunt Fortune, then, reading becomes a resolutely white, middle-class activity, and by extension, it becomes a very visible way to mark that class identity.[4]

Not surprisingly, conduct books also capitalized on the correlation between reading and class distinctions, and Fortune's character continues to provide an interesting counterpoint to the advice manuals' seamless representation of a normative middle-class reading dynamic. According to Jane E. Rose, conduct books were not premised on a fluid notion of class identity, nor did they promote a self-interested advance through the social ranks.[5] Instead, conduct books worked to define, so-

lidify, and sustain the values and behaviors of the middle class as both the nation's and God's chosen people.[6] Holding to this socioeconomic niche, Farrar directs her conduct book to women beginning their careers as "young ladies" (2), and Child's *The Mother's Book* speaks to the "wants of the middling class in our own country" (1). As they address this implied readership, conduct books invest middle-class courtesy, domesticity, and values with the power to elevate the nation as they elevate the individual. What is interesting about this investment in middle-class mores is that it ultimately transcends socioeconomic status.[7] Indeed, middle-class virtue is the conduct books' holy grail, and advice manuals hold out the possibility that regardless of economic realities, working-class readers can attain it. Actual social mobility within the advice manual is subordinate to the solidification and popularization of an idealized middle-class existence. Fortune's caustic comments to the contrary, conduct books intimate that this middle-class state of being is one into which every woman can—and should—read herself.

As *The Wide, Wide World* dramatizes it, the conduct of reading is so invested in middle-class subjectivity that as Ellen attempts to mother the reading of others, the novel reveals how reading was supposed to colonize the under-classes and bring this bourgeois woman into being. With the gift of a Bible, Ellen hopes to regenerate and reform Nancy—the wild, unrestrained, poor girl who exists outside the bounds of true womanhood in the novel. Unlike Ellen, Nancy is able-bodied, athletic, and unchecked by standards of courtesy: she lights nimbly over fences and creeks that leave Ellen torn, wet, and muddy; when Ellen falls ill, she gamely rifles through her things despite Ellen's protestations. Nancy represents an uninhibited self, and unlike her middle-class counterpart, she says what she thinks and does what she likes. Having come to know this ungoverned girl, Ellen believes that if Nancy would only read the Bible, the practice could bring Nancy into the fold of (middle-class) ideality, making her domesticated, subdued, and self-sacrificing. "'What did you give this to me for, Ellen?'" Nancy asks. "'Because I wanted to give you something for New Year,'" Ellen explains, "'and I thought it would be the best thing,—if you would only read it,—it would make you so happy and good'" (333). From Mrs. Montgomery and Alice, Ellen has learned the reading postures that distinguish a specific breed of womanhood, and, more important, she has learned to value them so wholeheartedly that she wishes to mother them into her social inferior. Ellen is sure that the Bible will engender "goodness" in Nancy because her own reading experiences are a testament to that fact. With the gift of the Bible and the reading practices that Ellen assumes always already go with it, Ellen is attempting to foster the binding emotional connections, moral imperatives, and ideological holds that mothered reading nurtured in her own character. With this textual exchange, the conduct of reading (and the ideal womanhood it cultivates) takes on an omnipresent power, one that pervades the social stratosphere to cultivate legions of reading women who are middle class in mind and manner, if not in economic means.

FATHERED READING

Were it taken to its logical extreme, this power might have created a very different woman reader and a very different *Wide, Wide World,* one in which networks of women nurture each other through matriarchal literary practices. Certainly, that is the plot line supported by conduct books' call for maternal sanction of a daughter's reading. "[E]ach woman in proportion to her mental and moral qualifications possesses a useful influence over all those within her reach," writes *The Young Lady's Mentor* (145). But *The Wide, Wide World* resists the mother-reign at key intervals and seemingly breaks with the conduct of reading through its emphasis on the importance of paternal scrutiny and direction. In actuality, whenever Alice's brother, John, returns to the parsonage, he supersedes Alice's authority in Ellen's studies, and after Alice's death, Ellen reads entirely under his tutelage.

Interestingly enough, John's command of Ellen's reading practices becomes a psychological and bodily engagement that Ellen both welcomes and desires, and *The Wide, Wide World* presents Ellen's movement into John's paternal regulation as an evolution or a progression—a kind of graduation. In the process, the novel intimates that her mother readers have not nurtured or addressed the embodied dimensions of the reading experience. In truth, Ellen's mother readers die. Consumptive, frail, and piously devout, Alice and Mrs. Montgomery seem more spiritual than corporeal, and the reading postures they model subordinate lived reality to divine principles. Even their texts are sacred. Under John's direction, however, Ellen's reading engages this world and the next one, and his surveillance takes hold of her body as well as her mind and spirit. With John, therefore, reading mediates emotional *and physical* connections; deploying psychosomatic tactics, his surveillance of Ellen's reading habits enacts an erotics of discipline that gives the conduct of female reading flesh. In consequence, the novel graphically portrays what remains latent in the advice manual: women read within a highly eroticized body, a body that must be regulated within a heterosexual power structure if it is going to assume the countenance of true womanhood.

John achieves this requisite regulation through a scrupulous and unrelenting attention to Ellen's reading habits. More pointedly, John selects the books that Ellen reads, prohibits her from reading fiction or novels, schools her in reading aloud, and shapes her responses to texts. Even in his absences, "He arranged what books she should read, what studies she should carry on" (484). John not only dictates an acceptable curriculum for Ellen's reading, he also opens the production of meaning to his evaluative judgment, requiring that Ellen provide written and spoken records of her interpretative conclusions. In the midst of this regimen, Ellen's attraction and deference to John reinforce his status as a more effective interpreter and teacher than Alice or even Mrs. Montgomery. "In her eagerness to please and satisfy her teacher," the narrative records, "[Ellen's] whole soul was given to the performance of whatever he wished her to do. The effect was all that [John] looked for" (351). While advice books privileged a mother's selection and interpretation of texts, *The Wide, Wide World* privileges paternal power over the woman reader. In this privileging, Ellen's reading moves from a maternal order where reading nurtures ties between women and the word to a paternalistic realm where reading becomes an exhibition of obedience before an earthly father.

Literally. Between John and Ellen reading literally stands as an exhibition of submission. Ellen habitually reads in John's presence, under his watchful gaze, and often aloud at his request. John uses these oral textual performances as a medium for exacting Ellen's compliance to his dictates and cultivating true womanhood within her. As he guides her elocution, for example, John "manages" Ellen psychically and physically: "[John] often read to her, and every day made her read aloud to him. This Ellen disliked very much at first, and ended with as much liking it. She had an admirable teacher. He taught her how to manage her voice and how to manage the language . . ." (464). Because reading aloud epitomized appropriate female reader activity within the conduct of reading, John's instruction is essential to Ellen's character development. According to advice writers, women were not only uniquely equipped to read aloud—"[T]he keynote of poetry," writes Anna U. Russell in *The Young Lady's Elocutionary Reader* (1851), "seems to have been lent to woman" (10)—but reading aloud to husbands, children, parents, or siblings was also the woman reader's special charge. Even "talk-[ing] about a book," according to Sedgwick, made an individual woman's reading "a social blessing" (244). A "social blessing" because reading aloud takes the activity of reading out of the individual psyche, renders it a public performance, and pre-empts any privacy or autonomy the woman reader might claim. Given that reading aloud fixes the activity of reading entirely within a domestic milieu, it is not surprising that John makes it a daily instructive ritual.

In a provocative move, however, *The Wide, Wide World* reverses the gendered paradigm which grounds Ellen's aptitude for elocution: in the end, John's oral performance (not Ellen's) best exemplifies the power of cultivated tones, and the female voice does not remain the sole conveyance for the text. In this reversal, *The Wide, Wide World* documents the embodied reality of reading aloud and, more important, enlists the body in the cultivation of female ideality, turning reading into an erotic interplay of discipline and desire. Interestingly enough, as he reads *Pilgrim's Progress* to Ellen, John's lips and voice rival the written word in inspiring her response to the text: "[Ellen's] attention was nailed; the listless, careless mood in which she sat down was changed for one of rapt delight; she devoured every word that fell from the reader's lips; indeed, they were given their fullest effect by a very fine voice and singularly fine reading" (351). In this exchange, Ellen connects with both the reading and the reader, and the impact of the words is intensified by the lips that speak them. When John reads aloud to Ellen, his hold on her attention crystallizes, and as his voice and lips absorb her, his body becomes an emblem and a vehicle of heterosexual intimacy and instruction.

In this way, reading between John and Ellen comes to mediate a sexually charged relationship.[8] As Ellen reads while John paces the room or studies or draws, reading becomes a medium through which John solidifies and sexualizes his dominance. In one instance, Ellen sits reading by the window late in the evening. "'Too late for you, Ellie,'" John commands. Ellen promises to stop reading in "two minutes," but "in a quarter of that time she had lost every thought of stopping, and knew no longer that it was growing dusk. Somebody else, however, had not forgotten it. The two minutes were not ended, when a hand came between her and the page and quietly drew the book away" (476). John's hand obstructing the page forces a tangible break in Ellen's reading process, and his physical removal of the book makes his paternalistic surveillance of Ellen's reading a very material reality. Ellen's reading, therefore, is positioned entirely within a space that John both defines and surveys.

After he removes the book, optical surveillance turns to even more invasive and sensual modes of discipline. With her book in hand, John clasps Ellen's arm and asks if she has taken any exercise that day. "'No,'" Ellen admits, "'. . . and I did not decide that I would not go . . . just as I did about reading a few minutes ago. I meant to stop, but I forgot it, and I should have gone on I don't know how long if you had not stopped me. I very often do so'" (477). John pauses, then returns, "'You must not do so any more, Ellie'" (477). As John delivers this prohibition, he brings Ellen into an emotional state that is as sensual as it is submissive: his "tone, in which there was a great deal of both love and decision, wound round Ellen's heart, and constrained her to answer immediately" with obedient resolve (477). John's corporeal command of Ellen's reading practices works through "love and decision," and the coagulation between these two forces constitutes a disciplinary

erotic that enables John to fully command Ellen—her mind and body.[9]

In essence, John appropriates the more sensual realm of the reading experience to achieve a physical and psychological hold on the woman who reads within the range of his vision, one that is intimate, controlling, and made that much more potent in the erotics of his grip. This power becomes so potent that John is able to maintain his hold on Ellen's mind, behavior, and reading even when Ellen moves beyond his eye-line. Indeed, after John has shaped her reading, the book in Ellen's head is not the only constraint on her behavior (as it was at the Marshman household); rather, the word joins forces with a censorious paternalistic gaze to punish and modify her behavior. For example, to gain Mr. Lindsay's leave to go to church, Ellen misrepresents her motivation, saying she wishes to see Edinburgh. When she chides herself for that falsification, *both* John's persona and a relevant scripture propel her self-examination and self-correction. "'Oh, how could I say that[,] how could I say that[.] Oh, what *would* John have thought of me if he had heard it. . . . "If ye love me, keep my commandments,"—I have not!'" (532). Ellen has learned to occupy more than just Biblical passages; she has also internalized John's disciplining vision—his way of evaluating thought and action against the sacred gauges of ideal womanhood. Still, Ellen welcomes John's judgments, and the sensual attraction between them seems to soften the strictures he places upon her mind, body, and reading behaviors. Sincerely interested in Ellen's well being, John acts out of the same love and concern that motivates Alice and Mrs. Montgomery.

But Mr. Lindsay's more tyrannical authority complicates the implications of the paternal discipline that John exercises, and for that reason, it is worth tracing Ellen's troubled relationship to her uncle and the role that reading plays within it. Ellen comes to know Mr. Lindsay when she learns of her mother's desire that she assume her place in her maternal grandmother's heart and home (489). In compliance with this wish, Ellen becomes the "darling possession" and "dear plaything" of her aristocratic Scottish relations—her grandmother, Mrs. Lindsay, her aunt, Lady Keith, and her uncle, Mr. Lindsay (538). But it is Mr. Lindsay whom Ellen loves, and it is Mr. Lindsay who consistently and physically intervenes in her reading habits. Like John, Mr. Lindsay positions his authority over Ellen (and the way she reads) within patrilineal designations: "'I will not have you call me "uncle,"'" he declares to Ellen, "'I am your father;—you are my own little daughter, and must do precisely what I tell you'" (510). Like John's dominance, Mr. Lindsay's authority works through love, decision, and physical holds: "She could not help loving her uncle; for the lips that kissed her were very kind as well as very peremptory; and if the hand that pressed her cheek was, as she felt it was, the hand of power, its touch was also exceedingly fond" (510). Both John and Mr. Lindsay intertwine the hand of power and the touch of fondness in effecting Ellen's compliance and submission, and that hand forces material censorship of Ellen's reading habits. When Mr. Lindsay discovers that Ellen has been reading *Pilgrim's Progress* to the housekeeper, for example, he takes "the book she still held" and quietly leaves the room (551). Ellen's reading to Mrs. Allen troubles Mr. Lindsay because it encourages Ellen to recall "old times" or her life outside his estate; equally, it troubles him because the book was a gift from John: "'I hardly know [what the book is],'" he later says to his mother, "'except it is from that person that seems to have obtained such an ascendency [sic] over her—it is full of his notes—it is a religious work'" (551). Ellen's reading disturbs Mr. Lindsay because it forges a space and a connection that supersedes his mastery and, ultimately, his ownership of her. When Ellen argues her claim to the book, saying "'it is mine!'" Mr. Lindsay asserts his claim to her, "'and you are mine, you must understand'" (553). As Mr. Lindsay's possession, Ellen can no more lay claim to a book or a reading of her own than she could as John's protégé. Unlike the emotional cadences of Ellen's apprenticeship in the Humphreys household, however, there is a measure of cruelty in Mr. Lindsay's discipline that does not enter John's governance: Mr. Lindsay speaks with anger to Ellen on more than one occasion, and he literally touches her lips to silence her. Nevertheless, Mr. Lindsay's harshness does not mediate the fact that his power colludes with John's command of Ellen's mind, behavior, and reading habits. In fact, his relative cruelty comments on both modes of paternalistic regulation: "John's was a higher style of kindness," the narrative qualifies, "that entered into all her innermost feelings and wants; and his was a higher style of authority too . . . an authority Ellen always felt it was utterly impossible to dispute" (538-39). The power that John employs with solicitous hands, erotic discipline, and soft-spoken dictates is only one step removed from Mr. Lindsay's more heavy-handed authority, and, thus, the novel begs the questions: What sort of commentary does Mr. Lindsay's despotism make on the conduct of female reading? Why does reading assume such a visible and contentious role in that despotism?

In the most obvious sense, the conduct of reading licenses the exercise of Mr. Lindsay's authority. Trained as the woman reader to know her place, Ellen would be ill-equipped to defy Mr. Lindsay's commandments. Or so one might assume. The novel will resist that assumption in the successive power plays it stages between Ellen and her uncle, but in *The Wide, Wide World,* Ellen's reading encompasses a contested ground wherein competing paternalistic powers duel for possession and control of a prized womanly identity.

In this literary context, women's reading exists in a mimetic relation with female subjectivity. To regulate a woman's reading was to regulate the woman, and implicitly, that is the appropriate conclusion to the female reading behaviors as the conduct of reading defined them: reading with purpose or with self-application, reading within a surveying network of family relations—they all premise the conclusion that a woman *is* what and how she reads, and thus it follows that reading becomes a constitutive mechanism for shaping and creating the female self, a mechanism of which John Humphreys and Mr. Lindsay take full advantage.

Touching Her Nationality: Reading and a Sacred National Identity

Gender, race, and class are not the only identity markers that are at issue in this creation. In fact, Mr. Lindsay's governance of Ellen's reading habits operates within his larger mandate that Ellen "forget that [she was] American" (510), and both her *national* and *religious* identities come under attack in the Lindsay stronghold. The regulation of Ellen's reading habits figures as a primary arm of that attack—the Lindsays out-flank Ellen's reading preferences with the micro-management of her daily movements and her privacy. As Ellen struggles to retain her right to read, the conduct of women's reading becomes a discretely American code of behavior; its very viability depends on a sacred democratic sociopolitical system. Ultimately, in the formation of Republican mothers and daughters, the conduct of women's reading reproduces that system, and in consequence, women read with the weight of the nation on their shoulders.

There is, of course, a certain power in that burden, and as noted above, critics of *The Wide, Wide World* and historians of domesticity have underscored the proto-feminist leanings extant here. Because "the home provided a touch-stone of values for reforming the entire society" (Matthews 35), the women who kept it ranked as safeguards of a national consciousness. Thus, middle-class women enjoyed the power that came from such an ardent faith in a woman's influence on an evolving American character. Yet given its investment in domestic hierarchies, the conduct of reading has to find a way to circumvent that influence, and the limits of the discourse are just as telling as its more empowering possibilities. Interestingly enough, while the conduct of reading can foster intense nationalism and forge a uniquely American identity—an identity literally founded on revolution—it cannot embrace the revolutionary facets of that consciousness. Commenting on the limits of republicanism itself, the resolutely social uses of women's reading work to pacify individual resistance—even justified resistance to more despotic power dynamics. With a paradoxical simultaneity, the conduct of women's reading generates a sacred national identity that at once sanctions and subdues Ellen's revolt against the Lindsays' oppressive regulation. In the end, Ellen's efforts to retain the reading habits that buoy her religious and national character reveal the indiscriminate relationship between despotism and democracy for women. Regardless of the political topography, the ideal woman reader cannot read without paternal sanction, and in the final analysis, national, class, and religious allegiances are second to domestic power structures.

When Mr. Lindsay takes Ellen's cherished copy of *Pilgrim's Progress* and "hardly know[s] what the book is," his ignorance distances him from Ellen's national, religious, and class origins. From its inception in 1678, *Pilgrim's Progress* was a dissenter's book—"the prose epic of English Puritanism"—and a middle-class manifesto; its author, John Bunyan, has been labeled the "poet-apostle of the English middle-classes" (Swaim 1). More important, *Pilgrim's Progress* became a seminal text in American culture, encompassing the religious beliefs and the reading practices of the Puritans who settled New England; most influential were its emphasis on spiritual autobiography, its tradition of meditation, and its reliance on scriptural paradigms and providential workings.[10] For two centuries after its publication, Bunyan's narrative circulated among politically radical or intensely devout segments of the laboring and middle classes.[11] The Lindsays occupy another geography altogether: they are not American, not middle class, and although they are practicing Protestants, they are by no means ardently religious. (They go to church only *once* on Sundays; Ellen, in contrast, is accustomed to attending two services.[12]) When he takes *Pilgrim's Progress* from her hands, then, Mr. Lindsay implicitly confiscates those aspects of Ellen's identity that the book represents, and in the process, he attempts to reconfigure Ellen's national, class, and religious character.

However, Ellen's reading has functioned as formative mortar in nation building, and against this aristocratic Scottish censor, it bolsters a distinctly American identity. As they debate the justification for the American revolution, for example, Mr. Lindsay maintains that Americans forfeited "good character" in the break from England, but Ellen returns, "[I]t was King George's fault, uncle; he and the English forfeited their characters first" (506). Ellen's reading serves her well as she struggles to maintain her national allegiance: her "strange notions about the Americans," Ellen explains, come from reading "'Two lives of Washington, and some in the Annual Register, and part of Graham's United States; and one or two other things'" (506). Her reading in history and biography, therefore, has not only advanced the cultivation of her own character, it has also enabled her to defend her nation's character when pitted against an antithetical point of view. In this

sense, the conduct of reading has empowered Ellen to resist Mr. Lindsay's invasion of her interpretive judgments and her patriotic reading identity.

In like manner, character, class, and nation formation also converge in the conduct of women's reading, and so it can illuminate Ellen's capacity for resistance in the Lindsay household. "Think, my dear young friends," writes Sedgwick, "of the difference that is made in the character of a human being, simply by reading" (232). For Sedgwick, this difference immediately assumes national and class connotations: "Compare an Irish girl, who comes to this country at fifteen or sixteen, who has never been taught to read, with one of your own countrywomen, in the humblest condition, of the same age, who '*loves to read,*' and who has read the books within her reach" (232-33). In the absence of economic gain, reading enables the approximation of a middle-class identity; more important, it distinguishes the Irish immigrant from her American counterpart. As if Warner's novel was meant to serve as a veritable testing ground for Sedgwick's theory, when Ellen reluctantly emigrates to Scotland, her reading becomes a measure of her difference, grounding a strong sense of nationalism. Nourished by a national literature, Ellen is a Republican Daughter, a child of both liberty and literacy.[13] Thus, when Mr. Lindsay questions her national character—"'You have an extraordinary taste for freedom! And pray, are all the American children as strong republicans as yourself?'"—Ellen responds, "'I hope so'" (515).

Significantly, Ellen's single and most vehement acts of resistance to the conduct of reading occur when she moves outside American national boundaries. Ellen not only rebelliously asserts her ownership of *Pilgrim's Progress* when Mr. Lindsay takes it from her, she also covets her "precious hour alone" with her "little Bible" before the rest of the family rises (540). When her grandmother learns of this practice, she directs Ellen to come to her immediately upon rising each morning. From Mrs. Lindsay's vantage, "Ellen was spoiling herself for life and the world by a set of dull religious notions that were utterly unfit for a child" (542-43). Countering her grandmother's direction, Ellen insists on her right to read and defies the conduct of reading that checked women's reading habits within a network of domestic obedience and submission.

Paradoxically, although conduct book edicts sanction Ellen's resistance to the Lindsays' imperialism, they cannot promise her resounding victory over their tyranny or a room of her own, so to speak, in which to read. In her *Treatise on Domestic Economy*, Catharine Beecher writes, "[T]he democratic institutions in this country are in reality no other than the principles of Christianity carried into operation" (27). These principles, Beecher continues, "tend to place woman in her true position in society . . . in fact, they have secured to American women a lofty and fortunate position, which, as yet, has been attained by the women of no other nation" (27). The American republic, according to Beecher's logic, is religion in practice, and it secures a unique position and identity for American women. The Lindsay household seeks to undermine that identity, and the loss of her "greatest comfort"—her solitude, her hour, her Bible-reading—serves as an instrument of both religious and national oppression. Thus, Ellen's rebellion against such curtailment is authorized and enabled in the convergence of the American political and religious precedents that Beecher articulates. Beecher, however, also recognizes that women's subordination is essential to the workings of republicanism: "[I]n order to secure her the more firmly in all these privileges, it is decided, that, in the domestic relation, she take a subordinate station" (27). In "civil and political concerns," she writes, women's interests are entrusted to men, their fathers, brothers, husbands, and "the inferior is to yield obedience" (27, 26).

With heightened awareness of that power dynamic, Ellen understands that once she has called Mr. Lindsay "father," she is "'bound to obey him'" (519). Because Ellen owes Mr. Lindsay a "child's duty," she throws "herself upon her knees" and apologizes for arguing his claim to her *Pilgrim's Progress* (554, 547); she regains the time and space to read her Bible only with his intercession. Ultimately, the Lindsays successfully constrain Ellen's reading through an economy of time and social obligation. "'I have read so little lately,'" Ellen admits to John in the final (unpublished) chapter, "'Because I had not time. I could not help it. . . . They filled up my days and nights with engagements which I had no means of avoiding, unless I would have provoked scenes that would have done them and me more hurt than any loss I was suffering'" (576).[14] The conduct of women's reading subordinates reading to a nexus of womanly duty and social responsibility, and given Ellen's idealized status within this ideology, she cannot read outside that nexus. To do so requires a display of temper, a resistance to temporal regulation, and an assertion of self that the conduct of reading forecloses. In Scotland, Ellen confronts the limits of the ideology that has licensed and regulated her relationship to texts, and in the process, she confronts the violence inherent in the woman reader's deference to domestic obligations and her ready submission to the censor and surveillance of her reading habits.

The Woman Reader Becomes a Wife

In the concluding, unpublished chapter of the novel, Ellen returns to America as John's wife. More pointedly, she returns to the national, class, and gender terrain that premises the conduct of women's reading, and thus it follows that she regains the sanction and space to read. John has furnished a "private room" for her, and as he opens the door, Ellen surveys a chamber filled with "the appliances of comfort and ease and literary and studious wants"—fine paintings and engravings, marble and bronze statues, easy chairs, footstools, lounges, and bookcases (574). "'What a delicious place for reading!'" she proclaims, and the room itself is "delightfully private" (576, 577). Still, the room joins John's study, is *entered through* his study, and while Ellen may open, close, even lock the door at will, the room's privacy is qualified by its proximity to John's room. Ellen "read[s] next door to [John]," the novel relates, and John will "pilot" her reading when Ellen "dare not trust [her] own navigation" (577). Again, Ellen's perceptions, movements, and reading habits are contained within an arena that John has ordered and defined. Nevertheless, with her marriage and her return to America, Ellen reassumes her status as an ideal woman reader. Although her reading will be effectively husbanded, she repossesses the narrow space and time to read which the conduct of women's reading affords. The original manuscript ends as Ellen lays claim to a site of middle-class comfort and qualified isolation, a room especially suited to appropriate female readerly desires.

However, the novel—even with the original ending intact—never consummates that desire. It does not image Ellen reading alone, enveloped in solitude before her window, the door locked. Moreover, the exchange analyzed above does not appear in the original or subsequent editions of the text. The novel's nineteenth-century manifestations absent reading from Ellen's fate altogether. In the original ending, the woman reader becomes a wife, and reading is effaced in the revelation of her idyllic domestic relations: "[Ellen] went back to spend her life with the friends and guardians she best loved, and to be to them, still more than she had been to her Scottish relations, 'the light of the eyes'" (569). In the end, the novel privileges a wifely woman, not a reading one. Paradoxically, for Ellen, reading herself into ideality ultimately means not reading; it means letting go of the text and assuming her position within the domestic fold.

Thus, even as **The Wide, Wide World** reinscribes and reinforces the conduct of reading, it simultaneously reveals the limits of the discourse. Republican daughters of reading were supposed to become mother readers, and as they read alone or aloud within the domestic circle, they were supposed to reproduce the norms of a middle-class national identity. Yet, in the mimetic relationship between female reading and female subjectivity, the conduct of reading creates a hierarchy of identity-markers; it subordinates a woman's national or class identity to her position within heterosexual, domestic disciplines. Democratic or tyrannical geographies, middle-class or aristocratic spaces—those distinctions collapse in the conduct of reading, subsumed by a husband's privilege. In both *The Wide, Wide World* and the conduct of reading, reading is a mechanism—a vehicle of ideality, and once ideality is achieved, the true woman relinquishes her books.

Notes

1. As Michel Foucault asserts, where power works through individual habits, daily practices, the organization and regulation of time and space, "there is no need for arms, physical violence, material constraints. Just a gaze. An inspecting gaze, a gaze which each individual under its weight will end by interiorizing to the point that he is his own overseer, each individual thus exercising this surveillance over, and against himself" (155). Instructed to occupy the text as a catalyst to self-examination, the woman reader becomes her own overseer, and reading becomes a mechanism of social conditioning.

2. Warner herself taught Bible classes to West Point cadets for years, and as John A. Calabro has shown, she firmly believed in a "right" way of reading it; so much so that one cadet comments, "Miss Warner is . . . very sure that she is in the full light and all who do not accept Christ as she has, remain in darkness" (Calabro 49).

3. This reading experience reinforces the power of what Brodhead terms "disciplinary intimacy, or simply discipline through love" (15). Ellen's love for her mother, Brodhead writes, "makes Ellen, in and of herself, want to do and be what her mother would require of her"—morally and spiritually (33). Ellen's desire to emulate her mother's relationship to scripture reveals the significance of women's reading in producing and advancing the moral imperatives that disciplinary intimacy enacted. In other words, reading figures as a point of both communion and discipline between Ellen and her mother.

4. Reflecting this class identity, the space that houses Alice's reading, her bedroom, likewise houses white dimity curtains, white floorboards, and a vanity draped with snow-white muslin. Roger Chartier reminds us that "reading is always a practice embodied in acts, spaces, and habits" (3); Alice mothers Ellen's reading habits in a space of white, middle-class womanhood.

5. Rose asserts that conduct books did not explicitly concern themselves with class mobility. As a genre, the conduct book remains distinct from etiquette or courtesy manuals. Etiquette manuals emphasized the rules and standards of polite society, and their primary purpose was to advance the individual's social status. Conduct books, in contrast, advanced the moral and intellectual stature of American women as the signpost of an advancing nation. As Rose notes, conduct books advocated "cultivating one's full potential, thereby meeting the components of ideal womanhood: serving God and the Republic by raising virtuous children, and ministering to one's husband . . ." (39).

6. Of course, this contention does not exclude the possibility that working-class readers read conduct books as etiquette books, as a guide to the protocols of middle-class identity, or as a reference manual for social advancement. Equally, this contention does not exclude the possibility that some conduct of life books were explicitly directed toward working-class readers. Sedgwick's *Means and Ends,* for instance, revolves around images of working-class existence—a soldier's wife's solitary condition, a blacksmith's quest for knowledge, a mechanic's lack of leisure to devote to reading.

7. John Kasson implicates all instructional literature at this time in the "spread of gentility" or "the cultivation of bourgeois manners" (43).

8. Attraction, fascination, and fear occupy the same relational space between John and Ellen, and Ellen's erotic connection to John is intimately allied with his power and dominance. Although the novel designates him "brother," the sensual attraction between them is apparent upon their first meeting when John "kisses her gravely on the lips" (274). Previously repulsed at Mr. Van Brunt's moves to claim a kiss from her, Ellen's rising color and her placid acceptance of John's kiss betray her attraction to him. However, that attraction is immediately qualified. Although "Ellen's eyes sought the stranger as if by fascination," she "was quite sure from that one look into his eyes that he was a person to be feared" (275).

9. In light of John's tactile and psychic hold on Ellen's reading processes, his prohibitions against fiction and novel reading discussed previously resonate differently: John forbids novel reading because that embodied and intensely emotional reading experience would pre-empt the erotic space that is his exclusive domain; and in a more holistic sense, the conduct of reading prohibits and punishes fiction reading because it can be a libidinal object, rendering women sexually independent and liberating them from the heterosexual dynamic that founds domesticity.

10. In John Bunyan's lifetime, *Pilgrim's Progress* sold one hundred thousand copies (Swaim 2). Bunyan's narrative spoke to a Protestant readership, portraying "a life made out of Scripture and bound by Scripture" (Johnson 210).

11. William J. Gilmore ranks *Pilgrim's Progress* among the most widely read texts in northeastern American family libraries well into the 1830s. Additionally, in the nineteenth century, as Barbara A. Johnson notes, *Pilgrim's Progress* was "spurned by the upper classes" (7).

12. For more on the relationship between Ellen's Protestantism and her bids for power in the Lindsay household, see Isabelle White's "Anti-Individualism, Authority, and Identity."

13. This distinction reflects and advances an ideology of Republican Motherhood that demarcated the political and social responsibilities of women in post-revolutionary America. As Linda K. Kerber writes, in addition to domestic and religious duties, Republican Motherhood required that a woman be "an informed and virtuous citizen." (235). According to Kerber, well-governed reading practices ensured the transmission of virtue to husbands and children of the new nation.

14. As Jane Tompkins writes in her "A Note on the Text" in the Feminist Press edition of the novel,

> The final chapter . . . was omitted from the original edition and all subsequent editions. Mabel Baker published it in 1978 as an appendix to her biography of Warner. . . . An unsigned note in the papers of the Constitution Island Association suggests that the manuscript had gone to Putnam without the last chapter and that Putnam urged omitting it since the book had run longer in the galleys than he had expected and the last chapter, in his opinion, did not contribute substantially to the novel.

([8])

Works Cited

Alcott, William. *The Young Woman's Guide.* 1836. 13th ed. Boston: C. H. Pierce, Binney, and Otheman, 1847.

Arthur, T. S. *The Mother's Rule; Or, the Right Way and the Wrong Way.* Philadelphia: H. C. Peck & Theo. Bliss, 1858.

Baym, Nina. *Woman's Fiction: A Guide to Novels by and About Women in America, 1820-1870.* 2nd ed. Urbana: U of Illinois P, 1993.

Beecher, Catharine. *Treatise on Domestic Economy.* New York: T. H. Webb, 1842.

Brodhead, Richard H. *Cultures of Letters: Scenes of Reading and Writing in Nineteenth-Century America.* Chicago: U of Chicago P, 1993.

Calabro, John A. "Susan Warner and Her Bible Classes." *Legacy* 4.2 (1987): 45-52.

Chartier, Roger. *The Order of Books: Readers, Authors, and Libraries in Europe between the Fourteenth and Eighteenth Centuries.* Trans. Lydia G. Cochrane. Stanford: Stanford UP, 1994.

Child, Lydia Maria. *The Mother's Book.* 1831. New York: Arno, 1972.

Coxe, Margaret. *The Young Lady's Companion, and Token of Affection, in a Series of Letters.* Columbus: I. N. Whiting, 1846.

Dobson, Joanne. "The Hidden Hand: Subversion of Cultural Ideology in Three Mid-Nineteenth-Century American Women's Novels." *American Quarterly* 38 (1986): 223-42.

De Witt, William Radcliffe. *Her Price Above Rubies, Woman: Her Excellence and Usefulness.* Harrisburg: n.p., 1841.

Farrar, Eliza Ware. *The Young Lady's Friend.* Boston: American Stationers, 1837.

Flint, Kate. *The Woman Reader 1837-1914.* New York: Oxford UP, 1993.

Foster, Shirley, and Judy Simon. *What Katy Read: Feminist Re-Readings of "Classic" Stories for Girls.* Iowa City: U of Iowa P, 1995.

Foucault, Michel. "The Eye of Power." *Power—Knowledge: Selected Interviews and Other Writings, 1972-77.* Ed. and Trans. C. Gordo. New York: Pantheon, 1980. 146-65.

Gilmore, William J. *Reading Becomes a Necessity of Life: Material and Cultural Life in Rural New England 1780-1835.* Knoxville: U of Tennessee P, 1989.

Halttunen, Karen. *Confidence Men and Painted Women: A Study of Middle-Class Culture in America, 1830-1870.* New Haven: Yale UP, 1982.

Harris, Susan K. *19th-Century American Women's Novels: Interpretive Strategies.* Cambridge: Cambridge UP, 1990.

Hart, John D. *The Popular Book: A History of America's Literary Taste.* New York: Oxford UP, 1950.

Hiatt, Mary. "Susan Warner's Subtext: The Other Side of Piety." *Journal of Evolutionary Psychology* 8 (1987): 250-61.

Hovet, Grace Ann, and Theodore R. Hovet. "Identity Development in Susan Warner's *The Wide, Wide World*: Relationship, Performance and Construction." *Legacy* 8 (1991): 3-16.

———. "*Tableaux Vivants*: Masculine Vision and Feminine Reflections in Novels by Warner, Alcott, Stowe, and Wharton." *American Transcendental Quarterly* 7 (1993): 335-56.

Johnson, Barbara A. *Reading* Piers Plowman *and* The Pilgrim's Progress: *Reception and the Protestant Reader.* Carbondale: Southern Illinois UP, 1992.

Kasson, John F. *Rudeness & Civility: Manners in Nineteenth-Century Urban America.* New York: Hill and Wang, 1990.

Kelley, Mary. "The Making of Learned Women in Antebellum America." *Journal of American History* 83 (1996): 401-22.

——. *Private Woman, Public Stage: Literary Domesticity in Nineteenth-Century America.* New York: Oxford UP, 1984.

Kerber, Linda K. *Women of the Republic: Intellect and Ideology in Revolutionary America.* Chapel Hill: U of North Carolina P, 1980.

Newcomb, Harvey. *Newcomb's Young Lady's Guide to the Harmonious Development of Christian Character.* 7th ed. Boston: J. B. Dow, 1846.

Newton, Sarah Emily. "Wise and Foolish Virgins: 'Usable Fiction' and the Early American Conduct Tradition." *Early American Literature* 25 (1990): 139-67.

O'Connell, Catharine. "'We must sorrow': Silence, Suffering, and Sentimentality in Susan Warner's *The Wide, Wide World.*" *Studies in American Fiction* 25 (1997): 21-39.

Rose, Jane E. "Conduct Books for Women, 1830-1860: A Rationale for Women's Conduct and Domestic Role in America." *Nineteenth-Century Women Learn to Write.* Ed. Catharine Hobbs. Charlottesville: UP of Virginia, 1995. 37-58.

Russell, Anna U. *The Young Lady's Elocutionary Reader, Containing a Selection of Reading Lessons.* Boston: J. Munroe & Company, 1851.

Sanderson, Dorothy Hurlbut. *They Wrote for A Living: A Bibliography of the Works of Susan Bogert Warner and Anna Bartlett Warner.* Washingtonville: Spear, 1976.

Schnog, Nancy. "The Psychological Work of *The Wide, Wide World.*" *Genders* 4 (1989): 11-25.

Sedgwick, Catharine Maria. *Means and Ends, or, Self-Training.* London: Charles Tilt, 1839.

Sicherman, Barbara. "Sense and Sensibility: A Case Study of Women's Reading in Late-Victorian America." *Reading in America: Literature and Social History.* Ed. Cathy Davidson. Baltimore: Johns Hopkins UP, 1989. 201-25.

Stewart, Veronica. "The Wild Side of *The Wide, Wide World.*" *Legacy* 11 (1994): 1-16.

Swaim, Kathleen M. *Pilgrim's Progress, Puritan Progress: Discourses and Contexts.* Urbana: U of Illinois P, 1993.

Tompkins, Jane. *Sensational Designs: The Cultural Work of American Fiction, 1790-1860.* New York: Oxford UP, 1985.

——. Afterword. *The Wide, Wide World.* By Susan Warner. Ed. Jane Tompkins. New York: Feminist, 1987. 584-608.

Warner, Susan. *The Wide, Wide World.* 1850. Ed. Jane Tompkins. New York: Feminist, 1987.

Warren, Joyce W. "Domesticity and the Economics of Independence: Resistance and Revolution in the Work of Fanny Fern." *The (Other) American Traditions: Nineteenth-Century Women Writers.* Ed. Joyce W. Warren. New Brunswick: Rutgers UP, 1993. 54-72.

White, Isabelle. "Anti-Individualism, Authority, and Identity: Susan Warner's Contradictions in *The Wide, Wide World.*" *American Studies* 31.2 (1990): 31-41.

Wise, Daniel. *The Young Lady's Counselor; or Outlines & Illustrations of the Sphere, the Duties, & the Dangers of Young Women.* Cincinnati: Swormstedt & Poe, 1855.

The Young Lady's Mentor: A Guide to the Formation of Christian Character. . . . 1851. Philadelphia: H. C. Peck & T. Bliss, 1853.

Zboray, Ronald. *A Fictive People: Antebellum Economic Development and the American Reading Public.* New York: Oxford UP, 1993.

Zboray, Ronald, and Mary Sarcino Zboray. "Books, Reading, and the World of Goods in Antebellum New England." *American Quarterly* 48 (1996): 587-622.

——. "'Have You Read . . . ?': Real Readers and Their Responses in Antebellum Boston and Its Regions." *Nineteenth-Century Literature* 52 (1997): 139-70.

Elizabeth Fekete Trubey (essay date fall 2001)

SOURCE: Trubey, Elizabeth Fekete. "Imagined Revolution: The Female Reader and *The Wide, Wide World.*" *Modern Language Studies* 31, no. 2 (fall 2001): 57-74.

[*In the following essay, Trubey evaluates the portrayal of women's reading in* The Wide, Wide World *as an instructional but potentially subversive activity.*]

The act of reading plays an important thematic role throughout Susan Warner's 1850 bestseller, ***The Wide, Wide World.***[1] Ellen Montgomery, the novel's heroine, is often depicted with book in hand, turning to the Bible and other moralizing texts for comfort, edification, and direction. Warner relates Ellen's method of approaching texts, as well as the titles of the works she reads, in extensive detail. Indeed, books and readership are integral to the novel's sentimental message. They teach the young girl morality and Christ-like submission; however, almost counter-intuitively, books also open up for Ellen the possibility of imagined acts of rebellion. In as far as Ellen is a behavioral model for Warner's female readers,[2] the cultural work performed by the girl's many interactions with texts is vital to an understanding of both Warner's contradictory vision of women's inner thoughts and outward behavior and the way Warner wanted her vast audience to approach *The Wide, Wide World.*

For the past fifteen years, *The Wide, Wide World* has been central to feminist critics' revival of nineteenth-century women's fiction. Because the text is so archetypal of sentimental novels, it has been the focal point of a scholarly discussion of the cultural work performed by this genre that began with Jane Tompkins' groundbreaking *Sensational Designs.*[3] Whereas earlier critics like Henry Nash Smith and Ann Douglas had focused on the conservatism of Warner's novel, especially its millennial Christian vision,[4] Tompkins' persuasive discussion of the empowering nature of female passivity changed the critical landscape. By calling Ellen's submission to authority a "self-willed act of conquest of one's passions" and, therefore "an assertion of autonomy," Tompkins spawned a critical discourse that focuses on the potential for female resistance within the outwardly repressive world Warner creates for her heroine (152). Joanne Dobson, for instance, determines that the self-sacrifice the novel mandates merely covers a subtext of "strong, repressed anger at enforced feminine powerlessness" (227). Similarly, Catharine O'Connell compellingly suggests that the novel's emphasis on female pain and restriction "grants narrative authority to the anger and suffering of the powerless, and implicitly questions the rightful authority of the powerful who cause such suffering" (29). Such critical perspectives emphasize the radical impulses buried within a conservative overplot; they find evidence of subversive female emotions, thoughts and actions that push against the oppressive force of religious and earthly patriarchy.

Scholarship studying hidden radicalism has opened up the study of Warner's work and her thoughts on the nature of womanhood; however, its use of terms like "subversive" and "conservative" to describe the conflicting forces in the novel limit its impact. Critics often argue that the novel fits perfectly their definition of either "radical" or "repressive" instead of taking Warner's work on its own, politically slippery terms. As Nicola Diane Thompson explains:

> The ideological agendas of twentieth-century feminism are incompatible with the unstable, fluid, and fundamentally *different* positions of . . . women writers on the woman question. Very often, the heroines of these popular novels, created against the backdrop of shifting nineteenth-century debates about the woman question, stubbornly resist approbation by twentieth-century critics as subversive role models for women.

(1-2)

Indeed, in their efforts to assert Warner's radicalism, feminist scholars continually point to submerged moments of female empowerment without adequately accounting for the novel's many repressive impulses. In these cases, the revival of the so-called submissive elements of the novel and the elision of its more conservative themes prevent the full exploration of the conflicted nature of the text and in effect circumscribe our understanding of the role for women imagined by *The Wide, Wide World.*

If, instead of searching for instances of radicalism or conservatism, one examines the novel on its own—often frustrating and contradictory—terms, one gets a clearer picture of the vision of female "power" and the nature of womanhood that Warner espouses.[5] A study of the act of readership as described in the novel enables a fuller understanding of Warner's notion of women's place. Several other critics have discussed the different ways in which the Bible figures in Ellen's life: as a physical reminder or talisman of maternal love that guides Ellen in times of need,[6] as a means to bond with other women,[7] as an expression of patriarchal authority that is subverted into a mechanism of resistant female self-control.[8] My own reading focuses not on the symbolic function of the text itself but on the impact of the method by which Ellen approaches it; the book is at once a conveyor of a widely-accepted notion of womanhood and, simultaneously, a vehicle that teaches women a method of reading that is potentially disruptive to this concept of women's place. Rather than searching for signs of power in the self-abnegation Ellen learns from the Bible, I argue that the text serves more as a reading primer that, when used to interpret John Bunyan's *Pilgrim's Progress* and Mason Weem's *The Life of Washington,* opens new imaginative doors for Ellen Montgomery that reveal an inner space where women actually can rebel against authority and assert their wills. The conservative force of Christian patriarchy, notably, is never erased completely from the novel—it remains the dominant part of Warner's message. However, the instances of imagined female strength offer up a different, stronger womanhood that pushes the limits of Victorian gender norms.

In order to interpret Warner's representation of women's reading, it is necessary to understand prevailing Victorian notions of what women should read and what female readership *does.* As both Cathy N. Davidson and Susan K. Harris have noted, although women read a variety of types of books—religious texts, biographies, histories, conduct books, and in the case of highly educated women, classical and Renaissance works—the most popular imaginative texts among women were sentimental novels like *The Wide, Wide World.* Reading texts of this sort primarily was a tool for female education, teaching women about new subjects and, more important, about their proper gendered role. Harris suggests that consumers of sentimental fiction were discerning readers interested in exploring their place in American society; novels like Warner's that focused on the struggles and successes of women's lives at once allowed women to imagine a variety of social possibilities while overtly advocating a traditional, domestic feminine ideal.[9]

Despite the potential educative value of sentimental fiction, as the novel grew in prominence as a literary form through the eighteenth and early nineteenth centuries, anxieties about the pernicious effects reading novels could have on "true women" were prevalent. Davidson quotes an 1802 jeremiad titled, "Novel Reading, a Cause of Female Depravity," as an example of such thinking:

> Without the position instilled [by novels] into the blood, females in ordinary life would never have been so much the slaves of vice . . . It is no uncommon thing for a young lady who has attended her dearest friend to the altar, a few months after a marriage which, perhaps, but for *her,* had been a happy one, to fix her affections on her friend's husband, and by artful blandishments allure him to herself. Be not staggered, moral reader, at the recital! Such serpents are really in existence . . . I have seen two poor disconsolate parents drop into premature graves, miserable victims to their daughter's dishonour, and the peace of several relative families wounded never to be healed again in this world.

(quoted in Davidson 45-6)

The language the author uses points toward fears that fiction-reading will unnaturally stimulate female readers' bodies. Novels are "poisonous" to women's blood, arousing uncontrollable sexual passion that unsexes the readers. The woman who is moved by reading to violate the sanctity of marriage ceases to be a "young lady," becoming instead a "serpent" who drives her parents to early graves. The concern expressed here is that, as the imagination is stimulated by fiction, so will be the body to the extent that the reader is no longer recognizably "feminine"; the excesses of novel-reading, it is feared, will not only ruin otherwise true women, but entire families and communities. Although this anti-novel discourse was declining by the middle of the nineteenth century, concerns about the effects of certain types of sensational fiction would have on the health and virtue of female readers remained common. For example, at the end of *The Wide, Wide World,* John Humphreys, Warner's voice of moral authority, warns Ellen not to read any novels. The girl implicitly understands his concern that such texts carry the potential to derail his teachings and demurs. Given this anxiety about the propriety of women and girls reading novels, many female writers refused to categorize their works as fiction, instead emphasizing, as for example Warner does, the religious and educative qualities of the book.[10]

Considering her protestations that *The Wide, Wide World* was not a novel *per se,* it is not surprising that Warner devotes a large portion of her book to discussing the proper way for women to approach texts. Warner treats reading foremost as a means to an end: instructing women in how to achieve true womanhood and Christian salvation. Within *The Wide, Wide World,* the message of piety and submission expressed in the Bible is of central importance. Indeed, readings such as Henry Nash Smith's that stress the conformity and submission learned from the Bible are repeatedly borne out in the course of the novel; Ellen's Bible-reading primarily teaches her to stifle her passions when she is upset. For example, as she begins to realize that her separation from her mother may well be permanent, Ellen reads a hymn that discusses the resignation of the soul to Christ: "Open my heart, Lord, enter in; / Slay every foe, and conquer sin. / Here now to thee I all resign,— / My body, my soul, and all are thine" (75). Before looking at the hymn, Ellen had been sobbing passionately, railing against the difficult fate facing her; once she reads it, however, the words help her make up her mind to "begin to follow [her] Saviour, and to please him" (75). Ellen learns from the Bible that her own desires and feelings must be secondary to divine will. She must suppress her own pain and resentment at losing her mother and instead submit to God's authority.

As she gets older, Ellen continues to have difficulty controlling her passions and imitating Christ's meekness. Alice and John Humphreys work hard to teach the girl to submit to authority; they constantly advise her to turn to the Bible for guidance. The restrictions Ellen's guardian, Aunt Fortune, places on Ellen's activities move the girl to constant, predictable, passionate outbursts; however, the Bible teaches her to control her anger:

> Strong passion—strong pride,—both long unbroken; and Ellen had yet to learn that many a prayer and many a tear, much watchfulness, much help from on high, must be hers before she could be thoroughly dispossessed of these evil spirits. But she knew her sickness; she had applied to the Physician;—she was in a fair way to be well.

(181)

Here, Ellen's rebellious nature is treated as a disease; indeed, John later tells Ellen that she is "'very, very weak—quite unable to keep [her]self right without constant help'" (296). It is the Bible that provides her with a cure from her "illness," a model of passivity to emulate. Alice, for instance, instructs her to "'see with how much patience and perfect sweetness of temper [she] can forbear; [to] see if [she] cannot win [Fortune] over by untiring gentleness, obedience, and meekness'" (241).

Tompkins has suggested that although this heavy moralizing "presents an image of people . . . [who] learn to transmute rebellious passion into humble conformity to others' wishes, their powerlessness becomes a source of strength"; the meek, she argues, by learning to master themselves, will inherit the earth (165). While this indeed may be true, the overarching model of womanhood that Warner represents through Ellen's Bible-reading is overwhelmingly traditional. The girl must learn to subsume her passionate and rebellious feelings under more lady-like, submissive comportment. Indeed, the entire purpose of Mrs. Montgomery, Alice and especially John's instruction has been to train Ellen to be the ideal domestic wife: she must be, as Barbara Welter has put it, pious, passive, and most of all submissive if she is to mature into a woman worthy of marrying John (152).[11] Even if Warner's support for this traditional feminine ideal is, as some suggest, tempered by the depiction of the toll Ellen's attempt to change herself takes,[12] the novel still espouses female behavior that is outwardly obedient and docile. More to the point, in her teachers' eyes Ellen's transformation cannot be simply a matter of changing her outward behavior; she must come to believe the words on the page. In large part, she does so. Over the course of *The Wide, Wide World* Ellen absorbs the Bible's lesson of submission: she is able to "temper and beautify her Christian character" and is proud of her hard-earned willingness to obey those who show her love (569).

This "conversion" to proper womanhood ultimately is made possible not simply by reading the Bible, but by learning to read it *correctly*. Ellen must master a specific way of approaching the text—delving deeply into the meaning of each word and phrase, learning them all by heart—in order to believe in the supremacy of God's message. There are several key aspects to the proper method of reading the Bible that she is taught. First, when perusing the Bible, her attention turns "entirely from herself" and instead focuses on the text and its message: "though, when she began [to read], her own little heart was full of excitement, in view of the day's plans, and beating with hope and pleasure, the sublime beauty of the words and thoughts, as she went on, awed her into quiet" (27). The act of reading turns Ellen's attention from the excitement of everyday life to the sublimity of the phrases. Her daily routine—doing chores, making tea, and occasionally going shopping—seems to vanish when she reads the Bible so that she focuses only on the meaning of the passages. As important as learning domestic skills is in the novel, these earthly trappings of woman's place are insignificant compared to the broader concerns of salvation and Christian love.

Second, the method of reading that Ellen learns is based on obsessive explication. The Bible's message must be pored over and closely read until every last drop of meaning has been gleaned. Ellen desired to "talk over" hymns, to read them "over and explain [them]"; she and Alice pick through the verses word by word, methodically explicating their meaning (238-9). Indeed, the Bible cannot be understood fully by mere perusal, Warner suggests. One must be a careful, focused reader in order to absorb God's message. This ideal Bible-reader becomes utterly lost in the words, entering into an emotional state of openness to the text's meaning. The effect of this kind of reading is similar to the experience that Georges Poulet describes in "Criticism and the Experience of Interiority"; as one reads, the text as object "is no more . . . It has become a series of words, or images, of ideas which in their turn begin to exist. And where is this new existence? . . . [In one's] innermost self" (42). In other words, because of the closeness of this mode of reading, the reader's identity and the words she encounters merge; the thoughts expressed in writing seem to originate not in the book but in the person who is holding it. The subject-object division is blurred, and thus it temporarily becomes possible for the reader to absorb and identify with experiences described in the text.[13]

Early in the novel, Ellen's mother serves as an example of this kind of reader; when reading the Twenty-third Psalm, Mrs. Montgomery clearly finds great comfort and solace in the words. The girl, on the other hand, seems more concerned with the possibility of losing her mother than she is with the meaning of the words, a state which she must learn to remedy: her "eyes were full, and her heart too. 'If only I could *feel* these words as mamma does!'" she thinks (15; emphasis mine). Ellen longs for the type of emotional absorption into the text that her mother has; indeed, she wants to read so that the passage is not merely something to believe in, but rather a thought or feeling that seems to originate within herself.

Ellen quickly learns to read in this fashion. The girl comes to seek comfort in the Bible that is inscribed by and thus identified with her mother. While on the ferry that takes her to Aunt Fortune's, Ellen and the kindly Mr. Marshman read hymns together. She has a deep and sustained reaction to the words, yearning truly to be able to give her "body, soul, and all" to Christ (75). She frequently has emotional reactions of this sort to the Biblical passages she reads; for example, she says "[hymns] make me happy; I love them dearly" (215). This is the third key quality of Ellen's reading: the words come to life for her, and she loves them as if they were alive, as if they themselves were her friends or family. Because of this, she takes every word she reads to heart as an example of how she should behave. For instance, she relates a reading of the eighteenth chapter of Matthew, specifically verses about Christ's infinite capacity to forgive trespasses, directly to herself and a fight she had had with her aunt: "'That means me,' she thought . . . 'I thought I was forgiven [by Christ], but how can I be, for I feel I have not forgiven aunt Fortune'" (157). Because Ellen's response to the Bible is emotional and personal, she is better able to incorporate the text's meaning, to believe in the reality of its power, and to emphasize with Christ and his love for others.

It is this detailed, emotional, personalized, identification-based mode of reading that makes the Bible's words so pertinent to the readers in *The Wide, Wide World.* When applied to Scripture, this method enables Ellen to absorb completely and to believe in the repressive passivity that the text emphasizes. Because she identifies her own thoughts with those expressed in the hymns and parables she peruses, Ellen comes to believe in the model of submissive, Christ-like womanhood promoted by the Bible, and she modifies her behavior accordingly. It is important to remember that Warner does not outwardly criticize this concept of woman's place; the sentimental plot of *The Wide, Wide World* revolves around Ellen's successful maturation into a pious woman ultimately worthy of marriage to a patriarchal figure. There is nothing insincere in Warner's representation of the value of female humility, submission, and docility. Even if one reads power into Ellen's passivity, this feminine strength does not in itself challenge the domestic womanly ideal. Rather, it is absolutely reliant upon a traditional concept of womanhood.

This is not to say, however, that Warner's ultimate promotion of one particular model of femininity is her final word on the subject. The scenes of Ellen's reading again hold the key to unpacking Warner's treatment of proper femininity. The obsessive, identification-based method of reading that Warner describes, while ostensibly pointing Ellen down the narrow path to salvation, notably resembles the interactions with the texts that anti-novel advocates labeled "dangerous." Likewise, the self-indulgence implicit in Ellen's relating every event about which she reads to herself challenges the self-denying, self-abnegating notion of womanhood promoted elsewhere in the novel. Indeed, for all its traditionalism, *The Wide, Wide World* might best be described as an "exploratory" text, one that imagines new roles for women while ultimately opting for the culturally dominant one.[14] While the behavior Ellen learns from reading the Bible is on the whole conservative, the interpretive skills she gains through reading that text, when applied to other books, open doors to intellectual and imaginative acts of rebellion. In other words, a method of reading that is largely responsible for the perpetuation of a traditional notion of womanhood also becomes a source of rebellion, at least in the mind of the female reader.

As Ellen begins to broaden her horizons by studying history, science and philosophy, she continues to read books in the personal, repetitive fashion in which she reads Scripture: "Alice insisted that when Ellen had fairly begun a book she should go through with it; not capriciously leave it for another, nor have half a dozen at a time. But when Ellen had read it once she commonly wanted to go over it again, and seldom laid it aside until she had sucked the sweetness all out of it" (335). Just as when she reads the Bible, when examining secular materials Ellen's mind is focused only on the text in front of her and nothing else, and she closely reads each book several times. Ellen's emotional reactions to these other books are also similar to those she has to Bible verses: "how delightful it was . . . to go with Alice, in thought, to the south of France . . . ; or run over the Rock of Gibraltar with the monkeys; or at another time . . . to forget the kitchen and supper with her bustling aunt, and sail round the world with Captain Cook" (336). Ellen's reading blocks out the intrusions of day-to-day life and her imagination allows her to become a part of the action about which she reads. Through focused acts of imagination, then, Ellen can escape from the daily minutiae of female duty and imagine herself actually out in the wide world, freely engaging in all sorts of "unwomanly" activities to which she does not otherwise have access. This escapism is a small-scale exercise of mental rebellion against the domestic lot the world has set for her.

This sort of imaginative resistance to the confines of womanhood runs through much of Ellen's extra-Biblical reading. She examines many secular and quasi-secular texts throughout the novel, but two are of particular importance to her: Bunyan's *Pilgrim's Progress* and Mason Weems' *The Life of Washington.* The first book provides an example of Biblical reading practices apply to "secular" texts and the conflicted messages Ellen gleans from such study; the second demonstrates more specifically how Ellen's mode of reading holds the key to potential female rebellion within a text that, on the whole, supports a traditional, restrictive notion of women's place.

Ellen reads Bunyan's late seventeenth-century allegory *Pilgrim's Progress* at several points throughout the book. On the surface, the text serves to further the girl's connection with John Humphreys, her future husband. John tries throughout *The Wide, Wide World* to reshape Ellen's passionate behavior into more womanly, submissive conduct, and he uses Bunyan as a teaching tool. He wants her to see *Pilgrim's Progress* as an exemplar like the Bible, and the first time he reads to her from the book, her reaction is very much like the one that she would have to hearing the Bible read: "Her attention was nailed; the listless, careless mood in which she sat down was changed for one of rapt delight; she devoured every word that fell from the reader's lips; indeed they were given their fullest effect by a fine voice and singularly fine reading" (351). Ellen's attention turns from worldly thoughts to the text at hand, and her emotional state is one of rapturous joy that nearly defeats John's intentions. He reads to Ellen in order to contain her emotions, but the girl's reaction is more akin to being seduced both by the words and their reader. The physicality of Ellen's response recalls contemporary fears that reading fiction would unnaturally arouse and excite susceptible women, but ultimately Warner suggests that this unsanctioned pleasure enables John's tutelary purposes. Ellen's mind forms a pleasurable connection between the book itself and the man reading it,—one brings to mind the lessons taught by the other.

This link between man and text is further heightened by John's gift of a personally annotated edition of *Pilgrim's Progress*. The notes allow him to shape Ellen's reading process even when he is not with her: "she found all through the book, on the margin or at the bottom of the leaves, in John's beautiful handwriting, a great many notes—simple, short, plain, exactly what was needed to open the whole book to her and make it of the greatest possible use and pleasure" (370). John had been Ellen's teacher, instructing her to find a paradigm of proper behavior in her Bible-reading; his annotations ensure that Ellen will read *Pilgrim's Progress* in the same fashion. The shadow of John's authoritative presence looms over the text, and his comments control her interpretations, ultimately furthering the education in "proper" femininity she receives at his hands. *Pilgrim's Progress* becomes his primary tool for teaching Ellen that "'what God orders let us quietly submit to'" (565). Indeed, Ellen does find the same meaning in Bunyan as in the Bible. Just as God's words comfort her in times of loss, teaching her acceptance and passivity in the face of challenge, reading about the death of Christian in *Pilgrim's Progress* consoles Ellen when her mother dies. Ellen becomes fascinated by Christian's ascension to heaven: "she pored over that scene with untiring pleasure until she almost had it by heart. In short never was a child more comforted and contented with a book than Ellen was with the 'Pilgrim's Progress'" (353). By reading obsessively, identifying with Christian's travails and finding personal instruction in them, Ellen can take comfort in Bunyan as she does in the Bible. The book teaches her the supremacy of God's will and her own need to submit to it.

Interestingly, the path that Ellen takes throughout *The Wide, Wide World* follows a trajectory similar to that of the first book of *Pilgrim's Progress*. As Dobson notes, "The heroine's progress is from individuality to self-renunciation, from energy to stasis. This 'progress' reflects the pattern of living and aspiration that social authority prescribed for women" (226). Also intriguing is the fact that Ellen is not shown reading the second half

of Bunyan's allegory, the section that details a woman's—Christiana's—journey to salvation. Rather than point to a female heroine for Ellen to imitate, Warner sets her up to identify with a male role model. This readerly cross-dressing is often inconsequential in the scheme of the novel: Ellen, just like Christian, learns the universal message of rejecting worldly goods and focusing instead on the hereafter. However, the gender difference between Warner's heroine and the hero she emulates becomes central in the rarely discussed last portion of the novel when Ellen lives in Scotland with her uncle Lindsay.[15] As Judith Fetterley, among others, has pointed out, the experience of identifying with male rather than female characters is common among women readers: when Ellen identifies with Christian, she "is co-opted into participation in an experience from which she is explicitly excluded" (xii). However, instead of emphasizing Ellen's exclusion from Christian's pious, yet masculine bravery, Warner uses this moment of identification to empower Ellen. Embedded within Christian's trip down the path of righteousness are several bloody battles; he must engage physically with monsters such as Apollyon if he wishes to enter the kingdom of heaven. While Warner never mentions reading these scenes in particular, Ellen's behavior towards the novel's end suggest that these moments of fighting for one's beliefs made an impression on her. In spite of John's intentions for the text, in Scotland Ellen begins to exhibit rebellious, "unwomanly" qualities that she has learned through *Pilgrim's Progress*.

The last section of ***The Wide, Wide World*** signals a shift in the novel's focus. The story seems to start over again as Ellen feels "strangely that she was in the midst of new scenes indeed, entering upon a new stage of life" (500). Whereas the bulk of the novel deals with Ellen's efforts to find true piety through friendship, in Scotland she must learn to maintain her faith without the influence of her friends. Moreover, in a sort of reverse colonial pilgrimage, Ellen moves from America to Great Britain, from relative freedom to strict (albeit loving) confinement. The issue of autonomy is prominent in this portion of the novel, as Uncle Lindsay repeatedly reminds Ellen of his authority over her, telling her that she "'belong[s] to [him] entirely'" (504). Ellen "'must have no nationality'" beyond that of her adoptive family; she must not "speak of those [American] friends, nor allude to them, especially in any way to show how much of her heart was out of Scotland"; she must hide her faith from adults who "insisted that Ellen was spoiling herself for life and the world by a set of dull religious notions that were utterly unfit for a child" (505, 528, 542-3).

In Scotland, *Pilgrim's Progress* serves to comfort Ellen in her separation from her loved ones, and at least for a while helps her to be passive and meek in the face of her uncle's rules. However, when the Lindsays try her by taking away her copy of the book, her reaction to authority is not, as before, to cry uncontrollably (although she certainly does shed tears) but rather to argue with her uncle. Deprived of *Pilgrim's Progress,* that symbol of Christian trial and of John's regulating presence, Ellen loses her self-control and is "surprised and half-frightened at herself . . . to find the strength of the old temper suddenly roused" (553). Indeed, without *Pilgrim's Progress* her ability to control her passions begins to diminish; in effect, her hard-won "feminine" passivity and submissiveness vanish without the containing presence of the book. But even while she violates prescribed womanly behavior by fighting with her uncle instead of simply accepting his authority, her actions nonetheless have been inspired by reading Bunyan. Ellen feels that by taking away the text her uncle is inexplicably and wickedly preventing her from attaining salvation; similarly, Christian must fight the monster Apollyon who blocks the path to heaven. Although she must ultimately accede to her uncle's wishes, Ellen temporarily imagines a new role for herself, one based in resistance and defense of her faith—the traits of a Christian hero—instead of in more feminine passive acceptance of higher authority. Because she has learned to identify with the male characters she reads about and to take their exploits as personal models, reading Bunyan has inspired Ellen's "improper" and unladylike behavior; rather than simply obey, she momentarily imitates Christian, challenging those who would take away her faith.

The Christian-as-soldier archetype that reading *Pilgrim's Progress* teaches Ellen provides her with short-term means to resisting her uncle's will. Her historical reading, specifically *The Life of Washington,* enables Ellen to assert her autonomy on a larger scale. Mason Weems' biography of George Washington is part of the literary movement that mythologized the president, and historians have considered its accuracy suspect since its first publication in 1800.[16] The book was largely responsible for the propagation of legends about Washington's life such as the cherry tree incident and is filled with anecdotes about his early years and military service. The basic thrust of his work is to present Washington's greatness as being a result of mother-love, piety, and patriotism. Weems claims that the president's "GREAT TALENTS, CONSTANTLY GUIDED AND GUARDED BY RELIGION [sic]" lead to his early victories, an argument for success clearly in keeping with Warner's *modus operandi* and with Bunyan's stories of Christian heroism (172).[17] In Washington, Weems stresses two types of behavior, both of which are familiar to Ellen: the president is at once full of religious and sentimental feelings—loving like Christ or even a sentimental heroine—at the same time as he is depicted as a strong and righteous crusader—heroic like Christian.

Given this attractive combination of meekness and strength, it comes as no surprise that Ellen is drawn in by *The Life of Washington* and treats the book as if it were as sacred to her as the Bible or *Pilgrim's Progress.* She becomes totally absorbed in the text, taking in every word as if it were the gospel truth:

> Whatever she had found within the leaves of the book, she had certainly lost herself. An hour passed. Ellen had not spoken or moved except to turn over the leaves . . .
>
> . . . The pleasure of that delightful book, in which she was wrapped the whole day; even when called off . . . to help . . . in fifty little matters of business or pleasure. These were attended to, and faithfully and cheerfully, but *the book* was in her head all the while . . . Even when she went to be dressed her book went with her, and was laid on the bed within sight, ready to be taken up the moment she was at liberty.
>
> (329-30)

Just as when she reads the Bible, Ellen's attention turns entirely to the book at hand when reading Weems. Worldly matters are merely distractions that keep her from reading further. Reading *The Life of Washington* is for Ellen a "wonderful pleasure": "Wiems' Life of Washington [sic] was read, and read, and read over again, till she almost knew it by heart" (335). Ellen memorizes the president's life so that, like the words of God the Father, the life of the father of the country is always in the front of her mind, permanently etched into her memory.

Although Ellen reads *The Life of Washington* in America, it is not until she is in Lindsay's thrall that the text becomes symbolically important. When she butts up against her uncle's many prejudices, she refers to Weems' book, engaging him in arguments about freedom and rebellion. For example, when the Lindsays make disparaging comments about Americans, calling them a "'parcel of rebels who have broken loose from all loyalty and fealty, that no good Briton has any business to like,'" Ellen's frustrations are expressed not by tears but by the employment of knowledge that clearly has come from *The Life of Washington*:

> "Are you one of those that make a saint of George Washington?" [Lindsay asked, amused].
>
> "No," said Ellen,—"I think he was a great deal better than some saints. But I don't think the Americans were rebels."
>
> "You are a little rebel yourself. Do you mean to say you think the Americans were right?"
>
> "Do you mean to say you think they were wrong, uncle?"
>
> "I assure you," said he, "if I had been in the English army I would have fought them with all my heart."

"And if I had been in the American army I would have fought *you* with all my heart, uncle Lindsay."

"Come, come," said he laughing;—"*you* fight! you don't look as if you would do battle with a good-sized mosquito."

"Ah, but I mean if I had been a man," said Ellen.

(506)

In this passage, Ellen's uncle, asking if she is "one of those that make a saint" of Washington, refers to Weems and other biographers of that ilk who portray the president as holy and nearly infallible. Ellen, having read "'Two lives of Washington, and some in the Annual Register, and part of Graham's United States,'" has absorbed these texts' representations of the American Revolution as something of a holy war. Her "'extraordinary taste for freedom'" has been cultivated by reading and memorizing quasi-historical texts (506, 515). Ellen reads these books, like everything she reads, in the same fashion as she reads the Bible, and the message of piety and freedom that she takes from them is just as central to her being as the word of God.

Because of this method of reading, Washington has become an exemplar for Ellen. She identifies with him as she does all the heroes about whom she reads, allying herself with his political and symbolic position. Washington, she claims, "'always did right,'" and she accepts his perfection with the blind faith with which she reads the Bible: "'If it had not been right,'" she claims, "'Washington would not have done it . . . [W]hen a person *always* does right, if he happen to do something that I don't know enough to understand, I have good reason to think it is right, even though I cannot understand it'" (515). Even if some of Washington's actions appear questionable, Ellen dismisses her qualms as a sign of her ignorance, not of Washington's moral failing. She must simply believe and follow his example. Ellen in fact treats the biography like *Pilgrim's Progress* or the Bible: a practical guide for her own life and not simply a lesson about the past.

Perhaps the most interesting moment in the long passage I quote above occurs when Ellen claims that if she had been a man she would have fought for her independence against Lindsay and the British. While as a young girl Ellen is necessarily barred from physical combat, her desire to engage the enemy signals the existence of her remaining sparks of intellectual resistance. In spite of having been taught again and again the value of passivity, submission, and obedience to authority—"though we *must* sorrow, we must not rebel," her mother tells her in a lesson that Ellen has, by this point in the novel, learned thoroughly (12)—the story of George Washington has inspired her. Washington is another paragon of Christian duty, someone whose motives are unquestioned and whose actions are always just. Surely, if a pious and righteous man such as he can fight with God's blessing on his side, Ellen should be able to resist her uncle, a "tyrant" who "governs" her tongue (530). And indeed, in making Ellen "forget" her nationality, taking away her freedom to worship as she pleases, forbidding her to speak freely, and constantly reminding her that she is owned by him, Lindsay is likened to a tyrant on the level of King George III. Uncle Lindsay represses Ellen as England did America; in fact, he takes away those very "American" freedoms established by the Bill of Rights. In the face of these actions, Ellen, having long learned from the Bible to emulate and imitate the great men she reads about in books, "becomes" Washington. As a girl, she cannot fight physically, but she can engage in intellectual warfare, fighting against her uncle for imaginative independence.

Although Ellen's attempts to struggle against her uncle's repression are largely futile (he indulges her whims, but she ultimately remains subject to his control), that she even has recourse to this kind of intellectual debate is significant. Positioning herself as a sort of female Washington fighting on the home front, Ellen argues the cause of liberty; specifically, she waxes rhapsodic about freedom fighters like Robert the Bruce and the Marquis de Lafayette. She also attempts to use "American" arguments for freedom and autonomy against her uncle. While, as a girl, she cannot fight against her "enemy," she at least has the abilities, gained through extensive and obsessive reading practices, to imagine herself possessing the same freedoms as a man and to use her intellectual acuity to fight, on some level, for her self-control.

But the strength that she gains through reading texts such as *The Life of Washington* is different in kind than any "power" she gains from reading the Bible. Rather than finding her resolve in being Christ-like and passive, Ellen learns from Weems how to be Washington-like, at once faithful and rebellious, willing to go to war to defend political and religious beliefs. Even *Pilgrim's Progress,* which John uses to promote passive, obedient, Biblical values, encourages Ellen to fight against those who would keep her from true faith just as Christian fights monsters who block his access to heaven. The ultimate futility of Ellen's efforts make this intellectual rebellion all the more important: because she cannot enact her freedom in the physical world, she must cling to the power she has in her imagination, a power gained through using proper reading techniques in what might be called "improper" ways. Because she has learned to read all texts with the same set of interpretive tools that she uses with the Bible, Weems' depiction of pious rebellion is at the very heart of her understanding of the world around her. Because she is a good reader, Ellen can gain access to the *idea* of freedom and rebellion if not actual freedom itself.

Warner does not promote a wholesale revision of traditional, passive, womanhood in *The Wide, Wide World,* but she also does not accept this role uncritically. Rather, she uses the novel to imagine a different model of femininity, one based not in docility but in strength and assertiveness, while ultimately opting to defend a safer, more traditional place for women. More specifically, what Warner does is suggest that even though Ellen ultimately accedes to submission and domesticity, she possesses the all-important ability to imagine a new position for herself. Using the very skills with which she interprets the Bible, she can think herself out of her home and into the world. Ellen may not be able to enact her visions of Washingtonian command, but she can fantasize about a world where girls can battle against tyrants and can fight for their beliefs and rights.

When at the end of *The Wide, Wide World* John instructs Ellen to "Read no novels" (564), Warner's readers are put in a curious position, being about to finish doing exactly that. Having learned through Ellen that John's moralizing is to be obeyed, how can readers justify their attachment to the book in hand? After all, this book prompted such readerly identification with Ellen and Warner that one woman wrote to Warner, "I feel as if I knew you and you were my personal friend," and another exclaimed that no author has "ministered to the highest and noblest feelings of my nature *so much as yourself*" (qtd. in Williams 573). Tompkins has suggested that Warner wanted readers to understand John's statement as proof that Warner thought of her book as a "story" that functioned in the same way as Biblical parables (149); O'Connell alternately claims that John's comment is ironized and is intended to undermine his authority (135). I would suggest that the decree appears to serve both purposes. It does not merely express disapproval of novels that could potentially corrupt the female mind and body. John is once again promoting a method of approaching texts which favors moral instruction rather than readerly pleasure. This notion of the value of reading comes out of Bunyan's own Puritan tradition and is the link between Ellen's interactions with the Bible, *The Life of Washington,* and Pilgrim's *Progress,* as well as the audiences experience of *The Wide, Wide World.*[18] In particular, each text places the responsibility for personal reform squarely within the reader and requires its (female) readers to contain and control themselves. At the same time, the power of John's stricture is undercut by both Ellen's frequent experience of the emotional pleasures of reading and her identification with a more heroic female role. Even though she tells John that she stays away from novels, it seems impossible for her to avoid "novel-reading"; while she finds moral instruction in texts, her imagination is stimulated to the point that she can fancy herself in positions that push at the edges of the cultural order she is taught.

Because the novel is shaped so that its audience is encouraged to identify with Ellen's suffering and successes, they also learn to approach *The Wide, Wide World* as Ellen does the books she reads. Ellen is herself a model for the girls who read *The Wide, Wide World*; like Christian and Washington she has the power to influence by example. While I am not suggesting that Warner's female audience was prompted by the novel to start radically questioning their place in the world, I do claim that she teaches them a mode of reading that enables a potential challenge to dominant notions of gender. By privileging an active, empathetic mode of readership, Warner fosters sympathy for imaginative exploration of the woman question. The final result of this exploration is outward passivity, but in women's inner minds, there is still room for vividly imagined acts of female rebellion and resistance. The strength is not in the decision to submit, but rather in the ability to imagine alternatives.

Notes

1. An earlier version of this essay was delivered at the NEMLA conference in Buffalo, NY, on April 8, 2000.

2. Almost all critical discussions of *The Wide, Wide World* depend on the assumption that Warner's readers are meant to identify with and emulate Ellen. Catharine O'Connell is most direct about the link between heroine and audience. She explains that the narrative "appeals to and constructs the reader as a domestic woman, one who is expected to identify with Ellen and whose own emotional experiences are implicitly validated by the narrative attention given to Ellen's" (22).

3. Before Tompkins, Nina Baym had discussed *The Wide, Wide World* in a feminist context in *Woman's Fiction: A Guide to Novels by and About Women in America, 1820-1870.* It was *Sensational Designs: The Cultural Work of American Fiction, 1790-1860* that established the terms on which the novel would be evaluated in the following years. Indeed, Tompkins' examination of the novel's cultural work—the way in which the text "engaged in solving a problem or a set of problems specific to the time in which it was written" (38)—shifted critic's focus from the literary value (or lack thereof) of *The Wide, Wide World* to the novel's discussion of woman's nature and role.

4. See Smith, 51; Douglas, 13.

5. My method for interpreting the often-contradictory gender politics of *The Wide, Wide World* has been influenced by Susan K. Harris' discussion of "exploratory" women's novels in *19th-Century American Women's Novels: Interpretive Strategies.* Looking at the "Janus-face" of popular fiction

(19), Harris examines texts' middle portions that establish "an area of female independence, competence, emotional complexity, and intellectual acumen" within a cover story of dependence and submission (21).

6. See Tompkins, 163-5; Barnes 104-9.

7. Schnog, 19-21.

8. Tompkins, 164-5, 171-3. Nearly all recent feminist interpretations of the novel make use of Tompkins' work in some way.

9. Harris writes that mid-nineteenth-century letters and diaries indicate that women readers were particularly interested in books that told historical or fictional stories of exceptional women, that provided intellectual substance which would give them "power in the world of ideas," and, more specifically, that featured heroines who had to become professionally or emotionally self-sufficient (30). Davidson, although she discusses republican sentimentalism, similarly stresses the imaginative possibility of such fiction, suggesting that "sentimental novels fulfilled the social function of testing some of the possibilities of romance and courtship—testing better conducted in the world of fiction than in the world of fact" (113).

10. This practice of criticizing novels within novels was so common that one frustrated reviewer wrote in *Godey's Lady's Book,* "This species of disingenuousness, be it said, is a common thing with novel-writers. Is it not an affectation of humility? Or does each novel-writer, who condemns that sort of work, consider his or her novel an exception to the rule?" (quoted in Noble 116).

11. Welter determines that of the four attributes of womanhood (piety, passivity, submissiveness and domesticity) submission—the virtue for which Ellen must strive the hardest and is most rewarded—"was perhaps the most feminine virtue expected of women" (158).

12. See O'Connell 30-6, for a discussion of John's efforts to shape Ellen's behavior, the costs of his actions on the girl, and the rhetorical significance of her pain.

13. Wolfgang Iser, responding to Poulet, uses the subject-object relationship to describe the reading process: "It is true [as Poulet claims] that [books] consist of ideas thought out by someone else, but in reading the reader becomes the subject that does the thinking. Thus there disappears the subject-object division that otherwise is a prerequisite for all knowledge and all observation, and the removal of this division puts reading in an apparently unique position as regards the possible absorption of new experiences" (66).

14. See Harris, 20.

15. Critics tend to gloss over the Scotland section and the ensuing changes in Ellen's behavior. Baym discusses the role of Ellen's nationalism in Scotland (xxiv-xxv). Tompkins, ignoring Ellen's moments of resistance to her uncle's will, notes that "The final chapters of *The Wide, Wide World* require of the heroine an extinction of personality so complete that there is literally nothing of herself that she can call her own" (179). O'Connell discusses the struggle between John and Lindsay for control of Ellen without accounting for the girl's own actions (33-4). Dobson names Lindsay as an authority figure (230), and Schnog parses out Ellen's attempts to maintain her link to absent friends (21). However, none of these critics launch sustained readings of this important segment of the novel.

16. Tompkins mentions that sentimental fiction worked to demonstrate national unity in a time of sectional strife (149-50); Julia A. Stern has pointed out that from the 1790's on, the "national fetishization of Washington" made it "possible for Americans to disavow the reality of increasing political conflict" (144). I would suggest that Warner's use of Washington as a role model and of Weems' biography as a key text are part of this literary-political trend.

17. Indeed, the similarities between Weems' vision of success and Warner's lends credence to Henry Nash Smith's theory about the "cosmic success story" in sentimental fiction.

18. Linda K. Kerber suggests that the legacy of Puritanism for American women in the nineteenth century is Bunyan's message of renunciation and self-control; she argues that Bunyan's rhetoric "provides [women with] a way of defining the limits on their behavior, what they may *not do,* rather than what they might" (175).

Works Cited

Barnes, Elizabeth. *States of Sympathy: Seduction and Democracy in the American Novel.* New York: Columbia University Press, 1997.

Baym, Nina. *Woman's Fiction: A Guide to Novels by and about Women in America, 1820-1870.* Second edition. Chicago: University of Illinois Press, 1993.

Davidson, Cathy N. *The Revolution and the Word: The Rise of the Novel in America.* New York: Oxford University Press, 1986.

Dobson, Joanne. "The Hidden Hand: Subversion of Cultural Ideology in Three Mid-Nineteenth-Century American Women's Novels." *American Quarterly* 38:2 (Summer 1986): 223-242.

Douglas, Ann. *The Feminization of American Culture.* Second edition. New York: Anchor Books, 1988.

Fetterley, Judith. *The Resisting Reader: A Feminist Approach to American Fiction.* Bloomington: Indiana University Press, 1978.

Harris, Susan K. *19th-Century American Women's Novels: Interpretive Strategies.* New York: Cambridge University Press, 1990.

Iser, Wolfgang. "The Reading Process: A Phenomenological Approach." *Reader-Response Criticism: From Formalism to Post-Structuralism.* Ed. Jane Tompkins. Baltimore: The John Hopkins University Press, 1980. 50-69.

Kelley, Mary. *Private Woman, Public Stage: Literary Domesticity in Nineteenth Century America.* New York: Oxford University Press, 1984.

Kerber, Linda K. "Can a Woman Be an Individual? The Limits of Puritan Tradition in the Early Republic." *Texas Studies in Literature and Language* 25:1 (Spring 1983): 165-178.

Noble, Marianne. *The Masochistic Pleasures of Sentimental Literature.* Princeton, NJ: Princeton University Press, 2000.

O'Connell, Catharine. "'We *Must* Sorrow': Silence, Suffering, and Sentamentality in Susan Warner's *The Wide, Wide World.*" *Studies in American Fiction* (Spring 1997): 21-39.

Poulet, Georges. "Criticism and the Experience of Interiority." *Reader-Response Criticism: From Formalism to Post-Structuralism.* Ed. Jane Tompkins. Baltimore: The Johns Hopkins University Press, 1980. 41-49.

Schnog, Nancy. "Inside the Sentimental: The Psychological Work of *The Wide, Wide World.*" *Genders* 4 (Spring 1989): 11-25.

Smith, Henry Nash. "The Scribbling Women and the Cosmic Success Story." *Critical Inquiry* 1:1 (September 1974): 47-70.

Stern, Julia A. *The Plight of Feeling: Sympathy and Dissent in the Early American Novel.* Chicago: University of Chicago Press, 1997.

Thompson, Nicola Diane. "Responding to the woman questions: rereading noncanonical Victorian women novelists." *Victorian Women Writers and the Woman Question.* Ed. Nicola Diane Thompson. New York: Cambridge University Press, 1999. 1-23.

Tompkins, Jane. *Sensational Designs: The Cultural Work of American Fiction, 1790-1860.* New York: Oxford University Press, 1985.

Warner, Susan. *The Wide, Wide World.* Ed. Jane Tompkins. New York: The Feminist Press, 1987.

Weems, Mason. *The Life of Washington.* Ed. Mason Cunliffe. Cambridge: Harvard University Press, 1962.

Welter, Barbara. "The Cult of True Womanhood: 1820-1860." *American Quarterly* 18:2 (Summer 1966): 151-174.

Williams, Susan S. "Widening the World: Susan Warner, Her Readers, and the Assumption of Authorship." *American Quarterly* 42:4 (December 1990): 565-86.

Jan L. Argersinger (essay date June 2002)

SOURCE: Argersinger, Jan L. "Family Embraces: The Unholy Kiss and Authorial Relations in *The Wide, Wide World.*" *American Literature* 74, no. 2 (June 2002): 251-85.

[*In the following excerpt, Argersinger probes Warner's use of "authorial seduction" in* The Wide, Wide World, *a process of subtly eroticizing familial and power relations in the novel so as to draw in readers.*]

In the originally unpublished final chapter of Susan Warner's ***The Wide, Wide World,*** Ellen and her new husband, John Humphreys, stand together before a painting of the Madonna and child and consider its meaning. This ideal woman's beauty, John declares, exists as a mere transparency through which the viewer may perceive the light of transcendent truth, the Word of the divine Father. After briefly challenging this reading, Ellen evidently capitulates—but at the same time she tells another story about the painting directly to the reader, unheard by the ravishingly masterful husband:

> It was merely two heads, the Madonna and child, . . . yet how much! The mother's face in calm beauty bent over that of the infant as if about to give the kiss her lips were already pouting for; the expression of grave maternal dignity and love; but in the child's uplifted deep blue eye there was a perfect heaven of affection, while the little mouth was parted, it might be either for a kiss or a smile, ready for both.[1]

In Ellen's narrative, mother and child are poised in the moment of yearning before a kiss, and the invisible paternal presence that presides over John's reading, and incarnates itself in him, seems to dissolve into absence. This scene, in its contemplation of Ellen as storyteller, caught up in spinning a private tale of family embrace, consummates a subtext that runs through the published version of the novel (1850), twining together the tropes of familial and eroticized relation to tell a story of Warner's coming-of-age as an author. That Warner permitted, and possibly sanctioned, the omission of the chapter in which the climactic expression of this subtext appears becomes part of that story.[2]

Many readers of Warner's unexpected bestseller, from its first appearance through much of the twentieth century, have regarded it, above all, as a religious book, one that wholeheartedly embraces the values of piety, self-discipline, and (female) submission central to the revivalistic Protestantism that dominated the antebellum era. In 1852, anthologist John Hart hailed *The Wide, Wide World* as the only novel "in which real religion, at least as understood by evangelical Christians, is exhibited with truth"; for Hart, as for legions of Warner's admiring contemporaries, the author and her text succeeded by giving passage to the Author and His Text, by turning as transparent as the painted Madonna that Warner herself proffers as possible exemplar in the novel's intended conclusion.[3] Not so for such renowned dissenters as Hawthorne and Melville, whose dismissal of what seemed to them shallow-brained scribblings rather than new pages of Holy Writ—contemptible for the commonplace piety that broke sales records in an undiscriminating marketplace—set the tone for critics in the next century. "What can be said of the intrinsic merit of the books themselves?" asks one scholar, writing in the 1940s about "the vogue of the domestic novel" in which *The Wide, Wide World* participated. The answer he hastens to supply epitomizes the kind of judgment that kept Warner's novel and others like it out of serious scholarly sight for decades: "Very little. Obviously they are in no cases the product of first-rate writers." Such inferior books were wildly popular, popular enough to provoke Hawthorne, this scholar explains, because they appealed to the religious emotionalism of the era and because they were crafted well enough to impersonate "good" literature, despite an abysmal lack of originality.[4]

In the latter half of the twentieth century, scholars interested in reclaiming undervalued episodes in the history of women's experience began to look at Warner's text with different eyes. Nina Baym and Jane Tompkins, to cite two influential examples, argue that compelling portraits of female selfhood can be found in the pages of Warner's novel and others like it—if their merits are appreciated within nineteenth-century limits. Baym sees in Ellen a "pragmatic" if "unspectacular" feminism, reflecting deep concern with the question of how to survive and grow as an integral self when social and spiritual power is out of reach, in other (largely masculine) hands. For Tompkins, Warner and her sister novelists address this question—again, without making a dramatic break through cramped borders—by reconstituting the little space of home and heart as, in fact, a center of spiritual power. Tompkins, like Baym, discerns in Warner's text a program of self-reform meant to inspire world reform. This vision of meaningful female identity demands, however, that the self, with its private, unruly desires, be strenuously disciplined, even at the cost of great pain—a cost that both Tompkins and Baym do find intimated in *The Wide, Wide World,* though overshadowed by a more strongly voiced consciousness of the benefits conferred by self-denial.[5]

In the wake of these pioneering studies, recent feminist treatments by such scholars as Susan Williams and Veronica Stewart have described a Warner more sharply at odds with Christian ideologies of the feminine. Warner's iconoclastic impulses become visible, Williams and Stewart contend, only when the time-honored conflation of the author of *The Wide, Wide World* and the virtuous jewel-in-the-making at its center, Ellen Montgomery, is pulled apart.[6] I would like to enlarge upon these treatments by looking, critically, both backward and forward: by reexploring the freshly challenged but, I believe, especially vital connection between Warner and her protagonist, between the new author's deeply conflicted sense of herself as a female Christian writer and the dissenting current that runs beneath her sentimental narrative of a young girl's training in submissive piety. As Warner wrestles with issues of power, compliance, and transgression that confronted mid-nineteenth-century women seeking to construct creative identities, she gives voice to a sustained subtext that approaches the proportions of a *Künstlerroman*—which, in the final accounting, resists containment with more vigor, and particularly more sexual vigor, than usually supposed.

To read *The Wide, Wide World,* in tandem with the biographical record of letters and journals, as a story of authorial experience is to return to the assumption of Warner's alliance with Ellen that underlies early feminist recoveries (as it does previous unsympathetic readings)—but with a difference, an intensification. Baym and Tompkins tap into the broad cultural resonance of the Warner-Ellen story and those features it shares with other popular women's fiction in order to contest a criterion by which it was typically judged a creative failure: the equating of literary worth with originality, with the expression of "things counter, original, spáre, strange."[7] This recuperative tactic did its work well, bringing a disregarded genre back into critical view and in the process, perhaps paradoxically, opening the way for further forays into its human particularities. Reading Ellen not simply as Warner's mouthpiece for relatively monologic, culture-bound views but more intensively as a figure for Warner as author, whose story works as a richly shaded *Künstlerroman,* throws into relief a vividly felt, almost Hopkinsian, individuality. Warner and her text are certainly meshed in a network of cultural identities—she writes within large interlocking circles defined by gender, class, race, and religion, as well as within more localized discursive communities (which for Warner often contracted to her small family in an isolated farmhouse on a Hudson River island).[8] But amid the welter of cultural influences, a distinctive—and, in nineteenth-century terms, heretical—sensibility refuses to be crowded out.

What makes itself obliquely known is a driving, eroticized passion for power, actualized and satisfied in the very medium that makes it known: words. Several recent studies of veiled eroticism in Warner's novel convincingly challenge its reputation for primness, but by concentrating on submissive, even masochistic, tendencies, they uncover only one side of the picture.[9] On the other side, sexual dominance is, for Warner, profoundly connected to a form of narrative authority that she clandestinely and with towering ambition desires. Trying on a range of possible authorial selves, including the Madonna and other female figures both quiescent and resistant, she shows herself in startling affinity with a celebrated nineteenth-century "masculine" type: the ravishing evangelist, agent of the Father's Word, whose persuasive prowess verges on the sadistic. Warner's evangelical narrative, read slant, speaks of power illicitly enjoyed by way of the lips.

* * *

While Warner's protagonist is more than a simple incarnation of her creator—more than the flesh made Word—she emerges through a web of textuality that invites us to read her career as a camouflaged version of Warner's entry into authorship.[10] Ellen is an eager consumer and producer of language: the dynamics of naming continually intrigue her. She insists, for example, that a bee for putting up apples and sausages ought to be called a hive—a label that better conveys its collective busyness (237). Like the young Susan Warner, she hungrily reads a wide range of texts—the Bible, history, natural philosophy, biography, and especially (though with guilty pleasure) novels and *Blackwood's Magazine* stories. She pens numerous letters using a writing desk lovingly outfitted by her mother, an event Warner represents in elaborate detail (32-36). And she spends hours learning, discussing, and singing hymns. Perhaps most significantly, however, Ellen shapes her own behavior as a text to be read. Struggling toward selfless Christian perfection, she offers herself as an evangelical narrative meant to persuade those empowered to judge her as well as those in need of redemption themselves—a reflection of Warner, who holds up to the public eye a textual image of her desire to win believers by making her own piety manifest.

Projecting an emergent authorial self in her first novel intended for publication, Warner moves Ellen through a series of family groupings that configure ways in which a writer might relate herself to literary authority as well as to her general audience. The novel opens as Ellen learns she will be parted from her beloved mother, whose grave illness requires (at least according to Ellen's unfeeling father) that she travel overseas. Beginning in circumstances typical of the "overplot" that Baym distills from what she calls "woman's fiction,"[11] the heroine finds herself orphaned, at first in a practical and soon in a real sense; the novel subsequently charts her quest to domesticate the wide, wide world by winning its embraces, placing herself in family relation to the strangers she meets—a figurative domestication of authorship that at first glance seems to stay neatly within the bounds of sentimental piety. A few potential family members resist Ellen—most notably the nonmaternal Aunt Fortune, who grudgingly takes charge of the abandoned child—but the majority welcome her as one of their own: John and Alice Humphreys provide a haven from Aunt Fortune and make her their adoptive "sister," though they act more as parents; their father, a pastor, is one in a procession of kindly paternal characters who treat her as a cherished daughter; and her Scottish relatives insist that she join their family circle and address her Uncle Lindsay as "father."

In Warner's subtextual *Künstlerroman,* parental characters (particularly fathers) often stand as figures for the merger of literary and religious authority, guiding Ellen's textual production and reading the results, whether written, sung, or performed, as a theatrical demonstration of growth in her character. Fatherly authority concentrates most potently in Ellen's supposed "brother" John, who embodies the omnipresent, omnipotent Father and is aligned through his biblical first name with the creative power of the Word.[12] The exacting John oversees Ellen's thinking, reading, painting, writing, and self-presentation and then sits as judge of their worth—an enactment of the tightly closed circle prescribed for the (female) Christian author, whose self-effacing creativity originates and ends in the Father's will. The story of Mr. Van Brunt, a kindly farm manager eventually won to Christ by Ellen's performance of virtue, follows this prescription: Warner's text, it suggests, must devote itself solely to such conversion of its readers, stifling (like Ellen) any more private aspirations and appetites. The familial logic of Warner's allegory appears to demand that both she and her fictional surrogate accept the role of the perpetual child, who transparently channels the Father's text (like the painted Madonna of John's exegesis) and relies on His readerly approval alone, forgoing the worldly pleasure of personal power over both the text and a wider audience. As the novel suggests, Warner has "'always one hearer . . . of so much dignity, that it sinks the rest into great insignificance'" (474).

This vision of authorship dominates *The Wide, Wide World*—as well as the Warner family's stories about the novel's genesis. According to Anna Warner, her sister Susan wrote "in closest reliance upon God: for thoughts, for power, and for words . . . and the Lord's blessing has followed it, down to this day. How many of whom even I have heard, trace their heart conversion straight to . . . the '*Wide, Wide World.*'" In the familiar Christian rhetoric that Warner herself typically uses to frame her lifelong struggle with an extraordinarily "imperious" self-will, right living and right authorship both demand that she humble herself as a "child of God," laying her own desires at the feet of the Father.[13] And according to many passages in her letters and journals, the faith that requires such sacrifice brings genuine solace into a life fraught with difficulties.

But alternative Warners push against the borders of this vision. The family allegory of *The Wide, Wide World* sets up, at least in passing, possibilities for relations based on parity. An outspoken champion of American democracy, Ellen invites readers both inside and outside the text to join what promises to be an egalitarian fellowship of God's children, of author and audience drawn together as sisters and brothers; she tries, in the words of her antirepublican Scottish uncle, to "'fraternize with all the world'" (530). Such fellowship takes on a homosocial cast in the persuasive readings of Tompkins and Nancy Schnog, who propose that the text's maternalized, Christocentric image of deity challenges the Father's rule by promoting a community of sympathy among women.[14] This model of relation finds a real-life corollary in the authorial habits of the Warner sisters: they often collaborated and, even when writing singly, met in the evening with their Aunt Fanny to appraise the pages composed during the day.[15] Finally, in another iteration of sibling ties within the novel, Ellen's spiritual guides, Alice and John, insistently figure as her adoptive "sister" and "brother," looking toward an authorial family united in mutual, democratic exchange. Images of interdependency in *The Wide, Wide World*, however, are unstable and transient, despite their appeal; they tend to slide into inversions of power. Although Ellen opens her arms in sisterly welcome to a wide circle of would-be converts (reader figures), she regulates the warmth of her embrace according to her perception of their social and intellectual standing. The sympathetic communion of women survives only temporarily: mothers and sisters must depart or die, in a feminized version of Bloomian literary inheritance, so that Ellen can find voice and ascendancy in text as well as home. And the brother is really a future husband who will master her words in fatherly fashion, unless she wrests power from him.

The eroticized relation of power and submission intimated in these relations enters the implicit *Künstlerroman* in the gesture of the kiss, which is nearly as pervasive as the weeping that alternately repulses and intrigues modern readers. Although kisses are generally better appreciated by applying some less mechanical measure than counting, it is significant that in the not-quite-600 pages of the novel the gesture of the kiss, metonymic locus of both language and sexuality, appears 161 times. Like recent critics who remark the number of times Ellen cries, I suspect that such an abundance, or even excess, marks a rupture in the plot's compliant surface.[16] Kissing, like crying, demarcates a site of contested power for the woman author. Through the kisses that her fictional double craves, bestows, and

withholds, Warner violates proper family boundaries and betrays her attraction to an illicit version of authorial relations that empowers the female writer: winning over the reader—whether figured as father, mother, sister, or brother—becomes an act of seduction, of orphic or sirenic enthrallment that revels in its own potency. And at one extreme, engaging with literary authority becomes a contest with a male lover, whom the woman author may defy by withholding erotic embrace. Startlingly, the character at the center of Warner's seduction narrative is a child—a girl of ten when the story begins and only about thirteen when it officially ends. Leslie Fiedler argues that the dangerous Richardsonian seducer had disappeared so completely from the sentimental tradition by Warner's time that novels like hers could sell as children's fiction. But in Warner's text, I suggest, the seducer is revenant *in* the adolescent female child—the girl-provocateur who stands in for the author herself.[17]

* * *

Ellen the child-seducer does, at several points, offer up what appear to be chaste, sisterly kisses that define relationships of equality with others who may become children of God. Nancy Vawse, an unruly country girl whose bold, dark-eyed stares have long offended Ellen, eventually receives from her what Warner explicitly calls the "kiss of peace" (264). In this salutation, granted as the "bad girl" begins to come under the sway of the supposedly "good girl," Warner evokes the ritual Christian greeting by which brethren symbolically unite with each other and God through a holy kiss, a long-standing practice probably instituted by apostles Paul and Peter.[18] Mr. Van Brunt is similarly favored; although Ellen recoils when the working-class Dutchman first demands a kiss in exchange for making her a swing (116), she later relents in the interest of evangelism. Passionately desiring that he enter "'[t]he fold of Christ's people,'" she works on him with the redoubled power of a kiss and a tear, to which he later traces his conversion: Ellen "carried the great brown hand to her lips before she let it go. He . . . looked at a little tear she had left on the back of it . . . till one of his own fell there to keep it company" (216, 569).

Such scenes suggest an impulse, on Warner's part, to kiss "the great brown hand" of the masses, to fight down her sharp sensitivity to class and reach out in selfless Christian good will, through Ellen, to readers of all levels. But signs of an unabated will to superiority unsettle this authorial democracy. In a scene following Alice's death, Ellen throws her arms around the Humphreys' housekeeper, Marjery, who responds to her caresses "most affectionately" but, Warner finds it necessary to add, "respectfully" (457). And as late as the unpublished conclusion, when Ellen returns unexpectedly from Scotland as John's wife and surprises Marjery with an exuberant kiss and hug, the speechless housekeeper finally finds her voice but can "hardly," of course, "return the embrace" (572). Aristocratic members of Ellen's extended "family," moreover, receive consistently different treatment. Genteel fatherly characters, in particular, inspire in Ellen an openly insatiable craving; she must have kisses, as many as possible, from John, from his friend the wealthy Mr. Marshman, and from Uncle Lindsay, even though her uncle's loving tyranny demands, in exchange, that she muffle her loyalties to John, his God, and American democracy—and she painfully feels the lack of these caresses when denied.

When Ellen's social delicacy raises its head at Aunt Fortune's bee, Alice gives her a gentle rebuke that calls her honesty—and Warner's—into question: "'[I]t's very funny what a notion people have for kissing,'" Ellen complains, alluding to several young men who are decidedly not gentlemen; "'I've run away from three kisses already, and I'm so afraid somebody else will try next.'" "'You don't seem very bitterly displeased,'" the perceptive Alice observes, as the girl blushes (255). Later in the evening, Ellen joins in a boisterous game called "the fox and the goose," and when the fox captures her, she must give up yet another kiss, which the fox provocatively terms, without elucidation, "'the worst kind'" (260-61). In the face of such popular entertainments, genteel etiquette manuals of midcentury raise scandalized eyebrows. Expressing the general dismay, the *Pocket Manual of Republican Etiquette* registers "an earnest protest against the promiscuous kissing which sometimes forms part of the performances in . . . these games." As if to confirm the danger, a nineteenth-century discussion of kissing reports that a game of "drop the handkerchief" played by the youth of a Massachusetts Baptist church caused such uproar that the minister resigned. The "'church was built for a house of God,'" the minister admonishes, "'and not for kissing-parties.'"[19] Kissing, it seems, is not automatically sanctified by a holy setting—whether a church or Warner's evangelical novel. Human appetites and distastes intrude.

The Ellen that Alice's remark unveils is something less—or more—than perfectly virtuous: she plays elaborate kissing games, acting out a complex pattern of authorial desire and guilt as Warner flirts with proper and improper significations for the gesture of the kiss. Ellen sometimes grants and sometimes withholds the egalitarian embrace. She brings herself to offer to Nancy and Van Brunt the kiss of Christian love—the kiss of peace she feels she ought to give freely but secretly resists—while she coquettishly runs, at the bee, from promiscuous embraces not hallowed by the evangelical impulse—kisses she should not want but secretly does. Underlying both scenarios is Warner's suspicion that reaching for a wide, undifferentiated audience is, in

fact, promiscuous, whether motivated by Christian feeling or not, because it violates the "laws of acquaintanceship" intricately codified in antebellum conduct manuals and carefully followed, according to Karen Halttunen, by a burgeoning affluent class that wished to draw clear borders around its gentility.[20] Warner considered herself part of this genteel circle, even after the financial panic of 1837 permanently destroyed her life of privilege, and she mirrors this class affiliation in Ellen's beautiful manners; the good breeding with which Warner's other characters constantly credit the young heroine may indeed, Warner suspects, be synonymous with good morals and godliness—as advice manuals insist again and again.[21]

Yet while Warner through Ellen condescends to "inferiors" and worries back and forth over her social trespass on the one hand and her un-Christian sense that it *is* a trespass on the other, she at the same time implicitly hungers for the broad, promiscuous embrace that sweeps away such considerations for the sake of authorial power over readers of every kind. Warner and Ellen want to influence the wide, wide world, and this evangelical desire shades over into an improper lust for mastery, for the ability to win over all who witness their performance of virtue. As Tompkins remarks, "The enormous amount of attention Ellen receives"—much of it in the form of kisses and lavish approbations of her goodness—"is one of the most seductive features of her story."[22] Projecting such a reception for her book, Warner exults as much in the effect of her own Word as she does in the effect of God's. And the wicked thrill of this seductive power, which Ellen experiences as a throb at the heart, arises largely out of its theatricality. The human heart is "deceitful," John warns (352), sounding in explicitly religious tones the chord that, according to Halttunen, dominates the prescriptive literature of the antebellum period: the urgent call for sincerity, or "transparency," and the corresponding diatribe against hypocrisy—the latter a threat to the American social order embodied in such figures as the confidence man and his female counterpart, the painted woman.[23] Because the show of virtue that Warner stages in Ellen covers a heart throbbing with an unrighteous love of sway, the kiss of brotherly love can look, at times, like the kiss of Judas—a symbol, in Christian writing and iconography, for deceit of the worst kind, because it feigns what should be an open-hearted expression of spiritual unity; in St. Augustine's view, Nicolas Perella explains, this kiss stands as "the prototype of a lack of correspondence between the lips and the heart."[24]

And Warner, like Judas, trades her less-than-holy kiss for money, seeking to win readers out of the imperative need to support her family and perhaps even restore something of their lost affluence[25]—a motivation that complicates her vision of authorship as divine mission. In *The Wide, Wide World,* the gesture of the kiss often goes hand-in-hand with tropes of exchange, bringing the act of authorial seduction into relation with the literary marketplace that Warner intends to enter. After indignantly refusing the kiss Van Brunt demands as payment for a swing but then pressing her lips to his hand in God's name, Ellen repeats the pattern with the more genteel Mr. Marshman; in a scene that casts the eleven-year-old as an adept seducer, her kisses provoke an explicit offer of money. Believing that Ellen has courted his affection out of cupidity, the paternal Mr. Marshman hides a new banknote under her napkin on New Year's Day, a "detested" gift that she publicly returns with painful blushes and tears, along with a corrective reading of her desires: "'I had rather never have any thing in the world than that you should think what you thought about me'" (327). "'I will never think any thing of you,'" the "old gentleman" responds, "'but what is the very tip-top of honourable propriety. . . . [Y]ou must give me half-a-dozen kisses at least to prove that you have forgiven me for making so great a blunder.' 'Half-a-dozen is too many at once,'" Ellen says "gayly; 'three now and three to-night'" (328).[26] The negotiations with Van Brunt and Marshman are differentiated by class status, but in both, Ellen professes herself ready to trade kisses only for righted readings of her character. Money, the decorous and devout Warner seems to insist through Ellen, is immaterial; what matters is a public that reads her properly and is thereby persuaded into God's family.

But as Ellen demonstrates in her transaction with Marshman by provocatively granting and, in the same breath, deferring kisses, the authorial embrace of inclusive, disinterested evangelism doubles as a less righteous gesture of seduction that really gives less than it offers—of taking in the reader by a show of goodness that, Warner fears, is more theatrical than genuine. And this performance takes on a doubly illicit coloring because, despite Ellen's demurral, it seduces for profit. Victorian manuals of proper conduct repeatedly insist that kissing and fondling—whether within families or between friends or courting lovers—be kept private,[27] yet Warner tenders kiss after symbolic kiss in the emphatically public space of the literary marketplace. In *The Wide, Wide World* the bliss of proper, democratic family ties between the author and her sisters and brothers in Christ tends to give way to prospective bliss of a less proper kind: the duplicitous pleasure of swaying an audience and getting paid for it, by telling a story that publicly disavows that very pleasure.

* * *

A feminized, homosocial version of the democratic family, extending outward from the mother to enfold women in the sympathetic care she fosters, exists in Warner's novel as a less inclusive alternative to the communion that includes brothers as well as sisters.

The maternal ethic that informs domestic fiction generally—whether read as the reflection of a patriarchal ideology that confines women, and women authors, at home or as an image transvalued by women for their own benefit—clearly has a strong magnetic pull in *The Wide, Wide World.* Scenes of affective unity between Ellen and her mother, and between Ellen and Alice (who supplies the place of the lost mother), unfold in profuse detail, and Ellen's grief over the loss of both overflows page after page with painful intensity. But by insisting on the loss of the mother's embrace, the narrative—and particularly the authorial parable—suggests that Warner gravitates toward another center. Her allegiance to the mother, and metonymically to the literary tradition she inhabits, develops fault lines at points where Ellen's career as her stand-in seems to be furthered by the withholding of maternal kisses. Although Mrs. Montgomery specifically links maternity with textuality by providing Ellen's writing desk, thereby calling up in the epistolary exchange a strongly mutual rendering of author-audience relations, it is the absence not only of her person but also of her letters that promotes her daughter's textual performance. The cold aunt, whose failure to offer a welcoming kiss mortifies Ellen, compounds the absence of the maternal embrace by keeping Mrs. Montgomery's letters from her daughter. Yet by suppressing one side of the epistolary conversation, she paradoxically helps to give Ellen's writing pride of place in the narrative: because the mother's responses do not appear for long stretches of time and so cannot be reproduced in the narrative, Ellen's own letters have representational primacy.

When the maternal absence becomes permanent, in the deaths first of Mrs. Montgomery and then of Alice, Ellen advances into the space they have left. In a scene immediately following Alice's death that is pivotal to the novel's domestic ideology, John asks Ellen to sing hymns for the grief-stricken Humphreys men, and she agrees; standing in the library, surrounded by books belonging to John's father, the Reverend Mr. Humphreys, Ellen sings with increasing poise, working her way up to the favorite hymns of the lost mothers—and as she sings she takes possession of the room, holding the men rapt in "breathless silence" (451-54). This passage marks, on one layer of the narrative, the rite of succession by which Ellen takes on her shoulders the cultural and literary mantle of true womanhood, becoming the home's spiritual center; but the telltale "strong throb of pleasure" that comes when she sees the spellbinding effect of her song points to another layer of meaning: her attraction to an unsanctioned model of woman's storytelling that Warner codes as dominantly masculine and embodies in the charismatic John. In him, she projects an alternate self who holds sovereignty over the Word, and through the Word, over the reader; killing off the mothers (particularly Alice, who holds first place in the heart of John, the Fatherly brother) becomes a subtle act of deposal whereby Warner, through Ellen, takes possession of the Father—a double seduction in which she appears to make love to the Father's will yet at the same time revolts by appropriating his linguistic power.

While for modern readers like Noble and Tompkins Ellen's ecstatic prostration before John brings to mind the submissive protagonist from *The Story of O,* I would argue that Warner obliquely invests her surrogate with an equal desire for dominance.[28] Ellen watches in envious admiration as John, an autocratic but much-loved minister as well as a skilled horse-breaker, imposes his will on others without sacrificing either their affection or respect. When he visits the haughty Scottish relatives with whom she is staying, she sits "with charmed ears, seeing her brother overturning all [their] prejudices, and making his own way to their respect at least, in spite of themselves. . . . 'I knew he would do what he pleased,' she said to herself,—'. . . but I did not dream he would ever make them *like* him'" (568). His ravishing word is her law, too, a mastery she appears to crave, though her compliance has a touch of theatrics about it: "[W]hat John told her *was done.* . . . In her eagerness to please and satisfy her teacher her whole soul was given to the *performance* of whatever he wished her to do" (351, second emphasis mine). His penetrating eyes seem to read her very soul: he knows when anything is "not right" with her; but this is a "censorship," Warner claims, that she "rather love[s] than fear[s]" (461). And John's linguistic dominion extends to a broader audience in his ministry: professing to care only that his sermons have their intended evangelical effect and not that they win personal regard, he succeeds at both. "'It gives me small gratification,'" he declares, "'to see the bowing head of the grain that yet my sickle cannot reach'"—a missionary zeal that betrays human arrogance and even sadism but that nonetheless enraptures his parishioners (474-75).

The magnetic John evokes the breed of revivalist preacher that Halttunen suggestively relates to the antebellum confidence man, himself a variant of the wicked seducer who dominates sentimental plots of the postrevolutionary period. Righteous persuasion here shades over into irresistible but ruthless seduction, the violation of one human will by another that is stronger; this is "the type of minister who attempts to ravish his congregation into heaven," as R. McClure Smith observes in his reading of Dickinson's poem "He fumbles at your Soul."[29] John's kind of oratory bears a strong resemblance to the preaching style that Warner's letters and journals say "please[s]" her "best," though these renderings soften the sadistic edge. "Impressive delivery," more than "excellence of . . . matter," makes a sermon "*tell,*" in Warner's view.[30] A prime exemplar of such rhetorical force for Warner was her minister, Thomas Harvey Skinner, a proponent of the revivalist movement that surged through American Protestantism in a

series of "Awakenings" from the early nineteenth century until the end of the Civil War, powered by such evangelists as Lyman Beecher and the famously compelling, incendiary Charles Grandison Finney. Finney, the New York revivalist whose "magnetic eye drew thousands to rebirth in Jesus" in Warner's home state (particularly during the 1830s) aspired not to dry theological complexity but to what he called a "'gushing, impressive, and persuasive oratory'" that would move the heart.[31] Halttunen numbers him among an elite group of heroes cum confidence men who "held the fascinated attention of the American people" by "us[ing] the power of charisma to bend others to their will." Recognizing a darkly erotic side to this potency, Ann Douglas observes that another modern characterization of the "dynamic and imperious," even "'demonic,'" evangelist "come[s] close to equating religious and sexual prowess."[32] Although a man of gentler fire, as Warner and her sister describe him, Skinner shows himself a worthy compatriot for such celebrated reapers of souls as Finney and Beecher, impressing Warner with the "*beautiful exhibition*" of his "countenance" and a "perfectly infectious" manner that demands from her, as if against her will, "an answering smile" that soon "turn[s] to weeping." After delivering what Warner praises as a "most excellent effective discourse on the words 'Turn you at my reproof,'" Skinner remarks with satisfaction that "he felt he had the minds of the congregation in his hands." Musing on the effect of his oratory, Warner observes: "[W]hat a difference there is between being, as it were, borne up on eagle's wings toward the sky when I hear him preach . . . , and being left to myself, as it were, on the ground, struggling to rise a little way by flapping my own untrained and unpracticed pinions. Alas! what a difference. But I ought not to say 'alas,' but to be glad that I have the teaching and stimulus of his example."[33]

Exclaiming "Alas!" Warner betrays her desire for oratorical force to match Skinner's, a force she "ought not" want but does—a force that, according to the accounts of those who heard her tell stories, she did in fact possess in good measure. A family friend recollects a scene that testifies to the writer's narrative power:

> I had always heard of Miss Susan's ability in telling stories, and the enjoyment she had in doing this, but I had no idea of the vividness and captivating interest that she gave to these stories. . . . [O]ne of the men of the family much given to outdoor life and usually impatient of a long afternoon indoors sat with us, and Miss Susan began to relate [a] true story. . . .
>
> . . . We were deeply impressed with [her] wonderful ability in telling this story, and sat until the evening came on and we were obliged to disperse to dress for dinner.[34]

Warner's tale, as suggestively summarized in this memoir, is one of attempted seduction: staging a confidence game, an Italian makes himself "intimate" in the home of a newly married couple, apparently murders the husband, and then courts the wife; the "ardent suitor" is later "struck by lightning" and "killed."[35] In this scenario, Warner as seductive storyteller relates a story of seduction with grave consequences—indirectly anticipating, perhaps, that her own unsanctioned mastery of language could call down the Father's wrath.

A "feminine" version of ecclesiastical oratory does speak in Warner's novel, through Alice, who regularly and persuasively "preaches" to homebound members of her father's congregation. When Miss Fortune remarks that she ought to be a minister, Alice demurs and says that she prefers to "'preach without taking orders'" (217); with this choice of phrase, Warner intimates that a woman may find liberation in unlicensed preaching even while she feels guilty about overstepping boundaries—and further, Warner allows something yet more unhallowed to slip through the interstices of language: the woman who preaches need not be nun-like. As Douglas observes in her treatment of the "uneasy" and competitive "alliance of ministers and women" who, she contends, sentimentalized American Protestantism in the mid-nineteenth century, female writers like Warner "could and did bypass clerical sanction even while they usurped clerical authority."[36] Ellen does try to fill Alice's office after she dies, but the rhetorical style to which the young heroine elsewhere aspires—a style figured by her spellbinding performance in the library— more strongly recalls the magnetic John than the gentle Alice. Moreover, while Warner manifests through Ellen her lust to preach like a man, her transgression goes deeper: she wants to tell stories like a novelist, stories not dissimilar to those John prohibits Ellen herself from reading.[37]

As Warner's romantic tale of the lightning-struck seducer suggests, and as the appetite for novels shared by the author and her heroine seems to confirm, Warner would like to co-opt the Father's linguistic power in order to convert readers not only to Christianity but also to the conviction of her novelistic gifts, her place in the canon of literature as well as church. And this power she allows herself and Ellen to enjoy in some measure, at the level of discourse, by reinvoking the eroticized gesture of the withheld kiss. In the novel's published ending, Warner conspicuously has her heroine insist on calling the intended husband "brother" to the very last, and she chooses to glance over the marriage toward which the sentimental plot has been building by refusing to name it except through artful innuendo that leads only to a dismissive final paragraph (569). In both refusals, the author sets herself above the authority of tradition and audience expectation: Ellen challenges John's dominion by denying him, through language, the erotic connection connoted by the status of fiancé, and Warner realizes the figurative potency of this gesture by refusing to fulfill what the sentimental genre requires.[38] Be-

cause Ellen implicitly will marry John, these refusals can also look like compliance; however, while she and Warner offer a submissive embrace to that imperious representative of God, they stop provocatively short of consummation, effecting a moment of suspension that carries through into the deferred kiss pictured in the novel's unpublished last chapter.

* * *

In Warner's original conclusion, Ellen seems to accept John's paternal exegesis of the painting of Madonna with child, conceding that her spiritualized beauty surpasses the voluptuous beauty of the Correggio Magdalen that hangs in a frame nearby. As John has declared, comparing the two images mounted above a window in the private room he has prepared for his new wife, "'[T]his is moral beauty, that is merely physical; *there* is only the material outside, with indeed all the beauty of delineation, *here* is the immaterial soul'" (578). John's reading rehearses the familiar nineteenth-century polarity: a "basically Protestant ethic," as feminist scholar Susan Haskins describes it, "recreated the old [Catholic] duality of madonna and magdalen," casting a sensualized Mary Magdalen as the "antithesis" of the Victorian "angel in the house."[39] John's critical focus on contrasting modes of artistic representation, however, doubles the scene's prescriptive force, showing Ellen-Warner what she should and should not aspire to be, not only as a woman but also as an author. Pursuing his relentless program to discipline Ellen's taste, John insists that Spirit *matters* most, that in properly self-erasing Christian artistry, "excellence" of spiritual "matter" must supersede "[i]mpressive delivery" or any "beauty of delineation" that is humanly crafted; he thus overturns the preference that Ellen in the narrative and Warner in her private letters and journal entries about sermon style have expressed.

But in the dissenting story of the two "painted women" that the protagonist and her author tell directly to the supposed reader, circumventing John's narrative authority, the alluring Magdalen breaks out of her own frame and infiltrates the other: the lips of Ellen's holy mother are "pouting" in readiness to kiss her child, and in a manner that is disconcertingly nonmaternal—suggesting a Madonna who is Magdalenlike in her seductiveness. While paying lip service to hegemonic dictates for which John is the mouthpiece, Warner in this final kiss—climactically unconsummated—blurs the boundary between his two Marys, secretly entertaining an attraction to the traditionally opposed pair at a point where their characters overlap. Through the erotic gesture that links them, Warner offers a glimpse of an alternative woman (who might inhabit the third frame, the prospect through the window that opens out beneath the two paintings), one who is alive to related forms of oral pleasure and power.[40]

Warner's sense of the Magdalen and the Madonna would have been shaped not only by her Christian training and intensive scripture reading but also by her education in visual art, begun by Henry Warner at an earlier stage in his daughter's life. The "recumbent Magdalen" of Correggio, a "fine copy" of which the author elects to have John display in Ellen's claustrophobic retreat (578), probably first came before the young Warner's eyes in the *Musée de peinture et de sculpture,* a collection of engraved black-and-white reproductions of European artworks issued in installments, many of which Henry brought home for Susan and Anna's edification.[41] In the renowned and much-imitated *Mary Magdalen Reading in a Landscape* (c. 1522), Correggio arranges a graceful young figure in languorous repose on the ground in a secluded dell, gown draped to bare the shapely curves of arms, shoulders, breasts, and just a teasing hint of nipples. This Magdalen is part of a Renaissance tradition that takes up an earlier Christian tableau, the "penitent in her grotto," and re-dresses (or undresses) its subject to create a Venus-Magdalen, in whom are blended the vestigial glories of pagan fertility goddesses and early-sixteenth-century strains of Platonic love.[42]

Mary Magdalen as the sensual icon of redeemed yet still seductive carnality in Correggio's time—and of unregenerate womanhood (specifically, prostitution) in Warner's—derives from centuries-old but questionable conflations of the figure scripturally identified as the Magdalen with sexual sinners who appear, unnamed, elsewhere in the Gospels. Most strongly, Mary Magdalen became associated with the wayward woman who, according to Luke's story, intrudes on a Pharisee's dinner party to kiss and anoint Jesus' feet, after a bath of tears wiped away with her hair—an act of loving humility that wins forgiveness of her many sins, typically assumed to be sexual (Luke 7:36-39). An eroticized myth, gradually coalescing in the early centuries of the Christian era and finally receiving sanction from Gregory the Great in the late sixth century, put the Magdalen in the service of an evolving Church patriarchy fearful of the flesh—especially female flesh.

The figure of the penitent prostitute, still prevalent today, thus came to eclipse a rather different character: in those biblical passages that explicitly name Mary Magdalen, she is always a close companion of Christ and a devoted member of his retinue, often in company with his mother, and most compellingly for Warner's clandestine project, she takes a central role in the Easter drama (especially in the renderings of John and Mark) as the primary witness to the resurrection and the first charged with evangelism, as apostle to the apostles.[43] This privileged relation to the Word, which challenged Peter's exclusive priority as founder of the Church (and thereby the male succession of popes), did not give way entirely to the sexualized myth but resurfaced over the centuries in persistent incarnations of the Magdalen as preacher. According to early medieval traditions of the East, for example, she preached with John the Evangelist in Ephesus; in later legend, she traveled farther afield to convert the heathens in Gaul; and in the sixteenth century she appeared in a Flemish altarpiece painting entitled *Mary Magdalen Preaching.* This evangelistic figure, inspirited by her special bond with Jesus, harks back to the Magdalen glorified in the apocryphal texts of Gnosticism (expanding on her role in the canonical Gospels) as the Savior's "consort," his "counterpart" and "chief interlocutrix . . . , who brings *gnosis* to the other disciples."[44]

How much of this representational history specifically entered Warner's thought is uncertain, but legends of Mary Magdalen as evangelist did circulate in the mid-nineteenth century,[45] and the potential for a Magdalen charged with verbal and spiritual power is more than latent in the Gospels that Warner knew intimately. Furthermore, determined attempts to rescue the biblical figure from her house of ill repute continued in Warner's time, giving latter-day evidence of the Magdalen as a "vessel," in Marjorie Malvern's words, enduringly "capable of holding controversial ideas."[46] Several of Warner's contemporaries in the evangelical Protestant movement put forward the biblical ("unmythologized") Magdalen—the faithful companion and favored witness to the events of Easter—as a model for Christian women, who calls them to make their influence actively felt in social reform and mission work.[47] And in the *Musée* itself, commentator Jean Duchesne strenuously dissents from the received notion of the "unific Magdalen," complaining often (in his remarks about Correggio's Magdalen, which Warner likely read, as well as in other entries) about artists' "mistaken" conflation of pious saint and repentant sinner; however, what discomposes him is not the degrading of a vital female exemplar but more fundamentally the interpenetration of holy and carnal, the "scarcely credible" possibility that "Jesus would have admitted . . . into the society of the Virgin and apostles, a woman whose previous conduct had been so reprehensible."[48]

But interpenetration—the cohabiting of a potent evangelical voice with a sensual persona—is just the possibility that Warner, as she experiments with the features of an authorial self-portrait, dares to envision. In Correggio's rendering, the voluptuous penitent in fact engrosses herself in a text, presumably though not visibly scripture—an iconographical attribute that connotes a humble desire for divine solace and forgiveness but that at the same time can signify the Gospel figure's privileged access to the Word. In Warner's scene this potential is made real—she transforms the passive to the active—by means of an adroit displacement: conspicuously, she and her protagonist omit any mention of the Magdalen's book, a focal element of the painting; spiriting this image of text out of Correggio's frame, where woman appears as object, she quietly, without fanfare, relocates the contest over woman's right to textual control to the level of discourse, to her own narrative frame, where she becomes the storytelling subject and subtly but effectively undermines the semidivine John and his reading of the two male-authored Marys.

The sexual gesture on which Ellen-Warner's retelling turns thereby becomes closely imbricated with the power of language; by coupling the kiss and the act of storytelling, she sets into vibration an intertextual web that reveals, in representations of the two Marys, points of kinship centered on a lover-like relationship with Jesus, the Word Incarnate. Figurations of the Madonna, like those of Mary Magdalen (though not to the same libidinous extreme), slide back and forth between the heavenly and the earthy, a push and pull out of which emerges, for Warner's use, a muse of seductively potent religious rhetoric: both women appear persistently as versions of Venus, among other earth goddesses, and typologically as the new Eve, and both are repeatedly identified with the mystically symbolic yet openly sensual Bride of Christ in the *Song of Songs* (the Madonna as mother-bride and the Magdalen as sister-bride).[49] From this special intercourse, this extraordinary liaison to divine truth, issue two women big with the potential for preeminent voice: the Magdalen as apostle to the apostles, the first Christian commissioned with spreading the good news, and the Madonna (wedded figuratively to two manifestations of the Godhead) as poet of the rapturous Magnificat and also as apostle, the "bearer of the divine Word" who enjoys "privileged access to the Holy Spirit" as well as the Son.[50]

* * *

In Warner's novel, the passive conduit for transcendent truth pictured in John's Madonna and the passively absorbed reader in Correggio's painting (who seems oblivious to her audience and undesirous of effect, an enactment of coyness when seen in retrospect, given her famously sensual sway over both artistic imitators and the viewing public)[51] thus exist in tandem with a Mary capable of her own dazzling rhetoric, brought into sub-rosa relation through Ellen's description of the Madonna's Magdalenian kiss. This multiveiled authorial figure carries implications at least as seditious as those of the mid-nineteenth-century American novels by women that Susan Harris terms "exploratory," including in her category Warner's second novel, *Queechy,* but not what she seems to view as the more conservative ***Wide, Wide World.***[52] Warner's painted Marys capture in tableau a twofold tension that runs through the novel, not only between the fledgling writer's impulse toward Christian subjection of self and her urgent ambition for authority but also between her rival ambitions for liter-ary authority of two casts, the spiritual and the secular. She slips over the border into secular narrative and stakes her claim there by telling the countertale of the two Marys in language that uses remarkably few explicit religious referents (as does the Correggio Magdalen itself, which in the absence of its title could pass as any young woman reading a novel) but that attends with some care to matters of aesthetic effect. The eroticized mother bending to kiss her baby is enclosed, Ellen reports with adjectival flourish, in "a little antique heavily carved oval frame"; and "'the perfect graceful repose'" of the Magdalen "'figure,'" the "'natural abandonment of every limb,'" paradoxically bespeaks "'a wonderful art'" that, she declares twice, she doubts "'anything'" could "'surpass'" (578)—anything, that is, except her own wonderful art/ifice, which prostrates the authorial self humbly, chastely, before the Father even as it demonstrates its own virtuosity, even as it stages, in its agile dissimulations, a masterpiece of seduction. Eve-like, Lucifer-like, Warner discovers the dissembling power of language.[53]

Looking toward modern feminist attempts to rehabilitate the Magdalen without divesting her of sexuality,[54] Warner surreptitiously fashions her own muse (or deific self-image) out of a conjunction of the sensual and the verbal. However, writing "through the body" from within religious and literary institutions that operate not a little like Sade's schools of discipline, as Jane Gallop describes and as Ellen and John enact, Warner writes through to the "masculine" position of mastery—precisely not the position that Hélène Cixous and Luce Irigaray would come to dream of for authors of *écriture féminine.* Cixous, Gallop finds, "affirm[s]" a feminine "model of writing as oral love," a Warneresque notion, but on one layer of Warner's narrative, her seductive orality thrusts toward a model of writing as penetrative or devouring ravishment, aiming to take over a role that these French theorists identify as male (as does the nineteenth-century novelist) and that they eschew for women writers.[55] In this reading, the Father is absent from Warner-Ellen's version of the painting of Madonna and child because his linguistic authority has been assimilated; through John's kisses, always mouth-to-mouth, Ellen has, on Warner's behalf, absorbed his power over language—subverting the venerable Christian tradition of the religio-erotic kiss, which symbolizes the passing of the Father's Word to the human soul.[56]

Yet the lips that entice and swallow up the Father are *not one,* do not speak—or kiss—univocally. Able to act several parts at once, to inhabit conflicting subject positions in her authorial parable (a capacity that R. McClure Smith theorizes as a defining feature of subversive masochistic fantasy in women's writing), Warner-Ellen expresses a fluidity that Irigaray might applaud, though the author's own pride in her prowess runs side by side with a sense of wrongdoing.[57] Strikingly, the "pouting" kiss of Ellen's reconceived Madonna is not only Magdalen-like but also child-like. Erotic provocation and childlikeness here converge, reproducing the doubleness, the multiplicity, of Ellen herself—whose elusive nature has sparked an unresolved debate in the novel's latter chapters (continuing into the unpublished ending, which finds her at age sixteen or seventeen) about whether she is woman or child. While Warner's richly multivalent portrait of a promised maternal kiss may be read as her embrace of the religious sentimental genre centered in the mother, that embrace is not fully realized; conjoined in the pouting kiss, Magdalen, Madonna, and child (the Word made flesh) also stand as a composite image of the female self as writer. The most compelling figure of authorship in *The Wide, Wide World* is finally the seductive little girl, a girlish Madonna-Magdalen, whose eroticized relations with family show Warner either submitting to paternal authority or trying to substitute ties of mutuality, but at the same time leaning irresistibly toward fatherly dominance herself. By projecting the writer as child, Warner assumes a Christian humility she wants to desire; but by investing that child with a surprisingly sexual sway over admirers, she at the same time covertly identifies with the charismatic male preacher.

* * *

The scene over which Warner's Madonna-Magdalen presides did not reach its intended audience, a fact that complicates its status as a denouement to the covert story Warner has been telling about herself. The initial decision to cut the last chapter, and the author's part in it, is sparsely and equivocally documented. The "Note on the Text" that prefaces the 1987 edition can report only this: "An unsigned note in the papers of The Constitution Island Association suggests that the manuscript had gone to Putnam without the last chapter and that Putnam urged omitting it since the book had run longer in galleys than he had expected and the last chapter, in his opinion, did not contribute substantially to the novel" (8). The publisher's worries about the unwieldiness of the project do find their way into Warner's journal; she writes in November 1850, "I got my last proof today, the *end,* as a note on the margin from the printer considerately informed me," and continues, "Mr. Putnam told father he was afraid the book would be too large still; a pleasant and inspiriting kind of remark, seeing that in the first place it is all set up, and in the second place if it were not, it would be impossible to abridge it much except by horrible mutilation."[58] The chagrin Warner privately expresses over the general need to shorten her manuscript and the specific need to end it prematurely, perhaps, is suggestive but not decisive (the adverb "still" may point to the excision of passages other than the final chapter);[59] available records do not clearly indicate how she reacted to the dispos-

ability of her conclusion or whether, as a first-time author anxious to publish and in need of income, she would have ventured to oppose "urgings" from Putnam even if she felt particular cuts did violence to authorial design.

Scholarly accounts of Warner's role in shaping the conclusion that her first readers experienced are necessarily speculative, but according to Susan Williams, the mark of her hand in later editions is more distinct: "[D]espite frequent requests from Warner's readers that she amplify the ending," neither Warner, Putnam, nor Anna Warner (after her sister's death) offered up the omitted chapter as a complement to one of the many subsequent editions or as part of a sequel. This determined refusal, Williams proposes—as well as the original suppression, she implies, of Ellen's reentry into a life of wealth and aesthetic pleasure—is part of a pattern of revision and mediation in which Warner consciously tailored her book to the market for religious sentimentalism by suppressing worldlier passages.[60] Williams's persuasive reading of the publication history throws into relief an under-explored aspect of Warner's complex temperament, yet given the final chapter's multifaced figurations of female selfhood and authorship, other readings of Warner's decision to withhold it are possible. Warner had what her public clamored for, what the conspicuously foreshortened, tantalizing end to the circulated version invited her readers to desire, but she chose over the years not to satisfy that desire; this posture of invitation and denial works powerfully as a projection of the endlessly deferred consummation pictured in the Madonna-Magdalen's promised kiss, moving seduction beyond the text into the more immediate marketplace intercourse between author and audience.

The authorial seductiveness that Warner stages on a subtextual level of *The Wide, Wide World* and brings to arresting nonclimax in her intended last chapter thus had its way with the reading public, or so the novel's unprecedented popularity suggests. It took in readers of both sexes and all ages and classes who embraced Ellen's piety, crediting her creator with heart-changing power, as well as those who applauded the novel's literary merit.[61] The seduced apparently included T. W. Higginson, who describes in an 1851 letter a bedtime reading ritual that eerily replays Warner's scene of the child-provocateur. Referring to a six-year-old girl who visited his household, Higginson exclaims:

> I cannot tell you how I enjoy Greta; she is the most noble & highminded child I ever knew, & yet a perfect child. I read her a little bit of the *Wide Wide World* every night after tea, selecting only what she can understand, & I lose my place sometimes in looking up at her beautiful glowing eyes. And every night after she goes to bed I go up to kiss her & she puts her arms around my neck so that I have to struggle to get away.[62]

A twin to Warner's duplicitous Ellen, Greta can be maturely "noble & highminded," perfectly childlike, and seductive—all in the same paragraph. Distracting Higginson from his John-like censorship of the woman's text with beguiling looks and embraces, she points with Ellen toward an empowered version of female authorship that Warner imagines as both alluring and transgressive. In *The Wide, Wide World,* Warner, like the eloquent Skinner, the minister she longs to rival, and like Ellen's irresistible John, does indeed hold her hearers in her hands.

Notes

1. [Susan Warner], *The Wide, Wide World* (1850; reprint, New York: Feminist Press, 1987), 578; further references will be to this edition and will be cited parenthetically in the text.

2. Warner's original conclusion was not published as part of the novel until the 1987 edition; see "A Note on the Text" in that edition (8).

3. John Hart, *The Female Prose Writers of America* (Philadelphia: E. H. Butler, 1852), 387. For excerpts from responses comparable to Hart's, see Edward Foster, *Susan and Anna Warner* (Boston: Twayne, n.d.), 35, 47-48; and Anna Warner, *Susan Warner* (New York: Putnam's, 1909), 344, 354, 355. For a recent analysis of such responses, see Susan Williams, "Widening the World: Susan Warner, Her Readers, and the Assumption of Authorship," *American Quarterly* 42 (December 1990): especially 569 and 573-74.

4. Alexander Cowie, "The Vogue of the Domestic Novel, 1850-1870," *South Atlantic Quarterly* 41 (October 1942): especially 422-23; see also Henry Smith, "The Scribbling Women and the Cosmic Success Story," *Critical Inquiry* 1 (September 1974): especially 50-51; and John Frederick, "Hawthorne's 'Scribbling Women,'" *New England Quarterly* 48 (June 1975): 231-32, 235. On the wrinkling of critical noses over Warner's novel, see Jane Tompkins's overview in *Sensational Designs: The Cultural Work of American Fiction, 1790-1860* (New York: Oxford Univ. Press, 1985), 147-49.

5. Nina Baym, *Woman's Fiction: A Guide to Novels by and about Women in America, 1820-1870* (Ithaca, N.Y.: Cornell Univ. Press, 1978), especially 18-19, 144-46; and Tompkins, *Sensational Designs,* 147-85.

6. See Williams, "Widening the World"; and Veronica Stewart, "The Wild Side of *The Wide, Wide World,*" *Legacy* 11.1 (1994): 1-16.

7. Gerard Manley Hopkins, "Pied Beauty," in *The Oxford Authors: Gerard Manley Hopkins,* ed.

8. See Richard Brodhead, *Cultures of Letters: Scenes of Reading and Writing in Nineteenth-Century America* (Chicago: Univ. of Chicago Press, 1993).

9. See G. M. Goshgarian, *To Kiss the Chastening Rod: Domestic Fiction and Sexual Ideology in the American Renaissance* (Ithaca, N.Y.: Cornell Univ. Press, 1992), 76-120; and Marianne Noble, *The Masochistic Pleasures of Sentimental Literature* (Princeton, N.J.: Princeton Univ. Press, 2000), 94-125. Mining a vein similar to the one I explore, Goshgarian contends that "domestic novels" are suffused with sexuality despite—or more precisely by virtue of—their determined refusal of it; Goshgarian uncovers intersections between profane familial relations in *The Wide, Wide World* and its creator's emerging sense of her writing project but implies that Warner's submission to the Father's Word is confirmed through Ellen. In Noble's well-wrought account, the masochistic pleasure that Warner's heroine finds in suffering and subjection is channeled through the "twin discourses" of "true womanhood" and "providential Calvinism" (95).

10. On biographical resonances, see Stewart, "Wild Side," 1, 13 n. 1; Jane Tompkins, afterword to *Wide, Wide World* (1987), 586-96, 601-3; and Williams, "Widening the World," 565-66.

11. Baym, *Woman's Fiction,* 11-12, 22.

12. See Goshgarian, *Chastening Rod,* 114-15.

13. Anna Warner, *Susan Warner,* 264. For references to Warner's penchant for domination, see, for instance, 34, 199, and 104-5, the latter offering the elderly Anna's account, in a tone of lingering enchantment touched with indignation, of her sister's teenaged storytelling practices. Presiding over Anna and two cousins, the older Susan would allow for certain democratic freedoms in their collective spinning of "silken, golden, impossible visions," but "hers was always the ruling hand," the one that held "certain particular charms which like a master key dominated the rest." For counterposed passages from Susan's journal that show her striving to be a humble "child of God," see 211, 353, 475.

14. Tompkins, *Sensational Designs,* 163-65; Nancy Schnog, "Inside the Sentimental: The Psychological Work of *The Wide Wide World,*" *Genders* 4 (spring 1989): 11-25.

15. See Anna Warner, *Susan Warner,* 264, 338-39 (quoting Susan's journal entry of 7 January 1850), 377; and Mabel Baker, *Light in the Morning: Memories of Susan and Anna Warner* (West Point, N.Y.: Constitution Island Association, 1978), 44, 68.

Catherine Phillips (Oxford, Eng.: Oxford Univ. Press, 1986), 133.

16. Tompkins and Baym see Ellen's stormy weeping spells as inarticulate eruptions of rage over powerlessness (*Sensational Designs,* 173, 178; *Woman's Fiction,* 144). For a tear count of 245, offered in a disparaging tone typical of earlier assessments, see Fred Pattee, *The Feminine Fifties* (1940; reprint, Port Washington, N.Y.: Kennikat, 1966), 57.

17. See Leslie Fiedler, *Love and Death in the American Novel* (New York: Criterion, 1960), 52; see also Baym, *Woman's Fiction,* 26. Elizabeth Barnes also sees in Warner's text a survival of the eighteenth-century seduction tale but from a different perspective. In her provocative reading, the mother whose profound influence shapes the sentimental heroine's coming-of-age "seduces" her daughter into reenacting the tight patterns of stricture that have made up her own history, thwarting the younger woman's quest for autonomy by highly textual means (see *States of Sympathy: Seduction and Democracy in the American Novel* [New York: Columbia Univ. Press, 1997], 100-110).

18. See Nicolas Perella, *The Kiss Sacred and Profane: An Interpretative History of Kiss Symbolism and Related Religio-Erotic Themes* (Berkeley and Los Angeles: Univ. of California Press, 1969), especially 25-26, 12-13.

19. See [Samuel Wells], *How to Behave: A Pocket Manual of Republican Etiquette. . . .* (New York: Fowler and Wells, 1856), 91; see also [Eliza Farrar], *The Young Lady's Friend* (Boston: American Stationers' Company, 1837), 293. For the Baptist anecdote, see Charles C. Bombaugh, *The Literature of Kissing, Gleaned from History, Poetry, Fiction, and Anecdote* (Philadelphia: Lippincott, 1876), 89-90.

20. Karen Halttunen, *Confidence Men and Painted Women: A Study of Middle-Class Culture in America, 1830-1870* (New Haven: Yale Univ. Press, 1982), 101, 111-16.

21. See, for instance, Mme. Celnart, *The Gentleman and Lady's Book of Politeness. . . . ,* 5th American ed. (Philadelphia: Grigg and Elliot, 1840), 9; Farrar, *Young Lady's Friend,* 10; Mrs. Manners, *At Home and Abroad. . . .* (New York: Evans and Brittan, 1853), 8. On the aristocratic life that Warner enjoyed well into her teens, see Foster, *Susan and Anna Warner,* 56-58. Warner's class consciousness appears to have begun early and persisted long after the family's financial decline; see Anna Warner, *Susan Warner,* 109, 427-28. Compare Jennifer Mason, "Animal Bodies: Corporeality, Class, and Subject Formation in *The Wide, Wide World,*" *Nineteenth-Century Literature* 54 (March 2000): 503-33.

22. Tompkins, afterword, *Wide, Wide World,* 597.

23. Halttunen, *Confidence Men,* especially xiv-xvi.

24. Perella, *Kiss Sacred and Profane,* 28.

25. See Anna Warner, *Susan Warner,* 261-63, 346, 351-52.

26. Mary Hiatt also notices that Ellen is "strikingly seductive" in this scene ("Susan Warner's Subtext: The Other Side of Piety," *Journal of Evolutionary Psychology* 8 [August 1987]: 257).

27. See Manners, *At Home and Abroad,* 63-64; Farrar, *Young Lady's Friend,* 269; Celnart, *Book of Politeness,* 14-15; and John Young, comp., *Our Deportment; or, The Manners, Conduct and Dress of the Most Refined Society. . . .* (Chicago: Union Publishing, 1881), 51.

28. See Noble, *Masochistic Pleasures,* especially 219 n. 3; and Tompkins, afterword, *Wide, Wide World,* 599-600. My reading of Warner's eroticized relation to readers as a rhetorical variety of "masculine" sadism that masquerades as "feminine" masochism is indebted to Leland Person, "Sadomasochism, Prince Amerigo, and *The Golden Bowl*" (paper presented at the American Literature Association Conference, Baltimore, May 1997; published as "Jamesian Sadomasochism: The Invisible [Third] Hand of Manhood in *The Golden Bowl,*" in *Questioning the Master: Gender and Sexuality in Henry James's Writings,* ed. Peggy McCormack [Newark, N.J.: Univ. of Delaware Press, 2000], 149-75).

29. Halttunen, *Confidence Men,* 23-24; R. McClure Smith, "'He Asked If I Was His': The Seductions of Emily Dickinson," *ESQ* 40 (first quarter 1994): 49, 54, 64 n. 23.

30. Susan Warner, quoted in Anna Warner, *Susan Warner,* 275 (letter of 18 April 1848) and 499.

31. Halttunen, *Confidence Men,* 24; and Charles Grandison Finney, quoted in Perry Miller, *The Life of the Mind in America* (New York: Harcourt, Brace, 1965), 31 (see also 26).

32. Halttunen, *Confidence Men,* 24; Ann Douglas, *The Feminization of American Culture* (New York: Knopf, 1978), 18 (quoting from Miller, *Life of the Mind,* 23).

33. Anna Warner, *Susan Warner,* 218-19, 237, 236 (quoting an undated journal entry and letter of Susan's). On Susan's moorings in evangelical Christianity and her near-idolatrous admiration for Skinner, see Foster, *Susan and Anna Warner,* 22, 27-31, 39. According to Foster, the form of evangelical belief espoused by Skinner's Mercer Street

Church in New York, where Susan and Anna became members in 1844, was "New School" Presbyterianism, which looked for salvation in heartfelt conversion rather than close compliance with doctrine; for Skinner, as for Finney, religion was "a matter of emotions or sensibility," an act of "absolute submission to divine will" accomplished in the heart rather than the intellect (29, 39). On the centrality of masterful sermonizing, in which the irresistible will of God and of human orator seem to merge—of "impressive delivery" more than "excellence of . . . matter"—to this evangelical cause, see Miller, *Life of the Mind,* 60-63; for a textual rendering of such eloquence, see Foster, *Susan and Anna Warner,* 30. On the revivalist movement generally, see Miller, *Life of the Mind,* 3-95.

34. Olivia Phelps Stokes, *Letters and Memories of Susan and Anna Bartlett Warner* (New York: Putnam's Sons, 1925), 9-11.

35. Ibid., 9, 10.

36. Douglas, *Feminization,* 79, 86. Douglas argues that in the nineteenth-century, liberal male ministers and female Christian writers, similarly cloistered in church and home, entered into the emerging mass market for popular literature as an avenue to spiritual and cultural power (77 and 80-117). These nonevangelical ministers, who eschewed rhetorical bombast and whom Douglas depreciatively labels "feminine" (91), are not, however, of the breed that sets Warner on fire. Awe-inspiring pulpit effects, in a style that both Warner and Douglas define as "masculine," were more characteristic of preachers in Warner's revivalist wing of liberal Protestantism. On women writers as "counterparts" to evangelical pulpiteers, see also Tompkins, *Sensational Designs,* 149; Mary Kelley, *Private Woman, Public Stage: Literary Domesticity in Nineteenth-Century America* (New York: Oxford Univ. Press, 1984), 285-315, especially 294; and Elaine Showalter, *Sister's Choice: Tradition and Change in American Women's Writing* (Oxford, Eng.: Clarendon, 1991), 11.

37. "[C]urrent opinion forbade a clergyman or a woman to publish a work concerned with thoroughly secular themes or informed by secular ambitions for artistic excellence" (Douglas, *Feminization,* 84).

38. On the conventional marriage ending, see Donna Campbell, "Sentimental Conventions and Self-Protection: *Little Women* and *The Wide, Wide World,*" *Legacy* 11.2 (1994): 123; and Joanne Dobson, "The Hidden Hand: Subversion of Cultural Ideology in Three Mid-Nineteenth-Century American Women's Novels," *American Quarterly* 38 (summer 1986): 225-26.

39. Susan Haskins, *Mary Magdalen: Myth and Metaphor* (New York: Harcourt, Brace, 1993), 319.

40. For a complementary angle on Warner's critique of the female "transparency" that John tries to inculcate, see Grace Hovet and Theodore Hovet, "*Tableaux Vivants*: Masculine Vision and Feminine Reflections in Novels by Warner, Alcott, Stowe, and Wharton," *ATQ* [*American Transcendental Quarterly*] 7 (December 1993): 335-56, especially 337-42.

41. See Anna Warner, *Susan Warner,* 132-33, 149 (quoting Susan's November-December journal and a journal entry of 8 February 1836); and *Musée de peinture et de sculpture,* etchings by [Etienne Achille] Réveil, 17 vols. (Paris: Audot; London: Bossange, Barthés, and Lowell, 1828-1834). On the first occasion that Anna recalls seeing the pamphlet, in 1834 or 1835, Susan was about fifteen. (Volume 1, which includes Correggio's reclining Magdalen as plate 97, initially appeared in 1828.) In the novel, when John leads Ellen to his painted copy, she remarks: "'I have seen that before, . . . in an engraving—not in colours'" (578).

42. The summary of the Magdalen's representational career in this and following paragraphs derives, except where noted, from Haskins, *Mary Magdalen* (see 304 for a reproduction of Correggio's painting); and Marjorie Malvern, *Venus in Sackcloth: The Magdalen's Origins and Metamorphoses* (Carbondale: Southern Illinois Univ. Press, 1975). In Haskins's view, the Gospel Magdalen's potential as a liberating example for Christian women has been stifled beneath layers of mythic accretion.

43. Mary Magdalen appears by name in Matthew 27:56-61, 28:1-10; Mark 15:40, 47, 16:1-11; Luke 8:1-3, 24:1-11; and John 19:25, 20:1, 11-18. Her inclusion with the Virgin Mary in the circle of intimates around Jesus is imaged often in European visual art; volume 1 of the *Musée* collection, which features the recumbent figure that attracts Warner's notice, reproduces several such groupings (plates 27, 44, 464).

44. Haskins, *Mary Magdalen,* 40, 38; Malvern, *Venus in Sackcloth,* 55; and Perella, *Kiss Sacred and Profane,* 20-21.

45. See, for example, Mrs. Jameson, *Sacred and Legendary Art,* 2 vols. (London: Longman, Brown, Green, and Longmans, 1848), 1:337, 364, 371.

46. Malvern, *Venus in Sackcloth,* 15.

47. See Haskins, *Mary Magdalen,* 365, 331-33, 327, citing Warner's contemporaries Clara Lucas Balfour, *The Women of Scripture* (London, 1847), and

John Angell James, *Female Piety: or, The Young Woman's Friend and Guide through Life to Immortality* (London, 1852).

48. [Jean] Duchesne, in *Musée,* vol. 1, plate 97. See also vol. 3, plate 287; and vol. 4, plate 396.

49. In addition to detailing Mary Magdalen's alliances with these figures, Malvern and Haskins mention parallel associations for the Virgin Mary (*Venus in Sackcloth,* 67; and *Mary Magdalen,* 56, 66-67, 40, 141, 238). The holy mother takes center stage in John Gatta's *American Madonna: Images of the Divine Woman in Literary Culture* (New York: Oxford Univ. Press, 1997), an insightful look at her "countercultural" appeal for Protestant writers in America (3); on the Madonna's sensuous incarnations, especially in the texts of three Warner contemporaries, see 7 and 10-71.

50. Gatta, *American Madonna,* 11, 40; see also 6, 7, and 57.

51. See Haskins, *Mary Magdalen,* 236, 307-8.

52. See Susan Harris, *Nineteenth-Century American Women's Novels: Interpretative Strategies* (Cambridge, Eng.: Cambridge Univ. Press, 1990), 12-13, 20, 64, 135.

53. On Eve, Satan, and the seductive "uses of rhetoric," see Smith, "Seductions of Emily Dickinson," 34-42. Weaving her own spell of words, Warner finds a narrative means of resistance and escape (see, in contrast, David Leverenz, *Manhood and the American Renaissance* [Ithaca, N.Y.: Cornell Univ. Press, 1989], 188).

54. For a (disparaging) digest of such attempts, see Haskins, *Mary Magdalen,* 367, 382-86, 391.

55. See Jane Gallop, *Thinking through the Body* (New York: Columbia Univ. Press, 1988), 3, 42-53, 165; Hélène Cixous, "The Laugh of the Medusa," trans. Keith Cohen and Paula Cohen, *Signs* 1 (summer 1976): 887; and Luce Irigaray, *This Sex Which Is Not One,* trans. Catherine Porter with Carolyn Burke (Ithaca, N.Y.: Cornell Univ. Press, 1985), 32-33.

56. Perella, *Kiss Sacred and Profane,* 21-23, 38. On the danger that the mystical Christian kiss may edge into carnality, see 29-31.

57. See R. McClure Smith, "Dickinson and the Masochistic Aesthetic," *Emily Dickinson Journal* 7 (fall 1998): 1, 8-9, 14-15; see also Irigaray, *This Sex.*

58. Anna Warner, *Susan Warner,* 326 (quoting Susan's journal entry of 7 November 1850).

59. See Susan Roberson, "Ellen Montgomery's Other Friend: Race Relations in an Expunged Episode of Warner's *Wide, Wide World,*" *ESQ* 45 (first quarter 1999): 1-31.

60. Williams, "Widening the World," 577.

61. On the novel's broad appeal, see Anna Warner, *Susan Warner,* 345, 354-55, 387 (quoting Susan's journal entry of 23 February 1859). For the response to its literary qualities, see Foster, *Susan and Anna Warner,* 48-49; and Dobson, "Hidden Hand," 240 n. 7.

62. T. W. Higginson to Louisa Higginson, 30 October 1851, Thomas W. Higginson Collection, bMS Am 784 (374); quoted by permission of the Houghton Library, Harvard University. I thank Judy Breedlove for pointing me to this letter.

FURTHER READING

Criticism

Barnes, Elizabeth. "Mothers of Seduction." In *States of Sympathy: Seduction and Democracy in the American Novel,* pp. 100-14. New York: Columbia University Press, 1997.

> Includes an investigation of Ellen's internalization of motherly love and authority in *The Wide, Wide World* as part of a wider discussion of maternal power and the mother-daughter bond depicted in the nineteenth-century sentimental novel.

Baym, Nina. "Susan Warner, Anna Warner, and Maria Cummins." In *Woman's Fiction: A Guide to Novels by and about Women in America, 1820-1870,* pp. 140-74. Ithaca, N.Y.: Cornell University Press, 1978.

> Examines the novels *The Wide, Wide World, Queechy,* and *The Hills of Shatemuc,* focusing on the attempts of Warner's protagonists to adapt to a lack of control over their own lives.

Blair, Andrea. "Landscape in Drag: The Paradox of Feminine Space in Susan Warner's *The Wide, Wide World.*" In *The Greening of Literary Scholarship: Literature, Theory, and the Environment,* edited by Steven Rosedale, pp. 111-30. Iowa City: University of Iowa Press, 2002.

> Offers a semiotic analysis of feminized metaphors of landscape in *The Wide, Wide World.*

Brusky, Sarah. "Beyond the Ending of Maternal Absence in *A New-England Tale, The Wide, Wide World,* and *St. Elmo.*" *ESQ* 46, no. 3 (2000): 149-76.

> Considers the pattern of narrative self-empowerment adopted by the motherless, female protagonists of three representative nineteenth-century sentimental

novels, including Ellen Montgomery of Warner's *The Wide, Wide World.*

Chantell, Claire. "The Limits of the Mother at Home in *The Wide, Wide World* and *The Lamplighter.*" *Studies in American Fiction* 30, no. 2 (autumn 2002): 131-53.

Concentrates on the superfluity of "sentimental materialism" associated with the maternal education of young children illustrated in *The Wide, Wide World* and Maria Cummins's *The Lamplighter.*

"Tears, Idle Tears." *The Critic,* no. 558 (29 October 1892): 236-37.

Lists the myriad ways in which Warner describes the heroine's frequent crying in *The Wide, Wide World.*

Hart, John S. "Elizabeth Wetherell (Susan Warner)." In *The Female Prose Writers of America: With Portraits, Biographical Notices, and Specimens of Their Writings,* pp. 421-23. Philadelphia: E. H. Butler & Co., 1866.

Describes Warner as principally a religious writer and briefly summarizes the qualities of several of the characters in *The Wide, Wide World.*

Henning, Martha L. "Susan Warner's *The Wide, Wide World*: Becoming the Christian Model." In *Beyond Understanding: Appeals to the Imagination, Passions, and Will in Mid-Nineteenth-Century American Women's Fiction,* pp. 49-81. New York: Peter Lang, 1996.

Endeavors to place *The Wide, Wide World* within its proper rhetorical context in order to explain discrepancies between the generally favorable nineteenth-century reception of the work and twentieth-century critical dismissal of the novel.

Mason, Jennifer. "Animal Bodies: Corporeality, Class, and Subject Formation in *The Wide, Wide World.*" *Nineteenth-Century Literature* 54, no. 4 (March 2000): 503-33.

Applies the metaphor of horseback riding (a subject frequently depicted or alluded to in *The Wide, Wide*

World) to an understanding of the novel's depiction of Ellen's maturation, identity formation, and acculturation.

Mott, Frank Luther. "American Fiction of the Fifties." In *Golden Multitudes: The Story of Best Sellers in the United States,* pp. 122-32. New York: Macmillan, 1947.

Notes the extraordinary popularity of *The Wide, Wide World* in the United States during the 1850s.

Noble, Marianne. "An Ecstasy of Apprehension: The Gothic Pleasures of Sentimental Fiction." In *American Gothic: New Interventions in National Narrative,* edited by Robert K. Martin and Eric Savoy, pp. 163-82. Iowa City: University of Iowa Press, 1998.

Studies the theory of sentimental fiction articulated in *The Wide, Wide World,* observing the novel's subversion of gothic horror and its accompanying sadomasochistic tendencies.

Papashvily, Helen Waite. "All Women-All Enchained-All Enchanted." In *All the Happy Endings: A Study of the Domestic Novel in America, the Women Who Wrote It, the Women Who Read It, in the Nineteenth Century,* pp. 1-14. New York: Harper & Brothers Publishers, 1956.

Surveys the early publication history and reception of *The Wide, Wide World.*

Review of *The Wide, Wide World, Queechy,* and *Dollars and Cents. North American Review* 76, no. 159 (January 1853): 104-23.

Admires Warner's *The Wide, Wide World* and *Queechy,* as well as her sister Anna's novel *Dollars and Cents,* for their religious qualities and "appeal to universal human sympathy."

Roberson, Susan L. "Ellen Montgomery's Other Friend: Race Relations in an Expunged Episode of Warner's *The Wide, Wide World.*" *ESQ* 45, no. 1 (1999): 1-31.

Studies a previously unpublished episode of *The Wide, Wide World* in which Ellen meets a young black girl in order to evaluate the place of race in the Christian ethos of the sentimental novel.

Additional coverage of Warner's life and career is contained in the following sources published by Thomson Gale: *Dictionary of Literary Biography,* **Vols. 3, 42, 239, 250, 254;** *Literature Resource Center*; **and** *Nineteenth-Century Literature Criticism,* **Vol. 31.**

How to Use This Index

The main references

Calvino, Italo
    1923-1985 .... **CLC 5, 8, 11, 22, 33, 39,**
                                    73; SSC 3, 48

---

list all author entries in the following Gale Literary Criticism series:

AAL = *Asian American Literature*
BG = *The Beat Generation: A Gale Critical Companion*
BLC = *Black Literature Criticism*
BLCS = *Black Literature Criticism Supplement*
CLC = *Contemporary Literary Criticism*
CLR = *Children's Literature Review*
CMLC = *Classical and Medieval Literature Criticism*
DC = *Drama Criticism*
HLC = *Hispanic Literature Criticism*
HLCS = *Hispanic Literature Criticism Supplement*
HR = *Harlem Renaissance: A Gale Critical Companion*
LC = *Literature Criticism from 1400 to 1800*
NCLC = *Nineteenth-Century Literature Criticism*
NNAL = *Native North American Literature*
PC = *Poetry Criticism*
SSC = *Short Story Criticism*
TCLC = *Twentieth-Century Literary Criticism*
WLC = *World Literature Criticism, 1500 to the Present*
WLCS = *World Literature Criticism Supplement*

The cross-references

See also CA 85-88, 116; CANR 23, 61;
DAM NOV; DLB 196; EW 13; MTCW 1, 2;
RGSF 2; RGWL 2; SFW 4; SSFS 12

---

list all author entries in the following Gale biographical and literary sources:

AAYA = *Authors & Artists for Young Adults*
AFAW = *African American Writers*
AFW = *African Writers*
AITN = *Authors in the News*
AMW = *American Writers*
AMWR = *American Writers Retrospective Supplement*
AMWS = *American Writers Supplement*
ANW = *American Nature Writers*
AW = *Ancient Writers*
BEST = *Bestsellers*
BPFB = *Beacham's Encyclopedia of Popular Fiction: Biography and Resources*
BRW = *British Writers*
BRWS = *British Writers Supplement*
BW = *Black Writers*
BYA = *Beacham's Guide to Literature for Young Adults*
CA = *Contemporary Authors*
CAAS = *Contemporary Authors Autobiography Series*
CABS = *Contemporary Authors Bibliographical Series*
CAD = *Contemporary American Dramatists*
CANR = *Contemporary Authors New Revision Series*
CAP = *Contemporary Authors Permanent Series*
CBD = *Contemporary British Dramatists*
CCA = *Contemporary Canadian Authors*
CD = *Contemporary Dramatists*
CDALB = *Concise Dictionary of American Literary Biography*
CDALBS = *Concise Dictionary of American Literary Biography Supplement*
CDBLB = *Concise Dictionary of British Literary Biography*

CMW = *St. James Guide to Crime & Mystery Writers*

CN = *Contemporary Novelists*

CP = *Contemporary Poets*

CPW = *Contemporary Popular Writers*

CSW = *Contemporary Southern Writers*

CWD = *Contemporary Women Dramatists*

CWP = *Contemporary Women Poets*

CWRI = *St. James Guide to Children's Writers*

CWW = *Contemporary World Writers*

DA = *DISCovering Authors*

DA3 = *DISCovering Authors 3.0*

DAB = *DISCovering Authors: British Edition*

DAC = *DISCovering Authors: Canadian Edition*

DAM = *DISCovering Authors: Modules*

   DRAM: *Dramatists Module;* **MST:** *Most-studied Authors Module;*

   MULT: *Multicultural Authors Module;* **NOV:** *Novelists Module;*

   POET: *Poets Module;* **POP:** *Popular Fiction and Genre Authors Module*

DFS = *Drama for Students*

DLB = *Dictionary of Literary Biography*

DLBD = *Dictionary of Literary Biography Documentary Series*

DLBY = *Dictionary of Literary Biography Yearbook*

DNFS = *Literature of Developing Nations for Students*

EFS = *Epics for Students*

EXPN = *Exploring Novels*

EXPP = *Exploring Poetry*

EXPS = *Exploring Short Stories*

EW = *European Writers*

FANT = *St. James Guide to Fantasy Writers*

FW = *Feminist Writers*

GFL = *Guide to French Literature,* Beginnings to 1789, 1798 to the Present

GLL = *Gay and Lesbian Literature*

HGG = *St. James Guide to Horror, Ghost & Gothic Writers*

HW = *Hispanic Writers*

IDFW = *International Dictionary of Films and Filmmakers: Writers and Production Artists*

IDTP = *International Dictionary of Theatre: Playwrights*

LAIT = *Literature and Its Times*

LAW = *Latin American Writers*

JRDA = *Junior DISCovering Authors*

MAICYA = *Major Authors and Illustrators for Children and Young Adults*

MAICYAS = *Major Authors and Illustrators for Children and Young Adults Supplement*

MAWW = *Modern American Women Writers*

MJW = *Modern Japanese Writers*

MTCW = *Major 20th-Century Writers*

NCFS = *Nonfiction Classics for Students*

NFS = *Novels for Students*

PAB = *Poets: American and British*

PFS = *Poetry for Students*

RGAL = *Reference Guide to American Literature*

RGEL = *Reference Guide to English Literature*

RGSF = *Reference Guide to Short Fiction*

RGWL = *Reference Guide to World Literature*

RHW = *Twentieth-Century Romance and Historical Writers*

SAAS = *Something about the Author Autobiography Series*

SATA = *Something about the Author*

SFW = *St. James Guide to Science Fiction Writers*

SSFS = *Short Stories for Students*

TCWW = *Twentieth-Century Western Writers*

WLIT = *World Literature and Its Times*

WP = *World Poets*

YABC = *Yesterday's Authors of Books for Children*

YAW = *St. James Guide to Young Adult Writers*

Literary Criticism Series
Cumulative Author Index

al-Hariri, al-Qasim ibn 'Ali Abu Muhammad al-Basri
1054-1122 .... **CMLC 63**
See also RGWL 3

Ali, Ahmed 1908-1998 .... **CLC 69**
See also CA 25-28R; CANR 15, 34; EWL 3

Ali, Tariq 1943- .... **CLC 173**
See also CA 25-28R; CANR 10, 99

Alighieri, Dante
See Dante

Allan, John B.
See Westlake, Donald E(dwin)

Allan, Sidney
See Hartmann, Sadakichi

Allan, Sydney
See Hartmann, Sadakichi

Allard, Janet .... **CLC 59**

Allen, Edward 1948- .... **CLC 59**

Allen, Fred 1894-1956 .... **TCLC 87**

Allen, Paula Gunn 1939- ..... **CLC 84; NNAL**
See also AMWS 4; CA 112; 143; CANR 63, 130; CWP; DA3; DAM MULT; DLB 175; FW; MTCW 1; RGAL 4

Allen, Roland
See Ayckbourn, Alan

Allen, Sarah A.
See Hopkins, Pauline Elizabeth

Allen, Sidney H.
See Hartmann, Sadakichi

Allen, Woody 1935- .... **CLC 16, 52, 195**
See also AAYA 10, 51; CA 33-36R; CANR 27, 38, 63, 128; DAM POP; DLB 44; MTCW 1

Allende, Isabel 1942- ... **CLC 39, 57, 97, 170; HLC 1; SSC 65; WLCS**
See also AAYA 18; CA 125; 130; CANR 51, 74, 129; CDWLB 3; CLR 99; CWW 2; DA3; DAM MULT, NOV; DLB 145; DNFS 1; EWL 3; FW; HW 1; INT CA-130; LAIT 5; LAWS 1; LMFS 2; MTCW 1, 2; NCFS 1; NFS 6, 18; RGSF 2; RGWL 3; SSFS 11, 16; WLIT 1

Alleyn, Ellen
See Rossetti, Christina (Georgina)

Alleyne, Carla D. .... **CLC 65**

Allingham, Margery (Louise)
1904-1966 .... **CLC 19**
See also CA 5-8R; 25-28R; CANR 4, 58; CMW 4; DLB 77; MSW; MTCW 1, 2

Allingham, William 1824-1889 ...... **NCLC 25**
See also DLB 35; RGEL 2

Allison, Dorothy E. 1949- .... **CLC 78, 153**
See also AAYA 53; CA 140; CANR 66, 107; CSW; DA3; FW; MTCW 1; NFS 11; RGAL 4

Alloula, Malek .... **CLC 65**

Allston, Washington 1779-1843 .... **NCLC 2**
See also DLB 1, 235

Almedingen, E. M. .... **CLC 12**
See Almedingen, Martha Edith von
See also SATA 3

Almedingen, Martha Edith von 1898-1971
See Almedingen, E. M.
See also CA 1-4R; CANR 1

Almodovar, Pedro 1949(?)- .... **CLC 114; HLCS 1**
See also CA 133; CANR 72; HW 2

Almqvist, Carl Jonas Love
1793-1866 .... **NCLC 42**

al-Mutanabbi, Ahmad ibn al-Husayn Abu al-Tayyib al-Jufi al-Kindi
915-965 .... **CMLC 66**
See also RGWL 3

Alonso, Damaso 1898-1990 .... **CLC 14**
See also CA 110; 131; 130; CANR 72; DLB 108; EWL 3; HW 1, 2

Alov
See Gogol, Nikolai (Vasilyevich)

al'Sadaawi, Nawal
See El Saadawi, Nawal
See also FW

Al Siddik
See Rolfe, Frederick (William Serafino Austin Lewis Mary)
See also GLL 1; RGEL 2

Alta 1942- .... **CLC 19**
See also CA 57-60

Alter, Robert B(ernard) 1935- .... **CLC 34**
See also CA 49-52; CANR 1, 47, 100

Alther, Lisa 1944- .... **CLC 7, 41**
See also BPFB 1; CA 65-68; CAAS 30; CANR 12, 30, 51; CN 7; CSW; GLL 2; MTCW 1

Althusser, L.
See Althusser, Louis

Althusser, Louis 1918-1990 .... **CLC 106**
See also CA 131; 132; CANR 102; DLB 242

Altman, Robert 1925- .... **CLC 16, 116**
See also CA 73-76; CANR 43

Alurista .... **HLCS 1**
See Urista (Heredia), Alberto (Baltazar)
See also DLB 82; LLW 1

Alvarez, A(lfred) 1929- .... **CLC 5, 13**
See also CA 1-4R; CANR 3, 33, 63, 101; CN 7; CP 7; DLB 14, 40

Alvarez, Alejandro Rodriguez 1903-1965
See Casona, Alejandro
See also CA 131; 93-96; HW 1

Alvarez, Julia 1950- .... **CLC 93; HLCS 1**
See also AAYA 25; AMWS 7; CA 147; CANR 69, 101, 133; DA3; DLB 282; LATS 1:2; LLW 1; MTCW 1; NFS 5, 9; SATA 129; WLIT 1

Alvaro, Corrado 1896-1956 .... **TCLC 60**
See also CA 163; DLB 264; EWL 3

Amado, Jorge 1912-2001 ... **CLC 13, 40, 106; HLC 1**
See also CA 77-80; 201; CANR 35, 74; CWW 2; DAM MULT, NOV; DLB 113; EWL 3; HW 2; LAW; LAWS 1; MTCW 1, 2; RGWL 2, 3; TWA; WLIT 1

Ambler, Eric 1909-1998 .... **CLC 4, 6, 9**
See also BRWS 4; CA 9-12R; 171; CANR 7, 38, 74; CMW 4; CN 7; DLB 77; MSW; MTCW 1, 2; TEA

Ambrose, Stephen E(dward)
1936-2002 .... **CLC 145**
See also AAYA 44; CA 1-4R; 209; CANR 3, 43, 57, 83, 105; NCFS 2; SATA 40, 138

Amichai, Yehuda 1924-2000 .. **CLC 9, 22, 57, 116; PC 38**
See also CA 85-88; 189; CANR 46, 60, 99, 132; CWW 2; EWL 3; MTCW 1

Amichai, Yehudah
See Amichai, Yehuda

Amiel, Henri Frederic 1821-1881 .... **NCLC 4**
See also DLB 217

Amis, Kingsley (William)
1922-1995 ...... **CLC 1, 2, 3, 5, 8, 13, 40, 44, 129**
See also AITN 2; BPFB 1; BRWS 2; CA 9-12R; 150; CANR 8, 28, 54; CDBLB 1945-1960; CN 7; CP 7; DA; DA3; DAB; DAC; DAM MST, NOV; DLB 15, 27, 100, 139; DLBY 1996; EWL 3; HGG; INT CANR-8; MTCW 1, 2; RGEL 2; RGSF 2; SFW 4

Amis, Martin (Louis) 1949- .... **CLC 4, 9, 38, 62, 101**
See also BEST 90:3; BRWS 4; CA 65-68; CANR 8, 27, 54, 73, 95, 132; CN 7; DA3; DLB 14, 194; EWL 3; INT CANR-27; MTCW 1

Ammianus Marcellinus c. 330-c. 395 .... **CMLC 60**
See also AW 2; DLB 211

Ammons, A(rchie) R(andolph)
1926-2001 ...... **CLC 2, 3, 5, 8, 9, 25, 57, 108; PC 16**
See also AITN 1; AMWS 7; CA 9-12R; 193; CANR 6, 36, 51, 73, 107; CP 7; CSW; DAM POET; DLB 5, 165; EWL 3; MTCW 1, 2; PFS 19; RGAL 4

Amo, Tauraatua i
See Adams, Henry (Brooks)

Amory, Thomas 1691(?)-1788 .... **LC 48**
See also DLB 39

Anand, Mulk Raj 1905- .... **CLC 23, 93**
See also CA 65-68; CANR 32, 64; CN 7; DAM NOV; EWL 3; MTCW 1, 2; RGSF 2

Anatol
See Schnitzler, Arthur

Anaximander c. 611B.C.-c. 546B.C. .... **CMLC 22**

Anaya, Rudolfo A(lfonso) 1937- ...... **CLC 23, 148; HLC 1**
See also AAYA 20; BYA 13; CA 45-48; CAAS 4; CANR 1, 32, 51, 124; CN 7; DAM MULT, NOV; DLB 82, 206, 278; HW 1; LAIT 4; LLW 1; MTCW 1, 2; NFS 12; RGAL 4; RGSF 2; WLIT 1

Andersen, Hans Christian
1805-1875 .... **NCLC 7, 79; SSC 6, 56; WLC**
See also AAYA 57; CLR 6; DA; DA3; DAB; DAC; DAM MST, POP; EW 6; MAICYA 1, 2; RGSF 2; RGWL 2, 3; SATA 100; TWA; WCH; YABC 1

Anderson, C. Farley
See Mencken, H(enry) L(ouis); Nathan, George Jean

Anderson, Jessica (Margaret) Queale
1916- .... **CLC 37**
See also CA 9-12R; CANR 4, 62; CN 7

Anderson, Jon (Victor) 1940- .... **CLC 9**
See also CA 25-28R; CANR 20; DAM POET

Anderson, Lindsay (Gordon)
1923-1994 .... **CLC 20**
See also CA 125; 128; 146; CANR 77

Anderson, Maxwell 1888-1959 .... **TCLC 2, 144**
See also CA 105; 152; DAM DRAM; DFS 16, 20; DLB 7, 228; MTCW 2; RGAL 4

Anderson, Poul (William)
1926-2001 .... **CLC 15**
See also AAYA 5, 34; BPFB 1; BYA 6, 8, 9; CA 1-4R; 181; 199; CAAE 181; CAAS 2; CANR 2, 15, 34, 64, 110; CLR 58; DLB 8; FANT; INT CANR-15; MTCW 1, 2; SATA 90; SATA-Brief 39; SATA-Essay 106; SCFW 2; SFW 4; SUFW 1, 2

Anderson, Robert (Woodruff)
1917- .... **CLC 23**
See also AITN 1; CA 21-24R; CANR 32; DAM DRAM; DLB 7; LAIT 5

Anderson, Roberta Joan
See Mitchell, Joni

Anderson, Sherwood 1876-1941 .. **SSC 1, 46; TCLC 1, 10, 24, 123; WLC**
See also AAYA 30; AMW; AMWC 2; BPFB 1; CA 104; 121; CANR 61; CDALB 1917-1929; DA; DA3; DAB; DAC; DAM MST, NOV; DLB 4, 9, 86; DLBD 1; EWL 3; EXPS; GLL 2; MTCW 1, 2; NFS 4; RGAL 4; RGSF 2; SSFS 4, 10, 11; TUS

Andier, Pierre
See Desnos, Robert

Andouard
See Giraudoux, Jean(-Hippolyte)

MULT, POET, POP; DFS 3, 11, 16; DLB 5, 7, 16, 38; DLBD 8; EWL 3; MTCW 1, 2; PFS 9; RGAL 4; TUS; WP

Baratynsky, Evgenii Abramovich 1800-1844 .... **NCLC 103**
See also DLB 205

Barbauld, Anna Laetitia 1743-1825 .... **NCLC 50**
See also DLB 107, 109, 142, 158; RGEL 2

Barbellion, W. N. P. .... **TCLC 24**
See Cummings, Bruce F(rederick)

Barber, Benjamin R. 1939- .... **CLC 141**
See also CA 29-32R; CANR 12, 32, 64, 119

Barbera, Jack (Vincent) 1945- .... **CLC 44**
See also CA 110; CANR 45

Barbey d'Aurevilly, Jules-Amedee 1808-1889 .... **NCLC 1; SSC 17**
See also DLB 119; GFL 1789 to the Present

Barbour, John c. 1316-1395 .... **CMLC 33**
See also DLB 146

Barbusse, Henri 1873-1935 .... **TCLC 5**
See also CA 105; 154; DLB 65; EWL 3; RGWL 2, 3

Barclay, Bill
See Moorcock, Michael (John)

Barclay, William Ewert
See Moorcock, Michael (John)

Barea, Arturo 1897-1957 .... **TCLC 14**
See also CA 111; 201

Barfoot, Joan 1946- .... **CLC 18**
See also CA 105

Barham, Richard Harris 1788-1845 .... **NCLC 77**
See also DLB 159

Baring, Maurice 1874-1945 .... **TCLC 8**
See also CA 105; 168; DLB 34; HGG

Baring-Gould, Sabine 1834-1924 ... **TCLC 88**
See also DLB 156, 190

Barker, Clive 1952- .... **CLC 52; SSC 53**
See also AAYA 10, 54; BEST 90:3; BPFB 1; CA 121; 129; CANR 71, 111, 133; CPW; DA3; DAM POP; DLB 261; HGG; INT CA-129; MTCW 1, 2; SUFW 2

Barker, George Granville 1913-1991 .... **CLC 8, 48**
See also CA 9-12R; 135; CANR 7, 38; DAM POET; DLB 20; EWL 3; MTCW 1

Barker, Harley Granville
See Granville-Barker, Harley
See also DLB 10

Barker, Howard 1946- .... **CLC 37**
See also CA 102; CBD; CD 5; DLB 13, 233

Barker, Jane 1652-1732 .... **LC 42, 82**
See also DLB 39, 131

Barker, Pat(ricia) 1943- ...... **CLC 32, 94, 146**
See also BRWS 4; CA 117; 122; CANR 50, 101; CN 7; DLB 271; INT CA-122

Barlach, Ernst (Heinrich) 1870-1938 .... **TCLC 84**
See also CA 178; DLB 56, 118; EWL 3

Barlow, Joel 1754-1812 .... **NCLC 23**
See also AMWS 2; DLB 37; RGAL 4

Barnard, Mary (Ethel) 1909- .... **CLC 48**
See also CA 21-22; CAP 2

Barnes, Djuna 1892-1982 .... **CLC 3, 4, 8, 11, 29, 127; SSC 3**
See Steptoe, Lydia
See also AMWS 3; CA 9-12R; 107; CAD; CANR 16, 55; CWD; DLB 4, 9, 45; EWL 3; GLL 1; MTCW 1, 2; RGAL 4; TUS

Barnes, Jim 1933- .... **NNAL**
See also CA 108; 175; CAAE 175; CAAS 28; DLB 175

Barnes, Julian (Patrick) 1946- . **CLC 42, 141**
See also BRWS 4; CA 102; CANR 19, 54, 115; CN 7; DAB; DLB 194; DLBY 1993; EWL 3; MTCW 1

Barnes, Peter 1931-2004 .... **CLC 5, 56**
See also CA 65-68; CAAS 12; CANR 33, 34, 64, 113; CBD; CD 5; DFS 6; DLB 13, 233; MTCW 1

Barnes, William 1801-1886 .... **NCLC 75**
See also DLB 32

Baroja (y Nessi), Pio 1872-1956 .... **HLC 1; TCLC 8**
See also CA 104; EW 9

Baron, David
See Pinter, Harold

Baron Corvo
See Rolfe, Frederick (William Serafino Austin Lewis Mary)

Barondess, Sue K(aufman) 1926-1977 .... **CLC 8**
See Kaufman, Sue
See also CA 1-4R; 69-72; CANR 1

Baron de Teive
See Pessoa, Fernando (Antonio Nogueira)

Baroness Von S.
See Zangwill, Israel

Barres, (Auguste-)Maurice 1862-1923 .... **TCLC 47**
See also CA 164; DLB 123; GFL 1789 to the Present

Barreto, Afonso Henrique de Lima
See Lima Barreto, Afonso Henrique de

Barrett, Andrea 1954- .... **CLC 150**
See also CA 156; CANR 92

Barrett, Michele .... **CLC 65**

Barrett, (Roger) Syd 1946- .... **CLC 35**

Barrett, William (Christopher) 1913-1992 .... **CLC 27**
See also CA 13-16R; 139; CANR 11, 67; INT CANR-11

Barrie, J(ames) M(atthew) 1860-1937 .... **TCLC 2**
See also BRWS 3; BYA 4, 5; CA 104; 136; CANR 77; CDBLB 1890-1914; CLR 16; CWRI 5; DA3; DAB; DAM DRAM; DFS 7; DLB 10, 141, 156; EWL 3; FANT; MAICYA 1, 2; MTCW 1; SATA 100; SUFW; WCH; WLIT 4; YABC 1

Barrington, Michael
See Moorcock, Michael (John)

Barrol, Grady
See Bograd, Larry

Barry, Mike
See Malzberg, Barry N(athaniel)

Barry, Philip 1896-1949 .... **TCLC 11**
See also CA 109; 199; DFS 9; DLB 7, 228; RGAL 4

Bart, Andre Schwarz
See Schwarz-Bart, Andre

Barth, John (Simmons) 1930- ... **CLC 1, 2, 3, 5, 7, 9, 10, 14, 27, 51, 89; SSC 10**
See also AITN 1, 2; AMW; BPFB 1; CA 1-4R; CABS 1; CANR 5, 23, 49, 64, 113; CN 7; DAM NOV; DLB 2, 227; EWL 3; FANT; MTCW 1; RGAL 4; RGSF 2; RHW; SSFS 6; TUS

Barthelme, Donald 1931-1989 ... **CLC 1, 2, 3, 5, 6, 8, 13, 23, 46, 59, 115; SSC 2, 55**
See also AMWS 4; BPFB 1; CA 21-24R; 129; CANR 20, 58; DA3; DAM NOV; DLB 2, 234; DLBY 1980, 1989; EWL 3; FANT; LMFS 2; MTCW 1, 2; RGAL 4; RGSF 2; SATA 7; SATA-Obit 62; SSFS 17

Barthelme, Frederick 1943- ...... **CLC 36, 117**
See also AMWS 11; CA 114; 122; CANR 77; CN 7; CSW; DLB 244; DLBY 1985; EWL 3; INT CA-122

Barthes, Roland (Gerard) 1915-1980 .... **CLC 24, 83; TCLC 135**
See also CA 130; 97-100; CANR 66; DLB 296; EW 13; EWL 3; GFL 1789 to the Present; MTCW 1, 2; TWA

Bartram, William 1739-1823 .... **NCLC 145**
See also ANW; DLB 37

Barzun, Jacques (Martin) 1907- ..... **CLC 51, 145**
See also CA 61-64; CANR 22, 95

Bashevis, Isaac
See Singer, Isaac Bashevis

Bashkirtseff, Marie 1859-1884 .... **NCLC 27**

Basho, Matsuo
See Matsuo Basho
See also PFS 18; RGWL 2, 3; WP

Basil of Caesaria c. 330-379 .... **CMLC 35**

Basket, Raney
See Edgerton, Clyde (Carlyle)

Bass, Kingsley B., Jr.
See Bullins, Ed

Bass, Rick 1958- .... **CLC 79, 143; SSC 60**
See also ANW; CA 126; CANR 53, 93; CSW; DLB 212, 275

Bassani, Giorgio 1916-2000 .... **CLC 9**
See also CA 65-68; 190; CANR 33; CWW 2; DLB 128, 177, 299; EWL 3; MTCW 1; RGWL 2, 3

Bastian, Ann .... **CLC 70**

Bastos, Augusto (Antonio) Roa
See Roa Bastos, Augusto (Antonio)

Bataille, Georges 1897-1962 .... **CLC 29; TCLC 155**
See also CA 101; 89-92; EWL 3

Bates, H(erbert) E(rnest) 1905-1974 .... **CLC 46; SSC 10**
See also CA 93-96; 45-48; CANR 34; DA3; DAB; DAM POP; DLB 162, 191; EWL 3; EXPS; MTCW 1, 2; RGSF 2; SSFS 7

Bauchart
See Camus, Albert

Baudelaire, Charles 1821-1867 . **NCLC 6, 29, 55; PC 1; SSC 18; WLC**
See also DA; DA3; DAB; DAC; DAM MST, POET; DLB 217; EW 7; GFL 1789 to the Present; LMFS 2; PFS 21; RGWL 2, 3; TWA

Baudouin, Marcel
See Peguy, Charles (Pierre)

Baudouin, Pierre
See Peguy, Charles (Pierre)

Baudrillard, Jean 1929- .... **CLC 60**
See also DLB 296

Baum, L(yman) Frank 1856-1919 .. **TCLC 7, 132**
See also AAYA 46; BYA 16; CA 108; 133; CLR 15; CWRI 5; DLB 22; FANT; JRDA; MAICYA 1, 2; MTCW 1, 2; NFS 13; RGAL 4; SATA 18, 100; WCH

Baum, Louis F.
See Baum, L(yman) Frank

Baumbach, Jonathan 1933- .... **CLC 6, 23**
See also CA 13-16R; CAAS 5; CANR 12, 66; CN 7; DLBY 1980; INT CANR-12; MTCW 1

Bausch, Richard (Carl) 1945- .... **CLC 51**
See also AMWS 7; CA 101; CAAS 14; CANR 43, 61, 87; CSW; DLB 130

Baxter, Charles (Morley) 1947- . **CLC 45, 78**
See also CA 57-60; CANR 40, 64, 104, 133; CPW; DAM POP; DLB 130; MTCW 2

Baxter, George Owen
See Faust, Frederick (Schiller)

Baxter, James K(eir) 1926-1972 .... **CLC 14**
See also CA 77-80; EWL 3

Baxter, John
See Hunt, E(verette) Howard, (Jr.)

Bayer, Sylvia
See Glassco, John

Baynton, Barbara 1857-1929 .... **TCLC 57**
See also DLB 230; RGSF 2

Benet, Juan 1927-1993 .... **CLC 28**
See also CA 143; EWL 3

Benet, Stephen Vincent 1898-1943 ... **SSC 10;
TCLC 7**
See also AMWS 11; CA 104; 152; DA3;
DAM POET; DLB 4, 48, 102, 249, 284;
DLBY 1997; EWL 3; HGG; MTCW 1;
RGAL 4; RGSF 2; SUFW; WP; YABC 1

Benet, William Rose 1886-1950 ..... **TCLC 28**
See also CA 118; 152; DAM POET; DLB
45; RGAL 4

Benford, Gregory (Albert) 1941- ..... **CLC 52**
See also BPFB 1; CA 69-72, 175; CAAE
175; CAAS 27; CANR 12, 24, 49, 95;
CSW; DLBY 1982; SCFW 2; SFW 4

Bengtsson, Frans (Gunnar)
1894-1954 .... **TCLC 48**
See also CA 170; EWL 3

Benjamin, David
See Slavitt, David R(ytman)

Benjamin, Lois
See Gould, Lois

Benjamin, Walter 1892-1940 .... **TCLC 39**
See also CA 164; DLB 242; EW 11; EWL
3

Ben Jelloun, Tahar 1944-
See Jelloun, Tahar ben
See also CA 135; CWW 2; EWL 3; RGWL
3; WLIT 2

Benn, Gottfried 1886-1956 .. **PC 35; TCLC 3**
See also CA 106; 153; DLB 56; EWL 3;
RGWL 2, 3

Bennett, Alan 1934- .... **CLC 45, 77**
See also BRWS 8; CA 103; CANR 35, 55,
106; CBD; CD 5; DAB; DAM MST;
MTCW 1, 2

Bennett, (Enoch) Arnold
1867-1931 .... **TCLC 5, 20**
See also BRW 6; CA 106; 155; CDBLB
1890-1914; DLB 10, 34, 98, 135; EWL 3;
MTCW 2

Bennett, Elizabeth
See Mitchell, Margaret (Munnerlyn)

Bennett, George Harold 1930-
See Bennett, Hal
See also BW 1; CA 97-100; CANR 87

Bennett, Gwendolyn B. 1902-1981 .... **HR 2**
See also BW 1; CA 125; DLB 51; WP

Bennett, Hal .... **CLC 5**
See Bennett, George Harold
See also DLB 33

Bennett, Jay 1912- .... **CLC 35**
See also AAYA 10; CA 69-72; CANR 11,
42, 79; JRDA; SAAS 4; SATA 41, 87;
SATA-Brief 27; WYA; YAW

Bennett, Louise (Simone) 1919- .... **BLC 1;
CLC 28**
See also BW 2, 3; CA 151; CDWLB 3; CP
7; DAM MULT; DLB 117; EWL 3

Benson, A. C. 1862-1925 .... **TCLC 123**
See also DLB 98

Benson, E(dward) F(rederic)
1867-1940 .... **TCLC 27**
See also CA 114; 157; DLB 135, 153;
HGG; SUFW 1

Benson, Jackson J. 1930- .... **CLC 34**
See also CA 25-28R; DLB 111

Benson, Sally 1900-1972 .... **CLC 17**
See also CA 19-20; 37-40R; CAP 1; SATA
1, 35; SATA-Obit 27

Benson, Stella 1892-1933 .... **TCLC 17**
See also CA 117; 154, 155; DLB 36, 162;
FANT; TEA

Bentham, Jeremy 1748-1832 .... **NCLC 38**
See also DLB 107, 158, 252

Bentley, E(dmund) C(lerihew)
1875-1956 .... **TCLC 12**
See also CA 108; DLB 70; MSW

Bentley, Eric (Russell) 1916- .... **CLC 24**
See also CA 5-8R; CAD; CANR 6, 67;
CBD; CD 5; INT CANR-6

ben Uzair, Salem
See Horne, Richard Henry Hengist

Beranger, Pierre Jean de
1780-1857 .... **NCLC 34**

Berdyaev, Nicolas
See Berdyaev, Nikolai (Aleksandrovich)

Berdyaev, Nikolai (Aleksandrovich)
1874-1948 .... **TCLC 67**
See also CA 120; 157

Berdyayev, Nikolai (Aleksandrovich)
See Berdyaev, Nikolai (Aleksandrovich)

Berendt, John (Lawrence) 1939- ...... **CLC 86**
See also CA 146; CANR 75, 93; DA3;
MTCW 1

Beresford, J(ohn) D(avys)
1873-1947 .... **TCLC 81**
See also CA 112; 155; DLB 162, 178, 197;
SFW 4; SUFW 1

Bergelson, David (Rafailovich)
1884-1952 .... **TCLC 81**
See Bergelson, Dovid
See also CA 220

Bergelson, Dovid
See Bergelson, David (Rafailovich)
See also EWL 3

Berger, Colonel
See Malraux, (Georges-)Andre

Berger, John (Peter) 1926- .... **CLC 2, 19**
See also BRWS 4; CA 81-84; CANR 51,
78, 117; CN 7; DLB 14, 207

Berger, Melvin H. 1927- .... **CLC 12**
See also CA 5-8R; CANR 4; CLR 32;
SAAS 2; SATA 5, 88; SATA-Essay 124

Berger, Thomas (Louis) 1924- .. **CLC 3, 5, 8,
11, 18, 38**
See also BPFB 1; CA 1-4R; CANR 5, 28,
51, 128; CN 7; DAM NOV; DLB 2;
DLBY 1980; EWL 3; FANT; INT CANR-
28; MTCW 1, 2; RHW; TCWW 2

Bergman, (Ernst) Ingmar 1918- ...... **CLC 16,
72**
See also CA 81-84; CANR 33, 70; CWW
2; DLB 257; MTCW 2

Bergson, Henri(-Louis) 1859-1941 . **TCLC 32**
See also CA 164; EW 8; EWL 3; GFL 1789
to the Present

Bergstein, Eleanor 1938- .... **CLC 4**
See also CA 53-56; CANR 5

Berkeley, George 1685-1753 .... **LC 65**
See also DLB 31, 101, 252

Berkoff, Steven 1937- .... **CLC 56**
See also CA 104; CANR 72; CBD; CD 5

Berlin, Isaiah 1909-1997 .... **TCLC 105**
See also CA 85-88; 162

Bermant, Chaim (Icyk) 1929-1998 ... **CLC 40**
See also CA 57-60; CANR 6, 31, 57, 105;
CN 7

Bern, Victoria
See Fisher, M(ary) F(rances) K(ennedy)

Bernanos, (Paul Louis) Georges
1888-1948 .... **TCLC 3**
See also CA 104; 130; CANR 94; DLB 72;
EWL 3; GFL 1789 to the Present; RGWL
2, 3

Bernard, April 1956- .... **CLC 59**
See also CA 131

Bernard of Clairvaux 1090-1153 .. **CMLC 71**
See also DLB 208

Berne, Victoria
See Fisher, M(ary) F(rances) K(ennedy)

Bernhard, Thomas 1931-1989 ..... **CLC 3, 32,
61; DC 14**
See also CA 85-88; 127; CANR 32, 57; CD-
WLB 2; DLB 85, 124; EWL 3; MTCW 1;
RGWL 2, 3

Bernhardt, Sarah (Henriette Rosine)
1844-1923 .... **TCLC 75**
See also CA 157

Bernstein, Charles 1950- .... **CLC 142,**
See also CA 129; CAAS 24; CANR 90; CP
7; DLB 169

Bernstein, Ingrid
See Kirsch, Sarah

Berriault, Gina 1926-1999 .... **CLC 54, 109;
SSC 30**
See also CA 116; 129; 185; CANR 66; DLB
130; SSFS 7,11

Berrigan, Daniel 1921- .... **CLC 4**
See also CA 33-36R, 187; CAAE 187;
CAAS 1; CANR 11, 43, 78; CP 7; DLB 5

Berrigan, Edmund Joseph Michael, Jr.
1934-1983
See Berrigan, Ted
See also CA 61-64; 110; CANR 14, 102

Berrigan, Ted .... **CLC 37**
See Berrigan, Edmund Joseph Michael, Jr.
See also DLB 5, 169; WP

Berry, Charles Edward Anderson 1931-
See Berry, Chuck
See also CA 115

Berry, Chuck .... **CLC 17**
See Berry, Charles Edward Anderson

Berry, Jonas
See Ashbery, John (Lawrence)
See also GLL 1

Berry, Wendell (Erdman) 1934- ... **CLC 4, 6,
8, 27, 46; PC 28**
See also AITN 1; AMWS 10; ANW; CA
73-76; CANR 50, 73, 101, 132; CP 7;
CSW; DAM POET; DLB 5, 6, 234, 275;
MTCW 1

Berryman, John 1914-1972 ... **CLC 1, 2, 3, 4,
6, 8, 10, 13, 25, 62**
See also AMW; CA 13-16; 33-36R; CABS
2; CANR 35; CAP 1; CDALB 1941-1968;
DAM POET; DLB 48; EWL 3; MTCW 1,
2; PAB; RGAL 4; WP

Bertolucci, Bernardo 1940- ...... **CLC 16, 157**
See also CA 106; CANR 125

Berton, Pierre (Francis Demarigny)
1920- .... **CLC 104**
See also CA 1-4R; CANR 2, 56; CPW;
DLB 68; SATA 99

Bertrand, Aloysius 1807-1841 .... **NCLC 31**
See Bertrand, Louis oAloysiusc

Bertrand, Louis oAloysiusc
See Bertrand, Aloysius
See also DLB 217

Bertran de Born c. 1140-1215 .... **CMLC 5**

Besant, Annie (Wood) 1847-1933 ..... **TCLC 9**
See also CA 105; 185

Bessie, Alvah 1904-1985 .... **CLC 23**
See also CA 5-8R; 116; CANR 2, 80; DLB
26

Bestuzhev, Aleksandr Aleksandrovich
1797-1837 .... **NCLC 131**
See also DLB 198

Bethlen, T. D.
See Silverberg, Robert

Beti, Mongo .... **BLC 1; CLC 27**
See Biyidi, Alexandre
See also AFW; CANR 79; DAM MULT;
EWL 3; WLIT 2

Betjeman, John 1906-1984 ...... **CLC 2, 6, 10,
34, 43**
See also BRW 7; CA 9-12R; 112; CANR
33, 56; CDBLB 1945-1960; DA3; DAB;
DAM MST, POET; DLB 20; DLBY 1984;
EWL 3; MTCW 1, 2

Bettelheim, Bruno 1903-1990 .... **CLC 79;
TCLC 143**
See also CA 81-84; 131; CANR 23, 61;
DA3; MTCW 1, 2

Brink, Andre (Philippus) 1935- . **CLC 18, 36, 106**
See also AFW; BRWS 6; CA 104; CANR 39, 62, 109, 133; CN 7; DLB 225; EWL 3; INT CA-103; LATS 1:2; MTCW 1, 2; WLIT 2

Brinsmead, H. F(ay)
See Brinsmead, H(esba) F(ay)

Brinsmead, H. F.
See Brinsmead, H(esba) F(ay)

Brinsmead, H(esba) F(ay) 1922- ...... **CLC 21**
See also CA 21-24R; CANR 10; CLR 47; CWRI 5; MAICYA 1, 2; SAAS 5; SATA 18, 78

Brittain, Vera (Mary) 1893(?)-1970 . **CLC 23**
See also CA 13-16; 25-28R; CANR 58; CAP 1; DLB 191; FW; MTCW 1, 2

Broch, Hermann 1886-1951 .... **TCLC 20**
See also CA 117; 211; CDWLB 2; DLB 85, 124; EW 10; EWL 3; RGWL 2, 3

Brock, Rose
See Hansen, Joseph
See also GLL 1

Brod, Max 1884-1968 .... **TCLC 115**
See also CA 5-8R; 25-28R; CANR 7; DLB 81; EWL 3

Brodkey, Harold (Roy) 1930-1996 .. **CLC 56; TCLC 123**
See also CA 111; 151; CANR 71; CN 7; DLB 130

Brodsky, Iosif Alexandrovich 1940-1996
See Brodsky, Joseph
See also AITN 1; CA 41-44R; 151; CANR 37, 106; DA3; DAM POET; MTCW 1, 2; RGWL 2, 3

Brodsky, Joseph . **CLC 4, 6, 13, 36, 100; PC 9**
See Brodsky, Iosif Alexandrovich
See also AMWS 8; CWW 2; DLB 285; EWL 3; MTCW 1

Brodsky, Michael (Mark) 1948- .... **CLC 19**
See also CA 102; CANR 18, 41, 58; DLB 244

Brodzki, Bella ed. .... **CLC 65**

Brome, Richard 1590(?)-1652 .... **LC 61**
See also DLB 58

Bromell, Henry 1947- .... **CLC 5**
See also CA 53-56; CANR 9, 115, 116

Bromfield, Louis (Brucker) 1896-1956 .... **TCLC 11**
See also CA 107; 155; DLB 4, 9, 86; RGAL 4; RHW

Broner, E(sther) M(asserman) 1930- .... **CLC 19**
See also CA 17-20R; CANR 8, 25, 72; CN 7; DLB 28

Bronk, William (M.) 1918-1999 .... **CLC 10**
See also CA 89-92; 177; CANR 23; CP 7; DLB 165

Bronstein, Lev Davidovich
See Trotsky, Leon

Bronte, Anne 1820-1849 ..... **NCLC 4, 71, 102**
See also BRW 5; BRWR 1; DA3; DLB 21, 199; TEA

Bronte, (Patrick) Branwell 1817-1848 .... **NCLC 109**

Bronte, Charlotte 1816-1855 ...... **NCLC 3, 8, 33, 58, 105; WLC**
See also AAYA 17; BRW 5; BRWC 2; BRWR 1; BYA 2; CDBLB 1832-1890; DA; DA3; DAB; DAC; DAM MST, NOV; DLB 21, 159, 199; EXPN; LAIT 2; NFS 4; TEA; WLIT 4

Bronte, Emily (Jane) 1818-1848 ... **NCLC 16, 35; PC 8; WLC**
See also AAYA 17; BPFB 1; BRW 5; BRWC 1; BRWR 1; BYA 3; CDBLB 1832-1890; DA; DA3; DAB; DAC; DAM MST, NOV, POET; DLB 21, 32, 199; EXPN; LAIT 1; TEA; WLIT 3

Brontes
See Bronte, Anne; Bronte, Charlotte; Bronte, Emily (Jane)

Brooke, Frances 1724-1789 .... **LC 6, 48**
See also DLB 39, 99

Brooke, Henry 1703(?)-1783 .... **LC 1**
See also DLB 39

Brooke, Rupert (Chawner) 1887-1915 ..... **PC 24; TCLC 2, 7; WLC**
See also BRWS 3; CA 104; 132; CANR 61; CDBLB 1914-1945; DA; DAB; DAC; DAM MST, POET; DLB 19, 216; EXPP; GLL 2; MTCW 1, 2; PFS 7; TEA

Brooke-Haven, P.
See Wodehouse, P(elham) G(renville)

Brooke-Rose, Christine 1926(?)- ..... **CLC 40, 184**
See also BRWS 4; CA 13-16R; CANR 58, 118; CN 7; DLB 14, 231; EWL 3; SFW 4

Brookner, Anita 1928- ... **CLC 32, 34, 51, 136**
See also BRWS 4; CA 114; 120; CANR 37, 56, 87, 130; CN 7; CPW; DA3; DAB; DAM POP; DLB 194; DLBY 1987; EWL 3; MTCW 1, 2; TEA

Brooks, Cleanth 1906-1994 . **CLC 24, 86, 110**
See also CA 17-20R; 145; CANR 33, 35; CSW; DLB 63; DLBY 1994; EWL 3; INT CANR-35; MTCW 1, 2

Brooks, George
See Baum, L(yman) Frank

Brooks, Gwendolyn (Elizabeth) 1917-2000 ... **BLC 1; CLC 1, 2, 4, 5, 15, 49, 125; PC 7; WLC**
See also AAYA 20; AFAW 1, 2; AITN 1; AMWS 3; BW 2, 3; CA 1-4R; 190; CANR 1, 27, 52, 75, 132; CDALB 1941-1968; CLR 27; CP 7; CWP; DA; DA3; DAC; DAM MST, MULT, POET; DLB 5, 76, 165; EWL 3; EXPP; MAWW; MTCW 1, 2; PFS 1, 2, 4, 6; RGAL 4; SATA 6; SATA-Obit 123; TUS; WP

Brooks, Mel .... **CLC 12**
See Kaminsky, Melvin
See also AAYA 13, 48; DLB 26

Brooks, Peter (Preston) 1938- .... **CLC 34**
See also CA 45-48; CANR 1, 107

Brooks, Van Wyck 1886-1963 .... **CLC 29**
See also AMW; CA 1-4R; CANR 6; DLB 45, 63, 103; TUS

Brophy, Brigid (Antonia) 1929-1995 .... **CLC 6, 11, 29, 105**
See also CA 5-8R; 149; CAAS 4; CANR 25, 53; CBD; CN 7; CWD; DA3; DLB 14, 271; EWL 3; MTCW 1, 2

Brosman, Catharine Savage 1934- ..... **CLC 9**
See also CA 61-64; CANR 21, 46

Brossard, Nicole 1943- .... **CLC 115, 169**
See also CA 122; CAAS 16; CCA 1; CWP; CWW 2; DLB 53; EWL 3; FW; GLL 2; RGWL 3

Brother Antoninus
See Everson, William (Oliver)

The Brothers Quay
See Quay, Stephen; Quay, Timothy

Broughton, T(homas) Alan 1936- ..... **CLC 19**
See also CA 45-48; CANR 2, 23, 48, 111

Broumas, Olga 1949- .... **CLC 10, 73**
See also CA 85-88; CANR 20, 69, 110; CP 7; CWP; GLL 2

Broun, Heywood 1888-1939 .... **TCLC 104**
See also DLB 29, 171

Brown, Alan 1950- .... **CLC 99**
See also CA 156

Brown, Charles Brockden 1771-1810 .... **NCLC 22, 74, 122**
See also AMWS 1; CDALB 1640-1865; DLB 37, 59, 73; FW; HGG; LMFS 1; RGAL 4; TUS

Brown, Christy 1932-1981 .... **CLC 63**
See also BYA 13; CA 105; 104; CANR 72; DLB 14

Brown, Claude 1937-2002 ... **BLC 1; CLC 30**
See also AAYA 7; BW 1, 3; CA 73-76; 205; CANR 81; DAM MULT

Brown, Dee (Alexander) 1908-2002 .... **CLC 18, 47**
See also AAYA 30; CA 13-16R; 212; CAAS 6; CANR 11, 45, 60; CPW; CSW; DA3; DAM POP; DLBY 1980; LAIT 2; MTCW 1, 2; NCFS 5; SATA 5, 110; SATA-Obit 141; TCWW 2

Brown, George
See Wertmueller, Lina

Brown, George Douglas 1869-1902 .... **TCLC 28**
See Douglas, George
See also CA 162

Brown, George Mackay 1921-1996 ... **CLC 5, 48, 100**
See also BRWS 6; CA 21-24R; 151; CAAS 6; CANR 12, 37, 67; CN 7; CP 7; DLB 14, 27, 139, 271; MTCW 1; RGSF 2; SATA 35

Brown, (William) Larry 1951- .... **CLC 73**
See also CA 130; 134; CANR 117; CSW; DLB 234; INT CA-134

Brown, Moses
See Barrett, William (Christopher)

Brown, Rita Mae 1944- .... **CLC 18, 43, 79**
See also BPFB 1; CA 45-48; CANR 2, 11, 35, 62, 95; CN 7; CPW; CSW; DA3; DAM NOV, POP; FW; INT CANR-11; MTCW 1, 2; NFS 9; RGAL 4; TUS

Brown, Roderick (Langmere) Haig-
See Haig-Brown, Roderick (Langmere)

Brown, Rosellen 1939- .... **CLC 32, 170**
See also CA 77-80; CAAS 10; CANR 14, 44, 98; CN 7

Brown, Sterling Allen 1901-1989 ...... **BLC 1; CLC 1, 23, 59; HR 2; PC 55**
See also AFAW 1, 2; BW 1, 3; CA 85-88; 127; CANR 26; DA3; DAM MULT, POET; DLB 48, 51, 63; MTCW 1, 2; RGAL 4; WP

Brown, Will
See Ainsworth, William Harrison

Brown, William Hill 1765-1793 .... **LC 93**
See also DLB 37

Brown, William Wells 1815-1884 ...... **BLC 1; DC 1; NCLC 2, 89**
See also DAM MULT; DLB 3, 50, 183, 248; RGAL 4

Browne, (Clyde) Jackson 1948(?)- ... **CLC 21**
See also CA 120

Browning, Elizabeth Barrett 1806-1861 ... **NCLC 1, 16, 61, 66; PC 6; WLC**
See also BRW 4; CDBLB 1832-1890; DA; DA3; DAB; DAC; DAM MST, POET; DLB 32, 199; EXPP; PAB; PFS 2, 16; TEA; WLIT 4; WP

Browning, Robert 1812-1889 . **NCLC 19, 79; PC 2; WLCS**
See also BRW 4; BRWC 2; BRWR 2; CDBLB 1832-1890; CLR 97; DA; DA3; DAB; DAC; DAM MST, POET; DLB 32, 163; EXPP; LATS 1:1; PAB; PFS 1, 15; RGEL 2; TEA; WLIT 4; WP; YABC 1

Browning, Tod 1882-1962 .... **CLC 16**
See also CA 141; 117

Brownmiller, Susan 1935- .... **CLC 159**
See also CA 103; CANR 35, 75; DAM NOV; FW; MTCW 1, 2

Brownson, Orestes Augustus 1803-1876 .... **NCLC 50**
See also DLB 1, 59, 73, 243

Bustos Domecq, H(onorio)
See Bioy Casares, Adolfo; Borges, Jorge Luis

Butler, Octavia E(stelle) 1947- .. **BLCS; CLC 38, 121**
See also AAYA 18, 48; AFAW 2; AMWS 13; BPFB 1; BW 2, 3; CA 73-76; CANR 12, 24, 38, 73; CLR 65; CPW; DA3; DAM MULT, POP; DLB 33; LATS 1:2; MTCW 1, 2; NFS 8; SATA 84; SCFW 2; SFW 4; SSFS 6; YAW

Butler, Robert Olen, (Jr.) 1945- ...... **CLC 81, 162**
See also AMWS 12; BPFB 1; CA 112; CANR 66; CSW; DAM POP; DLB 173; INT CA-112; MTCW 1; SSFS 11

Butler, Samuel 1612-1680 .... **LC 16, 43**
See also DLB 101, 126; RGEL 2

Butler, Samuel 1835-1902 .... **TCLC 1, 33; WLC**
See also BRWS 2; CA 143; CDBLB 1890-1914; DA; DA3; DAB; DAC; DAM MST, NOV; DLB 18, 57, 174; RGEL 2; SFW 4; TEA

Butler, Walter C.
See Faust, Frederick (Schiller)

Butor, Michel (Marie Francois)
1926- .... **CLC 1, 3, 8, 11, 15, 161**
See also CA 9-12R; CANR 33, 66; CWW 2; DLB 83; EW 13; EWL 3; GFL 1789 to the Present; MTCW 1, 2

Butts, Mary 1890(?)-1937 .... **TCLC 77**
See also CA 148; DLB 240

Buxton, Ralph
See Silverstein, Alvin; Silverstein, Virginia B(arbara Opshelor)

Buzo, Alex
See Buzo, Alexander (John)
See also DLB 289

Buzo, Alexander (John) 1944- .... **CLC 61**
See also CA 97-100; CANR 17, 39, 69; CD 5

Buzzati, Dino 1906-1972 .... **CLC 36**
See also CA 160; 33-36R; DLB 177; RGWL 2, 3; SFW 4

Byars, Betsy (Cromer) 1928- .... **CLC 35**
See also AAYA 19; BYA 3; CA 33-36R, 183; CAAE 183; CANR 18, 36, 57, 102; CLR 1, 16, 72; DLB 52; INT CANR-18; JRDA; MAICYA 1, 2; MAICYAS 1; MTCW 1; SAAS 1; SATA 4, 46, 80; SATA-Essay 108; WYA; YAW

Byatt, A(ntonia) S(usan Drabble)
1936- .... **CLC 19, 65, 136**
See also BPFB 1; BRWC 2; BRWS 4; CA 13-16R; CANR 13, 33, 50, 75, 96, 133; DA3; DAM NOV, POP; DLB 14, 194; EWL 3; MTCW 1, 2; RGSF 2; RHW; TEA

Byrne, David 1952- .... **CLC 26**
See also CA 127

Byrne, John Keyes 1926-
See Leonard, Hugh
See also CA 102; CANR 78; INT CA-102

Byron, George Gordon (Noel)
1788-1824 ..... **DC 24; NCLC 2, 12, 109; PC 16; WLC**
See also BRW 4; BRWC 2; CDBLB 1789-1832; DA; DA3; DAB; DAC; DAM MST, POET; DLB 96, 110; EXPP; LMFS 1; PAB; PFS 1, 14; RGEL 2; TEA; WLIT 3; WP

Byron, Robert 1905-1941 .... **TCLC 67**
See also CA 160; DLB 195

C. 3. 3.
See Wilde, Oscar (Fingal O'Flahertie Wills)

Caballero, Fernan 1796-1877 .... **NCLC 10**

Cabell, Branch
See Cabell, James Branch

Cabell, James Branch 1879-1958 .... **TCLC 6**
See also CA 105; 152; DLB 9, 78; FANT; MTCW 1; RGAL 4; SUFW 1

Cabeza de Vaca, Alvar Nunez
1490-1557(?) .... **LC 61**

Cable, George Washington
1844-1925 .... **SSC 4; TCLC 4**
See also CA 104; 155; DLB 12, 74; DLBD 13; RGAL 4; TUS

Cabral de Melo Neto, Joao
1920-1999 .... **CLC 76**
See Melo Neto, Joao Cabral de
See also CA 151; DAM MULT; LAW; LAWS 1

Cabrera Infante, G(uillermo) 1929- . **CLC 5, 25, 45, 120; HLC 1; SSC 39**
See also CA 85-88; CANR 29, 65, 110; CD-WLB 3; CWW 2; DA3; DAM MULT; DLB 113; EWL 3; HW 1, 2; LAW; LAWS 1; MTCW 1, 2; RGSF 2; WLIT 1

Cade, Toni
See Bambara, Toni Cade

Cadmus and Harmonia
See Buchan, John

Caedmon fl. 658-680 .... **CMLC 7**
See also DLB 146

Caeiro, Alberto
See Pessoa, Fernando (Antonio Nogueira)

Caesar, Julius .... **CMLC 47**
See Julius Caesar
See also AW 1; RGWL 2, 3

Cage, John (Milton, Jr.)
1912-1992 .... **CLC 41; PC 58**
See also CA 13-16R; 169; CANR 9, 78; DLB 193; INT CANR-9

Cahan, Abraham 1860-1951 .... **TCLC 71**
See also CA 108; 154; DLB 9, 25, 28; RGAL 4

Cain, G.
See Cabrera Infante, G(uillermo)

Cain, Guillermo
See Cabrera Infante, G(uillermo)

Cain, James M(allahan) 1892-1977 .. **CLC 3, 11, 28**
See also AITN 1; BPFB 1; CA 17-20R; 73-76; CANR 8, 34, 61; CMW 4; DLB 226; EWL 3; MSW; MTCW 1; RGAL 4

Caine, Hall 1853-1931 .... **TCLC 97**
See also RHW

Caine, Mark
See Raphael, Frederic (Michael)

Calasso, Roberto 1941- .... **CLC 81**
See also CA 143; CANR 89

Calderon de la Barca, Pedro
1600-1681 .... **DC 3; HLCS 1; LC 23**
See also EW 2; RGWL 2, 3; TWA

Caldwell, Erskine (Preston)
1903-1987 .... **CLC 1, 8, 14, 50, 60; SSC 19; TCLC 117**
See also AITN 1; AMW; BPFB 1; CA 1-4R; 121; CAAS 1; CANR 2, 33; DA3; DAM NOV; DLB 9, 86; EWL 3; MTCW 1, 2; RGAL 4; RGSF 2; TUS

Caldwell, (Janet Miriam) Taylor (Holland)
1900-1985 .... **CLC 2, 28, 39**
See also BPFB 1; CA 5-8R; 116; CANR 5; DA3; DAM NOV, POP; DLBD 17; RHW

Calhoun, John Caldwell
1782-1850 .... **NCLC 15**
See also DLB 3, 248

Calisher, Hortense 1911- ..... **CLC 2, 4, 8, 38, 134; SSC 15**
See also CA 1-4R; CANR 1, 22, 117; CN 7; DA3; DAM NOV; DLB 2, 218; INT CANR-22; MTCW 1, 2; RGAL 4; RGSF 2

Callaghan, Morley Edward
1903-1990 ..... **CLC 3, 14, 41, 65; TCLC 145**
See also CA 9-12R; 132; CANR 33, 73; DAC; DAM MST; DLB 68; EWL 3; MTCW 1, 2; RGEL 2; RGSF 2; SSFS 19

Callimachus c. 305B.C.-c.
240B.C. .... **CMLC 18**
See also AW 1; DLB 176; RGWL 2, 3

Calvin, Jean
See Calvin, John
See also GFL Beginnings to 1789

Calvin, John 1509-1564 .... **LC 37**
See Calvin, Jean

Calvino, Italo 1923-1985 .... **CLC 5, 8, 11, 22, 33, 39, 73; SSC 3, 48**
See also AAYA 58; CA 85-88; 116; CANR 23, 61, 132; DAM NOV; DLB 196; EW 13; EWL 3; MTCW 1, 2; RGSF 2; RGWL 2, 3; SFW 4; SSFS 12

Camara Laye
See Laye, Camara
See also EWL 3

Camden, William 1551-1623 .... **LC 77**
See also DLB 172

Cameron, Carey 1952- .... **CLC 59**
See also CA 135

Cameron, Peter 1959- .... **CLC 44**
See also AMWS 12; CA 125; CANR 50, 117; DLB 234; GLL 2

Camoens, Luis Vaz de 1524(?)-1580
See Camoes, Luis de
See also EW 2

Camoes, Luis de 1524(?)-1580 . **HLCS 1; LC 62; PC 31**
See Camoens, Luis Vaz de
See also DLB 287; RGWL 2, 3

Campana, Dino 1885-1932 .... **TCLC 20**
See also CA 117; DLB 114; EWL 3

Campanella, Tommaso 1568-1639 .... **LC 32**
See also RGWL 2, 3

Campbell, John W(ood, Jr.)
1910-1971 .... **CLC 32**
See also CA 21-22; 29-32R; CANR 34; CAP 2; DLB 8; MTCW 1; SCFW 4; SFW 4

Campbell, Joseph 1904-1987 .... **CLC 69; TCLC 140**
See also AAYA 3; BEST 89:2; CA 1-4R; 124; CANR 3, 28, 61, 107; DA3; MTCW 1, 2

Campbell, Maria 1940- .... **CLC 85; NNAL**
See also CA 102; CANR 54; CCA 1; DAC

Campbell, (John) Ramsey 1946- ..... **CLC 42; SSC 19**
See also AAYA 51; CA 57-60; CANR 7, 102; DLB 261; HGG; INT CANR-7; SUFW 1, 2

Campbell, (Ignatius) Roy (Dunnachie)
1901-1957 .... **TCLC 5**
See also AFW; CA 104; 155; DLB 20, 225; EWL 3; MTCW 2; RGEL 2

Campbell, Thomas 1777-1844 .... **NCLC 19**
See also DLB 93, 144; RGEL 2

Campbell, Wilfred .... **TCLC 9**
See Campbell, William

Campbell, William 1858(?)-1918
See Campbell, Wilfred
See also CA 106; DLB 92

Campion, Jane 1954- .... **CLC 95**
See also AAYA 33; CA 138; CANR 87

Campion, Thomas 1567-1620 .... **LC 78**
See also CDBLB Before 1660; DAM POET; DLB 58, 172; RGEL 2

Camus, Albert 1913-1960 ...... **CLC 1, 2, 4, 9, 11, 14, 32, 63, 69, 124; DC 2; SSC 9, 76; WLC**
See also AAYA 36; AFW; BPFB 1; CA 89-92; CANR 131; DA; DA3; DAB; DAC; DAM DRAM, MST, NOV; DLB 72; EW

Chappell, Fred (Davis) 1936- .... **CLC 40, 78, 162**
See also CA 5-8R, 198; CAAE 198; CAAS 4; CANR 8, 33, 67, 110; CN 7; CP 7; CSW; DLB 6, 105; HGG

Char, Rene(-Emile) 1907-1988 .... **CLC 9, 11, 14, 55; PC 56**
See also CA 13-16R; 124; CANR 32; DAM POET; DLB 258; EWL 3; GFL 1789 to the Present; MTCW 1, 2; RGWL 2, 3

Charby, Jay
See Ellison, Harlan (Jay)

Chardin, Pierre Teilhard de
See Teilhard de Chardin, (Marie Joseph) Pierre

Chariton fl. 1st cent. (?)- .... **CMLC 49**

Charlemagne 742-814 .... **CMLC 37**

Charles I 1600-1649 .... **LC 13**

Charriere, Isabelle de 1740-1805 .. **NCLC 66**

Chartier, Alain c. 1392-1430 .... **LC 94**
See also DLB 208

Chartier, Emile-Auguste
See Alain

Charyn, Jerome 1937- .... **CLC 5, 8, 18**
See also CA 5-8R; CAAS 1; CANR 7, 61, 101; CMW 4; CN 7; DLBY 1983; MTCW 1

Chase, Adam
See Marlowe, Stephen

Chase, Mary (Coyle) 1907-1981 .... **DC 1**
See also CA 77-80; 105; CAD; CWD; DFS 11; DLB 228; SATA 17; SATA-Obit 29

Chase, Mary Ellen 1887-1973 .... **CLC 2; TCLC 124**
See also CA 13-16; 41-44R; CAP 1; SATA 10

Chase, Nicholas
See Hyde, Anthony
See also CCA 1

Chateaubriand, Francois Rene de
1768-1848 .... **NCLC 3, 134**
See also DLB 119; EW 5; GFL 1789 to the Present; RGWL 2, 3; TWA

Chatterje, Sarat Chandra 1876-1936(?)
See Chatterji, Saratchandra
See also CA 109

Chatterji, Bankim Chandra
1838-1894 .... **NCLC 19**

Chatterji, Saratchandra .... **TCLC 13**
See Chatterje, Sarat Chandra
See also CA 186; EWL 3

Chatterton, Thomas 1752-1770 .... **LC 3, 54**
See also DAM POET; DLB 109; RGEL 2

Chatwin, (Charles) Bruce
1940-1989 .... **CLC 28, 57, 59**
See also AAYA 4; BEST 90:1; BRWS 4; CA 85-88; 127; CPW; DAM POP; DLB 194, 204; EWL 3

Chaucer, Daniel
See Ford, Ford Madox
See also RHW

Chaucer, Geoffrey 1340(?)-1400 .. **LC 17, 56; PC 19, 58; WLCS**
See also BRW 1; BRWC 1; BRWR 2; CD-BLB Before 1660; DA; DA3; DAB; DAC; DAM MST, POET; DLB 146; LAIT 1; PAB; PFS 14; RGEL 2; TEA; WLIT 3; WP

Chavez, Denise (Elia) 1948- .... **HLC 1**
See also CA 131; CANR 56, 81; DAM MULT; DLB 122; FW; HW 1, 2; LLW 1; MTCW 2

Chaviaras, Strates 1935-
See Haviaras, Stratis
See also CA 105

Chayefsky, Paddy .... **CLC 23**
See Chayefsky, Sidney
See also CAD; DLB 7, 44; DLBY 1981; RGAL 4

Chayefsky, Sidney 1923-1981
See Chayefsky, Paddy
See also CA 9-12R; 104; CANR 18; DAM DRAM

Chedid, Andree 1920- .... **CLC 47**
See also CA 145; CANR 95; EWL 3

Cheever, John 1912-1982 ..... **CLC 3, 7, 8, 11, 15, 25, 64; SSC 1, 38, 57; WLC**
See also AMWS 1; BPFB 1; CA 5-8R; 106; CABS 1; CANR 5, 27, 76; CDALB 1941-1968; CPW; DA; DA3; DAB; DAC; DAM MST, NOV, POP; DLB 2, 102, 227; DLBY 1980, 1982; EWL 3; EXPS; INT CANR-5; MTCW 1, 2; RGAL 4; RGSF 2; SSFS 2, 14; TUS

Cheever, Susan 1943- .... **CLC 18, 48**
See also CA 103; CANR 27, 51, 92; DLBY 1982; INT CANR-27

Chekhonte, Antosha
See Chekhov, Anton (Pavlovich)

Chekhov, Anton (Pavlovich)
1860-1904 ...... **DC 9; SSC 2, 28, 41, 51; TCLC 3, 10, 31, 55, 96; WLC**
See also BYA 14; CA 104; 124; DA; DA3; DAB; DAC; DAM DRAM, MST; DFS 1, 5, 10, 12; DLB 277; EW 7; EWL 3; EXPS; LAIT 3; LATS 1:1; RGSF 2; RGWL 2, 3; SATA 90; SSFS 5, 13, 14; TWA

Cheney, Lynne V. 1941- .... **CLC 70**
See also CA 89-92; CANR 58, 117; SATA 152

Chernyshevsky, Nikolai Gavrilovich
See Chernyshevsky, Nikolay Gavrilovich
See also DLB 238

Chernyshevsky, Nikolay Gavrilovich
1828-1889 .... **NCLC 1**
See Chernyshevsky, Nikolai Gavrilovich

Cherry, Carolyn Janice 1942-
See Cherryh, C. J.
See also CA 65-68; CANR 10

Cherryh, C. J. .... **CLC 35**
See Cherry, Carolyn Janice
See also AAYA 24; BPFB 1; DLBY 1980; FANT; SATA 93; SCFW 2; SFW 4; YAW

Chesnutt, Charles W(addell)
1858-1932 .... **BLC 1; SSC 7, 54; TCLC 5, 39**
See also AFAW 1, 2; BW 1, 3; CA 106; 125; CANR 76; DAM MULT; DLB 12, 50, 78; EWL 3; MTCW 1, 2; RGAL 4; RGSF 2; SSFS 11

Chester, Alfred 1929(?)-1971 .... **CLC 49**
See also CA 196; 33-36R; DLB 130

Chesterton, G(ilbert) K(eith)
1874-1936 . **PC 28; SSC 1, 46; TCLC 1, 6, 64**
See also AAYA 57; BRW 6; CA 104; 132; CANR 73, 131; CDBLB 1914-1945; CMW 4; DAM NOV, POET; DLB 10, 19, 34, 70, 98, 149, 178; EWL 3; FANT; MSW; MTCW 1, 2; RGEL 2; RGSF 2; SATA 27; SUFW 1

Chiang, Pin-chin 1904-1986
See Ding Ling
See also CA 118

Chief Joseph 1840-1904 .... **NNAL**
See also CA 152; DA3; DAM MULT

Chief Seattle 1786(?)-1866 .... **NNAL**
See also DA3; DAM MULT

Ch'ien, Chung-shu 1910-1998 .... **CLC 22**
See Qian Zhongshu
See also CA 130; CANR 73; MTCW 1, 2

Chikamatsu Monzaemon 1653-1724 ... **LC 66**
See also RGWL 2, 3

Child, L. Maria
See Child, Lydia Maria

Child, Lydia Maria 1802-1880 .. **NCLC 6, 73**
See also DLB 1, 74, 243; RGAL 4; SATA 67

Child, Mrs.
See Child, Lydia Maria

Child, Philip 1898-1978 .... **CLC 19, 68**
See also CA 13-14; CAP 1; DLB 68; RHW; SATA 47

Childers, (Robert) Erskine
1870-1922 .... **TCLC 65**
See also CA 113; 153; DLB 70

Childress, Alice 1920-1994 . **BLC 1; CLC 12, 15, 86, 96; DC 4; TCLC 116**
See also AAYA 8; BW 2, 3; BYA 2; CA 45-48; 146; CAD; CANR 3, 27, 50, 74; CLR 14; CWD; DA3; DAM DRAM, MULT, NOV; DFS 2, 8, 14; DLB 7, 38, 249; JRDA; LAIT 5; MAICYA 1, 2; MAIC-YAS 1; MTCW 1, 2; RGAL 4; SATA 7, 48, 81; TUS; WYA; YAW

Chin, Frank (Chew, Jr.) 1940- ...... **CLC 135; DC 7**
See also CA 33-36R; CANR 71; CD 5; DAM MULT; DLB 206; LAIT 5; RGAL 4

Chin, Marilyn (Mei Ling) 1955- .... **PC 40**
See also CA 129; CANR 70, 113; CWP

Chislett, (Margaret) Anne 1943- ...... **CLC 34**
See also CA 151

Chitty, Thomas Willes 1926- .... **CLC 11**
See Hinde, Thomas
See also CA 5-8R; CN 7

Chivers, Thomas Holley
1809-1858 .... **NCLC 49**
See also DLB 3, 248; RGAL 4

Choi, Susan 1969- .... **CLC 119**
See also CA 223

Chomette, Rene Lucien 1898-1981
See Clair, Rene
See also CA 103

Chomsky, (Avram) Noam 1928- ..... **CLC 132**
See also CA 17-20R; CANR 28, 62, 110, 132; DA3; DLB 246; MTCW 1, 2

Chona, Maria 1845(?)-1936 .... **NNAL**
See also CA 144

Chopin, Kate .... **SSC 8, 68; TCLC 127; WLCS**
See Chopin, Katherine
See also AAYA 33; AMWR 2; AMWS 1; BYA 11, 15; CDALB 1865-1917; DA; DAB; DLB 12, 78; EXPN; EXPS; FW; LAIT 3; MAWW; NFS 3; RGAL 4; RGSF 2; SSFS 17; TUS

Chopin, Katherine 1851-1904
See Chopin, Kate
See also CA 104; 122; DA3; DAC; DAM MST, NOV

Chretien de Troyes c. 12th cent. - . **CMLC 10**
See also DLB 208; EW 1; RGWL 2, 3; TWA

Christie
See Ichikawa, Kon

Christie
See Ichikawa, Kon

Christie, Agatha (Mary Clarissa)
1890-1976 .. **CLC 1, 6, 8, 12, 39, 48, 110**
See also AAYA 9; AITN 1, 2; BPFB 1; BRWS 2; CA 17-20R; 61-64; CANR 10, 37, 108; CBD; CDBLB 1914-1945; CMW 4; CPW; CWD; DA3; DAB; DAC; DAM NOV; DFS 2; DLB 13, 77, 245; MSW; MTCW 1, 2; NFS 8; RGEL 2; RHW; SATA 36; TEA; YAW

Christie, Philippa .... **CLC 21**
See Pearce, Philippa
See also BYA 5; CANR 109; CLR 9; DLB 161; MAICYA 1; SATA 1, 67, 129

Christine de Pizan 1365(?)-1431(?) .... **LC 9**
See also DLB 208; RGWL 2, 3

Chuang Tzu c. 369B.C.-c.
286B.C. .... **CMLC 57**

Chubb, Elmer
See Masters, Edgar Lee

Chulkov, Mikhail Dmitrievich
1743-1792 .... **LC 2**
See also DLB 150
Churchill, Caryl 1938- .... **CLC 31, 55, 157;
DC 5**
See Churchill, Chick
See also BRWS 4; CA 102; CANR 22, 46,
108; CBD; CWD; DFS 12, 16; DLB 13;
EWL 3; FW; MTCW 1; RGEL 2
Churchill, Charles 1731-1764 .... **LC 3**
See also DLB 109; RGEL 2
Churchill, Chick 1938-
See Churchill, Caryl
See also CD 5
Churchill, Sir Winston (Leonard Spencer)
1874-1965 .... **TCLC 113**
See also BRW 6; CA 97-100; CDBLB
1890-1914; DA3; DLB 100; DLBD 16;
LAIT 4; MTCW 1, 2
Chute, Carolyn 1947- .... **CLC 39**
See also CA 123
Ciardi, John (Anthony) 1916-1986 . **CLC 10,
40, 44, 129**
See also CA 5-8R; 118; CAAS 2; CANR 5,
33; CLR 19; CWRI 5; DAM POET; DLB
5; DLBY 1986; INT CANR-5; MAICYA
1, 2; MTCW 1, 2; RGAL 4; SAAS 26;
SATA 1, 65; SATA-Obit 46
Cibber, Colley 1671-1757 .... **LC 66**
See also DLB 84; RGEL 2
Cicero, Marcus Tullius
106B.C.-43B.C. .... **CMLC 3**
See also AW 1; CDWLB 1; DLB 211;
RGWL 2, 3
Cimino, Michael 1943- .... **CLC 16**
See also CA 105
Cioran, E(mil) M. 1911-1995 .... **CLC 64**
See also CA 25-28R; 149; CANR 91; DLB
220; EWL 3
Cisneros, Sandra 1954- .... **CLC 69, 118, 193;
HLC 1; PC 52; SSC 32, 72**
See also AAYA 9, 53; AMWS 7; CA 131;
CANR 64, 118; CWP; DA3; DAM MULT;
DLB 122, 152; EWL 3; EXPN; FW; HW
1, 2; LAIT 5; LATS 1:2; LLW 1; MAI-
CYA 2; MTCW 2; NFS 2; PFS 19; RGAL
4; RGSF 2; SSFS 3, 13; WLIT 1; YAW
Cixous, Helene 1937- .... **CLC 92**
See also CA 126; CANR 55, 123; CWW 2;
DLB 83, 242; EWL 3; FW; GLL 2;
MTCW 1, 2; TWA
Clair, Rene .... **CLC 20**
See Chomette, Rene Lucien
Clampitt, Amy 1920-1994 .... **CLC 32; PC 19**
See also AMWS 9; CA 110; 146; CANR
29, 79; DLB 105
Clancy, Thomas L., Jr. 1947-
See Clancy, Tom
See also CA 125; 131; CANR 62, 105;
DA3; INT CA-131; MTCW 1, 2
Clancy, Tom .... **CLC 45, 112**
See Clancy, Thomas L., Jr.
See also AAYA 9, 51; BEST 89:1, 90:1;
BPFB 1; BYA 10, 11; CANR 132; CMW
4; CPW; DAM NOV, POP; DLB 227
Clare, John 1793-1864 .. **NCLC 9, 86; PC 23**
See also DAB; DAM POET; DLB 55, 96;
RGEL 2
Clarin
See Alas (y Urena), Leopoldo (Enrique
Garcia)
Clark, Al C.
See Goines, Donald
Clark, (Robert) Brian 1932- .... **CLC 29**
See also CA 41-44R; CANR 67; CBD; CD
5
Clark, Curt
See Westlake, Donald E(dwin)

Clark, Eleanor 1913-1996 .... **CLC 5, 19**
See also CA 9-12R; 151; CANR 41; CN 7;
DLB 6
Clark, J. P.
See Clark Bekederemo, J(ohnson) P(epper)
See also CDWLB 3; DLB 117
Clark, John Pepper
See Clark Bekederemo, J(ohnson) P(epper)
See also AFW; CD 5; CP 7; RGEL 2
Clark, Kenneth (Mackenzie)
1903-1983 .... **TCLC 147**
See also CA 93-96; 109; CANR 36; MTCW
1, 2
Clark, M. R.
See Clark, Mavis Thorpe
Clark, Mavis Thorpe 1909-1999 ...... **CLC 12**
See also CA 57-60; CANR 8, 37, 107; CLR
30; CWRI 5; MAICYA 1, 2; SAAS 5;
SATA 8, 74
Clark, Walter Van Tilburg
1909-1971 .... **CLC 28**
See also CA 9-12R; 33-36R; CANR 63,
113; DLB 9, 206; LAIT 2; RGAL 4;
SATA 8
Clark Bekederemo, J(ohnson) P(epper)
1935- .... **BLC 1; CLC 38; DC 5**
See Clark, J. P.; Clark, John Pepper
See also BW 1; CA 65-68; CANR 16, 72;
DAM DRAM, MULT; DFS 13; EWL 3;
MTCW 1
Clarke, Arthur C(harles) 1917- .... **CLC 1, 4,
13, 18, 35, 136; SSC 3**
See also AAYA 4, 33; BPFB 1; BYA 13;
CA 1-4R; CANR 2, 28, 55, 74, 130; CN
7; CPW; DA3; DAM POP; DLB 261;
JRDA; LAIT 5; MAICYA 1, 2; MTCW 1,
2; SATA 13, 70, 115; SCFW; SFW 4;
SSFS 4, 18; YAW
Clarke, Austin 1896-1974 .... **CLC 6, 9**
See also CA 29-32; 49-52; CAP 2; DAM
POET; DLB 10, 20; EWL 3; RGEL 2
Clarke, Austin C(hesterfield) 1934- .. **BLC 1;
CLC 8, 53; SSC 45**
See also BW 1; CA 25-28R; CAAS 16;
CANR 14, 32, 68; CN 7; DAC; DAM
MULT; DLB 53, 125; DNFS 2; RGSF 2
Clarke, Gillian 1937- .... **CLC 61**
See also CA 106; CP 7; CWP; DLB 40
Clarke, Marcus (Andrew Hislop)
1846-1881 .... **NCLC 19**
See also DLB 230; RGEL 2; RGSF 2
Clarke, Shirley 1925-1997 .... **CLC 16**
See also CA 189
Clash, The
See Headon, (Nicky) Topper; Jones, Mick;
Simonon, Paul; Strummer, Joe
Claudel, Paul (Louis Charles Marie)
1868-1955 .... **TCLC 2, 10**
See also CA 104; 165; DLB 192, 258; EW
8; EWL 3; GFL 1789 to the Present;
RGWL 2, 3; TWA
Claudian 370(?)-404(?) .... **CMLC 46**
See also RGWL 2, 3
Claudius, Matthias 1740-1815 .... **NCLC 75**
See also DLB 97
Clavell, James (duMaresq)
1925-1994 .... **CLC 6, 25, 87**
See also BPFB 1; CA 25-28R; 146; CANR
26, 48; CPW; DA3; DAM NOV, POP;
MTCW 1, 2; NFS 10; RHW
Clayman, Gregory .... **CLC 65**
Cleaver, (Leroy) Eldridge
1935-1998 .... **BLC 1; CLC 30, 119**
See also BW 1, 3; CA 21-24R; 167; CANR
16, 75; DA3; DAM MULT; MTCW 2;
YAW
Cleese, John (Marwood) 1939- .... **CLC 21**
See Monty Python
See also CA 112; 116; CANR 35; MTCW 1

Cleishbotham, Jebediah
See Scott, Sir Walter
Cleland, John 1710-1789 .... **LC 2, 48**
See also DLB 39; RGEL 2
Clemens, Samuel Langhorne 1835-1910
See Twain, Mark
See also CA 104; 135; CDALB 1865-1917;
DA; DA3; DAB; DAC; DAM MST, NOV;
DLB 12, 23, 64, 74, 186, 189; JRDA;
LMFS 1; MAICYA 1; NCFS 4; NFS 1,
20; SATA 100; SSFS 16; YABC 2
Clement of Alexandria
150(?)-215(?) .... **CMLC 41**
Cleophil
See Congreve, William
Clerihew, E.
See Bentley, E(dmund) C(lerihew)
Clerk, N. W.
See Lewis, C(live) S(taples)
Cleveland, John 1613-1658 .... **LC 106**
See also DLB 126; RGEL 2
Cliff, Jimmy .... **CLC 21**
See Chambers, James
See also CA 193
Cliff, Michelle 1946- .... **BLCS; CLC 120**
See also BW 2; CA 116; CANR 39, 72; CD-
WLB 3; DLB 157; FW; GLL 2
Clifford, Lady Anne 1590-1676 .... **LC 76**
See also DLB 151
Clifton, (Thelma) Lucille 1936- .... **BLC 1;
CLC 19, 66, 162; PC 17**
See also AFAW 2; BW 2, 3; CA 49-52;
CANR 2, 24, 42, 76, 97; CLR 5; CP 7;
CSW; CWP; CWRI 5; DA3; DAM MULT,
POET; DLB 5, 41; EXPP; MAICYA 1, 2;
MTCW 1, 2; PFS 1, 14; SATA 20, 69,
128; WP
Clinton, Dirk
See Silverberg, Robert
Clough, Arthur Hugh 1819-1861 ... **NCLC 27**
See also BRW 5; DLB 32; RGEL 2
Clutha, Janet Paterson Frame 1924-2004
See Frame, Janet
See also CA 1-4R; 224; CANR 2, 36, 76;
MTCW 1, 2; SATA 119
Clyne, Terence
See Blatty, William Peter
Cobalt, Martin
See Mayne, William (James Carter)
Cobb, Irvin S(hrewsbury)
1876-1944 .... **TCLC 77**
See also CA 175; DLB 11, 25, 86
Cobbett, William 1763-1835 .... **NCLC 49**
See also DLB 43, 107, 158; RGEL 2
Coburn, D(onald) L(ee) 1938- .... **CLC 10**
See also CA 89-92
Cocteau, Jean (Maurice Eugene Clement)
1889-1963 ...... **CLC 1, 8, 15, 16, 43; DC
17; TCLC 119; WLC**
See also CA 25-28; CANR 40; CAP 2; DA;
DA3; DAB; DAC; DAM DRAM, MST,
NOV; DLB 65, 258; EW 10; EWL 3; GFL
1789 to the Present; MTCW 1, 2; RGWL
2, 3; TWA
Codrescu, Andrei 1946- .... **CLC 46, 121**
See also CA 33-36R; CAAS 19; CANR 13,
34, 53, 76, 125; DA3; DAM POET;
MTCW 2
Coe, Max
See Bourne, Randolph S(illiman)
Coe, Tucker
See Westlake, Donald E(dwin)
Coen, Ethan 1958- .... **CLC 108**
See also AAYA 54; CA 126; CANR 85
Coen, Joel 1955- .... **CLC 108**
See also AAYA 54; CA 126; CANR 119
The Coen Brothers
See Coen, Ethan; Coen, Joel

Cooper, Douglas 1960- .... **CLC 86**

Cooper, Henry St. John
See Creasey, John

Cooper, J(oan) California (?)- .... **CLC 56**
See also AAYA 12; BW 1; CA 125; CANR 55; DAM MULT; DLB 212

Cooper, James Fenimore
1789-1851 .... **NCLC 1, 27, 54**
See also AAYA 22; AMW; BPFB 1; CDALB 1640-1865; DA3; DLB 3, 183, 250, 254; LAIT 1; NFS 9; RGAL 4; SATA 19; TUS; WCH

Cooper, Susan Fenimore
1813-1894 .... **NCLC 129**
See also ANW; DLB 239, 254

Coover, Robert (Lowell) 1932- ...... **CLC 3, 7, 15, 32, 46, 87, 161; SSC 15**
See also AMWS 5; BPFB 1; CA 45-48; CANR 3, 37, 58, 115; CN 7; DAM NOV; DLB 2, 227; DLBY 1981; EWL 3; MTCW 1, 2; RGAL 4; RGSF 2

Copeland, Stewart (Armstrong)
1952- .... **CLC 26**

Copernicus, Nicolaus 1473-1543 .... **LC 45**

Coppard, A(lfred) E(dgar)
1878-1957 .... **SSC 21; TCLC 5**
See also BRWS 8; CA 114; 167; DLB 162; EWL 3; HGG; RGEL 2; RGSF 2; SUFW 1; YABC 1

Coppee, Francois 1842-1908 .... **TCLC 25**
See also CA 170; DLB 217

Coppola, Francis Ford 1939- ... **CLC 16, 126**
See also AAYA 39; CA 77-80; CANR 40, 78; DLB 44

Copway, George 1818-1869 .... **NNAL**
See also DAM MULT; DLB 175, 183

Corbiere, Tristan 1845-1875 .... **NCLC 43**
See also DLB 217; GFL 1789 to the Present

Corcoran, Barbara (Asenath)
1911- .... **CLC 17**
See also AAYA 14; CA 21-24R, 191; CAAE 191; CAAS 2; CANR 11, 28, 48; CLR 50; DLB 52; JRDA; MAICYA 2; MAIC-YAS 1; RHW; SAAS 20; SATA 3, 77; SATA-Essay 125

Cordelier, Maurice
See Giraudoux, Jean(-Hippolyte)

Corelli, Marie .... **TCLC 51**
See Mackay, Mary
See also DLB 34, 156; RGEL 2; SUFW 1

Corinna c. 225B.C.-c. 305B.C. ...... **CMLC 72**

Corman, Cid .... **CLC 9**
See Corman, Sidney
See also CAAS 2; DLB 5, 193

Corman, Sidney 1924-2004
See Corman, Cid
See also CA 85-88; 225; CANR 44; CP 7; DAM POET

Cormier, Robert (Edmund)
1925-2000 .... **CLC 12, 30**
See also AAYA 3, 19; BYA 1, 2, 6, 8, 9; CA 1-4R; CANR 5, 23, 76, 93; CDALB 1968-1988; CLR 12, 55; DA; DAB; DAC; DAM MST, NOV; DLB 52; EXPN; INT CANR-23; JRDA; LAIT 5; MAICYA 1, 2; MTCW 1, 2; NFS 2, 18; SATA 10, 45, 83; SATA-Obit 122; WYA; YAW

Corn, Alfred (DeWitt III) 1943- .... **CLC 33**
See also CA 179; CAAE 179; CAAS 25; CANR 44; CP 7; CSW; DLB 120, 282; DLBY 1980

Corneille, Pierre 1606-1684 ... **DC 21; LC 28**
See also DAB; DAM MST; DLB 268; EW 3; GFL Beginnings to 1789; RGWL 2, 3; TWA

Cornwell, David (John Moore)
1931- .... **CLC 9, 15**
See le Carre, John
See also CA 5-8R; CANR 13, 33, 59, 107, 132; DA3; DAM POP; MTCW 1, 2

Cornwell, Patricia (Daniels) 1956- . **CLC 155**
See also AAYA 16, 56; BPFB 1; CA 134; CANR 53, 131; CMW 4; CPW; CSW; DAM POP; DLB 306; MSW; MTCW 1

Corso, (Nunzio) Gregory 1930-2001 . **CLC 1, 11; PC 33**
See also AMWS 12; BG 2; CA 5-8R; 193; CANR 41, 76, 132; CP 7; DA3; DLB 5, 16, 237; LMFS 2; MTCW 1, 2; WP

Cortazar, Julio 1914-1984 ... **CLC 2, 3, 5, 10, 13, 15, 33, 34, 92; HLC 1; SSC 7, 76**
See also BPFB 1; CA 21-24R; CANR 12, 32, 81; CDWLB 3; DA3; DAM MULT, NOV; DLB 113; EWL 3; EXPS; HW 1, 2; LAW; MTCW 1, 2; RGSF 2; RGWL 2, 3; SSFS 3, 20; TWA; WLIT 1

Cortes, Hernan 1485-1547 .... **LC 31**

Corvinus, Jakob
See Raabe, Wilhelm (Karl)

Corwin, Cecil
See Kornbluth, C(yril) M.

Cosic, Dobrica 1921- .... **CLC 14**
See also CA 122; 138; CDWLB 4; CWW 2; DLB 181; EWL 3

Costain, Thomas B(ertram)
1885-1965 .... **CLC 30**
See also BYA 3; CA 5-8R; 25-28R; DLB 9; RHW

Costantini, Humberto 1924(?)-1987 . **CLC 49**
See also CA 131; 122; EWL 3; HW 1

Costello, Elvis 1954- .... **CLC 21**
See also CA 204

Costenoble, Philostene
See Ghelderode, Michel de

Cotes, Cecil V.
See Duncan, Sara Jeannette

Cotter, Joseph Seamon Sr.
1861-1949 .... **BLC 1; TCLC 28**
See also BW 1; CA 124; DAM MULT; DLB 50

Couch, Arthur Thomas Quiller
See Quiller-Couch, Sir Arthur (Thomas)

Coulton, James
See Hansen, Joseph

Couperus, Louis (Marie Anne)
1863-1923 .... **TCLC 15**
See also CA 115; EWL 3; RGWL 2, 3

Coupland, Douglas 1961- .... **CLC 85, 133**
See also AAYA 34; CA 142; CANR 57, 90, 130; CCA 1; CPW; DAC; DAM POP

Court, Wesli
See Turco, Lewis (Putnam)

Courtenay, Bryce 1933- .... **CLC 59**
See also CA 138; CPW

Courtney, Robert
See Ellison, Harlan (Jay)

Cousteau, Jacques-Yves 1910-1997 .. **CLC 30**
See also CA 65-68; 159; CANR 15, 67; MTCW 1; SATA 38, 98

Coventry, Francis 1725-1754 .... **LC 46**

Coverdale, Miles c. 1487-1569 .... **LC 77**
See also DLB 167

Cowan, Peter (Walkinshaw)
1914-2002 .... **SSC 28**
See also CA 21-24R; CANR 9, 25, 50, 83; CN 7; DLB 260; RGSF 2

Coward, Noel (Peirce) 1899-1973 . **CLC 1, 9, 29, 51**
See also AITN 1; BRWS 2; CA 17-18; 41-44R; CANR 35, 132; CAP 2; CDBLB 1914-1945; DA3; DAM DRAM; DFS 3, 6; DLB 10, 245; EWL 3; IDFW 3, 4; MTCW 1, 2; RGEL 2; TEA

Cowley, Abraham 1618-1667 .... **LC 43**
See also BRW 2; DLB 131, 151; PAB; RGEL 2

Cowley, Malcolm 1898-1989 .... **CLC 39**
See also AMWS 2; CA 5-8R; 128; CANR 3, 55; DLB 4, 48; DLBY 1981, 1989; EWL 3; MTCW 1, 2

Cowper, William 1731-1800 ..... **NCLC 8, 94; PC 40**
See also BRW 3; DA3; DAM POET; DLB 104, 109; RGEL 2

Cox, William Trevor 1928-
See Trevor, William
See also CA 9-12R; CANR 4, 37, 55, 76, 102; DAM NOV; INT CANR-37; MTCW 1, 2; TEA

Coyne, P. J.
See Masters, Hilary

Cozzens, James Gould 1903-1978 . **CLC 1, 4, 11, 92**
See also AMW; BPFB 1; CA 9-12R; 81-84; CANR 19; CDALB 1941-1968; DLB 9, 294; DLBD 2; DLBY 1984, 1997; EWL 3; MTCW 1, 2; RGAL 4

Crabbe, George 1754-1832 .... **NCLC 26, 121**
See also BRW 3; DLB 93; RGEL 2

Crace, Jim 1946- .... **CLC 157; SSC 61**
See also CA 128; 135; CANR 55, 70, 123; CN 7; DLB 231; INT CA-135

Craddock, Charles Egbert
See Murfree, Mary Noailles

Craig, A. A.
See Anderson, Poul (William)

Craik, Mrs.
See Craik, Dinah Maria (Mulock)
See also RGEL 2

Craik, Dinah Maria (Mulock)
1826-1887 .... **NCLC 38**
See also Craik, Mrs.; Mulock, Dinah Maria
See also DLB 35, 163; MAICYA 1, 2; SATA 34

Cram, Ralph Adams 1863-1942 ..... **TCLC 45**
See also CA 160

Cranch, Christopher Pearse
1813-1892 .... **NCLC 115**
See also DLB 1, 42, 243

Crane, (Harold) Hart 1899-1932 .... **PC 3; TCLC 2, 5, 80; WLC**
See also AMW; AMWR 2; CA 104; 127; CDALB 1917-1929; DA; DA3; DAB; DAC; DAM MST, POET; DLB 4, 48; EWL 3; MTCW 1, 2; RGAL 4; TUS

Crane, R(onald) S(almon)
1886-1967 .... **CLC 27**
See also CA 85-88; DLB 63

Crane, Stephen (Townley)
1871-1900 ...... **SSC 7, 56, 70; TCLC 11, 17, 32; WLC**
See also AAYA 21; AMW; AMWC 1; BPFB 1; BYA 3; CA 109; 140; CANR 84; CDALB 1865-1917; DA; DA3; DAB; DAC; DAM MST, NOV, POET; DLB 12, 54, 78; EXPN; EXPS; LAIT 2; LMFS 2; NFS 4, 20; PFS 9; RGAL 4; RGSF 2; SSFS 4; TUS; WYA; YABC 2

Cranmer, Thomas 1489-1556 .... **LC 95**
See also DLB 132, 213

Cranshaw, Stanley
See Fisher, Dorothy (Frances) Canfield

Crase, Douglas 1944- .... **CLC 58**
See also CA 106

Crashaw, Richard 1612(?)-1649 .... **LC 24**
See also BRW 2; DLB 126; PAB; RGEL 2

Cratinus c. 519B.C.-c. 422B.C. ..... **CMLC 54**
See also LMFS 1

Craven, Margaret 1901-1980 .... **CLC 17**
See also BYA 2; CA 103; CCA 1; DAC; LAIT 5

Dahlberg, Edward 1900-1977 .. **CLC 1, 7, 14**
See also CA 9-12R; 69-72; CANR 31, 62;
DLB 48; MTCW 1; RGAL 4
Daitch, Susan 1954- .... **CLC 103**
See also CA 161
Dale, Colin .... **TCLC 18**
See Lawrence, T(homas) E(dward)
Dale, George E.
See Asimov, Isaac
Dalton, Roque 1935-1975(?) ..... **HLCS 1; PC 36**
See also CA 176; DLB 283; HW 2
Daly, Elizabeth 1878-1967 .... **CLC 52**
See also CA 23-24; 25-28R; CANR 60;
CAP 2; CMW 4
Daly, Mary 1928- .... **CLC 173**
See also CA 25-28R; CANR 30, 62; FW;
GLL 1; MTCW 1
Daly, Maureen 1921- .... **CLC 17**
See also AAYA 5, 58; BYA 6; CANR 37,
83, 108; CLR 96; JRDA; MAICYA 1, 2;
SAAS 1; SATA 2, 129; WYA; YAW
Damas, Leon-Gontran 1912-1978 .... **CLC 84**
See also BW 1; CA 125; 73-76; EWL 3
Dana, Richard Henry Sr.
1787-1879 .... **NCLC 53**
Daniel, Samuel 1562(?)-1619 .... **LC 24**
See also DLB 62; RGEL 2
Daniels, Brett
See Adler, Renata
Dannay, Frederic 1905-1982 .... **CLC 11**
See Queen, Ellery
See also CA 1-4R; 107; CANR 1, 39; CMW
4; DAM POP; DLB 137; MTCW 1
D'Annunzio, Gabriele 1863-1938 ... **TCLC 6, 40**
See also CA 104; 155; EW 8; EWL 3;
RGWL 2, 3; TWA
Danois, N. le
See Gourmont, Remy(-Marie-Charles) de
Dante 1265-1321 .... **CMLC 3, 18, 39, 70; PC 21; WLCS**
See also DA; DA3; DAB; DAC; DAM
MST, POET; EFS 1; EW 1; LAIT 1;
RGWL 2, 3; TWA; WP
d'Antibes, Germain
See Simenon, Georges (Jacques Christian)
Danticat, Edwidge 1969- .... **CLC 94, 139**
See also AAYA 29; CA 152, 192; CAAE
192; CANR 73, 129; DNFS 1; EXPS;
LATS 1:2; MTCW 1; SSFS 1; YAW
Danvers, Dennis 1947- .... **CLC 70**
Danziger, Paula 1944-2004 .... **CLC 21**
See also AAYA 4, 36; BYA 6, 7, 14; CA
112; 115; CANR 37, 132; CLR 20; JRDA;
MAICYA 1, 2; SATA 36, 63, 102, 149;
SATA-Brief 30; WYA; YAW
Da Ponte, Lorenzo 1749-1838 .... **NCLC 50**
Dario, Ruben 1867-1916 .... **HLC 1; PC 15; TCLC 4**
See also CA 131; CANR 81; DAM MULT;
DLB 290; EWL 3; HW 1, 2; LAW;
MTCW 1, 2; RGWL 2, 3
Darley, George 1795-1846 .... **NCLC 2**
See also DLB 96; RGEL 2
Darrow, Clarence (Seward)
1857-1938 .... **TCLC 81**
See also CA 164; DLB 303
Darwin, Charles 1809-1882 .... **NCLC 57**
See also BRWS 7; DLB 57, 166; LATS 1:1;
RGEL 2; TEA; WLIT 4
Darwin, Erasmus 1731-1802 .... **NCLC 106**
See also DLB 93; RGEL 2
Daryush, Elizabeth 1887-1977 ...... **CLC 6, 19**
See also CA 49-52; CANR 3, 81; DLB 20
Das, Kamala 1934- .... **CLC 191; PC 43**
See also CA 101; CANR 27, 59; CP 7;
CWP; FW

Dasgupta, Surendranath
1887-1952 .... **TCLC 81**
See also CA 157
Dashwood, Edmee Elizabeth Monica de la Pasture 1890-1943
See Delafield, E. M.
See also CA 119; 154
da Silva, Antonio Jose
1705-1739 .... **NCLC 114**
Daudet, (Louis Marie) Alphonse
1840-1897 .... **NCLC 1**
See also DLB 123; GFL 1789 to the Present;
RGSF 2
d'Aulnoy, Marie-Catherine c.
1650-1705 .... **LC 100**
Daumal, Rene 1908-1944 .... **TCLC 14**
See also CA 114; EWL 3
Davenant, William 1606-1668 .... **LC 13**
See also DLB 58, 126; RGEL 2
Davenport, Guy (Mattison, Jr.)
1927- .... **CLC 6, 14, 38; SSC 16**
See also CA 33-36R; CANR 23, 73; CN 7;
CSW; DLB 130
David, Robert
See Nezval, Vitezslav
Davidson, Avram (James) 1923-1993
See Queen, Ellery
See also CA 101; 171; CANR 26; DLB 8;
FANT; SFW 4; SUFW 1, 2
Davidson, Donald (Grady)
1893-1968 .... **CLC 2, 13, 19**
See also CA 5-8R; 25-28R; CANR 4, 84;
DLB 45
Davidson, Hugh
See Hamilton, Edmond
Davidson, John 1857-1909 .... **TCLC 24**
See also CA 118; 217; DLB 19; RGEL 2
Davidson, Sara 1943- .... **CLC 9**
See also CA 81-84; CANR 44, 68; DLB
185
Davie, Donald (Alfred) 1922-1995 .... **CLC 5, 8, 10, 31; PC 29**
See also BRWS 6; CA 1-4R; 149; CAAS 3;
CANR 1, 44; CP 7; DLB 27; MTCW 1;
RGEL 2
Davie, Elspeth 1919-1995 .... **SSC 52**
See also CA 120; 126; 150; DLB 139
Davies, Ray(mond Douglas) 1944- ... **CLC 21**
See also CA 116; 146; CANR 92
Davies, Rhys 1901-1978 .... **CLC 23**
See also CA 9-12R; 81-84; CANR 4; DLB
139, 191
Davies, (William) Robertson
1913-1995 .... **CLC 2, 7, 13, 25, 42, 75, 91; WLC**
See Marchbanks, Samuel
See also BEST 89:2; BPFB 1; CA 33-36R;
150; CANR 17, 42, 103; CN 7; CPW;
DA; DA3; DAB; DAC; DAM MST, NOV,
POP; DLB 68; EWL 3; HGG; INT CANR-
17; MTCW 1, 2; RGEL 2; TWA
Davies, Sir John 1569-1626 .... **LC 85**
See also DLB 172
Davies, Walter C.
See Kornbluth, C(yril) M.
Davies, William Henry 1871-1940 ... **TCLC 5**
See also CA 104; 179; DLB 19, 174; EWL
3; RGEL 2
Da Vinci, Leonardo 1452-1519 ..... **LC 12, 57, 60**
See also AAYA 40
Davis, Angela (Yvonne) 1944- .... **CLC 77**
See also BW 2, 3; CA 57-60; CANR 10,
81; CSW; DA3; DAM MULT; FW
Davis, B. Lynch
See Bioy Casares, Adolfo; Borges, Jorge
Luis

Davis, Frank Marshall 1905-1987 ...... **BLC 1**
See also BW 2, 3; CA 125; 123; CANR 42,
80; DAM MULT; DLB 51
Davis, Gordon
See Hunt, E(verette) Howard, (Jr.)
Davis, H(arold) L(enoir) 1896-1960 . **CLC 49**
See also ANW; CA 178; 89-92; DLB 9,
206; SATA 114
Davis, Rebecca (Blaine) Harding
1831-1910 .... **SSC 38; TCLC 6**
See also CA 104; 179; DLB 74, 239; FW;
NFS 14; RGAL 4; TUS
Davis, Richard Harding
1864-1916 .... **TCLC 24**
See also CA 114; 179; DLB 12, 23, 78, 79,
189; DLBD 13; RGAL 4
Davison, Frank Dalby 1893-1970 ..... **CLC 15**
See also CA 217; 116; DLB 260
Davison, Lawrence H.
See Lawrence, D(avid) H(erbert Richards)
Davison, Peter (Hubert) 1928- .... **CLC 28**
See also CA 9-12R; CAAS 4; CANR 3, 43,
84; CP 7; DLB 5
Davys, Mary 1674-1732 .... **LC 1, 46**
See also DLB 39
Dawson, (Guy) Fielding (Lewis)
1930-2002 .... **CLC 6**
See also CA 85-88; 202; CANR 108; DLB
130; DLBY 2002
Dawson, Peter
See Faust, Frederick (Schiller)
See also TCWW 2, 2
Day, Clarence (Shepard, Jr.)
1874-1935 .... **TCLC 25**
See also CA 108; 199; DLB 11
Day, John 1574(?)-1640(?) .... **LC 70**
See also DLB 62, 170; RGEL 2
Day, Thomas 1748-1789 .... **LC 1**
See also DLB 39; YABC 1
Day Lewis, C(ecil) 1904-1972 . **CLC 1, 6, 10; PC 11**
See Blake, Nicholas
See also BRWS 3; CA 13-16; 33-36R;
CANR 34; CAP 1; CWRI 5; DAM POET;
DLB 15, 20; EWL 3; MTCW 1, 2; RGEL
2
Dazai Osamu .... **SSC 41; TCLC 11**
See Tsushima, Shuji
See also CA 164; DLB 182; EWL 3; MJW;
RGSF 2; RGWL 2, 3; TWA
de Andrade, Carlos Drummond
See Drummond de Andrade, Carlos
de Andrade, Mario 1892-1945
See Andrade, Mario de
See also CA 178; HW 2
Deane, Norman
See Creasey, John
Deane, Seamus (Francis) 1940- ...... **CLC 122**
See also CA 118; CANR 42
de Beauvoir, Simone (Lucie Ernestine Marie Bertrand)
See Beauvoir, Simone (Lucie Ernestine
Marie Bertrand) de
de Beer, P.
See Bosman, Herman Charles
de Brissac, Malcolm
See Dickinson, Peter (Malcolm)
de Campos, Alvaro
See Pessoa, Fernando (Antonio Nogueira)
de Chardin, Pierre Teilhard
See Teilhard de Chardin, (Marie Joseph)
Pierre
Dee, John 1527-1608 .... **LC 20**
See also DLB 136, 213
Deer, Sandra 1940- .... **CLC 45**
See also CA 186
De Ferrari, Gabriella 1941- .... **CLC 65**
See also CA 146

de Filippo, Eduardo 1900-1984 ... **TCLC 127**
See also CA 132; 114; EWL 3; MTCW 1;
RGWL 2, 3

Defoe, Daniel 1660(?)-1731 .... **LC 1, 42, 108;
WLC**
See also AAYA 27; BRW 3; BRWR 1; BYA
4; CDBLB 1660-1789; CLR 61; DA;
DA3; DAB; DAC; DAM MST, NOV;
DLB 39, 95, 101; JRDA; LAIT 1; LMFS
1; MAICYA 1, 2; NFS 9, 13; RGEL 2;
SATA 22; TEA; WCH; WLIT 3

de Gourmont, Remy(-Marie-Charles)
See Gourmont, Remy(-Marie-Charles) de

de Gournay, Marie le Jars
1566-1645 .... **LC 98**
See also FW

de Hartog, Jan 1914-2002 .... **CLC 19**
See also CA 1-4R; 210; CANR 1; DFS 12

de Hostos, E. M.
See Hostos (y Bonilla), Eugenio Maria de

de Hostos, Eugenio M.
See Hostos (y Bonilla), Eugenio Maria de

Deighton, Len .... **CLC 4, 7, 22, 46**
See Deighton, Leonard Cyril
See also AAYA 6; BEST 89:2; BPFB 1; CD-
BLB 1960 to Present; CMW 4; CN 7;
CPW; DLB 87

Deighton, Leonard Cyril 1929-
See Deighton, Len
See also AAYA 57; CA 9-12R; CANR 19,
33, 68; DA3; DAM NOV, POP; MTCW
1, 2

Dekker, Thomas 1572(?)-1632 ..... **DC 12; LC
22**
See also CDBLB Before 1660; DAM
DRAM; DLB 62, 172; LMFS 1; RGEL 2

de Laclos, Pierre Ambroise Franois
See Laclos, Pierre Ambroise Francois

Delacroix, (Ferdinand-Victor-)Eugene
1798-1863 .... **NCLC 133**
See also EW 5

Delafield, E. M. .... **TCLC 61**
See Dashwood, Edmee Elizabeth Monica
de la Pasture
See also DLB 34; RHW

de la Mare, Walter (John)
1873-1956 . **SSC 14; TCLC 4, 53; WLC**
See also CA 163; CDBLB 1914-1945; CLR
23; CWRI 5; DA3; DAB; DAC; DAM
MST, POET; DLB 19, 153, 162, 255, 284;
EWL 3; EXPP; HGG; MAICYA 1, 2;
MTCW 1; RGEL 2; RGSF 2; SATA 16;
SUFW 1; TEA; WCH

de Lamartine, Alphonse (Marie Louis Prat)
See Lamartine, Alphonse (Marie Louis Prat)
de

Delaney, Franey
See O'Hara, John (Henry)

Delaney, Shelagh 1939- .... **CLC 29**
See also CA 17-20R; CANR 30, 67; CBD;
CD 5; CDBLB 1960 to Present; CWD;
DAM DRAM; DFS 7; DLB 13; MTCW 1

Delany, Martin Robison
1812-1885 .... **NCLC 93**
See also DLB 50; RGAL 4

Delany, Mary (Granville Pendarves)
1700-1788 .... **LC 12**

Delany, Samuel R(ay), Jr. 1942- .... **BLC 1;
CLC 8, 14, 38, 141**
See also AAYA 24; AFAW 2; BPFB 1; BW
2, 3; CA 81-84; CANR 27, 43, 115, 116;
CN 7; DAM MULT; DLB 8, 33; FANT;
MTCW 1, 2; RGAL 4; SATA 92; SCFW
4; SUFW 2

De la Ramee, Marie Louise (Ouida)
1839-1908
See Ouida
See also CA 204; SATA 20

de la Roche, Mazo 1879-1961 .... **CLC 14**
See also CA 85-88; CANR 30; DLB 68;
RGEL 2; RHW; SATA 64

De La Salle, Innocent
See Hartmann, Sadakichi

de Laureamont, Comte
See Lautreamont

Delbanco, Nicholas (Franklin)
1942- .... **CLC 6, 13, 167**
See also CA 17-20R, 189; CAAE 189;
CAAS 2; CANR 29, 55, 116; DLB 6, 234

del Castillo, Michel 1933- .... **CLC 38**
See also CA 109; CANR 77

Deledda, Grazia (Cosima)
1875(?)-1936 .... **TCLC 23**
See also CA 123; 205; DLB 264; EWL 3;
RGWL 2, 3

Deleuze, Gilles 1925-1995 .... **TCLC 116**
See also DLB 296

Delgado, Abelardo (Lalo) B(arrientos)
1930-2004 .... **HLC 1**
See also CA 131; CAAS 15; CANR 90;
DAM MST, MULT; DLB 82; HW 1, 2

Delibes, Miguel .... **CLC 8, 18**
See Delibes Setien, Miguel
See also EWL 3

Delibes Setien, Miguel 1920-
See Delibes, Miguel
See also CA 45-48; CANR 1, 32; CWW 2;
HW 1; MTCW 1

DeLillo, Don 1936- ..... **CLC 8, 10, 13, 27, 39,
54, 76, 143**
See also AMWC 2; AMWS 6; BEST 89:1;
BPFB 1; CA 81-84; CANR 21, 76, 92,
133; CN 7; CPW; DA3; DAM NOV, POP;
DLB 6, 173; EWL 3; MTCW 1, 2; RGAL
4; TUS

de Lisser, H. G.
See De Lisser, H(erbert) G(eorge)
See also DLB 117

De Lisser, H(erbert) G(eorge)
1878-1944 .... **TCLC 12**
See de Lisser, H. G.
See also BW 2; CA 109; 152

Deloire, Pierre
See Peguy, Charles (Pierre)

Deloney, Thomas 1543(?)-1600 .... **LC 41**
See also DLB 167; RGEL 2

Deloria, Ella (Cara) 1889-1971(?) ..... **NNAL**
See also CA 152; DAM MULT; DLB 175

Deloria, Vine (Victor), Jr. 1933- ...... **CLC 21,
122; NNAL**
See also CA 53-56; CANR 5, 20, 48, 98;
DAM MULT; DLB 175; MTCW 1; SATA
21

del Valle-Inclan, Ramon (Maria)
See Valle-Inclan, Ramon (Maria) del

Del Vecchio, John M(ichael) 1947- .. **CLC 29**
See also CA 110; DLBD 9

de Man, Paul (Adolph Michel)
1919-1983 .... **CLC 55**
See also CA 128; 111; CANR 61; DLB 67;
MTCW 1, 2

DeMarinis, Rick 1934- .... **CLC 54**
See also CA 57-60, 184; CAAE 184; CAAS
24; CANR 9, 25, 50; DLB 218

de Maupassant, (Henri Rene Albert) Guy
See Maupassant, (Henri Rene Albert) Guy
de

Dembry, R. Emmet
See Murfree, Mary Noailles

Demby, William 1922- .... **BLC 1; CLC 53**
See also BW 1, 3; CA 81-84; CANR 81;
DAM MULT; DLB 33

de Menton, Francisco
See Chin, Frank (Chew, Jr.)

Demetrius of Phalerum c.
307B.C.- .... **CMLC 34**

Demijohn, Thom
See Disch, Thomas M(ichael)

De Mille, James 1833-1880 .... **NCLC 123**
See also DLB 99, 251

Deming, Richard 1915-1983
See Queen, Ellery
See also CA 9-12R; CANR 3, 94; SATA 24

Democritus c. 460B.C.-c. 370B.C. . **CMLC 47**

de Montaigne, Michel (Eyquem)
See Montaigne, Michel (Eyquem) de

de Montherlant, Henry (Milon)
See Montherlant, Henry (Milon) de

Demosthenes 384B.C.-322B.C. ...... **CMLC 13**
See also AW 1; DLB 176; RGWL 2, 3

de Musset, (Louis Charles) Alfred
See Musset, (Louis Charles) Alfred de

de Natale, Francine
See Malzberg, Barry N(athaniel)

de Navarre, Marguerite 1492-1549 ..... **LC 61**
See Marguerite d'Angouleme; Marguerite
de Navarre

Denby, Edwin (Orr) 1903-1983 .... **CLC 48**
See also CA 138; 110

de Nerval, Gerard
See Nerval, Gerard de

Denham, John 1615-1669 .... **LC 73**
See also DLB 58, 126; RGEL 2

Denis, Julio
See Cortazar, Julio

Denmark, Harrison
See Zelazny, Roger (Joseph)

Dennis, John 1658-1734 .... **LC 11**
See also DLB 101; RGEL 2

Dennis, Nigel (Forbes) 1912-1989 ...... **CLC 8**
See also CA 25-28R; 129; DLB 13, 15, 233;
EWL 3; MTCW 1

Dent, Lester 1904-1959 .... **TCLC 72**
See also CA 112; 161; CMW 4; DLB 306;
SFW 4

De Palma, Brian (Russell) 1940- ...... **CLC 20**
See also CA 109

De Quincey, Thomas 1785-1859 ..... **NCLC 4,
87**
See also BRW 4; CDBLB 1789-1832; DLB
110, 144; RGEL 2

Deren, Eleanora 1908(?)-1961
See Deren, Maya
See also CA 192; 111

Deren, Maya .... **CLC 16, 102**
See Deren, Eleanora

Derleth, August (William)
1909-1971 .... **CLC 31**
See also BPFB 1; BYA 9, 10; CA 1-4R; 29-
32R; CANR 4; CMW 4; DLB 9; DLBD
17; HGG; SATA 5; SUFW 1

Der Nister 1884-1950 .... **TCLC 56**
See Nister, Der

de Routisie, Albert
See Aragon, Louis

Derrida, Jacques 1930- .... **CLC 24, 87**
See also CA 124; 127; CANR 76, 98, 133;
DLB 242; EWL 3; LMFS 2; MTCW 1;
TWA

Derry Down Derry
See Lear, Edward

Dersonnes, Jacques
See Simenon, Georges (Jacques Christian)

Desai, Anita 1937- .... **CLC 19, 37, 97, 175**
See also BRWS 5; CA 81-84; CANR 33,
53, 95, 133; CN 7; CWRI 5; DA3; DAB;
DAM NOV; DLB 271; DNFS 2; EWL 3;
FW; MTCW 1, 2; SATA 63, 126

Desai, Kiran 1971- .... **CLC 119**
See also BYA 16; CA 171; CANR 127

de Saint-Luc, Jean
See Glassco, John

de Saint Roman, Arnaud
See Aragon, Louis

Donaldson, Stephen R(eeder)
1947- .... **CLC 46, 138**
See also AAYA 36; BPFB 1; CA 89-92;
CANR 13, 55, 99; CPW; DAM POP;
FANT; INT CANR-13; SATA 121; SFW
4; SUFW 1, 2

Donleavy, J(ames) P(atrick) 1926- .... **CLC 1,
4, 6, 10, 45**
See also AITN 2; BPFB 1; CA 9-12R;
CANR 24, 49, 62, 80, 124; CBD; CD 5;
CN 7; DLB 6, 173; INT CANR-24;
MTCW 1, 2; RGAL 4

Donnadieu, Marguerite
See Duras, Marguerite

Donne, John 1572-1631 ... **LC 10, 24, 91; PC
1, 43; WLC**
See also BRW 1; BRWC 1; BRWR 2; CD-
BLB Before 1660; DA; DAB; DAC;
DAM MST, POET; DLB 121, 151; EXPP;
PAB; PFS 2, 11; RGEL 3; TEA; WLIT 3;
WP

Donnell, David 1939(?)- .... **CLC 34**
See also CA 197

Donoghue, P. S.
See Hunt, E(verette) Howard, (Jr.)

Donoso (Yanez), Jose 1924-1996 ... **CLC 4, 8,
11, 32, 99; HLC 1; SSC 34; TCLC 133**
See also CA 81-84; 155; CANR 32, 73; CD-
WLB 3; CWW 2; DAM MULT; DLB 113;
EWL 3; HW 1, 2; LAW; LAWS 1; MTCW
1, 2; RGSF 2; WLIT 1

Donovan, John 1928-1992 .... **CLC 35**
See also AAYA 20; CA 97-100; 137; CLR
3; MAICYA 1, 2; SATA 72; SATA-Brief
29; YAW

Don Roberto
See Cunninghame Graham, Robert
(Gallnigad) Bontine

Doolittle, Hilda 1886-1961 . **CLC 3, 8, 14, 31,
34, 73; PC 5; WLC**
See H. D.
See also AMWS 1; CA 97-100; CANR 35,
131; DA; DAC; DAM MST, POET; DLB
4, 45; EWL 3; FW; GLL 1; LMFS 2;
MAWW; MTCW 1, 2; PFS 6; RGAL 4

Doppo, Kunikida .... **TCLC 99**
See Kunikida Doppo

Dorfman, Ariel 1942- .... **CLC 48, 77, 189;
HLC 1**
See also CA 124; 130; CANR 67, 70; CWW
2; DAM MULT; DFS 4; EWL 3; HW 1,
2; INT CA-130; WLIT 1

Dorn, Edward (Merton)
1929-1999 .... **CLC 10, 18**
See also CA 93-96; 187; CANR 42, 79; CP
7; DLB 5; INT CA-93-96; WP

Dor-Ner, Zvi .... **CLC 70**

Dorris, Michael (Anthony)
1945-1997 .... **CLC 109; NNAL**
See also AAYA 20; BEST 90:1; BYA 12;
CA 102; 157; CANR 19, 46, 75; CLR 58;
DA3; DAM MULT, NOV; DLB 175;
LAIT 5; MTCW 2; NFS 3; RGAL 4;
SATA 75; SATA-Obit 94; TCWW 2; YAW

Dorris, Michael A.
See Dorris, Michael (Anthony)

Dorsan, Luc
See Simenon, Georges (Jacques Christian)

Dorsange, Jean
See Simenon, Georges (Jacques Christian)

Dorset
See Sackville, Thomas

Dos Passos, John (Roderigo)
1896-1970 ... **CLC 1, 4, 8, 11, 15, 25, 34,
82; WLC**
See also AMW; BPFB 1; CA 1-4R; 29-32R;
CANR 3; CDALB 1929-1941; DA; DA3;
DAB; DAC; DAM MST, NOV; DLB 4,
9, 274; DLBD 1, 15; DLBY 1996; EWL
3; MTCW 1, 2; NFS 14; RGAL 4; TUS

Dossage, Jean
See Simenon, Georges (Jacques Christian)

Dostoevsky, Fedor Mikhailovich
1821-1881 .. **NCLC 2, 7, 21, 33, 43, 119;
SSC 2, 33, 44; WLC**
See Dostoevsky, Fyodor
See also AAYA 40; DA; DA3; DAB; DAC;
DAM MST, NOV; EW 7; EXPN; NFS 3,
8; RGSF 2; RGWL 2, 3; SSFS 8; TWA

Dostoevsky, Fyodor
See Dostoevsky, Fedor Mikhailovich
See also DLB 238; LATS 1:1; LMFS 1, 2

Doty, M. R.
See Doty, Mark (Alan)

Doty, Mark
See Doty, Mark (Alan)

Doty, Mark (Alan) 1953(?)- .... **CLC 176; PC
53**
See also AMWS 11; CA 161, 183; CAAE
183; CANR 110

Doty, Mark A.
See Doty, Mark (Alan)

Doughty, Charles M(ontagu)
1843-1926 .... **TCLC 27**
See also CA 115; 178; DLB 19, 57, 174

Douglas, Ellen .... **CLC 73**
See Haxton, Josephine Ayres; Williamson,
Ellen Douglas
See also CN 7; CSW; DLB 292

Douglas, Gavin 1475(?)-1522 .... **LC 20**
See also DLB 132; RGEL 2

Douglas, George
See Brown, George Douglas
See also RGEL 2

Douglas, Keith (Castellain)
1920-1944 .... **TCLC 40**
See also BRW 7; CA 160; DLB 27; EWL
3; PAB; RGEL 2

Douglas, Leonard
See Bradbury, Ray (Douglas)

Douglas, Michael
See Crichton, (John) Michael

Douglas, (George) Norman
1868-1952 .... **TCLC 68**
See also BRW 6; CA 119; 157; DLB 34,
195; RGEL 2

Douglas, William
See Brown, George Douglas

Douglass, Frederick 1817(?)-1895 ..... **BLC 1;
NCLC 7, 55, 141; WLC**
See also AAYA 48; AFAW 1, 2; AMWC 1;
AMWS 3; CDALB 1640-1865; DA; DA3;
DAC; DAM MST, MULT; DLB 1, 43, 50,
79, 243; FW; LAIT 2; NCFS 2; RGAL 4;
SATA 29

Dourado, (Waldomiro Freitas) Autran
1926- .... **CLC 23, 60**
See also CA 25-28R; 179; CANR 34, 81;
DLB 145; HW 2

Dourado, Waldomiro Autran
See Dourado, (Waldomiro Freitas) Autran
See also CA 179

Dove, Rita (Frances) 1952- . **BLCS; CLC 50,
81; PC 6**
See also AAYA 46; AMWS 4; BW 2; CA
109; CAAS 19; CANR 27, 42, 68, 76, 97,
132; CDALBS; CP 7; CSW; CWP; DA3;
DAM MULT, POET; DLB 120; EWL 3;
EXPP; MTCW 1; PFS 1, 15; RGAL 4

Doveglion
See Villa, Jose Garcia

Dowell, Coleman 1925-1985 .... **CLC 60**
See also CA 25-28R; 117; CANR 10; DLB
130; GLL 2

Dowson, Ernest (Christopher)
1867-1900 .... **TCLC 4**
See also CA 105; 150; DLB 19, 135; RGEL
2

Doyle, A. Conan
See Doyle, Sir Arthur Conan

Doyle, Sir Arthur Conan
1859-1930 .... **SSC 12; TCLC 7; WLC**
See Conan Doyle, Arthur
See also AAYA 14; BRWS 2; CA 104; 122;
CANR 131; CDBLB 1890-1914; CMW
4; DA; DA3; DAB; DAC; DAM MST,
NOV; DLB 18, 70, 156, 178; EXPS;
HGG; LAIT 2; MSW; MTCW 1, 2; RGEL
2; RGSF 2; RHW; SATA 24; SCFW 2;
SFW 4; SSFS 2; TEA; WCH; WLIT 4;
WYA; YAW

Doyle, Conan
See Doyle, Sir Arthur Conan

Doyle, John
See Graves, Robert (von Ranke)

Doyle, Roddy 1958(?)- .... **CLC 81, 178**
See also AAYA 14; BRWS 5; CA 143;
CANR 73, 128; CN 7; DA3; DLB 194

Doyle, Sir A. Conan
See Doyle, Sir Arthur Conan

Dr. A
See Asimov, Isaac; Silverstein, Alvin; Silverstein, Virginia B(arbara Opshelor)

Drabble, Margaret 1939- ...... **CLC 2, 3, 5, 8,
10, 22, 53, 129**
See also BRWS 4; CA 13-16R; CANR 18,
35, 63, 112, 131; CDBLB 1960 to Present;
CN 7; CPW; DA3; DAB; DAC; DAM
MST, NOV, POP; DLB 14, 155, 231;
EWL 3; FW; MTCW 1, 2; RGEL 2; SATA
48; TEA

Drakulic, Slavenka 1949- .... **CLC 173**
See also CA 144; CANR 92

Drakulic-Ilic, Slavenka
See Drakulic, Slavenka

Drapier, M. B.
See Swift, Jonathan

Drayham, James
See Mencken, H(enry) L(ouis)

Drayton, Michael 1563-1631 .... **LC 8**
See also DAM POET; DLB 121; RGEL 2

Dreadstone, Carl
See Campbell, (John) Ramsey

Dreiser, Theodore (Herman Albert)
1871-1945 .... **SSC 30; TCLC 10, 18, 35,
83; WLC**
See also AMW; AMWC 2; AMWR 2; BYA
15, 16; CA 106; 132; CDALB 1865-1917;
DA; DA3; DAC; DAM MST, NOV; DLB
9, 12, 102, 137; DLBD 1; EWL 3; LAIT
2; LMFS 2; MTCW 1, 2; NFS 8, 17;
RGAL 4; TUS

Drexler, Rosalyn 1926- .... **CLC 2, 6**
See also CA 81-84; CAD; CANR 68, 124;
CD 5; CWD

Dreyer, Carl Theodor 1889-1968 ...... **CLC 16**
See also CA 116

Drieu la Rochelle, Pierre(-Eugene)
1893-1945 .... **TCLC 21**
See also CA 117; DLB 72; EWL 3; GFL
1789 to the Present

Drinkwater, John 1882-1937 .... **TCLC 57**
See also CA 109; 149; DLB 10, 19, 149;
RGEL 2

Drop Shot
See Cable, George Washington

Droste-Hulshoff, Annette Freiin von
1797-1848 .... **NCLC 3, 133**
See also CDWLB 2; DLB 133; RGSF 2;
RGWL 2, 3

Drummond, Walter
See Silverberg, Robert

Drummond, William Henry
1854-1907 .... **TCLC 25**
See also CA 160; DLB 92

Eagleton, Terry
See Eagleton, Terence (Francis)
Early, Jack
See Scoppettone, Sandra
See also GLL 1
East, Michael
See West, Morris L(anglo)
Eastaway, Edward
See Thomas, (Philip) Edward
Eastlake, William (Derry)
1917-1997 .... **CLC 8**
See also CA 5-8R; 158; CAAS 1; CANR 5,
63; CN 7; DLB 6, 206; INT CANR-5;
TCWW 2
Eastman, Charles A(lexander)
1858-1939 .... **NNAL; TCLC 55**
See also CA 179; CANR 91; DAM MULT;
DLB 175; YABC 1
Eaton, Edith Maude 1865-1914 .... **AAL**
See Far, Sui Sin
See also CA 154; DLB 221; FW
Eaton, (Lillie) Winnifred 1875-1954 .... **AAL**
See also CA 217; DLB 221; RGAL 4
Eberhart, Richard (Ghormley)
1904- .... **CLC 3, 11, 19, 56**
See also AMW; CA 1-4R; CANR 2, 125;
CDALB 1941-1968; CP 7; DAM POET;
DLB 48; MTCW 1; RGAL 4
Eberstadt, Fernanda 1960- .... **CLC 39**
See also CA 136; CANR 69, 128
**Echegaray (y Eizaguirre), Jose (Maria
Waldo)** 1832-1916 .... **HLCS 1; TCLC 4**
See also CA 104; CANR 32; EWL 3; HW
1; MTCW 1
Echeverria, (Jose) Esteban (Antonino)
1805-1851 .... **NCLC 18**
See also LAW
Echo
See Proust, (Valentin-Louis-George-Eugene)
Marcel
Eckert, Allan W. 1931- .... **CLC 17**
See also AAYA 18; BYA 2; CA 13-16R;
CANR 14, 45; INT CANR-14; MAICYA
2; MAICYAS 1; SAAS 21; SATA 29, 91;
SATA-Brief 27
Eckhart, Meister 1260(?)-1327(?) ... **CMLC 9**
See also DLB 115; LMFS 1
Eckmar, F. R.
See de Hartog, Jan
Eco, Umberto 1932- .... **CLC 28, 60, 142**
See also BEST 90:1; BPFB 1; CA 77-80;
CANR 12, 33, 55, 110, 131; CPW; CWW
2; DA3; DAM NOV, POP; DLB 196, 242;
EWL 3; MSW; MTCW 1, 2; RGWL 3
Eddison, E(ric) R(ucker)
1882-1945 .... **TCLC 15**
See also CA 109; 156; DLB 255; FANT;
SFW 4; SUFW 1
Eddy, Mary (Ann Morse) Baker
1821-1910 .... **TCLC 71**
See also CA 113; 174
Edel, (Joseph) Leon 1907-1997 .. **CLC 29, 34**
See also CA 1-4R; 161; CANR 1, 22, 112;
DLB 103; INT CANR-22
Eden, Emily 1797-1869 .... **NCLC 10**
Edgar, David 1948- .... **CLC 42**
See also CA 57-60; CANR 12, 61, 112;
CBD; CD 5; DAM DRAM; DFS 15; DLB
13, 233; MTCW 1
Edgerton, Clyde (Carlyle) 1944- ...... **CLC 39**
See also AAYA 17; CA 118; 134; CANR
64, 125; CSW; DLB 278; INT CA-134;
YAW
Edgeworth, Maria 1768-1849 .... **NCLC 1, 51**
See also BRWS 3; DLB 116, 159, 163; FW;
RGEL 2; SATA 21; TEA; WLIT 3
Edmonds, Paul
See Kuttner, Henry

Edmonds, Walter D(umaux)
1903-1998 .... **CLC 35**
See also BYA 2; CA 5-8R; CANR 2; CWRI
5; DLB 9; LAIT 1; MAICYA 1, 2; RHW;
SAAS 4; SATA 1, 27; SATA-Obit 99
Edmondson, Wallace
See Ellison, Harlan (Jay)
Edson, Margaret 1961- .... **DC 24**
See also CA 190; DFS 13; DLB 266
Edson, Russell 1935- .... **CLC 13**
See also CA 33-36R; CANR 115; DLB 244;
WP
Edwards, Bronwen Elizabeth
See Rose, Wendy
Edwards, G(erald) B(asil)
1899-1976 .... **CLC 25**
See also CA 201; 110
Edwards, Gus 1939- .... **CLC 43**
See also CA 108; INT CA-108
Edwards, Jonathan 1703-1758 ...... **LC 7, 54**
See also AMW; DA; DAC; DAM MST;
DLB 24, 270; RGAL 4; TUS
Edwards, Sarah Pierpont 1710-1758 .. **LC 87**
See also DLB 200
Efron, Marina Ivanovna Tsvetaeva
See Tsvetaeva (Efron), Marina (Ivanovna)
Egeria fl. 4th cent. - .... **CMLC 70**
Egoyan, Atom 1960- .... **CLC 151**
See also CA 157
Ehle, John (Marsden, Jr.) 1925- ...... **CLC 27**
See also CA 9-12R; CSW
Ehrenbourg, Ilya (Grigoryevich)
See Ehrenburg, Ilya (Grigoryevich)
Ehrenburg, Ilya (Grigoryevich)
1891-1967 .... **CLC 18, 34, 62**
See Erenburg, Il'ia Grigor'evich
See also CA 102; 25-28R; EWL 3
Ehrenburg, Ilyo (Grigoryevich)
See Ehrenburg, Ilya (Grigoryevich)
Ehrenreich, Barbara 1941- .... **CLC 110**
See also BEST 90:4; CA 73-76; CANR 16,
37, 62, 117; DLB 246; FW; MTCW 1, 2
Eich, Gunter
See Eich, Gunter
See also RGWL 2, 3
Eich, Gunter 1907-1972 .... **CLC 15**
See Eich, Gunter
See also CA 111; 93-96; DLB 69, 124;
EWL 3
Eichendorff, Joseph 1788-1857 .... **NCLC 8**
See also DLB 90; RGWL 2, 3
Eigner, Larry .... **CLC 9**
See Eigner, Laurence (Joel)
See also CAAS 23; DLB 5; WP
Eigner, Laurence (Joel) 1927-1996
See Eigner, Larry
See also CA 9-12R; 151; CANR 6, 84; CP
7; DLB 193
Eilhart von Oberge c. 1140-c.
1195 .... **CMLC 67**
See also DLB 148
Einhard c. 770-840 .... **CMLC 50**
See also DLB 148
Einstein, Albert 1879-1955 .... **TCLC 65**
See also CA 121; 133; MTCW 1, 2
Eiseley, Loren
See Eiseley, Loren Corey
See also DLB 275
Eiseley, Loren Corey 1907-1977 .... **CLC 7**
See Eiseley, Loren
See also AAYA 5; ANW; CA 1-4R; 73-76;
CANR 6; DLBD 17
Eisenstadt, Jill 1963- .... **CLC 50**
See also CA 140
Eisenstein, Sergei (Mikhailovich)
1898-1948 .... **TCLC 57**
See also CA 114; 149

Eisner, Simon
See Kornbluth, C(yril) M.
Ekeloef, (Bengt) Gunnar
1907-1968 .... **CLC 27; PC 23**
See Ekelof, (Bengt) Gunnar
See also CA 123; 25-28R; DAM POET
Ekelof, (Bengt) Gunnar 1907-1968
See Ekeloef, (Bengt) Gunnar
See also DLB 259; EW 12; EWL 3
Ekelund, Vilhelm 1880-1949 .... **TCLC 75**
See also CA 189; EWL 3
Ekwensi, C. O. D.
See Ekwensi, Cyprian (Odiatu Duaka)
Ekwensi, Cyprian (Odiatu Duaka)
1921- .... **BLC 1; CLC 4**
See also AFW; BW 2, 3; CA 29-32R;
CANR 18, 42, 74, 125; CDWLB 3; CN
7; CWRI 5; DAM MULT; DLB 117; EWL
3; MTCW 1, 2; RGEL 2; SATA 66; WLIT
2
Elaine .... **TCLC 18**
See Leverson, Ada Esther
El Crummo
See Crumb, R(obert)
Elder, Lonne III 1931-1996 ..... **BLC 1; DC 8**
See also BW 1, 3; CA 81-84; 152; CAD;
CANR 25; DAM MULT; DLB 7, 38, 44
Eleanor of Aquitaine 1122-1204 ... **CMLC 39**
Elia
See Lamb, Charles
Eliade, Mircea 1907-1986 .... **CLC 19**
See also CA 65-68; 119; CANR 30, 62; CD-
WLB 4; DLB 220; EWL 3; MTCW 1;
RGWL 3; SFW 4
Eliot, A. D.
See Jewett, (Theodora) Sarah Orne
Eliot, Alice
See Jewett, (Theodora) Sarah Orne
Eliot, Dan
See Silverberg, Robert
Eliot, George 1819-1880 ...... **NCLC 4, 13, 23,
41, 49, 89, 118; PC 20; SSC 72; WLC**
See Evans, Mary Ann
See also BRW 5; BRWC 1, 2; BRWR 2;
CDBLB 1832-1890; CN 7; CPW; DA;
DA3; DAB; DAC; DAM MST, NOV;
DLB 21, 35, 55; LATS 1:1; LMFS 1; NFS
17; RGEL 2; RGSF 2; SSFS 8; TEA;
WLIT 3
Eliot, John 1604-1690 .... **LC 5**
See also DLB 24
Eliot, T(homas) S(tearns)
1888-1965 ...... **CLC 1, 2, 3, 6, 9, 10, 13,
15, 24, 34, 41, 55, 57, 113; PC 5, 31;
WLC**
See also AAYA 28; AMW; AMWC 1;
AMWR 1; BRW 7; BRWR 2; CA 5-8R;
25-28R; CANR 41; CDALB 1929-1941;
DA; DA3; DAB; DAC; DAM DRAM,
MST, POET; DFS 4, 13; DLB 7, 10, 45,
63, 245; DLBY 1988; EWL 3; EXPP;
LAIT 3; LATS 1:1; LMFS 2; MTCW 1,
2; NCFS 5; PAB; PFS 1, 7, 20; RGAL 4;
RGEL 2; TUS; WLIT 4; WP
Elizabeth 1866-1941 .... **TCLC 41**
Elkin, Stanley L(awrence)
1930-1995 .. **CLC 4, 6, 9, 14, 27, 51, 91;
SSC 12**
See also AMWS 6; BPFB 1; CA 9-12R;
148; CANR 8, 46; CN 7; CPW; DAM
NOV, POP; DLB 2, 28, 218, 278; DLBY
1980; EWL 3; INT CANR-8; MTCW 1,
2; RGAL 4
Elledge, Scott .... **CLC 34**
Elliott, Don
See Silverberg, Robert
Elliott, George P(aul) 1918-1980 .... **CLC 2**
See also CA 1-4R; 97-100; CANR 2; DLB
244

Elliott, Janice 1931-1995 .... **CLC 47**
  See also CA 13-16R; CANR 8, 29, 84; CN 7; DLB 14; SATA 119

Elliott, Sumner Locke 1917-1991 ..... **CLC 38**
  See also CA 5-8R; 134; CANR 2, 21; DLB 289

Elliott, William
  See Bradbury, Ray (Douglas)

Ellis, A. E. .... **CLC 7**

Ellis, Alice Thomas .... **CLC 40**
  See Haycraft, Anna (Margaret)
  See also DLB 194; MTCW 1

Ellis, Bret Easton 1964- ...... **CLC 39, 71, 117**
  See also AAYA 2, 43; CA 118; 123; CANR 51, 74, 126; CN 7; CPW; DA3; DAM POP; DLB 292; HGG; INT CA-123; MTCW 1; NFS 11

Ellis, (Henry) Havelock
  1859-1939 .... **TCLC 14**
  See also CA 109; 169; DLB 190

Ellis, Landon
  See Ellison, Harlan (Jay)

Ellis, Trey 1962- .... **CLC 55**
  See also CA 146; CANR 92

Ellison, Harlan (Jay) 1934- ... **CLC 1, 13, 42, 139; SSC 14**
  See also AAYA 29; BPFB 1; BYA 14; CA 5-8R; CANR 5, 46, 115; CPW; DAM POP; DLB 8; HGG; INT CANR-5; MTCW 1, 2; SCFW 2; SFW 4; SSFS 13, 14, 15; SUFW 1, 2

Ellison, Ralph (Waldo) 1914-1994 .... **BLC 1; CLC 1, 3, 11, 54, 86, 114; SSC 26; WLC**
  See also AAYA 19; AFAW 1, 2; AMWC 2; AMWR 2; AMWS 2; BPFB 1; BW 1, 3; BYA 2; CA 9-12R; 145; CANR 24, 53; CDALB 1941-1968; CSW; DA; DA3; DAB; DAC; DAM MST, MULT, NOV; DLB 2, 76, 227; DLBY 1994; EWL 3; EXPN; EXPS; LAIT 4; MTCW 1, 2; NCFS 3; NFS 2; RGAL 4; RGSF 2; SSFS 1, 11; YAW

Ellmann, Lucy (Elizabeth) 1956- ..... **CLC 61**
  See also CA 128

Ellmann, Richard (David)
  1918-1987 .... **CLC 50**
  See also BEST 89:2; CA 1-4R; 122; CANR 2, 28, 61; DLB 103; DLBY 1987; MTCW 1, 2

Elman, Richard (Martin)
  1934-1997 .... **CLC 19**
  See also CA 17-20R; 163; CAAS 3; CANR 47

Elron
  See Hubbard, L(afayette) Ron(ald)

El Saadawi, Nawal 1931- .... **CLC 196**
  See also al'Sadaawi, Nawal; Sa'adawi, al-Nawal; Saadawi, Nawal El; Sa'dawi, Nawal al-
  See also CA 118; CAAS 11; CANR 44, 92

Eluard, Paul .... **PC 38; TCLC 7, 41**
  See Grindel, Eugene
  See also EWL 3; GFL 1789 to the Present; RGWL 2, 3

Elyot, Thomas 1490(?)-1546 .... **LC 11**
  See also DLB 136; RGEL 2

Elytis, Odysseus 1911-1996 .... **CLC 15, 49, 100; PC 21**
  See Alepoudelis, Odysseus
  See also CA 102; 151; CANR 94; CWW 2; DAM POET; EW 13; EWL 3; MTCW 1, 2; RGWL 2, 3

Emecheta, (Florence Onye) Buchi
  1944- .... **BLC 2; CLC 14, 48, 128**
  See also AFW; BW 2, 3; CA 81-84; CANR 27, 81, 126; CDWLB 3; CN 7; CWRI 5; DA3; DAM MULT; DLB 117; EWL 3; FW; MTCW 1, 2; NFS 12, 14; SATA 66; WLIT 2

Emerson, Mary Moody
  1774-1863 .... **NCLC 66**

Emerson, Ralph Waldo 1803-1882 . **NCLC 1, 38, 98; PC 18; WLC**
  See also AMW; ANW; CDALB 1640-1865; DA; DA3; DAB; DAC; DAM MST, POET; DLB 1, 59, 73, 183, 223, 270; EXPP; LAIT 2; LMFS 1; NCFS 3; PFS 4, 17; RGAL 4; TUS; WP

Eminescu, Mihail 1850-1889 .. **NCLC 33, 131**

Empedocles 5th cent. B.C.- .... **CMLC 50**
  See also DLB 176

Empson, William 1906-1984 ... **CLC 3, 8, 19, 33, 34**
  See also BRWS 2; CA 17-20R; 112; CANR 31, 61; DLB 20; EWL 3; MTCW 1, 2; RGEL 2

Enchi, Fumiko (Ueda) 1905-1986 ..... **CLC 31**
  See Enchi Fumiko
  See also CA 129; 121; FW; MJW

Enchi Fumiko
  See Enchi, Fumiko (Ueda)
  See also DLB 182; EWL 3

Ende, Michael (Andreas Helmuth)
  1929-1995 .... **CLC 31**
  See also BYA 5; CA 118; 124; 149; CANR 36, 110; CLR 14; DLB 75; MAICYA 1, 2; MAICYAS 1; SATA 61, 130; SATA-Brief 42; SATA-Obit 86

Endo, Shusaku 1923-1996 ..... **CLC 7, 14, 19, 54, 99; SSC 48; TCLC 152**
  See Endo Shusaku
  See also CA 29-32R; 153; CANR 21, 54, 131; DA3; DAM NOV; MTCW 1, 2; RGSF 2; RGWL 2, 3

Endo Shusaku
  See Endo, Shusaku
  See also CWW 2; DLB 182; EWL 3

Engel, Marian 1933-1985 .... **CLC 36; TCLC 137**
  See also CA 25-28R; CANR 12; DLB 53; FW; INT CANR-12

Engelhardt, Frederick
  See Hubbard, L(afayette) Ron(ald)

Engels, Friedrich 1820-1895 .. **NCLC 85, 114**
  See also DLB 129; LATS 1:1

Enright, D(ennis) J(oseph)
  1920-2002 .... **CLC 4, 8, 31**
  See also CA 1-4R; 211; CANR 1, 42, 83; CP 7; DLB 27; EWL 3; SATA 25; SATA-Obit 140

Enzensberger, Hans Magnus
  1929- .... **CLC 43; PC 28**
  See also CA 116; 119; CANR 103; CWW 2; EWL 3

Ephron, Nora 1941- .... **CLC 17, 31**
  See also AAYA 35; AITN 2; CA 65-68; CANR 12, 39, 83

Epicurus 341B.C.-270B.C. .... **CMLC 21**
  See also DLB 176

Epsilon
  See Betjeman, John

Epstein, Daniel Mark 1948- .... **CLC 7**
  See also CA 49-52; CANR 2, 53, 90

Epstein, Jacob 1956- .... **CLC 19**
  See also CA 114

Epstein, Jean 1897-1953 .... **TCLC 92**

Epstein, Joseph 1937- .... **CLC 39**
  See also CA 112; 119; CANR 50, 65, 117

Epstein, Leslie 1938- .... **CLC 27**
  See also AMWS 12; CA 73-76, 215; CAAE 215; CAAS 12; CANR 23, 69; DLB 299

Equiano, Olaudah 1745(?)-1797 . **BLC 2; LC 16**
  See also AFAW 1, 2; CDWLB 3; DAM MULT; DLB 37, 50; WLIT 2

Erasmus, Desiderius 1469(?)-1536 ..... **LC 16, 93**
  See also DLB 136; EW 2; LMFS 1; RGWL 2, 3; TWA

Erdman, Paul E(mil) 1932- .... **CLC 25**
  See also AITN 1; CA 61-64; CANR 13, 43, 84

Erdrich, Louise 1954- .... **CLC 39, 54, 120, 176; NNAL; PC 52**
  See also AAYA 10, 47; AMWS 4; BEST 89:1; BPFB 1; CA 114; CANR 41, 62, 118; CDALBS; CN 7; CP 7; CPW; CWP; DA3; DAM MULT, NOV, POP; DLB 152, 175, 206; EWL 3; EXPP; LAIT 5; LATS 1:2; MTCW 1; NFS 5; PFS 14; RGAL 4; SATA 94, 141; SSFS 14; TCWW 2

Erenburg, Ilya (Grigoryevich)
  See Ehrenburg, Ilya (Grigoryevich)

Erickson, Stephen Michael 1950-
  See Erickson, Steve
  See also CA 129; SFW 4

Erickson, Steve .... **CLC 64**
  See Erickson, Stephen Michael
  See also CANR 60, 68; SUFW 2

Erickson, Walter
  See Fast, Howard (Melvin)

Ericson, Walter
  See Fast, Howard (Melvin)

Eriksson, Buntel
  See Bergman, (Ernst) Ingmar

Eriugena, John Scottus c.
  810-877 .... **CMLC 65**
  See also DLB 115

Ernaux, Annie 1940- .... **CLC 88, 184**
  See also CA 147; CANR 93; NCFS 3, 5

Erskine, John 1879-1951 .... **TCLC 84**
  See also CA 112; 159; DLB 9, 102; FANT

Eschenbach, Wolfram von
  See Wolfram von Eschenbach
  See also RGWL 3

Eseki, Bruno
  See Mphahlele, Ezekiel

Esenin, Sergei (Alexandrovich)
  1895-1925 .... **TCLC 4**
  See Yesenin, Sergey
  See also CA 104; RGWL 2, 3

Eshleman, Clayton 1935- .... **CLC 7**
  See also CA 33-36R, 212; CAAE 212; CAAS 6; CANR 93; CP 7; DLB 5

Espriella, Don Manuel Alvarez
  See Southey, Robert

Espriu, Salvador 1913-1985 .... **CLC 9**
  See also CA 154; 115; DLB 134; EWL 3

Espronceda, Jose de 1808-1842 ..... **NCLC 39**

Esquivel, Laura 1951(?)- ... **CLC 141; HLCS 1**
  See also AAYA 29; CA 143; CANR 68, 113; DA3; DNFS 2; LAIT 3; LMFS 2; MTCW 1; NFS 5; WLIT 1

Esse, James
  See Stephens, James

Esterbrook, Tom
  See Hubbard, L(afayette) Ron(ald)

Estleman, Loren D. 1952- .... **CLC 48**
  See also AAYA 27; CA 85-88; CANR 27, 74; CMW 4; CPW; DA3; DAM NOV, POP; DLB 226; INT CANR-27; MTCW 1, 2

Etherege, Sir George 1636-1692 . **DC 23; LC 78**
  See also BRW 2; DAM DRAM; DLB 80; PAB; RGEL 2

Euclid 306B.C.-283B.C. .... **CMLC 25**

Eugenides, Jeffrey 1960(?)- .... **CLC 81**
  See also AAYA 51; CA 144; CANR 120

Fraser, Antonia (Pakenham) 1932- . **CLC 32, 107**
    See also AAYA 57; CA 85-88; CANR 44, 65, 119; CMW; DLB 276; MTCW 1, 2; SATA-Brief 32
Fraser, George MacDonald 1925- ...... **CLC 7**
    See also AAYA 48; CA 45-48, 180; CAAE 180; CANR 2, 48, 74; MTCW 1; RHW
Fraser, Sylvia 1935- .... **CLC 64**
    See also CA 45-48; CANR 1, 16, 60; CCA 1
Frayn, Michael 1933- . **CLC 3, 7, 31, 47, 176**
    See also BRWC 2; BRWS 7; CA 5-8R; CANR 30, 69, 114, 133; CBD; CD 5; CN 7; DAM DRAM, NOV; DLB 13, 14, 194, 245; FANT; MTCW 1, 2; SFW 4
Fraze, Candida (Merrill) 1945- .... **CLC 50**
    See also CA 126
Frazer, Andrew
    See Marlowe, Stephen
Frazer, J(ames) G(eorge) 1854-1941 .... **TCLC 32**
    See also BRWS 3; CA 118; NCFS 5
Frazer, Robert Caine
    See Creasey, John
Frazer, Sir James George
    See Frazer, J(ames) G(eorge)
Frazier, Charles 1950- .... **CLC 109**
    See also AAYA 34; CA 161; CANR 126; CSW; DLB 292
Frazier, Ian 1951- .... **CLC 46**
    See also CA 130; CANR 54, 93
Frederic, Harold 1856-1898 .... **NCLC 10**
    See also AMW; DLB 12, 23; DLBD 13; RGAL 4
Frederick, John
    See Faust, Frederick (Schiller)
    See also TCWW 2
Frederick the Great 1712-1786 .... **LC 14**
Fredro, Aleksander 1793-1876 .... **NCLC 8**
Freeling, Nicolas 1927-2003 .... **CLC 38**
    See also CA 49-52; 218; CAAS 12; CANR 1, 17, 50, 84; CMW 4; CN 7; DLB 87
Freeman, Douglas Southall 1886-1953 .... **TCLC 11**
    See also CA 109; 195; DLB 17; DLBD 17
Freeman, Judith 1946- .... **CLC 55**
    See also CA 148; CANR 120; DLB 256
Freeman, Mary E(leanor) Wilkins 1852-1930 .... **SSC 1, 47; TCLC 9**
    See also CA 106; 177; DLB 12, 78, 221; EXPS; FW; HGG; MAWW; RGAL 4; RGSF 2; SSFS 4, 8; SUFW 1; TUS
Freeman, R(ichard) Austin 1862-1943 .... **TCLC 21**
    See also CA 113; CANR 84; CMW 4; DLB 70
French, Albert 1943- .... **CLC 86**
    See also BW 3; CA 167
French, Antonia
    See Kureishi, Hanif
French, Marilyn 1929- .. **CLC 10, 18, 60, 177**
    See also BPFB 1; CA 69-72; CANR 3, 31; CN 7; CPW; DAM DRAM, NOV, POP; FW; INT CANR-31; MTCW 1, 2
French, Paul
    See Asimov, Isaac
Freneau, Philip Morin 1752-1832 .. **NCLC 1, 111**
    See also AMWS 2; DLB 37, 43; RGAL 4
Freud, Sigmund 1856-1939 .... **TCLC 52**
    See also CA 115; 133; CANR 69; DLB 296; EW 8; EWL 3; LATS 1:1; MTCW 1, 2; NCFS 3; TWA
Freytag, Gustav 1816-1895 .... **NCLC 109**
    See also DLB 129
Friedan, Betty (Naomi) 1921- .... **CLC 74**
    See also CA 65-68; CANR 18, 45, 74; DLB 246; FW; MTCW 1, 2; NCFS 5

Friedlander, Saul 1932- .... **CLC 90**
    See also CA 117; 130; CANR 72
Friedman, B(ernard) H(arper) 1926- .... **CLC 7**
    See also CA 1-4R; CANR 3, 48
Friedman, Bruce Jay 1930- ...... **CLC 3, 5, 56**
    See also CA 9-12R; CAD; CANR 25, 52, 101; CD 5; CN 7; DLB 2, 28, 244; INT CANR-25; SSFS 18
Friel, Brian 1929- .... **CLC 5, 42, 59, 115; DC 8; SSC 76**
    See also BRWS 5; CA 21-24R; CANR 33, 69, 131; CBD; CD 5; DFS 11; DLB 13; EWL 3; MTCW 1; RGEL 2; TEA
Friis-Baastad, Babbis Ellinor 1921-1970 .... **CLC 12**
    See also CA 17-20R; 134; SATA 7
Frisch, Max (Rudolf) 1911-1991 ... **CLC 3, 9, 14, 18, 32, 44; TCLC 121**
    See also CA 85-88; 134; CANR 32, 74; CD-WLB 2; DAM DRAM, NOV; DLB 69, 124; EW 13; EWL 3; MTCW 1, 2; RGWL 2, 3
Fromentin, Eugene (Samuel Auguste) 1820-1876 .... **NCLC 10, 125**
    See also DLB 123; GFL 1789 to the Present
Frost, Frederick
    See Faust, Frederick (Schiller)
    See also TCWW 2
Frost, Robert (Lee) 1874-1963 .. **CLC 1, 3, 4, 9, 10, 13, 15, 26, 34, 44; PC 1, 39; WLC**
    See also AAYA 21; AMW; AMWR 1; CA 89-92; CANR 33; CDALB 1917-1929; CLR 67; DA; DA3; DAB; DAC; DAM MST, POET; DLB 54, 284; DLBD 7; EWL 3; EXPP; MTCW 1, 2; PAB; PFS 1, 2, 3, 4, 5, 6, 7, 10, 13; RGAL 4; SATA 14; TUS; WP; WYA
Froude, James Anthony 1818-1894 .... **NCLC 43**
    See also DLB 18, 57, 144
Froy, Herald
    See Waterhouse, Keith (Spencer)
Fry, Christopher 1907- .... **CLC 2, 10, 14**
    See also BRWS 3; CA 17-20R; CAAS 23; CANR 9, 30, 74, 132; CBD; CD 5; CP 7; DAM DRAM; DLB 13; EWL 3; MTCW 1, 2; RGEL 2; SATA 66; TEA
Frye, (Herman) Northrop 1912-1991 .... **CLC 24, 70**
    See also CA 5-8R; 133; CANR 8, 37; DLB 67, 68, 246; EWL 3; MTCW 1, 2; RGAL 4; TWA
Fuchs, Daniel 1909-1993 .... **CLC 8, 22**
    See also CA 81-84; 142; CAAS 5; CANR 40; DLB 9, 26, 28; DLBY 1993
Fuchs, Daniel 1934- .... **CLC 34**
    See also CA 37-40R; CANR 14, 48
Fuentes, Carlos 1928- .. **CLC 3, 8, 10, 13, 22, 41, 60, 113; HLC 1; SSC 24; WLC**
    See also AAYA 4, 45; AITN 2; BPFB 1; CA 69-72; CANR 10, 32, 68, 104; CD-WLB 3; CWW 2; DA; DA3; DAB; DAC; DAM MST, MULT, NOV; DLB 113; DNFS 2; EWL 3; HW 1, 2; LAIT 3; LATS 1:2; LAW; LAWS 1; LMFS 2; MTCW 1, 2; NFS 8; RGSF 2; RGWL 2, 3; TWA; WLIT 1
Fuentes, Gregorio Lopez y
    See Lopez y Fuentes, Gregorio
Fuertes, Gloria 1918-1998 .... **PC 27**
    See also CA 178; 180; DLB 108; HW 2; SATA 115
Fugard, (Harold) Athol 1932- . **CLC 5, 9, 14, 25, 40, 80; DC 3**
    See also AAYA 17; AFW; CA 85-88; CANR 32, 54, 118; CD 5; DAM DRAM; DFS 3, 6, 10; DLB 225; DNFS 1, 2; EWL 3; LATS 1:2; MTCW 1; RGEL 2; WLIT 2

Fugard, Sheila 1932- .... **CLC 48**
    See also CA 125
Fukuyama, Francis 1952- .... **CLC 131**
    See also CA 140; CANR 72, 125
Fuller, Charles (H.), (Jr.) 1939- .... **BLC 2; CLC 25; DC 1**
    See also BW 2; CA 108; 112; CAD; CANR 87; CD 5; DAM DRAM, MULT; DFS 8; DLB 38, 266; EWL 3; INT CA-112; MTCW 1
Fuller, Henry Blake 1857-1929 .... **TCLC 103**
    See also CA 108; 177; DLB 12; RGAL 4
Fuller, John (Leopold) 1937- .... **CLC 62**
    See also CA 21-24R; CANR 9, 44; CP 7; DLB 40
Fuller, Margaret
    See Ossoli, Sarah Margaret (Fuller)
    See also AMWS 2; DLB 183, 223, 239
Fuller, Roy (Broadbent) 1912-1991 ... **CLC 4, 28**
    See also BRWS 7; CA 5-8R; 135; CAAS 10; CANR 53, 83; CWRI 5; DLB 15, 20; EWL 3; RGEL 2; SATA 87
Fuller, Sarah Margaret
    See Ossoli, Sarah Margaret (Fuller)
Fuller, Sarah Margaret
    See Ossoli, Sarah Margaret (Fuller)
    See also DLB 1, 59, 73
Fulton, Alice 1952- .... **CLC 52**
    See also CA 116; CANR 57, 88; CP 7; CWP; DLB 193
Furphy, Joseph 1843-1912 .... **TCLC 25**
    See Collins, Tom
    See also CA 163; DLB 230; EWL 3; RGEL 2
Fuson, Robert H(enderson) 1927- .... **CLC 70**
    See also CA 89-92; CANR 103
Fussell, Paul 1924- .... **CLC 74**
    See also BEST 90:1; CA 17-20R; CANR 8, 21, 35, 69; INT CANR-21; MTCW 1, 2
Futabatei, Shimei 1864-1909 .... **TCLC 44**
    See Futabatei Shimei
    See also CA 162; MJW
Futabatei Shimei
    See Futabatei, Shimei
    See also DLB 180; EWL 3
Futrelle, Jacques 1875-1912 .... **TCLC 19**
    See also CA 113; 155; CMW 4
Gaboriau, Emile 1835-1873 .... **NCLC 14**
    See also CMW 4; MSW
Gadda, Carlo Emilio 1893-1973 ...... **CLC 11; TCLC 144**
    See also CA 89-92; DLB 177; EWL 3
Gaddis, William 1922-1998 ... **CLC 1, 3, 6, 8, 10, 19, 43, 86**
    See also AMWS 4; BPFB 1; CA 17-20R; 172; CANR 21, 48; CN 7; DLB 2, 278; EWL 3; MTCW 1, 2; RGAL 4
Gaelique, Moruen le
    See Jacob, (Cyprien-)Max
Gage, Walter
    See Inge, William (Motter)
Gaiman, Neil (Richard) 1960- .... **CLC 195**
    See also AAYA 19, 42; CA 133; CANR 81, 129; DLB 261; HGG; SATA 85, 146; SFW 4; SUFW 2
Gaines, Ernest J(ames) 1933- .. **BLC 2; CLC 3, 11, 18, 86, 181; SSC 68**
    See also AAYA 18; AFAW 1, 2; AITN 1; BPFB 2; BW 2, 3; BYA 6; CA 9-12R; CANR 6, 24, 42, 75, 126; CDALB 1968-1988; CLR 62; CN 7; CSW; DA3; DAM MULT; DLB 2, 33, 152; DLBY 1980; EWL 3; EXPN; LAIT 5; LATS 1:2; MTCW 1, 2; NFS 5, 7, 16; RGAL 4; RGSF 2; RHW; SATA 86; SSFS 5; YAW
Gaitskill, Mary (Lawrence) 1954- .... **CLC 69**
    See also CA 128; CANR 61; DLB 244

Gee, Maurice (Gough) 1931- .... **CLC 29**
    See also AAYA 42; CA 97-100; CANR 67,
    123; CLR 56; CN 7; CWRI 5; EWL 3;
    MAICYA 2; RGSF 2; SATA 46, 101
Geiogamah, Hanay 1945- .... **NNAL**
    See also CA 153; DAM MULT; DLB 175
Gelbart, Larry (Simon) 1928- .... **CLC 21, 61**
    See Gelbart, Larry
    See also CA 73-76; CANR 45, 94
Gelbart, Larry 1928-
    See Gelbart, Larry (Simon)
    See also CAD; CD 5
Gelber, Jack 1932-2003 ...... **CLC 1, 6, 14, 79**
    See also CA 1-4R; 216; CAD; CANR 2;
    DLB 7, 228
Gellhorn, Martha (Ellis)
    1908-1998 .... **CLC 14, 60**
    See also CA 77-80; 164; CANR 44; CN 7;
    DLBY 1982, 1998
Genet, Jean 1910-1986 .. **CLC 1, 2, 5, 10, 14,**
    44, 46; TCLC 128
    See also CA 13-16R; CANR 18; DA3;
    DAM DRAM; DFS 10; DLB 72; DLBY
    1986; EW 13; EWL 3; GFL 1789 to the
    Present; GLL 1; LMFS 2; MTCW 1, 2;
    RGWL 2, 3; TWA
Gent, Peter 1942- .... **CLC 29**
    See also AITN 1; CA 89-92; DLBY 1982
Gentile, Giovanni 1875-1944 .... **TCLC 96**
    See also CA 119
Gentlewoman in New England, A
    See Bradstreet, Anne
Gentlewoman in Those Parts, A
    See Bradstreet, Anne
Geoffrey of Monmouth c.
    1100-1155 .... **CMLC 44**
    See also DLB 146; TEA
George, Jean
    See George, Jean Craighead
George, Jean Craighead 1919- .... **CLC 35**
    See also AAYA 8; BYA 2, 4; CA 5-8R;
    CANR 25; CLR 1; 80; DLB 52; JRDA;
    MAICYA 1, 2; SATA 2, 68, 124; WYA;
    YAW
George, Stefan (Anton) 1868-1933 . **TCLC 2,**
    14
    See also CA 104; 193; EW 8; EWL 3
Georges, Georges Martin
    See Simenon, Georges (Jacques Christian)
Gerald of Wales c. 1146-c. 1223 ... **CMLC 60**
Gerhardi, William Alexander
    See Gerhardie, William Alexander
Gerhardie, William Alexander
    1895-1977 .... **CLC 5**
    See also CA 25-28R; 73-76; CANR 18;
    DLB 36; RGEL 2
Gerson, Jean 1363-1429 .... **LC 77**
    See also DLB 208
Gersonides 1288-1344 .... **CMLC 49**
    See also DLB 115
Gerstler, Amy 1956- .... **CLC 70**
    See also CA 146; CANR 99
Gertler, T. .... **CLC 34**
    See also CA 116; 121
Gertsen, Aleksandr Ivanovich
    See Herzen, Aleksandr Ivanovich
Ghalib .... **NCLC 39, 78**
    See Ghalib, Asadullah Khan
Ghalib, Asadullah Khan 1797-1869
    See Ghalib
    See also DAM POET; RGWL 2, 3
Ghelderode, Michel de 1898-1962 ..... **CLC 6,**
    11; DC 15
    See also CA 85-88; CANR 40, 77; DAM
    DRAM; EW 11; EWL 3; TWA
Ghiselin, Brewster 1903-2001 .... **CLC 23**
    See also CA 13-16R; CAAS 10; CANR 13;
    CP 7

Ghose, Aurabinda 1872-1950 .... **TCLC 63**
    See Ghose, Aurobindo
    See also CA 163
Ghose, Aurobindo
    See Ghose, Aurabinda
    See also EWL 3
Ghose, Zulfikar 1935- .... **CLC 42**
    See also CA 65-68; CANR 67; CN 7; CP 7;
    EWL 3
Ghosh, Amitav 1956- .... **CLC 44, 153**
    See also CA 147; CANR 80; CN 7; WWE
    1
Giacosa, Giuseppe 1847-1906 .... **TCLC 7**
    See also CA 104
Gibb, Lee
    See Waterhouse, Keith (Spencer)
Gibbon, Edward 1737-1794 .... **LC 97**
    See also BRW 3; DLB 104; RGEL 2
Gibbon, Lewis Grassic .... **TCLC 4**
    See Mitchell, James Leslie
    See also RGEL 2
Gibbons, Kaye 1960- .... **CLC 50, 88, 145**
    See also AAYA 34; AMWS 10; CA 151;
    CANR 75, 127; CSW; DA3; DAM POP;
    DLB 292; MTCW 1; NFS 3; RGAL 4;
    SATA 117
Gibran, Kahlil 1883-1931 . **PC 9; TCLC 1, 9**
    See also CA 104; 150; DA3; DAM POET,
    POP; EWL 3; MTCW 2
Gibran, Khalil
    See Gibran, Kahlil
Gibson, William 1914- .... **CLC 23**
    See also CA 9-12R; CAD 2; CANR 9, 42,
    75, 125; CD 5; DA; DAB; DAC; DAM
    DRAM, MST; DFS 2; DLB 7; LAIT 2;
    MTCW 2; SATA 66; YAW
Gibson, William (Ford) 1948- ... **CLC 39, 63,**
    186, 192; SSC 52
    See also AAYA 12, 59; BPFB 2; CA 126;
    133; CANR 52, 90, 106; CN 7; CPW;
    DA3; DAM POP; DLB 251; MTCW 2;
    SCFW 2; SFW 4
Gide, Andre (Paul Guillaume)
    1869-1951 ..... **SSC 13; TCLC 5, 12, 36;**
    WLC
    See also CA 104; 124; DA; DA3; DAB;
    DAC; DAM MST, NOV; DLB 65; EW 8;
    EWL 3; GFL 1789 to the Present; MTCW
    1, 2; RGSF 2; RGWL 2, 3; TWA
Gifford, Barry (Colby) 1946- .... **CLC 34**
    See also CA 65-68; CANR 9, 30, 40, 90
Gilbert, Frank
    See De Voto, Bernard (Augustine)
Gilbert, W(illiam) S(chwenck)
    1836-1911 .... **TCLC 3**
    See also CA 104; 173; DAM DRAM, POET;
    RGEL 2; SATA 36
Gilbreth, Frank B(unker), Jr.
    1911-2001 .... **CLC 17**
    See also CA 9-12R; SATA 2
Gilchrist, Ellen (Louise) 1935- .. **CLC 34, 48,**
    143; SSC 14, 63
    See also BPFB 2; CA 113; 116; CANR 41,
    61, 104; CN 7; CPW; CSW; DAM POP;
    DLB 130; EWL 3; EXPS; MTCW 1, 2;
    RGAL 4; RGSF 2; SSFS 9
Giles, Molly 1942- .... **CLC 39**
    See also CA 126; CANR 98
Gill, Eric 1882-1940 .... **TCLC 85**
    See Gill, (Arthur) Eric (Rowton Peter
    Joseph)
Gill, (Arthur) Eric (Rowton Peter Joseph)
    1882-1940
    See Gill, Eric
    See also CA 120; DLB 98
Gill, Patrick
    See Creasey, John
Gillette, Douglas .... **CLC 70**

Gilliam, Terry (Vance) 1940- .... **CLC 21, 141**
    See Monty Python
    See also AAYA 19, 59; CA 108; 113; CANR
    35; INT CA-113
Gillian, Jerry
    See Gilliam, Terry (Vance)
Gilliatt, Penelope (Ann Douglass)
    1932-1993 .... **CLC 2, 10, 13, 53**
    See also AITN 2; CA 13-16R; 141; CANR
    49; DLB 14
Gilman, Charlotte (Anna) Perkins (Stetson)
    1860-1935 ...... **SSC 13, 62; TCLC 9, 37,**
    117
    See also AMWS 11; BYA 11; CA 106; 150;
    DLB 221; EXPS; FW; HGG; LAIT 2;
    MAWW; MTCW 1; RGAL 4; RGSF 2;
    SFW 4; SSFS 1, 18
Gilmour, David 1946- .... **CLC 35**
Gilpin, William 1724-1804 .... **NCLC 30**
Gilray, J. D.
    See Mencken, H(enry) L(ouis)
Gilroy, Frank D(aniel) 1925- .... **CLC 2**
    See also CA 81-84; CAD; CANR 32, 64,
    86; CD 5; DFS 17; DLB 7
Gilstrap, John 1957(?)- .... **CLC 99**
    See also CA 160; CANR 101
Ginsberg, Allen 1926-1997 .... **CLC 1, 2, 3, 4,**
    6, 13, 36, 69, 109; PC 4, 47; TCLC
    120; WLC
    See also AAYA 33; AITN 1; AMWC 1;
    AMWS 2; BG 2; CA 1-4R; 157; CANR
    2, 41, 63, 95; CDALB 1941-1968; CP 7;
    DA; DA3; DAB; DAC; DAM MST,
    POET; DLB 5, 16, 169, 237; EWL 3; GLL
    1; LMFS 2; MTCW 1, 2; PAB; PFS 5;
    RGAL 4; TUS; WP
Ginzburg, Eugenia .... **CLC 59**
    See Ginzburg, Evgeniia
Ginzburg, Evgeniia 1904-1977
    See Ginzburg, Eugenia
    See also DLB 302
Ginzburg, Natalia 1916-1991 .... **CLC 5, 11,**
    54, 70; SSC 65; TCLC 156
    See also CA 85-88; 135; CANR 33; DFS
    14; DLB 177; EW 13; EWL 3; MTCW 1,
    2; RGWL 2, 3
Giono, Jean 1895-1970 .... **CLC 4, 11; TCLC**
    124
    See also CA 45-48; 29-32R; CANR 2, 35;
    DLB 72; EWL 3; GFL 1789 to the
    Present; MTCW 1; RGWL 2, 3
Giovanni, Nikki 1943- ...... **BLC 2; CLC 2, 4,**
    19, 64, 117; PC 19; WLCS
    See also AAYA 22; AITN 1; BW 2, 3; CA
    29-32R; CAAS 6; CANR 18, 41, 60, 91,
    130; CDALBS; CLR 6, 73; CP 7; CSW;
    CWP; CWRI 5; DA; DA3; DAB; DAC;
    DAM MST, MULT, POET; DLB 5, 41;
    EWL 3; EXPP; INT CANR-18; MAICYA
    1, 2; MTCW 1, 2; PFS 17; RGAL 4;
    SATA 24, 107; TUS; YAW
Giovene, Andrea 1904-1998 .... **CLC 7**
    See also CA 85-88
Gippius, Zinaida (Nikolaevna) 1869-1945
    See Hippius, Zinaida (Nikolaevna)
    See also CA 106; 212
Giraudoux, Jean(-Hippolyte)
    1882-1944 .... **TCLC 2, 7**
    See also CA 104; 196; DAM DRAM; DLB
    65; EW 9; EWL 3; GFL 1789 to the
    Present; RGWL 2, 3; TWA
Gironella, Jose Maria (Pous)
    1917-2003 .... **CLC 11**
    See also CA 101; 212; EWL 3; RGWL 2, 3
Gissing, George (Robert)
    1857-1903 .... **SSC 37; TCLC 3, 24, 47**
    See also BRW 5; CA 105; 167; DLB 18,
    135, 184; RGEL 2; TEA
Giurlani, Aldo
    See Palazzeschi, Aldo

Gladkov, Fedor Vasil'evich
See Gladkov, Fyodor (Vasilyevich)
See also DLB 272

Gladkov, Fyodor (Vasilyevich)
1883-1958 .... **TCLC 27**
See Gladkov, Fedor Vasil'evich
See also CA 170; EWL 3

Glancy, Diane 1941- .... **NNAL**
See also CA 136, 225; CAAE 225; CAAS
24; CANR 87; DLB 175

Glanville, Brian (Lester) 1931- .... **CLC 6**
See also CA 5-8R; CAAS 9; CANR 3, 70;
CN 7; DLB 15, 139; SATA 42

Glasgow, Ellen (Anderson Gholson)
1873-1945 .... **SSC 34; TCLC 2, 7**
See also AMW; CA 104; 164; DLB 9, 12;
MAWW; MTCW 2; RGAL 4; RHW;
SSFS 9; TUS

Glaspell, Susan 1882(?)-1948 ..... **DC 10; SSC
41; TCLC 55**
See also AMWS 3; CA 110; 154; DFS 8,
18; DLB 7, 9, 78, 228; MAWW; RGAL
4; SSFS 3; TCWW 2; TUS; YABC 2

Glassco, John 1909-1981 .... **CLC 9**
See also CA 13-16R; 102; CANR 15; DLB
68

Glasscock, Amnesia
See Steinbeck, John (Ernst)

Glasser, Ronald J. 1940(?)- .... **CLC 37**
See also CA 209

Glassman, Joyce
See Johnson, Joyce

Gleick, James (W.) 1954- .... **CLC 147**
See also CA 131; 137; CANR 97; INT CA-
137

Glendinning, Victoria 1937- .... **CLC 50**
See also CA 120; 127; CANR 59, 89; DLB
155

Glissant, Edouard (Mathieu)
1928- .... **CLC 10, 68**
See also CA 153; CANR 111; CWW 2;
DAM MULT; EWL 3; RGWL 3

Gloag, Julian 1930- .... **CLC 40**
See also AITN 1; CA 65-68; CANR 10, 70;
CN 7

Glowacki, Aleksander
See Prus, Boleslaw

Gluck, Louise (Elisabeth) 1943- .. **CLC 7, 22,
44, 81, 160; PC 16**
See also AMWS 5; CA 33-36R; CANR 40,
69, 108, 133; CP 7; CWP; DA3; DAM
POET; DLB 5; MTCW 2; PFS 5, 15;
RGAL 4

Glyn, Elinor 1864-1943 .... **TCLC 72**
See also DLB 153; RHW

Gobineau, Joseph-Arthur
1816-1882 .... **NCLC 17**
See also DLB 123; GFL 1789 to the Present

Godard, Jean-Luc 1930- .... **CLC 20**
See also CA 93-96

Godden, (Margaret) Rumer
1907-1998 .... **CLC 53**
See also AAYA 6; BPFB 2; BYA 2, 5; CA
5-8R; 172; CANR 4, 27, 36, 55, 80; CLR
20; CN 7; CWRI 5; DLB 161; MAICYA
1, 2; RHW; SAAS 12; SATA 3, 36; SATA-
Obit 109; TEA

Godoy Alcayaga, Lucila 1899-1957 .. **HLC 2;
PC 32; TCLC 2**
See Mistral, Gabriela
See also BW 2; CA 104; 131; CANR 81;
DAM MULT; DNFS; HW 1, 2; MTCW 1,
2

Godwin, Gail (Kathleen) 1937- ..... **CLC 5, 8,
22, 31, 69, 125**
See also BPFB 2; CA 29-32R; CANR 15,
43, 69, 132; CN 7; CPW; CSW; DA3;
DAM POP; DLB 6, 234; INT CANR-15;
MTCW 1, 2

Godwin, William 1756-1836 .. **NCLC 14, 130**
See also CDBLB 1789-1832; CMW 4; DLB
39, 104, 142, 158, 163, 262; HGG; RGEL
2

Goebbels, Josef
See Goebbels, (Paul) Joseph

Goebbels, (Paul) Joseph
1897-1945 .... **TCLC 68**
See also CA 115; 148

Goebbels, Joseph Paul
See Goebbels, (Paul) Joseph

Goethe, Johann Wolfgang von
1749-1832 .... **DC 20; NCLC 4, 22, 34,
90; PC 5; SSC 38; WLC**
See also CDWLB 2; DA; DA3; DAB;
DAC; DAM DRAM, MST, POET; DLB
94; EW 5; LATS 1; LMFS 1:1; RGWL 2,
3; TWA

Gogarty, Oliver St. John
1878-1957 .... **TCLC 15**
See also CA 109; 150; DLB 15, 19; RGEL
2

Gogol, Nikolai (Vasilyevich)
1809-1852 .... **DC 1; NCLC 5, 15, 31;
SSC 4, 29, 52; WLC**
See also DA; DAB; DAC; DAM DRAM,
MST; DFS 12; DLB 198; EW 6; EXPS;
RGSF 2; RGWL 2, 3; SSFS 7; TWA

Goines, Donald 1937(?)-1974 ... **BLC 2; CLC
80**
See also AITN 1; BW 1, 3; CA 124; 114;
CANR 82; CMW 4; DA3; DAM MULT,
POP; DLB 33

Gold, Herbert 1924- ... **CLC 4, 7, 14, 42, 152**
See also CA 9-12R; CANR 17, 45, 125; CN
7; DLB 2; DLBY 1981

Goldbarth, Albert 1948- .... **CLC 5, 38**
See also AMWS 12; CA 53-56; CANR 6,
40; CP 7; DLB 120

Goldberg, Anatol 1910-1982 .... **CLC 34**
See also CA 131; 117

Goldemberg, Isaac 1945- .... **CLC 52**
See also CA 69-72; CAAS 12; CANR 11,
32; EWL 3; HW 1; WLIT 1

Golding, Arthur 1536-1606 .... **LC 101**
See also DLB 136

Golding, William (Gerald)
1911-1993 ..... **CLC 1, 2, 3, 8, 10, 17, 27,
58, 81; WLC**
See also AAYA 5, 44; BPFB 2; BRWR 1;
BRWS 1; BYA 2; CA 5-8R; 141; CANR
13, 33, 54; CDBLB 1945-1960; CLR 94;
DA; DA3; DAB; DAC; DAM MST, NOV;
DLB 15, 100, 255; EWL 3; EXPN; HGG;
LAIT 4; MTCW 1, 2; NFS 2; RGEL 2;
RHW; SFW 4; TEA; WLIT 4; YAW

Goldman, Emma 1869-1940 .... **TCLC 13**
See also CA 110; 150; DLB 221; FW;
RGAL 4; TUS

Goldman, Francisco 1954- .... **CLC 76**
See also CA 162

Goldman, William (W.) 1931- ...... **CLC 1, 48**
See also BPFB 2; CA 9-12R; CANR 29,
69, 106; CN 7; DLB 44; FANT; IDFW 3,
4

Goldmann, Lucien 1913-1970 .... **CLC 24**
See also CA 25-28; CAP 2

Goldoni, Carlo 1707-1793 .... **LC 4**
See also DAM DRAM; EW 4; RGWL 2, 3

Goldsberry, Steven 1949- .... **CLC 34**
See also CA 131

Goldsmith, Oliver 1730-1774 .... **DC 8; LC 2,
48; WLC**
See also BRW 3; CDBLB 1660-1789; DA;
DAB; DAC; DAM DRAM, MST, NOV,
POET; DFS 1; DLB 39, 89, 104, 109, 142;
IDTP; RGEL 2; SATA 26; TEA; WLIT 3

Goldsmith, Peter
See Priestley, J(ohn) B(oynton)

Gombrowicz, Witold 1904-1969 .... **CLC 4, 7,
11, 49**
See also CA 19-20; 25-28R; CANR 105;
CAP 2; CDWLB 4; DAM DRAM; DLB
215; EW 12; EWL 3; RGWL 2, 3; TWA

Gomez de Avellaneda, Gertrudis
1814-1873 .... **NCLC 111**
See also LAW

Gomez de la Serna, Ramon
1888-1963 .... **CLC 9**
See also CA 153; 116; CANR 79; EWL 3;
HW 1, 2

Goncharov, Ivan Alexandrovich
1812-1891 .... **NCLC 1, 63**
See also DLB 238; EW 6; RGWL 2, 3

Goncourt, Edmond (Louis Antoine Huot) de
1822-1896 .... **NCLC 7**
See also DLB 123; EW 7; GFL 1789 to the
Present; RGWL 2, 3

Goncourt, Jules (Alfred Huot) de
1830-1870 .... **NCLC 7**
See also DLB 123; EW 7; GFL 1789 to the
Present; RGWL 2, 3

Gongora (y Argote), Luis de
1561-1627 .... **LC 72**
See also RGWL 2, 3

Gontier, Fernande 19(?)- .... **CLC 50**

Gonzalez Martinez, Enrique
See Gonzalez Martinez, Enrique
See also DLB 290

Gonzalez Martinez, Enrique
1871-1952 .... **TCLC 72**
See Gonzalez Martinez, Enrique
See also CA 166; CANR 81; EWL 3; HW
1, 2

Goodison, Lorna 1947- .... **PC 36**
See also CA 142; CANR 88; CP 7; CWP;
DLB 157; EWL 3

Goodman, Paul 1911-1972 ..... **CLC 1, 2, 4, 7**
See also CA 19-20; 37-40R; CAD; CANR
34; CAP 2; DLB 130, 246; MTCW 1;
RGAL 4

GoodWeather, Harley
See King, Thomas

Googe, Barnabe 1540-1594 .... **LC 94**
See also DLB 132; RGEL 2

Gordimer, Nadine 1923- ...... **CLC 3, 5, 7, 10,
18, 33, 51, 70, 123, 160, 161; SSC 17;
WLCS**
See also AAYA 39; AFW; BRWS 2; CA
5-8R; CANR 3, 28, 56, 88, 131; CN 7;
DA; DA3; DAB; DAC; DAM MST, NOV;
DLB 225; EWL 3; EXPS; INT CANR-28;
LATS 1:2; MTCW 1, 2; NFS 4; RGEL 2;
RGSF 2; SSFS 2, 14, 19; TWA; WLIT 2;
YAW

Gordon, Adam Lindsay
1833-1870 .... **NCLC 21**
See also DLB 230

Gordon, Caroline 1895-1981 . **CLC 6, 13, 29,
83; SSC 15**
See also AMW; CA 11-12; 103; CANR 36;
CAP 1; DLB 4, 9, 102; DLBD 17; DLBY
1981; EWL 3; MTCW 1, 2; RGAL 4;
RGSF 2

Gordon, Charles William 1860-1937
See Connor, Ralph
See also CA 109

Gordon, Mary (Catherine) 1949- .... **CLC 13,
22, 128; SSC 59**
See also AMWS 4; BPFB 2; CA 102;
CANR 44, 92; CN 7; DLB 6; DLBY
1981; FW; INT CA-102; MTCW 1

Gordon, N. J.
See Bosman, Herman Charles

Gordon, Sol 1923- .... **CLC 26**
See also CA 53-56; CANR 4; SATA 11

Gordone, Charles 1925-1995 .. **CLC 1, 4; DC 8**
See also BW 1, 3; CA 93-96; 180; 150; CAAE 180; CAD; CANR 55; DAM DRAM; DLB 7; INT CA-93-96; MTCW 1

Gore, Catherine 1800-1861 .... **NCLC 65**
See also DLB 116; RGEL 2

Gorenko, Anna Andreevna
See Akhmatova, Anna

Gorky, Maxim .... **SSC 28; TCLC 8; WLC**
See Peshkov, Alexei Maximovich
See also DAB; DFS 9; DLB 295; EW 8; EWL 3; MTCW 2; TWA

Goryan, Sirak
See Saroyan, William

Gosse, Edmund (William)
1849-1928 .... **TCLC 28**
See also CA 117; DLB 57, 144, 184; RGEL 2

Gotlieb, Phyllis (Fay Bloom) 1926- .. **CLC 18**
See also CA 13-16R; CANR 7; DLB 88, 251; SFW 4

Gottesman, S. D.
See Kornbluth, C(yril) M.; Pohl, Frederik

Gottfried von Strassburg fl. c.
1170-1215 .... **CMLC 10**
See also CDWLB 2; DLB 138; EW 1; RGWL 2, 3

Gotthelf, Jeremias 1797-1854 .... **NCLC 117**
See also DLB 133; RGWL 2, 3

Gottschalk, Laura Riding
See Jackson, Laura (Riding)

Gould, Lois 1932(?)-2002 .... **CLC 4, 10**
See also CA 77-80; 208; CANR 29; MTCW 1

Gould, Stephen Jay 1941-2002 .... **CLC 163**
See also AAYA 26; BEST 90:2; CA 77-80; 205; CANR 10, 27, 56, 75, 125; CPW; INT CANR-27; MTCW 1, 2

Gourmont, Remy(-Marie-Charles) de
1858-1915 .... **TCLC 17**
See also CA 109; 150; GFL 1789 to the Present; MTCW 2

Gournay, Marie le Jars de
See de Gournay, Marie le Jars

Govier, Katherine 1948- .... **CLC 51**
See also CA 101; CANR 18, 40, 128; CCA 1

Gower, John c. 1330-1408 .... **LC 76; PC 59**
See also BRW 1; DLB 146; RGEL 2

Goyen, (Charles) William
1915-1983 .... **CLC 5, 8, 14, 40**
See also AITN 2; CA 5-8R; 110; CANR 6, 71; DLB 2, 218; DLBY 1983; EWL 3; INT CANR-6

Goytisolo, Juan 1931- .... **CLC 5, 10, 23, 133; HLC 1**
See also CA 85-88; CANR 32, 61, 131; CWW 2; DAM MULT; EWL 3; GLL 2; HW 1, 2; MTCW 1, 2

Gozzano, Guido 1883-1916 .... **PC 10**
See also CA 154; DLB 114; EWL 3

Gozzi, (Conte) Carlo 1720-1806 .... **NCLC 23**

Grabbe, Christian Dietrich
1801-1836 .... **NCLC 2**
See also DLB 133; RGWL 2, 3

Grace, Patricia Frances 1937- .... **CLC 56**
See also CA 176; CANR 118; CN 7; EWL 3; RGSF 2

Gracian y Morales, Baltasar
1601-1658 .... **LC 15**

Gracq, Julien .... **CLC 11, 48**
See Poirier, Louis
See also CWW 2; DLB 83; GFL 1789 to the Present

Grade, Chaim 1910-1982 .... **CLC 10**
See also CA 93-96; 107; EWL 3

Graduate of Oxford, A
See Ruskin, John

Grafton, Garth
See Duncan, Sara Jeannette

Grafton, Sue 1940- .... **CLC 163**
See also AAYA 11, 49; BEST 90:3; CA 108; CANR 31, 55, 111; CMW 4; CPW; CSW; DA3; DAM POP; DLB 226; FW; MSW

Graham, John
See Phillips, David Graham

Graham, Jorie 1951- .... **CLC 48, 118; PC 59**
See also CA 111; CANR 63, 118; CP 7; CWP; DLB 120; EWL 3; PFS 10, 17

Graham, R(obert) B(ontine) Cunninghame
See Cunninghame Graham, Robert (Gallnigad) Bontine
See also DLB 98, 135, 174; RGEL 2; RGSF 2

Graham, Robert
See Haldeman, Joe (William)

Graham, Tom
See Lewis, (Harry) Sinclair

Graham, W(illiam) S(idney)
1918-1986 .... **CLC 29**
See also BRWS 7; CA 73-76; 118; DLB 20; RGEL 2

Graham, Winston (Mawdsley)
1910-2003 .... **CLC 23**
See also CA 49-52; 218; CANR 2, 22, 45, 66; CMW 4; CN 7; DLB 77; RHW

Grahame, Kenneth 1859-1932 ...... **TCLC 64, 136**
See also BYA 5; CA 108; 136; CANR 80; CLR 5; CWRI 5; DLB 34; DLBD 34, 141, 178; FANT; MAICYA 1, 2; MTCW 2; NFS 20; RGEL 2; SATA 100; TEA; WCH; YABC 1

Granger, Darius John
See Marlowe, Stephen

Granin, Daniil 1918- .... **CLC 59**
See also DLB 302

Granovsky, Timofei Nikolaevich
1813-1855 .... **NCLC 75**
See also DLB 198

Grant, Skeeter
See Spiegelman, Art

Granville-Barker, Harley
1877-1946 .... **TCLC 2**
See Barker, Harley Granville
See also CA 104; 204; DAM DRAM; RGEL 2

Granzotto, Gianni
See Granzotto, Giovanni Battista

Granzotto, Giovanni Battista
1914-1985 .... **CLC 70**
See also CA 166

Grass, Guenter (Wilhelm) 1927- ... **CLC 1, 2, 4, 6, 11, 15, 22, 32, 49, 88; WLC**
See Grass, Gunter (Wilhelm)
See also BPFB 2; CA 13-16R; CANR 20, 75, 93, 133; CDWLB 2; DA; DA3; DAB; DAC; DAM MST, NOV; DLB 75, 124; EW 13; EWL 3; MTCW 1, 2; RGWL 2, 3; TWA

Grass, Gunter (Wilhelm)
See Grass, Guenter (Wilhelm)
See also CWW 2

Gratton, Thomas
See Hulme, T(homas) E(rnest)

Grau, Shirley Ann 1929- .... **CLC 4, 9, 146; SSC 15**
See also CA 89-92; CANR 22, 69; CN 7; CSW; DLB 2, 218; INT CA-89-92; CANR-22; MTCW 1

Gravel, Fern
See Hall, James Norman

Graver, Elizabeth 1964- .... **CLC 70**
See also CA 135; CANR 71, 129

Graves, Richard Perceval
1895-1985 .... **CLC 44**
See also CA 65-68; CANR 9, 26, 51

Graves, Robert (von Ranke)
1895-1985 .. **CLC 1, 2, 6, 11, 39, 44, 45; PC 6**
See also BPFB 2; BRW 7; BYA 4; CA 5-8R; 117; CANR 5, 36; CDBLB 1914-1945; DA3; DAB; DAC; DAM MST, POET; DLB 20, 100, 191; DLBD 18; DLBY 1985; EWL 3; LATS 1:1; MTCW 1, 2; NCFS 2; RGEL 2; RHW; SATA 45; TEA

Graves, Valerie
See Bradley, Marion Zimmer

Gray, Alasdair (James) 1934- .... **CLC 41**
See also BRWS 9; CA 126; CANR 47, 69, 106; CN 7; DLB 194, 261; HGG; INT CA-126; MTCW 1, 2; RGSF 2; SUFW 2

Gray, Amlin 1946- .... **CLC 29**
See also CA 138

Gray, Francine du Plessix 1930- ..... **CLC 22, 153**
See also BEST 90:3; CA 61-64; CAAS 2; CANR 11, 33, 75, 81; DAM NOV; INT CANR-11; MTCW 1, 2

Gray, John (Henry) 1866-1934 ...... **TCLC 19**
See also CA 119; 162; RGEL 2

Gray, Simon (James Holliday)
1936- .... **CLC 9, 14, 36**
See also AITN 1; CA 21-24R; CAAS 3; CANR 32, 69; CD 5; DLB 13; EWL 3; MTCW 1; RGEL 2

Gray, Spalding 1941-2004 .... **CLC 49, 112; DC 7**
See also CA 128; 225; CAD; CANR 74; CD 5; CPW; DAM POP; MTCW 2

Gray, Thomas 1716-1771 .... **LC 4, 40; PC 2; WLC**
See also BRW 3; CDBLB 1660-1789; DA; DA3; DAB; DAC; DAM MST; DLB 109; EXPP; PAB; PFS 9; RGEL 2; TEA; WP

Grayson, David
See Baker, Ray Stannard

Grayson, Richard (A.) 1951- .... **CLC 38**
See also CA 85-88, 210; CAAE 210; CANR 14, 31, 57; DLB 234

Greeley, Andrew M(oran) 1928- ...... **CLC 28**
See also BPFB 2; CA 5-8R; CAAS 7; CANR 7, 43, 69, 104; CMW 4; CPW; DA3; DAM POP; MTCW 1, 2

Green, Anna Katharine
1846-1935 .... **TCLC 63**
See also CA 112; 159; CMW 4; DLB 202, 221; MSW

Green, Brian
See Card, Orson Scott

Green, Hannah
See Greenberg, Joanne (Goldenberg)

Green, Hannah 1927(?)-1996 .... **CLC 3**
See also CA 73-76; CANR 59, 93; NFS 10

Green, Henry .... **CLC 2, 13, 97**
See Yorke, Henry Vincent
See also BRWS 2; CA 175; DLB 15; EWL 3; RGEL 2

Green, Julian (Hartridge) 1900-1998
See Green, Julien
See also CA 21-24R; 169; CANR 33, 87; CWW 2; DLB 4, 72; MTCW 1

Green, Julien .... **CLC 3, 11, 77**
See Green, Julian (Hartridge)
See also EWL 3; GFL 1789 to the Present; MTCW 2

Green, Paul (Eliot) 1894-1981 .... **CLC 25**
See also AITN 1; CA 5-8R; 103; CANR 3; DAM DRAM; DLB 7, 9, 249; DLBY 1981; RGAL 4

Greenaway, Peter 1942- .... **CLC 159**
See also CA 127

Greenberg, Ivan 1908-1973
See Rahv, Philip
See also CA 85-88

Greenberg, Joanne (Goldenberg)
1932- .... **CLC 7, 30**
See also AAYA 12; CA 5-8R; CANR 14,
32, 69; SATA 25; YAW

Greenberg, Richard 1959(?)- ...... **CLC 57**
See also CA 138; CAD; CD 5

Greenblatt, Stephen J(ay) 1943- ...... **CLC 70**
See also CA 49-52; CANR 115

Greene, Bette 1934- .... **CLC 30**
See also AAYA 7; BYA 3; CA 53-56; CANR
4; CLR 2; CWRI 5; JRDA; LAIT 4; MAI-
CYA 1, 2; NFS 10; SAAS 16; SATA 8,
102; WYA; YAW

Greene, Gael .... **CLC 8**
See also CA 13-16R; CANR 10

Greene, Graham (Henry)
1904-1991 .... **CLC 1, 3, 6, 9, 14, 18, 27,
37, 70, 72, 125; SSC 29; WLC**
See also AITN 2; BPFB 2; BRWR 2; BRWS
1; BYA 3; CA 13-16R; 133; CANR 35,
61, 131; CBD; CDBLB 1945-1960; CMW
4; DA; DA3; DAB; DAC; DAM MST,
NOV; DLB 13, 15, 77, 100, 162, 201,
204; DLBY 1991; EWL 3; MSW; MTCW
1, 2; NFS 16; RGEL 2; SATA 20; SSFS
14; TEA; WLIT 4

Greene, Robert 1558-1592 .... **LC 41**
See also BRWS 8; DLB 62, 167; IDTP;
RGEL 2; TEA

Greer, Germaine 1939- .... **CLC 131**
See also AITN 1; CA 81-84; CANR 33, 70,
115, 133; FW; MTCW 1, 2

Greer, Richard
See Silverberg, Robert

Gregor, Arthur 1923- .... **CLC 9**
See also CA 25-28R; CAAS 10; CANR 11;
CP 7; SATA 36

Gregor, Lee
See Pohl, Frederik

Gregory, Lady Isabella Augusta (Persse)
1852-1932 .... **TCLC 1**
See also BRW 6; CA 104; 184; DLB 10;
IDTP; RGEL 2

Gregory, J. Dennis
See Williams, John A(lfred)

Grekova, I. .... **CLC 59**
See Ventsel, Elena Sergeevna
See also CWW 2

Grendon, Stephen
See Derleth, August (William)

Grenville, Kate 1950- .... **CLC 61**
See also CA 118; CANR 53, 93

Grenville, Pelham
See Wodehouse, P(elham) G(renville)

Greve, Felix Paul (Berthold Friedrich)
1879-1948
See Grove, Frederick Philip
See also CA 104; 141, 175; CANR 79;
DAC; DAM MST

Greville, Fulke 1554-1628 .... **LC 79**
See also DLB 62, 172; RGEL 2

Grey, Lady Jane 1537-1554 .... **LC 93**
See also DLB 132

Grey, Zane 1872-1939 .... **TCLC 6**
See also BPFB 2; CA 104; 132; DA3; DAM
POP; DLB 9, 212; MTCW 1, 2; RGAL 4;
TCWW 2; TUS

Griboedov, Aleksandr Sergeevich
1795(?)-1829 .... **NCLC 129**
See also DLB 205; RGWL 2, 3

Grieg, (Johan) Nordahl (Brun)
1902-1943 .... **TCLC 10**
See also CA 107; 189; EWL 3

Grieve, C(hristopher) M(urray)
1892-1978 .... **CLC 11, 19**
See MacDiarmid, Hugh; Pteleon
See also CA 5-8R; 85-88; CANR 33, 107;
DAM POET; MTCW 1; RGEL 2

Griffin, Gerald 1803-1840 ..... **NCLC 7**
See also DLB 159; RGEL 2

Griffin, John Howard 1920-1980 ..... **CLC 68**
See also AITN 1; CA 1-4R; 101; CANR 2

Griffin, Peter 1942- .... **CLC 39**
See also CA 136

Griffith, D(avid Lewelyn) W(ark)
1875(?)-1948 .... **TCLC 68**
See also CA 119; 150; CANR 80

Griffith, Lawrence
See Griffith, D(avid Lewelyn) W(ark)

Griffiths, Trevor 1935- .... **CLC 13, 52**
See also CA 97-100; CANR 45; CBD; CD
5; DLB 13, 245

Griggs, Sutton (Elbert)
1872-1930 .... **TCLC 77**
See also CA 123; 186; DLB 50

Grigson, Geoffrey (Edward Harvey)
1905-1985 .... **CLC 7, 39**
See also CA 25-28R; 118; CANR 20, 33;
DLB 27; MTCW 1, 2

Grile, Dod
See Bierce, Ambrose (Gwinett)

Grillparzer, Franz 1791-1872 .... **DC 14;
NCLC 1, 102; SSC 37**
See also CDWLB 2; DLB 133; EW 5;
RGWL 2, 3; TWA

Grimble, Reverend Charles James
See Eliot, T(homas) S(tearns)

Grimke, Angelina (Emily) Weld
1880-1958 .... **HR 2**
See Weld, Angelina (Emily) Grimke
See also BW 1; CA 124; DAM POET; DLB
50, 54

Grimke, Charlotte L(ottie) Forten
1837(?)-1914
See Forten, Charlotte L.
See also BW 1; CA 117; 124; DAM MULT,
POET

Grimm, Jacob Ludwig Karl
1785-1863 .... **NCLC 3, 77; SSC 36**
See also DLB 90; MAICYA 1, 2; RGSF 2;
RGWL 2, 3; SATA 22; WCH

Grimm, Wilhelm Karl 1786-1859 .. **NCLC 3,
77; SSC 36**
See also CDWLB 2; DLB 90; MAICYA 1,
2; RGSF 2; RGWL 2, 3; SATA 22; WCH

**Grimmelshausen, Hans Jakob Christoffel
von**
See Grimmelshausen, Johann Jakob Christoffel von
See also RGWL 2, 3

**Grimmelshausen, Johann Jakob Christoffel
von** 1621-1676 .... **LC 6**
See Grimmelshausen, Hans Jakob Christof-
fel von
See also CDWLB 2; DLB 168

Grindel, Eugene 1895-1952
See Eluard, Paul
See also CA 104; 193; LMFS 2

Grisham, John 1955- .... **CLC 84**
See also AAYA 14, 47; BPFB 2; CA 138;
CANR 47, 69, 114, 133; CMW 4; CN 7;
CPW; CSW; DA3; DAM POP; MSW;
MTCW 2

Grosseteste, Robert 1175(?)-1253 . **CMLC 62**
See also DLB 115

Grossman, David 1954- .... **CLC 67**
See also CA 138; CANR 114; CWW 2;
DLB 299; EWL 3

Grossman, Vasilii Semenovich
See Grossman, Vasily (Semenovich)
See also DLB 272

Grossman, Vasily (Semenovich)
1905-1964 .... **CLC 41**
See Grossman, Vasilii Semenovich
See also CA 124; 130; MTCW 1

Grove, Frederick Philip .... **TCLC 4**
See Greve, Felix Paul (Berthold Friedrich)
See also DLB 92; RGEL 2

Grubb
See Crumb, R(obert)

Grumbach, Doris (Isaac) 1918- . **CLC 13, 22,
64**
See also CA 5-8R; CAAS 2; CANR 9, 42,
70, 127; CN 7; INT CANR-9; MTCW 2

Grundtvig, Nicolai Frederik Severin
1783-1872 .... **NCLC 1**
See also DLB 300

Grunge
See Crumb, R(obert)

Grunwald, Lisa 1959- .... **CLC 44**
See also CA 120

Gryphius, Andreas 1616-1664 .... **LC 89**
See also CDWLB 2; DLB 164; RGWL 2, 3

Guare, John 1938- .... **CLC 8, 14, 29, 67; DC
20**
See also CA 73-76; CAD; CANR 21, 69,
118; CD 5; DAM DRAM; DFS 8, 13;
DLB 7, 249; EWL 3; MTCW 1, 2; RGAL
4

Guarini, Battista 1537-1612 .... **LC 102**

Gubar, Susan (David) 1944- .... **CLC 145**
See also CA 108; CANR 45, 70; FW;
MTCW 1; RGAL 4

Gudjonsson, Halldor Kiljan 1902-1998
See Halldor Laxness
See also CA 103; 164

Guenter, Erich
See Eich, Gunter

Guest, Barbara 1920- .... **CLC 34; PC 55**
See also BG 2; CA 25-28R; CANR 11, 44,
84; CP 7; CWP; DLB 5, 193

Guest, Edgar A(lbert) 1881-1959 ... **TCLC 95**
See also CA 112; 168

Guest, Judith (Ann) 1936- .... **CLC 8, 30**
See also AAYA 7; CA 77-80; CANR 15,
75; DA3; DAM NOV, POP; EXPN; INT
CANR-15; LAIT 5; MTCW 1, 2; NFS 1

Guevara, Che .... **CLC 87; HLC 1**
See Guevara (Serna), Ernesto

Guevara (Serna), Ernesto
1928-1967 .... **CLC 87; HLC 1**
See Guevara, Che
See also CA 127; 111; CANR 56; DAM
MULT; HW 1

Guicciardini, Francesco 1483-1540 ..... **LC 49**

Guild, Nicholas M. 1944- .... **CLC 33**
See also CA 93-96

Guillemin, Jacques
See Sartre, Jean-Paul

Guillen, Jorge 1893-1984 . **CLC 11; HLCS 1;
PC 35**
See also CA 89-92; 112; DAM MULT,
POET; DLB 108; EWL 3; HW 1; RGWL
2, 3

Guillen, Nicolas (Cristobal)
1902-1989 .... **BLC 2; CLC 48, 79; HLC
1; PC 23**
See also BW 2; CA 116; 125; 129; CANR
84; DAM MST, MULT, POET; DLB 283;
EWL 3; HW 1; LAW; RGWL 2, 3; WP

Guillen y Alvarez, Jorge
See Guillen, Jorge

Guillevic, (Eugene) 1907-1997 .... **CLC 33**
See also CA 93-96; CWW 2

Guillois
See Desnos, Robert

Guillois, Valentin
See Desnos, Robert

Guimaraes Rosa, Joao 1908-1967 .... **HLCS 2**
See Rosa, Joao Guimaraes
See also CA 175; LAW; RGSF 2; RGWL 2, 3

Guiney, Louise Imogen
1861-1920 .... **TCLC 41**
See also CA 160; DLB 54; RGAL 4

Guinizelli, Guido c. 1230-1276 ...... **CMLC 49**

Guiraldes, Ricardo (Guillermo)
1886-1927 .... **TCLC 39**
See also CA 131; EWL 3; HW 1; LAW; MTCW 1

Gumilev, Nikolai (Stepanovich)
1886-1921 .... **TCLC 60**
See Gumilyov, Nikolay Stepanovich
See also CA 165; DLB 295

Gumilyov, Nikolay Stepanovich
See Gumilev, Nikolai (Stepanovich)
See also EWL 3

Gump, P. Q.
See Card, Orson Scott

Gunesekera, Romesh 1954- .... **CLC 91**
See also CA 159; CN 7; DLB 267

Gunn, Bill .... **CLC 5**
See Gunn, William Harrison
See also DLB 38

Gunn, Thom(son William)
1929-2004 . **CLC 3, 6, 18, 32, 81; PC 26**
See also BRWS 4; CA 17-20R; 227; CANR 9, 33, 116; CDBLB 1960 to Present; CP 7; DAM POET; DLB 27; INT CANR-33; MTCW 1; PFS 9; RGEL 2

Gunn, William Harrison 1934(?)-1989
See Gunn, Bill
See also AITN 1; BW 1, 3; CA 13-16R; 128; CANR 12, 25, 76

Gunn Allen, Paula
See Allen, Paula Gunn

Gunnars, Kristjana 1948- .... **CLC 69**
See also CA 113; CCA 1; CP 7; CWP; DLB 60

Gunter, Erich
See Eich, Gunter

Gurdjieff, G(eorgei) I(vanovich)
1877(?)-1949 .... **TCLC 71**
See also CA 157

Gurganus, Allan 1947- .... **CLC 70**
See also BEST 90:1; CA 135; CANR 114; CN 7; CPW; CSW; DAM POP; GLL 1

Gurney, A. R.
See Gurney, A(lbert) R(amsdell), Jr.
See also DLB 266

Gurney, A(lbert) R(amsdell), Jr.
1930- .... **CLC 32, 50, 54**
See Gurney, A. R.
See also AMWS 5; CA 77-80; CAD; CANR 32, 64, 121; CD 5; DAM DRAM; EWL 3

Gurney, Ivor (Bertie) 1890-1937 ... **TCLC 33**
See also BRW 6; CA 167; DLBY 2002; PAB; RGEL 2

Gurney, Peter
See Gurney, A(lbert) R(amsdell), Jr.

Guro, Elena (Genrikhovna)
1877-1913 .... **TCLC 56**
See also DLB 295

Gustafson, James M(oody) 1925- ... **CLC 100**
See also CA 25-28R; CANR 37

Gustafson, Ralph (Barker)
1909-1995 .... **CLC 36**
See also CA 21-24R; CANR 8, 45, 84; CP 7; DLB 88; RGEL 2

Gut, Gom
See Simenon, Georges (Jacques Christian)

Guterson, David 1956- .... **CLC 91**
See also CA 132; CANR 73, 126; DLB 292; MTCW 2; NFS 13

Guthrie, A(lfred) B(ertram), Jr.
1901-1991 .... **CLC 23**
See also CA 57-60; 134; CANR 24; DLB 6, 212; SATA 62; SATA-Obit 67

Guthrie, Isobel
See Grieve, C(hristopher) M(urray)

Guthrie, Woodrow Wilson 1912-1967
See Guthrie, Woody
See also CA 113; 93-96

Guthrie, Woody .... **CLC 35**
See Guthrie, Woodrow Wilson
See also DLB 303; LAIT 3

Gutierrez Najera, Manuel
1859-1895 .... **HLCS 2; NCLC 133**
See also DLB 290; LAW

Guy, Rosa (Cuthbert) 1925- .... **CLC 26**
See also AAYA 4, 37; BW 2; CA 17-20R; CANR 14, 34, 83; CLR 13; DLB 33; DNFS 1; JRDA; MAICYA 1, 2; SATA 14, 62, 122; YAW

Gwendolyn
See Bennett, (Enoch) Arnold

H. D. .... **CLC 3, 8, 14, 31, 34, 73; PC 5**
See Doolittle, Hilda

H. de V.
See Buchan, John

Haavikko, Paavo Juhani 1931- .. **CLC 18, 34**
See also CA 106; CWW 2; EWL 3

Habbema, Koos
See Heijermans, Herman

Habermas, Juergen 1929- .... **CLC 104**
See also CA 109; CANR 85; DLB 242

Habermas, Jurgen
See Habermas, Juergen

Hacker, Marilyn 1942- ...... **CLC 5, 9, 23, 72, 91; PC 47**
See also CA 77-80; CANR 68, 129; CP 7; CWP; DAM POET; DLB 120, 282; FW; GLL 2; PFS 19

Hadewijch of Antwerp fl. 1250- ... **CMLC 61**
See also RGWL 3

Hadrian 76-138 .... **CMLC 52**

Haeckel, Ernst Heinrich (Philipp August)
1834-1919 .... **TCLC 83**
See also CA 157

Hafiz c. 1326-1389(?) .... **CMLC 34**
See also RGWL 2, 3

Hagedorn, Jessica T(arahata)
1949- .... **CLC 185**
See also CA 139; CANR 69; CWP; RGAL 4

Haggard, H(enry) Rider
1856-1925 .... **TCLC 11**
See also BRWS 3; BYA 4, 5; CA 108; 148; CANR 112; DLB 70, 156, 174, 178; FANT; LMFS 1; MTCW 2; RGEL 2; RHW; SATA 16; SCFW; SFW 4; SUFW 1; WLIT 4

Hagiosy, L.
See Larbaud, Valery (Nicolas)

Hagiwara, Sakutaro 1886-1942 .... **PC 18; TCLC 60**
See Hagiwara Sakutaro
See also CA 154; RGWL 3

Hagiwara Sakutaro
See Hagiwara, Sakutaro
See also EWL 3

Haig, Fenil
See Ford, Ford Madox

Haig-Brown, Roderick (Langmere)
1908-1976 .... **CLC 21**
See also CA 5-8R; 69-72; CANR 4, 38, 83; CLR 31; CWRI 5; DLB 88; MAICYA 1, 2; SATA 12

Haight, Rip
See Carpenter, John (Howard)

Hailey, Arthur 1920- .... **CLC 5**
See also AITN 2; BEST 90:3; BPFB 2; CA 1-4R; CANR 2, 36, 75; CCA 1; CN 7; CPW; DAM NOV, POP; DLB 88; DLBY 1982; MTCW 1, 2

Hailey, Elizabeth Forsythe 1938- ..... **CLC 40**
See also CA 93-96, 188; CAAE 188; CAAS 1; CANR 15, 48; INT CANR-15

Haines, John (Meade) 1924- .... **CLC 58**
See also AMWS 12; CA 17-20R; CANR 13, 34; CSW; DLB 5, 212

Hakluyt, Richard 1552-1616 .... **LC 31**
See also DLB 136; RGEL 2

Haldeman, Joe (William) 1943- .... **CLC 61**
See Graham, Robert
See also AAYA 38; CA 53-56, 179; CAAE 179; CAAS 25; CANR 6, 70, 72, 130; DLB 8; INT CANR-6; SCFW 2; SFW 4

Hale, Janet Campbell 1947- .... **NNAL**
See also CA 49-52; CANR 45, 75; DAM MULT; DLB 175; MTCW 2

Hale, Sarah Josepha (Buell)
1788-1879 .... **NCLC 75**
See also DLB 1, 42, 73, 243

Halevy, Elie 1870-1937 .... **TCLC 104**

Haley, Alex(ander Murray Palmer)
1921-1992 ...... **BLC 2; CLC 8, 12, 76; TCLC 147**
See also AAYA 26; BPFB 2; BW 2, 3; CA 77-80; 136; CANR 61; CDALBS; CPW; CSW; DA; DA3; DAB; DAC; DAM MST, MULT, POP; DLB 38; LAIT 5; MTCW 1, 2; NFS 9

Haliburton, Thomas Chandler
1796-1865 .... **NCLC 15**
See also DLB 11, 99; RGEL 2; RGSF 2

Hall, Donald (Andrew, Jr.) 1928- ...... **CLC 1, 13, 37, 59, 151**
See also CA 5-8R; CAAS 7; CANR 2, 44, 64, 106, 133; CP 7; DAM POET; DLB 5; MTCW 1; RGAL 4; SATA 23, 97

Hall, Frederic Sauser
See Sauser-Hall, Frederic

Hall, James
See Kuttner, Henry

Hall, James Norman 1887-1951 ..... **TCLC 23**
See also CA 123; 173; LAIT 1; RHW 1; SATA 21

Hall, Joseph 1574-1656 .... **LC 91**
See also DLB 121, 151; RGEL 2

Hall, (Marguerite) Radclyffe
1880-1943 .... **TCLC 12**
See also BRWS 6; CA 110; 150; CANR 83; DLB 191; MTCW 2; RGEL 2; RHW

Hall, Rodney 1935- .... **CLC 51**
See also CA 109; CANR 69; CN 7; CP 7; DLB 289

Hallam, Arthur Henry
1811-1833 .... **NCLC 110**
See also DLB 32

Halldor Laxness .... **CLC 25**
See Gudjonsson, Halldor Kiljan
See also DLB 293; EW 12; EWL 3; RGWL 2, 3

Halleck, Fitz-Greene 1790-1867 .... **NCLC 47**
See also DLB 3, 250; RGAL 4

Halliday, Michael
See Creasey, John

Halpern, Daniel 1945- .... **CLC 14**
See also CA 33-36R; CANR 93; CP 7

Hamburger, Michael (Peter Leopold)
1924- .... **CLC 5, 14**
See also CA 5-8R, 196; CAAE 196; CAAS 4; CANR 2, 47; CP 7; DLB 27

Hamill, Pete 1935- .... **CLC 10**
See also CA 25-28R; CANR 18, 71, 127

Hamilton, Alexander
1755(?)-1804 .... **NCLC 49**
See also DLB 37

Hamilton, Clive
See Lewis, C(live) S(taples)

Hamilton, Edmond 1904-1977 .... **CLC 1**
See also CA 1-4R; CANR 3, 84; DLB 8; SATA 118; SFW 4

Hamilton, Eugene (Jacob) Lee
See Lee-Hamilton, Eugene (Jacob)

Hamilton, Franklin
See Silverberg, Robert

Hamilton, Gail
See Corcoran, Barbara (Asenath)

Hamilton, (Robert) Ian 1938-2001 . **CLC 191**
See also CA 106; 203; CANR 41, 67; CP 7; DLB 40, 155

Hamilton, Jane 1957- .... **CLC 179**
See also CA 147; CANR 85, 128

Hamilton, Mollie
See Kaye, M(ary) M(argaret)

Hamilton, (Anthony Walter) Patrick
1904-1962 .... **CLC 51**
See also CA 176; 113; DLB 10, 191

Hamilton, Virginia (Esther)
1936-2002 .... **CLC 26**
See also AAYA 2, 21; BW 2, 3; BYA 1, 2, 8; CA 25-28R; 206; CANR 20, 37, 73, 126; CLR 1, 11, 40; DAM MULT; DLB 33, 52; DLBY 01; INT CANR-20; JRDA; LAIT 5; MAICYA 1, 2; MAICYAS 1; MTCW 1, 2; SATA 4, 56, 79, 123; SATA-Obit 132; WYA; YAW

Hammett, (Samuel) Dashiell
1894-1961 .... **CLC 3, 5, 10, 19, 47; SSC 17**
See also AAYA 59; AITN 1; AMWS 4; BPFB 2; CA 81-84; CANR 42; CDALB 1929-1941; CMW 4; DA3; DLB 226, 280; DLBD 6; DLBY 1996; EWL 3; LAIT 3; MSW; MTCW 1, 2; RGAL 4; RGSF 2; TUS

Hammon, Jupiter 1720(?)-1800(?) .... **BLC 2; NCLC 5; PC 16**
See also DAM MULT, POET; DLB 31, 50

Hammond, Keith
See Kuttner, Henry

Hamner, Earl (Henry), Jr. 1923- ...... **CLC 12**
See also AITN 2; CA 73-76; DLB 6

Hampton, Christopher (James)
1946- .... **CLC 4**
See also CA 25-28R; CD 5; DLB 13; MTCW 1

Hamsun, Knut .... **TCLC 2, 14, 49, 151**
See Pedersen, Knut
See also DLB 297; EW 8; EWL 3; RGWL 2, 3

Handke, Peter 1942- .... **CLC 5, 8, 10, 15, 38, 134; DC 17**
See also CA 77-80; CANR 33, 75, 104, 133; CWW 2; DAM DRAM, NOV; DLB 85, 124; EWL 3; MTCW 1, 2; TWA

Handy, W(illiam) C(hristopher)
1873-1958 .... **TCLC 97**
See also BW 3; CA 121; 167

Hanley, James 1901-1985 ..... **CLC 3, 5, 8, 13**
See also CA 73-76; 117; CANR 36; CBD; DLB 191; EWL 3; MTCW 1; RGEL 2

Hannah, Barry 1942- .... **CLC 23, 38, 90**
See also BPFB 2; CA 108; 110; CANR 43, 68, 113; CN 7; CSW; DLB 6, 234; INT CA-110; MTCW 1; RGSF 2

Hannon, Ezra
See Hunter, Evan

Hansberry, Lorraine (Vivian)
1930-1965 ... **BLC 2; CLC 17, 62; DC 2**
See also AAYA 25; AFAW 1, 2; AMWS 4; BW 1, 3; CA 109; 25-28R; CABS 3; CAD; CANR 58; CDALB 1941-1968;

CWD; DA; DA3; DAB; DAC; DAM DRAM, MST, MULT; DFS 2; DLB 7, 38; EWL 3; FW; LAIT 4; MTCW 1, 2; RGAL 4; TUS

Hansen, Joseph 1923- .... **CLC 38**
See Brock, Rose; Colton, James
See also BPFB 2; CA 29-32R; CAAS 17; CANR 16, 44, 66, 125; CMW 4; DLB 226; GLL 1; INT CANR-16

Hansen, Martin A(lfred)
1909-1955 .... **TCLC 32**
See also CA 167; DLB 214; EWL 3

Hansen and Philipson eds. .... **CLC 65**

Hanson, Kenneth O(stlin) 1922- .... **CLC 13**
See also CA 53-56; CANR 7

Hardwick, Elizabeth (Bruce) 1916- . **CLC 13**
See also AMWS 3; CA 5-8R; CANR 3, 32, 70, 100; CN 7; CSW; DA3; DAM NOV; DLB 6; MAWW; MTCW 1, 2

Hardy, Thomas 1840-1928 .... **PC 8; SSC 2, 60; TCLC 4, 10, 18, 32, 48, 53, 72, 143, 153; WLC**
See also BRW 6; BRWC 1, 2; BRWR 1; CA 104; 123; CDBLB 1890-1914; DA; DA3; DAB; DAC; DAM MST, NOV, POET; DLB 18, 19, 135, 284; EWL 3; EXPN; EXPP; LAIT 2; MTCW 1, 2; NFS 3, 11, 15, 19; PFS 3, 4, 18; RGEL 2; RGSF 2; TEA; WLIT 4

Hare, David 1947- .... **CLC 29, 58, 136**
See also BRWS 4; CA 97-100; CANR 39, 91; CBD; CD 5; DFS 4, 7, 16; DLB 13; MTCW 1; TEA

Harewood, John
See Van Druten, John (William)

Harford, Henry
See Hudson, W(illiam) H(enry)

Hargrave, Leonie
See Disch, Thomas M(ichael)

Hariri, Al- al-Qasim ibn 'Ali Abu Muhammad al-Basri
See al-Hariri, al-Qasim ibn 'Ali Abu Muhammad al-Basri

Harjo, Joy 1951- ..... **CLC 83; NNAL; PC 27**
See also AMWS 12; CA 114; CANR 35, 67, 91, 129; CP 7; CWP; DAM MULT; DLB 120, 175; EWL 3; MTCW 2; PFS 15; RGAL 4

Harlan, Louis R(udolph) 1922- .... **CLC 34**
See also CA 21-24R; CANR 25, 55, 80

Harling, Robert 1951(?)- .... **CLC 53**
See also CA 147

Harmon, William (Ruth) 1938- .... **CLC 38**
See also CA 33-36R; CANR 14, 32, 35; SATA 65

Harper, F. E. W.
See Harper, Frances Ellen Watkins

Harper, Frances E. W.
See Harper, Frances Ellen Watkins

Harper, Frances E. Watkins
See Harper, Frances Ellen Watkins

Harper, Frances Ellen
See Harper, Frances Ellen Watkins

Harper, Frances Ellen Watkins
1825-1911 ..... **BLC 2; PC 21; TCLC 14**
See also AFAW 1, 2; BW 1, 3; CA 111; 125; CANR 79; DAM MULT, POET; DLB 50, 221; MAWW; RGAL 4

Harper, Michael S(teven) 1938- ... **CLC 7, 22**
See also AFAW 2; BW 1; CA 33-36R, 224; CAAE 224; CANR 24, 108; CP 7; DLB 41; RGAL 4

Harper, Mrs. F. E. W.
See Harper, Frances Ellen Watkins

Harpur, Charles 1813-1868 .... **NCLC 114**
See also DLB 230; RGEL 2

Harris, Christie
See Harris, Christie (Lucy) Irwin

Harris, Christie (Lucy) Irwin
1907-2002 .... **CLC 12**
See also CA 5-8R; CANR 6, 83; CLR 47; DLB 88; JRDA; MAICYA 1, 2; SAAS 10; SATA 6, 74; SATA-Essay 116

Harris, Frank 1856-1931 .... **TCLC 24**
See also CA 109; 150; CANR 80; DLB 156, 197; RGEL 2

Harris, George Washington
1814-1869 .... **NCLC 23**
See also DLB 3, 11, 248; RGAL 4

Harris, Joel Chandler 1848-1908 ..... **SSC 19; TCLC 2**
See also CA 104; 137; CANR 80; CLR 49; DLB 11, 23, 42, 78, 91; LAIT 2; MAI-CYA 1, 2; RGSF 2; SATA 100; WCH; YABC 1

Harris, John (Wyndham Parkes Lucas) Beynon 1903-1969
See Wyndham, John
See also CA 102; 89-92; CANR 84; SATA 118; SFW 4

Harris, MacDonald .... **CLC 9**
See Heiney, Donald (William)

Harris, Mark 1922- .... **CLC 19**
See also CA 5-8R; CAAS 3; CANR 2, 55, 83; CN 7; DLB 2; DLBY 1980

Harris, Norman .... **CLC 65**

Harris, (Theodore) Wilson 1921- .... **CLC 25, 159**
See also BRWS 5; BW 2, 3; CA 65-68; CANR 11, 27, 69, 114; CD-WLB 3; CN 7; CP 7; DLB 117; EWL 3; MTCW 1; RGEL 2

Harrison, Barbara Grizzuti
1934-2002 .... **CLC 144**
See also CA 77-80; 205; CANR 15, 48; INT CANR-15

Harrison, Elizabeth (Allen) Cavanna
1909-2001
See Cavanna, Betty
See also CA 9-12R; 200; CANR 6, 27, 85, 104, 121; MAICYA 2; SATA 142; YAW

Harrison, Harry (Max) 1925- .... **CLC 42**
See also CA 1-4R; CANR 5, 21, 84; DLB 8; SATA 4; SCFW 2; SFW 4

Harrison, James (Thomas) 1937- ...... **CLC 6, 14, 33, 66, 143; SSC 19**
See Harrison, Jim
See also CA 13-16R; CANR 8, 51, 79; CN 7; CP 7; DLBY 1982; INT CANR-8

Harrison, Jim
See Harrison, James (Thomas)
See also AMWS 8; RGAL 4; TCWW 2; TUS

Harrison, Kathryn 1961- .... **CLC 70, 151**
See also CA 144; CANR 68, 122

Harrison, Tony 1937- .... **CLC 43, 129**
See also BRWS 5; CA 65-68; CANR 44, 98; CBD; CD 5; CP 7; DLB 40, 245; MTCW 1; RGEL 2

Harriss, Will(ard Irvin) 1922- .... **CLC 34**
See also CA 111

Hart, Ellis
See Ellison, Harlan (Jay)

Hart, Josephine 1942(?)- .... **CLC 70**
See also CA 138; CANR 70; CPW; DAM POP

Hart, Moss 1904-1961 .... **CLC 66**
See also CA 109; 89-92; CANR 84; DAM DRAM; DFS 1; DLB 7, 266; RGAL 4

Harte, (Francis) Bret(t)
1836(?)-1902 ... **SSC 8, 59; TCLC 1, 25; WLC**
See also AMWS 2; CA 104; 140; CANR 80; CDALB 1865-1917; DA; DA3; DAC; DAM MST; DLB 12, 64, 74, 79, 186; EXPS; LAIT 2; RGAL 4; RGSF 2; SATA 26; SSFS 3; TUS

Highway, Tomson 1951- ...... **CLC 92; NNAL**
See also CA 151; CANR 75; CCA 1; CD 5;
DAC; DAM MULT; DFS 2; MTCW 2

Hijuelos, Oscar 1951- .... **CLC 65; HLC 1**
See also AAYA 25; AMWS 8; BEST 90:1;
CA 123; CANR 50, 75, 125; CPW; DA3;
DAM MULT, POP; DLB 145; HW 1, 2;
LLW 1; MTCW 2; NFS 17; RGAL 4;
WLIT 1

Hikmet, Nazim 1902(?)-1963 .... **CLC 40**
See also CA 141; 93-96; EWL 3

Hildegard von Bingen 1098-1179 . **CMLC 20**
See also DLB 148

Hildesheimer, Wolfgang 1916-1991 .. **CLC 49**
See also CA 101; 135; DLB 69, 124; EWL
3

Hill, Geoffrey (William) 1932- ...... **CLC 5, 8,**
18, 45
See also BRWS 5; CA 81-84; CANR 21,
89; CDBLB 1960 to Present; CP 7; DAM
POET; DLB 40; EWL 3; MTCW 1; RGEL
2

Hill, George Roy 1921-2002 .... **CLC 26**
See also CA 110; 122; 213

Hill, John
See Koontz, Dean R(ay)

Hill, Susan (Elizabeth) 1942- ...... **CLC 4, 113**
See also CA 33-36R; CANR 29, 69, 129;
CN 7; DAB; DAM MST, NOV; DLB 14,
139; HGG; MTCW 1; RHW

Hillard, Asa G. III .... **CLC 70**

Hillerman, Tony 1925- .... **CLC 62, 170**
See also AAYA 40; BEST 89:1; BPFB 2;
CA 29-32R; CANR 21, 42, 65, 97; CMW
4; CPW; DA3; DAM POP; DLB 206, 306;
MSW; RGAL 4; SATA 6; TCWW 2; YAW

Hillesum, Etty 1914-1943 .... **TCLC 49**
See also CA 137

Hilliard, Noel (Harvey) 1929-1996 ... **CLC 15**
See also CA 9-12R; CANR 7, 69; CN 7

Hillis, Rick 1956- .... **CLC 66**
See also CA 134

Hilton, James 1900-1954 .... **TCLC 21**
See also CA 108; 169; DLB 34, 77; FANT;
SATA 34

Hilton, Walter (?)-1396 .... **CMLC 58**
See also DLB 146; RGEL 2

Himes, Chester (Bomar) 1909-1984 .. **BLC 2;**
CLC 2, 4, 7, 18, 58, 108; TCLC 139
See also AFAW 2; BPFB 2; BW 2; CA 25-
28R; 114; CANR 22, 89; CMW 4; DAM
MULT; DLB 2, 76, 143, 226; EWL 3;
MSW; MTCW 1, 2; RGAL 4

Hinde, Thomas .... **CLC 6, 11**
See Chitty, Thomas Willes
See also EWL 3

Hine, (William) Daryl 1936- .... **CLC 15**
See also CA 1-4R; CAAS 15; CANR 1, 20;
CP 7; DLB 60

Hinkson, Katharine Tynan
See Tynan, Katharine

Hinojosa(-Smith), Rolando (R.)
1929- .... **HLC 1**
See Hinojosa-Smith, Rolando
See also CA 131; CAAS 16; CANR 62;
DAM MULT; DLB 82; HW 1, 2; LLW 1;
MTCW 2; RGAL 4

Hinton, S(usan) E(loise) 1950- .. **CLC 30, 111**
See also AAYA 2, 33; BPFB 2; BYA 2, 3;
CA 81-84; CANR 32, 62, 92, 133;
CDALBS; CLR 3, 23; CPW; DA; DA3;
DAB; DAC; DAM MST, NOV; JRDA;
LAIT 5; MAICYA 1, 2; MTCW 1, 2; NFS
5, 9, 15, 16; SATA 19, 58, 115; WYA;
YAW

Hippius, Zinaida (Nikolaevna) .... **TCLC 9**
See Gippius, Zinaida (Nikolaevna)
See also DLB 295; EWL 3

Hiraoka, Kimitake 1925-1970
See Mishima, Yukio
See also CA 97-100; 29-32R; DA3; DAM
DRAM; GLL 1; MTCW 1, 2

Hirsch, E(ric) D(onald), Jr. 1928- .... **CLC 79**
See also CA 25-28R; CANR 27, 51; DLB
67; INT CANR-27; MTCW 1

Hirsch, Edward 1950- .... **CLC 31, 50**
See also CA 104; CANR 20, 42, 102; CP 7;
DLB 120

Hitchcock, Alfred (Joseph)
1899-1980 .... **CLC 16**
See also AAYA 22; CA 159; 97-100; SATA
27; SATA-Obit 24

Hitchens, Christopher (Eric)
1949- .... **CLC 157**
See also CA 152; CANR 89

Hitler, Adolf 1889-1945 .... **TCLC 53**
See also CA 117; 147

Hoagland, Edward 1932- .... **CLC 28**
See also ANW; CA 1-4R; CANR 2, 31, 57,
107; CN 7; DLB 6; SATA 51; TCWW 2

Hoban, Russell (Conwell) 1925- ... **CLC 7, 25**
See also BPFB 2; CA 5-8R; CANR 23, 37,
66, 114; CLR 3, 69; CN 7; CWRI 5; DAM
NOV; DLB 52; FANT; MAICYA 1, 2;
MTCW 1, 2; SATA 1, 40, 78, 136; SFW
4; SUFW 2

Hobbes, Thomas 1588-1679 .... **LC 36**
See also DLB 151, 252, 281; RGEL 2

Hobbs, Perry
See Blackmur, R(ichard) P(almer)

Hobson, Laura Z(ametkin)
1900-1986 .... **CLC 7, 25**
See Field, Peter
See also BPFB 2; CA 17-20R; 118; CANR
55; DLB 28; SATA 52

Hoccleve, Thomas c. 1368-c. 1437 ...... **LC 75**
See also DLB 146; RGEL 2

Hoch, Edward D(entinger) 1930-
See Queen, Ellery
See also CA 29-32R; CANR 11, 27, 51, 97;
CMW 4; DLB 306; SFW 4

Hochhuth, Rolf 1931- .... **CLC 4, 11, 18**
See also CA 5-8R; CANR 33, 75; CWW 2;
DAM DRAM; DLB 124; EWL 3; MTCW
1, 2

Hochman, Sandra 1936- .... **CLC 3, 8**
See also CA 5-8R; DLB 5

Hochwaelder, Fritz 1911-1986 .... **CLC 36**
See Hochwalder, Fritz
See also CA 29-32R; 120; CANR 42; DAM
DRAM; MTCW 1; RGWL 3

Hochwalder, Fritz
See Hochwaelder, Fritz
See also EWL 3; RGWL 2

Hocking, Mary (Eunice) 1921- .... **CLC 13**
See also CA 101; CANR 18, 40

Hodgins, Jack 1938- .... **CLC 23**
See also CA 93-96; CN 7; DLB 60

Hodgson, William Hope
1877(?)-1918 .... **TCLC 13**
See also CA 111; 164; CMW 4; DLB 70,
153, 156, 178; HGG; MTCW 2; SFW 4;
SUFW 1

Hoeg, Peter 1957- .... **CLC 95, 156**
See also CA 151; CANR 75; CMW 4; DA3;
DLB 214; EWL 3; MTCW 2; NFS 17;
RGWL 3; SSFS 18

Hoffman, Alice 1952- .... **CLC 51**
See also AAYA 37; AMWS 10; CA 77-80;
CANR 34, 66, 100; CN 7; CPW; DAM
NOV; DLB 292; MTCW 1, 2

Hoffman, Daniel (Gerard) 1923- . **CLC 6, 13,**
23
See also CA 1-4R; CANR 4; CP 7; DLB 5

Hoffman, Eva 1945- .... **CLC 182**
See also CA 132

Hoffman, Stanley 1944- .... **CLC 5**
See also CA 77-80

Hoffman, William 1925- .... **CLC 141**
See also CA 21-24R; CANR 9, 103; CSW;
DLB 234

Hoffman, William M(oses) 1939- ..... **CLC 40**
See Hoffman, William M.
See also CA 57-60; CANR 11, 71

Hoffmann, E(rnst) T(heodor) A(madeus)
1776-1822 .... **NCLC 2; SSC 13**
See also CDWLB 2; DLB 90; EW 5; RGSF
2; RGWL 2, 3; SATA 27; SUFW 1; WCH

Hofmann, Gert 1931- .... **CLC 54**
See also CA 128; EWL 3

Hofmannsthal, Hugo von 1874-1929 ... **DC 4;**
TCLC 11
See also CA 106; 153; CDWLB 2; DAM
DRAM; DFS 17; DLB 81, 118; EW 9;
EWL 3; RGWL 2, 3

Hogan, Linda 1947- ..... **CLC 73; NNAL; PC**
35
See also AMWS 4; ANW; BYA 12; CA 120,
226; CAAE 226; CANR 45, 73, 129;
CWP; DAM MULT; DLB 175; SATA
132; TCWW 2

Hogarth, Charles
See Creasey, John

Hogarth, Emmett
See Polonsky, Abraham (Lincoln)

Hogg, James 1770-1835 .... **NCLC 4, 109**
See also DLB 93, 116, 159; HGG; RGEL 2;
SUFW 1

Holbach, Paul Henri Thiry Baron
1723-1789 .... **LC 14**

Holberg, Ludvig 1684-1754 .... **LC 6**
See also DLB 300; RGWL 2, 3

Holcroft, Thomas 1745-1809 .... **NCLC 85**
See also DLB 39, 89, 158; RGEL 2

Holden, Ursula 1921- .... **CLC 18**
See also CA 101; CAAS 8; CANR 22

Holderlin, (Johann Christian) Friedrich
1770-1843 .... **NCLC 16; PC 4**
See also CDWLB 2; DLB 90; EW 5; RGWL
2, 3

Holdstock, Robert
See Holdstock, Robert P.

Holdstock, Robert P. 1948- .... **CLC 39**
See also CA 131; CANR 81; DLB 261;
FANT; HGG; SFW 4; SUFW 2

Holinshed, Raphael fl. 1580- .... **LC 69**
See also DLB 167; RGEL 2

Holland, Isabelle (Christian)
1920-2002 .... **CLC 21**
See also AAYA 11; CA 21-24R; 205; CAAE
181; CANR 10, 25, 47; CLR 57; CWRI
5; JRDA; LAIT 4; MAICYA 1, 2; SATA
8, 70; SATA-Essay 103; SATA-Obit 132;
WYA

Holland, Marcus
See Caldwell, (Janet Miriam) Taylor
(Holland)

Hollander, John 1929- .... **CLC 2, 5, 8, 14**
See also CA 1-4R; CANR 1, 52; CP 7; DLB
5; SATA 13

Hollander, Paul
See Silverberg, Robert

Holleran, Andrew 1943(?)- .... **CLC 38**
See Garber, Eric
See also CA 144; GLL 1

Holley, Marietta 1836(?)-1926 .... **TCLC 99**
See also CA 118; DLB 11

Hollinghurst, Alan 1954- .... **CLC 55, 91**
See also CA 114; CN 7; DLB 207; GLL 1

Hollis, Jim
See Summers, Hollis (Spurgeon, Jr.)

Holly, Buddy 1936-1959 .... **TCLC 65**
See also CA 213

Holmes, Gordon
See Shiel, M(atthew) P(hipps)

James, William 1842-1910 .... **TCLC 15, 32**
See also AMW; CA 109; 193; DLB 270, 284; NCFS 5; RGAL 4

Jameson, Anna 1794-1860 .... **NCLC 43**
See also DLB 99, 166

Jameson, Fredric (R.) 1934- .... **CLC 142**
See also CA 196; DLB 67; LMFS 2

Jami, Nur al-Din 'Abd al-Rahman
1414-1492 .... **LC 9**

Jammes, Francis 1868-1938 .... **TCLC 75**
See also CA 198; EWL 3; GFL 1789 to the Present

Jandl, Ernst 1925-2000 .... **CLC 34**
See also CA 200; EWL 3

Janowitz, Tama 1957- .... **CLC 43, 145**
See also CA 106; CANR 52, 89, 129; CN 7; CPW; DAM POP; DLB 292

Japrisot, Sebastien 1931- .... **CLC 90**
See Rossi, Jean-Baptiste
See also CMW 4; NFS 18

Jarrell, Randall 1914-1965 .... **CLC 1, 2, 6, 9, 13, 49; PC 41**
See also AMW; BYA 5; CA 5-8R; 25-28R; CABS 2; CANR 6, 34; CDALB 1941-1968; CLR 6; CWRI 5; DAM POET; DLB 48, 52; EWL 3; EXPP; MAICYA 1, 2; MTCW 1, 2; PAB; PFS 2; RGAL 4; SATA 7

Jarry, Alfred 1873-1907 .... **SSC 20; TCLC 2, 14, 147**
See also CA 104; 153; DA3; DAM DRAM; DFS 8; DLB 192, 258; EW 9; EWL 3; GFL 1789 to the Present; RGWL 2, 3; TWA

Jarvis, E. K.
See Ellison, Harlan (Jay)

Jawien, Andrzej
See John Paul II, Pope

Jaynes, Roderick
See Coen, Ethan

Jeake, Samuel, Jr.
See Aiken, Conrad (Potter)

Jean Paul 1763-1825 .... **NCLC 7**

Jefferies, (John) Richard
1848-1887 .... **NCLC 47**
See also DLB 98, 141; RGEL 2; SATA 16; SFW 4

Jeffers, (John) Robinson 1887-1962 .. **CLC 2, 3, 11, 15, 54; PC 17; WLC**
See also AMWS 2; CA 85-88; CANR 35; CDALB 1917-1929; DA; DAC; DAM MST, POET; DLB 45, 212; EWL 3; MTCW 1, 2; PAB; PFS 3, 4; RGAL 4

Jefferson, Janet
See Mencken, H(enry) L(ouis)

Jefferson, Thomas 1743-1826 . **NCLC 11, 103**
See also AAYA 54; ANW; CDALB 1640-1865; DA3; DLB 31, 183; LAIT 1; RGAL 4

Jeffrey, Francis 1773-1850 .... **NCLC 33**
See Francis, Lord Jeffrey

Jelakowitch, Ivan
See Heijermans, Herman

Jelinek, Elfriede 1946- .... **CLC 169**
See also CA 154; DLB 85; FW

Jellicoe, (Patricia) Ann 1927- .... **CLC 27**
See also CA 85-88; CBD; CD 5; CWD; CWRI 5; DLB 13, 233; FW

Jelloun, Tahar ben 1944- .... **CLC 180**
See Ben Jelloun, Tahar
See also CA 162; CANR 100

Jemyma
See Holley, Marietta

Jen, Gish .... **AAL; CLC 70**
See Jen, Lillian
See also AMWC 2

Jen, Lillian 1956(?)-
See Jen, Gish
See also CA 135; CANR 89, 130

Jenkins, (John) Robin 1912- .... **CLC 52**
See also CA 1-4R; CANR 1; CN 7; DLB 14, 271

Jennings, Elizabeth (Joan)
1926-2001 .... **CLC 5, 14, 131**
See also BRWS 5; CA 61-64; 200; CAAS 5; CANR 8, 39, 66, 127; CP 7; CWP; DLB 27; EWL 3; MTCW 1; SATA 66

Jennings, Waylon 1937- .... **CLC 21**

Jensen, Johannes V(ilhelm)
1873-1950 .... **TCLC 41**
See also CA 170; DLB 214; EWL 3; RGWL 3

Jensen, Laura (Linnea) 1948- .... **CLC 37**
See also CA 103

Jerome, Saint 345-420 .... **CMLC 30**
See also RGWL 3

Jerome, Jerome K(lapka)
1859-1927 .... **TCLC 23**
See also CA 119; 177; DLB 10, 34, 135; RGEL 2

Jerrold, Douglas William
1803-1857 .... **NCLC 2**
See also DLB 158, 159; RGEL 2

Jewett, (Theodora) Sarah Orne
1849-1909 .... **SSC 6, 44; TCLC 1, 22**
See also AMW; AMWC 2; AMWR 2; CA 108; 127; CANR 71; DLB 12, 74, 221; EXPS; FW; MAWW; NFS 15; RGAL 4; RGSF 2; SATA 15; SSFS 4

Jewsbury, Geraldine (Endsor)
1812-1880 .... **NCLC 22**
See also DLB 21

Jhabvala, Ruth Prawer 1927- . **CLC 4, 8, 29, 94, 138**
See also BRWS 5; CA 1-4R; CANR 2, 29, 51, 74, 91, 128; CN 7; DAB; DAM NOV; DLB 139, 194; EWL 3; IDFW 3, 4; INT CANR-29; MTCW 1, 2; RGSF 2; RGWL 2; RHW; TEA

Jibran, Kahlil
See Gibran, Kahlil

Jibran, Khalil
See Gibran, Kahlil

Jiles, Paulette 1943- .... **CLC 13, 58**
See also CA 101; CANR 70, 124; CWP

Jimenez (Mantecon), Juan Ramon
1881-1958 .... **HLC 1; PC 7; TCLC 4**
See also CA 104; 131; CANR 74; DAM MULT, POET; DLB 134; EW 9; EWL 3; HW 1; MTCW 1, 2; RGWL 2, 3

Jimenez, Ramon
See Jimenez (Mantecon), Juan Ramon

Jimenez Mantecon, Juan
See Jimenez (Mantecon), Juan Ramon

Jin, Ha .... **CLC 109**
See Jin, Xuefei
See also CA 152; DLB 244, 292; SSFS 17

Jin, Xuefei 1956-
See Jin, Ha
See also CANR 91, 130; SSFS 17

Joel, Billy .... **CLC 26**
See Joel, William Martin

Joel, William Martin 1949-
See Joel, Billy
See also CA 108

John, Saint 10(?)-100 .... **CMLC 27, 63**

John of Salisbury c. 1115-1180 ..... **CMLC 63**

John of the Cross, St. 1542-1591 .... **LC 18**
See also RGWL 2, 3

John Paul II, Pope 1920- .... **CLC 128**
See also CA 106; 133

Johnson, B(ryan) S(tanley William)
1933-1973 .... **CLC 6, 9**
See also CA 9-12R; 53-56; CANR 9; DLB 14, 40; EWL 3; RGEL 2

Johnson, Benjamin F., of Boone
See Riley, James Whitcomb

Johnson, Charles (Richard) 1948- .... **BLC 2; CLC 7, 51, 65, 163**
See also AFAW 2; AMWS 6; BW 2, 3; CA 116; CAAS 18; CANR 42, 66, 82, 129; CN 7; DAM MULT; DLB 33, 278; MTCW 2; RGAL 4; SSFS 16

Johnson, Charles S(purgeon)
1893-1956 .... **HR 3**
See also BW 1, 3; CA 125; CANR 82; DLB 51, 91

Johnson, Denis 1949- . **CLC 52, 160; SSC 56**
See also CA 117; 121; CANR 71, 99; CN 7; DLB 120

Johnson, Diane 1934- .... **CLC 5, 13, 48**
See also BPFB 2; CA 41-44R; CANR 17, 40, 62, 95; CN 7; DLBY 1980; INT CANR-17; MTCW 1

Johnson, E. Pauline 1861-1913 .... **NNAL**
See also CA 150; DAC; DAM MULT; DLB 92, 175

Johnson, Eyvind (Olof Verner)
1900-1976 .... **CLC 14**
See also CA 73-76; 69-72; CANR 34, 101; DLB 259; EW 12; EWL 3

Johnson, Fenton 1888-1958 .... **BLC 2**
See also BW 1; CA 118; 124; DAM MULT; DLB 45, 50

Johnson, Georgia Douglas (Camp)
1880-1966 .... **HR 3**
See also BW 1; CA 125; DLB 51, 249; WP

Johnson, Helene 1907-1995 .... **HR 3**
See also CA 181; DLB 51; WP

Johnson, J. R.
See James, C(yril) L(ionel) R(obert)

Johnson, James Weldon 1871-1938 .. **BLC 2; HR 3; PC 24; TCLC 3, 19**
See also AFAW 1, 2; BW 1, 3; CA 104; 125; CANR 82; CDALB 1917-1929; CLR 32; DA3; DAM MULT, POET; DLB 51; EWL 3; EXPP; LMFS 2; MTCW 1, 2; PFS 1; RGAL 4; SATA 31; TUS

Johnson, Joyce 1935- .... **CLC 58**
See also BG 3; CA 125; 129; CANR 102

Johnson, Judith (Emlyn) 1936- .... **CLC 7, 15**
See Sherwin, Judith Johnson
See also CA 25-28R; 153; CANR 34

Johnson, Lionel (Pigot)
1867-1902 .... **TCLC 19**
See also CA 117; 209; DLB 19; RGEL 2

Johnson, Marguerite Annie
See Angelou, Maya

Johnson, Mel
See Malzberg, Barry N(athaniel)

Johnson, Pamela Hansford
1912-1981 .... **CLC 1, 7, 27**
See also CA 1-4R; 104; CANR 2, 28; DLB 15; MTCW 1, 2; RGEL 2

Johnson, Paul (Bede) 1928- .... **CLC 147**
See also BEST 89:4; CA 17-20R; CANR 34, 62, 100

Johnson, Robert .... **CLC 70**

Johnson, Robert 1911(?)-1938 .... **TCLC 69**
See also BW 3; CA 174

Johnson, Samuel 1709-1784 .... **LC 15, 52; WLC**
See also BRW 3; BRWR 1; CDBLB 1660-1789; DA; DAB; DAC; DAM MST; DLB 39, 95, 104, 142, 213; LMFS 1; RGEL 2; TEA

Johnson, Uwe 1934-1984 .. **CLC 5, 10, 15, 40**
See also CA 1-4R; 112; CANR 1, 39; CD-WLB 2; DLB 75; EWL 3; MTCW 1; RGWL 2, 3

Johnston, Basil H. 1929- .... **NNAL**
See also CA 69-72; CANR 11, 28, 66; DAC; DAM MULT; DLB 60

Johnston, George (Benson) 1913- .... **CLC 51**
See also CA 1-4R; CANR 5, 20; CP 7; DLB 88

Kanin, Garson 1912-1999 .... **CLC 22**
See also AITN 1; CA 5-8R; 177; CAD;
CANR 7, 78; DLB 7; IDFW 3, 4
Kaniuk, Yoram 1930- .... **CLC 19**
See also CA 134; DLB 299
Kant, Immanuel 1724-1804 ..... **NCLC 27, 67**
See also DLB 94
Kantor, MacKinlay 1904-1977 .... **CLC 7**
See also CA 61-64; 73-76; CANR 60, 63;
DLB 9, 102; MTCW 2; RHW; TCWW 2
Kanze Motokiyo
See Zeami
Kaplan, David Michael 1946- .... **CLC 50**
See also CA 187
Kaplan, James 1951- .... **CLC 59**
See also CA 135; CANR 121
Karadzic, Vuk Stefanovic
1787-1864 .... **NCLC 115**
See also CDWLB 4; DLB 147
Karageorge, Michael
See Anderson, Poul (William)
Karamzin, Nikolai Mikhailovich
1766-1826 .... **NCLC 3**
See also DLB 150; RGSF 2
Karapanou, Margarita 1946- .... **CLC 13**
See also CA 101
Karinthy, Frigyes 1887-1938 .... **TCLC 47**
See also CA 170; DLB 215; EWL 3
Karl, Frederick R(obert)
1927-2004 .... **CLC 34**
See also CA 5-8R; 226; CANR 3, 44
Karr, Mary 1955- .... **CLC 188**
See also AMWS 11; CA 151; CANR 100;
NCFS 5
Kastel, Warren
See Silverberg, Robert
Kataev, Evgeny Petrovich 1903-1942
See Petrov, Evgeny
See also CA 120
Kataphusin
See Ruskin, John
Katz, Steve 1935- .... **CLC 47**
See also CA 25-28R; CAAS 14, 64; CANR
12; CN 7; DLBY 1983
Kauffman, Janet 1945- .... **CLC 42**
See also CA 117; CANR 43, 84; DLB 218;
DLBY 1986
Kaufman, Bob (Garnell) 1925-1986 . **CLC 49**
See also BG 3; BW 1; CA 41-44R; 118;
CANR 22; DLB 16, 41
Kaufman, George S. 1889-1961 ...... **CLC 38;
DC 17**
See also CA 108; 93-96; DAM DRAM;
DFS 1, 10; DLB 7; INT CA-108; MTCW
2; RGAL 4; TUS
Kaufman, Sue .... **CLC 3, 8**
See Barondess, Sue K(aufman)
Kavafis, Konstantinos Petrou 1863-1933
See Cavafy, C(onstantine) P(eter)
See also CA 104
Kavan, Anna 1901-1968 .... **CLC 5, 13, 82**
See also BRWS 7; CA 5-8R; CANR 6, 57;
DLB 255; MTCW 1; RGEL 2; SFW 4
Kavanagh, Dan
See Barnes, Julian (Patrick)
Kavanagh, Julie 1952- .... **CLC 119**
See also CA 163
Kavanagh, Patrick (Joseph)
1904-1967 .... **CLC 22; PC 33**
See also BRWS 7; CA 123; 25-28R; DLB
15, 20; EWL 3; MTCW 1; RGEL 2
Kawabata, Yasunari 1899-1972 ..... **CLC 2, 5,
9, 18, 107; SSC 17**
See Kawabata Yasunari
See also CA 93-96; 33-36R; CANR 88;
DAM MULT; MJW; MTCW 2; RGSF 2;
RGWL 2, 3

Kawabata Yasunari
See Kawabata, Yasunari
See also DLB 180; EWL 3
Kaye, M(ary) M(argaret)
1908-2004 .... **CLC 28**
See also CA 89-92; 223; CANR 24, 60, 102;
MTCW 1, 2; RHW; SATA 62; SATA-Obit
152
Kaye, Mollie
See Kaye, M(ary) M(argaret)
Kaye-Smith, Sheila 1887-1956 .... **TCLC 20**
See also CA 118; 203; DLB 36
Kaymor, Patrice Maguilene
See Senghor, Leopold Sedar
Kazakov, Iurii Pavlovich
See Kazakov, Yuri Pavlovich
See also DLB 302
Kazakov, Yuri Pavlovich 1927-1982 . **SSC 43**
See also Kazakov, Iurii Pavlovich; Kazakov,
Yury
See also CA 5-8R; CANR 36; MTCW 1;
RGSF 2
Kazakov, Yury
See Kazakov, Yuri Pavlovich
See also EWL 3
Kazan, Elia 1909-2003 .... **CLC 6, 16, 63**
See also CA 21-24R; 220; CANR 32, 78
Kazantzakis, Nikos 1883(?)-1957 .... **TCLC 2,
5, 33**
See also BPFB 2; CA 105; 132; DA3; EW
9; EWL 3; MTCW 1, 2; RGWL 2, 3
Kazin, Alfred 1915-1998 ..... **CLC 34, 38, 119**
See also AMWS 8; CA 1-4R; CAAS 7;
CANR 1, 45, 79; DLB 67; EWL 3
Keane, Mary Nesta (Skrine) 1904-1996
See Keane, Molly
See also CA 108; 114; 151; CN 7; RHW
Keane, Molly .... **CLC 31**
See Keane, Mary Nesta (Skrine)
See also INT CA-114
Keates, Jonathan 1946(?)- .... **CLC 34**
See also CA 163; CANR 126
Keaton, Buster 1895-1966 .... **CLC 20**
See also CA 194
Keats, John 1795-1821 ...... **NCLC 8, 73, 121;
PC 1; WLC**
See also AAYA 58; BRW 4; BRWR 1; CD-
BLB 1789-1832; DA; DA3; DAB; DAC;
DAM MST, POET; DLB 96, 110; EXPP;
LMFS 1; PAB; PFS 1, 2, 3, 9, 17; RGEL
2; TEA; WLIT 3; WP
Keble, John 1792-1866 .... **NCLC 87**
See also DLB 32, 55; RGEL 2
Keene, Donald 1922- .... **CLC 34**
See also CA 1-4R; CANR 5, 119
Keillor, Garrison .... **CLC 40, 115**
See Keillor, Gary (Edward)
See also AAYA 2; BEST 89:3; BPFB 2;
DLBY 1987; EWL 3; SATA 58; TUS
Keillor, Gary (Edward) 1942-
See Keillor, Garrison
See also CA 111; 117; CANR 36, 59, 124;
CPW; DA3; DAM POP; MTCW 1, 2
Keith, Carlos
See Lewton, Val
Keith, Michael
See Hubbard, L(afayette) Ron(ald)
Keller, Gottfried 1819-1890 .... **NCLC 2; SSC
26**
See also CDWLB 2; DLB 129; EW; RGSF
2; RGWL 2, 3
Keller, Nora Okja 1965- .... **CLC 109**
See also CA 187
Kellerman, Jonathan 1949- .... **CLC 44**
See also AAYA 35; BEST 90:1; CA 106;
CANR 29, 51; CMW 4; CPW; DA3;
DAM POP; INT CANR-29

Kelley, William Melvin 1937- .... **CLC 22**
See also BW 1; CA 77-80; CANR 27, 83;
CN 7; DLB 33; EWL 3
Kellogg, Marjorie 1922- .... **CLC 2**
See also CA 81-84
Kellow, Kathleen
See Hibbert, Eleanor Alice Burford
Kelly, M(ilton) T(errence) 1947- ...... **CLC 55**
See also CA 97-100; CAAS 22; CANR 19,
43, 84; CN 7
Kelly, Robert 1935- .... **SSC 50**
See also CA 17-20R; CAAS 19; CANR 47;
CP 7; DLB 5, 130, 165
Kelman, James 1946- .... **CLC 58, 86**
See also BRWS 5; CA 148; CANR 85, 130;
CN 7; DLB 194; RGSF 2; WLIT 4
Kemal, Yasar
See Kemal, Yashar
See also CWW 2; EWL 3
Kemal, Yashar 1923(?)- .... **CLC 14, 29**
See also CA 89-92; CANR 44
Kemble, Fanny 1809-1893 .... **NCLC 18**
See also DLB 32
Kemelman, Harry 1908-1996 .... **CLC 2**
See also AITN 1; BPFB 2; CA 9-12R; 155;
CANR 6, 71; CMW 4; DLB 28
Kempe, Margery 1373(?)-1440(?) ... **LC 6, 56**
See also DLB 146; RGEL 2
Kempis, Thomas a 1380-1471 .... **LC 11**
Kendall, Henry 1839-1882 .... **NCLC 12**
See also DLB 230
Keneally, Thomas (Michael) 1935- ... **CLC 5,
8, 10, 14, 19, 27, 43, 117**
See also BRWS 4; CA 85-88; CANR 10,
50, 74, 130; CN 7; CPW; DA3; DAM
NOV; DLB 289, 299; EWL 3; MTCW 1,
2; NFS 17; RGEL 2; RHW
Kennedy, A(lison) L(ouise) 1965- ... **CLC 188**
See also CA 168, 213; CAAE 213; CANR
108; CD 5; CN 7; DLB 271; RGSF 2
Kennedy, Adrienne (Lita) 1931- .... **BLC 2;
CLC 66; DC 5**
See also AFAW 2; BW 2, 3; CA 103; CAAS
20; CABS 3; CANR 26, 53, 82; CD 5;
DAM MULT; DFS 9; DLB 38; FW
Kennedy, John Pendleton
1795-1870 .... **NCLC 2**
See also DLB 3, 248, 254; RGAL 4
Kennedy, Joseph Charles 1929-
See Kennedy, X. J.
See also CA 1-4R, 201; CAAE 201; CANR
4, 30, 40; CP 7; CWRI 5; MAICYA 2;
MAICYAS 1; SATA 14, 86, 130; SATA-
Essay 130
Kennedy, William 1928- ... **CLC 6, 28, 34, 53**
See also AAYA 1; AMWS 7; BPFB 2; CA
85-88; CANR 14, 31, 76; CN 7; DA3;
DAM NOV; DLB 143; DLBY 1985; EWL
3; INT CANR-31; MTCW 1, 2; SATA 57
Kennedy, X. J. .... **CLC 8, 42**
See Kennedy, Joseph Charles
See also CAAS 9; CLR 27; DLB 5; SAAS
22
Kenny, Maurice (Francis) 1929- ..... **CLC 87;
NNAL**
See also CA 144; CAAS 22; DAM MULT;
DLB 175
Kent, Kelvin
See Kuttner, Henry
Kenton, Maxwell
See Southern, Terry
Kenyon, Jane 1947-1995 .... **PC 57**
See also AMWS 7; CA 118; 148; CANR
44, 69; CP 7; CWP; DLB 120; PFS 9, 17;
RGAL 4
Kenyon, Robert O.
See Kuttner, Henry
Kepler, Johannes 1571-1630 .... **LC 45**

Klabund 1890-1928 .... TCLC 44
See also CA 162; DLB 66
Klappert, Peter 1942- .... CLC 57
See also CA 33-36R; CSW; DLB 5
Klein, A(braham) M(oses)
1909-1972 .... CLC 19
See also CA 101; 37-40R; DAB; DAC;
DAM MST; DLB 68; EWL 3; RGEL 2
Klein, Joe
See Klein, Joseph
Klein, Joseph 1946- .... CLC 154
See also CA 85-88; CANR 55
Klein, Norma 1938-1989 .... CLC 30
See also AAYA 2, 35; BPFB 2; BYA 6, 7,
8; CA 41-44R; 128; CANR 15, 37; CLR
2, 19; INT CANR-15; JRDA; MAICYA
1, 2; SAAS 1; SATA 7, 57; WYA; YAW
Klein, T(heodore) E(ibon) D(onald)
1947- .... CLC 34
See also CA 119; CANR 44, 75; HGG
Kleist, Heinrich von 1777-1811 ...... NCLC 2,
37; SSC 22
See also CDWLB 2; DAM DRAM; DLB
90; EW 5; RGSF 2; RGWL 2, 3
Klima, Ivan 1931- .... CLC 56, 172
See also CA 25-28R; CANR 17, 50, 91;
CDWLB 4; CWW 2; DAM NOV; DLB
232; EWL 3; RGWL 3
Klimentev, Andrei Platonovich
See Klimentov, Andrei Platonovich
Klimentov, Andrei Platonovich
1899-1951 .... SSC 42; TCLC 14
See Platonov, Andrei Platonovich; Platonov,
Andrey Platonovich
See also CA 108
Klinger, Friedrich Maximilian von
1752-1831 .... NCLC 1
See also DLB 94
Klingsor the Magician
See Hartmann, Sadakichi
Klopstock, Friedrich Gottlieb
1724-1803 .... NCLC 11
See also DLB 97; EW 4; RGWL 2, 3
Kluge, Alexander 1932- .... SSC 61
See also CA 81-84; DLB 75
Knapp, Caroline 1959-2002 .... CLC 99
See also CA 154; 207
Knebel, Fletcher 1911-1993 .... CLC 14
See also AITN 1; CA 1-4R; 140; CAAS 3;
CANR 1, 36; SATA 36; SATA-Obit 75
Knickerbocker, Diedrich
See Irving, Washington
Knight, Etheridge 1931-1991 ... BLC 2; CLC
40; PC 14
See also BW 1, 3; CA 21-24R; 133; CANR
23, 82; DAM POET; DLB 41; MTCW 2;
RGAL 4
Knight, Sarah Kemble 1666-1727 .... LC 7
See also DLB 24, 200
Knister, Raymond 1899-1932 .... TCLC 56
See also CA 186; DLB 68; RGEL 2
Knowles, John 1926-2001 ... CLC 1, 4, 10, 26
See also AAYA 10; AMWS 12; BPFB 2;
BYA 3; CA 17-20R; 203; CANR 40, 74,
76, 132; CDALB 1968-1988; CLR 98; CN
7; DA; DAC; DAM MST, NOV; DLB 6;
EXPN; MTCW 1, 2; NFS 2; RGAL 4;
SATA 8, 89; SATA-Obit 134; YAW
Knox, Calvin M.
See Silverberg, Robert
Knox, John c. 1505-1572 .... LC 37
See also DLB 132
Knye, Cassandra
See Disch, Thomas M(ichael)
Koch, C(hristopher) J(ohn) 1932- .... CLC 42
See also CA 127; CANR 84; CN 7; DLB
289
Koch, Christopher
See Koch, C(hristopher) J(ohn)

Koch, Kenneth (Jay) 1925-2002 .... CLC 5, 8,
44
See also CA 1-4R; 207; CAD; CANR 6,
36, 57, 97, 131; CD 5; CP 7; DAM POET;
DLB 5; INT CANR-36; MTCW 2; PFS
20; SATA 65; WP
Kochanowski, Jan 1530-1584 .... LC 10
See also RGWL 2, 3
Kock, Charles Paul de 1794-1871 . NCLC 16
Koda Rohan
See Koda Shigeyuki
Koda Rohan
See Koda Shigeyuki
See also DLB 180
Koda Shigeyuki 1867-1947 .... TCLC 22
See Koda Rohan
See also CA 121; 183
Koestler, Arthur 1905-1983 ... CLC 1, 3, 6, 8,
15, 33
See also BRWS 1; CA 1-4R; 109; CANR 1,
33; CDBLB 1945-1960; DLBY 1983;
EWL 3; MTCW 1, 2; NFS 19; RGEL 2
Kogawa, Joy Nozomi 1935- ...... CLC 78, 129
See also AAYA 47; CA 101; CANR 19, 62,
126; CN 7; CWP; DAC; DAM MST,
MULT; FW; MTCW 2; NFS 3; SATA 99
Kohout, Pavel 1928- .... CLC 13
See also CA 45-48; CANR 3
Koizumi, Yakumo
See Hearn, (Patricio) Lafcadio (Tessima
Carlos)
Kolmar, Gertrud 1894-1943 .... TCLC 40
See also CA 167; EWL 3
Komunyakaa, Yusef 1947- .. BLCS; CLC 86,
94; PC 51
See also AFAW 2; AMWS 13; CA 147;
CANR 83; CP 7; CSW; DLB 120; EWL
3; PFS 5, 20; RGAL 4
Konrad, George
See Konrad, Gyorgy
Konrad, Gyorgy 1933- .... CLC 4, 10, 73
See also CA 85-88; CANR 97; CDWLB 4;
CWW 2; DLB 232; EWL 3
Konwicki, Tadeusz 1926- .... CLC 8, 28, 54,
117
See also CA 101; CAAS 9; CANR 39, 59;
CWW 2; DLB 232; EWL 3; IDFW 3;
MTCW 1
Koontz, Dean R(ay) 1945- .... CLC 78
See also AAYA 9, 31; BEST 89:3, 90:2; CA
108; CANR 19, 36, 52, 95; CMW 4;
CPW; DA3; DAM NOV, POP; DLB 292;
HGG; MTCW 1; SATA 92; SFW 4;
SUFW 2; YAW
Kopernik, Mikolaj
See Copernicus, Nicolaus
Kopit, Arthur (Lee) 1937- ...... CLC 1, 18, 33
See also AITN 1; CA 81-84; CABS 3; CD
5; DAM DRAM; DFS 7, 14; DLB 7;
MTCW 1; RGAL 4
Kopitar, Jernej (Bartholomaus)
1780-1844 .... NCLC 117
Kops, Bernard 1926- .... CLC 4
See also CA 5-8R; CANR 84; CBD; CN 7;
CP 7; DLB 13
Kornbluth, C(yril) M. 1923-1958 .... TCLC 8
See also CA 105; 160; DLB 8; SFW 4
Korolenko, V. G.
See Korolenko, Vladimir Galaktionovich
Korolenko, Vladimir
See Korolenko, Vladimir Galaktionovich
Korolenko, Vladimir G.
See Korolenko, Vladimir Galaktionovich
Korolenko, Vladimir Galaktionovich
1853-1921 .... TCLC 22
See also CA 121; DLB 277
Korzybski, Alfred (Habdank Skarbek)
1879-1950 .... TCLC 61
See also CA 123; 160

Kosinski, Jerzy (Nikodem)
1933-1991 .... CLC 1, 2, 3, 6, 10, 15, 53,
70
See also AMWS 7; BPFB 2; CA 17-20R;
134; CANR 9, 46; DA3; DAM NOV;
DLB 2, 299; DLBY 1982; EWL 3; HGG;
MTCW 1, 2; NFS 12; RGAL 4; TUS
Kostelanetz, Richard (Cory) 1940- .. CLC 28
See also CA 13-16R; CAAS 8; CANR 38,
77; CN 7; CP 7
Kostrowitzki, Wilhelm Apollinaris de
1880-1918
See Apollinaire, Guillaume
See also CA 104
Kotlowitz, Robert 1924- .... CLC 4
See also CA 33-36R; CANR 36
Kotzebue, August (Friedrich Ferdinand) von
1761-1819 .... NCLC 25
See also DLB 94
Kotzwinkle, William 1938- ..... CLC 5, 14, 35
See also BPFB 2; CA 45-48; CANR 3, 44,
84, 129; CLR 6; DLB 173; FANT; MAI-
CYA 1, 2; SATA 24, 70, 146; SFW 4;
SUFW 2; YAW
Kowna, Stancy
See Szymborska, Wislawa
Kozol, Jonathan 1936- .... CLC 17
See also AAYA 46; CA 61-64; CANR 16,
45, 96
Kozoll, Michael 1940(?)- .... CLC 35
Kramer, Kathryn 19(?)- .... CLC 34
Kramer, Larry 1935- .... CLC 42; DC 8
See also CA 124; 126; CANR 60, 132;
DAM POP; DLB 249; GLL 1
Krasicki, Ignacy 1735-1801 .... NCLC 8
Krasinski, Zygmunt 1812-1859 .... NCLC 4
See also RGWL 2, 3
Kraus, Karl 1874-1936 .... TCLC 5
See also CA 104; 216; DLB 118; EWL 3
Kreve (Mickevicius), Vincas
1882-1954 .... TCLC 27
See also CA 170; DLB 220; EWL 3
Kristeva, Julia 1941- .... CLC 77, 140
See also CA 154; CANR 99; DLB 242;
EWL 3; FW; LMFS 2
Kristofferson, Kris 1936- .... CLC 26
See also CA 104
Krizanc, John 1956- .... CLC 57
See also CA 187
Krleza, Miroslav 1893-1981 .... CLC 8, 114
See also CA 97-100; 105; CANR 50; CD-
WLB 4; DLB 147; EW 11; RGWL 2, 3
Kroetsch, Robert 1927- ... CLC 5, 23, 57, 132
See also CA 17-20R; CANR 8, 38; CCA 1;
CN 7; CP 7; DAC; DAM POET; DLB 53;
MTCW 1
Kroetz, Franz
See Kroetz, Franz Xaver
Kroetz, Franz Xaver 1946- .... CLC 41
See also CA 130; CWW 2; EWL 3
Kroker, Arthur (W.) 1945- .... CLC 77
See also CA 161
Kropotkin, Peter (Aleksieevich)
1842-1921 .... TCLC 36
See Kropotkin, Petr Alekseevich
See also CA 119; 219
Kropotkin, Petr Alekseevich
See Kropotkin, Peter (Aleksieevich)
See also DLB 277
Krotkov, Yuri 1917-1981 .... CLC 19
See also CA 102
Krumb
See Crumb, R(obert)
Krumgold, Joseph (Quincy)
1908-1980 .... CLC 12
See also BYA 1, 2; CA 9-12R; 101; CANR
7; MAICYA 1, 2; SATA 1, 48; SATA-Obit
23; YAW

Lang, Andrew 1844-1912 .... **TCLC 16**
See also CA 114; 137; CANR 85; CLR 101;
DLB 98, 141, 184; FANT; MAICYA 1, 2;
RGEL 2; SATA 16; WCH

Lang, Fritz 1890-1976 .... **CLC 20, 103**
See also CA 77-80; 69-72; CANR 30

Lange, John
See Crichton, (John) Michael

Langer, Elinor 1939- .... **CLC 34**
See also CA 121

Langland, William 1332(?)-1400(?) ..... **LC 19**
See also BRW 1; DA; DAB; DAC; DAM
MST, POET; DLB 146; RGEL 2; TEA;
WLIT 3

Langstaff, Launcelot
See Irving, Washington

Lanier, Sidney 1842-1881 . **NCLC 6, 118; PC 50**
See also AMWS 1; DAM POET; DLB 64;
DLBD 13; EXPP; MAICYA 1; PFS 14;
RGAL 4; SATA 18

Lanyer, Aemilia 1569-1645 .... **LC 10, 30, 83; PC 60**
See also DLB 121

Lao-Tzu
See Lao Tzu

Lao Tzu c. 6th cent. B.C.-3rd cent.
B.C. .... **CMLC 7**

Lapine, James (Elliot) 1949- .... **CLC 39**
See also CA 123; 130; CANR 54, 128; INT
CA-130

Larbaud, Valery (Nicolas)
1881-1957 .... **TCLC 9**
See also CA 106; 152; EWL 3; GFL 1789
to the Present

Lardner, Ring
See Lardner, Ring(gold) W(ilmer)
See also BPFB 2; CDALB 1917-1929; DLB
11, 25, 86, 171; DLBD 16; RGAL 4;
RGSF 2

Lardner, Ring W., Jr.
See Lardner, Ring(gold) W(ilmer)

Lardner, Ring(gold) W(ilmer)
1885-1933 .... **SSC 32; TCLC 2, 14**
See Lardner, Ring
See also AMW; CA 104; 131; MTCW 1, 2;
TUS

Laredo, Betty
See Codrescu, Andrei

Larkin, Maia
See Wojciechowska, Maia (Teresa)

Larkin, Philip (Arthur) 1922-1985 ... **CLC 3, 5, 8, 9, 13, 18, 33, 39, 64; PC 21**
See also BRWS 1; CA 5-8R; 117; CANR
24, 62; CDBLB 1960 to Present; DA3;
DAB; DAM MST, POET; DLB 27; EWL
3; MTCW 1, 2; PFS 3, 4, 12; RGEL 2

La Roche, Sophie von
1730-1807 .... **NCLC 121**
See also DLB 94

La Rochefoucauld, Francois
1613-1680 .... **LC 108**

**Larra (y Sanchez de Castro), Mariano Jose
de** 1809-1837 .... **NCLC 17, 130**

Larsen, Eric 1941- .... **CLC 55**
See also CA 132

Larsen, Nella 1893(?)-1963 .... **BLC 2; CLC 37; HR 3**
See also AFAW 1, 2; BW 1; CA 125; CANR
83; DAM MULT; DLB 51; FW; LATS
1:1; LMFS 2

Larson, Charles R(aymond) 1938- ... **CLC 31**
See also CA 53-56; CANR 4, 121

Larson, Jonathan 1961-1996 .... **CLC 99**
See also AAYA 28; CA 156

La Sale, Antoine de c. 1386-1460(?) . **LC 104**
See also DLB 208

Las Casas, Bartolome de
1474-1566 .... **HLCS; LC 31**
See Casas, Bartolome de las
See also LAW

Lasch, Christopher 1932-1994 .... **CLC 102**
See also CA 73-76; 144; CANR 25, 118;
DLB 246; MTCW 1, 2

Lasker-Schueler, Else 1869-1945 ... **TCLC 57**
See Lasker-Schuler, Else
See also CA 183; DLB 66, 124

Lasker-Schuler, Else
See Lasker-Schueler, Else
See also EWL 3

Laski, Harold J(oseph) 1893-1950 . **TCLC 79**
See also CA 188

Latham, Jean Lee 1902-1995 .... **CLC 12**
See also AITN 1; BYA 1; CA 5-8R; CANR
7, 84; CLR 50; MAICYA 1, 2; SATA 2,
68; YAW

Latham, Mavis
See Clark, Mavis Thorpe

Lathen, Emma .... **CLC 2**
See Hennissart, Martha; Latsis, Mary J(ane)
See also BPFB 2; CMW 4; DLB 306

Lathrop, Francis
See Leiber, Fritz (Reuter, Jr.)

Latsis, Mary J(ane) 1927-1997
See Lathen, Emma
See also CA 85-88; 162; CMW 4

Lattany, Kristin
See Lattany, Kristin (Elaine Eggleston)
Hunter

Lattany, Kristin (Elaine Eggleston) Hunter
1931- .... **CLC 35**
See also AITN 1; BW 1; BYA 3; CA 13-
16R; CANR 13, 108; CLR 3; CN 7; DLB
33; INT CANR-13; MAICYA 1, 2; SAAS
10; SATA 12, 132; YAW

Lattimore, Richmond (Alexander)
1906-1984 .... **CLC 3**
See also CA 1-4R; 112; CANR 1

Laughlin, James 1914-1997 .... **CLC 49**
See also CA 21-24R; 162; CAAS 22; CANR
9, 47; CP 7; DLB 48; DLBY 1996, 1997

Laurence, (Jean) Margaret (Wemyss)
1926-1987 . **CLC 3, 6, 13, 50, 62; SSC 7**
See also BYA 13; CA 5-8R; 121; CANR
33; DAC; DAM MST; DLB 53; EWL 3;
FW; MTCW 1, 2; NFS 11; RGEL 2;
RGSF 2; SATA-Obit 50; TCWW 2

Laurent, Antoine 1952- .... **CLC 50**

Lauscher, Hermann
See Hesse, Hermann

Lautreamont 1846-1870 .. **NCLC 12; SSC 14**
See Lautreamont, Isidore Lucien Ducasse
See also GFL 1789 to the Present; RGWL
2, 3

Lautreamont, Isidore Lucien Ducasse
See Lautreamont
See also DLB 217

Lavater, Johann Kaspar
1741-1801 .... **NCLC 142**
See also DLB 97

Laverty, Donald
See Blish, James (Benjamin)

Lavin, Mary 1912-1996 . **CLC 4, 18, 99; SSC 4, 67**
See also CA 9-12R; 151; CANR 33; CN 7;
DLB 15; FW; MTCW 1; RGEL 2; RGSF
2

Lavond, Paul Dennis
See Kornbluth, C(yril) M.; Pohl, Frederik

Lawler, Ray
See Lawler, Raymond Evenor
See also DLB 289

Lawler, Raymond Evenor 1922- .... **CLC 58**
See Lawler, Ray
See also CA 103; CD 5; RGEL 2

Lawrence, D(avid) H(erbert Richards)
1885-1930 .... **PC 54; SSC 4, 19, 73; TCLC 2, 9, 16, 33, 48, 61, 93; WLC**
See Chambers, Jessie
See also BPFB 2; BRW 7; BRWR 2; CA
104; 121; CANR 131; CDBLB 1914-
1945; DA; DA3; DAB; DAC; DAM MST,
NOV, POET; DLB 10, 19, 36, 98, 162,
195; EWL 3; EXPP; EXPS; LAIT 2, 3;
MTCW 1, 2; NFS 18; PFS 6; RGEL 2;
RGSF 2; SSFS 2, 6; TEA; WLIT 4; WP

Lawrence, T(homas) E(dward)
1888-1935 .... **TCLC 18**
See Dale, Colin
See also BRWS 2; CA 115; 167; DLB 195

Lawrence of Arabia
See Lawrence, T(homas) E(dward)

Lawson, Henry (Archibald Hertzberg)
1867-1922 .... **SSC 18; TCLC 27**
See also CA 120; 181; DLB 230; RGEL 2;
RGSF 2

Lawton, Dennis
See Faust, Frederick (Schiller)

Layamon fl. c. 1200- .... **CMLC 10**
See Laзamon
See also DLB 146; RGEL 2

Laye, Camara 1928-1980 ..... **BLC 2; CLC 4, 38**
See Camara Laye
See also AFW; BW 1; CA 85-88; 97-100;
CANR 25; DAM MULT; MTCW 1, 2;
WLIT 2

Layton, Irving (Peter) 1912- .... **CLC 2, 15, 164**
See also CA 1-4R; CANR 2, 33, 43, 66,
129; CP 7; DAC; DAM MST, POET;
DLB 88; EWL 3; MTCW 1, 2; PFS 12;
RGEL 2

Lazarus, Emma 1849-1887 ...... **NCLC 8, 109**

Lazarus, Felix
See Cable, George Washington

Lazarus, Henry
See Slavitt, David R(ytman)

Lea, Joan
See Neufeld, John (Arthur)

Leacock, Stephen (Butler)
1869-1944 .... **SSC 39; TCLC 2**
See also CA 104; 141; CANR 80; DAC;
DAM MST; DLB 92; EWL 3; MTCW 2;
RGEL 2; RGSF 2

Lead, Jane Ward 1623-1704 .... **LC 72**
See also DLB 131

Leapor, Mary 1722-1746 .... **LC 80**
See also DLB 109

Lear, Edward 1812-1888 .... **NCLC 3**
See also AAYA 48; BRW 5; CLR 1, 75;
DLB 32, 163, 166; MAICYA 1, 2; RGEL
2; SATA 18, 100; WCH; WP

Lear, Norman (Milton) 1922- .... **CLC 12**
See also CA 73-76

Leautaud, Paul 1872-1956 .... **TCLC 83**
See also CA 203; DLB 65; GFL 1789 to the
Present

Leavis, F(rank) R(aymond)
1895-1978 .... **CLC 24**
See also BRW 7; CA 21-24R; 77-80; CANR
44; DLB 242; EWL 3; MTCW 1, 2;

Leavitt, David 1961- .... **CLC 34**
See also CA 116; 122; CANR 50, 62, 101;
CPW; DA3; DAM POP; DLB 130; GLL
1; INT CA-122; MTCW 2

Leblanc, Maurice (Marie Emile)
1864-1941 .... **TCLC 49**
See also CA 110; CMW 4

Lebowitz, Fran(ces Ann) 1951(?)- ... **CLC 11, 36**
See also CA 81-84; CANR 14, 60, 70; INT
CANR-14; MTCW 1

Mandelshtam, Osip
See Mandelstam, Osip (Emilievich)
See also EW 10; EWL 3; RGWL 2, 3

Mandelstam, Osip (Emilievich)
1891(?)-1943(?) .... **PC 14; TCLC 2, 6**
See Mandelshtam, Osip
See also CA 104; 150; MTCW 2; TWA

Mander, (Mary) Jane 1877-1949 ... **TCLC 31**
See also CA 162; RGEL 2

Mandeville, Bernard 1670-1733 .... **LC 82**
See also DLB 101

Mandeville, Sir John fl. 1350- ...... **CMLC 19**
See also DLB 146

Mandiargues, Andre Pieyre de .... **CLC 41**
See Pieyre de Mandiargues, Andre
See also DLB 83

Mandrake, Ethel Belle
See Thurman, Wallace (Henry)

Mangan, James Clarence
1803-1849 .... **NCLC 27**
See also RGEL 2

Maniere, J.-E.
See Giraudoux, Jean(-Hippolyte)

Mankiewicz, Herman (Jacob)
1897-1953 .... **TCLC 85**
See also CA 120; 169; DLB 26; IDFW 3, 4

Manley, (Mary) Delariviere
1672(?)-1724 .... **LC 1, 42**
See also DLB 39, 80; RGEL 2

Mann, Abel
See Creasey, John

Mann, Emily 1952- .... **DC 7**
See also CA 130; CAD; CANR 55; CD 5;
CWD; DLB 266

Mann, (Luiz) Heinrich 1871-1950 ... **TCLC 9**
See also CA 106; 164, 181; DLB 66, 118;
EW 8; EWL 3; RGWL 2, 3

Mann, (Paul) Thomas 1875-1955 .... **SSC 5,
70; TCLC 2, 8, 14, 21, 35, 44, 60;
WLC**
See also BPFB 2; CA 104; 128; CANR 133;
CDWLB 2; DA; DA3; DAB; DAC; DAM
MST, NOV; DLB 66; EW 9; EWL 3; GLL
1; LATS 1:1; LMFS 1; MTCW 1, 2; NFS
17; RGSF 2; RGWL 2, 3; SSFS 4, 9;
TWA

Mannheim, Karl 1893-1947 .... **TCLC 65**
See also CA 204

Manning, David
See Faust, Frederick (Schiller)
See also TCWW 2

Manning, Frederic 1882-1935 .... **TCLC 25**
See also CA 124; 216; DLB 260

Manning, Olivia 1915-1980 .... **CLC 5, 19**
See also CA 5-8R; 101; CANR 29; EWL 3;
FW; MTCW 1; RGEL 2

Mano, D. Keith 1942- .... **CLC 2, 10**
See also CA 25-28R; CAAS 6; CANR 26,
57; DLB 6

Mansfield, Katherine . **SSC 9, 23, 38; TCLC
2, 8, 39; WLC**
See Beauchamp, Kathleen Mansfield
See also BPFB 2; BRW 7; DAB; DLB 162;
EWL 3; EXPS; FW; GLL 1; RGEL 2;
RGSF 2; SSFS 2, 8, 10, 11; WWE 1

Manso, Peter 1940- .... **CLC 39**
See also CA 29-32R; CANR 44

Mantecon, Juan Jimenez
See Jimenez (Mantecon), Juan Ramon

Mantel, Hilary (Mary) 1952- .... **CLC 144**
See also CA 125; CANR 54, 101; CN 7;
DLB 271; RHW

Manton, Peter
See Creasey, John

Man Without a Spleen, A
See Chekhov, Anton (Pavlovich)

Manzoni, Alessandro 1785-1873 ... **NCLC 29,
98**
See also EW 5; RGWL 2, 3; TWA

Map, Walter 1140-1209 .... **CMLC 32**

Mapu, Abraham (ben Jekutiel)
1808-1867 .... **NCLC 18**

Mara, Sally
See Queneau, Raymond

Maracle, Lee 1950- .... **NNAL**
See also CA 149

Marat, Jean Paul 1743-1793 .... **LC 10**

Marcel, Gabriel Honore 1889-1973 . **CLC 15**
See also CA 102; 45-48; EWL 3; MTCW 1,
2

March, William 1893-1954 .... **TCLC 96**
See also CA 216

Marchbanks, Samuel
See Davies, (William) Robertson
See also CCA 1

Marchi, Giacomo
See Bassani, Giorgio

Marcus Aurelius
See Aurelius, Marcus
See also AW 2

Marguerite
See de Navarre, Marguerite

Marguerite d'Angouleme
See de Navarre, Marguerite
See also GFL Beginnings to 1789

Marguerite de Navarre
See de Navarre, Marguerite
See also RGWL 2, 3

Margulies, Donald 1954- .... **CLC 76**
See also AAYA 57; CA 200; DFS 13; DLB
228

Marie de France c. 12th cent. - ..... **CMLC 8;
PC 22**
See also DLB 208; FW; RGWL 2, 3

Marie de l'Incarnation 1599-1672 ...... **LC 10**

Marier, Captain Victor
See Griffith, D(avid Lewelyn) W(ark)

Mariner, Scott
See Pohl, Frederik

Marinetti, Filippo Tommaso
1876-1944 .... **TCLC 10**
See also CA 107; DLB 114, 264; EW 9;
EWL 3

Marivaux, Pierre Carlet de Chamblain de
1688-1763 .... **DC 7; LC 4**
See also GFL Beginnings to 1789; RGWL
2, 3; TWA

Markandaya, Kamala .... **CLC 8, 38**
See Taylor, Kamala (Purnaiya)
See also BYA 13; CN 7; EWL 3

Markfield, Wallace 1926-2002 .... **CLC 8**
See also CA 69-72; 200; CAAS 3; CN 7;
DLB 2, 28; DLBY 2002

Markham, Edwin 1852-1940 .... **TCLC 47**
See also CA 160; DLB 54, 186; RGAL 4

Markham, Robert
See Amis, Kingsley (William)

Markoosie .... **NNAL**
See Patsauq, Markoosie
See also CLR 23; DAM MULT

Marks, J
See Highwater, Jamake (Mamake)

Marks, J.
See Highwater, Jamake (Mamake)

Marks-Highwater, J
See Highwater, Jamake (Mamake)

Marks-Highwater, J.
See Highwater, Jamake (Mamake)

Markson, David M(errill) 1927- .... **CLC 67**
See also CA 49-52; CANR 1, 91; CN 7

Marlatt, Daphne (Buckle) 1942- .... **CLC 168**
See also CA 25-28R; CANR 17, 39; CN 7;
CP 7; CWP; DLB 60; FW

Marley, Bob .... **CLC 17**
See Marley, Robert Nesta

Marley, Robert Nesta 1945-1981
See Marley, Bob
See also CA 107; 103

Marlowe, Christopher 1564-1593 . **DC 1; LC
22, 47; PC 57; WLC**
See also BRW 1; BRWR 1; CDBLB Before
1660; DA; DA3; DAB; DAC; DAM
DRAM, MST; DFS 1, 5, 13; DLB 62;
EXPP; LMFS 1; RGEL 2; TEA; WLIT 3

Marlowe, Stephen 1928- .... **CLC 70**
See Queen, Ellery
See also CA 13-16R; CANR 6, 55; CMW
4; SFW 4

Marmion, Shakerley 1603-1639 .... **LC 89**
See also DLB 58; RGEL 2

Marmontel, Jean-Francois 1723-1799 .. **LC 2**

Maron, Monika 1941- .... **CLC 165**
See also CA 201

Marquand, John P(hillips)
1893-1960 .... **CLC 2, 10**
See also AMW; BPFB 2; CA 85-88; CANR
73; CMW 4; DLB 9, 102; EWL 3; MTCW
2; RGAL 4

Marques, Rene 1919-1979 .. **CLC 96; HLC 2**
See also CA 97-100; 85-88; CANR 78;
DAM MULT; DLB 305; EWL 3; HW 1,
2; LAW; RGSF 2

Marquez, Gabriel (Jose) Garcia
See Garcia Marquez, Gabriel (Jose)

Marquis, Don(ald Robert Perry)
1878-1937 .... **TCLC 7**
See also CA 104; 166; DLB 11, 25; RGAL
4

Marquis de Sade
See Sade, Donatien Alphonse Francois

Marric, J. J.
See Creasey, John
See also MSW

Marryat, Frederick 1792-1848 .... **NCLC 3**
See also DLB 21, 163; RGEL 2; WCH

Marsden, James
See Creasey, John

Marsh, Edward 1872-1953 .... **TCLC 99**

Marsh, (Edith) Ngaio 1895-1982 .. **CLC 7, 53**
See also CA 9-12R; CANR 6, 58; CMW 4;
CPW; DAM POP; DLB 77; MSW;
MTCW 1, 2; RGEL 2; TEA

Marshall, Garry 1934- .... **CLC 17**
See also AAYA 3; CA 111; SATA 60

Marshall, Paule 1929- .. **BLC 3; CLC 27, 72;
SSC 3**
See also AFAW 1, 2; AMWS 11; BPFB 2;
BW 2, 3; CA 77-80; CANR 25, 73, 129;
CN 7; DA3; DAM MULT; DLB 33, 157,
227; EWL 3; LATS 1:2; MTCW 1, 2;
RGAL 4; SSFS 15

Marshallik
See Zangwill, Israel

Marsten, Richard
See Hunter, Evan

Marston, John 1576-1634 .... **LC 33**
See also BRW 2; DAM DRAM; DLB 58,
172; RGEL 2

Martel, Yann 1963- .... **CLC 192**
See also CA 146; CANR 114

Martha, Henry
See Harris, Mark

Marti, Jose
See Marti (y Perez), Jose (Julian)
See also DLB 290

Marti (y Perez), Jose (Julian)
1853-1895 .... **HLC 2; NCLC 63**
See Marti, Jose
See also DAM MULT; HW 2; LAW; RGWL
2, 3; WLIT 1

Martial c. 40-c. 104 .... **CMLC 35; PC 10**
See also AW 2; CDWLB 1; DLB 211;
RGWL 2, 3

DAB; DAC; DAM MST, MULT, NOV, POP; DLB 143, 175, 256; EWL 3; EXPP; INT CANR-14; LAIT 4; LATS 1:2; MTCW 1, 2; NFS 10; PFS 2, 11; RGAL 4; SATA 48; SATA-Brief 30; WP; YAW

Monette, Paul 1945-1995 .... **CLC 82**
See also AMWS 10; CA 139; 147; CN 7; GLL 1

Monroe, Harriet 1860-1936 .... **TCLC 12**
See also CA 109; 204; DLB 54, 91

Monroe, Lyle
See Heinlein, Robert A(nson)

Montagu, Elizabeth 1720-1800 .... **NCLC 7, 117**
See also FW

Montagu, Mary (Pierrepont) Wortley
1689-1762 .... **LC 9, 57; PC 16**
See also DLB 95, 101; RGEL 2

Montagu, W. H.
See Coleridge, Samuel Taylor

Montague, John (Patrick) 1929- ..... **CLC 13, 46**
See also CA 9-12R; CANR 9, 69, 121; CP 7; DLB 40; EWL 3; MTCW 1; PFS 12; RGEL 2

Montaigne, Michel (Eyquem) de
1533-1592 .... **LC 8, 105; WLC**
See also DA; DAB; DAC; DAM MST; EW 2; GFL Beginnings to 1789; LMFS 1; RGWL 2, 3; TWA

Montale, Eugenio 1896-1981 ... **CLC 7, 9, 18; PC 13**
See also CA 17-20R; 104; CANR 30; DLB 114; EW 11; EWL 3; MTCW 1; RGWL 2, 3; TWA

Montesquieu, Charles-Louis de Secondat
1689-1755 .... **LC 7, 69**
See also EW 3; GFL Beginnings to 1789; TWA

Montessori, Maria 1870-1952 ...... **TCLC 103**
See also CA 115; 147

Montgomery, (Robert) Bruce 1921(?)-1978
See Crispin, Edmund
See also CA 179; 104; CMW 4

Montgomery, L(ucy) M(aud)
1874-1942 .... **TCLC 51, 140**
See also AAYA 12; BYA 1; CA 108; 137; CLR 8, 91; DA3; DAC; DAM MST; DLB 92; DLBD 14; JRDA; MAICYA 1, 2; MTCW 2; RGEL 2; SATA 100; TWA; WCH; WYA; YABC 1

Montgomery, Marion H., Jr. 1925- .... **CLC 7**
See also AITN 1; CA 1-4R; CANR 3, 48; CSW; DLB 6

Montgomery, Max
See Davenport, Guy (Mattison, Jr.)

Montherlant, Henry (Milon) de
1896-1972 .... **CLC 8, 19**
See also CA 85-88; 37-40R; DAM DRAM; DLB 72; EW 11; EWL 3; GFL 1789 to the Present; MTCW 1

Monty Python
See Chapman, Graham; Cleese, John (Marwood); Gilliam, Terry (Vance); Idle, Eric; Jones, Terence Graham Parry; Palin, Michael (Edward)
See also AAYA 7

Moodie, Susanna (Strickland)
1803-1885 .... **NCLC 14, 113**
See also DLB 99

Moody, Hiram (F. III) 1961-
See Moody, Rick
See also CA 138; CANR 64, 112

Moody, Minerva
See Alcott, Louisa May

Moody, Rick .... **CLC 147**
See Moody, Hiram (F. III)

Moody, William Vaughan
1869-1910 .... **TCLC 105**
See also CA 110; 178; DLB 7, 54; RGAL 4

Mooney, Edward 1951-
See Mooney, Ted
See also CA 130

Mooney, Ted .... **CLC 25**
See Mooney, Edward

Moorcock, Michael (John) 1939- ...... **CLC 5, 27, 58**
See Bradbury, Edward P.
See also AAYA 26; CA 45-48; CAAS 5; CANR 2, 17, 38, 64, 122; CN 7; DLB 14, 231, 261; FANT; MTCW 1, 2; SATA 93; SCFW 2; SFW 4; SUFW 1, 2

Moore, Brian 1921-1999 ... **CLC 1, 3, 5, 7, 8, 19, 32, 90**
See Bryan, Michael
See also BRWS 9; CA 1-4R; 174; CANR 1, 25, 42, 63; CCA 1; CN 7; DAB; DAC; DAM MST; DLB 251; EWL 3; FANT; MTCW 1, 2; RGEL 2

Moore, Edward
See Muir, Edwin
See also RGEL 2

Moore, G. E. 1873-1958 .... **TCLC 89**
See also DLB 262

Moore, George Augustus
1852-1933 .... **SSC 19; TCLC 7**
See also BRW 6; CA 104; 177; DLB 10, 18, 57, 135; EWL 3; RGEL 2; RGSF 2

Moore, Lorrie .... **CLC 39, 45, 68**
See Moore, Marie Lorena
See also AMWS 10; DLB 234; SSFS 19

Moore, Marianne (Craig)
1887-1972 .... **CLC 1, 2, 4, 8, 10, 13, 19, 47; PC 4, 49; WLCS**
See also AMW; CA 1-4R; 33-36R; CANR 3, 61; CDALB 1929-1941; DA; DA3; DAB; DAC; DAM MST, POET; DLB 45; DLBD 7; EWL 3; EXPP; MAWW; MTCW 1, 2; PAB; PFS 14, 17; RGAL 4; SATA 20; TUS; WP

Moore, Marie Lorena 1957- .... **CLC 165**
See Moore, Lorrie
See also CA 116; CANR 39, 83; CN 7; DLB 234

Moore, Thomas 1779-1852 .... **NCLC 6, 110**
See also DLB 96, 144; RGEL 2

Moorhouse, Frank 1938- .... **SSC 40**
See also CA 118; CANR 92; CN 7; DLB 289; RGSF 2

Mora, Pat(ricia) 1942- .... **HLC 2**
See also AMWS 13; CA 129; CANR 57, 81, 112; CLR 58; DAM MULT; DLB 209; HW 1, 2; LLW 1; MAICYA 2; SATA 92, 134

Moraga, Cherrie 1952- ...... **CLC 126; DC 22**
See also CA 131; CANR 66; DAM MULT; DLB 82, 249; FW; GLL 1; HW 1, 2; LLW 1

Morand, Paul 1888-1976 .... **CLC 41; SSC 22**
See also CA 184; 69-72; DLB 65; EWL 3

Morante, Elsa 1918-1985 .... **CLC 8, 47**
See also CA 85-88; 117; CANR 35; DLB 177; EWL 3; MTCW 1, 2; RGWL 2, 3

Moravia, Alberto .... **CLC 2, 7, 11, 27, 46; SSC 26**
See Pincherle, Alberto
See also DLB 177; EW 12; EWL 3; MTCW 2; RGSF 2; RGWL 2, 3

More, Hannah 1745-1833 ...... **NCLC 27, 141**
See also DLB 107, 109, 116, 158; RGEL 2

More, Henry 1614-1687 .... **LC 9**
See also DLB 126, 252

More, Sir Thomas 1478(?)-1535 .... **LC 10, 32**
See also BRWC 1; BRWS 7; DLB 136, 281; LMFS 1; RGEL 2; TEA

Moreas, Jean .... **TCLC 18**
See Papadiamantopoulos, Johannes
See also GFL 1789 to the Present

Moreton, Andrew Esq.
See Defoe, Daniel

Morgan, Berry 1919-2002 .... **CLC 6**
See also CA 49-52; 208; DLB 6

Morgan, Claire
See Highsmith, (Mary) Patricia
See also GLL 1

Morgan, Edwin (George) 1920- .... **CLC 31**
See also BRWS 9; CA 5-8R; CANR 3, 43, 90; CP 7; DLB 27

Morgan, (George) Frederick
1922-2004 .... **CLC 23**
See also CA 17-20R; 224; CANR 21; CP 7

Morgan, Harriet
See Mencken, H(enry) L(ouis)

Morgan, Jane
See Cooper, James Fenimore

Morgan, Janet 1945- .... **CLC 39**
See also CA 65-68

Morgan, Lady 1776(?)-1859 .... **NCLC 29**
See also DLB 116, 158; RGEL 2

Morgan, Robin (Evonne) 1941- .... **CLC 2**
See also CA 69-72; CANR 29, 68; FW; GLL 2; MTCW 1; SATA 80

Morgan, Scott
See Kuttner, Henry

Morgan, Seth 1949(?)-1990 .... **CLC 65**
See also CA 185; 132

Morgenstern, Christian (Otto Josef Wolfgang) 1871-1914 .... **TCLC 8**
See also CA 105; 191; EWL 3

Morgenstern, S.
See Goldman, William (W.)

Mori, Rintaro
See Mori Ogai
See also CA 110

Moricz, Zsigmond 1879-1942 .... **TCLC 33**
See also CA 165; DLB 215; EWL 3

Morike, Eduard (Friedrich)
1804-1875 .... **NCLC 10**
See also DLB 133; RGWL 2, 3

Mori Ogai 1862-1922 .... **TCLC 14**
See Ogai
See also CA 164; DLB 180; EWL 3; RGWL 3; TWA

Moritz, Karl Philipp 1756-1793 .... **LC 2**
See also DLB 94

Morland, Peter Henry
See Faust, Frederick (Schiller)

Morley, Christopher (Darlington)
1890-1957 .... **TCLC 87**
See also CA 112; 213; DLB 9; RGAL 4

Morren, Theophil
See Hofmannsthal, Hugo von

Morris, Bill 1952- .... **CLC 76**
See also CA 225

Morris, Julian
See West, Morris L(anglo)

Morris, Steveland Judkins 1950(?)-
See Wonder, Stevie
See also CA 111

Morris, William 1834-1896 . **NCLC 4; PC 55**
See also BRW 5; CDBLB 1832-1890; DLB 18, 35, 57, 156, 178, 184; FANT; RGEL 2; SFW 4; SUFW

Morris, Wright 1910-1998 .. **CLC 1, 3, 7, 18, 37; TCLC 107**
See also AMW; CA 9-12R; 167; CANR 21, 81; CN 7; DLB 2, 206, 218; DLBY 1981; EWL 3; MTCW 1, 2; RGAL 4; TCWW 2

Morrison, Arthur 1863-1945 .... **SSC 40; TCLC 72**
See also CA 120; 157; CMW 4; DLB 70, 135, 197; RGEL 2

Morrison, Chloe Anthony Wofford
See Morrison, Toni
Morrison, James Douglas 1943-1971
See Morrison, Jim
See also CA 73-76; CANR 40
Morrison, Jim .... **CLC 17**
See Morrison, James Douglas
Morrison, Toni 1931- ..... **BLC 3; CLC 4, 10, 22, 55, 81, 87, 173, 194**
See also AAYA 1, 22; AFAW 1, 2; AMWC 1; AMWS 3; BPFB 2; BW 2, 3; CA 29-32R; CANR 27, 42, 67, 113, 124; CDALB 1968-1988; CLR 99; CN 7; CPW; DA; DA3; DAB; DAC; DAM MST, MULT, NOV, POP; DLB 6, 33, 143; DLBY 1981; EWL 3; EXPN; FW; LAIT 2, 4; LATS 1:2; LMFS 2; MAWW; MTCW 1, 2; NFS 1, 6, 8, 14; RGAL 4; RHW; SATA 57, 144; SSFS 5; TUS; YAW
Morrison, Van 1945- .... **CLC 21**
See also CA 116; 168
Morrissy, Mary 1957- .... **CLC 99**
See also CA 205; DLB 267
Mortimer, John (Clifford) 1923- ..... **CLC 28, 43**
See also CA 13-16R; CANR 21, 69, 109; CD 5; CDBLB 1960 to Present; CMW 4; CN 7; CPW; DA3; DAM DRAM, POP; DLB 13, 245, 271; INT CANR-21; MSW; MTCW 1, 2; RGEL 2
Mortimer, Penelope (Ruth) 1918-1999 .... **CLC 5**
See also CA 57-60; 187; CANR 45, 88; CN 7
Mortimer, Sir John
See Mortimer, John (Clifford)
Morton, Anthony
See Creasey, John
Morton, Thomas 1579(?)-1647(?) .... **LC 72**
See also DLB 24; RGEL 2
Mosca, Gaetano 1858-1941 .... **TCLC 75**
Moses, Daniel David 1952- .... **NNAL**
See also CA 186
Mosher, Howard Frank 1943- .... **CLC 62**
See also CA 139; CANR 65, 115
Mosley, Nicholas 1923- .... **CLC 43, 70**
See also CA 69-72; CANR 41, 60, 108; CN 7; DLB 14, 207
Mosley, Walter 1952- .... **BLCS; CLC 97, 184**
See also AAYA 57; AMWS 13; BPFB 2; BW 2; CA 142; CANR 57, 92; CMW 4; CPW; DA3; DAM MULT, POP; DLB 306; MSW; MTCW 2
Moss, Howard 1922-1987 . **CLC 7, 14, 45, 50**
See also CA 1-4R; 123; CANR 1, 44; DAM POET; DLB 5
Mossgiel, Rab
See Burns, Robert
Motion, Andrew (Peter) 1952- .... **CLC 47**
See also BRWS 7; CA 146; CANR 90; CP 7; DLB 40
Motley, Willard (Francis) 1909-1965 .... **CLC 18**
See also BW 1; CA 117; 106; CANR 88; DLB 76, 143
Motoori, Norinaga 1730-1801 .... **NCLC 45**
Mott, Michael (Charles Alston) 1930- .... **CLC 15, 34**
See also CA 5-8R; CAAS 7; CANR 7, 29
Mountain Wolf Woman 1884-1960 . **CLC 92; NNAL**
See also CA 144; CANR 90
Moure, Erin 1955- .... **CLC 88**
See also CA 113; CP 7; CWP; DLB 60
Mourning Dove 1885(?)-1936 .... **NNAL**
See also CA 144; CANR 90; DAM MULT; DLB 175, 221

Mowat, Farley (McGill) 1921- .... **CLC 26**
See also AAYA 1, 50; BYA 2; CA 1-4R; CANR 4, 24, 42, 68, 108; CLR 20; CPW; DAC; DAM MST; DLB 68; INT CANR-24; JRDA; MAICYA 1, 2; MTCW 1, 2; SATA 3, 55; YAW
Mowatt, Anna Cora 1819-1870 ..... **NCLC 74**
See also RGAL 4
Moyers, Bill 1934- .... **CLC 74**
See also AITN 2; CA 61-64; CANR 31, 52
Mphahlele, Es'kia
See Mphahlele, Ezekiel
See also AFW; CDWLB 3; DLB 125, 225; RGSF 2; SSFS 11
Mphahlele, Ezekiel 1919- ... **BLC 3; CLC 25, 133**
See Mphahlele, Es'kia
See also BW 2, 3; CA 81-84; CANR 26, 76; CN 7; DA3; DAM MULT; EWL 3; MTCW 2; SATA 119
Mqhayi, S(amuel) E(dward) K(rune Loliwe) 1875-1945 .... **BLC 3; TCLC 25**
See also CA 153; CANR 87; DAM MULT
Mrozek, Slawomir 1930- .... **CLC 3, 13**
See also CA 13-16R; CAAS 10; CANR 29; CDWLB 4; CWW 2; DLB 232; EWL 3; MTCW 1
Mrs. Belloc-Lowndes
See Lowndes, Marie Adelaide (Belloc)
Mrs. Fairstar
See Horne, Richard Henry Hengist
M'Taggart, John M'Taggart Ellis
See McTaggart, John McTaggart Ellis
Mtwa, Percy (?)- .... **CLC 47**
Mueller, Lisel 1924- .... **CLC 13, 51; PC 33**
See also CA 93-96; CP 7; DLB 105; PFS 9, 13
Muggeridge, Malcolm (Thomas) 1903-1990 .... **TCLC 120**
See also AITN 1; CA 101; CANR 33, 63; MTCW 1, 2
Muhammad 570-632 .... **WLCS**
See also DA; DAB; DAC; DAM MST
Muir, Edwin 1887-1959 . **PC 49; TCLC 2, 87**
See Moore, Edward
See also BRWS 6; CA 104; 193; DLB 20, 100, 191; EWL 3; RGEL 2
Muir, John 1838-1914 .... **TCLC 28**
See also AMWS 9; ANW; CA 165; DLB 186, 275
Mujica Lainez, Manuel 1910-1984 ... **CLC 31**
See Lainez, Manuel Mujica
See also CA 81-84; 112; CANR 32; EWL 3; HW 1
Mukherjee, Bharati 1940- ..... **AAL; CLC 53, 115; SSC 38**
See also AAYA 46; BEST 89:2; CA 107; CANR 45, 72, 128; CN 7; DAM NOV; DLB 60, 218; DNFS 1, 2; EWL 3; FW; MTCW 1, 2; RGAL 4; RGSF 2; SSFS 7; TUS; WWE 1
Muldoon, Paul 1951- .... **CLC 32, 72, 166**
See also BRWS 4; CA 113; 129; CANR 52, 91; CP 7; DAM POET; DLB 40; INT CA-129; PFS 7
Mulisch, Harry (Kurt Victor) 1927- .... **CLC 42**
See also CA 9-12R; CANR 6, 26, 56, 110; CWW 2; DLB 299; EWL 3
Mull, Martin 1943- .... **CLC 17**
See also CA 105
Muller, Wilhelm .... **NCLC 73**
Mulock, Dinah Maria
See Craik, Dinah Maria (Mulock)
See also RGEL 2
Munday, Anthony 1560-1633 .... **LC 87**
See also DLB 62, 172; RGEL 2
Munford, Robert 1737(?)-1783 .... **LC 5**
See also DLB 31

Mungo, Raymond 1946- .... **CLC 72**
See also CA 49-52; CANR 2
Munro, Alice 1931- .... **CLC 6, 10, 19, 50, 95; SSC 3; WLCS**
See also AITN 2; BPFB 2; CA 33-36R; CANR 33, 53, 75, 114; CCA 1; CN 7; DA3; DAC; DAM MST, NOV; DLB 53; EWL 3; MTCW 1, 2; RGEL 2; RGSF 2; SATA 29; SSFS 5, 13, 19; WWE 1
Munro, H(ector) H(ugh) 1870-1916 .... **WLC**
See Saki
See also AAYA 56; CA 104; 130; CANR 104; CDBLB 1890-1914; DA; DA3; DAB; DAC; DAM MST, NOV; DLB 34, 162; EXPS; MTCW 1, 2; RGEL 2; SSFS 15
Murakami, Haruki 1949- .... **CLC 150**
See Murakami Haruki
See also CA 165; CANR 102; MJW; RGWL 3; SFW 4
Murakami Haruki
See Murakami, Haruki
See also CWW 2; DLB 182; EWL 3
Murasaki, Lady
See Murasaki Shikibu
Murasaki Shikibu 978(?)-1026(?) ... **CMLC 1**
See also EFS 2; LATS 1:1; RGWL 2, 3
Murdoch, (Jean) Iris 1919-1999 ... **CLC 1, 2, 3, 4, 6, 8, 11, 15, 22, 31, 51**
See also BRWS 1; CA 13-16R; 179; CANR 8, 43, 68, 103; CDBLB 1960 to Present; CN 7; CWD; DA3; DAB; DAC; DAM MST, NOV; DLB 14, 194, 233; EWL 3; INT CANR-8; MTCW 1, 2; NFS 18; RGEL 2; TEA; WLIT 4
Murfree, Mary Noailles 1850-1922 .. **SSC 22; TCLC 135**
See also CA 122; 176; DLB 12, 74; RGAL 4
Murnau, Friedrich Wilhelm
See Plumpe, Friedrich Wilhelm
Murphy, Richard 1927- .... **CLC 41**
See also BRWS 5; CA 29-32R; CP 7; DLB 40; EWL 3
Murphy, Sylvia 1937- .... **CLC 34**
See also CA 121
Murphy, Thomas (Bernard) 1935- ... **CLC 51**
See also CA 101
Murray, Albert L. 1916- .... **CLC 73**
See also BW 2; CA 49-52; CANR 26, 52, 78; CSW; DLB 38
Murray, James Augustus Henry 1837-1915 .... **TCLC 117**
Murray, Judith Sargent 1751-1820 .... **NCLC 63**
See also DLB 37, 200
Murray, Les(lie Allan) 1938- .... **CLC 40**
See also BRWS 7; CA 21-24R; CANR 11, 27, 56, 103; CP 7; DAM POET; DLB 289; DLBY 2001; EWL 3; RGEL 2
Murry, J. Middleton
See Murry, John Middleton
Murry, John Middleton 1889-1957 .... **TCLC 16**
See also CA 118; 217; DLB 149
Musgrave, Susan 1951- .... **CLC 13, 54**
See also CA 69-72; CANR 45, 84; CCA 1; CP 7; CWP
Musil, Robert (Edler von) 1880-1942 .... **SSC 18; TCLC 12, 68**
See also CA 109; CANR 55, 84; CDWLB 2; DLB 81, 124; EW 9; EWL 3; MTCW 2; RGSF 2; RGWL 2, 3
Muske, Carol .... **CLC 90**
See Muske-Dukes, Carol (Anne)
Muske-Dukes, Carol (Anne) 1945-
See Muske, Carol
See also CA 65-68, 203; CAAE 203; CANR 32, 70; CWP

Orton, John Kingsley 1933-1967
    See Orton, Joe
    See also CA 85-88; CANR 35, 66; DAM
    DRAM; MTCW 1, 2
Orwell, George ...... **SSC 68; TCLC 2, 6, 15,
    31, 51, 128, 129; WLC**
    See Blair, Eric (Arthur)
    See also BPFB 3; BRW 7; BYA 5; CDBLB
    1945-1960; CLR 68; DAB; DLB 15, 98,
    195, 255; EWL 3; EXPN; LAIT 4, 5;
    LATS 1:1; NFS 3, 7; RGEL 2; SCFW 2;
    SFW 4; SSFS 4; TEA; WLIT 4; YAW
Osborne, David
    See Silverberg, Robert
Osborne, George
    See Silverberg, Robert
Osborne, John (James) 1929-1994 .... **CLC 1,
    2, 5, 11, 45; TCLC 153; WLC**
    See also BRWS 1; CA 13-16R; 147; CANR
    21, 56; CDBLB 1945-1960; DA; DAB;
    DAC; DAM DRAM, MST; DFS 4, 19;
    DLB 13; EWL 3; MTCW 1, 2; RGEL 2
Osborne, Lawrence 1958- .... **CLC 50**
    See also CA 189
Osbourne, Lloyd 1868-1947 .... **TCLC 93**
Osgood, Frances Sargent
    1811-1850 .... **NCLC 141**
    See also DLB 250
Oshima, Nagisa 1932- .... **CLC 20**
    See also CA 116; 121; CANR 78
Oskison, John Milton
    1874-1947 .... **NNAL; TCLC 35**
    See also CA 144; CANR 84; DAM MULT;
    DLB 175
Ossian c. 3rd cent. - .... **CMLC 28**
    See Macpherson, James
Ossoli, Sarah Margaret (Fuller)
    1810-1850 .... **NCLC 5, 50**
    See Fuller, Margaret; Fuller, Sarah Margaret
    See also CDALB 1640-1865; FW; LMFS 1;
    SATA 25
Ostriker, Alicia (Suskin) 1937- .... **CLC 132**
    See also CA 25-28R; CAAS 24; CANR 10,
    30, 62, 99; CWP; DLB 120; EXPP; PFS
    19
Ostrovsky, Aleksandr Nikolaevich
    See Ostrovsky, Alexander
    See also DLB 277
Ostrovsky, Alexander 1823-1886 .. **NCLC 30,
    57**
    See Ostrovsky, Aleksandr Nikolaevich
Otero, Blas de 1916-1979 .... **CLC 11**
    See also CA 89-92; DLB 134; EWL 3
O'Trigger, Sir Lucius
    See Horne, Richard Henry Hengist
Otto, Rudolf 1869-1937 .... **TCLC 85**
Otto, Whitney 1955- .... **CLC 70**
    See also CA 140; CANR 120
Otway, Thomas 1652-1685 ... **DC 24; LC 106**
    See also DAM DRAM; DLB 80; RGEL 2
Ouida .... **TCLC 43**
    See De la Ramee, Marie Louise (Ouida)
    See also DLB 18, 156; RGEL 2
Ouologuem, Yambo 1940- .... **CLC 146**
    See also CA 111; 176
Ousmane, Sembene 1923- ... **BLC 3; CLC 66**
    See Sembene, Ousmane
    See also BW 1, 3; CA 117; 125; CANR 81;
    CWW 2; MTCW 1
Ovid 43B.C.-17 .... **CMLC 7; PC 2**
    See also AW 2; CDWLB 1; DA3; DAM
    POET; DLB 211; RGWL 2, 3; WP
Owen, Hugh
    See Faust, Frederick (Schiller)

Owen, Wilfred (Edward Salter)
    1893-1918 ... **PC 19; TCLC 5, 27; WLC**
    See also BRW 6; CA 104; 141; CDBLB
    1914-1945; DA; DAB; DAC; DAM MST,
    POET; DLB 20; EWL 3; EXPP; MTCW
    2; PFS 10; RGEL 2; WLIT 4
Owens, Louis (Dean) 1948-2002 .... **NNAL**
    See also CA 137, 179; 207; CAAE 179;
    CAAS 24; CANR 71
Owens, Rochelle 1936- .... **CLC 8**
    See also CA 17-20R; CAAS 2; CAD;
    CANR 39; CD 5; CP 7; CWD; CWP
Oz, Amos 1939- ...... **CLC 5, 8, 11, 27, 33, 54;
    SSC 66**
    See also CA 53-56; CANR 27, 47, 65, 113;
    CWW 2; DAM NOV; EWL 3; MTCW 1,
    2; RGSF 2; RGWL 3
Ozick, Cynthia 1928- .... **CLC 3, 7, 28, 62,
    155; SSC 15, 60**
    See also AMWS 5; BEST 90:1; CA 17-20R;
    CANR 23, 58, 116; CN 7; CPW; DA3;
    DAM NOV, POP; DLB 28, 152, 299;
    DLBY 1982; EWL 3; EXPS; INT CANR-
    23; MTCW 1, 2; RGAL 4; RGSF 2; SSFS
    3, 12
Ozu, Yasujiro 1903-1963 .... **CLC 16**
    See also CA 112
Pabst, G. W. 1885-1967 .... **TCLC 127**
Pacheco, C.
    See Pessoa, Fernando (Antonio Nogueira)
Pacheco, Jose Emilio 1939- .... **HLC 2**
    See also CA 111; 131; CANR 65; CWW 2;
    DAM MULT; DLB 290; EWL 3; HW 1,
    2; RGSF 2
Pa Chin .... **CLC 18**
    See Li Fei-kan
    See also EWL 3
Pack, Robert 1929- .... **CLC 13**
    See also CA 1-4R; CANR 3, 44, 82; CP 7;
    DLB 5; SATA 118
Padgett, Lewis
    See Kuttner, Henry
Padilla (Lorenzo), Heberto
    1932-2000 .... **CLC 38**
    See also AITN 1; CA 123; 131; 189; CWW
    2; EWL 3; HW 1
Page, James Patrick 1944-
    See Page, Jimmy
    See also CA 204
Page, Jimmy 1944- .... **CLC 12**
    See Page, James Patrick
Page, Louise 1955- .... **CLC 40**
    See also CA 140; CANR 76; CBD; CD 5;
    CWD; DLB 233
Page, P(atricia) K(athleen) 1916- ...... **CLC 7,
    18; PC 12**
    See Cape, Judith
    See also CA 53-56; CANR 4, 22, 65; CP 7;
    DAC; DAM MST; DLB 68; MTCW 1;
    RGEL 2
Page, Stanton
    See Fuller, Henry Blake
Page, Stanton
    See Fuller, Henry Blake
Page, Thomas Nelson 1853-1922 .... **SSC 23**
    See also CA 118; 177; DLB 12, 78; DLBD
    13; RGAL 4
Pagels, Elaine Hiesey 1943- .... **CLC 104**
    See also CA 45-48; CANR 2, 24, 51; FW;
    NCFS 4
Paget, Violet 1856-1935
    See Lee, Vernon
    See also CA 104; 166; GLL 1; HGG
Paget-Lowe, Henry
    See Lovecraft, H(oward) P(hillips)
Paglia, Camille (Anna) 1947- .... **CLC 68**
    See also CA 140; CANR 72; CPW; FW;
    GLL 2; MTCW 2

Paige, Richard
    See Koontz, Dean R(ay)
Paine, Thomas 1737-1809 .... **NCLC 62**
    See also AMWS 1; CDALB 1640-1865;
    DLB 31, 43, 73, 158; LAIT 1; RGAL 4;
    RGEL 2; TUS
Pakenham, Antonia
    See Fraser, Antonia (Pakenham)
Palamas, Costis
    See Palamas, Kostes
Palamas, Kostes 1859-1943 .... **TCLC 5**
    See Palamas, Kostis
    See also CA 105; 190; RGWL 2, 3
Palamas, Kostis
    See Palamas, Kostes
    See also EWL 3
Palazzeschi, Aldo 1885-1974 .... **CLC 11**
    See also CA 89-92; 53-56; DLB 114, 264;
    EWL 3
Pales Matos, Luis 1898-1959 .... **HLCS 2**
    See Pales Matos, Luis
    See also DLB 290; HW 1; LAW
Paley, Grace 1922- .. **CLC 4, 6, 37, 140; SSC
    8**
    See also AMWS 6; CA 25-28R; CANR 13,
    46, 74, 118; CN 7; CPW; DA3; DAM
    POP; DLB 28, 218; EWL 3; EXPS; FW;
    INT CANR-13; MAWW; MTCW 1, 2;
    RGAL 4; RGSF 2; SSFS 3, 20
Palin, Michael (Edward) 1943- .... **CLC 21**
    See Monty Python
    See also CA 107; CANR 35, 109; SATA 67
Palliser, Charles 1947- .... **CLC 65**
    See also CA 136; CANR 76; CN 7
Palma, Ricardo 1833-1919 .... **TCLC 29**
    See also CA 168; LAW
Pamuk, Orhan 1952- .... **CLC 185**
    See also CA 142; CANR 75, 127; CWW 2
Pancake, Breece Dexter 1952-1979
    See Pancake, Breece D'J
    See also CA 123; 109
Pancake, Breece D'J .... **CLC 29; SSC 61**
    See Pancake, Breece Dexter
    See also DLB 130
Panchenko, Nikolai .... **CLC 59**
Pankhurst, Emmeline (Goulden)
    1858-1928 .... **TCLC 100**
    See also CA 116; FW
Panko, Rudy
    See Gogol, Nikolai (Vasilyevich)
Papadiamantis, Alexandros
    1851-1911 .... **TCLC 29**
    See also CA 168; EWL 3
Papadiamantopoulos, Johannes 1856-1910
    See Moreas, Jean
    See also CA 117
Papini, Giovanni 1881-1956 .... **TCLC 22**
    See also CA 121; 180; DLB 264
Paracelsus 1493-1541 .... **LC 14**
    See also DLB 179
Parasol, Peter
    See Stevens, Wallace
Pardo Bazan, Emilia 1851-1921 .... **SSC 30**
    See also EWL 3; FW; RGSF 2; RGWL 2, 3
Pareto, Vilfredo 1848-1923 .... **TCLC 69**
    See also CA 175
Paretsky, Sara 1947- .... **CLC 135**
    See also AAYA 30; BEST 90:3; CA 125;
    129; CANR 59, 95; CMW 4; CPW; DA3;
    DAM POP; DLB 306; INT CA-129;
    MSW; RGAL 4
Parfenie, Maria
    See Codrescu, Andrei
Parini, Jay (Lee) 1948- .... **CLC 54, 133**
    See also CA 97-100; CAAS 16; CANR 32,
    87
Park, Jordan
    See Kornbluth, C(yril) M.; Pohl, Frederik

Pendennis, Arthur Esquir
See Thackeray, William Makepeace
Penn, William 1644-1718 .... **LC 25**
See also DLB 24
PEPECE
See Prado (Calvo), Pedro
Pepys, Samuel 1633-1703 ... **LC 11, 58; WLC**
See also BRW 2; CDBLB 1660-1789; DA;
DA3; DAB; DAC; DAM MST; DLB 101,
213; NCFS 4; RGEL 2; TEA; WLIT 3
Percy, Thomas 1729-1811 .... **NCLC 95**
See also DLB 104
Percy, Walker 1916-1990 .... **CLC 2, 3, 6, 8,
14, 18, 47, 65**
See also AMWS 3; BPFB 3; CA 1-4R; 131;
CANR 1, 23, 64; CPW; CSW; DA3;
DAM NOV, POP; DLB 2; DLBY 1980,
1990; EWL 3; MTCW 1, 2; RGAL 4;
TUS
Percy, William Alexander
1885-1942 .... **TCLC 84**
See also CA 163; MTCW 2
Perec, Georges 1936-1982 .... **CLC 56, 116**
See also CA 141; DLB 83, 299; EWL 3;
GFL 1789 to the Present; RGWL 3
**Pereda (y Sanchez de Porrua), Jose Maria
de** 1833-1906 .... **TCLC 16**
See also CA 117
Pereda y Porrua, Jose Maria de
See Pereda (y Sanchez de Porrua), Jose
Maria de
Peregoy, George Weems
See Mencken, H(enry) L(ouis)
Perelman, S(idney) J(oseph)
1904-1979 .. **CLC 3, 5, 9, 15, 23, 44, 49;
SSC 32**
See also AITN 1, 2; BPFB 3; CA 73-76;
89-92; BPFB 3; CA 73-76;
89-92; CANR 18; DAM DRAM; DLB 11,
44; MTCW 1, 2; RGAL 4
Peret, Benjamin 1899-1959 .... **PC 33; TCLC
20**
See also CA 117; 186; GFL 1789 to the
Present
Peretz, Isaac Leib 1851(?)-1915
See Peretz, Isaac Loeb
See also CA 201
Peretz, Isaac Loeb 1851(?)-1915 ...... **SSC 26;
TCLC 16**
See Peretz, Isaac Leib
See also CA 109
Peretz, Yitzhok Leibush
See Peretz, Isaac Loeb
Perez Galdos, Benito 1843-1920 ..... **HLCS 2;
TCLC 27**
See Galdos, Benito Perez
See also CA 125; 153; EWL 3; HW 1;
RGWL 2, 3
Peri Rossi, Cristina 1941- .. **CLC 156; HLCS
2**
See also CA 131; CANR 59, 81; CWW 2;
DLB 145, 290; EWL 3; HW 1, 2
Perlata
See Peret, Benjamin
Perloff, Marjorie G(abrielle)
1931- .... **CLC 137**
See also CA 57-60; CANR 7, 22, 49, 104
Perrault, Charles 1628-1703 .... **LC 2, 56**
See also BYA 4; CLR 79; DLB 268; GFL
Beginnings to 1789; MAICYA 1, 2;
RGWL 2, 3; SATA 25; WCH
Perry, Anne 1938- .... **CLC 126**
See also CA 101; CANR 22, 50, 84; CMW
4; CN 7; CPW; DLB 276
Perry, Brighton
See Sherwood, Robert E(mmet)
Perse, St.-John
See Leger, (Marie-Rene Auguste) Alexis
Saint-Leger

Perse, Saint-John
See Leger, (Marie-Rene Auguste) Alexis
Saint-Leger
See also DLB 258; RGWL 3
Perutz, Leo(pold) 1882-1957 .... **TCLC 60**
See also CA 147; DLB 81
Peseenz, Tulio F.
See Lopez y Fuentes, Gregorio
Pesetsky, Bette 1932- .... **CLC 28**
See also CA 133; DLB 130
Peshkov, Alexei Maximovich 1868-1936
See Gorky, Maxim
See also CA 105; 141; CANR 83; DA;
DAC; DAM DRAM, MST, NOV; MTCW
2
Pessoa, Fernando (Antonio Nogueira)
1888-1935 ..... **HLC 2; PC 20; TCLC 27**
See also CA 125; 183; DAM MULT; DLB
287; EW 10; EWL 3; RGWL 2, 3; WP
Peterkin, Julia Mood 1880-1961 ...... **CLC 31**
See also CA 102; DLB 9
Peters, Joan K(aren) 1945- .... **CLC 39**
See also CA 158; CANR 109
Peters, Robert L(ouis) 1924- .... **CLC 7**
See also CA 13-16R; CAAS 8; CP 7; DLB
105
Petofi, Sandor 1823-1849 .... **NCLC 21**
See also RGWL 2, 3
Petrakis, Harry Mark 1923- .... **CLC 3**
See also CA 9-12R; CANR 4, 30, 85; CN 7
Petrarch 1304-1374 .... **CMLC 20; PC 8**
See also DA3; DAM POET; EW 2; LMFS
1; RGWL 2. 3
Petronius c. 20-66 .... **CMLC 34**
See also AW 2; CDWLB 1; DLB 211;
RGWL 2, 3
Petrov, Evgeny .... **TCLC 21**
See Kataev, Evgeny Petrovich
Petry, Ann (Lane) 1908-1997 .. **CLC 1, 7, 18;
TCLC 112**
See also AFAW 1, 2; BPFB 3; BW 1, 3;
BYA 2; CA 5-8R; 157; CAAS 6; CANR
4, 46; CLR 12; CN 7; DLB 76; EWL 3;
JRDA; LAIT 1; MAICYA 1, 2; MAIC-
YAS 1; MTCW 1; RGAL 4; SATA 5;
SATA-Obit 94; TUS
Petursson, Halligrimur 1614-1674 .... **LC 8**
Peychinovich
See Vazov, Ivan (Minchov)
Phaedrus c. 15B.C.-c. 50 .... **CMLC 25**
See also DLB 211
Phelps (Ward), Elizabeth Stuart
See Phelps, Elizabeth Stuart
See also FW
Phelps, Elizabeth Stuart
1844-1911 .... **TCLC 113**
See Phelps (Ward), Elizabeth Stuart
See also DLB 74
Philips, Katherine 1632-1664 . **LC 30; PC 40**
See also DLB 131; RGEL 2
Philipson, Morris H. 1926- .... **CLC 53**
See also CA 1-4R; CANR 4
Phillips, Caryl 1958- .... **BLCS; CLC 96**
See also BRWS 5; BW 2; CA 141; CANR
63, 104; CBD; CD 5; CN 7; DA3; DAM
MULT; DLB 157; EWL 3; MTCW 2;
WLIT 4; WWE 1
Phillips, David Graham
1867-1911 .... **TCLC 44**
See also CA 108; 176; DLB 9, 12, 303;
RGAL 4
Phillips, Jack
See Sandburg, Carl (August)
Phillips, Jayne Anne 1952- .... **CLC 15, 33,
139; SSC 16**
See also AAYA 57; BPFB 3; CA 101;
CANR 24, 50, 96; CN 7; CSW; DLBY
1980; INT CANR-24; MTCW 1, 2; RGAL
4; RGSF 2; SSFS 4

Phillips, Richard
See Dick, Philip K(indred)
Phillips, Robert (Schaeffer) 1938- .... **CLC 28**
See also CA 17-20R; CAAS 13; CANR 8;
DLB 105
Phillips, Ward
See Lovecraft, H(oward) P(hillips)
Philostratus, Flavius c. 179-c.
244 .... **CMLC 62**
Piccolo, Lucio 1901-1969 .... **CLC 13**
See also CA 97-100; DLB 114; EWL 3
Pickthall, Marjorie L(owry) C(hristie)
1883-1922 .... **TCLC 21**
See also CA 107; DLB 92
Pico della Mirandola, Giovanni
1463-1494 .... **LC 15**
See also LMFS 1
Piercy, Marge 1936- .... **CLC 3, 6, 14, 18, 27,
62, 128; PC 29**
See also BPFB 3; CA 21-24R, 187; CAAE
187; CAAS 1; CANR 13, 43, 66, 111; CN
7; CP 7; CWP; DLB 120, 227; EXPP;
FW; MTCW 1, 2; PFS 9; SFW 4
Piers, Robert
See Anthony, Piers
Pieyre de Mandiargues, Andre 1909-1991
See Mandiargues, Andre Pieyre de
See also CA 103; 136; CANR 22, 82; EWL
3; GFL 1789 to the Present
Pilnyak, Boris 1894-1938 . **SSC 48; TCLC 23**
See Vogau, Boris Andreyevich
See also EWL 3
Pinchback, Eugene
See Toomer, Jean
Pincherle, Alberto 1907-1990 ...... **CLC 11, 18**
See Moravia, Alberto
See also CA 25-28R; 132; CANR 33, 63;
DAM NOV; MTCW 1
Pinckney, Darryl 1953- .... **CLC 76**
See also BW 2, 3; CA 143; CANR 79
Pindar 518(?)B.C.-438(?)B.C. .... **CMLC 12;
PC 19**
See also AW 1; CDWLB 1; DLB 176;
RGWL 2
Pineda, Cecile 1942- .... **CLC 39**
See also CA 118; DLB 209
Pinero, Arthur Wing 1855-1934 .... **TCLC 32**
See also CA 110; 153; DAM DRAM; DLB
10; RGEL 2
Pinero, Miguel (Antonio Gomez)
1946-1988 .... **CLC 4, 55**
See also CA 61-64; 125; CAD; CANR 29,
90; DLB 266; HW 1; LLW 1
Pinget, Robert 1919-1997 .... **CLC 7, 13, 37**
See also CA 85-88; 160; CWW 2; DLB 83;
EWL 3; GFL 1789 to the Present
Pink Floyd
See Barrett, (Roger) Syd; Gilmour, David;
Mason, Nick; Waters, Roger; Wright, Rick
Pinkney, Edward 1802-1828 .... **NCLC 31**
See also DLB 248
Pinkwater, Daniel
See Pinkwater, Daniel Manus
Pinkwater, Daniel Manus 1941- .... **CLC 35**
See also AAYA 1, 46; BYA 9; CA 29-32R;
CANR 12, 38, 89; CLR 4; CSW; FANT;
JRDA; MAICYA 1, 2; SAAS 3; SATA 8,
46, 76, 114; SFW 4; YAW
Pinkwater, Manus
See Pinkwater, Daniel Manus
Pinsky, Robert 1940- .... **CLC 9, 19, 38, 94,
121; PC 27**
See also AMWS 6; CA 29-32R; CAAS 4;
CANR 58, 97; CP 7; DA3; DAM POET;
DLBY 1982, 1998; MTCW 2; PFS 18;
RGAL 4
Pinta, Harold
See Pinter, Harold

Putnam, Arthur Lee
See Alger, Horatio, Jr.
Puzo, Mario 1920-1999 .... **CLC 1, 2, 6, 36, 107**
See also BPFB 3; CA 65-68; 185; CANR 4, 42, 65, 99, 131; CN 7; CPW; DA3; DAM NOV, POP; DLB 6; MTCW 1, 2; NFS 16; RGAL 4
Pygge, Edward
See Barnes, Julian (Patrick)
Pyle, Ernest Taylor 1900-1945
See Pyle, Ernie
See also CA 115; 160
Pyle, Ernie .... **TCLC 75**
See Pyle, Ernest Taylor
See also DLB 29; MTCW 2
Pyle, Howard 1853-1911 .... **TCLC 81**
See also AAYA 57; BYA 2, 4; CA 109; 137; CLR 22; DLB 42, 188; DLBD 13; LAIT 1; MAICYA 1, 2; SATA 16, 100; WCH; YAW
Pym, Barbara (Mary Crampton)
1913-1980 .... **CLC 13, 19, 37, 111**
See also BPFB 3; BRWS 2; CA 13-14; 97-100; CANR 13, 34; CAP 1; DLB 14, 207; DLBY 1987; EWL 3; MTCW 1, 2; RGEL 2; TEA
Pynchon, Thomas (Ruggles, Jr.)
1937- ...... **CLC 2, 3, 6, 9, 11, 18, 33, 62, 72, 123, 192; SSC 14; WLC**
See also AMWS 2; BEST 90:2; BPFB 3; CA 17-20R; CANR 22, 46, 73; CN 7; CPW 1; DA; DA3; DAB; DAC; DAM MST, NOV, POP; DLB 2, 173; EWL 3; MTCW 1, 2; RGAL 4; SFW 4; TUS
Pythagoras c. 582B.C.-c. 507B.C. . **CMLC 22**
See also DLB 176

Q
See Quiller-Couch, Sir Arthur (Thomas)
Qian, Chongzhu
See Ch'ien, Chung-shu
Qian, Sima 145B.C.-c. 89B.C. .... **CMLC 72**
Qian Zhongshu
See Ch'ien, Chung-shu
See also CWW 2
Qroll
See Dagerman, Stig (Halvard)
Quarrington, Paul (Lewis) 1953- ..... **CLC 65**
See also CA 129; CANR 62, 95
Quasimodo, Salvatore 1901-1968 .... **CLC 10; PC 47**
See also CA 13-16; 25-28R; CAP 1; DLB 114; EW 12; EWL 3; MTCW 1; RGWL 2, 3
Quatermass, Martin
See Carpenter, John (Howard)
Quay, Stephen 1947- .... **CLC 95**
See also CA 189
Quay, Timothy 1947- .... **CLC 95**
See also CA 189
Queen, Ellery .... **CLC 3, 11**
See Dannay, Frederic; Davidson, Avram (James); Deming, Richard; Fairman, Paul W.; Flora, Fletcher; Hoch, Edward D(entinger); Kane, Henry; Lee, Manfred B(ennington); Marlowe, Stephen; Powell, (Oval) Talmage; Sheldon, Walter J(ames); Sturgeon, Theodore (Hamilton); Tracy, Don(ald Fiske); Vance, John Holbrook
See also BPFB 3; CMW 4; MSW; RGAL 4
Queen, Ellery, Jr.
See Dannay, Frederic; Lee, Manfred B(ennington)
Queneau, Raymond 1903-1976 ..... **CLC 2, 5, 10, 42**
See also CA 77-80; 69-72; CANR 32; DLB 72, 258; EW 12; EWL 3; GFL 1789 to the Present; MTCW 1, 2; RGWL 2, 3
Quevedo, Francisco de 1580-1645 .... **LC 23**

Quiller-Couch, Sir Arthur (Thomas)
1863-1944 .... **TCLC 53**
See also CA 118; 166; DLB 135, 153, 190; HGG; RGEL 2; SUFW 1
Quin, Ann (Marie) 1936-1973 .... **CLC 6**
See also CA 9-12R; 45-48; DLB 14, 231
Quincey, Thomas de
See De Quincey, Thomas
Quindlen, Anna 1953- .... **CLC 191**
See also AAYA 35; CA 138; CANR 73, 126; DA3; DLB 292; MTCW 2
Quinn, Martin
See Smith, Martin Cruz
Quinn, Peter 1947- .... **CLC 91**
See also CA 197
Quinn, Simon
See Smith, Martin Cruz
Quintana, Leroy V. 1944- ...... **HLC 2; PC 36**
See also CA 131; CANR 65; DAM MULT; DLB 82; HW 1, 2
Quiroga, Horacio (Sylvestre)
1878-1937 .... **HLC 2; TCLC 20**
See also CA 117; 131; DAM MULT; EWL 3; HW 1; LAW; MTCW 1; RGSF 2; WLIT 1
Quoirez, Francoise 1935- .... **CLC 9**
See Sagan, Francoise
See also CA 49-52; CANR 6, 39, 73; MTCW 1, 2; TWA
Raabe, Wilhelm (Karl) 1831-1910 . **TCLC 45**
See also CA 167; DLB 129
Rabe, David (William) 1940- .. **CLC 4, 8, 33; DC 16**
See also CA 85-88; CABS 3; CAD; CANR 59, 129; CD 5; DAM DRAM; DFS 3, 8, 13; DLB 7, 228; EWL 3
Rabelais, Francois 1494-1553 .... **LC 5, 60; WLC**
See also DA; DAB; DAC; DAM MST; EW 2; GFL Beginnings to 1789; LMFS 1; RGWL 2, 3; TWA
Rabinovitch, Sholem 1859-1916
See Aleichem, Sholom
See also CA 104
Rabinyan, Dorit 1972- .... **CLC 119**
See also CA 170
Rachilde
See Vallette, Marguerite Eymery; Vallette, Marguerite Eymery
See also EWL 3
Racine, Jean 1639-1699 .... **LC 28**
See also DA3; DAB; DAM MST; DLB 268; EW 3; GFL Beginnings to 1789; LMFS 1; RGWL 2, 3; TWA
Radcliffe, Ann (Ward) 1764-1823 ... **NCLC 6, 55, 106**
See also DLB 39, 178; HGG; LMFS 1; RGEL 2; SUFW; WLIT 3
Radclyffe-Hall, Marguerite
See Hall, (Marguerite) Radclyffe
Radiguet, Raymond 1903-1923 ...... **TCLC 29**
See also CA 162; DLB 65; EWL 3; GFL 1789 to the Present; RGWL 2, 3
Radnoti, Miklos 1909-1944 .... **TCLC 16**
See also CA 118; 212; CDWLB 4; DLB 215; EWL 3; RGWL 2, 3
Rado, James 1939- .... **CLC 17**
See also CA 105
Radvanyi, Netty 1900-1983
See Seghers, Anna
See also CA 85-88; 110; CANR 82
Rae, Ben
See Griffiths, Trevor
Raeburn, John (Hay) 1941- .... **CLC 34**
See also CA 57-60
Ragni, Gerome 1942-1991 .... **CLC 17**
See also CA 105; 134

Rahv, Philip .... **CLC 24**
See Greenberg, Ivan
See also DLB 137
Raimund, Ferdinand Jakob
1790-1836 .... **NCLC 69**
See also DLB 90
Raine, Craig (Anthony) 1944- .. **CLC 32, 103**
See also CA 108; CANR 29, 51, 103; CP 7; DLB 40; PFS 7
Raine, Kathleen (Jessie) 1908-2003 .. **CLC 7, 45**
See also CA 85-88; 218; CANR 46, 109; CP 7; DLB 20; EWL 3; MTCW 1; RGEL 2
Rainis, Janis 1865-1929 .... **TCLC 29**
See also CA 170; CDWLB 4; DLB 220; EWL 3
Rakosi, Carl .... **CLC 47**
See Rawley, Callman
See also CAAS 5; CP 7; DLB 193
Ralegh, Sir Walter
See Raleigh, Sir Walter
See also BRW 1; RGEL 2; WP
Raleigh, Richard
See Lovecraft, H(oward) P(hillips)
Raleigh, Sir Walter 1554(?)-1618 .... **LC 31, 39; PC 31**
See Ralegh, Sir Walter
See also CDBLB Before 1660; DLB 172; EXPP; PFS 14; TEA
Rallentando, H. P.
See Sayers, Dorothy L(eigh)
Ramal, Walter
See de la Mare, Walter (John)
Ramana Maharshi 1879-1950 .... **TCLC 84**
Ramoacn y Cajal, Santiago
1852-1934 .... **TCLC 93**
Ramon, Juan
See Jimenez (Mantecon), Juan Ramon
Ramos, Graciliano 1892-1953 .... **TCLC 32**
See also CA 167; EWL 3; HW 2; LAW; WLIT 1
Rampersad, Arnold 1941- .... **CLC 44**
See also BW 2, 3; CA 127; 133; CANR 81; DLB 111; INT CA-133
Rampling, Anne
See Rice, Anne
See also GLL 2
Ramsay, Allan 1686(?)-1758 .... **LC 29**
See also DLB 95; RGEL 2
Ramsay, Jay
See Campbell, (John) Ramsey
Ramuz, Charles-Ferdinand
1878-1947 .... **TCLC 33**
See also CA 165; EWL 3
Rand, Ayn 1905-1982 ...... **CLC 3, 30, 44, 79; WLC**
See also AAYA 10; AMWS 4; BPFB 3; BYA 12; CA 13-16R; 105; CANR 27, 73; CDALBS; CPW; DA; DA3; DAC; DAM MST, NOV, POP; DLB 227, 279; MTCW 1, 2; NFS 10, 16; RGAL 4; SFW 4; TUS; YAW
Randall, Dudley (Felker) 1914-2000 . **BLC 3; CLC 1, 135**
See also BW 1, 3; CA 25-28R; 189; CANR 23, 82; DAM MULT; DLB 41; PFS 5
Randall, Robert
See Silverberg, Robert
Ranger, Ken
See Creasey, John
Rank, Otto 1884-1939 .... **TCLC 115**
Ransom, John Crowe 1888-1974 .. **CLC 2, 4, 5, 11, 24**
See also AMW; CA 5-8R; 49-52; CANR 6, 34; CDALBS; DA3; DAM POET; DLB 45, 63; EWL 3; EXPP; MTCW 1, 2; RGAL 4; TUS

Rao, Raja 1909- .... **CLC 25, 56**
See also CA 73-76; CANR 51; CN 7; DAM NOV; EWL 3; MTCW 1, 2; RGEL 2; RGSF 2

Raphael, Frederic (Michael) 1931- ... **CLC 2, 14**
See also CA 1-4R; CANR 1, 86; CN 7; DLB 14

Ratcliffe, James P.
See Mencken, H(enry) L(ouis)

Rathbone, Julian 1935- .... **CLC 41**
See also CA 101; CANR 34, 73

Rattigan, Terence (Mervyn)
1911-1977 .... **CLC 7; DC 18**
See also BRWS 7; CA 85-88; 73-76; CBD; CDBLB 1945-1960; DAM DRAM; DFS 8; DLB 13; IDFW 3, 4; MTCW 1, 2; RGEL 2

Ratushinskaya, Irina 1954- .... **CLC 54**
See also CA 129; CANR 68; CWW 2

Raven, Simon (Arthur Noel)
1927-2001 .... **CLC 14**
See also CA 81-84; 197; CANR 86; CN 7; DLB 271

Ravenna, Michael
See Welty, Eudora (Alice)

Rawley, Callman 1903-2002
See Rakosi, Carl
See also CA 21-24R; CANR 12, 32, 91

Rawlings, Marjorie Kinnan
1896-1953 .... **TCLC 4**
See also AAYA 20; AMWS 10; ANW; BPFB 3; BYA 3; CA 104; 137; CANR 74; CLR 63; DLB 9, 22, 102; DLBD 17; JRDA; MAICYA 1, 2; MTCW 2; RGAL 4; SATA 100; WCH; YABC 1; YAW

Ray, Satyajit 1921-1992 .... **CLC 16, 76**
See also CA 114; 137; DAM MULT

Read, Herbert Edward 1893-1968 ..... **CLC 4**
See also BRW 6; CA 85-88; 25-28R; DLB 20, 149; EWL 3; PAB; RGEL 2

Read, Piers Paul 1941- .... **CLC 4, 10, 25**
See also CA 21-24R; CANR 38, 86; CN 7; DLB 14; SATA 21

Reade, Charles 1814-1884 .... **NCLC 2, 74**
See also DLB 21; RGEL 2

Reade, Hamish
See Gray, Simon (James Holliday)

Reading, Peter 1946- .... **CLC 47**
See also BRWS 8; CA 103; CANR 46, 96; CP 7; DLB 40

Reaney, James 1926- .... **CLC 13**
See also CA 41-44R; CAAS 15; CANR 42; CD 5; CP 7; DAC; DAM MST; DLB 68; RGEL 2; SATA 43

Rebreanu, Liviu 1885-1944 .... **TCLC 28**
See also CA 165; DLB 220; EWL 3

Rechy, John (Francisco) 1934- ...... **CLC 1, 7, 14, 18, 107; HLC 2**
See also CA 5-8R, 195; CAAE 195; CAAS 4; CANR 6, 32, 64; CN 7; DAM MULT; DLB 122, 278; DLBY 1982; HW 1, 2; INT CANR-6; LLW 1; RGAL 4

Redcam, Tom 1870-1933 .... **TCLC 25**

Reddin, Keith .... **CLC 67**
See also CAD

Redgrove, Peter (William)
1932-2003 .... **CLC 6, 41**
See also BRWS 6; CA 1-4R; 217; CANR 3, 39, 77; CP 7; DLB 40

Redmon, Anne .... **CLC 22**
See Nightingale, Anne Redmon
See also DLBY 1986

Reed, Eliot
See Ambler, Eric

Reed, Ishmael 1938- ..... **BLC 3; CLC 2, 3, 5, 6, 13, 32, 60, 174**
See also AFAW 1, 2; AMWS 10; BPFB 3; BW 2, 3; CA 21-24R; CANR 25, 48, 74, 128; CN 7; CP 7; CSW; DA3; DAM MULT; DLB 2, 5, 33, 169, 227; DLBD 8; EWL 3; LMFS 2; MSW; MTCW 1, 2; PFS 6; RGAL 4; TCWW 2

Reed, John (Silas) 1887-1920 .... **TCLC 9**
See also CA 106; 195; TUS

Reed, Lou .... **CLC 21**
See Firbank, Louis

Reese, Lizette Woodworth 1856-1935 . **PC 29**
See also CA 180; DLB 54

Reeve, Clara 1729-1807 .... **NCLC 19**
See also DLB 39; RGEL 2

Reich, Wilhelm 1897-1957 .... **TCLC 57**
See also CA 199

Reid, Christopher (John) 1949- .... **CLC 33**
See also CA 140; CANR 89; CP 7; DLB 40; EWL 3

Reid, Desmond
See Moorcock, Michael (John)

Reid Banks, Lynne 1929-
See Banks, Lynne Reid
See also AAYA 49; CA 1-4R; CANR 6, 22, 38, 87; CLR 24; CN 7; JRDA; MAICYA 1, 2; SATA 22, 75, 111; YAW

Reilly, William K.
See Creasey, John

Reiner, Max
See Caldwell, (Janet Miriam) Taylor (Holland)

Reis, Ricardo
See Pessoa, Fernando (Antonio Nogueira)

Reizenstein, Elmer Leopold
See Rice, Elmer (Leopold)
See also EWL 3

Remarque, Erich Maria 1898-1970 . **CLC 21**
See also AAYA 27; BPFB 3; CA 77-80; 29-32R; CDWLB 2; DA; DA3; DAB; DAC; DAM MST, NOV; DLB 56; EWL 3; EXPN; LAIT 3; MTCW 1, 2; NFS 4; RGWL 2, 3

Remington, Frederic 1861-1909 ..... **TCLC 89**
See also CA 108; 169; DLB 12, 186, 188; SATA 41

Remizov, A.
See Remizov, Aleksei (Mikhailovich)

Remizov, A. M.
See Remizov, Aleksei (Mikhailovich)

Remizov, Aleksei (Mikhailovich)
1877-1957 .... **TCLC 27**
See Remizov, Alexey Mikhaylovich
See also CA 125; 133; DLB 295

Remizov, Alexey Mikhaylovich
See Remizov, Aleksei (Mikhailovich)
See also EWL 3

Renan, Joseph Ernest 1823-1892 . **NCLC 26, 145**
See also GFL 1789 to the Present

Renard, Jules(-Pierre) 1864-1910 .. **TCLC 17**
See also CA 117; 202; GFL 1789 to the Present

Renault, Mary .... **CLC 3, 11, 17**
See Challans, Mary
See also BPFB 3; BYA 2; DLBY 1983; EWL 3; GLL 1; LAIT 1; MTCW 2; RGEL 2; RHW

Rendell, Ruth (Barbara) 1930- .. **CLC 28, 48**
See Vine, Barbara
See also BPFB 3; BRWS 9; CA 109; CANR 32, 52, 74, 127; CN 7; CPW; DAM POP; DLB 87, 276; INT CANR-32; MSW; MTCW 1, 2

Renoir, Jean 1894-1979 .... **CLC 20**
See also CA 129; 85-88

Resnais, Alain 1922- .... **CLC 16**

Revard, Carter (Curtis) 1931- .... **NNAL**
See also CA 144; CANR 81; PFS 5

Reverdy, Pierre 1889-1960 .... **CLC 53**
See also CA 97-100; 89-92; DLB 258; EWL 3; GFL 1789 to the Present

Rexroth, Kenneth 1905-1982 .... **CLC 1, 2, 6, 11, 22, 49, 112; PC 20**
See also BG 3; CA 5-8R; 107; CANR 14, 34, 63; CDALB 1941-1968; DAM POET; DLB 16, 48, 165, 212; DLBY 1982; EWL 3; INT CANR-14; MTCW 1, 2; RGAL 4

Reyes, Alfonso 1889-1959 .... **HLCS 2; TCLC 33**
See also CA 131; EWL 3; HW 1; LAW

Reyes y Basoalto, Ricardo Eliecer Neftali
See Neruda, Pablo

Reymont, Wladyslaw (Stanislaw)
1868(?)-1925 .... **TCLC 5**
See also CA 104; EWL 3

Reynolds, John Hamilton
1794-1852 .... **NCLC 146**
See also DLB 96

Reynolds, Jonathan 1942- .... **CLC 6, 38**
See also CA 65-68; CANR 28

Reynolds, Joshua 1723-1792 .... **LC 15**
See also DLB 104

Reynolds, Michael S(hane)
1937-2000 .... **CLC 44**
See also CA 65-68; 189; CANR 9, 89, 97

Reznikoff, Charles 1894-1976 .... **CLC 9**
See also CA 33-36; 61-64; CAP 2; DLB 28, 45; WP

Rezzori (d'Arezzo), Gregor von
1914-1998 .... **CLC 25**
See also CA 122; 136; 167

Rhine, Richard
See Silverstein, Alvin; Silverstein, Virginia B(arbara Opshelor)

Rhodes, Eugene Manlove
1869-1934 .... **TCLC 53**
See also CA 198; DLB 256

R'hoone, Lord
See Balzac, Honore de

Rhys, Jean 1894(?)-1979 ...... **CLC 2, 4, 6, 14, 19, 51, 124; SSC 21, 76**
See also BRWS 2; CA 25-28R; 85-88; CANR 35, 62; CDBLB 1945-1960; CD-WLB 3; DA3; DAM NOV; DLB 36, 117, 162; DNFS 2; EWL 3; LATS 1:1; MTCW 1, 2; RGEL 2; RGSF 2; RHW; TEA; WWE 1

Ribeiro, Darcy 1922-1997 .... **CLC 34**
See also CA 33-36R; 156; EWL 3

Ribeiro, Joao Ubaldo (Osorio Pimentel)
1941- .... **CLC 10, 67**
See also CA 81-84; CWW 2; EWL 3

Ribman, Ronald (Burt) 1932- .... **CLC 7**
See also CA 21-24R; CAD; CANR 46, 80; CD 5

Ricci, Nino (Pio) 1959- .... **CLC 70**
See also CA 137; CANR 130; CCA 1

Rice, Anne 1941- .... **CLC 41, 128**
See Rampling, Anne
See also AAYA 9, 53; AMWS 7; BEST 89:2; BPFB 3; CA 65-68; CANR 12, 36, 53, 74, 100, 133; CN 7; CPW; CSW; DA3; DAM POP; DLB 292; GLL 2; HGG; MTCW 2; SUFW 2; YAW

Rice, Elmer (Leopold) 1892-1967 ...... **CLC 7, 49**
See Reizenstein, Elmer Leopold
See also CA 21-22; 25-28R; CAP 2; DAM DRAM; DFS 12; DLB 4, 7; MTCW 1, 2; RGAL 4

Rice, Tim(othy Miles Bindon)
1944- .... **CLC 21**
See also CA 103; CANR 46; DFS 7

Stein, Gertrude 1874-1946 .... **DC 19; PC 18; SSC 42; TCLC 1, 6, 28, 48; WLC**
See also AMW; AMWC 2; CA 104; 132; CANR 108; CDALB 1917-1929; DA; DA3; DAB; DAC; DAM MST, NOV, POET; DLB 4, 54, 86, 228; DLBD 15; EWL 3; EXPS; GLL 1; MAWW; MTCW 1, 2; NCFS 4; RGAL 4; RGSF 2; SSFS 5; TUS; WP

Steinbeck, John (Ernst) 1902-1968 ... **CLC 1, 5, 9, 13, 21, 34, 45, 75, 124; SSC 11, 37; TCLC 135; WLC**
See also AAYA 12; AMW; BPFB 3; BYA 2, 3, 13; CA 1-4R; 25-28R; CANR 1, 35; CDALB 1929-1941; DA; DA3; DAB; DAC; DAM DRAM, MST, NOV; DLB 7, 9, 212, 275; DLBD 2; EWL 3; EXPS; LAIT 3; MTCW 1, 2; NFS 1, 5, 7, 17, 19; RGAL 4; RGSF 2; RHW; SATA 9; SSFS 3, 6; TCWW 2; TUS; WYA; YAW

Steinem, Gloria 1934- .... **CLC 63**
See also CA 53-56; CANR 28, 51; DLB 246; FW; MTCW 1, 2

Steiner, George 1929- .... **CLC 24**
See also CA 73-76; CANR 31, 67, 108; DAM NOV; DLB 67, 299; EWL 3; MTCW 1, 2; SATA 62

Steiner, K. Leslie
See Delany, Samuel R(ay), Jr.

Steiner, Rudolf 1861-1925 .... **TCLC 13**
See also CA 107

Stendhal 1783-1842 .. **NCLC 23, 46; SSC 27; WLC**
See also DA; DA3; DAB; DAC; DAM MST, NOV; DLB 119; EW 5; GFL 1789 to the Present; RGWL 2, 3; TWA

Stephen, Adeline Virginia
See Woolf, (Adeline) Virginia

Stephen, Sir Leslie 1832-1904 .... **TCLC 23**
See also BRW 5; CA 123; DLB 57, 144, 190

Stephen, Sir Leslie
See Stephen, Sir Leslie

Stephen, Virginia
See Woolf, (Adeline) Virginia

Stephens, James 1882(?)-1950 .... **SSC 50; TCLC 4**
See also CA 104; 192; DLB 19, 153, 162; EWL 3; FANT; RGEL 2; SUFW

Stephens, Reed
See Donaldson, Stephen R(eeder)

Steptoe, Lydia
See Barnes, Djuna
See also GLL 1

Sterchi, Beat 1949- .... **CLC 65**
See also CA 203

Sterling, Brett
See Bradbury, Ray (Douglas); Hamilton, Edmond

Sterling, Bruce 1954- .... **CLC 72**
See also CA 119; CANR 44; SCFW 2; SFW 4

Sterling, George 1869-1926 .... **TCLC 20**
See also CA 117; 165; DLB 54

Stern, Gerald 1925- .... **CLC 40, 100**
See also AMWS 9; CA 81-84; CANR 28, 94; CP 7; DLB 105; RGAL 4

Stern, Richard (Gustave) 1928- ... **CLC 4, 39**
See also CA 1-4R; CANR 1, 25, 52, 120; CN 7; DLB 218; DLBY 1987; INT CANR-25

Sternberg, Josef von 1894-1969 .... **CLC 20**
See also CA 81-84

Sterne, Laurence 1713-1768 .... **LC 2, 48; WLC**
See also BRW 3; BRWC 1; CDBLB 1660-1789; DA; DAB; DAC; DAM MST, NOV; DLB 39; RGEL 2; TEA

Sternheim, (William Adolf) Carl 1878-1942 .... **TCLC 8**
See also CA 105; 193; DLB 56, 118; EWL 3; RGWL 2, 3

Stevens, Mark 1951- .... **CLC 34**
See also CA 122

Stevens, Wallace 1879-1955 . **PC 6; TCLC 3, 12, 45; WLC**
See also AMW; AMWR 1; CA 104; 124; CDALB 1929-1941; DA; DA3; DAB; DAC; DAM MST, POET; DLB 54; EWL 3; EXPP; MTCW 1, 2; PAB; PFS 13, 16; RGAL 4; TUS; WP

Stevenson, Anne (Katharine) 1933- .. **CLC 7, 33**
See also BRWS 6; CA 17-20R; CAAS 9; CANR 9, 33, 123; CP 7; CWP; DLB 40; MTCW 1; RHW

Stevenson, Robert Louis (Balfour) 1850-1894 ...... **NCLC 5, 14, 63; SSC 11, 51; WLC**
See also AAYA 24; BPFB 3; BRW 5; BRWC 1; BRWR 1; BYA 1, 2, 4, 13; CD-BLB 1890-1914; CLR 10, 11; DA; DA3; DAB; DAC; DAM MST, NOV; DLB 18, 57, 141, 156, 174; DLBD 13; HGG; JRDA; LAIT 1, 3; MAICYA 1, 2; NFS 11, 20; RGEL 2; RGSF 2; SATA 100; SUFW; TEA; WCH; WLIT 4; WYA; YABC 2; YAW

Stewart, J(ohn) I(nnes) M(ackintosh) 1906-1994 .... **CLC 7, 14, 32**
See Innes, Michael
See also CA 85-88; 147; CAAS 3; CANR 47; CMW 4; MTCW 1, 2

Stewart, Mary (Florence Elinor) 1916- .... **CLC 7, 35, 117**
See also AAYA 29; BPFB 3; CA 1-4R; CANR 1, 59, 130; CMW 4; CPW; DAB; FANT; RHW; SATA 12; YAW

Stewart, Mary Rainbow
See Stewart, Mary (Florence Elinor)

Stifle, June
See Campbell, Maria

Stifter, Adalbert 1805-1868 .. **NCLC 41; SSC 28**
See also CDWLB 2; DLB 133; RGSF 2; RGWL 2, 3

Still, James 1906-2001 .... **CLC 49**
See also CA 65-68; 195; CAAS 17; CANR 10, 26; CSW; DLB 9; DLBY 01; SATA 29; SATA-Obit 127

Sting 1951-
See Sumner, Gordon Matthew
See also CA 167

Stirling, Arthur
See Sinclair, Upton (Beall)

Stitt, Milan 1941- .... **CLC 29**
See also CA 69-72

Stockton, Francis Richard 1834-1902
See Stockton, Frank R.
See also CA 108; 137; MAICYA 1, 2; SATA 44; SFW 4

Stockton, Frank R. .... **TCLC 47**
See Stockton, Francis Richard
See also BYA 4, 13; DLB 42, 74; DLBD 13; EXPS; SATA-Brief 32; SSFS 3; SUFW; WCH

Stoddard, Charles
See Kuttner, Henry

Stoker, Abraham 1847-1912
See Stoker, Bram
See also CA 105; 150; DA; DA3; DAC; DAM MST, NOV; HGG; SATA 29

Stoker, Bram . **SSC 62; TCLC 8, 144; WLC**
See Stoker, Abraham
See also AAYA 23; BPFB 3; BRWS 3; BYA 5; CDBLB 1890-1914; DAB; DLB 304; LATS 1:1; NFS 18; RGEL 2; SUFW; TEA; WLIT 4

Stolz, Mary (Slattery) 1920- .... **CLC 12**
See also AAYA 8; AITN 1; CA 5-8R; CANR 13, 41, 112; JRDA; MAICYA 1, 2; SAAS 3; SATA 10, 71, 133; YAW

Stone, Irving 1903-1989 .... **CLC 7**
See also AITN 1; BPFB 3; CA 1-4R; 129; CAAS 3; CANR 1, 23; CPW; DA3; DAM POP; INT CANR-23; MTCW 1, 2; RHW; SATA 3; SATA-Obit 64

Stone, Oliver (William) 1946- .... **CLC 73**
See also AAYA 15; CA 110; CANR 55, 125

Stone, Robert (Anthony) 1937- ... **CLC 5, 23, 42, 175**
See also AMWS 5; BPFB 3; CA 85-88; CANR 23, 66, 95; CN 7; DLB 152; EWL 3; INT CANR-23; MTCW 1

Stone, Ruth 1915- .... **PC 53**
See also CA 45-48; CANR 2, 91; CP 7; CSW; DLB 105; PFS 19

Stone, Zachary
See Follett, Ken(neth Martin)

Stoppard, Tom 1937- ... **CLC 1, 3, 4, 5, 8, 15, 29, 34, 63, 91; DC 6; WLC**
See also BRWC 1; BRWR 2; BRWS 1; CA 81-84; CANR 39, 67, 125; CBD; CD 5; CDBLB 1960 to Present; DA; DA3; DAB; DAC; DAM DRAM, MST; DFS 2, 5, 8, 11, 13, 16; DLB 13, 233; DLBY 1985; EWL 3; LATS 1:2; MTCW 1, 2; RGEL 2; TEA; WLIT 4

Storey, David (Malcolm) 1933- . **CLC 2, 4, 5, 8**
See also BRWS 1; CA 81-84; CANR 36; CBD; CD 5; CN 7; DAM DRAM; DLB 13, 14, 207, 245; EWL 3; MTCW 1; RGEL 2

Storm, Hyemeyohsts 1935- ... **CLC 3; NNAL**
See also CA 81-84; CANR 45; DAM MULT

Storm, (Hans) Theodor (Woldsen) 1817-1888 .... **NCLC 1; SSC 27**
See also CDWLB 2; DLB 129; EW; RGSF 2; RGWL 2, 3

Storni, Alfonsina 1892-1938 . **HLC 2; PC 33; TCLC 5**
See also CA 104; 131; DAM MULT; DLB 283; HW 1; LAW

Stoughton, William 1631-1701 .... **LC 38**
See also DLB 24

Stout, Rex (Todhunter) 1886-1975 ..... **CLC 3**
See also AITN 2; BPFB 3; CA 61-64; CANR 71; CMW 4; DLB 306; MSW; RGAL 4

Stow, (Julian) Randolph 1935- ... **CLC 23, 48**
See also CA 13-16R; CANR 33; CN 7; DLB 260; MTCW 1; RGEL 2

Stowe, Harriet (Elizabeth) Beecher 1811-1896 .... **NCLC 3, 50, 133; WLC**
See also AAYA 53; AMWS 1; CDALB 1865-1917; DA; DA3; DAB; DAC; DAM MST, NOV; DLB 1, 12, 42, 74, 189, 239, 243; EXPN; JRDA; LAIT 2; MAICYA 1, 2; NFS 6; RGAL 4; TUS; YABC 1

Strabo c. 64B.C.-c. 25 .... **CMLC 37**
See also DLB 176

Strachey, (Giles) Lytton 1880-1932 .... **TCLC 12**
See also BRWS 2; CA 110; 178; DLB 149; DLBD 10; EWL 3; MTCW 2; NCFS 4

Stramm, August 1874-1915 .... **PC 50**
See also CA 195; EWL 3

Strand, Mark 1934- .... **CLC 6, 18, 41, 71**
See also AMWS 4; CA 21-24R; CANR 40, 65, 100; CP 7; DAM POET; DLB 5; EWL 3; PAB; PFS 9, 18; RGAL 4; SATA 41

Stratton-Porter, Gene(va Grace) 1863-1924
See Porter, Gene(va Grace) Stratton
See also ANW; CA 137; CLR 87; DLB 221; DLBD 14; MAICYA 1, 2; SATA 15

Straub, Peter (Francis) 1943- ... **CLC 28, 107**
　　See also BEST 89:1; BPFB 3; CA 85-88;
　　CANR 28, 65, 109; CPW; DAM POP;
　　DLBY 1984; HGG; MTCW 1, 2; SUFW
　　2

Strauss, Botho 1944- .... **CLC 22**
　　See also CA 157; CWW 2; DLB 124

Strauss, Leo 1899-1973 .... **TCLC 141**
　　See also CA 101; 45-48; CANR 122

Streatfeild, (Mary) Noel
　　　1897(?)-1986 .... **CLC 21**
　　See also CA 81-84; 120; CANR 31; CLR
　　17, 83; CWRI 5; DLB 160; MAICYA 1,
　　2; SATA 20; SATA-Obit 48

Stribling, T(homas) S(igismund)
　　　1881-1965 .... **CLC 23**
　　See also CA 189; 107; CMW 4; DLB 9;
　　RGAL 4

Strindberg, (Johan) August
　　　1849-1912 ... **DC 18; TCLC 1, 8, 21, 47;**
　　　WLC
　　See also CA 104; 135; DA; DA3; DAB;
　　DAC; DAM DRAM, MST; DFS 4, 9;
　　DLB 259; EW 7; EWL 3; IDTP; LMFS
　　2; MTCW 2, 3; TWA

Stringer, Arthur 1874-1950 .... **TCLC 37**
　　See also CA 161; DLB 92

Stringer, David
　　See Roberts, Keith (John Kingston)

Stroheim, Erich von 1885-1957 ..... **TCLC 71**

Strugatskii, Arkadii (Natanovich)
　　　1925-1991 .... **CLC 27**
　　See Strugatsky, Arkadii Natanovich
　　See also CA 106; 135; SFW 4

Strugatskii, Boris (Natanovich)
　　　1933- .... **CLC 27**
　　See Strugatsky, Boris (Natanovich)
　　See also CA 106; SFW 4

Strugatsky, Arkadii Natanovich
　　See Strugatskii, Arkadii (Natanovich)
　　See also DLB 302

Strugatsky, Boris (Natanovich)
　　See Strugatskii, Boris (Natanovich)
　　See also DLB 302

Strummer, Joe 1953(?)- .... **CLC 30**

Strunk, William, Jr. 1869-1946 ...... **TCLC 92**
　　See also CA 118; 164; NCFS 5

Stryk, Lucien 1924- .... **PC 27**
　　See also CA 13-16R; CANR 10, 28, 55,
　　110; CP 7

Stuart, Don A.
　　See Campbell, John W(ood, Jr.)

Stuart, Ian
　　See MacLean, Alistair (Stuart)

Stuart, Jesse (Hilton) 1906-1984 ... **CLC 1, 8,**
　　　11, 14, 34; SSC 31
　　See also CA 5-8R; 112; CANR 31; DLB 9,
　　48, 102; DLBY 1984; SATA 2; SATA-
　　Obit 36

Stubblefield, Sally
　　See Trumbo, Dalton

Sturgeon, Theodore (Hamilton)
　　　1918-1985 .... **CLC 22, 39**
　　See Queen, Ellery
　　See also AAYA 51; BPFB 3; BYA 9, 10;
　　CA 81-84; 116; CANR 32, 103; DLB 8;
　　DLBY 1985; HGG; MTCW 1, 2; SCFW;
　　SFW 4; SUFW

Sturges, Preston 1898-1959 .... **TCLC 48**
　　See also CA 114; 149; DLB 26

Styron, William 1925- .... **CLC 1, 3, 5, 11, 15,**
　　　60; SSC 25
　　See also AMW; AMWC 2; BEST 90:4;
　　BPFB 3; CA 5-8R; CANR 6, 33, 74, 126;
　　CDALB 1968-1988; CN 7; CPW; CSW;
　　DA3; DAM NOV, POP; DLB 2, 143, 299;
　　DLBY 1980; EWL 3; INT CANR-6;
　　LAIT 2; MTCW 1, 2; NCFS 1; RGAL 4;
　　RHW; TUS

Su, Chien 1884-1918
　　See Su Man-shu
　　See also CA 123

Suarez Lynch, B.
　　See Bioy Casares, Adolfo; Borges, Jorge
　　Luis

Suassuna, Ariano Vilar 1927- .... **HLCS 1**
　　See also CA 178; HW 2; LAW

Suckert, Kurt Erich
　　See Malaparte, Curzio

Suckling, Sir John 1609-1642 . **LC 75; PC 30**
　　See also BRW 2; DAM POET; DLB 58,
　　126; EXPP; PAB; RGEL 2

Suckow, Ruth 1892-1960 .... **SSC 18**
　　See also CA 193; 113; DLB 9, 102; RGAL
　　4; TCWW 2

Sudermann, Hermann 1857-1928 .. **TCLC 15**
　　See also CA 107; 201; DLB 118

Sue, Eugene 1804-1857 .... **NCLC 1**
　　See also DLB 119

Sueskind, Patrick 1949- .... **CLC 44, 182**
　　See Suskind, Patrick

Suetonius c. 70-c. 130 .... **CMLC 60**
　　See also AW 2; DLB 211; RGWL 2, 3

Sukenick, Ronald 1932-2004 ..... **CLC 3, 4, 6,**
　　　48
　　See also CA 25-28R; 209; CAAE 209;
　　CAAS 8; CANR 32, 89; CN 7; DLB 173;
　　DLBY 1981

Suknaski, Andrew 1942- .... **CLC 19**
　　See also CA 101; CP 7; DLB 53

Sullivan, Vernon
　　See Vian, Boris

Sully Prudhomme, Rene-Francois-Armand
　　　1839-1907 .... **TCLC 31**
　　See also GFL 1789 to the Present

Su Man-shu .... **TCLC 24**
　　See Su, Chien
　　See also EWL 3

Sumarokov, Aleksandr Petrovich
　　　1717-1777 .... **LC 104**
　　See also DLB 150

Summerforest, Ivy B.
　　See Kirkup, James

Summers, Andrew James 1942- .... **CLC 26**

Summers, Andy
　　See Summers, Andrew James

Summers, Hollis (Spurgeon, Jr.)
　　　1916- .... **CLC 10**
　　See also CA 5-8R; CANR 3; DLB 6

Summers, (Alphonsus Joseph-Mary
　　　Augustus) Montague
　　　1880-1948 .... **TCLC 16**
　　See also CA 118; 163

Sumner, Gordon Matthew .... **CLC 26**
　　See Police, The; Sting

Sun Tzu c. 400B.C.-c. 320B.C. ...... **CMLC 56**

Surrey, Henry Howard 1517-1574 ...... **PC 59**
　　See also BRW 1; RGEL 2

Surtees, Robert Smith 1805-1864 .. **NCLC 14**
　　See also DLB 21; RGEL 2

Susann, Jacqueline 1921-1974 .... **CLC 3**
　　See also AITN 1; BPFB 3; CA 65-68; 53-
　　56; MTCW 1, 2

Su Shi
　　See Su Shih
　　See also RGWL 2, 3

Su Shih 1036-1101 .... **CMLC 15**
　　See Su Shi

Suskind, Patrick .... **CLC 182**
　　See Sueskind, Patrick
　　See also BPFB 3; CA 145; CWW 2

Sutcliff, Rosemary 1920-1992 .... **CLC 26**
　　See also AAYA 10; BYA 1, 4; CA 5-8R;
　　139; CANR 37; CLR 1, 37; CPW; DAB;
　　DAC; DAM MST, POP; JRDA; LATS
　　1:1; MAICYA 1, 2; MAICYAS 1; RHW;
　　SATA 6, 44, 78; SATA-Obit 73; WYA;
　　YAW

Sutro, Alfred 1863-1933 .... **TCLC 6**
　　See also CA 105; 185; DLB 10; RGEL 2

Sutton, Henry
　　See Slavitt, David R(ytman)

Suzuki, D. T.
　　See Suzuki, Daisetz Teitaro

Suzuki, Daisetz T.
　　See Suzuki, Daisetz Teitaro

Suzuki, Daisetz Teitaro
　　　1870-1966 .... **TCLC 109**
　　See also CA 121; 111; MTCW 1, 2

Suzuki, Teitaro
　　See Suzuki, Daisetz Teitaro

Svevo, Italo .... **SSC 25; TCLC 2, 35**
　　See Schmitz, Aron Hector
　　See also DLB 264; EW 8; EWL 3; RGWL
　　2, 3

Swados, Elizabeth (A.) 1951- .... **CLC 12**
　　See also CA 97-100; CANR 49; INT CA-
　　97-100

Swados, Harvey 1920-1972 .... **CLC 5**
　　See also CA 5-8R; 37-40R; CANR 6; DLB
　　2

Swan, Gladys 1934- .... **CLC 69**
　　See also CA 101; CANR 17, 39

Swanson, Logan
　　See Matheson, Richard (Burton)

Swarthout, Glendon (Fred)
　　　1918-1992 .... **CLC 35**
　　See also AAYA 55; CA 1-4R; 139; CANR
　　1, 47; LAIT 5; SATA 26; TCWW 2; YAW

Swedenborg, Emanuel 1688-1772 ..... **LC 105**

Sweet, Sarah C.
　　See Jewett, (Theodora) Sarah Orne

Swenson, May 1919-1989 ...... **CLC 4, 14, 61,**
　　　106; PC 14
　　See also AMWS 4; CA 5-8R; 130; CANR
　　36, 61, 131; DA; DAB; DAC; DAM MST,
　　POET; DLB 5; EXPP; GLL 2; MTCW 1,
　　2; PFS 16; SATA 15; WP

Swift, Augustus
　　See Lovecraft, H(oward) P(hillips)

Swift, Graham (Colin) 1949- ...... **CLC 41, 88**
　　See also BRWC 2; BRWS 5; CA 117; 122;
　　CANR 46, 71, 128; CN 7; DLB 194;
　　MTCW 2; NFS 18; RGSF 2

Swift, Jonathan 1667-1745 ..... **LC 1, 42, 101;**
　　　PC 9; WLC
　　See also AAYA 41; BRW 3; BRWC 1;
　　BRWR 1; BYA 5, 14; CDBLB 1660-1789;
　　CLR 53; DA; DA3; DAB; DAC; DAM
　　MST, NOV, POET; DLB 39, 95, 101;
　　EXPN; LAIT 1; NFS 6; RGEL 2; SATA
　　19; TEA; WCH; WLIT 3

Swinburne, Algernon Charles
　　　1837-1909 ... **PC 24; TCLC 8, 36; WLC**
　　See also BRW 5; CA 105; 140; CDBLB
　　1832-1890; DA; DA3; DAB; DAC; DAM
　　MST, POET; DLB 35, 57; PAB; RGEL 2;
　　TEA

Swinfen, Ann .... **CLC 34**
　　See also CA 202

Swinnerton, Frank Arthur
　　　1884-1982 .... **CLC 31**
　　See also CA 108; DLB 34

Swithen, John
　　See King, Stephen (Edwin)

Sylvia
　　See Ashton-Warner, Sylvia (Constance)

Symmes, Robert Edward
　　See Duncan, Robert (Edward)

MAICYA 1, 2; MTCW 1, 2; NFS 8; RGEL 2; SATA 2, 32, 100; SATA-Obit 24; SFW 4; SUFW; TEA; WCH; WYA; YAW

Toller, Ernst 1893-1939 .... **TCLC 10**
See also CA 107; 186; DLB 124; EWL 3; RGWL 2, 3

Tolson, M. B.
See Tolson, Melvin B(eaunorus)

Tolson, Melvin B(eaunorus)
1898(?)-1966 .... **BLC 3; CLC 36, 105**
See also AFAW 1, 2; BW 1, 3; CA 124; 89-92; CANR 80; DAM MULT, POET; DLB 48, 76; RGAL 4

Tolstoi, Aleksei Nikolaevich
See Tolstoy, Alexey Nikolaevich

Tolstoi, Lev
See Tolstoy, Leo (Nikolaevich)
See also RGSF 2; RGWL 2, 3

Tolstoy, Aleksei Nikolaevich
See Tolstoy, Alexey Nikolaevich
See also DLB 272

Tolstoy, Alexey Nikolaevich
1882-1945 .... **TCLC 18**
See Tolstoi, Aleksei Nikolaevich
See also CA 107; 158; EWL 3; SFW 4

Tolstoy, Leo (Nikolaevich)
1828-1910 . SSC 9, 30, 45, 54; TCLC 4, 11, 17, 28, 44, 79; WLC
See Tolstoi, Lev
See also AAYA 56; CA 104; 123; DA; DA3; DAB; DAC; DAM MST, NOV; DLB 238; EFS 2; EW 7; EXPS; IDTP; LAIT 2; LATS 1:1; LMFS 1; NFS 10; SATA 26; SSFS 5; TWA

Tolstoy, Count Leo
See Tolstoy, Leo (Nikolaevich)

Tomalin, Claire 1933- .... **CLC 166**
See also CA 89-92; CANR 52, 88; DLB 155

Tomasi di Lampedusa, Giuseppe 1896-1957
See Lampedusa, Giuseppe (Tomasi) di
See also CA 111; DLB 177; EWL 3

Tomlin, Lily .... **CLC 17**
See Tomlin, Mary Jean

Tomlin, Mary Jean 1939(?)-
See Tomlin, Lily
See also CA 117

Tomline, F. Latour
See Gilbert, W(illiam) S(chwenck)

Tomlinson, (Alfred) Charles 1927- .... **CLC 2, 4, 6, 13, 45; PC 17**
See also CA 5-8R; CANR 33; CP 7; DAM POET; DLB 40

Tomlinson, H(enry) M(ajor)
1873-1958 .... **TCLC 71**
See also CA 118; 161; DLB 36, 100, 195

Tonna, Charlotte Elizabeth
1790-1846 .... **NCLC 135**
See also DLB 163

Tonson, Jacob fl. 1655(?)-1736 .... **LC 86**
See also DLB 170

Toole, John Kennedy 1937-1969 ..... **CLC 19, 64**
See also BPFB 3; CA 104; DLBY 1981; MTCW 2

Toomer, Eugene
See Toomer, Jean

Toomer, Eugene Pinchback
See Toomer, Jean

Toomer, Jean 1894-1967 .. **BLC 3; CLC 1, 4, 13, 22; HR 3; PC 7; SSC 1, 45; WLCS**
See also AFAW 1, 2; AMWS 3, 9; BW 1; CA 85-88; CDALB 1917-1929; DA3; DAM MULT; DLB 45, 51; EWL 3; EXPP; EXPS; LMFS 2; MTCW 1, 2; NFS 11; RGAL 4; RGSF 2; SSFS 5

Toomer, Nathan Jean
See Toomer, Jean

Toomer, Nathan Pinchback
See Toomer, Jean

Torley, Luke
See Blish, James (Benjamin)

Tornimparte, Alessandra
See Ginzburg, Natalia

Torre, Raoul della
See Mencken, H(enry) L(ouis)

Torrence, Ridgely 1874-1950 .... **TCLC 97**
See also DLB 54, 249

Torrey, E(dwin) Fuller 1937- .... **CLC 34**
See also CA 119; CANR 71

Torsvan, Ben Traven
See Traven, B.

Torsvan, Benno Traven
See Traven, B.

Torsvan, Berick Traven
See Traven, B.

Torsvan, Berwick Traven
See Traven, B.

Torsvan, Bruno Traven
See Traven, B.

Torsvan, Traven
See Traven, B.

Tourneur, Cyril 1575(?)-1626 .... **LC 66**
See also BRW 2; DAM DRAM; DLB 58; RGEL 2

Tournier, Michel (Edouard) 1924- .... **CLC 6, 23, 36, 95**
See also CA 49-52; CANR 3, 36, 74; CWW 2; DLB 83; EWL 3; GFL 1789 to the Present; MTCW 1, 2; SATA 23

Tournimparte, Alessandra
See Ginzburg, Natalia

Towers, Ivar
See Kornbluth, C(yril) M.

Towne, Robert (Burton) 1936(?)- ..... **CLC 87**
See also CA 108; DLB 44; IDFW 3, 4

Townsend, Sue .... **CLC 61**
See Townsend, Susan Lilian
See also AAYA 28; CA 119; 127; CANR 65, 107; CBD; CD 5; CPW; CWD; DAB; DAC; DAM MST; DLB 271; INT CA-127; SATA 55, 93; SATA-Brief 48; YAW

Townsend, Susan Lilian 1946-
See Townsend, Sue

Townshend, Pete
See Townshend, Peter (Dennis Blandford)

Townshend, Peter (Dennis Blandford)
1945- .... **CLC 17, 42**
See also CA 107

Tozzi, Federigo 1883-1920 .... **TCLC 31**
See also CA 160; CANR 110; DLB 264; EWL 3

Tracy, Don(ald Fiske) 1905-1970(?)
See Queen, Ellery
See also CA 1-4R; 176; CANR 2

Trafford, F. G.
See Riddell, Charlotte

Traherne, Thomas 1637(?)-1674 .... **LC 99**
See also BRW 2; DLB 131; PAB; RGEL 2

Traill, Catharine Parr 1802-1899 .. **NCLC 31**
See also DLB 99

Trakl, Georg 1887-1914 .... **PC 20; TCLC 5**
See also CA 104; 165; EW 10; EWL 3; LMFS 2; MTCW 2; RGWL 2, 3

Tranquilli, Secondino
See Silone, Ignazio

Transtroemer, Tomas Gosta
See Transtromer, Tomas (Goesta)

Transtromer, Tomas (Gosta)
See Transtromer, Tomas (Goesta)
See also CWW 2

Transtromer, Tomas (Goesta)
1931- .... **CLC 52, 65**
See Transtromer, Tomas (Gosta)
See also CA 117; 129; CAAS 17; CANR 115; DAM POET; DLB 257; EWL 3; PFS 21

Transtromer, Tomas Gosta
See Transtromer, Tomas (Goesta)

Traven, B. 1882(?)-1969 .... **CLC 8, 11**
See also CA 19-20; 25-28R; CAP 2; DLB 9, 56; EWL 3; MTCW 1; RGAL 4

Trediakovsky, Vasilii Kirillovich
1703-1769 .... **LC 68**
See also DLB 150

Treitel, Jonathan 1959- .... **CLC 70**
See also CA 210; DLB 267

Trelawny, Edward John
1792-1881 .... **NCLC 85**
See also DLB 110, 116, 144

Tremain, Rose 1943- .... **CLC 42**
See also CA 97-100; CANR 44, 95; CN 7; DLB 14, 271; RGSF 2; RHW

Tremblay, Michel 1942- .... **CLC 29, 102**
See also CA 116; 128; CCA 1; CWW 2; DAC; DAM MST; DLB 60; EWL 3; GLL 1; MTCW 1, 2

Trevanian .... **CLC 29**
See Whitaker, Rod(ney)

Trevor, Glen
See Hilton, James

Trevor, William .. **CLC 7, 9, 14, 25, 71, 116; SSC 21, 58**
See Cox, William Trevor
See also BRWS 4; CBD; CD 5; CN 7; DLB 14, 139; EWL 3; LATS 1:2; MTCW 2; RGEL 2; RGSF 2; SSFS 10

Trifonov, Iurii (Valentinovich)
See Trifonov, Yuri (Valentinovich)
See also DLB 302; RGWL 2, 3

Trifonov, Yuri (Valentinovich)
1925-1981 .... **CLC 45**
See Trifonov, Iurii (Valentinovich); Trifonov, Yury Valentinovich
See also CA 126; 103; MTCW 1

Trifonov, Yury Valentinovich
See Trifonov, Yuri (Valentinovich)
See also EWL 3

Trilling, Diana (Rubin) 1905-1996 . **CLC 129**
See also CA 5-8R; 154; CANR 10, 46; INT CANR-10; MTCW 1, 2

Trilling, Lionel 1905-1975 ..... **CLC 9, 11, 24; SSC 75**
See also AMWS 3; CA 9-12R; 61-64; CANR 10, 105; DLB 28, 63; EWL 3; INT CANR-10; MTCW 1, 2; RGAL 4; TUS

Trimball, W. H.
See Mencken, H(enry) L(ouis)

Tristan
See Gomez de la Serna, Ramon

Tristram
See Housman, A(lfred) E(dward)

Trogdon, William (Lewis) 1939-
See Heat-Moon, William Least
See also CA 115; 119; CANR 47, 89; CPW; INT CA-119

Trollope, Anthony 1815-1882 .... **NCLC 6, 33, 101; SSC 28; WLC**
See also BRW 5; CDBLB 1832-1890; DA; DA3; DAB; DAC; DAM MST, NOV; DLB 21, 57, 159; RGEL 2; RGSF 2; SATA 22

Trollope, Frances 1779-1863 .... **NCLC 30**
See also DLB 21, 166

Trollope, Joanna 1943- .... **CLC 186**
See also CA 101; CANR 58, 95; CPW; DLB 207; RHW

Trotsky, Leon 1879-1940 .... **TCLC 22**
See also CA 118; 167

Trotter (Cockburn), Catharine
1679-1749 .... **LC 8**
See also DLB 84, 252
Trotter, Wilfred 1872-1939 .... **TCLC 97**
Trout, Kilgore
See Farmer, Philip Jose
Trow, George W. S. 1943- .... **CLC 52**
See also CA 126; CANR 91
Troyat, Henri 1911- .... **CLC 23**
See also CA 45-48; CANR 2, 33, 67, 117;
GFL 1789 to the Present; MTCW 1
Trudeau, G(arretson) B(eekman) 1948-
See Trudeau, Garry B.
See also CA 81-84; CANR 31; SATA 35
Trudeau, Garry B. .... **CLC 12**
See Trudeau, G(arretson) B(eekman)
See also AAYA 10; AITN 2
Truffaut, Francois 1932-1984 ... **CLC 20, 101**
See also CA 81-84; 113; CANR 34
Trumbo, Dalton 1905-1976 .... **CLC 19**
See also CA 21-24R; 69-72; CANR 10;
DLB 26; IDFW 3, 4; YAW
Trumbull, John 1750-1831 .... **NCLC 30**
See also DLB 31; RGAL 4
Trundlett, Helen B.
See Eliot, T(homas) S(tearns)
Truth, Sojourner 1797(?)-1883 ...... **NCLC 94**
See also DLB 239; FW; LAIT 2
Tryon, Thomas 1926-1991 .... **CLC 3, 11**
See also AITN 1; BPFB 3; CA 29-32R; 135;
CANR 32, 77; CPW; DA3; DAM POP;
HGG; MTCW 1
Tryon, Tom
See Tryon, Thomas
Ts'ao Hsueh-ch'in 1715(?)-1763 .... **LC 1**
Tsushima, Shuji 1909-1948
See Dazai Osamu
See also CA 107
Tsvetaeva (Efron), Marina (Ivanovna)
1892-1941 .... **PC 14; TCLC 7, 35**
See also CA 104; 128; CANR 73; DLB 295;
EW 11; MTCW 1, 2; RGWL 2, 3
Tuck, Lily 1938- .... **CLC 70**
See also CA 139; CANR 90
Tu Fu 712-770 .... **PC 9**
See Du Fu
See also DAM MULT; TWA; WP
Tunis, John R(oberts) 1889-1975 ..... **CLC 12**
See also BYA 1; CA 61-64; CANR 62; DLB
22, 171; JRDA; MAICYA 1, 2; SATA 37;
SATA-Brief 30; YAW
Tuohy, Frank .... **CLC 37**
See Tuohy, John Francis
See also DLB 14, 139
Tuohy, John Francis 1925-
See Tuohy, Frank
See also CA 5-8R; 178; CANR 3, 47; CN 7
Turco, Lewis (Putnam) 1934- ..... **CLC 11, 63**
See also CA 13-16R; CAAS 22; CANR 24,
51; CP 7; DLBY 1984
Turgenev, Ivan (Sergeevich)
1818-1883 ..... **DC 7; NCLC 21, 37, 122;**
SSC 7, 57; WLC
See also AAYA 58; DA; DAB; DAC; DAM
MST, NOV; DLB 238, 284; EW
6; LATS 1:1; NFS 16; RGSF 2; RGWL 2,
3; TWA
Turgot, Anne-Robert-Jacques
1727-1781 .... **LC 26**
Turner, Frederick 1943- .... **CLC 48**
See also CA 73-76; 227; CAAE 227; CAAS
10; CANR 12, 30, 56; DLB 40, 282
Turton, James
See Crace, Jim
Tutu, Desmond M(pilo) 1931- .. **BLC 3; CLC 80**
See also BW 1, 3; CA 125; CANR 67, 81;
DAM MULT

Tutuola, Amos 1920-1997 ..... **BLC 3; CLC 5, 14, 29**
See also AFW; BW 2, 3; CA 9-12R; 159;
CANR 27, 66; CDWLB 3; CN 7; DA3;
DAM MULT; DLB 125; DNFS 2; EWL
3; MTCW 1, 2; RGEL 2; WLIT 2
Twain, Mark .. **SSC 34; TCLC 6, 12, 19, 36, 48, 59; WLC**
See Clemens, Samuel Langhorne
See also AAYA 20; AMW; AMWC 1; BPFB
3; BYA 2, 3, 11, 14; CLR 58, 60, 66; DLB
11; EXPN; EXPS; FANT; LAIT 2; NCFS
4; NFS 1, 6; RGAL 4; RGSF 2; SFW 4;
SSFS 1, 7; SUFW; TUS; WCH; WYA;
YAW
Tyler, Anne 1941- . **CLC 7, 11, 18, 28, 44, 59, 103**
See also AAYA 18; AMWS 4; BEST 89:1;
BPFB 3; BYA 12; CA 9-12R; CANR 11,
33, 53, 109, 132; CDALBS; CN 7; CPW;
CSW; DAM NOV, POP; DLB 6, 143;
DLBY 1982; EWL 3; EXPN; LATS 1:2;
MAWW; MTCW 1, 2; NFS 2, 7, 10;
RGAL 4; SATA 7, 90; SSFS 17; TUS;
YAW
Tyler, Royall 1757-1826 .... **NCLC 3**
See also DLB 37; RGAL 4
Tynan, Katharine 1861-1931 .... **TCLC 3**
See also CA 104; 167; DLB 153, 240; FW
Tyndale, William c. 1484-1536 .... **LC 103**
See also DLB 132
Tyutchev, Fyodor 1803-1873 .... **NCLC 34**
Tzara, Tristan 1896-1963 ..... **CLC 47; PC 27**
See also CA 153; 89-92; DAM POET; EWL
3; MTCW 2
Uchida, Yoshiko 1921-1992 .... **AAL**
See also AAYA 16; BYA 2, 3; CA 13-16R;
139; CANR 6, 22, 47, 61; CDALBS; CLR
6, 56; CWRI 5; JRDA; MAICYA 1, 2;
MTCW 1, 2; SAAS 1; SATA 1, 53; SATA-
Obit 72
Udall, Nicholas 1504-1556 .... **LC 84**
See also DLB 62; RGEL 2
Ueda Akinari 1734-1809 .... **NCLC 131**
Uhry, Alfred 1936- .... **CLC 55**
See also CA 127; 133; CAD; CANR 112;
CD 5; CSW; DA3; DAM DRAM, POP;
DFS 11, 15; INT CA-133
Ulf, Haerved
See Strindberg, (Johan) August
Ulf, Harved
See Strindberg, (Johan) August
Ulibarri, Sabine R(eyes)
1919-2003 .... **CLC 83; HLCS 2**
See also CA 131; 214; CANR 81; DAM
MULT; DLB 82; HW 1, 2; RGSF 2
Unamuno (y Jugo), Miguel de
1864-1936 .. **HLC 2; SSC 11, 69; TCLC 2, 9, 148**
See also CA 104; 131; CANR 81; DAM
MULT, NOV; DLB 108; EW 8; EWL 3;
HW 1, 2; MTCW 1, 2; RGSF 2; RGWL
2, 3; SSFS 20; TWA
Uncle Shelby
See Silverstein, Shel(don Allan)
Undercliffe, Errol
See Campbell, (John) Ramsey
Underwood, Miles
See Glassco, John
Undset, Sigrid 1882-1949 ..... **TCLC 3; WLC**
See also CA 104; 129; DA; DA3; DAB;
DAC; DAM MST, NOV; DLB 293; EW
9; EWL 3; FW; MTCW 1, 2; RGWL 2, 3
Ungaretti, Giuseppe 1888-1970 ... **CLC 7, 11, 15; PC 57**
See also CA 19-20; 25-28R; CAP 2; DLB
114; EW 10; EWL 3; PFS 20; RGWL 2,
3

Unger, Douglas 1952- .... **CLC 34**
See also CA 130; CANR 94
Unsworth, Barry (Forster) 1930- .... **CLC 76, 127**
See also BRWS 7; CA 25-28R; CANR 30,
54, 125; CN 7; DLB 194
Updike, John (Hoyer) 1932- . **CLC 1, 2, 3, 5, 7, 9, 13, 15, 23, 34, 43, 70, 139; SSC 13, 27; WLC**
See also AAYA 36; AMW; AMWC 1;
AMWR 1; BPFB 3; BYA 12; CA 1-4R;
CABS 1; CANR 4, 33, 51, 94, 133;
CDALB 1968-1988; CN 7; CP 7; CPW 1;
DA; DA3; DAB; DAC; DAM MST, NOV,
POET, POP; DLB 2, 5, 143, 218, 227;
DLBD 3; DLBY 1980, 1982, 1997; EWL
3; EXPP; HGG; MTCW 1, 2; NFS 12;
RGAL 4; RGSF 2; SSFS 3, 19; TUS
Upshaw, Margaret Mitchell
See Mitchell, Margaret (Munnerlyn)
Upton, Mark
See Sanders, Lawrence
Upward, Allen 1863-1926 .... **TCLC 85**
See also CA 117; 187; DLB 36
Urdang, Constance (Henriette)
1922-1996 .... **CLC 47**
See also CA 21-24R; CANR 9, 24; CP 7;
CWP
Uriel, Henry
See Faust, Frederick (Schiller)
Uris, Leon (Marcus) 1924-2003 ... **CLC 7, 32**
See also AITN 1, 2; BEST 89:2; BPFB 3;
CA 1-4R; 217; CANR 1, 40, 65, 123; CN
7; CPW 1; DA3; DAM NOV, POP;
MTCW 1, 2; SATA 49; SATA-Obit 146
Urista (Heredia), Alberto (Baltazar)
1947- .... **HLCS 1; PC 34**
See Alurista
See also CA 45-48; 182; CANR 2, 32; HW
1
Urmuz
See Codrescu, Andrei
Urquhart, Guy
See McAlmon, Robert (Menzies)
Urquhart, Jane 1949- .... **CLC 90**
See also CA 113; CANR 32, 68, 116; CCA
1; DAC
Usigli, Rodolfo 1905-1979 .... **HLCS 1**
See also CA 131; DLB 305; EWL 3; HW 1;
LAW
Ustinov, Peter (Alexander)
1921-2004 .... **CLC 1**
See also AITN 1; CA 13-16R; 225; CANR
25, 51; CBD; CD 5; DLB 13; MTCW 2
U Tam'si, Gerald Felix Tchicaya
See Tchicaya, Gerald Felix
U Tam'si, Tchicaya
See Tchicaya, Gerald Felix
Vachss, Andrew (Henry) 1942- .... **CLC 106**
See also CA 118, 214; CAAE 214; CANR
44, 95; CMW 4
Vachss, Andrew H.
See Vachss, Andrew (Henry)
Vaculik, Ludvik 1926- .... **CLC 7**
See also CA 53-56; CANR 72; CWW 2;
DLB 232; EWL 3
Vaihinger, Hans 1852-1933 .... **TCLC 71**
See also CA 116; 166
Valdez, Luis (Miguel) 1940- ..... **CLC 84; DC 10; HLC 2**
See also CA 101; CAD; CANR 32, 81; CD
5; DAM MULT; DFS 5; DLB 122; EWL
3; HW 1; LAIT 4; LLW 1
Valenzuela, Luisa 1938- .... **CLC 31, 104; HLCS 2; SSC 14**
See also CA 101; CANR 32, 65, 123; CD-
WLB 3; CWW 2; DAM MULT; DLB 113;
EWL 3; FW; HW 1, 2; LAW; RGSF 2;
RGWL 3

Valera y Alcala-Galiano, Juan
1824-1905 .... **TCLC 10**
See also CA 106

Valerius Maximus fl. 20- .... **CMLC 64**
See also DLB 211

Valery, (Ambroise) Paul (Toussaint Jules)
1871-1945 .... **PC 9; TCLC 4, 15**
See also CA 104; 122; DA3; DAM POET;
DLB 258; EW 8; EWL 3; GFL 1789 to
the Present; MTCW 1, 2; RGWL 2, 3;
TWA

Valle-Inclan, Ramon (Maria) del
1866-1936 .... **HLC 2; TCLC 5**
See also CA 106; 153; CANR 80; DAM
MULT; DLB 134; EW 8; EWL 3; HW 2;
RGSF 2; RGWL 2, 3

Vallejo, Antonio Buero
See Buero Vallejo, Antonio

Vallejo, Cesar (Abraham)
1892-1938 .... **HLC 2; TCLC 3, 56**
See also CA 105; 153; DAM MULT; DLB
290; EWL 3; HW 1; LAW; RGWL 2, 3

Valles, Jules 1832-1885 .... **NCLC 71**
See also DLB 123; GFL 1789 to the Present

Vallette, Marguerite Eymery
1860-1953 .... **TCLC 67**
See Rachilde
See also CA 182; DLB 123, 192

Valle Y Pena, Ramon del
See Valle-Inclan, Ramon (Maria) del

Van Ash, Cay 1918-1994 .... **CLC 34**
See also CA 220

Vanbrugh, Sir John 1664-1726 .... **LC 21**
See also BRW 2; DAM DRAM; DLB 80;
IDTP; RGEL 2

Van Campen, Karl
See Campbell, John W(ood, Jr.)

Vance, Gerald
See Silverberg, Robert

Vance, Jack .... **CLC 35**
See Vance, John Holbrook
See also DLB 8; FANT; SCFW 2; SFW 4;
SUFW 1, 2

Vance, John Holbrook 1916-
See Queen, Ellery; Vance, Jack
See also CA 29-32R; CANR 17, 65; CMW
4; MTCW 1

**Van Den Bogarde, Derek Jules Gaspard
Ulric Niven** 1921-1999 .... **CLC 14**
See Bogarde, Dirk
See also CA 77-80; 179

Vandenburgh, Jane .... **CLC 59**
See also CA 168

Vanderhaeghe, Guy 1951- .... **CLC 41**
See also BPFB 3; CA 113; CANR 72

van der Post, Laurens (Jan)
1906-1996 .... **CLC 5**
See also AFW; CA 5-8R; 155; CANR 35;
CN 7; DLB 204; RGEL 2

van de Wetering, Janwillem 1931- ... **CLC 47**
See also CA 49-52; CANR 4, 62, 90; CMW
4

Van Dine, S. S. .... **TCLC 23**
See Wright, Willard Huntington
See also DLB 306; MSW

Van Doren, Carl (Clinton)
1885-1950 .... **TCLC 18**
See also CA 111; 168

Van Doren, Mark 1894-1972 .... **CLC 6, 10**
See also CA 1-4R; 37-40R; CANR 3; DLB
45, 284; MTCW 1, 2; RGAL 4

Van Druten, John (William)
1901-1957 .... **TCLC 2**
See also CA 104; 161; DLB 10; RGAL 4

Van Duyn, Mona (Jane) 1921- ...... **CLC 3, 7,
63, 116**
See also CA 9-12R; CANR 7, 38, 60, 116;
CP 7; CWP; DAM POET; DLB 5; PFS
20

Van Dyne, Edith
See Baum, L(yman) Frank

van Itallie, Jean-Claude 1936- .... **CLC 3**
See also CA 45-48; CAAS 2; CAD; CANR
1, 48; CD 5; DLB 7

Van Loot, Cornelius Obenchain
See Roberts, Kenneth (Lewis)

van Ostaijen, Paul 1896-1928 .... **TCLC 33**
See also CA 163

Van Peebles, Melvin 1932- .... **CLC 2, 20**
See also BW 2, 3; CA 85-88; CANR 27,
67, 82; DAM MULT

van Schendel, Arthur(-Francois-Emile)
1874-1946 .... **TCLC 56**
See also EWL 3

Vansittart, Peter 1920- .... **CLC 42**
See also CA 1-4R; CANR 3, 49, 90; CN 7;
RHW

Van Vechten, Carl 1880-1964 ... **CLC 33; HR
3**
See also AMWS 2; CA 183; 89-92; DLB 4,
9, 51; RGAL 4

van Vogt, A(lfred) E(lton) 1912-2000 . **CLC 1**
See also BPFB 3; BYA 13, 14; CA 21-24R;
190; CANR 28; DLB 8, 251; SATA 14;
SATA-Obit 124; SCFW; SFW 4

Vara, Madeleine
See Jackson, Laura (Riding)

Varda, Agnes 1928- .... **CLC 16**
See also CA 116; 122

Vargas Llosa, (Jorge) Mario (Pedro)
1939- .... **CLC 3, 6, 9, 10, 15, 31, 42, 85,
181; HLC 2**
See Llosa, (Jorge) Mario (Pedro) Vargas
See also BPFB 3; CA 73-76; CANR 18, 32,
42, 67, 116; CDWLB 3; CWW 2; DA;
DA3; DAB; DAC; DAM MST, MULT,
NOV; DLB 145; DNFS 2; EWL 3; HW 1,
2; LAIT 5; LATS 1:2; LAW; LAWS 1;
MTCW 1, 2; RGWL 2; SSFS 14; TWA;
WLIT 1

Varnhagen von Ense, Rahel
1771-1833 .... **NCLC 130**
See also DLB 90

Vasiliu, George
See Bacovia, George

Vasiliu, Gheorghe
See Bacovia, George
See also CA 123; 189

Vassa, Gustavus
See Equiano, Olaudah

Vassilikos, Vassilis 1933- .... **CLC 4, 8**
See also CA 81-84; CANR 75; EWL 3

Vaughan, Henry 1621-1695 .... **LC 27**
See also BRW 2; DLB 131; PAB; RGEL 2

Vaughn, Stephanie .... **CLC 62**

Vazov, Ivan (Minchov) 1850-1921 . **TCLC 25**
See also CA 121; 167; CDWLB 4; DLB
147

Veblen, Thorstein B(unde)
1857-1929 .... **TCLC 31**
See also AMWS 1; CA 115; 165; DLB 246

Vega, Lope de 1562-1635 .... **HLCS 2; LC 23**
See also EW 2; RGWL 2, 3

Vendler, Helen (Hennessy) 1933- ... **CLC 138**
See also CA 41-44R; CANR 25, 72; MTCW
1, 2

Venison, Alfred
See Pound, Ezra (Weston Loomis)

Ventsel, Elena Sergeevna 1907-2002
See Grekova, I.
See also CA 154

Verdi, Marie de
See Mencken, H(enry) L(ouis)

Verdu, Matilde
See Cela, Camilo Jose

Verga, Giovanni (Carmelo)
1840-1922 .... **SSC 21; TCLC 3**
See also CA 104; 123; CANR 101; EW 7;
EWL 3; RGSF 2; RGWL 2, 3

Vergil 70B.C.-19B.C. ... **CMLC 9, 40; PC 12;
WLCS**
See Virgil
See also AW 2; DA; DA3; DAB; DAC;
DAM MST, POET; EFS 1; LMFS 1

Vergil, Polydore c. 1470-1555 .... **LC 108**
See also DLB 132

Verhaeren, Emile (Adolphe Gustave)
1855-1916 .... **TCLC 12**
See also CA 109; EWL 3; GFL 1789 to the
Present

Verlaine, Paul (Marie) 1844-1896 .. **NCLC 2,
51; PC 2, 32**
See also DAM POET; DLB 217; EW 7;
GFL 1789 to the Present; LMFS 2; RGWL
2, 3; TWA

Verne, Jules (Gabriel) 1828-1905 ... **TCLC 6,
52**
See also AAYA 16; BYA 4; CA 110; 131;
CLR 88; DA3; DLB 123; GFL 1789 to
the Present; JRDA; LAIT 2; LMFS 2;
MAICYA 1, 2; RGWL 2, 3; SATA 21;
SCFW; SFW 4; TWA; WCH

Verus, Marcus Annius
See Aurelius, Marcus

Very, Jones 1813-1880 .... **NCLC 9**
See also DLB 1, 243; RGAL 4

Vesaas, Tarjei 1897-1970 .... **CLC 48**
See also CA 190; 29-32R; DLB 297; EW
11; EWL 3; RGWL 3

Vialis, Gaston
See Simenon, Georges (Jacques Christian)

Vian, Boris 1920-1959(?) .... **TCLC 9**
See also CA 106; 164; CANR 111; DLB
72; EWL 3; GFL 1789 to the Present;
MTCW 2; RGWL 2, 3

Viaud, (Louis Marie) Julien 1850-1923
See Loti, Pierre
See also CA 107

Vicar, Henry
See Felsen, Henry Gregor

Vicente, Gil 1465-c. 1536 .... **LC 99**
See also DLB 287; RGWL 2, 3

Vicker, Angus
See Felsen, Henry Gregor

Vidal, (Eugene Luther) Gore 1925- .. **CLC 2,
4, 6, 8, 10, 22, 33, 72, 142**
See Box, Edgar
See also AITN 1; AMWS 4; BEST 90:2;
BPFB 3; CA 5-8R; CAD; CANR 13, 45,
65, 100, 132; CD 5; CDALBS; CN 7;
CPW; DA3; DAM NOV, POP; DFS 2;
DLB 6, 152; EWL 3; INT CANR-13;
MTCW 1, 2; RGAL 4; RHW; TUS

Viereck, Peter (Robert Edwin)
1916- .... **CLC 4; PC 27**
See also CA 1-4R; CANR 1, 47; CP 7; DLB
5; PFS 9, 14

Vigny, Alfred (Victor) de
1797-1863 .... **NCLC 7, 102; PC 26**
See also DAM POET; DLB 119, 192, 217;
EW 5; GFL 1789 to the Present; RGWL
2, 3

Vilakazi, Benedict Wallet
1906-1947 .... **TCLC 37**
See also CA 168

Villa, Jose Garcia 1914-1997 .... **AAL; PC 22**
See also CA 25-28R; CANR 12, 118; EWL
3; EXPP

Villa, Jose Garcia 1914-1997
See Villa, Jose Garcia

Villarreal, Jose Antonio 1924- .... **HLC 2**
See also CA 133; CANR 93; DAM MULT;
DLB 82; HW 1; LAIT 4; RGAL 4

Villaurrutia, Xavier 1903-1950 ...... **TCLC 80**
See also CA 192; EWL 3; HW 1; LAW

Villaverde, Cirilo 1812-1894 .... **NCLC 121**
See also LAW

Villehardouin, Geoffroi de
1150(?)-1218(?) .... **CMLC 38**

Villiers, George 1628-1687 .... **LC 107**
See also DLB 80; RGEL 2

Villiers de l'Isle Adam, Jean Marie Mathias
Philippe Auguste 1838-1889 ... **NCLC 3;**
SSC 14
See also DLB 123, 192; GFL 1789 to the
Present; RGSF 2

Villon, Francois 1431-1463(?) . **LC 62; PC 13**
See also DLB 208; EW 2; RGWL 2, 3;
TWA

Vine, Barbara .... **CLC 50**
See Rendell, Ruth (Barbara)
See also BEST 90:4

Vinge, Joan (Carol) D(ennison)
1948- .... **CLC 30; SSC 24**
See also AAYA 32; BPFB 3; CA 93-96;
CANR 72; SATA 36, 113; SFW 4; YAW

Viola, Herman J(oseph) 1938- .... **CLC 70**
See also CA 61-64; CANR 8, 23, 48, 91;
SATA 126

Violis, G.
See Simenon, Georges (Jacques Christian)

Viramontes, Helena Maria 1954- .... **HLCS 2**
See also CA 159; DLB 122; HW 2; LLW 1

Virgil
See Vergil
See also CDWLB 1; DLB 211; LAIT 1;
RGWL 2, 3; WP

Visconti, Luchino 1906-1976 .... **CLC 16**
See also CA 81-84; 65-68; CANR 39

Vitry, Jacques de
See Jacques de Vitry

Vittorini, Elio 1908-1966 .... **CLC 6, 9, 14**
See also CA 133; 25-28R; DLB 264; EW
12; EWL 3; RGWL 2, 3

Vivekananda, Swami 1863-1902 .... **TCLC 88**

Vizenor, Gerald Robert 1934- .... **CLC 103;**
NNAL
See also CA 13-16R, 205; CAAE 205;
CAAS 22; CANR 5, 21, 44, 67; DAM
MULT; DLB 175, 227; MTCW 2; TCWW
2

Vizinczey, Stephen 1933- .... **CLC 40**
See also CA 128; CCA 1; INT CA-128

Vliet, R(ussell) G(ordon)
1929-1984 .... **CLC 22**
See also CA 37-40R; 112; CANR 18

Vogau, Boris Andreyevich 1894-1938
See Pilnyak, Boris
See also CA 123; 218

Vogel, Paula A(nne) 1951- ... **CLC 76; DC 19**
See also CA 108; CAD; CANR 119; CD 5;
CWD; DFS 14; RGAL 4

Voigt, Cynthia 1942- .... **CLC 30**
See also AAYA 3, 30; BYA 1, 3, 6, 7, 8;
CA 106; CANR 18, 37, 40, 94; CLR 13,
48; INT CANR-18; JRDA; LAIT 5; MAI-
CYA 1; MAICYAS 1; SATA 48, 79,
116; SATA-Brief 33; WYA; YAW

Voigt, Ellen Bryant 1943- .... **CLC 54**
See also CA 69-72; CANR 11, 29, 55, 115;
CP 7; CSW; CWP; DLB 120

Voinovich, Vladimir (Nikolaevich)
1932- .... **CLC 10, 49, 147**
See also CA 81-84; CAAS 12; CANR 33,
67; CWW 2; DLB 302; MTCW 1

Vollmann, William T. 1959- .... **CLC 89**
See also CA 134; CANR 67, 116; CPW;
DA3; DAM NOV, POP; MTCW 2

Voloshinov, V. N.
See Bakhtin, Mikhail Mikhailovich

Voltaire 1694-1778 .... **LC 14, 79; SSC 12;**
WLC
See also BYA 13; DA; DA3; DAB; DAC;
DAM DRAM, MST; EW 4; GFL Begin-
nings to 1789; LATS 1:1; LMFS 1; NFS
7; RGWL 2, 3; TWA

von Aschendrof, Baron Ignatz
See Ford, Ford Madox

von Chamisso, Adelbert
See Chamisso, Adelbert von

von Daeniken, Erich 1935- .... **CLC 30**
See also AITN 1; CA 37-40R; CANR 17,
44

von Daniken, Erich
See von Daeniken, Erich

von Hartmann, Eduard
1842-1906 .... **TCLC 96**

von Hayek, Friedrich August
See Hayek, F(riedrich) A(ugust von)

von Heidenstam, (Carl Gustaf) Verner
See Heidenstam, (Carl Gustaf) Verner von

von Heyse, Paul (Johann Ludwig)
See Heyse, Paul (Johann Ludwig von)

von Hofmannsthal, Hugo
See Hofmannsthal, Hugo von

von Horvath, Odon
See von Horvath, Odon

von Horvath, Odon
See von Horvath, Odon

von Horvath, Odon 1901-1938 .... **TCLC 45**
See von Horvath, Oedoen
See also CA 118; 194; DLB 85, 124; RGWL
2, 3

von Horvath, Oedoen
See von Horvath, Odon
See also CA 184

von Kleist, Heinrich
See Kleist, Heinrich von

von Liliencron, (Friedrich Adolf Axel)
Detlev
See Liliencron, (Friedrich Adolf Axel) De-
tlev von

Vonnegut, Kurt, Jr. 1922- . **CLC 1, 2, 3, 4, 5,**
8, 12, 22, 40, 60, 111; SSC 8; WLC
See also AAYA 6, 44; AITN 1; AMWS 2;
BEST 90:4; BPFB 3; BYA 3, 14; CA
1-4R; CANR 1, 25, 49, 75, 92; CDALB
1968-1988; CN 7; CPW 1; DA; DA3;
DAB; DAC; DAM MST, NOV, POP;
DLB 2, 8, 152; DLBD 3; DLBY 1980;
EWL 3; EXPN; EXPS; LAIT 4; LMFS 2;
MTCW 1, 2; NFS 3; RGAL 4; SCFW;
SFW 4; SSFS 5; TUS; YAW

Von Rachen, Kurt
See Hubbard, L(afayette) Ron(ald)

von Rezzori (d'Arezzo), Gregor
See Rezzori (d'Arezzo), Gregor von

von Sternberg, Josef
See Sternberg, Josef von

Vorster, Gordon 1924- .... **CLC 34**
See also CA 133

Vosce, Trudie
See Ozick, Cynthia

Voznesensky, Andrei (Andreievich)
1933- .... **CLC 1, 15, 57**
See Voznesensky, Andrey
See also CA 89-92; CANR 37; CWW 2;
DAM POET; MTCW 1

Voznesensky, Andrey
See Voznesensky, Andrei (Andreievich)
See also EWL 3

Wace, Robert c. 1100-c. 1175 .... **CMLC 55**
See also DLB 146

Waddington, Miriam 1917-2004 .... **CLC 28**
See also CA 21-24R; 225; CANR 12, 30;
CCA 1; CP 7; DLB 68

Wagman, Fredrica 1937- .... **CLC 7**
See also CA 97-100; INT CA-97-100

Wagner, Linda W.
See Wagner-Martin, Linda (C.)

Wagner, Linda Welshimer
See Wagner-Martin, Linda (C.)

Wagner, Richard 1813-1883 ..... **NCLC 9, 119**
See also DLB 129; EW 6

Wagner-Martin, Linda (C.) 1936- .... **CLC 50**
See also CA 159

Wagoner, David (Russell) 1926- .... **CLC 3, 5,**
15; PC 33
See also AMWS 9; CA 1-4R; CAAS 3;
CANR 2, 71; CN 7; CP 7; DLB 5, 256;
SATA 14; TCWW 2

Wah, Fred(erick James) 1939- .... **CLC 44**
See also CA 107; 141; CP 7; DLB 60

Wahloo, Per 1926-1975 .... **CLC 7**
See also BPFB 3; CA 61-64; CANR 73;
CMW 4; MSW

Wahloo, Peter
See Wahloo, Per

Wain, John (Barrington) 1925-1994 . **CLC 2,**
11, 15, 46
See also CA 5-8R; 145; CAAS 4; CANR
23, 54; CDBLB 1960 to Present; DLB 15,
27, 139, 155; EWL 3; MTCW 1, 2

Wajda, Andrzej 1926- .... **CLC 16**
See also CA 102

Wakefield, Dan 1932- .... **CLC 7**
See also CA 21-24R, 211; CAAE 211;
CAAS 7; CN 7

Wakefield, Herbert Russell
1888-1965 .... **TCLC 120**
See also CA 5-8R; CANR 77; HGG; SUFW

Wakoski, Diane 1937- ...... **CLC 2, 4, 7, 9, 11,**
40; PC 15
See also CA 13-16R, 216; CAAE 216;
CAAS 1; CANR 9, 60, 106; CP 7; CWP;
DAM POET; DLB 5; INT CANR-9;
MTCW 2

Wakoski-Sherbell, Diane
See Wakoski, Diane

Walcott, Derek (Alton) 1930- ... **BLC 3; CLC**
2, 4, 9, 14, 25, 42, 67, 76, 160; DC 7;
PC 46
See also BW 2; CA 89-92; CANR 26, 47,
75, 80, 130; CBD; CD 5; CDWLB 3; CP
7; DA3; DAB; DAC; DAM MST, MULT,
POET; DLB 117; DLBY 1981; DNFS 1;
EFS 1; EWL 3; LMFS 2; MTCW 1, 2;
PFS 6; RGEL 2; TWA; WWE 1

Waldman, Anne (Lesley) 1945- .... **CLC 7**
See also BG 3; CA 37-40R; CAAS 17;
CANR 34, 69, 116; CP 7; CWP; DLB 16

Waldo, E. Hunter
See Sturgeon, Theodore (Hamilton)

Waldo, Edward Hamilton
See Sturgeon, Theodore (Hamilton)

Walker, Alice (Malsenior) 1944- .... **BLC 3;**
CLC 5, 6, 9, 19, 27, 46, 58, 103, 167;
PC 30; SSC 5; WLCS
See also AAYA 3, 33; AFAW 1, 2; AMWS
3; BEST 89:4; BPFB 3; BW 2, 3; CA 37-
40R; CANR 9, 27, 49, 66, 82, 131;
CDALB 1968-1988; CN 7; CPW; CSW;
DA; DA3; DAB; DAC; DAM MST,
MULT, NOV, POET, POP; DLB 6, 33,
143; EWL 3; EXPN; EXPS; FW; INT
CANR-27; LAIT 3; MAWW; MTCW 1,
2; NFS 5; RGAL 4; RGSF 2; SATA 31;
SSFS 2, 11; TUS; YAW

Walker, David Harry 1911-1992 ...... **CLC 14**
See also CA 1-4R; 137; CANR 1; CWRI 5;
SATA 8; SATA-Obit 71

Walker, Edward Joseph 1934-2004
See Walker, Ted
See also CA 21-24R; 226; CANR 12, 28,
53; CP 7

Walker, George F. 1947- .... **CLC 44, 61**
See also CA 103; CANR 21, 43, 59; CD 5;
DAB; DAC; DAM MST; DLB 60

Walker, Joseph A. 1935- .... **CLC 19**
See also BW 1, 3; CA 89-92; CAD; CANR
26; CD 5; DAM DRAM, MST; DFS 12;
DLB 38

Walker, Margaret (Abigail)
1915-1998 .... **BLC; CLC 1, 6; PC 20;**
TCLC 129
See also AFAW 1, 2; BW 2, 3; CA 73-76;
172; CANR 26, 54, 76; CN 7; CP 7;
CSW; DAM MULT; DLB 76, 152; EXPP;
FW; MTCW 1, 2; RGAL 4; RHW

Walker, Ted .... **CLC 13**
See Walker, Edward Joseph
See also DLB 40

Wallace, David Foster 1962- ... **CLC 50, 114;**
SSC 68
See also AAYA 50; AMWS 10; CA 132;
CANR 59, 133; DA3; MTCW 2

Wallace, Dexter
See Masters, Edgar Lee

Wallace, (Richard Horatio) Edgar
1875-1932 .... **TCLC 57**
See also CA 115; 218; CMW 4; DLB 70;
MSW; RGEL 2

Wallace, Irving 1916-1990 .... **CLC 7, 13**
See also AITN 1; BPFB 3; CA 1-4R; 132;
CAAS 1; CANR 1, 27; CPW; DAM NOV,
POP; INT CANR-27; MTCW 1, 2

Wallant, Edward Lewis 1926-1962 ... **CLC 5,**
10
See also CA 1-4R; CANR 22; DLB 2, 28,
143, 299; EWL 3; MTCW 1, 2; RGAL 4

Wallas, Graham 1858-1932 .... **TCLC 91**

Waller, Edmund 1606-1687 .... **LC 86**
See also BRW 2; DAM POET; DLB 126;
PAB; RGEL 2

Walley, Byron
See Card, Orson Scott

Walpole, Horace 1717-1797 .... **LC 2, 49**
See also BRW 3; DLB 39, 104, 213; HGG;
LMFS 1; RGEL 2; SUFW 1; TEA

Walpole, Hugh (Seymour)
1884-1941 .... **TCLC 5**
See also CA 104; 165; DLB 34; HGG;
MTCW 2; RGEL 2; RHW

Walrond, Eric (Derwent) 1898-1966 .... **HR 3**
See also BW 1; CA 125; DLB 51

Walser, Martin 1927- .... **CLC 27, 183**
See also CA 57-60; CANR 8, 46; CWW 2;
DLB 75, 124; EWL 3

Walser, Robert 1878-1956 ..... **SSC 20; TCLC**
18
See also CA 118; 165; CANR 100; DLB
66; EWL 3

Walsh, Gillian Paton
See Paton Walsh, Gillian

Walsh, Jill Paton .... **CLC 35**
See Paton Walsh, Gillian
See also CLR 2, 65; WYA

Walter, William Christian
See Andersen, Hans Christian

Walters, Anna L(ee) 1946- .... **NNAL**
See also CA 73-76

Walther von der Vogelweide c.
1170-1228 .... **CMLC 56**

Walton, Izaak 1593-1683 .... **LC 72**
See also BRW 2; CDBLB Before 1660;
DLB 151, 213; RGEL 2

Wambaugh, Joseph (Aloysius), Jr.
1937- .... **CLC 3, 18**
See also AITN 1; BEST 89:3; BPFB 3; CA
33-36R; CANR 42, 65, 115; CMW 4;
CPW 1; DA3; DAM NOV, POP; DLB 6;
DLBY 1983; MSW; MTCW 1, 2

Wang Wei 699(?)-761(?) .... **PC 18**
See also TWA

Warburton, William 1698-1779 .... **LC 97**
See also DLB 104

Ward, Arthur Henry Sarsfield 1883-1959
See Rohmer, Sax
See also CA 108; 173; CMW 4; HGG

Ward, Douglas Turner 1930- .... **CLC 19**
See also BW 1; CA 81-84; CAD; CANR
27; CD 5; DLB 7, 38

Ward, E. D.
See Lucas, E(dward) V(errall)

Ward, Mrs. Humphry 1851-1920
See Ward, Mary Augusta
See also RGEL 2

Ward, Mary Augusta 1851-1920 ... **TCLC 55**
See Ward, Mrs. Humphry
See also DLB 18

Ward, Peter
See Faust, Frederick (Schiller)

Warhol, Andy 1928(?)-1987 .... **CLC 20**
See also AAYA 12; BEST 89:4; CA 89-92;
121; CANR 34

Warner, Francis (Robert le Plastrier)
1937- .... **CLC 14**
See also CA 53-56; CANR 11

Warner, Marina 1946- .... **CLC 59**
See also CA 65-68; CANR 21, 55, 118; CN
7; DLB 194

Warner, Rex (Ernest) 1905-1986 ...... **CLC 45**
See also CA 89-92; 119; DLB 15; RGEL 2;
RHW

Warner, Susan (Bogert)
1819-1885 .... **NCLC 31, 146**
See also DLB 3, 42, 239, 250, 254

Warner, Sylvia (Constance) Ashton
See Ashton-Warner, Sylvia (Constance)

Warner, Sylvia Townsend
1893-1978 .. **CLC 7, 19; SSC 23; TCLC**
131
See also BRWS 7; CA 61-64; 77-80; CANR
16, 60, 104; DLB 34, 139; EWL 3; FANT;
FW; MTCW 1, 2; RGEL 2; RGSF 2;
RHW

Warren, Mercy Otis 1728-1814 ..... **NCLC 13**
See also DLB 31, 200; RGAL 4; TUS

Warren, Robert Penn 1905-1989 .. **CLC 1, 4,**
6, 8, 10, 13, 18, 39, 53, 59; PC 37; SSC
4, 58; WLC
See also AITN 1; AMW; AMWC 2; BPFB
3; BYA 1; CA 13-16R; 129; CANR 10,
47; CDALB 1968-1988; DA; DA3; DAB;
DAC; DAM MST, NOV, POET; DLB 2,
48, 152; DLBY 1980, 1989; EWL 3; INT
CANR-10; MTCW 1, 2; NFS 13; RGAL
4; RGSF 2; RHW; SATA 46; SATA-Obit
63; SSFS 8; TUS

Warrigal, Jack
See Furphy, Joseph

Warshofsky, Isaac
See Singer, Isaac Bashevis

Warton, Joseph 1722-1800 .... **NCLC 118**
See also DLB 104, 109; RGEL 2

Warton, Thomas 1728-1790 .... **LC 15, 82**
See also DAM POET; DLB 104, 109;
RGEL 2

Waruk, Kona
See Harris, (Theodore) Wilson

Warung, Price .... **TCLC 45**
See Astley, William
See also DLB 230; RGEL 2

Warwick, Jarvis
See Garner, Hugh
See also CCA 1

Washington, Alex
See Harris, Mark

Washington, Booker T(aliaferro)
1856-1915 .... **BLC 3; TCLC 10**
See also BW 1; CA 114; 125; DA3; DAM
MULT; LAIT 2; RGAL 4; SATA 28

Washington, George 1732-1799 .... **LC 25**
See also DLB 31

Wassermann, (Karl) Jakob
1873-1934 .... **TCLC 6**
See also CA 104; 163; DLB 66; EWL 3

Wasserstein, Wendy 1950- ... **CLC 32, 59, 90,**
183; DC 4
See also CA 121; 129; CABS 3; CAD;
CANR 53, 75, 128; CD 5; CWD; DA3;
DAM DRAM; DFS 5, 17; DLB 228;
EWL 3; FW; INT CA-129; MTCW 2;
SATA 94

Waterhouse, Keith (Spencer) 1929- . **CLC 47**
See also CA 5-8R; CANR 38, 67, 109;
CBD; CN 7; DLB 13, 15; MTCW 1, 2

Waters, Frank (Joseph) 1902-1995 .. **CLC 88**
See also CA 5-8R; 149; CAAS 13; CANR
3, 18, 63, 121; DLB 212; DLBY 1986;
RGAL 4; TCWW 2

Waters, Mary C. .... **CLC 70**

Waters, Roger 1944- .... **CLC 35**

Watkins, Frances Ellen
See Harper, Frances Ellen Watkins

Watkins, Gerrold
See Malzberg, Barry N(athaniel)

Watkins, Gloria Jean 1952(?)- .... **CLC 94**
See also BW 2; CA 143; CANR 87, 126;
DLB 246; MTCW 2; SATA 115

Watkins, Paul 1964- .... **CLC 55**
See also CA 132; CANR 62, 98

Watkins, Vernon Phillips
1906-1967 .... **CLC 43**
See also CA 9-10; 25-28R; CAP 1; DLB
20; EWL 3; RGEL 2

Watson, Irving S.
See Mencken, H(enry) L(ouis)

Watson, John H.
See Farmer, Philip Jose

Watson, Richard F.
See Silverberg, Robert

Watts, Ephraim
See Horne, Richard Henry Hengist

Watts, Isaac 1674-1748 .... **LC 98**
See also DLB 95; RGEL 2; SATA 52

Waugh, Auberon (Alexander)
1939-2001 .... **CLC 7**
See also CA 45-48; 192; CANR 6, 22, 92;
DLB 14, 194

Waugh, Evelyn (Arthur St. John)
1903-1966 .. **CLC 1, 3, 8, 13, 19, 27, 44,**
107; SSC 41; WLC
See also BPFB 3; BRW 7; CA 85-88; 25-
28R; CANR 22; CDBLB 1914-1945; DA;
DA3; DAB; DAC; DAM MST, NOV,
POP; DLB 15, 162, 195; EWL 3; MTCW
1, 2; NFS 13, 17; RGEL 2; RGSF 2; TEA;
WLIT 4

Waugh, Harriet 1944- .... **CLC 6**
See also CA 85-88; CANR 22

Ways, C. R.
See Blount, Roy (Alton), Jr.

Waystaff, Simon
See Swift, Jonathan

Webb, Beatrice (Martha Potter)
1858-1943 .... **TCLC 22**
See also CA 117; 162; DLB 190; FW

Webb, Charles (Richard) 1939- .... **CLC 7**
See also CA 25-28R; CANR 114

Webb, Frank J. .... **NCLC 143**
See also DLB 50

Webb, James H(enry), Jr. 1946- ...... **CLC 22**
See also CA 81-84

Webb, Mary Gladys (Meredith)
1881-1927 .... **TCLC 24**
See also CA 182; 123; DLB 34; FW

Webb, Mrs. Sidney
See Webb, Beatrice (Martha Potter)

Williams, Hiram King
See Williams, Hank
See also CA 188

Williams, Hugo (Mordaunt) 1942- ... **CLC 42**
See also CA 17-20R; CANR 45, 119; CP 7;
DLB 40

Williams, J. Walker
See Wodehouse, P(elham) G(renville)

Williams, John A(lfred) 1925- . **BLC 3; CLC 5, 13**
See also AFAW 2; BW 2, 3; CA 53-56, 195;
CAAE 195; CAAS 3; CANR 6, 26, 51,
118; CN 7; CSW; DAM MULT; DLB 2,
33; EWL 3; INT CANR-6; RGAL 4; SFW
4

Williams, Jonathan (Chamberlain)
1929- .... **CLC 13**
See also CA 9-12R; CAAS 12; CANR 8,
108; CP 7; DLB 5

Williams, Joy 1944- .... **CLC 31**
See also CA 41-44R; CANR 22, 48, 97

Williams, Norman 1952- .... **CLC 39**
See also CA 118

Williams, Sherley Anne 1944-1999 ... **BLC 3; CLC 89**
See also AFAW 2; BW 2, 3; CA 73-76; 185;
CANR 25, 82; DAM MULT, POET; DLB
41; INT CANR-25; SATA 78; SATA-Obit
116

Williams, Shirley
See Williams, Sherley Anne

Williams, Tennessee 1911-1983 . **CLC 1, 2, 5, 7, 8, 11, 15, 19, 30, 39, 45, 71, 111; DC 4; WLC**
See also AAYA 31; AITN 1, 2; AMW;
AMWC 1; CA 5-8R; 108; CABS 3; CAD;
CANR 31, 132; CDALB 1941-1968; DA;
DA3; DAB; DAC; DAM DRAM, MST;
DFS 17; DLB 7; DLBD 4; DLBY 1983;
EWL 3; GLL 1; LAIT 4; LATS 1:2;
MTCW 1, 2; RGAL 4; TUS

Williams, Thomas (Alonzo)
1926-1990 .... **CLC 14**
See also CA 1-4R; 132; CANR 2

Williams, William C.
See Williams, William Carlos

Williams, William Carlos
1883-1963 .... **CLC 1, 2, 5, 9, 13, 22, 42, 67; PC 7; SSC 31**
See also AAYA 46; AMW; AMWR 1; CA
89-92; CANR 34; CDALB 1917-1929;
DA; DA3; DAB; DAC; DAM MST,
POET; DLB 4, 16, 54, 86; EWL 3; EXPP;
MTCW 1, 2; NCFS 4; PAB; PFS 1, 6, 11;
RGAL 4; RGSF 2; TUS; WP

Williamson, David (Keith) 1942- ..... **CLC 56**
See also CA 103; CANR 41; CD 5; DLB
289

Williamson, Ellen Douglas 1905-1984
See Douglas, Ellen
See also CA 17-20R; 114; CANR 39

Williamson, Jack .... **CLC 29**
See Williamson, John Stewart
See also CAAS 8; DLB 8; SCFW 2

Williamson, John Stewart 1908-
See Williamson, Jack
See also CA 17-20R; CANR 23, 70; SFW 4

Willie, Frederick
See Lovecraft, H(oward) P(hillips)

Willingham, Calder (Baynard, Jr.)
1922-1995 .... **CLC 5, 51**
See also CA 5-8R; 147; CANR 3; CSW;
DLB 2, 44; IDFW 3, 4; MTCW 1

Willis, Charles
See Clarke, Arthur C(harles)

Willy
See Colette, (Sidonie-Gabrielle)

Willy, Colette
See Colette, (Sidonie-Gabrielle)
See also GLL 1

Wilmot, John 1647-1680 .... **LC 75**
See Rochester
See also BRW 2; DLB 131; PAB

Wilson, A(ndrew) N(orman) 1950- .. **CLC 33**
See also BRWS 6; CA 112; 122; CN 7;
DLB 14, 155, 194; MTCW 2

Wilson, Angus (Frank Johnstone)
1913-1991 . **CLC 2, 3, 5, 25, 34; SSC 21**
See also BRWS 1; CA 5-8R; 134; CANR
21; DLB 15, 139, 155; EWL 3; MTCW 1,
2; RGEL 2; RGSF 2

Wilson, August 1945- ... **BLC 3; CLC 39, 50, 63, 118; DC 2; WLCS**
See also AAYA 16; AFAW 2; AMWS 8; BW
2, 3; CA 115; 122; CAD; CANR 42, 54,
76, 128; CD 5; DA; DA3; DAB; DAC;
DAM DRAM, MST, MULT; DFS 3, 7,
15, 17; DLB 228; EWL 3; LAIT 4; LATS
1:2; MTCW 1, 2; RGAL 4

Wilson, Brian 1942- .... **CLC 12**

Wilson, Colin 1931- .... **CLC 3, 14**
See also CA 1-4R; CAAS 5; CANR 1, 22,
33, 77; CMW 4; CN 7; DLB 14, 194;
HGG; MTCW 1; SFW 4

Wilson, Dirk
See Pohl, Frederik

Wilson, Edmund 1895-1972 .. **CLC 1, 2, 3, 8, 24**
See also AMW; CA 1-4R; 37-40R; CANR
1, 46, 110; DLB 63; EWL 3; MTCW 1, 2;
RGAL 4; TUS

Wilson, Ethel Davis (Bryant)
1888(?)-1980 .... **CLC 13**
See also CA 102; DAC; DAM POET; DLB
68; MTCW 1; RGEL 2

Wilson, Harriet
See Wilson, Harriet E. Adams
See also DLB 239

Wilson, Harriet E.
See Wilson, Harriet E. Adams
See also DLB 243

Wilson, Harriet E. Adams
1827(?)-1863(?) .... **BLC 3; NCLC 78**
See Wilson, Harriet; Wilson, Harriet E.
See also DAM MULT; DLB 50

Wilson, John 1785-1854 .... **NCLC 5**

Wilson, John (Anthony) Burgess 1917-1993
See Burgess, Anthony
See also CA 1-4R; 143; CANR 2, 46; DA3;
DAC; DAM NOV; MTCW 1, 2; NFS 15;
TEA

Wilson, Lanford 1937- ... **CLC 7, 14, 36, 197; DC 19**
See also CA 17-20R; CABS 3; CAD; CANR
45, 96; CD 5; DAM DRAM; DFS 4, 9,
12, 16, 20; DLB 7; EWL 3; TUS

Wilson, Robert M. 1941- .... **CLC 7, 9**
See also CA 49-52; CAD; CANR 2, 41; CD
5; MTCW 1

Wilson, Robert McLiam 1964- .... **CLC 59**
See also CA 132; DLB 267

Wilson, Sloan 1920-2003 .... **CLC 32**
See also CA 1-4R; 216; CANR 1, 44; CN 7

Wilson, Snoo 1948- .... **CLC 33**
See also CA 69-72; CBD; CD 5

Wilson, William S(mith) 1932- .... **CLC 49**
See also CA 81-84

Wilson, (Thomas) Woodrow
1856-1924 .... **TCLC 79**
See also CA 166; DLB 47

Wilson and Warnke eds. .... **CLC 65**

Winchilsea, Anne (Kingsmill) Finch
1661-1720
See Finch, Anne
See also RGEL 2

Windham, Basil
See Wodehouse, P(elham) G(renville)

Wingrove, David (John) 1954- .... **CLC 68**
See also CA 133; SFW 4

Winnemucca, Sarah 1844-1891 .... **NCLC 79; NNAL**
See also DAM MULT; DLB 175; RGAL 4

Winstanley, Gerrard 1609-1676 .... **LC 52**

Wintergreen, Jane
See Duncan, Sara Jeannette

Winters, Janet Lewis .... **CLC 41**
See Lewis, Janet
See also DLBY 1987

Winters, (Arthur) Yvor 1900-1968 .... **CLC 4, 8, 32**
See also AMWS 2; CA 11-12; 25-28R; CAP
1; DLB 48; EWL 3; MTCW 1; RGAL 4

Winterson, Jeanette 1959- .... **CLC 64, 158**
See also BRWS 4; CA 136; CANR 58, 116;
CN 7; CPW; DA3; DAM POP; DLB 207,
261; FANT; FW; GLL 1; MTCW 2; RHW

Winthrop, John 1588-1649 .... **LC 31, 107**
See also DLB 24, 30

Wirth, Louis 1897-1952 .... **TCLC 92**
See also CA 210

Wiseman, Frederick 1930- .... **CLC 20**
See also CA 159

Wister, Owen 1860-1938 .... **TCLC 21**
See also BPFB 3; CA 108; 162; DLB 9, 78,
186; RGAL 4; SATA 62; TCWW 2

Wither, George 1588-1667 .... **LC 96**
See also DLB 121; RGEL 2

Witkacy
See Witkiewicz, Stanislaw Ignacy

Witkiewicz, Stanislaw Ignacy
1885-1939 .... **TCLC 8**
See also CA 105; 162; CDWLB 4; DLB
215; EW 10; EWL 3; RGWL 2, 3; SFW 4

Wittgenstein, Ludwig (Josef Johann)
1889-1951 .... **TCLC 59**
See also CA 113; 164; DLB 262; MTCW 2

Wittig, Monique 1935(?)-2003 .... **CLC 22**
See also CA 116; 135; 212; CWW 2; DLB
83; EWL 3; FW; GLL 1

Wittlin, Jozef 1896-1976 .... **CLC 25**
See also CA 49-52; 65-68; CANR 3; EWL
3

Wodehouse, P(elham) G(renville)
1881-1975 . **CLC 1, 2, 5, 10, 22; SSC 2; TCLC 108**
See also AITN 2; BRWS 3; CA 45-48; 57-
60; CANR 3, 33; CDBLB 1914-1945;
CPW 1; DA3; DAB; DAC; DAM NOV;
DLB 34, 162; EWL 3; MTCW 1, 2;
RGEL 2; RGSF 2; SATA 22; SSFS 10

Woiwode, L.
See Woiwode, Larry (Alfred)

Woiwode, Larry (Alfred) 1941- ... **CLC 6, 10**
See also CA 73-76; CANR 16, 94; CN 7;
DLB 6; INT CANR-16

Wojciechowska, Maia (Teresa)
1927-2002 .... **CLC 26**
See also AAYA 8, 46; BYA 3; CA 9-12R;
183; 209; CAAE 183; CANR 4, 41; CLR
1; JRDA; MAICYA 1, 2; SAAS 1; SATA
1, 28, 83; SATA-Essay 104; SATA-Obit
134; YAW

Wojtyla, Karol
See John Paul II, Pope

Wolf, Christa 1929- .... **CLC 14, 29, 58, 150**
See also CA 85-88; CANR 45, 123; CD-
WLB 2; CWW 2; DLB 75; EWL 3; FW;
MTCW 1; RGWL 2, 3; SSFS 14

Wolf, Naomi 1962- .... **CLC 157**
See also CA 141; CANR 110; FW

Literary Criticism Series
Cumulative Topic Index

This index lists all topic entries in Gale's *Children's Literature Review* (CLR), *Classical and Medieval Literature Criticism* (CMLC), *Contemporary Literary Criticism* (CLC), *Drama Criticism* (DC), *Literature Criticism from 1400 to 1800* (LC), *Nineteenth-Century Literature Criticism* (NCLC), *Short Story Criticism* (SSC), and *Twentieth-Century Literary Criticism* (TCLC). The index also lists topic entries in the Gale Critical Companion Collection, which includes the following publications: *The Beat Generation* (BG), and *Harlem Renaissance* (HR).

Topic Index

Topic Index

NCLC Cumulative Nationality Index

AMERICAN

Adams, John **106**
Alcott, Amos Bronson **1**
Alcott, Louisa May **6, 58, 83**
Alger, Horatio Jr. **8, 83**
Allston, Washington **2**
Apess, William **73**
Arnold, Matthew **126**
Audubon, John James **47**
Barlow, Joel **23**
Bartram, William **145**
Beecher, Catharine Esther **30**
Bellamy, Edward **4, 86**
Bird, Robert Montgomery **1**
Boker, George Henry **125**
Boyesen, Hjalmar Hjorth **135**
Brackenridge, Hugh Henry **7**
Brentano, Clemens (Maria) **1**
Brown, Charles Brockden **22, 74, 122**
Brown, William Wells **2, 89**
Brownson, Orestes Augustus **50**
Bryant, William Cullen **6, 46**
Calhoun, John Caldwell **15**
Channing, William Ellery **17**
Child, Lydia Maria **6, 73**
Chivers, Thomas Holley **49**
Cooke, John Esten **5**
Cooke, Rose Terry **110**
Cooper, Susan Fenimore **129**
Cooper, James Fenimore **1, 27, 54**
Cranch, Christopher Pearse **115**
Crèvecoeur, Michel Guillaume Jean de **105**
Crockett, David **8**
Cummins, Maria Susanna **139**
Dana, Richard Henry Sr. **53**
Delany, Martin Robinson **93**
Dickinson, Emily (Elizabeth) **21, 77**
Douglass, Frederick **7, 55, 141**
Dunlap, William **2**
Dwight, Timothy **13**
Emerson, Mary Moody **66**
Emerson, Ralph Waldo **1, 38, 98**
Field, Eugene **3**
Foster, Hannah Webster **99**
Foster, Stephen Collins **26**
Frederic, Harold **10**
Freneau, Philip Morin **1, 111**
Hale, Sarah Josepha (Buell) **75**
Halleck, Fitz-Greene **47**
Hamilton, Alexander **49**
Hammon, Jupiter **5**
Harris, George Washington **23**
Hawthorne, Nathaniel **2, 10, 17, 23, 39, 79, 95**
Hayne, Paul Hamilton **94**
Holmes, Oliver Wendell **14, 81**
Horton, George Moses **87**
Irving, Washington **2, 19, 95**
Jackson, Helen Hunt **90**
Jacobs, Harriet A(nn) **67**
James, Henry Sr. **53**
Jefferson, Thomas **11, 103**

Kennedy, John Pendleton **2**
Kirkland, Caroline M. **85**
Lanier, Sidney **6, 118**
Lazarus, Emma **8, 109**
Lincoln, Abraham **18**
Longfellow, Henry Wadsworth **2, 45, 101, 103**
Lowell, James Russell **2, 90**
Madison, James **126**
Melville, Herman **3, 12, 29, 45, 49, 91, 93, 123**
Mowatt, Anna Cora **74**
Murray, Judith Sargent **63**
Osgood, Frances Sargent **141**
Parkman, Francis Jr. **12**
Parton, Sara Payson Willis **86**
Paulding, James Kirke **2**
Pinkney, Edward **31**
Poe, Edgar Allan **1, 16, 55, 78, 94, 97, 117**
Rowson, Susanna Haswell **5, 69**
Sedgwick, Catharine Maria **19, 98**
Shaw, Henry Wheeler **15**
Sheridan, Richard Brinsley **5, 91**
Sigourney, Lydia Howard (Huntley) **21, 87**
Simms, William Gilmore **3**
Smith, Joseph Jr. **53**
Solomon, Northup **105**
Southworth, Emma Dorothy Eliza Nevitte **26**
Stowe, Harriet (Elizabeth) Beecher **3, 50, 133**
Taylor, Bayard **89**
Tenney, Tabitha Gilman **122**
Thoreau, Henry David **7, 21, 61, 138**
Timrod, Henry **25**
Trumbull, John **30**
Truth, Sojourner **94**
Tyler, Royall **3**
Very, Jones **9**
Warner, Susan (Bogert) **31, 146**
Warren, Mercy Otis **13**
Webster, Noah **30**
Webb, Frank J. **143**
Whitman, Sarah Helen (Power) **19**
Whitman, Walt(er) **4, 31, 81**
Whittier, John Greenleaf **8, 59**
Wilson, Harriet E. Adams **78**
Winnemucca, Sarah **79**

ARGENTINIAN

Echeverria, (Jose) Esteban (Antonino) **18**
Hernández, José **17**
Sarmiento, Domingo Faustino **123**

AUSTRALIAN

Adams, Francis **33**
Clarke, Marcus (Andrew Hislop) **19**
Gordon, Adam Lindsay **21**
Harpur, Charles **114**
Kendall, Henry **12**

AUSTRIAN

Grillparzer, Franz **1, 102**
Lenau, Nikolaus **16**
Nestroy, Johann **42**
Raimund, Ferdinand Jakob **69**
Sacher-Masoch, Leopold von **31**
Stifter, Adalbert **41**

CANADIAN

Crawford, Isabella Valancy **12, 127**
De Mille, James **123**
Haliburton, Thomas Chandler **15**
Lampman, Archibald **25**
Moodie, Susanna (Strickland) **14, 113**
Richardson, John **55**
Traill, Catharine Parr **31**

CHINESE

Li Ju-chen **137**

COLOMBIAN

Isaacs, Jorge Ricardo **70**
Silva, José Asunción **114**

CUBAN

Avellaneda, Gertrudis Gómez de **111**
Casal, Julián del **131**
Martí (y Pérez), José (Julian) **63**
Villaverde, Cirilo **121**

CZECH

Macha, Karel Hynek **46**

DANISH

Andersen, Hans Christian **7, 79**
Grundtvig, Nicolai Frederik Severin **1**
Jacobsen, Jens Peter **34**
Kierkegaard, Søren **34, 78, 125**

ENGLISH

Ainsworth, William Harrison **13**
Arnold, Matthew **6, 29, 89**
Arnold, Thomas **18**
Austen, Jane **1, 13, 19, 33, 51, 81, 95, 119**
Bagehot, Walter **10**
Barbauld, Anna Laetitia **50**
Barham, Richard Harris **77**
Barnes, William **75**
Beardsley, Aubrey **6**
Beckford, William **16**
Beddoes, Thomas Lovell **3**
Bentham, Jeremy **38**
Blake, William **13, 37, 57, 127**
Bloomfield, Robert **145**
Borrow, George (Henry) **9**
Bowles, William Lisle **103**
Brontë, Anne **4, 71, 102**
Brontë, Charlotte **3, 8, 33, 58, 105**
Brontë, Emily (Jane) **16, 35**
Brontë, (Patrick) Branwell **109**

ISBN 0-7876-8630-1

90000

9 780787 686307